ERNEST HEMINGWAY

ERNEST HEMINGWAY

A BIOGRAPHY

Mary V. Dearborn

ALFRED A. KNOPF · NEW YORK 2017

This Is a Borzoi Book Published by Alfred A. Knopf

Copyright © 2017 by Mary V. Dearborn
All rights reserved. Published in the United States by Alfred A. Knopf,
a division of Random House LLC, New York, and distributed in Canada
by Random House of Canada, a division of Penguin Random House
Canada Limited, Toronto.
www.aaknopf.com

Knopf, Borzoi Books, and the colophon are registered trademarks of
Penguin Random House LLC.

Library of Congress Cataloging-in-Publication Data
Names: Dearborn, Mary V., author.
Title: Ernest Hemingway : a biography / Mary V. Dearborn.
Description; 1st ed. | New York : Knopf, 2017. | Includes bibliographical references.
Identifiers: LCCN 2016015837 | ISBN 9780307594679 (hardcover)
ISBN 9781101947982 (ebook)
Subjects: LCSH: Hemingway, Ernest, 1899–1961. | Authors, American—
20th century—Biography.
Classification: LCC PS3515.E37 Z5849 2017 | DDC 813/.52 [B]—dc23
LC record available at https://lccn.loc.gov/2016015837

Front-of-jacket photograph: Ernest Hemingway Collection,
John F. Kennedy Presidential Library and Museum
Jacket design by Janet Hansen

Manufactured in the United States of America
First Edition

FOR ERIC AND FOR BETH

Contents

ERNEST HEMINGWAY   3

Acknowledgments   629

Notes   631

Bibliography   697

Index   707

ERNEST HEMINGWAY

Prologue

One evening in the mid-1990s I attended a panel on Ernest Hemingway and his work at New York's Mercantile Library. The Mercantile was known for lively programming arranged by its then director, Harold Augenbraum, and this evening was no exception. Hemingway had been somewhat under fire of late. A controversial 1987 biography by Kenneth Lynn had left Hemingway fans reeling with the revelation that Ernest had been dressed as a girl in his early years, which Lynn argued had shaped the author's psyche and sexuality.

The previous year Hemingway's posthumously published novel, *The Garden of Eden,* had revealed a writer seemingly obsessed with androgyny, its hero and heroine cutting and dyeing their hair to become identical, beyond gender—just as in the explicit sex scenes they move beyond traditionally male and female roles. At roughly the same time, Hemingway and his place in the Western literary tradition came under full-on attack, as readers, scholars, educators, and activists urgently questioned what "dead white males" like Hemingway had to say to us in a multicultural era that no longer accords them automatic priority. The so-called Hemingway code—a tough, stoic approach to life that seemingly substitutes physical courage and ideals of strength and skill for other forms of accomplishment—increasingly looked insular and tiresomely macho.

That night at the Mercantile Library, these issues were roiling the waters. Should we still read Hemingway? Are his concerns still relevant? Was Hemingway gay? (The short answer is no.) Why could he not create a complicated female heroine? Does Hemingway have anything at all to say to people of different races and ethnicities? On the plus side, does his intense feeling for the natural world take on greater significance at a time of growing environmental consciousness? If we were to continue to read Hemingway, we needed to take note of *how* we read him, it seemed.

The discussion after the panel was animated. The moderator called on a burly man with a peppery crew cut. I recognized him as a professor and critic who wrote about the literature of the 1920s, especially Hemingway's friend F. Scott Fitzgerald. "I just want to say one thing," he stood up and announced. "Hemingway made it possible for me to do what I do."

I thought about what he said for a long time afterward. He seemed to mean something very specific and personal—something to do with reading literature and writing about it as a vocation. He was not talking about teaching or making money. He was talking about whether writing was an acceptable occupation for a man, both on his terms and the world's. Hemingway, not only in his extraliterary pursuits as a marlin fisherman, a big game hunter, a boxer, and a bullfight aficionado but also in his capacity as an icon of American popular culture, was the very personification of virility—*and he was a writer.* Any taint of femininity or aestheticism attached to writing had been wiped clean.

I was reminded of a rather extraordinary statement made late in life by the writer Harold Loeb, the model for Robert Cohn in Hemingway's first full-length novel, *The Sun Also Rises*—the lover of Lady Brett Ashley who proves himself a wet blanket during the Pamplona bullfighting fiesta. It was hardly a flattering portrayal, but Loeb had not forgotten why he, like so many others, had been drawn to Hemingway when they both were young: "I admired his combination of toughness and sensitiveness. . . . I had long suspected that one reason for the scarcity of good writers in the United States was the popular impression—that artists were not quite virile. It was a good sign that men like Hemingway were taking up writing."

As I went on to think and write about Hemingway myself in the period following this panel, I thought I understood the critic's remarks that evening. But I couldn't account for the risky, emotional, and highly personal nature of his confession. What I couldn't understand was his *passion.* It seemed to me that something was being said here about being a man and a writer, and it made me feel excluded.

There is no shortage of Ernest Hemingway biographies—one of them runs to five volumes. His first biographer, Carlos Baker, set the bar in 1969, and the efforts of most of those who followed have been impressively researched and, for the most part, insightful. There has not yet been a biography written by a woman. This doesn't necessarily mean that much; mainly, I find that I am interested in different aspects of Hemingway's life from the ones that drew his previous (male) biographers. I shrink from describing what aspects those are: I'd rather not encourage the notion that men and women see things in fundamentally different ways. By definition, studying Hemingway is about the rough opposite, the cultural construction of gender—how sex roles are determined by the forces around us rather than our genes. It is through figures like Hemingway that masculinity gets defined—even if that same cultural construction affects him in turn.

Before turning to Hemingway, I wrote biographies of two major writers who also helped define American masculinity through both their lives and their fiction: Henry Miller and Norman Mailer. Himself a (later) expatriate in Paris. Miller curiously never spoke of Hemingway, though Miller, like Hemingway, lived—from the outside, that is—a life that is the stuff of many a male fantasy. Mailer was a great admirer of both Miller and Hemingway; while he may have enjoyed Miller's work more, he considered Hemingway easily "America's greatest living writer." Yet he seemed to recognize that somewhere along the way, Hemingway's work and life became one—that without Hemingway's image of a ruggedly physical man of action, the work would not be the same. Mailer asked us to acknowledge how "silly" *A Farewell to Arms* or *Death in the Afternoon* "would be if . . . written by a man who was five-four, wore glasses, spoke in a shrill voice, and was a physical coward." A valid point, perhaps, but how useful is this really?

As I began to consider writing my own biography of Hemingway, I asked myself whether a woman could bring something to the subject that previous biographers had not. But perhaps the point was what I *did not* bring in tow.

I have no investment in the Hemingway legend. No doubt I come to him with my own baggage, but I cannot see what the legend has to offer to a female reader. I am not interested in the issue of who said what about whose hair on whose chest, the occasion for some thrown punches between Hemingway and Max Eastman in the Scribner's offices in 1937. I think we should look away from what feeds into the legend and consider what formed this remarkably complex man and brilliant writer.

* * *

I thought once that I might begin to understand Hemingway if I understood what it was like to know him when he was beginning his career in Paris in the 1920s, before we knew what we now know, before he was enveloped in the cloak of fame. I came up with a way to think about him that worked for me: I imagined a handsome young man who came out of nowhere and was dropped into Greenwich Village, perhaps, or, more likely these days, into Williamsburg or Bushwick or Red Hook, probably living over a very interesting shop or other workplace. This young man would be rangy and darkly handsome, his presence so arresting that heads would turn when he walked into a room. He would always have a sheaf of manuscripts in his inside coat pocket, which he would pull out in cafés and scribble on—but he would always spring up if you came over to his table, ever happy to see you, happy to make time for you. The word would be that he had a book out, printed on a little hand press in Brooklyn, and that a big New York publisher had picked it up and was soon to release it. He would have a whole new way of writing—stunningly simple, seemingly effortless. Of course there would be a book party—an enchanted evening, an occasion everyone would remember.

He would be madly in love with his wife too, a beautiful, serene-looking redhead who put you at ease instantly, whom you felt you could talk to about anything, who plainly adored her husband. As a couple they would *glow.* Everyone would be drawn to this young man—eager to be part of his energy field. He would be more curious than anyone you'd met. The life before him would seem to take on the outlines of a great adventure. It would be intoxicating to know him. Then, as part of my effort to understand my subject better, I picked this dazzling writer up and dropped him mentally into Montparnasse in the early 1920s, with F. Scott Fitzgerald, Gertrude Stein, John Dos Passos, Ezra Pound for companions.

Imagined this way, Hemingway's life took on the animation it must have if I were to see it clearly. The landscape he occupied gained color and dimension, and it seemed as if the world did not stop noticing him—even after his tragic death in 1961. He became, willy-nilly, a symbol of male potentiality, man as it seemed he always had been and was made to be. (The culture demanded no less; it was as if he filled a need that no one knew existed.) Ever since he first appeared, grinning devilishly and waving a crutch from his hospital ward during World War I, in an early newsreel shown on movie screens across the country, Hemingway captured the public imagination. Yet always, it seemed, a different Hemingway. The callow, lanky chronicler of the Lost Generation gave way to the mustachioed and virile Hemingway of the 1930s, as people read of his exploits in the bullring, on the deep seas, and in the African bush. He morphed yet again, into the politically engaged reporter of the Spanish Civil War, then into the intrepid, fighting journalist of World War II, and finally into "Papa," the bearded, white-haired living legend of the postwar Cuban years. He published a string of novels and stories that made readers see the world, because of him, as a different place, more vibrant, more alive, more elemental, and at the same time more romantic.

Yet something began to go wrong. The potential for this eventuality was there all along—it was in his genes, and in his childhood in the eccentric Hemingway household. Perhaps the times or the public asked too much of him. Maybe he shut out the critical voices he needed to hear to produce his best work. At some point in the unfolding of his brilliant career, a tragedy began to take shape.

Ernest seemed to find it difficult to give and receive love, to be a faithful friend, and, perhaps most tragically, to tell the truth, even to himself. By the end of World War II, and while still in his forties, he had done himself out of many of the rewards of the good life: he had three failed marriages behind him, had few good friends, was not writing well, and had sur-rounded himself with flunkies and sycophants. He was burdened by serious physical injuries, including several concussions—which we would today call traumatic brain injuries, whose scope and variety are only beginning to be understood. The dangers of retrospective diagnosis duly acknowledged, it seems probable that Hemingway also suffered from mental illness that included mania and depression so severe it became at times psychotic. The son of a doctor, Hemingway was drinking too much and taking varying cocktails of prescribed pills, and he refused to follow his doctors' orders. His habits of mind, the limitations of the psychopharmacology of his day, and the desire to avoid embarrassing himself as a public figure made it impossible for him to get the help he needed. His later fiction indicated a persistent confusion about gender identity or, to put it more positively and progressively, an openness to fluidity in gender boundaries.

Worse, by the 1950s his talent was befuddling him. Even at his peak, sentimentality and a garrulous streak sometimes crept into his writing. He began to run repeatedly into dead ends with ambitious projects like *The Garden of Eden* and so published very little: even the most acclaimed works, like *The Old Man and the Sea*, lacked the ambition and passion of his earlier work. Things got worse, and his world shrank to the grounds of the Finca Vigía in Cuba, the property that became his own private fiefdom. Then, after it became virtually impossible to remain in Castro's Cuba, he took refuge in a big concrete house in Idaho. Soon, no longer able to get the enormous pleasure he had once taken from life, no longer believing in his ability to write, he took his own life.

What happened to Hemingway was a tragedy for him; a tragedy for his family, who had to endure it and were often damaged in the process; and a tragedy for us. It does no good to read (or write) his biography anew if we simply shine up the legend and find more ways to admire it—or if we reflexively debunk a literary legacy that has proved durably fascinating and inspiring for nearly a century. We need to understand what happened, in part because what was lost is incalculable. Hemingway was without ques-tion one of the greatest American prose writers. He changed the way we think, what we look for in literature, how we choose to lead our lives. He changed our language. He changed how we see Paris, the American West, Spain, Africa, Key West, Cuba, northern Michigan. Even his place of birth, Oak Park—though he very rarely wrote about it, this suburb, equidistant from Chicago and the wilderness of the Des Plaines River, was part of what made Hemingway, and we will always see it differently for his presence.

If we are to understand all of this, it is important that we look at how it unfolded, how his unique gift came into full flower, how he came undone, even if the spectacle is one from which we might prefer to look away. It is painful to contemplate how Hemingway ceased engaging with a world he made new for us, so that even following the *corrida* circuit in the last years of his life became a nightmarish palimpsest of what it had been when he was young.

Because he died so young, we have been left to imagine what Hemingway, if he had regained his full powers and denied the suicidal impulse, would have made of, say, the domestic upheavals of the 1950s and 1960s in the U.S., the revolutions that swept the so-called Third World, feminism, environmentalism, Watergate, Reagan. The New Journalism. His beloved Spain after Franco.

Harry, the narrator in one of Hemingway's most powerful stories, "The Snows of Kilimanjaro," is himself a writer who reviews his life and his career and who, while slowly dying, recognizes his failed mission. "There was so much to write," Harry thinks. "He had seen the world change. . . . He had been in it and he had watched it and it was his duty to write of it, but now he never would." Hemingway acknowledged that he, like Harry, had at times been derelict in his "duty" as a writer—perhaps an impossible standard. Indeed, it's hard to argue that a writer "failed" when he revealed to us so much about war and violence, nature, relations between men and women, trauma, the creative life.

There's something else. As the heated discussion that mid-1990s evening in the Mercantile Library began to deflate and cool, someone got the attention of the moderator and stood up to add something. Echoing the professor who had said earlier that Hemingway made it possible for him to *do* what he did, this person said, "I just want to say that Hemingway made it possible for me to *be* who I am." And sat down. It was difficult to determine the speaker's gender, only that it appeared to have recently changed.

In the years to come, I would learn, in my study of Hemingway's life, what she or he meant.

ONE

Adelaide Edmonds Hemingway, Ernest Hemingway's paternal grandmother, remembered shaking Abraham Lincoln's hand, and Ernest Hall, his mother's father, noted that at a parade in London, two couples passed him by: Queen Victoria and Prince Albert; Napoleon III and the Empress Eugénie. Their grandson would become the master of literary modernism, at once the harbinger and product of a new age. In many ways this disjuncture represented the battleground on which Hemingway forged his identity in his early years. It is commonly believed that he carried scars from his physical wounding in World War I and from his emotional wounding when the Red Cross nurse who tended him rejected him for another man. But other, more lasting scars reached further back than that.

Ernest Hemingway would lead a peripatetic and bohemian life, but his family were religious, hardworking, and solidly middle-class people, eminently respectable, just the kind of Midwestern folk who helped build that part of the country from prairies into an economic powerhouse in the decades before and after the Civil War. They were successful, morally straitlaced when that was the rule in their level of society, confident that their material success was the just reward for their virtuous private lives.

And yet several of his antecedents were strange. His mother's father assembled the family and the servants every morning to pray on their knees. Not so unusual, maybe, for the time (though it is odd to think of the ne plus ultra literary modernist beginning his days this way). But Ernest Hall prayed looking up with his arms stretched upward, as if locked in a face-to-face with God. The man cut a strange figure in suburban Oak Park, for he wore his clothes "much too large" because, according to his granddaughter, he could not abide clothing touching his skin, "lest he feel bound in any way." Born in Sheffield, England, in 1840, Hall was educated in London; when he was fifteen, his father brought his extended family to

America, eventually settling in Dyersville, Iowa, probably because he had family or friends from England in the area.

Another English family, the Hancocks, had settled nearby in Iowa, and Ernest Hall always remembered that he met his future wife, Caroline Hancock, on an occasion that evoked their dual allegiances: a cricket match held in Dyersville on the Fourth of July. Originally from Somerset County in the U.K., Alexander Hancock was a sea captain who lost a young wife. Immigrating with his three children—Caroline, Annie, and Benjamin Tyley—to Australia after taking them around the world on his ship, the *Elizabeth,* he found he didn't like Australia and brought his children to Iowa in 1854. Caroline, born in 1843, had to wait for Ernest Hall when the Civil War intervened. Hall fought with the 1st Iowa Cavalry for under a year, discharged "for wounds" in 1862 in Butler, Missouri; he had taken an enemy minié ball in his thigh, one of the most damaging weapons in the Confederate arsenal. (His grandson would carry fragments from enemy weapons in *his* leg.) Before the war Ernest Hall had journeyed down the Mississippi as far as Louisiana; after marrying Caroline in 1865, they moved to Chicago, where they had two children, Leicester, born in 1874 and Grace, Ernest Hemingway's mother, born in 1872. After establishing, with his brother-in-law, William Randall, a wholesale cutlery firm in Chicago, Ernest Hall moved his family to the new Chicago suburb of Oak Park, eventually settling at 439 North Oak Park Avenue.

Across the street from the Halls' Victorian house stood a similar large home, where lived Anson and Adelaide Hemingway, Ernest Hemingway's paternal grandparents. Ernest Hall, a pillar of Grace Episcopal Church, boasted about his English stock. Anson Hemingway was descended from Ralph Hemingway, who came to America with the Great Migration, and through him from a line of Puritan and Congregationalist ministers. Ernest Hemingway's sister Marcelline, the family historian, wrote that it was rumored that a Hemingway was the first student at Yale, and indeed, a Jacob Hemingway was the first to enter the new college in 1672.

Anson Hemingway's father, Allen Hemingway, had come to Chicago from East Plymouth, Connecticut, in 1854, saying he wanted to find a farm for his boys. In Connecticut he had worked for a clock manufacturer, which in 1853 became the Seth Thomas Clock Company; possibly he resolved to go west when it became clear he would not have an advantageous place in the newly incorporated company. He had fathered five children with his first wife, Marietta; after her death he and Harriet Louisa Tyler had one son, Anson. The only Hemingway son who survived the Civil War, Anson fought in the bloody Battle of Vicksburg in 1863 with the 72nd Illinois

Regiment; he later received a commission and served as first lieutenant—at the age of twenty—in Company H of the Colored 70th Regiment. On his discharge he signed on with the Freedmen's Bureau in Natchez, finding work for freed slaves on Southern plantations. He came north in 1866 and attended Wheaton Academy (later Wheaton College), founded by Wesleyan abolitionists. A devout Christian who had undergone a conversion experience in 1859, Anson met Adelaide Edmonds, three years older than he, his first night at Wheaton at a prayer meeting; they married two years later. Adelaide, a schoolteacher when she married, would become the only grandmother Ernest Hemingway knew, fondly remembered for telling him that the only regrets she had in life were the things she hadn't done.

After Wheaton, Anson Hemingway opened a small real estate office in Chicago, settling into a house in Oak Park at the corner of Oak Park Avenue and Superior Street when children began to arrive. He sold real estate for eight years, but put most of his energies into religion, in 1878 leaving real estate to become general secretary of the Chicago YMCA. He had been involved in the YMCA, an organization founded in 1844, for several years. His first Civil War regiment, quartered at Camp Douglas outside Chicago, had been known as the "YMCA regiment" for its association with evangelist and YMCA official Dwight Moody, who saw the Civil War as an opportunity to proselytize among the new recruits. Anson Hemingway's great friendship with Moody, president of the Chicago YMCA from 1865 to 1870, and his tenure at the YMCA confirmed his deeply felt spirituality. Typically for a devout Christian of his day, he was opposed to such habits as smoking, drinking, dancing, and card playing, among other things. Though most of Anson and Adelaide's children were born before he took the YMCA job, evidently evangelical work was not financially feasible for a man with a growing family, for Anson left to reopen his real estate practice in 1888, with an office at 189 LaSalle Street in the city, now announcing that he specialized in suburban properties. At this point area real estate was becoming a big business: Chicago was enjoying a boom as the nation's largest railroad hub and the center for grain and livestock processing and shipping, and the real estate business was equally vibrant. By the time of the birth of Ernest Hemingway's father, Clarence, in 1871, Anson's business was thriving. He was able eventually to send all six of his children to Oberlin College in Ohio.

Anson Hemingway was a handsome man, but he had a pigeon breast, or a protrusion of the sternum and rib cage. A slight deformity common in his time, it often appeared with mitral valve prolapse—a bad heart, from which Anson suffered. The condition was said to be caused by rickets.

Whether this contributed to his son Clarence's decision to become a doctor is not known, but Dr. Hemingway would notably make a point of insisting that his patients (and his family) eat lots of vegetables to avert the rickets that caused pigeon breast. Ernest's father, Clarence, known as Ed, himself matured to be a good-looking, bearded man with an intense gaze who stood straight and tall. Prompted, perhaps, by his mother, who studied botany and astronomy at Wheaton College, Ed grew up with strong feelings about nature and the out-of-doors. His children remembered him talking about a period of some months spent with the Sioux in South Dakota and a month spent cooking for a government surveying team in the Smoky Mountains—which he particularly enjoyed. His youngest daughter, Carol, with some pride, later wrote, "Here are the things my father could do:

> He could saw down a tree and let it drop exactly where he wanted. He could chop wood and make a good fire under any weather circumstances, with a minimum of fuss. He could milk a cow, hitch up and drive a horse, pitch hay, clean a chicken or any other animal, and clean and cook the fish he caught. He made pickles, jam, and sauerkraut in the summer months and special shore dinners.

Ed spent three years at Oberlin, which had become the Hemingway family's favorite college. During this time he began his long association with the Agassiz Club, a fellowship that followed the teachings of the Swiss-born Harvard professor and naturalist Louis Agassiz, including the precept that amateurs (especially children) could best learn about the life and earth sciences by getting outside and studying nature firsthand. Ed delivered two papers on "The Extermination of the American Buffalo" before the Oberlin chapter of the Agassiz Club; he would later open an Oak Park chapter, whose meetings were religiously attended by all of his children, but especially Ernest. Ed's study at Oberlin was followed by enrollment at Rush Medical College in Chicago. A "Rush doctor" was highly esteemed in the nineteenth century, and Ed could expect a prosperous practice. He studied in Edinburgh in 1895, followed by a European tour, and after his graduation served an apprenticeship with local Oak Park doctor William R. Lewis.

With Dr. Lewis, Ed Hemingway tended the wife of his neighbor, Ernest Hall, when Caroline was diagnosed with cancer in 1894, at the age of forty-nine. At this point he renewed his acquaintance with Ernest's daughter, Grace Hall, now twenty, five feet eight inches tall, a buxom woman with beautiful "English" coloring: porcelain white skin with red cheeks and blue eyes. Among Ernest Hall's antecedents was Edward Miller, an eighteenth-century musician of some note, a church organist and composer. (His son, William Edward Miller, was also a talented professional musician for a time.) The Hall passion for music reached perhaps its highest expression in Grace Hall, who had an excellent voice and began to think as an adolescent of a serious singing career. Ernest Hall encouraged the musical education of his family; he had sent to England for his wife's parlor organ. The family often made music together. Ernest Hall was a baritone; his wife, Caroline, a soprano; Caroline's brother, Tyley (who lived with the family), a tenor; and the children had fine contralto voices. Grace took lessons in piano, violin, and voice. Ernest Hall regularly took Grace and her brother, Leicester, to the opera and other musical performances in Chicago.

In 1886, when Grace was fourteen, Ernest Hall moved his family to a substantial turreted house at 439 North Oak Park Avenue, equipped with a bathroom and a telephone, which were coming to be necessary accoutrements for the aspiring middle class. Her robust physique as an adult belied Grace's medical history, as she had nearly died from a run of childhood diseases that were leading causes of death among nineteenth-century children, but are now treatable with antibiotics. All derived from streptococci bacteria, which first laid her low with scarlet fever. In those days, the bacteria often led to rheumatic fever. The combination of scarlet and rheumatic fevers often led to sight impairment, and indeed Grace Hall often told the story of her blindness and the seemingly magical restoration of her sight. Rheumatic fever in children at that time often led as well, as it did with Grace, to St. Vitus's dance (now known as Sydenham's chorea); jerking limbs were this disease's more frightening symptoms—to the onlooker but also the patient. As a result of this barrage of disease, Grace's eyesight remained poor, and she was especially bothered by bright lights. (Later, her children remembered that the lights in the family home were kept dimmer than they might have been when they were growing up.)

Grace Hall and Clarence Hemingway had crossed each other's paths at Oak Park High School without particularly noticing each other. Grace later told her children that she found Ed—Clarence—thin and awkward, his well-mended clothes often outgrown. But Grace was writing to Ed in a teasing exchange as early as 1890, and a flirtatious 1893 letter from Grace assures him that she sees no "impropriety" in his writing to her father. Writing to Ed at the medical school, she apologizes for having used the word "butcher" in connection with doctoring, and asks Ed whether he can "prescribe for affection of the heart."

Though Grace would always be more permissive than Ed, both were devout, and they soon found they had much else in common. They exchanged letters when he went to Edinburgh to study in the spring of 1895, followed by a tour of the rest of Europe. Grace described how much she enjoyed the voice lessons she had recently started giving, and confided her hope to study in New York and pursue a career as an opera singer. In July she reported that she was probably leaving for New York, and she seems to have departed that fall. No letters from her year in New York survive, but there must have been correspondence, and it seems likely that Ed would steadily petition that she return to Oak Park.

Grace Hall and her family had followed the career of the Austrian-born singer Louisa Kapp-Young Cappiani, who had retired from the stage to give voice lessons, "known all over the country, as well as in Europe, as the great voice builder and teacher of perfect singing." Mme. Cappiani, as she was known, had appeared at the 1893 Columbian Exposition, or the Chicago World's Fair, and had lectured on the teaching of singing and training required of a musical hopeful. It seems clear that Grace met Mme. Cappiani at the Exposition and received some encouragement from her; at any rate, Grace made the journey to New York in the fall of 1895 to study with the teacher. She would always tell her family that she lived at the Art Students League during her time in the city, but records show that the League never accommodated residents. Her youngest son later noted that she settled "in upper Manhattan" for her music studies, and Grace's correspondence with a cousin, Mallinson Randall, indicates she stayed with him and his wife on West 130th Street, near St. Andrew's Church, where Randall was choirmaster.

During her New York year Grace made her singing debut at Madison Square Garden under the direction of Anton Seidl, the conductor of the Metropolitan Opera (as well as the musical director of the New York Philharmonic). Her reviews were said to have been excellent, but Grace remembered only that the stage lights so bothered her eyes that she was frightened off pursuing a singing career. It seems unlikely that this detail alone stood between her and the profession, but she never gave another explanation. It is likely, on the other hand, that Ed Hemingway was unremitting in his courtship of her by letter while she was in New York. Afterward, Ernest Hall took Grace on a whirlwind tour of Europe in the summer of 1896. From the ship, the R.M.S. *Campania,* she wrote Ed that she was flirting "with any person of the male persuasion," and made suggestive reference to "a tender sweet old red sofa." Grace returned to Oak Park and married Ed Hemingway on October 1.

Had Grace seriously considered a lifelong career as a musical performer?

When Mme. Cappiani spoke in Chicago at the 1893 World's Fair, her topic was "Voice Culture as a Means of Independence to Women," and, though she clearly laid out the steps a woman should take in pursuing a profession as a singer, she also clearly set forth what a woman trained in singing can bring to family life: "The musically well-educated woman in private life . . . becomes an anchor of hope and safety in case the husband is overtaken by sickness or other reverses. In such cases—and only in such [Mme. Cappiani cautioned], the wife will be the breadwinner. . . . Welfare and independence will then soon re-enter the threatened household; and all this by the acquired charm of music." Grace took this to heart. By the time of her marriage, she had a sizable roster of voice and musical instrument students and, she told her husband, loved the work: "You have no idea, how fond I am of my girls [her students], it is such a constant joy to feel that I have the power to mould them in some degree." In the early days of the marriage, when Ed was building his practice, her financial support was essential. The doctor only earned $50 in some months, though his obstetrical practice grew rapidly. Grace's contribution from the lessons was what enabled the Hemingways to take their place in the middle class.

As a music teaching professional, Grace seems to have had supreme self-confidence. She is said to have charged $8 an hour for her teaching, although that figure is surely too high. Similarly, she is said to have earned as much as a thousand dollars a month—again, an unlikely sum. Whatever her fees, she clearly brought in far more than did her husband. Though her son Ernest never cited this imbalance directly, his general complaint against his mother, that she had emasculated her husband, clearly had some of its beginnings here. He had a similar complaint about what he saw as his mother's extravagance, spending money on herself rather than her family. At the age of seven, Ernest would remember, he saw a bill for a hat his mother ordered from Marshall Field's department store in Chicago; it was $135, he noted—again, probably an absurdly elevated figure—but Ernest, ever one to nurse resentments, clung to this story as evidence of his mother's financial selfishness.

Grace *was* extravagant. She had a generous, expansive, and loving nature. Apparently her personal presence was extraordinary; when she entered a room, everyone was immediately aware of her. Her youngest daughter, Carol, said, "Living with Mother was a bit like living with someone on the stage." From her European tour she brought back thirty-five pairs of gloves, since duty fees were slapped onto three dozen pairs; she bragged that her wedding gown had ninety yards of organdy. Her energy was inexhaustible. She gave public musical performances all around the Chicago area (presumably in venues without the blinding footlights of Madison Square Garden) and composed numerous songs whose words and music a Chicago company published, bringing her modest royalties each year. Daughter Marcelline remembers waking up in the middle of the night and hearing her mother at the piano; the melodies often came to her in dreams, said Grace, and unless she got them down right away they were lost. Most striking, however, were the enthusiasm and high spirits she brought to the raising of the children, who began to arrive with some regularity a year after she and Ed married.

Marcelline Doris came first, in January 1898, and Ernest Miller (both his names were from Grace's family) a year and a half later, on July 21, 1899. Ursula (1902) and Madelaine (Sunny) would follow not long after, and the Hemingways would later have two more children, born seven years after Sunny's birth in 1904, Carol, born in 1911, and another son, Leicester, born in 1915. Grace's devotion to her children when they were young was extraordinary. For each child she created what she called baby books, not so different in ambition from the prefabricated ones common today among new parents—who generally tire of filling in the blanks after an initial burst of enthusiasm. Grace's baby books, or scrapbooks, were massive affairs, bursting with clippings, photographs, and Grace's handwritten descriptions and anecdotes. And they were multivolume: Ernest's took up five books, covering his birth to the age of eighteen (though Grace only filled the fifth book's earliest pages, so disappointed was she in his progress after his high school graduation). Such particulars as height and weight were recorded, along with notes on what he liked to eat, his sleeping habits, his earliest words, and so on. Entire pages are given over to Ernest's teeth, for example, at each stage of babyhood and childhood. Each gift delivered to the newborn was recorded, and the floral arrangements sent in honor of the new arrival were meticulously described down to the last lily. Grace later said she "burned the midnight oil to produce" the baby books, and indeed there is something more than a little excessive—perhaps manic—in her enterprise. Though she had servants to help with childcare, she breast-fed each child in turn. With children arriving so frequently, she had to have been exhausted for the first months of each child's life—especially given the needs and desires of the preceding children.

Grace's maternal energies were not called into play in the more quotidian aspects of childcare, however. "Beyond singing lullabies and breast-feeding," her son Leicester later wrote, "our mother lacked domestic talents. She abhorred didies [diapers], deficient manners, stomach upsets, house-cleaning, and cooking." Her mother had raised her that way: "There is no use any woman getting into the kitchen if she can help it," Caroline Hancock Hall had told her. Similarly, a playmate noted that Grace never learned to sweep, "and said she was never going to, because then she would have to do it." Grace seldom cooked, and the exceptions were notable, as when she successfully followed a recipe for teacake, a British favorite served with melted butter. She then baked the specialty for Boxing Day (observed in the Anglophile Hall/Hemingway household), but otherwise prepared food only when dire necessity demanded.

It was Ed who enjoyed cooking, having perfected his technique preparing food for the survey team in the Smokies. He especially loved to bake— he made excellent pies—and was famous for his doughnuts. Though the Hemingways employed a cook, and though Grace presumably was consulted about menus, it was Ed who saw to the family's significant food supplies: barrels of apples and potatoes, and jar after jar of vegetables, fruits, and other foodstuffs he had put up himself. Similarly, he took charge of the laundry, taking the dirty clothes to the laundress, and oversaw the child—for a long time it was Ernest's job—who sorted them into piles for the children to carry upstairs and stow. "My mother was exempt from household chores," said Carol, "because she must have time to practice her music." Their father's constant refrain was, "Don't disturb your mother."

Yet Grace Hemingway did her part to ensure that childhood was an uncommonly rich time for the young Hemingways. With her thrilling voice she read to them in the evenings: Dickens, Twain, Robert Louis Stevenson, *Pilgrim's Progress.* She took each child in turn on a trip east to see relatives and tour historic Boston, the centerpiece of the journey being a visit to Nantucket of a week or more, creating indelible, sunny memories of the sea and boats and the shore. It was a time for Grace and the children to get to know each other.

In these years, the American upper middle class was coming of age, discovering the ways in which prosperity could enable them to realize their economic, cultural, and social aspirations through their children. The young doctor and his cultured wife, both from eminently respectable families, were ideally situated to pursue this path, which led almost inevitably to the newly created American suburbs. Ed and Grace put a lot of thought into the raising of the children even before they began to arrive. Oak Park, Ed later wrote to his youngest daughter in a special birthday letter, seemed the ideal place to raise a family. "We planned a long time before our children were born," he wrote, "that our children should have good, healthy bodies and some good food and a nice place to live and grow up without all the naughty people of the cities to bother them." They were determined

The family, 1906. From left to right: Marcelline, Sunny, Ed, Grace, Ursula, and Ernest.

that their offspring make good use of the cultural resources of Chicago while they derived all the benefits of suburban living touted at the turn of the twentieth century: wholesome air, safe streets, plenty of young families to provide suitable playmates for their offspring.

Grace and Ed set the scene for vivid childhood memories in the summer of 1898, when they visited a Hall cousin near the north shore of Lake Michigan, at Bear Lake, later known as Walloon Lake, near Petoskey. The Hemingways bought a plot of land fronting the clear and cold, spring-fed lake from Henry Bacon, and made plans to build a cottage there the following summer, when Ernest was a newborn. By the summer of 1900 a small, two-bedroom cottage had been built, with a huge, seven-foot fireplace and a long screened porch looking out over the lake, as well as a dock where they tied up the family's succession of rowboats. Grace named the place Windemere, after the English lake of Wordsworth and Scott (the Hemingways left out the first of the two "r"s). At Windemere there was an outhouse and no bathtub, and in the kitchen, a wood stove for cooking and a hand pump in the sink. Great organization was required to move the growing Hemingway family en masse from Oak Park to Walloon Lake each year, involving several trains, a steamer, and finally a rowboat, but somehow they all got there with most of their belongings intact, ready to enjoy a summer of picnicking, boating, swimming, and fishing and hunting.

Ernest, who killed himself with a gun and whose father killed himself with a gun, was around guns from the very start. As a little baby, his mother said, she held him in her left arm while she shot a pistol with her right, Ernest shouting with delight at every report. Grace recorded his accomplishment in his baby book: before he was three, she wrote, "Ernest shoots well with his gun and loads it and cocks it himself." By his fourth birthday his grandfather Hall was asking about "that great hunter Ernest Miller." The Hemingway girls were taught about guns just as Ernest was, and every child learned the proper care of firearms and how to use them safely. As the children grew, target practice, held on Sundays, was the high point of the week; Ernest was an accomplished wing shot by the

About thirteen, with a good catch, ca. 1912

age of ten. He also developed a passion for fishing at a young age, going fishing with his father as a two-year-old, wrote Grace, and successfully landing the biggest fish of the day. Walloon Lake abounded in perch, large-mouth bass, pike, and bluegills, and the toddler Ernest learned to eat what he called "hish" with gusto. Ed Hemingway taught that it was wrong to shoot an animal or catch a fish unless it was to be eaten.

Dr. Hemingway taught his children about life outdoors. His son was an enthusiastic member of the Oak Park branch of the Agassiz Club. From Ed, Ernest learned how to survive in the wilderness, how to walk like an Indian, how to preserve and stuff animals after they were dead, how to tie flies to catch trout, and countless other lessons about the out-of-doors. The Agassiz Club was in his young mind even on his Nantucket trip, when he wrote his father asking him whether it would be worth the two dollars needed to buy the foot of an albatross for the club. In later years Ernest would make a point of learning the best way to do things—choosing a wine, for example, or writing in a café, or cooking a trout properly, or the art of bullfighting—indeed, some say Hemingway fetishized the proper ways of doing things at the expense of his emotions, especially as he grew older. (That is often his message, in fact, in many of the Nick Adams stories; for example, in "The Big Two-Hearted River." The horrors of mental turmoil and shell shock can be kept at bay by the mechanics of simple acts performed well, like hiking, packing a knapsack, fishing, and camp cooking.)

But Ernest commonly boasted, his mother wrote in his baby book, that he was "'fraid of nothing," which of course meant he knew fear, however much he could rise above it. Grace recorded other bits in the baby book that would embarrass any child: he sang "Fee blind mice / See how day run"; he had a dimple in each cheek, and a Cupid's bow of a mouth. "Ernest is a very loving boy," wrote Grace. "He cuddles round my neck and says, 'I'm Mama's little mink ain't I. Will you be my Mama Mink?'"

The photographs Grace pasted into Ernest's baby books show an infant and toddler in dresses, with bonnets and long hair, looking angelic. Grace described his "white lacey dress with Pink bows" in the caption. Sometimes he appeared in pink gingham frocks with Battenburg lace collars and crocheted bonnets; sometimes his hair was cut short, boyishly, while at other times it was long, or styled into a shoulder-length bob matching his sister Marcelline's. Of course many boys were dressed as girls at the turn of the century. The practice was an expression of a general sentimentalization of childhood, wherein innocence—associated with what was thought to be the gentler, fairer sex—was highly prized. Frances Hodgson Burnett's *Little Lord Fauntleroy* (1885) touched off a fad for shoulder-length curls, often rendering little boys indistinguishable from little girls. But after the first year boys were generally taken out of dresses and put in male clothing. What is remarkable in the case of Grace's firstborn children, however, is how often, after the first year, Marcelline and Ernest alternated between being dressed as girls and as boys.

For whether as girls or boys, Ernest and his older sister were dressed alike. For some reason of her own—perhaps in a determination to bring her often thwarted creativity to child-raising—Grace decided, soon after Ernest's birth, to treat him and his sister, eighteen months older, as twins. Later she would say she always wanted twins. Marcelline would remember that she and her brother had matching dolls and matching tea sets for their dolls, as well as matching air rifles. Grace wanted the children to *feel* like twins, so she encouraged them to do everything together: to fish and hike,

Ernest and his older sister, Marcelline, ca. 1901. Grace Hemingway
enjoyed dressing them alike—here, as girls.

to wheel their dolls in their dolls' carriages. Photographs of the pair at Windemere show them both in overalls with Dutch boy haircuts, cut straight across on the sides and back, with severe bangs.

Other photographs of Marcelline and Ernest around 1902 suggest that Grace had clothed them androgynously well after the children were old enough to know what was going on. The chubby toddler, his legs plump under a dress, did not look out of place, but the three-and-a-half-year-old Ernest displays long, slender legs in white stockings and Mary Jane–type shoes beneath his knee-length dress, sporting an outsize flowered hat on his head. The effect is decidedly odd—which is borne out by a remark Ernest made soon after these photographs were taken: "He was quite fearful before Christmas," Grace wrote in his baby book, "that Santa Claus would know he was a boy, because he wore just the same clothes as his sister."

Grace Hemingway, it seems, made much of hair. Ernest was blond at birth, with blue eyes, and remained so until about the age of five; Marcelline's hair was brown. Grace emphasized that Ernest, and later Sunny and the baby, Leicester, had Hall coloring—though Ernest's eyes would become brown about when his hair did. "His hair is yellow," noted Grace with satisfaction in one of his baby books, "worn in bangs, with curly ends round his head." Grace thought highly of blond hair, but especially prized red hair, and was disappointed that none of her children were redheads. "Mother always pointed it out to us as the most beautiful hair in the world," wrote Marcelline, noting that Ernest's first wife, Hadley, had hair the shade of auburn Grace most favored. Judging from the attention she paid to her two first children's hairstyles, she paid equal attention to the desirability of certain cuts, impressing on them, perhaps demonstrating on their younger siblings, the curve of a curl or the vulnerable spot at the nape of the neck, laid bare by a little boy's haircut such as those she had given both Ernest and his sister. It is not altogether surprising that Ernest would develop a fascination with hair—its color, its texture, its length—that became nothing less than an erotic fetish in the grown man. He would enact erotic scenarios regarding hair color and sex that each of his four wives would participate in. He and Hadley played out a drama in which he grew his hair while she kept hers trimmed until, when they were off on a skiing holiday and none of their city friends would see, their hair was the same length. In early drafts of *A Moveable Feast,* his memoir about his youth with Hadley in Paris, he writes of their exchanges about hair—and how their haircuts looked and felt—and alludes to the changes their gender-challenging haircutting wrought in their sexual practices—which they characterize as "secret pleasures" (*AMF,* 183–192).

The nature of what was going on in young Ernest's mind and psyche concerning androgynous clothing and hairstyles is by no means clear, however. It was overlaid with his apprehension of the ways his mother herself challenged traditional sex roles: with her profession and with what Ernest came to think was her dominance in their household—about which Ernest apparently had then and would demonstrably have later very mixed feelings.

To the two children, the twinning must have been at times pleasurable and at times annoying or embarrassing, especially as the practice continued. Marcelline was made to repeat her year in kindergarten so that she and Ernest could enter the first grade together. After Ernest's death in 1961, Marcelline would write a memoir about family life, and among the bits edited out was a protracted description of a friend's attempt to do something with Marcelline's Dutch boy haircut. The result was what one might expect from two little girls and a pair of scissors. Grace was not just dismayed by the state of her daughter's hair, she was enraged, the act somehow threatening her sense of propriety or even her dominion over her children. "I want you to remember this as long as you live," she told Marcelline, forcing her to wear a baby bonnet belonging to the youngest sibling, Sunny, until her hair grew out. After two weeks, Marcelline's second-grade teacher spoke up in the mortified girl's defense, and the punishment was ended. Shortly after, the same teacher recommended Marcelline be moved up into the third grade, and for the rest of grammar school she and Ernest were in separate grades. Between seventh and eighth grades, however, Marcelline was taken out of school for a year, thus entering high school with Ernest and graduating with him. The reasons Ed and Grace gave the girl for this action are at once practical and mystifying: they told her that, first of all, they wanted her to concentrate on music and gymnastic dance lessons; second, they had "strong-minded" theories, Marcelline said later, about child-rearing, "and one of them was that girls ought not to be kept in school and rushed through strenuous routines during the difficult maturing times of the early teens." For Marcelline and Ernest, the result was that through five difficult, adolescent years they were in the same classroom—with predictable social embarrassments and conflicts. They were Grace's favorite children, Marcelline because she was first and Ernest because he was the first boy—and competition between them was inevitable. Especially humiliating was Grace's insistence that Ernest escort Marcelline to the first high school dance they attended.

Marcelline and Ernest's relationship over the years was, as one might expect, fraught. They were extremely close as very young children and again in adolescence and immediately thereafter. Marcelline seems to have undergone a major personality change as she reached adulthood and married, seemingly adopting all of her mother's worst qualities, eventually becoming a clubwoman who dabbled in the arts. (Even her mother evidently came to dislike her.) Ernest would develop a violent hatred for his older sister, especially after a major quarrel following their father's death and a later disagreement about the fate of Windemere. The relationship with his sister touched chords in his emotional nature to which he reacted very strongly, suggesting how much the early twinning complicated his development.

Yet Ernest owed many of his best qualities to his mother: the youngest girl, Carol, thought Grace "was a very big and good influence on him in his early years." (Carol also remarked about her brother, "He's the one who's most like her.") For the first nine years of their marriage, Grace, Ed, and their growing brood lived in Ernest Hall's generously sized house at 439 North Oak Park Avenue, directly across from Anson and Adelaide Hemingway's home. Aside from the morning prayer regimen—conducted with the entire family on their knees—Ernest Hall was an easygoing, loving man. His brother-in-law, Benjamin Tyley Hancock, known as Uncle Tyley, lived there when he was not on the road selling Miller Hall bedsteads, and endeared himself to the young family. Marcelline, Ernest, Ursula, and Sunny were all born in the house's front bedroom. For his part, Ernest Hall was extremely solicitous about his family, especially in letters from the West Coast, where he went every winter, in part to see his other child, Leicester, who had settled there after a brief, mysteriously disastrous stint following the Gold Rush up to Alaska. Hall commented almost daily on the performance of stocks or bonds that either he or his daughter held, constantly urged the doctor (whom he addressed as "dear boy" and called "the blessed doctor") not to work so hard, commenting often, in a somewhat curious turn of phrase, that he hoped the children were "laying up stores of happy, sunshiney memories." Ernest Hall and his daughter initiated the custom of affixing to each letter "tussies," or hugs, symbolized by several circles at a letter's end; a dot in a circle meant a hug and a kiss. "I trust you are all well and the Doctor growing fat and sassy with the children growing like weeds," he wrote in the summer of 1901 on a trip to England.

But Ernest Hall returned from his trip west in 1904 with Bright's disease, a kidney ailment then almost uniformly fatal, and died in May 1905. Uncle Tyley and the Hemingways were rudderless, suddenly, and must have felt at loose ends living on in the Hall home. Moving was to be the least of the changes rung in the wake of the patriarch's death.

* * *

Fifty years later, Ernest Hemingway wrote to a young friend in the aftermath of his mother's death. He admitted that his feelings started to change toward his mother only after what he perceived was a change in how she treated his father; only then did he cease to love her. In any case, he said, it meant little now that she was dead. Perhaps written in a sentimental moment, this letter indicates a willingness to consider Grace's good qualities, which he otherwise almost never entertained. He knew that his hatred was unreasonable, but insisted that no one could speak as harshly as he was wont without cause. So he fixed a time when things soured. Before then the Hemingways lived in a sort of domestic Eden, insular and self-sufficient, fully functional.

Things began to fall apart, according to Ernest, around the time that Ernest Hall died—just when the boy was reaching the age at which he could form and keep memories. It is important to note that when Ernest spoke about his mother in later years he usually did so toward a particular end. It often served his purposes to present his father as a henpecked husband, dominated and hounded by an overbearing wife. He also had to make it sound as if his anger was justified, so found bases for it in what he presented as facts but really were imagination. One remark pinned the beginning of what he saw as the deterioration of his parents' marriage on the death of Ernest Hall. Everything between them before the death of his grandfather, he said, was fine, because he was strict with his daughter and "controlled her terrible selfishness and conceit." Ernest would later indulge in some fancy emotional footwork in childhood revisionism after his father's suicide. He blamed his mother for emasculating his father, wearing him down until he had no strength to weather crises of confidence. One such crisis, Ernest believed, led to his suicide.

There is no question, however, that the life of the Hemingway family was transformed with Ernest Hall's death, though hardly for the reasons Ernest later insisted on. It is true, in fact, that Grace came into her own at this juncture, though the transformation in her was hardly sinister. She inherited some money when her father died, and resolved to build a new house for her growing brood—one that could accommodate both her husband's practice and her own interests and professional activities. For "years," according to one biographer, Grace had been reading about architecture and specifically home design, and she had pronounced ideas on many aspects of the subject. She hired an architect and put her father's property on the market, moving her family to a rented house, and bought a lot on the corner of Kenilworth Avenue and Iowa Street. Construction began in spring 1906; in the fireplace stone was laid a collection of family keepsakes.

It is commonplace among Hemingway biographers to blame Grace Hemingway, when not for her "careerist zeal," for designing a house "that was much too grand for them" and strained the family finances, this despite the lack of any indication that the Hemingways ever quarreled about money. There is no evidence, for instance, that they went into debt to build the house. And the house was only as "grand" as was necessary for a family with two working parents, an uncle who was a regular boarder, six children, and one or two sleep-in servants. The family needed eight bedrooms; even at that, some of the girls would need to double up. Rather, Grace's involvement in the building of the house became a means for her to express herself creatively and to demonstrate her knack for imaginative practical solutions to domestic issues. The kitchen, for instance, was carefully thought out according to the latest trends in efficiency; counters, for example, were higher than usual to accommodate both Grace and Ed, both tall. The pantry was abolished as a thing of the past; food and cooking implements were stored in cupboards, themselves a kitchen novelty. Grace

The family's home after 1906, designed by Grace Hemingway,
at 600 North Kenilworth, Oak Park, Illinois

extended the kitchen to include areas in the basement that held built-in tubs for the wash, cement cabinets for preserved food, and a gas burner on which the doctor could both demonstrate the making of bullets for his children and, as one observer has noted, heat candy for taffy pulls.

The rooms for the doctor's office were separated from the living room by a door with a frosted panel on which was etched the Hemingway family crest, devised by Grace and Ed. Bookshelves lined his anteroom, filled both with books and examples of his taxidermy skills. A telephone occupied a place at the dining room table, in case patients called the doctor at mealtime. At the other end of the living room (which had what Marcelline described as a "severely modern" fireplace) was the house's most distinguishing feature: Grace's music room, designed according to the latest acoustical specifications. It was thirty feet square with a ceiling fifteen feet high, which could accommodate a balcony for spectators. On the radiators were placed large, galvanized containers of water, which Grace had read would keep the Steinway grand piano in tune (there was another piano in the dining room for the children's use). On a rug-draped platform Grace's students presented their performances, and on one wall, where Grace hoped one day to install a pipe organ, hung a portrait of the children's great-great-grandfather, William Edward Miller, who was, like his father, musical, but gave it up as a worldly pursuit when he became a Wesleyan minister late in life.

While the design of the Hemingway house was quite practical in its details, it seems to have been true that Oak Parkers believed that the house was too expensive for the family, and that they talked about it. A playmate of Marcelline's remembered just how large the house seemed, and the "unconventional" planning that appeared to have gone into it. "It had a touch of the grandiose," she observed, "which they evidently couldn't afford." The house was three full stories tall and drew neighborhood attention.

Ernest and Marcelline started first grade at the Lowell School while the house on Kenilworth Avenue was being built. They both learned to read quickly. Their rented house was next door to Oak Park's public library, called the Scoville Institute. Evidently the Hemingways no longer had a nursemaid, or if they had one her attentions were devoted to the younger girls, for brother and sister went every day after school to the Scoville, where they read books in small chairs at low tables until the librarian sent them home at dinnertime. In fall 1906, when the move into the new house was complete, the two eldest children transferred to the Oliver Wendell Holmes School.

The Oak Park house was not the Hemingways' only construction project. Around the time Ursula was born, they added a kitchen wing to the cottage at Walloon Lake; later, a separate three-bedroom structure was added. As the family grew, so did the responsibilities. Washday at Windemere was a good example. Ed had concocted a cleaning solution that he believed would clean clothes, linen, and bedding without soaping or rubbing. As this was added, loads of wash were boiled in two separate boilers. When a boiler had cooled a little, Ed and one of the children carried it precariously down to the lake, where the other children were waiting, standing waist-deep in the water, to rinse each item. Ed helped them wring out the washing and carry it up to the clothesline behind the cottage. As Marcelline later pointed out, the children may have gone barefoot and dressed only in overalls, but starched petticoats and ruffles, not to mention the considerable amount of bedding and linens (towels alone!), made for an enormous Windemere chore. Characteristically, Grace had devised a schedule that rotated the cooking duties, so that she had to cook only two nights in every eight. On the first two nights of a given period, she and her third daughter (Sunny) cooked; for the next two, the mother's helper (Ruth Arnold) and the youngest girl (Carol) cooked; on the next two, Marcelline and a school friend; and on the last two nights, Ed and Ernest. "Even at that age I realized it was a bit strange, the way things were done," remembered a family friend, who also noted, "there was no supervision of any kind in the kitchen."

Management of such a large family could border on the comical. Ed's bobwhite whistle summoned the children when they got separated in crowds, often on trips to the circus or state fairs or to Chicago's zoo or the Field Museum, a natural history museum opened in 1893 and a Hemingway favorite. The children were expected to assemble "instantly," said Marcelline. At Windemere the children received lifesaving lessons. Ed would take out the rowboat and rock it until it capsized, telling the children to swim to shore or to climb on top of the boat. Later, he dropped them off fully clothed in water over their heads and timed them as they removed shoes and clothes and swam to shore. The children were exceedingly competitive with each other.

Though outright rebellion wasn't to catch hold among the Hemingway children until adolescence, early on they chafed at parental restrictions that seemed straight out of the Victorian age. Ed, with his New England and Puritan ancestry, his upbringing by a follower of the evangelical Dwight Moody, and his exposure to Protestant strictness at Oberlin College, took a hard line when it came to what he would and would not allow for his family. In 1886 he had joined a group called the "Band of Hope," pledging he would not indulge in "wine, beer, intoxicating liquors, tobacco, and swearing." He also spoke against dancing, card playing, and gambling. Grace, who had asked Ed flirtatiously in an 1893 letter whether he frowned on theatergoing, was more lenient than her husband. Ernest Hall had a billiard table in his home and had taught his daughter to play what many saw as a morally suspect game. For the early years of their marriage, Grace's husband had accepted—willingly or not—her father's nightly pipe after supper, enjoyed with his brother-in-law, Uncle Tyley, behind closed doors in the parlor. Grace liked games in general and favored social dancing—the latter becoming a battleground when the girls reached adolescence.

Not surprisingly, Ed Hemingway was the disciplinarian of the family. Like many children, the Hemingway offspring knew that, rather than bringing major issues to their father and receiving an automatic no, they should, rather, work on their mother first, thus making it more likely that Ed would eventually agree. He felt free to spank for misbehaving, and often brought out his razor strop. (Grace used her hairbrush when necessary.) But the children found Ed's strict rules were less oppressive when they were aware of them. It was their father's moodiness that was the problem. "My father's dimpled cheeks and charming smile," wrote Marcelline, could change in an instant to the stern, taut mouth and piercing look which was his disciplinary self. Sometimes the change from being gay to being stern was so abrupt that we were not prepared for the shock that came, when one minute Daddy would have his arm around one of us or we would be sitting on his lap, laughing and talking, and a minute or so later—because of something we had said or done, or some neglected duty of ours he suddenly thought about—we would be ordered to our rooms and perhaps made to go without supper.

A spanking usually followed, after which Ed had the child kneel and ask God's forgiveness.

This very changefulness and its abrupt nature hinted at some underlying emotional struggle in the doctor, which became more pronounced as the children grew. The father who taught them how to walk like an Indian in the woods, who fried up delicious "hockies" (doughy treats) on special occasions, who taught them the names of wildflowers and the delights of green onions pulled directly from the woodland soil and eaten in an onion sandwich, could all too quickly metamorphose into a rigid, stern, and often enraged disciplinarian. As he got older, this moodiness revealed itself to be depression, the rapid cycling between light and dark aspects itself perhaps an indicator of manic-depressive illness.

Bewildering as this must have been to Ernest and his sisters, the family closed ranks around Ed. At different points as the children grew, they were given to understand that the doctor needed a rest. One such occasion was Ed's chance to pursue specialized training in obstetrics at New York City's Lying-in Hospital in the fall of 1908, a postgraduate course that would lead to his becoming chair of the obstetrics department at the Oak Park hospital. After the course, Ed sailed for New Orleans, a destination that had long fascinated him because of his father's descriptions of his trip down the Mississippi and the attractions of the Southern city. Grace's letters to Ed in New York City and New Orleans urged him to get some much needed rest: "Try to forget all about us," she wrote, "and rest the worry place in your brain." Oak Park had a local newspaper, *Oak Leaves,* that residents read avidly for local news and gossip. Evidently Ed asked Grace to send him some issues. She complied, but scolded him: "You know, dear, the way to rest is *not* to read Oak Leaves, and get into the old train of thought, but to give your mind a vacation." The newspaper had already said he was in New York for the residency; Ed wondered whether he should give them an update concerning his whereabouts. Grace said no. "Don't you think it perhaps wiser to let them keep the 1st idea in their minds that you are taking 'post grad' work in N.Y." She supported Ed's taking a rest, yet she worried what the neighbors would think. Ed returned home by steamboat up the Mississippi, retracing the route his father, Anson Hemingway, took in his rebellious youth when he was trying to escape from being a farmer.

If the trip brought him relief, it was only temporary. His depressions were very severe, to the point of immobility and worse, leading to paranoia and other symptoms of psychosis. Grace Hemingway had spells of nervousness, but these were as nothing compared to Ed's depressive episodes—which would only worsen with time, the depression before he committed suicide taking floridly psychotic form. Children tend to seek normalcy in the behavior of their parents, and Ernest was no exception: until late adolescence, he chose not to think about the periods in which his father was remote and his behavior bizarre.

Neighbors noticed. A contemporary of Ernest's later noted that Ed Hemingway was "a pretty wretched physician. . . . He was relatively unkempt, looked like the typical Country Doctor, drove a rattling Model-T, carried a disreputable bag. His office was pretty slovenly, too." A harsh picture, perhaps, but the element of eccentricity runs through most accounts of Ed and his family. Though it's problematic to read fiction for biographical evidence, John Dos Passos's *Chosen Country* (1951) supplies some details that, if they are accurate, are helpful concerning the Hemingway family. Dos Passos, later a close friend of Ernest's, married a childhood friend of his, Katy Smith, whose family was very close to the Hemingways in summers in Michigan. Ernest became incensed when he saw how much of his family was in Dos Passos's Warner family, suspecting (correctly) that Katy had provided her husband with revealing details. "The Warners are all peculiar," says the character Lulie, based on Katy, adding that Dr. Warner was considered a good doctor nonetheless. But Lulie resents the doctor for the "sarcastic curl" to his mouth and for how hard he was on his eldest son, the novel's Georgie: "Doc Warner had a knack of bringing tears to Georgie's eyes just by the tone of his voice," adding, "He seemed to enjoy doing it."

Religion was one of many battlegrounds that emerged as Ernest grew. At least into high school and to some extent beyond, Ernest internalized his parents' teachings on religion and comportment as fully as he did his father's instructions in woodcraft. He was baptized in the First Congregational Church by William E. Barton, a minister known today for the best seller by his son, Bruce Barton, *The Man Nobody Knows* (1925), about Jesus

Christ as an advertising man. Perhaps because of Grace's musical interests (she became a soloist and choirmaster in the new church), the family switched to the smaller Third Congregational Church, where Ernest and Marcelline were confirmed on Easter in 1911, at which time they received their First Communion. Ernest became a member of the Plymouth League, a group meeting on Sundays at five, which especially encouraged the participation of young people in church and community activities (a young Bruce Barton was president of the league).

At thirteen, Ernest was familiar enough with irony—or perhaps it's more accurate to say, he was old enough—to recognize the disparity between what he was taught and what he really felt. He spoke later of how you felt and how you were supposed to feel at religious rituals like the First Communion. Grace was vocal and enthusiastic about her faith; she expected committed church participation and practiced the integration of religious or spiritual talk in daily life. She tended to jump to conclusions about the "Christian" suitability of various influences—before the Oak Park school board she protested not once, but twice, for instance, that no "Christian" schoolchild should have to read *The Call of the Wild* in class. Grace could work herself up into an unstoppable rhetorical frenzy when it came to religion. She was explicit about the value she placed in certain Victorian ideals that she associated with being a good Christian. Not surprisingly, these differences would come to be at the heart of Ernest's differences with his mother when his books first began to appear.

But the picture was far more complicated than this. Ed was by far the more rigid and serious about his faith. Ernest later said that his father—like Ed's brother Willoughby, a successful missionary surgeon in China—had wanted to be a missionary in Guam or Greenland, but Grace had overridden him. When the children enlisted Grace on their side in a concerted campaign to allow them to take dancing lessons, Ed balked—and though all the children and Grace learned to dance, he held himself aloof, still believing dancing a heinous practice that opened the door to other, worse, sins.

It was not until Ernest was an adult that he was able to place his father's life into any kind of perspective, and even then he seemed obsessed with considerations about whether or not his father had shown courage. He remained profoundly ambivalent. The subject gave him some embarrassment. The father of Robert Jordan, the fictional hero of *For Whom the Bell Tolls,* shares many characteristics with Ed Hemingway, down to killing himself with a Civil War pistol. Robert Jordan remembers with some chagrin his first significant parting from his father: the older man kissed his son on both cheeks, murmuring, "May the Lord watch between thee and me, while we are absent one from the other." The passage, from Genesis 31:49, was a favorite of the Hemingway family, but more often expressed in letters. Hemingway's hero was clearly embarrassed by the remark's intimacy, and he noticed during their embrace that his father's mustache was damp with tears.

TWO

The substance of Ernest Hemingway's adolescence began much like that of any number of promising youths from good, solid, Midwestern families in his day: school, work, church, summer vacations in the country, and the first stirrings of interest in girls and a wider social life. It would come to a close much less conventionally. Instead of going to college, he would join a Kansas City newspaper as a cub reporter. Seven months later, frustrated in his efforts to enlist in the U.S. effort in World War I, he would leave for Italy as a Red Cross ambulance driver. On the surface, he was still a dutiful son of loving parents. Underneath, Ed and Grace suspected, not without reason, that there was something wayward about Ernest, some ambition or impulse they couldn't understand and they found deeply troubling.

An ongoing experience that shaped the man and the mature writer was his life at Windemere in northern Michigan. The family squeezed in as many days as possible at the lake every summer, the doctor usually joining the family for several weeks if not the whole summer (he saw patients in the area, including local Ojibway Indians). With his brothers and sisters, Ernest spent the days swimming or, more often, fishing. The summer he turned fourteen he slept in a tent pitched in the family yard, and as he got older he spent most of his time elsewhere, often staying with the Dilworths, a family in nearby Horton Bay. In the summer of 1905, Ed bought a forty-acre farm across the lake from Windemere; he and Grace called it Longfield, after a property in their favorite book, Dinah Mulock Craik's 1856 Victorian novel *John Halifax: Gentleman* (their third child, Ursula, was named after the book's heroine). As he got older, Ernest's chores increased with his allowance (once a week, he got pennies in the amount of his current age). While in Oak Park he delivered the weekly *Oak Leaves* and mowed lawns; in Michigan he was put to work at Longfield, where he often camped. He planted seeds, dug potatoes, and picked fruit from the orchards he and his father had planted. Ed and his son commonly exchanged businesslike letters about the quality of the produce and the numbers of bushels Ernest would sell locally as well as those he would ship back to Oak Park for the family. Ernest Hall had counseled Ed Hemingway, "Every man with some savings ought to have a farm," and the notion of feeding his large brood from his own land had a definite appeal to Ernest's father. But Ernest didn't like manual labor, even if it was outdoors, and as he grew older his evasion of his chores would become a point of contention in serious battles with his parents, which in turn would serve as a proving ground for his identity.

With other summer residents Lewis Clarahan, Ray Ohlsen, Carl Edgar, and brother and sister Bill and Katy Smith, Ernest took camping trips and got into the usual adolescent scrapes. One incident that had a lasting effect on him, however, occurred when he was out fishing with his sister Sunny, the fourth Hemingway child, born in 1904. Towing *Ursula of Windemere,* one of the family rowboats, he and Sunny walked and waded up to the head of Walloon Lake, toward a marshy area called the Cracken. Suddenly, Ernest caught sight of a blue heron. He raised his gun and shot it— definitely prohibited under local game laws—telling Sunny that their father would love to add it to his collection of stuffed birds and animals. While they went ashore to eat lunch, Ernest stowed the dead bird under the seat of the boat. When they returned it was gone. What happened next is not entirely clear; in one version Ernest encounters the game warden's son, who tells him his father is looking for him. It is clear, however, that the game warden did not encounter a warm reception when he went to Windemere in search of Ernest. Grace Hemingway drew herself up to her full height, turned the tables so that *she* was interrogating the game warden, and finally drove him off the property with a shotgun. Ernest, meanwhile, had fled. Accounts disagree again at this point, but the end result was that Ernest had to turn himself in and pay a stiff fine. He would later embroider this account, claiming that he narrowly missed being sentenced to reform school by the judge. He never forgot this brush with the authorities; evidently breaking the law left a significant impression on him. He was also impressed that Grace went to bat for him, even though she knew he was in the wrong. Her brandishing the shotgun became a favorite family story.

When Ernest entered Oak Park and River Forest High School side by side with his sister Marcelline, he had vague plans to become a doctor. These began to change with English classes and, later, courses in creative writing and, especially, journalism. Though he had not been an early reader, once he learned he was an enthusiastic one. Marcelline recalled that they both read extensively in sets of Scott, Dickens, Thackeray, Kipling, and Robert Louis Stevenson, and that Ernest took the lessons of the Horatio Alger novels with high seriousness. The family subscribed to lots of magazines, from *Good Housekeeping* to *Scribner's,* and the *Youth's Companion* and *St. Nicholas Magazine* came regularly for the children. At the Third Congregational Church he and his sister enrolled in a contest to be the first to read the complete King James Bible; even after Ernest's friend Harold Sampson won, Marcelline and Ernest went on and finished their reading.

In English I, in their freshman year, brother and sister read narrative poetry, tales from the Bible, and Greek and Roman myths with Frank Platt, chairman of the English Department. But Ernest would not really catch fire until later in his high school years, in classes with teachers Margaret Dixon and Fannie Biggs. Margaret Dixon, according to classmates interviewed by Hemingway scholar Charles Fenton, was an "outspoken liberal," a vigorous modern woman who, one classmate said, was a wonderful storyteller, the center of attention at any social gathering. Dixon took a special interest in Ernest and encouraged his earliest writing efforts.

But it was Fannie Biggs to whom Ernest came to feel especially close. A surviving letter he wrote her, not long after graduation, treats her as if she were another school chum, telling her about a practical joke and a brawl. Biggs wore her hair in a schoolmistress's bun and was tall and willowy, a well-read woman with an excellent sense of humor. Ernest came under her influence in a course on short fiction, which in turn led to Miss Biggs's elite Story Club, chosen at the end of junior year, in which both Ernest and Marcelline submitted short stories. The Story Club was essentially a fiction workshop, students circulating their work and critiquing it, with the guidance of the teacher. None of Ernest's high school efforts in this genre, most notably "The Judgment of Manitou" and "Sepi Jingam," published in the *Tabula,* the literary magazine, showed particular promise, except perhaps in a certain skill with dialogue. He would see five more stories appear there. It is interesting to note that not once during high school, or for that matter until about the age of twenty-four, did Ernest talk about writing a novel someday. Then, as now, many a genius manqué talks up his desire to write a novel while still in knee britches. It is a credit to Fannie Biggs, it could be argued, that Ernest, who would become one of the true masters of the short story, concentrated his focus on this genre—even when surrounded by other writers, as he would be in his early years in Paris.

It was journalism in which Ernest shone, and here Fannie Biggs was most influential, first through English VI, a course in journalism Ernest took in his junior year. As one biographer has noted, she ran the class "as though the classroom was a newspaper office." She appointed a rotating student editor to a hypothetical newspaper and assigned that person to different areas. Her reporters were taught the relatively novel but already classic "inverted pyramid" structure for news stories: they were told to put the whole story in the first paragraph, and then spin it out according to which details were the most salient, leaving the least important ones until the end, so an editor could cut the text easily. Students submitted sports stories, society columns, features, and even advertisements for imaginary products before signing on for the real thing, the popular and avidly read *Trapeze.* Ernest's first byline in the weekly paper appeared in January of his junior year. The following year both Marcelline and Ernest were chosen to be two among eight rotating editors of the paper.

Ernest had to snatch moments for activities like the *Trapeze* and the debating club, the young businessmen's club, and student plays away from his participation in sports, expected to be the major activity, after academics, for young boys. Ernest was never particularly fond of or good at team sports. Because he had shot up to five feet ten by his fifteenth birthday, and was large-boned, he went out for football, but didn't make the varsity team until he was a senior, and then did not shine. (Perhaps because in future so many of his readers and supporters expected him to have had a brilliant football career, Ernest couldn't help inventing one from time to time, once claiming to have been an extremely talented player under Bob Zuppke, who did in fact coach at Oak Park—though before Ernest attended—then going on to a legendary career at the University of Illinois.) In his last year he was on the varsity swimming team and was manager of the track team. He felt divided between his schoolwork and athletics, or perhaps rather thought he should feel divided, commenting later that Margaret Dixon and Fannie Biggs "were especially nice to me because I had to try to be an athlete as well as try to learn to write English." (This twin focus did look forward, however, to his immersion in both the worlds of writing and of sportsmanship in his adult life.)

Not surprisingly, he found it easiest to try his hand at sportswriting for the *Trapeze.* Almost from the start he turned out stories in the manner of Ring Lardner, whose work Ernest would have encountered in Lardner's syndicated sports column in the *Chicago Tribune* or in his 1916 collection *You Know Me Al,* which had been published piecemeal in *The Saturday Evening Post.* The latter consisted of fictional letters to a hometown friend, Al, from a lazy and dim-witted Chicago White Sox baseball player, Jack Keefe. Lardner specialized in a warm, subliterate vernacular in which the numbers of verbs and noun-verb agreement were all mixed up. In the spring of 1916 and the fall of 1917 Hemingway published several stories in the *Trapeze* that were announced in the headlines as being by "Our Ring

Lardner." Few of these pieces, however, imitated Lardner's style; rather, invoking Lardner's name gave Ernest license to be funny: "Hemingway is reported to be convalescing, but the Doctors Fear his mind is irreparably lost." The same piece, like several others, made him out to be the sports hero he most definitely was not: "The lightning fast Hemingway scored Oak Park's third touchdown, crossing the goal line by way of the Chicago avenue car line, transferring at Harlem and Lake." It wasn't until the spring of his senior year that Ernest adopted the epistolary mode and began to mimic, quite adeptly, Lardner's vernacular. "Dear Pashley," the article opened, "Well Pash since you have went and ast me to write a story about the swimming meet I will do it because if I didn't you might fire me off the papers."

The humor in these pieces is not exactly immortal. The point is, rather, that writing for the newspaper, and especially writing humorous stories for the newspaper, not only gave Ernest valuable journalistic experience but also made writing easy and enjoyable for him. For a boy of his era—expected to give at least equal time to athletics—English classes and short story writing, especially as a teacher's favorite, were somewhat dubious pastimes. And creative writing was not easy: Ernest undertook a play in his senior year, "No Worst than a Bad Cold," that he was unable to finish to his satisfaction. But writing about sports came easily, and won him popularity among his classmates, especially the boys.

Much of Ernest's time and energy in his high school years was given over to humorous pursuits—practical jokes, devising satiric language, enlisting his peers in fanciful fabrication. In what would prove to be a lifelong pattern, he bestowed nicknames on everyone he knew. He had nicknames for family members that he absolutely insisted on: Marcelline was known as Ivory, or Mazween; Ursula, Ernest's favorite as a boy, was called Uralegs; Madelaine, Sunny; Carol, Beefish or Beefy; and his youngest brother, born in 1915, Leicester, the Pester, Gasper, or, later, the Baron. (Marcelline dubbed him Dregs, which even Ernest thought went too far.) Ernest extended this practice to his friends. Trading on the genteel anti-Semitism that was no doubt a common prejudice in turn-of-the-century Oak Park, Ernest and his friends Ray Ohlsen and Lloyd Golder developed the conceit that they were pawnbrokers, drawing three circles with yellow chalk on their lockers and calling the spot the Three Ball Joint. Ernest took the name Hemingstein and dubbed Ohlsen Cohen and Golder Goldberg. He insisted on the nickname Hemingstein for years, often shortening it to Stein, which he liked for its punning reference to beer. (He often drew a brimming beer stein at the close of his letters.) He also called himself

Wemmedge, as well as the Brute. Devoting so much thought and care to renaming family members and friends—derivations of names like the Gasper were quite complex—is a way, of course, of naming one's universe, and thus controlling it.

Hemingway's friends, who in Oak Park included Morris Musselman (Mussie), Harold Sampson (Samp), and George Madill (Pickles), followed his lead in developing an elaborate lingo of their own, which they used religiously, evidently more in letters than in conversation, until they were well into their twenties. Some of this was derived from Mark Twain, some from Lardner, some from courtly language; a lot of it sounds like early Ezra Pound, though Ernest would not meet the poet until 1922. In these early years, he liberally salts his compositions with current slang. Creative spelling and bad punning give him "sitshooation" and "Alum Mattress" (for Alma Mater). Letters are "screeds" or "epistles"; Oak Park is "Oakus Parkus" and the sea is "the briny." In letters to Marcelline he proposes they "hie us to a spaghettery" or "allez to Chi," and asks, "Why is it I hear from you not?" as well as "Are you love smit by some youth yet?" Money is almost always "seeds," though sometimes it is "shekels" or "the jack." One "morts," and death is "mortage." Ernest would be announcing "some rather good additions to the Lingua": in cards, two queens were "monickered" "a double duo of Breasts" and kings "a Brace of the Monarchs" as late as 1919, when he was back from the war.

Again, nothing about this is terribly unusual, except for the energy Ernest put into the sustained use of this language from about 1916 to 1923—when well on his way in his serious fiction to the stripped-down, simple, and direct sentences that he would make famous. This lingo came easily to him, and it made his world seem insular, protected. He and his siblings, he and his friends, could understand each other. And, judging from the lavish use of nicknames in his adolescent letters to his parents, he expected them to fall in line as well. He would adopt this language with the woman he married, Hadley (Hash), and she would inevitably use it too. It is important to note that Ernest never used this language in his writing, except in his *Trapeze* columns in high school; its use made him adept at the slang that would appear in the vernacular narrative of "My Old Man" and the dialogue in such short stories as "The Killers" or "Fifty Grand." It also looked forward to the telegraphic, ungrammatical, and eccentric way of talking he developed in his late years, recorded in Lillian Ross's devastating *New Yorker* profile in 1950. At this youthful stage, however, this prose style, at once stilted and extremely loose, acted as a kind of lubricant for the writing that would enter and take over his life in just a few years.

For after high school Hemingway's momentous letter output, always fairly vigorous for a boy seldom separated from his family and friends, would begin to mount. For an adolescent, writing in satirical fashion and the heavy use of (heavy) irony come naturally, enabling the writer to put down words without self-consciousness or embarrassment. Beginning to write was like meeting a lifelong friend, and he eased naturally into the friendship through the language of satire.

Ernest was doing fairly well in his parents' eyes—with one significant exception, as Hemingway scholar Morris Buske has recently pointed out. One 1916 summer day at Windemere Ernest gave his mother a taste of what the next few years would bring. He and his friend Harold Sampson were at the kitchen table when Grace set down their lunch in front of them. Ernest complained, "Is this all we've got? This god damn slop." Grace asked him to leave the table and not come back until he apologized. Like most of the Hemingways, Ernest was very quick to take offense. Feeling he had been wronged, he summoned Harold and left the house for several days, staying with the Dilworths in Horton Bay. Touchiness is too mild a term for the quality in Ernest this incident brought forth. His mother and father tended to behave in the same way when criticized or misunderstood, as did most of his siblings. For Ernest it was but one instance in a lifelong pattern in which he would take great offense at a slight or an accusation, fly off the handle, and continue to be aggrieved regardless of how the matter ended. This particular incident—a more extreme banishment by his mother would follow in 1920—stayed with Hemingway for the rest of his life, and led him to claim several times that he had run away from home as a teenager and never returned.

It had made a great impression on the fifteen-year-old Ernest when Grace stood up to the game warden on his behalf, even running the interloping authority off the property with a shotgun. Another little-known incident, however, also brought to light recently by Buske, concerns a time when Ernest's parents, in equally indelible fashion, did not come to his defense. Perhaps carried away by their experience editing the high school newspaper and the literary magazine, Ernest and some other friends put together an underground publication of sorts called *The Jazz Journal,* the word "jazz" at that time just beginning to shift from its original meaning as sexual intercourse to describe a new kind of music. The writer-editors wrote up some dirty jokes and attributed them to various faculty members. There was only one copy of the magazine, with its editors given in a numbered list on the inside of the back cover; it was meant to be passed from one boy to another. Fellow editor Ray Ohlsen, who recounted this incident, found that the magazine was missing from his English book, where he had tucked it away. The next thing the boys knew they were called into the office of the principal, Marion McDaniel, who brandished the missing copy while haranguing them. Evidently their parents were notified, and, according to Ohlsen, their future at the high school hung in the balance. He credited Fannie Biggs for saving them from expulsion, surmising that she had stepped forward to explain that the boys had come to her for advice and then promised her that they would discontinue the magazine. The father of another classmate came to see the principal and "stoutly" stood up for his son, saying the school was being too severe.

Fannie Biggs would later describe the incident for Hemingway critic Charles Fenton in a letter that has since been lost. In another letter, she told Fenton that Ernest had said to her, "Neither of *my* parents would come to school for *me* no matter *how right* I was. I'd just have to take it." Ernest took great offense at his parents' refusal to come forward and take his part. Being called into the principal's office for a matter this serious, with expulsion threatened, was traumatic for the boy, who must have felt quite alone in the situation, thrown on his own devices and saved by the intercession of his favorite teacher. As the years went by he would build on these early resentments until they became cause to reject his parents and their world definitively. He wasn't always able to do so in their presence, and he remained close to his family and his parents for a longer time than his later comments about them allow. But he made up for this by using extremely colorful language to describe how much he hated his family. About his mother, he wrote late in life, "Isn't that . . . woman terrible? I don't know how I could have been whelped by her but evidently was."

Ernest's frequent truculence, his thin skin, and his irreverent humor, as well as his undeniable intelligence, set him apart from his peers. Among his close friends these qualities helped make him a leader and exemplar. But they didn't come from nowhere. Something set the whole Hemingway family apart from Oak Park society, with its acute class-consciousness and its bourgeois respectability, despite the clan's high position there. Fannie Biggs, however much an advocate of Ernest's while he was under her care, suggested some elements of this. Years later, when contacted by Hemingway scholar Charles Fenton, who was writing a book (much to Ernest's dismay) about his apprenticeship, Fannie found it necessary to establish the superiority of Oak Park and River Forest High School to other institutions of the day. (In fairness, the higher the quality of the school, the more superior she would seem as a teacher.) The school was meant to serve Oak Park children who would ordinarily have attended private school, she pointed out, citing the "poets, musicians, diplomats, critics, and newspapermen"—even, she added, the evangelist Billy Sunday—who appeared at assemblies. Parents sunk large sums into high school plays, which they attended, Biggs took pains to note, in evening wear. Yet Ernest "never had pocket money," she wrote disapprovingly (fifteen pennies did not go far), and she never saw his parents at venues like Oak Park country clubs or social clubs in Chicago. While this may have reflected the Hemingways' position in Oak Park at the time, it is unlikely that the Hemingways, a family of six good-looking and smart children, presided over by a well-respected doctor and his talented, impressive wife, living in one of Oak Park's largest houses, were shunned by wealthier or more socially connected families on this account; rather, they held a distinctive place in the town—their absence from social clubs notwithstanding.

This may not have been plain to Ernest, who in his high school years and immediately after was moving out of the concentric rings of his family and family friends. He had two girlfriends: first, Dorothy Davies, and later, Frances Coates; Frances had enchanted him in a performance of the German opera *Martha*. Little is known of these relationships, but they were evidently not serious, as Ernest went as Marcelline's date to the Junior-Senior Prom in May. He and Harold Sampson double-dated with Frances and Marcelline, sometimes canoeing on the Des Plaines River. Ernest at the time seems genuinely to have enjoyed Marcelline's company. Brother and sister united in efforts to bend or even change parental rules; Marcelline demanded dancing lessons after being embarrassed at a dance, over Ed's vigorous objections. Grace took her side, and the next fall her two oldest children attended Miss Ingram's dancing school on Saturday evenings (Ernest may have reminded himself to be careful what you wish for). Marcelline and Ernest passed on what they learned in family gatherings around the gramophone. All the children and Grace joined in, while Ed sat by sourly. Ernest was far more enthusiastic about boxing, which he took up as a high school junior. He later claimed to have learned the sport from old Chicago fighters like Jack Blackburn and Harry Greb, whom he may have encountered when he haunted notable Chicago wrestling gyms. The boxing milieu would always be important for his writing; indeed, it informed one of his high school story efforts, "A Matter of Colour."

Despite dancing lessons, there was something not entirely sociable about the Hemingways, including Ernest. Wilhelmina Corbett, a playmate who knew him in high school, noted that he "was no particular prize according to his contemporaries (female) because he never was 'sharp,' in fact was on the unkempt side." In Dos Passos's 1951 novel, in which the Warners stand in for the Hemingways, the heroine takes note of Georgie's "unbrushed hair in black spikes on his forehead like an Indian's and the line of grime round the open neck of his blue shirt," saying to herself, "my he's a lout." Dr. Hemingway, whom Wilhelmina also judged "unkempt," picked out his son's footwear, as he did for all the children, and the shoes "were never quite right." While Wilhelmina generally admired Grace Hemingway, she noted with disapproval that Grace was an "atrocious housekeeper," and "quite dominated the home scene." Ursula Hemingway would later remind her brother that the Oak Park house was a "slovenly mess." Ed Hemingway once discovered a pen that he had lost three years earlier underneath a sofa. Though her classmates found the Hemingway parents quite narrow in such matters as religion, classmate Lewis Clarahan found them "unconventional," a word Wilhelmina had used, not without admiration, to describe the Kenilworth Avenue house and its grand music room. Another classmate of Ernest's remembers thinking Mrs. Hemingway, with her white hair, looked like "Mrs. Santa Claus," and wore "very long" skirts, "so when paraded anywhere on Oak Park streets she was always noticed."

In the summer of 1916, up at Windemere, Ernest made two important friends, Bill and Katy Smith, also from an unconventional family. Their mother had died of tuberculosis in 1899, and their father was a university professor, an expert in mathematics, ancient Greek, and philosophy. (He was also an outspoken atheist.) With their considerably older brother Yeremiah Kenley (or Y.K., called Kenley), Bill and Katy had been brought up in St. Louis by their father, and lived in the summers in northern Michigan with their aunt and uncle, Mr. and Mrs. Joseph Charles ("Auntie" and "Unk"). Bill was twenty-one, Katy twenty-four—that is, considerably older than Ernest. Bill was studying agriculture at the University of Missouri, where Katy had studied journalism. Ernest and Bill had known each other as boys, but were reacquainted by mutual friend Carl Edgar, a Princeton graduate, that summer. Brother and sister were both widely read, and Katy was striking, with catlike eyes that some described as green, others, topaz. Bill and Ernest became solid fishing friends, and Ernest would be interested off and on over the next several years in courting Katy; in the meantime, he and she became fast friends.

In his senior year, Ernest reviewed his options for the immediate future. What plans he had included fishing at Horton Bay and hiking further into the wilds in upper Michigan in search of good fishing, where he hoped to live while working on his writing. He knew this wouldn't fly. His father wanted him to go to Oberlin, where Marcelline would enroll in fall 1917. In a letter to a schoolmate, Ernest noted that he was leaning toward applying to Cornell. He told his grandfather he would be going to the University of Illinois, and that's what his classmates understood as well. Ernest may not have liked any of these options, however. Friends of his near Horton Bay had been to impressive Eastern schools, some Ivy League, which decisively outflanked Oberlin, a small Ohio school built around social justice, abolition, and faith in God, while the University of Illinois was a very large Midwestern institution where male students were expected to focus on athletics. Ernest's interest in Cornell seemingly came out of nowhere and disappeared as quietly. What sounded best to him was apprenticing as a journalist at *The Kansas City Star*. Ed Hemingway's younger brother Tyler was successful in the lumber business and a man of some stature in Kansas City and an Oberlin classmate of Henry J. Haskell, chief editorial writer and Washington correspondent at the *Star*. Ed agreed to ask his brother to see if Haskell couldn't intercede for Ernest at the newspaper. Graduation intervened, Ernest delivering the Class Prophecy (a bit of clever balladeering) and Marcelline giving a speech on "The New Girlhood."

Ernest had hoped for a summer job at the *Star*, but instead the newspaper was willing to hire him full-time in the fall. The summer passed rapidly, for Ernest was working as hard as he ever had at outdoor manual labor. He was at Longfield, the family farm across the lake, almost all the time, often at his father's side. They hayed twenty acres, planted more fruit trees, moved an old farmhouse off the property, and built an icehouse, as well as tending the vegetable crops. Bill Smith lived on the Longfield side of Walloon Lake, and he and Ernest worked out a labor scheme: Bill helped pick beans and dig potatoes at Longfield in return for Ernest's help picking apples and chopping wood at Auntie Charles's. Relations with his mother were chilly, and Ernest spent most of his weeks camping out at Longfield and long weekends in Horton Bay, often staying with the Dilworths. He and Bill went fishing every moment they could find, as adulthood hovered.

* * *

Ernest would spend just over six months in Kansas City—a fast, intense apprenticeship—on *The Kansas City Star*, then arguably one of the best newspapers in the country. Kansas City was just over five hundred miles from Oak Park, but to Ernest it might as well have been a continent away. Kansas City represented the first time he had lived away from home for any period of time (except camping) without adult supervision, and it was a liberation. He would begin a lifetime habit of serious drinking, he would write every day except Sunday and be paid for it, and he would fall in love for the first time.

Hemingway's train arrived on October 15, 1917, at Kansas City's Union Station, where he was met by his friend Carl Edgar (nicknamed Odgar), an older man he knew from the previous summer in Horton Bay. Edgar, a friend of the Smiths' and a suitor of Katy Smith, managed the California Oil Burner Company and had been one of the boosters for Ernest's taking the Kansas City job. Edgar dropped him off at the large Victorian home of Ernest's Uncle Tyler Hemingway and Aunt Arabella on Warwick Boulevard; the next morning his uncle accompanied him to the *Star* offices on Grand Avenue, which took up an entire city block. There Ernest was almost immediately sent to George Longan, the city editor, who finalized such matters as hours (8:30 to 5:30), pay ($15 a week), and the month-long probation period. Longan wasted no time in turning Ernest over to assistant city editor C. G. Wellington, known as Pete, who would be his immediate boss.

Pete Wellington acquainted Ernest with the paper's house style, giving Ernest some galleys on which were printed the *Star*'s rules and recommendations for good writing. This style sheet was and is justifiably well known even outside the circle of Hemingway aficionados; Ernest himself later said the 110 directives were "the best rules I've ever learned for the business of writing. I've never forgotten them." The main precepts were "Use short sentences. Use short first paragraphs. Use vigorous English. Be positive, not negative." One example Ernest provided of the style sheet in action was that reporters were never to say anyone was "seriously injured. All injuries are serious. [The victim] was, as I recall, slightly injured or dangerously injured." Another dictum was to avoid adjectives, especially words like "gorgeous," "grand," or "marvelous." Similarly, "Slang to be enjoyable must be fresh." They were principles Ernest put into action in Kansas City and in his writing afterward. No writer, he said, "can fail to write well if he abides by them." For the time being, however, the greatest effect the *Star* had on his writing was to make him do it quickly, accurately, and economically—and to produce it in great quantity.

Wellington, whom Ernest characterized as "a stern disciplinarian, very just and very harsh," and who was responsible for the development of the style sheet, explained to Ernest his duties and responsibilities. Ernest would be on what the newspaper called "the short-stop run," which covered the police station on 15th Street; Union Station, where he was to note and interview, if possible, important people—even, to his delight, baseball players—passing through; and the emergency room of Kansas City's largest hospital, where "you got accidents and a double check on crimes of violence," Hemingway noted. As time went on, Wellington observed, Ernest

The newsroom of *The Kansas City Star*, where Ernest learned how to be a reporter, 1917

took "great pains" with his work, even stories that were just a paragraph long.

Meanwhile, the city lay at his feet; it could be argued that a city reporter starting at the bottom saw as much of the city's underside as did those who had lived in the heart of it for years. Kansas City had 300,000 inhabitants and was a major center for railroads, stockyards, and agricultural processing—an ideal place for an ambitious young reporter and writer to get started. But it was rough, and Ernest became acquainted not only with emergency room doctors, undertakers, and the cops, whether on the beat or running an investigation, but also with prostitutes, touts, con men, gamblers, thieves, and tramps. He needed to hear stories and get quotes from onlookers and authorities as well as the principals, and he made friends easily. A favorite doctor at General Hospital took him along to the jail where he provided shots of morphine for addicts in withdrawal. In a letter to his oldest sister, Ernest bragged that he had met and talked with military officers and senators and boxing champs, and that he had learned to "distinguish chianti, catawba, malvasia, Dago Red, claret and several others sans the use of the eyes." Working himself up, he concluded, "I can tell Mayors to go to Hell and slap Police commissioners on the Back!"

Pete Wellington observed that Hemingway "developed a friendship with all those on the staff with whom he came in contact." He made friends with Russel Crouse, Clifford Knight, Wilson Hicks, and Dale Wilson, all of whom went on to become prominent professionals. The man who influenced him most was, however, Lionel Moise—a "magnificently sensational" character, according to Ernest, straight out of *The Front Page*. Moise was a hard-drinking and colorful reporter and rewrite man, the most highly valued and paid reporter at the *Star*. (Wherever he worked, Moise would quit unless he was given the highest pay.) His reportorial skills were legendary. Ernest once observed that he could carry four stories in his head, take a phone call giving him material for a fifth, get off the phone, and write all five stories at great speed without a hitch. But in other reminiscences about Moise, Ernest downplayed him, saying he knew him only as an acquaintance, certainly not someone he looked up to. Moise, for instance, probably never worked one-on-one with Ernest on his writing—though he no doubt slashed plenty of Ernest's stories. And he never became a great friend, though Ernest picked up what he could from Moise's gruff directives about writing. Moise liked Twain, Conrad, and Kipling, saying, "Pure objective writing is the only true form of storytelling." He cautioned against shifting narrators and stream-of-consciousness *anything*—no tricks, he said summarily. Ernest listened to Moise when he could, but more often he was caught up in the drama of daily reporting. Perhaps Moise was important in Ernest's development not only as a mentor in becoming a writer, but also as a living legend, a colorful and brilliant eccentric—something to which Ernest could also aspire. Moise may not have been a hero to Hemingway, but he was a model of outrageous behavior.

Ernest's progress on the newspaper is hard to track, despite the best efforts of Hemingway scholars, as almost none of his stories were signed. To the degree that his competency is revealed by the long hours and hard work he put into his job, Ernest was well on his way to a promising career as a reporter. The fact that he was hired as a favor and his lack of real experience meant little to his employers after he was hired; they had a reputation for breaking in amateurs. Ernest responded with alacrity, making the grade and seemingly accepted very early on by some seasoned and very talented newspapermen.

In the midst of all this activity, Ernest managed to write regularly to his family and especially to Marcelline. He seemed to want his parents' approval, but more so to acquaint them with what his life was like in Kansas City so that he could still feel a member of the family—not an unusual pattern in adolescents leaving home for the first time. He tried to convey how it was. When Ed and Grace were understandably unable to imagine the true nature of his life, its pace and demands, and the changes he was undergoing, he got impatient. After several months on the job he felt that he had grown considerably and that his family wasn't giving him credit for that. He saw in one of the issues of the Oak Park local newspapers, which he—tellingly—had his family mail to him without fail, that his father had described him to one of the papers as "only 18." Somewhat comically, Ernest took offense, feeling he was old in experience if not in age. He might be just nineteen, he wrote his father, but he was keeping up a pace that would tax an older man. In fact, the letter to his father in which Ernest stakes his claim for respect (and begins a habit of nursing resentments) is a small masterpiece, even in a family of impressive letter writers, at setting the record straight; it also contains one of the best descriptions available of the reporting life. He doesn't need college, he tells his father. He's been cramming for exams his whole time in Kansas City: "Responsibility, absolute accuracy, thousands of dollars hinge on your statement, absolute truth and accuracy." Even a misspelled name might get the newspaper sued. It's exhausting, he says, working well into the early morning on deadline:

> Having to write a half column story remembering to use good style, perfect style in fact, and get all the facts and in the correct order, make it have snap and wallop and write it in fifteen minutes, five sentences at a time to catch an edition as it goes to press. To take a story over the phone and get everything exact see it all in your minds eye, rush over to a typewriter and write it a page at a time while ten other typewriters are going and the boss is hollerin at some one and a boy snatches the pages from your machine as fast as you write them.

He conveys beautifully the stress he is under, and leaves unsaid how much he has learned. Though the question of college would come up again, and in a manner very divisive to the family, Ernest makes clear that he does not need it. Newspapermen of the time had a somewhat raffish reputation, and Ernest wanted to convey that journalism was a profession, not a trade. He didn't care if his family found him raffish, but he felt they must respect the job he was doing. It seems funny, Ernest goes on to say in the letter to his father, that just a year before he had been writing "bunk and bull" for the Oak Park High School's *Trapeze*. "But it is so, and I am not telling you this because I think that I am any star or anything of the kind but just so you see the situation." Ernest was putting his father on notice that he was someone to be reckoned with, and first and foremost an adult. In the year to come he would prove it.

Not surprisingly, he loved the life he was leading. He had stayed only a few days with his aunt and uncle, moving to Grace Haynes's "respectable" boardinghouse further down Warwick Boulevard, where a few other reporters boarded. His family mailed him baked goods, some, alarmingly, made by Grace herself, and he sent his laundry home to Oak Park until he found a better arrangement. It was difficult for him to get back to the boarding house for the two meals allotted him, as he had only whatever time he could grab and often worked late, missing the evening meal. Before too long he moved into Carl Edgar's apartment on Agnes Street, where the men shared a large bedroom furnished with comfortable chairs and a sleeping porch, each paying $2.50 a week and boarding at restaurants. He made friends among his co-workers and Carl's. One good friend remembered coming over and drinking wine with Ernest and Carl; the hour grew late, and the friend lying on the floor grew sleepy, but Ernest kept at the bottles of "dago red," reading aloud from Robert Browning as his friend slipped into sleep.

Ernest wrote most of his letters to Marcelline, in her first year at Oberlin as a music student. They are cheerful and profane letters, couched in both family lingo and the weird language Ernest devised with his friends in "epistles." He kids her about boys; she kids him back about girls. In February, he chooses to make her his confidante about an unlikely relationship he had begun with a movie star passing through Kansas City. "I have got a bad case on Mae Marsh," Ernest writes Marcelline in a postscript to a letter written around February 12, 1918.

Ernest had met Mae in the twelve-story Hotel Muehlebach, Kansas City's best hotel, when she was on her way to the West Coast. The Muehlebach maintained a lavish press room, equipped with typewriters and phones, a full bath, and easy chairs for conversation and naps; Ernest once slept in the bathtub after a particularly trying day. Though one of his duties was to interview anyone important he saw in the hotel lobby, whether he and the actress met this way is not known. Mary Wayne Marsh was a relatively provincial girl, born in New Mexico in 1894—she was five years older than Ernest, establishing a pattern in his relationships with women—then at the height of her career. Her first starring role had been in *Ramona* in 1910, and she had proceeded to make films at the breakneck speed common in New York and Hollywood at the time. She had starred most prominently in D. W. Griffith's two great epics, *The Birth of a Nation* (1915) and *Intolerance* (1916), both of which Ernest reported seeing. While it is difficult at first to imagine a love affair between a brash young reporter and a bona fide movie star, the critic Pauline Kael, in a 1968 *New Yorker* piece, provided a recent description of Marsh's appeal that helps to explain why Ernest might have found her more approachable than most screen stars: "She is our dream not of heavenly beauty like [Lillian] Gish, but of earthly beauty, and sunlight makes her youth more entrancing. She looks as if she could be a happy, sensual, ordinary woman." On the other hand, Marsh had recently been signed by Goldwyn and was making $3,000 a week, which would have been nearly inconceivable to Ernest.

Though Ernest's relationship with Marsh very likely never progressed beyond friendship, he obviously saw it as a romance in his own imagination, and presented it in letters to friends and family as such. The friendship would continue in the months to come, and Ernest would see Marsh again when he got to New York City. Previous biographers, who did not have available the range of letters Ernest wrote, have treated the Mae Marsh episode as a joke, a bit of fantasy on Ernest's part. But Ernest wrote three letters to Marcelline, two letters and a telegram to his father, one to the family, and one to Dale Wilson, a friend from the *Star*, about the relationship, which have recently surfaced. These communications run from February 12 to May 19—a bit long for a sustained joke. It is entirely plausible that the actress made a stop in Kansas City on a train trip to Hollywood, and that Ernest met her while he was on the job. It is true, however, that no letters from Marsh exist; it also seems strange that he seems not to have engaged emotionally with the actress, and that there is no documentation for the end of their friendship—but perhaps the absence of these means rather that Ernest met and flirted with Marsh as she came through Kansas City, and then decided to spin out a fantasy about her. The romance, if indeed it was a romance, remains shrouded in mystery.

According to Ernest—perhaps just in his fantasy—they almost immediately were talking about marriage, Ernest calling Mae "the future Mrs. Hemingstein," and during the course of the romance, which lasted until Ernest went overseas as a member of the American Red Cross ambulance service in May, he persisted in speaking of Mae as a matrimonial prospect. No doubt this was due to the pervasive urgency that has always accompanied love affairs begun with war imminent, where marriage becomes a very real, and commonly exercised, option. In the same letter to his sister Ernest invoked the other feature common to such affairs, that the girl would "wait for" him. When he wrote Marcelline, Mae (whom he called Mary) had just left for the East Coast to make a film on location in Woods Hole, Massachusetts, but in the meantime she was writing him two or more letters a week, Ernest said, and she was to pass through Kansas City again on her way back to Hollywood. Three weeks later Ernest was anxious to learn whether Marcelline and her latest beau had seen Mae Marsh's recent *Beloved Traitor* (1918) and whether his sister agreed that "Mary" was "a wonder."

Any relationship Ernest had with Mae Marsh would have been very much a wartime romance. For although there was little time to think, much less to plan, in Ernest's months in Kansas City, between his apprenticeship and his romance with (or about) Marsh, he was also preoccupied with finding a way to serve in the Great War, which the U.S. had entered on April 6, 1917. In his senior year in high school, he would already have been aware of a not-so-subtle shift in the national psyche toward militarism. This found expression in preparedness parades in cities and towns across the country, advocating the buildup of a strong military in preparation for what many saw as the inevitable entrance of the U.S. into the conflict.

Woodrow Wilson had been reelected the previous November on a platform promising to keep the country out of the war in Europe, which had been raging since 1914, but it was becoming clear even at the time that the president and his advisers were only looking for a politically acceptable way to insert the U.S. into the war on the side of Britain and France. Aiding them was Germany's submarine offensive against all shipping, including merchant vessels, in what it declared to be a war zone in the northern Atlantic. Americans felt the full force of this starting with the German sinking of the Cunard liner RMS *Lusitania* in May 1915, which cost 128 American passengers their lives. The campaign continued with the torpedoing of seven American merchant ships just prior to U.S. entry into the war.

Increasingly, events of the war swept everything else off the front pages. But Ernest would have been aware also of the opposition to "intervention," especially in large cities like Chicago and Kansas City. This extended to antimilitarists of every stripe, but particularly those on the left who considered the war a means to break the international solidarity of the working class—and who detected a fundamental economic motive on the part of business interests that expected to profit from the conflict. To the extent that he thought about the issue at all, Ernest may have felt torn between a childhood and adolescent romance with soldiering and a temperamental tendency to side with the underdog, and perhaps a Chicagoan's admiration for Jane Addams, the leader of Chicago's settlement house movement and one of the strongest voices against the war. By the time Ernest arrived in Kansas City in the fall of 1917, however, the U.S. was already beginning to send troops to Europe, the American middle class was more or less fully committed to the cause, and the cub reporter was following war news with intense interest, soon hoping to join the American forces abroad.

The war itself, typified by a new and especially murderous kind of fighting called trench warfare, was reaching a different, more troubling phase for the U.S. and its new allies. While the western front in France was stalemated, Germany and its ally, Austria-Hungary, won a major victory over Italy at the Battle of Caporetto in October. Two months later, revolutionary Russia signed an armistice with Germany and left the war. The way was seemingly clear for Germany to throw its full strength into a new offensive against the French, British, and now American troops in northern France. Within a matter of weeks after his arrival in Kansas City in fall 1917, Ernest had signed up with the 7th Missouri Infantry of the National Guard, was issued a uniform (the appearance of which he detailed in letters to the family and, especially, to Marcelline), and was participating in regular drills. He was champing at the bit to enlist, but Ed Hemingway would not give his consent until Christmas 1917. Even then, father and son both knew that Ernest's poor eyesight, according to family legend inherited from his mother, would keep him out of any U.S. unit. Though he talked about enlisting in the Canadian Army, and spoke airily of joining the Marines or going in for aviation, his eyesight was a real sticking point.

Fellow reporter Ted Brumback, the son of a Kansas City judge, held out another possibility. Brumback had dropped out of Cornell when he lost an eye in a golfing accident and was thus ineligible for service. He enlisted with the American Field Service in 1917 and spent four months driving an ambulance in France prior to signing on at the *Star*. He was eager to return to the war, but the AFS had begun to require a stricter physical exam. The American Red Cross, however, had recently begun sending ambulances and drivers to the Italian front, and they were allowed to recruit *only* men otherwise ineligible for the armed services. The Italian army had recently suffered major defeats by the Austrians, most notably at Caporetto in October and November, with the result that ambulance drivers serving the front lines were in drastically short supply. The Red Cross was thus actively recruiting in 1918, and Brumback and Hemingway signed up, giving the *Star* notice that they would leave at the end of April.

* * *

His time in Kansas City gave Ernest the material for a sketch that would appear between chapters in his first book, *In Our Time;* it begins, "At two o'clock in the morning two Hungarians got into a cigar store at Fifteenth Street and Grand Avenue," and is about a policeman's killing of two Hungarians he believes to be "wops." Another sketch in the book, about a prison hanging, may also date from Kansas City. Events in Kansas City gave him material for the short story "A Pursuit Race," about a traveling bicycle racer in a burlesque show, sidelined in Kansas City by alcoholic defeatism. "God Rest Ye Merry Gentlemen" is set at Christmas in a Kansas City emergency room, where a doctor tells the story of a boy who pleaded for the doctor to castrate him, so troubled was he by lust, and who then went on to mutilate himself with a razor. "A Pursuit Race" would appear in his 1927 story collection, *Men Without Women,* while "God Rest Ye Merry Gentlemen" was included in *Winner Take Nothing,* his next collection, published six years later.

Neither story ranks among Hemingway's best, and in fact the *In Our Time* sketch (or sketches) is more relevant here, for it shows us that Hemingway, in seeing and noting incidents and storing them away until they were ready to be called forth, was learning already the undisputed power of simple observations, rendered in sentences in which not one word is wasted—if not yet transmuted into fiction. Witnessing, noting carefully, and writing economically—all skills he learned in Kansas City. The seven months in 1917 and 1918 at the *Star* was one of the best periods in Hemingway's life: when his personality, talent, and joy in living all came together felicitously, indelibly stamping him as a writer with a roaring appetite for experience.

He also came into his own as a young man. People noticed him. His looks were compelling (they would have to be, to attract a movie star), but his energy was what really grabbed people. Pete Wellington noted that he was "a big, good-natured boy with a ready smile." Ted Brumback later wrote that his first impression of Ernest "was that of a big, handsome kid, bubbling over with energy. And this energy was really remarkable. He could turn out more copy than any two reporters. He never seemed to be tired at the end of the day." With the exception of the peevish letter to his father, who he didn't think fully appreciated the demands of his job, Ernest's letters are free of the egotism and self-justification that would come to characterize too much of his correspondence. Further, in the letters he wrote and the stories he told friends about the *Star,* Hemingway tells the truth and does not embroider the facts to improve his story or put himself in a more favorable light. It could be argued that the rough-and-tumble of Kansas City and his beat made lying unnecessary. But there was a fundamental innocence to Hemingway's storytelling at this juncture, an innocence that could be said to characterize his entire sojourn in Kansas City, however much he was surrounded by vice.

THREE

A band of brothers: few things, ever, made Ernest Hemingway happier than to be surrounded by a group of male friends. At almost every period of his life he collected like-minded souls to share fishing, hunting, and general sport—or, as became clear at this early juncture, going to war. In fact, there are some indications that he viewed war in the same general category as the other pursuits: he said much later in life that he had been such an "awful dope" at this first experience of war, that "I can remember thinking that we were the home team and the Austrians were the visiting team." (Paul Fussell has written about this tendency to see war as sport, citing British Captain W. P. Nevill, who, in the Somme attack, had his men dribble four soccer balls up to the Germans' front lines, promising a prize to the winner. "Nevill was killed instantly," notes Fussell.) By the end of his life the companions he sought were acolytes and camp followers, but as a young man he seemed to believe that comradeship put a sheen on an experience that it did not otherwise have. This goes a way toward understanding Ernest's somewhat anomalous approach to sports. He never liked team sports and did not excel in them. Though he would go through periods when he played a fair amount of tennis, he wasn't very good at it, so he did not particularly engage with it. He seems never to have considered golf, even though it had a great vogue in the 1920s. Boxing, which, like tennis, requires another person, was a lifelong favorite of his, as a spectator and an enthusiastic and talented participant. But he would come to engage passionately with, over and above any other sport and for his entire life, hunting and fishing—which he vastly preferred to indulge in with friends joining him. All this is not to say that Hemingway was not an individualist. He was a great believer in man alone as a philosophical principle, but he most enjoyed his experiences with a side of companions.

War was something men pursued in the company of other men, at once lawless and governed by the strictest of rules. Two people from *The Kansas City Star* were to accompany him in the Red Cross ambulance service in

Italy: Wilson Hicks, the *Star's* movie critic, and Ted Brumback. Ernest convinced Hicks, Brumback, and *Star* editor Charlie Hopkins to come along on a last fishing trip in northern Michigan; his Kansas City roommate, Carl Edgar, who had spent summers in Horton Bay, needed no persuasion. (Hopkins was shortly to join the Army and Edgar the Navy, and Hicks had to back out from both the fishing trip and the Red Cross.) Ernest and his friends had not been in the country long when word reached them from Dr. Hemingway in Oak Park that Ernest had received a telegram from the Red Cross telling him to report to New York City for transportation overseas.

Ernest wasted no time in leaving, stopping in Oak Park only briefly; Brumback would join him in New York. Ernest wrote letters both to his parents and grandparents from on board the train, telling them it turned out he was traveling with a bunch of other Red Cross volunteers from Chicago suburbs New Trier and Evanston. At the Hotel Earle in Greenwich Village, Ernest also met a number of Red Cross volunteers from Harvard who were coming for the summer only (most volunteers signed up for six months), and who, as it turned out, shipped overseas a week before the others. While in New York, he received about $200 worth of uniforms and related material, including everything from a trunk with his name and unit stenciled on it to "aviator's puttees." Ernest was at great pains to convey to his family that the uniforms were those of "regular United States army officers" and that they wore "full U.S. officers' insignia." Like many young men new to military life, Ernest quickly became very interested in gradations of rank (which in turn were reflected in uniforms). At first, he was delighted to learn that privates and noncommissioned officers had to salute them "smartly," explaining that because of a "new ruling" the Red Cross volunteers were officers, "kind of camouflaged" as first lieutenants.

Ernest wrote his family on May 14 that he was seeing Mae Marsh in New York City and that, seemingly taken by the name or charming appearance of the Little Church Around the Corner on East 29th Street, he was thinking of marrying her there, saying, "I've always planned to get married if I could ever get to be an officer you know." Grace and Ed reacted with real alarm, sending a barrage of letters and telegrams his way, asking for an explanation and urging that he reconsider. (Grace felt that she must have been "a very poor success as a mother" if he had failed to confide in her about his love life, and, rather more typically, warned that he did not realize "what a laughing stock" he would make of himself if he went ahead with his plans.) Ernest answered their desperate inquiries pretending that he hadn't understood their questions before finally relieving their distress with a telegram on May 19. Meanwhile, however, he let Dale Wilson know that Mae had told him she didn't care to be a "war widow" but would wait for him, saying she was sure he would become a great newspaperman someday. He told Wilson that he had taken $150 his father sent him and spent it on an engagement ring for the actress (in the same breath confiding that he had also spent $30 on a pair of "cordovan leather boots"), and warned Wilson not to tell the whole "gang" about his engagement—though it would be okay to tell *Star* co-worker George Wallace. It is unclear what happened to this relationship after Ernest left for Europe, for he made no further reference to her, and her side of the record is silent. Marsh married someone else that September, however, which may have been the deciding factor.

During his brief stay in New York City in the spring of 1918, Ernest was too caught up in exciting new events and the anticipation of going overseas to dwell on what in other times might have been a considerably weightier matter. The volunteers were kept busy securing passports, visas, and passes to the war zone. On visits to Grant's Tomb, the Battery and the aquarium, and the top of the Woolworth Tower, Ernest was as much occupied with how he appeared in his new uniform as he was by the sightseeing. He told his parents that being saluted was nice, but returning all the salutes less so. Still, he was very excited to appear front and center in a parade down Fifth Avenue to raise funds for the Red Cross. Before the parade he told his parents that as "corporal of the 1st Squad" he would lead the parade, though afterward he said he led "the 2nd Platoon out in the middle of the avenue all by himself" and saluted President Wilson and his wife at the reviewing stand in Union Square.

He sailed on a French Line steamship called the *Chicago*—the first of many memorable crossings on the French Line, his favorite boats—sometime in the third week in May. On the voyage he met another volunteer who would become a great friend. Bill Horne (inevitably called Horney) was six years older than Ernest and a 1913 graduate of Princeton; he would eventually become a roommate of Ernest's and a member of his wedding party; another new friend was Howell Jenkins, called Jenks or Fever, also from the Chicago area, who was to be a member of Ernest's ambulance unit, Section 4. The trip took ten days, and the passengers endured a memorable two-day storm after two clear days. Ernest and his friends (Ted Brumback was also on board) played craps and poker, especially enjoying the excellent French cooking and French wines. The ship docked at Bordeaux on June 1, and the volunteers took a train to Paris the next day. There they were housed in a hotel on the Place de la Concorde, and enjoyed their stature in the eyes of the French military, which was heightened by the recent American-led victory at Belleau Wood. The Germans were regularly shelling the city with their novel Big Bertha, and Ernest convinced Ted Brumback to join him in taxis speeding to wherever they thought the shells had hit. He behaved, Ted said, "as if he'd been sent on special assignment to cover the biggest story of the year." Indeed, this brash exuberance characterized Ernest's approach to new experiences in 1917 and 1918, and again, a certain innocence pervaded his attitude. On his last night in Paris he conveyed to his family his pleasure in completing his uniform with a "cocky cap" and a Sam Browne belt. He looked "like the proverbial million dollars," he assured them. "'Tis Ye Gay Life."

The Red Cross volunteers took a train for Milan several days after their arrival in Paris, Ernest duly impressed by crossing the Alps. Immediately on their arrival they were sent on an unexpected mission: to gather up bodies and parts of bodies from an explosion at a munitions factory in a nearby town. The volunteers were directed to collect as many dead bodies as they could, and then to remove remains attached to the barbed wire fence surrounding the factory. Ernest went at the job most likely with his heart in his mouth. He was fascinated by the carnage, transfixed by the sight of the scattered body parts; he would later say that the biggest shock was that most of the bodies were of women, recognizable by their long hair. The experience made a great impression. Later, in *Death in the Afternoon* (1932), his book on bullfighting, in itself a sustained tribute to the art of death, he would include a "Natural History of the Dead" that described his cleanup work at the munitions factory and went on to describe in detail the nature of the change in corpses over time. ("The color change in Caucasian races is from white to yellow, to yellow-green, to black.") This was not knowledge he, or anyone else, could integrate. It lodged in the memory, undigested.

On June 9, Section 4 departed for the front, traveling first to Vicena and then to the town of Schio in the foothills of the Dolomites. Less than a year before, the Italian forces had suffered a crushing defeat at Caporetto, a rout that forced the Italian army back to the other side of the Piave River, which fortuitously flooded just after the retreating soldiers crossed it, halting the Austrians. There Ernest and the other men took up their duties, which consisted of accompanying experienced men driving ambulances to dressing stations near the front, where they would collect the wounded and transport them to hospitals. The drivers were housed on the second floor of a woolen mill, above a mess at which they were served plates of spaghetti, sausage, bread, and as much red table wine as they wanted. Ernest and his friends Howell Jenkins and Bill Horne devoured the repasts and absorbed their experiences on the job like sponges. In their ten days at Schio they also swam in the river and played a little baseball. When the editor of a monthly four-page paper for the drivers called *Ciao* posted a notice soliciting new material, Ernest stepped up and delivered in the form of a letter to "Al," a Lardneresque, breezy piece on the Schio boys' doings ("This Trench life is hell Al").

But Hemingway and his friends itched for action. They were soon rewarded when their commander told them the Red Cross had established several rolling canteens near the Piave, then quite a hot spot. Men were needed there to run the canteens, which dispensed soup, coffee, candy, and tobacco in pleasant rooms decorated with flags. The Red Cross drivers' job was really to lift morale, and they wore uniforms that looked like those of American officers in order to foster the illusion that the American army stood with the Italians in their fight. On July 1, Ernest and the others chosen to man these canteens, who included Jenkins and Horne, made their way first to Mestre and from there to Fossalta, which was to be their base. There they came under the command of Jim Gamble, a Red Cross captain who was designated "Field Inspector of Rolling Canteens"; Gamble would become an important figure in this phase of Hemingway's life. Ernest, eager as ever to get as close to the action as he could, asked to bicycle up to the trenches to distribute supplies—cigarettes, candy, magazines, and the like. About six days passed as Ernest traveled to and from the trenches, making friends with Italian officers.

Rumor had it that the Italians were about to mount an offensive against the Austrians, and the first week of July along the Piave was tense. Around midnight on the 8th, Ernest was making his way to a listening post between the trenches and the Austrian line when the shelling began. A trench mortar sounded, "chuh-chuh-chuh-chuh," from the Austrian side, and as the Minenwerfer landed Ernest experienced an explosion he later compared to a furnace door blasting open. When the air cleared, there were sounds of screaming and machine gun fire. Ernest saw that one of the men next to him was dead, and another had his legs blown off. Lifting the body of a third, badly wounded soldier, Ernest's legs bleeding from shrapnel, he staggered 150 yards to the Red Cross dugout. Walking felt, he said, like he "had rubber boots full of water on." On the way machine gun bullets ripped into his right knee and right foot. He collapsed when he reached the dugout, his clothing so bloody from the wounds of the soldier he carried that he was at first assumed to be near death. He lay there for two hours, in and out of consciousness, before Red Cross drivers took him to the dressing station at Fornaci.

At Fornaci, Ernest, with the other wounded, was given extreme unction by a chaplain with the Italian army, Don Giuseppe Bianchi. Captain Gamble comforted Ernest just before an Italian surgeon cleaned and dressed his wounds, removing what large pieces of shrapnel he could. From there Ernest was shipped to a hospital in Treviso, where he spent five days recuperating. Through most of this time, Gamble was his only visitor, and the two struck up a friendship. Gamble, thirty-six, had moved to Florence in 1914 to live the good life and work at his painting; among the many topics the two men apparently discussed as the days passed was the promise life in Europe held out for the artist. If Ernest hoped to become a writer, Gamble told him, the great cities of Europe were the places to be. Gamble had lost a friend, another expatriate painter and Red Cross officer, to a shell in Fossalta three weeks before; Lieutenant Edward McKey's last words were said to have been, "How splendidly the Italians are fighting!" Gamble might have recognized his dead friend's spirited enthusiasm in Ernest.

Hemingway needed further medical attention, and Gamble eventually got him on a hospital train "complete with flies and gore," according to the patient. Gamble made the forty-eight-hour train ride with him, and Ernest did not forget the older man's kindness, later telling him, "That trip to Milan from the Piave had all the bad part smoothed out by you. I didn't do a thing except let you make me perfectly comfortable."

As soon as Ernest reached Milan, he cabled his parents that he had been wounded but was all right and would receive the "valor medal"; at about the same time, the Red Cross also sent them a cable. But the first details his parents would hear were from a letter that his friend Ted Brumback wrote on the 14th, after spending the day with Ernest in the hospital in Milan. Brumback's is the earliest account of Ernest's heroism:

> An enormous trench mortar bomb lit within a few feet of Ernest while he was giving out chocolate. The concussion of the explosion knocked him unconscious and buried him with earth. There was an Italian between Ernest and the shell. He was instantly killed while another, standing by a few feet away, had both his legs blown off. A third Italian was badly wounded and this one Ernest, after he had regained consciousness, picked up on his back and carried to the first dug-out. He says he does not remember how he got there nor that he had carried a man until the next day when an Italian officer told him all about it and said that it had been voted upon to give him a valor medal for the act.

The Silver Medal of Military Valor, which, according to some, was conferred on any American who had been wounded, described his act of heroism differently: "Gravely wounded by numerous pieces of shrapnel from an enemy shell, with an admirable spirit of brotherhood, before taking care of himself, he rendered generous assistance to the Italian soldiers more seriously wounded by the same explosion and did not allow himself to be carried elsewhere until after they had been evaluated." One account, then, has Ernest carrying a wounded comrade, while another has him refusing aid until his comrades were seen first. This was just the beginning of some colossal confusion as to Ernest Hemingway's wounds and the nature and degree of his heroism. Many versions of the story would surface in the weeks and months to come as he told, retold, and embellished the tale of his exploits. Indeed, he would return to his wounding and his hero-ism obsessively, for the rest of his life, changing his report as the occasion demanded. Previous biographers have catalogued these discrepancies, and they will come up again in the course of Hemingway's story. For now, it suffices to say that rumors included "a dark-eyed olive-skinned beauty" left behind in Italy and a sexual encounter with the infamous Mata Hari (the spy was executed in 1917).

Yet Hemingway would as often leave hints that would seem to indicate what may have been the real truth. In revisiting the scene in his novel about World War I, *A Farewell to Arms,* he rethought his claim that he had car-ried a wounded Italian 150 yards (as one critic points out, that's one and a half times the length of a football field). Lieutenant Rinaldi asks Frederic Henry if he has committed "any heroic act" that might merit a medal. Frederic says no, he was eating a piece of cheese when he was hit. Rinaldi asks him to think carefully: "Didn't you carry anybody on your back?" "I didn't carry anybody," Frederic answers. "I couldn't move." (Chronicler Humphrey Carpenter finds it "astonishing" that Hemingway's biographers have accepted the "carrying-a-man" story "without question.") And, in one of the details that makes "Soldier's Home" such a superb story, Krebs finds, on returning home from the war, that his audiences have been so inured to stories about atrocities that he has to lie to get them to listen. He comes to feel terrible because of all the lying. Previously Krebs had been able to remember his war experiences and the simplicity of his actions and "feel cold and clear inside himself." Now those memories lost "their cool, valu-able quality and then were lost themselves." Because of all the lies, Krebs is left with nothing, yet another source of the alienation and despair he feels in returning home after the war. In the story "In Another Country," the hero befriends some Italian soldiers in the hospital with him in Milan. All have medals, and the Italians are "very polite" about the hero's medals; the citations, which the hero shows his friends, were full of "fratellanza" and "abnegazione" (Hemingway's citation uses these words), but what the citations really said was "that I had been given the medals because I was American." This hero, unlike Krebs, knows that "I would never have done such things." This hero was, during the war, and is still, "very much afraid to die" (*CSS*, 208).

In this novel and these two stories, it is as if the writer were running up red flags about his own war experiences and the claims he has made for them. Of course we cannot take what seem to be autobiographical stories as sovereign truth. Hemingway as a writer was very much aware of this, and in these two stories, which are about lying and the war, he is saying something more profound about lies and fiction, about heroes in real life and heroes in stories. But it would be disingenuous to look the other way when Hemingway presents these lying, or false, heroes. He wants us at least to question whether he has told lies about his war experiences. The writer of fiction is lying and false as well, the stories seem to say. But what does that mean in the aftermath of war? Is there any more authenticity, or truth?

"Soldier's Home" and "In Another Country" are also about, however, the aftermath of war for the soldier. Because of his war experiences, the hero of "In Another Country" is afraid of what will happen when he returns to the front, and he is afraid to die. "Soldier's Home" is more fundamentally about the profound alienation Krebs feels on returning home. Krebs's mother asks him if he loves her and he tells her no, that he doesn't love anyone; he also refuses when she kneels down on the floor of the dining room and asks him to pray with her. Shell shock, a term introduced in World War I, first mentioned in the British medical publication *The Lancet* in 1916, referred to an apparently new condition among soldiers consisting of nervousness, fatigue, various kinds of mental instability, and an assortment of physical ills ranging from facial tics to diarrhea. Shell shock was thought to be an organic phenomenon resulting from "shock waves" transmitted by the explosion of shells very near to the affected soldier; later it was understood to be also a psychiatric disorder, brought on by the stress of modern warfare.

Much ink has been spilled as to whether Hemingway's heroes suffer from shell shock, particularly the postwar Nick Adams, who in various Hemingway stories and especially the stories "Now I Lay Me" and "Big Two-Hearted River" barely holds himself together by means of the rituals of fishing and outdoor survival. Speculation also abounds whether Nick's creator actually suffered from the condition. The evidence is inconclusive, for no contemporary medical accounts of Hemingway's wounding mention the phenomenon, with one not very convincing exception. A Boyne

City, Michigan, doctor who saw Hemingway the summer after his war experience told a researcher, "Ernest was badly shell-shocked when he came for treatment in the summer of 1919. . . . As a patient, he was brave but very nervous." Aside from the dubious evidence of his fiction, Hemingway freely admitted in letters that after the war he was unable to sleep without a light on.

Ernest spent just over a month in the service of the American Red Cross in Italy, just a week in the combat zone near the Piave, and just seven months in Europe. Yet the experience of being wounded was profound, probably not only leaving Ernest with shell shock, or what we might call today post-traumatic stress disorder, but also greatly changing him psychologically and philosophically. He had described his near-death experience: he had felt his life leave him like a sheer white handkerchief pulled out of a pocket, in fairly convincing fashion; he was, apparently, near death indeed, and he would never be the same again. But the letters he wrote home about the experience, when they touch on how it changed him, sound like airy clichés. In an October 18 letter he tells the family that all soldiers offer their bodies, but "only a few are chosen. . . . Dying is a very simple thing. I've looked at death, and really I know. If I should have died it would have been very easy for me." It becomes clear that he is enamored by his own rhetoric when he refers directly to his mother, not only acknowledging her "sacrifice" in letting her son go to war but in supplying the words of nobility for her: "When a mother brings a son into the world she must know that some day the son will die. And the mother of a son that has died for his country should be the proudest woman in the world, and the happiest." He tells his family confidentially, "It is an awfully satisfactory feeling to be wounded, it's getting beaten up in a good cause."

Yet much later in life Hemingway kicked up a major fuss when critic Philip Young published a scholarly book putting forth the "wound" theory of his life and work. Put most simply, this theory held that the Hemingway hero (whom Young finds to be a stand-in for the author) has never recovered from wounds received in battle, and that in order to fend off complete dissolution, he develops a code of behavior to which he must adhere rigidly. Young is best describing this in the Nick Adams stories: "The Hemingway hero, the big, tough, outdoor man, is also the wounded man, and descriptions of certain scenes in the life of Nick Adams have explained how he got that way. The man will die a thousand times before his death, but from his wounds he would never recover so long as Hemingway lived and recorded his adventures."

Young's book was the first of a trio of critical books, the others by Carlos Baker and Charles Fenton, and Hemingway bridled when he heard that Young was writing about his life by way of some sketchy biographical information but mostly through the evidence of Hemingway's fiction. Determined to guard his privacy, Ernest railed against biography of living figures—but especially biography that finds its facts in the fiction. Young's book barely got published, so many roadblocks did Hemingway throw in his path. Hemingway ridiculed the notion that a wound he received at the age of eighteen could affect him for life and be the predominant force behind his fiction. Writing to Harvey Breit, a writer friend, in 1956, he said, "Sure plenty trauma in 1918 but symptoms absent by 1928."

Hemingway's objections to biographies of living figures on the grounds of privacy are certainly understandable, as is his vigorous disapproval of taking the heroes of his fiction as direct extensions of himself. Furthermore, he would brook no talk of psychological wounds. It's as bad to say a man has a neurosis, he wrote to Carlos Baker, as it is to say he has a venereal disease. One of the pioneers of modernism, Hemingway was not a modern man when it came to psychology. His characters exhibit plenty of neuroses, imbalances, and derangements, but never seek psychological explanations. Ernest notably did not get psychiatric treatment or any kind of therapy until the last months of his life.

What Hemingway would do with his war wounds in his fiction was, however, far in the future in 1918, when he was recuperating in the Red Cross hospital in Milan. For the time his wounding was indeed the major fact of his shortened life; he would spend the majority of his fiction as a young man sorting it out. The war is a significant force behind his early work, but after about 1928—to use the date by which Hemingway said he no longer had symptoms of trauma—the war no longer informs Hemingway's fiction. There are plenty of other forces motivating Hemingway's fictional heroes, and it is certainly a mistake to reduce the man's life to the trauma he suffered in World War I. For the present, however, he was already telling and retelling the story of his wounding, often fictitiously, trying out scenarios of heroism. He did indeed need to make sense of what happened to him and how it altered his world.

* * *

Second only to the trauma of his wounds, it is commonly thought, was the emotional body blow Ernest sustained in his first love affair, with the American Red Cross nurse Agnes von Kurowsky. Biographer Peter Griffin has said, "I think the real explosion that affected Hemingway was the broken heart Kurowsky gave him, not so much . . . being blown up." The

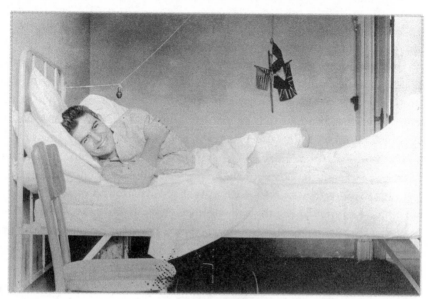

ABOVE: In a Milan hospital after being wounded near Fossalta. Summer 1918.

RIGHT: Ernest's wartime love, Agnes von Kurowsky, was a nurse at the Milan hospital; she was seven years his senior.

rejection, says his fellow Red Cross worker Henry Villard, writing with Hemingway scholar James Nagel, "had hurt him severely, so deeply that he wrote about it all his life." Ernest would indeed mention Agnes in the autobiographical segments of his 1936 short story "The Snows of Kilimanjaro," but almost nowhere else in his fiction—or, for that matter, in his letters, but for those written immediately after the love affair. There is, of course, a more famous exception: the love story in what is arguably his best novel, *A Farewell to Arms,* written in 1929. The heroine, Catherine Barkley, a nurse in the hospital where the hero, Frederic Henry, recuperates from his wounds, eventually becomes Henry's lover and dies while bearing his child. Hemingway changes not only details in the novel—Catherine is British, for instance, and nurses Henry in a British hospital—but fundamentals. Just as Frederic Henry fights in battles Ernest wished he had seen, like the Italian army's famous defeat at Caporetto, so too is Henry's love affair wishful thinking. Agnes von Kurowsky was bothered, she later told a biographer, the first time she read *A Farewell to Arms.* Then, hearing that it was said she was the basis for the heroine, she read it a second time—and became enraged. "Ernest never conceived the story [when I knew him] while he was in the hospital. He was much too busy enjoying the attention of friends and well-wishers to think about the plot of a novel; he invented the myth years later—built out of his frustration in love. The liaison [between Frederic Henry and Catherine Barkley] was all made up out of whole cloth."

Ernest met Agnes the second week he was in the hospital. The American Red Cross facility in Milan was brand-new and Ernest its first patient. The hospital was on the top floor of a four-story mansion-turned-pension, the nurses occupying the floor below. There were eighteen bedrooms, all "communicating," so in effect the hospital was a ward, but a luxurious one, half the rooms with balconies and the other half opening onto a large terrace.

Agnes von Kurowsky was born in Pennsylvania, seven years before Ernest, to a German father and an American mother. She had worked as a librarian before entering the nursing program at Bellevue Hospital in New York City and had arrived in Europe shortly after Ernest did, becoming one of the first nurses in the Milan hospital. She was tall and slim (Bill Horne, Ernest's ambulance service friend and fellow patient, remembered she had the smallest waist he'd ever seen) with dark brown hair and gray eyes—strikingly pretty, by all accounts, and exceptionally fun-loving, though a serious and competent nurse.

Ernest had struck up friendships with the other nurses before meeting Agnes, but he was immediately smitten with her, their relationship helped along by the hours an insomniac Ernest spent with her when she was on night duty. By late August, after two operations to remove material from his wounds, Ernest and Agnes were spending whatever time they could together, sightseeing and going to the races at San Siro on the afternoons when Ernest, now on a cane, was allowed out of the hospital. He wasn't alone in his admiration for Agnes: Bill Horne and Henry Villard were among a gaggle of men in the hospital all in love with her. She was undeniably a flirt and had left behind a fiancé, an older doctor, in New York; her most serious suitor while Ernest was in the hospital was a dashing one-eyed Italian officer, Captain Serena, of whom Ernest was very jealous. But she and Ernest were serious enough that they talked of getting married. In her diary Agnes called him Kid or Mr. Darling. She also wrote that he "is far too fond of me," and throughout their relationship, as far as can be judged from her diary and letters, she was seldom as serious as he was. Part of the reason was the seven-year age difference between them, on top of which Ernest was only barely an adult. Agnes did give him a ring of hers in September, however, and when she was sent for nursing duty in Florence in October and November, and then to Treviso in December, her letters to him, signed Mrs. Kid or Mrs. Hemingstein, were ardent.

Taken together, his wounding ("awfully satisfying") and his love for Agnes must have made life seem sweet indeed for Ernest. One nurse brought him martinis with castor oil floating on the surface, and Ernest sent the porter out for wine and liquor so often that the empty bottles in his room caused a major fracas. When Villard first met him, Ernest offered him "a swig" of cognac; Villard described watching Ernest in the room next to him "holding court," and noted how he "and a few other congenial souls formed a nucleus around the chief guest." Ernest was photogenic enough that a newsreel camera caught him in a wheelchair on the hospital porch waving a crutch for the camera, much to the delight of his older sister, who saw it unannounced before the feature in a Chicago movie theater (afterward, other family members repeatedly paid for the feature for the opportunity to see him on film). A photograph Ernest sent home showed him very handsome in his military cap in his hospital bed, rolled onto his side to face the photographer, his lips shaped in a cheerful whistle; the shot has become almost as iconic as the book jacket photo on Truman Capote's first novel, *Other Voices, Other Rooms* (1948). Then as now the picture seems evidence of near-heroic resiliency in the face of serious wounding and is taken as an example of Hemingway's fortitude, but it far more convincingly reflects the boyish fun that he was having with the frightening experience of war now behind him.

Yet Ernest's temperament while in the hospital was not as sunny as that photograph leads the viewer to believe. Villard has noted that "he was not an easy patient to handle . . . he could assert himself with no little authority if matters weren't exactly right or if he found the unrelenting discipline [of the hospital] too irksome." He had a temper, which he showed more during his hospital stay in Milan than he had ever before; it seems that his anger, previously never a real problem, was now becoming often ungovernable. He busied himself drinking, flirting with Agnes, and digging shrapnel out of his legs, putting the bits in a bowl by his bedside and giving them out freely as souvenirs. Much later, Agnes told Villard that she found Ernest "completely spoiled," that he "thrived on adulation" and "learned to play on the sympathy he received." With his wound stripes and medals, she said, he appeared "vainglorious." All decked out with his cane, wearing the Italian-made uniform he had specially ordered, complete with cape, he was a "laughing stock." While Agnes was clearly angry in this interview, her observations are not likely to have been fabricated. Villard agreed that Ernest was "overindulged" in the hospital, which "completely changed his fresh, boyish character and laid the foundation for a self-centeredness that saw himself in every action." There is no doubt that his experiences had marked him.

At any rate, he wanted to go back for more, and was elated when, at the end of October, he got permission to return to the front. It was an especially exciting time, as the Italians were about to rout the Austrians in the battle of Vittorio Veneto, but Ernest was disappointed when he came down with jaundice almost as soon as he arrived at the front and was sent straight back to the Red Cross hospital in Milan. He sorely missed being able to join the Italians at what would turn out to be the final, victorious battle in Italy, so much so that he often said he fought there. To the Hemingway family he claimed not only to have joined in that battle but to have been awarded the "Croix D'Guerre or Croce D'Guerra" for his actions there, a lie told with so little regard for being found out that his motivations seem downright bizarre. He was seeing his share of Italy and making plans to return in the near future, hoping that Agnes would be at his side as his wife. In September he had traveled to Lake Maggiore, where he met the diplomat Count Greppi, on whom he would base Count Greffi in *A Farewell to Arms*. In December he was in Treviso, seeing Agnes on the 9th for what would be the last time.

Just after Christmas he joined his Red Cross captain, Jim Gamble, for a week in Taormina, a charming and historically significant town on the east coast of Sicily, at a villa Gamble was renting. Little is known about this week, and some scholars have speculated that the two enjoyed a homo-sexual relationship during this time. Hemingway told recent acquaintance E. E. Dorman-Smith, a colorful Irish soldier Ernest knew as Chink, a story about his time in Sicily that raises more questions than it answers. Chink later related that Ernest told him he "had seen little of Italy, except from a bedroom window because his hostess in the first small hotel he had stopped in had hidden his clothes and kept him to herself for a week." But Ernest had nowhere near enough sexual sophistication to make an account like this believable. A different picture emerges in a letter Ernest wrote to Gamble in March 1919. "Every minute of every day I kick myself for not being at Taormina with you," the younger man writes. He recalls some of the characters they socialized with in the Sicilian town, including someone who called himself the Duke of Bronte and a couple of men called Woods and Kitsen. He evoked the memory of their time together, bemoaning the fact that he might still be there with Gamble: "When I think of old Taormina by moonlight and you and me, a little illuminated some times, but always just pleasantly so, strolling through that great old place and the moon path on the sea and Aetna fuming away and the black shadows and the moonlight cutting down the stairway back of the villa." It makes Ernest sick to think he might be there yet, he says.

What little is known about Gamble provides few clues to what might have been going on those moonlit Taormina nights. Born in 1882 and thus twelve years Ernest's senior, he was a scion of the wealthy Voorhees family of Williamsport, Pennsylvania; his grandfather was a railroad president. After Yale ('06) he studied at the Pennsylvania Academy of Fine Arts, and was painting in Florence when World War I started. After his service, Gamble was married briefly in Paris to a debutante from Philadelphia, and after that lived for the rest of his life with his sister in Philadelphia and at the family's summer cottage, Altamont, in Eagles Mere, on an Allegheny lake.

"You know how [Ernest] was," Agnes von Kurowsky later said to Carlos Baker, Hemingway's first biographer. "Men loved him. You know what I mean." Baker interpreted this to mean, "There were elements in his per-sonality that elicited a kind of hero worship." But surely another inter-pretation is that other men really did love him—or, rather, that they were sexually attracted to him. His first wife, Hadley, would later comment, "He was the kind of man to whom men, women, children, and dogs were attracted." Ernest was an extremely handsome young man, and his youth-ful enthusiasm and friendliness were catching and might easily have been misunderstood. He later complained about an Englishman who used to visit him in the hospital and bring him Marsala. Ernest liked him well enough, until the Englishman got "wet" and wanted to see his wounds dressed. "I didn't know well-brought up people were like that. I thought it was only tramps." (Later, he would note that from tramps he encountered as an adolescent he learned the homosexual saying, "Oh gash may be fine but one eye for mine.") He told the older man that he wasn't interested and gave him a bit of metal from the bowl next to his bed; the Englishman "left in tears." It seems clear enough that before the war Ernest avoided any boyhood skirmishes with homosexuality, to the extent that he recognized them as such. This trip to Europe was his introduction, and he reacted with fascination and perhaps an equal part horror.

We do know that Gamble invited Ernest to visit Madeira and the Canary Islands with him for two months, and Ernest was sorely tempted, as he told his family and friends. But he was thrown into great confusion and indecision by a far more tempting offer Gamble made to him: to travel with Gamble, living in Europe for a year, expenses paid. The idea of a free year in Europe, travel, and time to write greatly appealed to Ernest, so much so that he suppressed any knowledge he might have had of the kind of relationship seemingly sought by Gamble—whom, not incidentally, he apparently liked very much. Agnes, who had also witnessed the interest of the Englishman with the Marsala, was aware of Jim's invitation and knew what it meant, and felt it was her responsibility to do what she could to get Ernest back to the States quickly: "My idea was to get him home because he was very fascinating to older men. They all found him very interesting."

Evidently, however, Agnes was too inhibited by his innocence and her own lack of experience to broach the subject directly with Ernest. Still, she admitted to him that when she was with a fellow nurse, Elsie Jessup, she had wanted to do "all sorts of wild things—anything but go home." When Ernest was with Jim Gamble, she went on, he had felt "the same things." Thus cleverly establishing that she shared any ambivalence he might feel, she framed the issue as one of returning to the States: "But I think we have both changed our minds—& the old Etats-Unis are going to look tres tres bien to our world weary eyes." Perhaps she approved of the Taormina visit as the better of two evils—we can't know, as she evidently did not comment on it in her letters. She later told an interviewer that he would have accepted the invitation to the year abroad if she had not convinced him otherwise. "He really would have gotten to be a bum," she said, adding, "He had all the earmarks"—referring, most likely, not to any homosexual tendencies on Ernest's part but to what she perceived as a certain laziness or lack of ambition regarding conventional jobs. She said it was hard to convince Ernest to return to the U.S. because she recognized how tempting the offer was: "Leaving Europe wasn't easy to do because the man liked him very much and had money. [Ernest] wouldn't have to worry about a thing." In fact, with hindsight she felt she might have broken off their love affair but for this responsibility: "I had the feeling if I shoved him out then he would start off on that European tour."

In the end, Ernest resisted the offer, though Gamble would repeatedly make it and Ernest would repeatedly be tempted. The attraction between Gamble and Hemingway was far from over—though they would never, according to the record, see each other again. It is interesting to speculate, however, on the direction Hemingway's work might have taken if he had accepted the offer—and on what Hemingway's life might have been like.

There is no question that Ernest's friendship with Jim Gamble and his decision not to accept his friend's patronage was another turning point of a kind in his life. For it is true as well that Ernest's wounding on the Piave and his affair with Agnes (also by no means over) left an indelible mark, even if they were not as significant as his biographers have sometimes claimed. Ernest was only in Italy for seven months and in battle for less than a week. But something in his personality had changed, and it wasn't for the better. Not only had he lost a certain innocence, and with it much of his youthful good cheer, generosity, and expansiveness, but certain tendencies to impatience, irascibility when crossed, demand for attention, conceit, and dishonesty had been exacerbated, coming fully into play for the first time. What his friends saw as enthusiastic and friendly boyishness metamorphosed into a self-centered view of himself and events. Though his experience in Italy was one of several influences in his apprenticeship as a writer, it also contributed to Ernest's sense of his own importance.

FOUR

The word "charisma," overused today, originally had, and in some organized religions still has, a specific theological meaning: from the Greek, it means, roughly, "the gift of grace" or "a favor given." Max Weber first used the word to describe human relationships. "Charisma" has been widely used in its modern sense only since the 1950s, long after Ernest Hemingway's youth and young manhood, when he had it in abundance. The term retains several connotations: it carries the sense of something either given if not by divine forces then by the supernatural; it is not available to everyone and cannot be sought or acquired; it has something to do with leadership; and it is always a positive term, carrying meanings of kindness, attractiveness, and self-assurance.

The word describes the young Ernest. And Ernest got his charisma, without question, from a very human source: his mother. Like her, he had a commanding presence. As a young man, Ernest was "splendidly built," "robust, hulking, vivid"; as he aged he would become massive. He inherited his build from Grace: she was heavy-boned and strong and grew to have a massive bosom and upper arms, though her waist remained well proportioned. Her daughter Sunny stated, "When she entered a room everyone took note of her." Described as a "large, handsome woman," Grace was "formidable, statuesque." She was "unforgettable," according to one biographer.

But Grace apparently was commanding in ways that went far beyond her size or looks. Always curious about new experiences, as a young woman she had heard bicycling was "really just like flying," so she donned bloomers and tried riding her brother's new bicycle ("Of course such a costume is not graceful," she told Clarence, then courting her, "but it is sensible"). She seems to have had boundless energy and enthusiasm, whether for creating her children's baby books or pursuing her music. She collected royalties from several songs she composed (including "Lovely Walloona"). Later in life, when her voice had deteriorated to the extent that she could no longer give lessons, she took up art and taught that instead, as well as enjoying brisk sales of her paintings. She designed and built furniture. Later still, she had a lucrative career lecturing on such topics as Boccaccio, Aristophanes, Dante, and Euripides, and wrote poetry as well. Though there's no other evidence for this activity, which would have entailed an entirely new and difficult skill and finding access to some formidable equipment, she wrote Ernest in the late 1930s asking how he liked the tapestry she had woven for him. The vast amount of material relating to Grace's life in the primary repository of her papers, at the Harry Ransom Center in Austin, attests to this energy, and the scores of admiring letters from neighbors and other community members, from appreciative students and their mothers, speak to her charm and the contagious nature of her sheer zest for living.

Though Ernest never took up so dizzying a range of pursuits, not least because of his lifelong focus on writing, it is instructive in this light to consider his other activities in later years, from hunting and trout fishing on Western dude ranches, running with the bulls in Pamplona, covering two wars, fishing the Gulf Stream, and going on safari—twice—in Africa. His enthusiasm for these endeavors was, by all accounts and measures, so extreme as to be genuinely infectious. The number of friends and acquaintances he converted to deep-sea fishing alone is considerable. More than this, however, was the appetite for experience that he inherited from his mother, never more apparent than in his youth. Add to this the undeniable fact that—his claims about his upbringing aside—he grew up in a loving family with adoring parents and siblings, encouraged to believe that he could do almost anything he set his mind to, given his intelligence, talent, and physical presence, and it is no wonder that Ernest Hemingway in his adolescence and early adulthood seemed to all he met a young man of immense charm and potential. He virtually commanded affection, admiration, and attention. A natural leader, he was the center of any group, just as he had been when he "held court" in the Milan Red Cross hospital in 1918. The poet Archibald MacLeish would later say that Ernest was the only other man he knew besides FDR who "could exhaust the oxygen in the room just by walking into it."

If "charisma" carries a positive connotation, it also conveys a sense of power—power that the bearer can wield ruthlessly, to get his or her way, to dominate or intimidate. Grace was fully capable of this, and Ernest no doubt learned about this aspect of charisma from her. After the war, whether because of clinical shell shock or simply a considerable upheaval in his philosophical and psychological makeup and in his worldview, Ernest returned to Oak Park a changed person. It was not in his nature to simply come home and get on with the business of living, as another returning soldier might. Rather, Ernest spent several months enjoying the status of the conquering hero. If there is such a thing as a professional soldier, Ernest was a professional veteran. Even literally so, as he enjoyed a modest success lecturing on the war in the Chicago area, to the point that he had business cards made up advertising his skill. There was nothing cynical about this; Ernest was bursting with what he had seen, heard, and felt, eager to talk about it and share his enthusiasm. We might today say he was still high on his Italian experiences in love and war.

He was ready as soon as he hit American soil. Disembarking from the *Giuseppe Verdi* on January 21, 1919, he gave an interview to a reporter from the *New York Sun* who singled out from the other passengers the striking young man in cordovan boots and a cape lined in red satin over his officer's tunic. In a wildly error-ridden article titled "Has 227 Wounds, but Is Looking for Job: Kansas City Boy First to Return from the Italian Front," the reporter noted that the soldier had thirty-two pieces of shrapnel removed in Milan but had enough operations ahead of him to last "a year or more," that he probably had "more scars than any other man in or out of uniform," and that he had, after his recuperation, returned to the front until the armistice. In a burst of enthusiasm, Ernest told the journalist that he was looking for "a job on any New York newspaper that wants a man who is not afraid of work and wounds." The *Chicago Tribune* picked up the story and welcomed him back with the headline "Worst Shot-up Man in U.S. on Way Home."

Marcelline and her father were there to meet Ernest's train a few days later, after Ernest spent some time in New York City and stopped to see Bill Horne in Yonkers. Carol and Sunny were allowed to stay up late to greet their brother, and Leicester was woken at nine that evening to welcome Ernest, who promptly lifted his baby brother to his shoulders. The neighbors poured in with welcomes and congratulations. A few days later the *Oak Parker,* another local paper, printed an interview with Ernest in which he recounted how he carried his wounded comrade to safety after receiving his own wounds, now described as thirty-two bullets rather than shrapnel.

In the weeks following his return Ernest spent a lot of time recuperating in his third-floor bedroom, covered by a Red Cross quilt, one of many souvenirs he brought home. The others, far more exciting, included an Austrian helmet and revolver, and a pistol that shot off star shells, which he demonstrated in the backyard for Leicester and the neighborhood children. He hid a selection of liquor, including vermouth, cognac, grappa, and a bear-shaped bottle of Kümmel behind some books in his room, which he offered to his impressed sisters—though he claimed in a letter to a friend, not at all convincingly, that a newly tolerant Ed Hemingway "now chuckles at my tales of Cognac and Asti." One of the first letters he wrote was to Jim Gamble, bemoaning how he missed Italy and was sick about not being at Taormina with his friend. He said it drove him "to the camouflaged book case in my room [where I] pour out a very stiff tall one and add the conventional amount of aqua and . . . think of us sitting in front of the fire . . . and I drink to you Chief. I drink to you." For reasons of his own he evidently wanted to keep their friendship at a certain pitch, though the same letter is filled with news of Agnes as well.

Ernest later told a Fitzgerald biographer that he had trouble sleeping after his return from Italy, and that he became especially close to his sister Ursula during this period. He often found her waiting up for him on the staircase to his room. She had heard, she told him, that it was not good for anyone to drink alone, so she would join him in a drink. She not only stayed with him until he fell asleep but often slept in his room so he wouldn't wake up in the night and find himself alone. This difficulty sleeping was an emotional source for his masterful story "A Clean, Well-Lighted Place," in which a waiter at the well-lit café refers to "all those who need a light for the night," those who knew "it all was *nada y pues nada y nada y pues nada.*" Of course, Ernest's emotional response to his war experiences informed much of his best fiction in the 1920s and 1930s, but this was the only time he explicitly referred to his acute distress at nighttime.

After lying in bed mornings Ernest had lunch and then went for a stroll in the neighborhood, often to the library but far too often, for the neighbors' tastes, to the high school, where he waited for the closing bell to walk his sister Ursula home and flirt with some of the younger girls. By dint of the news reports about his service, and so to some extent the effectiveness of his exaggeration, Ernest was becoming a local celebrity. He soon received overtures from Italian Americans in Chicago who were eager to hear his stories and, most gratifyingly, take him into their community as one of their own. Not once but twice they brought a party— a "festa"—numbering close to a hundred guests to the Hemingway house, equipped with all kinds of foods, reported the *Oak Parker,* "from spaghetti to pasticerria," even supplying an Italian orchestra featuring a performance by a grand opera tenor straight from Italy. Wine flowed freely in the ordinarily teetotaling household—until after the second occasion Dr. Hemingway, never so tolerant as his son hoped, put his foot down and called off future gatherings. Ernest had made friends among the Italians by this time, and enjoyed trying to speak the language with them, especially a young man his own age named Nick Nerone. He and Nick frequented Italian restaurants in Chicago, as much for the pitchers of cheap red wine and for the pleasure of hearing Italian spoken as for the food. Ernest often brought along one or two of his pretty sisters on these occasions; Marcelline later remembered them all dancing the tarantella during one especially festive evening.

Ernest cut quite a figure in town, almost always dressing the military part on his afternoon walks, complete with his cape, uniform, and high, well-polished, cordovan boots. Marcelline, the sister with whom he was so close, later recalled this period in a memoir she published just after Ernest's death. Written when their complicated relationship had thoroughly soured, Marcelline introduces an incident in which some town gossips meanly comment on Ernest's appearance, particularly citing the ever-present boots. Marcelline indignantly interrupts one of the women, she wrote, telling her in no uncertain terms that Ernest wore them because the injuries to his legs gave him less trouble with the support the boots provided. Though Marcelline's motivations in including this story in her memoir are suspect, her reaction was indicative of her close relationship to Ernest at the time, and the way the family characteristically closed ranks

Chicago's Italian American community gathers in Grace Hemingway's music room to fête Ernest, home from the war.

around their son and brother. Possibly among themselves the family was amused by Ernest's pretensions, but they evidently felt they had to defend him from the calumny of outsiders.

Ernest was also dining out on his war stories. He lectured twice to rapt audiences at Oak Park High School, relaying stories about the Italian soldiers known as the Arditi, the so-called shock troops (the name comes from the Italian verb "to dare") reputedly made up of convicts who fought bare-chested with daggers and used cigarettes, according to Ernest, to plug up their wounds so they could continue to fight. He dramatically produced his bloodstained, shrapnel-shredded trousers and related in compelling detail the evening of his wounding, recalling his lack of sympathy with a wounded Italian who was crying for his mother in his pain. Ernest reported that he told the soldier repeatedly to shut up and then had to throw away his own revolver, so tempted was he to silence the soldier once and for all. (As one critic has pointed out, it's unlikely that a Red Cross worker would carry a revolver.) After his talk at the high school, in a bizarre apotheosis the students regaled him with a song composed by some unknown writer whose words ran, "Hemingway, we hail you the victor / Hemingway, ever winning the game." Ernest repeated his stories all over Oak Park—to the First Baptist Church, the Lamar Theater, the Southern Club, the Longfellow Women's Club.

Ernest was making some money from these lectures, and putting aside what he could against the day when he and Agnes, after their marriage, could return to Italy. Letters from her were arriving several times a week. (Ernest's side of the correspondence does not survive.) In retrospect it is all too easy to see warning signs in her letters. Her nickname for him, "Kid," began to seem suspect, as all too often she wrote down to him, as in one of the first letters that reached him in Chicago: "Dear Ernie, you are to me a wonderful boy, & when you add on a few years and some dignity & calm, you'll be very much worth while." Like Ernest, she was saving money—but for her leaves from nursing work and her "home coming clothes." She wrote of trying to decide "whether to come home, or apply for more foreign service," and, in the same letter, of a "tenente" giving her a "desperate rush."

The blow fell in a letter of March 7. She wrote that she was "still very fond of you," but "it is more as a mother than as a sweetheart"; she was "now and always will be too old." She brought up problems in their relationship that existed before he left Italy and pointed to developing features in his personality that seemed troubling. She referred to an occasion on which Ernest had acted "like a spoiled child." "For quite awhile before you left," she wrote, she was "trying to convince myself it was a real love affair" because they had so many fights, which ended all too often with her giving in "to keep you from doing something desperate." She had referred in earlier letters to similar threats, and, indeed, all too often in his relationships with women in the future, Ernest would threaten suicide.

The only way Ernest could take this in was in believing that Agnes was rejecting him for another man. For the letter closed with her saying that, as always, she hated to hurt him, and was able to do so now only because of the distance between them. "Then—& believe me when I say this is sudden for me, too—I expect to be married soon." She closed by assuring him she knew he would have a "wonderful career" and signed the letter "Ever admiringly & fondly/Your friend./Aggie."

Ernest's sister Marcelline remembered that on reading this letter Ernest took to his bed and actually ran a fever. In a letter written to Bill Horne just hours after he heard from Agnes, he blamed himself for leaving her in Italy where men were bound to make advances that the nurse, who "needs somebody to make love to her," could not withstand. Chivalry carried the day, and he said that he hoped her fiancé was "the best man in the world," and that while his first impulse was to invite Bill on a toot, he didn't want to do that because he loved Agnes too much to become bitter. Later, however, bitterness won out, and he wrote to Elsie MacDonald, a friend among the other Red Cross nurses in Milan, that he hoped that on Agnes's return to the States she would trip walking down the gangplank "and bust all her goddamn teeth." Many jilted lovers are bitter, but this remark seems especially pointed—perhaps because of the vivid image, which must have required some imaginative thought.

For Ernest was writing, and had been since his return from Italy, and his romantic setback barely occasioned a pause. In fact, he was beginning an intense apprenticeship that would last for some time—seeming to Ernest, in fact, to last way too long. He was letting it be known around Oak Park and among all his friends and acquaintances that he was embarking on a literary career and that he intended to make his living by his pen in any related fashion while he honed his craft. He noted to Bill Horne that he had been advised by Oak Park luminary Edgar Rice Burroughs, whose *Tarzan* books, recently made into a film that grossed over a million dollars, were enjoying a huge success, that he should write a book. Around this time Ernest sent out a story called "The Mercenaries," featuring an Italian soldier of fortune who recalls the moonlit nights in Taormina that Ernest had reminisced about to Jim Gamble, to *The Saturday Evening Post* and *Redbook,* both then among the best-paying outlets in the short story market. He also had great hopes for a story called "The Woppian Way," about a boxer named Pickles McCarthy, which he worked on for months and months and sent out repeatedly, without success.

The question of Ernest's future hung fire. He wanted only to work on his writing. He later said that after the war he felt he should not have to do anything for some time, and that his goal was to find a way to hunt and fish for a year or two. In his defense, he probably did require some time to rest and heal—not to mention to develop his craft if he was at all serious about a writing career. But his immediate future remained a concern, especially for his parents. The issue of college arose again around this time. Ernest would remain bitter about his lack of a college education for the rest of his life, blaming his family and his mother in particular for this omission. It grated on him that Marcelline had gone to Oberlin—even though she dropped out after her first semester. Significantly, she claimed that her parents told her that she couldn't return for the second semester because they didn't have the money. Other reports claim she left because she flunked out, but no doubt the family's finances were a factor—or, rather, Ed and Grace claimed they were a factor. Paying for college, refusing to pay for college, threatening not to pay for college: all were ways the parents could continue to control their offspring. Not that there was anything sinister in their motives; they may well have behaved this way out of a complex of emotions based on genuine love for their children. The children sensed something of the sort was going on, but that did not prevent them from feeling ill-used, and over time the role that college played in Ernest's and Marcelline's future—and perhaps their siblings' as well—became a hugely fraught issue.

Ernest went so far as to write Lawrence Barnett, a friend from the Red Cross days, about Barnett's experience at the University of Wisconsin, the college he said his parents were advocating at the time. The University of Illinois remained a possibility, as did Cornell, Ted Brumback's alma mater. But Ernest had said back in his Kansas City days that he didn't need college; the work he was doing was an education in itself. He did indeed exhibit some of the characteristics of the autodidact, especially in the wide range of his reading. Back from the war, however, he began to complain—as he would continue to do in later years—that he had to educate himself because college was closed off to him. In October he would enumerate the books he was reading, adding, "These are all things that are further along than Marcelline ever achieved so you see I have not been idle." Ernest's complaint about college took a more serious turn, however, in the summer of 1919, as his mother undertook a building project that threatened her marriage and the very future of the Hemingway family. He would always claim that she spent his college money on what he described as a folly, and he never forgave her for it.

* * *

Across Walloon Lake from Windemere, the Hemingways' summer cabin, was Longfield, the property Grace and Ed had bought in 1905, seven years after buying Windemere. On the property were a sizable stand of virgin timber, an old farmhouse, and some outbuildings. For a time the Washburns, tenant farmers, ran the farm "on shares," and at Dr. Hemingway's direction planted extensive fruit and nut trees and grew enough vegetables to supply the Hemingway family all winter. The only paying crops were fruits and nuts and sometimes a crop like potatoes. Ice was also cut there in the winter, stored in Longfield's icehouse, and sold in the warm weather. By 1919 the Washburns had moved on, the farm standing vacant for some time, and the Hemingways arranged for vegetable plantings that in recent years had increasingly become Ernest's responsibility.

Longfield had a centrally located hill, a favorite picnic spot, which the family dubbed Redtop Mountain after the reddish grass that grew there. Originally they thought to build a new family cottage there, but the children objected, preferring Windemere; Grace Hemingway, however, said she always wanted to build a cottage for herself there for its view and its seclusion. In turn, Dr. Hemingway always objected that the only water source was a hand pump at the base of the hill, and that it would be impractical to repeatedly carry food and water up the hill.

In 1919 Grace revived the plan. She had long complained that summers at Windemere involved more work than relaxation for her, and that even when other family members took up cooking duties, she spent far too much time in the rudimentary kitchen. As the four oldest children became noisy adolescents, she became more determined to find a refuge, reasoning that they needed her less and that Carol and Leicester, the two youngest, could be looked after by their siblings or join her at the new place she hoped to build atop Redtop Mountain.

Characteristically, Grace had learned a great deal from planning the new Oak Park house that the family moved into in 1906, and in the spring of 1919 she happily threw herself into a design for a simple cottage that could provide living on one story, with a loft added almost as an afterthought for visiting children. The combination kitchen and pantry she planned would be tiny, Grace reasoning that all she needed was space to make herself a cup of tea and a sandwich. "If you think I'm going to waste my time stirring up or baking anything, you're very much mistaken. I expect to enjoy this cottage," she said. After consulting some Petoskey builders she found that she could build such a cottage for a thousand dollars, a sum she could provide out of her own earnings from voice lessons.

Dr. Hemingway balked. He found the scheme foolish and impractical, and forbade Grace from going ahead with it. An exchange of letters between Grace and Ed details this story, as do Grace's letters to local builders. The letters include a remarkable chart that Grace drew up answering each of her husband's objections. A careful reading of this material yields the unmistakable conclusion that what Dr. Hemingway and the older children objected to was not the cottage itself, but the fact that Grace intended it as a refuge not only for herself but for her intimate friend, Ruth Arnold, herself almost a member of the Hemingway family.

Ruth had come to live with the Hemingways after taking voice lessons with Grace in 1906. Grace was thirty-four at the time, Ernest seven years old, and Ruth, quickly known to the family as Bobs or Bobbie, fifteen. Later she told Ernest that she remembered hunting and trout fishing with him in the summers at Horton Bay. "I was always a 'tomboy,'" she added. Ruth was a member of the Fippinger clan on her mother's side. The family had immigrated to the States in 1832 from Bavaria, while her father's family, also from Bavaria, arrived a little later. Ruth's older sister, Elizabeth, had a real musical gift, accompanying Grace on the piano in local concerts for many years. Ruth first cared for the Hemingway children in the summer of 1906, when, following her usual custom (and with her own money), Grace took the youngest Hemingway child—in this case, Sunny—on a trip to Nantucket. It is not clear why or how Ruth joined the household, though Grace referred later to Ruth's "unhappy and unsympathetic home life." Letters between Grace and Ruth during Grace's vacations away from the home indicate that Ruth played a part not unlike that of an au pair today, close to the children in age and often their friend as well as their caregiver. When the two younger children were born, Carol in 1911 and Leicester in 1915, Ruth took on many aspects of their care, playing more of a traditionally maternal role. She later told Grace, "I began loving them while you were carrying them." Letters between Grace and Ruth over these early years are freely affectionate; Ruth calls Grace "Sweet Muv," Grace calls her "Boofie."

But something had changed by the summer of 1919, when Grace was forty-seven and Ruth twenty-eight. Over Dr. Hemingway's objections, Grace had hired a local builder, Edwin Morford, and Grace Cottage went up early in the summer. Dr. Hemingway uncharacteristically stayed in Oak

Park that summer, which included a rare visit from China of his brother Willoughby and Willoughby's wife, Mary. Such a visit would traditionally have kept Grace in town as well, but this time it did not. Still, the reason for Ed's absence from Windemere in 1919 is not entirely clear, though Grace implied that she had urged him to stay home for "2 months rest from the family." She had "so hoped and prayed," she went on in an early August letter, "that the quiet would help you to readjust your mental attitude and find yourself with God's help in relation to your family." If he had not been able to "control" his "mental attitude," she asserted she would stand by him, but that her "dear blessed children" needed her, as did "the dear faithful Ruth, who has given me her youth and her loyal service for these many years." No one, she wrote, "can ever take my husband's place." Here, however, she added in the margin, evidently an afterthought, "unless he abdicates to play at petty jealousy with his wife's loyal girlfriend." In July Grace referred to herself and Ruth at the cottage, but by early August Ruth had evidently returned to Oak Park.

Dr. Hemingway always kept track of his correspondence, retaining carbons of letters sent. In the summer of 1919 he numbered the letters between himself and Grace, and there are two letters missing from the sequence, both from early August. Subsequent letters and replies make clear that he had banned Ruth Arnold from the Oak Park home.

That summer in Oak Park Marcelline had moved into a room near her new job at the Second Congregational Church, but she was still spending a lot of time at the Kenilworth Avenue house and making regular reports to her mother. She and Grace seem to have shared some long-standing criticisms of Ed Hemingway and, indeed, the whole Hemingway clan, whom Marcelline called "inquisitive and suspicious." There are indications that Dr. Hemingway's "nerves" were especially bad in 1919, and an almost conspiratorial tone characterizes letters between mother and daughter that summer. Marcelline longed for Grace's return from the lake, she said. "Dad does not *mean* to be irritable & exacting, and he does not even think that he is other than normal in any way, but the facts are that he is not normal at all in his disposition or attitude." She tried to talk to her father about other things, she said, "But Dad always gets back to his pet peeve—poor old Bobs." She told her mother about arranging to meet Ruth at the movies without the doctor's knowledge, and how Ruth asked Marcelline if she could see whether Ruth might be reinstated: "But Dad acts so insane on the subject, that I told her I couldn't for a while."

Meanwhile, Ruth was pouring her heart out to Grace: "I often wonder how I could have lived without your beautiful and genuine influence,"

Grace's friend Ruth Arnold (far left), age twenty-one, with the Hemingway children
(left to right), Sunny, Ursula, Marcelline, and Ernest, at Windemere, the Hemingway
family cottage on Lake Walloon, 1912. Ruth, known as Bobbie, came to live with
the family that year, and became involved in a relationship with Grace, which
became the subject of a feud between Grace and Ed Hemingway in 1919.

she wrote in August. "I want to stand with you physically, mentally, and spiritually—and will *always* want to help and do for you when ever I can." In another letter she said she had been thinking of Grace Cottage all day, picturing herself first at the kitchen table, and then in the living room, where she and Grace had worked on a rag rug together, "and then into your bedroom with a four-poster picture [?] bed which makes one long for bedtime." It was hard enough, she said, not being able to go to the Oak Park house, "but I could never, never give up you, or your love." She said in closing, "I wish I could do [your hair] and stroke your forehead as I enjoy doing each night that I could. Remember, I am loving you."

Except for Marcelline's conspiratorial whisperings with Grace, the Hemingway children's correspondence had been by and large silent on the subject of Ruth Arnold. There was one exception: around June 9, 1919, Ernest wrote his father that the hired hand over at Longfield was getting ready to "do the hauling"—apparently, moving Grace's belongings into Grace Cottage. He disingenuously asked his father if he was aware of what Grace was up to, letting his father know he thought it was just silliness. As time passed, the primary objection Ernest would make to Grace's building a refuge for herself and Ruth Arnold was his mother's "selfishness." His mother had pretty much hated him, he later told a Petoskey girl, "ever since I opposed her throwing two or three thousand seeds away to build a new cottage for herself when the Jack should have sent the kids to college." Never mind that none of "the kids" was ready for college in 1920; it sounded better than when he complained, as he would do increasingly, that his mother had prevented him from going to college through her "selfish" act.

What happened when the summer's contretemps subsided is unclear, for there are no further letters among family members extant until the summer of 1920, when it appears that Ruth and Grace were once again separated: "By the sound of your letter Muv I'm afraid you are lonesome," Ruth began. "Remember dearest 'every body is lonesome.' So am I *lonesome for you.* I have so much to be happy for up there. . . . Cheer up little Muv—when I get up I won't let you be lonesome. . . . How I wish I could put my arms around you and kiss you good night." It seems to have been agreed that Ruth would not go up that summer as long as the doctor was at the lake as well: "I suppose Dr. will be going up North soon. . . . If he stays all summer all right. I would be broken hearted not to get up—but would rather be, Dearest, than have any talk—So remember he comes first." The previous summer the tongues of what Grace called "the rocking chair brigade" had wagged all summer long, and neither wanted a repeat of that.

Years later Grace Hemingway spoke up about the Ruth Arnold affair, when word reached her through Ruth that two Petoskey residents, a "Miss Marjory Andree and Mrs. Clara Havell," had been talking about the events of the summer of 1919. She complained about the "repetition of an old malicious story (that Ruth separated Dr. Hemingway and his wife)":

> In the 1st place Ruth never had such thoughts; and in the 2nd place Dr. Hemingway and his wife were never separated. They were loving and sympathetic every day of their lives. No more understanding people could live together 32 years, through sunshine and shadow. Dr. Hemingway suffered mentally with that terrible disease, diabetes [diagnosed in the late 1920s]; but God never gave a woman a better husband than he was to me. As for Ruth; I have known her and loved her for nearly 30 years, and she has always been loyal and true to the Hemingway family.

The Hemingway family maintained an almost complete silence on the subject of Ruth Arnold until Grace's death in 1951. Ruth had married in 1926, but her husband died shortly after their marriage, and in 1932 Ruth came with her four-year-old daughter, Carol (whose godmother was Carol Hemingway), to live with Grace in the smaller home in nearby River Forest to which Grace had moved after Ed Hemingway's suicide in 1928. Grace does not seem to have mentioned Ruth in any of her letters to her children over the years (though she did tell Ernest when Ruth's husband died), a silence that is hard to reconcile with the presence of Ruth's daughter growing to adulthood in the household the two women shared.

It is impossible to tell how the Hemingway family viewed the relationship between Grace Hemingway and Ruth Arnold. Ernest clearly saw his mother's building Grace Cottage as a betrayal of his father and the family, though he focused on the money it cost her, money he thought would have been better spent or put aside for himself or the younger children. We simply don't know whether Ernest (or his siblings) saw the relationship between the two women as a lesbian one—though Ed Hemingway clearly did.

*   *   *

Ernest stayed on in northern Michigan after the summer of 1919, first at the Dilworths' in Petoskey, and later in a small room in a boardinghouse on State Street, where his landlady often surprised him with lunch and a thermos of hot cocoa. He was working on his writing and hoping to send out some stories, but he was frustrated that a Linotypists' strike had shut down most of the magazines. He had the beginning of "The Woppian Way" worked out and rewritten, ready to go. In the meantime he was reading a lot—Maupassant, Balzac, and historical novelist Maurice Hewlett. In the early fall he had been spending time with a high school girl, Marjorie Bump, flirting with her and taking her fishing, but she'd gone back to Chicago for school and he was lonely.

When Ernest gave his conquering-hero-home-from-the-wars speech at the Ladies Aid Society at the Petoskey Public Library, he attracted the interest of Dorothy Connable, a Toronto woman whose mother lived in the area. She was the wife of Ralph Connable, head of the F. W. Woolworth chain in Canada, and when she told her husband about Ernest, Connable met with him and presented an attractive job offer. The Connables and their adult daughter would be spending the winter in Palm Beach, but his nineteen-year-old son, Ralph Jr., disabled after a high forceps delivery at birth, would be staying behind in Toronto to go to school. Connable asked Ernest to be a companion to the boy, taking him to cultural and sporting events and teaching him some athletic activity that might give him more physical self-confidence (Ernest took this to mean that he should teach Ralph, who was lame, to box). Connable would give Ernest $50 a month and pay expenses, and Ernest boasted that the job "looks like the original Peruvian doughnuts," a term meaning an excellent idea, which first appeared in Harry Leon Wilson's popular *Ruggles of Red Gap* stories. (Ernest admired this kind of term extravagantly and used it in his short story "The Mercenaries.") Ralph Connable would give Ernest an introduction to his friend Arthur Donaldson, who worked in advertising for the *Toronto Star,* and Ernest had some hopes for a job there.

When Ernest arrived in Toronto in early January, the Connables had not yet left for Florida, and Ernest came to like all of them: Ralph Sr., with whom he played pool; his wife, Harriet, whom he praised extravagantly to his family, and twenty-six-year-old Dorothy, a Wellesley graduate who became a good friend and to whom Ernest gave advice on such subjects as playing roulette. He liked Ralph Jr. all right, though they never really hit it off. Before the Connables went south, Ralph Sr. brought him over to the *Star* offices, where Arthur Donaldson introduced him to Greg Clark, the features editor of the *Toronto Star Weekly.* Clark recognized a potentially fine journalist in Ernest, noting his solid experience at the excellent *Kansas City Star.*

The *Toronto Star*'s weekly publication, under the direction of the *Star*'s owner, Joseph Atkinson, was designed to entertain; it was the first Canadian paper to publish American colored comics and each issue was lavishly illustrated. J. Herbert Cranston, editor of the *Weekly,* was a big believer in the human interest story, saying later that the paper "aimed to give people largely what they wanted to read rather than what they ought to read." He noted Ernest's energy and his decidedly ironic style, and, since the weekly depended on freelancers whom they could pay cheaply, gave him free rein. "Hemingway," he said later, "could write in good, plain Anglo-Saxon, and had a certain much prized gift of humor."

Ernest's first piece, published in the *Weekly* on February 14, 1920, was about a scheme developed by a group of Toronto socialites to circulate works of art through their homes, thereby giving a favored group of artists exposure to well-heeled potential buyers and the women some interior decoration gratis. But the woman who ran the scheme wouldn't give Ernest the names of the artists or the women through whose houses the works would circulate, for fear, she said, of a fatal "taint of commercialism," which might attract less worthy people to try to join the scheme. Ernest brought all his irony to bear on his subject, which was supposedly the circulating scheme but obliquely the snobbery of the Toronto matrons: "It wouldn't be nearly so enjoyable to have one or two colorful joyous pictures in your home if you knew that any other responsible person might have them too," adding, with thick sarcasm, "Imagine the élan to be deprived from the public library if only a dozen or so persons were allowed to make use of it!" His second piece, appearing March 6, was about getting a free shave at a barber college and similar free services. He would write nine more articles before mid-May, earning a penny a word. When the Connables returned they let Ernest stay on, but by the end of May he yearned for another summer of fishing and hunting, and between times working on his writing.

Ernest's work for the *Star Weekly* was uneven. He turned out several stories about fishing and camping, drawing on an already honed talent for delivering instruction in how best to do things, a knack that would carry over into his fiction, with its frequent procedural detail. But these fine pieces, with descriptions that would not be out of place in his later Nick Adams stories set in the outdoors, were offset by too many glib and heavily ironic commentaries on the kinds of subjects that are staples of desperate newsmen: a piece on dentistry, for example, and another advising Canadians who had worked in American munitions factories how to hold their heads high on their return to Canada and blend in with the veterans by dressing like them. He tried out new techniques, however, which would work for him in the writing ahead of him. A piece about veterans who had not seen combat was written almost entirely in dialogue, whereas he adopted a terse, pared-down style and an insider's voice in a story about racketeers. This six-month period was a prelude to a four-year tenure on the *Toronto Star:* he would refine his craft, but he would also develop an ironic and cynical cast of mind that would occasionally get in his own way in the coming decade. And he would come to hate journalism, seeing it as a pitfall for a young writer—which, at this point, was what he felt he was.

FIVE

At twenty, Ernest was spoiling for a fight. His new self-image, that of a hard-boiled journalist-writer who broke women's hearts and drank a lot in Chicago dives—and its summer counterpart, that of the dedicated but fun-loving fisherman, always with a crowd of followers—demanded that, at twenty, he leave his family behind once and for all. His parents' religiosity, their intense belief in the moral life, their conservatism about sex and other essential activities, and mostly their middle-class values: all demanded that he reject them absolutely. When Ernest really wanted to attack his mother, he accused her of spending time with "moron literature" and of reading *The Atlantic Monthly* "just so someone would see [her] doing it." What he now saw as his mother's pretensions, her interests in art, music, and literature, were easy targets. Ernest's father had no comparable habits, though he invoked the Bible and cracked a harsh whip when it came to the children's pulling their weight around the house. This also won Ernest's disapproval—though on the whole his father evaded the wholesale rejection suffered by Grace.

The stage was set for a major conflict in the summer of 1920. Because family finances were shaky, Dr. Hemingway stayed in Oak Park for the summer, spending only two weeks in July at Windemere (Ruth Arnold delayed her journey to Longfield and Grace Cottage until after the doctor's vacation). Grace badly needed help with the heavy chores Ed Hemingway usually took care of: digging holes to bury garbage, killing and plucking the chickens, shooting the rabbits that were destroying the garden, and dragging the dock out onto the lake and securing it. Meanwhile Ernest, who intended to fully enjoy his summer up north, was staying in nearby Horton Bay. It could well be his last lake summer for some time, for he intended to ship off from San Francisco for India, China, and Japan the next winter in the company of Ted Brumback. He wanted to spend his vacation fishing and writing, not helping out around Windemere.

Word had also reached the Hemingways of their son's involvement with

Front row, left to right: Katy Smith, Marcelline, Ernest, and Bill Smith, ca. 1919

local girls, all much younger than he. On his return from the war, he had hung around some friends of his sisters'. During the summer and fall of 1919 he played at relationships with local Petoskey girls, including Grace Quinlan and the Bump sisters, Marjorie and her younger sister Georgiana. It's impossible to tell how serious—or rather, how sexual—these relationships were, especially because Ernest would later, in his fiction, describe Nick Adams and either his sexual initiation or that of the local girls up north. A series of letters Ernest wrote to the thirteen-year-old Grace are if not love letters then certainly very flirtatious pieces of writing, teasing her by bestowing and recalling his "love" when she misbehaves in some way, such as not writing often enough or by trading "cruel" gossip about him. A representative letter, written on the occasion of Grace's fourteenth birthday in September 1920, says how hurt Ernest had been to hear "you don't like me as well as you did. And because I did like you better than anybody else it hurt when I heard that you were saying things about me behind my back." The adolescent tone of these letters, and the immature tenor of these relationships, all indicate that Ernest regretted his inexperience with girls his own age at Oak Park and River Forest High School. He also regretted, of course, his rejection by Agnes. This rejection, in combination with his high school inexperience, could perhaps be said to have driven him to turn to younger girls to act out his nascent sexuality. Whatever the combination, it was too potent for Grace Hemingway, who took particular exception to his romances with young girls.

Another ingredient in the tense situation between Ernest and his family in the summer of 1920 was his refusal to look for a real job—instead, as his parents saw it, bumming around Petoskey and environs, unemployed but refusing to help out his mother. Ernest was to turn twenty-one in July, and it rankled Grace and Ed that he seemed to lack both the work ethic—writing did not count—and a sense of duty. Ed Hemingway wrote Grace from Oak Park all summer, telling her that he was praying "that [Ernest] will develop a sense of greater responsibility." As Ernest continued intransigent over the course of the summer, Ed despaired, he said, of finding the "means of softening his Iron Heart of selfishness." Both parents recognized that open conflict was imminent. Ed wrote Grace, "I think Ernest is trying to irritate us in some way, so as to have a witness in [Ted Brumback] in hearing us say we would be glad if he would go away and stay." Separately, the parents resolved to throw him out of the house.

Hemingway biographers have made much of the incidents that followed. Ernest's little brother, Leicester, at age five hardly aware of what was going on, would be largely responsible for the invention of Ernest's preferred version of the story; Leicester was the first to set it down in his *My Brother, Ernest Hemingway,* published a year after Ernest's death. Grace Hemingway threw Ernest out of Windemere, the story goes, the same night as his twenty-first birthday dinner, when she handed him a letter that dramatically ordered him off the premises. The letter was so good—Ed called it a "masterpiece"—that this version of events has won out. In the letter, Grace compared a mother's love to a bank account. As a baby and a toddler the child draws heavily on the account, but withdrawals properly become smaller and less frequent as the child grows up, learns to take care of himself, and, crucially, begins making deposits to the account by bringing Mother cards or flowers—she cited the Easter lily Ernest had brought her that spring—and attempts to soften Mother's load.

Not so Ernest and his "bank account" of his mother's love, despite the lily:

Unless you, my son Ernest, come to yourself; cease your lazy loafing and pleasure seeking; borrowing with no thought of returning; stop trying to graft a living off anybody and everybody . . . stop trading on your handsome face to fool little gullible girls, and neglecting your duties to God and your Savior, Jesus Christ; unless, in other words, you come into your manhood, there is nothing before you but bankruptcy—you have overdrawn.

Next to this ringing rebuke—an outstanding letter by the family standards, the Hemingways in general masters of letter writing—the actual letter throwing Ernest out came from Ed Hemingway and was but a pale imitation. Ed sent this letter to Grace with much fanfare, for her to read and pass on to Ernest. In fact, he sent Ernest via Grace not one but two letters telling him to leave the premises, one composed in mid-July, after he returned to Oak Park from two weeks at the lake, the second soon after. Ed described each one in letters to Grace that he sent along with them. "I have written Ernest," he wrote Grace on July 18, "I have advised him to go with Ted down Traverse City way and work at good wages and at least cut down his living expenses." Evidently the letters were so unspectacular that Ed uncharacteristically did not keep copies, while Grace's "bank account" letter to Ernest is preserved in many drafts and copies among her papers at the Harry Ransom Center at the University of Texas. Similarly, Hemingway biographers have chosen to go along with Leicester Hemingway's story—following Ernest's version—that has Grace Hemingway handing her son her inspired letter on the night of his birthday.

In all this hullabaloo, skillfully delineated by Hemingway scholar Max Westbrook, the occasion for Ernest's ejection from the family hearth is attributed to a single incident. Ursula, then eighteen, and Sunny, sixteen, had connived with two neighbor children, Bob and Elizabeth Loomis, to hold a midnight supper on the lake, to which they invited Ernest and Ted Brumback. When Mrs. Loomis found her offspring and a visiting friend missing in the middle of the night, she marched over to Windemere, where Ursula's and Sunny's beds were found to be empty. When Grace wrote to Ed describing the incident, she claimed that Mrs. Loomis said she would take her family back to Oak Park "unless we could do something to get rid of these grown men loafing around." This sounds suspiciously like Grace's complaints about the unseemliness of Ernest's being an adult among children that summer. She acknowledges that the picnic "was not wicked except in the deceit" and the "general lawlessness that Ernest instills into all young boys and girls. He is distinctly a *menace to youth,*" Grace wrote dramatically.

In fact, the letters that flew between the parents that summer indicate that the Hemingways were almost comically worried about the burgeoning sexuality of their daughters as well as their eldest son, driven to showdowns and curfews and improvised punishments. Ursula and Sunny were boy-crazy that summer, and their behavior horrified their parents, so much so that Grace chose to blame the influence of their "worldly" older brother (who in fact probably had little if any sexual experience as of the summer of 1920). Dr. Hemingway would take the girls in hand when they returned to Oak Park in the fall, he reported to Grace: "They will get into the game and do right or they will wish that they had." Otherwise he would make them go out and earn their own living. He commiserated with Grace in having such ungrateful daughters. Ironically, Marcelline, the sister to whom Ernest was very close, was beginning to show the hypocritical behavior for which Ernest would later vilify her almost as roundly as he would his mother. She had in some respects paved the way for her younger sisters with her courting behavior the previous summer. As she became more serious about a boy of whom her parents approved, she became their ally in keeping the younger children in line—so much so that Ed held her up to his wife as a happy example: "Do not worry about the girls. . . . I had just the same problems with the dear eldest daughter [Marcelline], now she would scarcely acknowledge it were possible."

In the wake of the midnight supper in July 1920 and the showdown with his mother, Ernest, rather understandably it seems in retrospect, "said he'd never open or read a letter from his pa or ma," Grace wrote in a letter to Ed July 28. She elaborated on his crimes, making clear that it was Ernest's rampant and blatantly awakened sexuality that so vexed her. Mrs. Dilworth had let her know, she said, that there were people in Petoskey who "had got his number" and were "disgusted with him—the way he lays himself out to make love to a girl until she is wild about him, and then goes off and leaves her for another." She added, "Oh! It is hard to have raised such a son."

Weeks later, Grace told Ed that she was planning with the Loomises a picnic supper on a Sunday for "the whole crowd," indicating the incident was smoothed over quickly enough. In fact, as the weeks wore on and Ernest was allowed back on the premises, if not forgiven, Ed grew alarmed, sensing that the family drama around the midnight supper and Grace's sensational letter was obscuring the real truth. Letters from Ernest seemed to indicate that the midnight picnic had not only been innocent but that Ernest and Ted had functioned more as chaperones than as conspirators. Ed urged Grace to "beg [Ernest's pardon] if she had 'falsely accused'" him, even if he had been guilty of other mistakes. "For false accusations," he wrote, "grow more sore all the time and separate many dear friends and relatives." Ernest had evidently convinced his father that in general he had been falsely maligned, accused of loafing when he had in fact been "doing the work of a 'hired man.'" "Let it go," Ed advised Grace, "if [Ernest] will only now stay away from irritating you." A pattern was being established in the Hemingways' relation to their eldest son, a pattern that would characterize their ways of dealing with him in the future, until Ed's death in 1928. Ed would maintain contact with Ernest even when Grace, in high dudgeon, wrote Ernest that she could not countenance his behavior, whether writing books with disreputable subject matter and language or divorcing his first wife. Ed would moralize and quote the Bible to Ernest, but he would also assert his pride in his son. Another, more serious stage was being set in the summer of 1920, on which Ernest sketched out a family drama in which his hectoring, shrewish mother drove his put-upon, innocent father to suicide.

Ernest wrote about the midnight picnic and his expulsion from the house in an August letter to thirteen-year-old Grace Quinlan. He set it in a context that reveals the architecture of the story he was concocting for himself: about what he saw as his mother's betrayal of the family, laying the groundwork to blame her for his lack of a college education, and later, and more meaningfully, for what he saw as her role in his father's death. Ernest explicitly made a connection between Grace Hemingway's actions of the summer to her actions the previous summer, when, over her husband's vigorous objections, she built Grace Cottage as a refuge for herself and Ruth Arnold, spending the money that should have been spent on his college education. He alluded to what he saw as the scandal associated with Grace Cottage: "That's another story," he said. "Fambly stuff. All famblys have skeletons in their closets. Maybe not the Quinlans," he added, "but the Steins [Hemingways] have heaps."

*   *   *

In retrospect, Ernest's life after his return from the war in 1919 does seem aimless if not feckless, but it may not have been very different from those of many a young man in his circumstances. He lingered up north for the fall duck season but was running out of money. He talked vaguely about going to work in the Hudson Bay oil fields, but his plans were as indefinite as his talk about shipping out on a freighter for the Far East proved to be. He boasted to his friend Howell Jenkins that he had a job offer from *The Kansas City Star* that would let him name his price; with his salary supplemented with pay from the *Toronto Star* for pieces he could write on the side, he hoped to save a lot of "the Jacksonian." For whatever reason he never did move to Kansas City. Then a letter came from Bill Horne, his friend from the ambulance corps, saying he intended to relocate to Chicago and that he had enough money to take a room and look for a job. Ernest jumped at the chance to join him. So desperate was he for a place to live that was not with his parents in Oak Park that he moved into a furnished room Bill was renting in a fourth-floor walk-up on North State Street. In the evenings they went to Kitsos, a Greek coffee shop on the corner of State and Division Streets where for 65 cents they could get a filling dinner.

Ernest was turning over various moneymaking schemes in his mind, as indicated by two job-seeking letters he sent to the *Chicago Daily Tribune* in the fall of 1920. One was in answer to a job opening advertised for a newspaperman looking to get into magazine work; Ernest drafted a response that claimed newspaper work back as far as 1916 (when he was on his high school paper). The other letter answered an ad for an advertising copywriter. Ernest wrote off in his cynical vein, saying that rather than writing a clever, eye-catching letter he would simply set forth his credentials (which included being twenty-four) and thus "overcome your sales resistance." Though there's no evidence he ever sent off the letter looking for a reporting job, he seems to have been a bit more serious about applying for the advertising job, the profession then as now thought to be a surefire way for writers to make a lot of money they could someday use to get their "real" writing done.

At roughly the same time a couple of members of the Smith family, his old friends from the lake, moved into a rambling, somewhat palatial apartment at 100 East Chicago Street, just a block away from Horne's rooming house. The apartment was leased from Mrs. Dorothy Aldis, a wealthy local woman, by Y. K. "Kenley" Smith and his wife, Doodles, a pianist. "Big-hearted Y.K.," said a colleague, "promptly moved all his indigent friends in to share the apartment." Bill Horne and Ernest both came, moving into a room together, as did Katy Smith, Kenley and Bill's younger sister, who was trying to break into magazine fiction and who shared a room with Edith Foley, another writer. Other roommates were Don Wright, who, like Kenley, was a successful advertising man, and sometimes Bobby Rouse, who worked for the Guaranty Trust. The residents seem to have been fanatical about playing bridge, soon to become a national fad. On nights out they frequented Italian restaurants like the Venice Café where they could buy red wine despite the onset of Prohibition in January, or *Bierstuben* on Halstead Street retooled as German restaurants, where they could usually find beer.

Ernest evidently applied to further jobs through the *Chicago Tribune,* and he finally landed a position. "He was pretty completely out of a job and money until this house organ editorship came along," said Bill Horne. *Co-operative Commonwealth* was the journal of the Co-operative Society of America, a trust set up by former *Tribune* executive Harrison Parker to which members subscribed with the promise of high returns on their investment; the investment allowed subscribers to "avail themselves of the advantages of co-operation as a welcome escape from the unconscionable profiteering of rapacious tradesmen." The scheme was as crooked as it sounds, and in fact Harrison Parker was a smaller-scale counterpart of Charles Ponzi, the scamster who was plying his trade in Boston at about the same time, though Parker's subscribers may have been fooled by the co-operative rhetoric behind the outfit. The magazine Hemingway edited—and, for the most part, wrote—was the prime vehicle for this rhetoric. Ernest himself was seduced at first, thinking "a cooperative thing was straight because they had tried to start one for marketing apples when I worked on the farm in Michigan." The job kept him very busy, though his schedule was his own and he wrote a lot of copy after eating lunch in the apartment, returning to the office around four. The responsibilities could become fairly oppressive when deadline approached.

Though he tried to make the best of it, Ernest knew the editing job had no future, and, in fact, the end was already near as far as Harrison Parker was concerned. The fraud's subscribers would sue him for their considerable losses in the fall of 1921. Among other things, it was learned that his wife was paid a salary of $500 a week and as an officer of the trust received over a million dollars in subscriptions. When Ernest's prospects looked especially bleak, Kenley Smith brought him up to Critchfield's, the advertising agency where he and Don Wright worked. Roy Dickey, Smith's copy chief, interviewed Ernest, taking note of "his dark hair trimmed to quite long sideburns like a matador," the first of many tonsorial styles he would affect in his twenties. Though nothing came of this meeting, advertising seemed to Ernest and his friends the easy way to make money. Those with jobs farmed out some assignments, like writing copy for Firestone tires or Hansen Gloves, to Ernest—or so he wrote in a letter to Grace Quinlan, possibly just to impress her.

A distinct cynicism permeated Ernest's milieu, the advertising work and the pedestrian, PR-related *Co-operative Commonwealth* job lending themselves all too well to a jaded worldview that the denizens of Kenley Smith's Near North Side apartment adopted with alacrity. The jargon Ernest and his friends used in letters, developed by Ernest in high school, became almost impenetrable to the uninitiated. "We had much fun after hours," Don Wright later said, "telling yarns about the scheming of the low grade morons who were our bosses in agencies and magazines." Ernest waxed heavily ironic about his job, though he did not immediately realize the co-operative scheme behind it was fraudulent. He and his roommates delighted in inventive, satiric play about advertising, Ernest, for example, thinking up a product, bottled blood from the stockyards, to be marketed as "Bull Gore for Bigger Babies."

But advertising could boast of real writers among its ranks, biding their time and producing ad copy for bucks. In Chicago, Sherwood Anderson was one such person, and Kenley Smith and Don Wright struck up a solid friendship with him. He was a frequent visitor to the apartment, sometimes accompanied by the poet Carl Sandburg, and Ernest studied Anderson carefully. The story of his dramatic beginning as a writer impressed Ernest terrifically; the older man had suffered a breakdown in 1912, disappearing for four days and deciding on his emergence to chuck his job as a Cleveland paint company executive and leave his wife and children to become a writer. He had published two novels, in 1916 and 1919, but when Ernest knew him he was forty-four and enjoying his first experience in the literary limelight as the author of *Winesburg, Ohio* (1919), a novel that was an amalgam of interrelated stories exposing the often twisted and emotionally impoverished ways of the residents of a small town. *Winesburg's* sexual frankness was widely discussed at the time, disapproved of by readers of conventional morality like Ernest's parents, a fact that would have very much impressed Ernest at the time.

Though Ernest learned a few lessons in literary style from Anderson, a realist who relied on laconic sentences to convey great emotion, he also drank in everything he could from Anderson about the life of a writer. For despite his rejection of small-town life and bourgeois values, Anderson was working for Critchfield's writing ad copy when *Winesburg* came out, and thus shared the cynicism of the younger men, who viewed advertising as a corrupt practice that nevertheless paid the bills.

Sandburg provided another example of a writer who made ends meet in a day job, writing for the *Chicago Daily News* to support his poetry. Though Sandburg's poem "Chicago" is remembered today as a hoary cliché, it is impossible to overstate its impact, along with the rest of Sandburg's *Chicago Poems,* published in 1916, on Chicagoans of an impressionable age, especially those who had aspirations to write. His apostrophe to Chicago as "Hog Butcher for the World, / Tool Maker, Stacker of Wheat, / Player with Railroads and the Nation's Freight Handler; / Stormy, husky, brawling, City of the Big Shoulders" was simply unforgettable.

In fact, though Ernest (or many an observer or participant, for that matter) did not know it at the time, Chicago was in the midst of a literary renaissance that had begun around 1912, represented by Edgar Lee Masters, Vachel Lindsay, and Theodore Dreiser as well as Anderson and Sandburg.

Sherwood Anderson, 1923

One Hemingway critic, Charles Fenton, has described literary Chicago as "a sort of cornbelt Florence." Ernest's and Kenley's friends could buy the latest of the little magazines and other interesting material at the nearby Radical Bookshop, on North Clark Street. Though Hemingway would never be associated with this movement, it is significant that he came of age in the midst of it, for Chicago writers were drawing on themes like the rejection of rural life, the increasing alienation of the modern industrialized worker, and the emergence of the teeming city as a new setting for moral conflict. Chicagoans Ben Hecht, Floyd Dell, Anderson, Dreiser, Sandburg, and Hemingway's early literary model, Ring Lardner, all started their careers as newspaper writers, another feature that would have encouraged Ernest at the start of his career. And the literary magazines that nurtured modernist literature, Harriet Monroe's *Poetry: A Magazine of Verse* and Margaret Anderson's *The Little Review,* were Chicago-based, both editors part of a salon that included Dell, Dreiser, and Anderson. Ernest, becoming friends with both Anderson and Sandburg, was in the thick of it, and the Chicago writers, perhaps as much for how they lived as how they wrote, impressed Ernest enormously. They were all to some degree controversial, both for their subject matter and their frankness, and Ernest learned from them that it was not important enough just to write, but that the writer must push the envelope, engage in nothing less than literary revolution, or, in the famous words of Ezra Pound (who would become another huge influence), "make it new."

Sherwood Anderson's biographer has written that Kenley Smith and his friends "could sit and listen to Anderson for hours. They enjoyed his flamboyance, the way he told his stories, the way he dressed." Anderson told his listeners about such professional matters as publishers, magazine editors, and writers' finances; he gossiped about other writers. He took Ernest out to Palos Park, the town outside Chicago where he did his writing, impressing on Ernest the need for a sacrosanct place to write, and he talked about Turgenev, Waldo Frank, and other writers, all new to Hemingway, who had influenced him. He told Ernest about a magazine in New Orleans, *The Double Dealer,* which was beginning to publish the works of the Southerners Jean Toomer and Allen Tate and was giving a big push for Anderson. Ernest submitted to the magazine, which accepted them, an ironic, fussy prose poem called "A Divine Gesture" and a decidedly strange, uncharacterizable, very short poem called "Ultimately." Ernest showed Marcelline, herself a frequent visitor to literary gatherings at the apartment, a "thin, pale-green paper-covered volume" that contained a poem of his; what Marcelline remembered was seeing in type "By Ernest M. Hemingway." Ernest would later say that at about this age everything he wrote sounded like Kipling, whom he inordinately admired at the time.

Hemingway scholar Charles Fenton has described the atmosphere at Kenley Smith's apartment on East Chicago Street (and another, equally palatial apartment on Division Street, to which Hemingway et al. moved en masse along with Kenley and Doodles) as characterized by "fraternity-type horseplay" though hardly "bohemian." Ernest thrived, as was his wont, on having a live-in cohort and audience; he would try to re-create this kind of situation for the rest of his life. By all accounts, he shone. "He was by far the most colorful of us," Kenley remembered, "and very witty." Perhaps Ernest was enjoying the equivalent of the college experience he was missing: dorm-style living, a fraternity atmosphere characterized by superficially clever, superficially sophisticated sexual conversation. Not yet ready to live on his own, and not a solitary type of person to begin with, Ernest experienced the Division Street apartment as a kind of halfway house to adult living. Of course, his acquaintances Anderson and Sandburg were showing him a new route that would successfully carry him through and beyond this collegiate phase.

Marcelline remembered that Kenley and Doodles Smith had a kind of open house on Sunday afternoons, perhaps a sort of ironic salon. One of Katy Smith's guests that Sunday was a "tall, auburn-haired" young woman from St. Louis. The date was sometime after October 1920, the guest was Hadley Richardson, and Ernest had just met the woman who would be his wife. Bill Horne would later remember that Hadley came up to Chicago "and boy, it was like being run over by a truck. There just wasn't any question about it: Ernie was gone."

*   *   *

Elizabeth Hadley Richardson was twenty-eight when she met Ernest, seven years older than he (as had been Agnes von Kurowsky), though neither realized this for some time. They were too busy losing themselves in each other as they fell precipitously in love. Hadley was a shy and uncertain young woman who spent her twenties almost in seclusion following a kind of breakdown that compelled her to quit college. Yet she also managed to separate herself from a very bad family situation that would probably have permanently crippled someone with less resilience.

Hadley was descended on both sides of her family from New Englanders who had made their way to the Midwest. Her father's father started out as a schoolteacher but went on to manage a grocery store, then founded the Richardson Drug Company, the largest pharmaceutical manufacturer west of the Mississippi. (No relation to the Lunsford Richardson Wholesale Drug Company founded in 1898, known for Vicks VapoRub.) Clifford Richardson outshone his younger brother James, Hadley's father. Clifford became a partner in the family drug business, while James worked there with so little enthusiasm that after a while he just stopped going in, spending most of his time drinking. When the company was divided between the two brothers after their father's death, Clifford used the proceeds to start what would become a leading St. Louis bank, while James gambled his share away in the stock market.

On her mother's side, Hadley's grandfather was also an educator, the founder of two preparatory schools. Florence, Hadley's mother, the only girl among three boys, showed a talent for music at a young age. Almost from the start, Florence, described by a relative as "a difficult, controlling woman," dominated her rather meek husband, though she confined her ambitions to the family as long as she kept bearing children. When Hadley was born in 1891, she had an older brother, Jamie, who was twelve (two other boys had died as infants); an eleven-year-old sister, Dorothea, who was Hadley's favorite sibling; and a two-year-old sister, Fonnie (for Florence). Hadley grew up in relative affluence in an outsize brick mansion on Cabanné Place in the West End of St. Louis, then a thriving metropolis rivaling Chicago. Like Grace Hemingway, Florence had a music room; hers had twin Steinway grand pianos. While Hadley was close to her sister Fonnie as a small child, Fonnie soon became her mother's favorite, and Hadley increasingly turned to her older sister, Dorothea, who all too soon married and left the family home. In the meantime, Hadley's father, alcoholic and depressed by his stock market losses, shot himself. Hadley was thirteen.

Florence Richardson had always been formidable, involving herself in cultural activities that helped to transform St. Louis, taking off the worst of its provincial edges. Increasingly she turned to spiritualist practices and especially to theosophy, an occult branch of religion and philosophy then quite a fad. Always a believer in the rights of women, Florence, with Fonnie, founded the St. Louis Equal Suffrage League in 1910, and mother and daughter threw themselves into its activities.

Though feminists have long had to endure being accused as man-haters, in the case of Florence and Fonnie this may have been a partial motivation for their women's rights activity. Her mother and her sister "both hated men," according to Hadley. Behind this seems to have been a hatred of sex. "My mother used to tell me," recalled Fonnie's daughter, "that if I enjoyed sex I was no better than a prostitute." Florence was adamantly opposed to birth control, which would seem anomalous except in light of her belief that without the fear of pregnancy as a check men would want sex all the time and marriage would degenerate into "one long orgy." She encouraged women to "revolt" against their husbands and deny them sex, which she called a "hateful, pernicious invasion of body and soul."

Hadley had no basis for disagreement, but she remained largely uninterested in the feminist cause. Her mother barely noticed. The attention Florence paid to her daughter was confined to treating her as an invalid—though nothing in particular bothered Hadley physically. "I know that in their way, my mother and sister loved me. But they were also out to ruin me."

After graduating from St. Louis's academically rigorous Mary Institute, Hadley had resolved to attend Bryn Mawr College in the fall of 1911. That summer, her favorite sister, Dorothea, died from burns following a domestic accident. Hadley was numb from grief, and never really adjusted to Bryn Mawr. She was taken up by a classmate, Edna Rapallo, who brought her to the family vacation house in Vermont. Hadley became close to Edna and to her mother, Constance. The sequence isn't entirely clear, but at some point Florence decided that both Rapallo women were lesbians and that Hadley had lesbian feelings for Constance Rapallo. Hadley later told Ernest that her mother had so confused her that she worried about her sexual orientation: "Being very suggestible, I began to imagine I had all this low sex feeling [for Constance] and she for me—quite certain now it was nothing but a very spoiling absorbing affection." The whole business rattled her, further undermining her already shaky self-confidence, and in May 1912 she dropped out of Bryn Mawr.

Returning to the house her mother now shared with Fonnie and Fonnie's young family, Hadley continued to suffer psychologically. Music was the only thing that allayed her depression. But her mother told her she lacked the stamina necessary for a musical career, and Hadley came to believe her. Living in near isolation, with only her mother and sister to advise her, Hadley grew suicidal. With World War I, she was able to get out of the house, thanks to a regular volunteer job in the public library, where she sorted books to send to soldiers, but whenever Hadley talked of getting a real job her mother angrily forbade it.

In 1920 Florence Richardson was diagnosed with Bright's disease, a kidney ailment then thought to be fatal. Hadley nursed her mother for months. Perhaps it is not so strange that as Florence weakened Hadley grew stronger, began to enjoy a social life, and even acquired beaus. Having been thrown on her own devices in a household where she got mostly abuse, Hadley was emerging as an amalgam of strong, independent thinking coupled with an understandable hesitancy and tendency to self-effacement. When Florence died at the age of sixty-five, Hadley, a genuine late bloomer, came into her own. She had been "starved for people [who] might really mean something" to her, she later told an interviewer. "I was ready to go. I was a very excited young woman" when she met Ernest. "I discovered that I was alive."

In October, Hadley began planning for a weekend in Chicago to visit her friend Katy Smith. Katy, still living in a hotel and not yet a resident of her brother's big apartment on East Chicago Street, arranged for Hadley to stay in a spare room there on her visit to the city. That night the apartment's inhabitants threw a party. Hadley noticed a young man with "a pair of very red cheeks and very brown eyes straddling the piano bench." She later told Ernest, "You surprised me I remember by seeming to appreciate me without my succeeding, from excitement, in doing anything to be appreciated." All evening she was aware of a "hulky, bulky, masculine" presence by her side; Ernest later said he knew that night that he wanted to marry her.

Hadley stayed in Chicago for three weeks, and during that time the two got to know each other well. Ernest often burst into the room where she was staying, reading aloud from something he had just written. Though Hadley didn't much like Hemingway's writing at this juncture, it was impossible not to believe in his future as a writer, given that he was so confident of it and so clearly could succeed at anything he put his hand to. "Ernest sort of knocked people over—rightfully so," Hadley later said. "His potential was right out in the open." After she returned to St. Louis, the two began a practice of writing daily or twice daily to each other. (Very few letters on Ernest's side have survived, but almost all of Hadley's were preserved.)

The sort of misunderstandings encountered by many young lovers plagued them: Ernest had been physically distant on the train platform when they parted; Hadley went to a St. Louis dance with someone else. The first real test of their relationship came around the holiday season in 1920. Hadley would never know the true nature of the test, but she passed her own small part in it with flying colors. It was occasioned by a letter Ernest received from Jim Gamble. He was leaving for Europe on the *Rochambeau* on January 4, Gamble said, though his plans after that were tentative and "can be formed according to your wishes." They had not been in touch since March 1919, and Gamble wrote, "What have you been doing since I heard last? Married? Writing?" Ernest composed a cabled reply almost immediately, of which survived a much emended draft. "Rather go to Rome with you than heaven Stop," the cable began. "But am broke stop," he wrote, even as he must have known that Gamble would also renew his offer to pay expenses. Twice in the cable draft he said he wasn't married, each time crossing it out, so that his marital status in the end went unmentioned.

"I'm liable to leave Tuesday for Rome, not Rome N.Y. the other one, on the biggest chance of my career," he wrote Hadley on December 29. "Career hell—I haven't had one—but I'm liable to with this Rome thing." Kenley Smith and Ed Hemingway both thought he ought to go, said Ernest. Hadley tried to be enthusiastic and said Rome sounded wonderful, adding, "I would miss you pretty frightfully unless I tho't it was going to be great gain to your work." A few days later she conceded that "it might be just as much fun" to write to him in Rome as Chicago. Hadley seemed to have no idea what was at stake, though comments she would make later in life indicate she was aware of Ernest's attractiveness to men. But Hadley's ignorance of the ramifications of Ernest's decision not to go to Rome with Jim Gamble in no way meant the decision was not a crucial one. Ernest was sure enough of his own eventual success as a writer that he could turn down what might have been a shortcut to that success. Was he uneasy that the trip would involve homosexual relations, about which he was very ambivalent, to say the least, even more so now that he was in love with Hadley? The decision concerned much more than a Roman holiday.

He was choosing to follow a more conventional life course—marriage and eventually a family of his own. Mostly, however, he was reluctant to leave Hadley, sure now that they had a future together. And so the crisis passed.

In early January, Ernest and Hadley began to talk about a wedding in the fall. They talked often of going to Italy, or, as they called it, Wopland, and both were buying up lira to take advantage of the exchange rate. Hadley was comfortable financially, as she gradually revealed to Ernest. Florence Richardson had recovered from her husband's financial losses with wise investments, so that her estate was worth $75,000 when she died, though the will was tied up in probate when Hadley and Ernest met. Hadley received the income from a $30,000 trust set up by James Richardson, Sr., her grandfather; eventually this, combined with the interest and other earnings from her mother's money, gave her an annual income of about $3,000, or about $37,000 today. (Hadley also would receive $8,000 outright from the estate of Arthur Wyman, her mother's brother, just after her wedding—a boon for the start of her married life.) Evidently Hadley's financial picture wasn't relevant to the couple during their courtship, though they did joke about her "filthy lucre and how we could with its aid and abetment go Woplandwards in November [1921]." But her income was a key piece in the unfolding of Hadley's independence after her years under the rule of her sister and mother. She was beholden to no one, and the effect on her confidence must have been considerable.

The two visited each other several times. At the Smith apartment they often slept on the roof after a good deal of petting, and they seem to have had sex there in July 1921, some eight or nine months after they met. Hadley wrote Ernest in August that she was "laid by the heels, yesterday, 19th, by that which all women agree in abhorring—but for which I praise the Lord." Hadley genuinely looked forward to married life: when her friend Georgia Riddle asked her if she didn't feel that being engaged was the greatest state of a young woman's life, Hadley said, "Why goodness no. . . . Seems to me everything lovely & wonderful is yet to come—sort of like the difference between studying the sun thru astronomical methods & simply and joyously living in a country saturated by light."

In fact, by all accounts, Hadley and Ernest seem to have been positively modern and healthy-minded as a couple. Hadley was worried about the word "obey" in her vows, and asked Ernest jokingly to give her some orders so she could practice it: "I ain't no good at it.—& I can't remember gettin' no orders from you anyway. . . . You write me an order a day and I'll begin trying to carry em out. Then—what do *you* do when I *don't* obey? Just quit lovin' or cherishin' or nothin'?" Both of them were reading Havelock Ellis.

Even with all the baby talk—Hadley called Ernest Oin or Nesto—Hadley recognized what they were doing. "Tremendous amount of maternals or paternals in our love for each other—you realize?" she wrote. Hadley could also evoke the loving times they spent together during their courtship: "a dark cool inside room of a German restaurant on a hot afternoon" or "moments of sitting near you in lobbys, street cars, rooms with other people just not talking or anything, just loving you so hard, so longing to get hold of you to love you with my arms and lips when a certain look came into your eyes."

They spent the weeks before the wedding apart, Hadley on a month-long trip to Wyoming with her friends Ruth Bradfield and George and Helen Breaker, and Ernest fishing on the Sturgeon River with Howell Jenkins and Charles Hopkins. The wedding was held on September 3 in the church at Horton Bay, the altar decorated with goldenrod and other wildflowers, balsam branches and bittersweet at the ends of each row of pews. Hadley's surviving sister, Fonnie, was maid of honor and her attendants were Helen Breaker, Ruth Bradfield, and Katy Smith; Ernest's were Bill Smith, Howell Jenkins, Carl Edgar, Jack Pentecost, and Art Meyer; Bill Horne was his best man. Though Sunny alone of the Hemingway family was not present at the wedding, no family members were in the wedding party. Excellent photos of the wedding survive: a grinning, relaxed Hadley and Ernest, a wreath on Hadley's auburn hair, damply dark from a pre-ceremony swim; Hadley and Ernest on a bench, Ernest, laughing, blurrily raising his hand to cover his mouth in a gesture unique to him; Ernest and his attendants linking arms, handsome in their dark jackets and white pants, Ernest in the middle standing a step in front of the others. After the wedding they drove a friend's Model T the four miles to Walloon Lake, where they climbed into a boat and rowed across the lake to Windemere, provided by Ernest's parents for the honeymoon.

*   *   *

In marrying Hadley, Ernest took an extremely important step. She believed in him utterly. When she heard Ernest was writing a novel in March she could barely contain her excitement. They talked a lot about writing, with Hadley giving him a Corona typewriter for his birthday and even introducing concepts that would become essential to his formulations about writing, in particular his so-called iceberg theory: "You have such a magnificent grip on the form back of your material, no matter how strange it is, like the icebergs," she wrote in August. Though she was still extremely serious about her piano playing, she said that it would "gladly be slid into a corner to keep out of his way." In another letter she asserted, "I'm wild to make a way for you to do your darndest, dear." Mostly, however, what Hadley brought to the marriage was a determination to succeed in love and work *together*. She knew that she was ready to share her future rather than to be alone; equally important, she intuited that Ernest was as well, even if he didn't yet know it himself. "The world's a jail," she told him, "and we're going to break it together." Ernest would not be the only rebel in the family, it seems, Hadley wanting out from her family and a conventional life as much as Ernest did.

The newlyweds returned to Chicago in October, the honeymoon less than an idyll because both had come down with colds and because Ernest insisted on taking Hadley around Petoskey to meet his old girlfriends; young as they were, Hadley was jealous. They got on the wrong side of Grace very quickly, deliberately or otherwise overlooking a note left at Windemere inviting them to lunch across the lake at Grace Cottage with the family; by the time they made their way there, the family had all gone back to Oak Park except Grace and Carol. Grace had gone to great trouble sprucing up Windemere and laying in supplies, and she was upset to arrive at the cottage after the newlyweds had left and find the place a mess, the mattresses still on the floor of the living room where Ernest and Hadley had dragged them. Though it seems unlikely that Hadley was capable of deliberate rudeness, and though she and Grace shared a love of music and of Ernest, Hadley's first allegiance was to her husband, and he seems to have predisposed her to keep Grace at arm's length. Hadley later told an interviewer, "He trained me to dislike her too."

Matters were not improved when Grace paid a visit to the small furnished apartment on the top floor of a walk-up building at 1239 North Dearborn Street that Ernest and Hadley had rented. Hadley later said the visit was "to teach me about love," Grace clasping Hadley's hands between hers "as in a trap." In October Grace and Ed celebrated their twenty-fifth wedding anniversary with a large party in Oak Park at which they also introduced their new daughter-in-law. Hadley refused to dress up, however, wearing an everyday dress. At a party the next week she wore a black evening dress, and when Ernest's friend Nick Nerone asked why she hadn't worn it for the Hemingway party, replied, "Well, I was just averse to that party." The family was offended. Again, Hadley's loyalty was to her husband, and it would have been disloyal to let Grace befriend her. It is also quite possible that Hadley's new sense of independence, compounded of her escape from the Richardson clan and her financial self-sufficiency, disinclined her to feel answerable to anyone, especially parents.

Before the wedding Ernest had drawn a floor plan of the Chicago apartment for Hadley, and they had worked out a budget down to the penny. But the place was a disappointment and Hadley at loose ends. Chicago was unfamiliar to her and Ernest was off all day at the *Co-operative Commonwealth*. But then scandal caught up with the Co-operative Society, and the magazine shut its doors in October, Parker indicted for making off with $13 million in subscribers' investments. Ernest had been corresponding with John Bone at the *Toronto Star*, negotiating a job. Now he offered to write for the *Star*, either in Toronto or on assignment in Italy.

But Hadley's and Ernest's plans were changing. Even after the buying of all those lira, after all their fantasies about "Wopland," after Ernest had decided to set his novel in Italy during the war—Italy was no longer their destination of choice for the jailbreak Hadley had spoken of. In the intervening weeks Ernest had seen Sherwood Anderson again, introducing him to Hadley. She had read *Winesburg, Ohio* and Anderson's latest novel, *Poor White* (1920), making, as it happens, a very trenchant remark about the man and his work: "Sherwood has the tenderest sympathy with inexpressive beings . . . people without an outlet and encased in nameless fear." (It's possible that Hadley recognized this quality in herself as she had been before meeting Ernest.) In the interim Anderson and his second wife, Tennessee, had been to Paris, and he could talk of little else. He told the younger couple that Paris—not Rome—was the best destination for the serious writer, particularly because of its low rents and cheap food, cafés welcoming the working writer, and the general romance of the city; moreover, Anderson could write him letters of introduction to two or three important Americans on the literary scene. Evidently Anderson's rhapsodies had their desired effect, for Ernest struck a deal with the *Toronto Star* that would pay him by the word for features on sports and politics from Paris, $75 a week for stories covered on assignment outside Paris. Ernest and Hadley booked passage to France for early December. In turn, Anderson wrote notes to his friends Ezra Pound and Gertrude Stein. He also wrote a letter on the Hemingways' behalf to Lewis Galantière, his French translator, a man about town who worked for the International Chamber of Commerce and who could offer practical suggestions for how an American could not just get by but live well in postwar Paris.

In Anderson's letter to Galantière he called Ernest "a young fellow of extraordinary talent [who], I believe, will get somewhere," a writer "instinctively in touch with everything worthwhile." In a sketch called "They Come Bearing Gifts," Anderson would remember Hemingway coming to visit him on the night before he was to leave for Europe, mounting the stairs of his apartment building, "a magnificent broad-shouldered figure of a man, shouting as he came," bearing an "enormous" knapsack that must have carried "a hundred pounds" of leftover canned goods, which Anderson thought a generous act for a "fellow scribbler." In fact, Anderson would not be alone among early Hemingway admirers in having as many good things to say about the man as about the writer: when he wrote a blurb for the American publication of Hemingway's first collection of stories, the quotation began, "Mr. Hemingway is young, strong, full of laughter, and he can write." As he had so often in his young life, Ernest in Paris would stand out, a leader among men, handsome, strong, charismatic. Now he began to show that he had writing talent to match. In the golden city at a golden time, he would appear a golden young man.

SIX

Ernest was constructing myths about himself before he got off the boat. He was having such an incredible time, he told Bill Smith in a letter written on board the *Leopoldina*, that Bill would think he was making it up. Hadley was the hit of the voyage with her piano playing, he wrote, but he was especially proud of having staged a boxing match between himself and a professional named Henry Cuddy to raise funds for a penniless French mother and child traveling in steerage. Cuddy, Ernest said, was a Salt Lake City fighter headed over to box in France, and was so impressed with Ernest's skill that he asked the young writer to fight with him professionally in Europe. According to Hemingway scholars Sandra Spanier and Robert Trogdon, however, Cuddy was fighting in Salt Lake City the day that Ernest wrote two letters describing the match, a bout documented in the Salt Lake City papers. Hadley mentioned a shipboard benefit boxing match in a letter of hers; Ernest's deception was in claiming it was with the well-known boxer.

The reasons for his fabrication are not immediately clear; he would start to accumulate enough experiences that really did seem fantastical—to him and to Hadley, at least—almost as soon as they arrived in Paris, a few days before Christmas 1921. They stayed at the Hôtel Jacob et d'Angleterre in the heart of the literary Left Bank. James Joyce and the poet Natalie Barney lived on the same street, the rue Jacob. The day after their arrival Ernest wrote to Sherwood Anderson from the *terrasse* at the Dôme café, warmed by a charcoal brazier, apparently unaware that his location was about to become a cliché as the meeting spot of choice for the American expatriates who were beginning to flood the city. Ernest and Hadley had found a letter from Sherwood Anderson welcoming them at the Jacob, where he had suggested they stay, and Ernest had a sheaf of letters of introduction the older writer had composed for him. He wrote Sherwood and his wife, Tennessee, that they'd found a restaurant on the corner of the rue Jacob and the rue Bonaparte called the Pré aux Clercs where they could get dinner with

With his first wife, Hadley Richardson, 1922, at Chamby, Switzerland

wine for the two of them for 12 francs, or about a dollar. Ernest reported to wartime friend Howell Jenkins that he had a row of spirits—rum, Asti Spumante, and vermouth—lined up on his hotel room windowsill.

The next day, Ernest told Sherwood, they were going to visit the Chicago-bred Frenchman Lewis Galantière and deliver Anderson's letter of introduction in person; perhaps he seemed the most approachable of Anderson's contacts, or perhaps they thought that as an employee of the International Chamber of Commerce Galantière might have some useful tips on the best places to eat in Paris and how to find a cheap place to live. They weren't disappointed—Galantière helped them find their first apartment—but there was an awkward moment at their first meeting. Ernest invited Galantière back to his hotel room to box, where he conveniently produced two pairs of regulation boxing gloves from one of his trunks. Galantière called a halt after one round, and was removing his gloves and replacing his glasses when Ernest, still shadow boxing energetically, jabbed his opponent in the face and broke his glasses.

The apartment Anderson's friend helped them find was at 74, rue du Cardinal Lemoine, a little street in the 5th Arrondissement, isolated because of the lack of a nearby Métro stop; the Hemingways would have to take a bus to cash a check at Morgan Guaranty. The apartment was really just two rooms, one occupied by a double bed and the other by a dining table, with room for a rented piano. The toilet was on the landing, and the building was next to a dance hall whose tunes they could hear tinkling all day and night, down the street from the decidedly plebeian Place de la Contrescarpe.

They had barely deposited their trunks at their new home when they fled Paris, perhaps discouraged by the dampness and cold. A friend or acquaintance had apparently recommended the resort town of Chamby in the Swiss Alps as a cheap refuge from Paris that offered all kinds of winter sports; Hadley and Ernest left Paris at nine at night and arrived in Montreux at ten the next morning. They found a little pension that offered cheap accommodations and spent their days riding a toy railway to the top of the Col de Sonloup, where they would ride luges or bobsleds four miles down the mountain, often reaching speeds of fifty miles per hour. The fresh air and the hearty breakfasts in bed provided by their hosts, the Gangwisches, so agreed with them that both were converted to winters in the Alps for as long as they were in Europe. Ernest wrote his friend Howell Jenkins, somewhat predictably, that with a lot of alcohol and winter sports, "It would be a paradise with the men along."

Back in Paris Ernest and Hadley settled into their Latin Quarter apartment. Ernest was already writing features for the *Toronto Star* and would contribute nineteen in 1922. He quickly saw that even with Hadley barely making a sound, he could not get much writing done in their cramped quarters, and rented a room in a hotel in the nearby rue Descartes where the poet Paul Verlaine had died twenty-five years before. He settled down to producing the journalism that he would more and more, over the coming year, come to resent. He tried to work on his own writing as well, but when he pulled out the war novel he had begun in Chicago, it didn't look very good to him, and he shelved it for the time being. Increasingly he just wrote sketches in his notebook, trying for accuracy in his fleeting observations. Instead of the novel, he picked up a story that he had started two years before, "Up in Michigan," about a young girl's sexual initiation on a lakeside dock.

Still finding life in Paris new and often disconcerting, Ernest and Hadley moved out beyond the ambit of the rue Cardinal Lemoine. Ernest had heard of one of literary Paris's heroes, James Joyce, before he crossed the Atlantic, and he had a letter of introduction from Anderson to Joyce's Paris publisher, the American Sylvia Beach. It did not take particular courage to follow up on Anderson's letter, for Beach could be found at her bookstore and lending library, Shakespeare and Company, on the rue de l'Odéon. Ernest later said he admired her lively, "very sharply cut face" and her "pretty legs"; how "kind, cheerful and interested" she was, adding, "No one that I ever knew was nicer to me" (AMF 31). (His likely exaggeration may have reflected just how happy he had been to find a sympathetic American soul in his earliest days in Paris.) Sylvia's bookstore was filled with English-language books and magazines, and black-and-white photographs of authors hung above the shelves. Perhaps because it was the only establishment the Hemingways had yet found in their earliest days where English was reliably spoken in the overwhelmingly new and foreign city, Shakespeare and Company became "a very special point of focus in our lives," according to Hadley. "We went there all the time." The Princeton, New Jersey–raised Beach was a minister's daughter who made her way to Paris for lack of a clear vocation or defined goal, where she had met and moved in with Adrienne Monnier, a Frenchwoman who ran another bookstore and lending library, Maison des Amis des Livres, this one stocked with French books. Beach and Monnier soon asked the Hemingways to dinner; they were to become one of two lesbian couples to whom Ernest and Hadley grew close in their first year in Paris.

While Shakespeare and Company housed a welcoming wood-burning stove, around which American expatriate writers could often be found gossiping, the real draw for Hadley and Ernest at this point was the lending library. From his first visit Ernest emerged with an armful of books by Turgenev, Lawrence, Dostoevsky, and Tolstoy; Sylvia had told him he could pay whenever it was convenient for him, no doubt told by Ernest that he and Hadley had little discretionary income. Ernest would later say his reading in his Paris years, in books provided by Sylvia Beach, was enormously important to him, citing Stephen Crane's stories, Maupassant, Ambrose Bierce, and Flaubert, though he still considered Kipling's stories a primary influence.

In fact, though Hemingway later told enormous whoppers about trapping pigeons in the Luxembourg Gardens for their dinner, Ernest and Hadley were not living the hand-to-mouth existence that he would describe with such nostalgia in *A Moveable Feast*. Ernest was making between $1,500 and $2,000 a year from his work for the *Toronto Star*, and Hadley had a trust fund that gave her $3,000 a year; she had as well the income from a recent inheritance of $8,000 from her uncle Arthur. In today's money, they would have had over $60,000 a year.

In Paris in the 1920s, this would have gone far indeed. The value of the franc was descending at a clip, and the dollar was currently at 14 francs; an average meal was about fifty cents. Marie Rohrbach (called Marie Cocotte), the *femme de ménage* Ernest and Hadley hired to clean their apartment and cook their dinner, cost about $12 a month. Their rent was 250 francs a month, or about $18. It was no wonder that the Hemingways would travel as frequently as they did in the 1920s; it seemed criminal not to take advantage of low prices throughout Europe.

The exchange rate was drawing Americans to Paris in droves. Paris promised sexual freedom, a rich cultural life, and an escape from the stuffy, traditionalist values Sinclair Lewis was brilliantly sending up in his two best sellers of the time, *Main Street* (1920) and *Babbitt* (1922). Of course Prohibition was a big factor, the attraction of legal liquor playing a central role for many of the expatriates. Ernest Hemingway was just one of many writers, John Dos Passos and E.E. Cummings among them, who had come to know European culture through experience in the Great War and, after suffering the disillusionment the war fostered, longed to reexperience French or Italian life. Greenwich Village was evacuating for Paris en masse.

Of course, this meant that among the genuinely talented artists and writers drawn to postwar Paris were a fair share of ersatz artists and poseurs. Hemingway himself called it "the mecca of fakers," and devoted a full *Star* feature to "American Bohemians in Paris":

The scum of Greenwich Village, New York, has been skimmed off and deposited in large ladleful on that section of Paris adjacent to the Café Rotonde. . . . The . . . scum has come across the ocean, somehow, and with its afternoon and evening levees has made the Rotonde the leading Latin Quarter show place for tourists in search of atmosphere.

Since "the good old days" when Baudelaire had "led a purple lobster on a leash through the same old Latin Quarter," good poetry has not been "written in cafés."

Hemingway all but stated for his Canadian readers that he was not part of this "scum," that he was not a tourist but a serious writer and resident of Paris. He himself could and did write in cafés, probably even poetry. When in his romanticized memoir he describes his writing at his favorite café, the Closerie des Lilas on Boulevard Montparnasse near rue d'Assas, he remembers himself as working on not poems but a short story about a trout pool in a river and a soldier back from the war—one of the Nick Adams stories for which he would become known. Perhaps one of the most effective aspects of Hemingway's writing, the specificity of authentic experience, the drive to write "one true sentence," grew from the need to differentiate his experience and his very being from the scum that washed up in the wrong Parisian cafés.

In the early months in Paris, Ernest was much busier tending a key element in a literary career: making connections. He was a little more hesitant to contact Ezra Pound than he had been to get in touch with Galantière, probably because Pound was already a writer of some accomplishments who seemed, if possible, even more connected than Sherwood Anderson. Born in Idaho twelve years before Ernest but raised in the East, Pound was very well educated, having entered the University of Pennsylvania at the age of fifteen and commenced work toward a PhD in Romance languages after receiving his MA in 1906. Though he broke off his studies, he was extremely erudite—if in some languages in which he claimed proficiency somewhat sketchy. His educational accomplishments would not be lost on any reader of his poetry, including Ernest, who might well have found himself immediately on the defensive on this score. An established poet, Pound was well known for his 1909 collection *Personae*. Ernest was probably most impressed, however, by his recent long poem, "Hugh Selwyn Mauberley" (1920), a complaint about the sterility of the modern world, in which Pound wrote, about the recent war, "There died a myriad, / And of the best, among them, / For an old bitch gone in the teeth, / For a botched civilization." Pound spoke for a new generation, profoundly disillusioned and traumatized by the Great War, searching for meaning and finding new ways to express meaning's seeming absence in the Western world.

Hemingway would also have heard, and no doubt had strong opinions about, Pound's role in founding Imagism, an artistic movement that called for direct treatment of the "thing itself," and was perhaps best understood

Ezra Pound in Paris, early 1920s

by something that had happened to the poet himself. One day in 1913 Pound was deeply impressed by the sensation he felt on seeing a series of faces floating toward him in the Paris Métro; after months of mulling it over, he wrote "In the Station of the Metro," which read, in its entirety: "The apparition of these faces in the crowd, / Petals on a wet, black bough." To a would-be writer of Hemingway's generation, raised on Victorian poets like Tennyson and Arnold, such a poem would have been a revelation. Imagism, helped along by Pound's good friend the poet Hilda Doolittle (HD), her poet husband, Richard Aldington, and the eccentric American poet Amy Lowell almost as soon as it became a literary movement, was just the sort of topic that would have been hotly debated in circles like the one that converged at Kenley Smith's Chicago apartment in 1921. (By then, however, Pound had renounced Imagism, dismissing it as "Amygism" after Lowell took it up.)

But Pound was also, more importantly to Hemingway at this juncture, a literary *macher*, if it's possible to use a Yiddish term to describe someone who would become infamous for his anti-Semitism. Before moving to Paris in 1920, Pound had spent twelve years in London, befriending writers like Yeats, James Joyce, and T. S. Eliot. In fact, he met his wife, Dorothy Shakespear, through her mother, Yeats's lover Olivia Shakespear; he helped Joyce with the publication of all his works up to and including *Ulysses*; and he got Harriet Monroe to publish Eliot's "The Love Song of J. Alfred Prufrock" in her journal *Poetry* in 1915, when all other English editors were dismissing it as the work of a crazy man. Pound was nominally the foreign editor of Harriet Monroe's Chicago-based *Poetry* but exercised greater influence than this suggests in shaping the journal's identity, and was no less instrumental to the other literary publications to which he also contributed poems: *The New Age* (where he was a columnist); *The New Freewoman; The Egoist;* and Wyndham Lewis's short-lived but significant *BLAST.* He would soon be receiving $750 a year (almost $10,000 today, a hefty sum for a little magazine) as Paris correspondent of Scofield Thayer's *The Dial,* a very influential periodical that would never publish Hemingway, thus incurring Ernest's great wrath.

But if Pound was a *macher,* he was a *macher* of the most open-minded and helpful sort. Though he could be contentious, and "made more enemies than friends," according to a London editor, his mission was the future of modern literature. As a young man, he wrote, he "resolved that at thirty I would know more about poetry than any man living," something he surely achieved, and as a poet and as an enabler of poets and writers he perhaps did more for literature than any man living in his time. Hemingway himself would write, in "Homage to Ezra Pound" in 1925, that Pound spent about a fifth of his time on his own poetry:

> With the rest of his time he tries to advance the fortunes, both material and artistic, of his friends. He defends them when they are attacked, he gets them into magazines and out of jail. He loans them money. . . . He introduces them to wealthy women. He gets publishers to take their books. He sits up all night with them when they claim to be dying . . . and dissuades them from suicide.

Hemingway knew whereof he spoke, as events would tell.

Ernest and Hadley arrived at Pound's studio in the rue Notre-Dame-des-Champs in late February 1922, invited for tea by Ezra and Dorothy. There they found a genuine eccentric—Thayer called Pound "a queer duck"— with a full head of unruly reddish hair. The writer Ford Madox Ford described him facetiously but apparently with some accuracy as approaching "with the step of a dancer, making passes with a cane at an imaginary opponent. He would wear trousers made of green billiard cloth, a pink coat, a blue shirt, a tie hand-painted by a Japanese friend . . . a flaming beard cut to a point, and a single, large blue earring." Sylvia Beach commented, "There was a touch of Whistler about him; his language, on the other hand, was Huckleberry Finn's." He also, she noted, made all his own furniture—an odd point of contact with Grace Hemingway. Ernest would find that Ezra's letter writing was in a lingo more impenetrable than the argot that characterized Ernest's own correspondence; in a characteristic piece of advice Pound later wrote, "HELL, I want stuufffff that'll END discussion. I want to say: me friend Hem, kin knock yew over the ropes."

Ezra Pound was also perhaps modern literature's best editor—Hemingway's famous editor, Max Perkins, included—having only recently done yeomanly work on Eliot's modernist epic "The Wasteland" (1922), to the extent that Eliot dedicated the poem "to Ezra Pound, *il miglior fabbro,*" the better craftsman. Ernest asked Pound to take a look at his poems and stories, and Pound responded with excellent, concrete advice. We don't know his exact words that particular day, but Hemingway would later say that Pound taught him to be leery of adjectives, a mistrust that would become an essential part of the Hemingway style. Pound's criticism of a later Hemingway story, "An Alpine Idyll," was characteristic: "This is a good story (Idyl) but a leetle literary and Tennysonian. I wish you wd. Keep your eye on the objek MORE and be less licherary. . . . Licherchure is mostly blanketing up a subject. Too much MAKINGS. The subject is always interesting enough without the blankets." No better advice for a young fiction writer, but especially Hemingway, whose current writing suffered from the self-conscious quality of would-be "licherchure."

Two matters related to Ernest's initial encounter with Pound require comment. First is Ernest's asking Ezra for help with his poetry—not his prose. Hemingway had been writing poetry probably as far back as childhood, and at times he saw himself as primarily a poet: when six of his poems were published (by Pound's agency) in *Poetry* in 1923, the contributor's note identified him, almost unrecognizably to our eyes, as "a young Chicago poet now abroad who will soon issue in Paris his first book of verse." As the editor of Hemingway's posthumously published *Complete Poems* has pointed out, most of his poems were written when he was in his twenties; of the eighty-eight poems attributed to Hemingway, seventy-three were completed by 1929. Most of the poems written before 1922 were about his war experiences or current events, especially war news.

A typical early poem, "Champs d'Honneur," leaves no question that the author is a realist, if not a cynic, in his worldview and does not shy away from graphic language or images. Perhaps this modernity is what Pound saw in the poem; it was one of the six that he took from Ernest and sent to *The Dial,* where Thayer rejected them; they ultimately appeared in *Poetry* magazine in 1923. Ernest had no such luck placing his other poems in literary journals; he complained that *Der Querschnitt* (*Cross-section*), an irreverent illustrated German magazine edited by Berliner Alfred Flechtheim and published by Hermann von Wedderkop, an acquaintance of Pound's, was the only publication that would take them. But what is interesting here is that Ernest persevered with poetry, despite the poor response or, indeed, deafening silence from almost everyone *but* Pound. He stayed at it even as he came to know the work of other, far better poets, including Pound himself, T. S. Eliot, and Archibald MacLeish, the last becoming a good friend. He seems to have lacked any critical acumen when it came to his poems—an absence that would crop up again in his career, most notably in the case of his dismal 1950 novel *Across the River and into the Trees,* but also in the case of some poems to his fourth wife that he wrote during World War II. Just after that war he would seriously and persistently urge Scribner's to publish these compositions in a volume of his poetry, and it was only with great difficulty and tact that the firm wriggled out of it.

In fact, Ernest's initial response to his encounter with Ezra was to write a scurrilous satire about the poet, bringing it to Lewis Galantière prior to dropping it off with Margaret Anderson and Jane Heap, the editors of the prestigious *Little Review.* Galantière told Hemingway's first biographer that the poem commented on Ezra's bohemianism, his wild hair and beard, and his poet's shirt. It was so scurrilous that Galantière told Ernest in no uncertain terms not to take it to *The Little Review,* where Pound was an unpaid and much respected editor. Ernest evidently put it away with his papers.

Ernest loved irony and satire, and never more so than as a young and somewhat reckless man. Though it's a commonplace in Hemingway biography that he seemed to need to bite the hand that fed him—or, more precisely, to hurt anyone who had helped him in any way—this impulse does not seem to have been at work here. Rather, he appears to have naively thought that publishing such a satire, thereby showing his acquaintance with the dean of modern poetry, Ezra Pound, would enhance his reputation.

And then Ernest must have thought his lines about Ezra were clever and very funny. In fact, Ernest was well known for his sense of humor, though it's not a quality contemporary readers think of in connection with Hemingway. Humor does not travel well; it is difficult to convey the sense of humor of historical characters. Moreover, Ernest seems to have thought his sense of humor extended to himself—that is, that he believed he could take any kind of ribbing or satire applied to himself—despite all evidence to the contrary. He was in fact oversensitive—"easily hurt," according to Hadley. His friend Mike Strater stated flatly, "He had no humor about himself." Though there would be far too many times when he did use satire or cruel humor to hurt others, including friends or mentors, when he wrote his satirical bit about Pound, he probably thought the older man would take it in the right spirit. Of course, it was all for the good that Galantière made sure Pound did not see it.

Shortly before meeting Pound, Hemingway had set out to visit the other writer on Anderson's list, Gertrude Stein. He and Hadley arrived at 27, rue de Fleurus, probably sometime in March, and were admitted to a large room that "was like one of the best rooms in the finest museum except there was a big fireplace and it was warm and comfortable and they gave you good things to eat and tea and natural distilled liqueurs made from purple plums, yellow plums or wild raspberries" (*AMF,* 23). The walls were hung with paintings reaching up to the ceiling, the works of Picasso, Cézanne, Renoir, and other, lesser-known painters like Bonnard who would also become modernist giants. But Stein's collecting days were for the most part over, as prices commanded by the modernists were now beyond her reach and that of most of her visitors. On this first visit, Gertrude sat Ernest down next to her and fixed her intense gaze on him, while her companion since 1907, Alice Toklas, dark-haired, hook-nosed, and with a faint but distinct mustache, conducted Hadley to another seating area and took out her needlepoint, as she always did with the wives of Gertrude's male visitors.

Stein herself was, in Scofield Thayer's description, "five feet high and two feet wide and has a dark brown face and small, wise old Jewess' eyes. . . . She possesses the homely finish of a brown buckram bean bag." Physically, except for her height, she resembled no one so much as Grace Hemingway, heavy-boned and stout, with beautiful eyes; in 1922 she still wore her hair in a bun that recalled Grace's. She shared Grace's bulk and the proud way she carried herself, and a visitor was immediately struck by her charisma, the quality Grace passed on to her son. Hemingway scholar Rose Marie Burwell has pointed out these and other similarities between Gertrude and Grace that go beyond appearance. Both were critical and controlling; both were narcissistic and egotistical. Stein's goal was to publish in the *Atlantic,* the same magazine Ernest accused his mother of taking to appear highbrow. Finally, Burwell notes that the famous line Ernest would attribute to Stein—"You are all a lost generation"—sounds like Grace, especially in the letter she wrote Ernest about his filial bank account being overdrawn.

Though he would have hated the idea, it was not a bad time in Ernest's life to adopt a maternal figure (Gertrude would serve as godmother to his first son), especially a writer who could mentor him as well.

Stein, who was born in 1874 in Oakland, California (about which she famously wrote, "There is no there there"), into a German American family, was educated at Radcliffe, where she studied with William James, and began medical school at Johns Hopkins before dropping out and leaving the country for Europe in 1903. By 1922, Stein had already made a name for herself with her notoriously difficult writing, which prompted a great deal of scoffing. James Thurber later called her "the most eminent of the idiots" writing in the "bizarre" modernist period. Her first published work, *Three Lives* (1909), had been relatively straightforward, however. The story "Melanctha" in that volume had won her considerable praise. Her 1914 *Tender Buttons,* decidedly experimental, would be called by later critics like Max Eastman "the ravings of a lunatic," but earlier writers found it inspirational; the American writer Bob Brown wrote that on reading it he "threw [his] typewriter up in the air and huzzahed." In 1922, when Stein's *Geography and Plays* appeared, Sherwood Anderson said in his introduction, "For me the work of Gertrude Stein consists in a rebuilding, an entirely new recasting of life, in the city of words." Evidently Anderson had waxed equally enthusiastic to Hemingway, as Ernest was predisposed to take Gertrude's work altogether seriously. In a frank letter to his old friend Bill Smith, he said he thought she'd written "swell stuff. . . . She's trying to get at the mechanics of language. Take it apart and see what makes it go. Maybe she don't get it together again. But she's always getting somewhere."

Ernest felt an affinity for Stein, her work, and her conversation almost immediately. Later, perhaps inevitably, he wrote, "I always wanted to fuck her and she knew it and it was a good healthy feeling." But aside from describing her "lovely, thick, alive, immigrant hair" (*AMF,* 24), nothing in the way of anti-Semitism found its way into his conversation about her. At their second meeting, when Stein and Toklas visited the rue Cardinal Lemoine apartment, Stein read Hemingway's poems and part of the war novel he had started in Chicago the year before while perched on the Hemingways' bed, which sat on the floor without a bedframe. She called the poems "direct and Kiplingesque" but said she did not think much of the novel—a viewpoint Ernest was beginning to share. She read "Up in Michigan," his graphic story about a sexual initiation, and called it *inaccrochable*—like a painting that cannot be displayed. While Hemingway repeated this criticism several times, he seems to have thought it revealed Stein's essential prudishness or was otherwise beside the point. The latter may have been true, but it can be argued that Stein was flattering Hemingway by speaking to him as one professional to another, advising him not to spend time on material that could not be printed. "There is no point in it," she said in exasperation, when Ernest said he was only writing in words that people actually used.

Hemingway nevertheless learned a great deal from Stein. In his letter to Bill Smith praising her writing, he also spoke highly of her editing: "Can always tell you what's wrong with your stuff when you don't know but only that it ain't right. She's sure given me straight dope." He visited Gertrude and Alice many times that spring and summer, usually without Hadley, telling Anderson, "Gertrude Stein and me are just like brothers." At the end of the same letter he added, "We love Gertrude Stein." For her part, Gertrude told Anderson, "He is a delightful fellow and I am teaching him to cut his wife's hair." Gertrude was most likely unaware of Hemingway's fixation on hair and could not have known how tantalizing this act would be for him.

One of the pieces of advice she gave Hemingway that he did not dispute was that he would need to give up journalism if he wanted to be a writer. Reporting was occupying almost all of his time in 1922; he was contributing about two articles a week to the *Toronto Star,* either the daily or (more often) the weekly. He wrote about fishing in Vigo, Spain; the value of the German mark; travel in Switzerland; and so forth, features that he could write from Paris based on trips he had previously made or news he had picked up in the local papers. He first traveled as a reporter in late April to Genoa, on the occasion of an international conference about the European economies and Western relations with Russia in the aftermath of the Great War; Hemingway filed fifteen stories about the conference, which extended into May. While there he met several journalists and came to know better a few whom he'd met earlier in Paris. Among them were foreign correspondents George Seldes of the *Chicago Tribune* and Sam Spewack of the *New York World;* the sculptor Jo Davidson (there to make sketches for busts of the foreign leaders); Paris-based newsmen George Slocombe of the (Communist) *British Daily Herald;* Bill Bird of the Consolidated Press (Bird later becoming a good friend); and freelancers Max Eastman and Lincoln Steffens. The latter spoke as glowingly about Hemingway as he had about another journalist *wunderkind,* John Reed, whom he told, when Reed confided to Steffens he wanted to write, "You can do anything you want to." Steffens praised Hemingway's story "My Old Man" to the skies; his biographer writes that of other Paris figures, Hemingway seemed to

Steffens "to have the surest future, the most buoyant confidence, and the best grounds for it."

Others shared Steffens's observations; it seemed Hemingway, on his appearance in Paris in 1922, was bathed in a kind of golden light. His physical presence was undeniable: "He was an extraordinarily good-looking young man," Gertrude Stein would later observe. Almost immediately on meeting Pound, Hemingway offered him boxing lessons. Wyndham Lewis describes first meeting Hemingway in mid-lesson, when Lewis walked into Pound's studio: "A splendidly built young man, stript to the waist, and with a torso of dazzling white, was standing not far from me. . . . The young man was Hemingway." William Shirer, a foreign correspondent with the *Chicago Tribune,* said, "He was big and athletic, with bright, lively eyes," and Max Eastman said he had "the most beautiful row of teeth I ever saw in man, woman, or child": every aspect of Hemingway's appearance, demeanor, and personality attracted superlatives. His dress drew attention, not always positive, for he wore sweatshirts and sneakers at a time when such attire signaled poverty more than it did bohemianism. Shirer noted, "Robust, hulking, handsome, vivid, [Hemingway] is probably the slouchiest figure in Montmartre. Throughout the seasons he wears canvas shoes; in summer, tennis trousers and sports shirts; in winter, tweeds and brown, flannel blouses; almost always, a Basque beret." Shirer went on to dispel any impression that Hemingway's appearance was studied: "This fashion of dress is not an affectation; it is a naturalism." Similarly, Ernest drew praise for his unassuming nature, seemingly at odds with his commanding presence. Shirer went on to say, "I was struck by his directness and modesty." Hadley told a biographer that Ernest was "a priceless person that people were really crazy about. Not only his talent, but also his personality and his looks were really marvelous. . . . Ernest sort of knocked people over."

As Ernest became known in the Latin Quarter, his reputation grew in the expatriate community. Yet just as he would differentiate himself from the "scum" of expatriate writers who "washed up" in Montparnasse, so too were his early champions eager to assert his difference from these clichéd characters. Burton Rascoe said that Ernest had told him he lived in Paris for three reasons: it was cheap; it provided a change of scene; and he liked wine with his meals.

Rascoe was not denying that Ernest's was a familiar presence on the *terrasses* frequented by Americans. Malcolm Cowley, a writer who knew Ernest in Paris, wrote indelibly about passing a café like the Dôme with him. (Cowley's story shows as well how quickly a circle of friends and acquaintances formed around Ernest.) Someone at a table would hail him, and Ernest would look to see who it was:

> Then suddenly his beautiful smile appeared that made those watching him also smile. And with a will and an eagerness he put out both his hands and warmly greeted his acquaintances, who, overcome by this reception, simply glowed and returned with him to the table as if with an overwhelming prize.

And everyone was struck by how happy he was with Hadley. The following summer Aunt Arabella would report back to Grace and Ed from Paris: Ernest was "splendid looking" and so happy he fairly "radiates" it, using the adverbial form of the word in the next sentence: "Hadley is adorable and so radiantly happy with Ernest. I doubt if married people ever were happier than they are, each so gentle and deferential but such rollicing [sic] good pals withal." Arabella was a little carried away, adding, "Each considers the other absolutely perfect."

Hadley and Ernest felt good about their marriage and let others know it. Their nonsensical nicknames were well known to their Paris friends: Ernest was Tatie, Hadley was Feather Kitty or Bones. Ernest seemed to think these details should be shared, telling Sherwood Anderson, for instance, in a March 1922 letter: "Bones is called Binney now. We both call each other Binney. I'm the male Binney and she is the female Binney." It is perplexing to think what Anderson might make of this, but it is clear that Ernest considered this important, informing family members and others of the name change. One evening back in Kenley Smith's apartment in Chicago, before they left for Paris, Ernest put his arm around Hadley and announced to their friends that "they were prince and princess." Hadley was mortified.

However embarrassing Hemingway's confidence in his own charm may have been, it is important to note the huge advantage it gave him in his writing career. He once told his third wife, Martha, that it had never occurred to him that he would not be a great writer. And those around him could not imagine his failure either. Nor could they dislike him, no matter how they might have tried. It is well to recall this in considering odd details of his behavior, such as inventing a bout with a professional boxer en route to France, or hitting Galantière and knocking off his glasses, or abusing friends who had helped him. Nobody cared if he acted strangely or ungraciously, or noticed if he wrote some bad poems. In the eyes of the world, or rather Hemingway's world, which was that of Paris and the American Midwest, he simply could do no wrong.

Meanwhile, Ernest and Hadley were exploring the countryside around Paris, hiking energetically whenever Ernest could take time off from his writing. They planned extremely ambitious expeditions, thinking nothing of covering between twelve and twenty miles a day, depending on the terrain. In May they set out on a hike of close to one hundred miles, starting in Chantilly; they walked forty miles to Compiègne, passing through Senlis, which boasted a twelfth-century Gothic cathedral and walls dating to Roman times; they planned to go on to Soissons and then on to Reims, home to a thirteenth-century cathedral that was once the coronation site for France's kings. But the weather became rainy, and no respite was forecast; this on top of one of Ernest's sore throats forced them to cut their trip short in Compiègne. Ernest noted the forests they passed through, teeming with game. The couple ate the region's wild boar twice, cooked in a delectable pastry with carrots and onions and mushrooms.

Ernest and Hadley were attracted to energetic activity; hikes like these as well as the winter sports they loved had left them in splendid physical shape, and they wanted to spend more time in the dramatically beautiful mountains of Europe. In mid-May they arranged a climb over the Alps from Switzerland to Italy in the company of a friend who had first met Ernest in 1918, Eric Dorman-Smith, always called Chink.

Ernest's and Chink's first meeting, in a café in Milan a week before the Armistice, had been marked by another of Ernest's inventions. As Chink later told Carlos Baker, "this harmless looking Red Cross youngster" said he had been wounded "leading Arditi storm troops up Mount Grappa," Chink learning the truth only much later. Born in 1895 in County Cavan, Ireland, Chink was a Sandhurst graduate and a member of the Northumberland Fusiliers, and was embarked on what would become an impressive if somewhat erratic military career. Buck-toothed and unprepossessing-looking, Chink had what some considered a certain intellectual arrogance, as well as a biting wit that would have appealed to Ernest.

Ernest and Hadley met up with Chink in Chamby, where the three stayed in the same pension that the Hemingways had occupied the previous winter. There they laid plans: they would send their luggage ahead to Milan and make their way over the western Alps through the St. Bernard Pass. They set out carrying knapsacks, Chink's the heaviest because he volunteered to carry Hadley's cumbersome toilet articles, which Ernest wanted her to leave behind. The first day's hike was a steep eight miles to the monastery-run hospice established by Saint Bernard in the sixteenth century, where they would stay overnight. Ernest later told Gertrude Stein that he made the last mile only with the help of Hadley and Chink and a shot of cognac every two hundred yards. Chink later said that Ernest was suffering from mountain sickness, a very real malady that strikes some hikers when they ascend too steeply too quickly; Chink had to carry both Hadley's and Ernest's backpacks, ferrying two of them at a time. The next day, Ernest having acclimated himself to the altitude, they continued the hike to Aosta, a twenty-mile trek, intending to make it to Milan the next day, from which Ernest hoped to show Hadley the scenes of his war service. But Hadley was hiking all those miles in the snow in sturdy-looking but completely inadequate oxfords, and her blistered feet eventually made them give up the trek. (Evidently Hadley had ridden bobsleds and skied months before without proper boots, perhaps as a false economy. It seems odd that Hemingway, so concerned with doing things well, with the proper gear and the proper attitude—especially in outdoor activity—would have allowed Hadley to attempt the hike without appropriate footwear.)

They left Chink in Milan and continued on to Schio and then Fossalta, where the battlefields Ernest had known were grassed over, unrecognizable. He was sorely disappointed; in fact, he seems to have been shaken by history itself. "Don't go back to visit the old front," Hemingway told the *Toronto Star*'s readers. "It is like going into the empty gloom of a theater where the charwomen are scrubbing." It had been a trip, made part of the way in the company of a soldier friend who did not know Ernest's real war experience, to battlefields that bore no trace of fighting, making the war seem unreal.

Later that summer Ernest, together with his journalist friend Bill Bird, hatched a plan for another hike, or rather a walking tour, in the Black Forest. They enlisted Lewis Galantière and his fiancée, Dorothy Butler, and Sally Bird would join her husband. Ernest and Bill got wind of inexpensive tickets for journalists for transit on a Franco-Romanian Aero Company airplane that made a stop in Strasbourg on the way to Bucharest. The others demurred, arranging to travel by train and rendezvous in Strasbourg, but the Hemingways bought 120-franc tickets (about $10), which was less than train tickets cost. The trip could be made in two and a half hours as opposed to ten. Not only did Ernest and Hadley register no trepidation at trying this new mode of transportation, they claimed Hadley slept during the entire flight. Though they did have to arise at four in the morning to get to Le Bourget for the flight, and though both were told to stuff their ears with cotton, it is hard to believe that anyone could sleep through the deafening roar of an interwar biplane, even if she were indifferent to the novelty of traveling at a little over a mile above the earth. Ernest later wrote about the flight for the *Star*, noting the resemblance of the checkered farmland below to a cubist painting.

Though they were not at all disappointed by prices in the Black Forest region—it was possible to live for about a dollar a day, and Ernest wrote two *Star* columns about the exchange rate, which was about a trillion marks to a dollar—the Hemingway party was put off by the Germans, whom they found brutish and unfriendly. Trout fishing was difficult, for it was hard to locate permits, and the Black Forest was not the secluded and remote mountainous landscape Ernest had looked forward to. One day out hiking Ernest tripped and fell on his back. Evidently it knocked the wind out of him and hurt quite badly, for he insisted on returning to his room, where he spent the day in bed, refusing to emerge for supper. He had evidently regained his sense of humor by the following morning, however, for Galantière later told Carlos Baker that Ernest said he would probably die while the rest of them went out hiking again. The prolonged humorlessness of the day before, on the other hand, indicated a rather alarming capacity for petulance.

Seeing their companions off to Paris from Frankfurt, the Hemingways traveled down the Rhine by boat to Cologne, where Chink Dorman-Smith was stationed. According to Ernest's later memories, Chink "had been my best friend and then our best friend for a long time," and Hadley commented, "When you and Chink talked I was included. It wasn't like being a wife at Miss Stein's" (*AMF,* 46–47). Ernest and Hadley celebrated their first anniversary on the trip, happy that Chink could be with them.

While Hemingway was in Germany, events were coming to a head in the Greco-Turkish War, and by the time he and Hadley returned to Paris he began to make plans to journey to Constantinople for the *Star.* This conflict, which broke out over Greece's efforts to seize territories in Anatolia with large Greek populations during the postwar disintegration of the Ottoman Empire, was one of the bloodiest and most atrocity-ridden of the chaotic postwar period. In 1922, the Turks, under their military leader Mustafa Kemal, or Atatürk, had begun a major westward offensive against Greece at the end of August, defeating the Greek army decisively at the Battle of Dumlupinar, retaking and burning Smyrna, and, by mid-September, pushing the Greeks out of Anatolia. Ernest left Paris on September 25 after duplicitously arranging to send cables to the International News Service's Frank Mason, who would publish Ernest's stories under the name John Hadley, as well as to John Bone, his editor at the *Star.* After a trip through Bulgaria on the Orient Express, he arrived in Constantinople on September 30.

Hemingway's coverage of the end of the Greco-Turkish War would yield not only fourteen articles for the *Star*, but three vignettes and a short story called "On the Quai at Smyrna" for what would soon be his first book, *In Our Time*. The Greek retreat from Thrace was a crucial element in the flashbacks of "The Snows of Kilimanjaro" and in the retreat from Caporetto in *A Farewell to Arms*. Perhaps because of his recent attempts at writing, in which he sought concrete images that were exactly accurate to convey what he meant to say in fiction, Ernest seemingly wrote down everything. He met two British officers, a Captain Wittal and Major Johnson, who helped him "see" major events that he had missed, describing for him Greek soldiers who were so poorly led that in one confrontation the artillery had fired on and killed many of their own. Clipped British voices rang in his head when he composed the *In Our Time* pieces, the stereotypical "stiff upper lip" of his narrators lending just the right tone of detachment and irony to his lean narratives of gruesome events.

His *Star* pieces were tremendously evocative. He described the dust and, when it rained, the mud everywhere in "old Constan," where rats and drunks swarmed the streets and alleys of the city, in marked contrast to the traditionally "oriental" aspects of the city: "In the morning when you wake and see a mist over the Golden Horn with the minarets rising out of it slim and clean towards the sun and the muezzin calling the faithful to prayer in a voice that soars and dips like an aria from a Russian opera, you have the magic of the East." When Hemingway arrived, the city was still occupied by Allied troops; the inhabitants expected a harsher and drabber regime under Atatürk and were making the most of their freedom while they could. They did not eat until after nine, when the smells of "hot sausage, fried potato and roast chestnut" filled the air. The theaters opened at ten, and the nightclubs would not open until two and the after-hours clubs around four in the morning.

Hemingway was indelibly marked by the sight of a seemingly endless line of Greek and other Christian refugees walking from Eastern Thrace through Adrianople:

It is a silent procession. Nobody even grunts. It is all they can do to keep moving. Their brilliant peasant costumes are soaked and draggled. Chickens dangle by their feet from the carts. . . . An old man marches bent under a young pig, a scythe and a gun, with a chicken tied to his scythe. A husband spreads a blanket over a woman in labor in one of the carts to keep off the driving rain. She is the only person making a sound.

It was a "ghastly procession," he wrote, earning the adjective. He also exhibited some political acumen. The key element in the background of the war was the relationship of the Allies and Greece during and after World War I. The Allies, especially the British, promised Greece large territorial gains from the Ottoman Empire. After the war, when it became clear that the Turks would continue to battle against this land grab, the Allies gradually withdrew their support, and the Turks far overtook the Greeks, sending a steady stream of refugees out of Eastern Thrace toward Bulgaria and what would become the modern Greek republic. By the time Hemingway arrived in the area, the war had been settled. His observations, as absolutely crystalline and masterful as they were, were made during the aftermath of the war.

But nothing was simple for Hemingway during his time in the contested area. He had had an enormous, protracted argument with Hadley before he left. She had uncharacteristically (her biographer claims it was "very unlike her") opposed his going to Constantinople, despite the fact that his job required that he go. Hadley explained it simply: "Ernest was the only thing I had in Paris, and I dreaded being alone again." The couple enjoyed playing at being small children, and Hadley may have been acting out a childish behavior. More seriously, their relationship was built on Ernest's fundamental intuitive understanding of Hadley's past. Her mother's treatment of her as an invalid, denigrating her as inferior to her sister Fonnie, with whom Florence Richardson had allied herself, as well as Fonnie's continued ill treatment of her after their mother's death, had combined to burden Hadley with a deep feeling of mistrust of others, a lack of confidence in herself, and a belief that love always led to loss. Today we might speak of separation anxiety and intimacy issues. Ernest knew the source of Hadley's unreasonable feelings and probably sympathized with her. But the necessity of his departure trumped her desire to keep him at home, and they clashed, finally lapsing into a furious silence that lasted three days, and was not broken when Ernest boarded the Orient Express.

Ernest rivaled Hadley's separation anxiety with a complicated mix of fear and fantasy about marital infidelity, imagined mostly, but with some basis in reality. The autobiographical reminiscences of the authorial stand-in in Hemingway's masterful "The Snows of Kilimanjaro" include the narrator's memories of wartime in Constantinople, memories that were decidedly erotic and had much to do with the end of Ernest's wartime relationship with Agnes, the nurse in Italy who threw him over. The narrator writes that he corresponded with the Agnes figure while in Constantinople—which

Ernest evidently did not do. Experiencing his own kind of separation anxiety, Hemingway apparently—if we take the story as autobiographical, which is problematic—replayed his earlier separation from, or desertion by, his first love. But the narrator also remembered about Turkey, "He had whored the whole time." He describes a night with "a hot Armenian slut" who "slung her belly against him so it almost scalded." It is hard to locate truth in this part of the story; the vivid details could support arguments either for its veracity or that the Armenian woman was a fantasy.

Another piece of the erotic puzzle is Ernest's Constantinople encounter with an unforgettable woman, the journalist Louise Bryant. A top correspondent with the Hearst papers and the author of *Six Red Months in Russia,* a personal account of the Russian Revolution that she wrote alongside the better-known (but not necessarily better) account by her husband, John Reed—*Ten Days That Shook the World.* After Reed's death from typhus in Russia in 1920, Louise had persevered in her journalistic career, specializing in the Near East and filing stories with Hearst's International News Service. A stunning beauty, Louise was ardently pursued, she coyly stated, by such colorful figures as the Turkish leader Enver Pasha and the Italian adventurer poet Gabriele d'Annunzio. When she was in Constantinople in 1922, her most persistent suitor was the diplomat and journalist William Bullitt, a man of considerable fortune who was taking the decade off after a period of service in the Wilson administration that ended with the disillusionment of the Treaty of Versailles. He seems to have followed Louise's trail to Constantinople.

Though Louise Bryant's friendship with Hemingway in 1920s Paris is well documented, we know of their encounter in Constantinople only from a furious response he would later write to Archibald MacLeish, then living in Conway, Massachusetts, where MacLeish was a neighbor of William Bullitt—who had recently married Louise Bryant. MacLeish teased Hemingway that Louise said she knew all about him, though it's not clear whether Louise had insinuated romantic knowledge or whether MacLeish was nosing about a possible relationship. At any rate, Ernest exploded: "As for Mrs. Bullet [sic] knowing all about me the bitch where in hell does she get that stuff. . . . I did know her when her hair was blonde but that was in Constantinople and besides the wench was surrounded by naval officers." His overreaction suggests either that such a relationship existed or, more likely, that Ernest had been attracted to Bryant in the fall of 1922 but was frustrated by an inability to make inroads. What we know about Hemingway and his fetishism about hair and, especially, about blond hair, bears out the impression she made on him in Constantinople. And, as the next weeks and months would show, he would have good reason to resent her professional successes.

No letters between Hadley and Ernest during their month-long separation survive, which is in itself remarkable, given how often they wrote each other when apart. Hadley told an early biographer that she felt terribly guilty for having "lacerated" Ernest, and she surely wrote to tell him so. (Hadley later destroyed all of Ernest's letters to her.) When he returned he brought her a beautiful antique necklace, but neither of them would forget their protracted quarrel, thus far the worst of their married life. Ernest's later fiction and his comments on Louise Bryant indicate that infidelity was certainly on his mind in Constantinople. If he did not act on his feelings, he may well have felt guilty for them, given how close he and Hadley had been up to this point.

Though an armistice between Greece and Turkey had gone into effect in mid-October, it was not until the following July that a treaty would be signed. In November the Turkish government, led by Ismet Inönü, met in Lausanne with leaders from France, Italy, and Great Britain; Lord Curzon, then foreign secretary, declared himself president of the conference. The *Star* evidently did not put Hemingway on the story, perhaps because of his double-dealing when in Constantinople; indeed, he would publish only two pieces from Lausanne in the Toronto paper. Both features rather than news stories, they would not run in the *Star* for over a month. One of them, "Mussolini: Biggest Bluff in Europe," supplied his impressions of the dictator, who had seized power at the end of October, thus bringing him to the conference table.

His mind may have been elsewhere, for Lausanne was the scene of what Ernest came to see as the greatest tragedy of his young life: Hadley, en route to join him on the train from Paris, lost his manuscripts when the valise containing them disappeared. He would never forgive her, and he would never forget the incident. Nor would she.

It all began with Hadley and Ernest making plans to return to Chamby for the winter, with Chink Dorman-Smith to meet them there on December 16. Chicago friend Isabelle Simmons (later Godolphin), and Hadley's friends Mab Phelan and her daughter Janet, they hoped, would meet them soon after. Hemingway at the time had in mind leaving journalism altogether, encouraged by Gertrude Stein but also by William Bolitho Ryall, a South African reporter whom Ernest had just met at the conference. Ryall, called by one Hemingway biographer "the newsman's Nietzsche," was very well grounded in international politics and was a thoroughgoing cynic as well, and he urged Ernest to leave journalism while he was still young. Ernest had no immediate plans to quit, even though the *Star* had not assigned him to cover the Lausanne Conference. Instead, Ernest was there for the two Hearst agencies, the International News Service and the Universal News Service, answering to Frank Mason, whom he had immediately disliked.

Because Lausanne was so close to Chamby, Ernest and Hadley agreed in advance that she should join him in Lausanne whenever she could get away so they could travel together to Chamby; for the time being she was entertaining a St. Louis friend and then came down with a bad cold. Wires and a letter to Hadley, now addressed as Wicky Poo, indicated Ernest's frustration at his low pay (he complained that Mason had "kiked me so on money" that he had to forgo taxis and walk or take a streetcar). The $60 a week the INS and Universal News paid him was $15 less than what the *Star* had paid, and they were more exacting about expenses. Because reporters were barred from actual sessions at the conference, Ernest was run ragged going from one press conference to another and having to file stories both in the morning and at night. Essentially he was on call at all hours, which a cable to Mason reveals that he hadn't understood when he signed on.

Besides Ryall, Ernest spent time with the usual crew of reporters, including Guy Hickok and George Slocombe. Lincoln Steffens was also present, and Steffens was an important figure in Hemingway's writing life at this juncture. Following their meeting at Genoa, Ernest had sent Steffens "My Old Man," a horse-racing story he had completed that summer, and Steffens admired it so much he immediately sent it to Ray Long at *Cosmopolitan*. (The magazine would ultimately reject it, but Steffens's regard for the story was the first in a series of accolades it would receive; Ernest got a great deal of mileage out of Steffens's championship.) In Lausanne, Ernest showed Steffens his story from Adrianople about the bedraggled stream of refugees from Thrace, together with a copy of the cable he had sent to the INS. Steffens was impressed with the story, and rightly so, but Ernest became impatient and urged Steffens to look at the language of the cables. Ernest had become fascinated by cablese, which he used casually in letters at the time; he composed one cable to Frank Mason, in response to Mason's query about his expenses and the account books, that has earned Hemingway the undying affection of journalists everywhere: "SUGGEST YOU UPSTICK BOOKS ASSWARDS HEMINGWAY." Steffens got it. He asked to read other dispatches and whatever stories or poems Ernest had on hand; what he saw made him "sure of Hemingway." He admired the way Hemingway walked along the street shadow boxing or otherwise illustrating his stories with physical antics. "Nobody noticed," he wrote, "except to smile with this big, handsome boy, squaring off to phantom-fight you. . . . And he was straight, hard-boiled honest, too."

Hemingway amused himself waiting for Hadley by taking notes that he soon after turned into a poem, "They Made Peace—What Is Peace?" commenting scurrilously that the leaders present at the conference, Lord Curzon, George Chicherin, and Atatürk, liked "young boys." He concocted a little exercise in recording his doings at the conference in free verse. He obviously liked the result, for he sent it off to *The Little Review,* which would publish it the following April. He admitted writing it, however, while avoiding filing his morning story en route from Paris to Lausanne.

In the interim, Hadley arrived in Lausanne absolutely stricken. Knowing that Steffens was present at the conference and reading whatever work Ernest had, Hadley packed a valise with all of Ernest's writing to date—poems, short stories, a partially completed novel, and the short prose sketches he was experimenting with. In the Gare de Lyon Hadley gave the valise, along with her other luggage, to a porter, but when her baggage caught up with her in her compartment, she found the valise was missing. (Another version of the story describes her leaving the luggage in the compartment while she went to find a newspaper or magazine.) She alerted the conductor and searched what parts of the train she could, but it was clear the valise had disappeared—surely stolen. Steffens accompanied Ernest to the station to meet Hadley. When she emerged on the platform she was nearly frantic with worry and remorse.

Many years later, when Hemingway described the loss of his manuscripts in *A Moveable Feast,* his memoir about the Paris years, he presented himself as calm and collected when he got the news, worried only by Hadley's distress: "She . . . cried and cried and could not tell me [what had happened]. I told her that no matter what the dreadful thing was that had happened nothing could be that bad, and whatever it was, it was all right and not to worry. We would work it out" (*AMF,* 70). When she finally told him the manuscripts were lost, together with all the carbons that she had unfortunately packed as well, he didn't believe her and hastened back to Paris to see for himself.

From this point on Hemingway's version of what happened after he learned of the loss becomes questionable. While his passport indicates that he did indeed take a train back to Paris almost at once, on December 3, things unfolded in a less dramatic, messier fashion than he relates in *A Moveable Feast.* To begin with, he did not go to Gertrude Stein's the next day for a consoling lunch, as he claimed; Stein and Toklas were in Provence for the winter. In Ernest's dramatic retelling, he did not believe Hadley also packed his carbons; he made the trip to check—and confirmed they were indeed gone. In a more unrestrained memory of the incident, in an unpublished novel written in the late 1940s and early 1950s, excerpted as a short story, "A Strange Country," he wrote, "I felt almost as though I could not breathe when I saw there really were no folders with originals, nor folders with typed copies, nor folders with carbons" (*CSS*, 647). In fact, in this version of the story, he found on returning to Paris that Hadley had packed, and thus lost, not only his writing but his paper clips, pencils, erasers, and a pencil sharpener shaped like a fish; his "envelopes with the typed return address in the upper left-hand corner," and the international postage coupons that he enclosed when he sent his stories out. In this version, Hadley was trying to put Ernest out of business—to use one of his favorite phrases.

On the heels of Ernest's quick trip to Paris and back—six days afterward—Guy Hickok and Lincoln Steffens helped investigate the loss, both of them traveling to Paris and looking in one of the city's Lost and Found Bureaus (or perhaps it was the railway station's), and reporting to Ernest that it was hopeless. They also consulted Bill Bird, who suggested placing an ad in various newspapers, but Bird said it would not be worth the cost of the ad unless Ernest was willing to promise a large reward. Bird didn't think Ernest would do this, and indeed Bird told Steffens and Hickok that he'd in the meantime received a letter from Ernest authorizing him to pay 150 francs as a reward—or about $10. Evidently that's all he thought the lost valise was worth.

Furthermore, there were mitigating factors. "Up in Michigan" turned up in the Hemingways' Paris apartment, while Steffens had sent out "My Old Man," so that was saved, and Harriet Monroe had at least six poems he had sent to her for *Poetry* magazine. Pages from the war novel he was working on were lost for good, however. It seems likely that some of his best work, what he called his Paris sketches, was etched indelibly in his brain, so carefully had he chosen his words—and thus not impossible to re-create. Furthermore, he turned his Lausanne notes into his lighthearted and scurrilous five-finger exercise in poetry, "They Asked for Peace—What Is Peace?" on the train back to Lausanne after searching for his manuscripts, hardly the action of a desperate man.

Hemingway said that Gertrude Stein was very sympathetic to his loss; no doubt she was, when he saw her the following February, after she returned to Paris. Lincoln Steffens, reporting on his and Guy Hickok's findings after a search in Paris, wrote, "I'm afraid the stuff is lost, Hem." Ezra Pound put the whole thing in the proper perspective. It was an "act of Gawd," he said. "No one is *known* to have lost anything by *suppression* of early work."

So he didn't lose much—and he gained a great deal. In the coming year Robert McAlmon, an American writer living in Paris, would publish, with his Contact Press, Hemingway's *Three Stories and Ten Poems*—not, that is, a large output for a young writer. In the future, when his stories began to be accepted and his future looked rosy, it gave Ernest an out when a novel was expected from him; his first novelistic effort had been traumatically lost. It was a dramatic, even a romantic, story, and it was seamlessly absorbed into the saga of Ernest's nascent career, becoming a legend about the legend.

SEVEN

Almost everyone they knew heard the story about Hadley losing Ernest's manuscripts. The painter Mike Strater recalls that Ernest said to him in early 1923, "You know, Mike, if you had those manuscripts in your trunk, you would not have left them to go and get something to read." Explaining, Strater added, that Ernest was "very upset because it showed how little she valued what he was doing." But Hadley's first biographer, on sound information, concluded that she "was incapable of being artful." No doubt Hadley feared just such an interpretation, especially from her husband. Her grief at the loss of his manuscripts was deeply felt and lifelong, and Ernest held it against her for the rest of his life. It was not a question of forgiveness. It was a question of never letting her forget that he had not forgotten. As one Hemingway biographer wrote, "Whatever happened between them, he would always have this edge."

On the 11th of December Ernest had gone with Hadley to Chamby for a little skiing, and they intended to leave Lausanne by the 16th. Negotiations at the conference were by no means over. Lord Curzon was threatening to leave in the face of what he considered Turkish intransigence around December 13, so Ernest shut down his wire service work at a relatively crucial time. (A treaty was not signed until July 24, 1923.) Frank Mason would find someone to take Ernest's place easily enough, and no doubt at lower pay: at this point Ernest was earning $90 a week and billing for $35 in expenses.

Chink joined Hadley and Ernest in Switzerland December 16, as did the O'Neil family from St. Louis. Dave O'Neil, the patriarch, made his money in lumber but really wanted to write poetry, an aspiration that Ernest mocked rather viciously in letters to Ezra Pound, calling O'Neil a "Celto-Kike." Dave had a "system" of writing poetry, which was "to write a few words about something he does not understand. The less he understands it the more 'magic,' the better the poem." On January 2 Isabelle Simmons arrived, and soon after that a mother and daughter from

St. Louis appeared in Paris as well. The women began to style themselves "the Harem," with Ernest a sultan. He enlisted all the guests in bobsledding and skiing, making the O'Neils' teenage sons, George and Horton, his aides-de-camp. In the afternoon they took a railway to Les Avants and from there to the ski run and bobsled courses at the Col de Sonloup. Ernest loved skiing, which was fast and dangerous, and required a good deal of physical exertion; railways and trams could get skiers only partway up the mountain; inevitably, they would need to climb, attaching sealskins to the bottoms of their skis for traction.

Mornings were given over to writing. Almost every word Ernest produced at about this time was right, and his reputation would be built on how he strung them together. He was producing with seeming effortlessness short prose-poems collectively titled "Paris 1922," building on fragments he remembered from his lost manuscripts; six of these would appear in the February issue of *The Little Review* in a special "Exiles" number. Two short stories (not vignettes) that date from this period are "Cat in the Rain" and "Cross-Country Snow." Both are stories of regret, "Cross-Country Snow" about the losses associated with marrying and having a family.

In "Cat in the Rain" a husband, another George, and his American wife, unnamed, are at an Italian hotel when the wife sees a cat outside looking for cover in the rain. When she goes out looking for the cat, it is gone, and she is disconsolate. For an unspecified reason she regrets the things she's lost: sitting at a candlelit table with her own silver, some new clothes, hair long enough to put up. And a cat: "If I can't have long hair or any fun, I want a cat." Though the cat is eventually produced, longing and loss suffuse the story.

An interesting feature of "Cat in the Rain" reflects on a curious stage in Hadley and Ernest's marriage. The wife wants to let her hair grow out; George likes it cut short, "the back of her neck, clipped close like a boy's," and says he likes it the way it is. But she is sick of short hair: "I get so tired of looking like a boy" (*CSS*, 131). This casual allusion to hair length reveals (while it also masks) Ernest's deep-seated preoccupation, anything connected with haircuts and hair color an obsessive interest. The idea that women and men could explore different sexual roles excited him terribly, as did the role that hair could play in such a drama. In two of Hemingway's best-known novels, *A Farewell to Arms* and *For Whom the Bell Tolls,* hero and heroine talk about growing and/or cutting their hair to the same length. Out of context these conversations are not remarkable—just a little unexpected. But Hemingway's obsessive interest in hair is obvious to any reader of his late fiction, especially *The Garden of Eden,* where husband and wife embark on a period of trying out different gender roles in bed, and at the same time a course of cutting their hair and dyeing it with henna or bleach to match each other's. Hemingway seems to have been specifically aroused by the back of the neck of a woman with a boyish haircut, though this should not be taken to suggest any homosexual impulse on Ernest's part. It was far more complicated.

Of late, this subject has been explored at great length by Hemingway scholars. Critics like Debra Moddelmog, Mark Spilka, Carl Eby, and Rose Marie Burwell have pointed out that Hemingway was hardly conventional in his sexuality, opening up an aspect of his life that directly touches on the work of many contemporary scholars, particularly those engaged in feminist and queer studies.

This may seem far afield of Hemingway's life in Paris in the 1920s, but a controversial new edition of Hemingway's Paris memoir, *A Moveable Feast,* shows abundant early evidence of his fetish, suggesting that Ernest was acting on it in Paris with his first wife a willing partner. The edition contains other chapters of the memoir that did not appear in the 1964 edition, which was posthumously selected and edited by Mary Hemingway, the author's fourth wife. In 2009, Seán Hemingway, Ernest's grandson, revised the text of the 1964 volume and added ten new "sketches" as well as other fragments of manuscript; the new material was found among Ernest's papers at the Hemingway Collection at the JFK Library, and includes a fascinating sketch called "Secret Pleasures," about the role of Ernest's hair fetish in his first marriage.

The sketch is about Ernest's desire to wear his hair long. Ernest had been extremely impressed by the long hair sported by some Japanese painters he had met at Ezra Pound's studio; the sketch goes on to re-create a conversation he had with Hadley on the subject. Husband and wife discuss Ernest's growing his hair long while Hadley, who then had close-cropped hair, said she would cut hers periodically so that their hair would be the same length. The whole notion arouses Ernest, and when she returns from the hairdresser the next day he is very excited: "I put my arm around her and felt our hearts beating through our sweaters and I brought my right hand up and felt her neck smooth and the hair thick against it under my fingers that were shaking." He feels the blunt haircut against her neck and says "something secret." Hadley replies, "Afterwards."

The sketch describes a conversation later in the year but refers to events in Switzerland, where "nobody cared how you dressed or how you cut your hair," from the winter of 1922–23. The editors of the revised edition of *A Moveable Feast* make note of a fragment cut from this new sketch:

When we lived in Austria we would cut each other's hair and let it grow to the same length. One was dark and the other dark red gold and in the dark in the night one would wake the other swinging the heavy dark or the heavy silken red gold across the others lips in the cold dark in the warmth of the bed. You could see your breath if there was moonlight. (*AMF,* 183–89)

The specific nature of this language is reminiscent of Hemingway's descriptive writing at its best, yet this style, along with the repetitions of "dark" and "heavy," characterizes all of Hemingway's later writing about hair and sexuality to an extent that suggests the specificity and repetitions of pornography. Indeed, Ernest's letters about her hair to his fourth wife, Mary, with whom he freely enjoyed acting out sexual fantasies about haircuts and hair dyeing, are frankly pornographic; he admits that writing about her hair and its color hugely excites him.

"Secret Pleasures" conveys to the reader a sense of the sexual excitement and experimentation that characterized Ernest's first marriage; when he and Hadley were apart, letters between them dwelled on how happy they would be when sleeping together again. And certainly Ernest, objectively speaking, found Hadley's hair very attractive, as did most observers. It was beautiful when it was waist length, and it was beautiful when she had it bobbed in New York City just before the couple sailed for Europe in December 1921. Grace Hemingway had always admired red hair, and it seemed right that Hadley's hair was a reddish gold of the sort Ernest had come to admire. Letters showed a solicitude about her hair that might otherwise be unremarkable but for the context of his lifelong hair fetish. Just before they married Ernest apparently showed some concern over how her hair might look at the September wedding; Hadley reassured him that she was washing it with Castile shampoo, drying it in the sun, and then applying Brilliantine to it, which was said to soften hair and bring out its shine. "It looks a thousand times better," she assured him. All descriptions of the wedding by those present mention Hadley's long, thick hair, still damp from swimming earlier that day. Her hair was a critical component of Hadley's attractiveness—especially to her husband.

*   *   *

On February 7 Ernest and Hadley left Chamby by train, stopping in Milan and then going on to the seaside town of Rapallo, where Ezra Pound was living with his wife, Dorothy, and writing cantos about Sigismondo Malatesta, the Renaissance patron of the arts and soldier of fortune. Pound urged Ernest and Hadley to come to Rapallo and join him on a walking tour to uncover more information about Malatesta. By the time they arrived, however, Pound was about to set out on another literary mission of some kind. He managed to convince the Hemingways to stay at Rapallo while he was away and begin the promised tour with the Pounds when he returned.

While in Rapallo, Hadley came to believe she was pregnant, and told her husband sometime during February. Although they must have discussed having a child, Ernest was shocked by her news.

"I am too young to be a father," Ernest complained "with great bitterness" to Gertrude Stein, who found his remark so amusing she quoted it to Hadley. "He felt deeply sorry for himself at times," remembered Hadley later. But he came around to the idea and resolved anew to bring money in by his writing. In the meantime, Hadley did not let her pregnancy slow her down at all; she felt "exuberant" and "realized what I'd been born for." She would visit a doctor a few weeks later in Milan, who confirmed the pregnancy and told her she could pursue any activity she wanted "as long as I promised I wouldn't fall down," she told a biographer.

In Pound's absence, Ernest and Hadley were delighted to spend some time with Mike Strater and his wife, also in Rapallo. Mike was a graduate of Princeton, where he had known F. Scott Fitzgerald; he appeared as Burne Holiday in Fitzgerald's *This Side of Paradise* (1920). Ernest had met Mike at the end of 1922 in Pound's Paris studio; the two struck up a friendship and frequently boxed together. In Rapallo, where Mike was ensconced with his wife, Maggie, and their child, Ernest hoped Mike could box with him or at least replace Pound as a tennis partner, but Mike had sprained his ankle. Mike was an accomplished artist who had studied at the École Julien in Paris, and he had painted a portrait of Ernest two months before. Now he painted another, which made Ernest look, Hadley thought, like Balzac; Ernest sported a mustache and his hair was long, presumably because the *Star* wasn't sending him anywhere in the near future where it would matter how he looked.

In *A Moveable Feast* Ernest would write of his Rapallo stay, "It was a bad time and I did not think I could write any more then" (*AMF,* 70). He was possibly referring in part to Hadley's loss of his manuscripts and in part to her pregnancy, arguably holding her responsible for his failure to start writing again. But if her pregnancy had stalled his writing momentarily, it had not checked his ambition. He felt financial pressure, no doubt, to come up with a steady means of support for his growing family, but he also seems to have felt that if he was old enough to have a child he was old enough to be launched as a successful young writer.

Ernest's journalist friend Bill Bird had by this time announced that he would publish a Hemingway collection as a book in a six-part series edited by Pound, importantly described as "an inquest into the state of contemporary English prose." The previous October Bird had bought a seventeenth-century printing press on the Île St.-Louis and intended to produce finely printed editions for his Three Mountains Press. In February and March Ernest was just sending off to Jane Heap at *The Little Review* the short journalistic sketches that he had been working over for the past six months: a description of the execution of six Greek cabinet members during the war with Turkey, an account of a bullfight (though he hadn't yet seen one), and a description of the Greek refugees passing through Adrianople (from his *Star* story), among others.

Ernest was immensely proud of these sketches, and they would eventually also appear as interchapters in the commercially published *In Our Time*. But he knew that on their own they added up to a rather thin book. Though Pound's imprimatur would help, he felt sure, he had little hope that Bird's publication of his first book would do anything for him financially. And even if copies found their way into influential hands, practically speaking Bird was unable to print enough to ensure a wide readership.

But in his short stay in Rapallo Hemingway had two encounters that would give his career a spectacular boost. When Hadley and Ernest first got to Rapallo, the Pounds had taken them on a hike to the top of Montallegro, Rapallo's mountain. A brisk six-hundred-meter climb took them to the top, which commanded a view of the village and the Bay of Tigullio beyond. Sitting at a table in the Hotel Ristorante Montallegro, Pound spotted Edward O'Brien, a writer and editor who was staying at a mountaintop monastery to devote himself to his work.

Born in 1890, O'Brien was "a gentle, shy man, pale, with pale blue eyes," according to Hemingway. Perhaps they discussed their hair, for Ernest noted O'Brien had "straight lanky hair he cut himself" (*AMF*, 69–70). Among O'Brien's published work were two volumes of poetry and a fictional diary called *The Forgotten Threshold* (1919), and in a few years he would begin to write literary criticism. He was best known, however, for his annual compilations of the best stories of the previous year, published by Small, Maynard since 1915, when O'Brien began the series with *The Best American Short Stories of 1914*. He was known to work "heroically," claiming he read eight thousand stories a year, and the anthology was widely admired, publishing such authors as Ring Lardner, William Faulkner, F. Scott Fitzgerald, and Dorothy Parker.

Ernest could see immediately that O'Brien was someone to cultivate, and he set out to impress him, telling him his life story to date—the dramatic version, full of untruth. O'Brien was immediately impressed. Later, in a 1929 critical book about short stories, *The Dance of the Machines* (1929), he wrote that he had met Ernest "some years ago on top of an Italian mountain," when Ernest "told me some of his war experiences." He explained, "During the war he joined the Italian Army. He was a brave member of the *Arditi*. He was made an officer. He had never seen life before. He was to see it now." O'Brien's thesis was that the coming of "the machine," or modern mechanized life, caused a great disillusionment, especially among writers and artists: Hemingway "went into the war a pious boy. Then he witnessed the spiritual destructiveness of machinery." He wanted to see anything Ernest had written so that he could consider it for inclusion in *The Best American Short Stories of 1923*.

Ernest gave him one of the two finished short stories he had in his possession, "My Old Man," a racetrack tale about a boy who learns with bitterness that his father, a jockey, is dishonest; the story is commonly said to be derivative of Sherwood Anderson's work, both in its subject (Anderson wrote racetrack stories) and the youthful naïveté of the protagonist. O'Brien liked Hemingway and the story so much that he accepted it on the spot and, in an extremity of feeling, asked Ernest if he could dedicate the volume to him. (O'Brien printed the story as by "Ernest Hemenway," but in the dedication his name was spelled correctly.) Moreover, he agreed to write a letter of support when Ernest submitted the story to Arthur Vance of the *Pictorial Review;* Vance rejected it, and Ernest had to write an awkward letter to O'Brien asking whether the letter had gone astray. The story was never accepted by a magazine, but "My Old Man" would be published in the book Bill Bird was putting out in 1923, so it would indeed qualify as a published story for O'Brien's anthology. Moreover, O'Brien's promise was certain enough that Ernest felt he could trumpet this triumph to any interested party, and did.

Ernest accomplished as much in this chance meeting, careerwise, as he had done in all his reportage to date. He seemed to have a magic touch. "Believe me, he's going places," wrote Robert McAlmon, another writer who also made a powerful connection with Hemingway in Rapallo. McAlmon was born in a small town in Kansas, one of ten children of a Presbyterian minister and his wife. His family moved often, always further west, eventually landing in California, where McAlmon grew up. He worked as a farmhand and merchant seaman, and served in the Air Service in the Great War, though he never saw combat. He began writing, poems originally, and migrated to Chicago and then New York, where he supported himself as a nude model. In New York he formed a lifelong friendship with the poet William Carlos Williams, and with Williams started a journal called *Contact*, which would publish Pound, Wallace Stevens, Marianne Moore, and H.D.

McAlmon was dark and angular, often wearing a turquoise earring that matched his eyes. He seems to have been bisexual, and when he was a young man, a rich man wanted to adopt him, in an echo of Ernest's relationship with Jim Gamble. McAlmon's life took a dramatic turn when, in New York City, he met the Imagist poet H.D. and her companion, Bryher, whose real name was Winifred Ellerman. Bryher, also a writer, was the daughter of British shipping magnate Sir John Ellerman, who supported his daughter with a generous allowance. H.D. and Bryher were lovers, and wanted to continue living and traveling together. Sir John was threatening to "come after" Bryher, according to her friend Marianne Moore, because he did not approve of her traveling in Europe and America "without an escort." Bryher proposed a marriage of convenience to McAlmon: she would share her allowance with him, while he was to be what is known as a beard.

Their "marriage of convenience" was to become a favorite story of the literary 1920s, especially among the Paris expatriates. It served both parties cleverly, was sexually bohemian, and carried an added element of sticking it to the rich. And the money the marriage made available launched McAlmon's career as a publisher, which would take off when he founded Contact Editions, an important modernist imprint that published the newest and most talented of the expat writers. Bryher would later say, bluntly, "We neither of us felt the slightest attraction to each other, but remained perfectly friendly."

The real story, however, was slightly different and far more interesting, and helps to explain this complicated character and his role in Hemingway's life. When Bryher and McAlmon first met, in September 1921, she gave McAlmon a copy of her novel, *Development* (1920). Upon reading it, McAlmon felt he had met a kindred bohemian soul. But Bryher left *in medias res* for a stay in California; soon after, McAlmon wrote to tell her he was going to ship off to China. Evidently Bryher then returned in haste and made her proposal. McAlmon and Bryher were married on Valentine's Day 1921, and both soon departed, separately, for Europe.

There are indications that all was not as it seemed; Bryher and McAlmon evidently felt a mutual attraction when they met, though Bryher withdrew quickly because of her relationship with H.D. McAlmon seems not to have really understood the terms of the agreement, and was initially embarrassed and ashamed that he had entered into the marriage without full knowledge of Bryher's expectations. "Maintaining that he chose to marry Bryher because he loved her," a McAlmon biographer writes, he "repeatedly asserted that he had been surprised and distressed by her refusal to consummate their union." Indeed, he would later break off his friendship with Williams when the poet said in his *Autobiography* that the marriage was unconsummated. It seems that McAlmon genuinely wanted a marriage with Bryher, sexually and otherwise.

Furthermore, Bryher was not in fact receiving a very large allowance from her father; it was £600 a year, or roughly $38,000 today, and had to support her as well as her husband. It was enough, maybe, for McAlmon to pay for his drinks, but not much more. The Ellermans, however, were without a doubt very rich; McAlmon later said he hadn't really known how rich until he saw the family's mansion in London. On this visit Bryher and McAlmon masqueraded as loving bride and groom; Bryher genuinely did not want to displease her parents. McAlmon, whose personal charm was considerable, struck up separate friendships with Lady Hannah Ellerman, who loved the nightlife of London (her husband didn't) and often went to nightclubs with her new son-in-law; and the Ellerman butler, who could be counted on to let McAlmon into the house late at night and generally cover for him when necessary. But the most important friendship he formed was with Sir John himself. "The fact of my being a minister's son impressed him from the first moment, and he feared I might disapprove of his serving wines and whisky at and before meals," a theory, McAlmon said, that was soon "discredited." Ellerman knew of and even took an interest in McAlmon's plans for supporting and publishing artists, and in the winter of 1922–23 conferred an outright gift of $70,000 on his son-in-law. The equivalent of $750,000 today, this gift was what made McAlmon's writing and publishing career possible, not the relatively small part of Bryher's allowance she had promised him in exchange for marrying her.

When Ernest and McAlmon met in Rapallo in February 1922, McAlmon was riding high. He had published a book of poems, *Explorations,* with the prestigious (if small) Egoist Press in London, and *A Hasty Bunch,* a book of short stories (the title suggested by his friend James Joyce). In 1923 he would publish two titles, a book of stories called *A Companion Volume,* and an autobiographical novel called *Post-Adolescence.* He was considered to have great promise; Ernest Walsh, the editor of *This Quarter,* would call McAlmon "the most honest and authentically American of our writers, and the only one who can seriously compete with Joseph Conrad and James Joyce." T. S. Eliot, who met him in London, spoke of him as "a very charming man of lively intelligence and amiable personality." Hemingway himself wrote McAlmon, shortly after the two met, that his not yet published novel *Village* was "absolutely first-rate and damned good reading." And Hemingway would continue to champion McAlmon's work throughout the 1920s.

McAlmon was also riding a wave of social success. He was "certainly the most popular member of 'The Crowd,' as he called it," observed Sylvia Beach in her memoir. Moreover everyone took their cues from him. Beach continued, "Somehow he dominated whatever group he was in. What-

The writer Robert McAlmon, Ernest's first publisher. McAlmon was Ernest's companion at his first bullfight, in June 1923.

ever café or bar McAlmon patronized at the moment was the one where you saw everybody."

In the winter of 1922–23 McAlmon had decided to start a publishing company to be called Contact Editions, its name recalling the literary magazine he had edited with William Carlos Williams in Greenwich Village. The first two books to roll off the press were his own, but in a remarkably short time he arranged to publish works by Mina Loy, Marsden Hartley, Williams, and Bryher. The outright gift from Sir John Ellerman in mid-1923 would ease finances considerably, enabling McAlmon to follow through on his expansive plans for the press.

Sometime in early 1923, perhaps as early as February, when he was with the Hemingways in Rapallo, McAlmon decided to take on a book by Hemingway, at this date designated only as "Short Stories." There was one immediate awkwardness or difficulty that quickly turned into a happy coincidence: Bill Bird's projected Hemingway book. Part of the series on prose to be edited by Pound, the book was listed as "Blank," because when the series was announced it was not clear what Hemingway would be supplying Bird. (Evidently Ernest sent a copy of Bird's prospectus back home, for two separate orders came in from Oak Park: letters from both parents on their respective letterheads, each ordering five copies of "Blank.")

McAlmon esteemed each of the authors printed by Contact Editions in 1923, Marsden Hartley especially—though no critic publicly noticed Hartley, otherwise a well-known painter. Mina Loy's *Lunar Baedecker* (misspelled by McAlmon) was highly thought of, and Williams was well launched on his career as a major modernist poet. McAlmon was taking a bit of a chance on Hemingway, though the news of his part in O'Brien's anthology of 1923 short stories no doubt made him feel more certain. McAlmon was very discerning, though of course he made some bad calls. He was dead-on, however, when it came to Hemingway. When he said Ernest was "going places," he added, "[He's] got a natural talent for the public eye, has that boy. He's the original limelight kid, just you watch him for a few months. Wherever the limelight is, you'll find Ernest with his big lovable boyish grin, making hay."

Ernest and Hadley spent only a couple of evenings with McAlmon and the Straters before Ezra returned and the Hemingways set off on a walking tour of sites associated with Malatesta. Ernest showed a particular interest in the battlegrounds where the condottiero's military campaigns were carried out, while Hadley remembered, "This was . . . a rucksack trip, and we always lunched from our sacks on some hillside—native cheese, figs, and wine." The couples went their separate ways at Sirmione, Ernest and Hadley going on to Cortina for some spring skiing. There the *Star's* John Bone telegraphed Ernest, declaring his intention to send him on a month-long tour of the French-occupied Ruhr, Germany's industrial heartland. Ernest agreed to go for ten days only, and left Hadley in Cortina while he went briefly to Paris to get a visa and the necessary letters to get him into Germany, which was strangely difficult. He then climbed aboard a Strasbourg-bound train. He wrote ten articles for the *Star* about Franco-German relations and the Ruhr occupation, but three of these were filed from Paris. He was not a particularly astute critic of the occupation and the crisis surrounding war reparations. Indeed, this would be his last sustained foreign trip for the *Star*, for after the summer Ernest and Hadley were returning to Toronto, where Hadley would have her child and Ernest would work full-time for the newspaper. They preferred to have the baby closer to the U.S. Ernest evidently thought that as a newly domesticated family man, he should be working full-time.

In the summer of 1923 Hemingway discovered Spain, and he discovered the bullfight, both life-changing developments. While in Rapallo, Mike Strater had waxed rhapsodic about Spain and bullfighting, and Ernest had already been hearing about the bullfights from Gertrude Stein, herself a bit of an *aficionada*. (She had written a poem, included in her 1922 *Geography and Plays,* which Ernest had read, called "I Must Try to Write the History of Belmonte," about the matador Juan Belmonte.) In his own bullfighting bible, *Death in the Afternoon* (1932), Hemingway would say he had heard Stein talking about the matador Joselito and seen photographs of her and Toklas at a bullfight. Citing his memory of the Greeks' torturous treatment of their pack animals, he would add that he had murmured something about not wanting to see the horses injured—often disemboweled—by the bulls.

With the advantage of hindsight, Hemingway analyzed why he thought it was important for him to see a bullfight at this juncture in his life. His remarks were extremely insightful and, as it happens, fairly accurate: "The only place that you could see life and death, *i.e.* violent death now that the wars were over, was in the bull ring and I wanted very much to go to Spain where I could study it. I was trying to learn to write, commencing with the simplest things," adding, "and one of the simplest things of all and the most fundamental is violent death" (*DIA,* 91). It might be contemporary hindsight alone that makes his remarks seem accurate, for we are now used to the idea—having read our Hemingway—that the writer who portrays life the most simply and fundamentally works from close observation and consideration of violent death. At the time that Hemingway wrote, however, this was by no means a commonplace. It could be argued that he well knew the contradictions in his argument, and that was the reason he would write a full-length book (and, late in life, a second one, *A Dangerous Summer*) about the subject. It *was* strange to associate violent death with writing, and it speaks to some remarkable features of Hemingway's character. Hemingway remarked to Bill Horne about bullfighting, "It's just like having a ringside seat at the war with nothing to happen to you."

Bob McAlmon, whom Ernest spent some time with when he returned to Paris in May, was planning a trip to Spain. In McAlmon's memoir of the period, *Being Geniuses Together,* written a decade later, he reports that he, Ernest, and Bill Bird talked about taking such a trip for a week before agreeing that Ernest and Bob would travel together, Bird joining them in Madrid, for the first two weeks in June. Somewhere along the line it became clear that McAlmon would be footing the bills.

McAlmon was a heavy drinker, but Ernest could match him drink for drink (no account reveals Bird's habits), and they were already "well lubricated with whiskey" when they boarded the train. At one point en route to Madrid occurred the incident of the dead dog, familiar to all readers of Hemingway biographies. McAlmon told the story in *Being Geniuses Together*. In a rail yard, their train pulled up to a flatcar on an adjacent platform on which lay the maggot-ridden carcass of a dog. McAlmon looked away, but "Hemingway gave a dissertation on facing reality," McAlmon wrote. Ernest told Bob that he had seen in the war the stacked corpses of men, maggot-eaten in a similar way. He advised a detached and scientific attitude toward the corpse of the dog. He explained that those of their generation must inure themselves to the sight of grim reality. McAlmon continued his account by adding that Ernest had then asked, "Hell Mac, you write like a realist. Are you going to go romantic on us?" McAlmon concluded his description with the remark that he took himself off to the bar car "with an oath"; he had seen plenty of maggot-eaten corpses himself and he had no need to look upon a dead dog in the name of literature.

McAlmon's sarcastic reasoning is seductive, though in almost all accounts of this incident Hemingway is seen as having the upper hand, carrying the argument. Again, this is only with the benefit of hindsight. Given what we know of Hemingway's achievements in the line of looking unflinchingly at death, it is seductive to see him as triumphant over McAlmon's jaded cynicism in the service of a higher truth. The incident served as emblematic of their whole experience in Spain, where Ernest emerged as the only one of the three men who could really appreciate the profound tragedy of the bullfight and of its centrality not just to experience but to art.

In Madrid, Ernest had somehow divined at which pension the matadors and their *cuadrillo*s stayed, and there Bird joined the two men. They saw several *novillado*s in Madrid, and then they went on to Seville and saw their first really full-scale bullfight, or *corrida*. Though Hemingway was never able to convey exactly what bothered him about McAlmon's response to the Seville bullfight, he did give it a lot of thought, so that he was still trying to figure it out eight years later, when he included a description of McAlmon's reaction in *Death in the Afternoon*. McAlmon, called X. Y., became one in a category of "types" who watched bullfights:

X. Y. — 27 years old; American; male; college education; ridden horses on farm as boy. Took flask of brandy to his first bullfight — took several drinks at ring — when bull charged picador and hit horse X. Y. gave sudden screeching intake of breath — took drink of brandy — repeated this on each encounter between bull and horse. Seemed to be in search of strong sensations. Doubted genuineness of my enthusiasm for bullfights. Declared it was a pose. He felt no enthusiasm and declared no one else could. Still convinced fondness for bullfights in others is a pose. Does not care for sport of any sort. Does not care for games of chance. Amusements and occupation drinking, night life and gossip. Writes. Travels about. (*DIA*, 466)

Hemingway's contempt is unmistakable.

Considerable tension between the two men had surfaced, based on opposing reactions to profound experiences or about the ability to stomach pretty strong stuff—as well as on McAlmon's sexuality. Late in life, McAlmon supplied Yale professor and H.D. scholar Norman Holmes Pearson (whom he knew through Bryher) with some almost certainly imagined details about Hemingway making a sexual advance in their hotel room on this trip, supposedly pretending he was having a dream: "[In Hemingway's dream] I was Vicky, the buxom, tough and beautiful tart of the cabaret of the night before."

McAlmon no doubt manufactured this story about Hemingway's closeted homosexuality when he wrote to Pearson in 1952, probably because he was tired of being asked about Hemingway's sexual tendencies over the intervening thirty years. Yet it is hard to avoid the sense that sexual currents contributed to the tension between the men on the Spanish trip. First, though, it is important to state that McAlmon was attracted to women as well as men (to his wife Bryher, for one) and, as a contemporary noted, "It was clear he was far from being the kind of invert whose predilection shapes his whole personality." The most likely scenario is that the subject came up, not because either man made any kind of pass at the other, but simply because they were two handsome men whose looks appealed to gay men, because they moved in a setting in which homosexuality was commonplace, or because each had seriously considered attaching himself to an older homosexual to further his career.

Another difficulty had to do with the fact that McAlmon was paying the bills and Ernest was not being especially gracious about it. Whatever the cause, the tension between Hemingway and McAlmon was noticeable to Bill Bird when he arrived. He later said that he found Ernest speaking to Bob "only in snarls," while McAlmon was, when Ernest was present, acting indifferent and remaining very quiet. Kay Boyle, in her contrapuntal, often annoying, contribution to McAlmon's narrative in the later edition of *Being Geniuses Together*, notes Bill Bird's long-ago remark to her regarding the trip to Spain about "Hem making Bob the goat of that trip. All the bills were paid by Bob, of course. . . . Hem had to have his bottles of Johnnie Walker, or whatever the brand was, even in Spain, and at Bob's expense. The price of them was enough to ruin a millionaire, and Bob was never that." This pettiness, coalescing into resentment of anyone who had been generous to him, was revealing itself to be a distressingly recurring pattern in Ernest's twenties.

More important, because more closely related to his complicated psyche and his complicated approach to writing, was the emergence of a certain possessiveness Ernest took toward bullfighting. Bird continued bitterly to Kay Boyle, "When a choice of seats came up at a bullfight, Hem would throw his stalwart honor to the wind and have to have the one good seat left, down by the ring, because he was 'studying the art of it' while Bob and I, not knowing anything, I suppose, about art in any shape or form, could just as well sit in the bleachers."

With Bird and McAlmon, Hemingway saw bullfights in, besides Madrid and Seville, Ronda, Granada, Toledo, and Aranjuez. In July, Ernest went back to Spain with Hadley to see more bullfights. They went to Pamplona for the Fiesta of San Fermín, which began July 6—a red-letter day for *aficionado*s. Every morning the bulls stormed down the streets of Pamplona to the bullring, accompanied by a group of rowdy young men in blue shirts with red handkerchiefs tied around their necks; festivities—food, drink, music, and dancing in the cafés and streets—continued all day, the contests starting in the afternoon. Rain delayed the events this July, dampening spirits but bringing anticipation to a fever pitch. When the fights began, Hadley was relieved (as was Ernest) that she did not find them difficult to watch; she brought her knitting, and during particularly gruesome interludes concentrated on that. In his catalogue of spectators' reactions to bullfights in *Death in the Afternoon,* in which he described McAlmon, or "X. Y.," as suspicious of poseur fans, he described Hadley as "Mrs. E. R.," whose favorite author (like Hadley's) was Henry James. He noted with satisfaction that "she was not shocked nor horrified by [the deaths of] horses and enjoyed it as a part of bullfight which she enjoyed greatly first time and became great admirer and partisan of" (*DIA,* 467). Hadley observed and learned together with her husband the styles and skills of each matador, coming to appreciate nuances in the fights, which Ernest was absorbing at an amazing rate.

By the time they left Pamplona, Ernest was a true *aficionado* and could talk of little else. Some friends became fascinated by his descriptions and signed on for future tours, especially the July fiesta in Pamplona with the

Hemingways. Others quickly tired of his enthusiasm. McAlmon observed that Ernest, who when walking the streets with a companion energetically shadow boxed, was now more likely to be shadow-bullfighting, brandishing an imaginary cape and demonstrating imaginary sword thrusts into an imaginary bull's shoulders. Like many tourists who have made exciting discoveries, he was both eager and reluctant to pass on his experiences in Pamplona. Soon he became downright proprietary about it. Filling in for the absent editor of *the transatlantic review,* a publication read avidly by the Paris expatriates, he would write, about the Festival of San Fermín, "The less publicity it has, the better," because almost everyone "who deserved to be at Pamplona" had been there. "The more people that think it is a terrible, brutal, degrading relic of etc. the better." It is not clear whom he considered his audience for these observations.

Meanwhile, Hemingway was producing several more of his short "pieces," or vignettes, to build on those he had published in *The Little Review* in February, which he was carefully revising. Several were about bullfighting, including one about the death of the matador Maera, whom he had seen in Pamplona, that mixed fact and fiction—for Maera was not gored and killed until the following year. When the earlier vignettes were accepted by *The Little Review,* he had titled them "In Our Time," after the verse from the Book of Common Prayer: "Give peace in our time, O Lord," and he told Bird he wanted to keep that title.

Bill Bird's Three Mountains collection was supposed to come out that year, but in the meantime proofs arrived for the Contact Editions' *Three Stories and Ten Poems* from McAlmon's press. With his fiction and poetry thus spoken for, Ernest began sending his vignettes to Bird. When he received bound copies of *Three Stories and Ten Poems* in August, he was pleased by the looks of the book, a slim, pocket-sized volume with the titles of the stories and poems printed on the front cover. He exuberantly described Contact Editions to his old friend Bill Horne as "the same gang that published Ulysses," but the book appeared initially to critical silence; the scant reviews would not appear until the fall. Gertrude Stein had promised to review it, however, so Ernest was hopeful.

The Hemingways were due to sail for Toronto on August 17, but their ship was delayed for over a week. Hadley was enormous and often did not feel well, but they managed to squeeze in a boxing match and a visit or two to the horse races, which had become one of their favorite activities in France. They made the rounds of their Parisian universe; at Shakespeare and Company Sylvia Beach loaned them $100 and gave them some copies of *Ulysses* that they had agreed to smuggle into the States. When they called on Pound at his studio he gave Hadley a velvet and brocade smoking jacket (which she would wear for years as a bathrobe) and took her aside to say, "Well I might as well say good-bye to you here and now because [the child] is going to change you completely." Ernest feared the same would be true of him.

* * *

Hemingway sent Pound the first letter he wrote from their new home in Toronto, declaring, "It couldn't be any worse," referring to any "of that stuff about America, Tom Mix, Home and Adventure in search of beauty." His job at the *Star* was made nearly impossible by his immediate supervisor, Harry Hindmarsh, the assistant editor of the *Daily Star*. In France he had worked under Herbert Cranston, the editor of the *Star Weekly,* and he was in the good graces of John Bone, the managing editor of the daily edition. But Hindmarsh seemed determined to humiliate Ernest with trivial assignments of middle-of-the-night inconvenience, quickly becoming Hemingway's bête noire.

Hadley wrote her in-laws, Ed and Grace, about Ernest's overwork: "So many trips, no sleep and countless unimportant assignments." The young reporter Morley Callaghan, who noted the "sweetness in [Ernest's] smile and a wonderful availability," remembered that he was "appalled" when he looked at the assignment lists and saw the "piddling" events Ernest was ordered to cover: "just junk assignments."

Ernest and Hadley lived in a hotel for almost three weeks before they found an apartment at 1599 Bathurst Street, and even then Ernest was out of town on assignment and unavailable for the move. A railroad flat overlooking a ravine, beautiful with fall foliage, the apartment had a Murphy bed in the bedroom, which was squeezed between the kitchen and living room. The baby was due in early October, yet it was not until September that Ernest told his parents. Hadley explained that the expectant parents hadn't wanted to cause worry, and pleaded with the Hemingways to understand if they didn't hear from Ernest often.

On October 5 Ernest left for a six-day trip to New York City to cover the arrival of former prime minister David Lloyd George in the U.S. and to join him on a train trip to Toronto and then across Canada, which practically assured that Ernest would miss the birth of his child. When he arrived back in Toronto on October 10, a *Star* employee met the train and told him that Hadley had given birth to a son, but could give no report on her condition. Ernest rushed to her side. By that time Hadley was quite recovered—her labor lasted less than three hours—and calm. It was Ernest who broke down. "Ernest came in about 9 the next morning and wept—he was frightened too, poor lamb—they didn't break it to him very gently and he was bitter about having been sent away just at that time too." She told Isabelle Simmons (now Godolphin) that he "quite broke down for a while from fatigue and strain," though she added that he "pulled together" and "was as sweet as you and I know he can be." Certainly Ernest was wracked by worry and elation—and fatigue, to be sure, and anger at his boss. But perhaps his breakdown and distress owed something as well to the exclusive attention paid to Hadley and the newborn.

They named the boy John Hadley Nicanor—Nicanor for the matador Nicanor Villalta—and reported to Isabelle Simmons that he was a "corker," with Ernest's eyes and nose and a thatch of dark brown hair. Ernest reported that when the baby nursed, "he makes a noise like a little baby pig," noting, "He is perfect and his body is very beautiful." They found they were calling him Bumby "because of the round, solid feel of him."

Ernest and Hadley began planning to leave Toronto and return to Paris while Hadley and the baby were still in the hospital, and Ernest made the decision final when he returned to the newspaper and Hindmarsh scolded him for not coming to the office before going to the hospital. Luckily, he was transferred to the *Star Weekly* office at the end of October. On the *Weekly* he went back to writing features, many of which harked back to his stay in Europe; he filed articles on bullfighting and on trout fishing in Spain, Germany, and Switzerland. After setting a January 1 departure date he produced a storm of stories, on subjects ranging from nightlife in Europe to the bookies of Toronto. He wrote three entirely frivolous articles on how Christmas was celebrated in Switzerland, Italy, and France, respectively.

It was impossible for Hemingway to spend any time on his own writing, and the disjuncture between his life in Paris and the drudgery of his journalistic work began to feel almost surreal. He worried about his state of mind and its effects on his writing. As he wrote Pound, "Feel that I'm so full of hate and so damned, bitchingly, sickeningly tired that anything I do will be of little value." He officially resigned in December and collected a final paycheck on New Year's Eve. Several legends circulate about his resignation and his revenge on Hindmarsh, probably because his fellow reporters took vicarious pleasure in imagining a confrontation. Nobody liked Hindmarsh.

Over Christmas Ernest paid a quick visit to Oak Park. The family's delight at seeing the long-absent son and brother was tempered by their disappointment over missing Hadley and John Hadley Nicanor. Ed Hemingway told Ernest, "I feel like running away from here and going to Toronto and New York to see him. Wish I had the chance." Hadley and Ernest slunk out of the Bathurst Street apartment, for they were breaking their lease. Even as a new parent and an unemployed writer, Ernest must have been enormously relieved to shake the dust from his heels and board, on January 14, the steamship *Antonia*, bound for France.

EIGHT

When the Hemingway family arrived in France, Ernest found a place to live at 113, rue Notre-Dame-des-Champs. It was on the second floor of a two-story house, in back of which there was a large courtyard and a sawmill. When the noise of the saws died down it was a very pleasant place, redolent with the smell of wood. Ernest could not resist telling his parents, "We have about the nicest place in Paris." His journalist friend Guy Hickok visited Ernest, Hadley, and the "fat" baby "in a funny little house in the tree-shaded courtyard of a sawmill in the Latin Quarter." There was a small room for Ernest to write in, but the commotion of infant care—Marie Cocotte had agreed to return to keep house and take care of Bumby—often drove him to a café to work, usually the nearby Closerie des Lilas. The sawmill owners, the Chautards, who were also their landlords, lived below them. An American friend gave them a cat, which they named Mr. Feather Puss (Hadley was still, sometimes, Feathercat).

Ernest told a friend that Hadley ran the place "like a Rolls Royce," saying, "Hash and I had and have a damned good time. We pastime the fights and the concerts, skiing, bull fights and the finnies. She fishes not with the usual feminine simulation but like one of the men, she's as intelligent about fights as she is about music, she drinks with a male without remorse." Moreover, she "hasn't lost any looks and gets better all the time."

To Howell Jenkins he reported the same thing, adding, "She is keeping her piano up . . . and is always ready to go out and eat oysters at the café and drink a bottle of Pouilly before supper."

Hadley was equally glad to be back in Paris, especially with her young son, who glowed with good health and happiness; he was an unusually sunny baby. Even out on the streets of Paris, having Bumby with her assuaged her previous loneliness: "People were happy [to talk to me] as the mother of this enchanting child." Though they had no room for a piano in their apartment, Ernest found one to rent in a bakery on the boulevard du Montparnasse; when Bumby was home with Marie Cocotte, Hadley

Ernest's new friend Gertrude Stein, a godmother
to his son Jack, or Bumby, ca. 1924

bundled up and went to the bakery to play, probably relishing the time to herself and the warmth of the bakery as much as her music.

Theirs was a vastly different age in childcare customs: Hadley and Ernest would leave Bumby in the apartment with the cat while they went out—though seldom for very long—with Madame Chautard looking in on him every hour. In the early mornings, Ernest would often let Hadley sleep and get up early to prepare Bumby's bottle and feed him. On March 10, they took the child to St. Luke's Episcopal Chapel to be christened, with the visiting Chink Dorman-Smith as godfather and Gertrude Stein and

Alice Toklas as godmothers. (Gertrude suggested the church.) A month later, at a birthday celebration of Bumby's six-month mark, Stein and Toklas brought a silver christening cup, and in general they were delighted with their position, often calling Bumby "Goddy," for Godson.

Ernest responded to this domestic tranquility, and perhaps more directly to his freedom from a demanding staff position on a newspaper, as well as freedom from writing journalism for money, with an amazing fecundity, writing eight or nine of his finest short stories in the coming year. Understandably, he was impatient to get his work properly published and acknowledged. His publications with Bird and McAlmon were a start, but what Ernest knew he needed, for professional success, was a volume published by a commercial New York City publisher. He wanted it desperately.

Ernest approached every endeavor in a determined but graceful spirit, mastering such doings as trout fishing, game hunting, choosing wine, boxing, skiing, and food preparation, believing there was a right way to do things that must be followed. When he became fascinated by bullfighting he learned everything on the subject, attending scores of bullfights and giving serious thought to how he might face the bulls in the ring himself. As his friend John Dos Passos later noted, "He had an extraordinary dedication to whatever his interest was at the moment. . . . He stuck like a leech till he had every phase of the business in his blood."

As for writing, Ernest knew two things: how to write, and how to be a writer. Learning how to write happened on many different levels and by means of many different methods. He would try to write one true sentence, he vowed in the early days in Paris. He would avoid adjectives. He would work on the iceberg principle, meaning that if the writer knew much more than what actually made its way into the story, or the part of the iceberg that is below the water, and wrote in the right fashion, what was unseen would inform the story, the part that was above water, without the writer voicing it. Writing was a craft, and it had rules, which, if they had to be reduced to a single concept, dictated that the writer be genuine.

His stories and prose pieces and even, to some extent, his poems affected most readers (what readers there were), but most of them would be hard put to pin down just how this happened. McAlmon's wife, Bryher, remembered a remark that Adrienne Monnier, Sylvia Beach's partner, made in a discussion with some others of the literary scene in Paris. "Hemingway will be the best known of you all," she said. Bryher went on, "She spoke in French and some of the others did not understand her but I had a great respect for her critical judgment and asked her in some surprise why she felt he was better than we were. 'He cares,' she said, 'for his craft.' (I imagine she used the word *métier.*)" He had, in fact, *found* his *métier.* He felt passionate about writing and, like any superior craftsman, learned what worked and what didn't. He sought out the best teachers—Anderson, Pound, and Stein—and took their advice (though often only when it suited him).

For the most part, learning *how to write* came relatively easily to Ernest because of his natural talent and the instincts of an inveterate reader. He was an equally good learner when it came to *how to be a writer*, a subject that engaged him concurrently. In the early 1920s, he was mounting a campaign to get his name known and his work published. Ezra Pound was part of the plan: he could help to arrange publication—though not in the commercial outlets Ernest knew he needed for his career. At the outset, Ernest's work had been rejected by all the commercial magazines to which he had sent it—*The Saturday Evening Post, Everybody's Magazine,* the *Atlantic.* He had already been sending material to those magazines back in the days of "The Woppian Way." One of his first contacts in this world was Edwin Balmer, a thirty-five-year-old editor and writer of detective and science fiction short stories, who was visiting Walloon Lake when Ernest met him in 1919; Balmer gave Ernest encouragement as well as the names of the editors to contact at several popular magazines. When Ernest reported to Balmer that winter that he had not met with any luck, Balmer sent the stories out himself with cover letters recommending the work. That way, he told Ernest, he could at least find out the editor's opinion, even if the stories were rejected. Ernest would never forget his kindness, and would somewhat uncharacteristically write him in 1934 thanking him for his early help (Ernest could at that point write for any magazine for large fees, and he had no need of the good opinion of Balmer, who was then editor of *Redbook*). He would later tell editor Arnold Gingrich, extravagantly, that his respect for Balmer was equal to his respect for his father.

Up until 1923, Ernest had only one sure outlet, a New Orleans magazine called *The Double Dealer,* through the recommendation of Sherwood Anderson. In the May and June 1922 issues of the magazine his fable "A Divine Gesture" and a poem called "Ultimately" appeared, which was his first appearance in print since the Oak Park High School's literary magazine, the *Tabula.* Hemingway evidently wasn't paid as promptly as he would have liked—though it is interesting that he expected a literary magazine to pay at all, surely an uncommon practice. He wrote the editor, John McClure, calling him a "son of a bitch" and saying he had just figured out what the title of the magazine meant—that the editor was the double-dealer, in not paying him promptly. (In Ernest's defense, the title *is* strange.)

Ernest evidently never sent the letter, deciding it was unwise. This kind of strategizing occupied him in the early 1920s to the exclusion of much else. He didn't get much guidance in this sort of thing: whom he should treat as an enemy, whom he should treat as a friend. His seriously competitive nature seems to have overtaken him, prompting him to keep a kind of crib sheet detailing how to handle other writers. This can be seen in his treatment of T. S. Eliot, to take but one example. Eliot was a real comer, already so well established that it wouldn't do to ridicule him in most company. Perhaps unwisely, given Pound's massive job of editing Eliot's masterpiece, *The Wasteland*, Hemingway sent gibes Eliot's way in letters to Pound, referring to the poet often, and inexplicably, as Major Elliot [*sic*], and disparaging Eliot's journal, *The Criterion*. In October he would gratuitously and bizarrely malign Eliot in the pages of a Paris literary magazine. In a tribute to Joseph Conrad, who had recently died, Hemingway wrote that if he could grind up "Mr. Eliot" into a dust that he could then sprinkle on Conrad's corpse and thus bring Conrad back to life, he would "leave for London tomorrow morning with a sausage-grinder." Possibly Ernest publicly put him into the enemy camp because Eliot was making his name in poetry, a field that Ernest at this point had vacated. Also, Eliot's reputation was made in London, as part of a literary coterie that included Bloomsbury, a venue that held no interest for Hemingway. And Eliot had gone to Harvard, which predisposed Hemingway to dislike him. As John Dos Passos later noted, Ernest "was a moody kind of fellow. . . . Sorry for himself. One of the things he'd get sorriest for himself about was not having been to college."

Another literary scene drew Ernest's public dismissal, again no doubt carefully calculated. He took a dislike to *The Dial*'s editor, Scofield Thayer (aka "Scofield Buggering Thayer," as Ernest called him—again unaccountably, for Thayer preferred women, the younger the better), because *The Dial* rejected Hemingway's poems when Pound brought them to him, and also seemingly because Thayer was a rich Harvard graduate. Gilbert Seldes, just beginning his career as a critic, came in for similar treatment because he had been on the staff of *The Dial* when Hemingway's poems were rejected; Hemingway referred to his "sphincter muscle" losing its "attractive tautness." Hemingway's abuse of Seldes was lifelong.

In marked contrast was Hemingway's treatment of those he wanted to cultivate in the service of his career. Among these was Edward O'Brien, whom he had met and cultivated in Rapallo. When he wrote O'Brien seeking his help with a story he had submitted to the *Pictorial Review* he stated, baldly, "And yet I want, like hell, to be published." The *Pictorial Review* was a far cry from *The Double Dealer* or other little magazines. For one thing, it paid and paid well. Ernest was soon to meet F. Scott Fitzgerald, who made thousands of dollars for stories he placed in *The Saturday Evening Post,* a market Hemingway never would crack. As it turned out, he wouldn't need to make his way in the literary world with stories in commercial magazines. In fact, publication in journals like *Poetry* and *The Little Review* served his purposes better in 1923 and 1924, as his career was taking shape. But the slim volumes that McAlmon and Bill Bird brought out in those years, *Three Stories and Ten Poems* and *in our time,* did not reach enough people, and Ernest was finding it difficult to get his name and work properly circulating. He made getting a New York publisher his highest priority.

* * *

Ernest had gotten in the habit of dropping by for Thursday literary teas at the home of Ford Madox Ford, the eminent British novelist. *The English Review,* which Ford founded in 1908, published such British writers as H. G. Wells, John Galsworthy, Thomas Hardy, and Henry James; the work of D. H. Lawrence and Wyndham Lewis first appeared in its pages. Hemingway may have had little interest in the British literary scene, but Ford had recently moved to Paris and, with Joyce's patron John Quinn, launched a new literary journal, *the transatlantic review.* Now a cultural force in Anglophone Paris, Ford set up an office on the property of Bird's Three Mountains Press, on the Quai d'Anjou, and held court with his current mistress, the painter Stella Bowen, once a week for tea, and later, dances on Fridays.

Hemingway and Ford had first met at Ezra Pound's studio. At fifty, Ford seemed an old man to Ernest, and he was unattractive. Identifying him as a mouth breather, Ernest noted his "stained" mustache, "washed-out" blue eyes, and bad teeth, noting that the overweight Ford held himself upright "as an ambulatory, well clothed, up-ended hogshead" (*AMF,* 75). Ernest made these remarks toward the end of his life, but he was saying bad things about Ford all along; the critic Allen Tate remembered Ernest's gratuitously telling him Ford was impotent.

When Ford was mapping out *the transatlantic review* the previous fall, Pound had advised him to take Hemingway on as a deputy editor, called by the British a subeditor, telling Ford, "He's an experienced journalist. He writes very good verse and he's the finest prose stylist in the world . . . He's disciplined too" [Pound's ellipsis]. Ford said Hemingway reminded him of an "Eton-Oxford, husky-ish young captain of a mainland regiment of his Britannic Majesty," the first and last time Hemingway would be compared to an Englishman, though the point about his husky self-possession is well taken. Hemingway joined the board of the magazine, along with Joyce, Pound, and Quinn. For the first few months in 1924 Hemingway read submissions and edited pieces for publication, often "rewriting" some, he claimed, "for fun." The *review* only paid writers 30 francs a page, and Ernest was not paid at all as a subeditor; he later told Carlos Baker it was forced labor that, in retrospect, had given him a huge leg up. Determined to make the job worth his while, he took on as his first real task at the *transatlantic* convincing Ford to serialize Gertrude Stein's *The Making of Americans.*

Stein wrote *The Making of Americans,* her massive epic about the Hersland family, German immigrants to America whose story in some ways reflected that of the Stein family, between 1903 and 1911, calling it simply "the long book." Years later, in his Paris memoir, which was for the most part very negative about Stein, Hemingway remembered, "The book began magnificently, went on very well for a long way with stretches of great brilliance," but unfortunately, he wrote, "went on endlessly in repetitions that a more conscientious and less lazy writer would have put in the waste basket" (*AMF,* 27). Though "lazy" is an odd word to describe a work that demanded nothing if not perseverance, Hemingway was accurate about the net effect of Stein's book, and in particular about the difficulty of sustaining the reader's interest in such a work over many installments. While he was able to offer Stein payment for the first installment, he could not convince Ford to pay her for those that followed it, which infuriated Stein, which in turn left Ernest in the uncomfortable middle.

The first installment of Stein's epic appeared in the April 1924 issue. That issue also contained Hemingway's masterful story, "Indian Camp," about the visit of Nick Adams and his doctor father to attend an Indian woman in a very difficult childbirth, culminating in a cesarean section performed with a jackknife. After the trauma of watching the birth Nick also sees, in the upper bunk, the body of the baby's father, who has silently slit his throat during the ordeal. "Indian Camp" was one of the stories that Hemingway produced on his return to Paris from Toronto; it was as if a dam had broken, they came that quickly and with such profound assurance.

The second publication in book form of Hemingway's writing, Bill Bird's *in our time,* was in March, and received its first review in the same issue of the *transatlantic* as "Indian Camp" and the first section of *The Making of Americans,* putting Ernest's stamp on the issue. The journal's secretary, Marjorie Reid, called attention to the punch packed by the vignettes' minimalist, heightened language: Hemingway "projects the moments when life is condensed and clean-cut and significant, presenting them in minute narratives that eliminate every useless word."

While this was to be expected from an in-house review, the other comments that *in our time* received elsewhere were also favorable. That is, what there were of them. *Three Stories and Ten Poems* had gone virtually unremarked by American readers and reviewers. The exception was the young American critic Edmund Wilson, who would closely follow Ernest's career, for good or ill, from this point on. Ernest saw an item in the *New York Tribune* by Burton Rascoe, the literary editor, noting that Edmund Wilson had recommended Hemingway's short prose sketches in *The Little Review* to him. Ernest seems to have sensed that Wilson was or would become an important critic; as an editor at the sophisticated magazine *Vanity Fair*, the twenty-eight-year-old Wilson already held one of the most important positions in literary New York.

Ernest saw Rascoe's column while still in Toronto in late 1923. As soon as it was published, he sent Wilson a copy of *Three Stories and Ten Poems*, along with a respectful and naive-sounding letter. He said that the book had not yet garnered a review in the U.S., though he had had a letter from Gertrude Stein saying she had "done" a review. He asked a favor: he wanted Wilson to send him the names of four or five people to whom he could send the book to be reviewed—almost certainly hoping Wilson would write about it himself. Somewhat surprisingly, Wilson wrote back. He seems to have told Ernest (the letter is missing) that he would write about *Three Stories* in the "Briefer Mention" column in *The Dial*, for Ernest dissuaded him, asking him to wait until Ernest could send him a copy of *In Our Time* as well (Ernest was still capitalizing the title at this point) and review the two books together. This might mark the point at which Hemingway first considered combining the two books, looking forward, of course, to the 1925 Boni and Liveright publication of *In Our Time*.

Ernest told Wilson that his was "the only critical opinion in the States I have any respect for," and he went on in a familiar vein about E.E. Cummings, Gertrude Stein, and Willa Cather. (Wilson, in the September *Vanity Fair*, had written approvingly of Stein's 1922 *Geography and Plays*.) He told Wilson about the inclusion of "My Old Man" in Edward O'Brien's *Best Short Stories of 1923* and the dedication of that volume to himself. O'Brien, Ernest said, had asked him whether he had enough material for a short story collection that Boni and Liveright could publish, and Ernest in turn asked Wilson, somewhat disingenuously, whether he thought O'Brien "could get them to publish it."

When Ernest passed through New York on the way to Paris in early January 1924, the two men met. Wilson recorded that Hemingway seemed "one of the glibbest and slickest and most knowing young newspapermen" he had ever come across. Almost alone among critics, Wilson could respond in this way to the man and yet write fairly about his work. Wilson did as Hemingway asked, reviewing both *Three Stories and Ten Poems* and *in our time,* his review appearing in the September *Dial.*

It was all that a young writer could ask. Wilson dismissed Hemingway's poetry in the first half of the first sentence, but continued with nearly unqualified praise. First, he objected to the lowercasing of the title *in our time* as having "grown common and a bore." (Ernest would promptly tell Wilson he thought this practice "very silly and affected.") "His prose is of the first distinction," Wilson wrote, citing especially "the dry compressed little vignettes" of *in our time,* quoting the passage about the firing squad and the cabinet ministers in its entirety. He wrote that he was "inclined to think that his little book has more artistic dignity than anything else that has been written by an American" about the period of the war.

Ernest responded gratefully to Wilson's review on October 18, writing that he was "awfully glad" Wilson liked it, sending Hadley's "best regards to you and Mrs. Wilson." But Hemingway went on to sound a curious note. He was grateful, he said, that Wilson's review was "cool and clear minded and decent and impersonal and sympathetic. Christ how I hate this personal stuff. Do you remember my writing from Toronto wanting some reviews and publicity? And then got some and it turned me sick." As John Raeburn has pointed out in his study of Hemingway as a public figure, of the three reviews Hemingway's work had received to this point—one of which was Gertrude Stein's in the *Chicago Tribune,* too gnomic to count for much—none was less than favorable, and none included any remarks about Hemingway's personal life. He had received no personal "publicity" at all, despite what he told Wilson. Yet this was only the first in a series of lifelong complaints he would make about the public's invasion of his privacy. As Raeburn goes on to point out, Hemingway courted publicity at almost every stage of his writing life, giving a great deal of thought to his image and, as time went on, his legend. At this early stage, however, he must have realized that complaining about the nosiness of reviewers was part and parcel of being an important writer—which he hoped desperately to be taken for.

The three favorable reviews, the excitement surrounding Hemingway as a visible American in Paris, the high regard in which he was held by Pound, McAlmon, and O'Brien—all this contrasted dramatically with the response from Oak Park. Ernest had let his family know that the Three Mountains Press book, of which Grace and Ed had both ordered five copies, was forthcoming, and had bragged in November 1923 that they would be able to buy it in McClurg's, Chicago's best-known bookstore. Given that only 170 copies (of an edition intended to be of 250 copies) were published, as Ernest knew, the boast was born out of his desire to please his parents, particularly his father. But Ernest's sister Marcelline, in a memoir written after his death, describes a visit she paid to her parents in 1924, after the books had arrived, noting her father's "grim look." Later she came upon him wrapping up two packages of books, which he was sending back to the publisher. They were "shocked and horrified at some of the contents," writes Marcelline. They were especially distressed by a brief vignette, later titled "A Very Short Story," that gives a thumbnail sketch of a romance modeled on his relationship with Agnes, here called Luz. What Grace and Ed objected to was the story's last line, "A short time after he contracted gonorrhea from a sales girl in a loop department store while riding in a taxicab through Lincoln Park" (*IOT,* 66). Marcelline reports that her father, "incensed," wrote to Ernest "that no gentleman spoke of venereal disease outside a doctor's office." (No such letter survives.) Grace, Marcelline records, wanted to keep just one copy, but Ed would not allow her: "He would not tolerate such filth in his home, Dad declared." Ernest, says Marcelline, "bitterly resented" their response, and "simply stopped writing the family for a time." Two things are remarkable in this response: that his father objected more strenuously than his mother, when his father was traditionally the warmer and more demonstrably affectionate parent, and that the passage they cited concerns sex in their very backyard, in Chicago, in the Loop. In a taxicab. Their humiliation was complete.

Meanwhile, Ernest was becoming an ever more prominent fixture of expatriate life in Paris. *The transatlantic review* was foremost in his thoughts in spring 1924, his best opportunity to shape the literary scene invested in its pages. He contributed a series of "notes" in each issue (the magazine appeared monthly in 1924), about such matters as the return of Mike Strater and his family to the U.S., the boxing matches of Eugène Criqui, and the presence in the Latin Quarter of American writer Djuna Barnes, who had a story in the April issue. He published a play by Ring Lardner. And he griped about Ford, mostly to Ezra Pound. His difference with his boss, he told Pound, was not "personal." It was "literary." He complained that Ford would not publish his work from timidity about its sexual content. "Goddam it he hasn't any advertisers to offend or any subscribers to discontinue why not shoot the moon?"

Ernest gave his friends a forum in the *review*'s pages. Bob McAlmon contributed stories, and the magazine ran reviews of his novel and story collections. *The transatlantic review* published the poems of H.D. and those of her partner, Bryher. During 1923 and 1924 Ernest made other friends and was delighted to place their work in Ford's journal. Among these friends was Evan Shipman, who would remain a friend until his death in 1957. Shipman's first poems appeared in the last issue of *the transalantic review;* he would eventually publish a novel with Scribner's through Maxwell Perkins, by then Hemingway's editor. Shipman would appear in Ernest's Paris memoir as a sweet, poverty-stricken poet, a friend to waiters and a horse lover, with whom Ernest whiles away many happy hours in cafés. Nathan Asch was another friend; he placed three stories in the *review,* part of his first novel, *The Office,* published in 1925. Asch's name comes up repeatedly in Hemingway's correspondence, most often as a writer with talent he respected—but, as Hemingway nastily said, "You couldn't tell. Jews go bad quickly." The friendship didn't survive Asch's return to the States in 1927.

Asch and Shipman were part of an expatriate circle of American writers and journalists that included Josephine Herbst and her boyfriend (and later husband) John Herrmann, Malcolm Cowley, Donald Ogden Stewart, and John Dos Passos. Ernest met several of these at Ford's literary teas; later, no longer wanting to entertain at home, at dances Ford held at a *bal musette*—as it happens, the very one on the same street where the Hemingways first lived in Paris. Herrmann was from Michigan, and he and Ernest talked often about the landscape of the northern part of the state; Herrmann and Herbst, both political radicals, would remain friends with Hemingway into the 1930s only to part acrimoniously. Cowley, who would later document the lives of the 1920s expatriates in his *Exile's Return* (1933), was a fixture at the Dôme and won infamy in expat Paris for starting a fight at the Rotonde that quickly became a brawl, ending in Americans' arrests. Like Hemingway, he had been an ambulance driver in World War I; so had E.E. Cummings, then spending a couple of years in Paris, briefly marrying Elaine Orr, with whom he fathered a child and then stole from Scofield Thayer. Cummings wrote a book about his three months' imprisonment in a French detention camp, *The Enormous Room,* published in 1922 to much acclaim. This would have been reason enough to make Ernest too jealous to acknowledge his work, but Ernest was also wary because of the Thayer connection and because Cummings was a Harvard graduate.

John Dos Passos, who drove ambulances in the same unit as Cummings, would also become a long-term friend—though not without some serious hitches. Dos Passos was the illegitimate son of a Portuguese-descended

John Dos Passos, also assigned to an ambulance unit in Italy in World War I. He and Ernest became friends in Paris in 1924.

lawyer and his Southern mistress, extremely well educated (Choate, private tutors, Harvard) and well traveled; he had studied art in Spain. Although only twenty-eight, he had already written five novels by the time he and Ernest became friends, among them *One Man's Initiation: 1917* (1920) and *Three Soldiers* (1920), both well received, achievements later topped by his 1925 *Manhattan Transfer* and his *U.S.A.* trilogy (1930–1936), which quickly became classics. Though his output was distinctly uneven, Dos Passos was, as this account makes clear, already prolific. Ordinarily, these factors would make Ernest deeply suspicious. But Dos, as Ernest came to call him, was friendly and unpretentious, as well as extremely serious about his art. Hadley would later comment on this friendship, saying that Ernest "was always looking for someone who could really talk with him and on his level, and with the same interests. . . . They had a lot to say to each other."

Ernest had actually met Dos Passos briefly in 1918, in Italy, and perhaps again (according to Dos Passos) in 1922, but they didn't form a friendship until 1924. Dos thought it must have been in the spring, because they were sitting outside at the Closerie des Lilas, and he noted with amusement that a lilac was in bloom. In those days Ernest was an enthusiast of prizefights at the Cirque de Paris, the six-day bicycle races at the Vélodrome d'Hiver, horse racing, and of course bullfighting, and Dos noted the "evangelistic streak" that led Ernest to try to "convert" his friends to the pastime of the moment. Inevitably, there was friction between the two men, as Dos Passos noted in his autobiography: "Now and then he would remember that I was a rival wordfellow and clam up, or warn me sharply that I mustn't do any writing about [for instance] bicycle racing." Dos Passos's story "July" appeared in the August number of *the transatlantic review.*

On any given day, Ernest would put in an hour or two at the *review* office, spend a few hours at a café writing, and in the late afternoon perhaps do some boxing, usually in the basement gym of the American Club. He often played tennis, usually with Pound or Harold Loeb, a new friend, and with William Carlos Williams when he came through Paris. Harold and he sometimes played against Bill Bullitt and an architect friend, Paul Smith, with whom Ernest also boxed. Loeb wrote, "He was hindered by a trick knee and a bad eye," which Ernest led him to believe were "relics of wounds he had received while in Italy while serving with the Red Cross." Loeb noted that in tennis, Ernest tried very hard and got a lot of pleasure out of a good shot.

Ernest seems to have singled out the tennis-playing Harold Loeb for special favor. Loeb, a tall and good-looking Princeton graduate, was related to the wealthy Guggenheims and for a time helped to run the Sunwise Turn, a New York bookstore and gathering place frequented by writers and other bohemians. Loeb moved to Europe in 1921 and with Alfred Kreymborg published a literary magazine, *Broom*, first out of Rome and later from Berlin. In 1924 *Broom* folded and Loeb turned up in Paris; when Ernest first met him Loeb had just signed a contract for his first novel, *Doodab*, with the New York publishers Boni and Liveright. With his experiences at Sunwise Turn and in editing *Broom*, Harold was very well connected, which did not escape Ernest's notice. In turn, Harold found Ernest "unaffected." The more Harold saw of Ernest, the more he liked him. Later he made a wise observation about what it meant to him that a man like Ernest was a writer. Loeb noted that, after the days of "Oscar Wilde and his lily," it boded well that men like Hemingway had become writers, freeing the profession from any "taint" of femininity, homosexuality, and decadence. Though Loeb was perhaps among the first to make this observation, it would be voiced off and on by male writers throughout the twentieth century. The decadence and aestheticism of the 1890s were not far behind modernism, and it was still necessary for the male writer to dissociate himself from this "unmanly" movement.

Loeb's girlfriend, Kitty Cannell, on the other hand, didn't think much of Ernest. She felt he had another, more sensitive side to him, and that he hid it by "overact[ing] the part of a ruthless, hairy-chested, unintellectual he-man." Loeb reported that their disagreement was exacerbated when Ernest bought a painting he admired, *The Farm*, from the painter Joan Miró. A tall, blond, well-dressed dance and fashion writer, Cannell objected to spending money on a painting when Hadley was unfashionably dressed in last year's clothes. "And it's her money," Cannell added.

Since Ernest remained anxious about finding a commercial publisher for his work, it must have rankled that so many of his friends seemed either to have published books or have book contracts. Donald Ogden Stewart, a humorous writer associated with the Algonquin Round Table, was just sending off his second book after a considerable success four years earlier with a parody of H. G. Wells's *The Outline of History* (1920). An amiable Midwesterner, Stewart was good friends with John Dos Passos and some other people he told Ernest about, including the poet Archibald MacLeish and his singer wife, Ada, and the fabulous Gerald and Sara Murphy, legendary hosts and high-livers who would become important friends.

Ernest had managed to interest this whole range of Paris expats in the bullfight, and Dos Passos, Stewart, and Loeb signed on, as did his old friends Bob McAlmon and Bill Bird and his wife, Sally, when Ernest announced that he and Hadley were going back to Pamplona in July for the running of the bulls. Chink Dorman-Smith and family friend George O'Neil rounded out the party. This summer's journey was a happy dress rehearsal for the tumultuous 1925 Pamplona trip soon to be the subject of Hemingway's first novel—this trip sunnier and more jovial all-around. "The godamdest wild time and fun you ever saw," Ernest wrote his Chicago friend Howell Jenkins about the trip. "Everybody in the town lit for a week."

Don Stewart may have spoken for all of the men in the group when he wrote that he was apprehensive about the bullfight, having heard Ernest dismiss those who didn't like it. But, said Stewart, in the "around-the-clock wine-drinking, street dancing gaiety" he discovered that he "liked bullfighting almost as much as Ernest did." Each morning, after racing ahead of the bulls stampeding down the cobblestoned streets, one or two of the men, usually Stewart and Chink, joined Ernest in the actual arena before the fights, when amateurs were allowed to practice against small bulls with padded horns. When one young bull charged his tormentor, breaking through the fence and into the first rows of seats, Dos Passos managed to jump out of the way but Stewart somehow was driven into the ring, where he was promptly "gored" by a bull. Though Hemingway managed to save him from severe injury, Stewart found out the hard way that grappling with an angry animal weighing nearly a ton could be painful, padded horns or not. He got away with a couple of broken ribs. The whole exploit would be written up a week later in the *Chicago Tribune* and from there migrated into the ether of literary gossip, Hemingway morphing into the hero of the day. This bit of legend was helped along by a bragging letter Hemingway provided to the *Toronto Star*, gratis.

Ernest and Hadley would never forget the bucolic, peaceful end to their Spanish stay. They had stayed in Pamplona until the very end of the *feria*, then joined the Birds and McAlmon in Burguete, a Basque village in the

Pyrenees close to the Irati River. The trout fishing was superb, and Ernest savored the icy water of the river and the beech forests in the countryside near Roncevaux, the landscape virtually untouched by modern civilization. The experience cemented his lifelong love of Spain. "The wildest damn country," Ernest called it in his letter to Howell Jenkins. Some of the party went on to hike the upper Pyrenees to Andorra, a two-week trip that Ernest hated to miss. But he and Hadley were expected back by their *femme de ménage* and her husband, who were taking care of the young Bumby.

In Paris, Ernest again turned his attention to *the transatlantic review.* In May, Ford had recognized that the *review* needed an infusion of cash to survive, and with that end in mind he had gone to New York with an eye to appealing to Joyce's patron, John Quinn. He had left Hemingway in charge of the shop; for the July issue Ernest added a Dos Passos story, along with two poems by Bryher and two more by the exceedingly eccentric Baroness Elsa von Freytag-Loringhoven, who sometimes wore a coal scuttle for a hat. (Ford had consistently refused to publish the Baroness's work, and Ernest hugely enjoyed overriding him.) The August issue had pieces by Stewart, Asch, and Guy Hickok and a review of McAlmon's work by William Carlos Williams; Ernest pointedly suspended the serialization of Ford's novel *Some Do Not.* In an issue published that fall, Ford was forced to apologize for Ernest's nasty remarks about T. S. Eliot in the Joseph Conrad memorial supplement.

Unfortunately, Ford was not successful in getting funding from Quinn. When Ernest got back from Spain, he suggested Ford contact Krebs Friend, a war veteran who had worked at *Co-operative Commonwealth,* the shady Chicago publication that Ernest had edited in 1920 and 1921. Friend had recently married a much older heiress and led a luxurious life on the Right Bank. He immediately agreed to give Ford $200 every month for six months, for which he was made a "president" of *the transatlantic review.* The infusion of money didn't bring an end to the headaches involved with the magazine, however. Friend's wife, Elizabeth, became involved as well, insisting that the funds be used to retire the *transatlantic's* debts before any went to pay contributors. If contributors received any money at all, that is—some writers, Gertrude Stein most audibly, were raising a ruckus about their pay.

Meanwhile, Ernest complained to Ezra Pound that "the Transatlantic killed my chances of having a book published this fall." He was "going to have to quit writing," he said, "because we haven't any money." This time, unfortunately, he was on firmer ground when he pleaded poverty. In 1923 Ernest had asked George Breaker, the husband of Hadley's St. Louis friend Helen, to invest $19,000 that Hadley had previously held in railroad bonds. The bonds had been dropping in value and Ernest wanted Breaker to sell them before they declined further. Breaker had big plans for the roughly $10,000 the bonds yielded, and sent Ernest and Hadley reports of various concerns in which he had invested. Records showed, however, that he had only put a little over a thousand dollars back in Hadley's account after the original sale. Ernest spent the spring and summer of 1924 chasing down Breaker, who evaded his letters and telegrams. Though Hadley said they were somehow able to recover some of the money, the loss of this chunk of her trust came as a bitter blow. The railway bonds had added about $760 to the Hemingways' annual income, money they could not spare. Excursions like Pamplona were summarily ruled out. Unless, that is, he found a publisher for his book. His "real" book.

*　*　*

In 1924, the year he turned twenty-six, Ernest seemed to have boundless energy. Finances notwithstanding, he and Hadley not only enjoyed a month in Spain on the bullfight circuit, but they took a skiing vacation in Austria at the end of the year. Ernest was forging new friendships, some of them with those who knew important people and others who would become important people themselves, like Dos Passos. He was an editor of one of the most influential of the modernist little magazines, *the transatlantic review.* Hadley and he were enjoying nights out and days at the racetrack or the bike races, thanks to Marie Cocotte. When friends from Chicago showed up they took the time to show them Paris, and not just the tourist sights. They were able to show their visitors the literary Paris they knew, making stops at Sylvia Beach's Shakespeare and Company and the Friday night dances that Ford Madox Ford hosted. Ernest showed them the *review* offices, and made the rounds of the cafés, from the Closerie des Lilas to the ever-popular Dôme, where their guests ran a better than even chance of seeing someone they knew from back home.

In the midst of all this activity, Ernest was producing some of the most important work of his career, including "Cat in the Rain," about an American wife's unmet desires, and "The End of Something," another story about Nick Adams, here ending an adolescent relationship because "it isn't fun any more." The writer subtly conveys why, Nick telling Marjorie, "I feel as though everything was gone to hell inside of me" (*CSS,* 81). "The Three-Day Blow," in which Nick has a long conversation with his friend Bill around a fireplace while they get drunk, seems in part a coda to the previous story, but it is itself a profoundly moving story about loss:

what was lost when the relationship with Marjorie ended, and that could never be regained, no matter how drunk he and Bill got, or however many hunting trips they could safely make now that Nick and Marjorie were through. It is in some ways about the limitations of male friendships, as if to remind readers that Hemingway was not to be understood too quickly. In "Cross-Country Snow," Nick, in what might as well be another epoch, is skiing in Switzerland with his friend George (probably George O'Neil) and tells George that his wife, Helen, will soon have a baby. George responds, "It's hell, isn't it?" Not exactly, Nick says. After they agree that good skiing is impossible in the States, George wonders whether they'll ever ski together again. "We've got to," answers Nick. "It isn't worth while if you can't" (*CSS*, 146). Again the emotion underlying the conversation between male friends is a profound sense of loss, this time partly the loss of male friendship but more a loss of everything that has come before this moment, not least Nick's youth and innocence.

Hemingway began his best-known Nick Adams story, "Big Two-Hearted River," in June, leaving it to jell while he and Hadley went to Spain. It was the longest story he had yet written, and he would eventually divide it into two parts. Based on a fishing trip he had made to the Fox River in 1919, the story opens in the burned-over, desolate countryside near the town of Seney on Michigan's Upper Peninsula. When Nick reaches the river, called the "Big Two-Hearted River" because the name "is poetry," as Hemingway said later, the countryside is intact, the trees uncut, and Nick gives himself over to searching for grasshoppers for bait, fishing for trout, preparing beans and spaghetti over a campfire for dinner and flapjacks for breakfast the next day. We are told only that Nick "felt he had left everything behind, the need for thinking, the need to write, other needs. It was all back of him" (*CSS*, 164). There is more behind this, the reader senses, which is confirmed by other Nick Adams stories, in which it becomes clear that Nick has been profoundly affected by his experiences in the war. Ernest would reveal, in "The Art of the Short Story," an essay written close to the end of his life, that "Big Two-Hearted River" is an excellent example of his iceberg principle, that Nick's backstory is that he was badly damaged in the war; the damage is sensed by the reader despite the fact that "the war, all mention of the war, anything about the war, is omitted."

Though the Nick Adams stories are based on Hemingway's own experiences, he was at pains to state that they were completely fictional. In the well-known passage in a letter to Gertrude Stein in which he somewhat mystifyingly says he has been trying to "do the country like Cezanne," he asserted that "I made it all up, so I see all of it." Originally, however, the story was directly autobiographical, as indicated by Nick's eleven-page interior monologue closing this draft of the story. Nick reflects on previous fishing trips with Bill Smith (for the most part, real names are used), summers on Walloon Lake, and the bullfights in Pamplona that summer. Most notably, Nick has Ernest's writing history, and ruminates on "Indian Camp" and "My Old Man" (real names used here too), as well as contemporaries like McAlmon and Joyce. By November, however, he had cut this whole section, telling McAlmon he had decided "all that mental conversation . . . is the shit" and that he had received "a hell of a shock" when he "realized how bad it was." Now he had "finished it off the way it ought to have been all along. Just the straight fishing."

Another story composed in this creative outpouring was again directly autobiographical. Called "The Doctor and the Doctor's Wife," the subject of the piece, set in northern Michigan, was his parents' marriage. The doctor negotiates with some Indians about sawing logs cast up on the beach. This ends in a quarrel, and the job is left unfinished. After the doctor goes inside and tells his wife, who is lying on her bed in a darkened room with a headache, about the quarrel, he goes outside and tells his son, here again called Nick, that his mother wants to see him. Nick says he would rather stay with his father, and they walk away, Nick telling his father he knows where to see some black squirrels. A very small detail suggests the principle of the iceberg is again at work here, for this detail informs the entire import of the emotions back of the story. Ernest made no secret of the fact that he had always blamed his mother for what he saw as her emasculation of his father. This emasculation, he seems to have believed, manifested itself in big ways and less obvious ones, but if one had to sum it up, he felt that his mother did not believe in his father. The detail, the only one Hemingway invented in "The Doctor and the Doctor's Wife," is that the doctor's wife is a Christian Scientist, with a copy of Mrs. Eddy's *Science and Health* on her bedside table with her Bible. Christian Scientists do not believe in treating people with medicine, relying instead on God's healing powers. They do not believe in doctors.

NINE

I t was no accident that Ernest responded as he did to his first Festival of San Fermín in Pamplona in 1923; the seven-day period was a constant round of feverish activity—which matched his mood. The running of the bulls every morning and the bullfights every afternoon; the Riau-riau and the drumming and piping waltz music that accompanied it; parades and processions every afternoon; the heightened sexual atmosphere encouraged by drinking and dancing in the streets, not to mention the eroticized dance with death of the matador in his tight-fitting suit of lights. Drinking wasn't confined to the traditionally vinous and prolonged lunches and dinners but went on pretty much around the clock, the traditional bota bag, or leather wineskin, making cheap red wine accessible at all times.

Ernest had immediately fallen in love both with the Spanish people and the bullfight, and this love was what brought him back to Pamplona and other Spanish towns and cities year after year. But he responded to the Fiesta de San Fermín with an enthusiasm remarkable even in someone with the seemingly boundless energy of Ernest in the 1920s. Participants—for one did not watch, but was a part of, the festival—stayed up for days on end, even the traditional siesta forgone by many.

For Ernest, the fiesta distilled the way he was living and would live for much of his twenties and thirties. He was a naturally high-spirited and vital young man whose energy level at times reached the extraordinary. In these years, Ernest showed a certain amount of what would in retrospect seem to be manic behavior, classic symptoms of which include excessive energy and grandiosity, racing thoughts, irritability, and self-destructive tendencies. At this time, however, his depressions, during which he found it difficult to write and sometimes mentioned suicide, were relatively mild and spaced far apart. It was the mania that dominated: he seemed to need very little sleep, and exercised relentlessly: he hiked, biked, boxed, played tennis, and skied—in addition to hunting and fishing. He recognized his own talent and convinced other people of it, even before he had much to show for it, as in the early 1920s. This could be called grandiosity, though grandiosity was less a symptom in Ernest's case than a personality trait. Yet symptoms of mania like irritability or hair-trigger temper marked these periods in Ernest's life. He was irritable to the point of combativeness, writing angry letters in which he slammed others, including Scofield Thayer, Lewis Galantière, George Seldes, and Marianne Moore. His insults were graphic and nasty—witness his remarks about George Seldes's "sphincter muscle" in a letter to Pound. In fact, his attacks constituted a kind of grandiosity in reverse: his talent, character, and actions were so great that all those around him were puny or pitiful.

The sheer creative energy, manic or not, that Ernest expended in this period was remarkable: he wrote eight short stories in three months, stories that are among the greatest of his career: "Cat in the Rain," "The Undefeated," "Soldier's Home," "The Three-Day Blow," "Cross-Country Snow," "The Doctor and the Doctor's Wife," "The End of Something," and "Mr. and Mrs. Elliot." Creative bursts like these were fairly typical of the way he worked. Two examples from the same period help to make the case: his first novel, *The Torrents of Spring,* a parody of Sherwood Anderson, took him a little more than a week to write. And he wrote his first "real" novel, *The Sun Also Rises,* in just over six weeks.

As the years went on, these manic episodes became more and more marked. And Ernest's down periods would become far more serious, probably exacerbated by several traumatic brain injuries and alcohol use, and were marked by inability to work, feelings of worthlessness, talk about suicide. Inklings of the terrible depressions and serious manic episodes of his fifties were already present in these early years.

* * *

Christmas 1924 found Ernest, Hadley, and Bumby in Austria for two months of skiing. They had heard of an excellent pension, the Hotel Taube, in Schruns, in Vorarlberg; he rented two rooms for $30, which was a bargain—especially after they managed to sublet their apartment in Paris. Mathilde Braun, a young woman who lived next to the hotel, took care of Bumby for a pittance. Ernest decided to grow a beard and forswear cutting his hair. The beard came in black and full, and with his flowing locks the villagers took to calling him "The Black Christ." The snow held off in December and the weather was warm, but when the snows came Ernest went with a ski school led by Walther Lent further up in the mountains, usually up the Madlener Haus, where for days at a time they stayed in snug huts heated by amazingly efficient porcelain-coated brick stoves.

Hadley often joined him; when she didn't she stayed in the village playing with Bumby, skiing on less dramatic slopes, and passing the time with girlfriends.

Harold Loeb was supposed to join the party in the mountains, but at the last minute he canceled, deciding to journey to New York to see his novel, *Doodab,* into press. And, Ernest hoped, Harold was to see about *his* book, a collection incorporating elements from both the Contact Press's *Three Stories and Ten Poems* and Three Mountains Press's *in our time.* His best hope, as it shook out, was Boni and Liveright, Loeb's publishers. Horace Liveright, called by his biographer a "firebrand," was indeed eager to sign up the moderns; he published Eliot's *The Wasteland,* Faulkner's *Soldier's Pay,* and Hart Crane's *The Bridge,* among others. Much good writing seemed to be coming out of Europe, and to be in touch with the most exciting new writers Liveright had two European book scouts: Ezra Pound and Leon Fleischman. Pound, his anti-Semitism aside, spoke of the Jewish Liveright as a "pearl among publishers." Liveright had been paying Pound $500 a year since 1922 to send worthy American writers his way. For some reason, however, Pound had nothing to do with getting his friend Ernest Hemingway in Liveright's stable. At least not officially. No doubt Pound had mentioned Ernest and even urged Liveright to publish him, but Ernest had simply not had enough stories together to think of a commercial publisher until the end of 1924.

A meeting with Liveright's other European book scout, Leon Fleischman, who was a friend of Loeb's, went badly. Loeb, who with Kitty Cannell went with Ernest to Fleischman's apartment, was dismayed when after the meeting Ernest bitterly referred to Fleischman as a "low kike." Ernest did agree to give Fleischman his manuscript to send to the publisher. Don Stewart also had a copy, which he showed first to George H. Doran and Company, the firm that had published Stewart's humorous book about the Haddocks in Europe. The word was that George Doran felt it had too much sex in it, though his real reason, which Ernest conveyed to Loeb, was that they would prefer to publish a novel before they issued the short stories. But Doran hadn't said no yet, so Ernest still had hopes. Meanwhile, Stewart also showed the manuscript to H. L. Mencken in the hopes of Mencken's interesting Knopf in its publication; Mencken passed on it (which earned him Ernest's lifelong antipathy). Ernest reckoned that it was unlikely he would hear anything from a publisher until well after the holidays, and his letters from Schruns dwell on skiing and weather news rather than book publishing.

He was continuing to send out stories, however, hoping to get them into a wide range of publications. He sent a new bullfighting story, "The Undefeated," to George Horace Lorimer at *The Saturday Evening Post;* he admitted in a cover letter that the details were somewhat technical, but he noted that everything was eventually explained by the end of the story. He had learned to tailor his submissions, writing that he hoped the story did for bullfighting what Charles E. Van Loan, a prolific *Post* writer, had done for prizefighting. (Lorimer didn't buy it, and it appeared in Hemingway's reliable German outlet, *Der Querschnitt.*) He sent "Big Two-Hearted River" to a new journal he had high hopes for, *This Quarter,* run by the sometime-poet Ernest Walsh and his older girlfriend, the painter Ethel Moorhead—the latter providing the funds. (The story would appear in the journal's spring 1925 issue.)

Fresh from his stint at *the transatlantic review,* Hemingway had lots of advice for Walsh, most of it given in talks they shared the previous fall at the Hotel Venezia, some of it in letters from Schruns. He had recommended that the magazine do everything in its power to pay writers, which Ernest saw as crucial. He also suggested Walsh and Moorhead look into publishing a whole range of his writer friends, including Josephine Herbst and her husband, John Herrmann; Nathan Asch; Bob McAlmon; Don Stewart; William Carlos Williams; Lewis Galantière; and even Edmund Wilson. Walsh had tuberculosis (which would kill him in October 1926), so he and Moorhead were spending the winter in Cambo, a French town near Spain, where the climate was milder. Soon they would announce a prize for the best contribution in the first four quarterlies of *This Quarter;* Walsh told Hemingway he was a shoo-in. When the magazine gave the prize to someone else, Walsh too earned his lasting contempt.

Ernest sent off some letters to his oldest friend, Bill Smith, once his constant companion in Horton Bay summers. A lot of water had flowed under that bridge. The previous spring Ernest's old friend (and Bill's brother) Y. K. "Kenley" Smith, his landlord during his stay in Chicago, had been part of a rather sordid scandal. Kenley, then living in Palos Park, a Chicago suburb, had been having an affair, and his mistress, evidently deranged, came to his home in order to kill Kenley and his wife, Doodles. Kenley was out, but the mistress fired her gun at Doodles, missing each time, and then at the Smiths' caretaker, whom she killed. She went on the run to New York and then to Detroit, where she killed herself in a hotel room. Ed and Grace Hemingway sent a clipping about the business to Ernest, which no doubt made a great impression. The Smiths had been very much on his mind when Ernest received a letter from Bill Smith near the end of 1924. He had not heard from Bill since 1921. Toward the end of his time in Chicago, Kenley had gotten wind of some gossip Ernest was spreading about Doodles, and the quarrel extended to include Bill, who laid claim to blood as being thicker than water; besides, Bill had said, he didn't like the 1922 version of Ernest. Over two years later, friendship won out.

Ernest was delighted to hear from him in 1924, and he told Bill so in a long letter on December 6. "I haven't felt so damn good since we used to pestle them on the Black [River]." The overarching theme of the letter was that Bill must join him in Europe. Along the way he decried recent marriages that had befallen the old gang, alluded to the Kenley and Doodles Smith scandal, passed on the news about Hadley losing his manuscripts, and conveyed his sympathy for the loss of Bill's aunt. He constructed a scenario in which Bill would join him in Paris, where a literary job would await him, and travel to Spain the next summer, where they could take in the bullfights and fish for trout in the Irati River. He urged Bill to come, saying it would be good for him physically: "High and cool nights and swell hot days. No bugs." He described his life with Hadley and Bumby, his new friends Dos Passos and Stewart, the racing and the prizefights in Paris, all with an eye to showing Bill the paradise that could be his if he would only come to Europe. Ernest immediately began looking for jobs for his friend. He had Dossie Johnston, also at Schruns at the time, ask her father, William Dawson Johnston, then the director of the American Library in Paris, whether he would take on Bill Smith, a college graduate with an agriculture degree, as a secretary. Failing that, he asked Ernest Walsh to hire Bill at 1,000 francs a month. Walsh flatly refused this peremptory request, which ushered in bad feelings between the two Ernests.

All the good writing he had produced was about Michigan—fishing and courting local girls, Ernest wrote to Bill. Those experiences were ineradicable, he went on, and would only be spoiled if they went back and tried to relive them. "But we can go on," wrote an excited Ernest, "and get some new ones and some damn fine ones. Like over here and Spain and Austria up in the mts. in the winter time." He was thrilled that "we will have some of the old genuwind together again." Though Ernest had some fine friends (each of whom he described glowingly), there weren't that many of the "real" kind, he said, and he valued Bill very highly. This initial exchange of letters with Bill was full of promise—hope that Ernest could assemble a team of men to share experiences as he had in Michigan, with Bill Smith first and foremost.

The Hemingways grew browner each day, positively radiating health. Ernest and Hadley were skiing on the upper reaches of the Alps when important news reached them. Don Stewart and Harold Loeb each cabled

Ernest to tell him that Horace Liveright had accepted his manuscript for Boni and Liveright. Ernest immediately wrote Harold, saying he couldn't believe it at first when the cables reached him in the hut on Madlener Haus. He'd been so excited he'd been unable to sleep. But the first paragraph of the letter was given over not to the news but to the glacier skiing, a recent blizzard, and the number of kilometers they'd logged on skis, both climbing and descending various mountains. Ernest then told Harold how wonderful it would be if he were with them. Only then did he question Harold as to details of publication: whether the book would have to be cut, and how much money he would get. He casually asked about a detail that would loom very large for him: would it be coming out in the fall, like Harold's?

When Ernest came down from the mountains, he found a cable from Boni and Liveright stating that they wanted to publish the stories and could promise a $200 advance against royalties. Ernest immediately cabled back acceptance. However, Horace Liveright himself followed this with a letter, which said that the house could not publish "Up in Michigan" because of the obscenity laws, and that some phrases in "Mr. and Mrs. Elliot" would have to be changed for the same reason. Ernest immediately set about producing a story to replace "Up in Michigan." He came up with "The Battler," a brutal and stark story about Nick Adams, who is riding freight trains when he meets a crazy ex-pugilist. Ernest sent the story along to Boni and Liveright, and proceeded with the business of telling everyone his news. At the end of his stay in Schruns, Hemingway devoted himself to contributing a generous tribute to Ezra Pound for the first volume of *This Quarter,* which Walsh had decided would be a Festschrift for the poet.

Hemingway signed the contract the publisher sent, which also gave Liveright the option on his next three books, on March 31. By then he and Hadley and Bumby were back in Paris, Ernest spending a lot of time helping Ernest Walsh and Ethel Moorhead with *This Quarter.* One of the first things he and Hadley did on their return to Paris was to celebrate the acceptance of what would become *In Our Time* (capitalized) with the man who had helped the deal along, Harold Loeb. In fact, when Harold filled Ernest in on the details of what had happened at Boni and Liveright, Ernest said he felt wonderful that they had taken it and "simultaneously kicked in the balls." As it turned out, the manuscript had nearly missed being rejected. Fleischman had in fact sent it on to Liveright back in October, without reading it, he claimed. Isidor Schneider, a New York–based friend of Malcolm Cowley's whom Harold knew as a contributor to *Broom,* had somehow gotten wind of the manuscript's progress and told Loeb that

Bea Kaufman, the wife of the playwright George Kaufman, was reading the manuscript for Boni and Liveright. When Harold contacted her, she told him she had the manuscript packed up and ready to return to Fleischman. Loeb insisted that it be unpacked and reconsidered. His intervention with the publisher was bolstered by a phone call to Horace Liveright from Sherwood Anderson, who had just become a Boni and Liveright author.

It's no surprise that Hemingway would never tell the story of the book's near rejection, and in fact all of Hemingway's biographers have overlooked Loeb's story. It is true that Loeb provided these details, but he had no reputation as a fabulist and was painfully honest about himself when he later wrote about Hemingway. The details Loeb provided in this story—the roles of Isidor Schneider and Bea Kaufman, in particular—militate against Loeb having concocted the story himself. But it was not in Hemingway's interest to have the tale of his obligation to his friend—or the fact that his first book came so close to being rejected—bruited about, and evidently his biographers followed his lead. The publication of *In Our Time* was made possible, then, through the intervention of two people: Harold Loeb and Sherwood Anderson. Within the next year, Ernest would respond to this kindness in two markedly unkind books.

* * *

When he might have been happy, Ernest was fulminating about other writers and critics. In a February 14 letter to Bill Smith, he complained about the "fairies" who find publication easy, delivering a diatribe against the American writer Glenway Wescott, who was said to have switched allegiance from women to men when a rich man financed his trip to Europe. (If this reminded Ernest of Jim Gamble's offers to bankroll him for a year in Europe, it might account for the scabrous tone of the letter. Wescott, as Hemingway may have seen it, chose the path that he did not.) "There's a homosexual claque that make a guy overnight," he commented. They were organized, said Ernest, "like the Masons." The way to succeed as a writer, he said crudely, is "through the entrance to the Colon."

Writing to Sherwood Anderson, he set forth his position on another literary set, this one the critics. At this juncture in Ernest's life critics had paid scant attention to him, with the exception of the Edmund Wilson review in the October 1924 *Dial*, an unsigned (generally positive) review in *The Kansas City Star*, and the in-house piece in *the transatlantic review*. But all this had been encouraging, though Wilson's review had a few quibbles—and as his career progressed Hemingway would seldom take even the smallest criticisms well.

Thus it is difficult to say from where a letter Ernest wrote Anderson derives. Critics were worthless, he said: "camp following eunochs of literature. They won't even whore," he went on to say. "They're all virtuous and sterile. And how well meaning and high minded." Granted, Hemingway was writing these comments apropos of a criticism he made of Anderson's most recent novel, *Many Marriages* (1923), though he made these remarks in a very positive review of Anderson's memoir, *A Story Teller's Story* (1924). Even so, it is difficult to know whether Ernest was voicing these complaints because that's what he thought professional writers did, or because he was bracing himself against receiving negative reviews in the future. Whatever the source, the remarks seem especially vehement, particularly at this early date.

Ernest was also sensitive to how *In Our Time* (Boni and Liveright capitalized the title) would be received in Oak Park, given the fact that Ed and Grace had returned all ten copies of *in our time* to Bill Bird at Three Mountains Press (in this edition, the title was lowercased). Before Ernest had to deal with this, he got a letter from his father on March 8, right around the time of his negotiations with Liveright. Somehow Ed had read Ernest's "The Doctor and the Doctor's Wife," which had been published by *the transatlantic review* in November 1924—the only place it had appeared thus far. Ed said he had seen the story "by accident." He commented only on the part of the story dealing with the doctor's negotiations with two local Indian workers over sawing up some logs on his property, overlooking the damning characterizations of both the doctor and his wife. Ed said that he had always known his son had a great memory, and commented on his skill in evoking that episode, dating to when Ernest was twelve: "I saw that old log on the beach as I read your story." He wanted to see more of his son's stories, he said.

Certainly this letter would have brought Ernest much pleasure and pride. He no longer consciously sought his mother's approval, but his father's always had and always would have great importance to him. Ernest constructed a painstaking defense of his work in his return letter to his father. His goal, he said, was to re-create life itself, in all its dimensions. "You cant do this without putting in the bad and the ugly as well as the beautiful," he said. Ed and "Mother" should remember that when they came across a story of his that they found objectionable, the odds were good that they would next read a story that pleased them. Ernest hadn't sent on any of his work because of the copies of the Three Mountains book that they returned, he explained. He was not forthcoming, however, in sending his father any stories in this letter (or any other), and 1925 would be a difficult year requiring quite a juggling act in communicating with his family.

An event that would become almost epochal in retrospect was a tea given by Kitty Cannell and Harold Loeb in Kitty's apartment to celebrate Liveright's acceptance of *In Our Time*. The principals have told the story in different ways, but the upshot is the same. Perhaps Kitty Cannell's version is the least trustworthy, because she had a genuine aversion to Ernest. Something about his build made her wary, she later said, not very helpfully. But when Cannell heard Ernest dismiss Fleischman as a "kike" after Harold had taken Ernest to meet him, she immediately mistrusted him. According to Kitty, Harold was stunned by Ernest's remark, but when Kitty brought up the subject after Ernest left, Harold hastily made the odd comment, "If Hem thought of me as a Jew he wouldn't have spoken that way in front of me." Kitty held Hemingway's anti-Semitic slur very much against him; it contributed to her feeling that he had treated Harold badly almost from the start.

Kitty was fond of Hadley, however. They went antiquing together in Paris, looking for affordable earrings mostly, and they often played tennis, sometimes with Harold and Ernest. (Kitty had also supplied Hadley and Ernest with the cat they called Mr. Feather Puss, Ernest's fondness for cats a mark in his favor to Kitty.) Cannell had long wanted to introduce Hadley to two sisters from St. Louis, Virginia and Pauline Pfeiffer; somehow their paths had not crossed each other in the Midwestern city, despite their similar backgrounds and a friend they shared, Bill Smith's sister, Katy. Ironically, as it turns out, Katy had been instrumental in bringing Ernest and Hadley together. Kitty asked the Pfeiffer sisters to join them at the tea.

Kitty Cannell remembers the pair as "petite with bright black eyes and black bobbed hair cut straight across the forehead like Japanese dolls." Jinny Pfeiffer was visiting her older sister in Paris and trying to figure out what she wanted to do with her life, while Pauline worked for Paris *Vogue*, which explained her fashionable chipmunk coat, which Ernest later said he admired. Both were good-looking and known for their wit; Kitty observed that Pauline, then thirty, was the funnier of the two, while Jinny, just twenty-three, was the prettier. The sense of twinship or interchangeability prompted Ernest to remark, after they'd left, that he'd like to take Jinny out in Pauline's coat; Hadley cannot have been amused. The next time Kitty saw the sisters they had called on Hadley and Ernest on rue Notre-Dame-des-Champs. They had been entertained only by Hadley; Ernest was visible in the next room, lying on the bed reading, and he struck the Pfeiffer sisters as "coarse," they told Kitty. They liked Hadley, and agreed with Kitty that Ernest clearly did not give her enough money to enable

Archibald MacLeish, a longtime friend,
shown here with his wife, Ada, 1916

her to dress fashionably or even presentably. Both sisters would soon become good friends of Hadley's, and Pauline soon saw Ernest and Hadley together frequently, becoming friends of both.

Ernest made other, equally important new friends in 1924 and 1925. He was passing the time at Shakespeare and Company, browsing and talking to Sylvia, when a good-looking man came in. Sylvia promptly introduced Ernest to Archibald—always Archie—MacLeish, a young man from, like Ernest, a Chicago suburb, who had graduated from Yale and Harvard Law School. Six years older than Ernest, Archie had volunteered in the First World War as an ambulance driver, which no doubt mitigated those academic credits in Ernest's estimation. Archie was before long transferred to the artillery, and saw action in France. He was a poet as well, and had quit the Boston firm where he was practicing law (on the day he made partner) and brought his entire family—his wife, Ada, and a son and daughter—to Paris to write poetry. Archie and Ernest got on immediately and soon he and Hadley met Ada as well. "Ada was a dandy," wrote John Dos Passos. She was an extremely talented musician, a concert singer, and was performing and working on her voice in Paris. High spirits reigned whenever the four met. Archie boxed with Ernest a few times, though he was thirty pounds lighter, making the matches rather uneven. He also occasionally rode bicycles with Ernest, then thoroughly taken up with six-day bicycle races. Ernest wore the striped jerseys favored by the racers and rode around the outskirts of Paris with, according to Dos Passos, "his knees to his ears and his chin between the handlebars" (Dos was highly amused). According to MacLeish's biographer, Archie "compulsively" raced against Ernest that spring; Archie was almost as competitive as Ernest, which would in future cause tension between the two men.

The most important, and the most tumultuous, friendship of Ernest's life, with the writer F. Scott Fitzgerald, began in 1925. The two met at the Dingo bar around May 1. That much is all that is known definitively about their meeting, further details furnished only by Hemingway's posthumously published memoir, *A Moveable Feast*. For reasons that go right to the heart of his character, Hemingway painted Fitzgerald, whose reputation was then being restored, as a neurotic fool, a facile writer, a chronic alcoholic, and a fawning acolyte. To start, Ernest said that Duncan Chaplin, a fellow Princeton graduate of Scott's, was present at the meeting, but Chaplin was not in Europe in 1925. At their initial meeting, Hemingway tells us, Scott was intimidated by Ernest's military experience and his serious approach to writing.

In Hemingway's telling, Fitzgerald was the neophyte and he the established writer, when actually the situation was quite the opposite. Fitzgerald, another son of the Midwest, was born in St. Paul, Minnesota, in 1896, to another upper-middle-class family headed by a rather ineffectual father. Scott started writing very early; at Princeton, he hastily wrote a draft of what would become *This Side of Paradise* and then dropped out to join the Army, fully expecting to die in the war. While stationed near Montgomery, Alabama (he was never sent to the front), Scott met Zelda Sayre, a beautiful and brilliant Montgomery debutante with a strong character and considerable charm. She agreed to marry Scott, but she broke it off when she very practically noticed he did not have enough money to support her properly—a decision to which Scott understandingly acquiesced, though he didn't like it. After Scribner's accepted *This Side of Paradise* in 1919, Scott's financial future looked bright, and he and Zelda moved to New York to be married in 1920. They had a daughter they named Frances Scott Fitzgerald, called Scottie. In 1924 the family moved to Europe, living in the south of France, then in Rome, before settling in Paris.

Unlike Ernest's, Scott's literary career had been spectacular seemingly overnight. From the first, Scott entered easily into the lucrative market of short fiction for popular magazines. Approaching his writing career as a businessman (not a very good one, for he was always improvident), Fitzgerald kept elaborate ledgers detailing the large sums he received from magazines, especially *The Saturday Evening Post*, for popular and critically admired stories like "Bernice Bobs Her Hair" and "The Diamond as Big as the Ritz." Magazines paid him a couple of thousand dollars a piece, two or three stories a year providing a handsome income, especially on top of book royalties. (Unfortunately, he did not keep as close an eye on money going out as on money coming in.) He and Zelda won renown (and infamy) as avatars of the Jazz Age—the era of youthful irresponsibility, the flapper, and the unre-

F. Scott Fitzgerald and his wife, Zelda. Ernest said Scott's face was "between handsome and pretty." Zelda, he said, "had hawk's eyes."

strained expatriate life in Paris. Scott's first novel had been extremely successful, as was his second, *The Beautiful and Damned,* published in 1922, and two collections of stories published in 1921 and 1922. *The Great Gatsby* had been published on April 11, 1925; the novel would eventually bring Scott lasting fame, but when he met Hemingway less than a month later, he already sensed the novel was, by his standards (which his publisher had come to share), a commercial failure.

Fitzgerald's fellow writers recognized the achievement of *Gatsby* immediately, though the novel would not really win widespread recognition as a classic until after his death. When it first came out, T. S. Eliot wrote him that the novel seemed to him "the first step that American fiction has taken since Henry James." Gertrude Stein, who felt his first book "really created for the public the new generation," also wrote an admiring letter, as did Willa Cather and Edith Wharton. But Hemingway gave *The Great Gatsby* a decidedly backhanded compliment in *A Moveable Feast:* "When I had finished the book I knew that no matter what Scott did, nor how preposterously he behaved, I must know it was like a sickness and be of any help I could to him and try to be a good friend" (*AMF,* 151).

Ernest had taken an instant dislike to Zelda—while admitting to having had an "erotic dream" about her the night they met—and blamed her from the very start for almost all of his friend's troubles. He thought Zelda "had hawk's eyes" (*AMF,* 154), titling a chapter about Scott's marriage in *A Moveable Feast* "Hawks Do Not Share." She was "jealous," he said, of Scott's work, though the word was ill-chosen; she may have resented the time he spent on it, and entertained writing aspirations herself (though not until much later), but she had a healthy respect for Scott's talent as well as the money he made by it. She encouraged him to drink and to waste his time at parties, thought Ernest, which was perhaps true, but then these pursuits were the order of the times—indulged in, rather preeminently, by Ernest himself. Ernest professed to be not at all surprised when Zelda began to show signs of schizophrenia at the end of the decade. He liked to tell the story of her leaning in to him and confiding "her great secret," rhetorically asking him, "Ernest, don't you think Al Jolson is greater than Jesus?" Zelda, who most likely meant the remark either as a joke or as a comment on the celebrity culture of the 1920s, did not think much of Ernest either.

After their first, somewhat inebriated meeting in the Dingo, Ernest and Scott had a good, writerly talk at the Closerie des Lilas. They came to know each other better on a trip to Lyon to retrieve the Fitzgerald car, a trip hilariously evoked in Hemingway's Paris memoir, with emphasis on Scott's hypochondria and general foolishness. After the trip, Scott and Zelda invited Ernest and Hadley to lunch in their apartment on the rue de Tilsitt, on the Right Bank near the Champs-Élysées. Zelda claimed to have disliked Ernest immediately, telling a mutual friend she thought he was "bogus," and telling Ernest that "nobody is as male as all that." Her biographer wrote that she said to Hadley, "I notice that in the Hemingway family you do what Ernest wants," a mostly true statement that Ernest cannot have liked very much.

At the time they met, Fitzgerald was still reveling in the great good fortune of being a successful writer who had just written a nearly perfect novel. He was enjoying prosperity and the flush of youth with a lovely and lively wife. A fundamentally generous person, he wanted his friend to share in the writing bounty and not only talked to Ernest at great length about technique and what to charge for stories (he pulled out his ledger at the rue de Tilsitt lunch), he wanted very badly for Ernest to sign up with his publisher, Scribner's, and repeatedly told his editor there, Maxwell Perkins, to sign Hemingway.

Max Perkins did not need persuasion. He had just missed signing Hemingway for *In Our Time,* because a mistaken mailing address caused the editor's first letter to go awry. He had written Ernest that he had found a copy of Bird's *in our time* only with great difficulty. Though he greatly admired it, he told Ernest, its slenderness would prevent booksellers from earning a profit on it, thus making the book a challenging sell for Scribner's. But Perkins would consider anything Ernest had to offer for publication, he said, hinting that a novel would be most welcome. Hemingway was so elated that when he ran into Max Eastman on a Paris street he made Eastman come back to the apartment with him to see the letter. Ernest's answer to Perkins said that Boni and Liveright would have an option for his next book. He wrote that he very much regretted not being able to sign up with Scribner's. Hemingway and Eastman walked away with various ideas for getting Ernest into Max Perkins's stable.

Ernest was feeling pressure to write a novel, and not only from Max Perkins and Scribner's. Though Horace Liveright's first letter to Ernest does not survive, apparently the publisher told him that story collections did not sell, for Ernest responded that he didn't see *In Our Time* as a lost cause (and predicted that *In Our Time* would be read by highbrows *and* lowbrows). But because Perkins admitted a similar bias, he had to address it, telling Perkins, lamely, that he didn't "care about writing a novel," and thought the novel "an awfully artificial and worked out form."

The flood of short stories in 1924 and into 1925 had slowed to a trickle; Ernest wrote "The Undefeated" in November 1924 and "The Battler" in March 1925. The truth was he had no idea what to write next, and clearly saw that something more ambitious was expected of him. In the meantime he was toying with several ideas for *Der Querschnitt;* the musician George Antheil, who lived above Shakespeare and Company, was its Paris scout. The cultural journal was edited by Berlin gallery owner Alfred Flechtheim— one of the first to publish Hemingway. Though it would often print pieces he could not publish elsewhere, it was more than a dumping ground for poor-quality work. It did publish some strange pieces of his, including the six-part, heavily Gertrude Stein–influenced, prose-ish poem called "The Soul of Spain with McAlmon and Bird the Publishers," which appeared in the magazine in 1924. It listed his dislikes in a formulaic litany that began "Dictators are the shit," and listed Mencken, Waldo Frank, *Broom,* Dada, and Jack Dempsey, each individually being "the shit" (*Complete Poems,* 70). The magazine also published his "Lady Poets with Foot Notes," which contained scurrilous references to Edna St. Vincent Millay and Amy Lowell, among others, illustrated with a Matisse sketch of an odalisque. *Der Querschnitt* was known in Europe for paying writers well.

In April 1924 Ernest wrote Dos Passos that he had "an order" from the German magazine every month and that they were paying him handsomely. He bragged that *Der Querschnitt*—they "got all the fun there was out of that name," according to Dos—was going to publish a book of his "dirty poems," to be illustrated by Pascin, the Bulgarian artist whom Ernest later profiled in "With Pascin at the Dôme" in *A Moveable Feast.* Though nothing ever came of this, he talked for a month or two about writing a book about bullfighting in which he had interested Flechtheim, which had grown out of Flechtheim's intention to publish Ernest's bullfighting story, "The Undefeated," with illustrations by Picasso. That did not transpire, but, as Ernest told Dos, Flechtheim ("a swell Spanish Jew") was an *aficionado* who gave him an advance for a book about bullfighting, the third in a series, one thus far on horses and another on boxing. Picasso and Gris, among others, would illustrate it, but the book would also have copious photographs, the latter a feature that Ernest determined early on was a necessity in any book on the subject. This too did not transpire, though here was the kernel of his later *Death in the Afternoon.*

In the spring of 1925, the subject that interested Ernest most, after his own career, was bullfighting. Bill Smith had arrived in France at last, perhaps the person Ernest most wanted to introduce to the sport. In his February letter he had described the bullfight at some length for Bill, closing, "It ain't a moral spectacle and if a male looks at it for a moral standpoint there isnt any excuses. But if a male takes it as it comes. Gaw what a hell of a wonderful show." He was brimming with enthusiasm, enough so that he wrote Horace Liveright that the publisher would have to go to Spain with Hadley and him sometime. In the meantime, he wrote, Robert Benchley and Don Stewart "and a good gang" were going to Pamplona with the Hemingways in July for the Festival of San Fermín. Pamplona was shaping up to be a road trip and occasion for male comraderie, especially enjoyable because it would be preceded by some fishing on the primordially beautiful Irati River. Hadley would be along too, of course. And Lady Duff Twysden.

Hemingway was never in love with Duff—or, if he had been, he recovered before they all reached Spain. She was too much of a spectacle—not the kind of woman who attracted him. In fact, Ernest was a serial monogamist who was not given to affairs. Hemingway mythmakers have tended to add womanizing to the masculinity mix because it seems to belong, not from any real evidence. Because he would marry four times, it's taken as a given that he was a ladies' man. But he was more romantic in nature than most womanizers are. It is not known, of course, whether this applied to Duff Twysden; the most compelling evidence for his feelings is found in the character of Lady Brett Ashley in *The Sun Also Rises*—a bitch who refuses to be a bitch, loved by Jake Barnes, the hero without a penis.

There is no question that Lady Duff Twysden was alluring, and that Ernest took notice—after all, most of expatriate Paris did. In her mid-thirties in the spring of 1925, Duff was striking without being pretty: she wore her dark hair closely cut to her head and slicked back away from her face. (The hairstyle alone would have interested Ernest.) She culti-vated a mannish look, or what we would today call a preppy style: tweed skirts, worn with sweaters under blazers with an Eton collar opened over the lapels. (The look depended on an excellent figure under all that wool.) She often wore hats, either berets, soft felt hats, or Scottish tams. She spoke in a tony English accent, and her habit of calling men "chaps" caught on in her circle. Furthermore, Duff came with a very romantic backstory—one that sounds slightly sordid in retrospect, but that trailed behind her like a mist. She made much of her Scottish (bourgeois rather than upper-crust) origins; her father was a Yorkshire merchant. Duff, a recent war bride, caught the attention of Sir Roger Thomas Twysden, a baronet. Against the wishes of his family, they married (after Duff's divorce from her first husband, with another man named as co-respondent), and had a son. Even then, Sir Roger's family accused her of promiscuity and excessive drinking, while Duff maintained that her husband was a mean drunk who from time to time made her sleep on the floor. He also sometimes slept with his sword on the marital bed, a detail that embellished Duff's story and fascinated Ernest. (Did they sleep with the sword between them, as in the tales of medieval knights and ladies? If so, he further wondered, wasn't it easy to roll over it, the sword presumably lying flat on the bed?) Duff often fled England with her son, frequently to Paris or her grandmother's house in Scotland. Here a lover entered the picture: Pat Guthrie, a Scottish cousin about whom little else is known—except that he seems to have been finan-cially strapped and a serious alcoholic. The two dashed off to Paris, leaving Duff's child to be raised by her parents, and settled in Montparnasse, each dependent on checks from home that did not reliably appear. When funds reached them, they decked themselves out, went to the Ritz, and feasted on caviar and champagne until their money ran out. They became a legend-ary couple who, it seemed, had sacrificed everything for their love. Jimmie Charters, the bartender at the Dingo, later said, "They were very much in love, and as a result everyone treated them with special consideration and attention."

If the legend surrounding her is any indication, Duff must have been a charmer. She stood for the triumph of love over convention, of life lived to the hilt in defiance of society's expectations. Struck by her sense of (androgynous) style and the drama of her past, Paris's expatriates were drawn into her orbit—particularly gay men. A well-known homosexual couple, the artists Sir Cedric Morris (another baronet) and Lett Haines, were often seen in attendance on Duff. When she and Pat (Mike Campbell in *The Sun Also Rises*) swept into Paris nightspots with her entourage, everyone present paid attention. But because of her romantic liaison and her identification with gay men, few Americans or Englishmen openly pursued her. In fact, as Bernice Kert discovered, Hadley herself appreciated Duff's seeming adherence to a code by the terms of which husbands were off limits. Hadley also enjoyed Duff's sense of humor. "When she laughed, the whole of her went into that laughter," Hadley observed. "Lots of broad language, certainly, but it went over with all kinds of people."

Ernest's friend Harold Loeb fell decisively in love with Duff. He met her in early June at the Select, her legend having preceded her, and Harold was tongue-tied in her presence, though he did manage to get her into bed. Meanwhile, he and Kitty Cannell were in the throes of breaking up, and Kitty had conveniently gone off for England, as had Pat Guthrie, who was visiting his mother. In their absence, Harold and Duff left Paris: they took a *wagon-lit* on a train to St.-Jean-de-Luz, where they spent three days before moving to a country village near a town called Ascain. Two weeks passed, blissfully, it seems, for both parties. At one point Duff raised the possibility of going to South America together, leaving their old lives behind; Harold, according to his version of the story, said no.

When Duff returned to Paris, Harold stayed on in St.-Jean-de-Luz to do some writing; also, he was joining Ernest and company in Pamplona in early July to fish and go to the Festival of San Fermín, and St.-Jean was already partway there. A letter from Duff in Paris reached him there, saying she was miserable without him and their time together had been a wonderful dream. "Now for doubtful glad tidings," she wrote. "I am coming on the Pamplona trip with Hem and your lot. Can you bear it? With Pat of course." She offered to get out of it, but added that seeing and being able to talk to him in Spain was better than nothing.

Meanwhile Ernest had been planning the trip, renting rooms for the group first in Burguete for the trout fishing and then at the Hotel Quintana in Pamplona. He knew the proprietor of the hotel, he told his friends,

Juanito Quintana, himself an *aficionado*. Matadors stayed there, Ernest notified them. Originally the whole group—Duff, Pat, Harold, Don Stewart, Bob Benchley, Bill Smith, and Ernest and Hadley—were going fishing, and Ernest told Harold that Pat had sent off to the U.K. for rods and Duff for funds. Bill had brought along his best trout flies. Evidently Ernest did not know about Duff and Harold—in particular, that they had gone off together to the south of France—for he innocently wrote Harold, "As far as I know Duff is not bringing any fairies with her." But members of the party peeled off at the last minute, Benchley canceling completely, and Pat, Duff, and Harold arranging to meet the others in Pamplona, skipping the fishing. In fact, Pat and Duff, for reasons that remain elusive, arranged to travel to St.-Jean-de-Luz, meet Harold there, and proceed from there on to Spain.

Ernest may have been unaware of any intrigue going into the trip—in fact, that was probably what most angered him later about the experience—but Pat was catching on, right from the moment Harold met their train at St.-Jean. In a moment alone at the bar, Duff explained to Harold that things had changed, saying, "Pat broke the spell. He worked hard at it." Harold had already decided for himself that he and Duff had no future together, but the tension between the two remained and Pat was simmering.

Meanwhile the pre-bullfight fishing was a disaster. Their landlady warned the party—Ernest and Hadley, Bill Smith, and Don Stewart—that loggers had come through the valley, ruining the countryside—and the fishing. She was right. In the loggers' wake, the Irati was a mess, full of signs of timbering, the pools that once harbored trout now vanished, and in four days they did not catch a single fish. Their spirits were dampened, but the bullfights were the real point of the trip. Ernest wanted to show his friends the world of bullfighting, from its arcane detail to the multiplicity of its meanings. It was, in fact, his favorite kind of situation: taking a trip with his buddies to do some serious celebrating, then getting to explain to them an exciting subject in technical detail. He had not counted on romantic intrigue and was slightly proprietary about Duff. She was a phenomenon in Paris that spring, and Ernest had met her before the others had.

In Pamplona, when the romantic intrigue surfaced and the tensions among Pat, Duff, and Harold became apparent to all, it was Ernest who simmered. He hated being the last to know anything. Even though he had no plans to sleep with Duff himself, that didn't mean, according to his logic, that she was fair game for Harold. Not long after their arrival in Pamplona, Bill Smith took Harold aside and told him that Ernest knew about Harold and Duff's romantic escape (Ernest had become suspicious when Harold begged off the fishing trip) and was not pleased. "You mean he's in love with Duff?" Harold asked. "I didn't say that," said Bill, leaving everything ambiguous.

Don Stewart later said he thought the problem was Ernest's Puritan nature. He was equally naive himself, he later said, refusing to admit anything might be wrong between Ernest and Hadley, "and I wondered in my innocence why Ernest and Hadley brought in these strangers." He could tell that Ernest felt Harold had somehow betrayed him. Everything seemed changed on this trip, in contrast to the idyll the year before. The previous trip had been like "a college reunion," he told Hemingway's first biographer. In 1925, "The Garden of Eden wasn't the same." Ernest evidently felt a letdown too, judging from the emotions that would animate his novel about the experience, *The Sun Also Rises*. A snake had slithered in—a snake that Ernest identified as Harold Loeb.

On the first day, after the running of the bulls, Bill, Harold, and Ernest entered the ring for the amateur fights before the big event, and Harold somehow managed to grab on to the bull's horns, hanging on while the bull carried him the length of the arena. Ernest felt overshadowed—not a good sign. This is not to say they didn't enjoy themselves: they reveled in the streets, pouring wine into their mouths from a wineskin, sitting endlessly in cafés, drinking and listening to the Spanish music, and enjoying the fireworks—figurative and literal—in the evenings. They debated the finer points of the bullring, and discussed the spectacle, which Ernest kept calling a tragedy, at great length. Bill and Don were enthusiastic about the fights, while Harold and Duff disliked the deaths of the horses and the bulls. The hero of the hour was the matador Cayetano Ordóñez, a nineteen-year-old from Ronda, but Brett Ashley's relationship with the young Pedro Romero in *The Sun Also Rises* was entirely imagined. Duff made no connection with Ordóñez.

The tensions among the group of five, however, were very real. One set of problems, according to Don Stewart, was that Pat Guthrie revealed well into the festival that he and Duff did not have any money. The group had to pay for Duff and Pat, and consequently felt "betrayed," said Don. Another set had to do with sexual jealousy. The silence of Hadley on the subject of Duff, in letters and in discussions with her first biographer, Alice Sokoloff, seems to support Loeb's contention that Duff and Ernest never had an affair. (It was Hadley, not Duff, who would be given the ear of a killed bull by the admiring matador Niño de la Palma, at a bullfight in Madrid after Pamplona.) According to Harold, Duff spent some time with him one evening, and then she went off alone to join some revelers at a private club. When she appeared at lunch the next day with a bruised face and a black eye, Harold asked her, in front of the others, what happened. Ernest said she had fallen against a railing, and Harold became furious. (It's not clear how she got injured.) That evening, after a drizzly afternoon, Ernest and the others persisted in baiting Harold. Pat Guthrie was fairly direct in making clear to Harold that his attentions to Duff were unwanted. Harold later said that the situation became intolerable to him when Ernest joined in the teasing—for Ernest had arranged the whole trip and was the one who had invited Pat and Duff after Harold had already signed on. Guthrie insisted that Harold leave Pamplona as he was not wanted there. Duff demurred, and Ernest said something about Harold hiding behind a woman. At that Harold challenged Ernest to a fight, even though he knew full well Ernest was forty pounds heavier and would win any match. Outside, Harold took off his glasses and put them in his jacket pocket, explaining that he couldn't get them fixed in Spain if they were to break. Ernest, smiling, asked if Harold wanted him to hold the jacket, and Harold answered, "If I may hold yours." The fight was averted.

The next morning Harold found a note from Ernest in his mailbox at the hotel, Ernest apologizing for insulting him, saying he had been drunk. He hated to have the fiesta end on this note, he said, and he was ashamed of the part he had played in humiliating Harold—proving that he could behave decently. Readers of *The Sun Also Rises* might be disappointed that the real-life festival expedition fizzled rather than ending with a bang. In the novel, Bill Gorton (Smith) is a proven enemy of Robert Cohn (Loeb). In fact, however, Harold and Bill followed up the fiesta by going on a hiking trip together. Before setting out, they rented a car and drove Duff and Pat to Bayonne, putting the lie to any enmity among them. Don Stewart, also a model for Bill Gorton, left for the south of France; he later maintained that the fiesta ended badly when Duff and Pat did not pay for their rooms at the Hotel Quintana, where Ernest was such good friends with the *aficionado* owner. (*The Sun Also Rises* makes much of the code of paying one's debts.) Ernest and Hadley took a train to Madrid, where they stayed again in the Pension Aguilar and took in more bullfights, alternating with trips to the Prado, Ernest's lifelong favorite among museums. They were again impressed by Ordóñez, Ernest vowing to make him a centerpiece of his current piece of fiction.

Without really intending to, Ernest had slipped into the writing of a novel. He later said he began it on his birthday, July 21, because he was sick of hearing everyone around him talk about the novels they'd written.

It took him just six weeks to write, though he would revise it for several months. By August, however, he was confident of his success, writing to Jane Heap that the novel was almost done, written very simply. "I think it will be a knockout," he said, "and will let these bastards who say yes he can write very beautiful little paragraphs know where they get off at."

Don Stewart, as Ernest was all too aware, had very recently published his humorous novel, *Mr. and Mrs. Haddock Abroad,* and was already known for *A Parody Outline of History.* Ernest did not begrudge him these successes, as they were in a genre that Ernest felt was not his turf (though he would turn to parody in his next book). But because Stewart's publisher, Doran, had recently rejected Hemingway's *In Our Time,* Ernest could not help but resent Stewart. (In *The Sun Also Rises,* Bill Gorton is a published writer.) But it was the success of Harold Loeb and Bob McAlmon that he most resented. McAlmon seemed content to reach only small audiences with his writing; he was strangely impervious to Ernest's jockeying for literary position, thereby dodging Ernest's competitive aggression. But Harold had great hopes for *Doodab,* and the novel had come out in May—while Ernest's wasn't due out until October. Ernest complained to Horace Liveright about the publisher's objection to the phrase "son of a bitch," which he had noted in Harold's proofs of *Doodab.* Seeing a prepublication copy of Loeb's book prompted Ernest's inserting him into his novel as the impossible Robert Cohn, called a Jew by every member of the party, and told to leave Pamplona because he wasn't wanted.

Harold Loeb wrote about his experiences in Spain in his 1959 memoir, *The Way It Was,* and later contributed two essays to a collection edited by Bertram Sarason, *Hemingway and the Sun Set* (1972). "[*The Sun Also Rises*] hit like an upper-cut," he remembered after nearly fifty years. He was simply unable to understand why Hemingway turned on him in this way. Why could Ernest not have done a bit more to camouflage events rather than just changing the names of his friends? Harold came up with a number of possible reasons: Ernest envied and was suspicious of rich people and Ivy League schools; his war wound scarred him for life; he had an uncontrollable temper; various experiences from his early years had made him quick to take offense, seeing persecution where it was not. Though Harold wrote about publishing *Doodab* in these autobiographical accounts, he did not recognize that this might have been a factor in Hemingway's attack as well.

Harold Loeb's detection of a certain delusional component to Hemingway's thinking is a fairly good read of what was going on toward the end of Ernest's life, but it does not explain Hemingway's motives in casting "that kike Cohn" as the villain of his novel. One of the things that puzzled Harold most was that he had thought he and Ernest were very good friends. They had boxed together, they played tennis together, they talked about writing. Letters between the two are marked by a warmth and intimacy that is rare in Ernest's correspondence. Harold rescued *In Our Time* from the returns pile at Liveright; he fought for the book, and he was instrumental in getting it published. But that was enough to damn him in Ernest's eyes. Ernest had a terrible time accepting favors. He did not like the feeling of being beholden to someone, certainly not uncommon. What is uncommon is the way Ernest lashed back. "Hemingway came to distort all his kind friends," Harold concluded. He could see nothing in his relationship with Ernest that justified the abuse.

Somewhat fittingly, Donald Ogden Stewart offered perhaps the most satisfactory observation on the subject. Don's relationship with Ernest survived the summer week in Pamplona, though he would later break with Ernest over Ernest's brutal behavior toward a mutual friend. Yet Don saw what Ernest was doing to those around him, Harold in particular. He had a mean streak, said Stewart:

> The mean streak was a booby trap kind of thing. There's no explaining it particularly, it was just part of his character along with the rest of him. It wasn't any dark secret known only to a few. People talked about it. To look at it in a more charitable way, if Hem had been just plain mean you wouldn't have noticed it. But he wasn't mean, he was charismatic; and it was for this very reason that the mean streak startled you so when it came to the surface. The important thing to remember is that he didn't have to have a reason to be mean. It was more of a mood thing.

Stewart recognized Hemingway's charisma as tied inextricably to his character. Simply put, people wanted him to like them, so he got away with more than other people did. His charisma protected him from the consequences of his more outrageous actions.

Ernest was a visionary writer in that he saw more than others did, recognizing people, places, and things that he could draw from in his fiction. Every writer does this, of course, but Ernest was unique in transforming these elements into a literary whole that worked on many levels. He changed names—mostly, that is. (Name changes would be an issue throughout his dealings with editors.) The novel he was writing, soon to be titled *The Sun Also Rises*, signaled the beginning of a lifelong pattern of Ernest's using his fiction for revenge. He changed his friends' names and he did, to a degree, camouflage them, modifying certain of their traits. Harold Loeb, for instance, was never "the middleweight boxing champion of Princeton"; that was Ernest's invention. But because it suited his purposes—he wanted Harold to pay for helping get his first fiction published, for publishing his own novel first, for presuming that he was a suitable mate for the ineffable Lady Duff Twysden—because Ernest was in the *mood* to see Harold as a pretender, an obnoxious love-struck puppy, a kike, he transfigured Harold Loeb into Robert Cohn.

TEN

After Pamplona '25, Ernest and Hadley went on to take in still more bullfights, first in Madrid, during an unusual spell of cold weather there, and then in Valencia. Ernest's novel, for the time being called "Fiesta," was well under way, 1,200 words a day issuing from his typewriter. By August 7, he had eight chapters. Meanwhile, Ernest and Hadley moved around restlessly: back to Madrid, now gripped by a heat wave, then to San Sebastián and from there to Hendaye.

Hadley was reading Ernest's pages every afternoon. In this early draft, he was using real names; the narrator, later Jake Barnes, was "Hem," for instance, and the character who would become Lady Brett Ashley was Duff Twysden. No doubt it was a strange sensation for Hadley, reading about events very recently experienced, especially given that she was the only member of the party who did not appear in her husband's manuscript. There was no trace of her, nor would there be in the finished book; it was as if she did not exist. On August 11, Hadley returned to Paris, eager to see Bumby (and, one imagines, to take a break from bullfights; she enjoyed them, but not as much as her husband did). Ernest stayed in Hendaye because his work was going so well, only returning to Paris on the 17th. Even then he continued to write ceaselessly, using the second bedroom in the apartment over the sawmill as an office. He was "working very hard," Hadley remembered, "disappearing every morning and night into that little room." Evidently he did not want to risk the disruptions working in a café might bring him.

The wake of the Pamplona trip saw new alliances formed, old ones broken up. Ernest went through the motions of being Harold Loeb's friend, Harold aware of the chill but of course with no idea of Ernest's future treachery. Harold and Bill Smith had formed what turned out to be a lifelong friendship, from Pamplona going on to a cycling trip in the Black Forest. They had both booked passage to New York on September 5. On the eve of their trip, the remnants from the Festival of San Fermín, minus

Duff, Pat, and Don Stewart, reunited for a dinner given by Kitty Cannell at the Nègre de Toulouse. Harold and Kitty both wrote about the night, but only Kitty's account of her conversation with Ernest survives, and she was not always a reliable narrator. According to an account she gave Carlos Baker, Kitty and Ernest lagged behind as they all left the restaurant. Ernest told her he was writing a novel. "I'm putting everyone in it," he said, "and that kike Loeb is the villain. But you're a wonderful girl, Kitty, and I wouldn't do anything to annoy you." In *The Sun Also Rises*, Kitty appears as the grasping Frances Clyne, desperately hanging on to her boyfriend, Robert Cohn, whom she leads around by the nose, ignorant that his affections are elsewhere.

Ernest put the manuscript aside for a few days only to pick it up again and take it with him on one of several trips he would make to Chartres in the years to come. In Sherwood Anderson's autobiography, *A Story Teller's Story*, published in 1924, Chartres is the location for a 1921 epiphany about Anderson's calling as an artist. Ernest had recently read the book, but it is impossible to know whether this was on his mind. He did comment on Chartres's meaning to Anderson in a later letter to Wyndham Lewis in which he took Anderson to task for not crediting D. H. Lawrence as an influence. "In [*A Story Teller's Story*], you find, he was formed through contemplation of the cathedral of Chartres! Accompanied, of course, by Jewish gentlemen." This last was a reference to the critic Paul Rosenfeld, who took Anderson to Europe with him as his guest in 1921. The day spent with Rosenfeld at Chartres, writes Anderson's biographer, "was among the happiest of his life."

By the time Ernest returned to Paris, *In Our Time* was published, and his entire life was changing. By the end of 1926 he would have written, on top of *In Our Time*, two new stories, both among his best—"Ten Indians" and "Fifty Grand." More important, he would have written two novels, one a tossed-off parody but the other a novel that would define an epoch. And he would have fallen in love again. With Pauline Pfeiffer, the woman who would become his second wife.

* * *

It is impossible to overstate how much of a departure from the usual debut story collection Hemingway's *In Our Time* represented. Though many factors influenced early critics and readers, most notably Ernest's charm, his achievement was unmistakable. In some lights the collection appeared to be no more than a reshuffled compendium of his early journalism with some stories thrown in. Those journalistic pieces, however, were extraordinary, deriving from Hemingway's eye for unsettled—and unsettling—situations, his knack for being in the right place at the right time. And *In Our Time* is not a compendium, it is an organic whole, the intermingled vignettes at once setting off and complementing the stories. Hemingway's vignettes of war and its violent aftermath function as counterpoint to and commentary on the lives of the characters in the stories, lives he examines and presents microscopically, giving the impression that he is presenting real conversations, not re-creations of them. The war becomes something that overshadows and affects everything else; the stories all relate back to it in some fashion. The book's effect is in its shards and how they combine into a brilliant whole.

The early notices for *In Our Time* were scant; important critical notice would not come until Allen Tate's review in *The Nation* the following February and Fitzgerald's admittedly partisan piece in *The Bookman* that May. D. H. Lawrence's review in the influential British journal *Calendar of Modern Letters* did not appear until April 1927. But the *New York Times* review appeared on October 18 and was all Ernest could wish for: "Ernest Hemingway has a lean, pleasing, tough resilience," wrote the reviewer. "His language is fibrous and athletic, colloquial and fresh, hard and clean, his very prose seems to have an organic being of his own." *Time* said, "Ernest Hemingway is somebody, a new, honest, un-'literary' transcriber of life—a Writer," but *Time* did not so pronounce until January 18, 1926. It was Paul Rosenfeld, Sherwood Anderson's companion at Chartres, who wrote the first critical essay, in *The New Republic* in November 1925, and it was uniformly favorable, though in Rosenfeld's turgid and dense style. Rosenfeld was the music critic at the journal, and while Edmund Wilson at *The New Republic* may have recommended *In Our Time* to him, it is a good bet that Anderson had spoken to his friend about the book's publication. Not surprisingly, then, Rosenfeld noted the influence of Anderson, as well as Gertrude Stein. "Horseshit review by Paul Rosenfeld," Hemingway wrote Bill Smith, "very favourable and plenty of length but nauseating to read."

It may well have seemed that Anderson was dogging Hemingway's heels, especially when Grace sent her son the Rosenfeld clipping along with an *Atlantic Monthly* piece on Anderson by Ernest's new friend Archibald MacLeish. In a December 14 letter thanking her, Ernest affected the jaded author: "What a lot of Blah Blah that N. Republic review was. Still I'm always glad to read them." Perhaps he was more eager to hear what his own family thought than *The New Republic*. Writing to his mother on October 29, after asking her ten days earlier whether she had seen the book, he said that the publication date was October 10 and that she had "doubtless" seen it by then. In a letter to his Oak Park friend Isabelle Simmons Godolphin of December 3, he said that he thought his family was praying over what to say to him about it. Then he casually asked her, "What have your family written to you about it if anything? Oak Park re-actions are swell."

With the exception of his father's compliment on Ernest's good memory after reading "The Doctor and the Doctor's Wife," he had heard nothing from his family about his work since the copies of Bill Bird's *in our time* had been returned to the publisher. "I wonder what was the matter," Ernest wrote sardonically to his family, "whether the pictures were too accurate and the attitude toward life not sufficiently sentimentally distorted."

Ernest's letter to Grace about the Rosenfeld review almost certainly crossed over the Atlantic two letters in early December from Ed to his son. On December 2, Ed wrote to Ernest, Hadley, and Bumby that he had bought a copy of *In Our Time* and read it "with interest." It was not until a letter dated December 9 that the other shoe dropped. Ed opened by saying that he had heard many compliments for *In Our Time*. "Trust you will see and describe more of humanity of a different character in future volumes," Ed went on. "The brutal you have surely shown the world. Look for the joyous, uplifting, and optimistic and spiritual in character. . . . Remember God holds us each responsible to do our best." And Ernest may not have received this letter when he wrote at some length to his father on December 15, saying that he had received his mother's clippings: "I know what I'm doing and it doesn't make any difference either way what anybody says about it. Naturally it is nice to have people like it. But it is inside yourself that you have to judge. . . . You have to be your own worst critic." With this, all parties seem to have suspended further discussion of the topic for some months.

This does not mean that Ernest kept news from his parents. On December 8, 1925, he wrote his mother, "Hadley is better looking and huskier than ever." The following May Ernest wrote to his father that he, Hadley, and Bumby would be spending the following winter in Piggott, Arkansas, news that must have left Ed Hemingway completely mystified. Pauline Pfeiffer appeared regularly in his letters home by that time; in 1925 he announced that she would be spending the holidays in Schruns with Ernest and family. He didn't seem to be able to keep her out of his letters to Bill Smith. On December 3 he wrote that he and Pauline had done some "A1 drinking." The two of them, he reported, on a Sunday "killed" five bottles of wine (two Beaunes, two Chambertins, and a Pommard); with Dos Passos's help, a quart of Haig whiskey; and a quart of heated Kirsch brandy, with or without outside help. Presumably he was showing off for Bill, both his capac-

With Hadley and Bumby, in Schruns, Austria, 1926

ity and his knowledge of wines, but even with that in mind it is obvious that a serious drinking bout took place, in which the Hemingways' new friend enthusiastically participated. What he was trying to communicate to Bill beyond boasting is not clear. By now, however, Pauline, a rich young woman from Piggott, Arkansas, was an established feature in his emotional landscape.

Years later, when Hemingway wrote about the advent of Pauline in his life in *A Moveable Feast,* he had a very complicated agenda and numerous scores to settle. What he chose to focus on, however, was Pauline's wealth and the advent of other people with wealth in his life at the same time. He spoke of the last season he spent in Schruns as a "nightmare," one disguised as huge fun. It was the year the rich showed up, he said.

Somewhat inexplicably, he blamed his friend Dos Passos, calling him the "pilot fish" who swims ahead as a scout, sends signals to those behind him, and then moves on. Hemingway was referring to a new and golden—and undeniably rich—couple, Gerald and Sara Murphy, who had also entered the Hemingways' lives that fall and winter. But he was also referring to Pauline, although she had nothing at all to do with Dos Passos or the Murphys at that time. In fact, she probably had not even met Dos Passos yet and probably only met the Murphys that December. In the Paris memoir, Hemingway seems to have been conflating people and events in the interests of showing causality—and assigning blame. Leaving his first wife for the second was not his fault, he insisted.

Don Stewart, a friend of the Hemingways and the Murphys, said that any description of Gerald and Sara should begin, "There once was a prince and a princess." They had an exquisite talent for life, bringing to life the Spanish proverb "Living well is the best revenge"—the title, in fact, of the first of several books about the Murphys and their circle. Gerald, ten years older than Ernest, was a Yale graduate, a classmate and friend of Cole Porter's; he was the heir to the Mark Cross leather goods fortune, a business he took up only briefly and left in order to study landscape architecture at Harvard, eventually tiring of that as well. He was an extremely talented painter, turning out meticulous works depicting everyday objects like razors or matchboxes in a colorful Cubist-inspired idiom. He worked as if he was something he wasn't—that is, a dilettante, in that he produced very few paintings and stopped painting once he saw what he could accomplish. He and his wife were both gifted aesthetes, bringing verve and imagination to everything from clothing and house decoration to the unique menus for their famous dinner parties. Sara, born in 1883, was five years older than Gerald, and they had three children, Baoth, Patrick, and Honoria, fiercely protected by Sara but exposed to the passions of their parents in cultural activities and social life. In Paris, the Murphys gave a party for the corps of the Diaghilev ballet at their apartment on the quai des Grands-Augustins; in 1923 they rented a barge on the Seine for an opening party for Stravinsky's startlingly modernist ballet *Les Noces*. Guests at these parties included their friend Fernand Léger; Picasso; Cole and Linda Porter; Tristan Tzara; Jean Cocteau; Scott and Zelda Fitzgerald; and Don Stewart, among many others. Ernest and Hadley had been living in a cultural wasteland compared to the world of the Murphys, one of the many ways in which their lives would change at this time.

The Murphys were renovating a house in Cap d'Antibes that they would call the Villa America, which would be a magical place inside and out.

The Riviera had previously been a winter destination for tourists, usually Germans, but thanks to trendsetters like the Murphys, summering in the seaside towns of the south of France became the height of chic in the 1920s. Despite their considerable sophistication the Murphys were kind and generous to their friends; Sara had an endearing, down-to-earth quality that won her many admirers, among them Hemingway, who became a friend of hers for life. Gerald was introspective and could often be moody, almost certainly bisexual yet deeply in love with his wife.

Dos Passos was indeed the first of the Hemingways' expatriate American circle to meet the Murphys. In the spring of 1923 he was painting sets for *Les Noces* with Gerald. Illegitimate and raised by his mother in a series of hotel rooms, Dos particularly liked spending time with the Murphys and their children. "I had never had a proper family life and was developing an unexpressed yearning for it," he later wrote. "Their three little towheads were constantly amusing." He and the MacLeishes, close friends since 1923, had told Scott Fitzgerald about the Murphys when Scott and Zelda were leaving for France in the spring of 1924. The Fitzgeralds planned to live on the Riviera, where Scott, with characteristic improvidence, thought they could live more cheaply. (He would publish a humorous piece in *The Saturday Evening Post* that July about life in the south of France called "How to Live on Practically Nothing a Year.")

The Murphys and Fitzgeralds became intimate almost immediately that summer. When Scott and Zelda went back to Paris soon afterward, Gerald wrote a rather extraordinary letter that speaks to that immediate closeness. "There *really* was a great sound of tearing heard in the land as your train pulled out," Gerald wrote. "Ultimately, I suppose, one must judge the degree of one's love for a person by the hush and the emptiness that descends on the day,—after the departure. We heard the tearing because it was there,—and because we were'nt able to talk about how much we do love you two." The children were part of the magic: when four-year-old Scottie Fitzgerald said she wanted to get married, Gerald asked her to marry him and mounted a mock wedding. Scottie dressed up in a white dress and a veil, and Gerald took her for a ride in his Renault, which he had bedecked with flowers, and then gave her a dime store ring, whereupon a lot of cake was consumed.

Hadley and Ernest were swept up into the Murphys' orbit. Sara loved Ernest from the outset, but Gerald was a little cooler, as was his nature. He found Ernest charismatic but overwhelming: "He was such an enveloping personality, so physically huge and forceful, and he overstated everything and talked so rapidly and so graphically and so well that you just found yourself agreeing with him." Hadley, in turn, was a bit overwhelmed herself, finding Sara "exquisite." She added, however, with characteristic reserve, "Sara and Gerald were impressive friends, you know; they were both very good looking, fine featured and blond. Somehow they matched each other." Hadley, so admired by most, did not impress Sara, who remembered her as "a nice, plain girl," perhaps noting Hadley's meager wardrobe; she added, inexplicably, that she thought Hadley "not very bright." Perhaps Sara was responding to Hadley's difficulty in just keeping up with the repartee in the conversations of the Murphys and their circle: Dos Passos later remarked, "Conversation in the early twenties had to be one wisecrack after another. Cracks had to fly back and forth continually like the birds in badminton." Ernest could be quite funny, as could Dos Passos, and Gerald and Sara were quick to respond; it would be remarkable for most people *not* to lag in such company.

Ernest was proud of his sense of humor. This was one factor in the strange complex of motivations that led him to turn his hand to a book-length satire in the second half of November 1925. Some of his friends believed—and Hemingway did little to discourage their belief—that he wrote *The Torrents of Spring* in order to extricate himself from his contract with Liveright and sign instead with Scribner's. Certainly he regretted that the letter of interest in his work from Scribner's editor Maxwell Perkins came *after* he had signed a contract with Boni and Liveright. While *In Our Time* was on press, his new friend Scott Fitzgerald had taken up the cudgels for Ernest with Perkins, his own editor.

Perkins, who would become Ernest's editor at Scribner's, let Ernest know that he was standing by to read whatever he wrote next—especially if, as had been rumored, it was a novel. Perkins was full of praise for Ernest's work, and managed to find a copy of the already scarce *in our time* volume when Ernest said he did not own a single copy. Meanwhile Ernest let Perkins know that Boni and Liveright held the option to publish his next three books, so Ernest was bound to them—unless they should reject his next book.

It is unclear whether that last clause was what Ernest had in mind when he began his satire. If he could write something that Boni and Liveright would reject, went the logic, he would be free to sign a contract with another publisher. This argument ignores the many other factors that went into the writing of *The Torrents of Spring;* certainly there are easier ways to get out of a contract than by writing a book-length satire. (Presumably Hemingway could have submitted any book-length manuscript, however negligible, to Liveright, but his pride, and the spirit of the contract, would not allow him to do this.) Ernest told a correspondent in 1953, when he had no reason to lie, that he submitted the satire hoping it would be rejected simply because he didn't like Liveright. But he had very definitely written it with publication in mind.

Ernest had a target for his satire, and that was his mentor, Sherwood Anderson. When he described his action later, he said that he was disgusted by Sherwood's latest book, *Dark Laughter*, published earlier that year. As he later told the story (to Anderson, of all people), he and Hadley had lunch one fall day in Paris with Dos Passos, to whom he had just lent his copy of *Dark Laughter.* "He'd read it and we talked about it," Ernest wrote mildly. After lunch, he said, he went right home and began writing and didn't stop for seven days. The result was a 28,000-word tale set in Petoskey, Michigan, the small town closest to Lake Walloon and the Hemingways' summer place. The hero is Scripps O'Neill, and the subject the disruption of his marriage to an aging waitress (from England's Lake District), with a complicated backstory involving a French general, told by a younger waitress, Mandy. The other protagonist is Yogi Johnson, an American veteran who has lived in Paris. Throughout are references to Dos Passos, Fitzgerald, Mencken, *Vanity Fair* and *The Dial;* one chapter is called, in dubious homage to Gertrude Stein, "The Passing of a Great Race and the Making and Marring of Americans" (*TOS*, 81). Ernest's title came from Turgenev (though what he was trying to say with this gesture is elusive), and he provided an epigram on satire from eighteenth-century novelist Henry Fielding.

Ernest was immensely pleased with the result and read it to all his friends, later telling Bill Smith that Fitzgerald, Dos Passos, and novelist Louis Bromfield all found it "OK." One evening he read it to the Murphys, Hadley, and Pauline Pfeiffer. Pauline, who had a reputation as a wit, laughed uproariously, as did the Murphys. But Hadley begged him not to publish it, saying it would be unfair to Anderson. (Hadley, in direct contrast to Pauline, had never liked Ernest's humorous writing, observing, in the early days of their marriage, that his "funny stuff" lacked "vitality.") Dos Passos later wrote that he found the material in *Torrents* very funny, especially the portrayals of the Michigan Indians who stood in for Anderson's black folk given to "dark laughter." But he couldn't understand quite what Hemingway was up to, he later confessed. "Was he deliberately writing stuff that Liveright, as Sherwood Anderson's publisher and friend, couldn't possibly print, or was it just a heartless boy's prank?" Dos didn't think it stood up as parody, "and that *In Our Time* had been so damn good he ought to wait until he had something really smashing to follow it with."

Fitzgerald may have thought *Torrents* was "OK," but after Ernest sent it off on the *Mauretania* on December 8, Scott wrote a distinctly odd letter to Liveright. Part of its strangeness was his frank admission that he hoped Liveright wouldn't like the book, "because I am something of a ballyhoo man for Scribner's and I'd someday like all of my generation . . . that I admire rounded up in the same coop." Even so, he told Liveright he thought *The Torrents of Spring* was "about the best comic book ever written by an American," comparing it to *Alice in Wonderland*. The likeliest explanation is that Scott could not contain his enthusiasm for his new friend and his work; however inappropriate it may now seem for Fitzgerald to have written in this way to Hemingway's publisher, he could not resist a plug for his new friend.

Hemingway had almost convinced himself that *The Torrents of Spring* ought to be published by Boni and Liveright, judging from the December letter he wrote the publisher. He led off with some airy words about Fielding and the great tradition of satire in English literature. He went on in an offensively chummy manner about the correct length for such a book, as "You do not want it too long." He advised wide margins and judicious chapter breaks and spacing. If Boni and Liveright took it, he went on, they would have to push it, doing what he felt they had not for *In Our Time*. The letter does not refer to Anderson until about two thirds of the way through, when Hemingway addresses what he says might be the firm's fear of offending "Sherwood." In any case, Ernest felt, it was important for him to differentiate himself as a writer from Anderson (indeed, probably an underlying reason for writing the book), and Boni and Liveright "might as well" have both authors in the same house. "And any one who has ever read a word by Anderson will feel strongly about it— one way or the other." As if taunting Liveright with something he could not have, he told him *Torrents* was not the "long novel" he was working on, which he was calling *The Sun Also Rises*.

The reasoning that Ernest offered for his action—that Anderson had written a very bad book and that it was his duty to point it out—was particularly specious. As he explained in a condescending letter to Anderson the following May, "You see I feel that if among ourselves we have to pull our punches, if when a man like yourself who can write great things writes something that seems to me (who have never written anything great but am anyway a fellow craftsman) rotten, I ought to tell you so." If he really felt that way, why didn't he just tell Anderson so, as he said? Why did he need to publish a book-length satire of the man's work? In an essay written late in his life Ernest brought a more seasoned perspective to his action: "I thought [Anderson] was going to pot the way he was writing and that I could kid him out of it by showing him how awful it was." But he understood that he had been "cruel" and observed, "What the hell business of mine was it if he wanted to write badly? None."

Anderson had followed Ernest's career from the start, bringing him along with advice and praise before he was published; writing glowing letters of introduction to some of the most influential writers in Europe; making a call at the right time to his own publisher, Liveright, to save Ernest's manuscript from the slush pile; providing a generously worded blurb for it; and likely facilitating a lengthy, warm, and insightful review of the book in *The New Republic.* Like Harold Loeb, Anderson had ensured that *In Our Time* was properly published and Hemingway's brilliant career effectively launched. Yet Hemingway was making Harold Loeb a clueless, pitiable character, a "kike," in *The Sun Also Rises,* and he was making Sherwood Anderson the subject of a parody submitted for publication to Anderson's own publisher.

On December 30 Liveright wrote Hemingway a letter of rejection that Liveright's biographer calls "a model of firmness, restraint, and good sense." The publisher said that there was not a market for an "intellectual travesty" such as Hemingway submitted. As for the "Sherwood Anderson angle," he wrote, "it would be in extremely rotten taste, to say nothing of being horribly cruel, should we have wanted to publish it." He still very much wanted Hemingway's first "real" novel, however, so when he mailed the letter he also sent along a telegram: "REJECTING TORRENTS OF SPRING PATIENTLY AWAITING SUN ALSO RISES WRITING FULLY." "So I'm loose," Hemingway crowed.

* * *

Following their usual winter practice, Ernest, Hadley, and Bumby decamped for Schruns in mid-December, hoping to spend several months there. With Gerald and Sara Murphy they had made elaborate skiing plans: together they were to charter a plane, stock it with food and fine wines, fly to the Silvretta glacier, which was much higher than Schruns, and ski down from there—an extreme plan, to be sure. And the Murphys were paying. Ernest and Hadley, meanwhile, had invited Pauline Pfeiffer to Schruns for Christmas. Pauline's sister Jinny had gone back to Piggott for the winter, and Pauline had no other plans, so she said yes. Skiing on the glacier did not transpire, but the Murphys would come to Schruns in March.

Pauline, unlike Hadley, was comfortable with the Murphys. For one thing, as a *Vogue* correspondent and assistant to Main Bocher, the managing editor (and later the designer), her clothes were lovely, and she could appreciate what Sara and Gerald wore. But more than anything else she was like the Murphys in that she had plenty of money and the same easy air about it that they did. Pauline was independently wealthy; her father, Paul Pfeiffer, from a German immigrant family, originally went into the drugstore business with his five brothers, including Pauline's generous and childless Uncle Gus. The brothers, making up the Pfeiffer Drug Company, had acquired the Richard A. Warner Company, a pharmaceutical firm, and then the Richard Hudnut Company, which manufactured cosmetics and perfumes, and moved the headquarters to New York. (The company later bought a company called Lambert, which made Lis-

Pauline Pfeiffer, Ernest's second wife, a writer for Paris *Vogue* when he met her in 1925

terine, and eventually became the Warner-Lambert Pharmaceutical Company.) Then one day, the family story went, Paul Pfeiffer's train broke down in Piggott, Arkansas. While he was waiting for it to be repaired, he disembarked and took a look around. He saw a lot of recently cleared land that he thought could support a number of crops, cotton, mainly, and also soybeans. He would eventually buy about sixty thousand acres and parcel them out to tenant farmers. Soon, he owned the one cotton gin and the one bank in Piggott, but he was a benevolent despot, ensuring that each tenant family had, in addition to a fair contract, a house, barn, chicken house, smokehouse, outdoor toilet, corncrib, and wooded lot. (As might be expected, there were those who disagreed, according to Pauline's biographer.)

The Pfeiffers were observant Catholics; their eldest child, Pauline, went to the Academy of the Visitation in St. Louis, and her parents waited for her to graduate before making the move to Piggott. But her mother, Mary, refused to move from St. Louis to Piggott unless her husband could assure her she could get to Sunday Mass. For a time she took the train to a town further south on Sundays. Then Paul converted a downstairs room into a chapel, where the priest who served the area could celebrate Mass. The chapel was in their recently built Colonial Revival house on a hill in the town; it had five bedrooms upstairs, and a generous porch wrapped around three sides of the house. The town school was right across the street, conveniently located for the younger children, Karl, Virginia, and Max. After graduating from the convent school, Pauline went to the University of Missouri, where she earned a journalism degree, among the first awarded in the U.S. Graduating in 1918, the year of the influenza epidemic, Pauline returned home to nurse her younger brother Max, who soon died.

Uncle Gus and his wife, Louise, lived in a New York City apartment, and were happy to watch out for Pauline when she came to the city for a job with the *New York Morning Telegraph*. (Her colleagues there included the gossip columnist Louella Parsons and the legendary Wild West lawman Bat Masterson, now a sportswriter.) By 1921 she had taken a job with *Vanity Fair*, and from there she went on to *Vogue*, which, according to one account, was at the time governed by the "Elevated Eyebrow School of Journalism." In between her work and trips to Europe, Pauline became engaged to a cousin, Matthew Herrold, and planned to marry him in Italy in the summer of 1924. In the meantime, however, *Vogue* gave her a temporary assignment with their Paris bureau, which had opened in 1922. The position soon became permanent. Pauline's time in Paris was the heyday of *haute couture*, with designers like Paul Poiret, Fortuny, and Chanel dressing the "new women" of the 1920s. Pauline was near the center of that world. She moved into a Right Bank apartment with a strict French Catholic family and put off her marriage.

It is easy to construct a scenario, as Hemingway later did, in which Pauline was in league with some vaguely defined "rich," determined to upturn his happy life and come between him and his wife. The paragraph in which he set down his version of what happened has been widely quoted:

Before these rich had come we had already been infiltrated by another rich using the oldest trick there is. It is that an unmarried woman becomes the temporary best friend of another young woman who is married, goes to live with the husband and wife and then unknowingly, innocently and unrelentingly sets out to marry the husband. (*AMF*, 211)

The account is not only mendacious but also muddled. The words "unknowingly" and "innocently" suggest a lack of intentionality on Pauline's part, a mark in her favor. But to couple those adverbs with "unrelentingly" suggests determined intentionality, an interpretation bolstered by other words in the passage: "trick," "temporary best friend," and "sets out." Perhaps Ernest was, at the time he wrote these words, ambivalent about Pauline and willing to give her some benefit of the doubt. One thing is clear, however, and this is the most important feature of his statement: At neither time—not years later, when he was writing about it, nor at the time to which it refers—did Ernest acknowledge any agency of his own in the breakup of his marriage over another woman.

Kitty Cannell ran into Pauline on a Paris street wearing a chic suit and struggling with a pair of skis she had evidently just bought. When Pauline told Kitty she was going to Schruns to join the Hemingways on holiday, Kitty was surprised, for she had not previously thought Pauline and the couple were good enough friends to spend the holidays together. Pauline had indeed made friends with Hadley first, but as she came to know Ernest better they realized they were on the same wavelength intellectually. Pauline thought *The Torrents of Spring*, for instance, extremely funny, and encouraged Ernest to send it to Liveright. (She may have been flirting, however, and almost certainly voiced her opinion without knowledge of Ernest's previous friendship with Sherwood Anderson.) Pauline was a very funny woman; the poet Elizabeth Bishop later said she was the "wittiest person, man or woman, I have ever known."

The visual contrast between Hadley and Pauline was striking. Ernest described Hadley in late 1925 as "huskier"; photographs from the period show excess weight that probably dated back to Bumby's birth. Max Eastman was quite critical of her appearance: "Hadley was a likable though not alluring girl, rather on the square side, and vigorously muscular and independent; I think of her as a natural born 'hiker.'" Pauline, on the other hand, was small and attractive and always immaculately dressed. Martha Sauer, a later friend, said Pauline was "very sociable, congenial," and that in appearance "she was trim, neat, kind of birdlike with bright eyes and an inquiring look, as though she were inquisitive and wanting to know what was coming next."

Chink Dorman-Smith, by now an old friend to both Ernest and Hadley, said bluntly, "[Hadley] was nice but Hem outgrew her." The Murphys' fondness for Pauline suggests that they too thought it was time for Ernest to move on. Ernest was now a renowned author with a brilliant future, and some observers thought he needed a more fashionable and up-to-the-minute companion, self-assured and witty in conversation. None of this puts Ernest in a very good light, nor does the possibility that he was probably drawn to Pauline partly because of her money. In a much later story, "The Snows of Kilimanjaro," Hemingway sketches in the "rich bitch" wife of his hero and how her money corrupted him and stole his power to write. The wife is a composite of several women, Pauline just one of them, but Hemingway reveals that he was at least familiar with the argument that could be mounted about his marriage to a rich woman. He speaks of the wife's "acquiring" the hero, who he says had traded away his old life. "He had traded it for security, for comfort too, there was no denying that. . . . She would have bought him anything he wanted" (*CSS,* 46). Pauline's biographer believes that money was a big factor in Ernest's attraction to Pauline, and notes that "perhaps not coincidentally," Pauline's Uncle Gus around this time increased the size of her trust fund to $60,000, which gave her $250 a month.

Ernest conveyed the confusion between the part of his character that was changing and the part that had stayed the same when he wrote, in *A Moveable Feast,* "When you have two people who love each other, are happy and gay and really good work is being done by one or both of them, people are drawn to them as surely as migrating birds are drawn at night to a powerful beacon." But these lucky people often do not know how to respond to those they attract: "They do not always learn about the good, the attractive, the charming . . . the generous, understanding rich who have no bad qualities and who give each day the quality of a festival and who, when they have passed and taken the nourishment they needed, leave everything deader than the roots of any grass Attila's horses' hooves have ever scoured" (*AMF,* 28). Putting aside whether or not this characterization is fair to the Murphys or the Pfeiffers, it seems clear that Ernest resented them, perhaps for forcing him to see himself as playing a role in a moral dilemma. In the passage, he both admits and denies that he was changed by the advent of the rich in his life. He cannot in good conscience deny that they affected him as they passed through his life like, perhaps "Attila's horses" (a description that hardly fits the Murphys). But to admit that they had had such an effect would be to admit that, on some level, he had "sold out," succumbed to them. It was a complicated turn of affairs, and no one acted blamelessly.

Hadley later told her biographer that Ernest held himself aloof from "the adulation of the Murphys and this rich, worldly crowd." He did not want all they offered him. Eventually, however, she said, "Ernest changed. He became terribly fond of the best of everything . . . the best in fishing gear, the best in guns and boats." At the end of 1925 Ernest wrote to his old friend Isabelle Simmons Godolphin, discussing plans for the future, "Have an idea will be making quite a little dough soon. Feel it in the bones."

* * *

On Pauline's visit to the Hemingways at Schruns that winter, she got to know Hadley better, usually passing the morning with her and Bumby while Ernest wrote. Ernest gave her some ski lessons, but Pauline generally preferred to stay where she was and read while Hadley skied with Ernest. In the evenings the three of them usually talked or played three-handed bridge, and Pauline heard all about Ernest's plans for his writing and his future. Ernest welcomed her into the nickname family, calling himself Drum; Hadley was Dulla and Pauline Doubladulla. On January 5 the three left Bumby with a nurse and went further up the Alps to the Hotel Rossle at Gaschurn for four days of glacier skiing. Soon after, Pauline left Schruns and returned to Paris. By this time she had probably fallen in love with Ernest, perhaps at first against her will. She was a devout, practicing Catholic and considered adultery a sin, but passion has rules of its own, and Pauline could no sooner stop what was happening to her than she could a freight train. Ernest seemed to be succumbing as well. As he went on to say in his account of the husband, the wife, and the third (rich) party, in *A Moveable Feast:*

> When the husband is a writer and doing difficult work so that he is occupied much of the time and is not a good companion to his wife for a big part of the day, the arrangement has advantages until you know how it works out. The husband has two attractive girls around when he has finished work. One is new and strange and if he has bad luck he gets to love them both. (*AMF,* 209–10)

Back in Paris, Pauline wrote Hadley and Ernest copious letters, addressing them as "My dears, my very dears." She busied herself running errands for them, offering, for instance, to return any books left in their apartment to Shakespeare and Company. Ernest had almost finished revising *The Sun Also Rises,* which Pauline wanted to read. He began to plan a trip to New York to deliver his manuscript and meet his new publishers. On the way, he would need to visit Paris for a few days to tie up various loose ends. Though Hadley planned to stay in Schruns while he was in New York, at first she thought she might come with him to Paris for a brief visit. Writing Hadley in support of that idea, Pauline used language that would seem, in retrospect, highly charged: "Better brood well over the you coming to Paris idea. I am not a woman to be trifled with and I shall behave badly if trifled with by you." When Hadley decided to forgo Paris, Pauline wrote in disappointment ("We wooda had a good time"). She was "overjoyed" that Ernest would be in Paris soon, she said. "I feel he should be warned that I'm going to cling to him like a millstone and old moss, and [illegible; winter?] ivy." In Paris over those few days Pauline and Ernest almost certainly became lovers. The Hemingway apartment was still sublet, so Ernest stayed at the Hotel Venetia in Montparnasse.

* * *

It was not obvious that Ernest needed to go to New York in January 1926, and it was quite possible that he made the trip partly to consummate his relationship with Pauline in Paris. He had needed to make some answer to Liveright's cable rejecting *Torrents* and saying he was "awaiting" *The Sun Also Rises.* Ernest wrote Horace Liveright on January 19 that he considered himself released from their contract. (The contract did not insist that the next work be a full-length novel, he argued in circular fashion, and even if it did, *The Torrents of Spring* was a full-length novel.) Given the letter's sarcasm, it is somewhat surprising that Ernest said he looked forward to meeting Liveright when he arrived in New York. Yet he went to Liveright's office immediately after the *Mauretania* docked on February 9. The meeting was sufficiently cordial that the two went out to a speakeasy for a couple of drinks afterward.

Negotiations with Scribner's were ongoing, with Scott Fitzgerald in the middle, receiving cables from Perkins and then cabling on to Ernest from Paris to Schruns. Scott had sprung into action as soon as Liveright turned down *Torrents.* Whatever he might have said to Liveright in praise of the book, he had revealed that he was aware of the real lay of the land, as he often was in publishing matters. He had sent a wire to Maxwell Perkins at Scribner's: "YOU CAN GET HEMINGWAYS FINISHED NOVEL PROVIDED YOU PUBLISH UNPROMISING SATIRE." Scott had told Max that Hemingway had received a definite offer from Harcourt (which probably was not true) and added, "WIRE IMMEDIATELY WITHOUT QUALIFICATIONS." Perkins had evidently wanted to qualify his acceptance, wiring Scott, "PUBLISH NOVEL AT FIFTEEN PERCENT AND ADVANCE IF DESIRED. ALSO SATIRE UNLESS OBJECTIONABLE OTHER THAN FINANCIALLY." Perkins's preoccupation with the work's legality would repeat itself with almost every book Ernest submitted to Scribner's. The legendary editor did not change or allow to be changed a word of Hemingway's writing, however. Ernest made this a precondition of publishing with the firm, a hard and fast rule he had first set when Liveright accepted *In Our Time*. (The only changes he would allow were spelling and punctuation corrections, matters he knew were beyond his ken.) Max's job consisted mostly of holding the author's hand, an extremely fraught duty that included timing the publication of his work, encouraging him on some writing projects and discouraging him from others, and giving personal advice only under certain circumstances, and then only with great delicacy and tact. But Perkins's first duty, as he saw it, was to ensure that what Hemingway submitted for publication with Scribner's was legally viable; that is, not defamatory or otherwise libelous, and not censorable on the grounds of obscenity. The latter would prove a lively subject over which Max and Ernest came to ritually battle. It was hardly a trivial matter, since an important aspect of Hemingway's modernism—as of Joyce's and others'—was an insistence on addressing earthy and unpleasant subjects such as abortion and divorce; the demands of modernity and of free speech had to be met. Thus the quarrels over four-letter words were important. What Perkins did not do to Ernest's work, however, is line editing. Max's job as Thomas Wolfe's editor would be very different; part of his genius was in knowing what each writer needed from him.

And Max Perkins knew to suspend legal considerations when wooing an author was the uppermost goal. He followed up the cable that qualified the acceptance of *Torrents* on legal grounds, cabling on January 11 (again, to Scott instead of Ernest), "CONFIDENCE ABSOLUTE. KEEN TO PUBLISH HIM." When Fitzgerald had let Max know that Hemingway had other offers, he was not basing his remarks on any bluff on Ernest's part. Ernest spent his first night in the U.S., after getting "slightly tight," worried about whether he should go to Scribner's or accept another offer. Harcourt, Brace had made clear that they wanted to sign Hemingway, on the advice of one of their authors, Louis Bromfield.

But Ernest was swayed by Fitzgerald's recommendation of Perkins, and by Perkins's letters to him the previous winter. His second day in New York, Ernest signed a contract with Scribner's advancing him $1,500 for both *The Torrents of Spring* and *The Sun Also Rises* against a royalty of 15 percent. (In the interval, Max had presumably read *Torrents*.) Fitzgerald continued to worry even after Hemingway had signed, telling Max that Ernest was "temperamental in business," the result of dealing with "bogus publishers" in the U.S. (the only editor to whom this could refer was the editor of *The Double Dealer*, who published him back in 1922). He urged Max to "*get a signed contract*" for *The Sun Also Rises*. Scott's letter crossed one of Max's thanking Scott for his role in the negotiations.

Fitzgerald had all along been coaching Perkins from the sidelines, as it were. Even after Ernest signed with Scribner's, Scott was urging him to offer to place one of Hemingway's stories in *Scribner's Magazine*. Scott had already sent the editor Ernest's "Fifty Grand," commenting to Max that "to [his] horror"—Scott considered it a writer's duty to charge high fees for magazine publication—Ernest had sold a story to an "arty" magazine in Paris (*This Quarter*) for $40. By this time Fitzgerald's role seems to have changed from that of a scout to that of author's agent.

Scribner's Magazine would months later reject "Fifty Grand" because it was too long and Ernest could not or would not cut it down further than he already had. Eager to keep Ernest happy as Scott recommended, the magazine also considered the story "Alpine Idyll." In that story, a peasant keeps his wife's frozen body over the winter in a toolshed, hanging a lantern from her open jaw to see by. The magazine decided it could not publish it, *Scribner's* editor Robert Bridges claiming it was "too terrible, like certain stories by Chekhov and Gorky." *Scribner's* finally published a Hemingway story later that year, when Perkins forwarded "The Killers," paying him, however, only $200. (If Scott knew the price, he would not have approved.) Thus commenced a long relationship between the author and the magazine. *Scribner's Magazine* would later pay Hemingway the highest fee they had ever paid, $16,000, for the serial rights to his *A Farewell to Arms*. (Eventually they could no longer afford him, despite the fact that he was one of the publishing house's best sellers.)

Scott's role in launching Ernest's career was far from over. Perkins may not have edited Hemingway's writing in the technical sense, but Scott did—with decidedly mixed consequences.

* * *

Ernest returned from New York in mid-February. He would later write dramatically about his passage through Paris and his arrival back in Schruns. We do not know how long he lingered in Paris, where he saw "the girl [he] was in love with" then. We only know that he did not take the first train, or the second or the third, but the one after that. He had been prevented from traveling immediately because of "the terrible remorse" that he felt, which could only be assuaged when he spent enough time with Pauline that their love blotted it out. Later he wrote a dramatic (if awkwardly worded) coda about the arrival of his train in Schruns: "When I saw my wife again standing by the tracks as the train came in by the piled logs at the station, I wished I had died before I loved anyone but her" (*AMF,* 218).

ELEVEN

By the time Ernest rejoined Hadley and Bumby in Schruns, he was wrung out by the complications involved in loving two women at the same time. The sense of divided loyalties bothered him as much as or more than lying to either of them: he would no sooner convince himself of the charms of one when the other's would entice him. It must have seemed a relief when Dos Passos and the Murphys came to ski in late March. By then Schruns had not had much fresh snow for some time, so they took the train to a higher elevation and stayed in Gaschurn, where they had last been at Christmas with Pauline. Ernest enthusiastically gave them all skiing lessons, which they took with good grace. Dos's eyesight was so bad that the safest course he could take was straight down the hill, sitting down when a tree loomed ahead, while Gerald, who had skied as an adolescent in the Adirondacks, diligently practiced his stem Christies. The first time down the mountain—higher than any he had skied down before—Gerald was elated when he reached the bottom. Ernest was waiting there and asked whether Gerald had been afraid. Gerald said yes, and Ernest told him that he had decided courage was simply grace under pressure. Dos, who remembered Schruns as "the last unalloyed good time" they all had together, said they laughed so hard at mealtimes that it was an effort to stop long enough to eat (usually "vast quantities of trout"), but that they drank plenty of hot kirsch and slept "like dormice" under great featherbeds. When the holiday ended, Dos wrote, "We were all like brothers and sisters," adding, with sadness, "It was a real shock to hear a few months later that Ernest was walking out on Hadley."

Hadley found out about Pauline in April, soon after the Hemingways returned to Paris. Ernest and Pauline had been trysting secretly by that time, but Hadley, somewhat unbelievably, suspected nothing. Pauline and her sister, Jinny, invited Hadley on a driving trip to the Loire valley to visit chateaus. Because she had never been, Hadley was eager to go; in retrospect, she believed that the Pfeiffers had invited her to break the news about Pauline and Ernest. On the trip Pauline seemed moody and unusually bad-tempered. Alone with Jinny at one point, Hadley asked her if she didn't agree that Pauline and Ernest got on "awfully well" with each other. In response, Jinny said carefully that she believed the two were "very fond" of one another. "It was the way she said it," Hadley recalled. "It was like an announcement. I seized the situation. Suddenly it was immediately clear for me."

Right after the trip, which proceeded awkwardly indeed after this revelation, Hadley confronted Ernest. His response, incredible by any measure, was anger at Hadley. She should not have brought it up, he said, but rather let them continue as before, Ernest with his mistress on the side. In the ensuing fight Ernest insisted that it would all have continued to go smoothly if only Hadley had not broached the subject. "Why can't

With Gerald Murphy (left) and John Dos Passos in Schruns, March 1926

we go on the way we are?" he asked Hadley. Not unreasonably, Hadley demurred, and the fight continued, on and off for days on end. While Hadley reported this argument to her biographer, her version of it was borne out by some remarks Ernest made to his old Chicago friend Isabelle Simmons Godolphin soon after. Adopting the tone of a veteran adulterer and exaggerating the time period involved for effect, he wrote that he had been enjoying more than one woman for "years" and now was in a terrible mess over it. Hadley should not have said anything, he added. Because she had, the whole rotten situation was her fault. These circumstances allowed Ernest, incredibly, to cast himself as the injured party. It could be argued that this was the only way for him to tolerate such ambiguity, but it could also be said that this was the only way he could deal with his guilt. It was part of a continuing and escalating pattern in which Ernest would lay the blame for anything that went wrong in his life, even things for which he was responsible, at the doors of others.

With few friends of her own and for family only a sister she disliked, Hadley was moored to Ernest and their child. Hers had been a happy marriage until this. At this juncture she did not so much choose a course of action as she decided not to decide. She would let things go on as they were (did she remember Zelda saying, "I notice that in the Hemingway family you do what Ernest wants"?). She may not have expected the affair to continue, under wraps, as it were, but it did. In retrospect, she could see that she had known when she learned of the affair that her marriage had no future. Ernest did not commit adultery lightly. If he strayed, it would be a momentous matter. Meanwhile, Pauline's Catholic upbringing, with its strict moral worldview, would have ensured that Ernest shared her very serious view of the situation. Their eventual marriage was all but understood.

So everyone carried on as before. Not only did it suit Ernest's sense of himself (and his convenience) to pretend he and Pauline had never been found out, it meant that Hadley could cling to a hope that the affair might burn itself out. She later said that Pauline requested that they meet and talk things over, but that she declined, fearing the clever Pauline would best her in any discussion. Soon, thankfully for Hadley, Pauline departed for a visit to a Pfeiffer uncle and his family in Italy. In the meantime, Ernest left for Madrid as planned, expecting Hadley to join him there soon after. For a variety of reasons, including somewhat freakish snowy weather, the bullfights he had hurried to Madrid to see were canceled, and instead he passed his time writing in bed. The drama between husband and wife had yet to play itself out.

* * *

In the meantime, Ernest's writing life was continuing its now vigorous course. May was a turbulent month in this regard. He wrote two of his best stories, "Ten Indians" and "The Killers," in his Madrid hotel bed, but also turned out the painfully bad one-act play *Today Is Friday,* about three Roman soldiers drinking together the night after the Crucifixion. He was anticipating the May 28 publication of his previous effort, *The Torrents of Spring,* when he felt the need to write to Sherwood Anderson, his onetime mentor and the subject of his parody. The letter, dated May 21—almost the latest possible date to extend the courtesy of telling Anderson about the parody before it appeared publicly—is a remarkable document. Ernest moved from the offensive to the defensive from sentence to sentence and even within sentences. "[*Torrents*] is a joke and it isn't meant to be mean," he said, "it is absolutely sincere." With convoluted logic, he tried to persuade Anderson that he understood how it looked ("of course," he said) that he was lining up with Ben Hecht and "the smart jews" in criticizing Anderson's latest novel. Acknowledging that Anderson had always been "swell" to him, and helped "like the devil" with *In Our Time,* Ernest said that he was acting out "an irresistible need to push you in the face with true writer's gratitude." After bumbling on with further contradictory explanations, he added feebly that he hoped Anderson would find *Torrents* funny, and sent along his best wishes to Mrs. Anderson from Hadley and himself. Anderson later said he thought it "possibly the most self-conscious and patronizing" letter ever written from one writer to another.

As might be expected, *The Torrents of Spring* had a mixed reception, though comments were generally favorable. Allen Tate, writing in *The Nation* in July, was extravagant in his praise: "'In Our Time' proved Hemingway to be the master of . . . irony. It is an irony pre-eminently fitted for sustained satire of the sort conspicuous in Defoe and Swift, and Hemingway's success with it in 'Torrents of Spring' is a triumph, not a surprise." Tate acknowledged that the book was a parody of *Dark Laughter* and reported in the first sentence of his review that Hemingway wrote it in ten days, but his admiration was undimmed. Harry Hansen at the *New York World* thought Hemingway had missed the mark, concluding, "He is better as a writer of short stories"—not the last time this complaint would be registered. Some other remarks Hansen made were a bit more troublesome. He noted that Anderson was Hemingway's target, and also that the book was published by Scribner's, not "Mr. Liveright," picking up on what may have been Hemingway's object in leaving Liveright: "Ergo, Mr. Scribner is able to announce that he will publish Hemingway's first novel in the fall." Evidently the success of the book preoccupied Ernest when he extravagantly assured his father that *Torrents,* while a parody of someone he and Grace wouldn't have read, had gotten more than a hundred reviews, all positive.

Clearly a great deal was riding on the novel that Scribner's was to publish in the fall. Ernest had sent the manuscript, now titled *The Sun Also Rises,* to the publisher in late April. It evidently wasn't yet in final production, however, because Ernest would turn in a significant revision at the proof stage, after an extremely fraught exchange with Scott Fitzgerald, who wrote him a long letter in June objecting in the strongest possible terms to the first sixteen pages of the book. All evidence suggests that Fitzgerald performed a crucial role in guiding the editing of the manuscript. With the instinctive talent of a top-notch writer and an excellent reader, he saw what was wrong with *The Sun Also Rises* immediately. Telling Ernest, however, would be half the battle.

Scott began the letter with a general statement that honest responses to a writer's work were invaluable—that in writing his latest book he had listened to advice from Bunny Wilson, Max Perkins, and his St. Paul friend Katherine Tighe, none of whom had written a novel themselves; he seems to have been giving his friend to understand that it was commonplace for writers to receive strongly worded criticism of their work. Having established that, and admitting that in his own work he had a tendency to preserve "fine writing" when it had better be jettisoned, he went on to tell Ernest that parts of *The Sun* "are careless & ineffectual," especially the opening pages, in which "you . . . envelope or . . . embalm an anecdote or joke that's casually appealed to you," citing the "condescending *casualness*" of the novel's opening pages.

The first draft of *The Sun Also Rises,* before Scott's intervention, had more in common with the satirical *Torrents of Spring* than it did with *In Our Time.* The brittle and even chatty tone of the manuscript-in-progress suggests that Hemingway saw himself as largely an ironist, even to his creation of a narrator, Jake Barnes, who is so removed from the action that Hemingway has neutered him, sidelining him with a war wound that made it impossible for him to have sex. Originally, the novel had been dedicated "TO MY SON/John Hadley Nicanor/This collection of Instructive Anecdotes," the phrase "instructive anecdotes" at once facetious and dismissive, much like the words "a highly moral story," which Ernest used to describe what would follow in his novel, and to which Fitzgerald objected as well. In the version Scott saw, Ernest had thus introduced Lady Brett Ashley:

This is a novel about a lady. Her name is Lady Ashley and when the story begins she is living in Paris and it is Spring. That should be a good setting for a romantic but highly moral story. As everyone knows, Spring in Paris is a very happy and romantic time. Autumn in Paris, although very beautiful, might give a note of sadness or melancholy that we shall try to keep out of this story.

The flippant, offhand tone of this introduction is, as Scott said, condescending; it isn't even good writing. The first twenty-eight pages, he said, showed "about 24 sneers, superiorities, and nose-thumbings-at-nothing that mar the whole narrative" up to the point of what would become the novel's famous beginning—Hemingway introducing Robert Cohn, "the middleweight boxing champion of Princeton." Scott illustrated just how dismayed he was by "these perverse and willfull non-essentials," by pointing out passages that any would-be writer should be ashamed of—the phrase "something or other" ("if you don't want to tell, why waste 3 wds. saying it"), for example. Ernest's language had a "snobbish" edge, moreover, especially the paragraphs that provide the details of Brett's background and remark on the fate of the British aristocracy after the First World War (not per se snobbish, said Scott, but "shopworn").

Fitzgerald knew how much was riding on this manuscript, which he was at pains to point out to Ernest: "You know the very fact that people have committed themselves to you will make them watch you like a cat." The dross in the novel's opening pages did not even have Hemingway's natural rhythms, Scott complained. The shoddy introduction, he pointed out, was especially galling coming from Ernest—"you, who allways believed in the superiority (the preferability) of the *imagined* to the *seen not to say to the merely recounted.*" Scott felt it important that Ernest understand the dismay and disappointment that "the beginning with its elephantine facetiousness" gave him. "When so many people can write well & the competition is so heavy I can't imagine how you could have done these first 20 pps. so casually," Scott went on, underscoring for Ernest the necessity to get it right this time, while he had everyone's attention.

Fitzgerald advised cutting at least 2,500 words out of the first 7,500, but he also pointed out the wisdom of having Robert Cohn appear without a lot of backstory, and the setting given without any ironic observations on Paris in the spring. We don't know what Ernest said to Scott in response to this letter, but evidently it was part of a larger dialogue, as the Fitzgerald and Hemingway families were practically neighbors in the south of France at the time. We also know what Ernest did in response: he told Max Perkins that when he sent back the proofs to Scribner's they would be marked as beginning on page sixteen: "There is nothing in those first sixteen pages," he said, "that does not come out, or is explained, or re-stated in the rest of the book—or is unnecessary to state." He added coolly, "Scott agrees with me," leaving Perkins the impression that cutting the manuscript had been Ernest's own idea. (Ernest saved Scott's letter advising the cuts, most likely out of habit—he saved every piece of paper that came his way.)

The major cut was exactly what the manuscript needed. But once again someone had made a crucial intervention in Ernest's career, just as Harold Loeb and Sherwood Anderson had done with Boni and Liveright. Once again, Ernest suffered a blow to his pride. Admitting that Scott had performed him an essential favor brought with it deep resentment. As soon as he wrote to Max saying that Scott "agreed" with him about the revision, Ernest began the undoing of what Scott had done. Fitzgerald had rescued Hemingway's novel, and Ernest would never forgive him for it.

A Moveable Feast, Hemingway's posthumous memoir of Paris, provides what he presents as good-natured memories of Fitzgerald: their first meeting when he saw in Scott's—between handsome and pretty—face a mouth that reminded him of a girl's, as well as a death's-head (*AMF,* 125); an amusing trip to Lyon to pick up the Fitzgerald car, during which Scott was floridly hypochondriacal; an exchange in which Scott consults Ernest about the size of his penis; Scott's drunken behavior on a train after a Princeton game (why this in a Paris memoir is not clear); an exchange with Scott's driver, who confides Scott's total ignorance about cars; and signs of Zelda's coming insanity. Some of these memories are positive; at their first meeting, for instance, Scott "asked questions and told me about writers and publishers and agents and critics and [*Saturday Evening Post* editor] George Horace Lorimer, and the gossip and economics of being a successful writer, and he was cynical and funny and very jolly and charming and endearing" (*AMF,* 129). In fact, a friend who provided him with the ins and outs of publishing and its "economics" was vital to Ernest's career at this point. Scott told him that *The Saturday Evening Post* gave him $3,000 for a story (though he clarified in a subsequent letter that the figure was $2,750); Ernest, who would soon sell his first story for just $200, was frankly envious. But in *A Moveable Feast* he is careful to add several sentences distinguishing his kind of writing from Scott's "whoring": "I said that I did not believe anyone could write any way except the very best they could write without destroying their talent. He said he had learned to write the stories for the *Post* so that they did him no harm at all" (*AMF,* 131).

What *A Moveable Feast* leaves out completely is how valuable Scott's help was when Ernest was publishing his first books—and especially, Scott's essential aid when Ernest was making corrections on *The Sun Also Rises* in proofs. In fact, in the memoir he explicitly denies Scott's help with this, saying Scott did not see "the completely rewritten and cut" version that Ernest had sent in to Scribner's at the end of April; at this stage, the essential editing—mostly, the excision of the first pages—had not been done yet *because* Scott had not seen it yet. Ernest writes that he does not remember when Scott saw that version with its supposed rewrites and cuts, but that when Scott did see them, "we discussed them. But I made the decisions. . . . I did not want his help while I was trying to [write]" (*AMF,* 158–59).

Like Harold Loeb, Fitzgerald considered himself a good friend of Hemingway's. "I can't tell you," Scott wrote to Ernest at the end of 1926, "how much your friendship has meant to me during this year and a half—it is the brightest thing in our trip to Europe for me." Returning to America, he told Ernest he would look out for his friend's interests in the U.S. in any way Ernest wanted while he was there. In two letters from these weeks Scott offered to lend him money. In the same letter in which he thanked Ernest for his friendship, Scott made an exceedingly ambiguous statement about the revisions to *The Sun Also Rises:* he told Ernest he was "delighted" to see the press the novel was getting, and added, "Did not realize you had stolen it all from me but am prepared to believe that it's true and shall tell everyone." It is hard to imagine to what he was referring with this amused observation if not his suggested cuts in the novel. And if he were serious, all the more reason for Ernest to deny it.

* * *

While beginning *The Sun Also Rises* with Robert Cohn and Jake Barnes *in medias res* had a refreshing clarity, nothing else in Ernest's life was clear at the time. He was revising the novel on which so much depended at the same time that *Torrents* was coming out, receiving notices coming so fast and furiously that he had a hard time keeping track of them—surely a cause of intense anxiety, given how closely he had managed his career up to this point. The British wanted to publish his work—a more welcome development. And he devoted several letters to extended discussion of "obscene" words and scenes in *The Sun Also Rises.*

Despite the turmoil in their marriage, Ernest had expected Hadley to join him in Spain and later in the south of France, but instead she went directly to Antibes with Bumby to stay with the Murphys while awaiting the arrival of her husband. Mother and child spent only one night in the

Villa America's private guesthouse, however; a doctor called in to check Sara's cold determined that the cough that had been bothering Bumby was in fact whooping cough. Sara, who had a horror of germs infecting her children, even washing coins they brought into the house, sent Hadley and Bumby to the nearest hotel. Scott and Zelda Fitzgerald saved the day, however. They had rented a nearby house, the Villa Paquita; finding it unsatisfactory, they had moved to another, and now offered the Villa Paquita to Hadley, Bumby, and Marie Cocotte, whom Hadley had summoned from Paris, at no cost. The Murphys provided their British doctor's services gratis for Bumby, Sara sent the chauffeur every day with fresh vegetables from her garden, and after spending their days on the beach the Murphys, Fitzgeralds, and MacLeishes came over in evening dress, shaking up cocktails they passed to Hadley through the gate.

Ernest was importuning Hadley to join him in Spain, pleading loneliness, and Hadley was all too aware that Pauline was the missing piece. She and Pauline were exchanging letters, debating whether they should both join Ernest in Madrid. Instead, Hadley had to stay with her sick child and, for reasons that can only be guessed at, asked Pauline—who had already had whooping cough—to join them at the Villa Paquita: "It would be a swell joke on tout le monde if you and [Pauline] and I spent the summer at Juan-les-Pins or hereabouts instead of Spain," she wrote Ernest. As it turned out, it would not be much of a joke.

Ernest was deeply unhappy in Madrid, resentful that Hadley could not join him, and lonely. He and Pauline were corresponding at the time, though few letters survive. In a letter to Ernest dated May 20, Pauline answered a question Ernest seems to have asked about the Catholic Church hierarchy—who the "Eucharists" were. She answered, patiently and carefully, that there wasn't any group of "Eucharists" per se, but that he perhaps meant the attendees at the Eucharistic Council in Chicago, a conference about Church practice held once every ten years. Pauline noted that a trip Ernest planned to the U.S. in the fall might bring him to Chicago during the convention, "and won't that be fine," she commented. Clearly, the two were closer to marriage than Hadley, or any of their friends, thought. Ernest was considering converting to Catholicism in order to marry Pauline in the Church. No doubt Pauline was researching the Church's requirements for marriage to a divorced man.

Hadley remained ignorant of their advance plans, as her letters to Ernest in Madrid make clear. She was growing tired of the awkward, painful situation, and Ernest's complaints about his unhappiness and lonesomeness did not help. She was miserable as well at the Villa Paquita, one of her letters to Ernest in Madrid telling him she was sorry about not being able to join him there. Bumby was still sick with the whooping cough and she did not want to leave him and Marie Cocotte alone in the house, the lease on which ran out in early June in any case. She assured Ernest that she was living inexpensively and not presuming on the Fitzgeralds' largesse beyond staying in their vacant villa; Ernest would most definitely have feared any more favors from Scott. Hadley's unhappiness was plain: "I work for the common good and am sorrier than I can say I haven't been able to expend myself more on you and not so much on [Bumby]. I probably have written Shit letters and that's the truth. My hand shakes writing most of them." Still naive, she hoped that Pauline's presence would cheer up her glum husband.

Pauline arrived May 26, and a few days later Ernest appeared. To celebrate his arrival, the Murphys had planned a champagne and caviar party at the casino at Juan-les-Pins. Pauline's presence made Hadley miserable, her smart, witty rival leaving her feeling especially dowdy and slow, she feared, in the eyes of Pauline and Sara. "I had a terrible time because I was so unhappy," Hadley later said. "Nobody liked me. My hair misbehaved, and my clothes misbehaved." She was picking up on something quite real, for Sara, Honoria Murphy later remembered, was "privately critical" of Hadley. When she learned of Hadley's confrontation with Ernest over his affair, Sara, incredibly, viewed it as Ernest did. Hadley should never have said anything when she did. "It put the idea in his head and made him feel guilty at the same time," Sara said.

The Fitzgeralds' lease on the Villa Paquita was up shortly after Ernest's arrival, and the Hemingways, Bumby's nurse, and Pauline moved to the Hôtel de la Pinède, where their rooms had their own little garden. Hadley described the scene for Hemingway's first biographer: "Here it was that the three breakfast trays, three wet bathing suits on the line, three bicycles were to be found. Pauline tried to teach me to dive, but I was not a success. Ernest wanted us to play bridge but I found it hard to concentrate, we spent all morning on the beach sunning or swimming, lunched in our little garden. After siesta time there were long bicycle rides along the Golfe de Juan." One day the Murphys took everyone out on their yacht, the *Picaflor;* they docked in Monte Carlo for lunch and a little gambling at the casino.

Their vigorous outdoor activity left Ernest, Hadley, and Pauline all looking terrific. Even the fair Hadley got a tan, later saying, "I came back from that awful summer absolutely in bloom with the best color I ever had." Pauline wanted an all-over tan, so she and Hadley sometimes lay naked in the sun. Some twenty years later, when Ernest was writing the unfinished *The Garden of Eden,* he drew on these heady days when the three of them were deeply tanned, everyone's hair lightening in the sun, the two women with close-cropped, boyish hair. In the novel, Catherine and her writer husband, David, tan themselves and cut and lighten their hair until they are often indistinguishable: when they are joined by a woman, Marita, the ménage becomes sexual. That scenario may have been in the minds of Pauline, Ernest, and Hadley in Juan-les-Pins in the summer of 1926; certainly the three were living in very close quarters and half undressed most of the time.

But Hadley was not likely to agree to such an arrangement—nor, for that matter, was Pauline. It was not Ernest's style, either, for any number of reasons, including his constitutional inclination to marital fidelity. Still, prurient observers, working out of received notions of what constitutes manly behavior (which assumes threesomes are a universal male fantasy), have insisted on seeing a sexual relationship when there was none. Hemingway biographer Peter Griffin, for example, describes (without giving a source) Pauline joining Ernest and Hadley in bed for breakfast every morning, climbing in with them—bizarrely, with her pajama top on but minus her pajama bottoms, he maintains. Pauline was "sexually spontaneous," writes Griffin, and "made it clear that these mornings in bed—the three of them together—was the way she hoped it would always be." (So much for Pauline's convent upbringing.) But a letter from Pauline to Ernest that fall confirms that not only did such an arrangement never exist, but that Hadley did not even know for sure that Ernest and Pauline were sleeping together at any time.

Gerald Murphy was in the habit of calling younger women "Daughter," using it more often for the diminutive Pauline than the more maternal Hadley. Ernest picked up the nickname as well, and Pauline entered into the spirit of things by using the name "Papa," first for Gerald and then for Ernest. That summer, "Papa" caught on as Ernest's nickname and spread like wildfire. Papa's mood was black, however. Archie MacLeish remembered that he could be stricken with "the horrors" at any time, even on a sunny beach, surrounded by friends. Archie knew that Ernest was filled with remorse for the inevitable uproar of the increasingly inevitable divorce. "I never saw a man go through the floor of despair as he did," observed MacLeish.

Nothing, however, could keep Ernest away from certain pleasures. In July, like clockwork, he and his friends went to Pamplona for the Fiesta de San Fermín, packing Bumby off with Marie Cocotte to visit her family in

Brittany. Again Ernest arranged for rooms at the Hotel Quintana, where the matadors stayed. Gerald bought everyone *barrera*—front-row—seats at the bullfights; Sara's stomach turned when a bull gored the horses, forcing her to leave. One morning Ernest got Gerald to participate in the morning's amateur bullfight; a terrified Gerald acquitted himself well. And one evening at a plaza in the middle of a dance Ernest started leading cheers for the Murphys to dance a Charleston—*Dansa Charles-ton,* called the excited crowd. Gerald and Sara, who had taken lessons in the popular dance at the Villa America, obliged the revelers with a polished but spirited rendition.

Though there were assuredly tensions in the group in Pamplona, they were of an entirely different order from those of the previous summer, perhaps because of the effervescent presence of the Murphys. Still, Hadley would have been relieved when the party split up, the Murphys and Pauline headed for Bayonne, Ernest and Hadley off to San Sebastián, where they stayed at the Hotel Suiza. There they received a somewhat strange letter from Gerald. This letter has been much quoted by biographers, perhaps because it evokes so keenly Ernest's energy and charm that summer. But Gerald directs his address to Ernest and Hadley together—and also melds their names into one, writing to "Hadern." He thanks them for showing him and Sara Pamplona, then continues: "As for you two children: you grace the earth. You're so right: because you're close to what's elemental. Your values are hitched up to the universe. We're proud to know you. Yours are the things that count." Surely Gerald was aware of the tatters of the Hemingway marriage just then, and he, like Sara, would take Pauline's side. It seems odd for him to address Hadley and Ernest at this point as "you two children" and evoke their celestial "values" when they had brought Ernest's mistress along with them to the fiesta. As events would bear out, he most likely recognized that Ernest, to whom he felt he owed his first loyalty, needed bucking up if he were to move forward out of the temporarily stalled situation.

That summer Ernest and Hadley crisscrossed Spain, attending bullfights in San Sebastián, Madrid, and Valencia. Letters from Pauline to the two of them arrived frequently, and presumably Ernest answered them (only letters from Pauline have survived). Hadley must have felt as if Pauline and Ernest were gloating together, as when Pauline wrote, "I'm going to get a bicycle and ride in the Bois. I am going to get a saddle too. I am going to get everything I want." It did not help that Pauline added, "Please write to me. This means YOU Hadley." It must have galled Hadley to realize that Pauline wanted them to remain friends.

On their way back to Paris, Hadley and Ernest stopped at the Villa

America to spend a few days more with the Murphys. Pauline was of course gone, back in Paris. With the MacLeishes and the Fitzgeralds, they had enjoyed a busy summer; as Scott noted, "everybody" was on the Riviera—the list he provided an old Princeton friend included, besides the Murphys and the MacLeishes, Anita Loos, Picasso, Don Stewart, "& so many others I can't enumerate." Zelda later commented, "The summer passed, one party after another"; Scott often so drunk that he did not come home after a night out. Ernest evidently spoke privately to Gerald, with the result that Gerald offered him the use of his Paris studio beginning on September 1. Ernest and Hadley took the train back to the city, the trip furnishing the closing line of the story "A Canary for One" (1926). It is a portrait of a couple on a train, the story ending with the sentence "We were returning from Paris to set up separate residences" (*CSS*, 261).

*   *   *

Pauline does not come off well in all this, though most of Ernest's friends saw her as a more suitable mate than Hadley. Late that summer or early fall, Gerald made clear that he and Sara approved of his new relationship with Pauline. As Gerald wrote, "We said to each other last night and we say to you now that: we love you, we believe in you in all your parts, we believe in what you're doing, in the way you're doing it." Sara added a few words: "In the end you will probably save us all,—by refusing . . . to accept any second-rate things places ideas or human natures—Bless you & don't ever budge."

Gerald buttressed Ernest further with the loan of his studio at 69, rue Froideaux. On their return from Antibes, Ernest and Hadley had visited the apartment on rue Notre-Dame-des-Champs to collect some belongings; Hadley's biographer claims they then got drunk and stayed overnight together in Gerald's studio. Hadley went on to the Hôtel Beauvoir on the avenue de l'Observatoire, where she rented two rooms for Bumby and herself, later moving to an apartment on the rue de Fleurus, near the Luxembourg Gardens.

Gerald discreetly put $400 in Ernest's bank account and wrote him another letter expressing his concern. It was a somewhat strange communication, and perhaps fueled the case Ernest later made that "the rich" had broken up his marriage to Hadley. Gerald worried, he said, that "Hadley's tempo" was slower than his, and urged Ernest against moving at her slow speed in ending the marriage. Should his sympathy for Hadley dictate that he proceed as she might want, even if "it deter[red] you from acting cleanly and sharply," Gerald would see it as "a betrayal of your nature." He tried to clarify, not very successfully: "Hadley and you, I feel, are out after two different kinds of truth." Specifically, he wrote, "For years conditions have allowed of Hadley's drawing on your personal energy to face the efforts of the day." Gerald closed by urging, "Your heart will never be at peace to live, work and enjoy unless you clean up and cut through." Pauline was not mentioned. A letter like this was perhaps unwise, because Ernest was deeply loving and loyal to Hadley even as he severed his marriage to her. His loyalty would persist until the end of his life. By the time he wrote *A Moveable Feast,* in his fifties, moreover, Ernest saw his marriage to Hadley bathed in an impossibly rosy light, and Gerald's well-intentioned advice would enable him to sentimentalize relations with his first wife and to cast "the rich" as the villains in the story.

At the time of their separation, however, the situation between Hadley and Ernest was decidedly awkward. Shortly after their return from the south of France, she presented him with a slip of paper that she made a flourish of signing before handing it to him. It was a statement that Ernest and Pauline would not see each other for one hundred days. If they still wanted to be married at the end of this cooling-off period, Hadley would grant Ernest a divorce. Ernest then signed it too. The hundred-day agreement was Hadley's offer of a solution to an insoluble situation. She later doubted the wisdom of this strategy, reasoning that if she had left the two alone they might have come to their senses eventually.

Most likely, the result would have been the same. But no member of the triangle knew the outcome when they made the hundred-day pact. Pauline and Ernest acquiesced right away; it is likely that all three were glad of an opportunity to put off a final decision. Ernest and Pauline told each other they were sure to get through the period with their love intact. Pauline decided that she would spend the next three-plus months in the U.S., first in New York seeing friends (and Ernest's publisher) and later staying with her family in Piggott. She booked passage on the liner *Pennland* for September 24. The night before, she and Ernest took a train to Boulogne, where they ate a dinner of sole and partridge and stayed at the Hôtel Meurice before he put her on the boat.

From the *Pennland,* Pauline quickly established a letter-writing strategy, writing Ernest almost every day. Evidently a little self-conscious about corresponding over the course of their separation, in a letter from the boat she warned Ernest that she would probably write about some "stupid" things. "By writing you everything I can keep you very close to me and very much in my life until I see you again." Once in the U.S., she became obsessed with the sailing dates of the liners that would carry her letters to Ernest, and the schedules of the trains that would carry her letters to the New York port. Early on, with nothing much else to report, Pauline devoted a good part of her letters to these details. Love letters were not her strong suit, as Ernest would learn (to his dismay).

Pauline must have known that spending three months with her family in Piggott meant she would have to tell her strictly observant Catholic mother that she had fallen in love and intended to marry an already married man—that, in fact, the man she loved was not only a husband but the father of a small child. She was in for an uphill battle, not least with herself—something Ernest perhaps did not understand. She wrote Hadley a conciliatory letter from New York, saying things must have happened so quickly in Hadley's eyes "that it would be very natural if you think that perhaps Ernest and I don't really love each other and that something permanent is being ended for something passing." Evidently worrying that Hadley had promised the divorce without really knowing her own mind, Pauline wrote, "I know I love Ernest and always will, but you may not be sure of this, and it's things people do when they aren't sure that they regret." She acknowledged at the end of the letter that "you don't think of me as a trustworthy person, I suppose," adding, "but you know what I always said about you—that you not only couldn't do a low thing, you didn't even think one, and I still feel the same way."

In Paris, it was clear that Hadley was indeed confused. She was not trying very hard to avoid Ernest, eating breakfast every day in his favorite café, the Closerie des Lilas. He generally visited her after dinner in her hotel rooms, and they alternated between tearful reveries and bruising arguments, to the point that Hadley had to write him a letter asking that they not see each other anymore. It was hard for both of them to keep to that agreement, however. Ernest continued to visit to pick up and deliver Bumby, though he often brought a friend along, usually Archie MacLeish. Hadley's biographer notes that Ernest was "always" sending along small gifts to her apartment—toys for Bumby, and books and bottles of wine—as well as money from their bank account.

Letters from Pauline were coming every day after the first of October. "I'm really just fold[ing] days up like sheets and putting them away," she wrote Ernest in mid-month. She continued to apologize for her "stupid" letters, regularly tallied the number of days remaining in their separation, and included in almost every one the evidently talismanic statement "Ernest is perfect." While this was probably a private joke, not one of Pauline's letters was without some words of extravagant praise of her betrothed. "Darling, you are very swell—funny and 'swell,'" she wrote on October 5;

on the 6th she wrote, "Oh you are lovely and a great classic beauty. And smart and perfect." On the 17th, she wrote that like himself, his letters were perfect. In an undated letter she colorfully elaborated, "You've always been like celery, and like the fresh still cold air, and like a Viking. My dear love, you are so clear and sharp . . . and swift and sure and wise and very, very kind and altogether lovely."

This flattery became habitual. Pauline was seeking to bolster Ernest's self-confidence and see him through what had become for him a very bad time. But something more was at work here. Pauline was mounting a campaign to stand behind Ernest absolutely, to compliment him constantly and see to his every need, to read and edit his work with enthusiasm, to make him feel he was the best lover a woman could ask for, and generally to arrange his life so that, to the extent it was possible, everything would go easily for him. In this sense the refrain "Ernest is perfect" represented her efforts to make him feel that everything he thought, said, and did was correct and could not be improved upon—in short, that he *was* perfect. But despite the obvious boost to his work life and his general well-being, this uncritical adulation did not do his character any good at all.

* * *

Ernest was suffering in Paris without the woman he loved, trying to adjust to the awkward new role he must play in the lives of Hadley and their son. Especially in Pauline's absence, it was hard to give up Hadley's many attentions, their pet names, and her flattering dependency. His writing, however, was not going badly; he made final revisions on the proofs of *The Sun Also Rises,* and that fall he wrote five new short stories; he and Max Perkins would soon be talking about assembling a new short story collection.

On October 11 he traveled to Zaragoza with Archie MacLeish to see the bullfights there. He and Archie had become quite close during this period; they frequently took long bike rides together, and Ernest came to the MacLeish apartment on the avenue du Bois almost every day for a meal, making great friends of the MacLeish children, especially young Mimi. Ernest and Archie may or may not have known in advance that their visit to Zaragoza coincided with the feast day of El Pilar, or Our Lady of the Pillar, a beautiful and boisterous festival. ("Pilar" was also a code name agreed to by Pauline and Ernest for their telegraphic contact; it became their favorite girl's name.) But the fiction writer and the poet would never do well when spending protracted time together. They enjoyed the bullfights and the El Pilar festivities, and they talked about Spanish art (they saw some excellent Goya etchings), divorce, and bullfighting. One night the discussion turned to James Joyce and his influence on a generation of writers. Ernest tried to dismiss the subject, but Archie replied that he thought reading Joyce might be a benefit to Ernest's own work. "I told him to relax a bit and give Joyce credit," MacLeish later told an interviewer. At this Ernest exploded. He thought Joyce's work was overrated and very far anyway from what he was attempting. Archie was no stranger to noisy quarrels, and the battle was on. It ended with their not speaking to each other for two days—a little awkward, observed Archie, given that they shared a hotel room.

In the meantime, however, Ernest was extremely dissatisfied with his and Pauline's correspondence. Despite her unremitting praise of him, he asked for constant reassurance that she loved him. She repeated many times what was apparently the loftiest statement of love between them: "We are the same guy." They were "cockeyed crazy in love," she assured him, "cockeyed" becoming their favorite expression for the next several years. Their future children, she wrote, "will be my jewels": hers will be the realm of "kinder, küche, kirche." This last might seem somewhat odd coming from a woman with a career; while Pauline had taken a leave of absence from her job, she had not given it up. In fact, she said she might work for *Vogue* in New York after Christmas—a statement that dismayed Ernest, since they had planned to be reunited in Europe by then.

Pauline was keeping to a strict schedule of self-improvement: drinking milk to put on some needed weight, exercising vigorously and taking long walks, studying Spanish, and getting up and going to bed early. Still, she had been unsuccessful in trying to stave off depression, especially after she told her mother about her plans. Mary Pfeiffer was heartbroken, as Pauline expected, her first sympathies for Hadley and the child. Mary saw the wisdom of the hundred-day separation, but more because it gave Pauline the time and opportunity to square her actions with her faith. They agreed that the news should be kept, for the immediate future, from Pauline's father, then in Memphis.

Her mother's response fed the considerable guilt that Pauline already felt, making her doubt herself and even her future with Ernest. Following her mother's lead, she began to put Hadley first in her mind. "We must be very good to each other, and to other people," she wrote Ernest on October 25, "because we have been very, very cruel to the people we love most." She believed they should give Hadley "any amount of money settlement." She thought Hadley had been "very wise to want to wait three months for all of us to think things over." On October 30 she wrote a letter looking back at their attempt to handle the situation: "We were so cock-eyed crazy about each other, and so very scared we might lose each other—at least I was—that Hadley got locked out." In the meantime, Hadley learned that Ernest and Pauline were corresponding—which came as a surprise, as she had assumed they would not be in touch with each other during the separation. When Pauline learned of this, she took her guilt to extremes, writing Ernest that they should stop corresponding and begin anew another hundred-day separation. "If at the end Hadley says three months more, we will go three months more."

Ernest did not take any of this well. Hadley was the center of Pauline's attention, it seemed, Ernest taking a secondary place, and he worked himself into high dudgeon over this. And Pauline was doing her best to behave nobly, which stole his thunder. Midway through a long letter in November he asserted that she had broken her promise. "You see when you went to Piggott you said that you were going to tell your mother and that if she didn't like it you would leave—or that she would have to come around to it—because it was us against the world and that we had to do our own thing and that you were going to rest and not worry and get healthy and strong and above all not worry." He added sarcastically, "Well and how did all that work out?" He had come to doubt their future, and accused Pauline of deserting their relationship: "You have given yourself and your heart as a hostage to your mother too and the whole thing seems so absolutely hopeless." He knew that "this is a lousy terribly cheap self pitying letter just wallowing in bathos."

But he continued in the same manipulative vein, going on to threaten suicide. In the fall, he reminded her, he had told her he would kill himself if the situation was not "cleared up" by Christmas. And then he promised he would not think about it or do anything under any circumstances until she returned to Paris. But now, he said, she had broken her promises, and "I should think that would let me out. . . . I'd rather die now while there is still something left of the world than to go on and have every part of it flattened out and destroyed and made hollow before I die."

Letter after letter to Pauline in the fall of 1927 was about Ernest's unhappiness. He lashed out where he could, and his lash fell on Pauline, who, he felt, was not paying him enough attention in this troubled time. She was worrying about the many elements in this overwhelming change in her life, and he picked up that he was no longer her primary (or only) focus, a situation that was intolerable to him. He would try to regain the spotlight, even if it meant threatening suicide.

Meanwhile, Mary Pfeiffer had come around, Pauline said, getting used to the idea that Pauline loved Ernest above everything else. Pauline began to speak of "when" they would marry, rather than "if." Things began to look up. In Paris, in early November, Hadley left Bumby with Ernest while she went to Chartres with a girlfriend. With some needed distance, she came to see that the problem was not hers, but rather Pauline's and Ernest's, and on November 16 she wrote to Ernest telling him so. "I am *not* responsible for your future welfare," she wrote, and she said she thought it was best if they keep all talk about the divorce in letters. Unfortunately, Ernest saw Hadley before he received this letter and they had another bruising quarrel. Afterward, Ernest told her, "I think your letter like everything you have ever done is very brave and altogether unselfish and generous." He also said that he would be turning over all proceeds from *The Sun Also Rises* to her and Bumby—which, as it turned out, would be an appreciable sum. He wrote that the best luck Bumby would ever enjoy was having Hadley for a mother, and closed by saying, "[You] are the best and truest and loveliest person that I have ever known." He put a copy of the letter in the mail to Pauline.

Jinny Pfeiffer, who had acted as a go-between throughout the affair and was as well a boon companion for Ernest, immediately sent a telegram to Pauline saying the separation had been called off at Hadley's request. "We are so lucky," Pauline wrote back. For some reason, however, they would not be reunited right away. Perhaps the reasons had more to do with the slower pace of travel in those times—plans to sail on a particular ship were necessarily set far in advance—than they did with their desire to see each other. Even in his telegram Ernest wrote "SUGGEST YOU SAIL AFTER CHRIST-MAS." In any case, Pauline did not change her plans. In fact, she started talking about taking the temporary *Vogue* job in New York, which would mean she wouldn't return until February.

This threatened delay may have informed another anguished letter Ernest sent to Pauline on December 3. Admitting that he had not been doing well lately, he complained of "the horrors" during the night and "black" depression. The separation of two people in love "works almost as bad as an abortion. . . . It isn't good for the head either." If you weren't careful, he said, you'd be up all night asking God to keep you from going crazy. He settled on a single complaint: her letters had been too cut-and-dried for him, and the one written after she got the cable announcing an end to the separation was insufficiently passionate: "I love you so . . . I want a letter from you—just about loving each other and no facts bulletins nor anything timely—because it has been a terrible long time since I had a letter like that nor one that wasn't written to catch a mail . . . and what I miss worse is not having any intimacy with you—nor any feeling of us against the others."

Pauline reassured him, and told him that *Vogue* had failed to meet her salary demands in any case. She was sailing, she announced, on December 30. They had withstood the test of time.

TWELVE

The Sun Also Rises, published in October 1926, was a huge success, absorbing at least as much of Ernest's attention as his marital troubles. The critic Malcolm Cowley called his notices "hat-in-the-air reviews."

Maxwell Perkins had known Scribner's had picked a winner as soon as the manuscript came in, writing Ernest that it seemed to him "a most extraordinary performance." The first reviews were from *The New York Times* and the *New York Herald Tribune.* The *Times* reviewer found it "a truly gripping story, told in a lean, hard, athletic prose that puts more literary English to shame." At the *Herald Tribune,* Conrad Aiken wrote, "The dialogue is brilliant. If there is better dialogue being written today I do not know where to find it. It is alive with the rhythms and idioms, the pauses and suspensions and innuendoes and short-hands, of living speech." Burton Rascoe, writing for the *New York Sun,* said, "Every sentence that [Hemingway] writes is fresh and alive."

The negative reviews of *The Sun Also Rises* were generally of the sort that sold more books. The characters were degenerate and immoral, ran the most common complaint. The *Dial* reviewer, confirming Ernest's view of the journal, said they were "as shallow as the saucers in which they stack their daily emotions." The *Chicago Tribune* reviewer, in a piece Grace cut out and mailed to her son, wrote, "*The Sun Also Rises* is the kind of book that makes this reviewer at least almost plain angry, not for the obvious reason that it is about utterly degraded people, but for the reason that it shows an immense skill. . . . Ernest Hemingway can be a distinguished writer if he wishes to be. He is, even in this book, but it is a distinction hidden under a bushel of sensationalism and triviality."

Ernest responded with healthy skepticism, if his frank correspondence with Maxwell Perkins is any indication. The trend in the reviews, he said, is "pretty interesting and there seems to be a difference of opinion about it—I've always heard that was good. . . . Aiken seemed to like it. . . . Maybe that will encourage some of the other boys to like it." He was particularly interested that Edmund Wilson, in an extremely positive letter he had written to the poet John Peale Bishop, said that he thought it was the "best novel by one of my generation." In another letter Ernest said, "I imagine, now that [the critics] seem to be rowing about it that The Sun may go very well." The reviewers got under his skin, however, and he seemed to want to argue with them—sort of like shadow boxing, in fact. If they said his characters were unattractive, he told Perkins, he'd give them "the people in, say, Ulysses, The Old Testament, Judge Fielding," writing the critics seemed to like.

But the reviews gave him a moment to pause and reconsider what he had achieved with *The Sun Also Rises.* Most of the time he was mildly bemused. "It's funny to write a book that seems as tragic as that," he wrote Perkins, "and have them take it for a jazz superficial story. If you went any deeper inside they couldn't read it because they would be crying all the time." The whole fuss was making him look down the road past a short story volume and a bullfighting book he hoped to publish to his next novel. People weren't all "as hollowed out as some of The Sun generation." In fact, he said, "There is, to me anyway, very great glamour in life—and places and all sorts of things and I would like sometime to get it into stuff." *The Sun Also Rises,* he thought, had a "dull" subject, and maybe someday he would produce a book with a subject not so dull, "and try to keep all the good qualities" of the novel.

He reflected as well on the novel's epigrams, which had caused a good deal of comment among critics. The first was a quotation from Gertrude Stein "in conversation," as Hemingway put it: "You are all a lost generation." He was pleased by a *Boston Transcript* review Perkins had sent him in which the reviewer expressed some doubts that Hemingway was taking Gertrude Stein entirely seriously. The second epigram was the passage from Ecclesiastes from which the title of the novel was taken. But Ernest had originally begun the quotation with verses two and three: "Vanity is vanity, saith the preacher, vanity of vanities, all is vanity? / What profit hath a man of all his labor, which he taketh under the sun?" He wanted to "lop off" that, and include instead just verses four through seven, beginning, "One generation passeth away, and another generation cometh, but the earth abideth forever." The point of the book, he told Perkins, "was that the earth abideth forever—having a great deal of fondness and admiration for the earth and not a hell of a lot for my generation and caring little about Vanities. . . . I didn't mean the book to be a hollow or bitter satire but a damn tragedy with the earth abiding for ever as the hero." His point is well taken. The reader is not to take away from the book any real belief in the values—or, mostly, the lack of them—of his characters, or even of the narrator, Jake Barnes. Hemingway is aiming for something more: the tragedy of such valueless individuals and the randomness of the world they inhabit, symbolized perhaps by the violent but contained anarchy of the bullfight.

The Sun Also Rises was a defining text for the so-called Lost Generation, both for its contemporary readers and for those who came after. Its brittle, darkly humorous characters came apart with dramatic suddenness in Spain, a more elemental culture, where death (via the bullfight) was an immediate reality, not a joke. It was also a kind of monument to a certain kind of existential pessimism engendered by the war, along with such works as Eliot's *The Wasteland* and Pound's "Hugh Selwyn Mauberley." Moreover, it was a novel that was not meant to be likable or familiar, which did not engage readers the way they were used to being engaged, and which refused to make any of its characters noble, even its "hero," Jake Barnes. *The Sun Also Rises* can be said to have marked a milestone in the maturation or evolution of the twentieth-century American novel.

The novel's reviews, and the critics' breathless admiration—or the spirited denunciation—of its author meant that Ernest's career was launched on a decidedly upward trajectory. He was writing about a new, amoral world and he was using language in such a way as to be revolutionary. He also began to become a legend, already with an element of machismo in the mix. Smith College girls were said to be adopting the attitudes of Lady Brett Ashley, and "hundreds of bright young men from the Middle West," said Malcolm Cowley, were making their way down city streets shadow boxing, as Hemingway was said to do, or waving imaginary red capes at imaginary charging bulls. Dorothy Parker, a new friend of Ernest's, said, "There was a time when you could go nowhere without hearing of *The Sun Also Rises*." The critic Richmond Barrett said that the American young "learned [*The Sun Also Rises*] by heart, deserting their families and running away from college, and immediately took ship to Paris to be the disciples of the new faith under the awnings of the Dôme and the Rotonde."

In Paris, meanwhile, Montparnassians were having a good time figuring out who was who in the novel, though there weren't any real mysteries. Scribner's had Ernest disguise some real people's names even further, so that, for instance, the expatriate writer Glenway Wescott, initially called Roger Prescott, became Roger Prentiss. Even though he was given the name Braddocks in the novel, everyone recognized Ford Madox Ford. Ernest told Scott, "There is a story around that I had gone to switzerland to avoid being shot by demented characters out of my books." He joked that he had learned Harold Loeb was after him with a gun. Ernest said that he had spread the word that he would be at the Lipp from two to four on Saturday so that Loeb or any other aggrieved party could meet him there at the time. Kitty Cannell, unbothered by her portrait as Frances Clyne, commented, "I'm really tougher than the big he man and I can stick up for myself," but she admitted she was angry about Loeb's portrayal as Robert Cohn. And Duff, who had since been abandoned by Pat Guthrie and had spirited her child out of England, told Ernest, "The only thing was she never had slept with the bloody bullfighter," according to a letter Ernest wrote Scott.

In the midst of this complex of circumstances, Ernest spent the first two and a half months of 1927, after her arrival in Europe on January 8, in Gstaad with Pauline, with Jinny along, they liked to say, as a chaperone. In March, he had brought Bumby up for a ten-day visit. On his return to Paris, he stayed just long enough to go before a judge with Hadley to finalize his divorce. He left France almost immediately for a trip to Italy with his old newspaper friend Guy Hickok in Guy's decrepit Ford. Ernest hoped, among other things, to find Don Giuseppe Bianchi, the priest who had given him extreme unction in 1918. (According to Catholic procedure, usually this rite was preceded by a contingent "emergency" baptism if the dying person was not Catholic, and Ernest needed to be Catholic to marry Pauline.) Leaving on March 15, they reached Rapallo on the 18th, where they stayed with Ezra and Dorothy Pound, and went from there to Pisa, Rimini, Bologna, Parma, and Genoa, a trip of over 1,800 miles. Along the way they took grim note of the ugly realities of life under Fascism. Ernest and Guy fought and did not speak to each other for two days, and when the car broke down outside Paris on the return leg, Pauline wryly called their trip the "Italian tour for the promotion of masculine society," noting that in future, "I'm very sure your wife is going to be opposed to [such trips]."

There is no evidence that Ernest returned with a baptismal certificate (perhaps swearing to his baptism sufficed), but plans for the wedding proceeded apace. Meanwhile, Pauline found them a luxurious apartment at 6, rue Férou next to St. Sulpice and near the Luxembourg Gardens. Though it only cost about 9,000 francs a year, or about $30 a month, they had to pay a large amount up front and a subletting fee to the tenant, Ruth Goldbeck, an American woman who, with her husband, the Greenwich Village–based portrait painter Walter Goldbeck, had recently joined the expatriate community in Paris; the Goldbecks were now living on the Riviera and agreed to rent to the couple. Gus Pfeiffer, Pauline's magnanimous rich uncle, was in town for the month of April to open a new Richard Hudnut branch, and he gladly stepped in to provide the cash to pay the Goldbecks. (Ernest later claimed Gus was sent to inspect the groom-to-be, said to be a drunk and a man with low associates: Gus cabled the family, Ernest said, that Pauline could marry "no better and finer citizen" after meeting with Ernest for just ten minutes.)

Ernest and Pauline were to be married in a civil as well as a religious ceremony. The archbishop of Paris granted dispensation for the annulment and marriage on April 25, and the banns were published on May 1. They married in the mayor's office on May 10 and went on to the St. Honoré church for the religious ceremony. Jinny Pfeiffer and Mike Ward, Ernest's banker, were the maid of honor and best man. Pauline and Ernest's wedding picture shows a very attractive and intelligent-looking couple. Both are looking off-camera, wearing slight smiles. Pauline's dark hair, parted on the side, is cut in boyish fashion but fuller on the top; she is wearing a modest strand of pearls and looks pert, but definitely not prim. Ernest is wearing a tweed three-piece suit and knit tie; he has a full mustache and his dark hair gleams. His face is a little fuller than usual, but he seems to be slim—unlike some other photos of this time in which he looks on the heavy side, his face a bit jowly. His eyes are amused. After the ceremony, Archibald and Ada MacLeish gave the couple a luncheon, though, as Ada later told Carlos Baker, they did not attend the ceremony because they did not approve of an annulment that declared his marriage to Hadley null and void. "To see this farce being solemnized by the Catholic Church was more than we could take," Ada commented. Many friends, like the Murphys, were glad the situation was eased. "It certainly is an immense relief to everyone who loves Ernest (like us)," Sara Murphy wrote to Pauline, "to think he is out of a lot of woods which must have been at least partly destructive, & a 100% cause of general confusion at best." Sara's affection for Pauline was unspoken. Gerald, too, wrote Ernest around this time, "Best to 'P the Pifer.' She looks finely. Is good chicken. And I'd like to see her get along."

After the wedding, Ernest and Pauline took a train to Le Grau-du-Roi, a tiny fishing town in the Camargue in the south of France, near Arles and the ancient walled town of Aigues-Mortes. They rode bikes and sunned, turning deeply tan. Ernest would much later use the ancient town and the fishing village as a setting for his *Garden of Eden,* in which Catherine and David obsess about looking alike and otherwise play with gender roles. Legend has it that one day Pauline and Ernest, hearing word of a nearby Gypsy festival, stained their faces with berries to disguise themselves as Gypsies and joined in the festival, a romantic-sounding but unlikely story.

The news about Ernest and Hadley and his remarriage to Pauline was not well received back in Oak Park. To Grace and Ed Hemingway, divorce did not exist; there is no evidence of any in their extended family before Ernest's in 1927. (Though if there had been any, it would not have been mentioned.) It was a year in which open discord broke out among the Hemingways. Ernest's marital trouble was only part of it.

Grace and Ed's son was becoming a public figure, and one consequence was that he could not keep his private life from Oak Park's attention. As far as Paris news went, little escaped notice in the Oak Park household. The Hemingways were privy to all manner of details about their son's private life, relatives and neighbors having all along made reports of Ernest in Paris.

Throughout this period, in fact, Ernest's feelings about his family were changing. He remained in close touch with them throughout his life—in direct contradiction to his remarks to other people on the subject, including reporters and biographers. In his eyes, his father could do no wrong, even when Ed registered disapproval of Ernest's actions or his writing with words that rivaled Grace's in old-fashioned moralizing. Remarkably, though, in the 1920s Ernest seems to have cared equally about his mother's reactions. He may have sneered at what he called Grace's hypocrisies to others and to her face, but he also was in communication with his mother steadily throughout his life.

As adolescents, the Hemingway children, while usually as secretive as most teenagers, often sought to include their parents in their doings. Ernest, for instance, sent his buddies from the war to visit his family in Oak Park when he was not there—even more remarkably, these friends did so, often forming independent relationships with Grace and Ed, as Ted Brumback and Bill Horne did. The Hemingways hosted a Thanksgiving dinner while Ernest was away in the war—a symbolic empty place at the table marking his absence—at which his Kansas City friends Howell Jenkins and Charlie Hopkins joined them; the Oak Park house had been the scene for elaborate parties the family gave for Ernest's friends from Chicago's Italian community.

Grace and Ed continued to meet Ernest's friends while he was in Paris in the early 1920s, sometimes to his discomfiture. Not always, however: when Don Stewart was to pass through Detroit in 1925, at Ernest's suggestion Don looked up and had lunch with his sister Marcelline, now living in Detroit with her husband. In 1927, Ernest's friend the novelist Louis Bromfield while in Chicago spoke at the Nineteenth Century Club, of which Grace was an enthusiastic member. She introduced herself to Bromfield after his lecture, asking if he didn't know her son. "I should think I do," he answered. "He's one of my best friends." And when Ford Madox Ford was in Chicago in January 1927, Ed noticed in the newspapers that Ford was staying at the Blackstone Hotel and invited him to dinner in Oak Park. Afterward, Ed Hemingway reported to his son, "Mother was so pleased with the Englishman."

This persistent closeness marked Ernest's relations with his siblings as well. His sisters and his brother left behind voluminous correspondence with their brother after their deaths. Ernest kept up with their marriages and children, their relationships with other siblings and their mother, and their often rocky finances. Though he sometimes did his share of kicking and screaming about it—he never ceased to plead poverty, even when his best-selling books sold to the movies—Ernest steadily loaned his sisters and brother money when they needed it, and was—intermittently—spontaneously generous. With Ursula, his favorite sister, Ernest was particularly confidential and frank in his correspondence. He developed especially close relationships with the youngest children, Carol and Leicester, assuming a parental role—often extremely disapproving and arbitrarily strict, almost comically replicating the behavior of his own parents. Remarkably, in the 1920s he was even close to the sister he would come to dislike the most, Marcelline, often writing to her and expressing interest in her life as he did with the other siblings, until his father's death in 1928. Even then they continued to correspond, though letters on both sides were huffy and judgmental. In 1927 and 1928, however, of all his sisters, Ernest was closest to Sunny. It was to her he would confide his marriage to Pauline, considerably before their parents knew, swearing her to secrecy.

The years 1926 and 1927 were difficult years for the family. Events such as Ernest's divorce from Hadley and remarriage to Pauline meant major family upheavals, almost as much as had openly rebellious behavior in his childhood and adolescence. This is hardly unusual, but what is striking is Ernest's flat denial that he cared what his family had to say about anything. He was frequently defensive, for instance, about his drinking, rumors of which reached his family an ocean away (such rumors arising, as Ernest rightly told them, about any public figure who drank). The same was true with his writing. Though he affected not to care about Ed's and Grace's reactions, both to others and to his parents themselves, their approval preoccupied him whenever one of his stories or books appeared.

Ernest was gaining greater public notoriety, as he divorced and remarried, and as he published a novel, *The Sun Also Rises,* full of frank and even obscene language and about characters whom readers like Ed and Grace would have found immoral and even degenerate. Reactions to Ernest's split with Hadley reverberated for over a year, long after he had married Pauline—probably because he gave the family so little information. Characteristically defensive in the face of criticism or expected criticism, he obfuscated and even denied rumors and published reports, and he did not tell them directly about his divorce until after his remarriage. His parents kept the issue alive in their letters long after the events had played out.

Reports about troubles in his marriage with Hadley made their way to Oak Park by December 1926, when Grace wrote to her son, "We have heard rumors of the cooling off of affections between you and Hadley," noting that this, combined with the fact that "you have not mentioned her in any recent letter," made her "worry a little concerning your happiness." Ed wrote, in a letter about the same time, "The gossip is about a serious domestic trouble" between Ernest and Hadley. He asked Ernest to write him right away "so I can deny the awful rumors that you and Hadley have had a break." Five days later, in a letter addressed to Ernest, Hadley, and Bumby, he wrote, "I am sure all the gossip is bunk"; few letters after this did not express this sentiment.

Grace seems to have been quicker to accept the situation than was her husband. In February 1927, she wrote that she was sorry to hear Ernest's marriage had gone "on the rocks," but, she said provocatively, "Most marriages ought to. I hold very modern and heretical views on marriage—but keep them under my hat." It is not clear why she chose to reveal her "very modern" thoughts to her son at this juncture, especially since the letters before and after it are written in high Victorian dudgeon.

By then newspapers were carrying the story of their son's marital problems, and clippings were being forwarded to Ed and Grace. On March 6 Ed wrote that he had seen articles from the *Detroit Free Press* (no doubt forwarded by Marcelline) and upstate Michigan's *Boyne City Citizen* saying that Hadley had been granted a divorce; later that month the *Chicago Tribune* carried such a story.

"Too bad!" said Ed. "Please tell me the truth."

Ernest was doing his best *not* to. As early as May 1925 Ernest cryptically wrote that he and Hadley would be spending the next winter in Piggott, Arkansas—a letter written when he had great hopes for including Pauline in his family's life. Then, not a word indicating any new developments for over a year, until December 1, 1926, when he wrote that they should not worry about Bumby's health as the boy was *not* living in a studio. (Ernest was living in Gerald Murphy's studio at the time, but he had not previously mentioned that to his parents, as it would indicate that he and Hadley were separated.) His son, he said, was living "in a comfortable, light, well heated apartment on the sixth floor with a lovely view and all modern comforts." He did not say that the apartment was Hadley's. In early February he acknowledged, "Hadley and I have not been living in the same house for some time," adding, nonchalantly, "by now Hadley may have divorced me." They remained close, he told his mother, and informed her that the proceeds of *The Sun Also Rises* were all going to Hadley.

Even then, however, Ernest said not one word about his plans to marry. Divorce was one thing, and divorce for cause was quite another. Grace and Ed Hemingway did not know the full story for another six months, by which time their son had married Pauline. Even more remarkably, on a trip to the U.S. made after Ernest married Pauline, Hadley visited Oak Park to introduce the Hemingways to their grandson—and even after her visit they did not know how things stood. In August, when Hadley had long since left, Ed Hemingway wrote his son at length:

> I hope you may [illegible] yourself and start aright to regain your wife soon. We are grieved and feel disgraced in a way you know not. . . . I wish all the "Love Pirates" were in Hell. Our family has never had such an incident before and trust you may still make your get-away from that individual who split your home. Oh Ernest how could you leave Hadley and Bumby? . . . Put on the armor of God and shun Evil companions. . . . Your mother and I have been heartbroken over your conduct.

The letter is proof that over the course of her visit Hadley did not tell Ed and Grace of Ernest's marriage to Pauline (perhaps reasoning that it was not her problem), for Ed closes the letter to Ernest, "Are you again married and to who?"

In a mostly honest letter written to his father in September 1927, Ernest attempted to sort this all out, admitting that it was time he come clean with his parents. He said that he and Hadley had split up but not because he deserted her or was committing adultery with anyone—though it was entirely his fault and was a private matter, he said. He alluded to his father's "Love Pirates" letter, saying that Ed had never had the misfortune of loving two women at once. The year had been a "tragedy" for him. Somewhat strangely, he said Hadley was the one who wanted the divorce (which may have technically been true, but did not reflect the emotional reality of the situation), and that she would have taken him back if he had wanted (perhaps a point of pride). He averred that he had never stopped loving Hadley and Bumby, but added valiantly, "I will never stop loving Pauline Pfeiffer to whom I am married." (It was the first time he told his parents his new wife's name.) He spoke as well of the difficulty of being somewhat in the public eye—a condition he had ostentatiously complained of much earlier, but that had genuinely started to bother him by this time.

The tone of this letter leaves no doubt that Ernest was concerned for his father's well-being. Ed was in fact deteriorating physically and mentally, on a downward spiral that would culminate in his suicide in December 1928. It is possible that the vehemence of the "Love Pirates" letter, not to mention his willful blindness in general about his son's marital situation, were early indications that Ed was growing mentally unbalanced. He had recently started to suffer from painful angina pectoris, and in 1927 would learn he was a diabetic. Ed's father, old Anson Hemingway, died in the fall of 1926, after which Ed became, according to his wife, "very depressed."

That fall, Ed and Grace were trying hard to sell their house—and, after Anson's death, to sell his as well. For two years now they had been making frequent trips to Florida, hoping to relocate there. The Florida land boom of the 1920s was reaching its peak—the *Miami Herald* was said to be the heaviest newspaper in the country, so thick was its real estate section—when Ed and Grace invested in land there, along with so many other hopeful middle-class Americans. As in most real estate bubbles, land was being valued not by its real worth but by the existence of buyers for it. Property was changing hands as many as ten times in a day. The boom saw its slow death begin in January 1926 when a freighter capsized and sank off the coast of Florida, effectively blocking Miami harbor for over a month and making it impossible for building supplies to get through to South Florida. Land stopped going up in value, and then, with the hurricane of September 1926, went downhill fast. It is not clear how much land Ed and Grace had bought, though one letter refers to five lots and another to property in Gulfport.

Whether Ernest's parents intended to build down south is not clear, but their letters to each other in brief separations over those two years were full of talk about Florida. Ed had received a license to practice medicine there in 1925, so they were not thinking of retirement, exactly—just an easier life in a warmer clime. Added to Ed Hemingway's depression in 1927 was his frustration at not being able to find a buyer for the Oak Park house, and his dismay as his Florida investments began to drop in value as the boom turned to bust.

Ernest's marital problems were another cross to bear, as was his new novel, *The Sun Also Rises,* which was not welcomed by the Oak Park household. From the first, Grace disapproved in the strongest possible terms. The reviews all seemed to be full of praise for his "terse style" and "success in word-painting," she wrote.

> But the decent ones regret that you should use such great gifts in so degraded a strata of humanity. . . . What is the matter? Have you ceased to be interested in loyalty, nobility, honor and fineness of life—Why life is more wonderful and beautiful. . . . If you are going through domestic disillusionment or drink has got you—throw off the shackles of these conditions and rise to be the man and the writer God meant you to be.

Every page of the novel, she said, "fills me with a sick loathing." In contrast, Ernest's father wrote him a letter at the end of December in which he said he was "so glad" of Ernest's success; their pastor, William Barton, who apparently kept up with the reviews, had told Ed Hemingway that Ernest's " 'technique' was wonderful & you had it all over the rest of modern writers."

Another piece of news from Oak Park, Grace's very recent discovery of another artistic calling, painting, had an influence on her response to Ernest's activities. When her voice finally gave out in her early fifties, Grace started painting, first copying works in the Chicago Art Institute, taking a course from an instructor there, and then producing canvases of her own, usually landscapes, which she signed Hall Hemingway. She was exceedingly proud of her work, winning several local prizes and asking $250 for a painting. In 1927 and 1928 she was very eager to show her work in Paris, and, she hoped, at the Paris Salon, or, failing that, "even a less important show." Grace was seeking Ernest's advice and help, then, at the same time that she was passing judgment on his writing and his marital life.

In a letter dated soon after she wrote to him of the "sick loathing" she had felt on reading his work, she included a flyer announcing the fourth annual exhibit of the Chicago Society of Artists, which included paintings of Grace Hall Hemingway. In the same letter she mentioned that she had read "The Undefeated" and that she had seen "The Killers" in *Scribner's Magazine*. "It's well written," she added. In fact, this letter inaugurated a new tolerance emanating from Oak Park. From this point on, Grace had very little to say about Ernest's work. Though she would never admit as much, she may have been afraid that to comment would mean losing him entirely.

In the September 1927 letter to his father finally confirming his marriage to Pauline (three months after the fact), Ernest stated plainly that he was sorry his father didn't like his writing. "I *know* that I am not disgracing you in my writing but rather doing something that some day you will be proud of." He said that his work meant more to him than anything else, writing, with some emotion, "You cannot know how it makes me feel" for his mother to be ashamed of him—perhaps the only explicit acknowledgment Ernest ever made that his mother's approval was important to him. He hoped that one day he, his father, and Bumby could go fishing together.

* * *

Ernest and Pauline returned to their apartment on the rue Férou for only a few weeks before they were off for the summer to Spain. They went to Pamplona as usual—one of very few times Ernest went without a crowd—and then on to see bullfights in Madrid, Valencia, San Sebastián, La Coruña, and Palencia, also spending over a week in the Catholic pilgrimage town Santiago de Compostela. In September they proceeded to Hendaye, just over the French border, where they spent two weeks at the beach.

The Hemingways were back in Paris when Ernest's short story collection, *Men Without Women,* was published on October 14. He had had almost enough stories for a volume to come out the previous spring, but both he and Max Perkins thought publication then might interfere with continuing sales of *The Sun Also Rises.* That book had sold 9,350 copies in 1926 alone, and sales continued strong in 1927, by the end of the year reaching a total of 18,530; it was also to come out in England from Jonathan Cape with the title *Fiesta.* Most of the stories in *Men Without Women* had been published before, but the most widely circulated magazines they had appeared in were *The Atlantic Monthly* ("Fifty Grand") and *Scribner's Magazine* ("In Another Country" and "Now I Lay Me"). The collection was looking skimpy for a while, but by July Ernest had added "A Banal Story," "Che Ti Dice La Patria" (really notes on Italy from his recent trip with Guy Hickok), and "Hills Like White Elephants." In determining the order in which the stories would appear, Perkins wanted to lead with the bullfight story, "The Undefeated"; he also decided on an illustration of a bull for the cover, hoping to make the connection with *The Sun Also Rises,* the novel that had introduced so many readers to bullfighting. Ernest originally dedicated the book to Jinny Pfeiffer, who had been such a good companion during his hundred-day separation from Pauline, but he realized that this might be deemed inappropriate on account of the title, and he dedicated it to his friend Evan Shipman instead. (It is not clear why he did not consider dedicating it to Pauline.)

The reviews of *Men Without Women* were decidedly mixed, yet they are of interest because the critics took the time to assess Hemingway's career thus far, usually with perspicacity. The first major notice was by Virginia Woolf in the *New York Herald Tribune Books*. Max warned Ernest about it, calling it an "enraging" review because it appeared a week too early, when he had explicitly asked the newspapers not to run a review before the publication date. But their editors all being women, Max said, their "promises [were] worthless." Max also complained because the reviewer was Virginia Woolf, who spent a lot of time talking about the function of criticism "instead of functioning as a critic," as Max neatly put it.

In a letter to Max, Ernest professed to be "irritated" with Woolf's review. First, he complained, she was a member of the Bloomsbury group, who were all over forty (Woolf was actually thirty-nine) and only liked others in their group. Secondly, he was bothered that she pointed out a flaw in the wording of the book description used in all its advertising: the stories were said in the ads to be of worlds in which "the softening feminine influence is absent—either through training, discipline, death, or situation." Woolf countered, "Whether we are to understand by this that women are incapable of training, discipline, death, or situation, we do not know." She criticized the book's title in a similar vein: "Tell a man that this is a woman's book, or a woman that this is a man's, and you have brought into play sympathies and antipathies which have nothing to do with art. The greatest writers lay no stress upon sex one way or the other." Beyond this, she complained that the characters were not fully realized, and the stories were marked by an overreliance on dialogue. But in the closing paragraph she called Hemingway courageous, candid, highly skilled. He showed "moments of bare and nervous beauty," but he was "self-consciously virile." She felt his talent has "contracted rather than expanded" in these stories, which were "a little dry and sterile" compared to *The Sun Also Rises*. "The deliberate twisting of the blurb was what angered me," Ernest told Max. Even though Scribner's advertising department had made up the offending description, it was attached to *his* book, and it was laughably wrong. But he could not forgive Woolf for pointing it out: "I would have enjoyed taking the clothes off Virginia Woolf this noon," he declared, "permitting her to walk down the Avenue de l'Opera."

Ernest asked Max if he'd mind having an assistant collect the reviews and send them to him at Christmastime, when he and Pauline would once again be skiing at Gstaad. "I'm working hard and the damned things are irritating and make you self-conscious." Some notices were downright infuriating. Joseph Wood Krutch complained, "In his hands the subject matter of literature becomes sordid little catastrophes in the lives of very vulgar people." Lee Wilson Dodd's review in *The Saturday Review of Literature* was titled "Simple Annals of the Callous," and observed that Hemingway was neither Shakespeare nor Tolstoy. The characters in the stories "are all very much alike."

But Ernest missed some good notices in telling Max to hold all the notices that appeared before Christmas—that is, thoughtful responses from intelligent critics who were beginning to see past the relative merits and demerits of individual works to Ernest's larger literary significance. In England, Cyril Connolly, writing for *The New Statesman,* wrote straight off, "With Mr. Hemingway, we at once enter the front line of modern literary warfare." Connolly went on to make a fairly obscure comparison to Gertrude Stein but concluded that Hemingway "remains easily the ablest of the wild band of Americans in Europe." He sensibly thought that comparisons to Joyce were meaningless, and that at present Hemingway was "more of a dark horse than a white hope."

Like some other reviewers, Connolly was interested in how Hemingway's career was unfolding. Edmund Wilson, for instance, wrote a long review in *The New Republic* in which he discussed Hemingway's talent as it emerged through *In Our Time* and *The Sun Also Rises,* and made some interesting statements about Ernest's worldview and the manner in which his stories revealed it. He was, like Connolly, a little apprehensive about a sentimentality he saw lurking in Hemingway's work (Connolly had noted the book's "ferocious virility," to which a "strong, silent sentimentality" clung). But Wilson went a little deeper. Hemingway's "drama almost always turns on some principle of courage, of pity, of honor—in short, of sportsmanship, in its largest human sense which he is able to bring to light in them." He went on to say, "His point of view, his state of mind, is a curious one . . . he seems so broken in to the human agonies, and, though even against his will, so impassively, so hopelessly, resigned to them, that the only protest, is, as it were, the grin and the curse of the sportsman who loses the game." But Wilson also caught how deeply engaged the writer was in his work, so engaged that he transmuted his characters and his landscape into a new, modern kind of art.

Men Without Women contains some of Ernest's very finest short stories: "In Another Country," "Hills like White Elephants," "The Killers," "The Undefeated," and "Now I Lay Me." "The Undefeated" fixes the bullfight as an essential element of Spanish culture (far more powerfully than the rambling and sometimes even inane *Death in the Afternoon* would do). "Hills like White Elephants" nakedly lays out a relationship of extraordinary complexity in a story that is pared down to its absolute essentials. "Fifty Grand," whether it is or is not the first example of American hard-boiled crime fiction, gives that whole genre a reason to exist. The autobiographical hero of "Now I Lay Me," one of Hemingway's most understated but powerful statements about the aftereffects of war, has a profound understanding of his damaged psyche and how to compensate for it even as he knows it is beyond repair. Yet some stories—"Che Ti Dice La Patria," "Banal Story," and the playlet "Today Is Friday"—give the impression of having been phoned in, as it were, striking an attitude but little more. While there are few "story collections" that are as beautifully stitched together as *In Our Time* (if that can be called a story collection), *Men Without Women* does not achieve the unity of the earlier book. Like many fiction writers, Ernest was somehow thinking through his novels while writing his short stories. (His next novel, *A Farewell to Arms,* began as a short story.)

Men Without Women also got a glowing review from Dorothy Parker. She observed what was happening to Ernest, how he was becoming a legend, fairly uncritically. With *The Sun Also Rises,* she wrote, he "was praised, adored, analyzed, best-sold, argued about, banned in Boston; all the trimmings were accorded him." She found *Men Without Women* "a truly magnificent work," though conceding the stories were "sad and terrible." She insightfully called "Hills like White Elephants," a slice of the life of a man and a woman and their relationship in which the man is trying to convince the woman to have an abortion, "delicate and tragic." She concluded, "His is, as any reader knows, a dangerous influence. The simple things he does look so easy to do. But look at the boys who try to do it."

The Algonquin humorist had a decided soft spot for Ernest. She had first met him when she and Robert Benchley crossed the Atlantic on the *Roosevelt* with him in February 1926, after Ernest had gone to New York to straighten out his publishing life after *In Our Time.* They had plenty of time to get to know each other, and Parker had met him again that November in Paris, when she was on her way home from Spain. "I was touched with your sweetness and sympathy," she said, and looking forward to reading the books he had given her on the crossing. Ernest did not feel the same way. Dorothy had told him details about a late-stage abortion she had recently undergone, about attempting suicide, and about some other recent bad luck in her life. What he was most offended by, or what his fury focused on, was her dislike of Spain. He genuinely loved Spain—not just the bullfighting but the warm people, the slow pace, the beautiful mountains—all of it. He seems to have taken her dislike personally.

Ernest wrote a long, cruel poem about Parker, not published until both were dead, called "To a Tragic Poetess," revealing the personal details she had evidently related during their most recent meeting. He referred to the dead fetus, noted that she had all too conveniently failed in her suicide attempts, and mocked her failures with men. He was pointedly mean about her being Jewish, referring to "the Jewish cheeks of your plump ass." "To a Tragic Poetess" is eighty-two lines long, and what has been previously quoted from it in Hemingway biographies are selections from the especially vituperative first forty lines. The second half of the poem consists of insults piled on Parker and others who, out of ignorance about it, do not appreciate Spain (inevitably, bullfighting comes up). Perhaps Parker said something to Ernest that suggested she had acted like a typical ugly American while in the country, passing too swift judgments on whole countries or peoples. But this was, as the existence of the stereotype shows, a common response among Americans abroad. F. Scott Fitzgerald, for instance, summarily dismissed all of Italy, and he didn't think much of France, either—until he came to love it. At any rate, Parker's reaction to Spain was a very small failing on which to hang such a vituperative piece of work.

Nothing quite explains Ernest's fury. It is hard to understand why he would bother composing such a long poem to make his point—whatever that point might have been. That seems to have been Pauline's reaction. Ernest had sent her the poem during their hundred-day separation, and Pauline, whose critical judgment won out over her partisanship, told him, "I don't like the Dotty poem too much Ernest." It was overkill, she said, "like ordering a lot of clothes for an elephant and putting them on a mouse." It is not clear who Ernest thought the audience of the poem to be; he cannot have hoped to publish it. Apparently he wanted to circulate it privately. Nothing explains, either, his motivations in reading the poem before a 1926 gathering at the MacLeishes', a crowd that included Don Stewart and his wife, close friends of Parker's. No doubt he thought the poem was funny. But the Stewarts ever after kept their distance from him. Ada and Archie MacLeish remained friends—but only against their better judgment—after what must have been a very uncomfortable evening.

THIRTEEN

By the time Ernest and Pauline arrived in Switzerland for a couple of months of skiing, Ernest had written fifty thousand words of a new novel, or about two hundred typescript pages. Despite his progress, it was a nonstarter. The novel opened with a train trip from northern Michigan to Chicago and on to New York. The protagonist is the fourteen-year-old Jimmy Crane, in a later version Jimmy House, and at one point Jimmy Breen. Jimmy is traveling through the postwar Midwest with his father, a soldier of fortune who has seen twelve revolutions and is headed to Europe to join another. Father and son stop briefly in Chicago, where they visit an Italian old man (evidently a mafioso), who gives Jimmy's father a fake passport. The novel details all the advice the father gives the son—providing him with information that he should already know, such as the facts about masturbation, and that his mother lives in Paris. Crane Sr. gives Jimmy his opinions on books and writers (lots of them are finished before they are thirty and by forty-five almost all of them are) and, when they get to New York (Hemingway never got them onto a ship to Europe), his observations on how to detect a homosexual—a subject that becomes a bit of an obsession in the manuscript. But all the action is filtered through Jimmy; at the outset Ernest found using the third person liberating, but a fourteen-year-old's point of view is still fairly limited. The novel was too talky, the characters did not engage him, and the story never really got off the ground. He had been trying to create a fictional world far removed from the expatriate set of *The Sun Also Rises,* which didn't interest him anymore. Indications were that he was reaching toward the autobiographical. But the imaginative landscape of the fledgling novel simply did not engage him. By the time Ernest, Pauline, and Jinny were ready to leave Gstaad in March 1928 Hemingway had abandoned it.

En route to Gstaad for skiing with the MacLeishes, Pauline, Ernest, Jinny, and Bumby stopped in Montreux, where, in their hotel room in the middle of the night, Ernest went to lift Bumby onto the pot; Bumby accidentally stuck his finger in Ernest's right eye, which Ernest said was his remaining good eye. A fingernail cut into his cornea, and he had to spend several days lying down in the dark. By this time Pauline knew she was pregnant, and like Hadley she wanted the baby born in America. Ernest had been scheduled to go to the United States with Hadley and Bumby until romantic events intervened, and he was eager to get there. He and Pauline booked ahead for a trip in March.

In mid-January Ernest complained that his eye injury had robbed him of all but three days of skiing since he had arrived at Gstaad. So when Pauline, Jinny, and Bumby returned to Paris on February 1, he stayed on for a skiing trip to Lenk and Adelboden, going back to Paris on February 12. Soon after, Ernest had a bloody 2 a.m. accident in the apartment bathroom caused by his confusion of the flush chain with the skylight chain; the skylight fell, the glass opening a nasty cut on his forehead. After trying to stop the bleeding, and unsure of the next course of action when it didn't stop, Pauline called Archie MacLeish, with whom they'd had dinner earlier that evening; Archie took him to the American hospital in Neuilly, where the wound was clumsily sewn up with nine stitches. In the aftermath, Ernest developed an ugly, frown-shaped, purple scar that was with him for the rest of his life, at first marring his good looks, later adding character to his face—but always visible. Shortly after, Hadley's old friend Helen Breaker, now a photographer, took a photo of Ernest to be used in publicity for his next book; Max told Ernest that Scribner's had to remove the scar, and Ernest assured him that it was fine to remove it, that it had bothered Breaker as well. This photograph established a pattern: in this and subsequent photos, his scar was usually airbrushed out.

Wherever Pauline went, it seemed, Jinny went too. They had been nearly inseparable since coming to Europe in 1924, despite the fact that Jinny was seven years younger. Ernest had long been an admirer of Jinny's, though he learned very quickly after meeting her that she preferred women. Pauline's biographer believes that Ernest and Jinny had a sexual relationship shortly after meeting and perhaps intermittently thereafter. It is true that Ernest was attracted to Jinny, but there was not necessarily any sexual spark; Ernest just liked lesbians, perhaps remembering his mother's inclinations and her relationship with Ruth Arnold. He was interested in Sylvia Beach's relationship with Adrienne Monnier and was of course good friends with Stein and Toklas; Janet Flanner was a friend as well. Through Jinny he met other lesbians, among them Clara Dunn (one of Jinny's early girlfriends), Djuna Barnes, and the bisexual Emily Coleman. Rose Marie Burwell, one of the preeminent critics of Hemingway's work, has written that there was significant evidence that "Hemingway was intrigued by the freedom that lesbians had achieved in their lives during the Paris years." And those around Jinny may have picked up on the stereotype of lesbian mannishness when they adopted androgynous terminology. Both Pauline and Ernest addressed women or women and men together as "you men"; when Dos Passos married Katy Smith, Ernest addressed the couple this way. Pauline wrote letters to Hadley and Ernest addressing them as "men." "We are the same guy," was a habitual way to say one was in love in this circle; the expression made its way into Hemingway's fiction as well. In no reductive way does this indicate anything about sexual preference, though there is no question it reflected Ernest's long ambivalence about and fascination with gender roles and sexuality, and a lifelong tendency toward androgyny. This tendency, which had its beginnings in his very early childhood twinning with Marcelline, in turn was one of the main reasons Ernest was so interested in lesbians. He told Archie MacLeish in the 1930s that he had met three lesbians in his life who impressed him with their thought processes: Stein, Janet Flanner, and the Italian musician Renata Borgatti.

Pauline's closeness to Jinny was of a piece with her constant devotion to her family. The Pfeiffers were especially close. Pauline was eager to return to Piggott, perhaps even more so now that she was pregnant. The Pfeiffers were very witty people and poked fun at Piggott, Arkansas—even the name was funny. But Pauline and Jinny both returned at least once a year, their brother Karl eventually building a house next door to their parents' and moving in with his wife, Matilda. It was understood that Pauline would visit the family soon and often in 1928, especially just before and after the baby was born in June. Ernest went along with the Piggott imperative with relatively little fuss, though he did complain to Max Perkins that it was a "christ offal"—Pauline's spelling—place, especially in the spring and summer months. It helped that the hunting—mostly for quail and duck—was excellent.

Ernest formed a special bond with Mary Pfeiffer, who shared his ironical sense of humor and his love for a cocktail after a long day. Paul was a little more distant—or perhaps just seemed so, busy with his land, his investments, his bank. The Pfeiffers were rich, and it would only be a slight exaggeration to say they owned the town of Piggott. Pauline had an income of about $6,000 and benefited in other ways from the Pfeiffer largesse. Gus, Paul Pfeiffer's brother, treated his nieces and nephew with great generosity, in large part because he and his wife, Louise, had lost a two-month-old son and had no more children. Back in Iowa, the Pfeiffers' home before St. Louis, Gus and Paul had moved their families into what was known as a mother-in-law house, a residence separated into two identical halves—another indication of the close-knit quality of the Pfeiffer clan. Uncle Gus would become a huge champion of Ernest's, and Ernest in turn quickly got on an intimate footing with Gus, whom he liked very much.

If it was understood that their ultimate destination in the U.S. was to be Piggott, the Hemingways were very excited about their first stop, Key West, the last in the long line of islands off Florida's southernmost tip, which Dos Passos had told them was like "something seen in a dream." They sailed for Havana from La Rochelle in southwest France on a ship called the *Orita,* of the U.K.'s Pacific Stream Navigation Company. It was a dreadful ship, the cabins extremely cramped. Out of Havana, they took the afternoon ferry to Key West, where they were to pick up a brand-new Model A Ford that Gus Pfeiffer had bought for them. When they docked at the pier, they found no trace of the car. Calling the Ford dealership on Simonton Street they learned that its shipment from Miami had been delayed a week; the Ford dealership found them an apartment in the same building, in the rear of the second floor. Pauline and Ernest set out to see what Dos had meant when he called the town "like no other place in Florida." With its palm-tree-shaded streets, most with girls' names, and its white frame Conch-style houses, all with generous porches, the town "had a faintly New England look," according to Dos. In other sections, pastel-colored houses bedecked with gingerbread hid behind bougainvillea, oleander, and jacaranda blossoms; the town was girded by the bright blue-green waters of the Bay of Mexico and the Atlantic, with the navy blue Gulf Stream beyond. The tip of the Florida Keys was ideally situated for the sunset, the most beautiful moment of the day—great news for observers of the cocktail hour like Ernest and Pauline, as well as for the somewhat louche locals who were immediately drawn to Ernest.

During these months Hemingway was writing his novel of love and war, *A Farewell to Arms,* which grew out of what he thought was a short story, displacing the sixty-thousand-word manuscript about a boy and his father. As late as May 31 Ernest was telling Max Perkins he was going back to the Jimmy Crane novel after he finished *A Farewell to Arms,* and in the same letter that it was hard for him to believe there was a time when it had been difficult for him to work. This despite considerable diversions, for Ernest had discovered deep-sea fishing, a real turning point in his life. He had been fishing off a pier near the No Name Key ferryboat dock when a local lawyer, George Brooks, struck up a conversation with him, recommending that if he liked fishing he should introduce himself to Charles

Thompson, who could be found at his hardware store on Caroline Street. Thompson became a fast friend, one of the very few who remained friends with Ernest through a long stretch of his life, and his wife, Lorine, a college-educated schoolteacher, befriended Pauline—another lasting bond. The next evening Ernest went out deep-sea fishing with Charles. In turn, Thompson introduced him to Bra Saunders, a white Bahamian immigrant who led fishing parties out to the Gulf Stream in search of sailfish, tarpon, and marlin—the last becoming a long obsession of Ernest's. Bra Saunders and Charles Thompson formed the nucleus of what Ernest would come to call his Mob, a circle of friends and, increasingly, hangers-on who shared the fun.

Ernest's first response to this island paradise with fishing attached was to invite his male friends to come down and see for themselves. Dos Passos arrived first; he would become an enthusiastic participant even if he did not catch the fishing bug himself. Bill Smith came down as well, along with his sister, Katy, familiar to Ernest from the summers on Lake Walloon. (Dos confessed "the only one he really had eyes for" was Katy.) Two friends from Paris also paid visits: Mike Strater and Waldo Peirce. Strater was a Princeton graduate, the model for Burne Holiday in Fitzgerald's *This Side of Paradise* (1920), a painter, and an avid sportsman. Peirce, also a painter, was the most colorful of the lot, sporting long mustaches and a full beard, a big man with a big belly and Rabelaisian attitudes and appetites.

Ernest wrote in the mornings and joined his companions for lunch and afternoon fishing. (The Hemingways put up their visitors at a local hotel—as they did all their guests, even after they owned their own home in Key West, a sage practice, given Key West's popularity with tourists and the likelihood of many would-be house guests.) Pauline, not yet an enthusiastic fisherman, came along a couple of times but she was too pregnant to exert herself much and usually spent her days with Lorine. She was happy that Ernest was content and writing, the goal toward which she would work throughout their marriage. His visible pleasure convinced her that Key West was a good place, a place to put down roots, a place where he could work and enjoy himself in equal measure. Pauline talked it up so to the Pfeiffers back in Piggott that her father decided to come down himself, perhaps hoping to accompany his daughter back to the Midwest for the delivery of her baby at the end of June. Meanwhile, Ernest was waxing ebullient about Key West to Archie MacLeish, saying that it was the place where his writing went most smoothly; in Key West you could swim all winter, speak Spanish with the locals just as if you were in another country, fish in the Gulf Stream seven miles out, and sail to uninhabited keys. Good

Spanish wine could be had from Cuba, whiskey $5 a quart, and Bacardi and Fundador for even less.

Meanwhile, Ernest learned that his parents, together with his uncle Will, Ed's missionary brother visiting from China, were in Florida, which struck all concerned as a huge coincidence. Ernest found out by way of a letter forwarded to him from Paris, which told him they would be staying at the Hotel Idlewild in St. Petersburg. Ernest sent a telegram addressed to his father (not to his father and mother) there, explaining the circumstances and inviting him to Key West to do some fishing. The doctor and his wife promptly took a train down to Key West along the famous line that ran magnificently along the high bridges stringing the keys together, the railroad built by developer Henry Flagler, which was responsible for the islands' lifeblood—increasingly, tourist dollars. Ernest and Pauline met Grace, Ed, and Will in their (finally delivered) Model A at the train station; when Ed spotted Ernest coming toward them, he sounded the bobwhite whistle that had once called all the Hemingway children together. Uncle Will took pictures of the four of them. Ernest, beaming, looks radiantly happy, though a large scar is visible over his left eye. Grace is florid in a big hat and generous dress, while Pauline is quite pregnant in a flowered dress, her face obscured by a fashionable cloche hat. There is no record of what transpired on the visit except that it was short; in an April 11 letter, Ed wrote about seeing him "last evening." Perhaps Ernest did not invite them to stay, or somehow gave the impression that they were not welcome. Or perhaps it was just that Ed Hemingway was eager to get on, already planning the trip back to Oak Park. He was "nervous" these days.

In photographs of that occasion, Dr. Hemingway does not look healthy. He seems to be swimming in his dark suit, visibly too thin, and his beard and hair have gone gray, his face gaunt. In a photograph of Ernest and his father, Ed looks proudly at Ernest, but a look of bafflement plays on his features. The last two or three years had been increasingly hard on the doctor. In February he had written to Grace, on her annual winter visit to her brother in California, "I surely need a vacation—so far I have not enjoyed a single *all* nights sleep in 1928," adding, however, that his practice had been profitable. But their Florida investment had continued to go sour—a big blow, for Ed had taken out a $15,000 mortgage on the Oak Park house to buy the Florida land. He had to make regular payments on the Florida properties; it was for a loan to cover these payments that he eventually would turn to his brother, George Hemingway, the real estate man. George would say that if Ed could not make the payments he should cut his losses and sell the properties for any price, trying to hold on to a few of the best ones. George would have plenty of advice for Ed Hemingway, but he would refuse the request for a loan.

Moreover, Ed's health was poor: angina increasingly troubled him, meaning he had to carry nitroglycerin with him at all times. He had recently diagnosed himself with diabetes, bringing home a scale on which to measure his food, for he would need to pay close attention to his diet for the rest of his life. The development of insulin, a substance derived from animal pancreas that lowered blood sugar, had emerged as the cornerstone of the treatment of diabetes as recently as 1922. Ed Hemingway no doubt injected himself with insulin, which along with a careful diet made the disease manageable. As a doctor, however, he had seen many diabetic patients in the years before insulin, when the diagnosis of diabetes was essentially a death sentence, the only treatment a starvation-level diet. Diabetics of that era succumbed soon after the disease's onset to heart attack, stroke, or kidney failure, and this may have been what Ed Hemingway envisioned for himself. Even with insulin, the disease was dangerous; diabetics could lose limbs to gangrene caused by the neuropathy that accompanies the disease.

Ed Hemingway, however, suffered from another potentially fatal disease, one that might induce him to view a diagnosis of diabetes in the darkest possible light: clinical depression. Hindsight, which includes our knowledge of his suicide as well as that of fully half his children, makes diagnosis of this disease clear to even a nonmedical observer. The depression that would envelop his oldest son provides a template, or a lens, onto or through which we can see what was happening to Ed Hemingway. Extremely severe depression came upon him insidiously, making him increasingly "nervous," paranoid, and irrational. "My father changed from his high-strung, active, determined, cheerful self . . . to an irritable, suspicious person," wrote Marcelline. He spent long hours in his office in the house on North Kenilworth, and came to lock up his things in his drawers and clothes closet. He distrusted everyone, which Marcelline observed was "agony" for her mother. His youngest son, Leicester, one of the two children remaining at home, became an obsession with Ed Hemingway. He took the boy on all his house calls, keeping Leicester around him at all times; Marcelline notes that he "even seemed to resent" the time Leicester spent in school. In the late fall of 1928, however, he would rapidly change his mind, refusing to let Leicester ride with him and barring all family members from riding in the car with him. Marcelline later said that the family came to realize that he feared he would suffer an angina attack while driving. It was just as likely to have been a paranoid delusion.

In 1928 Ed seized on a memory and vowed to revisit a time of great

With his father, Ed Hemingway, Key West, April 1928.
Ed killed himself eight months later.

happiness when, after his graduation from Oberlin College, he had joined
a geological expedition to the Smoky Mountains, during which he had
worked as the group's cook. Driving back from Florida in April, Ed, Grace,
and Will stopped in the Smokies, which awakened Ed's memories. Camping in the Smokies with his two sons, Ernest and Leicester, all fishing for
trout, became something Ed brought up in all of his letters that spring and
summer. He proposed a trip in the first week in October. But Ernest never
responded, and finally Ed gave up. Leicester would have had to miss school
to go and Grace didn't think she would be able to either (it's unclear when
she became part of the plan, in any case a feature that wasn't likely to sway
Ernest). Ed said in letters to his son that he feared he himself might have
too much work to make the trip. But, he added, unwilling to let go of it,
"If you can go, write right away."

After he had seen his son and his son's new wife in Florida so unexpectedly, Ed wrote Ernest the meeting had been "like a dream." He had not

seen his son in five years, and in the most recent couple of years relations between parents and son—and not just between Grace and Ernest, but between Ed and Ernest as well—had been decidedly rocky. The divorce had genuinely shocked and scandalized his parents in ways that it is hard to understand today. They loved Hadley and Bumby, and feared what would become of that relationship. Though Grace and Ed had very different responses to the divorce, it is fair to say that the Hemingways were dismayed to see what they considered changes in their son (*he* would deny any such changes); concerned about his well-being, both mental and spiritual; embarrassed when their son's shocking fiction became well known; and genuinely puzzled by his increasing fame.

Just after the meeting in Florida, Ernest wrote his father about his summer plans with Pauline. They had been planning for the baby's delivery in Kansas City, where Ernest had family and good recommendations for doctors, but then Ernest began to think about Windemere and Lake Walloon. The smoothness of the meeting in Florida perhaps made Ernest hope the family might see more of each other. Ernest asked if he and Pauline could come to northern Michigan. Could they stay at Windemere, or perhaps in the nearby Loomis cottage? Did Ed think they could hire a cook and a nurse up there, and could Pauline have the baby at the Petoskey hospital?

It's difficult to say why, but this letter put Ed off. His response to his son's request was a studied coldness. He would love to see Ernest and Pauline at Windemere, he wrote back, but he and Grace probably couldn't get to Lake Walloon until after the Fourth of July (after Pauline's due date), and it was said to be a "cool spring" up there anyway. Marcelline had recently bought the Loomis cottage, he said—and he couldn't say whether she would allow the couple to stay there or not. He did think Ernest and Pauline would have difficulty finding servants, and suggested that Pauline would be better off having the baby in St. Louis or Kansas City, the Petoskey hospital being only good for local emergencies (though he added, in the next breath, that Ernest's friend Wesley Dilworth and his wife had had twins there that spring). "If you want to have me attend your wife at the Oak Park Hospital," he added stiffly, "I am glad to offer you my services."

It is equally difficult to say why, in turn, this letter annoyed or offended Ernest. Evidently overlooking his father's willingness to deliver Pauline's baby in Oak Park (but not Petoskey), he chose to see his father's response as a "rejection," as he referred to it in his letters. In turn, his father may have thought Ernest was being disrespectful in not asking him to deliver Pauline's child in the first place; then, with Ernest's silence on the matter, he may have felt that Ernest was rejecting his offer to deliver it in Oak

Park. Windemere was a somewhat loaded issue itself, his family no doubt a bit perplexed or hurt that Ernest did not choose to spend time there as an adult when he had loved it so much as a boy. It must have stung Ernest that Marcelline had bought the Loomis cottage, and he may well have blamed his parents for this, however unjustly. As of May 31, Ernest was still telling Max Perkins he hoped to go to Michigan. Evidently Ed continued to invite Ernest to Windemere, for in a July letter to his parents, written after the baby was born, Ernest sent regrets that he couldn't come, adding, "I wrote to Dad . . . asking about getting a cottage at Walloon but was discouraged." A Hemingway never forgave a slight.

Meanwhile Ernest was getting to know his new in-laws. Pauline's father, Paul, came to Key West in May to see the place Pauline had been praising so extravagantly. He may have hoped to drive back to Piggott with his daughter, but at this stage in her pregnancy it seemed wisest for Pauline to go by train. It was left to Paul and Ernest to make the 1,400-mile drive themselves, the new Model A piled high with the couple's belongings. It took six days, a long time for new in-laws to spend together; Paul was somewhat remote, in marked contrast to Ernest's warm relations with Mary Pfeiffer. In Piggott, Ernest and Pauline settled in two weeks before moving on to Kansas City, where they had finally agreed Pauline would give birth. The baby was kicking, she said, "and I've taken to kicking back."

Setting up a table for writing in the barn, Ernest hoped to move his new novel along significantly before he and Pauline left for Kansas City in mid-June. He had been building up the setting of the war in Italy and developing the character of Frederic Henry, the American ambulance driver hero, who meets and falls in love with a British nurse, Catherine Barkley—a character with a lot of Agnes von Kurowsky in her. Frederic is wounded and recovers in Milan—like Hemingway—where he and Catherine become lovers. As Ernest wrote away in the Pfeiffer barn, which must have been oppressively hot that June, Catherine was three months pregnant and Frederic Henry was rejoining the Italian forces for the retreat from Caporetto.

Ernest made it clear to everyone in Piggott that his priority was to finish his book, and that after the baby's birth he would go somewhere out-of-doors to write as well as to do some fishing and shooting, the Piggott quail hunting only whetting his appetite. If not Michigan, he meant to go to Idaho; gradually he came around to the idea of Wyoming, and sent an invitation to his old war buddy, Bill Horne, to join him there in late June or July, whenever the baby was born and Ernest could get away. Mary Pfeiffer told him he was under no obligation to do anything beyond getting Pauline and the baby safely back to Piggott, at which time he could "hie away to the woods and streams or wherever the call of the wild beckons—and rest up and get back to normalcy."

Ernest and Pauline arrived in Kansas City on June 20, when the city was host to the Republican National Convention, which nominated Herbert Hoover. They stayed with Malcolm and Ruth White Lowry, relatives of Arabella Hemingway, the wife of Ernest's Uncle Tyler, who had helped to get Ernest his job at the *Kansas City Star* in 1917. (Uncle Tyler had died and Arabella had remarried, becoming neighbors of the Lowrys, who evidently were better equipped to host the couple.) The Lowrys found a doctor, Don Carlos Guffey, to deliver the baby at Research Hospital.

The Hemingways went to the hospital on July 27, Pauline's labor pains having begun. After eighteen hours of labor, Dr. Guffey came to Ernest and asked permission to perform a cesarean. On July 28 a boy was born, surprising the parents, who had expected a girl; they named him Patrick. He was a big baby, nine pounds; it would have been difficult for the slight, narrow-hipped Pauline to deliver him without the cesarean. She needed ten days to recover from surgery, and a week to rest in the hospital. After that she could return to Piggott with the baby but she would have to stay on the second floor, prohibited from climbing stairs or doing any lifting. Even with that, Ernest added, in a letter to Mary Pfeiffer, "The doctor said she shouldn't have another baby for three years if she did not want to become a cripple or a corpse." At various times he compared the operation to a can opener and said Pauline had to be opened up "like a picador's horse"—particularly gruesome ways to look at it.

They arrived back in Piggott July 20, and Ernest stayed just five days, going back to Kansas City by train, where he had arranged to meet Bill Horne. They set out in the Model A for Wyoming, where they had arranged to stay on Folly Ranch in the Bighorn Mountains, near Sheridan, joined there by Horne's fiancée. Dude ranches, or ranches that took paying guests, were destinations for those like Hemingway who wanted to fish and hunt in the West, often with the use of a guide; Ernest told Guy Hickok he was leaving for Wyoming, where he could finish work on his book and fish.

The Folly Ranch did not meet his expectations—evidently too crowded—so he spent four nights in Sheridan before winding up at Eleanor Donnelly's nearby Lower Ranch. On his first day there he wrote a huge chunk of manuscript, the long scene in which Ernest rows Catherine across Lake Maggiore to Switzerland. Like Pauline, Catherine was to deliver her baby by cesarean section—but Catherine's baby is dead and Catherine dies after the operation. It is a strange semiautobiographical detail, perhaps strangest in its timing (not to mention the fact that his heroine dies).

By the time Ernest wrote to Max Perkins on August 20, Pauline was with him out west, having left Patrick with her mother and Jinny in Piggott, and he was happy to report that the first draft of the—yet untitled—*A Farewell to Arms* was done. He would revise the manuscript over the winter in Key West, putting off their return to Paris until the spring. In the meantime, he and Pauline moved on to the Spear-O-Wigwam ranch near the Montana border, where they spent the days fishing for trout and hunting deer, elk, and antelope, prairie chickens, ducks, and grouse.

At the same time Ernest was thinking a lot about money. Though Pauline brought a healthy income to the marriage, he complained often about having a wife and children to support. He griped to his editor about the lack of advertising for his latest book, letting Perkins know he knew the tricks of the trade. He told the editor he wanted a big advance on his next book to ensure that Scribner's had a stake in advertising it widely. He complained that other writers were getting rich, while he was cashing few royalty checks—in part because the only ones he saw were for his two story collections, the proceeds from *The Sun Also Rises* going to Hadley, as promised. He cited Thornton Wilder (enjoying the success of his 1927 Pulitzer Prize–winning *Bridge of San Luis Rey*), Julien Green (an American writer who wrote mostly in French), and Glenway Wescott (author of the 1927 *The Grandmothers* and a particular bête noire of Ernest's), telling Perkins, "This bull market in beautiful letters isn't going to last forever." He wanted to make a "chunk" of money at one time so he could invest it, preferably buying bonds to ensure a $75-a-month or even $100-a-month income.

In late September Perkins offered him a $5,000 advance, which Ernest happily accepted, explaining that he hadn't yet cashed a $3,700 royalty check from Scribner's because he was trying to accumulate capital to invest. (He had no need for ready cash.) He confided to Max that he hoped to serialize *A Farewell to Arms* in *Scribner's Magazine*—despite having offered Ray Long at *Cosmopolitan* first crack at serial rights. He said he did not want to tell Long that he would prefer to publish in *Scribner's* because he feared Long would think he was trying to start a bidding war, "the last thing I want." (Clearly a bidding war was exactly what he wanted.) Whether *Scribner's* cooperated is not known. Perkins told Ernest the company very much wanted to serialize the book in its magazine, but he needed an assurance that there was no censorable material in the manuscript. The upshot was that Perkins guaranteed $10,000 for serial rights (presumably a high enough offer to outbid *Cosmopolitan*), and that *Scribner's Magazine* eventually paid Ernest $16,000 for the rights—more than the magazine had ever paid before.

Early in September Ernest and Pauline packed up the Ford and went on the road, their eventual destination Yellowstone Park. On the way they stopped in Shell, Wyoming, a tiny town at the base of the Bighorn Mountains, to look up Owen Wister, once a very popular writer of Western stories and a best-selling novel, *The Virginian* (1903), which remained a steady moneymaker. No doubt Ernest had read *The Virginian* in his adolescence or after, as the setting and certain plot sequences—practical jokes, gunfights, horsemanship—would have greatly appealed to him. The Virginian himself was a memorable character, noble and gallant yet tough when toughness was called for. "When you say that, *smile!*" became a widely quoted line, the equivalent, perhaps, of today's "Go ahead, make my day." Back in February, Ernest had told Perkins that he thought Wister's "The Right Honorable the Strawberries," which had appeared in Edward O'Brien's *Best Short Stories of 1927,* "the best story I've read in a hell of a time. . . . It was wonderfully good . . . and a lesson to our generation in how to write."

Ernest's first contact with Wister was indirect. In Paris Ernest had been friends with Barklie McKee Henry, the author of the 1924 novel *Deceit,* and husband of Gertrude Vanderbilt Whitney's daughter. Henry had some acquaintance with Wister, and had given him a copy of *In Our Time.* Wister had not particularly liked it but he showed interest in the younger writer, and Henry later sent him *The Sun Also Rises* and "Fifty Grand." Henry was pleased to tell Ernest that Wister had greatly admired the novel and story. "Were I thirty," Wister wrote Henry, "that's the way I should wish to write." Ernest was delighted, and told Henry he wasn't surprised that Wister had not been able to praise *In Our Time,* because "that was so much on the side of your and my generation that we couldn't expect anybody much older to get it."

Ernest was enormously impressed by everything he saw in the West, and he loved Wyoming, finding that the outdoor life offered in the U.S. had it over Europe (with the single, and at the time very significant, exception of skiing). So it is not surprising that on that basis alone he called on Wister in August. But he was also strangely drawn to the writer who had done so much to inscribe the figure of the cowboy in the national psyche. Wister was a good friend of Teddy Roosevelt's, who was instrumental in constructing a general romance of the West. The meeting between Wister and Hemingway was successful, and the two took a liking to each other, leading to several further meetings and a seven-year-long correspondence.

In August they talked mostly about Robert Bridges, the editor of *Scribner's Magazine*, whom they called "the old Dodo." Ernest knew that Bridges would be afraid of *A Farewell to Arms* running afoul of the censor, and Wister shared stories about Bridges's cutting his quotation of letters of Teddy Roosevelt in an article he had written for the magazine. Then Wister and Ernest drove out to the Snake River to fish, Wister's son Carl joining them. On the ride to the river, Wister introduced Ernest to the dubious practice of shooting prairie dogs with pistols from a car (which Ernest enjoyed for the rest of his time out west, sometimes using his twelve-gauge Winchester). Afterward, Ernest told Waldo Peirce he found Wister to be "a sweet old guy." Wister was even more enthusiastic. He had been a friend of Henry James's, of whom he often spoke in connection with Ernest: "I loved seeing you," Wister told him. "Not since I last talked to Henry James at Rye in 1914 have I opened up at such a rate." Wister referred to him as a "young phoenix" in a letter to Max. Wister was an extremely outspoken conservative who detested what he saw as the decline in morals and culture in the 1920s, and he may have persuaded himself that Hemingway, with his passion for the outdoors, was a winged hope, rising up out of the ashes. (Evidently he chose not to associate *The Sun Also Rises* with any such decline.)

Toward the third week of September Ernest and Pauline began the drive back to Piggott, stopping in Kansas City for Pauline to see her obstetrician. By the 25th they were in Piggott. Pauline was no doubt overjoyed to see her son after a separation of over a month. Patrick was more than amply cared for by his grandparents, the live-in housekeeper Lillie Jordan, and by Jinny, who had returned to the U.S. to attend him. Though it is generally accepted practice, eighty years later, that an infant not endure long separation from the mother during the first year, parenthood practices were very different in the 1920s and 1930s—witness Ernest and Hadley's habit of going out to cafés leaving Bumby home with the cat. Patrick was bottle-fed, and in his first month and a half established that he was a placid baby who seldom cried and had not been, as yet, colicky. But, as Pauline had reasoned from the start, her first loyalty was to Ernest, her fixed object to be the best wife she could, smoothing paths for him and ensuring that he could write. She made her priorities clear in a letter she wrote to him from Piggott, before she went out to Wyoming to join him. "With you away it seems as though I was just a mother, which is not very gripping," she wrote. "But in three weeks I'll . . . go to Wyoming, where I shall be just a wife."

In Piggott they learned that their son weighed twice his birth weight, which gave Ernest something to brag about. Mary Pfeiffer and Jinny left for a much needed two-week vacation, leaving the care of Patrick to Pauline, Ernest, and Lillie. Ernest was determined to delay revision of the manuscript of *A Farewell to Arms* until they were back in Key West, so he hung about Piggott helping with his son, trap shooting, and writing on the generous porch of the Pfeiffer home. He wrote a story called "The Wine of Wyoming," based on a French Catholic couple he met in Sheridan, Wyoming, who were unlikely bootleggers.

Ernest wasn't in Piggott long, leaving in the Ford for Oak Park by himself. Pauline would join him later at the Whitehall Hotel in Chicago. Though it has been believed that Ernest kept Pauline's presence in Chicago a secret, a newly surfaced letter reveals that Ernest brought her out to Oak Park, if only for a very brief visit. Pauline later wrote "Mother Hemingway," saying, "When I saw [Ed] in Oak Park I thought he was a very sick man and that he must suffer a great deal." The visit would likely have been a short one as Ernest and Pauline suspected that his family had taken Hadley to their hearts—where she remained, as the mother of Bumby—and thought Ed and Grace would accept Pauline only with time. Even so, their disappointment at not seeing their new grandson must have been profound, and would have been painful for Ernest to see, especially in his father, about whom he and his family were so worried. Ursula, now married, came by herself from Minnesota to see her brother. Sunny was still at home at twenty-four, working for a dentist and not very happy about it. Carol was seventeen and Leicester thirteen.

Grace was thriving in her new career—for she earned money with her paintings, and saw it as her work, not a hobby. She had won several competitions but had suffered her share of setbacks; in the beginning of 1928, when she was visiting her brother out west (and painting several landscapes), she had Ed send seven paintings for a juried competition at the Chicago Art Institute. Ed, extremely supportive of his wife (perhaps because he was becoming so emotionally dependent on her), referred to "the precious paintings of my darling Artist wife." When her work was not selected, he reassured her, "Keep up the good work and never mind what the jury didn't do." He wrote her another letter in the same vein, urging her to stay out there. "Let it all blow over and produce more painting."

Grace had put on a three-day "studio tea and exhibition" of Western paintings at the house on North Kenilworth just over two weeks before Ernest came to Oak Park in mid-October. The *Oak Leaves* article covering the show, probably to her annoyance, noted that her "claim for fame is not only for her art, but also she is the mother of Ernest." Perhaps, how-ever, this was the only way she could get coverage—which would not have pleased her either. A year earlier an article about her painting appeared in the *Chicago Daily News,* in which the reporter, Bertha Fenberg, allowed her to vent about "these young writers" and their pessimism. Grace said she thought the pendulum was swinging back to "normal." "Her way of expressing her own happy life," wrote Fenberg, is "'God's in His heaven, all's right with the world.'"

Ernest sneered about his mother's career to his siblings. Right after his visit he told Sunny he fully expected Grace to take up writing—since she'd taken care of music and art. But when he was in Paris Grace wrote him repeatedly for help showing her paintings there. (She had no doubts about her talent.) Ernest chose not to discourage her. In an undated letter prob-ably written in 1927, he carried on at great length over where she might show, providing arcane-sounding detail about pricing systems in galleries and salons. He'd be willing to take her paintings around, he said, but he strongly advised her to show in the U.S., partly because in France artists paid the cost of mounting a show. Also in 1927 Grace had sent Ernest a notice of a show of her work, and he answered that he'd prefer to see her paintings over anything else shown in Paris. This sounds unlike the Ernest of the earlier 1920s. The inescapable sense is that the family remained very close, despite all that had come between them, and it was easy for Ernest to slip into the rhythms familiar to childhood and early adolescence, offering Grace the extravagant praise on which she thrived.

Remarkably, for someone who wrote almost ten thousand letters in his lifetime, Ernest evidently wrote no letters while in Oak Park in 1928. It is difficult to imagine what it was like in the big house on North Kenilworth, with his father growing more and more gaunt and more and more para-noid. Grace seems to have swanned around with her usual confidence, busy with her art. Marcelline later said her mother was "frantic with worry," but it did not show in Grace's letters, for, Marcelline wrote, "She did not want any letter of hers to add to anyone's burdens." It must have been a tense and difficult time. In a letter written after Ernest left, Ed tried to show how proud he was of his son in a crude limerick:

> *I can't seem to think of a way*
> *To say what I'd most like to say*
> *To my very dear son*
> *Whose book is just done,*
> *Except give him my love and "HOORAY."*

After their visit to Chicago, Ernest and Pauline went on to Conway, Massachusetts, to visit the MacLeishes, and enjoyed it so much they stayed longer than expected, fitting in a Harvard football game as well. Archie and Ada had bought Cricket Hill Farm, soon rechristened Uphill Farm, which consisted of three hundred acres, a Revolutionary War–era house that could accommodate three children, and the various outbuildings of a working farm. Ernest had always been a favorite with the older children, Ken, now eleven, and Mimi, aged six. Mimi especially adored Ernest and for some reason spoke with him only in French. On this visit, Mimi detected Ernest's voice downstairs and ran to greet him. She stopped short to look at him and screamed. Archie later described the scene in verse:

> She ran to him,
> stopped, looked, screamed. It wasn't Ernest!
> wasn't Ernest! wasn't . . .
> She raced up the stair.

MacLeish's biographer believes Mimi was afraid of the livid scar on Ernest's forehead from the skylight incident, but evidently Ernest took this as, rather, the child's detection of a great change in him. Mimi's failure to recognize him, he thought, indicated that she blamed him for Hadley's absence—guilt about Hadley always just beneath the surface with Ernest. Later he went up to Mimi to say good night.

Pauline and Ernest went on to New York City, where they stayed in the Hotel Brevoort. Ernest met with Perkins while Pauline saw Uncle Gus, Aunt Louise, and various other relatives who came in from Connecticut. Ernest saw his Paris friend Waldo Peirce. On the 17th Ernest, Pauline, and Mike Strater went down to Princeton for the Princeton-Yale football game, meeting Scott and Zelda Fitzgerald there. They enjoyed the game, which Princeton won twelve to two. Everybody had remained fairly sober during the game, but afterward, on the train to Ellerslie, Scott and Zelda's palatial new home in Delaware, Scott became much drunker. The weekend was a nightmare.

The visit ended in a miserable comedy of errors, involving Scott and a policeman at the Philadelphia railway station on the Hemingways' trip back to New York. Ernest had evidently been agitated about getting to the train on time, and, in his words, "made a shall we say nuisance of myself," arriving long before the train pulled in. In the meantime Scott had apparently been taken to the local police station; Ernest said he called the arresting policeman at the station and said Scott was a great writer (Ernest may have been drinking as well), at which the cop responded, "He seems like a Dandy fellow." How it all turned out is lost to history, but Ernest told the story about the cop to Scott and Zelda, along with his apology about his behavior regarding the train, in a polite thank-you note. Fitzgerald's drinking was starting to become a serious problem at this time, as attested in letters between him and Max Perkins, and between Max and Ernest. For now, however, Ernest was genuinely solicitous about Fitzgerald's health and his work.

Ernest and Pauline, but especially Ernest, had been undertaking long trips almost every month they had been in the States, and their journey back to Key West from Delaware continued the pattern. They returned to Chicago first, where they picked up the Model A and Ernest's sister Sunny, who was going to make an extended visit to Key West to type the manuscript of *A Farewell to Arms* and help with the care of her new nephew. From there they went on to Piggott and to Key West, where a newly rented house at 1110 South Street awaited them. Found by Lorine Thompson, the four-bedroom house, near the beach, cost them $125 a month. There Ernest heard from Hadley that she had become concerned about Bumby's cough and his general health and thought he would do better in warm Key West. Hadley and Bumby were due to arrive in New York City on the *Île de France* on December 4. However delighted he was to be spending time with his five-year-old son, Ernest cannot have relished taking the train up to New York after just two days in Key West.

He met Bumby and Hadley at their train; as it turned out, Hadley had decided to send Bumby down without her, in his father's company. Hadley was now quite serious about the journalist and poet Paul Mowrer, another American in Paris, whom she was soon to marry, so it was just as well that the exes met only briefly in Penn Station, from where Ernest and Bumby got on the Havana Special to Key West.

They were only as far as Trenton when the porter brought Ernest a telegram from his sister Carol that read, "FATHER DIED THIS MORNING ARRANGE TO STOP HERE IF POSSIBLE." They were only about a half hour from Philadelphia, where Ernest could get off and take the next train to Chicago. He entrusted Bumby to the porter, to whom he gave money for the boy's expenses and, presumably, a sizable tip. Bumby had traveled with unrelated adults before, Marie Cocotte having shepherded him all over France. (Still, the next day, until late in the evening Ernest would be "frantic worrying" why a telegram from the train porter reporting on Bumby had not come. Finally, he would receive a wire saying, "The boy had a good night's sleep.") The same porter brought Ernest timetables and telegram forms for wires to be sent to Pauline, Hadley, and his mother.

Ernest was thinking and acting fast. Before the train reached Philadelphia, he sent a wire to Max Perkins telling him the news and asking him to wire money to the North Philadelphia station. As soon as the train pulled in, he said goodbye to Bumby. At the station he called Mike Strater in New York, but finding him out, called Scott Fitzgerald, who was home and agreed to wire Ernest money to the railroad station. The money came through quickly, and Ernest cabled Perkins again to say he no longer needed money.

It was not really a great surprise. Ed Hemingway, just fifty-seven years old, had turned to his brother George for financial help before the first of December, when he had to make some payments on the Florida lots, and George had told him to sell them at any price—and refused to loan him money. Ed had been almost paralyzed with depression in the weeks leading up to his suicide, much as his son would be in the weeks leading up to his own in 1961. The doctor was increasingly paranoid and secretive. Grace later wrote to an N. L. Bedford, possibly a creditor, about Ed's actions on December 6: "Dr. Hemingway was not in his right mind before his death and he destroyed valuable books & records, burned in the furnace the morning he took his own life." At breakfast he told Grace that he was bothered by a pain in his foot; any doctor knew what that might presage in a diabetic. He said he would get it checked at the Oak Park hospital that day. He came home at noon and asked after Leicester, who was home in bed with a cold. Grace said the boy was a lot better, but that he was probably asleep. Ed Hemingway went upstairs to his bedroom, and, using the Smith & Wesson .32 revolver that his father, Anson Hemingway, had carried in the Civil War, he put a bullet through his right temple. Ironically, it was Ruth Arnold, again a member of the household, who heard the shot and told Grace when she returned to the house after an errand. Grace went into Ed's bedroom and found the body and the gun.

Ed's widow and children made it through the funeral without incident. The wrangling began afterward. Grace was incapacitated by grief and bewildered by her plight in the wake of Ed's death—for once not able to rise to the occasion. While she was temporarily retired from the field, her two oldest children, Marcelline and Ernest—both long since moved out and with families of their own—vied for dominance; no doubt they were reliving some struggles of their childhood, especially their need to individuate themselves from each other after Grace's early practice of "twinning" them.

Marcelline had the temporary edge because she got to Oak Park first, but after Ernest arrived the real struggle began. She wrote publicly about the occasion twice, in *At the Hemingways,* a family memoir she published serially in 1962 in *The Atlantic Monthly* and in 1963 as a book. But she wrote about it passionately, with no holds barred, in a letter to her mother written in 1939. The letter was very angry because of a quarrel she was having with Ernest about the use of Windemere. The house had come to be symbolic of their idyllic early years, so it is easy to see in this later quarrel how much the argument between them reached back to childhood, easier than it is to discern the source in the wake of their father's death. The Windemere struggle was for high stakes emotionally as well, but in the quarrel after Ed's funeral, brother and sister acknowledged their long-buried anger at each other for the first time. The passion they brought to their argument may have surprised them both.

Ostensibly, the quarrel was about religion. In *At the Hemingways,* Marcelline says that as soon as the newly Catholic Ernest arrived he told the rest of the family he had had a Mass said for Ed. The doctor was laid out in the music room before the service at the First Congregational Church, she related, and Ernest led the family in the Lord's Prayer, much as Grandfather Hall, Grace's father, used to do every day, his eyes directed heavenward. It was only in the letter to Grace ten years later that Marcelline revealed her major objection (though once again it masked another, less governable emotion). She railed at Ernest for saying their father was going to purgatory because his suicide had been a mortal sin. Ernest said that because he had a "Heathen Family" it was impossible to offer enough prayers to get his soul into heaven. "Praying him out of purgatory," Marcelline said, "was a disgusting suggestion," and furthermore her father was hardly guilty of a mortal sin when he killed himself to spare his family. It is true that Ernest's younger brother, Leicester, said in his biography of his brother (published the same year as Marcelline's, right after Ernest's death) that Ernest had told him to pray as hard as he could for his father's soul to be released from purgatory. While Ernest was probably less than diplomatic about this particular issue (Marcelline notes quickly that he had said "cutting, sarcastic things" about, for example, her having gone to college when he had not), it is only fair to say that Ernest was, at least in the years after his conversion, a practicing Catholic (he went to Mass, fasted on Good Friday, and so forth), and he may have been feeling genuine distress about this point of Catholic doctrine. And, of course, in this difficult time he did no doubt turn to his faith, the teachings of his church serving as anchors in his grief. But Ernest's speech to his family about his father's soul and purgatory was a way for him to assert the patriarchal role he wanted to assume—a way to show he was in charge. Imposing his faith on his family was insensitive, to say the least, but he seems to have wanted to establish just how far he had come in being different from them.

For Ernest made it clear from the moment he arrived in Oak Park that he was now head of the family—not Marcelline, the eldest, and not his incapacitated mother. He claimed this place by virtue of being the eldest male. He began to act the part immediately, reassuring his grieving mother that she could rely on him emotionally ("Never worry because I will always fix things up") and that he was proud of her for the way she was handling everything. He would see to his father's estate, clearing up any financial problems, and he would very soon after take complete responsibility for his mother's finances, establishing a trust for her and for the two youngest children. He would discharge these duties without being asked and, for the most part, gracefully. But it was perhaps inevitable, given the way he felt about his mother and Marcelline, that he would often abuse his position, confusing responsibility with control. This extended to his younger siblings as well, Ernest seeming to relish behaving authoritatively with Carol and Leicester, ironically echoing how his mother and father had dealt with him so many years before.

Of course Ernest was at a time in his life when he was taking on a patriarchal role with his own wife and children, and with Hadley as well. He took his responsibilities toward Hadley very seriously; for instance, he met with Paul Mowrer (albeit at Mowrer's request) to discuss whether she was free to remarry. In his second marriage, Pauline deliberately placed him in a traditionally dominant role, subjugating her will to his and telling him so, repeatedly, as well as taking on all the childcare unless Ernest indicated he wanted otherwise (which, to be fair, he would do more often as the children grew older). He may have been encouraged to take up this role by the self-confidence he had discovered in his immediate response to his father's death, springing into action, briskly dispatching cables, giving orders, and deftly handling his oldest son's immediate care.

Ernest was proud of his relationship with his father, but it had been difficult, Ernest not always able to be honest with Ed or to show affection for him. Certainly he wished things had been different. He no doubt went over his most recent meetings with his father, wondering what he could have done differently. Perhaps he regretted missed opportunities, like Ed's repeated request to go camping in the Smokies with Ernest and Leicester that fall.

It may have been inevitable, given the way Ernest had come to react to instances of his own weakness or failure, that he tried to become a hero in this time of trial. His last letter to his father lay unopened on Ed's nightstand when he shot himself. Ernest told two stories about this letter, both designed to present himself in a nobly filial role. The story he told to Leicester was the more fanciful. Ernest said their father had turned to him "in desperation" after their uncle George refused to lend him money, asking frankly for Ernest's financial help. According to what Ernest told his little brother, he "immediately" answered, enclosing a check: "It lay unopened," Leicester wrote, "on top of Father's white-painted bed-side table. It had reached the house that very morning." His father had not opened the letter, Leicester wondering if he might not have been too "dazed and bewildered," perhaps "by lack of insulin" to do so. The story was tragic, of course, because if Ed Hemingway had opened his eldest son's letter, he would perhaps not have died.

Besides the unlikelihood of any such melodramatic turn of events, the story does not work because there is no trace of either letter. As one biographer has pointed out, Ernest seems to have saved every other letter his father sent him, so at least Ed's letter in this exchange should have survived. The check has not surfaced either.

The story Ernest told his mother-in-law, Mary Pfeiffer, was far more modest, not really untruthful. One detail needed to be explained for Ernest's role in the story to make sense. How to account for the telegram that reached Ernest en route to Florida with Bumby? How did Carol know what train her brother would be on? The answer, of course, was the letter he'd mailed Ed, the one on the bedside table, which gave his father details of what train he planned to take—the only thing we can be sure the letter contained, since it has not survived. In the account Ernest told Mary Pfeiffer a week after Ed Hemingway's death, he once again said he had written his father a letter about money matters (omitting, in this version, any mention of a letter his father sent to him asking for financial help). The drama in this account was more finely honed, for in this story the letter arrived twenty minutes after Ed died—too late to save his father's life.

FOURTEEN

Ernest's household in Key West buzzed with activity. He was revising *A Farewell to Arms* and handing manuscript pages to his sister Sunny to type, one page at a time; even Pauline took a seat at the typewriter when Sunny was occupied with Patrick and Bumby. (Sunny was in Florida that December when her father died and did not attend the funeral.) Then twenty-five, Sunny was the fourth-born of the six siblings; she was not the favorite sister—that was Ursula, or Nunbones—but she was enjoying a rare day in the sunlight of Ernest's favor. The house on South Street that the ménage rented for the first three months of 1929 was a cramped two-bedroom affair, "not impressive," according to Sunny; she shared a bedroom with Patrick and Bumby, finding that childcare occupied her more than she had expected.

Until a mid-January letter, Ernest had called his editor at Scribner's Mr. Perkins; he apologized for "mistering" him for so long and called him Max thenceforth. He was still proselytizing for the adventures his friends could have out fishing the Gulf Stream with him. Max had finally agreed to come when Ernest said his editor wasn't going to get *A Farewell to Arms* without claiming it in person. To an earlier invitation Max had said wistfully, "I would give anything to do that kind of thing." For once conquering inhibition, he joined Ernest at the end of January and stayed for a week. Ernest had finished the novel on January 22 and had been celebrating by staying out on the water all day every day fishing for kingfish and tarpon. Max discovered a part of himself that loved being in the open air, singlemindedly devoted to catching fish. He had yet to catch a tarpon—the real prize, the largest fish he had yet seen in those waters. Ernest hooked one and immediately thrust the rod at Max, who had no choice but to take it and hold on—for almost an hour, as it turned out. Ernest talked him through it, Max bringing the fish in and landing it on the deck. "I had one of the best times of my life with him," Max wrote Owen Wister afterward. It was the first of many trips.

With *Scribner's* editor Max Perkins, Key West, January 1929

In the evenings Max read *A Farewell to Arms*. He loved it and told Ernest so. He enjoyed it so much, in fact, that he reread it on the train back to New York, enjoying it differently now that he knew the story, he said. "It's a most beautiful book. . . . It's full of lovely things." It was all he could do not to buttonhole someone on the train and make them read it; as it was, he said he would take the bottle of absinthe Ernest had bestowed on him into the train's bathroom "& drink a lonely health to you."

He thought *Scribner's Magazine* would serialize it, the only obstacle (which was to loom large at times) being the language. Indeed, he wired Ernest on February 13 with the magazine's $16,000 offer. Ernest quickly accepted.

He needed the money in the aftermath of his father's death—as his mother was quick to tell him. Uncle George—who had refused to bail Ed out—paid for half of the funeral, Marcelline's husband, Sterling, paying the other half. (It's not clear why Ernest did not contribute; perhaps he wasn't asked.) Sounding desperate, Grace said she hoped to find more pupils or take in roomers, but she told Ernest she was sure her "blessed loyal children" would come through for her. She was left with the (mortgaged) North Kenilworth house, the cabin on Lake Walloon, the near-worthless Florida land, and a $25,000 insurance policy. (Ernest described this as "25,000 insurance"; no doubt he meant life insurance, but it's not clear if the insurance company would pay out in the case of a suicide.) Ernest reassured his mother that he would pay the taxes on the Florida land (doubled because delinquent, plus penalties) and would send her, for now, $100 a month. "You will never know," she told him, "what a relief it was to my poor worried head . . . to receive your letter yesterday. Why Ernest! It's like being reprieved when you expected to hang." On March 6 he sent a check for $500, and the next day sent another, larger one, along with a letter any mother would welcome: he was going to send her $100 a month for the next year, until he could set up a trust that would take care of her and the two minor children. He assured Grace he could and would solve all her problems. He wanted her to "*make*" Uncle George sell the house for a big profit. He told her that he was counting on additional money for her support to come from Marcelline and Sterling, because "they are rich" and (though he did not say this) because Marcelline was, after that funeral visit, now his mortal enemy.

Grace sent Ernest his father's watch. In a much misunderstood gesture, she also sent him the gun with which his father killed himself. She evidently had promised it to him right after Ed died. In a family that kept guns for hunting or historical purposes, the "Long John," carried by Anson Hemingway in the Civil War, was a family heirloom. Grace reminded Ernest of an old story he had liked as a child: "Old Long John was the pistol I learned to shoot with when you were a baby in my arms. You always loved to cuddle in my neck when the gun fired." It is hard to imagine that any baby, however precociously fond of guns or happy being held by his mother, would stay without protest in the arms of a mother learning to shoot, or that he would turn his face into his mother's neck "to cuddle" when the gun went off.

In any case, a family mythology had accrued to the gun, and Grace thought it should go to the eldest son, just like Ed's watch. She sent it off in the beginning of March by Railway Express, together with a roll of desert pictures she'd painted in 1928, a box of cookies for Sunny, a book for Bumby, salted nuts for Ernest, and a cake for Pauline. A back-and-forth ensued over where the gun would be the most safe and secure, and eventually Ernest sent it back to be kept in the local bank.

Ernest spent the months of February and March 1929 in almost uninterrupted fishing and drinking. He summoned Dos Passos, Mike Strater, and Waldo Peirce, all equally enthusiastic about the entertainment on offer, which included ten-plus rare bottles of Château Margaux, among other good things salvaged from a wreck on an offshore reef that January. "He was the best host and sportsman," said the reporter of a fishing magazine about Ernest, "and the most generous, always giving first chance to the visiting firemen and a more than even cut of Fundador." Though Peirce and Strater were artists (both produced portraits of Ernest), and Dos a fellow writer, there was little competitive spirit among the men—at least as far as their vocations went. Ernest's friendship with Dos seemed to be immune from the bad feelings and resentment that all too often were coming to characterize Ernest's relationships with other writers, even though Dos, who had been for a time another American in Paris, had a fine literary reputation. Ernest once told Hadley, "Dos Passos is the only writer I know that isn't more or less full of shit." Dos was now writing *The 42nd Parallel,* the first volume of his *U.S.A.* trilogy, which would bring him widespread acclaim, yet even when Ernest eventually did break with him, it was over politics, not literary standing. Meanwhile, Dos was forging another bond with Ernest by falling in love with his childhood friend, Katy Smith, Bill and Kenley Smith's sister, now a magazine writer; Katy (known as Possum) and Dos (Kingfish) would marry the following summer.

Ernest hated to leave the fishing in early April when he and Pauline, Sunny, Bumby, and Patrick took a boat over to Havana and from there embarked for Boulogne. They were back at the rue Férou apartment in Paris by the 21st. They had compelling immediate reasons to return to Europe, even though Ernest was determined, and Pauline game, to take up residence in Key West: they had to return Bumby to Hadley, and they had promised Sunny a European trip, for which she had been saving money for a year and a half. And they planned to spend the summer in Spain, going to the Festival of San Fermín in Pamplona as usual, then tracing the bullfight circuit around the country all summer and fall. Ernest was beginning to research and make notes for what he saw as his next book, a comprehensive volume about bullfighting—which would become *Death in the Afternoon* (1932). For rest and relaxation they would spend time at Hendaye in the fall.

Late that spring in Paris an old friend from Toronto looked Ernest up:

Morley Callaghan, a Canadian journalist, fiction writer, and law school graduate (who never practiced). He had been sending stories to Ernest for some time, when, in 1926, he sent him a just completed novella, "Blackwater." Ernest in turn recommended him highly to Robert McAlmon for Contact Editions; he even offered to go 50-50 with McAlmon to cover the costs. "He seems to me like a kid that is worth doing something about," Ernest said in a May letter to Bob. (McAlmon did not publish the novella, which later appeared as *An Autumn Penitent*.) In 1929, Morley was in France for several months with his wife, Loretto, a time he wrote about in his vivid 1964 memoir, *That Summer in Paris*. On the first meeting Ernest ascertained that Morley had boxing experience; he immediately produced boxing gloves, the two laced up,

Ernest clowning for Waldo Peirce on a Key West beach, late 1920s

and they went at it in the rue Férou living room, making a series of passes, swings, and lunges at each other. (Pauline did not object, and on the contrary seemed "interested," noted Morley.) Ernest spoke up and put an end to it, explaining to Morley that he had just wanted to make sure that he knew how to box. They set a date for the next day at the American Club. As it turned out, they were fairly well matched in the ring, Callaghan having a slight edge. Ernest was taller and in better shape, while Callaghan was five feet eight and a touch flabby. But Morley had more experience than Ernest, and he had boxed mostly with professional fighters, while Ernest had of late boxed with other amateurs like himself.

Morley noticed that Ernest sulked when he did poorly in the ring. One afternoon at the American Club, Morley wrote, "He did something that astonished me." Morley was repeatedly catching Ernest on the mouth with a quick left after Ernest threw a long left, Morley's left connecting before Ernest had time to catch Morley with his right. Ernest's mouth began to bleed, but they kept going, Morley catching him twice more on the mouth; Ernest loudly sucked in and swallowed the blood. Suddenly he spat at Morley, right in the face, a mouthful of blood. It covered Morley's face and his jersey as well. Morley was dumbfounded and dropped his hands to his sides. Then Ernest "solemnly" told him, "That's what the bullfighters do when they're wounded. It's a way of showing contempt." Afterward, Ernest seemed to have renewed goodwill toward his friend and they continued boxing. Morley remained mystified by Ernest's "unbridled impulse, so primitive and insulting."

The centerpiece of Callaghan's *That Summer in Paris* is the celebrated match between Ernest and Morley, with Scott Fitzgerald keeping time, at the American Club in June 1929. It is not quite clear why this particular fight was so important; in fact, the two memorable features revealed themselves outside of the ring. The rounds were three minutes long, a minute for rest in between. In the second round, Morley was beginning to tire, and both men were bloody. Morley caught Ernest with a punch on the jaw, and Ernest, reeling backward, fell solidly on his back. Morley observed, "If Ernest and I had been there alone I would have laughed," and Ernest would, in a moment, have laughed too, he said. Just as he was getting up they heard Scott cry, "Oh, my God, I let the round go to four minutes!" He looked stricken. "All right, Scott," Ernest said—"savagely," according to Callaghan—"If you want to see me getting the shit knocked out of me, just say so. But don't say you made a mistake." But all eventually was well, it seemed, and the three of them adjourned to the Falstaff for drinks, where everyone, according to Callaghan, was "jovial." Scott was all apologies, clearly innocent of malice—but Ernest never did apologize to him.

The match figured again in a quarrel that fall involving all three men. The *New York Herald Tribune*'s Isabel Paterson, in her column in the paper's Books section, stated that Hemingway criticized a boxing story Callaghan wrote and then challenged the Canadian to a match. Callaghan, Paterson wrote, knocked Hemingway out in one round. When Morley read the item, he was horrified, not least because the story made Ernest look so bad: "He had been made to look like a boastful bully whose bluff has been called." Callaghan immediately sent a letter denying the story to Paterson and received an apology from her and an assurance the paper would run his letter. Then the fur began to fly, starting with Scott (why he was involved is not clear) sending Morley a cable—collect—that said, "HAVE SEEN STORY IN HERALD TRIBUNE. ERNEST AND I AWAIT YOUR CORRECTION," ending with a letter from Ernest threatening to knock Morley's block off. Eventually, the following February, Morley got a strange, friendly letter from Ernest in which he acknowledged Morley's superiority in the ring, but asserted that he could beat Morley in a fight with two-minute rounds in which he would wear smaller gloves. "He sounded more like the boyish old Ernest," said Morley, who was finally able to laugh about it.

The Hemingway-Callaghan bout, as this indicates, quickly became the stuff of legend in Paris's American colony. (In his 1947 book called *Paris Was Our Mistress,* Samuel Putnam wrote that Morley had challenged Ernest to a match, in which *Ernest* knocked *Morley* out in the first round. Ernest never corrected it—never mentioned it.) *That Summer in Paris* concludes on a rather more thoughtful note, in fact. For Morley, the subject was really his friendship with Scott and Ernest. Eventually, he observed in his memoir, he came to see that the overarching issue that summer was the friendship between Scott and Ernest, and that he barely played a part in that story.

Callaghan happened to come to Paris at a time when the friendship between Scott and Ernest was undergoing a sea change. From colleagues exchanging publishing tips, drinking companions, partners in high jinks, manic talkers, they were moving toward a chilly détente that would last until Scott's death. (Actually, Ernest would continue his crusade against Scott until his own death, becoming particularly incensed by the revival of Fitzgerald's fiction in the late 1940s.) The events of 1929, especially that summer—that summer in Paris—marked the beginning of the end of what had been an extremely close and mutually rewarding friendship.

Scott had been exceedingly generous in his relations with Ernest, bringing Ernest into the Scribner's stable and saving *The Sun Also Rises* with a bold editorial intervention, lopping off the entire amateurish beginning. Ernest had established a pattern whereby anyone who came to his aid or did things for him eventually had to pay the price of his lost friendship. The more important the favor, and the more helpful to Ernest's career, the swifter and more sure the end would be. Ernest would abandon the friend, and perhaps betray him in some fashion—in Harold Loeb's case, caricaturing him in *The Sun Also Rises* as "that kike" Robert Cohn. A complicated mechanism was at work in Ernest's psyche, for an extremely naked vulnerability seems to have been at the heart of it—not a quality we usually think of in connection with Ernest Hemingway.

Between Christmas and New Year's in 1928 Scott had written to Ernest asking when he might expect Ernest's next book, or, as Scott maladroitly put it, "When will you save me from the risk of memorizing your works from over-reading them by finishing another?" signing himself "Your

Crony and Gossip." When Max told him in February that Ernest's book was now at Scribner's Scott was "delighted." Ernest, however, was becoming ever more irked with his friend—particularly by Scott's actions when drinking. In an April 3 letter, he told Perkins that he must not give Scott the Hemingways' Paris address before the Fitzgeralds came over in March. In his letter, Ernest referred to two previous incidents that showed how utterly essential it was that Scott not know where he lived. In the first, rather shadowy episode, Scott had brought his daughter, Scottie, on a visit to Ernest and Hadley's apartment on the rue Notre-Dame-des-Champs; when they reached the building the little girl needed to go to the bathroom, so Scott began to undress her. The landlord came out and told Scott there was a *cabinet de toilette* just up the stairs on the landing. Evidently Scott made a rude response; Ernest wrote in his Paris memoir that Scott had then threatened the landlord. Ernest later told Max that Scottie "pee-ed" on the "front porch," the porch an unlikely detail. Furthermore Scott had woken them at all hours, even, as Ernest told Max, trying to break down the door at three and four o'clock in the morning. Indeed, in a November 1925 letter Scott *had* apologized to Ernest for disturbing him and Hadley in the middle of the night, with some wit: "It is only fair to say that the deplorable man who entered your apartment Sat. morning *was not* me but a man named Johnston who has often been mistaken for me." But Ernest was every drinker's nightmare, for he not only would not forget (or let you forget) what you had done, he would tell anyone who would listen about your misadventures—and give them an ominous cast. So to Perkins, Ernest said that Scott had gotten them "kicked out" of one apartment and in trouble "all the time"—whether at that apartment or another is not clear. (Ernest and Hadley had never been evicted from one of their dwellings.)

In fact, Ernest's letter to Max Perkins is pitched to a near-hysterical tone. When he heard Scott was going to Paris, he said, it gave him "the horrors." He would see Scott, but not in his home, "where we're quiet and comfortable and found it with great difficulty and he would get us ousted by only one performance." He couldn't guarantee, in fact, that he wouldn't kill Scott, because it was the finest place he'd ever lived in, and Scott "would lose it for us without one thought."

It is clear that Ernest became more nervous as he wrote this letter, progressing from beating Scott up to "as a matter of fact" fearing he'd kill him. The most persuasive explanation is that this time Ernest was genuinely afraid that he and Pauline would lose their apartment. Perhaps the potential for social embarrassment was a factor as well, for the woman from whom they sublet their apartment was now a countess and traveled in more elevated circles than those in which the Hemingways and Fitzgeralds circulated—or hoped to.

In the interim, this woman, Ruth Goldbeck, had buried her husband, the painter Walter Goldbeck, and married, in January 1928, Paul Mance de Mores, Count de Vallombrosa. (Her elevation was all the more remarkable because she had been born Ruth Obre, the daughter of two servants living on the John Jacob Astor estate near Rhinebeck, New York.) She and her new husband were living on the Riviera, where Scott and Zelda saw them frequently. By this time Scott was not only aware of the Hemingways' address but also knew they sublet from the countess. Ernest had complained to Scott that prospective tenants had been shown the apartment; he was annoyed at the disruption but also feared it meant Ruth might lose the sublease and thus the Hemingways their apartment. Scott thought he was doing Ernest a favor when he told Ruth of Hemingway's complaints, but he had of course only roiled the waters between the Hemingways and the countess, whom they would prefer not to alienate.

Scott learned, somehow, that Ernest had withheld his address from him—knew, probably, that Ernest had directed Max Perkins not to reveal where he lived. In a letter to Zelda summarizing the events of their marriage, written to help with Zelda's psychiatric care, Scott wrote: "[That spring] Ernest and I met but it was a more irritable Ernest, apprehensively not telling me his whereabouts lest I come in on them tight and endanger his lease." Though he recognized by that point that others might need to treat him differently because of his severe alcoholism—that his drinking had consequences, which might include alienating a friend—Scott must have been very hurt. He would later tell Max Perkins that his friendship with Ernest had been one of "the great spots of [his] life."

The crisis might have been, in part, manufactured in order for Ernest to vent some of his complaints about Scott to Maxwell Perkins. In April, when Ernest wrote this letter, Scott was already back in Paris, living on the rue Palatine, which was a stone's throw from the rue Férou apartment the Hemingways were returning to. Fitzgerald may have already given Hemingway the address; even if he hadn't, Hemingway had to have known it was extremely unlikely he could have concealed his address from Fitzgerald. The friendship between Scott and Ernest was still very much in its active phase, as the jocular, often puerile letters they exchanged in 1928 attest. It is also possible that Ernest *wanted* word to get back to Scott—as it did. Ernest was moving into a phase in which he would repeatedly tell Scott he was a "rummy" who was squandering his talent. But the affection in the relationship would take a number of years to leach out.

Another, more significant factor entered the equation in 1929: Scott's criticism of *A Farewell to Arms*. It had been four years since Scott had provided crucial help with *The Sun Also Rises*. His and Ernest's careers were diverging dramatically at this point. Scott's masterpiece, *The Great Gatsby* (1925), had been largely a *succès d'estime,* and his new book was not getting off the ground. Ernest thought, not entirely wrongly, that the glowing reviews of *Gatsby*—even more than that, the high personal praise Scott got in letters from T. S. Eliot and Edith Wharton, among others—had raised the bar for the next novel so high that Scott found it hard to go forward. Moreover, while his fees for short stories were still very high, more and more Scott thought he had to dumb his stories down for wider audiences. He spent more than he earned; he did not know what to do about Zelda, who was showing signs of mental instability; he drank so much that he compromised his health, jeopardized his marriage, and alienated many people who cared for him. Meanwhile, Ernest's stock was soaring.

The first installment of *A Farewell to Arms* appeared in *Scribner's Magazine* on May 8; the publication schedule for the novel was a good bit later. Ernest and Pauline had dinner at Scott and Zelda's Paris apartment around May 18, when Ernest seems to have given Scott a typescript of the novel. Scott sent Ernest a ten-page typed letter in June, offering his advice.

At all times, Ernest was hypersensitive to criticism. He could sometimes distance himself from what reviewers said about his books (more often, he tried to but could not), but criticism from friends was an especially bitter pill. Increasingly, he could not take it from Max, with what would become disastrous consequences for his work. He especially hated receiving criticism when it was too late for him to do anything about it—hardly unusually—or when he could not act on it for other reasons.

A brouhaha involving the reaction of another friend, Owen Wister, to the novel when it was already in proofs added to Ernest's prickliness. Wister was unequivocal in his support for the young writer. After Ed Hemingway's death, Wister heard that Ernest was setting up a trust fund for his mother and the youngest children and sent him $500 (which Ernest returned); in an accompanying note, Wister said, "Not since I talked with Henry James at Rye in 1914 have I opened up at such a rate." Wister wanted to see his new novel, and Ernest told him Max would be sending galleys along. While Wister's first response was positive, he followed it up with a letter to Perkins saying he thought the ending was too "painful" and urged that it be softened. Max forwarded this letter to Ernest, and followed it with another that built on Wister's criticisms to advance some suggestions of his own, arguing that the love story and the wartime sections didn't work well together. This was entirely too much for Ernest, who fired off a letter to Perkins complaining that Max had sent the galleys to Wister without his permission, and that he cared nothing for the prudish observations of an old man. Actually, we can only surmise what the letter contained, because Ernest asked Max to burn it, which he evidently did; Perkins's response is contrite and Ernest wrote in answer that he was furious at what he perceived to be Wister's interference. The novel was done, to all intents and purposes, and he was not about to make changes to more closely associate the love and war plots. Adding to his vexation, he was still tinkering with the final paragraphs, which, try as he might, would not come right. By June, when Scott's ten pages of comments arrived, Ernest was in no mood to give the manuscript the thorough overhaul that would be needed were he to follow this fresh advice.

Scott was extremely enthusiastic about the book, far more than he had been about *The Sun Also Rises*; he called the novel "damn good" and closed his remarks with the exclamation, "A beautiful book it is!" He sprinkled compliments throughout his suggestions: the retreat from Caporetto was "marvelous"; the sequence in which Frederic buys the pistol "is a *wonderful* scene"; at another point he says, "Now here's a great scene." He brought up the justly famous passage that begins, "If people bring so much courage to this world the world has to kill them to break them, so of course it kills them" (*FTA,* 249), calling it "one of the best pages you've ever written."

But his criticisms would have required substantial revision. He wanted scenes cut: a long conversation with opera singers in a Milan bar, Catherine and Frederic's visit to a racetrack. Mostly he had problems with the character of Catherine: the pregnancy of an unwed mother was "an *old situation,*" the character "too glib," the quality of her conversations with Frederic too naive. But the flaw in the character of Catherine was more fundamental, he said. In "Cat in the Rain" and "Hills Like White Elephants," Fitzgerald said, "you were really listening to women—here you're only listening to yourself, to your own mind." This cut close to the bone. In the margin Ernest wrote, "Kiss my ass —EH."

Fitzgerald's criticisms came too late—according to Hemingway's clock—to be of use, and reading them simply annoyed the always touchy writer. But Ernest's communications to Max Perkins about why he wanted his address withheld from Scott signaled the beginning of an era in which Ernest would do everything he could to downplay his friend's achievement and to ruin—the word is not too harsh—his reputation. By the time 1929 was out, Ernest would effectively end his relationship with Scott; the two men, once the closest of friends, would meet face-to-face only four times before Scott's death in 1940.

* * *

On June 20 the most recent installment of *A Farewell to Arms* in *Scribner's Magazine* was banned in Boston. Max Perkins was of two minds about the resulting publicity—any attention was good, but there was a danger the presumed salaciousness would be all the public would hear about the book. The whole matter was extremely ticklish, Perkins fearful that he would alienate his colleagues, the press, and his star writer if too much attention was paid to the sensationalistic aspects of the book. Ernest, he knew, was not only sensitive to slights but understandably ready to explode in the face of what he saw as censorship. Max was privately a rather fastidious man, not given to using four-letter words himself, and his exchanges with Ernest about which words were objectionable at times approached the farcical. There were three such words in *A Farewell to Arms,* and Ernest thought they were "balls," "cocksucker," and "shit," while actually it was "fuck" rather than "shit" that was deemed unpublishable. After everyone approved some obvious substitutions, halfway measures were aired, but in the end Scribner's published the novel with long dashes in place of the offending words. It was all a distraction from what was, to Ernest, the real issue—the novel's ending.

In *Scribner's Magazine,* Ernest had chosen to end the novel with approximately 250 words following the death of Catherine and the baby in childbirth. Frederic Henry, the narrator, says that there are many more details he could provide: his meeting with the undertaker, his friend Rinaldi and the cure of his syphilis, the future of the priest under Fascism—or even his own actions the night after Catherine's death. The last sentence read, "I could tell what has happened since then but that is the end of the story." Most of Ernest's alternate endings—there were as many as forty-seven—ended with this sentence, but the material that came between Catherine's death and these last words changed with every telling. Perhaps Ernest was putting pressure on himself to equal the stunningly effective ending of *The Sun Also Rises.* In the penultimate version, that book ends when Lady Brett says ruefully that they could have "had such a damned good time together," and Jake Barnes replies, "Isn't it nice to think so?" In his final revision, Hemingway changed only one adjective, substituting the word "pretty" for "nice," and it made all the difference.

Meanwhile, Max Perkins was influenced by Owen Wister's reading of the manuscript of *A Farewell to Arms,* and Wister had trouble with the ending. Max did too, but for a different reason: Wister thought Catherine's death was too graphic a note to end on, while Max felt the war component of this love-and-war novel dropped away too completely; he wanted a final reference back to the war. And Fitzgerald had recommended moving the beautiful set piece that begins, "If people bring so much courage to this world . . ." to the very end.

Faced with these clashing recommendations, Ernest floundered. He wrote an ending in which Frederic and Catherine's baby lives. In another version he closed with Frederic hiring an undertaker. He tried ending on a religious note: "The thing is that there is nothing you can do about it. It is all right if you believe in God and love God" (*FTA,* 304). He toyed with what the editor of the 2012 revised edition of the novel, Seán Hemingway, called "The *Nada* Ending": "That is all there is to the story. Catherine died and you will die and I will die and that is all I can promise" (*FTA,* 303). In this mood, in which no version of the novel seemed right, he began dreaming up titles. The list includes the title he eventually chose, but also "If You Must Love," "In Praise of His Mistress," "One Event Happeneth to Them All," "The Sentimental Education of Frederic Henry," among others, some better and some worse. He crossed out "The Enchantment."

One thing he was sure of, Ernest told Max, and that was the dedication: To G. A. Pfeiffer. Ernest was very appreciative of Pauline's munificent Uncle Gus, and sincere in choosing to dedicate the book to him rather than Pauline. Gus had sent Ernest a very kind letter when his father died, saying he would have sent financial aid to Ed Hemingway if he had known of his plight. In the same letter he brought a refreshing reminder of some often forgotten truths about art, that whether the book was "popular" or not, it "remains an expression and part of yourself. . . . I know it's honest all the way through and that's what's important."

Pauline and Ernest spent most of the summer of 1929 in Spain, though Pauline did not come south until after the feast at Pamplona in early July. Jinny Pfeiffer and Guy Hickok joined Ernest for the fiesta. Ernest and Pauline then followed the matadors through Santiago de Compostela to such towns as Verín and Benavente, crossing the Guadarrama Mountains to Madrid on September 1, where they saw the American matador, Sidney Franklin (née Frumkin), in the ring. Though Ernest did not then go on the circuit for over a month with the self-styled bullfighter from Brooklyn, as Franklin claimed in his autobiography, the two spent several days together in early September, Ernest briefly joining Franklin's *cuadrilla.* A fringe benefit of these days on tour with Franklin was the access the matador gave him to the *callejón,* the zone between the arena and the stands, where one could see the action close up. The days the two men spent together saw the cementing of a warm friendship that would last through the Spanish Civil War. In 1933, when Franklin needed surgery for intestinal resection caused by a rectal goring, Ernest footed the bill.

Ernest was now gathering materials assiduously for a piece about bull-fighting, which had been a goal of his for some time. Immediately, he was writing a shorter article for Archie MacLeish, now at the new business magazine *Fortune;* this would appear in March 1930 as "Bullfighting, Sport and Industry." (Ernest was embarrassed to tell his friend what he thought he should get for the piece: $2,500. It's not clear what he was ultimately paid.) The longer work he envisioned would be much more ambitious, accompanied by photos of all phases of the bullfight.

In general, however, he was somewhat at a loss for what to write next, as he expressed in a letter to Max from Santiago, but he had a direction in mind: "Maybe it is punk—but started to write some things about fishing—hunting—about Bull fights and bull fighters—About eating and drinking—About different places—Mostly things and places." He feared that he might have the same trouble getting his new book off the ground that Scott was having. He was resolved to act. "I think that's Scott's trouble . . . to consciously write such a thing that had to be *great* just constipated him." In fact, however, he would not bring out another book—his bullfighting book, *Death in the Afternoon*—until 1932.

A Farewell to Arms came out on September 27—not the day of the stock market crash, which was a month later, on October 29, though Ernest later claimed that the book was published on Black Friday. He heard from his friends right away. Archie, after he read the serialized novel in *Scribner's Magazine,* told Ernest, "It is beautiful—beautiful beyond words. . . . I send you my complete praise & my profound respect. You become in one book the great novelist of our time." John Peale Bishop, a writer friend by way of Scott, wrote Ernest, "I should need to be strong and well fortified to give it all the praise I think it deserves. But let me say that no contemporary could have done better, and few in the past have surpassed its best stretches." And Dos Passos responded, "Dear Hem, do you realize that you're king of the fiction racket?"

The reviews were spectacular. "FIRST REVIEWS SPLENDID. PROSPECTS BRIGHT, " Max cabled Ernest on September 28. Perry Hutchison, writing for *The New York Times Book Review,* called it "a moving and beautiful book." T. S. Matthews, in his *New Republic* review, said, "The writings of Ernest Hemingway have very quickly put him in a prominent place among American writers, and his numerous admirers have looked forward with great impatience and great expectations to his second novel. They should not be disappointed. *A Farewell to Arms* is worthy of their hopes and of its author's promise." *Time* observed, "In its sustained, inexorable movement, its throbbing preoccupation with flesh and blood and nerves rather than the fanciful fabrics of intellect, it fulfills the prophecies that his most excited admirers have made about Ernest Hemingway." Mary Ross in the *Atlantic* noted in the novel "a wider and deeper range of emotion than Hemingway has dared before." The reviewer for the London *Times* observed, "Mr. Ernest Hemingway has found in the War a finer scope for his very powerful talent than he has ever found before. *A Farewell to Arms,* even in these days of many War novels, stands out as something entirely original." And Fanny Butcher, writing in the *Chicago Tribune,* where his mother would be sure to see it, called the book "the most interesting novel of the year. . . . Anyone who thus has watched American writing cannot but find in it a blossoming of a most unusual genius of our day."

Perhaps Edmund Wilson would prove the most perspicacious in referring to Hemingway as a "Bourdon gauge of morale," referring to his "barometric accuracy." *A Farewell to Arms* came out at an odd time—just before the Crash, in the last year of the 1920s, and eleven years after the end of the war. Critics weren't sure how to assess this timeliness (or lack of it). Malcolm Cowley, for instance, wanted to place it in terms of demobilization "draw[ing] slowly to its end"; more meaningfully, he saw the novel as Hemingway's "farewell to a period, an attitude and perhaps to a method also." Indeed, with its farewell to such words as glory and honor the novel unquestionably closed out a certain understanding of war; the modern sense of war had as much to do with bureaucratic mixups, failures in communications, or tedious waiting as it did with a series of heroic battles. At the same time, *A Farewell to Arms* is, like other poems, novels, and memoirs of the 1920s, very much a work about disillusioned youth, similar to the mood (and title) of Robert Graves's contemporaneous *Good-bye to All That.* In some senses Hemingway got the novel in under the wire, so to speak—before the economy crashed and the entire mood of the country changed. With that shift, demands came to be made that art reflect cultural shifts and that the writer be socially conscious.

Another feature that Cowley touched on in his review was a sense that the novel was a farewell to "a method," the emotions in the novel "more colored by thought," demanding "a subtler and richer prose." Hemingway's style in his previous book had been so distinctive that critics looked for it in his latest novel, sensitive to modifications and innovations. For the most part, they didn't find any new elaborations on the laconic style of his early work; instead they referred to the style as expressive of a nature behind it that was emotional and sensitive in the extreme ("a wider and deeper reach of emotion than Hemingway has dared before"), something that had not been said of him thus far. Bernard De Voto thought Hemingway in *A Farewell to Arms* "for the first time justifies his despair and gives it the dignity of a tragic emotion." (Emotion is, in fact, one of the aspects of the novel that makes it seem somewhat dated: Hemingway's prose expresses a lot of very traditional emotions, almost reinjecting concepts of honor and glory into Frederic's extremely romantic nature and the romanticism of the entire love plot.) The novel has not in the end the power his short stories have; there, emotions are stripped, obscured, buried, to reemerge to readers as they discover them; in *A Farewell to Arms* the only place that happens is the dialogues. Necessarily, the hero and heroine take on a certain cardboard quality, and the novel falls short of the magnificently complex characters created by, say, F. Scott Fitzgerald in *Gatsby* or even *Tender Is the Night*. Hemingway could be said to have traded complexity in return for a rip-roaring plot with recognizable emotions expressed in a more traditional aesthetic than his own brilliant short stories.

Rip-roaring plots win audiences. Ernest must have been gratified to hear that by the end of October Scribner's had sold 36,000 copies of *A Farewell to Arms,* as Max wrote Scott. (The editor had what must have been an annoying habit of keeping Scott informed of Ernest's sales numbers.) By Christmas it had sold nearly 70,000 copies. It topped most best-seller lists, the closest contender another war novel, Erich Maria Remarque's *All Quiet on the Western Front.* Ernest was worried, however, about the effect of the stock market crash and its aftermath on book sales—and rightly so; Max Perkins wrote, "The danger now is on account of the sudden and distinct depression in business that came with the Wall Street crash," though Max thought *A Farewell to Arms,* considered such a worthy book, might be spared.

But Ernest was caught up that fall in two troubling situations, in both of which Fitzgerald figured. The first was a misunderstanding involving Gertrude Stein, and the second a fracas that resulted when Bob McAlmon reappeared with a manuscript to sell.

Ernest had kept his distance from Stein since he and Hadley split up; Stein and Toklas were still Bumby's godparents, but the closeness they had all enjoyed was history. According to Stein, she had heard Ernest was back in Paris when she ran into him and brought him back to the rue Fleurus apartment for a long talk. Stein said that during that talk she accused him

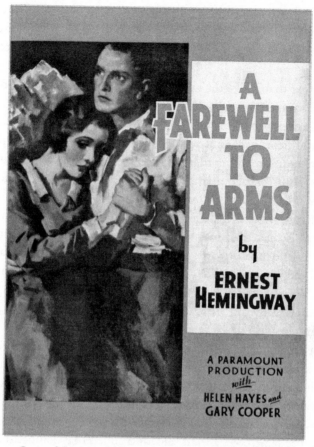

Cover of the tie-in for the 1932 movie, starring Gary Cooper

of being ninety percent Rotarian. Ernest asked if she could make it eighty percent, but Stein said she couldn't. (This was recounted in the 1933 *Autobiography of Alice B. Toklas,* a wonderful but untrustworthy document.) When Stein ran into Ernest again in October 1929, she asked him to come around the next evening and to bring Scott. Ernest encouraged Scott to come, telling him, "She claims you are the one of all us guys with the most talent etc." Stein was indeed an admirer of Fitzgerald's work, believing that *This Side of Paradise* "really created for the public the new generation." She said this was "equally true" of *The Great Gatsby* and predicted his work would be read, "when many of his well known contemporaries are forgotten."

When Ernest showed up at Stein's with Scott that Wednesday, they brought Pauline and Zelda; John and Margaret Bishop; and two new friends, the budding critic Allen Tate and Caroline Gordon, his novelist wife. At one point Gertrude and Ernest were deep in conversation about *A Farewell to Arms*. She was complimentary, but Ernest, aware of her excellent critical eye, wanted to hear what she *didn't* like. "She thinks the parts that fail," he told Scott in a letter the next day, "are where I remember visually rather than make up"; perhaps she meant that the realism or naturalism of his prose represented a step backward—because so different from her own. Ernest was a little disappointed—he already knew that, he said. At this point Scott walked up and joined the conversation. Gertrude evidently then said something that sent the two men into mental conniptions afterward about their comparative "flames." It is not clear which she felt burned the most brightly, and whether a bright flame was in fact preferable to a low flame that would then blow up in great bursts. What is abundantly clear is that Stein was forced to say something very tactful to the two men, who wanted to talk together about their respective talents. But Scott believed she had spoken slightingly of his "flame," and he brooded further as the Hemingways and Fitzgeralds walked home. Both men were quite drunk. Scott wrote Ernest a quick note the next morning apologizing for anything insulting he might have said on the way back.

With a hangover from the evening bad enough to remark on, Ernest answered Scott's note of apology the next day, saying he had not been insulted and tried to explain what he thought Stein had meant in her comments about their "flames." He observed, quite astutely, that she had set up a hare-and-tortoise race in which neither contender "won." Serious writers were all in the same boat, Ernest said, and added that competition between them was as silly as all "deck sports" were. He reminded Scott that she had said critical things about his work, and he didn't care: "When they bawl you out ride with the punches."

Ernest had seen or heard little from Bob McAlmon in the past few years, seemingly not giving him much thought lately. In a letter to Scott in 1925 he had called him "a son of a bitch with a mind like an ingrowing toe nail" and had seldom referred to him since. McAlmon and Bryher had been divorced in 1927, and in mid-1929 McAlmon had shut down Contact Editions and left for the U.S. Ernest had given McAlmon a letter of recommendation to bring to Max Perkins. Independently, he wrote Max that he thought McAlmon had been "unjustly treated," in that McAlmon's critics had never given his work serious consideration—though he added that much of Bob's work was "terrible." Evidently having some misgivings about sending such "damned gossip" to Perkins, he added that McAlmon had once spread a rumor (which seems to have arisen out of thin air) about Ernest beating Hadley when she was pregnant. Ernest appears to have had continued doubts that McAlmon would spread other rumors, true or not, about him, writing Max in November that with the "most purely inventive" gossips he knew in New York at the time, rumors about him might reach Max at Scribner's.

McAlmon visited Perkins sometime in October. Max, again not showing the greatest wisdom in telling Scott stories about Ernest, wrote Scott on the 30th that though Ernest had sent McAlmon to him with a letter, McAlmon had, that night at dinner, said "mean things about Ernest (this is absolutely between you and me) both as a man and as a writer." Scott wrote Max back that McAlmon was a "bitter rat" who had told both Ernest and Morley Callaghan that Ernest and Scott were "fairies," adding, "He's a pretty good person to avoid."

Ernest did not get wind of this until December 9, when Scott told him what Perkins had said. Ernest was furious, starting two different letters to Max before sending off the third. He had heard, he said, that McAlmon was spreading rumors that he was homosexual and that Pauline was a lesbian (this last was new). Ernest defended Scott to Max (he is "the soul of honor" when sober and "completely irresponsible" when drunk). He told Max, somewhat reproachfully, that McAlmon had told one of these stories in front of Ernest's friend Evan Shipman, who had hit McAlmon, calling him a liar.

McAlmon may well have been telling stories about what he believed to be Ernest's homosexuality ever since Ernest's first trip to Spain with him in 1923. Accusations of homosexuality were thick on the ground in Paris in the 1920s, and it is not entirely surprising many of them seemed to spring up around Ernest and Scott. Closer to home, Zelda apparently believed that her husband and Ernest had a homosexual relationship, accusing Scott one night during an argument on the rue Palatine. The accusations of others were no doubt malicious, fueled by envy of the writers' success, and probably unfounded; Zelda's remains opaque—but equally groundless. One of Scott's biographers points convincingly to a statement in Fitzgerald's *Notebooks* as being about Ernest and their relationship: "I really loved him, but of course it wore out like a love affair. The fairies have spoiled all that."

Whether it was the welter of gossip, Scott's criticisms of *A Farewell to Arms,* or Scott's instability and increasing drunkenness, Ernest was finding their relationship ever more vexing. Perhaps typically, the incident he kept returning to was the boxing match with Morley Callaghan, and Scott's failure to end the round on time. In a long letter to Scott on December 12, Ernest told Scott over and over again that he believed Scott when he said he did not do it purposefully: he believed Scott *implicitly.* Over the course of the letter he described many situations in which a timekeeper might deliberately not call time, but he insisted that he did not believe Scott, "the soul of honor," would do such a thing. In the end, he tried to understand. "I only wish to God you didn't feel so bum when you drink," he said in closing. "I know it's no damn fun but I know too everything will be fine when your book is done."

In *That Summer in Paris,* Morley Callaghan tried to put his finger on just what Scott so admired in Ernest:

> [Scott] began to tell me about all Ernest's exploits and his prowess and his courage. . . . It seemed to give him pleasure to be able to tell stories about a man whose life was so utterly unlike his own. He gave Ernest's life that touch of glamour that he alone could give, and give better than any man. Ernest and the war. His wound. The time when Ernest thought he was dead.

As he listened to Scott spin his tale, Morley became impatient. He said he had as much affection for Ernest as Scott had, but at the same time felt Scott was belittling his own life and work, as well as making excessive claims for the importance of courage.

The problem, Morley thought, was that the admiration was so one-sided. Scott, he said, "had some need of the kind of close friendship he thought he could get from Ernest. It seemed to me that Scott wanted to offer incredible loyalty to him." Yet for some reason that Morley could not fathom—whether it was something about Scott's work, or some troublesome past history—Ernest could not reciprocate. On balance, Morley concluded, "[Ernest] simply didn't want to be bothered with him."

FIFTEEN

The *Bourdonnais,* carrying the Hemingways back to Key West by way of Havana after nine months in Europe, stopped in New York City for two days in January 1930. With Archie, Don Stewart, and Dorothy Parker, Ernest and Pauline visited Ada MacLeish, in the hospital for an operation, and Ernest saw Max Perkins and Mike Strater. But Ernest and Pauline also saw lawyers and bankers, found for them by Uncle Gus, in order to establish a trust fund to take care of Grace Hemingway and the three youngest children. Ultimately, Pauline and Gus Pfeiffer together gave $20,000 for the trust, while Ernest would provide $30,000, which came directly out of his profits from *A Farewell to Arms.*

Ernest could be generous with his family, but it was a difficult process. Grace Hemingway remained a strong-willed and independent woman, unlikely to respond well to anyone's efforts to govern her, least of all her eldest strong-willed son's. When Grace wrote Ernest in December or January (Ernest did not keep the letter that he quoted from) that "justice demanded" he provide financial support for the younger children's college educations, he was quick to respond that she had better not talk to him about "justice" and what it "demanded," since he had accepted no money from home after high school, and certainly not for a college education. As a matter of fact, he told her, he was setting up a $50,000 trust for Carol, the youngest daughter, which would pay her $600 a year; he was giving Grace money for Leicester directly. The elaborate letter Ernest wrote his mother on January 27, with its refrain of what "justice demanded," recalls nothing so much as the letter his mother had sent him in 1919 about his overdrawn account in the bank of maternal love.

Not surprisingly, Grace bristled when she received this letter, and she immediately wrote Ernest saying that she did not appreciate being "threatened." She invoked the Heavenly Father and stated that she was a free soul not owned by any man—husband *or* son. Writing back on February 19 Ernest stated, unequivocally, that he did not make threats, and that his stipulations about how Grace spent or invested her resources were not made to "own" her. He still needed to clear up many financial matters, notably the unsold Florida land that was eating up her small capital in taxes. In his anger he was unable to refrain from sarcasm, writing, "It is beside the point to bring into this effort to give you economic stability any discussion of our Lord or our Heavenly Father. I am glad you are on such excellent terms with Him. It is one of the important things in life and I congratulate you, but that is not the point."

Ernest may have been happy to lord it over his mother in this way. More important, he was happy that he could provide amply for her and the children. But for emotional reasons of his own, Ernest liked to plead poverty—hardly unusual behavior. Giving money carried risks, of course, and mainly the risk that by doing so you would reveal that you had money to give. These letters to his mother are marked by this most basic contradiction—as well as the conflicting desire to brag about success and still plead poverty. In the January letter Ernest went into detail about his income, adding that he told her this only to show her how very poor he was: he had two sons and no house or other property. Evidently his mother sent him clippings about him, the novel, and plans for a movie and play, for Ernest wrote in February that he supposed she was trying to point out that he had made a lot of money from the movie and theatrical rights. This was not true, he wrote, providing ample details. When you give people a certain amount of money, he said, they tend to think you have more than that figure and don't understand how you can give them the smaller amount. Ernest, of course, was invoking a fundamental but no less bothersome habit of human behavior.

It was almost certainly no accident that just as he was writing letters that sounded like his mother's infamous overdrawn-bank-account letter, Ernest had begun to adopt a conservative—or worse, an intolerant, patronizing, and too often hypocritical—tone when taking an interest, or meddling, in the affairs of others. Naturally, this emerges most clearly in his letters to his younger siblings. He was already taking on a conventionally parental role in a letter to his youngest sister, Carol, in late 1929. He had seen Carol at his father's funeral in 1928 and thought she was wonderful, he told her. But he was not pleased with a recent letter she wrote him, which he thought did not sound like her and used too much slang. (He himself used the word "swell," he told her, only in dialogue in his fiction.) He sounded like a displaced Edwardian parent inveighing against flappers when he wrote Carol in late 1929 that he fervently hoped she "won't be corrupted by the cheapness, flipness, petting instead of love, complete self-absorption and cheap, cheap petting vacantness that has come to such a perfect flowering in Oak Park." In this context it is amusing that Carol would later note that Ernest did not really hate their mother; indeed, "He's the one who's most like her," she observed.

This kind of condescension also increasingly marked relations with some of his friends, when it touched on the hypocritical. Painter Waldo Peirce had visited Ernest in Key West in 1928 and found it most congenial, joining Ernest's fishing buddies. In early 1930, when his mistress, Alzira, soon to be his third wife, found herself pregnant, Peirce sent her to Key West to await his arrival. Ernest helped Alzira with some much needed cash, but cautioned Peirce that it would not be wise to join her in Key West unless he could marry her right away. "What's simple in Paris," he told his friend, was complicated in Key West. Guys "like you and me" might not care what people said, but matters were different for "merchants," who might personally worry, needing to maintain a certain standing in the town. These local businesspeople not only might have to endure nasty comments, Ernest told Peirce, but perhaps also see their businesses suffer if scandals involving Hemingway's friends were afoot.

It is doubtful that Ernest's closest friend among the "merchants," Charles Thompson, paid any attention to the marital status of Ernest's visitors—and Thompson was probably among the most respectable of the Key West "merchants" who became part of his Florida posse in the early 1930s. While characters like Arnold "Mice" Samuelson and Toby Bruce had not yet joined the ranks around Hemingway, he had already assembled quite a group. J. B. Sullivan, a Brooklyn-born Irishman known to all as Mr. Sully, had come to Key West after working on Henry Flagler's railroad in 1906 and now owned a Key West marine engine shop. Josie Russell, who would open Sloppy Joe's on Green Street in 1933, had a thriving business running rum in his thirty-two-foot cabin cruiser, the *Anita,* which Ernest frequently rented for deep-sea fishing. Three other men came from the charter boat fishing world: Burge Saunders, Bra Saunders's half brother, who often crewed on Bra's boat; Jakie Key, who also sometimes rented Ernest his boat; and Hamilton Adams, a Conch fisherman who sometimes worked for tourists as a guide.

In the early months of 1930 Ernest seemingly did nothing but fish. Indeed, in the entire year he wrote just one story, "Wine of Wyoming," though he was working intermittently on the bullfighting book. Max Perkins once again came to Key West to visit, though this time not in any editorial capacity, and Ernest rented a cabin cruiser for a trip out to the Dry Tortugas, a group of small islands about sixty-five miles west of Key

On the Gulf Stream, 1933

West, so named because they have no fresh water. Though a 1929 visit had been largely uneventful, on this trip Ernest, Max, Mike Strater, Archie MacLeish (on his first visit), and John Herrmann, whose wife, Josephine Herbst, was waiting it out on shore, were marooned by a tropical storm at Fort Jefferson on Garden Key for days. The men camped in a shed on the dock, fishing a bit during the lulls. They had a good supply of canned food but a finite amount of beer, coffee, and liquor and by the last days were eating only fish. The trip was memorable for Max Perkins, dubbed Deadpan by the group, who caught a fifty-eight-pound kingfish, one pound heavier than the current record, with a rod and reel.

Ernest had barely shaved and changed his clothes before he went out to the Tortugas again, this time with the newly married John and Katy Dos Passos. But it was April, and temperatures in Key West were rising. Ernest began to think of going elsewhere and hunting. He was already planning a remarkable trip, an African safari, which Uncle Gus was happy to bankroll in full. Ernest invited Mike, Archie, and Charles Thompson. He frequently said that Gus was paying their way too, but it seems more likely that guests would be responsible for transportation to and from Africa; all expenses once there, like guides, were already covered by Gus on Ernest's behalf. "You won't have to spend a sou after we leave New York," he told MacLeish. Various obstacles would interfere before the safari became a reality, but Ernest began preparations for it at once, reading everything he could about the continent and researching and buying guns. He expected a lot from it, telling Archie, "We'll go and purify ourselves with a little danger and not shoot the lions until we can smell their breath." Later, he would explain to Janet Flanner, "I like to shoot a rifle and I like to kill and Africa is where you do that."

More immediately, Ernest assembled what was needed for his and Pauline's summer hunting and fishing expedition. First he went to New York City to pick up Bumby, who would be spending the summer with him; Pauline went off to Piggott with Patrick and Henriette, his French nurse, the latter two staying on there. Ernest and Bumby picked up Pauline in Piggott and the three of them drove west. They found they did not much like the dude ranch where they had booked quarters and went instead to the L—T Ranch, only recently bought by the thirty-year-old Lawrence Nordquist and his wife, Olive. The L-Bar-T, as it was called, was in Cody, Wyoming, near the Clarks Fork, a branch of the Yellowstone River, and the Nordquists gave the Hemingways a double log cabin. With such features as huge flagstone fireplaces and leather hinges on the doors, and reached by a swaying plank bridge over a river, the ranch was becoming "one of the choice, invitational dude ranches in the country," according to a Wyoming historian, though Nordquist observed Ernest's wish for anonymity. Pauline and Bumby would spend the whole summer there, and Ernest would stay into the fall, when hunting replaced fishing as the primary activity.

Pauline suited up in blue jeans and a cowboy hat and dutifully mounted the horse provided for her. Her aim in life, she often said, was to be "a lovely unharried wife." She was the luckiest person in the world, she told Ernest. "Going to be a *very* good wife & you deserve *such* a good wife." This meant she would stay at his side all summer and take care of his son Bumby (now, at age seven, increasingly called Jack). Everybody liked Pauline; her ready wit sparkled. According to the ranch hands, Pauline was considered "a real good sport"—though at least one observer, the daughter of a neighboring dude rancher, did not like the way Ernest treated her. She put her husband's need to work first—and Ernest was trying to devote mornings working to the bullfighting book, now called *Death in the Afternoon*. Ernest relied on her editorial instincts completely; if it didn't get past Pauline, it didn't fly. Biographer Bernice Kert writes that Ernest "valued her literary judgment above anyone's," a fact notable in the light of his refusal to submit his works to editing—everything was to be published precisely as he turned it in, except for spelling and punctuation changes. She organized even Ernest's voracious reading; she first read the stacks of books he was always requesting from Scribner's to see if they were worth his time.

Ernest made some lasting friends among the ranch hands at the L-Bar-T, some of whom became, over the summers, the core of his Western posse. Munro Wogaman, known as "Mun," was a fair-haired but darkly tan Norwegian; Leland Stanford Weaver (known as Chub), an inveterate traveler from nearby Red Lodge, Montana; and the redheaded Ivan Wallace all became friends over the years, sometimes visiting him in Key West for a spot of fishing. In early August Ernest became absorbed in hunting down a bear that was killing a nearby rancher's cattle; he and Wallace shot a horse and left it for bait in the hills near the ranch. On the 23rd, when the horse was extremely fragrant, Ernest, Weaver, Wallace, and another hand named Smokey Royce found a brown bear feasting on the baited animal; Ernest killed him with one shot from his new Springfield rifle. Bill Horne and his wife, Bunny, visiting for two weeks in August, played no part in the bear hunt but were good listeners.

In mid-September, Pauline and young Jack (Bumby) left for Piggott and Key West, Ernest planning to stay until November 1 for the hunting. In September he and some hands went off into the mountains for a two-week hunt for elk, mountain sheep, and bear; he followed the kill of the August bear with a mountain ram and a bull elk—each of which he also brought down with one shot. In mid-October, Dos Passos joined Ernest for a ten-day hunting trip up in the mountains. Dos was too nearsighted to shoot but went along for the company and the scenery. He noted that Ernest had "the sense of topography that military technicians have," was always knowledgeable about whether the terrain ahead promised a valley or a cliff, and had a keen sense of smell, almost as accurate as that of the animals they tracked. Dos also noted that Ernest "had the ranch hands under his thumb. They thought he was the most wonderful guy they ever met."

On the night of November 1 (after they had been drinking, according to Dos, "right much bourbon"), Ernest, Dos, and ranch hand Floyd Allington were driving on the narrow gravel road to Billings when Ernest, blinded by the lights of an oncoming car about eighteen miles west of town, landed his car upside down in a ditch. Dos and Floyd were unhurt, but Ernest wound up in St. Vincent's Hospital in Billings with "an oblique spiral fracture, nearly compound" of his right arm, according to Carlos Baker. Pauline arrived by train, and afterward Ernest had surgery in which the torn muscles were bound by kangaroo tendons, a colorful detail he never failed to mention.

The break required that Ernest stay immobilized in bed for almost a month. His bent arm hung suspended over his body in a cast. For the time being, his right hand was paralyzed, but doctors hoped the nerves would heal themselves. Ernest had aimed to finish the bullfighting book by Christmas; he tried dictating it to Pauline, but found writing anything but letters that way impossible. Time passed slowly, and Ernest grew a huge dark beard and mustache, letting his hair grow as well. He was a bad patient; Key West's Lorine Thompson once observed, "He wasn't a very good invalid. When anything happened to him, he made an awful lot of it." Dos left and Archie MacLeish, summoned to Ernest's bedside by Pauline in a desperate attempt to cheer him up, arrived after what he called "the most hair-raising flight of my life." When he approached Ernest's bed, Ernest accused him of coming west only to watch him die. Eventually they calmed down (Ernest really had been angry),

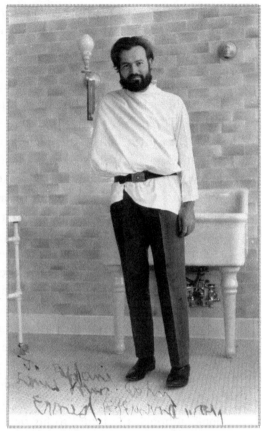

With broken arm after a car crash in Billings, Montana, November 1930. Autographed for Louis Cohn with his left hand.

passing the time with bourbon. Ernest had a standing order for a pint of "bonded" bourbon a day, prescribed in a different name each time and filled at a pharmacy; an old hand since Milan at drinking in hospitals, he hid the pint under his mattress. Finally, the bones knitted successfully and the use of his right hand was restored, though further recovery was slow. He and Pauline left for Christmas in Piggott.

The news of Ernest's accident had appeared in the newspapers, ensuring that he got a lot of mail, though he complained to Grace that aside from her he had heard from no other members of the family. Ernest by now was apprehensive of any press interest in his activities and behavior. He had to warn his mother repeatedly not to talk to reporters, and reprimand her when she did so. Say you don't give interviews, he told her. It was the only way he could keep personal things from becoming public. He did not say so, of course, but while he disliked the prying, he was far more nervous about what Grace herself might say.

Indeed, the year 1930 also saw a strange bit of publicity that Ernest does not seem to have been aware of but that would have borne out his concern; his mother and siblings did not mention it, so it is not clear whether the other children knew about it either. A "Talk of the Town" piece in *The New Yorker* titled "The Other Hemingways" reported that two unspecified Hemingway girls were sculptors (definitely Marcelline and either Ursula or Sunny); another daughter was a pianist (Ursula or Sunny); another girl was a writer (that would be Carol); and another son, age fifteen, was a violinist. The reporter also noted, in a detail that made clear where he or she got the story, that the Hemingways' mother said she gave none of her children middle names or even middle initials, encouraging them to take the name of a relative or someone else they admired when they were old enough. Ernest never chose one, she said. This was pure invention; three of her children had in fact been given middle names. Ernest's was Miller, for his great-uncle; he just chose, as an adult, not to use it. This piece of news was harmless, but its appearance made plain to any other inquiring gossip hounds that Grace Hemingway would provide any and all information the press might want, elaborately embroidered—exactly what her son feared.

Barely back in Key West in early 1931, Ernest was finishing the bullfight book, although the injury to his right arm and hand still prevented him from working too long at a time. He needed to get to Spain that summer to report on the season's bullfights and to lay claim to the photographs that would illustrate the technical points he was trying to make and also convey some small notion of the essence of the experience. Meanwhile, however, he wanted to fish, despite one of the stormiest winters ever known in Key West. His arm prevented him from reeling anything in, but he could hold the rod until he got a strike and then pass the rod—and the fish—over to someone else. He reported to Archie in March that he had shot twenty-seven out of thirty clay pigeons holding a shotgun in his left hand and raising it to his right shoulder, right arm by his side. "May never be a gt. writer but by Christ I am a hell of fine shot with shotgun," he wrote with satisfaction to Archie.

Pauline and Ernest were deluged with guests in early 1931, regardless of the weather. Jinny was visiting, but she was no trouble, and she could help with Uncle Gus and his wife, Louise, also guests. From Wyoming, Ernest's new friends Lawrence and Olive Nordquist took Ernest up on his invitation and came to fish. Chub Weaver, who had driven the Hemingway car south and east from Billings, went out on Ernest's rented boat several times; he would stay in Key West in the winter and return to Wyoming in the summer and fall, as Ernest would do over the next several years. Mike Strater came early and stayed late, always a welcome guest. His Paris friend Evan Shipman showed up (Shipman was an easy guest, wrote Ernest in a letter to Archie MacLeish complaining about being overwhelmed by visitors). Grace Hemingway came and stayed for a couple of days, very likely bringing Carol with her; Carol was now studying at Rollins College in Winter Park, near Orlando. Carol was a pretty girl and a talented writer. Her brother's proximity would prove a mixed blessing. Ernest was able to say, in a letter to Pauline's parents, that Grace and Pauline got along "splendidly."

The writers John Herrmann and Josephine Herbst were not visiting the Hemingways, exactly; they had rented a house nearby. Josephine, or Josie, was the more successful of the two. She had published short stories and two novels—Ernest had provided a blurb for her first novel, *Nothing Is Sacred,* in 1928—and she was just commencing her "Trexler trilogy," her most successful work. Herrmann—who found common ground with Ernest, summers spent in northern Michigan—had published a novel with McAlmon's Contact Editions in 1926. Both he and Josie were increasingly involved in radical politics as the 1930s began, a time that was ripe for left-wing ideas and action.

When Max Perkins showed up for his annual visit, Ernest assembled Herrmann, Strater, Bra's brother Burge, Chub Weaver, and a honeymooning couple, Pat and Maude Morgan, for a ten-day fishing expedition to the Dry Tortugas. Max was lucky enough to leave after only a few days, catching a ride to Key West on another fishing boat. Midway through the trip supplies ran low; most crucially, the party ran out of the ice that was refrigerating the catch—yellowtail, snapper, grouper, and a few kingfish. John Herrmann and Burge Saunders embarked in a small motorboat to pick up three hundred pounds of ice in Key West. Their trip took five days, as it turned out, because of engine trouble, rough water, and nautical misadventures; besides the ice they brought Josie Herbst back with them. By then, the fishermen were eager to get back to the mainland.

Ernest was livid when the two men and Josie returned with the ice; they were too late, and the fish had gone off. The entire party set out for home immediately. There was a lot of tension on board, and Ernest began to needle Herrmann, saying, as Josie later remembered it, "Look, the hero of Lake Michigan, stuck on a sandbar. Look, the famous handyman, can't even get the motor repaired." Ernest was shooting his pistol at birds during his harangue, and finally Josie said, "If you don't stop talking that stuff, Hem, I'll take your gun and shoot you." Ernest kept quiet for the rest of the trip, but once ashore he started up again. Josie began to cry and walked away, and Ernest followed her, claiming that his black mood was the fault of his hurt arm, which was giving him a lot of pain. They all made up the next day, and Ernest somewhat oddly tried to give Josie and John $100 for their car trip up the Keys to the mainland. John turned it down.

Josie Herbst was able to mend her relationship with Ernest (she and Herrmann divorced in 1934), but she never felt the same way about him after watching his performance during and after the Tortugas experience. Indeed, his older friends' general attitude toward Ernest was changing. The increasingly irascible disposition he had shown in his later years in Paris was turning into habitual domineering and a sense of entitlement. The writer Nathan Asch referred to him as "the Lord Mayor of Key West." The Murphys and Dos Passos took to calling Ernest "the Old Monster." The locals and his fishing friends, on the other hand, called him "Mahatma." They looked up to him and tried to please him, which was increasingly what he sought in his companions.

But he was also becoming known as a man with a temper. "As long as people around him were worshipful and adoring," Arnold Gingrich would later observe, "why then they were great. The minute they weren't, there was a tendency to find others who were." Ernest was recognizable on the Key West streets: a big, handsome man, usually in very casual clothes. In fact, he almost always wore shorts, using a knotted rope for a belt. On his feet he wore Indian moccasins (sent to him by Horton Bay friends). It could be worse: in Spain in 1930, Sidney Franklin later wrote, he made a habit of wearing "battered" bedroom slippers in the street. (Evidently he liked footwear he didn't have to bend down to put on.) Often, however, he went barefoot, said his boyhood friend Chub Weaver, who visited Ernest in the winter of 1930–31; he sometimes carried a "fish knife" stuck in his belt. He often went without undershorts and he had huge feet. As far back as his Red Cross exam before going to Italy with the ambulance corps, he had been told he needed glasses. After being fitted for a pair on his return from Italy, he avoided being seen wearing them; his mother was the same way. He also carried a comb in the back pocket of his shorts and compulsively combed his hair, especially before photographs were taken.

Key West was an extremely casual place at the time, and residents liked it that way; Ernest's clothing was not terribly unusual. But he treated the small settlement as his extended domicile, as if the town was under one big roof—his. He did not need to stand on ceremony there; indeed, many people he encountered in his walks around town were directly or indirectly in his employ. Key West was Ernest's personal fiefdom, and when it came time to leave it was quite difficult—but by then essential—to find a place to live that offered the same kind of feel to it.

In mid-March Ernest was able to report to MacLeish, "I am strong and healthy as a pig." He was making plans for a May departure for Spain, aiming to finish the book there. In the meantime Pauline had been house hunting. She was not constrained by finances, for Gus Pfeiffer had told Ernest and Pauline he would pay for it. She was looking for a place that had a secluded study for Ernest, reasonable living and sleeping space for the Hemingways and their servants, and a large yard that would provide some privacy. Pauline had just learned that she was pregnant again, and the baby was calculated to arrive in November. Ernest and Pauline made no secret of the fact that they wanted a girl this time.

Pauline wasn't able to find a house that met her requirements and that appealed to her tastes. The previous year she and Lorine Thompson had looked at a run-down, ramshackle house at the corner of Whitehead and Olivia Streets; plaster fell from the ceilings as they were walking through and they dubbed it the haunted house. Now Lorine suggested that Pauline look again at the old ruin. It needed a huge amount of renovation, but its bones were good. A Spanish colonial structure with wide porches on both levels, both with cast-iron railings, it had been built in 1851 by Asa Tift, a ship's captain with a large marine salvage business. The living room had floor-to-ceiling arched windows, as did the master bedroom above. Uncle Gus, conveniently, was just back from a fishing trip with Ernest. After he was given a tour of the place, he bought it outright for $8,000. The deal was inked on April 29, and Ernest celebrated by getting drunk at Sloppy Joe's (still a speakeasy), while Pauline and Lorine Thompson went for drinks at Pena's Garden of Roses, which had a large outdoor area that boasted the eponymous rose garden.

Despite the long list of renovations needed before they could move in, the Hemingways were off for Europe before any of the work was scheduled, Ernest on the *Volendam* from Havana to Spain, and Pauline following May 20 with Patrick and Henriette on the *President Harding* out of New York.

The general plan was for Pauline to vacate the Paris apartment, arranging to ship the furniture to Key West, and for the two of them to follow the bullfights in Spain. After Paris, Pauline would stay in Hendaye with Patrick and Henriette while Ernest took Jack, who would be eight in October, with him to Spain. Then Pauline would join Ernest as well, and they would

Pauline's generous uncle, Gus Pfeiffer, early 1930s

be back in the U.S. in October in plenty of time to travel to Kansas City, where Dr. Guffey would deliver the child.

Sidney Franklin remembered Jack with his father in Spain that summer. Because the boy was enthusiastic about learning cape work, at which he became quite proficient, Franklin had made him a silk work cape and *muleta* half the size of his own. Caresse Crosby, the colorful American widow of eccentric publisher Harry Crosby, who had recently died in a suicide pact with his mistress, was visiting Spain at the time. She remembered Jack listening to an elderly, retired bullfighter explaining a complicated maneuver with the cape, Ernest straddling a chair and looking on. "The boy had to repeat it again and again; his father was a harsh taskmaster, and [Jack's] face was puckered with apprehension." Caresse thought he was very close to tears. But Ernest painted quite a different picture in a letter to Archie, saying his eldest son wanted to be a bullfighter and showed signs of being a good one, adding that some of his teachers wanted to bring him to a ranch in Salamanca to train.

Much had changed in Spain since the summer of 1929, when Ernest and Pauline were last there. The past two decades had been turbulent. Several years of strikes, social agitation, and rural and industrial unrest preceded the dictatorship of Miguel Primo de Rivera, who took power in 1923. In January 1930, after losing the confidence of the military amidst widespread social unrest, he was forced to resign. In April 1931 King Alfonso XIII, discredited by his long association with Primo de Rivera, fled the country, and the Second Spanish Republic was declared. All this Ernest, a great reader of foreign newspapers, followed with interest.

He arrived in Madrid in June just before the national election on June 28, in which Republicans and Socialists prevailed. Madrid was under martial law. Tensions were growing between the mildly anticlerical new government and the powerful Catholic hierarchy. Some leaders of the Catholic Church were making for the borders. In July the primate, Pedro Cardinal Segura, was exiled. Civil ferment and strikes ruled the day. In some parts of Spain, like Catalonia and Navarra, the right was concentrating its power, anticipating the civil war that would follow in a few years.

As the summer of 1931 wore on, Ernest's interest in the budding conflict between the Republicans and Socialists, then in power, and the royalist and conservative opposition deepened. His new interest stood in sharp contrast to the distinctly apolitical lens through which he had observed the country he loved so much in the 1920s. Then, he had focused instead—in his writings, his letters, and the places he chose to frequent and the people he chose to spend time with—on what he saw as the fundamental, primal "essence" of the people of Spain, something in which Socialist, anarchist, and religious reactionary politics played no part. What he had told his readers about Spain in such stories and novels as "The Undefeated" and *The Sun Also Rises* was not at all false or dishonest. But it disclosed only one part of the country's reality, and perhaps not the most urgent.

This trip, the other side of Spain was compelling to him in a new way, and he was eager to understand it as well. He had to come to terms with it personally as well as politically. The budding conflict was revealing potential tensions within the new familial pattern he had established with Pauline and the Pfeiffers. As a Catholic and now a member of a very observant Catholic family, Ernest would have some sympathy with the conservative, traditionalist side in Spain, at least in the early days of this unrest. If he had any inclination to support the other side, he kept it to himself for the present.

That summer Ernest was feeling the itch to be a journalist again. He told Max Perkins he was following events as avidly as if he were a reporter, and wished there was "some market" for his views. For the time being, however, he was focused on his bullfighting book; regrettably, in those months, as he complained to Dos Passos, "Most bull displays lousy." Ernest's energies were concentrated on making sure that all his information was up-to-date. Not that much was time-sensitive, but he knew that every detail had to be right if the book were to have any authority—and it had to be authoritative, or the whole effort would fail. To him, "getting it right," in this endeavor as in so many others, was in the nature of a challenge he had to meet, or, perhaps, a kind of obsessive compulsion. His work was eased when Uncle Gus took it upon himself to spearhead an effort to find any and all printed material on Spanish bullfights; he had the manager of the Warner-Hudnut lab in Barcelona scour listings for bullfight libraries for sale and to take out ads himself listing the books and magazines Ernest wanted—with Gus paying the bills. Most of what Ernest had to say, however, was not to be found in books, but rather was based on what had now been several years of study. More than factual detail, he wanted to convey what he saw as the essence of bullfighting, a subject he dearly loved. *Death in the Afternoon* has no equal in the Hemingway canon in the passion he felt about what he was communicating.

While the book does get technical, *Death in the Afternoon* is far more than a guide to the mechanics of bullfighting. Rather, Hemingway takes up in turn various aspects of bullfighting that are necessary to understand before comprehending the whole. He explicates the bullfight rather than describing it, so that the reader learns why each element is important; thus there are chapters on cape work, on the placing of the *banderillas*, and on the *muleta*. He discusses various matadors and the qualities needed to make good ones. He moves on to subjects pertaining to bulls: the regions various bulls come from, the breeding and raising of them, at what age they should fight, and so forth. The book is a compendium, but it is also a narrative; it is as if he were speaking from his own notes, telling stories along the way. In every detail Ernest's passion for his subject is palpable. He provides an extended and invaluable glossary of bullfighting terms and concepts. The photographs are an essential part of the book; Ernest gathered over four hundred and Max Perkins and he nearly came to blows over how many would be included, Ernest eventually selecting eighty-one, picturing sixty different matadors. Hemingway provides detailed captions that show at every point along the way the salient features of the action photographed.

Some odd features distinguish the book: at one point he confesses that he cannot describe one fight in detail for they are all different, and so introduces a character called the Old Lady, with whom he has a cranky conversation for several chapters; she moves the story along and also asks questions that allow the narrator to discourse freely. More to the point, he reveals that he is using the device of the Old Lady to introduce dialogue into this work; he is known for his skillful dialogues, he says, so the book needs to have some. Another odd feature is an appendix giving little "case histories" of individual bullfight spectators; the reader familiar with Hemingway's history thus far can recognize his "examples": Hadley, Bill Smith, McAlmon, Chink Dorman-Smith, Don Stewart. The thumbnail sketches are so intriguing that it is an interesting section, though the point is not clear.

Another strange bit is inserted roughly in the middle of the book, in Chapter 12, as a separate section called "A Natural History of the Dead" (he sold it to Caresse Crosby to publish it separately, in fact, as a limited edition). It is a sort of taxonomy of the dead—the changes in color of corpses, the sex of corpses, what happens to bodies that are blown up (they aren't divided along anatomical lines); his tone is dryly humorous, even sarcastic. But while it is vividly presented, gripping in its horrible details, it is not entirely clear why it is here. Perhaps the reason is simple: death is central to understanding the bullfight.

*　*　*

Returning from Spain in September 1931, Pauline and Ernest found themselves on board the *Île de France* with Don Stewart and his wife. Relations with Don Stewart had been strained ever since Ernest had read his scurrilous poem about Dorothy Parker to a gathering in 1926. Since then, Don, who would become caught up in radical politics in the 1930s, had become friends with Jock Whitney, scion of the Whitney fortune, and Jock's sister Jean. Through Jock and Jean Whitney, the Stewarts rented what Stewart described as "a beautiful old white clapboard farmhouse" on the Payne Whitney estate on Long Island; Stewart acknowledged that he and his wife were accused by their friends of "going Whitney." On this crossing the Hemingways and the Stewarts put their differences aside. Through Don and Bea, Ernest and Pauline met a woman who was to be an important part of their lives for the next six or seven years.

Born in 1909, Jane Kendall Mason was born Jane Welsh, but when her adoptive mother remarried, she took the name of her stepfather, the wealthy Lyman Kendall. An accomplished equestrienne, she grew up in Washington, D.C., and on Kentsdale, a Maryland estate. At seventeen, she went to Paris to study painting. At a party at the White House in Jane's debut season a year later, Mrs. Calvin Coolidge called her "the prettiest girl who ever entered the White House"—that is, if we are to believe her testimonial in an advertisement for Pond's cold cream that appeared in magazines in 1928. The ad described her as a Botticelli beauty with "flawless skin as delicate as a wood anemone." Later, Hemingway would describe the Jane Mason character in an excised draft of his novel *To Have and Have Not* as "tall blonde, lovely, [with] perfect features . . . her shining copper-colored [*sic*] hair drawn back like some early Madonna . . . [a] swishing promise to any man." In 1927 Jane Kendall was married to G. Grant Mason, Jr., a Yale graduate and heir to the fortune of James Henry "Silent" Smith; Mason was at the time an executive with Pan American Airways based in Havana, Cuba. He and Jane had designed their own villa there, next to a country club in the exclusive suburb of Jaimanitas.

When the Hemingways met them, the Masons were returning from England, Jane with bland anecdotes about the Prince of Wales, a friend of her mother's. Her stories about Cuba and Africa were more interesting; she knew (and would soon have an affair with) Dick Cooper, a British army major who owned a coffee plantation in Tanzania. After returning to Havana, Jane had Cooper help Ernest and Pauline with their preparations for their 1933 African safari. For now, Ernest admired her very much. He had ongoing plans to take a fishing trip to Havana, an excursion he would make in spring 1932, when his relationship with Jane would begin.

At this point Pauline was seven months pregnant and Ernest still occupied with fine-tuning the bullfighting book. When they docked in New York City, Ernest met Max Perkins and gave him the photographs for *Death in the Afternoon,* which he hadn't wanted to entrust to the mails. From New York they went up to visit Archie and Ada at their farm in Conway, Massachusetts. Pauline returned to New York while Ernest went with Archie and Waldo Peirce to see a Harvard football game.

By October 14 Pauline and Ernest were in Kansas City expecting their child's arrival. Ernest was finishing *Death in the Afternoon,* writing the evocative final chapter, a lyrical paean to Spain. The book may have been informed by Hemingway's view of bullfighting as the most masculine of pursuits (there was no place for a woman in the bullfighting world, except to receive ears from matadors in the stands). But the last chapter made clear that Ernest loved Spain first, and loved bullfighting as a uniquely Spanish art. "If I could have made this enough of a book," he wrote in the concluding chapter's first sentence, "it would have had everything in it" (*DIA,* 270). He went on to enumerate the elements he had left out of the book, along the way, of course, adding them in—and describing them in tender language. By the last line of the chapter he invoked the inadequacy of the book ("It is not enough of a book," he writes) and modestly described what little he had done. "But still there were a few things to be said. There were a few practical things to be said" (*DIA,* 278). Ernest, a connoisseur of endings, wrote confidently to Archie that in the book he'd pulled off, again, a miraculous close.

SIXTEEN

Gregory Hancock Hemingway was born on November 12, 1931, the name Hancock that of Grace's mother, Caroline Hancock Hall, and Gregory after any number of popes, Ernest said; he liked the name because it reminded him of Greg Clark, a friend from the *Toronto Star* days. Pauline had gone into labor around 6 p.m., was taken to Kansas City's Research Hospital, and underwent twelve hours of very hard labor in hopes of a natural birth. A cesarean operation and Gregory's appearance followed; Ernest later said the boy did not breathe for the first twenty minutes—undoubtedly an exaggeration. Ernest wrote his mother that Pauline had suffered through agonies in labor. As Gregory (then a trained doctor) would later reconstruct it, the belief at the time was that if a woman had more then two cesarean sections, any further pregnancy "would cause her uterus to rupture." And so, while Ernest had desperately wanted a daughter, Greg's birth meant there could be no further children and no prospect of a daughter—with Pauline, at any rate. Patrick, born after Ernest's "volcanic" love affair with Pauline, became his mother's favorite son, "which is certainly no crime, but unfortunately was so construed by me," Greg would write.

After a brief stop in Piggott, the family was back in Key West for Christmas, moving into their new house on Whitehead Street, which was still undergoing renovation. Jinny Pfeiffer had been there looking after things with Ernest's sister Carol, on vacation from college. The two women, who quickly became friends, took delivery of and arranged the antique Spanish furniture Pauline and Ernest had bought in Europe. The house was still dilapidated, however, the plaster walls and ceilings crumbling; Pauline hung cheesecloth over the ceiling in the boys' room so nothing would fall on them in their cribs. The kitchen was still under construction. But in the two-story structure in back of the house, originally a carriage house, Ernest's second-floor studio was ready for occupancy. Housing all his manuscripts and his uniform and souvenirs from the First World War,

With Pauline in Key West, ca. 1932

the room was not yet decorated or fitted out, but Ernest installed a desk, chair, and typewriter, and settled down to finishing *Death in the Afternoon.* Nesting made both Ernest and Pauline extremely happy. Max Perkins once observed, "Hemingway is one of the most domestic people in the world, with an extraordinarily domestic wife." He got Pauline right—except that her version of domesticity was not maternal; her aim was always to make a home for her husband. (Ernest was not particularly paternal with the boys, for that matter.)

This winter, as during the last, there was no end of guests—all shunted off to a hotel or guesthouse to sleep, without exceptions. In January Dos and Katy visited on their way to Mexico. Afterward Dos read *Death in the Afternoon* and said he thought it "hellishly good." But he did not like it, he said, when Ernest intruded as a philosopher. Somewhat surprisingly, given Ernest's sensitivity to criticism, the friendship survived; Ernest wrote back with some editorial suggestions for Dos's *1919.* His old friend from the war, Bill Horne, also came, with his wife, Bunny. And Mike Strater and Archie MacLeish came for another, ever-eventful fishing trip to the Dry Tortugas.

This time out, Archie and Ernest quarreled and each evidently said some unforgivable things. Judging from a letter Archie wrote on April 7 and Ernest's reply (a couple of letters seem to be missing), what happened was this: a fire of some sort started when they were onshore and at one point threatened the fishing boat. It was a dangerous situation, and both men (and, presumably, Mike) had to make snap decisions and take action under pressure. Ernest barked orders and criticisms in a tone that implied he didn't think Archie knew what he was doing. Archie, himself extremely competitive since his days at Yale, felt the same way: that Ernest had taken what he did and said in fighting the fire as "in some way a criticism." Tactfully, Archie wrote that—with the single exception of biking in Paris—"there is nothing we have ever done together . . . in which I have not implicitly in myself acknowledged your superiority." Ernest acknowledged the misunderstanding at the time of the fire, saying he had been unduly complaining, but then became a little less gracious, justifying the rest of what he had said as "just practical suggestion[s]," and saying that he had been "just discussing technique for possible hurried performances." But Ernest made these somewhat churlish remarks in a long letter meant to salvage their friendship. He offered to help his friend out by advancing Archie money if he needed it, again referring to the expenses-paid African safari on which he hoped Archie would join him. Both letters between the men are awkward, difficult to decode; clearly neither was comfortable—nor did either of them claim or strive to be—talking about their feelings.

But it is clear that, for whatever reason, neither wanted to endanger their friendship. They wrote frequently to each other, bucking one another up, commiserating over bad reviews and plotting revenge for them, discussing family matters and romances, making elaborate plans for future shared adventures, and sometimes disagreeing. Archie was and would continue to be—with a hiatus or two—one of Ernest's closest friends. Not as close as Scott Fitzgerald, but that friendship seems to have been shelved at this point. It is hard to compare the relationship to Ernest's wartime friendships with Bill Horne or Howell Jenkins, or with his Michigan buddy Bill Smith, for most of those friendships had been burnished with nostalgia and now seemed somewhat ephemeral.

Archie would remind himself of his friend's loyalty and generosity "when Ernest seems insensitive." They were companions through the most turbulent and happy years, when they were marrying and finding their way as writers. As early as 1927 Archie was reminiscing about the smell of wet bark in Bayonne from their trip to Spain, melting snow on their pants at Gstaad, bicycling to Chartres. In a similar vein, Ernest remembered occasions on which Archie had showed himself a true friend: paying Ernest's way in Gstaad one winter, including buying him train tickets; Archie's coming out to Billings, Montana, when Ernest broke his arm; the way Archie and Ada welcomed and fed him as part of their family in their Paris apartment in 1926, after Ernest and Hadley separated.

Archie was not an especially tolerant man himself, or an easy friend, as his biographer points out. Like Ernest, he was cut from unusual cloth. He wore many different hats, as they say today: he was a poet, a playwright, a lawyer, later Librarian of Congress, undersecretary of state under FDR, professor, and part-time farmer. Like Ernest, he could be difficult. He was unable to hide his feelings if he didn't like someone, and he was, claims his biographer, subject to "crushes" on new people, "tremendous emotional outpouring followed by disillusionment"—though he sometimes relented and met the friend on a firmer, more lasting footing. It was on his trip to Spain with Ernest, MacLeish told Carlos Baker, that he learned he did not have the "temperament to be with someone else day and night"; it was partly on these grounds, and partly because of his fear of becoming too competitive with his friend, that Archie eventually declined to go on the African trip. He early on established a pattern of losing his temper at Ernest (unless Ernest lost *his* first) and forswearing their friendship. In most cases, it was Ernest who apologized and tried to reestablish the connection, as it was in 1932.

Their friendship was thus different from most of Hemingway's relationships: Ernest was quick to say he was sorry for being annoying and bullying, acknowledging that he was indeed, as Archie said, the first to perceive a slight. In the years to come he would insist that he had changed, dismissing his previous behavior as that of a mean bastard, once announcing the advent of a new self: "good, non-righteous, non-bragging, no-boasting, almost non-chicken-shit." In no other context than in his friendship with MacLeish was Hemingway able to show this kind of self-knowledge; in that respect, though the two men could behave very childishly with each other, the friendship brought out the best in them.

Ernest's constant refrain to Archie was to come visit wherever he was. In Wyoming, in Key West, in Cuba: Ernest said he would pay Archie's expenses round-trip, "New York to New York," time after time. Their writing, of course, was quite different: Archie wrote poetry, Ernest fiction. (Once, when Archie showed Ernest a short story he wrote about skiing, Ernest told him never to write about a subject he didn't know inside and out. If they ever discussed Ernest's poetry, the evidence has not survived.) Like many a poet, Archie was often short of funds. Though Ernest pleaded poverty with his own family and other friends, he was extremely generous to Archie. It could be argued that both men had a deep, if usually concealed, vein of snobbery, in that they spoke and acted as if money matters were beneath them as gentlemen, and as if there was plenty of money for everything. Archie predicated his inability to afford the expenses of the safari that Gus Pfeiffer was not covering (transportation to and from Africa) on the drying up of dividends from Carson Pirie Scott and Company, his father's dry goods firm; since Black Friday they had dwindled to the extent that Archie had to take a job at *Fortune* and would have to hold down jobs for the rest of his life. In fact, however, as Archie made clear in a letter in the conciliatory exchange in 1932, he had always been ambivalent about going on the safari, breaking the news to Ernest and repeating himself thus: "I suppose I have known it all along. I suppose I have always known that I really couldn't go." The trip to the Tortugas that year had been a nightmare, yet, Archie wrote, meaning to show enthusiasm, "Tortugas was just a taste of what Africa with you and Mike and Charles might have been." As Archie later told Carlos Baker, he knew he and Ernest would fight if they were together for that long a period. In April of 1932, once the two had buried their differences, Ernest told Archie he was keeping a place open for him on the coming African safari—which, in fact, he was postponing again.

After his early trips to the Tortugas, Ernest was interested in any location within striking distance of Key West. Because his beloved Gulf Stream flowed between Florida and Cuba, and because Havana was an exotic city and a destination likely to lure Pauline on a fishing trip, Ernest was eager to make the voyage over from Key West. Pauline and Ernest's new friendship with Cuba residents Grant and Jane Mason, whom they had met on board the *Île de France* the previous September, was also a factor; no doubt the Masons had been issuing invitations to the Hemingways for some months.

Jane Mason, accomplished in many different areas, seems to have been constantly busy. She and her husband, when designing their house in the posh Havana suburb of Jaimanitas, built a sculpture studio for her on the third floor. She admired and promoted Cuban art and craftwork, at one point opening a shop that showcased and sold it. She loved sports, gambling, shopping, and entertainment, roughly in that order. She and her husband were so widely known for their skill at the rumba that the floors in Havana nightclubs would clear when they stood up to dance. They were also known for their parties, some of them twenty-four-hour affairs; at one party white pigeons, dyed in bright colors, pecked around the guests' feet. By the end of 1932 the Masons had adopted two small boys, usually left at home with their English nanny (they had, as well, a veritable United

Nations of servants: a Haitian houseman, Italian butler, German gardener, Chinese cook, Jamaican maid, and Cuban chauffeur). An accomplished horsewoman, Jane also raised whippets.

Sports were Jane's passion, however. She was crazy for deep-sea fishing and for shooting pigeons, the commonest hunting prey in the countryside outside Havana. Moreover, Jane was known as a daredevil, which would have appealed to Ernest. According to Leicester Hemingway, Ernest's little brother, who would come to know Jane well in the 1930s, she "became another kid brother to my brother, especially on [Josie Russell's boat] the *Anita.*" In any sporting pastime with Ernest it would have been difficult for anyone not to play second fiddle in this way, and—not because of any special misogyny on Ernest's part—impossible for a woman to prevail.

While Key West fishermen sometimes caught marlin, this enormous fish proved to be Ernest's ruling piscine passion for the rest of his life, and it predominated in the waters off Cuba. On his first "trip across," to borrow the title of one of his later stories, he tried to learn everything there was to know about marlin. Josie Russell took Ernest, Charles Thompson, and Ernest's Kansas City cousin, Bud White. It was supposed to be a two-week affair, but they stayed longer, finding scores of marlin every day in the waters off Havana. Pauline took the ferry over and joined Ernest, and accompanied him on other trips to Cuba that spring, once bringing along Ernest's sister Carol.

Jane became a good friend to both Ernest and Pauline. On land, they gambled. She and Ernest played a game of chicken in her sports car, driving it off-road at top speed, the chicken the one who first told the other to slow down. The game was considerably modified when Ernest drove, for he took off the glasses he needed to drive because he feared they would break in a sudden impact. At one party at the Masons' Jaimanitas home, Jane organized a conga line that took over the adjoining golf course, the guests carrying torches to light the way.

Good judgment may have been in short supply in Cuba that spring, but it is clear that no affair between Jane and Ernest was in the cards, at least for the time being. The two definitely carried on a flirtation, reflected in a note in the *Anita*'s log in an unknown hand that says, "Ernest loves Jane"; whoever wrote it, it was certainly recorded in jest. It was not that Jane was particularly faithful to her husband; in fact, romantically speaking, she had her eye on Dick Cooper this spring. Grant Mason was something of a stick, and Ernest referred to him as a twerp. In May and June, however, the two couples were very friendly. Jane had already sent a pair of peacocks home with the Hemingways to wander around their lawn; for their fifth anniversary, May 10, she sent a pair of flamingos as company for the peacocks. A letter to Pauline dating from this period reads, "Pauline, you are the peak of funniness and I miss you terribly." That summer, when Jane was off for a short trip to Europe, she was considered such a close friend that a plan was made for her to shepherd Jack over on her way back for his summer visit to his father; though the plans changed, Jane seemed part of the extended family. And while Jane was eye-catching (especially her blond hair), Ernest and Pauline were still very much in love. Ernest would write to Guy Hickok that fall, "Well Pauline is cock-eyed beautiful—Figure lovely

Jane Mason, like the character Margaret Macomber, endorses a beauty product, *Ladies' Home Journal,* July 1929

after Greg born—never looked nor felt better." Ernest slept with other women only after falling in love with them.

This Havana connection promised much for the future, especially off-shore, but Pauline and Ernest were headed for Wyoming again, for their traditional summer fishing and fall shooting. They planned to drive to Piggott first to drop off Patrick and Gregory. But because there had been four cases of infantile paralysis in Key West, as Pauline told her Kansas City physician, Dr. Guffey, she sent them off with Jinny to Piggott with the new nurse, Ada Stern. Gregory was too young to travel easily and the ranch didn't offer much for children as young as the boys were. Still, it was somewhat callous to tell the doctor she was "shipping" the children north; perhaps she could not resist the edgy wit.

A middle-aged woman from Syracuse, New York, Ada seemed perfect for the Hemingways' needs. She was strict, which would be good for the boys, and Pauline thought she liked children (she may well have) and could provide the affection they would need with their parents away for such long stretches. Because of her later misdeeds, Patrick would say that

Ada was "a mean woman who could roast in hell," but for the time being he only objected to her bad cooking. Otherwise she seemed ideal, and in many ways she was. Perhaps most important, she didn't object to becoming part of the Hemingway entourage, managing the children's caravan without blinking an eye.

In any case, Pauline hurried up to Piggott soon after and spent the month of June there, awaiting Ernest, who arrived July 2. He was accompanied by Carol, who was taking a semester off from school and heading to Oak Park to take care of Leicester; Grace was out west herself, seeing her brother and painting landscapes from her car. Carol had made two new friends in Key West and Cuba; one was Jane Mason, who became a confidante in romantic matters, and the other was Jinny, a "great gal" whose sense of fun appealed to Carol, though she confessed to Jane that in her lights Jinny was a bit "too much of a man-hater." When Ernest arrived, she and Jinny had a surprise for him: Jinny had redone the loft of the Pfeiffer barn to make a two-room apartment, with a writing studio for Ernest.

Gerald and Sara Murphy, with their children Honoria and Baoth, joined Ernest and Pauline in Wyoming for three weeks in September. Life had changed drastically for the Murphys. In the fall of 1929 nine-year-old Patrick Murphy was diagnosed with tuberculosis, and the Murphys brought him to a sanitarium in Montana Vermala in the Swiss Alps, where the whole family would stay while Patrick received the quite painful treatments then known as the only effective measure for survival with TB. In the summer of 1932 Patrick was too sick to go out to Wyoming with the rest of his family. By 1932 Gerald's father had died and Gerald had begun to think of going to work in the family business, the Mark Cross Company, a leather goods concern, in New York. In the spring of 1932 the Murphys decided to move back to the U.S., and Gerald went to work in New York City. Ernest and Pauline had visited the Murphys in Switzerland at Christmas that year, but had not seen them since. Of the 1920s expats, Sara and Gerald were closer to the Dos Passoses and the MacLeishes than they were to the Fitzgeralds and Hemingways.

Honoria Murphy had nothing but good memories of the trip, and she was fifteen, old enough to pick up uneasiness among the adults. Each guest was assigned a horse. Honoria said the high point was a trip to a remote spot in the mountains where there was a lake teeming with trout; they rode up there with knapsacks and camped. They went out on the lake in pairs, as the boats each held two, and Honoria drew Ernest, which pleased her immensely. She remembered Ernest showing her how to clean her just caught trout, an operation she wanted no part of and said so. But Ernest, who had been fishing for and cleaning trout almost since birth, it seemed, and for whom it was as integral to living as washing one's hands, talked her through it, cataloguing each aspect of the fish as his knife deftly cleaned and gutted it—the gills that looked "like pink coral" and the feathery fins, which looked "like lace." He told her how clean the trout was, having lived in crystal clear waters, eating only bugs and plants. She never forgot it.

Honoria also recalled how delicious the trout were, roasted over a fire that night, but to Gerald something was lacking the whole time, including the food. Despite the abundance of fresh beef, Gerald found the meat they ate "tasteless," and the trout not cooked "respectably." He remembered far, far better meals eaten with friends, Gerald wrote Archie MacLeish: the ham and bread at Vézelay in the Burgundy region, cheese eaten at the foot of the Val de Mercy, some plums in Menton. Having spent so long in the Swiss Alps, Gerald was not impressed by the mountains of the American West. His was "only a good horse," "most indifferent to ride." In the same letter he emphasized to Archie how clearly fond of him and Ada the Hemingways were. But the visit crystallized something about his relationship with Ernest. He noticed that Ernest was never "difficult" with people he did not like—and Gerald felt he was in that category, as opposed to Sara, Ada, Archie, Dorothy Parker, and Dos, all of whom Ernest had wrangled with in some way. He found Ernest generally "more mellowed" and "more patient," which indicates Ernest was on his best behavior. But, said Gerald, "the line has been drawn very definitely between the people he admits to his life and those he does not." Gerald didn't really mind; he felt that he and Ernest were from "opposing worlds," but that the bond between Ernest and Sara remained very strong. Ernest would have been in full masculine plumage during these three weeks. Gerald went through periodic bouts of self-doubt, which increasingly seem to have concerned his sexuality. In another life, he might have been homosexual, but in this life, for now, he was very much in love with Sara and happy with his family. Ernest's full-on macho behavior would have been hard for Gerald to take in the best of times, and this September Gerald was going through a difficult period, made worse by his son's illness. The two men never really tried to be friends again. The Murphys would remain very close to Pauline, however, long after her marriage to Ernest ended several years later. Sara and Ernest exchanged warm letters, but they would meet only once or twice more.

Shortly after the Murphys left, Pauline went to Key West by way of Piggott, arriving in Florida in time to meet Jack. After she left Wyoming, Charlie Thompson arrived, and he and Ernest spent a couple of weeks in search of bear; Charlie got his right off, and when Ernest shot his, they left

Wyoming. A series of misadventures involving children's illnesses over the next two months kept Pauline and Ernest shuttling between Key West and Piggott.

Meanwhile, the reviews of *Death in the Afternoon* were coming in, and while some predictably dismayed Ernest, most were thoughtful, the reviewers seeming to understand what Hemingway was striving for and what he had accomplished, even in a work that was such a clear departure from what they had come to expect from him, and not only because it was nonfiction. Ben Redman, writing in *The Saturday Review of Literature*, said the book was "excellent reading . . . couched in a prose that must be called perfect because it states with absolute precision what it is meant to state . . . communicates to the reader the emotion with which it is so heavily charged. . . . No reader can put it down ignorant of the fact that bullfighting is a tragic art." Herschel Brickell in the *New York Herald Tribune* wrote, "It is a book teeming with life, vigorous, powerful, moving and consistently entertaining. In short it is the essence of Hemingway." But some critics were not as positive, or misunderstood the book. Robert Coates in *The New Yorker* found the Old Lady an artificial device, and felt that Hemingway "expresses some pretty bitter opinions on readers, writers, and things in general. There are passages in which his bitterness descends to petulance." Coates cited passages critical of Faulkner, T. S. Eliot, and Jean Cocteau, yet allowed "there are some passages of bright, appealing honesty." (Ernest corrected Coates on Faulkner; he had been, in fact, mildly positive about the writer.)

Ernest tried to adopt a sober view of the book's reception and sales, telling Archie that he hadn't expected sales to be high but that he had done the best he could. Scribner's had printed 10,300 copies—as Hemingway critic Leonard Leff points out, not a lot for a best-selling author, but optimistic for a book about bullfighting. Inevitably, however, the critics got to him, especially Seward Collins in *The Bookman* and Lincoln Kirstein in *Hound and Horn*. Kirstein had written a negative review of MacLeish's *The Hamlet of A. MacLeish* (1928) in the same magazine, and in his friend, Ernest had a sympathetic ear. Ernest wrote at some length, and with a bitterness that far surpassed the complaints Coates had singled out. These "little pricks" like Lincoln Kirstein only treat you well if you treat them badly. Go after them, he told Archie; it was the only way to get ahead in the "literary snot-eating contest" of writers and their critics. There is no evidence that Ernest ever went on the attack as he describes it here, but his contempt is plain; what the critics had to say about him or his work would continue to rankle.

In early December a series of unfortunate events in Piggott left some of the townspeople—and, perhaps, the Pfeiffers—a little dismayed by Ernest's behavior. The first debacle was the premiere of the film version of *A Farewell to Arms,* which Ernest flatly refused to attend—his attendance the entire point of opening the film in Piggott—and which threw the small town into a tizzy. Then the barn burned down. The fire was the result of the design of the heating system, which required a local high school student to stoke the fire in the morning and wake up the Hemingways so they could open the damper after the barn got warm. One morning, the student woke them up as he was supposed to do, but they fell back to sleep, and awoke to a fire in the next room. Ernest and Pauline got out safely, but Ernest lost not only some hunting clothes and guns, but also manuscripts and books (though many of the latter were salvaged). As Pauline's biographer records, Ernest was angry at everyone but himself, reserving a special tongue-lashing for the poor high school student. In turn, Jinny decided that it was Ernest's fault for not tending to the fire, and was furious about the waste of the work she had put in converting and decorating the loft.

The Hemingways' bad luck continued. A hunting expedition on a houseboat on the White River, south of Piggott, which Ernest had booked for the week before Christmas for himself, Pauline, Jinny, and Max Perkins, was made miserable by a blizzard that hit the day Max arrived at the Memphis airport, bringing record cold in its wake. Pauline and Jinny had caught the flu from the boys, so it was just Max and Ernest on the boat. Max later said that he experienced "some of the coldest hours of [his] life" on this trip, but he was transfixed by the wintry landscapes and the sight of an old-fashioned steamboat chugging down the river. Right before Christmas Pauline wrote Jane Mason a letter in which she summed up a "very bad fall": whooping cough; flu; fire; poor quail hunting in November because of terrible weather, including a destructive ice storm; and a "lousy" bird dog.

* * *

Despite the trying circumstances, Ernest had written three of his best short stories in the fall of 1932. "A Clean, Well-Lighted Place," another story set in Spain, is about two waiters and a deaf old man who is the last customer in a café, getting drunk; the younger waiter is eager to get home to his wife while the older waiter is sympathetic to the old man, who had tried to hang himself the week before but was cut down by his niece. The older waiter knows why it is important for there to be a clean, pleasant, quiet, and well-lighted café that is open late, for he understands the old man's despair. For all was "*nada y pues nada.*" He says to himself, "Our *nada* who art in *nada.* . . . Give us this *nada* our daily *nada* . . . deliver us from *nada; pues nada.* Hail nothing full of nothing, nothing is with thee" (*CSS,* 291). The submerged iceberg of this story was Hemingway's memory of the months after he returned from the war, when his sister Ursula would wait up for him and sleep in his room "so [he] would not be lonely in the night," always with the light left on until he fell asleep.

"Homage to Switzerland," not one of Hemingway's best-known stories, presents three short scenes, each with a different American customer in a Swiss café at a railroad station. "The Gambler, the Nun, and the Radio," then called "Give Us a Prescription, Doctor," was far more memorable. It was inspired by Hemingway's 1931 stay in the Billings hospital with his badly broken arm and by a local newspaper story Hemingway read at the time about a shooting. In the story, a Mexican gambler, Cayetano, is brought to the Catholic hospital with several gunshot wounds; Mr. Frazer is an onlooker who interprets for the Mexican and is addicted to the radio in his room; a nun who prays for everything, including the results of base-ball games, brings in some musicians to play Mexican music for Cayetano to keep him from being bored. Cayetano has told Mr. Frazer that religion is the opium of the people. This sets off a train of thought in Mr. Frazer's head; music is also the opium of the people, as is religion, or drink, or gam-bling, or ambition, or bread. Opium is also necessary to ease Mr. Frazer's pain.

"The Gambler, the Nun, and the Radio" was, like the other two stories, printed in *Scribner's Magazine.* This new spate of writing gave an impetus to the idea of another story collection to be published in the fall of 1933, containing such stories as "The Sea Change," "A Way You'll Never Be," "Wine of Wyoming," and "A Clean, Well-Lighted Place." For now it was called *After the Storm,* after the title of another recent story. The idea for this one Ernest had gotten from Bra Saunders by way of Pauline (who wrote down the gist of what Bra said), about a scavenger after a storm who is the first to dive for the treasures of a sunken Spanish liner. The story becomes spooky when he is unable to get into the submerged ship. Trying unsuccessfully to break a porthole, he looks inside a cabin and sees a dead woman floating inside, her hair undulating in the water. No bodies turn up after the wreck.

Once his family was again assembled in good health in Key West, Ernest set out by car to New York City. He had told Archie he needed to be in a city for a while. His first stop was to see Max Perkins; Ernest had tele-graphed his impending arrival from Knoxville. He signed a contract for the new story collection, which he was now calling *Winner Take Nothing,* after a completely invented quotation from a supposedly medieval source, which he used as an epigram: "Unlike all other forms of *lutte* or combat the conditions are that the winner shall take nothing, neither his ease, nor his pleasure, nor any notions of glory; nor, if he win far enough, shall there be any reward within himself." Perhaps making up sources from which to draw quotations for an epigram and title was accepted practice; it certainly was, in this case, creative.

When he arrived at the Scribner's offices, the first person he saw was the six-feet-six Thomas Wolfe, Max's other *wunderkind*, whose *Look Home-ward, Angel*, after heroic editorial work on Max's part, had appeared just weeks after *A Farewell to Arms* came out. Ernest had to have been suspicious. He cannot have liked Wolfe's size—so few people were bigger than he—and he worried that Wolfe was Max's favorite more than he worried that Wolfe was a competitor; in their writing, the two men were like chalk and cheese. Max took them to his usual restaurant, Cherio's, where Ernest monopolized the conversation. The two writers did not become friends. According to one account, Ernest also had lunch with Dorothy Parker, saw Sara Murphy, had dinner with Gus Pfeiffer, and met with Jane Mason's friend Dick Cooper, an old safari hand. He also paid the taxidermist who was making a bearskin rug out of his October bear, and he slunk into a movie theater to see *A Farewell to Arms*—the movie he had pointedly ignored in Piggott, so determined was he to buck the film's PR flacks.

He also met with Louis Henry Cohn, a book collector who wanted to issue one of his short stories as a limited edition. The last limited edition he had agreed to was for Caresse Crosby's imprint, an edition of "The Natural History of the Dead," a selection from *Death in the Afternoon*. Over the years Ernest would swear that he would no longer have anything to do with limited editions, favorite projects of book collectors that were just this side of unethical. Cohn wanted to publish "God Rest Ye Merry Gentlemen," the decidedly strange story, set in Kansas City, about a sixteen-year-old who asks his doctor to castrate him to banish his lustful urges.

Cohn introduced Ernest to another collector who was also a magazine editor, Arnold Gingrich. He had contacted Ernest not long before, asking him to sign his copy of *Death in the Afternoon*. Gingrich, who would become an important figure in Ernest's life, was currently publishing *Apparel Arts*, a magazine about men's fashion, and was starting, with David Smart and Henry Jackson, a new magazine for men to be called *Esquire*; he got the name from an envelope addressed to "Arnold Gingrich, Esq." The magazine, which at first was to be distributed only through men's hab-erdashery stores, would publish its first issue in October 1933, and Ernest would be a regular contributor for several years as the magazine grew in distribution, circulation, advertising pages, reputation, and influence.

Ernest had another meeting in New York that he expected to be unpleasant. It was. During her sophomore year at Rollins College Carol had met and fallen in love with a rather remarkable man, John Fentress Gardner, always called Jack. Born in Colorado in 1912, Gardner was accepted by Princeton at the age of fifteen, though he first studied for a year in Grenoble, France. At Princeton, he worked as a mover to support his studies; money was apparently scarce in the Gardner household, then located in Lake Wales, Florida, for John dropped out of Princeton and enrolled in Rollins College in nearby Winter Park. He had become interested in the ideas of anthroposophist Rudolf Steiner, whose teachings he and Carol would follow for the rest of their lives. Anthroposophy, sometimes described as a spiritual form of individualism, focused on finding and/or forging a link between science and mysticism, and helping the followers express themselves in the arts. Anthroposophy is dismissed by many as quackery today, but Steiner's ideas have been very influential in progressive education, especially informing the foundation of the Waldorf schools, based on a so-called holistic theory of child development.

Carol was now on a year-abroad program at the University of Vienna, with Ernest's approval. He does not seem to have heard of Jack until Gardner asked to meet him in New York. Gardner first comes up in related correspondence in a letter from Beefie (Carol's nickname) to Jane Mason, confiding that she was going to miss Jack awfully. By the time Ernest met him in New York City, matters had moved along enough that Gardner was telling (not asking) Ernest that he was going to marry Carol. Ernest was outraged at the very idea. One presumes he did not want her to marry while still in college, and that he did not appreciate hearing about it as something of a fait accompli. Both Jane Mason and Jinny, who was going to Europe herself in early 1933, were playing Cupid, helping the affair along: Pauline wisely did not weigh in. Ernest hated friends and family having secret knowledge or making plans behind his back.

Jack Gardner as a person did not impress him either. Despite his professed Catholicism, Ernest was impatient with religion, overt philosophizing, and what we would call today self-help. Gardner, as a follower of Steiner, was a proselytizer for all three, though he called religion "spirituality." Moreover, Gardner showed off his considerable erudition and may have bragged about his early acceptance at Princeton, which would have rankled Ernest. Gardner later told his daughter he called Ernest "an overgrown boy scout," which may have been true. Gardner also told Ernest confidently that in three months his putative brother-in-law would be as enamored of him as his sister was. Marcelline's disapproval must be discounted because of her distaste for anyone unconventional, but her remarks to Ernest about Gardner are of interest. He seems, she wrote, "the most superficial and conceited *young* egocentric I've encountered in years!" Gardner's daughter said that in later years, "My dad was mortified by how cocky he had been as a college student."

But the damage was done. A few years later, after Carol and Jack were married, Ernest wrote, in a seemingly drunk and unsent letter to his youngest sister that, thinking back on it, "Only thing to have done would have been to shoot John." He was enraged when he learned Gardner was on his way to Europe himself, where he would spend four months at the Goetheanum in Dornach, Switzerland, a Steiner study center. Gardner was accompanying a Yale student and fellow Steiner enthusiast who had recently suffered a breakdown. Ernest sent Carol a telegram:

WOULD APPRECIATE YOUR WIRING GARDNER NOT COME EUROPE NOW UNABLE UNDERTAKE HIS SUPPORT AT PRESENT YOU HAVENT ENOUGH FOR TWO BESIDES OTHER CONSIDERATIONS WRITING STOP YOU HAVE PLENTY TIME PLEASE BELIEVE KNOW WHAT TALKING ABOUT OLD BEEF JINNY ARRIVING SKI IN FEBRUARY WITH YOU LOVE CABLE ME CARE SCRIBNERS LOVE ERNIE.

As the telegram shows, Ernest was still on good terms with Carol, though she wrote to a friend that she felt stymied because of her financial dependence on her brother. She was trying to convince him she didn't expect him to support Gardner as well. A furious exchange of letters followed, correspondence that remains in private hands; a critic who has seen the letters says Ernest accused Carol of worshipping Gardner—practicing "Gardnerism." In his defense, if Carol was as avid a Steinerite as Gardner, it may have seemed that her behavior was suspiciously cultlike. Ernest claimed that it was his "duty" to point out that Gardner was a "pitiful psychopathic," a liar, and a fool.

Remarkable throughout this whole matter is Ernest's adoption of a parental role, stern, censorious, unforgiving: just the kind of thing he had objected to in Ed and Grace. Ernest scolded Carol for using "dirty" words, words he claimed he didn't use in his own writing—a patent falsity. Then, in rather a remarkable passage, he accused Carol of saving up money to get an abortion. Hemingway critic Gail Sinclair has read ten intimate letters Carol wrote at the time to two college friends, and found no evidence for this. Rollins College officials did know, however, that the couple were living together in the spring of 1932, which would keep Carol and Jack from being readmitted to the college after their marriage, and it is possible that Ernest as Carol's legal guardian would have been told about this. He believed, he told her, that abortion was "murder," not for religious but "biological" reasons. Interfering with pregnancy would be bad for her "spirit." Had Hadley or Pauline had an abortion, Jack, Patrick, and Gregory would have been "murdered." He compared Gardner to Nathan Leopold, as in Leopold and Loeb, who killed an innocent victim in quest of the perfect murder. Bizarrely, evidently thinking through what would happen if Carol had the supposed baby, Ernest said that afterward Jack and Carol could be sterilized, apparently to keep Gardner's genes from being passed on. Earlier, in his story "Hills Like White Elephants" (1927), Ernest had shown a thoughtful sensitivity about abortion: a young man tries to convince a woman—clearly, though it is not explicitly stated—to undergo an abortion, while she is reluctant. It is hard to believe this tale was written by the same person who voiced such brutal views to his youngest sister five years later.

It was money to which Carol's guardian circled back; as he had learned, since the death of his father, the paternal role and the power he wielded, the means by which he could control his mother's and his siblings' behavior, was bolstered by money, and it would prove to be so again and again as the years went by. He told Carol that she could of course marry legally, since she was twenty-one, but she would then receive only $50 per month from him. He asked her to fly from Europe to Key West to meet with him so he could talk to her; she refused.

Meanwhile, Jane Mason had seen Carol in Europe and brought her a letter from Jack, and Jinny provided moral support for Carol after she read Ernest's angriest letter. Ernest called Jinny a *sinvergüenza* (Spanish for a naughty imp; an insult in that language) for "bringing Gardner and Carol together." On March 4 Carol wrote Jane that she had made up her mind: "Ernie's done a great deal for me, but Jack's the man I'm going to be living with for many years." With Jinny's help, Carol and Jack made plans to marry in Salzburg. Ernest received a wire on March 17, he later wrote his mother, saying that Carol and Jack would be married March 25.

Ernest complained about the position Carol had forced him to take. He would never forgive her after she defied him; the break was permanent. (Ernest wrote a letter to Carol in 1945, in which he said he "hate[d] that guy like I hate the Nazis," but evidently the letter was unsent.) Carol later reported that her brother often lied about her; when someone asked about

Carol, he would say she had died or been divorced. Ernest also said that she had been raped at the age of twelve by a "sex pervert," a story Carol flatly denied. Ernest's motives in making this specific charge are difficult to fathom. It is not clear whether he continued to send her $50 a month; it is unlikely, for Ernest seldom passed up a chance to make a comment when he mailed a check to family members, and Carol said she had no further contact with him whatsoever. He would never forget her disobedience. The outright defiance Carol and Jack showed in marrying against his wishes simply enraged him.

Ernest was infuriated by another woman from his past in 1933: Gertrude Stein. *The Autobiography of Alice B. Toklas,* Stein's memoir masquerading as her companion's, began appearing in monthly installments in May in *The Atlantic Monthly.* The book, one of the great documents of literary and artistic Paris in the early twentieth century, was to make Stein famous.

Ernest was nervous from the moment he learned, in a piece by Janet Flanner in *The New Yorker,* about Stein's memoir and her plans to publish it. He had a specific fear: that Stein would say he was a homosexual. Flanner was a friend, so he wrote her on April 8 asking her to come to Havana, where he'd been doing a lot of fishing; his letter then meandered through domestic news before turning to Stein. The last time he saw Stein, he wrote, she told him she had heard of an incident "which proved me conclusively to be very queer indeed." She wouldn't tell him the story, but said it was "completely credible and circumstantial." (It is difficult to imagine Stein making these remarks; they do not sound in character, and the last time she and Ernest saw each other was an occasion in 1929 at which Pauline, Zelda and Scott Fitzgerald, Allen Tate and Caroline Gordon, and John and Margaret Bishop had been present—hardly a likely occasion or an appropriate audience.)

Ernest said that he had never cared about "what she did in and out of bed," but then returned to what he imagined was Stein's charge of homosexuality. He began with an old canard of his, that menopause had changed Stein for the worse. Afterward, he said, she got "patriotic"; in what followed it is clear that he used "patriotic" to mean loyal to homosexuality and homosexuals. She went through three phases of "patriotism," he said: "The first stage was nobody was any good that wasn't that way. The second was that anybody who was that way was good. The third was that anybody that was any good must be that way." Stein was in her third stage now, and Hemingway feared he was in her line of fire.

May came and the first installment of Stein's book appeared in *The Atlantic Monthly;* it was about her arrival in Paris, and she clearly had a great deal to cover before she reached the 1920s and her friendship with Ernest; what she wrote could be called gossipy, with lots of astringent views about what would later be called bold-faced names. It was not until August, the last installment, that she got to her friendship with Ernest. Here she talked about the arrival of this "extraordinarily good-looking man" in Paris and their friendship, being Bumby's godmother, and Hemingway's intervention in getting Stein's *The Making of Americans* published in Ford Madox Ford's *transatlantic review*, which would always cause her to remember him "with gratitude" (*AABT*, 261). But then she went on to discuss how she and Sherwood Anderson had "formed" Hemingway, "and they were both a little proud and a little ashamed of the work of their minds" (*AABT*, 265). She wrote, apropos of nothing, that she and Anderson "admitted" Hemingway was "yellow," a low, unsubstantiated blow. She also passed on Ernest the judgment that she had heard said about artist André Derain: "He looks like a modern and he smells of the museum." Here it is a little easier to see what she was getting at: that for all he had said about getting past such old, hollow terms (and concepts) as "valor" and "glory" in pared-down, minimal language, *A Farewell to Arms* was a highly romantic war novel.

It went on like that: Stein said Hemingway had learned about bullfighting from her, that he was fragile and accident-prone (a very good observation at this early juncture; Hemingway was so accident-prone that an appendix in Jeffrey Meyers's Hemingway biography is devoted to a chart of Ernest's many injuries). She complimented Fitzgerald and bestowed a backhanded compliment on McAlmon (who was likely the source of any gossip she might have heard about Ernest and homosexuality). Yet she confessed to "a weakness" for Hemingway (*AABT*, 271), perhaps because she saw him somewhat through a parent's eyes. All this was nevertheless enough to rouse Ernest's ire, forming the foundation for a lifetime's worth of resentment of the woman he had once praised so highly. "I always loved her very much," he would tell Stein biographer W. G. Rogers in 1948. He had written to Anderson in 1921, saying, "Gertrude Stein and me are just like brothers."

Stein never makes reference to Hemingway's sexuality—overtly, at least. She does, however, allude to something mysterious that she and Sherwood talked about: "What a book, they both agreed, would be the real story of Hemingway, not those he writes but the confessions of the real Ernest Hemingway. It would be for another audience than the audience Hemingway now has but it would be very wonderful" (*AABT*, 265–66). While it is tempting to credit Stein with admirable insight in at least suggesting something more complicated in Ernest's sexuality, the fact is that she did seem to be suggesting simple homosexuality, which really was not fair (or true). It is not surprising that Ernest had dreaded what she might say about him, or that he was furious when he read the final product. Hers was an insinuation against which it was impossible for him to defend himself.

Stein's assessment of Hemingway—both as an artist and a person—was, however, very much in step with the time. The early 1930s were seeing a kind of backlash against him, and, in a sense, the whole Lost Generation mystique. (Fitzgerald's *Tender Is the Night,* a serious novel about the era, was published two years later and failed, critically and commercially.) Hemingway had not published a major work since his great success of *A Farewell to Arms,* just before the stock market crash. The romantic fatalism of the 1920s was no longer in fashion, and Stein showed commercial acumen in treating Hemingway, now its most conspicuous avatar, with brittle irony, distancing herself from the literary phenomenon she had helped to nurture.

Doomed artists, bullfights, and the intimate lives of expatriate couples no longer seemed fascinating and romantic as the desperate years of the Depression dragged on. Nor did the flirtation with death that was the bullfight seem quite so urgent as Fascism engulfed more and more of Europe and battle lines were drawn between Nazis and Marxists and Social Democrats. Politics was again becoming more and more important to Hemingway, much as it had when he first arrived in Europe as a correspondent. And yet his major work of the 1930s, thus far, was a lengthy nonfiction treatise on bullfighting.

The critical vultures were definitely circling, and Hemingway's resentment of them, always latent, was growing much sharper. One reason, however, was that the attacks on him took a more personal tone, perhaps, than did criticism about other writers. Hemingway's work conveyed not just stories "in our time," but, implicitly, his own attitudes, personality, and values. He was a celebrity, his movements tracked in the press. The virile sportsman seemed, in the public imagination, to be one with protagonists of his fiction. Some of this was insightful: Clifton Fadiman called Hemingway "the American Byron" and recognized the "real contemporary hero-myth" that had sprung up around the writer, thus capturing some of the tenor of contemporary criticism of Hemingway. But in general the trend was not a happy one: Hemingway commentators often could not help critiquing the man—or at least his presumed personality—along with the work. This Stein certainly did in *The Autobiography of Alice B. Toklas.*

So too did a belated review in *The New Republic* of *Death in the Afternoon* by Max Eastman, which appeared in June 1933. This piece so provoked Ernest that, a few years later, when he and Eastman next met, fisticuffs ensued. Cleverly titled "Bull in the Afternoon," the article seems at first to be tongue-in-cheek, but Eastman for the most part was deadly serious in condemning bullfighting on the well-worn grounds of its cruelty and injustice. "A bullfight—foolishly so-called by the English, since it does not . . . resemble a fight—is real life," he wrote. "It is men tormenting and killing a bull. . . . You see this beautiful creature, whom you despise for his stupidity and admire because he is so gorgeously equipped with power for wild life, trapped in a ring where his power is nothing, and you see him put forth his utmost in vain to escape death at the hands of these spryer and more flexible monkeys. . . . That is what a bullfight is, and that is all it is." Ernest would have been enraged by this lengthy attack on the spectacle he so loved, especially because Eastman's attack was very well reasoned.

But it was his attack on Hemingway himself that was, and still is, also well reasoned—yet totally unfair. Eastman purported to be interested in why the brave veteran of a terrible war should be drawn to bullfighting, and along the way called Hemingway, among other things, a sensitive poet; his argument was that many people (like children) of a delicate nature and vulnerability emerge from experiences like the "barbaric slaughter" of the war finding themselves transformed. And then, "It is of course a commonplace that anyone who protests his manhood lacks the serene confidence that he *is* made out of iron." (It is "of course" *not* a commonplace that this is so.) It is this and the line in which Eastman calls Hemingway's a literary style "of wearing false hair on the chest" that were then and are today the most wounding, in part because in their pithiness they are so eminently quotable.

Ernest was at a loss how to respond. Anything he said, he complained to Archie, would be construed as defensiveness and thus would provide further ammunition for one of Eastman's most damning points: that defending one's integrity is itself defensiveness about one's virility. Since he couldn't very well answer, he asked Archie to. Archie dutifully wrote to the editor of *The New Republic* protesting the attack on his friend; he was outraged on Ernest's behalf. But as far as Ernest was concerned, the damage was done; he felt he was being accused of homosexuality, though he said so on paper only to MacLeish. Eastman, he said, was trying to pass him off as another Glenn Anders—the star of the short-lived 1930 Broadway production of *A Farewell to Arms,* who was evidently rumored to be homosexual. It was not easy to defend against insinuations of homosexuality without seeming to protest too much. Whatever we might think of Ernest's reaction to the suggestion, given the very different social norms of a later period, Eastman had gone over the top; Ernest was not unjustified in reacting to the personal nature of the attack against him.

SEVENTEEN

By mid-April 1933 Ernest was deeply absorbed in his love affairs with Cuba and the marlin—Cuba being the best place for catching marlin he had yet encountered. He left around the 12th to spend over two months fishing the Cuban coast around Havana with Joe Russell in his *Anita,* with Cuban fisherman Carlos Gutiérrez aboard as guide. Sometimes Ernest spent the night on the boat; other nights, especially when he wanted to sample the celebrated Havana nightlife or attend parties at the Masons' place outside Havana, he would stay in the Hotel Ambos Mundos at the corner of Obispo and Mercaderes. The hotel, built in the 1920s in the heart of colonial Havana, was shaped like New York's Flatiron Building, and provided rooms for only two dollars a night.

Though Ernest's son Jack would say later that his father told him that Jane tried to climb over the transom of his Ambos Mundos room, his boast was not only logistically unlikely (the story probably had its origins in a joke) but inconsistent with the nature of the friendship between Ernest and Jane at this time. Jane was supremely content fishing with Ernest, and it is indeed true that she was unhappy in her marriage. She and Grant had a small adopted son, Tony, and later adopted another, but motherhood did not provide definition to her life either. "Talents too many, not enough of any" would later literally be carved on her gravestone, but her plight was no laughing matter. Ernest later said that he wrote the Nick Adams story "A Way You'll Never Be," set in 1918 Italy, to show her what he said in the story's title: Jane would never be like Nick, unhinged not only by war but by life itself.

But Jane did come unhinged that spring in Havana. First, she was in a car with Jack, Patrick, and her son Tony when some photos she had on her lap blew out the window; in the confusion she drove off the road. The car rolled over as it slipped off the road, gaining momentum all the way down an embankment. The doors were jammed shut, but the children and Jane crawled out through an open window; all were unhurt. Afterward she spent a few days on the *Anita* with Ernest and his friends. Soon after, at her Jaimanitas home, she jumped out a low window and was badly injured, breaking her back. After a stay in a Havana hospital where she was treated for "nervous shock" and her back injury, Grant Mason sent her to Doctors Hospital in New York City.

Jane's stay in the hospital in New York, where she was enclosed in a body cast for two months and then fitted with an iron brace she would need to wear for a year, was the occasion for some strange letters between Ernest and Archie MacLeish. At Ernest's request Archie had visited Jane in a New York hospital on a previous stay; in two different June letters to Archie, Ernest asked his friend to look in on her again. Something sexually competitive between them was sparked, apparently by the irresistible combination of a blonde and a bed. It seems that Jane and Archie had some kind of sexual encounter, though a relatively chaste one because of her cast. A confused letter from a seemingly drunken Ernest to Archie, written three years later, makes erotic but puzzling reference to Jane.

Overall, though, any eroticism associated with Jane was in connection with Archie, not Ernest. Hemingway genuinely worried about her up there alone in the hospital, urging Archie to visit her and bring "Mrs. Parker." But the reason Ernest did not at least attempt a fling with the attractive and compelling, high-strung Jane was really quite simple: in 1933, he was deeply in love with his wife. Indeed, they were having a sort of second honeymoon centered around his persistent sexual fetish, hair. Both he and Pauline would share their hair-coloring escapades by letter with Jane, whose blond hair seems to have set off the sex play.

First Ernest bleached or dyed his. Josephine Merck, a friend from Montana, visited Ernest and Pauline in 1933 and remembered Ernest's hair "bleached by the sun"; it was highly unlikely that the sun "bleached" his dark hair. She also saw it just after, when his hair was red, and when she asked him about it, he got annoyed. A letter from Pauline to her husband cleared up what color his hair was that spring: "About your hair," she wrote him, "don't know how to turn red to gold. What about straight peroxide—or better what's the matter with red hair. Red hair lovely on you." Evidently Ernest felt some regret, if not for dyeing his hair in the first place, then for choosing the wrong color: "Ernest is a little subdued, though not much, by his haircut," wrote Pauline to Jane, "his hair turned bright gold on the boat in Havana . . . and he cut it to the roots in a frenzy."

Pauline became a blonde. She had done it once before, on their honeymoon in Hendaye, just before they left for Valencia; it had excited Ernest terribly. Hair dyes were different then: nasty-smelling and chemically noxious, they were very hard on the hair, and achieving just the right shade was always a problem, especially for blondes. Pauline had trouble keeping her blond hair from getting too pink. More interesting to Ernest was the variety of shades of blond available to work with. At one point Pauline's hair was "pale gold," another time a "deep gold," and this summer "ash blonde." Each conjured up a different woman. Over time, just writing about the shades of hair color would become almost unbearably exciting to him; he would catalogue them with obvious erotic pleasure.

Ernest told his friends about this only when it was over, and Pauline had gone back to her normal brunette hair. Pauline is wonderful, he told Jane. She dyed her hair for him and no one could believe it wasn't always that way. To Archie Ernest wrote, using Bumby's nickname for Pauline (derived from hearing so often "Pauline knows") that "Paulinoes" had been a gorgeous blonde but was now brown-haired again; when she was blond her looks had rivaled those of Ada MacLeish, on whom Ernest had a long-standing crush. The summer, with his blond wife coming and going between Havana and Key West, had been lovely, and if he missed Jane Mason it was only as a friend. In a rare moment of self-awareness, Ernest acknowledged in the same letter to Archie that though he loved his wife he wasn't always the best of husbands, especially when he drank too much.

In the meantime Ernest began his long arrangement with Arnold Gingrich and the nascent *Esquire.* The magazine's publishers had deep enough pockets that with the second, November issue the magazine would change from a quarterly to a monthly, and go on sale at all the usual outlets, not just men's clothing stores. *Esquire* did not set out on the firmest footing, editorially speaking, but Gingrich made it worth Ernest's while to become a regular contributor whose name would draw in other heavy hitters, including Ezra Pound and Theodore Dreiser, and after that a whole raft of twentieth-century male literary eminences. Gingrich snagged Ernest as a contributor by agreeing to pay him twice the going rate, which quickly ascended with *Esquire*'s fortunes. Ernest missed journalism and liked writing nonfiction, especially about places and activities he loved. He suggested a series of "letters" from wherever he happened to be; perhaps he was following the example of his friend Janet Flanner, whose "Paris Letter" had been a popular feature in *The New Yorker* since 1925. Ernest's first article, accordingly, published that fall, was a "Cuban Letter," called "Marlin off the Morro," referring to the castle fortress at the entrance to the Havana bay.

Gingrich wanted the letter to appear regularly each month as soon as possible, but Ernest agreed only to submit articles when he felt like it. The editor tried to sweeten the pot with offers of merchandise from his advertisers; Ernest obligingly communicated his collar (17½), jacket ("44 OK, but 46 better"), shoes (11 wide), and trousers (33 waist, 34 length) sizes. If Gingrich sent anything, Ernest promised to "wear it out." He may have been making a wisecrack, however, contrasting his casual-to-unkempt attire to Gingrich's own natty, always impeccable wardrobe. With Ernest, a discouraged Gingrich observed, "The general effect is that of items left over from a rummage sale."

One of Gingrich's most appealing traits, as far as Ernest was concerned, was his reluctance to edit his writers. His motto was said to be, "He edits best who edits least." In a specific description he later wrote of editing Hemingway's copy for *Esquire,* Gingrich said, "We . . . always operated on the basis that I would make no changes of any kind, but would suggest changes, by wire or telephone, only if impelled to do so by considerations of libel, invasion of privacy, obscenity." Thus Gingrich, like Horace Liveright and Max Perkins, joined the ranks of legendary editors who never touched Ernest's stuff. Like them, he was doing his prickly author no favors. As time went on Ernest more and more would need a good editor who was not afraid to be tactless, to give his work a good line editing, and to warn him when it was moving in the wrong direction.

Ernest and Joe Russell did not return to Key West until July 20, one day before Ernest turned thirty-four. His departure for the African expedition was imminent. By now Mike Strater had joined MacLeish in bowing out of the trip, both men pleading poverty but actually fearful that their friendship with Ernest would not survive the trip. Charlie Thompson was still coming, and at the last minute Pauline, who had been planning to spend the summer in New York with her sister, perhaps going on to Paris in the fall, signed on, mindful that Ernest would not be satisfied with only Charles as companion and audience. On August 4, the Hemingways arrived in Havana with Jack and Patrick, Gregory having been dispatched to spend the summer with his nurse, Ada, in her native Syracuse, New York. Patrick's old French nurse, Henriette, looked after Patrick and Jack in her home in Bordeaux before delivering Jack to Paris for school in the fall. Ernest and Pauline spent the next month and a half in Spain with Jinny before the two sisters themselves departed for Paris in early fall. Ernest did not attend a bullfight until the last day of August, according to his "Letter from Spain" for the January 1934 issue of *Esquire.* He was helping his friend Sidney Franklin with a translation of a Spanish novel for Scribner's, reading Spanish newspapers avidly as much for political information (the right would win the November election) as for news of the up-and-coming matadors, and spending many hours in the Prado and in his favorite cafés in Madrid.

When it came time to write his "Letter from Paris" for the next issue, Ernest spent most of the allotted space on a bull moose he encountered in Montana the year before, also describing several prizefights between French boxers. At the end of the essay he wrote about possible war on the horizon in Europe. "What makes you feel bad [to be in Paris]," he wrote, "is the perfectly calm way everyone speaks about the next war." And finally, he acknowledged that Paris was "very beautiful" and "a fine place to be quite young in," writing, "We all loved it once." But Paris, he wrote, is like "a mistress who does not grow old and she has other lovers now. . . . [Paris] is always the same age and she always has new lovers."

Charles Thompson joined Pauline and Ernest in Paris in the exalted position of gun bearer, bringing all the new weapons he and Ernest had bought for the safari. Ernest met him at the train station wearing a beret and clutching a magnum of champagne, and immediately whisked his friend off on a taxi tour of Paris. On their last night there, Ernest, Pauline, and Charles entertained James and Nora Joyce for dinner, whom Ernest had known only slightly when he lived in the city. For some elusive reason Ernest told the story of this meeting repeatedly throughout his life. He said that Joyce worried his writing was too "suburban," and Nora said it would be good for her husband to shoot a lion, a feat Joyce said was impossible for him because of his poor eyesight. Perhaps Joyce was picking up on Ernest's suggestions that Joyce's subjects were tame in comparison to his own, which would only become more exciting on safari. But Ernest made an excellent impression on the preeminent modernist writer, who later wrote, "We like him. He's a big, powerful peasant, strong as a buffalo. A sportsman. And ready to live the life he writes about."

On November 22, the Hemingways and Charles boarded the *General Metzinger* bound from Marseilles to Port Said. Traveling through the Suez Canal, Ernest wrote in a letter to Patrick, they went right through the desert, with palm trees and Australian pines just like the trees in the yard at Key West, and then on through the Red Sea into the Gulf of Aden. The boat then followed the coastline to Mombasa, where the party disembarked. A friend of Thompson's later described the group: Ernest, he said, had produced a brown felt hat with a wide brim, and looked sporting in his shirtsleeves, while Charles was sweating in coat and tie. Pauline was all in white, from her frilly parasol to her ankle-length dress and gloves. "Pauline and I looked like missionaries," Charles later said, "while Ernest had the distinct look of a whiskey drummer."

After taking the train to Nairobi, where they stayed in the luxurious New Stanley Hotel (whose comforts Pauline was soon to long for, she said),

Philip Percival, "Great White Hunter," 1934

the party traveled to Machakas, where Philip Percival had a farm. A legendary "white hunter," Percival had taken Theodore Roosevelt on safari back in 1909, an outing that embedded these adventures in the popular imagination. Safari guides were celebrities of sorts in the 1930s, enterprising and often from British families who either had no money or had other reasons to leave England. These romantic figures specialized in showing people *with* money around an exotic part of the world where they could feel as if they were taking risks—which, as it turns out, they often were. Life in camp was rustic yet comfortable; the principals slept in large tents and bathed in canvas bathtubs. Like the Hemingways, the adventurers went to Abercrombie & Fitch to be outfitted before their trip in khaki clothes, belted safari jackets, and pith helmets or soft-brimmed hats. (The look was considerably more exotic then than it seems today.)

With two others, Philip Percival had very recently started Tanganyika Guides, Ltd.; it was Jane Mason's friend Dick Cooper who had sent them to Percival, whom Hemingway would later, in his 1935 *Green Hills of Africa*, immortalize as "Pop." Charles Thompson would be Karl, and Pauline P.O.M., short for Poor Old Mama. (Later, when Ernest complained about cold nights at the L-Bar-T in Wyoming, Pauline dubbed him P.O.P.) Percival, in turn, called Ernest Pop. He won Ernest's admiration not only for his hunting prowess and bravery, but because he was a notorious womanizer, cynic, and bon vivant. He would inform the character of Robert Wilson in "The Short Happy Life of Francis Macomber," who sleeps with his female clients.

The Hemingways and Thompson stayed at the farmhouse in Machakas waiting for Percival to join them, making forays onto the Kapiti Plain with African guides, shooting gazelles for meat and impalas for their trophy heads. On December 20, now under Percival's guidance, they headed for the Serengeti Plain, with Mount Kenya to the northeast of them and Mount Kilimanjaro to the southwest.

Theirs was a big entourage, consisting of two trucks bearing supplies and a vehicle for the hunters, essentially a large platform. Numerous Africans accompanied them to help with the cooking and other camp duties, as well as porters, game skinners, and gun bearers, and a mechanic. Ernest came to love the shape of their days: they would breakfast in the dark, setting out at sunrise to hunt in the relative cool of the morning, and between noon and four have drinks, eat lunch, and then sleep or read in the shade, often cooled by a light breeze. After drinks and dinner, they spent evenings in canvas chairs around a fire, drinking whiskey and telling stories. The next day, Ernest observed with satisfaction, they "sweated out" the alcohol of the night before. Ernest could not imagine having come without Pauline: "The only person I really cared about, except the children, was with me," he wrote later, "and I had no wish to share this life with any one who was not there, being completely happy to live it and quite tired" (*GHOA*, 55). The Kenyans, especially one called M'Cola, took a liking to Pauline, and there came to be a general feeling that she should shoot the party's first lion. They sighted the prey near dusk in early January, and Pauline knelt, aimed her Mannlicher rifle, and shot; at the same instant Ernest fired as well, killing the beast. The party gave all credit to Pauline, who accepted the acclaim gracefully, later writing in her diary that she wished she *had* been the one to kill it. The party celebrated Christmas with a feast of roast gazelle.

Just two weeks into the safari, around New Year's Day, Ernest came down with amoebic dysentery. By the middle of the month he was passing a frightening amount of blood, his intestine alarmingly slipping partway out. Percival got word to a pilot with a small, two-passenger plane that took Ernest to Nairobi. Because of the lack of real hospitals, Ernest was treated with emetine injections in his bed at the New Stanley Hotel.

During his week-long recuperation in Nairobi he made the acquaintance of another legendary white hunter, Baron Bror von Blixen-Finecke, one of Percival's business partners. Blixie, as Ernest came to call him, was a Swedish-born aristocrat widely known in connection with his first wife, Karen, who wrote under the pen name Isak Dinesen; his hunting clients included the prince of Wales. With him at the New Stanley when Ernest met him was Alfred Vanderbilt, about to go on safari with Blixie. Ernest took a liking to Vanderbilt, then in his twenties and refreshingly modest. They talked about going deep-sea fishing in the Indian Ocean after their safaris.

On the 24th of January Ernest rejoined the hunting party, which had moved to a second base camp near the Ngorongoro Crater. Before Ernest came down with dysentery, both he and Thompson had bagged numerous wild animals, among them leopards, cheetahs, eland, and oryx. They had shot four black-maned lions, but now they were after sable, rhinoceros, and kudu, Percival taking them south near Kijungu. They especially sought the greater kudu bull, which resembles a gazelle but was sought after for its curved spiral horns, making it a very desirable trophy. To Ernest's consternation, for every beast he killed it seemed Thompson downed a larger specimen of the same animal. Though Ernest would write about their rivalry in *Green Hills of Africa* and render it humorous, anyone who knew him would see that the situation was hardly laughable. But Charles resolutely refused to rise to the bait, remaining serene and friendly throughout. When Ernest brought down a kudu bull bigger than Thompson's, Charles came back the same day with a finer, larger specimen. Charles shot a rhinoceros whose smaller horn was bigger than the primary horn on Ernest's specimen. Even the heat of Ernest's competitive nature, however, seemed to dim his happiness in Africa only slightly.

The safari was over in mid-February, and Thompson and the Hemingways moved on to Malindi on the Kenyan coast, checking in to the fairly luxe Palm Beach Hotel. They met Blixen-Finecke and Vanderbilt there and could not resist a few more days hunting with Blixen-Finecke in the coastal hills near Lushoto. Ernest had convinced Philip Percival to try out deep-sea fishing, so he joined the party on the *Xanadu* out of Malindi. The expedition was enjoyable but unexciting, for they never even saw any of the giant sailfish, tuna, and marlin they had hoped for, catching instead dolphin, kingfish, grouper, amberjack, and only modest-sized sailfish.

The stamina of moneyed travelers before widespread airline travel was considerable, but that of the Hemingways was heroic. After two months in Africa they took the *Gripsholm,* Blixen-Finecke and Vanderbilt both on board, to Palestine, where they met Lorine Thompson, who had sailed from Key West, meeting them at Haifa, then going on a day excursion to the Sea of Galilee. On the boat back to France they disembarked at Villefranche for a little gambling in Monte Carlo, before taking the train from Nice to Paris. Lorine got in only a few days of Paris life before she and Charles had to return to Key West, but Ernest and Pauline stayed in the city for another nine days.

Lorine had brought with her some photos of Greg and Patrick, which almost made Pauline cry, believing that their faces showed how much they missed her. That fall, Gregory remained with Ada in Syracuse, New York; Jinny had sailed for the U.S. with Patrick in October, bringing him to Piggott for Thanksgiving and Christmas. Then the boys were watched over in Key West by Ada, Jinny, and Ursula with her daughter, Gale.

While in Paris Pauline and Ernest saw Joyce again for dinner at Michaud's, this time with Janet Flanner and her friend, Solita Solano. But Joyce was evidently drunk and nearly mute. One afternoon they were visiting Sylvia Beach in her bookshop when Ernest came upon an essay about himself called "The Dumb Ox," by Wyndham Lewis. The piece made Ernest so angry that he turned abruptly and upset a vase of tulips, in some versions merely knocking them over, in others punching the vase. (Noel Riley Fitch said he delivered a "right uppercut.") He had to give Sylvia a check for 1,500 francs to cover the damage.

Lewis and Hemingway had only met once, in Pound's studio in July 1922, when the two writers were boxing. But Lewis had followed his career with characteristic vitriol. Well-known in the 1920s, Lewis, a painter and writer, was thought to be a bigot and political conservative; his best-known work, *The Apes of God* (1930), was a scathing attack on the London literary world, and found by many readers to be anti-Semitic. Lewis's essay on Hemingway appeared in the June 1934 edition of *The American Review.* At Shakespeare and Company Ernest read the essay with mounting rage, his face turning "purple," according to Fitch. The qualities to which the title referred were a certain anti-intellectualism—to the point of stupidity, Lewis said. The Hemingway hero, according to Lewis, is "a dull-witted, bovine, monosyllabic simpleton. . . . [a] constipated, baffled, frustrated . . . leaden-witted, heavy-footed, loutish and oafish marionette." Ernest probably hadn't been called stupid since the sandbox. But what really riled him was how closely Lewis tied his work to Gertrude Stein's. Referring to the "steining of Hemingway," an early period in his career, Lewis maintained that the writing of Hemingway and Stein was so similar that the only way passages from the two writers could be distinguished from each other was the subject matter: if it was prizefighting, war, or bullfighting, it was Hemingway's. In the process of "steining," Hemingway had stolen from Stein "lock, stock, and barrel." Thus, Lewis wrote, "It is difficult to know where Hemingway proper begins and Stein leaves off."

Ernest had read the last installment of Stein's *Autobiography of Alice B. Toklas* just the past August, in Spain, which had enraged him anew. Being compared to a woman who in many particulars resembled no one so much as Grace Hall Hemingway infuriated him, and it was mortifying to have his work called derivative of (or stolen from) a writer who had been published only in little magazines and privately printed books. That is, until her *Autobiography* appeared in *The Atlantic Monthly* (the same magazine he had accused his mother of buying to appear highbrow) and, later, as a book published by Harcourt, Brace. *The Autobiography of Alice B. Toklas* at the same time became a best seller and a hit with critics such as Edmund Wilson—which, as Hemingway well knew, was quite a feat. She was about to make her celebrated American tour, which made her truly famous, a name recognized in many American households.

Wyndham Lewis's remarks about the "steining" of Hemingway were like salt on an open and infected wound. Ernest never saw Lewis again, but later remembered him in *his* (posthumous) memoir, *A Moveable Feast,* as a "nasty" man whose face reminded him of a frog. Walking home, he tried to think what Lewis reminded him of: "toe-jam," he thought. He tried to recall Lewis's face under his black, wide-brimmed hat, but all he could remember were the eyes. When Ernest first saw them, he said, they had been those of "an unsuccessful rapist" (*AMF,* 88–89). Unfortunately, Wyndham Lewis died in 1957, thus missing the imaginative insult.

* * *

Ernest and Pauline had an interesting crossing on the *Île de France* in late March. Among the passengers was the actress Marlene Dietrich, who was on board with her eight-year-old daughter, Maria. Legend has it that the actress was joining a party in the dining room when she saw that she would be the thirteenth member of the party. Superstitious, she said she had to decline, but Hemingway stepped forward and said he would be the fourteenth. This was the beginning of a lifelong friendship between Ernest and the woman he always referred to as "the Kraut." She called him Papa and he addressed her as Daughter and made a great show of declaring his love for her on multiple occasions and in every letter he wrote her. Yet the relationship was chaste.

Also on board was the twenty-seven-year-old Katharine Hepburn, who had recently starred in the 1932 drama *A Bill of Divorcement;* she had also just failed quite badly in the Broadway production of *The Lake.* While Hepburn and Ernest seem not to have become close, they bantered on the dock in New York for the press, Ernest telling Hepburn on parting, she said, "Don't be a mug." According to a Hepburn biographer, however, she was the mystery woman whom Hemingway described as the inspiration for the "rich bitch" in "The Snows of Kilimanjaro" who offered, he said, to bankroll a second safari for him, with her and Pauline both accompanying him. He demurred; likely the offer was casual and not serious—paying for three people on a safari was beyond almost anyone's reach in the Depression (except, perhaps, Uncle Gus). It's somewhat more interesting, however, that Ernest turned this slight encounter—without identifying the woman—into a jumping-off point for one of his best short stories. It is interesting as well that he did not go on to be friends with Hepburn. Perhaps she was simply too independent—not daughterly enough.

When the *Île de France* docked in New York, Pauline took the train on to Key West while Ernest transacted some important business. He wanted a boat. After some research, he had seen the model he wanted in the Wheeler Shipyard catalogue and made his way to Brooklyn to look at their stock, choosing a thirty-eight-foot cabin cruiser in the Playmate line. He arranged for a $3,000 advance from *Esquire,* later adding $2,500 from Scribner's toward the $7,495 price—all of it paid for with his own money, not Pauline's or Gus Pfeiffer's. He would name her the *Pilar,* after the code name he had used for Pauline during their hundred-day separation. Made of several different woods, most notably Canadian fir and mahogany from Honduras, the *Pilar* was painted black rather than the usual white. The boat, which could sleep six, had a 75-horsepower Chrysler Crown engine, as well as a backup, a 40-horsepower Lycoming. Ernest's other specifications included a well of ocean water to store bait and smaller fish, four 75-gallon fuel tanks to enable longer trips, and a lowered transom to allow for reeling in large fish; later he would add a flying bridge. He took delivery in late April in Miami and brought the boat down to Key West with Bra Saunders and a Wheeler representative on board. Everything he did reflected plans for a fishing future; on the way down to Miami he stopped in Philadelphia and met Charles Cadwalader, the director of the Philadelphia Academy of Natural Sciences, who was very interested in the study of game fish, especially the marlin. Ernest agreed to meet Cadwalader and Henry Fowler in Cuba that summer to observe marlin.

Ernest's younger brother, Leicester, then nineteen, surfaced in February, sending word that he was coming to Key West by boat. Like Carol, Leicester had been a trial to his older brother, who became even more parental when Leicester seemed to be loafing. Just a year after their father had shot himself, Ernest was demanding that Leicester pull his weight. Writing to Carol about the Baron, as Les was known, Ernest made up an account of how he himself had contributed to the family fortunes while still in school: he had delivered the local newspaper, *Oak Leaves;* he had worked in the high school lunchroom; and he had worked every summer (at unspecified jobs). Leicester had to get a job, Ernest told his mother in 1930, or risk a spanking. He reminded his mother that the family didn't lack an authority figure, and that he could easily come to Oak Park and take Leicester in hand. Leicester dreamed of seeing the world, and had started young, spending his freshman year of high school in Hawaii with his aunt (Ed's sister), Grace Livingston, and her family. He made plans to enter the University of Michigan, but he was elsewhere when the time came to enroll, and he never tried to go to college again. Like his older brother, Leicester saw himself as a writer, and would eventually make his living, such as it was, in journalism.

Leicester had built a seventeen-foot sailboat called the *Hawkshaw,* by himself, for $600, and planned to sail it all the way to South America. He arrived with Al Dudek, a friend from Petoskey, full of stories about his journey from Mobile, Alabama, during which he had weathered seven major storms, he said, each time having to lower the sails and drag the anchor. Ernest, who noted that Key West had enjoyed a string of temperate days, was dubious, but happy to take on a genuine little brother after the younger friends he had treated as such. The latest was Arnold Samuelson, a twenty-two-year-old admirer who had ridden freight trains from Minneapolis to meet Ernest, hoping to learn how to be a writer. Ernest said he would pay him a dollar a day plus meals if he would sleep aboard the *Pilar* and help out as a hand on fishing trips.

Samuelson later wrote about his year on the *Pilar,* and described in some detail one early fishing excursion. Ernest's Model A approached the dock with a large chunk of ice strapped to its rear bumper. Ernest handed down to Samuelson the ice; a box full of beer; lunch; a bottle of gin and one of whiskey; mullet wrapped in newspaper to be used for bait; wicker chairs borrowed from the Hemingway house to be used on deck; and the fishing rods and tackle. On board were Charles and Lorine Thompson; Pauline, Archie MacLeish, Leicester and Al Dudek, and Bra Saunders. It was Pauline's first trip on the boat, and Ernest kept asking her how she liked it. She would reply that it was "lovely," "marvelous," or, when really pressed, "perfect." Ernest pointed out to Samuelson the different colors of the water, indicating the nature of the bottom below, and showed him how the birds could be seen along the dark purple waters of the Gulf Stream; the birds and flying fish almost always indicated the Stream. The party was delighted when a sailfish leapt into the air, dancing on its tail and shaking its bill. Archie caught two cero mackerel and Thompson a bonito and a twenty-pound barracuda. Later they were surrounded by a school of yellow-green dolphinfish, or mahi-mahi, swimming right on the surface, and Ernest and company landed eighteen of them in five minutes. They would be used as fertilizer for Pauline's flowerbeds.

It was his "belle epoch," Ernest told his brother. In the mornings he worked on a project that started as a short story about Africa and quickly became an account of the safari—not fiction, but shaped like fiction. He was trying to write about the experience "truly," to use a word that would crop up again and again in his speech and prose. This entailed such stratagems as changed names, composite characters, flashbacks, and an omniscient first-person narrator. Very much as he had with *Death in the Afternoon,* Ernest took note of whatever occurred to him, to be edited later; with this book, however, he at least had a linear story to tell. Both books are full of Hemingway, and both exert considerable charm. But Ernest was careless in both of them—going on for too long on certain subjects, making much of his own observations, sometimes overwriting. With discipline, both *Death in the Afternoon* and what would become *Green Hills of Africa* could have been great works rather than the somewhat aimless, discursive, uneven (though often charming) accounts that they are. With discipline, Ernest could have mapped out and produced two "nonfiction novels," anticipating Norman Mailer's efforts in *Armies of the Night* (1968) and *The Executioner's Song* (1979) some thirty and forty years later.

But Ernest worked at *Green Hills of Africa* with his left hand, as it were. Arnold Samuelson wrote of the spring and summer of 1934, "Fishing had become our business and our way of life." They had planned to go over to Cuba in May to catch the marlin season, as Ernest had told the "scientificos" from Philadelphia. But Carlos Gutiérrez, the Cuban Ernest was going to hire as his navigator and fishing adviser, sent word on the ferry that significant marlins were not running, and Ernest did not go over until mid-July. Cuba had been roiled by unrest and attempted revolution in the early 1930s, and dictator Gerardo Machado had fled the country in August 1933. Almost immediately thereafter, however, the military, in the so-called Sergeants' Revolt, took the reins, headed by Fulgencio Batista. The situation in Cuba was precarious; when Dos Passos and Hemingway were there on May Day snipers fired on marching radicals, causing a riot.

Americans like Grant and Jane Mason simply laid low and waited for the dust to settle. The Depression was no easier in Cuba than it was in Key West; Charlie Thompson remembered a big knot of hungry people often awaiting the return of the sport fishing boats, hoping that the fishermen, who had no use for much of their catch, would give some away.

Except their catches that summer turned out to be small, after high hopes initially. In mid-July, having received word that the marlin were running, Ernest and the *Pilar* arrived at Havana's San Francisco dock. Soon he was fishing every day; the "scientificos" joined him for ten days, later stretching to two weeks and then to thirty days, taking photographs and samples of tuna and marlin; on his last day out, Cadwalader finally had a strike. Hooking the largest marlin the *Pilar's* crew had seen that year, the scientist lost him when the fish cut the line with its tail; he told Ernest that nonetheless the experience was "a thrill of a lifetime." But the fishing season that year was "disastrous," according to Arnold Samuelson; he recorded only twelve marlin in three months. By the time the *Pilar* and its crew made their way into Key West harbor in the fall, hurricane season was upon them, making anything longer than a day trip out impossible. Arnold Gingrich and Dos Passos nevertheless came down for some fall fishing.

But Ernest was relieved, feeling slightly guilty about being away from his writing for so long. The exception was his articles for *Esquire,* which were appearing, if not regularly, at least without gaps of more than two months between them. From the start, the *Esquire* pieces won him a large readership. About fishing or shooting and, sometimes, politics, the "letters" did much to establish him as a hard-living, hard-drinking, fearless, adventurous sort who was living a life most (male) readers wished was their own—for better or worse. As the 1930s wore on and critical demand for socially conscious fiction—the "proletarian novel"—grew louder, Ernest would come to see that this image did not always work to his advantage. Too often he appeared interested in activities like deep-sea fishing or big game hunting that were far beyond the reach of the Depression-era reader. Ernest would come to view this kind of criticism of what he did as envy, referring to the critics who "foam at the mouth . . . at the idea that I ever have any fun or any right to have fun." Another consideration, which worried Max if it did not worry Ernest, was that fans of this image of Hemingway did not always view him as a serious writer or his work as serious fiction.

At this point, it seemed his only course was to turn his attention again to the African book, and he piled up pages of it fairly regularly that fall. But after *Death in the Afternoon* and *Winner Take Nothing,* Ernest's 1933

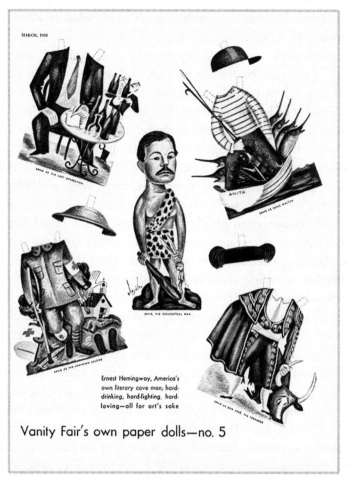

Ernest Hemingway, America's own literary cave man; hard-drinking, hard-fighting, hard-loving—all for art's sake

Vanity Fair's own paper dolls—no. 5

Paper dolls, *Vanity Fair*, March 1934

volume of short stories, Perkins wanted a novel—and Hemingway knew it. With "One Trip Across," a story about Harry Morgan, a fishing boat owner forced in the Depression, when sport fishermen were scarce, into criminal activity—which sold to *Cosmopolitan* for $5,500, the most Ernest had earned for a short story—Ernest thought he might have the beginnings of a novel. Further, he thought of the African book—which started as a short story that grew and grew—as a "long bitch," bearing similarities to a novel.

He structured *Green Hills* as such, beginning with the hunt—late in their safari—for greater kudu bulls, when Ernest was trying desperately to outshoot and bag larger specimens than his friend Karl (Charles Thompson). Because this effort was doomed to failure, the reader is immediately signaled that this narrative—nonfiction, if that's what it was—will not be the boasting, vainglorious account the subject matter might suggest. Though there is abundant self-importance in the finished book, Ernest succeeded in stepping back from himself, and with the new distance was able even to laugh at himself. The Pauline character—P.O.M.—is generously given a lot of humorous turns, and the narrator's affection for her is abundantly clear; the ribbing here, at Pauline's expense at any rate, is of the gentlest sort. The narrator engages the others, including Kandisky, a character based on an Austrian hunter the party met on their travels, in literary discussions, pronouncing Henry James, Stephen Crane, and Mark Twain the best American authors. One literary observation, "All modern American literature comes from one book by Mark Twain called *Huckleberry Finn*" (*GHOA*, 22), is certainly one of Hemingway's most famous. But he also sounds off characteristically against the critics, calling them "angleworms in a bottle, trying to derive knowledge and nourishment from their own contact and from the bottle" (*GHOA*, 21).

The book opens with Hemingway's narrator at an unsuccessful point in his hunting, and ends with him finally shooting a kudu bull, only to find that Karl, or Charles, has brought down a bull with even larger horns, just as Karl had previously bested him in a rhino hunt. "Poisoned with envy" (*GHOA*, 291), he nevertheless brings himself to compare their kudus together and tells Pop (Philip Percival), "I'm really glad he has him. Mine'll hold me" (*GHOA*, 293). For Hemingway to address the subject of competition and acknowledge himself bested suggests he had reached a point where his supreme confidence could allow him to cede ground. The narrator of *Green Hills of Africa* is a rarity in Hemingway works: a happy man.

While certainly not an achievement on the order of *The Sun Also Rises* or *A Farewell to Arms*, *Green Hills of Africa*, like *Death in the Afternoon*, is an entertaining piece of nonfiction that reveals a man passionate about his subject and surprisingly self-revealing and self-deprecating. Ernest was not at all modest, however, in assessing what he had written. He was elated to be finished, and told Max Perkins, "It is a swell thing . . . I think the best Ive written." He understood that Max had been expecting a novel, perhaps because of his references to "this long thing" or "the long bitch." He had started writing a short story, but the momentum of the plot carried him along until he'd written the whole story of the safari. He was a little nervous about how to characterize it exactly: "Then we will have to figure how to handle it—I suppose 70,000 words is a little long for a story—It can be a book by its-self *Is*!" Still, he thought of "throw[ing] it in free" with the collection of fifty-four stories he and Max had been talking about publishing. "True narrative that is exciting and still is literature is very rare. . . . You have to *make* the country—not describe it. It is as hard to do as paint a Cezanne—and I'm the only bastard right now who can do it." To his relief, Max wanted it to stand alone as a book rather than added on to a short story collection—though he too worried. He wanted it to seem more of a story than a travel book: his hope, he told Ernest, was "that the book has the quality of an imaginative work, is something utterly different from a mere narrative of an expedition." The "imaginative" element not only made it more pleasurable reading, but would help it sell more copies than a travel book, or a piece of nonfiction about Africa. At the same time, Perkins did not have high expectations for *Green Hills,* referring to it and *Death in the Afternoon* as "minor" works in a letter to Scott Fitzgerald. Just as well, Perkins feared, because from his perspective Hemingway was still going through a lull in the halls of public opinion ("The tide runs against him strongly").

Ernest turned in *Green Hills of Africa* in February 1935. The Hemingways had spent the holidays in Piggott, finding on their return that Ernest was having a recurrence of dysentery that required hospitalization. He was back on his feet in time to welcome Max Perkins and his wife to Key West and, on a separate trip, Sara Murphy. The Murphys had returned to America for good in 1932, and Gerald took up running the family business, the Mark Cross leather goods company, at the end of 1934. Patrick Murphy's tuberculosis had returned in his other lung, and he spent months in Doctors Hospital in New York City; he would later be moved to a sanitarium on Saranac Lake in the Adirondacks.

Tragedy struck the Murphys in an unexpected quarter in early 1935. After a bout with measles, Baoth Murphy, the eldest son—the "healthy" one—developed a mastoid condition that required surgery; in the aftermath, Baoth contracted meningitis, which killed him, after an agonizing ten days, on March 17. The Dos Passoses and the Hemingways responded with such generosity of spirit that the Murphys wired them back thanks, saying, "WE TRY TO BE LIKE WHAT YOU WANT US TO BE KEEP THINKING OF US PLEASE."

Amanda Vaill, the Murphys' biographer, writes that Ernest's letter to Gerald and Sara was perhaps the most moving and perceptive of all the friends' letters. "It is not as bad for Baoth," Ernest wrote, "because he had a fine time, always, and he has only done something now that we all must do. He has just gotten it over with." Making the crude but inevitable analogy to how he would feel if Jack died, he continued, "It is *your* loss [Hemingway's emphasis]: more than it is his so it is something that you can, legitimately, be brave about. But I cant be brave about it and in my heart I am sick for you both." He imagines the Murphys and their friends on a boat together, which they know now will never reach port. Since there's to be no landfall, the people on board must endure all kinds of weather on their journey. "We must keep the boat up very well and be very good to each other. We are fortunate we have good people on the boat." In the wake of Baoth's death, Ernest redoubled his efforts to hearten Patrick Murphy in the Adirondacks sanitarium, sending him the mounted head of an impala for his sickroom. The plight of the Murphy children moved him to a new tenderness in his continued friendship with Sara (his connection to Gerald had painlessly withered).

Katy Dos Passos had recently remarked on a change she was sure she had been seeing in Ernest lately; rather than being "irascible" and "truculent," he is "just a big cage of canaries" followed around by "a crowd of Cuban zombies" who treated him like a "conquistador." But he still had, she noted, "a tendency to be an Oracle," and really needed "some best pal" and "severe critic" to tear off "those long white whiskers"—the white whiskers still figurative.

Katy and Dos had rented a house in Key West that winter, noting that the town had filled up with New Dealers and that the Hemingway house on Whitehead Street had become a tourist attraction. They had taken to calling Ernest "the Old Master" because he was always laying down the law, or "Mahatma" for the towel he often wrapped around his head to keep off the sun. "He had more crotchety moments than in the old days," observed Dos, "but he was a barrel of monkeys when he wanted to be." Dos seems not to have had a competitive bone in his body and enjoyed Ernest's battles with the big fish.

Not that fishing with Ernest was easy. In early April, he set out for Bimini, in the Bahamas, on the advice of his old friend Mike Strater, who said giant tuna roamed the waters off the island. With Mike, Dos and Katy, and two locals, Bread Pinder and Hamilton Adams, joining him on the 175-mile trip, they had barely left the harbor when Ernest hooked a large shark. Bringing the fish alongside the boat, he tried to gaff it with his left hand while holding a loaded pistol in his right, which he commonly used to shoot sharks that interfered with big fish he had hooked. In this maneuver, the gaff broke off and a piece hit the pistol, which in turn fired two shots right into each of Ernest's legs. The bullets hit fleshy areas, but the wounds needed medical attention, and the *Pilar* had to reverse direction and return to Key West. Katy Dos Passos was livid at Ernest's carelessness in handling the gun and refused to speak to him.

Gregory, Jack (Bumby), and Patrick Hemingway, ca. 1935

Bimini was a rare find for Ernest, however, and he would spend months at a time there over the next three years. A small island, smack in the Gulf Stream, it enjoys a constant cool breeze; the water is so clear, he told Sara Murphy, that you think you'll run aground when you have ten fathoms beneath your boat. There were several thatched huts on the island, a few houses, a small hotel, and a store-cum-barroom. Pauline flew over in late April, noting a seven-mile-long beach for swimming, and rented a house for herself and the boys for the summer. For Jack, Patrick, and Gregory it turned into a magical interlude, the setting for *Islands in the Stream,* the only one of Hemingway's novels in which his sons would appear as characters.

The drawback to Bimini was a large shark population; a dramatic scene in *Islands in the Stream* would involve the rescue of Thomas Hudson's middle son from attacking sharks. The sharks made big game fishing difficult, as they could "apple-core" fish on the line, leaving just the head and the vertebrae. Ernest's solution was to shoot them; the challenge was the small size of the shark brain, for the only way to stop a shark was to shoot it in the brain. Frustrated, Ernest borrowed a Thompson submachine gun from another yachtsman who eventually out and out gave it to him, seeing Ernest liked it so much that he clearly would not return it anytime soon. Katy Dos Passos described a shark attack with Ernest and his tommy gun:

They come like express trains and hit the fish like a planing mill—shearing off twenty-five and thirty pounds at a bite. Ernest shoots them with a machine gun, *rrr*—but it won't stop them—It's terrific to see the bullets ripping into them—the shark thrashing in blood and foam—the white bellies and fearful jaws—the pale cold eyes—I was really aghast but it's very exciting.

The tommy gun cost him a friend: one afternoon on board the *Pilar* Mike Strater had hooked a fourteen-foot black marlin and Ernest immediately got out the gun, ready to aim it at any predators. Ultimately, he did shoot a shark; unfortunately, so much blood was released that the scene attracted more sharks, and Mike's fish was mutilated. It weighed five hundred pounds even *after* being cored. It was the largest black marlin caught off Bimini. Mike and Ernest, aware that the fish's size would excite envy from all the sports fishermen frequenting Bimini, had the fish weighed and measured on the dock, and then posed for photographs, Ernest as the boat owner and Strater as the fishing hero.

The only problem was that in all the photos a proud, grinning Ernest stands closer to the fish than does Mike, with a proprietary hand raised up and placed on one of the fish's remaining fins. After several pictures a photographer asked if he couldn't get some of the angler and his catch—without Ernest. Later, when one of the first photographs was reproduced in *Time,* the magazine wrote as if it were Ernest's catch—and he did not correct this impression. Mike blamed Ernest, first, for unleashing a feeding frenzy by machine-gunning the shark; and second, for trying to take credit for the mutilated but still record-breaking marlin that Mike eventually reeled in. In a July 1935 column in *Esquire* headlined "The President Vanquishes"—Strater was the president of the Maine Tuna Club, a title Ernest was evidently poking fun at—Hemingway makes no mention of tommy-gunning the shark and the subsequent feast, and in fact says he had to spell a tiring Strater during the battle with the marlin—a claim Mike disputed later. Though the two men continued to exchange letters over the years, the friendship was effectively over.

Ernest's fervid pursuit of the big fish reached a new intensity when he discovered Bimini. And when he discovered the rich, who likewise were attracted to the island for the fish. Ernest formed bonds with several of these particular denizens over their shared passion, but when they got to know one another, differences emerged. Most of the anglers, for one thing, had boats significantly bigger than the *Pilar.* Kip Farrington, one of the first yachtsmen Ernest met that spring and summer on Bimini, had been an extremely successful stockbroker who got out of the market just in time before the Crash and then became a preeminent writer on fishing. He was the first sportsman to catch a marlin off Bimini, in 1933, other wealthy anglers following in his wake. Another new friend, Mike Lerner, owned a chain of women's clothing stores. He and his wife, Helen, were both avid anglers; they owned one of the most comfortable houses on Bimini, with screened porches on three sides. Lerner would loan or rent the house to Ernest many times; it would serve as a model for Thomas Hudson's house in *Islands in the Stream.* Lerner also became a serious researcher in the field of marine biology. He was one of game fishing's pioneers, becoming a founding member of the International Game Fish Association at the Museum of Natural History in New York, the IGFA soon making Ernest an officer. Tommy Shevlin, who was to become an important friend to Ernest, came from a family that made a fortune in lumber on the West Coast. He was an excellent hunter (including big game), golfer, and polo player; he visited the L-Bar-T Ranch to hunt grizzly, elk, and antelope with Ernest. Tall, handsome, and charming, Shevlin was another pioneer, having built the first house on the nearby Bimini island Cat Cay. He was only twenty-one, so he filled the role of the little brother whom Ernest loved to have around.

Ernest was pleased to be able to introduce a real white hunter to this crowd of well-endowed, competitive anglers. He had stayed in touch with Bror Blixen-Finecke and his thirty-year-old second wife, Eva, and effusively invited them to Bimini. There was a rumor at the time that Ernest slept with Eva, who was known as a bit of an adventuress; one evening most of the party, including Bror, slept on the deck of the *Pilar,* while only Ernest and Eva had rooms belowdecks. It was no doubt just a rumor, one of many that circulated among the small yachting community, the locals, and the natives. Eva was a beautiful blonde, but Pauline was now a blonde as well, and this summer she had her husband transfixed by changing her hair's hue to ash blond. Ernest wrote to Jane Mason, now back in Cuba, about Pauline, "She looks simply marvelous; sweller looking all the time . . . can't think of herself as anything but a blonde. Me I can think of her plenty of ways and all marvelous." Pauline made sure that she was in Bimini when the Blixen-Fineckes visited.

Ernest wasted no time in making himself cock of the Bimini walk. He issued a challenge: he could knock out any man on the island by the third round. He is reported to have had a couple of takers, both of whom he beat handily. Later that summer he boxed a few "exhibition" rounds with Tom Heeney, an out-of-shape heavyweight who had once fought Gene Tunney.

Outside the ring, Ernest knocked out one of his fellow yachtsmen, Joseph Fairchild Knapp, of the Fairchild magazine fortune. Knapp had told Ernest and a group of late-night revelers to quiet down, calling him, "You big fat slob . . . You phony, you faker . . . You rotten writer." Ernest downed him with four quick punches. The fight became a legend, the subject of a local calypso song whose words included, "The big fat slob's in the harbor," Ernest being the slob.

By way of contrast, Ernest found himself, at the end of this Bimini summer spent with rich anglers, contributing an article to the Marxist-oriented *New Masses*. The magazine, in fact, had previously had it in for him, faulting him for refusing to engage politically; because he did not take up "proletarian literature," he was an enemy of the worker, the magazine's writers argued—Granville Hicks suggesting in the *New Masses'* pages that Hemingway write a novel about a strike.

On September 2 a hurricane swept through the Florida Keys, largely sparing Key West but hitting with full force the Upper and Lower Matecumbe Keys. A bridge and a highway connecting the keys with the mainland was a current project of the Civilian Conservation Corps, and seven hundred CCC workers, all war veterans, and their families were camping in crude housing on the two keys while the vets worked. Though there was ample notice of the coming hurricane and its path, the government had done nothing to protect these people. The hurricane's twenty-foot storm surge flattened the camps, and over five hundred people lost their lives. Ernest joined a rescue effort whose participants donned gloves and gas masks to collect the bodies, fast disintegrating in the tropical sun. Ernest was incensed; the government had dispatched a train to rescue the workers, but not in time; the workers had been housed in flimsy wood-and-cardboard shacks that could not withstand even the mildest hurricane season; and Washington did not send adequate numbers of rescue workers or material aid. When the *New Masses* cabled Hemingway for a story, he at first dismissed it, as he did most requests from magazines that did not pay him top dollar. But he decided that this event was above politics—or, rather, that an article asking who killed the vets (which would become the article's title) could be a powerful indictment of the way some things were run in Washington.

After he sent it off he had second thoughts. There seems to have been no conversation about pay; the magazine either did not pay or paid a pittance for its stories, a sum so low that they might have feared it would insult Hemingway. In any case he did not ask for payment. He was so unaccustomed to selfless acts that he could not resist bragging about having written the *New Masses* article for free. He wrote to Sara Murphy, a friend he so much admired that he always sought a chance to get in her good graces, that the *New Masses* "had better" print the following disclaimer: "We disapprove of Mr. H. and do not want anyone to ever be sucked in by anything else he may ever write but he is a very expensive reporter who happened to be on the spot and because he does not believe in making money out of murder he has written this for us for nothing."

The *New Masses* printed no such disclaimer. Only Sara Murphy and the other friends he may have told ever knew that he wrote the article for free. From polo players to the magazine for the proletariat, it had been a strange summer.

EIGHTEEN

It was probably inevitable that Hemingway would talk one day about the size of Scott Fitzgerald's penis. His friendship with Scott was a defining feature of his life and his literary career. Scott had been instrumental early on, bringing Ernest to Scribner's and roughly licking the first quarter of *The Sun Also Rises* into shape. In their lives the two men emblematized Paris in the 1920s, and in their fiction they both spoke for and inspired a whole new generation of writers. Between the two, they pretty much covered the waterfront. By 1933, however, Ernest was looking to terminate his actual contact with Scott.

Scott dated the demise of the friendship fairly accurately when he wrote in his *Notebooks,* in 1929, "Ernest—before he began to walk over me with cleats." After 1930 the two men met four times—though on the last occasion, in Hollywood in 1937, they only said hello to each other. And another time they were said to have met, when they repaired to the toilet in Michaud's for Ernest to see the size of Scott's penis, probably never happened. Ernest told the story of this inspection toward the very end of his life in *A Moveable Feast,* his memoir about Paris in the 1920s, placing it sometime after Zelda had her first mad spell, which was April 1930; he seems to have been suggesting a meeting in the fall of 1931. The first difficulty arises here; the two men were in Paris at the same time for less than a week that year, in mid-September. Zelda was released from the Swiss clinic, Prangins, on September 15, and she and Scott sailed for the U.S. for good on the *Aquitania* on September 19. Ernest traveled to Paris from Spain at the end of August, and he and Pauline sailed for America on the *Île de France* on September 23.

Hemingway's biographers, with the exception of Kenneth Lynn, have taken him at his word when he describes the scene at Michaud's for readers of *A Moveable Feast.* Scott said that his only sexual partner had been Zelda—which is possible—and that she said Scott's penis was not large enough to satisfy her. Ernest told Scott to meet him in the "office"—*le water,* he clarified—where Ernest mutely examined Scott's penis. When both men returned to their table, Ernest told Scott that looking at one's penis from above is misleading, as the organ is foreshortened from such a perspective. Scott's penis was normal, he said, and Zelda was just trying to "put [him] out of business" (*AMF,* 162).

Ernest added that the size when erect was what mattered, and that Scott could use pillows in bed to modify angles of penetration—masculine lore Fitzgerald would have almost certainly already known. According to Hemingway, when Scott remained doubtful, Ernest took him off to the Louvre to look at Greek statues with penises of various sizes. Such an excursion seems wildly improbable.

What really happened was likely far more mundane. Ernest probably never inspected Scott's penis. But to judge from accounts of the next meeting of the two men, in January 1933, Scott was indeed concerned about his ability to satisfy Zelda. Ernest had agreed to meet Edmund Wilson and Scott Fitzgerald at the Aurora Restaurant in midtown Manhattan. Scott was drunk when he got there, and Ernest must have been, for he arrived in a hansom cab, saying he wanted to do something good for horses, since he patronized so many bullfights where they were killed. He was on a bit of a tear, easily persuaded to sing a couple of bawdy Italian songs for the waiters. Scott spent a good part of the evening with his head on the table—like the dormouse at the Mad Tea Party, Wilson said—and lying down underneath the table, from which vantage point he occasionally joined in the conversation. Wilson wrote that Ernest said Scott had been asking him whether Scott's penis was normal size; John Peale Bishop had already informed Wilson that this was now a dinner table topic of Scott's. Ernest tried to convey to Wilson the point about the foreshortening of the penis when seen from above, but Wilson did not really understand what he was saying. It was probably this meeting, in fact, that would contribute to Wilson's impression that while a great writer, "as a person [Ernest] was a real all-American S.O.B., mean and curmudgeonist, quarrelsome and extremely egocentric, and in many ways virtually a psychopathic case." Certainly it was churlish to wholesale Scott's penis size concerns. Edmund was also struck by Scott's behavior vis-à-vis Ernest, writing, "Hemingway was now a great man and Scott was so overcome by his greatness that he embarrassed me by his self abasement." Scott saw his own behavior a little differently, judging by a letter of apology he wrote to Wilson shortly afterward. "With Ernest I seem to have reached a state where when we drink together I half bait, half truckle to him." He also reported to Max Perkins that he had been on "a terrible bat," something he said he knew Ernest had tried to conceal from Max.

The two writers would not see each other for four more years, but their correspondence was lively. Fitzgerald's flawed masterpiece, *Tender Is the Night,* appeared in the spring of 1934, after appearing serially in *Scribner's Magazine* from January through April. In May he still had not heard from Ernest, and bluntly asked for his opinion: "Did you like the book? For God's sake drop me a line and tell me one way or the other." Ernest, for his part, had been sounding off to all and sundry, but especially to Perkins, that Scott had got himself all balled up trying to write the book his critics expected of him, complicated by the fact that Scott was a "rummy" and that Zelda was out to destroy him. Scott was also coming closer to Ernest's material with *Tender Is the Night.* The main characters, Dick and Nicole Diver, in part autobiographical, are also modeled in part on Gerald and Sara Murphy. The novel raises issues about wealth and the wealthy—long a Fitzgerald topic, but one about which Ernest was more ambivalent, and increasingly so as he began to live in the world of the rich in places like Bimini and Havana.

"I liked it and I didn't like it," Ernest wrote at the outset of his letter to Scott about *Tender Is the Night.* "It started off with that marvelous description of Sara and Gerald. . . . Then you started fooling with them, making them come from things they didn't come from, changing them into other people and you can't do that, Scott." The letter became even more confused here; Ernest didn't know whether he was angry that Scott used real people as characters or that he wasn't completely true to the real-life models. At the same time he complained that Scott had invented characters but hadn't invented *enough* of them, taking too much from life. Halfway through, however, the letter became friendly, as if Ernest were giving Scott his undivided attention after tuning him out for so long: "For Christ sake write and don't worry about what the boys will say nor whether it will be a masterpiece nor what." Good advice, perhaps, but given a little too late. He told Scott to put Zelda, his "personal tragedy," aside. And he got down to cases: "I'd like to see you and talk about things with you sober. You were so damned stinking in N.Y. we didn't get anywhere." Again, good advice, but with a catch all its own: the pot was calling the kettle a rummy. And he found himself praising Scott: "You can write twice as well now as you ever could," adding, "I'm damned fond of you."

The letter was "skyophreniac," to borrow a term Ernest used to describe himself in a letter to Sara Murphy. Ernest was really of two minds about Scott, just as he would prove to be about Scott's achievement in *Tender Is the Night.* Though for whatever reason he could not praise the novel when it came out, he was able to do so just five years later, not long before Scott's death, when it would do his friend little good—and then in a letter to Max Perkins, not Scott himself: "It's amazing how *excellent* much of [the novel] is," Ernest wrote. "How I wish he would have kept on writing. Is it really all over or will he write again?" Perhaps because he believed Scott had left the field, as it were, he offered Max a psychological snapshot of their friendship. "I always had a very stupid little boy feeling of superiority about Scott—like a tough little boy sneering at a delicate but talented little boy," he wrote parenthetically in a postscript, adding, using a well-chosen word, "Reading that novel much of it was so good it was frightening."

Ernest and Scott had exchanged letters in December 1935, Ernest inviting Scott to go with him to see a prizefight in Havana. Scott had evidently not been enthusiastic enough about *Green Hills of Africa,* so Ernest became abusive: "Was delighted from the letter to see you don't know any more about when a book is a good book or what makes a book bad than ever," he wrote, a comment that suggests Ernest was still keen to dismiss the good work Scott had done on *The Sun Also Rises.* In another letter to Scott five days later Ernest started out solicitous, commiserating over insomnia, the ravages of drinking, and so forth. But he then turned on Scott in what he may well have meant as black humor. The conceit was that Scott should get himself heavily insured and come with him to Cuba where he could get killed in the revolution. Hemingway's and Scott's other friends could then give Scott's liver to the Princeton Club, one lung to Max Perkins, and the other to *Saturday Evening Post* editor George Horace Lorimer. If they could find his balls they could be taken on the *Île de France* to Paris and then to Antibes, where they could be thrown in the sea at Eden Roc with MacLeish reading some profound verses. Ernest was so taken with the conceit that he even provided some lines for such a poem. He eviscerated his friend as neatly as he might gut a trout.

In the meantime, Scott had written and was about to publish a series of three essays in *Esquire,* the first of which was called "The Crack-Up." Appearing in January, February, and March 1936, the essays would be collected in a 1945 volume of the same title, edited posthumously by Edmund Wilson. They began with Fitzgerald's perception that he was a plate that had cracked, and analyzed how that had happened and how he might go on with his life from there. The essays are small classics, laying the groundwork for the intense, self-examining memoirs that would flourish decades later, and they provided some of the most memorable sentences in American prose, among them "In the real dark night of the soul it is always three o'clock in the morning, day after day." After the nakedly confessional memoirs that were to follow, the "Crack-Up" essays have now lost some of

August. 1936

27

The Snows of Kilimanjaro

A Long Story

by ERNEST HEMINGWAY

Kilimanjaro is a snow covered mountain 19,710 feet high, and is said to be the highest mountain in Africa. Its western summit is called by the Masai "Ngàje Ngài," the House of God. Close to the western summit there is the dried and frozen carcass of a leopard. No one has explained what the leopard was seeking at that altitude.

Let's not quarrel any more. No matter how nervous we get. Maybe they will be back with another truck today. Maybe the plane will come."

"I don't want to move," the man said. "There is no sense in moving now except to make it easier for you."

"That's cowardly."

I mean by giving up. It says it's bad for you. I know it's bad for you."

"No," he said. "It's good for me."

So now it was all over, he thought. So now he would never have a chance to finish it. So this was the way it ended in a bickering over a drink. Since the gangrene started in his right leg he had no pain and with the

This 1936 *Esquire* story provided a rueful run-through of Hemingway's life thus far.

their original power, but at the time, readers and critics reacted strongly to their personal revelations—Ernest among them. It was as if Scott had done something unnatural. "He seems to almost take a pride in his shamelessness of defeat," Ernest told Max after the first two essays appeared.

Ernest took the occasion to enumerate his complaints about Scott. He had long maintained that "he couldn't think—he never could," and that he should work well and stop "whin[ing] in public." He thought that it would have been better if Scott had gone overseas in the war, rather than staying stateside in a desk job—then he would have been "shot for cowardice." He supplied a couple of reasons for Scott's arriving at such a pass: he had written too many times for the marketplace (while elsewhere Ernest had said that Scott's problem was writing for the critics); and he had loved youth so much that losing it spooked him thoroughly—this last a rather more perceptive comment.

In "The Snows of Kilimanjaro," the masterly short story Ernest began to write in April 1936, the month after the "Crack Up" pieces, he would fire the opening salvo in a campaign to bury Scott and his reputation in a flood of misinformation—and defamation.

* * *

In the first half of 1936, Ernest's writing energies were devoted to one of his worst novels and two of his best short stories. *To Have and Have Not* was cobbled together out of "The Tradesman Returns," which appeared in February 1936 in *Esquire,* and "One Trip Across," published in *Cosmopolitan* in May. Ernest was already thinking about a story collection that would feature these two stories, along with the two Africa stories he was also finishing that spring, "The Snows of Kilimanjaro" (first published in *Esquire* in August) and "The Short Happy Life of Francis Macomber" (first published in *Cosmopolitan* in September).

As this complicated publishing history attests, Ernest was doing a lot of thinking about career moves in this period. Both he and Max Perkins were engaged in mid- to long-range planning, and the next object seemed to be another short story volume, this one what was then called an "omnibus." He and Max foresaw a collection to be called "The First Forty-eight" or "The First Forty-nine," depending on which stories they would include, a decision complicated by the fact that such a collection would have both "some *damned* good [stories] to end . . . with," as Ernest put it, and one to open with. He and Max would move the stories around like chess pieces between January 1936 and October 1938, when *The Fifth Column and the First Forty-nine Stories* appeared.

Max, spotting no novel—the most desirable Hemingway "product"—on the horizon, suggested taking all four of these new stories and publishing them as a collection along with some of the best of Ernest's *Esquire* letters, including a long one, "Wings over Africa," about Italian dictator Benito Mussolini's war in Ethiopia. But Ernest nixed that, loath to include hunting and fishing pieces and run the risk of being vilified by the critics, who he felt didn't believe his sporting life had any social or literary value. Critics have assumed that Ernest was referring to the left-wing critics then in the ascendancy, demanding "proletarian," or nonfrivolous, subject matter, and he may well have been (especially since Perkins proposed including his *New Masses* piece about the veterans in Matecumbe), but Ernest also knew that he was running the danger of appearing an international adventurer of sorts, a type with which he was now familiar from his time in Bimini.

Arnold Gingrich broke the stalemate in June 1936 when he came down to Bimini and convinced Ernest he had a novel on his hands—welcome news indeed to Ernest, who knew how much this information would please his readers and his publisher. The *Esquire* editor complicated matters by having an affair with Jane Mason during his stay and, afterward, in New York City (they would not marry for twenty years and after several intervening marriages to others). Ernest knew something was going on, though he could hardly make a territorial claim, muttering, "God damn editor comes down to Bimini and sees a blonde, and hasn't been the same since."

Gingrich thought Ernest could cobble together "One Trip Across" and "The Tradesman's Return," his two stories with Harry Morgan as the hero or antihero; he envisioned a long novella, the equivalent of three chapters, to be added to these for a novel in five chapters. This manageable project had great appeal to Ernest, for he increasingly thought he wanted to go to Spain to cover the civil war heating up there, and thus he might not be writing much fiction in the near future. Not only would the two stories count toward the novel, but also, he thought, somewhat strangely, that he could rework the *New Masses* article and include it in the novel as well (which did not transpire). He devoted himself to adding material that would fill out his story, especially the parts Gingrich had urged him to expand on—those about Helene Bradley, a rich woman who takes up with Richard Gordon, a politically committed writer.

Unfortunately, the characters Helene Bradley and Richard Gordon were closely modeled on real people, Jane Mason and John Dos Passos, both later additions to the novel. Ernest may well have been eager to expand on Richard Gordon, the politicized writer, because for the first time in his life he felt competitive with Dos Passos. Dos was, of course, a longtime friend; for one thing, he was more easygoing than friends like MacLeish. He didn't care if Ernest caught a bigger fish or made more money. He also seemed unfazed by Ernest's literary career and growing fame. Ernest had, until 1936, never felt threatened by Dos Passos as a writer. Dos had been prolific, publishing eight volumes in the 1920s. Only two of those, *Three Soldiers* (1920) and *Manhattan Transfer* (1925), had been critical successes; none of his books had sold well and his readership seemed confined to a small, educated coterie. But by 1936 this had begun to change.

Another factor in Ernest's invention of the Dos Passos character in *To Have and Have Not* was payback. Five years before, Dos had made the mistake of reading and offering comment on the manuscript of *Death in the Afternoon*—just as Scott Fitzgerald had offered Ernest book-saving advice on *The Sun Also Rises*. Ernest let Dos read the manuscript in the winter of 1932, in part because of Dos's knowledge of Spain. Half Portuguese, Dos had spent a lot of time in Spain, living there for about eight months in 1919 and 1920. He had published, in 1922, a volume of essays on the country called *Rosinante to the Road Again*. Moreover, Dos saw his first bullfight four years before Ernest saw his. Yet Dos never lorded it over Ernest because of his experience; he was part of the gang who went to Pamplona on Ernest's second trip there in 1924 and was an enthusiastic reveler and bullfight observer (though never an *aficionado*). Still, Ernest knew, when he allowed Dos to see the manuscript of his book on bullfighting in February 1932, his friend would give it an informed reading.

Dos Passos's letter to Ernest about *Death in the Afternoon* was extremely positive, calling it "absolutely the best thing [that] can be done on the subject," "damn swell," "hellishly good"—"I'd say way ahead of anything of yours yet." He was critical, however, of the device of the Old Lady, and didn't in general approve when Ernest proceeded to get down to brass tacks and "give the boys the lowdown," spilling "all the secrets of the profession" and not playing fair, like a boxer who loads his gloves with plaster of Paris before a bout. Ernest seemed to take the criticism well, making some attempt to "cut the shit" as Dos had recommended, adding, "You were damned good to take so much trouble telling me." (In the same letter he called *1919*, the second book in Dos's *U.S.A.* trilogy, "bloody splendid.") By the end of May he could write that he had "cut out all you objected to (seemed like the best to me God damn you if it really was) cut 4 ½ galleys of philosophy and telling the boys." Ernest, a great believer in the effective ending ("Isn't it pretty to think so?"), thus cut the original ending, which had moved on from bullfighting to a discussion of authorship and the art of writing. The excised portion builds to a section in which Hemingway makes observations on the danger of writing for commercial ends; if a writer tailors his work for the marketplace, he no longer has any claims to be an artist.

While Dos's suggestions no doubt improved the book, his advice was also an unforgivable offense, and Ernest struck the first blows by putting Dos into *To Have and Have Not* as Gordon, a proletarian writer who is working on a novel about a strike in a textile mill. The portrait is masked somewhat; Gordon has previously slept with Helene Bradley, the character based on Jane Mason. But Arnold Gingrich, for one, was hardly fooled when he saw the manuscript. He had come to like Ernest and to feel protective of Jane, and he believed both she and Dos were libeled in *To Have and Have Not*. Gingrich flew down to Bimini, where he fought tooth and nail each evening with Ernest and his lawyer, Maurice Speiser—although they happily laid aside their differences to spend the days out in the *Pilar* fishing. With his attention now focused on getting to Spain to cover the civil war, Ernest was no longer very interested in the slapped-together novel, and agreed to almost all of what Gingrich said had to be cut. Gingrich later wrote, however, that he was dismayed to find Ernest "chopping whole hunks out of a book and not bothering to put one word back in." Gingrich felt *To Have and Have Not* "was rather malformed as the result of . . . major excisions without any sort of replacement of the deleted elements."

Perhaps partly for this reason, the Dos Passos figure is thinly realized, recognizable mainly in references the character makes to things "bourgeois." But this suggests the nub of the problem. As concern about the Fascist threat began to spread from the left to the general public, Dos was becoming a larger figure in the cultural landscape; he was praised for the same reason Ernest was dismissed, at least in some circles: his politics. Ernest, who at this time of his life was not particularly interested in the workers' struggle, knew that the critical battles over the place of the proletariat in literature had no reference to his work. But criticism was criticism, and he hated it.

In 1936 Dos Passos published the concluding volume of the *U.S.A.* trilogy, which at last made his reputation. The novels were experimental in form, demonstrating that it was possible to combine literary modernism—at least some elements of it—with politically committed, accessible narrative fiction. Readers found the trilogy spoke powerfully to the plight of the workers and dispossessed, especially in these years of the Depression. One of the most powerful passages was the description of the trial and execution of immigrant anarchists Sacco and Vanzetti, in which Dos Passos concluded, famously, "All right we are two nations America." Dos's single biggest offense in Ernest's eyes, however, was appearing on the cover of *Time* magazine in July 1936, something Ernest had yet to achieve, despite his fame. (The article compared Dos Passos to Tolstoy and Joyce, which would not have escaped Ernest's notice.)

It is unlikely that Ernest's competitive nature was roused by Dos Passos's sales; the biggest seller of the trilogy, *The Big Money,* sold just twenty thousand copies the year it came out. Dos Passos was not even able to get Harcourt, Brace to publish the trilogy in one set of covers until 1938. He seemed, however, to be the new darling of the intellectual left wing—a group vocal in criticizing Hemingway's lack of political engagement over the past decade; this despite the *New Masses* article about the hurricane and the veterans. Ernest thus felt he had received neither the credit he thought he deserved or the payment he was so conscious of forgoing.

Though Ernest affected to care little about what the left thought about him, he was pleased when his Russian translator, Ivan Kashkin, sent him a 1935 article called "Ernest Hemingway: A Tragedy of Craftsmanship," which spoke admiringly of the moral code of the Hemingway hero. In a letter to Kashkin, Ernest wrote: "I cannot be a communist now because I believe in only one thing: liberty. First I would look after myself and do my work. Then I would care for my family. Then I would help my neighbor. But the state I care nothing for." Back in 1933 he had told one young writer that he saw the state as little more than a get-rich-quick scheme. Though he would never valorize the state, his views were about to change, as the civil war in Spain began to awaken his political consciousness.

Yet contemporary politics had little place in two of Hemingway's strongest and most revealing short stories, "The Short Happy Life of Francis Macomber" and "The Snows of Kilimanjaro," published the same year. Both made use of his safari experience, the first featuring characters lifted from life, seemingly without changing a whisker. Robert Wilson, the great white hunter, is obviously based on Philip Percival, the Hemingways' guide, while Margot is clearly based on Jane Mason. Hemingway writes of her, recalling Jane's endorsement of Pond's cold cream, "She was an extremely handsome and well-kept woman of the beauty and social position which had, five years before, commanded five thousand dollars as the price of endorsing, with photographs, a beauty product which she had never used" (*CSS*, 5–6).

The story opens after Macomber has been carried into camp in triumph, after supposedly shooting a lion, the desired trophy of the safari; in reality, Macomber had panicked when he saw the charging lion, leaving Wilson to shoot the beast and allow Macomber to claim the kill, retaining the shreds of his pride. The scene in the camp seems to indicate that Margot has been sleeping with Wilson, dealing Macomber further humiliation. When the party goes out to shoot buffalo, the two men bring down two, but the third bull retreats, wounded, just as the lion had. Then, like the lion, the animal charges. Macomber stands his ground and shoots at the buffalo, missing; Wilson fires the killing shot, but at the same time Margot has fired, seemingly at the buffalo charging her husband—but her shot is right to Macomber's head. The story does not resolve whether Margot intentionally or coincidentally shot her husband. "The Short Happy Life of Francis Macomber" plays on several elements from Hemingway's life and psyche. It questions everything from courage itself to the ethics of hunting practices (like shooting from a moving car). Hemingway powerfully projects himself even into the consciousness of the lion, briefly describing what the hunted animal sees. But the story asks at the same time in which character the narrative consciousness lies: with the hunter Wilson, brave and principled, though compromised by the demands of his job; Macomber, whose very weakness and cowardice arouse the sympathy of the reader, for watching his humiliation is not easy; or even Margot, who seems to put herself on an altogether different plane with her desperate action. Who is really brave and who is not?

"The Snows of Kilimanjaro" is a story essential to any understanding of Hemingway the man and the shape of his life after his early years in Paris. Harry is a writer on safari who is dying of gangrene from a minor cut, the story consisting of his musings, reminiscences, and conversations with his rich wife. She is different in factual detail from Pauline, but there are enough emotional similarities that Pauline would have recognized herself and found the story hurtful indeed, for the character believes Harry loves her and the reader knows he doesn't really. Harry slips in and out of consciousness, remembering the experiences he has not written about and now never will. We learn of these experiences in lyrically rendered passages set in italics: many of these are part of Hemingway's past, some of them amplified and made more dramatic—just as Ernest's were in actuality. Among them are his childhood at the lake; his experiences in Italy in the war (amplified to include much combat); covering the Greco-Turkish War; winters skiing in Schruns, sleeping on mattresses stuffed with beech leaves by night and making dramatic runs downhill by day; fishing in the Black Forest; summers hunting and fishing in Wyoming. But most of the memories that come to Harry are of Paris, the city as Ernest had experienced it in the early days with Hadley, when life was at once urgent and sweet. Harry has by and large stopped writing before the story opens, for which he partly blames his wife's money, which has made it unnecessary for him to work. But he also blames himself: "He had destroyed his talent by not using it, by betrayals of himself and what he believed in, by drinking so much that he blunted the edge of his perceptions, by laziness, by sloth, and by snobbery" (*CSS*, 45). (The reference to drinking in itself is telling, for this is one of a handful of times in his life Ernest—through the character of Harry—admitted he drank too much.) Harry is almost overwhelmed by how much he has to write, and, in an interesting detail, by the responsibility that went with it: "He had seen the world change. . . . He had been in it and he had watched it and it was his duty to write of it, but now he never would" (*CSS*, 49).

It was with "The Snows of Kilimanjaro," also, that Hemingway first sounded a near-obsession in his correspondence from this point until his death: that he might "use up" and thus be unable to write about certain experiences that he had always known would make fit subjects for fiction. As public curiosity about Ernest grew and criticism of his work in these years became increasingly biographical, he feared that those who wrote about his life would somehow take those experiences away from him as well. After Malcolm Cowley wrote a long biographical essay about him in *Life* magazine in 1948, Hemingway would lament that he had "lost" the experiences Cowley wrote about, complaining to a fan that it bothered him to lose things he once thought a lot of. In "Snows," Harry berates himself for not "using" his experiences in his work. About what is clearly the Nordquist ranch in Wyoming, he wrote, "[Harry] knew at least twenty good stories from out there and he had never written one," adding, as if questioning himself, "Why?" (*CSS*, 53).

With "The Snows of Kilimanjaro" Ernest, at age thirty-seven, reached a watershed in his career. This brilliant short story also serves as a reminder of and a rejoinder to his own behavior in allowing Gingrich to eviscerate *To Have and Have Not* without troubling to rewrite it into something worthwhile—or abandon it. He no longer wrote for himself, he seemed to fear, but only for others—and, increasingly, for the marketplace—exactly what he had warned against in the passages from *Death in the Afternoon* about the demands of art, passages, ironically, that he had cut on Dos Passos's advice. "The Snows of Kilimanjaro" is in part his apologia.

Comments about Scott Fitzgerald in the story mark another turning point, this one in his relations with friends: almost an announcement that he had no further scruples about people in his past. "The Snows of Kilimanjaro" first appeared in *Esquire* in August 1936—just five months after the last of the "Crack-Up" essays, suggesting that Gingrich did not show the same tender concern for Fitzgerald's reputation as he did for Jane Mason's and Dos Passos's. The passage used Scott's real name in wholesaling an incident regarding the rich that made his friend look ridiculous:

> The rich were dull and they drank too much, or they played too much backgammon. They were dull and they were repetitious. He remembered poor Scott Fitzgerald and his romantic awe of them and how he had started a story once that began, "The very rich are different from you and me." And how someone had said to Scott, Yes, they have more money. But that was not humorous to Scott. He thought they were a special glamorous race and when he found they weren't it wrecked him just as much as any other thing that wrecked him. (*CSS*, 53)

Ernest may have thought that a story about a writer undone by his association with the rich was an appropriate forum in which to raise such a question, but there was no need to use the name of a real person in a piece of fiction. The point he was making, that Scott was naive and even stupid in not seeing through the rich as he did, suggests an exculpation for the narrator of "Snows": however misguided he may have been, there was at least one other famous writer who was more so. The gesture was hardly a kind one.

But rearranging the anecdote so that Scott was the butt of it, when in actuality Ernest had been, was underhanded in the extreme. Scott had actually used the phrase in his 1926 story "The Rich Boy," one of the most sharply observed portraits of the rich in fiction: "Let me tell you about the very rich," Scott wrote. "They are different from me and you." But the exchange comes from a totally different incident. Max Perkins and Ernest had been having lunch in New York with the writer Mary Colum. It was Ernest who provided the opening for the line. He said, "I am getting to know the rich," and Colum got off the reply: "The only difference between the rich and other people is that the rich have more money." Ernest simply transferred the mild humiliation inflicted on him by a woman writer to Scott, in doing so also taking the credit for a shrewd observation and a funny remark.

Scott wrote him a short, to-the-point note about the matter, which began, bluntly, "Please lay off me in print," adding, "And when you incorporate it (the story) in a book would you mind cutting my name?" When the manuscript of *The First Forty-nine Stories* came in to Scribner's in August 1937, Max Perkins noted that Ernest had simply cut Scott's last name. Max told Ernest this wasn't enough, and in the end Ernest substituted the name Julian.

But this contretemps marked a final turn in the Hemingway-Fitzgerald relationship, as exemplified by Scott's response to Ernest's latest high jinks—his much anticipated confrontation with Max Eastman. A year later, in August 1937, in Max Perkins's office, Ernest encountered Eastman, whose jaw he had been threatening to break ever since Eastman, in his scathing review of *Death in the Afternoon,* accused him of having false hair on his chest. Ernest bared his chest and pulled open Eastman's shirt to reveal his. Eastman picked up a copy of the book in which his review appeared, and Ernest slammed the book into his face. Blows were exchanged right there in the Scribner's office, though it is unclear who bested whom. In one telling the meeting ended with the two men on the floor in a clinch, Eastman on top, but Ernest vigorously disputed this version, supplying reporters with his own, which held that Eastman had attacked him "like a woman," clawing at his face with open hands. The gossip columnists loved the story, calling Eastman the "Croton Mauler" and Hemingway "the Havana Kid."

Scott's response, when Max sent him a long account of the confrontation, indicated not only his distance from his friend's activities (when once he would have joined in the fray, had he been present) but his own keen perception of Ernest's increasing self-absorption and folly: "He is living at present in a world so entirely his own that it is impossible to help him."

Scott was not inclined to try, given the state of his friendship with Ernest at the time. "I like him so much, though," he went on, "that I wince when anything happens to him, and I feel rather personally ashamed that it has been possible for imbeciles to dig at him and hurt him." Scott noted that it was too bad that this kind of "yelping" attended the doings of the country's most eminent writer.

Another incident not long before indicated that Ernest was not assuming that preeminence in dignified fashion. He was very proud of a fracas he got into with the poet Wallace Stevens, though frustrated in his efforts to make the story known. One February evening Ursula Hemingway, who was visiting her brother in Key West, was at a cocktail party where she heard Stevens say something negative about her brother. She came back to the Whitehead Street house in tears. Ernest rushed over to the party and threw a punch at the insurance-executive-cum-poet, who was twenty years older than him but solidly built. Though only Ernest's version of what happened survives, Waldo Peirce saw Stevens the next day and reported that he came out of the brawl with a bruised face, a black eye, and a hand broken in two places. Ernest, in an exuberant outburst, told Sara Murphy that Stevens was confined to his hotel room for five days with a doctor and nurse "working on him." He told the story to Dos Passos as well, though he asked his friend to keep it quiet, as he had promised Stevens he wouldn't tell anyone. In his crowing letter to Sara, who was attending the tubercular Patrick at a sanitarium in the Adirondacks, he gave her Stevens's measurements (six feet two and 225 pounds, he asserted) so she could tell the story to her ailing son. Patrick was to be an exception, however. Ernest asked, begged, and ordered Sara not to tell anyone about it. Five times.

* * *

That summer and fall, which he spent as was his custom at the Nordquist ranch in Wyoming, Ernest was seriously thinking of how he might convey himself to Spain. "I've *got* to go to Spain," he told Max Perkins. He was burning to write about the civil war that had broken out between the Republican government and its supporters, including democratic moderates but also Communists, Socialists, anarchists, and other assorted leftists, collectively known as Loyalists, and the forces who called themselves Nationalists, made up of the church hierarchy, large landholders, the police, army officers, and other powerful right-wing groups and leaders.

Part of Ernest's sense of urgency grew naturally out of his deep affection for the country, reaching back to his earliest visits there in the 1920s. He loved the countryside and he loved the Spanish people. He loved the fishing, the bullfights, the Catholic shrines and cathedrals, the El Grecos at the Prado, the cafés in Barcelona, the beaches at San Sebastián in Basque country. He sought to make his friends believers in Spain, and not only by sending them to Pamplona to run with the bulls. He urged them to visit, and he took it as a mortal insult when they did not like the country or did not enjoy themselves there. Spain was also where Ernest made the emotional decision to become a Catholic. He was passionate about Spain's future, and feared for it.

What was going on in Spain was in no way a "good" war, Ernest wrote Harry Sylvester, a Brooklyn writer, in 1937; there wasn't a right or wrong side. He was trying to convince Sylvester to donate money for ambulances for the Republicans. The rebels, led by General Francisco Franco, were aligning themselves with the Fascist wave threatening to engulf Europe; Germany and Italy provided abundant planes, soldiers, and matériel. *They* had plenty of ambulances, Ernest told Sylvester, "but it's not very catholic or Christian to kill the wounded in the hospital in Toledo with handgrenades." He knew the Republicans had killed some priests, but he did not understand why the Catholics supported "the oppressors." He might have the ignorance of an outsider, he said, but "my sympathies are always for exploited working people against absentee landlords." He acknowledged that he was a friend to plenty of rich people who might themselves be on the side of, say, absentee landlords. "I drink around with the landlords and shoot pigeons with them," but, he added, a little disingenuously, he might prefer shooting the landlords.

The birth of Hemingway as a political being is a complicated matter. The Nationalist side too had claims on his consciousness, and these would trouble him persistently over the course of the war, and not just when he was shooting pigeons with landlords. The Pfeiffers, as devout Catholics, sided instinctively with the Nationalists, especially as reports of church burnings and murders of priests and nuns multiplied, but also by way of class feeling. Jinny Pfeiffer asked the writer Dawn Powell why "we" wanted to be Loyalists when it was the side waiters fought on. Ernest later told Pauline's parents that while he had been neutral at first, he soon had become "the leader of the Ingrates battalion on the wrong side." Worried that he must appear ungrateful, financially and otherwise, he shuddered to think how Gus Pfeiffer viewed the conflict. But as Fascist control of the Nationalist movement strengthened, Ernest found it easier to defend his position to the Pfeiffers, calling the conflict a "dress-rehearsal for the inevitable European war," though in 1937 such a war was not yet "inevitable."

Conscious political commitment was new to Ernest, who thus far had maintained a detached cynicism—although not entirely. While both sets of grandparents—and the Oak Park community in general—had been solid members of the Republican Party, Ed and Grace were mostly indifferent. Ed went to the Republican convention in Chicago in June 1920, when his wife and children were away at Windemere, and he saw Warren G. Harding elected on the tenth ballot. The Harding-Coolidge ticket went up against Democrats James Cox, governor of Ohio, and his running mate, a young Franklin Delano Roosevelt. This was the only presidential election in which Hemingway voted, and he cast his vote for Eugene V. Debs, the perennial Socialist candidate who in the election of 1920 campaigned from a jail cell. Ernest was then staying at Kenley Smith's apartment in Chicago, and communal living involved great programs of reading, Ernest trying to compensate for his elusive college degree. At Kenley's, he met Isaac Don Levine, a *Chicago Daily News* reporter who had covered the Russian Revolution, which sent him directly to one of Levine's books, *The Russian Revolution* (1917). No doubt the attention of the *wunderkind*-to-be was also sparked by reading about the *wunderkind* of the hour, John Reed, who had covered the Revolution in *Ten Days That Shook the World* (1919); Reed had died in October 1920 in a Russian hospital.

Ernest had never been anything like an activist, however; the cynicism he cultivated was a pose that dated from the scandals of the corrupt Harding administration. Part of his coming-to-consciousness as a modernist writer had been his growing realization that the war had been fought less "to make the world safe for democracy," as Woodrow Wilson had claimed, than to promote a political and economic status quo, a view reinforced by his reporting for the *Toronto Star* on European economics conferences in the 1920s. Ernest did make a rather mean-spirited comment on the Herbert Hoover–Roosevelt election of 1932, calling it a race between "The Syphilitic Baby" and "The Paralytic Demagogue." This was born out of his native cynicism more than it indicated real thinking about political issues.

Until the Spanish Civil War he believed the writer must be above politics. Just recently, he had repeatedly to respond to a constant barrage of criticism of him and his work for their *lack* of politics. He complained to Arnold Gingrich that in the proletarian 1930s writing about a strike was "automatically" considered literature. In other countries critics were not as hard on their writers, allowing them to write about shooting and fishing without being "a shit." "A writer is an outlier like a Gypsy," he said in his 1935 letter to translator Ivan Kashkin. He must not be class conscious if he has any talent as a writer; in good writing, he averred, "All classes are his province."

In his reportage in the 1920s, however, Ernest had proved himself an astute political observer. His coverage of Mussolini in that time, for example, revealed a sharp eye for detail and a cynicism that would, however, tend toward the dilettantish. At the dictator's first press conference Ernest was, like many reporters and observers at this stage, impressed, perhaps most so by Mussolini's description of himself as an "adventurer for all roads." By the next press conference, however, Ernest was sharply critical, as indicated by his piece's title: "Mussolini: Biggest Bluff in Europe." When the dictator invited the press into his office, he was seated at his desk reading a book; Ernest crept up and observed the book was a French-English dictionary—held upside down. His conclusion, however, was that "Mussolini is no fool and he is a great organizer." In the 1930s, when he did take note of world politics, Ernest was clear-headed and astute, especially about Italy, whose political developments he had been following since he was wounded there in the war. Thus, for instance, a September 1935 column for *Esquire* on Italy's fight against Ethiopia. He showed a sensitivity to the dynamics of appeasement and had no doubt that a larger war was looming. Even as he was criticized in the U.S. about his lack of political engagement, he was educating himself on world politics and forming sound views he could cogently express.

The development of Ernest's political consciousness, coming as it did in the midst of his awakening knowledge of events in civil war Spain, was swift and sure. By mid-December he was sending money to buy and outfit ambulances for the Spanish Republicans. In the same letter to the Pfeiffers in which he characterized himself as "the leader of the Ingrates," he presented his decision to go to Spain as a matter of conscience. He was sorry to have to go, he said, "but you can't preserve your happiness by . . . putting it away in mothballs" (which actually was pretty much what he planned to do). "For a long time me and my conscience both have known I have to go to Spain." He had tried to ignore his conscience, but he could no longer. He acknowledged that "the Reds" might look bad, but they represented the people against their oppressors in Spain and the Fascists elsewhere. Earlier, in 1935, and despite his carping at the fashion for proletarian fiction, Ernest had expressed his admiration for *Man's Fate,* André Malraux's celebrated 1933 novel about a failed revolution in 1927 Shanghai. Malraux was already in Spain, and Ernest was modeling his concept of the man *engagé* partly on Malraux (with whom he would go on to have a rather complicated relationship).

In November, Madrid was under siege. That month Walter Winchell mentioned Ernest's desire to go to Spain in his gossip column, and as a result he was offered a way to get there. NANA, the North American Newspaper Alliance, founded by John Wheeler in 1922, was a newspaper syndicate that serviced sixty American papers, including the *San Francisco Chronicle, The New York Times,* the *Chicago Daily News,* the *Los Angeles Times,* and Ernest's old employer, the *Kansas City Star.* Wheeler himself offered Hemingway a persuasive deal: he would get $500 for a cabled story and $1,000 for a 1,200-word story written and mailed, for a maximum of $1,000 a week. This represented the highest pay ever given to a war correspondent; other reporters were getting $15 or $25 an item.

Pauline opposed this new development. Ernest's plans to cover the Spanish Civil War filled her with dismay; it was the first plan of her husband's that she did not vehemently support. Her opposition had nothing to do with any family sympathy for the Nationalists. She simply did not want to lose her husband. And she feared she would lose him in the bloodshed in Spain.

Shortly after, Pauline found another reason to fear she would lose him. This fear had to do with a blonde Ernest met in a Key West bar in December 1936.

NINETEEN

W e two are great people. We can shake the world." So Hemingway claimed Martha Gellhorn had said to him in the early days of their relationship. Certainly Martha herself was, by all accounts, another natural talent. From St. Louis, like both Hadley and Pauline, Martha was born November 8, 1908, to George and Edna (Fischel) Gellhorn, the third of four children and the only girl. George Gellhorn was a German-born gynecologist with progressive views, and Martha's mother was active in the fight for women's suffrage, instrumental in the early days of the League of Women Voters. Martha attended Bryn Mawr, as had Hadley Hemingway, and, like Hadley, did not graduate. Extraordinarily independent, Martha worked as a cub reporter on an Albany, New York, newspaper, where she met and began a lifelong friendship with her mother's old friend Eleanor Roosevelt, whose husband was then governor. She returned to St. Louis after just six months, and, when she failed to land a job at the *St. Louis Post-Dispatch,* made her way to Europe, bartering an article for the trade magazine of the Holland America Line for her ticket. In Paris, Martha took a succession of jobs and began what turned out to be a rather frivolous novel with a nineteen-year-old heroine, *What Mad Pursuit,* supporting herself by writing fashion articles. Never part of any expatriate writing circles in Paris, Martha in the summer of 1930 became involved with the Frenchman Bertrand de Jouvenel, a left-leaning journalist who had enjoyed an affair, at sixteen, with Colette, his father's second wife, and was the model for her young fictional lover Chéri. Bertrand was married, the first of a lifelong string of married lovers, though, as Martha wrote to a friend years later, "I had one lifelong rule. . . . I never knew the wives; the same applied to any woman who was a friend—her man was hers." When the affair with Jouvenel was over, Martha returned to the States and took a research job with Harry Hopkins, the New Deal architect and relief administrator.

When Martha wrote a book of semifictional portraits gleaned from her

Martha Gellhorn, Finca Vigía, ca. 1939

research, which she titled *The Trouble I've Seen,* she got help finding a publisher from a new friend, the writer H. G. Wells, whom she had met in the White House. Martha always denied that she and Wells had an affair, telling his son Gip that hers had been the story of "a young woman being charming to an elderly important gent." Though the evidence is ambiguous, certainly Wells left the impression the relationship was intimate. *The Trouble I've Seen* was published by William Morrow in 1936 with a preface by Wells and quickly received excellent reviews. A glamorous photograph of the twenty-eight-year-old author appeared on the cover of *The Saturday Review of Literature* the last week of September.

In December 1936, Edna Gellhorn and the youngest Gellhorn children, Martha and her younger brother, Alfred, were at loose ends following Dr. Gellhorn's death earlier that year and decided to celebrate Christmas in Miami, moving on to Key West after they found they disliked Miami. Martha claimed later that she had never heard of the place before their trip there, and it is unlikely that any of Edna Gellhorn's friends were Key West enthusiasts. Though she also said she and her mother and brother had never heard of Sloppy Joe's, they ended up in the fabled Hemingway haunt, finding Ernest, "a large, dirty man in somewhat soiled white shorts and shirt," in Martha's telling, sitting at one end of the bar, drinking and reading his mail. She went over and introduced herself, and Ernest came back to the Gellhorns' table. Soon after, Edna and Alfred left, leaving Martha deep in conversation with Ernest.

An hour or so later, the two at first ignored Charles Thompson when Pauline sent him to find Ernest and bring him home to dinner. Eventually, describing Martha as a "literary fan," Ernest asked Charles to relay to Pauline the message that she and the Thompsons should come join him at Pena's Garden of Roses after dinner. Although Charles said Ernest was talking to a "beautiful blonde in a black dress," or perhaps *because* that's what he said, Pauline did join Ernest and Martha later at Pena's.

Rumor was that Martha had told a girlfriend she was going down to Florida to "get" Hemingway, come what may. It is possible that Martha deliberately put herself in Ernest's way, even to the point of going with her mother and brother to Sloppy Joe's, known to be Ernest's favorite bar. Her motives may have been innocent in any case; in her own work she was a great admirer of Ernest's writing. In general, however, her romantic ambitions did not escape notice. Meeting her soon after Ernest did, Archie MacLeish describes "watch[ing] Miss Gellhorn conduct her amazing and quite shameless attack on [Ernest's] marriage." Key Westers were immediately suspicious as well. One biographer's detective work, however, has revealed that Pauline and Ernest were in Miami from December 27 until New Year's, so many of the colorful recollections have to be discounted. Martha did evidently feel a connection had been made, because she sent her mother and brother home just after Christmas (after meeting Pauline and Ernest and being given a tour of the Whitehead Street house), deciding to stay another two weeks and work on a novel. On January 7, she took a ride offered by a family friend to Miami. Ernest, who was leaving for New York City within days anyway, hurried up to Miami where he had a steak dinner with Martha and the boxer Tom Heeney. The next day Ernest rode a northbound train with Martha as far as Jacksonville, where she transferred to a train to St. Louis. He kissed her goodbye on the forehead, saying "Goodbye daughter."

Back in St. Louis Martha promptly wrote a thank-you letter to Pauline. She was grateful that Pauline hadn't minded Martha becoming a fixture around the house ("like a kudu head"), noting that "Ernestino" was a "lovely guy"—in case Pauline hadn't already figured that out, she added. These potentially sharp edges were dulled by the two photographs of Bertrand de Jouvenel she enclosed, telling Pauline she was enclosing them "so you'd know"—indicating the two women had discussed their romantic affairs at some length. Martha asked for the photos back, and not only because they were all she had of Bertrand: she wanted to get a letter from Pauline when she returned them, she claimed.

In New York, Ernest met with Max Perkins, promising him the completed *To Have and Have Not* by June. (Gingrich wrote another letter critical of the manuscript to Ernest that reached him in the city.) But most of Ernest's time was spent in matters relating to the war in Spain. He signed his contract with NANA at a meeting with John Wheeler, and he closely questioned his friend Jay Allen, who had been covering the war as a freelance journalist after the *Chicago Tribune* fired him. He also spent some time working with a Spanish American writer, Prudencio de Pereda, putting together commentary for a film on the civil war called *Spain in Flames*.

Ernest was called back to the arms of family and friends in mid-January, when he went with Jinny Pfeiffer and Sidney Franklin to visit the very ill Patrick Murphy at Saranac Lake, where friends of the Murphys had gathered to help the family through the ordeal. Honoria Murphy remembered that Ernest managed to talk to Patrick about fishing in his bedroom but only with great difficulty; when he left the room Honoria heard him say, near tears, "Goddamn it, why does that boy have to be so sick?" When Patrick died on January 30, everyone in his orbit was devastated. Alice Lee Myers, a family friend, wrote a letter to Ernest that must have been wrenching: she said that Patrick had been working on an etching of Ernest at the very end, and that he had asked that the Hemingway boys be given his gun rack and two model train engines. Sara, she added, would like him to have, for his trophy room, the mounted animal heads he had sent Patrick for his sickroom.

Ernest may have been in Key West when word of Patrick's death reached him; he made a brief trip there at the end of January, for no discernible reason except perhaps to allay Pauline's fears. He had been able to ease some of these by convincing Sidney Franklin to travel with him; Pauline and Sidney were especially close friends. But that was not enough, and Pauline announced she would be coming to Spain with Ernest, something from which he dissuaded her only with great difficulty—perhaps in all innocence, fearing for her safety. By this time Ernest and Martha were supposedly corresponding, though evidently only two letters, from Martha to Ernest, survived. These letters have not been seen by any of the Hemingway or Gellhorn biographers, but only by Bernice Kert, who wrote a group portrait of the women in Hemingway's life. According to Kert, Martha wrote, "I hope we get on the same ark when the deluge begins" in a February 7 letter; by mid-month she was writing that they were "co-conspirators," and she had already outfitted herself with a beard and dark glasses to travel incognito. Though she closed the second letter by saying, "Hemingstein, I am very, very fond of you," she also asked him to give her love to Pauline (which surely was an empty gesture). Martha claimed that she did not see Hemingway between their goodbye in Florida and their reunion in Spain in March, but Gellhorn's biographer notes that the two were photographed together at the Stork Club and '21' in late February. Martha was not enough of a seasoned reporter to get an assignment to cover the Spanish war, though eventually she got a letter from a *Collier's* editor that she hoped would at least help her get a visa in Paris to cross the Spanish border. She paid her passage over by writing an article for *Vogue* called "Beauty Problems of the Middle-Aged Woman."

Back in New York, through John Dos Passos Ernest had gotten involved with a group called Contemporary Historians, of which Archie MacLeish was president. This group, dedicated to the Republican cause, hoped that Ernest, Dos, and writer Lillian Hellman would write the screenplay for a documentary film to be directed by the Dutchman Joris Ivens. MacLeish recommended that *Spain in Flames* be put aside in favor of this project. Ivens was drawn to Russia by the filmic advances of the Soviet avant-garde; he knew the cutting-edge Soviet director Sergei Eisenstein and had made two avant-garde documentaries, *Borinage* and *New Earth*. But Ivens had been a committed Communist before the war in Spain; one chronicler thinks Ivens was "almost certainly" the Soviets' "case officer" during the war, though Ivens always denied a direct connection to the Soviets in the making of what would become *The Spanish Earth*. Despite his doctrinaire Communism and his fiercely principled work, Ivens was, by all accounts, a very likable fellow, said by MacLeish to be "as mild as your grandmother, really quite a lovely guy." Dos Passos said Ivens reminded him of "a high school boy playing hookey."

The costs of making *The Spanish Earth* would run to about $18,000, raised primarily from among the Contemporary Historians group and their friends. While most gave $500, the North American Committee for Spain (part of a Paris-based international group formed by Comintern member Willi Münzenberg) and Hemingway each gave $4,000. The primary goal of the filmmaking project was to induce Western democracies to provide aid to Spain in spite of a nonintervention treaty—a pact that Germany and Italy ignored by providing military and financial support to the Nationalists, while Great Britain, France, and the U.S. chose to "honor" it.

Ernest sailed for France on the *Paris* on February 27, Max Perkins seeing him off at the pier; Sidney Franklin and Evan Shipman were also aboard (Shipman was to help convey ambulances from France to Spain). Ernest was forced to cool his heels in Paris for ten days because Sidney Franklin was delayed in getting his visa. In fact, Franklin's struggle was the subject of Hemingway's first dispatch for NANA, a "piece of fluff," according to one historian, which Ernest himself called "the dirtiest of dirty journalism," an easy and harmless way to collect a thousand dollars. Leaving Franklin to the bureaucracy, Ernest traveled with Joris Ivens, whom he had just met and already liked, to Toulouse. They drove down together to the Spanish border to see whether or not they could get across—an essential part of what both of them were documenting; indeed, they ran into trouble, and were told that they needed special French visas to cross. Instead, they simply flew to Barcelona, leaving the 16th.

Ernest arrived in Madrid ten days before Martha, and he was lonely. He would write of his loneliness in a letter to the Pfeiffers, of all people. "After the first two weeks in Madrid [I] had an impersonal feeling of having no wife, no house, no boat, nothing. The only way to function." He took the occasion (and nerve) to complain that Pauline's parents did not take this existential loneliness into account when they reminded him—far too often, by his lights—that his absence was hard on Pauline and the boys: "So don't point out how much harder it is on them because have a little

With Joris Ivens (right) filming *The Spanish Earth,* 1937

imagination too" in order to understand his plight. Though he had a lot more important things on his mind to communicate to the Pfeiffers, he could not give up pride of place to their daughter and grandchildren; he had it worse, he was saying, and they should feel sorry for him. Even as Martha Gellhorn joined him in Spain, Ernest was telling his in-laws that he thought their daughter was "well off" where she was, in Key West, for if she were in Europe he would "sort of worry about her."

Almost immediately on arrival in Madrid Ernest traveled to the battle-field in Guadalajara, where the Republicans had just won what he optimis-tically said was a "decisive" victory. It was indeed crucial, as it kept Madrid, already surrounded by Nationalist forces to the east, south, and west, out of Franco's hands. One of the less tangible spoils of the battle was con-siderable proof of Italy's intervention in the war, thought to be critical in convincing the Allies to jettison the nonintervention pact that was keeping them out of the war.

Shortly after Ernest returned to Madrid from Guadalajara, he was eat-ing dinner in the underground Gran Vía restaurant, the government-run haunt of journalists, when Martha walked in, accompanied by Sidney Franklin, who had driven her up from Valencia. Ernest laid a hand on the top of her head and said, "I knew you'd get here, daughter, because I fixed it so you could." While it is not entirely clear exactly how Martha made her way to Spain—she claimed, implausibly, to have crossed over on foot at Andorra—it *is* clear that Ernest had nothing to do with it. (The only conceivable way he helped was that Martha and Sidney invoked his name to get into the closely guarded restaurant, which was reserved for journal-ists and workers for the Republic, recalled Franklin.) Ernest knew Martha knew this, so he must have been performing for his many admirers in the Gran Vía.

Ernest did seem extraordinarily well connected, as his old friend Jose-phine Herbst, also reporting in Madrid, noticed; while most foreigners had no means of transport, he had not one but two cars at his disposal—probably for his work on *The Spanish Earth*. While others had a hotel room, he had a suite, and while food shortages were so widespread that crowds "more than once" tried to storm the closely guarded Gran Vía, Ernest had not only eggs and butter, which though plentiful in the countryside seldom could be found in the capital; he also had outright rarities like ham, coffee, jam, and all the Johnnie Walker available in Madrid, procured for him by Sidney Franklin. And while most correspondents were flying solo, Ernest had a leggy blonde on his arm and, after about two further weeks of court-ship, in his bed. The nature of their relationship was made clear when a bombardment hit the hotel's hot water tank, creating huge amounts of steam that forced their hotel's inhabitants from their rooms, and Martha and Ernest emerged from his suite in their nightclothes.

They were ensconced in the Hotel Florida on the Plaza de Callao on the Gran Vía, across the way from the Telefónica, a tall building used by the Republic as a communications center; it was there that the correspondents filed their stories, usually every night by nine. Shells intended for the Telefónica often hit the hotel, and many of its rooms were so damaged they were unusable. Ernest had room 108 on the second floor, connected to room 109, where Sidney Franklin as a kind of majordomo oversaw the armoire full of food and cooked meals on a hotplate for Ernest and Martha and a constant stream of visitors. The rooms were on the side and back, safer from shells.

A phonograph in Ernest's room was usually playing Chopin; in the nearby room of Sefton Delmer, a reporter for the *Daily Express,* Beethoven's Fifth was often playing. In Delmer's quarters, an alternate watering hole, journalist Virginia Cowles said the cast of characters included "idealists and mercenaries, scoundrels and martyrs; adventurers and *embusqués;* fanatics, traitors, and plain down-and-outs. . . . Dutch photographers, American airmen, German refugees, English ambulance drivers, Spanish picadors and Communists of every breed and nationality." The guests at the Hotel Florida included some whose presence was explicable and others whose presence was not: Claud Cockburn, who wrote for the *Daily Worker* as Frank Pitcairn; writer and airman Antoine de Saint-Exupéry; Herbert Matthews, a *New York Times* reporter who became a good friend of Ernest and Martha; the Duchess of Atholl; the actor Errol Flynn; as well as Cowles, Herbst, and, after his arrival in March to join Ernest and Joris Ivens on *The Spanish Earth,* John Dos Passos.

Dos Passos, in fact, was a player in an often told drama about loyalty, politics, and betrayal, with different tellers giving different emphasis to different parts of a portentous story that effectively ended the friendship between Dos and Ernest. Dos had spent a lot of time in Spain and was well respected in Republican circles, perhaps more so than, at this particular point, Ernest, because of Dos's long activism for social justice. He had become very close to José Robles Pazos, his Spanish translator, a professor of Spanish language and literature at Johns Hopkins. Robles had joined the Republicans, who gave him a War Ministry job that involved translating for the Russians. When Dos looked for him in the Loyalist capital, Valencia, he was unable to locate his friend. Dos began to be suspicious when Robles's wife told Dos her husband had been taken away.

Sometime in February or March, in fact, Robles had been executed as a traitor by Loyalist figures who were, most believe, part of the Comintern. Dos Passos did not learn this right away, however, and made known to the other Americans his frustration at his inability to find his friend. Josie Herbst, a friend to Communism who had visited the Soviet Union and written articles sympathetic to the Cuban revolution, learned fairly quickly, from a Loyalist official she never named, that Robles was dead. Soon after, she was having a drink with Ernest when he brought up Robles and Dos Passos, telling Josie he had been assured that Robles was safe and would be given a fair trial, asking what they could do to convince Dos to drop the subject. Dos's persistence "was going to throw suspicion on all of us and get us into trouble," as Herbst later wrote. She of course trumped Ernest's information with hers, and they fell into discussion about how to handle the matter. They eventually agreed that Hemingway would tell Dos Passos of Robles's death the next day, at a quasi-public luncheon given by the Russians—though what they feared from a private meeting is unclear.

In the meantime, Ernest and Dos had been quarreling about Robles, a quarrel that both started from and spiraled into matters large and small, all having to do with bravery. When Dos showed up at the Hotel Florida, Ernest asked him what he had with him in the way of smuggled-in food. Dos Passos had no food with him. Ernest, who set such store by the right way of doing things in all activities, told Dos this showed he was a poor hunter, thus ineffective in war. Extrapolating from this, he started to needle Dos for cowardice. Placing Robles in this context, Ernest proceeded to tell Dos to stop his inquiries. Robles was probably safe, he said, launching into a string of contradictory remarks. If anything had happened to Robles it was warranted; Ernest suggested Robles was probably a Fascist. It is impossible to avoid the sense that Ernest was telling Dos in the most condescending way imaginable that Dos was being nothing so much as *uncool.*

Of course it was more complicated than this. Dos was familiar with the ethical gradations among the Loyalists in a way that Ernest just wasn't. As Herbst later put it, Hemingway was getting involved in areas that were familiar to Dos and herself but new to him. "He seemed to be embracing on the simpler levels the current ideologies at the very moment when Dos Passos was urgently questioning them," she wrote. Dos believed it was impossible that Robles was a traitor; Hemingway's view was that it was wartime and only the most basic principles—like knowing how to hunt—pertained. Dos should leave it alone.

Josie observed Ernest telling Dos that Robles was dead at the luncheon the next day. Dos was "agitated," he said, and wanted to know why he could not speak with whoever gave Josie the news. (Josie did not record her answer.) Back at the Hotel Florida, Ernest "bolted" out of the car, and Josie and Dos, both still upset and at loose ends about what to do next, took a walk to the Plaza Mayor in the old section of Madrid.

Dos was in Valencia for most of April, still working for *The Spanish Earth,* but trying to find more information about his friend's death. He saw the American ambassador and did what he could to help Robles's family. Townsend Ludington, a Dos Passos biographer, says Ernest and Dos next met in Paris in early to mid-May; Katy was present. Dos was saying wildly that he was going back to the U.S. and would tell everyone about Robles and how he died. Ernest said, "You do that and the New York reviewers will kill you. They will demolish you forever." Ludington reports that Katy then made a remark about Ernest's opportunism. Although he and Ernest would never be friends again, their story was not yet over. But the story of Dos's left-wing politics was most definitely finished. He would have nothing more to do with the left, and he moved further and further to the right over the course of his life. That was it for Spain as well, at least for the duration of the war. Dos Passos made his way through Catalonia, where he met with George Orwell, disillusioned with the Republic in his own way. Stephen Koch, who has written a passionate account of Dos Passos, Hemingway, and the Robles affair, maintains convincingly that Dos never stopped believing in the Republic.

* * *

Josephine Herbst, in *The Starched Blue Sky of Spain,* her memoir about the war, used the words "crackling with generosity" and "busting with vigor" to describe Hemingway's presence in the Hotel Florida in 1937. He would "bustle around," she wrote, confiding in Josie that he had just shot a hare and a partridge that were being cooked on the hotplate in his room. "Part of his exuberance came from the success of his love affair," Herbst believed. He behaved a little strangely around Martha in the beginning. On her first night in the Hotel Florida he locked her into her room from the outside, something she discovered in the middle of the night when she sought company—perhaps Ernest himself—for comfort. She banged on the door and shouted, and someone finally let her out, whereupon she found Ernest playing poker. Martha told one chronicler that he said he did it "so no man could bother her"; she also said he told her the hotel was full of pimps and drunks and he didn't want her taken for a whore. Locking the door from the outside would also have prevented her from seeking him out in the middle of the night, which presumably he would have welcomed.

Gellhorn's biographer tells us that the two slept together for the first time about two weeks later. Pauline continued unaware, taking a trip to Mexico in March and suggesting to Ernest that they take the boys to a Mexican bull ranch that summer instead of to Wyoming. "I wish you were here," she said, bemoaning a rash of visiting friends and family, "sleeping in my bed and using my bathroom and drinking my whisky." He only wrote her once on this trip, but cabled several times.

Both Sidney Franklin and Josie Herbst, fans of Pauline, disapproved of Martha. Franklin, while conceding she wasn't hard to look at, described her ordering him around, at one point telling him, "Don't stand there like a dope," and generally acting entitled. Herbst described Martha as "sail[ing] in and out in beautiful Saks Fifth Avenue pants, with a green chiffon scarf wound around her head." Martha herself recorded in her diary bargains in the shops, noting that she and Ginny Cowles priced some silver fox furs and "got desperately greedy wanting them"; evidently she succumbed, for the following month she was seen in New York wearing a silver fox fur, even though it was June.

But Martha was soon writing her first feature for *Collier's,* and she toured four fronts with Ernest at the end of April. Meanwhile, he had been joining Joris Ivens to film battles in and around Madrid itself. Loyalist spirits remained high after the win at Guadalajara and in the relative holding pattern that prevailed in Madrid itself. A dispatch dated April 11 described twenty-two shells landing on Madrid on a Sunday, causing panic among strolling civilians; that afternoon Ernest, Herbert Matthews, and Virginia Cowles hid in a ruined building they called the Old Homestead, watching Loyalist groups in their third day of battle trying to repel the Nationalists from positions they had held since the previous November. His April 20 dispatch reported ten straight days of "indiscriminate" shelling of the city. As Hemingway critic Alex Vernon points out, Ernest took the occasion of that dispatch to wonder if the Nationalists were using all that ammunition to kill off the supposedly Red inhabitants of Madrid. In fact, he said, he knew of no one who had been executed since the war began. This was his way of saying that, for all the rumors about murdered priests and desecrated churches, he had not heard of one Republican missing or killed since the war began except in warfare. In all likelihood this remark was also in part a response to the execution of Dos Passos's friend Robles.

In the same dispatch Ernest mentions in passing the "press censor," a reference to Arturo Barea, who, with his companion, Ilse Kulcsar, ran the press office in the Telefónica, which with candor otherwise in short supply was called the office of the censor. As the filming of *The Spanish Earth* made clear every day, the Republic was determined to make the Allies understand what was going on in Spain—and, of necessity, to decide which events to relate. It was crucial to let the Allies know, as Ernest did in his ninth dispatch, that the Republicans had not committed any atrocities—though of course there are uncounted atrocities in every war, he added. So too propaganda and censorship were facts of life on both sides. The massacre at Guernica, which introduced the relatively new horror of aerial bombardment to the rest of the world, made explicit the grotesqueries of ethics in wartime. Martha often referred to journalism and "all that objectivity shit"; what she meant was that reporters of any integrity had to take sides within themselves. The only question was just how much this should (or could) affect their reporting. "Given that they longed for the republic to behave heroically and within the law," and "longed for the democracies to break the nonintervention pact and supply the republic with arms," asks a Gellhorn biographer, "how far consciously or unconsciously did they distort reality?" The nature of time during periods of war is such that decisions are made and sides chosen with lightning swiftness, without the luxury of thought; Ernest already knew this from his experience in his first war. Only with the passage of time, in fact, would he be able to realize the balanced consideration of the rights and wrongs of the Spanish Civil War in his *For Whom the Bell Tolls*, written in 1939, when the Spanish war proved itself to be only the first sally in the fight against Fascism. Alex Vernon, in his book on Hemingway and the Spanish Civil War, reminds us that the issue of "committed journalism" is still with us: "One man's truth is another man's propaganda."

In the last dispatch he would file from Spain on this visit, dated April 30, Ernest looked forward with some bleakness to the Fascists' assault on the northern port of Bilbao, a conflict to which the Republicans could send matériel but not men. On May 3 he and Martha left for Paris; the filming of *The Spanish Earth* was finished, and at this point both reporters could be more helpful to the cause in the U.S. In part to avert the Fascist attack the Loyalists staged a major offensive in the Guadarrama mountains, an offensive they would lose in a matter of days; Hemingway would set his novel in this place and period.

Ernest arrived back in New York on board the *Normandie* on May 18. Martha returned to the States at about the same time, but likely on a different boat, at a time when ships' manifests were public information. In New York he hung around Joris Ivens and the film's editors; he had agreed to write the film's narration, and he needed to know how the sequences in the film would appear in order to do so. But he was back in Key West by

May 26, when he took the *Pilar* out for an eagerly anticipated day of fishing. Pauline had a lot to show him on his return: she had installed a saltwater swimming pool and a pool house. In order to give the family some privacy, she had Toby Bruce, a Piggott man whom Ernest had recently hired as "driver, secretary, man-Friday, getaway-money-holder, and drinking companion," begin construction of a five-foot-high brick wall around the Whitehead Street property. Biographers are generally agreed that Pauline knew something was going on and that it probably involved Martha Gellhorn; correspondence between the two had stopped dead after the first exchange of letters. Nevertheless, the reunion was a happy one, and when Joris Ivens came down for a visit, Pauline enjoyed hearing another's account of her husband's doings in Spain. Pauline had planned a summer in Bimini with Ernest and the boys, and she hoped he would become caught up in his old life.

It was not to be. Ernest returned to New York City three times in the next two months—a fairly complicated procedure from Bimini. The first occasion was an address he was scheduled to give on June 4 at the Second American Writers' Congress, sponsored by the League of American Writers. A radicalized Donald Ogden Stewart was president of the league, and he would speak first, followed by Earl Browder, secretary of the Communist Party in the U.S.; Joris Ivens, showing clips from *The Spanish Earth;* Walter Duranty, a Pulitzer Prize winner until recently the Moscow Bureau Chief of *The New York Times;* and Ernest. MacLeish was chairing that evening at Carnegie Hall—invited, he thought, because of his ability to produce Ernest, but no doubt also for his role with the Contemporary Historians and his considerable charm.

Ernest was terrified of public speaking and had assiduously avoided it until that spring. While briefly in Paris in May, Sylvia Beach somehow convinced him to participate in a reading with the poet Stephen Spender, whom Ernest had met in Spain. He and Sylvia agreed he would read from *To Have and Have Not,* and he helped her write out invitations by hand to such Paris personages as Natalie Barney, William Bullitt, Romaine Brooks, Janet Flanner, André Maurois, Alain Duhamel, Paul Valéry, André Chamson, and Jean Paulhan. Beach later said that Ernest came in at least twice a day asking to be excused from the occasion. When the evening came, she supplied him with two beers and a bottle of White Horse scotch to bring to the podium. Even so, when he began reading from his second short story volume, *Winner Take Nothing,* he was so frozen that he whispered and audience members asked him to speak up. Thereafter, wrote the Paris *Herald Tribune,* he began to read "with the air of an innocent child and a strong American accent," adding, "[His] shyness could only make him seem more likable." Though he got through the experience, Ernest told Beach he would never again read in public—not even for her, of whom he was very fond.

Ernest was no less nervous on June 4 in Carnegie Hall—and this time, what the audience lacked in the way of intimidating French intellectuals, it made up in numbers: roughly 3,500 turned out for the program. He was nowhere to be found when the program began and later turned up, *Time* magazine observed, "inbibulated," and could be overheard backstage muttering, "Why the hell am I making a speech?" In a seven-minute address that the *New Masses* would publish in its entirety in the June 22 issue, Ernest included such remarks as, "It is very dangerous to write the truth in war, and the truth is also very dangerous to come by." The temperature in the hall soared, and Ernest's glasses fogged up. "Really good writers," he went on to say (in a sentiment with which not all writers would agree), "are always rewarded under almost any existing system of government that they can tolerate." The single form of government, he went on to say, under which writers could not work well was Fascism: "For fascism is a lie told by bullies. A writer who will not lie cannot live and work under fascism."

The applause was loud and long. But not everyone was equally impressed. Dawn Powell wrote to Dos Passos, the latter conspicuously absent at the evening, that the correspondents filed in, "each with his private blonde," and made a nasty comment about Martha's silver fox fur. The poet Louise Bogan, who had seemed to rather like Hemingway in previous years, was sympathetic to the Republicans, though skeptical about the Soviet involvement. Yet Ernest seemed to her "*too* noble." In this context, she missed the Hemingway the public knew through bullfights, two-fisted drinking, and African safaris, describing him as "all full of the milk of human kindness, and the virtues of the dear *peasants* and the brave civilians. I don't see him doing any labor and union helping at home, however. I suppose an automobile strike isn't colorful enough for him." What bothered her most, she said, huffy with indignation, was that "Hemingway was having such a hell of a good time, looking at a *War,* and being disgustingly noble about it."

Afterward, wrote Prudencio de Pereda, the audience was very enthusiastic, and Ernest "lapped up the warm acceptance." Perhaps, but he resolved never to speak in public again (and was by and large successful). The evening was a great success all around. Back in Bimini, Ernest received frequent telegrams from Ivens, saying that his presence was needed to provide the script for *The Spanish Earth,* so Ernest was again in New York (and with Martha) in mid-June, barely missing a beat. This time Pauline told him to stay as long as he needed to—evidently the arrivals and departures were getting a little predictable. She closed the letter, "Remember me to the comrades, and remember me yourself." In New York, Ivens sent Ernest back to the drawing board several times, mostly to cut the narration, not so much because it was too long but because most of it was unnecessary, the camerawork eloquent enough.

Orson Welles was hired to narrate for the soundtrack, his meeting with Ernest the subject of a widely publicized story. When Welles showed up to record, Hemingway was present with a bottle of whiskey. According to Welles, he found some of the lines pompous and did not hesitate to say so, whereupon Ernest said, "You effeminate boys of the theatre, what do you know about real war?" Welles could not resist saying that he responded by acting like a homosexual and lisping, "Mister Hemingway, how strong you are and how big you are!" The two scuffled but soon set aside the quarrel and had a drink together. The upshot, however, was that Hemingway himself narrated the film, though his high-pitched voice was a handicap.

In the meantime, Martha had been writing her friend Eleanor Roosevelt about Ernest, the war, and *The Spanish Earth,* and Mrs. Roosevelt responded just as Martha must have hoped, inviting Martha, Ernest, and Joris Ivens to show the film at the White House. Ernest learned of the invitation when he was back in Bimini after the film was finished—just the kind of lightning visit that Pauline had sought to avoid. In Washington, the Roosevelts were both appreciative, FDR suggesting that if more background were provided the film could make an even more effective anti-Fascist statement. Ernest, knowing the Pfeiffer family would love hearing the story of his White House visit, obliged by cabling Pauline "WHITE HOUSE STILL SAME COLOR BUT ENTHUSIASTIC WE CHARMED PAPA" and writing a long letter to Paul and Mary Pfeiffer that detailed such matters as how the president was moved from his wheelchair to a chair; those who knew of FDR's disability (it was kept hidden from the public as much as possible) were avidly curious about such matters. He said he found the first lady "enormously tall [and] very charming," the president "very Harvard charming and sexless and womanly," adding that the food was "the worst I've ever eaten," a judgment with which Washington insiders concurred. He referred to Martha as "the girl who fixed it up for Joris Ivens and I to go there," which may have fooled the Pfeiffers, but not those who read the newspapers the next day. All the same, he said to Mary Pfeiffer, "It was damn nice of the Roosevelts to have us there and to see the picture and I appreciate it."

Flush with this heady experience, Ernest returned to Bimini for ten days, where he made final revisions on the manuscript of *To Have and Have Not.* He then planned to travel with Ivens to the West Coast to show *The Spanish Earth* to actors and other film people, notorious for being politically (and financially) liberal. Pauline thought of joining him on the trip back to New York and then to California, even notifying Sara Murphy of her plans, but in the end she did not. Ivens and Hemingway screened the film at the home of actor Fredric March, and Ernest spoke again, but just for a minute or two, telling the audience that they could pay for an ambulance

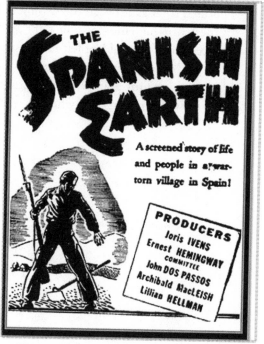

The Spanish Earth, 1937, narrated by Hemingway

for the Republic for a thousand dollars, an ambulance that would reach the front in just four weeks. Dorothy Parker bought an ambulance herself, having previously given $500 toward the film.

That afternoon, according to a letter Robert Benchley wrote to his wife, he had lunch with Scott Fitzgerald and Ernest. Though the old friends had met briefly in New York in early June, Scott had written Ernest a note afterward that revealed the gulf between them. "I wish we could meet more often," he wrote. "I don't feel I know you at all." Lunch with Benchley may have been their last meeting, for though we know Scott attended the screening (he sent Ernest a telegram the next day that read "THE PICTURE WAS BEYOND PRAISE AND SO WAS YOUR ATTITUDE"), we don't know whether they even exchanged greetings that evening. Scott told Max Perkins he detected a "nervous tensity" in Ernest, "something almost religious." Scott may have been commenting on the tension and intensity of Ernest's mien, and no doubt Ernest might have seemed almost religious in his reverence for the Republic. But this, put together with the strangely worded cable (About what did Ernest display an "attitude"? What does "beyond praise" mean exactly? Is it entirely positive?), indicates that there were still complicated feelings between the two men. In fact, it was just weeks later, after Ernest had his embarrassing fight with Max Eastman in the Scribner's offices, that Scott said he felt Ernest was living in a world entirely his own. He tried to explain to Max the distance he felt from Ernest; though he assured his editor that he "liked" Ernest a great deal, he did not feel close enough to him to be of any help—even if he could be helped.

TWENTY

Hemingway later said that the Spanish Civil War was lost as early as the summer of 1936, before he had even arrived there as a reporter covering the war. The Loyalists lost a key battle at Irún on September 3, which effectively cut off the overwhelmingly Republican Basque provinces from sympathetic French suppliers of men and matériel. When this informal traffic was interrupted, France cut off all official support as well, citing the nonintervention pact that England, France, and the U.S. had signed the month before. Moreover, with the victory at Irún, the Nationalist strategy of cutting off Madrid and the surrounding territories from Spain's borders and the sea appeared to be nearing fruition.

Hemingway, of course, was analyzing this stage of the war with hindsight; at the time, he had convinced himself the Republic would prevail over Franco's forces. "In a war you can never admit, even to yourself, that it is lost. Because when you admit it you will be beaten." At present, he was reporting the day-to-day doings in Spain in his NANA dispatches and his letters, in which his attitude about the Republican prospects sounded very optimistic. Later, he would write about the war with great power in *For Whom the Bell Tolls*, a novel that documents the real war through fictional characters, some based more directly than others on actual people. The novel shows a brilliant understanding of military tactics—an understanding Hemingway was still reaching during his time in Spain in 1937 and 1938. He also was able to sort out in the novel the Loyalists' many factions, which had been impossible to untangle in the midst of the war, and to evaluate intelligently the role of the Soviets and the strengths and shortcomings of various Soviet commanders. He could admit atrocities on the part of the Republicans, something he denied with vigor during the war. One wonders what Dos Passos made of his friend's book, which admitted moral ambiguities on both sides—though Dos was already beginning his own journey rightward.

After his first trip to Spain, in the late winter and spring of 1937, Ernest made three further visits later in 1937 and in 1938. The second, from September to late December 1937, was the longest. That summer, the Republic had lost a key battle at Brunete, west of Madrid, and launched an offensive in Aragon, which was not going well for its troops. In a September dispatch, which NANA separated into two stories, Ernest described an early conflict in this offensive, the battle at Belchite, at which the Republican forces prevailed, but only with massive loss of life. Meanwhile Franco had struck at and then taken Asturias, the last bit of coastline held by the Republic and a major supplier of its coal. When Ernest, Martha, and Herbert Matthews journeyed from Paris to Madrid, arriving on May 6, they immediately set out for the Aragon front. The major fighting there was over, however, and Ernest and Matthews made a three-day trip to Teruel, where it was feared the Nationalists would next strike. In this period of relative quiet, Ernest and Martha then settled in at the Hotel Florida, Ernest turning his attention to a play he was writing set in wartime Spain, *The Fifth Column*.

The play took its title from a remark made to reporters by Emilio Mola, a Fascist general, in 1936, describing the approach to Madrid of four columns of troops behind him. In the capital, he said, his army would be joined by a fifth column, made up of sympathizers within the city who were boring from within the Republican ranks. Suspicions of the existence of such a group were rife in the capital, a circumstance that provides telling context for the Robles affair.

In Hemingway's play, Philip Rawlings, a secret agent for the Republic, though ostensibly a war correspondent, is living in the Hotel Florida with Dorothy Bridges, a "tall, handsome blonde," according to the stage directions, a fellow journalist and a "bored Vassar bitch" (*Fifth Column*, 5). Early on he says he wants to marry Dorothy because she has "the longest, smoothest, straightest legs in the world" (*Fifth Column*, 60) and qualifies even negative statements with defenses of her good qualities. In a longish, quite bilious speech about American women abroad ("They're all the same"), he adds, "This one writes. Quite well too" (*Fifth Column*, 105–6). But even then he adds, "when she's not too lazy" (*Fifth Column*, 105–6). Such backhanded compliments recur throughout the play. "Granted she's lazy and spoiled, and rather stupid, and enormously on the make," Rawlings admits. "Still she's very beautiful, very friendly, and very charming and rather innocent—and quite brave" (*Fifth Column*, 68). By the play's end, however, he says, to her face, "You're uneducated, you're useless, you're a fool and you're lazy" (*Fifth Column*, 132). Rawlings mocks Dorothy's frivolity, signaled by her purchase of a silver fox fur cape—a great bargain—but he allows that he is at a point in his life when he wants to make "an absolutely colossal mistake." The clear, if rather sour, reference is to Ernest's budding relationship with Martha. Ernest later told Buck Lanham to read *The Fifth Column* if he wanted to know what life with Martha had been like: he had been in love with her, he said, but he had sometimes acted badly to her because he did not like her very much.

Rawlings, a hard-drinking, big-shouldered, combative double agent who clearly sprang from Hemingway's imagining himself as not just a writer, but an actual soldier working for the Republic (like the hero of *For Whom the Bell Tolls*), comes to see that devotion to the cause carries its own demands, calling for moral compromise. Antonio, a character based on Pepe Quintanilla, the so-called executioner of Madrid, a dedicated Communist who will do anything necessary for the cause, is a key figure in Rawlings's muddy ethics. By the end of the play Rawlings has broken off with Dorothy, who is not a suitable mate for a revolutionary: "Where I go now I go alone, or with others who go there for the same reason I go" (*Fifth Column*, 131), Rawlings declares, in one of the play's few memorable passages.

Ernest later elaborated on the conditions under which he wrote *The Fifth Column;* if the play was not any good, he said, it was because the Hotel Florida was hit by shells thirty-odd times during the period in which he wrote it. The front, he noted, was sometimes as close as 1,500 yards from the hotel. When he went out, he said mysteriously, he hid the manuscript of the play in the "inner hold"—it is not clear what he meant—of a rolled-up mattress, where he was always happy to find it on his return.

In an undated letter to *The New York Times,* discovered in 2008, which was evidently written to boost ticket sales for the first production of his play, Ernest said that he was very lucky to have two rooms in the Hotel Florida that were happily unreachable by shells: "The two rooms where we lived were in what is called by artillerymen a dead angle. Any place else in the hotel could be hit and was. But unless the position of the batteries on Garabitas Hill were changed; or unless they substituted howitzers for guns; rooms 112 and 113 could not be hit because of the position of three different houses across the street and across the square."

Despite his relatively secure berth, living in a hotel in the war zone seems to have aggravated some of Ernest's obsessive behaviors, one of them an inclination to hold others to higher standards of bravery than himself. Elinor Langer, in her biography of Josephine Herbst, reports strange behavior on Hemingway's part regarding the safety of his rooms. Apparently the reaction of the Hotel Florida's residents to shellings was of great interest to him. Herbst, in her memoir of Spain, records how in the course of one particular bombardment of the hotel, when the guests were clustered in the hall, she was mortified to discover that she had temporarily lost her voice; Hemingway's presence heightened her "shame." According to fellow resident William Pike, a doctor who volunteered his services for the Republic, after one particularly hair-raising shelling Ernest learned that several other residents, including a movie producer named Herb Klein, wanted to change their rooms in the front for "quieter" accommodations in the rear. Hemingway's response was to bully them into keeping their rooms, arguing that to give them up "would be running away from the enemy, capitulating to the Fascists." Later, according to one observer, he rode up with Klein in the elevator, called him a coward, and "jostled" him, saying, "I'd like to flatten your big Jewish nose." Hemingway associated the timing of Dos Passos's departure from Spain too with shelling of the Hotel Florida, later saying, "The very first time his hotel was bombed, Dos Passos packed up and hurried back to France." All this despite the fact that Ernest himself was living in one of the safer parts of the hotel.

If Martha was paying any attention to the play Ernest was writing, she most certainly would have noticed the hostility, or at least real ambivalence, that he applied to his characterization of Dorothy. He pursued the affair, however, from all other evidence enthusiastically, meanwhile vaguely trying to keep up appearances for the sake of Pauline and the children. Pauline, unconvinced, set out to join him in Spain, hoping, it seems, to report on the war herself; she was, after all, a trained journalist, with a degree in the subject and experience on a New York City newspaper as well as *Vogue*. She arrived in Paris on December 21, expecting further word from Ernest.

Meanwhile, on December 15, the Republicans struck at Teruel, now in Nationalist hands, and took the town over Christmas—a glorious victory that heartened everyone, though Franco's army would win it back by February. Word of the attack reached Ernest in Barcelona just as he was planning to leave for Paris, where he had promised to join Pauline for Christmas. Instead, he went off to Valencia, near Teruel, and from there drove to the front in Herbert Matthews's car on the 16th. Martha was not with him; she was in Paris in December, and in fact boarded the *Aquitania* on December 15. (As Amanda Vaill points out, her ship probably passed Pauline's on the Atlantic.) From Barcelona Ernest cabled Pauline that he would be delayed, and a frantic Pauline had tried to assemble the papers needed to join Ernest in Spain before the holiday; Ernest in turn wired NANA asking them to send correspondent credentials to Pauline in Paris. They did not arrive in time, however, and Pauline spent Christmas alone in her rooms at the Hôtel Élysée Park, where Ernest joined her around

December 28. Bill Bird, Ernest's old newspaper friend from the Paris days, came to visit them in the hotel (a Right Bank hotel, in contrast to all of Ernest's previous Paris addresses), found them miserable, and heard later that in the midst of a bitter fight Pauline had threatened to jump off the hotel balcony—a story that, while possible, would have been somewhat out of character for someone with Pauline's aplomb. They spent two weeks in Paris, where Ernest consulted a doctor for a "severe liver complaint," according to Carlos Baker, before leaving on the *Gripsholm* for New York on January 12, and they were back in Key West on the 29th.

Though his mind was not really on it, Ernest was hoping to keep his writing career purring along even as he devoted himself to journalism and a new love affair. *To Have and Have Not* had been published on October 15, and by the beginning of November it had sold 25,000 copies and was fourth on national best-seller lists, Perkins told Ernest. The reviews were mixed. Alfred Kazin and Malcolm Cowley took the occasion to talk about what a fine writer Hemingway was—while saying they disliked the novel. Three of his critics were especially negative. Cyril Connolly judged *To Have and Have Not* as "morally odious," noting that Hemingway had "alienated a great many people" with "his book on big-game hunting, his flashy he-man articles in *Esquire,* and his attitude to criticism." Delmore Schwartz, writing in *The Southern Review,* responded to the novel with a thoughtful essay on Hemingway's work, but concluded that *To Have and Have Not* "is a stupid and foolish book, a disgrace to a good writer, a book which should never have been printed." J. Donald Adams, in *The New York Times,* flatly said, "There is evidence of no mental growth whatever; there is no better understanding of life, no increase in his power to illuminate or even to present it. Essentially, this new novel is an empty book." What made the situation worse than just picking up some bad reviews was the way in which so many of his critics took the new book as an occasion to expound on Hemingway's entire career—with punishing results.

Ernest was still feeling the stings in a February exchange of letters with Max Perkins, in which he complained about what seemed to him the scantiness of advertising for the book. He apologized in a later letter, vowing that he was going to rejoin the "tough racket" that was writing; he had been too long away. He and Max were making plans again for an "omnibus" edition of Ernest's short stories and spent a lot of time going back and forth about such matters as the inclusion of the (still censorable, Max felt) "Up in Michigan," the order of the stories, possible titles, and whether *The Fifth Column* would be included.

He remained in the public eye, however—truly a small compensation.

Publication of *To Have and Have Not* was the occasion for a *Time* magazine cover story—on the heels of Dos Passos's cover and the accompanying story about the literary triumph of his *U.S.A.* trilogy. And Ernest had been roped in by a new publication begun by Arnold Gingrich and his publisher, David Smart, to be called *Ken*. It was to be another men's magazine, in this case with a mildly left-wing, anti-Fascist, and anti-Nazi perspective. Evidently in promotional material Gingrich and Smart had announced Ernest as an editor, for when the first issue hit the stands on April 14, it carried a note that Ernest was *not* an editor, as well as Ernest's essay "The Time Now, the Place Spain." He was to appear in the next fourteen issues of the biweekly magazine, receiving a paltry $200 a story—which indicates Gingrich had been extremely persuasive. An essay called "Treachery in Aragon," published on June 30, denounced Dos Passos as a friend to a traitor (Robles) and thus a traitor himself, but otherwise Ernest's pieces were of little interest.

In the same letter to Max in which he complained about his "tough racket," Ernest confided, "Am in such an unchristly gigantic jam of every bloody kind now that it's practically comic." There is no question that Ernest was referring to his romantic situation, and this remark is one of the few clues we have to the progress of the affair in the lives of the three most concerned: Ernest, Martha, and Pauline. Few letters from this period that document the entanglement survive; neither Ernest nor Pauline kept a journal, and Martha's largely details her movements in Spain, not any emotional imbroglios.

The available letters from Pauline to Ernest indicate that she was aware of the affair but was hoping she could either derail it or wait it out. (Perhaps she remembered how Hadley had infuriated Ernest and precipitated the end of her marriage simply by *bringing up* Ernest's infidelity.) A year before, Pauline had signed a letter, "All my love—I don't love anybody else," an odd closing given that there was never any question that *Pauline* would be unfaithful. On April 29, 1938, just after Ernest left on his third trip to Spain, she typed a letter saying, testily, "You can see that life here is going on just the same as when you were here and it was so unattractive to you, and it won't be any different when you get back, so if you are happy over there don't come back here to be unhappy." Perhaps because she feared she might be giving him an out, she added in a handwritten note, "but hope you can come back and we can both be happy." Ernest later told Martha that Pauline had found a picture of Martha in his luggage, implying that she had first learned of their affair in this way.

This time Ernest did not stay in Spain long. He was back in Key West by early June, but almost immediately decamped on a fishing trip to Cuba. His temper was short, as an incident in late June makes clear. He arrived back from a day on the *Pilar* unexpectedly, and when he was going to his study on the second floor of the pool house to do some work, he found the door locked and the key missing. When Pauline was unable to help him, he fired a .38 revolver at the ceiling of the main house and then returned to his study, where he shot the lock off the door. While he was in the study Pauline sent the children with the younger boys' nurse, Ada Stern, to stay overnight at the Thompsons'.

That evening Pauline went ahead with her plans to attend a costume party at the Havana Madrid nightclub, dressed scantily as a hula dancer, but shortly after her arrival asked Charles Thompson to go to the house to check on Ernest. Charles found him subdued and brought him to the party. In an altercation over a dancing partner, a drunken partygoer swung wildly at Ernest, who decked him with his first punch and eventually knocked him out, doing considerable damage to the nightclub in the process. Pauline joined the children and Ada at the Thompsons' that night after Ernest went off to Sloppy Joe's to continue drinking. The following morning, when a hungover Ernest collected his family at the Thompsons', Lorine Thompson recalled that Pauline was near tears and Ernest very glum.

The rest of the summer wasn't much better. In August Ernest and Pauline went back to Wyoming with Patrick and Jack, sending Greg to Syracuse with Ada Stern to visit her family. While out west Ernest went over page proofs of *The Fifth Column*. The Theatre Guild in New York was going to stage the play with Lee Strasberg directing and Franchot Tone as Rawlings, and Max had thought its publication should be timed to coincide with the production. But delays in mounting the play persisted, to Ernest's annoyance. He and Max began to discuss the idea of leading a collection of all his previous stories with the play. Published alone, *The Fifth Column* might not sit well with critics because of its politics, or because he was an inexperienced playwright, he thought. (Soon after he finished the play, however, he had cabled Max that *The Fifth Column* was not only a property for Scribner's to publish but most likely "BEST THING EYVE [I'VE] EVER WRITTEN." And he didn't have enough recent stories (he told Max he was saving up for a novel) for the story collection to be impregnable to critics who might want to report the demise of his career. Because he was also reading proofs for the story collection while in Wyoming, Scribner's was able to combine the play and stories in one volume and bring it out that

October as *The Fifth Column and the First Forty-nine Stories.* Predictably, reviews commented on the play (mostly negatively) and gave the stories only cursory attention.

Edmund Wilson, in *The Nation,* did not much like the play either, calling it "almost as bad" as *To Have and Have Not.* But he took the occasion to write about Hemingway's short stories, singling out "The Short Happy Life of Francis Macomber" as a classic. He judged *The Fifth Column and the First Forty-nine Stories* "one of the most considerable achievements of the American writing of our time." But his reaction to the play really stung. Wilson was suspicious of the role of the Russians on the Republican side, which Ernest took as evidence that Wilson was a traitor to the cause. He did acknowledge, in a letter that might not have been mailed, his great professional debt to Wilson, but went on to say, his words saturated with sarcasm, "I hope to live long enough to see John Dos Passos, Max Eastman, and yourself rightly acclaimed as the true heroes of the Spanish War and Lister, El Campesino, Modesto, Durán and all our dead put properly in their places as stooges of Stalin."

When Ernest was assembling *The Fifth Column and the First Forty-nine Stories,* he dedicated it "To Marty and Herbert with love," Herbert being Herbert Matthews, his colleague on *The New York Times.* Though he removed the dedication by the time of publication, Ernest clearly was at least thinking of making his liaison with Martha public. By September, Pauline and the children had seen the photo of him with Martha at the Stork Club taken the year before. Yet after Ernest left on his fourth and last trip to Spain on August 31—the family remaining in Wyoming would return to Key West via Piggott—Pauline was able to write honestly three days later: "I'm in fine shape," she wrote, "miss you much, but in a fine solid way founded on quiet confidence that everything is going to be fixed up good." During his absence this time, she rented an apartment for the fall in New York City, promising Ernest a "golden key" so he could "slip in any time."

On September 6 Ernest was in Paris with Martha. Almost immediately *Collier's* sent her to Prague, when it was becoming clear that Hitler meant to annex Czechoslovakia; about this time Martha began to misrepresent her whereabouts for the fall of 1938, in part because she and Ernest did not want any record to show they were together that fall, news that might reach Pauline. Ernest spent the rest of September, all of October, and most of November in Paris, where he worked on short stories about Spain, among them "Night Before Battle." He vowed to Max Perkins that he was not going to waste any material on reporting or on his articles for *Ken;* his experience had been "absolutely invaluable" for his writing. After making a brief trip to Spain that September, he told Max he had plans to "look in" on Barcelona in November, but spoke of "the mess everything's in, and the sort of letdown and carnival of treachery and rotten-ness that's going on." He seems to have been experiencing nostalgia for the clarity of *la causa*.

A world of changes had occurred since Ernest had returned from his third trip. Franco's forces had divided the Republic between Barcelona and Valencia and Franco was calling for the Republic's unconditional surrender. The Republicans, looking to regain the ground that divided their territory in two, crossed the Ebro River and won some crucial engagements. But the battle, launched at the end of July, dragged on, Franco reversing the Republican gains, and was still being fought when Ernest paid a brief visit to the Ebro front in September and saw it was going badly. He then retreated to Paris, returning to Barcelona on November 4, and then to the Ebro, where an incident occurred in which Hemingway was undeniably a hero. While the Republicans were making their retreat, General Hans Kahle, who was visiting the front, commandeered a boat and four oarsmen to cross the Ebro, shepherding Ernest, the photographer Robert Capa, and journalists Vincent Sheean, Herbert Matthews, and Henry Buckley. They were just above Mora, where Ernest had seen a bridge blown up in April. Those in the boat ran into trouble, finding themselves driven by the current and strong winds inexorably toward the bridgehead. Herbert Matthews described what happened next: "Hemingway . . . saw the danger we were in. He grabbed a spare oar, manipulating it on the left side and through sheer brute strength pulled us out of the predicament. If he hadn't we surely would have been dashed against the bridgehead, thrown in the water and drowned."

Though Martha Gellhorn described in a *Collier's* story the farewell parade of the departing International Brigades in Barcelona on October 28, she and Ernest were in fact in Paris at the time. The brigades had been disbanded by the Soviets, the various members about to decamp for their respective homelands. A third of the forty thousand who had served in the brigades had been killed. Jim Lardner, Ring's son, whom Martha and Ernest had met when he was on his way to the fighting, was one of these.

Shortly after, Ernest and Martha encountered Randolfo Pacciardi, the Italian officer who had led the Garibaldi Brigade, in their Paris hotel. He had left the brigade the year before when the Soviets merged it with one of the brigades they controlled. Pacciardi could not return to Fascist Italy and was living in France, a man without a state, money, or property. His story moved Ernest, further contributing to his disillusionment with the Soviets' behavior. That night, Martha heard Ernest crying, lamenting Pacciardi's fate and the brave face he was putting on it. He cried not just for Pacciardi but for all the volunteers, those going home or those, like Pacciardi, unable go home, and those who had died. Martha was moved by his grief.

Though Martha would, after their relationship was over, refuse to discuss Ernest with interviewers and acquaintances, she actually managed to say quite a lot about him anyway—most of it negative. She had unqualified admiration for his conviction and his courage during the Spanish Civil War, however. Citing the "tenderness for others" he showed during that time, she added, "I loved him then for his generosity to others and for his selfless concern for the Cause." In a somewhat self-serving remark in a letter to a later paramour, she said of Ernest, "In Spain, he was not tough, he was kind. . . . He was good to soldiers, to poor people. For a very short time, he tried to live up to the image I had made of him." More insightfully, she could see that the war brought out the best in him, and she could see why: "I think it was the only time of his life," she said, "when he was not the most important thing there was. He really cared about the Republic and he cared about that war," adding, "I believe I never would've gotten hooked otherwise." Actually, in these statements, Martha makes clear one of her own greatest faults: she liked to believe that she was noble and brave—as, indeed, she often was—and she measured people against her own high standards. But her observation about Ernest seems particularly apt. Somehow his enormous ego was brought down to reasonable size and put aside for the time being. What happened in Spain—to the people he loved, to the fight against Fascism—mattered more.

* * *

Ernest and Martha saw the beginning of the end for the Republic as they watched the tide of battle at the Ebro, so promising at first, begin to turn to the Nationalists' advantage. After Franco's soldiers defeated the Republicans there, they moved on to Catalonia, where they captured Tarragona, and, at the end of January 1939, Barcelona. The government went into exile, and France and the U.K. recognized the Nationalists as Spain's legitimate government. Franco declared the war over on April 24, long after the fact. By now, all that remained of the Republic were the hundreds of thousands of refugees who had scrambled across the border to France to escape the cleansing mission of Franco's regime. They were quickly condemned, indefinitely, to refugee camps, marginalized and, despite the best efforts of the Republic's friends in Europe and the U.S., nearly forgotten.

The broader public's attention was diverted by the rumblings of a larger war in Europe. In June Martha left Ernest in Paris to go to Prague, where *Collier's* sent her to cover the struggles of that state to stay alive. Ernest, however, was not ready to let go of the Republic and its role in the struggle against Fascism. In January he started what he thought would be several stories about the Spanish conflict, and believed what he was writing was excellent.

The Fifth Column, by contrast, was going nowhere. After arriving back in Key West in December, Ernest immediately turned around, heading for New York to observe the progress of his play. The Theatre Guild had hired Hollywood screenwriter Benjamin Glaser to rewrite it for the stage, and Ernest cabled Pauline that it was "ABSOLUTELY APPALLING STUPID CHILDISH IGNORANT SENTIMENTAL SILLY." By the end of January the play was being cast, but Ernest had lost interest. Martha had arrived in New York just after Christmas, and they were happy to be together for a brief interval. Ernest couldn't resist showing her off to his eldest son; when sixteen-year-old Jack came to New York from boarding school to see *The Spanish Earth,* Ernest greeted him at the theater with Martha on his arm, and Jack was duly impressed.

Although Pauline had known about Martha for some time, she remained hopeful that her marriage would survive. Friends told her about seeing Ernest with Martha. She tried to be game about it, writing to Ernest, the previous September, "If you want to keep a contented wife, see to it that she does not hear from strangers where her husband is and with whom." At the same time she had told him, "I miss you very much, but I feel surprisingly serene about the fate of you and me." Soon enough, however, she was referring to "this Einhorn business," her way of identifying Martha.

Pauline and Ernest put aside their differences when Grace Hemingway decided to visit her son's family in February 1939. Grace had raised the possibility of a visit, and the next thing they knew she had wired that she would be in Key West the next day. Ernest had broken a protracted silence with a letter to his mother at Christmas enclosing what she called a "generous" check. Writing in response, Grace noted that she had not heard from him for three years; five months earlier she had written that she had not heard from him for a year and a half. The latter is more likely, for in this communication Grace refers to "a very unkind and uncalled for letter." This letter has been lost, but in a letter to his sister Sunny in March 1936, a year and a half earlier, Ernest had stated sarcastically that he was a tad peeved to hear Grace had bought a new house, which would likely have occasioned a stern letter to his mother as well. Indeed, Grace had moved to a smaller house in nearby River Park. Her belongings barely fit in her new quarters, and her paintings covered every inch of wall space, up to the ceiling—much like the art at 27, rue de Fleurus, where Gertrude Stein lived. Grace now supported herself by teaching art as well as voice, and her new enthusiasms included spiritualism and, if a letter from Grace to Pauline is to be believed, weaving tapestries, one of which she'd recently sent to her son. Clearly, she remained vigorous in her old age.

Something had changed around Christmastime between Ernest's mother and her children. In 1935, Grace had deeded Windemere to Ernest, thereby revealing that she had some positive feelings for her eldest son despite the "filth" he had written. In fact, Grace and Ernest remained close—though correspondence between them runs about fifty-fifty—as many angry, hurt, or vengeful letters as loving, warm, and sunny letters—with very few letters in between. Meanwhile, Ernest and his older sister, Marcelline, had become sworn enemies. Marcelline, who was active in the local dramatics society and boasted that she and her husband were invited to be in the Detroit *Social Register,* had become just the kind of refined clubwoman that Ernest so detested—the kind he (wrongly) accused his mother of being.

To Grace's great dismay, Ernest had no real use for Windemere. Whatever charms the waters of Walloon Lake and the rivers around it possessed, he thought that in the minds of his young sons tuna caught off the coast of Bimini was far more exciting. The house was too small, with no room for servants. Whatever the reasons, it stood empty—until Marcelline wrote Ernest in the summer of 1937 from her own family's cottage on Walloon. She asked if her boys could use the Windemere rowboat, offering to return it caulked and painted; she also asked whether their visiting sister Sunny could retrieve her canoe from the boathouse. Finally she wanted to know whether Sunny could "perhaps" sleep there "if we should be crowded." Ernest hit the ceiling, expressly forbidding Marcelline to go anywhere near Windemere. He pointedly told her that Sunny, Ursula, and Leicester were all allowed to use the place and its boats, but she was not. The only concession he made was that her sons could use the rowboat if they returned it improved, as promised. He closed with a threat: "If you go into the house for any other purpose, except if you go there as a guest of the people I have given the right to use it, I will regard it as trespass and proceed accordingly." (Marcelline quietly ignored the threat, writing to Grace in 1942 that even though Ernest had told her to stay away, she had put in a "little" garden at Windemere—just *nine rows* of vegetables.)

Yet Ernest unbent at Christmas 1938, sending his sister, whom he addressed as Masween, her old nickname, a small check and offering an apology for what he had written a couple of summers back. Marcelline, in turn, took quick advantage of his changed feelings, trying to see him on a trip to New York in January 1939. Seeking publication of a play she had written (and, she added in a letter to Grace, to thank him for his Christmas check), she decided to ask Ernest for help with her play in person, perhaps fearing his response to a written request. Having learned from Leicester that Ernest was staying at the Hotel Barclay, Marcelline telephoned him there, twice leaving her name, a message, and her phone number and then leaving a message in person at his hotel. Clearly Ernest was stonewalling.

It was soon after that Grace arrived in Key West. She stayed in the Casa Marina for six long days, spending some time with Patrick and Gregory; she had not seen her youngest grandson, Greg, before this trip. Patrick said later that he found her intimidating and not especially grandmotherly. Grace gave him a penknife that she said belonged to his grandfather, but the nine-year-old Patrick had seen her buy it in a five-and-ten-cent store that morning and was not fooled, though he pretended otherwise. Nothing further of her stay was recorded.

There was a strange detail associated with Ernest's renewed relations with his mother that winter. Recently, when Martha Gellhorn was on a national tour lecturing about the Spanish Civil War, she spoke at the Nineteenth Century Club in Oak Park, of which Grace Hemingway was a longtime member. Grace sent a clipping reporting the speech to Ernest, remarking in a note how much she had enjoyed meeting Martha, making no further comment about what she might have made of the young woman.

Grace may have eyed Martha appraisingly, and not just because of her relationship with Ernest, for Grace had recently added lecturing to her activities, and now attended such talks with a critical ear. She spoke on any number of cultural topics, usually literary. She offered lectures on Aristophanes, the *Decameron,* Euripides, "The Music of Greece," "Three Patriarchs: Petrarch, Boccaccio, and Dante," and one titled simply "Poetry." These were no doubt informative and entertaining, to judge from admiring letters Grace received. Her lecture notes are among her papers at the Harry Ransom Center at the University of Texas, and most reveal themselves to be lifted from books dating to the 1870s that she would either have had at home or consulted at the library. For her Aristophanes lecture, she drew, from volume three (titled *Aristophanes*) in a handy series called *Ancient Classics for English Readers,* the thought that the Greek playwright was known "not only as a brilliant humorist but a high moral teacher"; he was, she said, "morality itself." These are the words of the translator (and editor of the series), the Rev. W. Lucas Collins, M.A. The words of translator Theodore Alois Buckley appear in any number of editions of Euripides' plays: "As if he took a delight in the black side of humanity, [Euripides] loves to show the strength of false reasoning, of sophistry antagonistic to truth, of cold expediency in opposition to natural human feelings." These were Grace Hemingway's words as well, lecturing on Euripides.

So she gathered various pieces from introductions to be found in any good reference work of the Victorian era, and cut and pasted them together—in those days passages were "pasted" together with straight pins—for a lucrative lecture in a Chicago suburb. Of course these written lectures may only have been intended as points of departure for Grace's talk—though why, then, bother to cut and pin passages? It may well be more rewarding, in any case, to look at the gist of many of these talks, by whatever Victorian gentleman had translated or edited them, rather than their wording. For Aristophanes, Euripides, and the *Decameron* were once widely thought to be scandalous and improper, although more discerning readers recognized them as great books—as Grace Hemingway/the Rev. W. Lucas Collins, M.A., said, Aristophanes was "morality itself." Ernest's mother had come a long way from rejecting her son's work for its "filth."

Grace's lecture repertoire included, along with these literary favorites, her own pet topics, seemingly worded entirely by herself. One, which she put together as a book, was comprised of typed pages bound together with light blue cords tied into two bows at the top. This was "The Analogy of Music and Color," based on the idea that certain notes have certain colors "attached" to them, a subject to which Grace returned many times in her life, bringing together, as the subject did, two of her passions, music and art. It was practical as well, for, as Grace told her listeners, "You may decorate your home and provide the things you live with according to definite musical harmony."

Grace's new career as a lecturer did not seem to be bringing in enough money to support her and her establishment in River Forest, which now included her friend Ruth Arnold, the one-time mother's helper whose relationship with Grace had caused such trouble in the Hemingway household back in 1919. Ruth had been widowed after five years of marriage to Harry William Meehan, who died in 1931 at the age of forty-one, and she went to live with Grace sometime after that. By mid-1939, Grace was needy enough that she was looking to sell some memorabilia relating to her famous son. She wrote to "Dutton" (presumably the publisher E. P. Dutton), saying that a Robert Hickox and his wife told her they were looking for copies of Ernest Hemingway's early writing. Grace told them she had two copies of *Tabula*, the Oak Park High School literary magazine, which included

Ernest's prophecy for the class of 1917. "Let me know," she wrote, "what you'll offer for one or both."

None of this was known to Ernest, who, the day after Grace left Key West, took the ferry to Havana. He had written several short stories about the war in Spain; one, "Night Before Battle," appeared in *Esquire* in February. After embarking on another, it quickly became clear that this new story could be a novel. And thus Ernest began work on *For Whom the Bell Tolls*.

He wrote in a rented room in the Hotel Ambos Mundos, a favorite haunt on earlier trips to Cuba. His mail arrived at the hotel as well, but Ernest stayed at another, the Sevilla-Biltmore, deliberately making himself hard to find. No doubt he had in mind Martha's joining him in Havana, though there is some controversy as to when that happened. Martha noted that she arrived in Havana on the 18th, just three days after Ernest, but his biographers generally say that she did not arrive in Cuba until mid-April. Martha's biographer suggests, plausibly, that it behooved the couple to appear to have stayed apart for the longer span of time.

They may have thought this necessary because Ernest's eventual divorce from Pauline was becoming a certainty. Martha had written a letter to her mother the previous spring, just after Ernest sailed for New York, returning to Pauline yet again. Martha was being, she told her mother, "what the French call 'reasonable': There isn't anything left to be, I have tried everything else." She wasn't sure Ernest and she would ever be together permanently, she said. "I believe he loves me, and he believes he loves me, but," she added dramatically, "I do not believe much in the way one's personal destiny works out." Letters between Ernest and Pauline, meanwhile, began to take on the tenor of communications between divorced parents, even though they were not yet legally separated. The children's plans were discussed at length, and various accusations about the other's duties toward them beginning to surface. Pauline was trying to find a summer camp to take the children and evidently Ernest accused her of wanting to dump them somewhere, for she replied, evenly, "Also sweetie I didn't just shove the children in camp to get rid of them as you seem to think." With Ernest in Havana while she was in Key West, Pauline sounded world-weary. When she decided to go to Europe that summer, she told him, "Relax and enjoy Miss Einhorn and here I am off your hands temporarily at least." Her feelings for Ernest had not changed, and this whole period must have been heartbreaking for her; she stalled for time as if she had a viable plan to repair the marriage. Over the next year she would accept the fact that no such plan would work, but she kept up a good front.

Ernest wrote *For Whom the Bell Tolls* over a period of a year and some months; he would deliver the manuscript to Scribner's in July 1940. By March 1939 he could report to Max Perkins that he had two chapters finished and was writing steadily. The novel was set in 1937—after the first, successful defense of Madrid from the Nationalists, when the Republican military efforts still revolved around strategies to win the war, rather than measures to prevent collapse. The central character, Robert Jordan, is an American academic and an expert in explosives working with a guerrilla band in the Guadarrama mountains, laying plans to dynamite a bridge as part of a major Loyalist offensive. Among the small band is Pilar, an older woman with the peasant equivalent of worldliness; Pablo, Pilar's paramour, a flawed partisan leader whom Jordan suspects of treachery; and Maria, a beautiful young woman who has been raped by the Fascists who killed her parents. Dramatic stories are studded through the novel: perhaps the most important is Pilar's account of the execution of Fascists in her village, tortured and forced to jump off a cliff at Pablo's command. Based on a massacre in the village of Ronda in 1936, the incident cast a very harsh light on the Republicans; Ernest was no longer so naive as to believe the Fascists were the only barbarians. Another of the novel's dramatic high points: the last-ditch resistance by another guerrilla band against a Nationalist battalion; and the desperate mission of Andrés, another guerrilla in Jordan's group, to the Soviet general Golz to call off the attack on the bridge when it is clear the Fascists know of their plan. Much of the dramatic tension focuses on Pablo's various duplicities, and his partial redemption at the novel's end, when, having jettisoned the dynamite meant for the bridge, he helps Jordan blow the bridge with materials at hand.

Although *For Whom the Bell Tolls* is Hemingway's longest novel, it is also his most tightly constructed, and his most straightforwardly written—its art is not so much in the "leaving out" as his other work. It contains many powerful narrative and descriptive passages, and is laced through with his love of Spain and Spaniards, exemplified by Pilar and other members of her band. But the book is riddled with melodramatic flaws and bad authorial decisions. The love story between Robert Jordan and the victimized Maria, though it made the novel enormously popular at the time, does not hold up well today. She is totally pliant, giving herself utterly to Jordan. They make love in his sleeping bag; afterward, he asks Maria, in a line that has spawned many a parody, "Did thee feel the earth move?" Hemingway spills far too much ink on Maria's shorn locks (her head was shaved by the Fascists) and the feel of her short hair.

Robert Jordan (he is never called "Robert" or "Jordan," always "Robert Jordan") is, of course, an idealized version of Hemingway himself. He never feels the doubts that increasingly bothered Ernest but is completely devoted to the Republican cause. Ernest's values are revealed in the contrast between the anarchists and Pablo, who with the trim, efficient, ironic Soviets is getting the job done. And Pablo is an example of, perhaps, how those at war might have to take measures against people who may not be actual traitors but who are unreliable—possibly a more reasoned response to the Robles affair. Jordan himself is a bit of a cipher; not sentimentalized exactly, but very much like a hero in a Western movie: laconic, no-nonsense, adhering to a strict ethical code, and withal comporting himself nobly as a lover. (Gary Cooper would play Jordan in the movie made from *For Whom the Bell Tolls,* and the casting was almost too perfect.) Like Ernest's, Jordan's father has killed himself. Suicide in the novel is a very real option for the guerrillas. Jordan does virtually kill himself at the novel's end when he forces the others to leave him behind, badly wounded, lying in ambush, awaiting a firefight with the Fascists that he cannot survive. Some of Ernest's ambivalence about killing himself as an option, and whether the suicide acts out of bravery or cowardice can be seen in Jordan's conclusion about the subject, which is deadpan to the point of being ironic: "You have to be awfully occupied with yourself to do a thing like that" (*FWTBT,* 338).

Several features of the novel seem unfortunate today, and do not bode well for the future of *For Whom the Bell Tolls* as a canonical work of literature. Ernest decided to use "thee" and "thou" in his dialogue, so as to reflect the use of the familiar form for "you" in Spanish, unfortunately making the talk seem stilted and thus less authentic rather than more, and giving rise to instances of unintended humor: "Dost thou want a sandwich?" is but one of these; inevitably too we read, "I am thee and thou art me." His decisions as to how to split the difference between his desire to capture the everyday speech of people like the characters he portrayed, and the need to keep to the right side of the censor, also come across awkwardly: "fuck" becomes "muck," "chickenshit" becomes "chicken-crut" (173). Otherwise, in another unfortunate choice he simply substituted the word "obscenity" every time another four-letter or profane word was called for. He rendered a common Spanish phrase repeatedly, with different objects, as "I obscenity in the milk of thy Republicanism," or "thy shame," or even "thy science." The point Ernest was making about "truly" rendered speech and issues relating to censorship is largely lost on readers today, familiar with literary works that deploy profanity pretty much constantly. And the effect on the dialogue is just as unfortunate as the use of "thee" and "thou."

Another troubling trend emerges in the composition of *For Whom the Bell Tolls:* his frequent use of the word "truly." Ernest had striven quasi-religiously for "one true sentence" since his earliest days in Paris, and "truly" is exactly what he means in the following, from *For Whom the Bell Tolls:* "All things truly wicked start in innocence." But when he writes, in a 1940 preface he wrote for the memoirs of Gustav Regler, a German friend injured in the Spanish war, "There are events which are so great that if a writer has participated in them his obligation is to write truly rather than assume the presumption of altering them with invention," he is beginning to use "truly" to mean a fuzzy sort of "reality." Martha complained, as would his fourth wife, that Ernest used the word "truly" constantly, especially when drinking and telling tall tales—when the word wasn't always appropriate. He was increasingly using the word as shorthand for a kind of emphasis by which he hoped to render his sentiments authentic. So when Robert Jordan asks Maria whether the earth had ever moved before for her, and she replies, "Nay, truly never," Ernest relies on the word as a fill-in for "really," for real, authentic activity—especially in connection with writing. Concerns about authenticity in writing, the authenticity of political commitment, the authenticity of love, and the authenticity of experience in general are no longer played out in his descriptive prose, or his fictional characters and their motivations, but shorthanded in the repeated use of the word "truly." Authenticity truly loses.

TWENTY-ONE

It was Martha Gellhorn who discovered the house on the hill that was to be Ernest's home for just about the rest of his life. At first, he did not take to it at all, flatly rejecting the run-down and overgrown property outside Havana. Yet he had already zeroed in on Cuba as a congenial spot: as temperate as Key West and as remote, but more exotic; providing a lively nightlife (in Havana) but sleepy during the daylight hours; offering all the piscine delights of the Gulf Stream; enabling a lifestyle at once luxurious and affordable; teeming with colorful characters and decidedly bohemian, but without the writers and artists whose affectations he increasingly found he disliked.

For someone who loved travel, Martha also thrived on nesting and would prove to be, over the years, exceedingly clever at spotting potential in unlikely real estate. The Finca Vigía—Spanish for Lookout Farm—was no exception. Eager to get out of Ernest's hotel rooms at the Ambos Mundos, she had enlisted the services of a real estate agent who drove her and Ernest around Havana and environs. Martha responded immediately to the Finca, a fifteen-acre hilltop property with a view of Havana, in the village of San Francisco de Paula, about twelve miles from the city. In great disrepair, the house had been uninhabited for some time, its swimming pool filled with rainwater and algae, the pink tennis court—made of crushed coral limestone—weedy and cracked. The house was nearly overtaken by vegetation—though of the most exotic sort, including bougainvillea, jacaranda, mango and tamarind trees, palms, frangipani, and a huge ceiba tree studded with orchids, its sculptural roots carving their way out of the house's marble steps. The one-story limestone house had earthenware tiled floors and featured a sixty-foot living room; it had been built in 1886 by Catalan architect Miguel Pascual y Baguer. The local scuttlebutt was that the Spanish army, after taking over the farm during the Spanish-American War, abandoned it and burned it to the ground—after which it had risen from the ashes.

Ernest vetoed taking the house, which seemed like a wreck to him; in any case, he was happy in the Ambos Mundos. But when he was off on a fishing trip, Martha rented it anyway, agreeing to pay 100 Cuban pesos a month (about $100) to its owner, a New Orleans native named Roger D'Orn. She hired an army of workers to clean and repair the house and grounds, and took on the arduous task of managing the staff. She had promised D'Orn to keep some of the servants on, though few lasted long; Martha was an imperious employer. A Jamaican, Luis, was the major-domo; the cook, María, was a short, stout Spaniard; and the white-haired and mustachioed Don Pedro was the head gardener (he would later drown himself in the property's well). While she happily directed renovations and cleaning, and bought kitchenware in town, Martha nevertheless had a moment of "acute depression bordering on despair," fearing that posses-sions and real estate, she wrote Eleanor Roosevelt, would impinge on her independence. But she "slept on it," she wrote, "and woke to look out my window at a saba [ceiba?] tree, so beautiful that you can't believe it, and hear the palms rattling in the morning wind, and the sun streaking over the tiled floors, and the house itself, wide and bare and clean and empty. Lying quiet all around me. And I am delighted."

When Ernest returned and saw the place anew, he too was delighted. Larger than the Key West house, with more extensive grounds and a sep-arate white frame structure that could accommodate guests and visiting sons, it allowed him room to expand, literally and figuratively. He found a nearby town, Cojimar, where he could moor the *Pilar*, and installed the first mate he had hired the year before, Gregorio Fuentes. "It is fine out here in the country," he wrote Max Perkins. "There are quite a lot of quail on the place and lots of doves."

But Ernest and Martha had yet to fully settle in, in part because matters with Pauline stood in the way. In 1945 Pauline would write Ernest regret-fully that they had sounded on the phone like "what we swore we would never be, 'Parents Fighting Over Their Children,'" and this had begun even before the divorce. Her biographer notes that Pauline, in a venge-ful moment, tore up a letter she had written to her husband document-ing complicated plans regarding the children. She then sealed the torn-up pieces in an envelope addressed to Ernest; to learn the details for the hand-off of their children, he would have to assemble the scraps.

The breakup of Ernest's second marriage was far more acrimonious and dispiriting than the end of his marriage to Hadley. On Pauline's side, she had devoted her life to him, very consciously, and giving up was very hard for her. Ernest, for his part, was now a serial cheater and home-breaker, and his sense of guilt spilled over into anger and efforts to blame Pauline for the split. Their marriage had lasted longer than had Ernest's first marriage; neither was any longer a twenty-something; two children were involved—there was simply more for both of them to be angry about or regret. Ernest would never write about the end of their marriage (though his anger at Pauline is palpable in "The Snows of Kilimanjaro"), while his marriage to Hadley inspired a lot of his fiction, and was the impetus, it seems at times, behind *A Moveable Feast,* his Paris memoir.

As he had with Hadley, however, Ernest agonized over the choice he had to make. Some of the time, with establishing his new base at the Finca, he behaved as if he was already starting a new life. At other times, he seemed to regret what he was giving up and wanted to believe he could walk back into his marriage. Pauline, for quite some time, hoped he would, which only raised the temperature on both sides when they attempted to live together again, if not reconcile.

In 1938 and 1939, Pauline would accept the fact that no such plan would work, but her wit never flagged. Ernest visited Key West briefly in July, when Pauline was absent, on his way to Wyoming where he would meet the boys for the usual hunting and fishing at the L-Bar-T Ranch; he dropped off Martha in St. Louis on the way for a visit with her mother. In September, Pauline, hastily cutting her European trip short because of war news, cabled Ernest that she would join him and the boys at the L-Bar-T. Unfortunately, she contracted a terrible cold en route, and she and Ernest had a miserable time together at the ranch. Ernest in turn cut *his* Wyoming trip short, since Pauline could now look after the boys there, and cabled Martha to join him in nearby Billings. They would go on to Sun Valley, Idaho, for fall hunting.

The marriage was obviously on its last legs. Just before joining him in Wyoming, Pauline had written Ernest a heartfelt letter that shows she knew the lay of the land while still harboring hopes for their future: "Oh Papa darling, what is the matter with you & if you are no longer the man I used to know get the hell out, but if you are stop being so stupid. Or maybe you are Mad and Madness I can understand." Not long before, Ernest had claimed in a letter to Pauline that he was unable to work while living with her, because of the "tongue lashing and the type of twenty four hours all night long bawling out" he had experienced on his last stay in Key West.

Pauline had suffered a cancer scare earlier in the summer, and Ernest told her he was ready to join her in New York immediately. It was a false alarm, and was woven into the fabric of their arguments in those months. Ernest was ambivalent, without question. In the same letter he told Pauline, "You are the finest, best, smartest, loveliest, most attractive, and all time glamourous and wonderful person that I have ever known." In fact, he would miss her critical eye for years to come. He told Max Perkins that she was the one person he trusted to give him an honest opinion about the Spanish Civil War novel he was embarked on: "Pauline hates me so much now she wouldn't read it and that is a damned shame as she has the best judgement of all." Whatever good feeling remained, however, would be lost. For the time, it was dissipated by recriminations and quarrels about money. Jinny Pfeiffer, whom Ernest saw as the villain of the piece that was the end of his marriage, had advised her sister to go after Ernest for whatever she could get in the way of alimony and child support, putting aside her actual financial situation. Jinny had been one of Ernest's earliest champions, and they enjoyed a warm relationship of their own, but that too was lost, in this case permanently, because of her outrage over Pauline's suffering. In the divorce settlement the following year Pauline would be granted what Ernest called "punitive" alimony—$500 a month. No amount was specified for child support; Ernest was tacitly expected to contribute proportionately to the boys' needs, which he did without much prompting, though seldom gracefully. Paying alimony rankled, however, especially when he thought of how much land Paul Pfeiffer owned in Piggott, or Uncle Gus's fortune. Ernest estimated that over ten years he would have paid Pauline $60,000, and swore that when the ten years were up, he would refuse to give another penny—let "them" come after him.

Meanwhile, Ernest would say that Pauline got what she deserved in losing him to another woman, since she had herself broken up a marriage—his with Hadley. He launched what would become a set piece, delivered almost every time Pauline's name came up: her Catholic faith had wrecked the marriage. His reasoning was arcane; her St. Louis doctor had warned her after her two difficult births that having another baby was unwise. Since the only birth control method open to her as a practicing Catholic—withdrawal—blunted his pleasure, the failure of the marriage was Pauline's fault. His son Greg, who heard this story many times, later pointed out that as a doctor's son, Ernest would have known to simply avoid Pauline's fertile days—something that would have been obvious to "any fool," Gregory observed.

It was hard for Ernest to let go of the Pfeiffer family. He had become quite close to them, especially Mary Pfeiffer and Uncle Gus. He worried that the souring of his relationship with Jinny would affect that closeness, for he believed Jinny was feeding the family her version of the breakup of the marriage. This moved Ernest to write a strange letter to Mary Pfeiffer that December. Addressed to "Mother Pfeiffer," the letter explained why he had not come to Piggott after the trip to Wyoming as planned. (He had actually left to go to Sun Valley with Martha, but he simply said his plans had changed.) He said he feared Mary might believe Jinny's side of the story. He promised her he would look after Pauline materially and that he would take good care of the children, and he told Mary he missed her very much. He also described the "lovely" time he was having writing his book. Pauline's mother answered very simply. "This is the saddest Christmas I have ever known," she wrote. "A broken family is a tragic thing, particularly so when there are children." Paul Pfeiffer wrote two letters to Ernest after receiving his, but both letters at the Hemingway archive are closed, evidently by Paul's grandson Patrick. It is not hard to imagine the tenor of them.

Matters were also complicated with Gus Pfeiffer, the rich, childless uncle who had grown very attached to Ernest. Judging by an entry in the writer Dawn Powell's diary, initially Gus "upbraid[ed]" Pauline for "not holding" Ernest, and declared himself ready and willing to meet her "supplantee"—who would be Martha. While it is not clear that this meeting actually took place, evidently Gus did maintain a foot in both camps, for he brokered part of the financial deal eventually agreed upon for the divorce: if Pauline were to sell the Key West house (Gus himself having provided the purchase price, as well as the funds for renovations), she would make a 60–40 deal with Ernest for the proceeds. (Ernest later claimed that Pauline had been awarded some land he owned in Idaho as well, and that she would be legally entitled to a share of his earnings from writing—neither of which was true.) Gus had been extremely generous with Ernest; in addition to buying the house in Key West, he had bankrolled the African safari and made large cash gifts freely and often. Not long after these proceedings Ernest gave the manuscript of the recently completed *For Whom the Bell Tolls* to Gus. The manuscript was quite valuable at the time, and would be even more so when Ernest much later undertook to retrieve it for his sons.

After Ernest's disastrous attempt at a Wyoming vacation with Pauline and the boys, he and Martha headed for Sun Valley, a new resort in the Sawtooth Mountains near Ketchum, Idaho, in what was once mining country. Averell Harriman, chairman of the Union Pacific Railroad, opened the resort in 1936 as a ski area, hoping to increase ridership on the railroad and tap into the burgeoning American interest in alpine skiing in the wake of the recent Lake Placid Olympics. The Sun Valley Lodge, the resort hotel he opened in 1937, had outdoor (heated) pools, as part of the developer's strategy to market the winter playground as a year-round resort as well. The resort publicist, Steve Hannagan, who had successfully promoted the latest destination success story, Miami Beach, named the place Sun Valley and engineered a story in *Life* magazine called "Sun Valley, Society's Newest Winter Playground"; over the next few years the resort attracted such celebrities as Claudette Colbert, Clark Gable, Gary Cooper, and Bing Crosby. By the time Sun Valley contacted Ernest about visiting as part of its ongoing promotion efforts, the publicist was Gene Van Guilder, and it had a full-time photographer, Lloyd "Pappy" Arnold, who would become Ernest's lifelong friend.

Ernest was drawn not by the winter sports—he had not skied since the winter of 1927–28 in Gstaad—but by what the resort offered in the fall, especially the promise of excellent duck, partridge, and pheasant hunting, as well as antelope and elk. Taylor Williams, the chief guide, a Kentucky native also known as "Beartracks" or "the Colonel," took Ernest and Martha out on horseback most afternoons, usually accompanied by the rest of what Ernest came to call the "Sun Valley Mob"—Arnold, Van Guilder (who would die within weeks in a hunting accident), another hunter named Bill Hamilton, and Spike Spackman, a stuntman in the movie industry. Martha was a willing pupil, and soon became very comfortable on a horse, if not with a shotgun. Mornings they spent writing—Martha on the short stories that she would later collect as *The Heart of Another*, Ernest on *For Whom the Bell Tolls*, then about 100,000 words. In the afternoon, they often stayed close by, playing tennis or swimming: at times they packed a lunch and rode into the hills without the usual entourage; other days they canoed in Silver Creek, hunting ducks or trout fishing.

The idyll was interrupted, and Ernest was given his first real taste of what life with—or, rather, without—Martha was to be like when *Collier's* contacted her in October about sending her to Finland, where Stalin's troops were expected to attack at any time. In an unguarded moment, when Pappy Arnold's wife, Tillie, told Martha that she wouldn't go if she were in Martha's shoes, Martha told her, "I'd rather have [the assignment] than anything else in the world," adding, "I guess it's just in my blood. I can't help it." Ernest affected to be unconcerned, announcing the formation of "Hemingstein's Mixed Vicing and Dicing Establishment" in suite 206—which, when he had shared it with Martha, had been known as Glamour House.

Martha left around the first of November. Writing Ernest from Helsinki, she took a high-minded tone that can only have gratified his vanity. In response to a disconsolate letter from her en route, he gallantly offered to join her in Finland. She knew that was how he would respond, she said, but he must instead stay where he was and write: "The book is what we have to base our lives on, the book is what lasts after us and makes all this war intelligible. Without the book our work is wasted altogether." Martha made a point of using this kind of exalted language, which nicely reflected (and in turn influenced) Hemingway's thinking at the time, particularly in connection with *For Whom the Bell Tolls.* Quite rightly, he saw the novel as the best use of his talents in the fight against Fascism. However, such an approach did not always make for the best writing, which in Ernest's case was at its best when concrete, finely observed, to-the-point.

Alone, Ernest claimed he was "stinko deadly lonely." He was at loose ends, once even shooting at coyotes from a low-flying plane, which he knew was not good sport. Christmas at Sun Valley, even with his mob keeping him company, began to look bleak. Key West, with its warm trade winds and comfortable home, began to seem enticing, and he resolved to spend the holidays with Pauline and his sons. When he called her, Pauline informed him, however, that if he planned to rejoin Martha after the holidays he was not welcome in Key West, and to make sure there would be no confrontations, she took Patrick and Gregory to New York to visit Jinny and her Uncle Gus and Aunt Louise. Ernest evidently thought she would relent. He summoned his general factotum, Toby Bruce, from Piggott to drive him to Florida. Bruce picked up "a much hungover" Ernest—Taylor Williams and Pappy Arnold had thrown him a going-away party, "a royal drunk"—the night before. Ernest felt sure, Toby later said, that Pauline and the boys were awaiting his arrival.

What awaited Ernest in Key West was an empty house. As usual when she was away, Pauline had the gardener and his family move into the pool house to act as caretakers, but she had given the other servants the holidays off—which meant Ernest had to forage for his meals. He rattled around the empty house for nine days, packing up his belongings—everything from his clothes to his guns, typewriters, trophy heads, and collected manuscripts and letters—and putting whatever he could in his Buick, storing the rest in a spare room at Josie Russell's saloon, Sloppy Joe's. When he got on the car ferry for Cuba on the day after Christmas, he was no longer under any illusion that there was a future for him and Pauline.

* * *

The new year began with a lot of silliness between Bongie (Ernest) and Mookie (Martha) that masked a serious fault line already appearing in the relationship. On January 19, the day she arrived back at the Finca, Martha drew up a "guaranty"—a tripartite agreement, in couple-speak, attesting that she thoroughly understood how miserable she had made him by going away, and promising never to do it again. She recognized, she said, that "a fine and sensitive writer cannot be left alone for two months and sixteen days." She vowed to make up for the "wretchedness" she had put him through, and that she would protect him from same in the future. She promised, "I will not leave my present and future husband not for nothing no matter what or anything." She signed her name three times, taking his each time: Martha Gellhorn Hemingway. (On the dust jacket of her Czechoslovakia novel, *A Stricken Field,* she would be identified as "Martha Gellhorn [now Mrs. Ernest Hemingway].")

To her surprise, Martha found Ernest's sons, who visited in March, an unexpected benefit: "I am now suddenly a mother of three," she told two old friends, "and I must say I love it. . . . E's three sons have turned out very very good." She had already seen Jack in New York City at the opening of *The Spanish Earth,* and admired him: he was taller than Ernest "and has a body like something the Greeks wished for, and to make you cry it is so lovely." She described Patrick and "Gigi," or Gregory, vividly as well, and drew deft characterizations of each of the boys' distinct personalities. They were all funny, she said, as funny as their father, "which is saying something." They called her "the Marty," she said, thinking her "a sort of colossal joke. . . . I think it all goes very fine." Meanwhile, the boys were of an age (Jack was sixteen, Patrick eleven, Gregory eight) to admire her beauty and appreciate her youth and informality. Jack noticed that Martha could say *fuck* "so naturally it didn't sound dirty, and, otherwise, talk like a trooper or a high-born lady, whatever suited the circumstances." Patrick considered her not so much as a stepmother but rather as his friend—and one he badly needed. And Gregory, the youngest and the most needy, adored her, later writing: "She could talk of anything—or nothing if you wished. . . . She'd talk to you like an equal, listen to your . . . opinions, and at least pretend to give them weight." He would always remember how she tossed her hair like "a filly in a pasture tossing her mane," and her "wonderfully abandoned, sinful, yet perfectly pure laugh."

Later, Jack Hemingway would recall life at the Finca with his father and Martha. You had to drive through terrible slums to get there, he said, but once you reached the hilltop, the situation was idyllic. The Finca was hung with his trophy heads, bullfight posters, and oil paintings, including Miró's 1921–22 *The Farm.* Ernest wrote at a desk in his nominal bedroom, which was lined with bookshelves, while Martha wrote in a "beautiful large bedroom" outfitted with a "giant" double bed, a desk that looked out on a courtyard, and a vanity made by Cuban carpenters. Ernest's little brother,

Leicester, visited Ernest in the summer of 1939 and remembered Ernest bragging about Martha's beauty. Drinking at poolside, Ernest gazed at Martha rising from the pool and reached for his drink, saying, "That's my mermaid. What a woman that one is."

Martha's *A Stricken Field* appeared in March, but she had already moved on and was completing her collection of short stories. She wrote an article, which *Collier's* subsequently rejected, on the Nazi presence in Cuba, where a potentially dangerous community of Germans and Spaniards promulgated Fascist ideology; both she and Ernest were on the alert to Nazism in the Caribbean, though they would respond to it in future very differently. In March, she was infuriated to read a piece in *Time* about her and Ernest in Cuba, which mentioned her friendship with the Roosevelts and Harry Hopkins and wholesaled gossip about her role in the breakup of Ernest's marriage to Pauline—who responded by forbidding the boys' visits to Cuba for the duration.

Meanwhile, Ernest was writing the last pages of *For Whom the Bell Tolls.* He'd told Hadley the previous November that he "had decided to write as good and big a novel as I can," and in April he felt confident enough of the manuscript that he could show some chapters around. Martha reported it was "the finest novel any of us will read in this decade"; Ernest was "writing smoothly, with ease and magic and like an angel." An ex-Marine friend, Ben Finney, thought it "was the best and most exciting book I'd ever written," and Ernest even bragged that Finney had twice called him into the room where he was reading to show Ernest that he had an erection from reading the sex scenes between Robert Jordan and Maria. Ernest also submitted a chunk of the manuscript to Harry Burton at *Cosmopolitan* for serialization—*Scribner's Magazine* had stopped publishing in 1937. In a departure from his usual practice, Ernest even sent some chapters to Max, who responded, most gratifyingly, with nothing short of amazement. He was "still in a kind of daze," he told Ernest. "I think this book has greater power, and larger dimensions, greater emotional force, than anything you have ever done, and I would not have supposed you could exceed what you had done before." He thought the title perfect; it came from John Donne's "Meditation XVII": "No man is an *Iland,* intire of itself. . . . Any man's death diminishes me, because I am involved in *Mankinde;* And therefore never send to know for whom the *bell* tolls; It tolls for thee."

An intrusive criticism from an old friend interrupted Ernest's unstoppable progress with his novel. Archie MacLeish had recently become Librarian of Congress, and in the run-up to war he was entering a patriotic phase, as indicated in his controversial 1939 poem, "America Was

Promises." Critic Morton Dauwen Zabel observed, "There isn't anybody smarter than Archie MacLeish when it comes to knowing how . . . to jump onto band wagons." Discovered in tears at his great desk after hearing of the fall of France, Archie was now an ardent interventionist. Besides turning out political poems, in a May 1940 speech MacLeish tasked his contemporaries, the writers who had made art of their disillusionment after World War I, with having created young readers who lacked the moral conviction to fight Fascism. He singled out Dos Passos's *Three Soldiers* and Hemingway's *A Farewell to Arms* not only for the authors' "contempt" for the convictions behind that earlier war but also for their influence in making readers believe that not only "the war issues, but *all* issues, all moral issues, were false—were fraudulent—were intended to deceive." In this and an earlier speech called "The Irresponsibles," MacLeish charged that the nation's writers had contributed to the atrophy of the moral sinews of the nation.

Justifiably angry—few Americans had fought against Fascism in Spain with more ardor than he—Ernest characteristically took Archie's remarks personally, and responded in *Life* magazine in an *ad hominem* vein, accusing his friend of "a very bad conscience." If MacLeish had been at the battles of Teruel, Guadalajara, and so on, "he might feel better," Ernest wrote. Perhaps his old friend deserved this. Ernest's closing words, however, unnecessarily twisted the knife: "Or do his high-sounding words blame us because we never advocated a Fascism to end Fascism?" It was, indeed, an irony that Archie would choose to tangle with his friend just when Ernest was finishing his great anti-Fascist novel, and the friendship between the two men again became strained.

Ernest sent the completed manuscript to Scribner's in August; the ending, as usual, gave him great trouble. He had written an epilogue that treated the aftermath of the blown bridge in a scene between the Russian journalist Karkov and Golz, the Soviet-trained officer, and another in which the guerrilla fighter Andrés Nin comes across the traces of Pablo and Pilar's camp and sees the exploded bridge below. After much thought, Ernest removed this conclusion, ending the novel as it began, with Robert Jordan lying on the pine needles in the forest, his heart beating loudly, now waiting for the arrival of the Fascists and his certain death. The ending seemed then as perfect as those of *The Sun Also Rises* and *A Farewell to Arms*—though all three were vastly different. Nowhere else is Hemingway's consummate skill so evident as in his instinct for dramatic endings.

Max was able to report in August that the Book-of-the-Month Club had taken *For Whom the Bell Tolls,* which of course promised greater profits. If this suggested an element of aesthetic compromise, nobody noticed the contradiction except Max, who wrote Scott Fitzgerald that the good news was "the stamp of bourgeois approval. [Ernest] would hate to think of it that way," but, he added, "It is a good thing, practically speaking."

Ernest was occupied most of the summer with the business of publishing the book, though he was diverted by his brother's visit and that of Edna Gellhorn, Martha's mother, of whom he was enormously fond. Martha, in a rare moment of perspicacity about herself, later said that Ernest loved her mother: "Both of my husbands," she said, "loved my mother, always . . . they loved her more than me . . . and they were absolutely right." Ernest had an evident weakness for older women, as his first two marriages made clear, as did his warm friendship with Mary Pfeiffer. No doubt this reflected his closeness, as a young child, to a larger-than-life woman, Grace Hemingway, before his ambivalence about such a figure had taken hold. Edna Gellhorn, on the other hand, was by all accounts a remarkable woman: loving, accomplished, witty, and independent while at the same time an excellent wife and mother in all respects.

Edna reciprocated Ernest's feelings—but she warned her daughter off him. Sometime during her summer visit the older woman told Martha that she felt sorry for Ernest. Martha was flabbergasted: what was there to pity? Edna may have sensed the unmooring Ernest was experiencing after the breakup of his family, or she may have intuited a deeper trouble. Martha later said that in retrospect it seemed possible that Edna had become aware of "an emotional instability" in Ernest, one that had perhaps not yet revealed itself clearly.

On September 1 the couple left, Ernest from Florida and Martha from St. Louis, for another season in Sun Valley, this time with a visit from the boys, who Ernest rightly predicted would love it. They were once again given the Glamour House, a $38-a-night suite for which Ernest and Martha paid a token dollar. That fall Robert Capa, their friend from Spain, came to photograph Ernest for a *Life* magazine piece on the author of *For Whom the Bell Tolls* (and—practically an open secret—his relationship with Martha). Capa drew Ernest's ire by allowing *Life* to caption a photograph of him cleaning his gun, stating that "Dead-Shot Hemingway, in ten days of hunting, never missed a bird." Ernest knew that hunters reading the caption would have a good laugh at his expense, as a good wing-shot averaged at best a seventy percent success—and more like sixty percent.

Ernest turned in his corrected proofs to Scribner's on September 10, a milestone he celebrated for weeks. This year rain made hunting impossible for almost a month, but his attention was diverted by a visit from Dorothy

Parker and her husband, Alan Campbell, and also the appearance at the resort of Gary Cooper and his wife, Rocky, who had first visited Sun Valley in 1938.

Though Ernest had disliked the movie version of *A Farewell to Arms,* in which Cooper had played Frederic Henry, he got to know Cooper and his wife while hunting in Sun Valley and came to value the actor's friendship; Cooper claimed Ernest was his best friend. Cooper and Hemingway, both tall, good-looking men who photographed beautifully, were both avid shooters. Cooper had gone on safari in Africa two years before Ernest had, killing sixty animals, including two lions; Ernest had thirty-one kills with three lions. Both converted to Catholicism in part for their Catholic wives, though Pauline was now an ex, and Cooper would not convert until 1954. Rumors of a film version of *For Whom the Bell Tolls* were circulating while Ernest was still writing the book in 1940; it was even bruited about, doubtless on no basis in fact, that Paramount wanted Ernest to take a screen test. But Ernest became convinced that Cooper was the right actor to play Robert Jordan. October saw progress on the film front, when Donald Friede, once a publisher and now a story agent in Hollywood, flew to Sun Valley to talk about the movie rights; Paramount eventually bought the property for $100,000, then a record. Increasingly, Ernest delegated most of this business to his lawyer, Maurice Speiser, whom he'd hired in 1933; Speiser handled the foreign and film rights to his books, Ernest never having hired a literary agent.

Many comments Ernest made while writing the book indicated that he understood that *For Whom the Bell Tolls* came at a crucial juncture in his career. He seemed to have almost no doubts about its quality; it was the first of his books in some time that he felt thoroughly enthusiastic about, and to some extent he was emotionally banking on its success. The book's publication date was October 21, and Ernest was so eager for reviews that he called his friend Jay Allen in the East and asked him to read the first notices to him over the phone. One of the most gratifying was by Edmund Wilson, who had stung him so badly in 1939, regretting his seeming transformation from a serious writer into a fixture of the social pages: "the Hemingway of the handsome photographs with the sportsman's tan and the outdoor grin, with the ominous resemblance to Clark Gable." Now, he wrote in *The New Republic,* "Hemingway the artist is with us again; and it is like having an old friend back." J. Donald Adams, reviewing the book for *The New York Times,* said summarily, "This is the best book Ernest Hemingway has written, the fullest, deepest, the truest." Not so surprisingly—not only were "true" and "truly" constantly on Hemingway's lips beginning around this

With Gary Cooper, Sun Valley, September 1940

time, just as in his writing—the *New Yorker* reviewer used the very word: "I do not much care whether or not this is a 'great' book. I feel that it is what Hemingway wanted it to be: a true book." It was all the more striking, then, when Ernest wrote Max Perkins that he was tired of the "lies" of the reviewers. That was the method of the critic: "When they want to destroy you they lie and distort and fake." Quite possibly, unscrupulous reviewers distort, but they seldom lie or fake for the obvious reason that they would not get very far. This puts Ernest's insistence on the "true" in a more shadowy light.

Scribner's published 75,000 copies of the novel, aside from the 135,000 books printed as the November selection for the Book-of-the-Month Club. By the end of the year 189,000 copies had been sold, and by the end of March 1941, 491,000. Because the peak months for its sales straddled 1940 and 1941, *For Whom the Bell Tolls* was fourth on the *Publishers Weekly* best-seller list for 1940 (number one was *How Green Was My Valley*) and fifth for the 1941 list, which was headed by A. J. Cronin's *The Keys of the Kingdom*. One biographer asserts that the cumulative sales figure by 1943 of 885,000, which included 100,000 in Great Britain, made the book the biggest seller since *Gone with the Wind*.

For Whom the Bell Tolls was thought to be a shoo-in for the Pulitzer Prize for fiction. Strangely enough, however, the prize was not given that year—though this was not unprecedented. The Pulitzers were awarded under the aegis of Columbia University, and university president Nicholas Murray Butler personally vetoed the giving of the fiction prize to Hemingway's novel, telling the board he hoped they would not award the prize for "a work of this nature," presumably because of Robert Jordan's radical politics and the explicit sex. Butler held enormous power for a college president, evidently so much so that no one on the board dared to oppose him; it is not clear why the board did not give the award when their first choice was rejected.

The smashing critical and popular reception of *For Whom the Bell Tolls*, nevertheless, cemented the "comeback" of Hemingway's reputation that had begun with the publication of *The Fifth Column and the First Forty-nine Stories*. As Robert Trogdon has said in a book on Hemingway's business relationship with Scribner's: "The miracle of *For Whom the Bell Tolls* might be the fact that everyone did the right thing while writing, editing, packaging, and selling the novel." Yet the credit did not belong only to Scribner's: Ernest had set out to write a conventionally satisfying novel, one whose meaning was—recalling the iceberg theory—above the waterline rather than below. With its sentimental love story it was meant to appeal to the same audiences who had responded so enthusiastically to *Gone with the Wind* the year before. Scribner's was helping out as best they could, and *For Whom the Bell Tolls* brought in $218,000 by 1945, roughly the equivalent of $2.8 million today. Ernest was not only handsome and fit, a young blonde at his side, and said by the critics to be writing better than ever—he was well heeled, and for the first time made enough to live on from sales of his writing. Now, taxes competed with reviews for his attention.

For Whom the Bell Tolls was the right book at the right time. It struck a nerve in any number of American readers. It was published very soon after the German invasion of France, when support for the fight against Fascism had taken hold and a character like Robert Jordan, giving up his life for the struggle, could be embraced—despite the novel's notes of sympathy for Communism. Gary Cooper had just won an Oscar for *Sergeant York* (1941), a movie that was a fairly explicit exhortation for Americans to eschew isolationism and join the good fight. Further, Hemingway's now habitual focus on practical, applied skill, embodied in Robert Jordan, made the novel (and the character) seem to be a roadmap to a way that Americans could make a difference in a world that needed fixing, without losing what made them distinctive. In fact, the way Jordan arrives in Pablo's guerrilla camp and is immediately recognized as a leader, and his reluctance to accept that role, would have flattered Americans' view of themselves.

It would have been surprising if Ernest did not feel on top of the world, even given the emotional toll of his marriage's end. In a much later letter to art critic Bernard Berenson, Ernest wrote that Martha had said to him around this time, "We were giants and could have had the world at our feet." There is no reason to doubt that she did; Martha was given to high-flown language and an idealized view of herself—and, at this stage, of her soon-to-be-husband. Ernest was sufficiently impressed, and gratified, to mention this flight of self-admiration years later; whatever were her words exactly, they were reminiscent of Ernest's telling Hadley, much to her embarrassment, that they were the "prince" and "princess" among their friends. Still, each with a book out (one a best seller); fresh from a war against Fascism that had fully engaged them; trim, tanned, vacationing at a glamorous resort: it is not surprising that Ernest and Martha felt as they did. Ernest's divorce from Pauline became final on November 4, and Ernest and Martha wasted no time, marrying seventeen days later in Cheyenne before a Justice of the Peace, Ernest saying that it was "wonderful to be legal" after their four years of cohabitation.

Yet the marriage began on shaky ground. There was that strange "guaranty" Martha had written for Ernest after her prolonged absence covering the Russian attack on Finland. Pauline had put all her considerable energy into her marriage; everything that did not concern her husband's comfort, happiness, or career—including the children—had taken second place in her universe. Martha's career did not take second place in *her* universe, though this was at times a matter of some ambivalence and confusion; at least at first, she did "guarantee" that she would put Ernest first, and indicated that when married she would take his name.

Meanwhile, Pauline might have derived some chilly comfort from the fact that Ernest would make some remarks acknowledging the harm he had done to her in leaving her for Martha. But these were made in the context of the continued campaign to revile Martha. Just as he had blamed Pauline for "stealing" him from Hadley, as if he played no part in the matter, so he would gripe (to Martha's mother, of all people) that his marriage to Martha became "just a bad joke that was played on me in the fall of 1936 and the point of the joke was I had to give up my children and 500 dollars a month for life to be the point of a bad joke." To Bernard Berenson, however, he would be more fair to Pauline, acknowledging that he knew at the time that he was deluded to leave Pauline and the boys for the sake of Martha.

Unfortunately, Martha and Ernest found quotidian life with each other fraught with endless adjustments and petty quarrels. Martha drank enthusiastically with Ernest (as had Pauline), but even so she was disturbed by his alcohol consumption. Martha had rented the Finca in part because she could not stand the mess Ernest made in his hotel room at the Ambos Mundos. One observer noted "piles of books and discarded newspapers on the floor" in a different room in another establishment in which Hemingway was staying, while another remembered, of another hotel room, "You have never seen—or been in—a room that was such a shambles." Ernest had not yet lived in one place long enough to be considered a hoarder, but he was well on his way; he saved every scrap of paper he saw. Evidently he got this habit from his father, and already in the Paris years he was in the habit of leaving trunks of papers behind him when he moved, with only vague plans for later retrieval. Later, when cleaning house at the Finca, Martha discovered ten or twenty lottery tickets amidst a pile of papers; she and Ernest cashed them in for $60. A later observer said of Ernest in his Cuban years that he "kept any and all printed material."

Martha came to call Ernest "the Pig" in letters to her friends; she meant it fondly at first. She was personally fastidious and spent a lot of time on her health and beauty regimen—for which Ernest came to mock her. Ernest was more often than not unkempt, his everyday wear even outside the Finca principally slippers or shoes flattened at the heel and grubby shorts held up by a rope. After Gary Cooper became a friend, Martha constantly compared Ernest's appearance to the actor's, encouraging Ernest to dress as smartly as Cooper did and to pay more attention to his grooming. As a matter of fact, Ernest seldom bathed, relying instead on alcohol sponge baths; besides, he said, in Cuba he was frequently in and out of the water in the swimming pool or off the *Pilar*. Yet in the eyes of the public, Ernest and Martha were a stylish, even glamorous couple.

In Sun Valley, they posed for a series of pictures taken by Pappy Arnold, which show a mustachioed, rugged Ernest, on the heavy side, with Martha a svelte and tanned blonde, confidently holding a shotgun. Gregory and Patrick joined them on a school vacation, the most memorable event a jackrabbit hunt on which the four of them bagged almost four hundred rabbits, the boys contributing some eighty each. Ed Hemingway's rule, that you ate what you killed, seems to have long since fallen by the wayside.

After the wedding, Ernest and Martha drove to New York for a honeymoon at the Barclay Hotel, and stayed around two weeks. Jack came down from the Storm King School on two weekends, and Ernest gave him a series of boxing lessons at George Brown's gym, recalling the boy's earlier tutoring in bullfighting. During one of the handoffs of the children the previous month, Ernest staged a meeting with Hadley and her husband, Paul Mowrer, on a trail near the L-Bar-T Ranch in Wyoming. Hadley, Paul, and Jack were hiking when Jack wandered off; when he returned to the trail he was "delighted" to see "Papa, Paul, and Mother" sitting beside the trail and talking. A variation on the fantasy of a child of divorce bringing his parents together again, the experience was moving for Jack: "It was wonderful for me to see my mother, my father, and Paul all together talking like that." It's just possible, however, that the afternoon was indelible to Jack because of something else that happened that day. It was September 1. As Ernest waited in his car at the place where he was to meet the Mowrers and Jack, he turned on the radio and heard the news. Germany had invaded Poland, and Britain and France had declared war on Germany. As the world went to war, further indelible moments were to follow, for both Jack and "Papa."

TWENTY-TWO

The friendship between Scott Fitzgerald and Ernest—so emblematic in the modern imagination of Paris in the 1920s, was effectively over by 1940. They had been distant for years, and their last exchange, in 1936, in which Ernest used Scott's name in a cheap shot in "The Snows of Kilimanjaro," had been extremely chilly. When Scott died of a heart attack in Hollywood on December 21, 1940, in Sheilah Graham's apartment, his work was in literary eclipse. Max Perkins thought that was about to change when he saw the manuscript of *The Last Tycoon*, which Scott had been working on at the time he died. "It is the most tragic thing that it wasn't finished," he wrote with excitement to Ernest. "For it broke into wholly new ground and showed Scott as advancing and broadening." He had a lot of plans for publishing it, with an introduction by Bunny Wilson, in a volume with a reissue of *The Great Gatsby* and Scott's best stories. He wanted to leave out material from the "Crack-Up" essays that Wilson might want to include—he hadn't liked those confessional pieces any more than Ernest had. *The Last Tycoon* "shows that except for the physical side of it he didn't crack up. He was just getting into a good state of mind." Ernest wasn't having any of this, and told Max he thought it too bad to publish something unfinished, implying Scott wouldn't like it, but then added, gruffly, "I suppose the worms won't mind"—worms being all he hoped was left of Scott.

But this was tough even by Ernest's standards, and he soon made it clear he didn't want to leave matters there. He gave a lot of thought to Scott's body of work over the next weeks—and years. He did, however, summarily reject the notion that *The Last Tycoon* had any worth: "Most of it has a deadness that is unbelievable from Scott"—a remark that could truly be called a backhanded compliment. In the same letter he said he thought *Tender Is the Night* was Scott's real masterpiece—a sentiment that would have done his old friend a world of good to hear.

"By the beginning of 1941, the Sino-Japanese war had been going on so long and was so far away that it ranked more as a historic fact than a war." So begins Martha Gellhorn's piece about her honeymoon in China in her amusing travel book, *Travels with Myself and Another,* published long after Hemingway's death. To most Americans, the brutal war that followed Japan's 1937 invasion of China south of Manchuria was already an old story; what made it new was the fact that Japan had joined the Axis powers in September 1940, giving the long-running conflict new significance. The U.S. was also very concerned about the ability of Chiang Kai-shek's Nationalists to win an ongoing civil war with Mao Tse-tung's Communists, and by 1940 the American establishment was already embarked on an agonizing debate as to whether the U.S. should intervene on behalf of the Nationalists. The same year as the Japanese invasion, Chiang and his photogenic, American-educated wife—a subject of fascination to many Westerners—were featured on *Time* magazine's cover as "Man and Wife of the Year."

In the aftermath of her reporting of the Spanish Civil War, *Collier's* assigned Martha a mission to cover the "Chinese army in action"; she also was asked to write about the status of the Burma Road, the trade route opened in 1938 by the British between Lashio in Burma and Kunming in China, now seen as a critical supply route in the event of British entry into the war. Martha was eager to go, her imagination fired since childhood with visions of the "Orient" à la Somerset Maugham, teeming with Fu Manchus and rickshaws. Ernest was another matter, his geopolitical attention firmly oriented toward Fascism in Europe. As Martha later wrote, he "was knowledgeable in exact detail about anything that interested him but China had not been on the list" (*TMA,* 53). In fact, her nickname for him in her later account of their travels in the East was U.C., for "Unwilling Companion."

Ernest was not entirely unwilling, however. He and Martha had been good traveling companions in Spain and worked well together as journalists. Though Ernest may have approached the North American Newspaper Alliance about covering the Far East for them, another opportunity arose that appealed to him more. The previous spring he and his brother Leicester had taken Ralph Ingersoll, long a *Time* editor and a founder of *Fortune,* out fishing on the *Pilar* in the waters off Cuba. Ingersoll was talking about starting a newspaper in New York to be called *PM,* which would be decidedly progressive—the first issue, proclaiming support for U.S. entry into the war, would trumpet, "We are against people that push other people around." He intended to sign editorials and sometimes run them on the front page, and the newspaper would be one of the first issued in a tabloid format. He was looking, moreover, for reporters with a well-honed sense of the drama of the story they were covering, unafraid to narrate with flair and make clear their point of view. Leicester signed on immediately. Ingersoll was really trying to recruit Ernest, of course, and pursued him to that end in a series of talks in the Barclay Hotel in July, when Ernest was in New York to deliver *For Whom the Bell Tolls* to Scribner's. Ernest did not sign on until that December, however, when Ingersoll agreed that he would cover the Chinese situation for the newspaper. Ernest should stay in the East and cover the story if any action broke out, but otherwise take notes and write when he returned, when he had, said Ingersoll, the distance and time to think about what he'd seen and thus to "render a report of more lasting value than day-to-day correspondence." Ernest's seven articles, and an interview with Ingersoll, would run the second and third weeks of June, after he was back in the U.S.

Martha and Ernest embarked for China by way of Hollywood, where Ernest talked with Gary Cooper and Ingrid Bergman about the upcoming film version of his novel, Ernest telling Bergman that she would have to cut her hair short to play Maria; he asked her to show him her ears, and he thought they would do. The next stop was Hawaii, where they were wined and dined not only by local bureaucrats but also by Ernest's relatives, namely his Aunt Grace (his father's sister) and her family; Ernest and Martha didn't know which was worse, the bureaucrats or the family. U.C. liked Hawaii better than she did, Martha wrote her mother, adding, "He was by no means on fire with impatience for the Orient" (*TMA*, 13).

Upon arrival in the Far East, Ernest and Martha spent a luxurious few weeks in Hong Kong, where they took a stylish suite at the Repulse Bay Hotel. While Martha made the trip to Burma and from there to Kunming (then regularly a target of Japanese shelling) and back to Hong Kong, Ernest, she noted, surrounded himself with a "mixed jovial entourage" made up of police and "crook-type" figures: local Chinese businessmen, unsavory millionaires, and the like. He always seemed to be busy, going to the races and other sporting events, hunting pheasant in the nearby hills, and spending hours drinking rice wine and telling stories; he loved Chinese food and seemed never to tire of setting off the ubiquitous firecrackers, especially in his and Martha's hotel rooms.

From Hong Kong, Ernest and Martha went together to Namyung and then to Shaokwan, the base of the 7th War Zone, where both of them took notes on the Chinese army. From there they traveled down the muddy North River in a rustbucket Chris-Craft, making numerous stops at which they were received with bewilderment. They wound up in the wartime capital, Chungking, where they had a three-hour meeting with Chiang Kai-shek and his formidable wife, "still a beauty and a famous vamp," according to Martha (*TMA*, 50). Shepherded by a tall blond Dutch woman, who approached them at a Chungking market, they went by a mysterious process and circuitous route to meet the Communist leader Chou Enlai.

Ernest would report on both meetings to Secretary of the Treasury Henry Morgenthau, Jr., who was evaluating U.S. funding of the Chinese Nationalists. As reporters covering countries at war, Martha and Ernest were naturally seeking war intelligence, which did indeed greatly interest some in the Roosevelt administration, whom Martha knew through her friendship with the president and his wife. This hardly qualifies their trip to China as a "spy mission," as the author of a recent book on their sojourn there claims. On the other hand, Ernest was establishing a pattern in agreeing to report to Morgenthau. During the Spanish Civil War, Claude Bowers, the American ambassador to Spain, had had a meeting with Hemingway on May 16, 1938, at St.-Jean-de-Luz, in which Ernest gave him a detailed analysis of the Republican army, evaluating, for example, their armaments and the strengths and weaknesses of such generals as Durán, Modesto, Pozas, and Miaja. Bowers reported this conversation in a letter to Secretary of State Cordell Hull. As in many such exchanges, it is not clear why (or whether) the secretary wanted such a report, and why or under what circumstances Hemingway provided it. It is probable that he was hoping to encourage American intervention on behalf of the Republican government, as many leading liberal types, such as his friend Archie MacLeish, were doing at the time. This does not make his sojourn in Spain a spy mission, especially because these events in Spain and China took place in the premodern days of foreign affairs, when many visitors to other countries, especially writers, with their superior powers of observation, functioned as "diplomats" or as "spies" in the sense that they came back to the U.S. and told those in power what they had seen.

Hemingway's reports to *PM* were competent but nothing special, however crucial a period it was in Far Eastern history. Ernest did seem to grasp what lessons could be learned in China that might help in any upcoming larger conflict. The U.S. must tell Generalissimo Chiang that it would not back a civil war in China. Chiang did want to beat Japan, he assured *PM* readers. He warned, "The Generalissimo is a military leader who goes through the motion of being a statesman," in contradistinction to Hitler, who "is a statesman who employs military force." He concluded the piece, called "U.S. Aid to China," with a clever if somewhat forced horse racing analogy: "At present Russia figures to win against the Japanese with the Generalissimo. She figures to place with the Chinese Communists." He concluded, portentously if somewhat lamely, "After this race is run it will be another and very different race."

Though their journalism in these months was unremarkable, Ernest and Martha's trip to China was, for all Martha's descriptions of it as a "super horror journey" (*TMA*, 10), in many respects a wonderful time for the two of them. They each had an incisive, nonstop sense of humor (though it seldom comes through in their major writings, or even the letters between them). Martha's description of her journey with the U.C. presents an invaluable portrait of a couple in love meeting great adversity (she doesn't seem to be exaggerating the appalling living conditions they encountered) and cracking unending jokes about it.

Martha's essay in *Travels with Myself and Another* is a fond and positively rollicking portrait of Ernest and their relationship. The running theme is that Martha was the one who started this whole thing, and now she is the one to complain: "Who brought us to China?" or "Who wanted to come to China?" are Ernest's running responses to Martha's gripes. Their repartee is witty, so much so that it is unlikely that Martha invented it some thirty years later. Martha: "I'd rather jump off the Empire State building in long underwear than come to China again." U.C.: "I put nothing past you. Nothing" (*TMA*, 38). Everything in China was way too dirty for the fastidious Martha: Ernest, her polar opposite in cleanliness, advises her against bathing in the murky and noxious-smelling water, saying that if she brushes her teeth with it, she is a "nutcase" (*TMA*, 26). When Martha learns, to her horror, that she has acquired a case of "jungle rot," an athlete's foot kind of fungus, on her hands, U.C. replies, "Honest to God, Martha. You brought this on yourself. I told you not to wash" (*TMA*, 54).

More meaningfully, Martha's essay shows a very unusual, for her, lack of self-consciousness. Or, perhaps, an indication of a sense of humor about herself—not much in evidence elsewhere in her work. Ernest made some dead-on comments about her that she reported almost forty years later. When Martha slipped away from a bull session in which Ernest was participating with an assortment of shady characters, Ernest said, "M. is going out to take the pulse of the nation" (*TMA*, 15). A random observation, when Martha complained about the diseased, poor, desperate people they were meeting on their travels: "M. loves humanity but can't stand people" (*TMA*, 48–49). At another juncture, on the same subject, U.C. says, "The trouble with you, M., is you think everybody is exactly like you. What you can't stand, they can't stand. How do you know what they feel about their lives?" If they were as badly off as she thought, he said, they'd commit suicide rather than endlessly produce children or set off firecrackers (*TMA*, 22–23). There's an insight in every one of these wisecracks, which Martha seems to have recognized at the time, not just when she recalled them many years later. In China in 1941, Martha and Ernest were having a ball.

They parted in Rangoon, Ernest heading back to Hong Kong while Martha left for the west coast of Burma to see yet more military installations. They met again in New York in late May or early June. Ernest was debriefed in Manila by Army Intelligence, and both he and Martha at the Office of Naval Intelligence (ONI) in Washington by Colonel John W. Thomason, Jr., before his scheduled meeting with Henry Morgenthau, who had a particular expertise in relations with China.

On their way back to Havana, the couple stopped in Key West to pick up Patrick and Gregory for their summer at the Finca. Later that month Ernest learned that "Mr. Josie," aka Joe Russell, the proprietor of Sloppy Joe's, had died of a heart attack. Ernest felt bereft. Josie was only fifty-three.

* * *

Ernest seems to have greatly admired John Thomason, who would prove to be a surprisingly important figure in his life for several years to come. Ernest had heard of the colonel long before they met. Thomason was a much decorated Marine veteran of World War I and a longtime successful author of military fiction. Perkins had urged a volume of Thomason's short stories, *Fix Bayonets!*, on Ernest back in 1926; Ernest told Max that he was "disappointed" in it—apparently because he did not like the idea of the bayonet, which lent itself too readily to "ornamental killing"—though he found the writing "often splendid." But Ernest was otherwise predisposed to Thomason, having been introduced to him by a longtime friend whom he greatly admired, Colonel Charles Sweeny, the soldier of fortune and adventurer who would eventually fight under five flags before his death in 1963.

Ernest had first met Sweeny in Istanbul in 1926, where Sweeny joined Atatürk's revolutionary army; his romantic military history and his sophisticated understanding of warfare quickly made him an object of fascination to Ernest. A ruddy-faced San Francisco native and graduate of West Point, Sweeny had in the First World War organized the Lafayette Escadrille, the celebrated crew of American pilots flying for France; he had transferred to the U.S. Army after American entry into the war. In the aftermath he had fought the Bolsheviks with the Polish Army. Ernest next ran across Sweeny in Spain, where the two men spent a great deal of time together. Ernest told Perkins that Sweeny showed up in Spain as a newspaper correspondent, bearing six bottles of cognac and three of absinthe as gifts for Ernest. Sweeny was really there to aid the Republican army, and participated in the planning for the battle at Teruel—the Republican defeat there was due in part to nobody's paying attention to Sweeny's recommendations, Ernest said. Ernest found Sweeny outspoken and arrogant, nearly impossible to work with, and believed he was almost the only one in Spain who could, but, he told Max, "I would rather listen to him on military things than anybody I have ever known."

Thomason and Sweeny seem to have known each other through a military elite with a common interest in intelligence work. Ernest and Martha's "debriefing" with Thomason after their China trip was no doubt only pro forma, perhaps even Ernest's first meeting with the colonel. But his interest in intelligence-related skullduggery was piqued, and Ernest was soon hatching schemes that resulted in one of the murkiest and most feckless projects of his career—a government-sanctioned campaign against Nazis in the Caribbean.

As Americans in Cuba, Ernest and Martha were of course more removed from the war than their compatriots stateside, yet at the same time they felt in some ways more in the thick of it. Havana was very much an international city where unaffiliated individuals of many nationalities were in close contact, providing a fertile ground for espionage. Cuba's location, at the edge of the Atlantic and as the closest of the Caribbean islands to the U.S., added to the possibilities for wartime intrigue.

The impetus behind Ernest's first intelligence effort may have been Martha's work on an article about possible Nazi spies in Cuba for *Collier's*. She had cleared the idea with editor Charles Colebaugh in advance; it was a great story, and one that Martha, with her knowledge of the role fifth columnists had played in Spain, was ideally situated to write. But when she sent it in, in July 1941, the magazine rejected the article. In protest, she reminded Colebaugh that Nazi sympathizers in Cuba had the ability to tip off German U-boats to the location of American ships carrying matériel to the U.K. There were almost eight hundred Germans in Cuba, she told him, and thirty thousand Falangists, or Fascist supporters of Franco (surely a wildly exaggerated figure). Martha thought the editor was foolish; *Collier's* was passing up a possible headline reading "Swastikas over Cuba!"

Martha and Ernest grumbled for months about the story, casually continuing to keep track of Cuba residents they believed were Fascist sympathizers. They each badly wanted to do something for the war effort, especially after the bombing of Pearl Harbor. Ernest had been following the buildup to war for some time; Pearl Harbor, he thought, only exposed the "laziness, criminal carelessness, and blind arrogance" that had made the devastating attack possible. Too old to enlist, he cast about for ways that he could help the Allied effort. His old friends Evan Shipman and John Herrmann had enlisted, and his son Jack was soon to leave Dartmouth for Officers' Candidate School.

Even young Leicester Hemingway was doing his part—though he was extremely clumsy at it. Ernest had not seen his little brother for any extended period of time since 1934, when Leicester and a friend had sailed across the Gulf of Mexico in a homemade boat, then made their way to Key West, where they stayed aboard the boat for three months, Leicester joining his big brother for many fishing trips aboard the *Pilar*.

In 1940 Leicester and a British friend, Tony Jenkinson, had cruised the Caribbean for several months in a schooner called the *Blue Stream,* on the lookout for any signs of Nazi activity. Once they found a cache of diesel fuel they believed was waiting to be pumped into German U-boats; another time they were approached suspiciously by someone they thought was asking them to run fuel to the Germans. When they docked in Puerto Rico they overzealously reported that they had overheard two men in a post office speaking German and saw them receiving mail with German postmarks. Several articles in the Baltimore *Sun* detailed Leicester's cruise on the *Blue Stream*. Ernest was skeptical. A year later, when John Thomason said he was interested in the possibility of Leicester making further patrols, Ernest lectured his brother on the difference between journalism and espionage—in the latter you reported *only* what you had seen or not seen, rather than looking for stories—and told Leicester to get a haircut and wash his face "good" before meeting Thomason.

In 1942, however, patrols like Leicester's had begun to seem like an integral line of defense in the wartime Caribbean. The attention of many Caribbean islanders was riveted to the presence in their waters of German U-boats, which were coming dangerously close to American shores and sinking U.S. ships in alarming numbers. In 1942 the U.S. was losing cargo ships at a horrific rate—251 were sunk in the Caribbean alone. By this time America was in the war and these vessels were carrying vital supplies to the U.K. and, perhaps more importantly, to Russia. A total of 1,508 Allied merchant ships were sunk in that one year. It is not surprising that Americans like Hemingway were eager to do anything they could do to stem these losses. And espionage was, by then, an essential kind of war work.

By early 1942 Ernest was in close touch with American officials in Havana involved in intelligence work. Though the sequence of events is not entirely clear, in the second half of March, Ernest and Martha spent two weeks in Mexico City, ostensibly on vacation. According to recently unclassified OSS documents from 1944, Ernest had been sent to Mexico City to investigate the possibility of raising an army of Republican exiles from Spain who would be shipped to North Africa to join Allied troops there, perhaps the American soldiers who would be landing there in May as part of Operation Torch, the first major counteroffensive against Germany. While in Mexico, Ernest and Martha spent time with Nathan "Bill" Davis and his wife, Emily; Ernest had met Davis in Sun Valley, later reminding Patrick that they had hunted jackrabbits with Davis in the fall of 1941. Davis was in years to come said to be driving a taxi in Mexico City at the time—which does not jibe with his own background as an aristocratic Peabody or his marriage to a wealthy woman, Emily, who, with her husband, would soon become an art collector of note, buying the first of a number of Jackson Pollock paintings the same year. Bill Davis would become an important friend of Ernest's, and Martha too became a warm friend of both, writing them several long, chatty letters over the next two months. (One, addressed "Dear Guys," began, "Ernest is asleep and I want to talk.")

Davis, himself an *aficionado* whose enthusiasm rivaled Ernest's, took Martha and Ernest to several bullfights while they were visiting in Mexico City. Though rumors would later surface that he was with the OSS, it is not clear that Ernest was discussing possible espionage with Davis at this time. He and Martha, however, were staying at the Hotel Reforma under assumed names; though Hemingway scholar Daniel Robinson suggests that they were simply avoiding publicity, there is no record that Ernest ever went by a different name for this purpose. Hemingway's activities in Mexico City at this time remain sketchy; it is known, however, that he met there with Gustav Regler, his friend from the Spanish Civil War. Regler, a Communist, had fled Nazi Germany and then joined the XIth International Brigade in Spain, where he was wounded at Guadalajara. He had recently left Communist ranks. Regler remembered that when he met Ernest and Martha at Tampico Club, a Mexico City restaurant, Ernest, for some reason "in an alarming state of emotional confusion," harangued him for leaving the party when Soviet Russia was the only hope for beating Germany; he could not understand why Regler had done so, evidently overlooking Stalin's purges or, for that matter, the Hitler-Stalin Pact of 1941.

Nothing came of the Mexico City visit, except perhaps that Ernest was more open to the idea of doing intelligence work in Cuba for the U.S. He and Martha had a number of friends at the American embassy in Havana, notably Bob Joyce, second secretary, and his wife Jane, who in turn introduced them to State Department secretary Ellis O. Briggs, first secretary. Perhaps they were talking over Martha's rejected *Collier's* story about the Nazi presence in Cuba. In any event the possibility of Ernest's taking on some type of intelligence project and reporting the results to embassy officials was floated, and Briggs and Joyce approached Spruille Braden, the American ambassador to Cuba. (In Braden's memoir, he claims he approached Ernest himself.) Bob Joyce later told Carlos Baker that Ernest said he had experience running an intelligence operation in Madrid in 1937. This was an invention, or perhaps an exaggeration of his debriefing about the Republican Army with Bowers.

The Montana-born Braden was a Yale graduate (as was Bob Joyce), a Latin American expert who had previously served as ambassador to Colombia. He created a position for Joyce as chief of intelligence, and told Ernest to report to Joyce any suspicious activity; the operation was called the "crime section," but Ernest quickly dubbed it the Crook Factory. Ernest asked for Gustavo Durán to be made his second in command; Durán was a Barcelona native who had fought in the Republican army before escaping to London and then the U.S., becoming a U.S. citizen and then securing a position with the American embassy in Cuba. Ernest described Durán as "an ideal man to conduct this work." Ernest then assembled a ragtag circle of operatives, consisting of a bartender at his favorite Havana boîte, the Floridita; Basque friends, many of them former bullfighters or jai-alai players; Spanish priests; rich Americans like Winston Guest and Tommy Shevlin; and what Braden later called "wharf rats."

The Crook Factory did not escape the notice of the FBI, which had had its eye on Ernest since his rabblerousing speech at the American Writers Congress in 1937. Its first report, an October memo from Raymond Leddy, the bureau's legal attaché, to J. Edgar Hoover, noted that "conferences" in August had discussed using Hemingway's "services" in intelligence operations, cautioning, however, that Ernest was no friend of the FBI, having introduced Leddy at a jai alai match as a "member of the Gestapo." Further memos flew, and that December Hoover himself weighed in, saying that he "of course" disapproved of the connection between Ernest and Braden, calling Hemingway "the last man, in my estimation, to be used in any such capacity." Hoover added that he believed Hemingway's "judgment is not of the best," and cited Ernest's drinking: "If his sobriety is the same as it was years ago, that is certainly questionable." The agency also doubted

Durán's loyalties, citing his previous Communist Party affiliation; in fact, in months to come the FBI would obsess about Durán.

Ernest in turn hated the FBI with a passion. He had heard it said that many FBI agents were Catholics and that the bureau was a known friend to the Church, concluding that FBI agents were automatic Franco sympathizers and calling the agency "Franco's Bastard Irish." When the local police arrested one of his "operatives" (presumably for an unrelated matter), Ernest exploded, marching off to Bob Joyce's apartment and insisting that the FBI had ordered the arrest.

The Crook Factory became defunct, in fact, when the confusion among different intelligence-gathering bodies in Cuba and elsewhere in Central America led Roosevelt to order that all such efforts be consolidated and run by the FBI. But the operation had largely been superseded in Ernest's life by another plan, in which he and his men would patrol the coast of Cuba in the *Pilar*, looking for U-boats.

The idea was not completely the fantasy of a middle-aged man eager to play at war. The Navy was camouflaging armed vessels as merchant ships; called Q-boats, these ships would lure aggressive U-boats to the surface, open fire with guns, then send down depth charges when the U-boats dove back underwater. Unfortunately, many of the Q-boats that did come across German submarines were inadequately armed. The *Pilar* was no match for a submarine either, unless the sub was riding on the surface and came within close range. But Ernest devised a modus operandi that would set his operation apart from the other civilian patrols. The *Pilar* would draw a sub as closely as possible, then open fire, at the same time lobbing grenades into the sub's conning tower and bombs into the forward hatch. (Ellis Briggs pointed out that the approaching sub could blow the *Pilar* and her crew out of the water.) It would be a grand adventure—an adventure by sea, involving the big guy vs. the little guy, played for grand stakes, not to mention considerable danger: it was to be a noble enterprise that could possibly encompass fishing as a peripheral activity and would definitely mean that, as Martha would later point out acidly, the *Pilar* could tap an unlimited supply of hard-to-get, otherwise strictly rationed gasoline.

Though Hemingway's U-boat hunting operation is often lumped in with the Crook Factory's activities, it was administered differently and run differently, and it grabbed Ernest's fancy in a way the Crook Factory never did. It was run under the same auspices as the Crook Factory—the American Embassy, under Braden, Joyce, and Briggs—with John Thomason at the Office of Naval Intelligence overseeing the project. Thomason, however, did not entirely approve the operation, telling Ernest he didn't think any vessel would get close enough that anyone could "throw beanbags down the hatch"; Ernest in turn called him Doubting Thomason. Ernest told Braden that Durán could take over the Crook Factory; he also airily stated that the Embassy should "pay" him for having started his spy ring by supporting his antisub patrol.

"Friendless"—as Ernest dubbed the U-boat scheme, after one of the Finca cats—would not come cheap: Ernest had a lot of demands. He wanted twin .50-caliber machine guns to be attached to the *Pilar's* wales. He requested a number of pistols, including a Smith & Wesson magnum for his own use; bazookas; additional machine guns; magnetic mines and dynamite chargers; and box upon box of grenades. (Ernest's son Patrick remembered "an unlimited supply" of grenades and machine guns.) The *Pilar* would tow a collapsible rubber boat (in bright orange, so it could be easily spotted from the air). More important, Ernest wanted radio equipment: a state-of-the-art shipborne HF/DF system (for high-frequency direction finder, called a Huff-Duff) that could detect where radio signals were being sent from, as well as a traditional radio, the bill for communications equipment alone running to $32,000.

Along the way the *Pilar's* engines were completely rebuilt. Ernest also had some steel plates that he considered "armor" installed in the hull, in spite of the excess weight they added. The crew was outfitted with olive green U.S. Navy jackets, presumably through Thomason's office, and, curiously, sombreros, worn against the sun. The embassy and/or the ONI also approved Ernest's request that his men, if killed, be considered war casualties for reasons of indemnification.

The gasoline supply was of utmost importance. According to the Hemingway servant René Villarreal, gardeners at the Finca had, at Ernest's instruction, dug a very large hole on the property near the swimming pool. Villarreal, the chauffeur, and two of the jai-alai players, in a comic and drunken misadventure, attempted to lower a large gas tank, the first of three, into the hole; the chain they were using to lower it snapped and the tank hurtled into the hole. Eventually all three tanks were buried, presumably attached to gas hoses for access—though it is not clear how the fuel was to be delivered to the *Pilar.*

For the Friendless patrols, the *Pilar* had a crew of anywhere from five to nine, whom Ernest dubbed his Hooligan Navy. The crew almost always consisted of Gregorio Fuentes, the *Pilar* captain and cook; Winston Guest, nicknamed Wolf, the American millionaire who eventually became the right-hand man in Friendless; Juan Duñabeitia, one of Ernest's Basque friends, given the nickname of Sinbad the Sailor because of his familiarity with the sea, shortened to Sinsky; Paxtchi Ibarlucia, a jai-alai player, one of several who joined the crew from time to time; Fernando Mesa, an exile from Catalonia who had worked as a waiter in Barcelona; Roberto Herrera, a Spanish Cuban whose brother Luis had been a surgeon attached to the Loyalists in the Civil War; and Don Saxon, a Marine sergeant attached to the embassy, a radio operator and expert in small arms supplied by Thomason at the ONI. In a letter to Martha, Ernest described an evening with his Hooligan Navy: "We were just twenty-one . . . and twenty-four bottles of wine were drunk. . . . Tommy Shevlin sang some wonderful songs and everybody threw bottles at Fernando as a form of applause. Chairs were thrown to express disapproval. . . . Thorwald [Sánchez, a sugar magnate] had taken the pistol of the soldado, who had fallen asleep, and was firing it. . . . Juan was hit on the ear by a loaf of bread and rendered hors du combat. . . . It was an all time high in Basque celebrations."

When Patrick and Gregory arrived for their summer visit in July they joined the crew, but Ernest told his brother Leicester that he left his sons at home when they were going to specific places—as opposed to aimless cruising—that suggested impending danger. Ernest also insisted that in those cases Fuentes, who had six children, be left ashore. Ernest described the strategic scenario for Operation Friendless to Leicester:

> We had a bomb with a short fuse and handles. We kept it topside, unleashed and ready to fling. The idea was to keep nosing around where we heard them talking [through the Huff-Duff radio system]. Eventually one would surface and order us alongside. Then Patche [Paxtchi] and his pal would arm the bomb, grab the handles, and, as we came abreast of the sub's conning tower, we figured to clean her decks with our guns while the [jai alai] players flung the bomb over the lip of the conning tower. It would either blast the watertight hatch or go down the hatch and explode in the periscope control area.

It should be noted that if any member of the crew believed this projected scenario, he would need considerable bravery to participate on the *Pilar's* patrols. Ernest drilled his shipmates in gun assembly and cleaning and in target practice, throwing everyday objects as they would throw a bomb or grenade. Fuentes remembered shooting at old fuel drums with painted faces, which they called Hitlers. Patrick Hemingway, who remembers the sub-hunting period as "probably the last really great, good time we all had together," recalls dropping hand grenades on turtles: "this was justified by the need to learn how long it was between when you pulled out the pin and when it went off."

Ernest got so caught up in the spirit of what he was doing that he proclaimed Operation Friendless a success. The *Pilar's* log, camouflaged in a 1941 *Warner's Calendar of Medical History,* contains fishing notations, gambling debts, and the like, and also records such activity as inspecting a cave on the Matanzas coastline in search of saboteurs or supply dumps. The FBI, who still had their eye on Ernest, supplied a record of Friendless's success rate in a memorandum dated June 13, 1943. Some of the reported activities ranged far from sub hunting; in a report to the embassy, Ernest noted that General Manuel Benítez, the chief of the Cuban police, was plotting to seize power when Fulgencio Batista, the dictator, was in Washington. Abundant details were provided, but events proved him wrong; the rifle training he observed with alarm was simply a regular feature of the National Police's program. FBI agent Leddy pointed out that alienating the Cuban police force was not a good idea.

Leddy recorded other schemes or plots Hemingway brought to the attention of the embassy or the ONI, many of them very confused in the way of much of this kind of intelligence works—one thinks, for example, of the role of the pumpkin patch in the Alger Hiss case. For instance, Hemingway closely followed the visit of the Italian Fascist Prince Camilo Ruspoli; he reported that Ruspoli, who had pleaded illness to delay his internment by the Cuban police, "was not really ill." Hemingway also reported what he thought was an exchange between a submarine and the Spanish *Marqués de Comillas* on December 9, 1942, but the legal attaché interviewed almost a hundred witnesses who denied seeing a submarine on the surface. Hemingway submitted another memo protesting that, even so, it would be a "tragedy" if saboteurs from the sub had boarded the ship and might thus land in the U.S. Perhaps the most absurd event was the investigation of a suspicious box found in the Basque Club, a bar frequented by that community, which had been brought to the embassy by one of Hemingway's friends; the box was found to contain a "cheap edition" of the *Life of Saint Teresa.* Some of these incidents involved the Crook Factory, not the Friendless operation. But, as Leddy pointed out, all of Hemingway's activities were of a piece; he noted that Ambassador Braden viewed Ernest as "a pet project of his own" and took "Hemingway's opinions as gospel." Leddy, perhaps not the most reliable narrator, also noted that "a clique of celebrity-minded hero worshippers" surrounded Hemingway, citing Guest; Shevlin; Cathleen Vanderbilt Arostegui, the socialite and half sister of Gloria Vanderbilt; and unnamed embassy officials. To them, Leddy cynically added, "Hemingway is a man of genius whose fame will be remembered with Tolstoy."

The *Pilar*'s first patrol went out in July 1942, less than two months from the date Ernest proposed the operation. Officially, Ambassador Braden announced that the Friendless operation was over as of April 1, 1943, though Hemingway was out chasing subs that summer and into the fall. In the meantime, Martha had embarked on a cruise around the Caribbean for *Collier's,* with the purpose of reporting preparations for war but, like her husband, submarine hunting. She told her editor that she was going to pack a lot of white dresses and Proust, and wrote Mrs. Roosevelt that she was tired of managing the servants and overseeing the housekeeping at the Finca. Martha would later write up her expedition in another winning and humorous piece in *Travels with Myself and Another,* describing her island-by-island tour as yet another "horror journey," albeit punctuated with naked swims off deserted white sand beaches. To justify her expense account, she told herself that she might well come across survivors from torpedoed ships—a not uncommon occurrence in the area—or find enemy supply caches or radio transmitters. Her "private dream," she wrote, was to sight a German submarine—"private" because she "had the sense to keep [it] to [her]self," as her husband did not (*TMA,* 61).

Martha later told an interviewer that she found Ernest's Q-boat operation "rot and rubbish." She urged him to drop his "shaming and silly" activities at sea and put his mind to how he could really help the war effort. Increasingly, she felt they would have to go to Europe to report from the front, but Ernest dragged his heels.

*   *   *

However bumbling, Ernest's wartime intelligence activities need to be reconsidered in light of recent discoveries that have shown he was at the same time doing intelligence work for the Soviet Union. The discoveries were reported in a 2009 book whose three authors included a former KGB officer who was given access to KGB records from the 1940s. The story began in early 1941, when Ernest was in New York on his way to China with Martha. He was contacted by Jacob Golos, an operative with the NKVD, the Soviet law enforcement agency whose intelligence unit was the precursor to the KGB. What actually occurred is not clear, but Golos reported that Hemingway was given a password for communications with another operative for future contact; "I am sure," Golos wrote, "that he will cooperate with us and will do everything he can" to aid the NKVD. Ernest's code name was Argo.

One historian calls Hemingway's acceptance of this pitch "stunning"; indeed, it is hard to reconcile with his iconoclastic individualism and, to the extent that he was political at all, his antagonism to totalitarianism whether on the right or the left. When Argo signed on, the Nazi-Soviet Pact was still in effect. For obvious reasons, this had caused a number of left-leaning people to denounce the Soviet Union—especially Jews. To many, the Moscow show trials of 1936–38, meant to root out dissenting Bolsheviks, had already confirmed Stalin's totalitarianism. But from where Ernest Hemingway sat, the view was slightly different.

First, the circumstances of the Spanish Civil War left Ernest inclined to give the Soviet Union the benefit of the doubt. After all, as Ernest himself pointed out in a preface to a Gustav Regler novel, "The Soviet Union was not bound by any pact with Hitler when the International Brigades fought in Spain." The alliance came into effect, he asserted, only after the Russians "lost any faith in the democracies." In such a view, the Soviet Union was in a terrible position; its leaders, unsure whether they could beat Germany in any war, for years had sought an entente with France and the U.K. According to this argument, Stalin had only decided to form an alliance with Germany—an alliance principally to delay the inevitable conflict between the two powers—when the democracies' refusal to come to the aid of Republican Spain against Fascism made clear that they were either blind or complicit when it came to Hitler and his allies.

Ernest was not an ideological person; the only ideology that ever sat well with him was anti-Fascism. He would not have seen any conflict in agreeing to help both the NKVD and the U.S. embassy in Cuba, so long as the purpose was to defeat the Axis. In both cases his personal contacts were key; if he trusted his interlocutor he would do whatever he was asked. In Madrid, Ernest had become good friends with Alexander Orlov, the NKVD station chief; Orlov enabled him to get to the front and made sure he had all the caviar and vodka he wanted. The developments in Ernest's friendship with John Dos Passos and the Robles affair suggest how blinkered his relationship with the Soviets could be, yet in *For Whom the Bell Tolls* Hemingway showed himself to have some awareness of the range of ideological positions available in the Spanish Civil War. And, as noted, in 1938 he gave information to Claude Bowers, the U.S. ambassador to Spain, providing details about the Republicans' military capacities—simply because he liked and trusted Bowers.

The NKVD connection never really bore fruit, however. An operative would be in touch with Ernest twice in the next few years, once in London in June 1944, and once in Havana in April 1945. But Ernest never made use of the password he was given for future meetings with an NKVD agent. The NKVD files carried the following assessment:

> Our meetings with "Argo" in London and Havana were conducted with the aim of studying him and determining his potential for our work. Throughout the period of his connection with us, "Argo" did not give us any polit. information, though he repeatedly expressed his desire and willingness to help us. "Argo" has not been studied thoroughly and is unverified.

It is important to note again that writers were important cultural figures then, and it was not uncommon for government figures to approach them for reports of what they saw when they returned from other countries.

What are we to make, however, of the totality of Ernest's political activity in these years—his embrace of the Loyalist cause and its most ruthless exponents in Spain; his dalliances with both American and Soviet intelligence; his sometimes comic misadventures attempting to run a quasi-independent anti-Nazi operation of his own in the early years of World War II? Ernest, with his international celebrity, his years living as a minor potentate, first in the quirkily independent "Conch Republic" of Key West and then as the leader of a ragtag entourage of hero worshippers in Cuba, had come to see himself as a political power unto himself, an existential actor who set his own political boundaries and agendas outside conventional ideological definitions. In this, he was part of a cultural tradition that was still very familiar in the 1930s and 1940s.

Many of the most celebrated writers of the literary period that nurtured Hemingway, such as Victor Hugo, Tolstoy, and Gabriele D'Annunzio, had operated in similar ways. Ernest's close attention to Italian politics during and after World War I would indicate he was aware of D'Annunzio's renunciation of the Paris Peace Conference and his filibustering expedition to seize the Adriatic island of Fiume; D'Annunzio was a befuddled idealist, at times a quasi-Fascist, who made his own rules, and that was increasingly how Hemingway saw himself—minus the Fascism. These writers could participate in politics when they were inclined to do so, but also, when it suited them, hold themselves aloof. Hemingway, having settled in Cuba while remaining a U.S. citizen, in fact would become enraged when asked, over the years, how he could live there without speaking out against the oppressive Batista regime. He could also protest his own naïveté when he felt it would keep him out of trouble, once writing to a Soviet poet, for instance, "Excuse me if I talk politics. I know that I am always supposed to be a fool when I do."

During the Spanish Civil War, Ernest was able to find political clarity at two different junctures—first, when he defended the Soviets to Dos Passos; anyone who could beat the Fascists had his support, and the Soviets ran a tight operation that had the best chance of doing so. The second time was when he created the character of Robert Jordan in *For Whom the Bell Tolls*, who supported the struggle of the band of guerrillas he found in the mountains, primarily because he liked, trusted, and admired them. Ernest had taken an ideological stand each time, and he felt that he had fought the good fight and had written a successful book, which is what a writer was expected to do for the cause. But the Spanish Civil War was the last time such clarity was attainable for him. Perhaps he disappointed the Soviets as Argo, and the Americans as a spymaster and U-boat hunter, in part because he no longer felt such clarity, and in part because global politics increasingly had no place for his kind of renegade activism.

TWENTY-THREE

Haven't written a line now for just over a year," Ernest wrote to Archie MacLeish in August 1943. He had turned in *For Whom the Bell Tolls* in July 1940. That was it for fiction for those three years. A remark he made to Max Perkins led his editor to start referring to an upcoming collection of stories; when Max explicitly asked about it several months later Ernest told Max he was working on two long stories, allowing Max to believe that otherwise the "collection" was complete. In fact, Ernest would not publish a new book of fiction until 1950.

He did publish some journalism in the 1940s: there had been his seven articles for *PM* about China in 1941, and he would publish six more about the war in Europe for *Collier's* in 1944. Odds and ends: In August 1942, he wrote a brief preface to an anthology he had a hand in editing called *Men at War.* In 1945 he would publish an article in *Holiday* magazine called "The Great Blue River," about fishing in the Gulf Stream.

For many reasons, Ernest seems not to have felt the need or desire to write fiction. *For Whom the Bell Tolls* had been a command performance. With his acute sensitivity to the desires of the reading public, he had packed the novel with all the ingredients of a book that would be both a best seller and a critical coup; it was even highly cinematic, bringing in a nice pile of money from Hollywood. He had sorted out to his satisfaction the political tangles of the Spanish Civil War—for which he rightly prided himself. He had managed to create a hero who is passionately committed to political ends, but who would offend few readers politically. It was not surprising that Ernest felt "limp" and "dead" after he wrote the last chapter, as he reported to his editor; he knew, he said, that he had to write a majestic ending. But it was "a hell of a book," he concluded with pride. He cannot be blamed for thinking he deserved a rest.

Looking back on his father's third marriage, Patrick Hemingway told a biographer, "He felt that he was entitled to stay behind [in Cuba], living in a place he liked, and enjoying himself." Patrick's brother Greg said his father told Martha in July 1942, when Ernest returned from a sub-hunting expedition, "You're the writer in the family now, Marty." Greg believed he meant it. "Jesus, he was tired of the lists, tired of competition," Greg wrote later. He was happy to be Martha's editor, Ernest said; both he and she thought she needed one.

But, as Greg was quick to point out, such an arrangement could never work: "His idea of making Marty the writer in the family was doomed to fail, not because of her lack of talent but because of my father's compulsion to be Number One." Indeed, soon afterward, Greg heard his father say something quite different: "I'll show you, you conceited bitch. They'll be reading my stuff long after the worms have finished with you."

Ernest's competitiveness with Martha would increase dramatically throughout 1942 and 1943. But that was only one aspect of the decline of their marriage, which, like the bankruptcy described by a character in *The Sun Also Rises,* happened gradually and then suddenly. And they both showed a painful awareness that they were in danger of losing something that had once been very important to them. "My man is another hell on wheels character," Martha told a friend. "Two people cannot live together, with any order or health, if they are both hell on wheels so for the mutual good, and the sake of the party, they must both calm themselves." In other words, Ernest and Martha had a tacit agreement that neither of them would pitch an emotional fit—because the other would just pitch an emotional fit in response. Even given Martha's penchant for addressing everyone as "darling" and her tendency to show much warmth in her letters, the correspondence between Ernest and Martha that has survived from this period is especially tender, fond, and often elegiac, expressing, strangely, a kind of nostalgia for the present. So Martha wrote Ernest a long letter in June 1943, addressing him as "Bug my dearest," saying that she longed to have been young and poor with him in Italy—something like how she felt the first winter with him in Madrid: "I wish we could stop it all now," she wrote, "the prestige, the possessions, the position . . . and that we could by a miracle return together under the arch at Milan, with you so brash in your motor cycle sidecar. . . . I would give every single thing there now is to be young and poor with you. . . . and the days hard but always with that shine on them that came of not being sure, of hoping, of believing in fact in just the things we now so richly have." She did not specify what exactly had changed after the first two years of their marriage. She did not need to.

The same month, Ernest wrote Martha a lonely, heartfelt letter, begging her not to give up on him. She had made clear her disapproval of the goings-on at the Finca—the sub patrols, his drinking, and most of all, his ceasing to write. Carlos Baker has noted that Ernest returned to serious drinking that summer. He would haunt the Floridita, where strangers would sometimes identify him and run out to buy a book for him to autograph. In his portrait of Thomas Hudson, the autobiographical hero of his posthumous *Islands in the Stream,* Hemingway described a day of Hudson's drinking:

> It had started at noon at the Floridita and he had drunk first with Cuban politicians that had dropped in, nervous for a quick one; with sugar planters and rice planters; with Cuban government functionaries, drinking through their lunch hour; with second and third secretaries of the Embassy, shepherding someone to the Floridita; with the inescapable FBI men. . . . He had drunk double frozen daiquiris, the great ones that Constante made, that had no taste of alcohol and felt, as you drank them, the way downhill glacier skiing feels.

He felt important at the Floridita, and he surrounded himself with people who made him feel that way. Greg described "just unbelievable drinking" in these years. One night Martha insisted on driving back to the Finca because Ernest was not in a condition to get behind the wheel; he slapped her face, and she slowed the car to ten miles an hour. Disgusted, she slowly and deliberately drove the car into a ditch, left Ernest there, and walked back to the Finca. Other nights, Greg said, "Papa would be just out of his mind, but able to do it because Juan (the chauffeur) would drive the car home. So he could get as drunk as he wanted." Greg said he never saw his father work in this period. That summer he would join the boys with a scotch and soda around ten in the morning. He allowed Patrick, then fifteen, and Greg, age twelve, to drink all they wanted, offering them Bloody Marys if they had overdone it the night before.

Martha noted his bragging and his spinning of tales, many of which she knew to be untrue, and many of which he repeated, tirelessly, over the course of an evening. His audience didn't mind; they increasingly expected the man they called Papa to produce tales of his own heroics. Besides, they were drunk as well. The jai-alai players rubbed shoulders with rich playboys like Winston Guest and Tommy Shevlin, whom he knew from the days in Bimini, all competing for Papa's favor. One later observer noted that Ernest "demanded in his leisure hours a kind of willing sycophancy from people—needed it, craved it, enjoyed it, reveled in it." When he did not get this attention, he increasingly became irascible. Arnold Gingrich, later his editor at *Esquire,* noted that "as long as people around him were

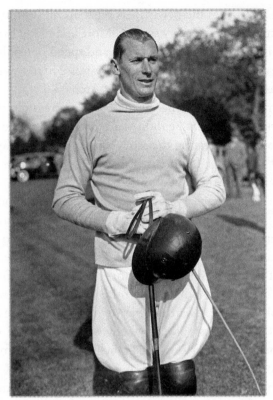

Winston Guest, Westbury, New York, May 1939

worshipping and adoring, why they were great. The minute they weren't, there was a tendency to find others who were." Martha was to speak about his need for attention and followers in a letter written much later. Ernest was interested in everyone, she said—but there was a catch. "He has the excessive need to be loved by everyone, and specially by all the strange passing people whom he ensnares with that interest . . . though in fact he didn't give a fart for them. So he would take people into camp; they became his adoring slaves (he likes adoring slaves) and suddenly, without warning, he would turn on them."

When Martha was away on reporting trips, life at the Finca would deteriorate. In letters from this period, Ernest not infrequently wrote of spending the night, with only the cats for company, on the living room floor, atop the Filipino straw matting he and Martha had brought home from the Far East. Martha complained the many cats were reproducing too fast and that their smells were becoming overpowering, but Ernest vowed that he would kill them before he did what Martha suggested and have the male cats fixed. The magazines and newspapers piled up, and empty wine bottles and glasses cluttered almost every surface. More and more, Ernest was content to return from his sub-hunting jaunts and spend hours listening to his fancy Capehart record player, entertaining his posse in the evenings. Often, though, he was "damned lonely," as he told Archie.

When Martha was in residence at the Finca, more often than not they fought. She complained that he didn't bathe and objected to his going all over Havana barefoot, wearing the same clothes day after day. He in turn accused her of being over-fastidious, a running joke of theirs on their trip to China—except now the good humor had leached out.

More often than not, however, their quarrels were about his refusal to participate in the war in any way, shape, or form. Patrick Hemingway remembered that his father was "very reluctant" to go away to the war "in any capacity." It was not that he had not given the matter some thought—that was what the Crook Factory and Operation Friendless were all about. But he was also looking into other ways he might serve. Around the time his sub-hunting adventures were falling off, he wrote to MacLeish, now Librarian of Congress, asking whether it was possible to be professionally attached as a writer to some branch of the armed forces. He was not speaking of propaganda, he said, but assigned to work "so as to have something good written" when the war was over. MacLeish knew just what he meant, citing Samuel Eliot Morison, whom the Navy took on as a historian. He volunteered to speak to John McCloy, the assistant secretary of state, about getting Ernest some such position, but neither Ernest nor Archie apparently followed through.

In September Martha was off to New York, on her way to London to cover the war for *Collier's*. She was reading proofs for her novel *Liana* (1944), set in the Caribbean; she had also very recently published a volume of short stories written during her time in Cuba, *The Heart of Another* (1941). She was held up in the city waiting for her passage to be booked, and escaped on weekends to Washington to visit the Roosevelts. She did not leave for London until the end of October. From there she wrote Ernest loving letters exhorting him to join her. In December she wrote about the appeal journalism held for her, while acknowledging that Ernest felt differently about it. But she had resolved, "I won't urge you any more to come, though I do think you will regret [not coming]."

Martha followed the fighting to Italy, where the Germans were counterattacking the Allies' landing at Salerno. There she encountered Bob Joyce, whom she knew from the American Embassy in Havana. Joyce was now with the OSS, the Office of Strategic Services, having found work with the new intelligence agency more appealing than his former labors at the Foreign Service. Martha confided in Joyce her difficulty convincing Ernest to leave Cuba and his sub-hunting activities. The sequence is unclear—whether Martha asked Joyce to do it or whether he volunteered—but he cabled the OSS, with the suggestion that office chief Bill Donovan and Whitney Shephardson, who was the head of Secret Intelligence (SI), the agency's espionage arm, might consider Ernest for service with the SI.

The suggestion threw the OSS into some confusion, reports Nicholas Reynolds, the writer whose investigation recently revealed this chapter in Hemingway's life. Memos evidently went out far and wide, for Lieutenant Commander Turner McWine, chief officer in the Middle East, wrote that he believed Hemingway's "prominence" and "reputed temperament" would make his employment with the OSS a difficult fit. Joyce wrote Shephardson a long memo in response, highlighting Ernest's unique experience in Spain, and, through his work there, his extensive knowledge of guerrilla warfare and "special operations." Joyce argued that facets of Hemingway's personal life—like his three marriages—were irrelevant to professional service with the OSS, and that he found Hemingway a man of "the highest integrity and loyalty." Joyce urged Shephardson to invite Ernest to Washington to discuss possible service, perhaps in Spain or Italy.

Shephardson sought further advice. Deputy Director Brigadier General John Magruder managed to cast aspersions on Joyce himself, deeming him "an extremely intelligent and somewhat temperamental individual who would not be improved by association with . . . Hemingway" [Reynolds's ellipsis]. Hemingway's file made its way to Morale Operations (MO), a division dedicated to so-called black propaganda, but authorities there felt that he was "too much of an individualist" for their ranks. When Shephardson finally let Joyce know that they weren't going to pursue taking Hemingway on, he gave the same reason: although Ernest had "conspicuous ability for this type of work," he was too much of a lone wolf to take orders.

This was not to be the end of Hemingway's association with the OSS—for one thing, his son Jack had recently joined the agency, parachuting into German-occupied France (equipped with his fly rod, in case of fishing opportunities)—but it marked the end of Martha's attempts to find a direct role for her husband in the war. That left the obvious route: he should cover the fighting as a foreign correspondent, just as he had the Spanish Civil War. She went so far as to recommend that Ernest propose a series to *Collier's*—the magazine that was currently her employer. If Ernest complied, his status would obviously outweigh hers. Because of a rule of the U.S. Press Corps, magazines were allowed only one front-line war correspondent apiece—and that correspondent, in this case, would be Ernest, not Martha.

He was still very reluctant, and his viewpoint remained unchanged. Martha returned to the Finca, for what would turn out to be the last time, in March 1944. She found Ernest with a thick and long grizzled beard, and full of talk about how "selfish" she was. He woke her up in the middle of the night to harangue her for being "insane," accusing her of wanting "excitement and danger," with no thought of her own responsibilities. He tried to involve Edna Gellhorn, Martha's mother, on his side; he seems to have thought that approval of this good woman, who, like Mary Pfeiffer before her, liked her son-in-law as much as he liked her, would give him the moral high ground. He wrote Edna that Martha was "just plain spoiled." Worse than that, she was "mentally unbalanced; maybe just borderline." Backing off, he concluded, weakly, "If it is just pure, straight, hard, unmoral selfishness then there is nothing to worry about." Martha came to her own conclusion: "My crime really was to have been at war when he had not."

Not only did Martha let Ernest take her place as *Collier's* sole war correspondent, she did all she could to arrange for Ernest to get to Europe. She appealed to Roald Dahl, a charming Englishman of Norwegian descent she had met in Washington. Dahl had been an RAF pilot and now worked in intelligence for the MI6; in early 1944 he was with the British embassy in D.C. Martha asked for his help getting Ernest a seat on a plane to Britain, which Dahl was able to provide. Ernest flew over on May 17. Martha assumed she would go over on the same plane, but Ernest said, flatly, "They only fly men." (Actresses Beatrice Lillie and Gertrude Lawrence were on the same plane.) Martha shipped out before Ernest, on May 13, as the only passenger on a Norwegian boat carrying amphibious landing machines and dynamite; it was an especially uncomfortable trip for her because the nature of the cargo meant she couldn't smoke.

Ernest was not happy about the prospect of gearing up to be a reporter again—nor of going to the front. Before departing for London, he made his feelings plain in a letter to Max Perkins: "Take not the slightest interest in where am going to go and feel no lilt nor excitement. Just feel like horse, old horse, good, sound, but old, being saddled again to race over the jumps because of unscrupulous owner. Will make same race as always, best that can make, but am neither happy, excited, nor interested."

Ernest and Martha's marriage was effectively over when they traveled separately to Europe in May 1944. The fundamental problem was that both were high-strung, emotionally needy, and not always honest with themselves or each other. Each was used to getting his or her way. They could not make themselves heard to each other, and they soon stopped trying. Martha was fed up with what she called Ernest's "Q-boat play-acting"; she hated the Cuban posse who seemed to have taken up residence in the Finca; and she was increasingly disgusted by her husband's personal slovenliness and dishonesty. Ernest was tired of Martha's highhandedness and pretensions (he complained about her posh, quasi-British accent); he felt threatened by her refusal to stay home and take care of his needs (perhaps as Pauline did); he objected to her pursuing a career, once cabling her, "ARE YOU A WAR CORRESPONDENT OR WIFE IN MY BED?"; and he had come to resent, deeply, her growing lack of respect for him. It was time to go their separate ways.

For all the pains Martha took to help Ernest get to the war, she arrived in London on May 28, twenty-four days after her ship sailed—and eleven days after her husband. By the time she arrived, in fact, he had already met the woman who was to replace her.

* * *

Ernest's arrival found London in the grip of invasion fever. The Blitz may have been over, but bombs were still raining on the city. The period between January and May 1944 was dubbed the Baby Blitz, the Germans sending 524 bombers over London and environs, partly to retaliate for recent Allied bombings of German cities. The Dorchester Hotel in fashionable Mayfair was a favorite of visiting American luminaries like General Dwight Eisenhower, U.S. ambassador Averell Harriman, and journalists Vincent Sheean and Ernie Pyle. Built in 1931, it was solidly constructed of reinforced concrete, thought to be strong enough to withstand direct hits. Ernest got a room that, like his room at the Hotel Florida in Madrid, was at a "safe angle," a concept Philip Rawlings explained to Dorothy Bridges—the Martha Gellhorn character in his play, *The Fifth Column*: "The room has an excellent angle, really. I mean it. I could show you from the street." When Dorothy questions whether "the angle [is] really safe," Rawlings replies that the room is as safe as any one could get in wartime. Weeks later, when Martha joined Ernest at "the Dorch," she too noted that his room was at a "safe angle."

He held court in the second-floor room, visited by Lewis Galantière, his first friend in Paris; Bob Capa and his girlfriend, Pinky; Lael Wertenbaker, a *Time* reporter whose husband, Charles, was the magazine's foreign editor; and Fred Spiegel, a journalist Ernest had known in Italy in the first war. Ernest was busy getting his ducks in a row, journalistically speaking. The RAF were the heroes of the hour, and had been ever since the Battle of Britain, when the U.K. pilots began to turn the tide in the air because of their skill in precision and nighttime bombing. The term "glamour boys" was actually coined in 1941 to describe RAF pilots; they were exemplars of dashing heroics—and genuine heroism—and Ernest naturally gravitated to them.

He intended to pursue them professionally as well; an RAF pilot in action made a natural story, ideal for mass consumption in *Collier's*. He wanted to fly with British pilots in nighttime bombing raids on German targets, and the RAF cooperated by sending a public relations team and an officer, John Macadam, to organize Ernest's flights. He did not make a good impression with these men. John Pudney, one of the RAF's PR team (and also a poet), remembered Ernest holding forth in a bar to some junior RAF officers, telling them their senior officers were "cowards" because they were not in the air flying over enemy territory. Pudney was "ashamed" for Ernest; senior pilots, in these weeks before D-Day, were grounded because they might be shot down behind enemy lines and forced to divulge the Allies' plans. "Set beside . . . a crowd of young men who walked so modestly and stylishly with death, [Hemingway] seemed a bizarre cardboard figure."

By then Ernest was treating the Dorchester like an outpost of the Finca, and the visiting journalists and RAF pilots like the jai-alai players who had been his comrades in sub hunting. He had made friends on his flight over, two Navy men who were in the OSS and would soon parachute behind enemy lines, Lieutenant Henry North and Lieutenant Michael Burke. The two officers became part of Ernest's retinue, accompanying him even when he went to Barclay's Bank to open a checking account. He asked them to wear their uniforms and sidearms for this mundane excursion, arguing that the bank management would take him more seriously with bodyguards thus arrayed.

Leicester Hemingway unexpectedly turned up at the Dorchester, part of the U.S. Corps, a film unit meant to document the European war, known as the Hollywood Irregulars. Headed by director George Stevens, the unit included William Saroyan, then at the height of his career as novelist and playwright; Irwin Shaw, at the time known mainly as an accomplished writer of plays and short stories; and the writer Ivan Moffat, son of the British socialite Iris Tree. Moffat, who turned up in Ernest's hotel room in Shaw's tow, reported that Ernest showed off "his collection of shotguns and rifles, pre-invasion rows of boots, and a portable canvas device that would enable him to cross rivers." Moffat noted, "I had wondered why he needed all that stuff as a war reporter." (Ernest later complained to writer Peter

Viertel that the film unit "was a lot like reading Proust"; that is, full of "fairies," which was inaccurate; as Mary Hemingway herself said at the time, "Shaw's no fairy.") Ernest, who never traveled with less than ten pieces of luggage, was evidently well prepared. Leicester had a similar memory: he visited the Dorchester bar with his brother, who solemnly showed him a letter from Spruille Braden stating that "the bearer . . . performed hazardous and valuable operations in the prosecution of the sea war against Nazi Germany that were of a highly confidential nature. The undersigned was highly cognizant of the value of these . . . and grateful for the manner in which they had been performed." Ernest was ready for anything.

Ernest traded gibes with Saroyan and Shaw, who were both enjoying early success, and, at least at the time, considered capable of great things, much like Ernest himself twenty years earlier. It cut no ice with Ernest that Shaw was responsible for introducing him to the reporter Mary Welsh Monks—the next woman in Ernest's life. If anything, he was jealous of Shaw, who had had an intimate relationship with Mary. Shaw made the introduction on May 22 at the Greek-owned White Tower restaurant in Soho, a favorite haunt of journalists. Mary, a small, braless blonde with blue eyes, a perky smile, and a tight sweater, was lunching with Shaw when a heavily bearded Ernest asked for an introduction. Mary noted that he looked overheated in a wool RAF uniform (why or how Ernest was wearing this remains a mystery). She agreed to a lunch date the next day; they ate outside at the same restaurant, struggling to hear each other over the traffic noise. Neither seemed especially excited about pursuing a friendship, or so it seemed.

Two nights later Ernest had an accident the effects of which would stay with him for the rest of his life. Robert Capa, delighted to find Ernest in London, decided to throw him a party, combining it with a tongue-in-cheek celebration of the successful appendectomy of his girlfriend Elaine Justin, known to all as Pinky. He had a "useless and very expensive" flat, a fully furnished penthouse at 26 Lowndes Square just made for parties—though penthouses were unpopular in wartime London, for obvious reasons. Pinky had somehow come up with ten bottles of scotch and eight of gin. Capa soaked some peaches in brandy for punch (the guests reached the peaches, he said, around four in the morning), found some champagne, and invited almost every English-speaking correspondent in London, among them *Life* picture editors Ed Thompson and John Morris and *Life* photographers Frank Scherschel and Dave Scherman. Morris remembered that Ernest was wearing a British battle dress jacket rather than the Eisenhower jacket most correspondents wore.

Also present was Bill Walton, a *Time* correspondent who had been training with the 82nd Airborne to parachute behind enemy lines after the invasion; Ernest learned that night that Walton had spent his summers in northern Michigan. (He later found out that Walton was a good friend of the blond woman who had caught Ernest's eye just days before at the White Tower.) Leicester Hemingway was present, and he and Ernest did a little boxing in the kitchen, Ernest then daring onlookers to hit him in his hard stomach. Mostly, though, Ernest talked to a British immunologist, Peter Gorer, and his German refugee fiancée, Gertrude, showing Gorer what he had been told was a benign skin cancer on his face, mostly covered by the beard he had grown to hide it. He also showed Gorer the same letter of commendation from Spruille Braden that he had showed Leicester in the Dorchester bar. Around three in the morning, the doctor offered Ernest and Lael Wertenbaker a ride back to the hotel. Wertenbaker declined, and Ernest was the only passenger as Gorer's car crept along the blacked-out streets. In less than half a mile the car solidly hit a metal water tower. Ernest's head hit the windshield, opening a huge gash in his skull and giving him a severe concussion; he also injured his knees. He was taken to nearby St. George's Hospital. Capa saw him in the emergency room, later reporting, "His skull was split wide open and his beard was full of blood."

He was soon moved to the London Clinic, a private hospital at the corner of Devonshire Place and the Marylebone Road, which he promptly turned into an outpost of his room at the Dorchester. Little had changed in that respect from his days in the Red Cross hospital in Milan in 1918: the bottles piled up around his hospital bed, and as with Agnes von Kurowsky, he did some serious courting, this time of Mary Welsh, who heard he was in the hospital and stopped by with a bouquet of tulips and daffodils.

Martha Gellhorn had heard of her husband's accident as soon as her boat docked—the story made the wire services—and appeared in his hospital room, only to burst out laughing at the sight of Ernest in a bandage wound many times around his head like a turban, looking, according to Robert Capa and Pinky, like "an Arab potentate." Martha doubted that he had even had a concussion, having observed him "drinking with his pals" in the hospital room. Indeed, it is not clear Ernest had a concussion, Carlos Baker reporting in 1969 that the injury was a "subdural hematoma." The distinction would be irrelevant except that the head injury Ernest received in May 1944 was life-changing. Either one would today be called a traumatic brain injury, or TBI, the severity and effects of which vary widely. This would be his second such injury after the concussion he suffered when wounded in Italy in 1918.

St. George's Hospital, London, after head trauma
suffered in a car accident, May 1944

Baker used the term "subdural hematoma" when he reviewed what Ernest's Cuban doctor, José Luis Herrera Sorolongo, told him about the injury and how it should have been treated when the doctor first saw him, which was on his return to Cuba after the war, in 1945. Herrera of course had not examined Ernest at the time of the injury, and was only addressing the symptoms Ernest described to him. We know of what the doctor said through a letter Ernest wrote to Mary Welsh about his injury in April 1945. "What should have been done [just after Ernest's accident] was open and drain the original hemmorage," Herrera said. This is, in fact, basically what is done for a subdural hematoma, which is a buildup of blood on the brain due to head injury. Diagnosis of this specific injury, however, has been possible only since the availability of MRIs and CT scans, beginning in the early 1970s. Baker concluded, from the treatment Herrera said Ernest *should* have received, that the injury was a subdural hematoma. Indeed, it probably was. The distinctions between a concussion and a subdural hematoma are in three areas: diagnosis; treatment; but perhaps most crucially here, severity.

Subdural hematomas are extremely serious injuries, often requiring drilling a hole in the skull to drain the blood. The symptoms Ernest reported to Herrera a year later were serious enough that Herrera believed he should have been treated for that condition. Ernest told Mary what he had told the doctor: that he experienced nearly constant headaches, ringing in the ears, slowness and inertia; he had trouble with his handwriting and he suffered a loss in verbal memory so that he often searched for words in conversation. These were all, Ernest reported that the doctor said, "symptoms of what had been done to head." He also told Mary that the difficulties experienced by Mr. Scrooby—their pet name for his penis—were the direct result of his condition. Dr. Herrera, Ernest said, told him he would not only have drained the blood from his brain at the time of the injury, but would have insisted upon three months' convalescence. Drinking, the doctor further said, was the worst thing for his condition.

The London Clinic, however, discharged Ernest on May 29, just four days after his accident. He told Mary that he lied to the doctors about how he felt so that he could be sure of covering the coming invasion, just days away. In any case, four days were wholly inadequate for recovery from a traumatic brain injury, even if it had been only a mild concussion. Ernest knew, and would not have needed a doctor to tell him, that drinking alcohol was a very bad idea, but he stocked his hospital room with liquor nonetheless. Perhaps because of his injury, he was operating against all common sense.

The consequences of his disregard were enormous.

* * *

At the time of his injury, Ernest's attention was on two things: the coming invasion (about which he knew few details until the early days of June) and this new blonde in his life, thirty-six-year-old Mary Welsh. After his discharge from the London Clinic, he saw her again when she and Irwin Shaw stopped by the Wertenbakers' suite at the Dorchester to have a drink. Mary and Connie Ernst, a friend who worked with the Office of War Information, had been unsettled enough by the Baby Blitz that they took a room together at the hotel; when Ernest told her he'd come see her in her room later, she hoped he wouldn't. He did nevertheless, entertaining her and Connie with stories of his upbringing in Oak Park and his strange family. He broke off his monologue to tell Mary that he wanted to marry her, and that he felt sure they would be married one day soon. When Mary protested that each was already married, Ernest persevered. Again, Mary remained unimpressed. Another lunch at the White Tower, this time with Charlie Wertenbaker present, marked the beginning of Mary's unbending. More lunches, visits to London nightclubs, and long talks at both venues brought her around completely; when Ernest said he would dedicate a book to her she asked if he would dedicate it with love. When he said yes, she was genuinely flattered. He was too big for her—in "both stature and status"—but she had fallen in love.

Like Hadley, Pauline, and Martha, Mary was a Midwesterner, though her background was quite different from theirs. Her beginnings were rough; she was born in 1908 in Walker, Minnesota, on Leech Lake, and grew up in the small town of Bemidji. Her father, Tom Welsh, worked as a logger and in the summers piloted a paddle boat called the *Northland* that took tourists out on the lakes for day trips, towing booms of logs when lumber abounded after storms brought down the white and Norway pines. Mary loved joining her father on his boat; her mother, Adeline, usually stayed behind in Bemidji. Mary attended the local teachers college after high school, but she had ambition and itched for big city life. Impressed by the editor of the Bemidji *Pioneer,* she went to Northwestern University, which offered a journalism degree and proximity to Chicago. She met her first husband there, a drama student named Lawrence Cook, and did not finish college, going to work instead for a trade magazine for florists. The marriage soon ended. She then parlayed a position with a "newspapering sweatshop" that published several free papers into a job assisting the society editor of the *Chicago Daily News.*

On her first trip to Europe, she knew only that she wanted to stay there, and asked Lord Beaverbrook himself for a job on the London *Daily Express.* When he asked her to sleep with him, she refused, but she eventually got the job, moved to London in 1938, and cultivated a lively social life, mostly with correspondents on Beaverbrook's other papers. These included Noel Monks, an Australian who wrote for the rival London *Daily Mail* (and covered the Spanish Civil War for that paper, according to Mary), whom she soon married. Mary worked for a time in Paris, and capital-hopped across Europe covering the coming of the war. She and Noel were often apart. Then, from Walter Graebner, an editor she knew from Chicago, Mary landed a job with the London bureau of the Luce publications—*Time, Life,* and *Fortune.* She began her job on July 10, 1940, the first day of the Battle of Britain.

Working for the Time-Life organization gave her a position of some prestige, and Mary was a respected reporter who weathered the vicissitudes of wartime London with professional agility as well as good cheer, mixing Churchill press conferences with weekends at British country houses. Irwin Shaw was just one of her many boyfriends, most drawn from the ranks of London-based reporters. She was also having an affair with a (married)

Mary Welsh, Ernest's fourth wife, in the early 1940s

brigadier general, Robert A. McClure, who had been since 1941 a military attaché to the American embassy in London. Around the time Mary met Ernest, McClure was made chief of intelligence for the entire European Theater of Operations (ETO), creating the Psychological Warfare Division of the Supreme Headquarters Allied Expeditionary Force (SHAEF). In early 1944 Mary had been in bed with Irwin Shaw when the general started pounding at her apartment door, ordering her to let him in. She and Shaw were both terrified, Irwin because he was "rank-conscious" and knew exactly what the general could do to him, and Mary because McClure was wildly jealous. She finally convinced the general to leave.

Meeting Ernest Hemingway, then forty-five, was in no way a remarkable event in the thirty-six-year-old Mary Welsh's life, then; beyond journalists—Beaverbook, after all, among them—she knew many successful writers. She was very aware of Martha Gellhorn, whom she would consider a colleague—never mind that Martha had also published fiction and was a good friend of Eleanor Roosevelt's. The playing field of prewar London was, as far as Mary was concerned, perfectly level, and she could easily replace Martha as the object of Ernest's affections.

Ernest himself had another preoccupation that accompanied his courtship of Mary, however. In a poem he wrote to Mary, the first of two poems that one biographer fairly convincingly argues are "the worst things he ever wrote," Ernest refers to the headache he'd been suffering from since his traumatic brain injury as if it were a person, characterizing it as a faithful friend. "First Poem to Mary" and "Second Poem to Mary," the first poetry he had written since 1935, suggest how much damage Ernest had suffered from his head injury. The first is hardly a poem at all; he uses line breaks only for the first eight lines, roughly one ninth of a piece that then is written without any further breaks—that is, as prose. It is an odd tribute "to Mary" in any case, for he refers to her only in the second-to-last paragraph, where he talks of the hour when he hears her coming into his hotel room, asking in a whisper whether she can come in. Otherwise, it is about the sub-hunting days, and how much he misses that time—his boat and his crew, and how he is "homesick" for men like Paxtchi, his jai-alai-playing crew member. Twice he invokes Winston Guest by his nickname "Wolfie": in fact, the last paragraph of the "poem" begins by telling Wolfie never to worry. Ernest writes that he never lets his headache know how long the intervals seem between his flights with the RAF, lest he hurt the headache's "feelings." But just as Martha ignored the evidence of how Ernest really felt about her in his depiction of Dorothy Bridges in his play *The Fifth Column,* so Mary seems to have heard no warning bells in this bizarre, self-pitying poem ostensibly written for her.

* * *

Only a scant handful of correspondents were allowed on the beaches of Normandy on D-Day and, for all their considerable journalistic chops, neither Mary, Martha, nor Ernest was among them. Martha came the closest, locking herself in the bathroom of a Red Cross ship bound for Normandy; she waded ashore at Omaha Red on June 7—day 2—to help bring wounded back to the ship. Mary, assigned to tour air bases during the invasion, consoled herself with having the only bylined story from the European Theater in *Life* magazine for the week of D-Day.

Ernest himself came within yards of the beaches of Normandy on the historic day. Late at night on the 5th, he boarded the *Dorothea M. Dix,* and around 2 a.m., leery of further damage to his injured knees, he was lowered in a bosun's chair onto another transport, the *Empire Anvil,* to observe the landing from shipboard. Shortly before the sun came up he climbed down from the boat, now trusting his knees—or perhaps reluctant to draw more attention to himself—onto an LCVP commanded by Lieutenant Bob Anderson. Behind it, the battleships *Texas* and *Arkansas* were firing toward shore, sounding "as though they were throwing whole railway trains across the sky," he later wrote. Ernest had studied his maps thoroughly, and as daylight leached into the scene, could see the landmarks that identified their target, the Fox Green section of Omaha Beach. Ashore, he could see tanks burning and the bodies of the wounded or dead littering the beaches; crafts of all sorts roiled the waters. Anderson tried to land the men, but drew heavy fire and stayed back. Ernest made out infantrymen climbing the bluffs with what seemed to be agonizing slowness. Mines on the beach and machine gun fire decimated the landing troops, but many German pillboxes blew under the fire of the destroyers at the rear of the LCVPs. Finally the landing craft disgorged its men onto a ramp to the shore, Ernest remaining aboard to be deposited back on the *Dix*.

He was back at the Dorchester that same day. While in the second sentence of his account of the invasion for *Collier's* he casually referred to "the day we took Fox Green beach," Ernest did not elaborate on anything "we" did after the landing. (He could well, of course, have been referring to Americans when he used "we.") But he told Leicester and Bill Van Dusen, another friend he had made on the flight from New York to London, otherwise, inventing for his brother a colorful account: he saw any number of men prone on the sand, that being their only way of avoiding fire; he had to kick a lieutenant lying next to him to get him to join him in moving up off the beach. He wrote his *Collier's* editor Henry La Cossitt in 1945 that when he landed on the beaches for the magazine he still had all those stitches in his head.

About ten days after the invasion Ernest again took up his assignment to write about the RAF. He went down to a testing site at Amesbury, near Stonehenge, to go up with the pilots of the Walker Tempests, refinements of the earlier Typhoons, which were the U.K.'s best flying hope against the German doodlebugs, or V-1 buzz bombs. While he was in Surrey, close to the coast of the English Channel, to see the 98th Squadron, a buzz bomb landed nearby and he and other reporters covering the squadron rushed out and took pieces of the exploded missile as souvenirs; Ernest got himself scolded and had to turn over the fragment he had picked up. He was frustrated by how physically far from the fighting he felt when he rode on bombing missions; once, Ernest asked a pilot to fly back over the sites he bombed so as to get a closer look. According to a pilot who talked to Carlos Baker, Ernest did enjoy a trip in a Mosquito fighter that actually tried to hit the V-1s, though the pilot had been strictly warned not to take him over enemy territory, let alone into a firefight; the pilot said that he was acting "against [his] better judgment"—a state he said was familiar to anyone who'd been around Ernest at such a time.

His admiration for the RAF notwithstanding, Ernest wanted to get to the front. On the way, he visited a villa in Cherbourg rented by Bill Walton, CBS correspondent Charles Collingwood, and John Palfrey, a British major, where visiting journalists held a sort of continuous party while covering the slow-moving front by day. Collingwood remembered that Ernest took a lot of notes, though no story appeared in *Collier's* from this period. After another visit to London, where he continued to court Mary Welsh, he decided to hook up with an armored division of General George Patton's Third Army, which had recently arrived in France. But when he did, the constant dust and mud irritated his throat and there was not enough action to suit him, for the division was well behind the front line. He was not interested in battles between armored tanks, nor did he like the general; his whole time with the division, he said, was an "abortion."

Instead, just after his forty-fifth birthday in July, he attached himself to the 4th Infantry Division, where he befriended General Raymond O. Barton. Tubby, as Barton's friends called him, became the subject of Ernest's article "The G.I. and the General," which would appear in the November *Collier's*. Meanwhile, Barton assigned Ernest a German motorcycle and sidecar, as well as a Mercedes convertible and a driver, Archie Pelkey, a twenty-nine-year-old redhead with a broken front tooth from Potsdam, New York, who would shepherd him all over France in the coming months. Correspondent Charles Collingwood observed about Ernest's ease with his superiors, "He spoke the same language as senior officers, and many of them sought his company and conceived a great respect and personal affection for him."

When Ernest met Colonel (later General) Charles "Buck" Lanham, his chances for getting a firsthand look at the fighting looked even brighter. Lanham was a short man, a West Point graduate from Washington, D.C., and a career soldier, just as were Ernest's good friends Charlie Sweeny and Chink Dorman-Smith. Buck first found out what Ernest was like on August 3 when he saw him standing on a street corner in the town of Villedieu-les-Poêles in Normandy. Ernest was watching the fighting when Buck caught sight of him, registering that Ernest was "standing poised as always on the balls of his feet. Like a fighter. Like a great cat. Easy. Relaxed. Absorbed. Intent. Watchful. Missing nothing." Buck would hear later how the town's inhabitants, mistaking Ernest for a colonel, had told him about some SS troops hiding in a farmhouse cellar behind the Allied line. Not knowing if anyone was really down there, Ernest called down orders to surrender, and then threw in three grenades. The relieved mayor called for two magnums of champagne in thanks.

Ernest was still experiencing severe symptoms of the traumatic brain injury he had suffered in the London car crash in May, including blurred vision, confusion, and constantly recurring headaches. On August 5 he suffered another head injury, said to be a possible concussion, which made his condition worse. Pelkey was driving him and Robert Capa in the motorcycle sidecar near St.-Pois when Pelkey made a wrong turn and drove right into the path of a German antitank gun. All three leapt out and into a

With General Charles "Buck" Lanham, Ernest's war
buddy, September 1944, Seigfried Line

ditch, when Ernest hit his head again. They were forced to remain in the
ditch until it was almost dark, when American gunfire made it safe for
them to emerge.

In a repeat of the house party at the Cherbourg villa, Ernest, Bill Walton,
and a crew of correspondents took up residence in the Hôtel de la Mère
Poulard at Mont-St.-Michel, where they went out to watch the war during
the days and at night ate superbly and drank copiously. Walton was becoming a good friend, as were several others among the journalists, a group that
included Shaw, Collingwood, Wertenbaker, and Capa; A. J. Liebling, covering the war for *The New Yorker;* Ira Wolfert, a NANA correspondent who
knew Ernest from Spain; Bill Stringer, a Reuters correspondent; and Helen
Kirkpatrick of the *Chicago Daily News.* The eminent film director John
Ford was another of the intimate group at Mont-St.-Michel; he was a Navy
commander and head of the photographic unit of the OSS. (Peter Viertel,
a Hollywood insider and friend of Ernest's, later admitted he found the
association of the film crew with the OSS "mysterious.") Ford shot film
of the correspondents in the unique setting and was responsible for some
of the only existing film footage of Ernest, which shows him walking across
the spit of land connecting the island to the mainland and poised against

the rocky outcrop and its monastery. Ernest was at his best on this brief working holiday, and his colleagues had mostly fond memories of him. Kirkpatrick, the only woman in the group, found him "good company, amusing, dogmatic and holding forth always on strategy and interpreting the next moves." Collingwood wrote, "When the mood was on him, as it usually was, he exuded good humor and charm. The mood was not always on him and he would lapse into periods of silence, or abruptness. . . . He could be a marvelous talker and raconteur and boon companion. . . . He did often dominate the conversation, out of sheer force of character and exuberance. But he was always willing to listen to others."

Ernest had other OSS contacts besides Ford. Outside of Chartres in late August, he ran into Colonel David Bruce, his old friend from the embassy in Cuba, harking back to the sub-hunting days. He persuaded Bruce to give him what turned out to be a valuable letter authorizing him to assume command of a group of Resistance fighters. Ernest had reached Chartres on his way south in the jeep driven by Red Pelkey, and, after a few nearby skirmishes, met Bruce in the village of Rambouillet, about twenty miles southwest of Paris, where Ernest had surrounded himself with French partisans. He commandeered a vacant hotel for several days to serve as a quasi-military headquarters, where he worked with Free French fighters in interrogating German prisoners and sending out intelligence patrols. He assembled a considerable stockpile of weapons in his room at the commandeered hotel.

Stories abound about Ernest's Rambouillet period. The best that can be done is to pick and choose from among them, since the veracity of each source is questioned by another, and it is difficult to ascertain what versions were, as Ernest would have it, "true." Carlos Baker, his first biographer, tried to integrate three wildly different accounts of Hemingway's actions at Rambouillet and the liberation of Paris. Frustrated beyond endurance, he asked his three sources, "Are you sure you were in the same war?" According to one source, an OSS officer, Ernest boasted that he could make a captive soldier talk. "Take his boots off," he reportedly ordered. "We'll grill his toes with a candle." Pinckney Ridgell, the cameraman for the Signal Corps unit who filmed the invasion and the fighting in Normandy, remembered Ernest striding around one of his two rooms in the hotel wearing no clothes while questioning French informers.

The two latter stories both seem out of character; they are almost certainly spurious. They are, however, good stories, and they are consistent with what many observers, especially correspondents, believed was Hemingway's character. Journalists liked Ernest. Not only did he make for good copy, but he also gave rise to colorful tales the correspondents could exchange, often at convivial meetings where alcohol flowed freely. The subject of these stories, moreover, was a fellow journalist, which made the stories of the bravery, irreverence, and toughness of "Papa" all the more appealing to his colleagues. Most of the correspondents at Rambouillet and in Paris during the liberation had also covered D-Day, many of them having landed on the beaches themselves, and they too were suffering from the trauma, dislocation, and hardships of war; believing in stories of Ernest's courage—and profane wit—under fire was both reassuring to them and flattering to their own self-image.

Moreover, Ernest may have felt under some pressure to provide good "material" for his colleagues, mainly because he liked them and wanted to help them. He may have felt pressure as well to perform for the camera, as it were. (Just as he had for photographers in Milan in his first war, grinning broadly in one shot, in the next attempting a carefree whistle.) Here, in the midst of a cataclysmic episode of world history and a critical period of the war, he was enveloped by his legend, which insisted on certain types of behavior. Acknowledging his own hopes and fears, assuming he had any, would have been difficult; it would have been equally so for him to have kept himself out of the limelight when he was used to an audience and knew how to charm them. Neither could he bring himself to do what he should have after his injury in London in May: seek out competent treatment, refrain from alcohol, and convalesce for several weeks as his doctors recommended. The legend had to be maintained, and in its service Ernest's truer self and his physical health were beginning to pay the price.

There is no question that Ernest played an important role in the Allied preparations to liberate Paris; Hemingway and his band of irregulars contributed by removing dangers on the route of General Philippe Leclerc and the Free French as they advanced on the capital. He later said he had mastered "the entire Kraut MLR," or Main Line of Resistance: he and his French partisans located mines, roadblocks, and any artillery lurking between the village and Paris. Bruce later spoke highly of Ernest and his operation, which the OSS officer joined enthusiastically in Rambouillet. But Ernest was blurring the line between reporting the war and waging it, going so far as to remove the correspondent's insignia from his uniform. In fact, he was acting in violation of the Geneva Conventions, which held that correspondents must stay out of combat—specifically, that they were not to bear arms. He was also annoying some of his fellow journalists, just as he impressed and entertained others. William Randolph Hearst, Jr., a correspondent for his father's newspapers, complained, "He was only a reporter the same as us, but he thought he was the Second Coming and acted like it." In the scant days before Leclerc's march on Paris, as correspondents converged on Rambouillet, several of them grew resentful about the number of rooms Ernest's operation was taking up when most reporters had no cover under which to sleep. Over dinner in the hotel dining room, Andy Rooney, then a *Stars and Stripes* reporter, described the beginnings of a fight between Ernest and Bruce Grant of the *Chicago Daily News*. An AP photographer, Harry Harris, inserted himself between the two men as things heated up. Ernest then stalked outside through a set of French doors; after cooling his heels for a minute he flung the doors open and asked Grant whether or not he was coming outside to fight. Rooney didn't record the denouement, only that he "could never take Hemingway seriously after that." As with so many of the World War II stories about Ernest, there is a contradictory report, which says that he walked up to Grant and knocked him to the floor with a punch.

Thousands of people who were present at Leclerc's triumphant liberation of Paris on August 25 have only the happiest memories of that day, and Ernest himself used the word "delirium" to describe it. The Resistance had already expelled the last German occupiers the day before, and Eisenhower agreed that Leclerc's 2nd French Armored Division should lead the march into the city. When Leclerc's men crossed the Seine, the bells of Notre Dame began to peal and Paris exploded with joy, greeting wave after wave of soldiers with passionate expressions of gratitude. The frenzy had not abated when the U.S. 4th Infantry Division arrived behind them, and Parisians hailed the Americans with champagne, embraces, and choruses of "La Marseillaise, " waving French flags brought out of long hiding. The day was chaotic. Pockets of Germans were still shooting and lobbing grenades and German tanks sat here and there, not all of them abandoned. Marching soldiers found it difficult to remain together in the crowds and were often carried off in the confusion.

Despite all the reporters and future historians present—including Brigadier General S. L. A. Marshall, chief historian of the European Theater of Operations—it is remarkably difficult to sort out all that happened that day. Different versions of Hemingway's actions vie with each other in color, intensity, and believability, as did his own, frequent retellings in later years. All too often he used the term "we" in speaking of the triumphant routing of the enemy from the city. By the end of his life he was telling his friend A. E. Hotchner that his little band of Free French irregulars had been the first into Paris, Hotch reporting that "Ernest and his boys had already liberated the Hôtel Ritz and were properly celebrating the event with magnums of champagne at the bar when . . . Leclerc came marching into Paris with what he thought was the first expeditionary force." One story claims that from a camp outside Paris, Ernest sent his Irregulars off to find a way into the city by way of a back road that wasn't rendered impassable by mines; he was said to be setting off when MPs surrounded the camp, and Patton himself announced that any journalist who made a move to get to Paris ahead of the American troops would be court-martialed. Again, the story, or parts of it, seems spurious.

The general shape of the legend that gradually came together is that Ernest and his band, its numbers in some stories inflated to two hundred or so, slipped into Paris by way of the Bois de Boulogne, where they came under fire, and fought stray Germans on the Champs-Élysées before drinking champagne atop the Arc de Triomphe. Next Ernest made his way to the Travellers Club, where he called for more drinks, finally pushing through the crowds at the Place de l'Opéra and "liberating" the Hôtel Ritz on the Place Vendôme, where he ordered a round of fifty martinis at the bar. That night, when Robert Capa arrived at the Ritz, Ernest's driver Archie Pelkey is said to have greeted him saying, "Papa took good hotel. Plenty stuff in cellar. You go up quick." By the next day, the last of the journalists had straggled in, most of them putting up at the nearby Hôtel Scribe or the Lancaster; Ernest entertained a large contingent of them for lunch at the Ritz, including Wolfert, Wertenbaker, Shaw, and Kirkpatrick. When Kirkpatrick announced that she had to leave to cover the victory parade, Ernest said, addressing her as Daughter, "Sit still and drink this good brandy. You can always watch parades, but you'll never again celebrate the liberation of Paris at the Ritz."

A curious gloss on the elusive nature of the truth in the days after the Allied invasion of France is provided, in fact, by the career trajectory of the Army's chief historian of the ETO, Brigadier General S. L. A. Marshall. The author of many best-selling accounts of World War II, Sam Marshall was a respected and acclaimed historian. Perhaps his wide popularity compromised his scholarship; his account of Hemingway in Paris was published in 1962 in the widely circulated *American Heritage* magazine with the not very scholarly title "How Papa Liberated Paris." In recent years, Marshall's accounts have been increasingly discredited, however; his grandson has written a memoir, *Reconciliation Road,* in which he describes coming to terms with Marshall's often inaccurate stories of the experiences of other soldiers, and his own, in World War II. One of the ironies of the metastory of Hemingway's actions in France after D-Day, in fact, is that

Marshall himself provided a dissenting view; he reported that Ernest did *not* liberate the Ritz.

As John Raeburn has pointed out, in a study of the formation and development of the Hemingway legend, the story of Ernest's liberation of Paris, or, for the nonbelievers of that story, his liberation of the Ritz, was colorful and dramatic enough to be "perfectly suited for journalists who wanted to convey the flavor of his personality." But the legend took shape at a point when reality, or, as Ernest might have it, the truth, was getting away from him, when his hold on reality was growing more and more tenuous, when stories were all he could catch hold of. The severe head injuries he sustained in the past four months; the enormous amount of alcohol he was consuming; the traumas of combat in the first war and the trauma ahead of him, in Hürtgenwald, in this one; his growing self-absorption, facilitated by sycophants—and what we might today call enablers—with whom he increasingly surrounded himself, made it harder and harder for him to see himself and the way before him clearly, never mind produce good work. His legend had begun to take on a life of its own with World War II, as reporters told their tales, and Ernest himself spun new stories like Rumpelstiltskin spinning straw into gold. Now, however, the stories were not gold, not creative efforts to be published by Scribner's as the new work of Ernest Hemingway. They were, nonetheless, still fictions.

TWENTY-FOUR

A certain fluidity characterizes not only Ernest's stories about World War II, but also the stories that other biographers and historians have told about his behavior during that time. To a great extent, this problem plagues any effort to write about war, since battlefield-level histories in particular rely a great deal on oral testimony. Every soldier has a story, and the term "war stories" has over the years come to carry a suggestion of inaccuracy—like fishing tales about "the one that got away." The Internet has only exacerbated this situation, so that stories of Hemingway's exploits in World War II continue to surface—including one description of Ernest, a brown-haired Illinois native, as a "red-headed Knickerbocker."

Undeniably, however, much of the legend building began with Ernest himself. Decades later, the comic/journalist Stephen Colbert memorably coined the term "truthiness" to recall the "gut feeling" that President George W. Bush used to justify the 2003 invasion of Iraq, a feeling Bush held seemingly in contradiction of all evidence or logic. Ernest could be said to have anticipated Colbert's point in the years immediately following the Second World War, when he began to pepper his writing with the words "true," "truth," "truly" and the phrase "to speak [or write] truly" with metronomic regularity— just as his ability to tell the truth seemed to begin a slow erosion. Ironically, this curious habit dovetailed with a diminution of his fictive powers, for after the war he would publish no more major fiction. It is true that Ernest had always been a bit cavalier with facts, especially when they were not flattering to him. But after the war, for many reasons, this tendency became more marked.

The erosion of Ernest's truth telling began with his traumatic brain injury in the car accident in London on May 24 and his subsequent concussion on August 5, which was the third such injury in his lifetime (the first having occurred with his wounding in Italy in 1918). Exacerbating the injury were drinking, war trauma, and the very male atmosphere in which he found himself during wartime. Daring and humor were valued above all else, journalists valorized for the risks they took. So-called war stories mushroomed, often contradicting themselves.

All this came at a particularly unfocused time in Ernest's life, when he was not writing fiction and not taking his journalistic duties very seriously either. He was ridding himself of a wife, who, as he saw it, humiliated him professionally, and he was in love with a new woman whom he intended to marry—not least because he sensed he might need a caretaker, if his confused thinking and various neurological problems were to continue (as would prove to be the case).

This new love affair began at a time when Ernest was having problems with his sexual potency—a common side effect of traumatic brain injury. Of course that problem fed on itself, undermining his confidence in an area that was for Ernest, with his fundamental, long-standing gender confusion, particularly fraught. His body was betraying him in other ways as well. He had thickened in the middle and would continue to do so; he was graying, and he had begun to assume—while only in his mid-forties—a grandfatherly mien. Ernest had been a hugely good-looking young man, and the disappearance of his youthful good looks may well have constituted another trauma, as it does in many such lives. He was aware of this at least on some level. The year before, he had written Martha, "I am ugly on the surface. When, I know now, everybody thought I was wonderful . . . looking in the mirror I never knew it or thought it."

A photo from 1939, taken in Sun Valley by Lloyd Arnold, shows a grinning Ernest with a paunch, a fishing rod attached to his belt, and a good-sized trout. His cheeks look like those of a squirrel storing nuts— a feature that shows up in several other photographs from his thirties and forties. He is wearing a wide-brimmed hat and resembles Teddy Roosevelt, his predecessor as America's great public outdoorsman. By the time the U.S. joined the war Ernest was markedly heavier. Because of sun exposure, which had already damaged his skin to the point of cancer—he said he was diagnosed with it, though it is not clear he was treated for it—he grew a long and bushy beard. Like many lonely men who grow facial hair when they are isolated and/or bored, he was not at all attached to his beard and cheerfully shaved it in 1944. With the beard he looked strangely different, almost another person; without it, age showed its inroads. Ernest was well on his way to the famous Papa visage of the 1950s—overweight, cheerful-looking, his (considerably more groomed) beard and thinning hair both white. In 1944–45, he had definitely reached middle age and looked, in fact, well past it.

This also coincided with a considerable decline in his charm. He retained his charisma, the quality he shared, somewhat to his dismay, with his mother, Grace Hall Hemingway, but his aura was changed. He projected a cheery, hail-fellow-well-met demeanor, but heavy drinking was increasingly a part of it. People wanted to get drunk with Papa—and the feeling was mutual. If he spun wild stories with little basis in fact, which he told and retold, with embellishments, over the course of a single evening, his companions, when they remembered such an evening themselves—well, that was Papa, a born storyteller. And he was cut a lot of slack for being drunk—which hardly anyone seemed to mind. His new persona was also becoming increasingly irascible and mean, no doubt owing to his brain injury.

If he talked about writing at all it was as a competition: he began to speak of going at it in the "ring" with partners like Tolstoy and Turgenev. His speech itself was changing, moving toward the clipped, telegraphic, and ungrammatical Indian-speak that Lillian Ross would re-create with such devastating accuracy in her *New Yorker* profile of 1950, just five or six years off. Peter Viertel remarked on this "limited" language, which "sounded like an affectation until you got used to it." It is tempting to see as symbolic a strange feature of this idiom: he no longer used the first-person singular. He almost never said "I."

* * *

As Ernest's relationship with Mary Welsh became more serious, some wreckage needed to be cleared away: Ernest's relationship with Martha. As it happened, Ernest was not against a divorce—quite the contrary. At this time, however, divorce was something over which he and Martha could fight—which they did, with great drama. By the time he met Mary again in Paris in late August, he had last seen Martha in the Dorchester after his traumatic brain injury. When she came into his hotel room at the hotel, Martha found him naked—evidently in order to discomfit her. She found him "shameful, arrogant, boastful, embarrassing." When she met him again in Paris in the fall, surrounded with his wartime posse of soldiers and reporters, he asked her to dinner with him. He was very aggressive, Martha said, treating her "like a cobra until the boys melted away with embarrassment." When she brought up getting a divorce, he became even meaner and borderline irrational, predicting that she would cause him to die in battle and leave his children "orphans." He threatened to shoot her before he would give her a divorce. Martha left in uncharacteristic tears.

Later that night, stopping by her room after his nightly poker game, Capa consoled her. Once she had established grounds for divorce, the photographer argued, Ernest would have to agree, so Capa recommended that she call Ernest's room and ask for Mary. Martha did, and Ernest became apoplectic in response. At Capa's prompting, she then said she knew all about Mary and thus he had to give her a divorce. Capa told her, "It will be all right now." In a scene shortly after, having heard Ernest go on about Mary, Capa said, "You know, Papa, you don't have to *marry* Mary." Ernest threw a bottle of champagne at him (and missed); their friendship was over.

At Christmastime, an officer friend talked Martha into visiting Ernest, then in Luxembourg with Buck Lanham's 22nd Infantry. It's unclear why Martha agreed, perhaps to convince him to agree to a divorce, perhaps simply because they were still married—though any hope of reconciliation had to have vanished. On Christmas Eve she joined Ernest in a late-night drink with General Barton for the general's fifty-fourth birthday. The next day they went to Rodenbourg, where Buck had his command post. Buck was unsympathetic to Martha in the extreme: "All hands despised her for her arrogance, her general snottiness," he said years later. That day, in front of Buck, Martha berated Ernest in French, ignorant of the fact that Buck had studied at the Sorbonne and knew the language well. Disgusted, Lanham later said, "She was a bitch from start to finish, and every member of my staff . . . thought so too." That night in Rodenbourg, Bill Walton met Martha for the first time and, finding her very attractive, asked her out to dinner. They then ran into Ernest, who invited himself along. During the drunken evening that followed, Ernest was so overtly mean to Martha that Walton remonstrated with him; Ernest replied, "Well, you can't shoot an elephant with a bow and arrow." After dinner, Bill witnessed an embarrassing display, as Ernest found a mop and bucket in a housekeeping closet at his Luxembourg hotel, put the bucket on his head and the mop over his shoulder like a weapon, and went off in search of Martha. Not for the first time when she found herself under the same roof as her husband, she locked the door to her room.

Buck had not met Mary, yet, given his dislike of Martha, was predisposed to like the newcomer, seeing she obviously made Ernest happier. All of September, when Ernest was with the 22nd, moving toward Germany and the Siegfried Line, he was writing Mary rapturous letters—and made a couple of trips back to Paris, once with a chest cold, where they spent long days in bed in the hotel, drinking, according to Mary, "a midmorning *quart de champagne*" and "a drink or two" at the Ritz bar before lunch. (She did not detail the drinks menu for the rest of the day.) He wanted Mary to see his Paris, taking her through Montparnasse and along the Seine, where they found all the bookstalls closed; the museums were closed as well.

Ernest wanted to show her, he said, the boxing matches at the Vel d'Hiv, the horse races at Auteuil, Montmartre, the Parc Montsouris, the Salon d'Automne, and, while they were at it, the Salon des Refusés—almost all of which would have been closed in wartime Paris. He wanted to show her New York: the Stork Club, El Morocco, the Colony (which he didn't like, he told her), and barrooms that were haunts of criminals. They could go to the Museum of Modern Art, the Met, the Museum of Natural History; they could walk in Central Park. Their talk was all of the future, as Ernest began to speak of Mary returning to Cuba with him after the war. After enumerating the nightclubs of Havana, he added that the best place, with the best food, was on the roof of the Pacifica. Going into great detail about the Finca routine, he described a typical morning: if Perrier-Jouet was not on ice, Scotch was for the morning, on arising; afterward, she could join him in a big breakfast that he described in detail. Now, in wartime, he was hungry all the time, he unnecessarily added.

But Mary had her doubts. One Paris afternoon he addressed her, "You goddamn, smirking, useless female war correspondent." When officers from the 22nd visited Paris, the cocktail hour in Mary and Ernest's suite at the Ritz went on too long, and at dinner one man passed out in his soup. Worse, Clare Boothe Luce, an accomplished woman whom Mary knew as the wife of the publisher of Time-Life—Mary's boss—was in the restaurant and came to sit with the Hemingway party. To Mary's horror, one soldier engaged her in insolent conversation, at one point telling her, "You ought to read a book, you dumb broad." Mary fled upstairs, where she found one of the officers had thrown up all over her bathroom; she cleaned it up and went to bed. When Ernest came up to the room he accused her of insulting his friends, after which Mary let him have it with both barrels. Ernest slapped her across the face. The fight continued, with Mary stooping to low tactics herself, baiting him to knock her head off and bring it on a platter to the regiment.

The next day they not only made up but went over their fight in frank detail. Ernest confessed that he had finally "discovered what went wrong" the night before. Ever alert when it came to a woman's hair, he asked whether Mary had gone to the hairdresser's the day before; when he learned she had, he confided, "Something she did to your hair made you look mean and malicious. She really changed the expression of your face. I didn't know what it was last night. But that was it." Martha had been Ernest's first blonde; her biographer said, "He took a close interest in her hair," once asking her to cut it in the current Hollywood look. Mary's hair was to become a total obsession with Ernest, possibly made more florid and pervasive as a result of his brain injury. She had intimations of this when she noticed his "favorite and most frequent song" was an old French folk tune whose lyrics ran: *"Auprès de ma blonde, qu'il fait bon dormir"* (Next to my blonde, it is so good to sleep).

Another quarrel was more serious in that it almost definitely revealed irrational, violent behavior that could well be a result of his brain injury. On a visit to Paris in the New Year, Buck Lanham brought Ernest a pair of German pistols in a velvet-lined case and a supply of ammunition. Ernest strutted about the suite—they were having a small gathering—with one of the loaded pistols under his arm. In the room was a photo of Mary and her then husband, Noel Monks (which Mary had inexplicably let him borrow, according to her story); showing it around and complaining about Monks's reluctance to give Mary a divorce, he placed it in the fireplace and took aim at it. Buck yanked Ernest's arm up, aborting what might have been, because of ricochets, a very dangerous shot. Ernest could not be stopped, however, and he took the photograph into the bathroom, put it in the toilet bowl, and fired at it six times. The shots caused a flood and destroyed the toilet, at a time when porcelain was virtually unobtainable. Once again, Mary fled. After another argument, Mary felt resigned, writing in hindsight, "I had never before been catapulted into the role of whipping boy, a part which I would play, unexpectedly, from time to time for years."

Mary's friends were sending her letters advising her not to marry Ernest. She evidently had her doubts, according to a story Irwin Shaw's biographer reports. One evening in the Ritz bar Mary and Irwin were having a long, intimate talk, when Mary interrupted and "flatly" asked Irwin to marry her. Irwin pointed out that they were both married, trying to turn her proposal into a joke. Instead, she flung back at him that if he wouldn't marry her she would marry Ernest. Shaw's biographer claims that Mary also "on at least one occasion" told Ernest that Irwin had a bigger penis.

Ernest pressed Mary for commitment, telling her that *he* was as committed "as an armored column in a narrow defile where no vehicle can turn and without parallel roads . . . and in favor of you sitting up straight in bed lovelier than any figurehead on the finest tallest ship." And on a night not long after, in bed, Ernest and she exchanged vows in their own marriage ceremony: "We would be faithful and true to each other, Ernest said. We would seek to understand and support each other in all times, troubles or triumphs. We would *never* lie to each other. We would love each other to the full extent of our capacities."

In a letter soon after, Ernest said he hoped neither of them would have to be journalists again, but for the time being he wanted to write a book, he told her, and he was going to do it first, not because he was selfish, but because it was his turn, much like, in his analogy, whose turn comes around first to use the bathroom. It was not clear what it was Mary wanted to "do," but whatever it was, Ernest, burned by his experience with Martha and her career, made clear that Mary's turn would come second, always. Similarly, apparently replying to a query from Mary about the nightlife in Havana, he dodged her question and said that he never drank or stayed up late when he was working. He intended to be the one who worked, he said—though he added that he would respect her wishes on the subject.

Surely Mary was smart enough to see that she would be quitting journalism. As a reporter, she had had only her salary to live on, and whatever remained from her peripatetic husband's paychecks. In this she was alone among Ernest's wives. Hadley and Pauline had their own separate incomes, and Martha was a well-paid writer. If Mary were to throw in her lot with Ernest, it would be for good, and she would have very little leverage in the relationship.

But the two of them, for the most part at this time, were tender with each other. In comparison to his correspondence with Martha, even while the marriage was doing very well, his letters to Mary were those of a happy man. Mary told him in a letter, not always articulately, why she loved him: for "your sudden sunny gaiety, uncalculated gaiety, wisdom, sincere craftsmanship, your love and generosity and kindness to your beasts, including me, your joy in small mortal things—sky birds, flowers, vegetables." They would have a boy and a girl, they agreed, and name them Tom and Bridget. He called her Kitten or Pickle; she called him Lamb.

In the meantime, the fighting in Europe continued, as the Allied forces made their way across Belgium and Luxembourg toward Germany. Buck Lanham and his 22nd were on the Belgian border, moving toward Liège, when Buck somewhat melodramatically cabled to Ernest a version of the rebuking words of King Henry V to the Duke of Crillon: "Go hang yourself, brave Hemingstein. We have fought at Landrecies and you were not there." Needless to say, Ernest rose to the occasion and made the dangerous trip north to rejoin Buck, spending three weeks there. One night he commandeered a deserted farmhouse nearby, where he and his friends conjured a meal of freshly killed chicken and quantities of wine; over the 22nd hung the beginning of the fighting along the Siegfried Line, and Buck ate and drank with relish, later telling Carlos Baker it was his happiest night of the war. Ernest thought that he had never been happier than in August and September 1944, comparing going into battle with starting off on a fox-hunt on a clear day. Two *Collier's* pieces came out of this period: the first, "The G.I. and the General," appeared in the November 4 issue, and the second, "War in the Siegfried Line," which described the horrific fighting at the Westwall on September 13 and 14, appeared on November 18.

In October, however, the inspector general of the U.S. Third Army in Nancy called Ernest for questioning about his activities in and near Rambouillet during the week of August 18–25. Other correspondents, no doubt including the reporter Bruce Grant, had registered complaints that Hemingway had violated the Geneva Conventions in bearing arms while acting as a correspondent. Were he to lose his case, he would be immediately sent back to the States and stripped of his accreditation as a correspondent. The colonel and OSS operative David Bruce, who wrote a letter of support that proved useful in the proceedings at Nancy, characterized the complaint: "There was considerable feeling displayed by a few of [the reporters] against Ernest, apparently for having been first on this particular scene. He was obliged . . . to push a couple of them around with the back of his hand." Bruce bemoaned "the lodging of jealous charges against" his friend, including removing the correspondent's insignia from his jacket (Ernest said he may have removed the jacket in the hot weather); making a colonel his chief of staff (Ernest claimed that he was a liaison man for the colonel, and that he himself was addressed by military titles only in an honorary way—as a man from Kentucky is a Kentucky colonel); stocking his room with arms and turning it into a map room (Ernest claimed he needed maps for his reportage, and his room was simply a convenient place for the military to store arms). Bruce's letter anticipated all these charges, casually mentioning, for instance, Ernest working "in shirtsleeves." The letter further stated, "Ernest, as a war correspondent, did not carry arms, but he had as workmanlike a lot of partisans under his informal command as one could wish for." Ernest, Bruce went on, "unites . . . that rare combination of advised recklessness and caution that knows how properly to seize upon a favorable opportunity which, once lost, is gone forever. He was a born leader of men, and, in spite of his strong independence of character, impressed me as a highly disciplined individual."

Ernest had to perjure himself answering these questions, and his interrogators probably knew it; the procedure was, most likely, only a formality. They were trying Ernest only because there had been complaints about his behavior from other journalists, and likely had no intention of finding him guilty or meting out punishment or censure. Ernest had plenty of support for his story, including another testimonial from Major James Thornton and from various witnesses who swore they never saw Ernest carrying a gun. The inspector general found "no violation by him of the existing regulations for war correspondents."

Ernest got off scot-free, which he took as permission to tell anyone and everyone that he did in fact fight in World War II. Years later he wrote to scholar Charles Fenton saying he had not wanted to become a commissioned officer in the war because he would have been put to work as a noncombatant writer. He explained that he had unofficially fought in the war, but said illogically that anyone could look up his official records. If they did, he continued, they would find he had been awarded a Bronze Star. He had not received the Distinguished Service Cross, he explained, only because "technically" a civilian.

In the last weeks of October he finally had news of Jack, who had been wounded, captured, hospitalized, and sent to a prisoner of war camp in Germany. Jack had had the great good luck of being recognized by the man who interrogated him prior to his medical treatment, an Austrian who had known Jack as a child at Schruns. The Austrian's girlfriend was Tiddy, Jack's nursemaid. Ernest learned this only much later, and, for the time being, because his plans were already set, he dispatched Mary to find out whatever she could about Jack, and was extremely grateful when she asked to be sent to the front line so she could bring back word.

That same month Ernest also became reacquainted with a woman whom he had first met on a crossing on the *Île de France* in 1934, when he and Pauline were on their way home from Africa. Marlene Dietrich had by now become another member of his stable of beautiful celebrities, which at this point included Ingrid Bergman and would expand to accommodate Ava Gardner and the socialite Slim Hayward, along with some lesser lights. To all these women Ernest professed his undying love; to his great disappointment, to a one they evidently chose not to notice his sexual attentions. Though they were drawn to Ernest by his charisma and charm, none of them seems to have wanted to sleep with him—a new wrinkle for the aging and overweight Ernest. He called them each Daughter, and they called him Papa, and that was the best he could do. He made the most of it, indulging in jests and verbal horseplay with Dietrich and asking her to sing to him—which she often did, according to Mary, perched on the edge of the bathtub as he shaved. It was Dietrich whom Ernest had sent as an envoy to Mary after the quarrel in which he hit her. His letters to Daughter, over the years (Dietrich was two years younger), are indistinguishable from passionate love letters, yet their relationship remained platonic; the same is true of his letters to the other women. That Dietrich was sometimes said

With Marlene Dietrich on board the *Normandie,* traveling from France to New York, 1938

to be bisexual or lesbian seems to have been part of the appeal. Ernest had always liked lesbians.

On November 3 Ernest left Paris again to rejoin the 22nd Regiment; the 4th Infantry Division was commencing a campaign to invade and win the Hürtgenwald, a heavily wooded region just south of Aachen and west of Bonn, the Allies' first incursion into Germany itself and, ultimately, across the Rhine. Ernest arrived November 9 in a jeep driven by his Free French friend Jean Decan and accompanied by Bill Walton. He would be with the 22nd from November 15 to December 4.

Hürtgenwald was a bloodbath, and there was no room for heroics on Ernest's part. In fact, the fighting seems to have humbled him. He told Mary that were it not for his witnessing this battle he would never have known the American people were so "wonderful." The soldiers saluted him and armed him, which made him proud, he told her. Ernest's letters to Mary in this period, almost every one of them, describe Hürtgenwald as one of the worst battles he had seen and one of the worst ever fought. In a five-day attack early in November Allied forces advanced only one and a half miles. Conditions were terrible—unrelenting rain, snow, and cold; over the three months of battle, nine thousand men died of pneumonia, trench foot, frostbite, and combat fatigue or shell shock. The Germans made the Americans pay for every inch of progress. They had left behind them in the forest mines and hidden bunkers housing German soldiers. Battle conditions were extremely unfavorable. Trees were everywhere, without even a firebreak that soldiers could use to advance. Their tanks could make no progress, and their bullets often ricocheted off trees, turning into friendly fire. Meanwhile the Germans were dropping shells that exploded in the treetops, sending down a rain of shrapnel and missiles of exploded tree that hit the GIs from above.

Ernest spent a lot of time in Buck's plywood trailer in the evenings; during the day he tried to stay out of the way. The nights were enjoyable, and Ernest held forth on everything from the mating habits of lions to bravery in combat. On one of these evenings J. D. Salinger and his friend Werner Kleeman decided to go look up Ernest. Salinger was a twenty-five-year-old who had risen to staff sergeant in the 12th Infantry, 4th Division, which had landed on D-Day, and an as yet scantily published writer. Ernest had met him in August in Paris, and Salinger had given him some stories to read. Ernest thought the young man was very talented, and they struck up a friendship. In Hürtgenwald, Salinger and Kleeman found Ernest in the PR office, a luxurious spot as it had its own generator; Ernest was reclining on a couch, wearing a sun visor, writing on a yellow pad. Ernest was glad to see Salinger and his friend and he broke out a bottle of champagne. One tall tale about the occasion has it that Ernest was idly chatting while handling a Luger when someone asked which was the better weapon, the German Luger or the Colt .45. Ernest thought the Luger was better, and to prove it, turned and shot the head off a chicken. The story is almost certainly apocryphal, as is a similar, even more unlikely account that has Ernest providing several chickens in this fashion for a feast he had assembled for Buck Lanham at the Westwall in September. As Seán Hemingway, Ernest's grandson—albeit not an eyewitness—points out, shooting the head off a chicken is actually very hard to do. Equally dubious is the contention that Salinger, who had an undescended testicle, "revealed" this fact to Ernest on one of these occasions—the verb is ambiguous, no doubt purposely. The story, like the well-known one about F. Scott Fitzgerald showing Ernest his genitals in the bathroom at Michaud's, *sounds* like a Hemingway story, but is almost certainly not true.

Ernest had another interesting encounter during his down time in Hürtgenwald. An Army psychiatrist whom Baker identifies as Major Maskin was brought in to examine the men for combat fatigue. The story Ernest told was that he had a great time with the psychiatrist, telling him he wanted to have intercourse with cats. Bill Walton remembered their inter-action differently, and didn't use Maskin's name; he also identified him as a colonel, not a major. The psychiatrist, in conversation with the two men, was scoffing at the idea of courage as a psychological state and predicted that Ernest, like the other men, would be broken by the stress of combat. As Walton told it, Ernest got beet red and pounded on the table, calling the psychiatrist "an ignoramus, an uneducated fool, a pervert, and enemy spy." Walton noted that he thought, "Something that was very deep in [Ernest] had been touched."

The incident stayed with Walton. He came to know Ernest very well during the war, more than perhaps anyone else then in Ernest's life except for Buck—and Buck could see no faults in his friend until well after the war. Walton found Ernest wonderful company: "He made me laugh more deeply than anyone else I've ever known. He had such a sense of the ridicu-lous." He believed a lot of Ernest's "silliness" during the war, like going after Martha with a mop and a bucket on his head, had as much to do with mental illness as with being drunk. Walton later was adamant about what he thought was wrong with Ernest: "He was a classic manic-depressive his whole life," he told Hemingway historian Denis Brian. "Certainly. Abso-lutely," he answered when Brian asked him if Ernest talked so frequently about death because of his condition. "I think he was perfectly aware of his own strain of madness, that he was a manic-depressive." The Army psychiatrist no doubt saw plenty of combat fatigue, and even Ernest would likely not have denied he felt it—even as a supposed observer—though he assuredly would not have admitted it to a psychiatrist.

American troops finally made their way through the Hürtgenwald in mid-December, Lanham's battalion taking the villages of Gey and Gross-hau, the latter in a bloody hand-to-hand battle in which Ernest was almost continuously under fire. By the time the shooting stopped, 24,000 Ameri-cans were killed, captured, or missing. With the tragic advantage of hind-sight, it was clear to many that the entire expedition was a mistake. The troops should never have advanced through the Hürtgen Forest, observers said. They should have gone around it.

* * *

Ernest's war was effectively over, though he made another trip to Luxem-bourg where the Germans were making what turned out to be an easily tamed counterattack; it was on this trip that Bill Walton saw him go after

Martha with a mop. It is a small miracle that Ernest got through the war unharmed, which came about for no particular reason. It was not as if he had stayed out of danger.

Otherwise, Ernest was in Paris, holding court in the Ritz again, though he was very ill with a chest cold for over a month. In December Paris's king and queen of the intellectual prom, Jean-Paul Sartre and Simone de Beauvoir, paid a visit to his sickbed. Ernest later told critic Charles Poore that he had a tryst with de Beauvoir that night but was unable to get an erection—he said nobody who had been through Hürtgenwald could. He did the best he could, he told Poore, and then collapsed, coughing and spitting up blood all over her, which he claimed "impressed" her.

Perhaps correspondingly, Ernest's capacity to find offense was as robust as ever. Around this time William Saroyan ran into Ernest, surrounded by a group of correspondents, outside the bar of the Hôtel Scribe. Saroyan remarked on Ernest's having shaved his beard, at which the older writer took umbrage. A few nights later, as Captain Peter Wykeham reported, Ernest saw Saroyan at the same bar and made a comment about "that lousy Armenian son of a bitch." Saroyan's friends took offense at *that*, and a brawl involving several men resulted, at which the management intervened and they all were thrown out, Ernest, Wykeham said, "laughing like a hyena."

All sorts of soldiers from the 22nd Regiment paid calls on Ernest, as did admirers Henry North and Michael Burke, who had met him on his plane from the U.S. in April 1944. Burke and North were charter members of a fantasy organization called the Valhalla Club. Because the U.S. president was the commander of the armed forces, all drinks ordered by the Valhallans were to be charged to him. North and Burke were among those to whom Ernest read several of his poems one night, as was David Bruce, the officer who testified for him at the proceedings in Nancy. Among them were the intimate "First Poem to Mary," "Second Poem to Mary," and "Now Sleeps He with That Old Whore Death." Later Ernest read these to the Wertenbakers and Bill Walton, followed by a scurrilous one entitled "To Martha Gellhorn's Vagina," which made a comparison to the baggy neck of a hot water bag, and which embarrassed everyone.

Ernest was tempted, he told Buck Lanham, to stick with the war until it was over—not so much to report on it, as he was no longer producing pieces for *Collier's*, but because he felt most alive when he was in the thick of combat. He likened this emotional sense to hearing one had inherited a huge sum of money, and compared it as well to the feeling of immortality he had experienced in his first war. He acknowledged that this elation made little sense, but he compared it to a liquor ration, and said he had so much for himself that he would split it with Buck just as he would liquor. His all-time favorite phrase in the war, in fact, was "ballroom bananas," a term of unknown but possibly British origin meant to convey the senselessness of war and, all too often, the bungling of military plans.

Meanwhile, Mary had asked Charles Wertenbaker, her boss at *Collier's,* to grant her a year's sabbatical as of the end of March, and managed to get travel orders that would take her across the Atlantic on a troopship. (Mary, in her words, "begged" to go by way of a British one, since their American counterparts were "desert dry.") Ernest meanwhile sailed on March 6, stopping off in London to visit Martha at the Dorchester, where she was sick in bed with the flu. They had long before agreed on a divorce, and this occasion was the last time he would see her. She wrote to her mother, "I simply never want to hear his name mentioned again; the past is dead and has become ugly. . . . A man must be a very great genius to make up for being such a loathsome human being."

Ernest made a number of nasty remarks about Martha in the wake of their relationship, but far fewer than his disposition might lead one to suspect and fewer than his biographers have claimed. Most of his complaints were about her absence from the Finca on reporting trips; what he called her poor writing; her competitiveness (she would compete with the fireman carrying her out of a burning building, he said); her vanity and reliance on beauty aids; what he called her phoniness and pretension; and her selfishness. Describing the Martha character to his beloved in *Across the River and into the Trees,* the Colonel: "She had more ambition than Napoleon and about the talent of the average High School Valedictorian. . . . She is too conceited ever to be sad, and she married me to advance herself . . . and have better contacts for what she considered her profession." He was especially mean when in the early 1950s he inscribed a copy of *For Whom the Bell Tolls* for collector Lee Samuels, apropos of Martha—and perhaps his enduring resentment of Gertrude Stein—"A cunt is a cunt is a cunt." Ernest almost never used this word.

He was capable of a bit more perspective on his failed third marriage, however. Not long after the marriage was over, Ernest wrote to Charles Scribner asking if he had any word from her (Martha had been a Scribner's writer, though she would soon move on to Doubleday), adding, thoughtfully, "Martha was a lovely girl though. I wish she hadn't been quite so ambitious and war crazy." (He got on the subject, however, by way of telling Scribner that he had a new maid called Martha and that he enjoyed giving her orders.) He would later give A. E. Hotchner a considered and quite fair assessment of what went wrong: "The last time with Miss Martha it was a break to break up on acct. no children, no love, she was making more money than I was and convinced she had a much better future without me and was probably right since our interests and tastes were not the same and I liked to write and could not match her in ambition."

Ernest would write a long and angry unsent letter to Martha in 1946 expressing great bitterness about the help he had given her with her writing, sometimes expressed in cruel exaggerations. But he also had written her a remarkably tender letter the year before. He began by giving her news about each of his sons, asserting that they loved her very much and talked of her "very affectionately." He reported on the cats ("cotsies") and described the damage to the Finca from a recent hurricane. Evidently they had agreed on a cover story when they last saw each other in London, and he assured her he was keeping to it. "Everybody friendly. Everybody respectful. No scandal. Two people been married and were busting up. Bout as dignified as could be." Those who had been friends with both, he went on, were not taking sides. He had packed her things at the Finca, he said, "with sad reverence." If she needed the divorce to go through quickly for any reason, he would see to it she got it, adding, "You have a right to anything you want." Finally, he wrote, "Also if you and [your] Mother ever want to use this place no reason why not." If he seldom called women by the crudest of terms, by the same token he seldom spoke so highly of anyone who had ever crossed him, or made such extravagant promises. The letter was, according to the editor who published it, probably—like the 1946 one—never sent.

*   *   *

Ernest saw his experiences in World War II in superlatives. Unfortunately, that was how he described them, time after time, to others. His tales caused real distress to two of the people whose opinions he most cared about, and whom he would probably count as his best friends: Archie MacLeish and Buck Lanham. In August 1948 Archie would receive a jovial, bloodthirsty letter from Ernest, probably written while drinking, noting the number of "Krauts" Ernest had killed: it was the letter of a braggart telling tall tales almost compulsively, an exaggeration or lie in nearly every sentence, the grimmest exploits described in glib, offhand fashion. MacLeish would seal the letter in his archives at the Library of Congress for fifty years—so damaging did he think it was to Ernest's reputation. It goes without saying that his view of Ernest was irreparably damaged as well. The same holds true for Buck Lanham, long a Hemingway stalwart who thought his friend could do no wrong, until he saw in the years after the war Ernest repeatedly mistreating his wife and telling stories Buck knew to be untrue. After Ernest's death, when Buck began to correspond with Carlos Baker about Ernest's actions in the war, he was "flattened" when Baker showed him an early draft of his biography and some of Ernest's letters to Mary, which were "full of chest-beating." He asked Baker, "Why of all people did he feel he had to inflate himself in this way?" Echoing MacLeish's response, he said he felt "almost physically ill" at the picture of his old friend that was emerging from the self-serving, bombastic untruths. By the end of the war, Ernest was becoming someone who could make his friends recoil.

TWENTY-FIVE

When he returned to Cuba from World War II in early March 1945, Ernest had not published anything significant since *For Whom the Bell Tolls,* five years earlier. As he wrote in his increasingly deployed verbal shorthand, he had been working hard on his writing, but "is difficult on acct. five years do opposite of writing." He had plenty of material, he told Max Perkins, though he did not have a war novel in mind. Rather, he intended a novel—surely his most ambitious yet—built around the three environments of the Sea, the Air, and the Land; specifically, the Air would be about the RAF, and the Land about Europe during the war. He had the Sea portion "ready to write" when he left for Europe, he said, indicating that he intended it to be about his sub-hunting adventures. Ernest would go on projecting the ambitious Sea-Air-Land work for the next ten years, although in the interim it morphed into several different novels that diverged from the original template. He also referred to it as the "Big Book." As the larger concept began to dissipate, he would drop references to the Air and Land enterprises and instead talk about the Sea book, though even that would break down into separate projects.

He had a hard time getting down to it, however. In April Ernest told Buck Lanham he didn't give a damn about writing; he wrote Mary that he wished he could hire some other people—like James Thurber—to do his writing for him. After several false starts, however, he was launched, and began with the Sea book; specifically, what would become the Bimini section of the tripartite novel *Islands in the Stream*—not the sub-hunting tale he'd planned. The novel was set in 1936, when Ernest first visited Bimini. The autobiographical persona of this story was Thomas Hudson, a painter who lives in Bimini with his three sons, unmistakably based on Jack, Patrick, and Gregory. (The Hudson persona would later be split into two parts, the second being Roger Davis, a good friend of Hudson's who is a writer; the identities of the three sons would be transposed and otherwise modified.) The Bimini section of the novel would conclude with the deaths of the two younger sons and their mother in a car accident; when "Cuba," the second part of the novel, opens, Hudson's eldest son, based on Jack, has been killed in the war. The profound parental ambivalence indicated by this fictional scheme reflected Ernest's own, extremely conflicted relations with Jack, Patrick, and Gregory.

The last news Ernest had of his son Jack had been in November 1944, when Mary Welsh, from her posting in the Vosges mountains near Germany, reported that Jack was in a German POW camp with nonserious wounds in his right arm and shoulder from grenade fragments and carbine fire. Later, Ernest learned that soldiers from the 4th Armored Division had freed him from a POW camp near Hammelberg; he was recaptured four days later and confined to a camp in Nuremberg. After V-E Day on May 8, Jack was released from the camp twenty-five pounds lighter; Ernest expected him to arrive at the Finca in June to recuperate. He was fairly bursting with pride over his son's exploits. He bragged to Max that although Jack's wound was serious enough that doctors had threatened to amputate his arm, his son was offhand about it, noting blithely that it had loosened up his tennis serve. Before Jack had left for the war Ernest had criticized him in a letter to Martha as too concerned with his tennis game and fly-fishing, cruelly noting that he was not stupid so much as "dazed." Jack had matriculated successfully enough at his boarding school, Storm King, that he had been admitted to Dartmouth, and now, after the war, would take up his studies again at the University of Montana, chosen in part for its proximity to excellent trout fishing. Though Ernest would later grow frustrated at Jack's search for a vocation and series of failures at jobs, in the aftermath of the war Jack was riding high in Ernest's estimation.

With Patrick and Gregory, things were a bit more complicated. In March, on his return from Europe, Ernest met Patrick's train in New York. After a few days in the city, during which Ernest brought Patrick to Abercrombie & Fitch to buy him a shotgun, George Brown, the owner of the boxing gym on West 47th Street where Ernest sparred, put father and son on the train to Miami; from there they would pick up Gregory in Key West. Pauline, angry at not being consulted about the boys' plans, said it was not convenient for Ernest to pick up Gregory at this time; she sent him to Cuba by himself a day or two later. Patrick was on vacation from the Canterbury School, located in New Milford, Connecticut, a lay Catholic boys school where he was a junior. (Pauline, who had raised Patrick and his brother as Catholics—both were altar boys—had initially sent them to parochial schools in Key West.) Canterbury was not as academically rigorous as some boys' prep schools, but it was in the first tier of Catholic boarding schools. Ernest was dubious about Canterbury, where the boys went daily to chapel, fearing that "the Church" was insidiously affecting Mousie (the family nickname for Patrick). Undoubtedly in part because Pauline chose it, Ernest professed to a full-on hatred of the school (which Gregory too would enter in the fall), calling it one of "those snot schools." Yet Ernest was proud of Patrick's football prowess at Canterbury, although the boy did not play varsity until he was a senior.

Gregory (known as Gigi or Giggy, pronounced with hard g's) was the son who would always arouse the strongest feelings in his father—for good or ill. One of the defining events in Gregory's life had been, without question, the end-of-season pigeon-shooting contest at Havana's Club de Cazadores del Cerro on July 26, 1942. In interviews and a book about his father, Greg would later provide many details about this contest, many of them inaccurate; Ernest would tell the story many times as well, just as unreliably—as would scholars and biographers. Ernest also made the contest a central incident in the story "I Guess Everything Reminds You of Something," probably written around 1955 and not published until after his death. In brief: Greg had learned to shoot that summer and had won some minor matches. Both Patrick and Ernest entered the tournament that summer as well, but were eliminated in an early round. Greg made it into the finals when he dramatically shot a certain number of birds without a single miss. Eventually, he lost. (How badly he lost is a matter for debate; accounts differ, and in his 1976 book, *Papa*, Greg leaves the impression he won.)

The salient facts are that the eleven-year-old made it into the final rounds of an international contest and acquitted himself brilliantly, making his father proud and giving himself a crucially important dose of self-confidence. The combination of his age and his performance made for some media attention in the Havana papers, and Patrick remembered that his brother was known as *El Pequeño Rey de la Escopeta* (The Little King of the Shotgun). "The shoot was the turn of the corner for Giggy," Ernest wrote reassuringly to Martha. He held the victory inside him, Ernest said, like it was money in the bank, telling Martha the children "are comeing along all right now."

Things were not "all right" as far as the children were concerned, however. Gregory in particular was a problem. As a young boy, Greg had been left with his nurse, Ada Stern, while his mother was away on frequent trips, the most notable his parents' African safari, which took them away for a full year; Greg turned two while they were gone. During his mother's absence, Ada apparently threatened to leave the boy as well whenever he misbehaved. Greg found that he derived enormous comfort at the time from taking his mother's stockings from her drawer and rubbing the silky material against his cheek.

By the time Gregory was ten, he found that other articles of women's clothing both soothed and excited him, especially if he put them on. It is not clear when Ernest first learned about this habit of Greg's, which he found most disturbing, nor is it clear when Pauline learned of it. Accounts vary. Biographer Jeffrey Meyers wrote in 1999 that Gregory was found with women's clothing in the summer of 1946, at age fifteen. According to this story, Mary found she was missing some French underwear, eventually firing the Cuban maid she believed responsible for its disappearance. But that fall, when Greg was away at school, Mary discovered the lingerie under the mattress of his bunk bed.

Other accounts put Ernest's discovery of Greg's tendency much earlier. Donald Junkins, a poet and friend of Greg's, told *Chicago Tribune* reporter Nara Schoenberg that when Greg was about ten, Ernest found him *wearing* his wife's underwear—only this time the wife was Martha, not Mary. Junkins says Ernest "went berserk" at this discovery. Reporter Gerald Clarke, in another account, wrote that Greg told him he was "about twelve years old" when Ernest walked in on him "trying on a pair of his mother's nylons." Greg told Clarke that his father had "a look of horror on his face," and that weeks later he said to his son, "Gigi, we come from a strange tribe, you and I."

Both accounts of Ernest's response—whether he "went berserk" or had an expression of "horror"—were recorded many years after the fact; it is difficult to say exactly what Ernest made of his discovery at the time. A letter that Ernest wrote Pauline in June of 1941 suggests that Junkins is correct that Greg was around ten when his father saw him with women's clothes: "Giggy is better all the time I think," Ernest wrote. "He has the biggest dark side in the family except me and you and I'm not in the family." If this is any indication, and if in fact it conveys in oblique fashion Ernest's discovery of Greg's behavior, it seems that he did not feel he had to tell Pauline specifically what he had seen. It also suggests that he did not draw any conclusions about Greg and his sexual or gender orientation—beyond finding such matters "dark"—and that he may have hoped the problem would go away. It is also interesting that Ernest felt a bond with Greg either in spite of or because of his son's proclivities. Not specifically—Ernest never dressed in women's clothing—but in the sense that he perceived that the "dark side" was not only the source for his own demons and those of his son, but that it was perhaps the source of their gifts as well.

Something of Ernest's feelings about Greg are revealed in a similar-sounding paragraph in the Sea manuscript that Ernest began sometime after the war, later incorporated in *Islands in the Stream*. In a description of Thomas Hudson's youngest son, Andrew, who bedevils his older brothers, Ernest wrote:

> The smallest boy was fair and looked like a pocket battleship. He was a copy of Thomas Hudson, physically. . . . He was a devil too, and dev-iled both his older brothers, and he had a dark side to him that nobody except Thomas Hudson could understand. Neither of them thought about this except that they recognized it in each other and knew it was bad and the man respected it and understood the boy's having it. . . . He was a boy born to be quite wicked who was being very good and he car-ried his wickedness around him transmuted into a sort of teasing gaiety. But he was a bad boy and the others knew it and he knew it. He was just being good while his badness grew inside him. (*IIS*, 50–51)

Here, noting that not only did Andrew, or Greg, have a dark side, Heming-way indicates that Thomas Hudson, and by extension himself, shared this dark side with his son. Of course, the usual caveats about reading fiction autobiographically apply.

Ernest's preoccupation with his son's problems of identity was compli-cated by a further development in his creative life. At the same time as he began writing what would become *Islands in the Stream,* he found himself commencing another, quite different novel, *The Garden of Eden*. In the lat-ter, a strange novel about androgyny, sexual doubling, and gender changes, often in fetishistic relation to hair, Ernest was admitting, if only in his fic-tion and if only to himself, his own "dark side," again with confusion over sexuality at the heart of it. In time, Greg would bravely, if tragically, con-front this "side" of himself. With Ernest, it was to be a very different story.

Ernest's confusion in these matters goes, of course, back to his child-hood, when Grace Hemingway dressed him and his sister Marcelline in the same outfits. Grace persisted with this sham twinhood even after the children were of school age. "We wore our hair exactly alike," added Mar-celline. Ernest did not get his first haircut until he was six. Grace paid a good deal of attention to the children's hair color and haircuts. Ernest internalized Grace's intense interest until it grew to be a private obsession, entangled with issues of gender, sexual identity, and sexuality.

Ernest was guarded about these preoccupations as an adolescent and young man, though he always took great interest in his wives' hair color and haircuts, often linking them to a certain gender fluidity that seemed to transfix him. Though Ernest would much later write, in a sketch cut from *A Moveable Feast,* just how lively a role Hadley's red-gold hair played in their sexual lives, it is difficult to read this as evidence, partly because of the date of composition—decades after the events described. The sketch records a conversation the two had about timing the growth of their hair and their haircuts so they could be identical. They were frightened and excited by the prospect, but resolved to ignore the opinions of others, acting in the service of their own pleasure. Again, it is difficult to know just how to evaluate this sketch; certainly Ernest is overstating Hadley's interest in haircut experiments, though most likely she would have gone along with his wishes.

The fiction that dates from the years of his marriage to Hadley, however, does not make hair and gender issues central concerns in the way his later writing would. In *The Sun Also Rises,* much is made of Lady Brett's mannishness, which in no way compromises her sexual attractiveness to Jake or the other men in the novel. "Her hair was brushed back like a boy's," Hemingway writes. "She started all that" (*SAR,* 22). Much has been made, in fact, of Brett's mannishness, particularly in relationship to Jake's war wound: it seems—the text is guarded—that Jake has lost his penis. Much has been made as well of Jake's wound as a symbol, though Hemingway is at pains in the novel to indicate that the wound affected Jake only in that he could not have intercourse; in other words, it seems to be Hemingway's intent that Jake's wound "mean" nothing. It is simply a plot point. If this aspect of Ernest's first major novel has received a good share of critical attention, the fact that it is indeed a plot point has not received enough. Why would Hemingway make this the most salient feature of the main character in his first real novel? Why, at the outset of his career, create a castrated hero? The move seems especially anomalous in light of the pains Ernest was already taking to cultivate the manliest of reputations. He never commented on or explained his decision to inflict on his fictional character this particular wound.

There are indications, however, that the idea of such wounds was a bit of an obsession in itself. He later said that he had been "nicked in the scrotum" in the First World War and said to several others he had spent time in the "genito-urinary" ward in the hospital after a mysterious "wool infection" set in and that his testicles were "swollen up like footballs." That's where he got the idea for Jake Barnes's wound, he said.

Indeed, it was perhaps not such a remarkable decision in a man so conflicted about basic questions of gender. Few would dispute that Jake Barnes in most respects stands in for the author, and Hemingway throughout his life and work explored obsessively such issues. But the autobiographical fallacy—that we must not take details from the fiction as evidence for the life—reminds us to read Jake's plight with caution; in fact, Ernest almost certainly was not at the time aware of any relation between Jake's plight and his own conflicts about assigning sexuality.

Ernest only began to write directly about these preoccupations after World War II. Yet already, in some of his major prewar writings, he was describing lovers who merged with each other, becoming one, in a state in which neither was male or female. Hemingway heroes and heroines commonly speak of wanting to be the other. In *A Farewell to Arms* Catherine Barkley tells Frederic Henry, after suggesting, in order that they "both be alike," that she should have her hair cut and he should let his grow: "I want you so much I want to be you too." Frederic answers, "You are. We're the same one" (*FTA,* 299). In *For Whom the Bell Tolls,* Robert Jordan asks Maria to have her very short hair (her head had been shaved by the Fascists) shaped by a coiffeur so they might look alike, and Pilar observes that they look like brother and sister. The lovers tell each other several times, "I am thee and thou art me," merged in such a way as to go beyond sexual difference. And such stories as "The Last Good Country," also written after the war, also treat of haircuts that make a boy and a girl the same. In this case, Nick Adams's sister, Littless, has joined her brother in flight in the woods after he has violated a game law by shooting a heron (as Ernest had in 1915, a traumatic memory). She cuts her hair off, telling Nick, "It's very exciting. Now I'm your sister but I'm a boy too." An undercurrent of incestuous danger runs throughout the story, Littless telling Nick she wants to marry him and have his children. He tells himself, "I guess those things straighten out. At least I hope so" (*CSS* 531, 535). The story ends with Nick reading aloud to his sister from *Wuthering Heights,* the romantic novel in which Catherine Earnshaw famously declares, "I am Heathcliff."

After the war, these concerns become central to almost all of Ernest's fiction. *The Garden of Eden,* which he began writing in late 1945, tells the story of several months in the marriage of David Bourne and his wife, Catherine, who are honeymooning on the Riviera in Le Grau-du-Roi— where Ernest and Pauline had honeymooned in 1927. Catherine has her hair cut to match her husband's, which sets off almost constant gender reversal, as husband and wife repeatedly cut and dye their hair. Ernest makes much of their platinum hair and brown skin, which becomes darker as they obsessively sunbathe. In this, the most explicit of Hemingway novels, Catherine becomes David's boy, calling herself Peter, while David becomes her girl, whom she calls Catherine; David reciprocates. Catherine finds a way to penetrate David anally: "He lay there and felt something and then her hand holding him and searching lower and he helped with his hands and then lay back in the dark and did not think at all and only felt the weight and strangeness inside and she said, 'Now you can't tell who is who, can you?'" (*GOE*, 17). Almost immediately, David senses danger, as Catherine takes their games further, to the point where she really cannot tell "who is who." She brings home a dark girl, Marita, with whom she is having a lesbian affair; she urges Marita on David, who falls in love with her as Catherine continues to disintegrate. The novel is in important ways about creativity, and David's writing career reflects and comments on Hemingway's own. Catherine's eventual descent into madness is signaled by her burning David's manuscripts, in an echo of Hadley's losing Ernest's stories at the train station in Paris in 1922. David is able to rewrite what has been lost, even improving on the originals, and he and Marita appear to find happiness together as Catherine departs, on her way, the text implies, to an asylum.

Why did these themes—of gender ambivalence, madness, and the shifting boundaries of monogamous heterosexual relationships, some of which had previously been undercurrents in Ernest's work—suddenly surface so insistently at this time? One factor may have been his new marriage to the boyish and short-haired Mary, who had had considerable sexual experience before their meeting and would show herself willing to join him in acting out his sexual and gender-related fantasies. Another may have been his preoccupation with the identity-related issues that his youngest son, the one with whom he felt the strongest emotional empathy, was wrestling with. Other factors—his traumatic brain injury, for example, or his relief that his humiliating marriage to Martha was over—might have been at work. Over and above this, Ernest had a perpetual compulsion to act out his desires, and not just sexual ones. The result was a fictional project whose subject matter was nearly unheard of in mainstream American literature at the time. The Kinsey Report on male sexuality was several years away at the time that Ernest began *The Garden of Eden,* as was the American publication of groundbreaking works like Henry Miller's *Tropic of Cancer.* Unlike novels such as *A Farewell to Arms* and *For Whom the Bell Tolls,* in which Ernest responded creatively to events and the zeitgeist, *The Garden of Eden* was generated internally, out of his nemeses and deepest preoccupations. In February 1946 he estimated he had written four hundred pages; by May, seven hundred; and in July, a thousand. By 1947 he was viewing the manuscript as a distinct book and in 1948 beginning to carve it out of the longer Sea book, telling Buck Lanham in June 1948 that his new book was about "the happiness of the garden that a man must lose."

The more urgently Ernest worked on the manuscript of *The Garden of Eden,* however, the less fit for publication it must have appeared to him. He never finished the book; various subplots developed along the way, including another set of characters, Nick and Barbara Sheldon, Nick an artist and another stand-in for Ernest (recalling Nick Adams as well). Included in Ernest's manuscript is a story David writes about an elephant hunt, but his creativity, clearly meant to be central to the novel, is never fully addressed. Ernest wrote several different endings, none satisfactory to himself. More important, perhaps, he had to know publication was precluded not just by the sexually explicit nature of the book, and its radical notions of gender transference, but by the contrast of the subject with his own, super-masculine image. If he knew his subject made the novel he was writing unpublishable, he still saw it as part of a longer work, and must have hoped that the rest of the projected novel would make his material more palatable. *The Garden of Eden* in no way provides any evidence that the author had homosexual desires, in fact. He may well have known, however, that readers might conclude from the novel that he was homosexual or otherwise sexually unconventional.

Given the times, there were really no other conclusions for anyone to draw. Transgenderism was almost unheard of among the general public at the time; the first widespread media coverage of gender reassignment surgery was in 1952, when George William Jorgensen became Christine Jorgensen. Almost everyone viewed this case as extremely bizarre; it was not until 1967, when Jorgensen published her autobiography, and 1968, when gay rights was born in the wake of the Stonewall Riots, that the issue of transgenderism even entered public discourse. And it was not until the turn of the last century that the specific issues associated with it got any acceptance. For a gender-ambivalent man born at the turn of the twentieth century, there was no escape from the binary, male-female notion of gender except through cross-dressing; role playing, both sexual and otherwise; and/or fetishism. Whether Ernest's desires went beyond sexual role playing and his hair fetish is unclear, and finally irrelevant; those were the only options open to him at the time.

Ernest was extremely brave to take up such issues in his fiction. As he wrote Buck in 1946, "If anyone knew what book was about would be attacked, pooped on, destroyed and copied long before out. All I can say is a long book." Against all these probable reactions, and what we can assume was the difficulty of admitting his gender issues even to himself, it is a tribute to Ernest's courage that he kept working on the manuscript. But his intense focus on the telling of this unusual story also suggests that Ernest grew increasingly comfortable about his gender identification and sexual desires after his return from the war. It was about this time that he began to refer frequently to "our one and only life," usually to Mary. Nearing fifty, he seems also to have awakened to his own mortality, coming to feel that if we only have one life, we should go after what we want, however our pursuit appears to others.

*   *   *

A new era was ushered in by Mary Welsh's arrival at the Finca in May 1945. In preparation, Ernest told all his correspondents, several times, that he was readying the place for her arrival, replanting trees and shrubs uprooted in the latest hurricane—replacing, for instance, all the mango trees. He was boxing up and shipping out Martha's things, though he kept a photograph of her on his desk, to Mary's later chagrin; he continued to see in Martha's good looks a trophy of sorts. Most important, he cut his drinking way back, although he offered competing explanations of how he was doing so, saying on the one hand that he had cut out all hard liquor, on the other that he had given up his morning and nighttime (after-dinner) drinking—which, as he later admitted, allowed him to drink before and during both lunch and dinner. Since his concussion, he had found through trial and error that he had bad reactions to both gin and brandy, so he had easily cut those out.

After Mary's arrival, Ernest reported to Buck Lanham that he was well pleased with her: she was good around a boat, adaptable, considerate, and loved the sea. Her skin was smooth and her legs and stomach trim; he commented especially on her tan, itself becoming a fetish, as the current pages of his manuscript attested. Ernest was sunbathing as well, wearing only a jockstrap to minimize tan lines. The two spoke of this time together as a visit, but it was readily apparent that Mary was making a permanent move; she left for Chicago in August to see to the details of her divorce from Noel Monks. Ernest was writing to her about plans to secure an apartment in Paris and a place in Kenya.

Mary sometimes found her environment otherworldly. Her life with Ernest was new and strange, but in the meantime it was warm and breezy on the Finca's hilltop, overlooking Havana. Every morning she took Spanish lessons from a local girl, Pilar, whom Ernest had picked because she spoke only the purest Castilian. Mary was learning the Spanish names for plants, and that yucca and sweet potatoes did better in the vegetable garden than spinach and tomatoes, which did not thrive under the blazing sun. Without Spanish, it was hard for her to oversee the servants: Juan, the chauffeur; Justo, the butler; Ramón Wong, the half-Chinese cook; Pancho, the carpenter; and a succession of maids and gardeners. The children arrived for the summer and Mary was captivated by them. They were old enough now that they had no need for a maternal presence, nor were they starstruck by her, as they had been by Martha, so it was possible to meet them on fairly level ground. Greg took her in hand and taught her how to shoot, starting with the great numbers of blackbirds that inexplicably swarmed into Havana each morning from nighttime perches in the country.

Soon after Mary arrived Juan drove her and Ernest to the nearby fishing village, Cojimar, where the *Pilar* was berthed, and she began learning the art and science of deep-sea fishing: she learned to navigate by means of a rusty sextant supplied by Gregorio, the boat's first mate, but soon gave it up. Ernest hired a manicurist, Lily, who also washed Mary's hair in rainwater from the cistern; at his diffident suggestion Mary went into Havana and had it bleached "as a present." Ernest wrote to Mary's aged parents, whose financial support he had generously assumed, that he and their daughter had "no debt, the March income tax paid and others provided for and us both healthy and happy," adding, "The boys love Mary very much and she is so good, thoughtful, friendly and wise with them." Mary wrote in her diary, "Papa has been kind, thoughtful and loving and has said several times that he was happier than ever before in his life."

Not everything went smoothly in the island paradise, however. Mary understood that she was to give up her career, and she didn't like the early financial arrangements with Ernest, in which money appeared only in the form of gifts from him. She didn't like not being included in his plans, financial and otherwise, and in general felt "I had been an entity; now I was an appendage." Though she was game about fishing and hunting, no one knew as much about those endeavors as Ernest, and Mary did not like feeling stupid. Furthermore, she was tired, she told him, of seeing Martha everywhere: the color schemes, the furniture, "the folkways and past" of Martha. The way Ernest was always telling her how much the children liked Martha, and his explanation for the photo of Martha on his desk—that he kept it there for the boys' sake—bothered her. Shortly after her arrival he began writing the first of many in-house letters to Mary; both of them would constantly write such notes, sometimes two a day, while Mary was recording everything in her diary. In one such letter, dated January 19, Ernest pleaded for mercy after she had accused him of keeping her from her friends. In exasperation he replied that he could no longer evaluate Mary's account of her life before she met him. He knew her side of the story of her marriage to Noel—but the accusations she was making against him suggested to him that maybe Noel had his own story to tell—and besides, it wasn't Ernest's fault that Mary was in bed with Shaw when the general came around (a reference to Mary's being caught in bed with Irwin Shaw by his then rival, General McClure). Mary had told Ernest this story during their courtship, never imagining he would recast it as an indictment of her promiscuity and fling it back at her, using it to close a letter that was a small masterpiece of passive aggression.

To Mary's further annoyance, before their wedding she had to sit through two long and painful sessions with lawyers, the marriage contract in Cuba being "straight out of the Napoleonic Code." (A Cuban marriage required the equivalent of a modern prenup, with each party, for instance, required to return all gifts in the event of divorce.) The wedding took place in the Havana apartment of Dick and Marjorie Cooper, Dick an old friend from Bimini days who had turned up in Africa during Ernest's safari in 1934. Winston Guest was Ernest's best man. On the drive back to the Finca, Ernest and Mary quarreled, erupting into an evening-long "small, furious earthquake of incrimination and abuse," with Ernest going to sleep in the middle of the fight and Mary packing her bags (though it is unclear where she could go).

More troubling on a day-to-day level was the boys' dormitory quality the Finca could take on when Ernest's buddies were around, which was constantly. Evidently Ernest thought Mary might prefer rich sportsman friends like Tommy Shevlin, another Bimini friend, and Winston Guest, or Wolfie, a comrade from the sub-hunting days. Like veterans everywhere, they wanted to celebrate their return from the war, and the Finca was an unbeatable location for a party. Gradually, what Ernest called the "veterans from the 12th Brigade," his Basque friends and their circle—including Father Andrés (Andrés Untzaín, also known as the Black Priest), Roberto Herrera, and Juan Duñabeitia (Sinsky)—who had manned the *Pilar* when he was hunting for German subs, began to make their appearance, despite Ernest's resolution, voiced to Buck Lanham in a March letter, not to resume his support of them. They filtered back in, in any case, and "parties often lasted for days," according to René Villarreal, a Cuban boy who grew to manhood at the Finca, eventually becoming majordomo and later caretaker. Mayito Menocal, the oldest son of an ex-president of Cuba, said Ernest always liked to number a "stooge" among his companions. Indeed, Ernest could be quite mean about various members of this group. When

Menocal complained to him that there was far too much "yes, Papa" going on at the Finca, Ernest joked that if he told Winston Guest (whom he called "the ideal subaltern") to jump out of a plane without a parachute and that one would be given to him on his way down, Winston would just say "yes, Papa," and proceed to jump.

Mary put up with these fixtures of the Finca as easily as she did the multitude of cats, but as the months passed it became clear that she did not always say yes to Papa. For the most part, she had walked into her new life with her eyes open and for as long as Ernest would have her, which she fully intended would be until death. She knew about his depressions—what he called his "Black Ass" moods—his drinking, his inability to be alone, his tempers, his insistence on getting his way, and his massive, blinkered egotism. But she knew as well his tender, loving qualities; his unalloyed enjoyment of life; the excitement of his companionship; his vulnerability, and his shy sexual secrets. She foresaw fights, adventures, and even caretaking, as Ernest grew less and less able to face down his demons.

Newly expansive in his contentment, Ernest was in a mood to regroup with far-flung friends from the past, many who had scattered in the war. Archie MacLeish was among them. There had been a wartime hiatus in their correspondence, reflecting an estrangement that dated back to their financial quarrel over *The Spanish Earth* in 1938. Archie, in a fit of patriotism, had accused Ernest of being "irresponsible" for writing negatively about war in his early fiction. Ernest had written Archie just six months later: "Can it be that I am becoming an Irresponsible?" He made the first of several references to his "chickenshit" behavior back in 1938. Vowing to Archie that he had changed and was no longer "self-righteous," he was repentant when he looked back on that part of his life. Archie did not respond directly to this particular point, and their warm correspondence recommenced.

As he had many times in the past, Ernest concluded a 1948 letter to Archie with a message of love to Ada, now freely confessing that he had always wanted to sleep with her. Archie, apparently unperturbed, sent Ernest "Years of the Dog," a poem about Paris, situating Ernest in the apartment over the sawmill on the rue Notre-Dame-des-Champs in 1924. What became of that early youth? asks the poet. "Fame became of him." Ernest managed to thank Archie gracefully for the poem, which he said he found very moving. He paid a visit to Archie in his Library of Congress office during the war, later reporting to Sara Murphy, "Archie was fine. I made all up with him because what are people doing nursing old rows at our age?" The two old friends would not see each other again until 1956, however. Toward the end of his life Archie commented on Ernest's tendency to destroy friendships—at least with his peers. To understand this, he said, "You have to be familiar with a bitterness of tongue which would break through all inhibitions on his part and do enormous damage."

Ernest was also trying to mend fences with John Dos Passos. But because he had broken with him over principles during the Spanish Civil War, he understandably feared reconciliation would mean compromise. No doubt Ernest was thinking of Dos when he reflected in a 1945 letter to Buck that he did not have many friends whom he both liked and respected, and that Spain had been the hardest on his friendships. He told Archie as early as 1943 that he would love to see Dos. He knew Dos wouldn't ever forgive him over "the boys" shooting Robles. Perhaps if Ernest had said this five years earlier the breach might have been avoided, but back then he had been unable to admit that "the boys"—in this case, the Soviets—could do wrong. Dos, for his part, never commented further about his friendship with Ernest, beyond a note he sent to Sara Murphy after seeing Ernest at a shipboard party to celebrate his friend's departure for Italy in 1948; he called Ernest the "good old Monster" and noted he "kept ordering up more giggle-water."

Yet Ernest told Archie he wanted to stay on good terms with Dos Passos because Dos was married to Ernest's boyhood friend Katy Smith. In 1947 Dos lost Katy in a tragic car accident. Dos had been driving into the evening sun when, momentarily blinded, he drove into a parked truck; Katy was nearly decapitated and Dos lost an eye. Ernest muttered that Dos should never have been driving with his poor eyesight. Later, when Dos drew on Katy's stories of her childhood to write about northern Michigan and Ernest in *Chosen Country* (1951), Ernest complained, "He's killed her off, and now he's stealing my material." Ernest sent a consoling telegram to his friend after the accident, however. He followed up with a forlorn letter that said, revealingly, that a huge part of his past had died with Katy. He never doubted, he said, that he and Dos would remain lifelong friends, putting the past well behind them.

A notable exception to Ernest's usual pattern of breaking off friendships, especially with those who had helped him, was Ezra Pound. The poet had been indicted for treason in July 1943 for his pro-Fascist, anti-Semitic radio broadcasts from Italy. They were shocking, even vile—he recommended *The Protocols of the Elders of Zion* and *Mein Kampf;* he spoke of the "60 kikes who started this war," and asserted, "The Jew is a savage." Archie MacLeish, like Ernest a longtime friend of Pound's, was dismayed. Archie was then Librarian of Congress, and Ernest and he corresponded at some length about what should be done about their friend. Ernest asked Archie for photostats of the transcripts of Ezra's broadcasts; reading them only confirmed his view. Calling the broadcasts "vile, absolutely idiotic drivel," he said Ezra "is obviously crazy." Though he knew it would be an unpopular stance, he believed Pound should plead insanity. As it turned out, MacLeish, Hemingway, and the poet and New Directions publisher James Laughlin (a disciple of Pound's) were instrumental in what happened: Ezra was adjudged insane and confined to St. Elizabeths in Washington, D.C., in early 1946. In fact, most of the credit for that quick and shrewd thinking was Ernest's. He owed a great debt to Pound, who took him up when he had hardly written anything at all, offered him passionate support and endorsement, and introduced him to all kinds of people who would be helpful to him.

Yet there was one friend whom Ernest still had to come to terms with: Scott Fitzgerald. In the mid-1940s, Fitzgerald was enjoying a bit of a boom. In 1945 Max Perkins brought out *The Crack-Up,* a compendium of Scott's essays, letters, and journals that was (and is today) very well regarded. Dorothy Parker made the selections for *The Portable F. Scott Fitzgerald* in 1945; it contained *Gatsby, Tender Is the Night,* and the best of his stories. In the introduction to the edition, novelist John O'Hara wrote, a little incoherently, "All he was was our best novelist, one of our best novella-ists, and one of our finest writers of short stories." Fitzgerald's biographer called the activity of the 1940s not so much a revival as a "resurrection." Ernest was not sure how to stop it.

He had been giving some thought to his friend's continuing reputation. When *The Last Tycoon* appeared in 1941, Ernest gave Max his strongly negative assessment. He was glad it got such a fine, prominent review in *The New York Times Book Review,* but the reviewer was unable to see that "the book has that deadness . . . as though it were a slab of bacon on which mold was grown. You can scrape off the mold," he continued, with some relish, "but if it has gone deep in the meat, there is nothing that can keep it from tasting like moldy bacon." He went on to make some more insightful observations: that reading the book was like watching a baseball pitcher whose arm is shot coming in for a few good innings before completely blowing the game. "The old magic was gone," Ernest observed.

If *The Last Tycoon* was not going to enhance Scott's posthumous reputation (and many felt differently), Ernest had some other ideas. He was thinking of writing something about Scott himself, he told Max: "I know [*sic*] him, through some time periods, better than anyone and would be glad to write a long, true, rich, detailed . . . account of the years I knew him." He would probably save it for his own memoirs (his first mention of writing these). He later elaborated, telling Max that no one could write the true story of Scott as long as Zelda was still alive. He called his old friend, with some truth, "completely uneducated," and observed, "He did everything wrong; and it came out right." (Doing everything wrong, of course, was a particular sin in Ernest's universe.) "Where other people were dazzled by him," he continued to Max, "we saw the good, the weakness and the great flaw that was always there."

TWENTY-SIX

Ernest could be a kind and giving person, his generosity heartfelt. His wives and children would probably have said he was generous when he cared to be—with all the ambiguity that carries with it. His friends would have said that he could be extremely generous—witness his offering to pay for Archie MacLeish's and Mike Strater's safaris (albeit with Gus Pfeiffer's money), or his agreeing to take on the support of Mary's aging parents—but they would also have added that sometimes his gifts were conditional. He was financially generous to his siblings and mother—depending on whom they married, for instance, as Carol, who broke with Ernest over John Gardner, could attest. He wasn't always the best father, but he would have given his children the moon if it had been in his power to steal it from the sky; he financed and would continue to finance a good part of the ventures, many dubious, that his three interesting children came up with. (This generosity, sadly, had strings attached.)

If he was mean to writer friends like Fitzgerald and Dos Passos, he was almost always generous with amateur writers who wrote in, free with advice and helpful with connections. And he had a special liking for journalists—especially foreign and war correspondents. In the midst of the massacre at Hürtgenwald he wrote to Mary that he felt a responsibility to the next generation of journalists: "I don't want to compete with the fine kids who have been through this and have the right—and will write wonderfully. The young, the new, the always comeing that we hope will write better and sounder than we can."

Another generation: the prospect moved him. Generosity and parenting were tangled in a sometimes nasty snarl that included selfishness, the need for gratitude and respect, a wonderful spirit of fun, and a great openness to adventure. When Ernest first married Martha, he wrote Max Perkins, who had five daughters, "Also would like to have a daughter. I guess that sounds funny to a man with five of them but I would like to have one very much." He had wanted a girl when Patrick was born. That meant that he (and Pauline, with him in everything) *really* wanted a girl when Gregory was born. It was obvious enough that Greg picked up on it—even before his father, in a mean mood, told him. And told him again, time after time. "My father had wanted a girl badly," wrote Greg in his memoir about Ernest.

Ernest did not know it when he married her, but Martha could not bear children, probably as the result of earlier abortions—one of which ended a pregnancy with Ernest's child. With Mary, Ernest hoped for a new start—and a daughter, which at this point he thought he "deserved." Mary was thirty-six and eager to bear either Bridget or Tom. When she announced her pregnancy in March 1947, very soon after her marriage, Ernest was thrilled, and set his sights on a little Bridget. It was not to be, however, and her pregnancy very nearly cost Mary her life. It was Ernest who saved it.

Ernest and Mary headed west that summer, Ernest eager to show Mary the hunting and fishing grounds in Wyoming, Montana, and Idaho that he so loved. Jack was driving Patrick and Greg across country, much to Ernest's dismay—his fantasies were transfigured into the automobile deaths of two of the hero's sons in the Sea novel he was then writing—and they all made plans to rendezvous in Sun Valley. For Ernest and Mary, it was a hot trip across the country on the now legendary Route 66; in Kansas City, it really was 120 degrees in the shade—Mary checked. Ernest disliked small-town hotels, claiming it was because he hated to carry loads of luggage upstairs, so he and Mary stayed in the increasingly common, low-priced motels and motor courts springing up along America's roadsides. (Mary later joked that she thought of writing a book called "Slumming Across God's Country.")

In a particularly bad specimen, the "ramshackle, linoleum-floored" Mission Motor Court in Casper, Wyoming, just as they were packing up to leave the next morning, Mary was hit by excruciating pain. At the local hospital, the chief of surgery was away on a hunting trip, but the staff rushed Mary into surgery, where it was determined that what had been an ectopic pregnancy led to a burst Fallopian tube. The staff pumped her full of the blood and plasma she was so rapidly losing, until that evening she passed out, her veins collapsed, her pulse disappeared, and the attending doctor told Ernest to say his goodbyes. Ernest, always at his best in an emergency, made an assistant open a vein and start a fresh tube to transmit plasma. He fed the plasma into the vein himself, doing it slowly, "milking" the bag and tilting it until it flowed freely; soon the doctor was able to operate, and the crisis passed. They had been fortunate; as Ernest wrote to Buck Lanham, "Lucky it was in Casper instead of up in the hills." Mary was lucky as well that her husband was so clear thinking, resourceful, and persistent.

Pappy and Tillie Arnold had set aside the largest cabin for Ernest and his party in the MacDonald Cabins in Ketchum, Idaho, a "resort" that would become a favorite Hemingway destination over the coming years. The cornfields, lowlands, and copses of cottonwood and aspen offered abundant pheasant, duck, quail, and other game birds, which Mary, with Tillie Arnold's help, soon learned to cook. Though Greg soon had to return to school, Patrick had graduated from Canterbury the previous year and was taking a year off; Jack was enrolled at the nearby University of Montana; the two of them were able to do a lot of shooting with their father and his new wife, who stayed on into late November.

Mary and Ernest arranged to spend Thanksgiving with her parents in New Orleans. In yet another tribute to his charm, Ernest got along very well with them, despite their disapproval of alcohol and profanity. From there he and Mary went on to New York, where they stayed at the Sherry-Netherland for most of December. Ernest was not at his best on this leg of the trip, however. Buck Lanham met them there for some hunting on Gardiners Island, which Winston Guest had rented for the occasion, but the shooting was poor. When Buck stopped at the hotel to pick up Ernest and Mary for an evening at the Stork Club, he was discomfited to find his friend unshaven, paunchy, and particularly poorly groomed, though Ernest said he was ready to go out. (Buck made him shave.) At the Stork Club, where they were guests of the owner, Sherman Billingsley, they sat with the gossip columnist Leonard Lyons and his wife; since about 1944 Ernest had become friends with not only Lyons but also columnist Earl Wilson. Why Ernest thought Buck might enjoy an evening spent in this fashion is not clear. When Ernest saw one of his favorite women, Ingrid Bergman, sitting at a nearby table with Charles Boyer, he had to be restrained from attacking Boyer.

It may have been on this trip to New York that Ernest finally got Gene Tunney to spar with him, probably at George Brown's gym on West 47th Street. According to Tunney, Ernest was persistent in trying to get Tunney to spar bare-fisted with him, but Tunney always said no. The fighter remembered that Jack Dempsey had refused to box with Ernest back in the 1920s in Paris, when Dempsey was heavyweight champion. Dempsey said he always refused to get in the ring with Ernest because he had sensed that Ernest "would come out of the corner like a madman," and feared that he would hurt Ernest, as he had Al Jolson in a "playful" sparring match. Tunney knew this story, and he had also heard that Ernest had boxed Tom

Heeney in Bimini in the 1930s on the sand, the fights so fierce Ernest said they ought to get paid to box for real. George Brown was skeptical, as one might expect. Ernest didn't always fight fair, Brown said, trying to knee him a couple of times; Ernest once brought his fist down on top of Brown's head when the two men were in a clinch. Yet Ernest kept trying, and Tunney finally agreed, thinking to cut it short. Ernest took a swing at Tunney's face, drawing blood, and then caught Tunney on his left elbow. Tunney wanted to stop there. "Do stop it please, Ernest," Tunney said. But Ernest kept punching. Tunney said to himself, "What Ernest needs is a good little liver punch." He proceeded to deliver one. Ernest crumpled and went gray in the face, but he didn't fall. "For the next few hours Ernest was perfectly charming," observed Tunney.

The year 1947 proved to be an annus horribilis for Ernest and his family. In April, Patrick was staying in the little house at the Finca while he studied for the College Board exams that month. For a break, he went over to join his little brother in Key West during Greg's spring vacation. Shortly after her fiftieth birthday in 1945, Pauline had bought herself a sportscar—a new Bantam convertible. Patrick, newly licensed, had evidently allowed Gregory to drive the car, and he promptly had an accident, driving off the road and into a tree near the Casa Marina. Greg hurt his knee and Patrick his head, but there seemed to be no ill effects, and the boys arrived at the Finca soon after. Shortly after his arrival, however, and on a day-long fishing jaunt with his brother and René Villarreal, Patrick began to behave strangely. Back at the Finca, he asked for a pot of hot water and some tea, and when René brought it to the little house, Patrick complained that the water was dirty. He began to shout loudly at the cook, Ramón—who wasn't present.

Later, accusations flew thick and fast as to which parent was most responsible for what happened to Patrick after he hit his head. But the damage had been done in the crash, not after. At the main house, Ernest put Patrick on a wicker chaise and stroked his head. Patrick was able to take the College Boards in Havana the next day, but later that day he grew more and more agitated, and Ernest called Dr. Carlos M. Kohly, known as Cucu, a deep-sea-fishing friend. The physician sedated Patrick, but the next day he was delirious and soon became violent, and it was necessary to restrain him.

There followed a dreadful ordeal for Patrick's family, as his sanity—and his life—hung in the balance. At the very start Mary had to leave, as her father was extremely ill in Chicago, having received Christian Science "treatments" for prostate cancer before collapsing completely. Ernest put Patrick in his own bed in the Finca, and slept just outside the door, on the straw mat in the living room, virtually nonstop for the next three months. Pauline came over from Key West in mid-April, and she and Ernest put aside their differences to care for their son.

At first, everyone hoped it would be at most a couple of weeks before Patrick was well again. Kohly was joined by Dr. José Herrera Sotolongo, and eventually doctors from all over the island were called in. Dr. Herrera deemed Patrick's condition "predemential" and said it was set off either by the strain of taking the exams or by a crisis involving his Catholic faith. Religion was, indeed, a large part of the content of Patrick's delirium; his other subject was *putas*. The local priest Don Andrés, who would become one of Patrick's primary caretakers, at first could not enter his room without being abused as the devil incarnate—the source of Don Andrés's subsequent nickname, the Black Priest. Ernest noted, not without pride, that Patrick's language was sometimes pure poetry.

Ernest and the doctors were initially concerned that they could not get near Patrick without being scratched or bitten. But he only got worse—more violent—and had to be constantly restrained. The otherwise worthless Sinsky (Juan Duñabeitia) proved his mettle with his stalwart aid in Patrick's care, as did the doctor's brother, Roberto Herrera; Don Andrés; and often Félix Areito, the jai-alai player known as Ermua. At first the doctors advised Ernest to get Patrick to a hospital, as it became clear that the boy was in for a siege. But Ernest was adamant that Patrick stay at home. In any kind of institutional setting, he said, attendants were likely to brutalize Patrick in retaliation for the injuries he might try to inflict on them. Nor did he feel that he could hire anyone to perform the duties that he, Pauline, and his friends took on. Ernest told Mary he was able to keep the restraining "calm and good," and he certainly had the strength and physical condition to tend to his son. He also swore everyone to secrecy, and himself showed great restraint in his letters, for the sake of Patrick's future; if made public, the episode might be difficult for the boy to explain, casting a shadow over his future.

Patrick refused to eat—Ernest thought he was imagining himself a captured Resistance fighter on hunger strike—and when he did he stored the food in his mouth to spit it out at his caretakers. He could not swallow his saliva. He would have ripped out any tubes designed to feed him nasally, so, five days after his illness began, his friends began feeding him rectally, a horrible procedure for which he had to be fully sedated and restrained. Patrick was fed drop by drop, a hundred drops to the minute, and the whole ordeal took an hour and a half. Even so, his weight dropped to eighty-eight pounds by the beginning of August.

Patrick recognized Pauline, but otherwise she could do little for him—she wasn't physically strong enough. She saw to some of the housekeeping duties and oversaw the menus and the cooking. Early on, because she was going to be away with her parents, Mary had written urging Pauline to take her bedroom and telling her where she might find clean shirts and shorts in the closet. By the time Mary returned on May 18, Pauline had flown over to Key West for a brief rest. When she came back to Cuba, the two women found they got along very well. They joked about being alumnae of Hemingway University, but Pauline seems to have meant it when she called Mary "the high grade wife Mr. Hemingway brought back from the war. I think she is tops as to looks, charm, intelligence and general appeal. She certainly appeals to me. Lovely girl." The two women were not at all the same type, but they found common ground, and not just Ernest. That summer, as Patrick's ordeal continued, Mary went to Key West to recuperate at Pauline's house from an intestinal virus, and she would meet regularly with Pauline as friends after Patrick had recovered.

Though he wrote to Mary frequently, Ernest left no record of his overview of the situation, so it is not known how he viewed his son's overall progress, or lack of it. He seldom voiced either hopes or fears about Patrick's recovery—or the possibility that there would be none. In Ernest's letters to Mary he recorded mostly how much sleep he had managed to get the previous night. (He seems to have functioned on less than four.) Every night Patrick's caretakers—usually Ernest, Sinsky, Don Andrés, and Dr. Herrera—gathered in the living room "with the liquor bottles necessary for what they called their own scientific treatment—'chemical compounds' that were mostly gin."

It was undeniable to all concerned that Patrick had become psychotic. Psychiatric diagnosis has come a long way since then, when it must have seemed that Patrick was schizophrenic, perhaps facing a lifetime of institutional care. In a much later letter, Ernest was extremely uncharitable about Pauline's role in Patrick's illness, blaming her for letting him play tennis and sleep outdoors after his concussion. More significantly, he wrote, "In Pauline's family the children, and there is a long history of it, tend to blow at adolescence. . . . P. probably would have blown anyway and the concussion just set it off." Ernest knew better—for one thing, he was well aware of his father's near-psychotic depression leading up to his suicide. But this was all later: during Patrick's illness he did not indulge in speculation or blame or recrimination—he just took care of his son.

Eventually, in July, a new doctor recommended a series of shock treatments. In the absence of antipsychotic drugs, at a time when some mentally ill patients were treated with lobotomies, electroshock seemed the only option remaining for a patient in Patrick's condition. The desperate parents gave permission. Patrick received the first one at the Finca, in an outbuilding by the swimming pool, but he was able to get to the local hospital for the remaining treatments. He had them Tuesdays, Thursdays, and Saturdays for six weeks. Ernest was able to report to Mary (then in Key West) that Patrick was "lucid" after the first treatment, which took about ten minutes. He was somewhat dazed, but walked up to the house, where he ate breakfast. These routine movements must have seemed nothing short of miraculous. Patrick's was the first of many experiences with shock treatment in the Hemingway family, and always they would remember how shock had made Patrick better when his case seemed hopeless.

It is risky to speculate on Patrick's diagnosis from a contemporary vantage point, though it is probable that he, like his father, had suffered a traumatic brain injury—the original concussion. These injuries cause any number of conditions, and psychosis is not uncommon. Electroshock is still administered in some cases, though most post-traumatic brain injury patients with psychosis are treated today with antipsychotic drugs. In Patrick's case, the electroshock brought him back. By November Pauline observed, "Patrick is wonderful, sweet, considerate, unegotistical and cheerful, like his old self." He was "a little slow" from time to time, "but most of the time it is hard to believe that horrible summer had anything to do with him." Pauline for once stilled her own sharp tongue, telling Ernest "what a source of strength you were," and "how unremittingly kind and considerate you were in every way." The way he had kept up "the morale of the troops" was absolutely indispensable in this time of crisis. Although Ernest sometimes indulged in self-pity, for the most part he submerged his ego and its demands as long as Patrick needed him.

Behind this is the fact that he floated all through Patrick's demanding care and his own frantic anxieties that summer on a sea of sexual fantasy. In his stream of letters to Mary, he indulged in many different fantasies about the color she might dye her hair when she was in Chicago, or when she was back in Cuba. He liked imagining her with silverish hair, her skin brown from the sun—a look he would soon be assigning to Catherine, the writer's wife in *The Garden of Eden*. He thought a lot about the color ash blond: was it a smoky quality that gave rise to the name? Mary had gone off to Chicago with a lemon cast to her hair that Ernest thought should be fixed. He wasn't sure about ash blond, however, and wondered whether "moonlight" blond might be better. He also researched the various hair dyes and their ill effects and constantly advised Mary on hot oil treatments, the dangers of chlorinated water, and the difficulty of making blond hair lighter ("maybe a kind of smoke silver?" he wondered) and how damaging it was to the hair. Just writing these words, and thinking of Mary's hair and what they called her "place," often made Mr. Scrooby stand at attention, he said.

He liked the notion of Mary's dyeing her hair red, and entertained the image for a while before rejecting it as too risky in the summer, given the amount of time she spent in the pool. (This did not keep him from fantasizing that she might make her hair red for his birthday.) He began to dream about his own now rapidly graying hair being dyed red—the color of leaves in the fall—and told Mary that "Katherine" was growing thinner and growing her/his hair longer.

One lonely night at the Finca, after Patrick had subsided for the evening, Ernest took the bold step of coloring his hair red. He was a little drunk, he admitted later, and when he woke up the next morning he was "spooked shitless." His hair was "as red as a French polished copper pot or a newly minted penny." He fleetingly wondered what the servants—or Sinsky and company—would think, he told Mary. But he had an analogy on hand that made him feel better: just as Custer grew his hair long and yet commanded the respect of his troops, so too did Ernest's "troops"—Sinsky and company—look up to him. Sounding slightly like an emphatic Grace Hemingway, he wrote, "If a girl has a right to make her hair red I have." Explaining the changed color, he told "the troops" that his coppery hair was the result of his mistakenly using a leftover bottle of Martha's shampoo. Ernest added that they said it took fifteen years off his age. He viewed it as such a success, in fact, that he began to toy with the idea of dying *his* hair blond, but Mary returned before that fantasy was realized.

Without question Mary improved Ernest's life by giving him space to air—and actualize—his fantasies, treating them seriously but not without humor and understanding. In her memoir she casually relates having her hair bleached when she first arrived in Cuba as a present to Ernest. She noted that he was "entranced" by the result. "Deeply rooted in his field of esthetics," she wrote, "was some mystical devotion to blondness, the blonder the lovelier, I never learned why." If he wanted to write her as Katherine, she was willing to respond as Pete.

* * *

In the midst of his ordeal with Patrick, on June 17 Ernest received a telegram from his publisher, Charles Scribner III, known as Charlie, relaying terrible news: Max Perkins had died. He had been run-down for some time, exhausted and driving himself too hard, so that when he came down with pleurisy and pneumonia he just slipped away. He had never been hale or hearty—at five feet ten he weighed only 150 pounds—and was just sixty-three when he died. His death left many Scribner's writers bereft. When Perkins biographer A. Scott Berg called Perkins "Editor of Genius," he was referring mostly to a trinity of America's best novelists: Fitzgerald, Hemingway, and Thomas Wolfe. But Perkins had many other authors under his wing, including Marjorie Kinnan Rawlings, Taylor Caldwell, Vance Bourjaily, James Jones, and Alan Paton, and many others whose names are no longer familiar.

A quick look at the collections of correspondence between Max and his authors is extremely revealing. With a writer like Wolfe, Max's job was multifaceted: primarily he cut, stanching the gush of Wolfe's florid prose until it was a manageable stream. He also participated imaginatively in Wolfe's universe, immersing himself in Wolfe's characters and stories so that he could help his author regain direction when Wolfe lost his own thread. He ministered to Wolfe's mental health as a kind of on-call therapist, and he was a fixer too, on occasion clearing up Wolfe's personal problems or managing his passage through the outside world—just as he managed Wolfe's manuscripts through the phases of the publishing process: copyediting, proofing, production, marketing, sales, and advertising.

Perkins's role with Fitzgerald was quite different, perhaps because, at least when it came to writing, Scott was a professional. He didn't need line editing or substantive editing; the most that was ever necessary was Perkins's gut reaction to whatever Scott was writing at the time: corrections when he was headed up a blind alley or encouragement when he was full of doubts about the worth of his current project. He was an excellent sounding board for titles. Max became a very close friend of Scott's, but he did not play the emotionally laden paternal role that he assumed with Wolfe.

With Ernest, Max had played yet another role: like Scott, Ernest became a very good friend. Max encouraged him when he was unsure and redirected him when he was off course. He shepherded Ernest's books through the publishing process just as smoothly as he did Wolfe's and Fitzgerald's—not an automatically smooth process with any of these testy authors. When Ernest asked him—but *only* when Ernest asked him—he weighed in with his opinion on titles or endings. But that is where his editing stopped. By and large, no one touched Ernest's prose—and that included Max Perkins. In a letter to Charlie Scribner just after Max's death, meant to reassure Charlie he would not be changing publishers, Ernest said that Max "never cut a paragraph of my stuff nor asked me to change one."

Ernest had directed his very first publisher, Horace Liveright, that no changes were to be made to the sentences in his first novel, *The Torrents of Spring*, without his explicit permission. Assuming a high-handed stance unusual for one of his age and station, he hectored Liveright, "The alteration of a word can throw an entire story out of key." He freely acknowledged that his punctuation and spelling had to be fixed; as he famously said, also to Liveright, "The game of golf would lose a great deal if croquet mallets and billiard cues were allowed on the putting green."

But that makes Ernest sound far more easygoing than he in fact was. Max told Marjorie Kinnan Rawlings what happened the one time he "ventured an important criticism of a Hemingway book." Ernest swore and barked, "Why don't you get Tom Wolfe to write it for me?" As Charlie Scribner, who functioned as Ernest's unofficial editor after Max's death, would learn to his eternal chagrin, you corrected any point in Ernest's fiction at your peril.

Arnold Gingrich, Ernest's editor at *Esquire*, recounted what it was like to edit a writer who believed his own press. One afternoon out on the *Pilar*, Ernest and Arnold were talking about how the use of real people in fiction sometimes flattered the originals. "It's a little like having Cezanne include your features in a village scene," Ernest observed. Gingrich thought he was kidding, and asked Ernest whether he wasn't mixing his métiers. "Not really," Ernest went on. "What I can't get through your Pennsylvania Dutch skull is that you're not dealing with some little penny-a-liner from the sports department of the Chicago *Daily News*. You're asking for changes in the copy of a man who *has* been likened to Cezanne, for bringing 'a new way of seeing' into American literature." Gingrich was speechless.

"When Max died I did not think I could stand it," Ernest wrote to another Scribner's editor. "We understood each other so well it was like having a part of yourself die." Max had been Ernest's friend for over twenty years. "You are my most trusted friend," Ernest had told him in 1943, and Max was one of the few Ernest never fell out with. With Max's death, Ernest lost his literary conscience; from this point on, he seemed to have no real idea what to write or what to publish, often making bad decisions about both. And with Max's death, Ernest lost his emotional mooring: Max had been more constant than family and more forgiving than friends. He seemed to understand Ernest as nobody else could, and Ernest could not replace him.

In the absence of such real friends, Ernest surrounded himself with his omnipresent Cuban posse, reliably responsive to his moods and whims, ready to indulge his fancies. To some extent, Ernest recognized this situation for what it was, and looked for real friendship elsewhere. Because he was unable to maintain relationships with anyone who was in any way an equal, he began, as he had at several earlier junctures in his life, to seek out young men who would function as surrogate kid brothers, figures of at least some accomplishment to whom he could show the ropes of fishing, shooting, writing, the treatment of women, and the correct way to do everything from choosing wines to naming cats.

One such, potentially, was his real kid brother, Leicester. Ernest hardly saw the youngest Hemingway, born in 1915, during Leicester's childhood or adolescence, until his younger brother turned up in Key West in 1934, where he spent several months. Ernest encountered him again in London during the war, when Leicester, a journalist, was in the Signal Corps; Irwin Shaw, also in the unit, would paint a vivid (and damning) portrait of Ernest and Leicester in his 1948 war novel, *The Young Lions*. Leicester, who wanted to write fiction, contacted Ernest after the war asking for help in finding a job working for *Time* in Cuba, and enclosed with the letter a draft of a wartime novel he had written. Ernest replied with a kind, generous letter that at the same time spoke directly about the strengths and weaknesses of his brother's writing. Ernest could not be of any help with a job, he said, but he offered to send Leicester a loan of any size at any time. Then he got to the novel: he felt that one part of it was first-rate and recommended that Leicester turn the incident at the heart of this section into a short story, which Ernest would then be glad to send to his magazine editor friends: he suggested only that Leicester change the hero's name from "Ric" in order to avoid confusion with his own Nick Adams character. But the rest of the novel needed a lot of work. The love story was "ng," almost "nbfg," and the whole novel was not "integrated" and needed rewriting. Leicester would persevere, writing four subsequent novels, one of which would be published in 1953.

Ernest was fundamentally unsympathetic to his younger brother, on balance. Strikingly handsome when young, Leicester looked like Ernest in height and girth, but he bore an unfortunate resemblance to Grace Hemingway that Ernest could not get beyond. Leicester had a booming voice and a lot of energy, and Ernest was embarrassed by his outsize enthusiasm. Ernest's letters to Buck Lanham indicate that he had been terribly worried Leicester would not acquit himself well in the war; when Leicester did nothing that made Ernest look bad, he was still hard on Leicester's war performance, probably because, unlike his son Jack, whose exploits filled him with pride, Leicester performed no heroic feats.

More fundamentally, however, unlike the other younger men with whom Ernest associated in the war years and after, Leicester had a sizable ego and was unable to assume the obliging, subtly subordinate position Ernest would have preferred. "Ernest was never very content with life unless he had a spiritual kid brother nearby," Leicester wrote later. "He needed someone he could show off to as well as teach. He needed uncritical admiration. If the kid brother could show a little worshipful awe, that was a distinct aid in the relationship." Leicester seems to have been aware that his presence vaguely annoyed his older brother.

Several strong candidates for the kid brother position appeared in the years after the war. One of the first was Peter Viertel, a handsome young, German-born screenwriter whose parents, writers Salka and Berthold Viertel, were Hollywood royalty. Salka, also an actress, held salons for the film colony's intelligentsia. Peter's stunning wife, Virginia, known as Jigee, had been born in Pittsburgh six years before him, had previously been married to writer Budd Schulberg, and was active among Hollywood's left. Peter and Jigee, on a ski vacation, first met Ernest at MacDonald's Cabins in Ketchum, Idaho, in the winter of 1947–48. Twenty years younger than Ernest, Peter remembered seeing him at the Hollywood showing of *The Spanish Earth* back in 1937. As a writer, Peter had long admired Ernest, and Robert Capa had alerted him that Ernest might be at Sun Valley too. Jigee met Ernest outside their cabin and they struck up a conversation, and introductions to spouses followed. Ernest and Mary invited the young couple along to a dinner with Gary Cooper and his wife; Ernest was unfazed when Jigee afterward criticized Cooper's "reactionary" politics, Ernest saying he himself disagreed with friends at either end of the political spectrum. The couples quickly became friends, although Peter was brought up short by some of Ernest's stories, especially one about a local guide who had asked Ernest why he wasn't skiing. Ernest (who had indeed, somewhat inexplicably, given up skiing) considered the question an affront, took the guide aside, and threatened to use his hunting knife to cut out the man's liver. Noting Ernest's odd verbal shorthand and "an element of testing" in their exchanges, Peter observed, "It was obvious that he lived in a special world of his own." Soon after their meeting, Peter sent Ernest a copy of his very successful first novel, *The Canyon* (1940), which Ernest told him he liked very much.

The two couples cemented their friendship five months later when Peter came to Cuba with another man with an outsize personality, John Huston, and Huston's wife, Evelyn. Viertel and Huston were developing a film, *China Valdez* (to be released as *We Were Strangers* in 1949), about a plot to kill the Cuban dictator Gerardo Machado; at a temporary impasse on the script, director and screenwriter decided on a working vacation scouting locations in Cuba. Huston and Viertel were basing their film on an actual incident in which conspirators set off a bomb in a Havana cemetery while Machado and his cabinet were attending a state funeral nearby. Ernest and Mary both recommended that they brush up on their Cuban politics, and Huston and Viertel, who had chosen the subject because it sounded like "a good yarn," were brought up short. As Peter expected, Hemingway and Huston were uneasy with each other, their massive egos preventing any real bond from forming. Peter twice had to prevent them from boxing.

Peter and Jigee, however, became fast friends with the Hemingways. Ernest was very attracted to Jigee, a flirtatious and charming brunette, but for now she became another member of his chaste stable to whom he constantly professed his love. He admired a lot about Peter's background, from his war experience first as a Marine and later as an officer in the OSS; his skiing and his general athleticism; his friendship with Marlene Dietrich and his ease with similar celebrities. Most immediately, Ernest was interested in Peter's literary efforts, and was distressed that Peter was writing for the movies, which he thought guaranteed ruin for a writer. The movies made from Ernest's books and stories had all disappointed him to varying degrees, and while he no doubt would have been welcomed had he decided to write for Hollywood himself, he chose to husband his resources and thought other writers should do the same.

Instead, Ernest came up with an idea for a book that he and Peter could write together. He sketched the plot out for his friend in some detail: a Q-boat, much like the *Pilar,* would come in contact with a German submarine, a vivid if lopsided battle to ensue. The idea was that Ernest would write the sections taking place aboard the Q-boat, while Peter would write the sections about the German sub. Ernest predicted a best seller, with the proceeds evenly split, which would make it possible for Peter never, he averred, "to whore for Hollywood again." While Peter was flattered and tempted, he doubted he could write believably, even with a lot of research, about a German submarine. More than that, he foresaw that collaboration would be extremely difficult—he was having a tough enough time with John Huston. Though he spent "a couple of sleepless nights" thinking about it, he wrote a letter turning Ernest down, finally anxious to preserve their friendship. Writing back, Ernest pretended he had not heard Peter decline to collaborate, looking forward to a meeting at which they could discuss the project further.

Shortly after the Viertels visited him, Ernest met another substitute son, in this case one who would become a lifelong friend and a veritable Boswell—a position in which he excited some controversy. Aaron Edward

Hotchner, known as Ed, was, like Ernest's first three wives, born in St. Louis, and was, like Peter Viertel, born in 1920. He graduated from Washington University (as had Pauline); he also earned a law degree there and briefly practiced as a lawyer, which would aid him in his future writing, editorial, and entrepreneurial career. When he met Ernest in May 1948, he was a staff writer with *Cosmopolitan,* then known as a publisher of outstanding fiction.

Cosmopolitan was planning an issue on the future, asking experts in diverse areas to weigh in on the subject in their fields, and dispatched Ed Hotchner to Havana to extract an article from Hemingway on the future of literature. Ernest agreed to meet Hotch, as he would call his new friend (Ed called him Papa from the start), at the Floridita, where he introduced the journalist to the Papa Doble, a daiquiri-type of drink he had invented, containing a double measure of rum frothed with ice, fresh grapefruit and lime juices, and *no sugar.* Hotch tried to keep pace with Ernest on Papa Dobles, and little business got done. After a fishing trip the next day on the *Pilar,* Ernest, when he heard that the magazine was offering a more than respectable $15,000 for the article, agreed to write it. Before long he was promising the magazine, through Hotch, two projected short stories and, not long after, rights to his next novel.

Hotch was not the most promising candidate for kid brother in Ernest's life; he was short and freckled and unprepossessing. The son of a traveling salesman, he had gotten off to a slow start, serving as a journalist with the Army in World War II (which Ernest and he seem not to have discussed); he would become a prolific book writer in his forties and beyond, but as a young man he had published very little. His deepening friendship with Ernest, however, helped Hotch establish a niche for himself, adapting Ernest's stories and novels for television and, sometimes, the theater and film. Hotch's many efforts on this front brought Ernest welcome money and exposure.

Hotch and Ernest began hatching plans for various projects as soon as they met, though the article on the future of literature was canceled. Hotch arranged for an advance on the two short stories (which never appeared in *Cosmopolitan*), but Ernest declined any advance for his novels-in-progress, *The Garden of Eden* and *Islands in the Stream,* saying he could not write with anyone breathing down his neck.

His writing plans were put on hold in September, when he and Mary sailed to Italy on a belated honeymoon on board the *Jagiello,* a small enough boat that he told Peter Viertel he hoped to fish off her stern, surely a misguided notion. They docked at Genoa and drove through Stresa and

Cortina, skirting Lake Maggiore—all old haunts that were featured in *A Farewell to Arms.* He found a very warm welcome among the northern Italians; Alberto Mondadori, one of his two Italian publishers, reported huge sales of his Italian editions.

This trip to Italy marked the beginning of Ernest's attraction to social advancement, something to which he had previously been immune, despite friendships with celebrities and playboys like Winston Guest and Tommy Shevlin. His new friends were a cut above this crew on the social scale: well-born members of old European aristocratic families. In Cortina, for instance, he met Count Federico Kechler, who shared his enthusiasm for hunting and fishing, whose friendship he cultivated. The Hemingways enjoyed Cortina so much that they arranged to rent, as of December, a house, the Villa Aprile, on the outskirts of the city. Mary had plans to ski while Ernest hunted and fished, as she had done in Sun Valley.

They reached Venice in late October. They stayed at the Gritti Palace and Ernest soon discovered Harry's Bar nearby. The city captivated them both. But Ernest also discovered quieter pleasures on the island of Torcello in the Venetian lagoon, where they stayed at the Locanda Cipriani; there Ernest spent the morning writing, the afternoons duck shooting, and the evenings eating extremely well in the inn's excellent restaurant. He was working on a story about a retired colonel enjoying just such hunts, and as it took shape he wondered whether it might turn into a novel. Mary spent part of the month of November in Fiesole, outside Florence, where she stayed with her friends Alan and Lucy Moorehead, and met Bernard Berenson—who would become an enthusiastic correspondent of Ernest's, though the two men never met. Ernest was enjoying himself so much that he stayed behind on Torcello.

Carlos Baker points out that in his several stays in northern Italy Ernest came to love Venice so much that he sometimes imagined that he had defended the city during the First World War. Fossalta was not far from Venice and Ernest went to see the place where he had been wounded, having seemingly forgotten he had made this trip before, in 1922. He was accompanied by Fernanda Pivano, who was then translating *A Farewell to Arms,* previously unavailable in Italian. Pivano interested Ernest greatly because she had been arrested shortly after undertaking this translation back in 1943 (at that time for the publisher Einaudi); Mussolini had banned the book because it was felt the novel made the Italian army look bad, especially in the description of the Battle of Caporetto. Ernest had decided that it was important for Pivano to see some of the places on which he had based various scenes in the novel. (Her translation would appear in 1949.) At Fossalta, he found the site greatly changed, an enormous disappointment. There was a crater where once was the battlefield he remembered. He had imagined defecating on the spot, an odd but perhaps understandable impulse. Instead, using that old substitute for shit, money (pace Freud), he dug a little hole and stuffed in it a $10,000 lira note—about $15. Rather than having been wounded in this nondescript spot, he much preferred the idea of himself defending Venice from an Austrian attack.

In December, the Hemingways met Federico Kechler's brother, Carlo, who took Ernest hunting for partridge in the marshes of the lower Tagliamento River, near the Adriatic coast, as well as fishing nearby, on the property of Carlo's friend Baron Nanuk (or Nanyuki) Franchetti (his father had given him and his sister, Afdera, African names, which would have intrigued Ernest). Carlo invited an eighteen-year-old family friend, Adriana Ivancich, to a shooting party one weekend at Franchetti's lodge. That Friday he and Ernest were to pick her up at a crossroads near the Ivancich home, but they lost track of time talking about World War I and kept her waiting in the rain. When they reached the Franchetti lodge Adriana took a seat by the fireplace to dry herself. Her luxurious long black hair was wet, and she did not have a comb. Ernest, in a gesture that must have seemed to him the height of romance, and the beginning of a lustful fantasy, broke his comb in two and gave half to Adriana.

Ernest was smitten. Though he was a year away from fifty, Ernest would proceed to act as though he had moved on to a new love. He had established a pattern, shedding a wife when a new woman came along—Scott Fitzgerald once said his friend moved on to a new woman with every book. Ernest seems to have expected that he would encounter absolutely no opposition in wooing Adriana—that this not-quite-adult Venetian would fall in love with him in return, and that her family would happily marry off the well-bred young Adriana to a middle-aged, eccentric American writer, who would by that time be four times divorced. Long used to desirable women becoming attracted to him, he was to have a very rude awakening, and one that deeply marked him.

Adriana later said that her first thought on climbing into Carlo's car was that Ernest was an old man—though when she looked more closely she realized he was probably not as old as he looked. The men offered her drinks from a flask, but she declined. Whatever transpired on that hunting weekend at the Franchettis' was not recorded, but in the months to come Ernest would see Adriana several times, becoming totally lovestruck.

Adriana Ivancich, the young Venetian woman
with whom Ernest fell in love in 1948

Almost immediately he saw that he could not very well lay siege to her as he might have done to earlier conquests, as she was almost always accompanied by her mother, Dora, or her brother, Gianfranco.

The Ivanciches were a very old family. They were from an island in Dalmatia, owners of merchant ships that traveled all over Europe, part of the great commerce of the Veneto. Anton Luigi Ivancich moved the family from Dalmatia to Venice in the seventeenth century, where they took their place in the Venetian aristocracy; they were said to be one of the city's five leading families. Adriana's grandfather, she said, owned the Grand Hotel when Queen Victoria stayed there, and had established his family in a century-old elegant palazzo in the Calle de Rimedio, near the Piazza San Marco. Adriana's father, Carlo, was given the title Grandissimo Ufficiale Dottore for his work on behalf of the city, especially bringing in electricity. In the recent war, when northern Italy was still held by the Germans, Carlo Ivancich had helped route supplies to Italians who were working underground with the Allies. Gianfranco, the oldest of Adriana's three brothers, had fought with Rommel in North Africa and been wounded in 1942, but had joined the American OSS and worked with the underground in Venice. Italy joined the Allies in September 1943, but the northern regions remained in the German grip and thus subject to air attacks. The Ivancich country estate in San Michele was destroyed in 1945 by Allied bombers aiming for a nearby bridge; Carlo and Gianfranco escaped by bicycle. Shortly after, Carlo was found mysteriously murdered in a San Michele alley, a victim of the tangled score settling between the partisans and their foes. This dramatic series of family tragedies, with their swashbuckling romantic overtones, piqued Ernest's interest.

Dora Ivancich did not know what to make of this American with a white beard who increasingly desired her daughter's time and attention, and she wasn't satisfied by Adriana's explanations. Adriana was flattered by the attention and warmed to Ernest—a feeling that would last for some time, though on her part the flirtation soon settled into a friendship. Her mother allowed her to go to lunch at Harry's Bar with Ernest when she heard Mary would be present. Adriana, who had made her debut in Venice the year before, had as sheltered an upbringing as was possible in wartime. She went to Catholic girls' schools and spent six months in school in Switzerland; despite this rather spotty education she was intelligent and talented, especially in art. And she was classically beautiful. Her clear green eyes set off her black hair, flawless olive skin, and prominent cheekbones, and her proportions were lovely. Her English was fair, but Ernest's eccentric speech patterns and his slang often confused her, and his tourist's Italian, while better than average, remained rusty.

Ernest's growing affection extended to the Ivanciches as a family, especially when he met Gianfranco, who had behaved so heroically in the war and suffered so profoundly. Gianfranco would soon begin a job with the Sidarma shipping company, which was, happily enough, based in Havana. He engaged both Mary and Ernest, but Mary would become especially close to him over the years. In her memoirs, she pointedly describes Gianfranco—"delightful . . . deep, dark eyes"—having barely mentioned Adriana. Mary was impressed by Ernest's desire to help the stricken family however he could, but she watched the flirtation between him and Adriana warily. She was less jealous than worried that Ernest would be hurt or humiliated. She thought, "Ernest was weaving a mesh which might entangle and pain him." She reasoned, however, that nothing she could say would deflect him from the relationship.

In May 1949 the Hemingways returned to Cuba, where they found three nests of paired mourning doves and a blooming star jasmine winding itself around the massive ceiba tree in front of the house. In their absence a tower, planned by Mary with a lot of help from Pauline, had been erected on the northwest side of the house. The first floor of the tower was given to the cats, who were ousted from their room in the house, which subsequently became a guest room. The second floor was dedicated to storing the Hemingways' massive collection of luggage, while the third floor, which commanded an impressive view of Havana, was to be Ernest's study. Mary planned to sun herself naked on the roof of the tower, one of her favorite activities. It proved to be a great relief to rid the house of the cats, now numbering over thirty. Some visitors had, not surprisingly, noted the fragrance of the litter boxes. But Ernest barely used his third-floor study. He told Mary he missed the everyday sounds of the household and found it hard to write without them.

Ernest toiled continuously at his typewriter, which was placed atop a bookcase in his bedroom so that he could type standing up, which he sometimes preferred. In the afternoons, as usual, he fished or puttered around the Finca. Buck Lanham visited in June. He left his wife, Mary, at home. (Everyone called Buck's wife Pete—also the name Mary Hemingway took in her sex play with Ernest.) Both Lanhams had visited the Finca just after the war, but Pete Lanham and Ernest had clashed repeatedly, over everything from bullfighting to Ernest's attitude toward women. Ernest stopped himself on the verge of throwing a wineglass in her face. So Buck came down from Washington alone. On this visit, he noted Ernest's often abusive treatment of Mary, who in turn looked on approvingly, with smiles, when Ernest started telling stories about his sexual exploits, most of which she knew to be false.

Early in June, Ernest received what should have been happy news: Jack was to be married to Byra "Puck" Whittlesey, a war widow he had met out west. But Ernest had been feuding with Jack for months over an incident involving his courtship of a different woman. Jack had met Nancy de Marigny, a young widow and family friend at the Finca, and when she left for her family's place in the Bahamas, he followed her, much to Ernest's inexplicable disgust. Ernest was so furious he threatened to disinherit his eldest son. This marked the start of a pattern: Ernest always violently opposed the women his sons were serious about, though he usually came around eventually. Over Ernest's protests, Jack married Puck in Paris on June 25; Julia Child was the matron of honor and Alice B. Toklas—Jack's remaining godmother, after Gertrude Stein's death in 1946—the hit of the reception, which was held in Hadley and Paul Mowrer's apartment. Ernest was mollified when their wedding photographs arrived, and by the time Joan, or Muffet, their first child, and Ernest's first grandchild, was born all was forgiven. Ernest would never be a doting grandfather—there are few mentions of grandchildren in his correspondence—and new difficulties between Ernest and Jack grew out of the fits and starts of his son's career.

That spring, Ernest had found that the story he was writing about an American colonel hunting in Venetian marshes had grown appreciably, taking shape as a novel—probably to his great relief, since there was no end in sight to *The Garden of Eden* or the Sea manuscript. The narrative's hero, Richard Cantwell, a West Point graduate, is a veteran of both world wars who had been in Spain during the civil war as an observer (much as had Charlie Sweeny, Ernest's much admired soldier-of-fortune friend) and was demoted in World War II after a disastrous battle. Cantwell is having a love affair with a beautiful eighteen-year-old Venetian countess whom Ernest first called Nicola and eventually Renata.

The story takes place in various Venetian settings, restaurants, and the Gritti Palace. Renata mysteriously gives or loans the colonel some family emeralds; they make love in a gondola. Mostly they talk through several meals at the Gritti, Hemingway describing in great detail Cantwell's friendship with the headwaiter. Cantwell talks at length to Renata (who periodically reassures him that yes, she is still listening) about his war experiences, based partly on Ernest's own war history but mostly that of Buck Lanham and his old friend Chink Dorman-Smith. Chink's military career, always controversial, had foundered after serving as chief of operations under Field Marshal Claude Auchinleck in North Africa, providing the basis for Cantwell's disgrace. Cantwell details the battle on the Piave River in World War I and includes stories from the next war about battles in Normandy and the Hürtgenwald, as well as the liberation of Paris.

Cantwell is ill, suffering from a heart condition and high blood pressure; Ernest himself had been severely warned about his own blood pressure just months before. The colonel is separated from his journalist wife, who is clearly modeled on Martha. The book opens with great promise, describing the colonel hunting ducks after dawn in a marsh near Venice. An elegiac tone prepares the reader for what is to come: Cantwell is just fifty—Ernest turned fifty while writing the book—yet he dies at the end, his heart giving out, alone in the backseat of his chauffeur-driven Buick, on his way to Trieste. Ernest gave the book another of his striking titles, *Across the River and into the Trees*, taken from the last words of Stonewall Jackson: "Let us cross over the river and rest under the shade of the trees."

It would be his weakest book.

TWENTY-SEVEN

Ernest liked animals and he liked cockfights—both of them quite a lot. His fondness for cats or "cotsies"—as he called them—is part of the legend, and, as such, frequently distorted. The story has it that Ernest had some kind of pod of cats in Key West that inbred unchecked, resulting in the tribe of six-toed cats that overrun the Hemingway house in Key West today. Patrick Hemingway has stated that the Hemingway family had no cats when they lived in Key West, and the cats there today have nothing to do with Ernest Hemingway or his family.

Cuba is where Ernest had the cats. As of 1947, there were twenty-two: Littless, Boise, Princesa, Uncle Willy, Bigotes, Uncle Wolfie, Spendy, Shopsky, Thrusty, and so on, each with its own distinct personality, the subject of countless conversations and speculations, always a feature of letters between Ernest and Mary—who also liked cats. Though she liked cats too, Martha took some male cats to be neutered to check the breeding, winning an outburst from Ernest. Mary designed the dedicated cat room on the ground floor of the Finca's newly built tower, with shelves for the cats to sleep on and floors that slanted toward a drain and could be easily hosed down. Ernest worried that the move would make the cats feel rejected, but everyone soon adjusted.

Something of the complicated nature of Ernest's feeling for animals is evident in a story he told to Bonte Durán, the wife of one of his Spanish Civil War heroes (Gustavo Durán would soon join the ranks of friends whom he turned on). A cat was missing, and Ernest feared a dog had killed it. This made him recall a bloody incident in which a local dog killed one of his cats, and Ernest "gut-shot" the dog, he told Bonte, so that the dog took three days to die. Ernest seemed to want approval, she told Carlos Baker, but instead she burst into tears.

Perhaps Ernest had been so angry about his cat's death that he entertained a fantasy of killing a dog in this way, and then invented a story that made it "true." It does not seem in character for him to have deliberately made a dog suffer. He owned dogs; in fact, a beloved black spaniel-like stray, Black Dog, was his constant companion; five other dogs, at Malcolm Cowley's 1948 count, had their homes at the Finca. And he was well known to endorse good hunting procedures, which held that if you wounded an animal you had to kill it, even though stalking the wounded beast might endanger your life—an ethos reinforced on his African safari.

Peter Viertel later told a story about shooting at beer bottles with Ernest and John Huston on board the *Pilar* in the spring of 1948. While the boat was anchored in a cove for lunch, an enormous iguana appeared on shore, a little too far away to see clearly. With Peter coaching him through binoculars, Ernest hit the iguana with his third shot, upon which it leaped into the air and ran away. Ernest would not allow the boat to leave the cove without dispatching the iguana. Swimming ashore with his gun held over his head to keep it dry, Ernest eventually found blood spots and the three men were able to track the animal to a cave, where Ernest shot it dead. Conversely, Tommy Shevlin's wife saw Ernest row a dinghy ashore from the *Pilar* when he saw two turtles mating. He parted them and took one for cat food. The other he flipped on his back, leaving it to die; she remembered it turning pink, then purple, and emitting a horrible smell before it died.

Still, he loved a good cockfight—a pastime with a venerable tradition in Cuba, dating to the indigenous Taino people, and in Ernest's time both cockfights and gambling on them were legal. Ernest was introduced to the sport in 1943 by his gardener, Pichilo, who bred cocks for fighting, and cockfighting became a fixture of life at the Finca, one that it is said Gary Cooper especially enjoyed. For cockfights, two "gamecocks," or male chickens bred for fighting, have their wattles, combs, and earlobes removed, as well as most of their feathers. The birds' natural spurs are often removed as well, in some traditions replaced by miniature silver spurs, though in Cuba the natural spurs are usually taken off, sharpened, and reattached. Two gamecocks are let loose in what is called a cockpit and allowed to fight each other to the death, sometimes for fifteen, and sometimes for thirty minutes. More than half of the fights are said to be over in the first five minutes. Gambling is a fundamental part of the ritual.

Ernest looked at cockfighting—the alleged cruelty to animals involved—much as he did bullfighting. The two activities are hardly comparable, to be sure; a *Death in the Afternoon* for the cockfight is not likely. Ernest's defense of the activity was forthright and simple, and has been quoted widely by fellow fans (*aficiones?*): "Some people put the arm on fighting cocks as cruel. But what the hell else does a fighting cock like to do?"

As Ernest pointed out in his defense of cockfighting, the same people who crusaded against fighting gamecocks also argued that pigeon hunting—another of Ernest's favored activities in Cuba—was cruel to animals. In fact, Ernest did any number of things in the name of sport that would arouse indignation among many animal lovers: he used submachine guns on sharks and blew them up with grenades; he shot coyotes from the air; sometimes, despite all his protestations to the contrary, he hunted big game from a jeep; he once used a dead 514-pound tuna, rigged aloft on a dock, as a punching bag.

And yet. As René Villarreal, the Cuban boy who grew up at the Finca, stated simply, "[Ernest] was a great lover of nature. Even though he was a hunter, I never saw him harm an animal. He always told us, 'Never even throw rocks at a bird.'" Ernest learned the rules for humans and the natural world at his father's knee, and he venerated these rules, making them part of the famous Hemingway code, which never changed. He also told one of his daughters-in-law that the one point on which he parted company with the Catholic Church was that he believed animals had souls.

If Hemingway did not see any contradictions in or dilemmas about where he stood vis-à-vis animals, that does not mean that his apprehension of the animal world was simple. In fact, it was fraught with any number of conflicting emotions. Nowhere is this clearer than in his relation to wild animals in captivity—usually in circuses, though sometimes in zoos. Starting around 1949, and coinciding with a lot of odd developments in his life, Ernest became fascinated with handling circus animals.

No doubt Ernest had gone to circuses as a child, and perhaps he had taken his children to one in Key West, but circuses did not seem to engage his admiration until his time in Cuba. Mostly ragtag affairs, run by would-be entrepreneurs with Cuban companies, circuses often set up in towns like San Francisco de Paula. A vacant lot just outside the Finca's gates became a frequent home to these traveling shows, and Ernest, with his omnipresent curiosity, became, after he visited the first of these, a habitué.

He had a particular affinity for the bear. Over the years he described several dreams of bears: once, he even dreamed he made love to a bear, as he wrote Mary in 1944, shaking hands with the bear afterward, noting the beautiful silver of its fur. As a boy, he said, bears always got along with him, to the point where he wondered if he smelled like a bear to another bear. A bear he "worked with" at a circus, which was not friends with anyone, once licked his hand and kissed him on the face, he said; he companionably put his hand in the bear's paw. He joked that given a couple more days this bear would leave the circus and go drinking with him at the Floridita. At another time he said it was wrong to kill black bears because they like to drink and to dance, and because they understood him better than other kinds of bears did. On the other hand, he told Ed Hotchner about an incident with an agitated, pacing polar bear on one of his visits to the circus between performances: the bear's keeper told Ernest he was mean, and Ernest admitted, "I should get through to him, but I haven't talked bear talk for some time and may be rusty." He moved as close to the bear as he could get through the bars and began murmuring to him "in a soft, musical breath." The bear stopped pacing, sat down and looked at Ernest, and made a number of sounds through its nose. "I'll be goddamned," said the keeper. "Bears like me," explained Ernest. "Always have."

But when the circus came to town in September 1949—a modest outfit, its tent pitched in a lot just to the right of the driveway leading up to the Finca—it was, not surprisingly, the big cats, or cotsies, that enchanted him. He made friends with Gonzalo, the lion tamer, and his co-workers. He was delighted to hear the lions' roaring at night, he told a friend. Tigers, he wrote to Mary, then in Chicago, were mean, while nobody had been able to train a leopard at all.

Ernest charmed and impressed Gonzalo enough that he allowed Ernest to come into the large performance cage with the lions. Ernest reported that he "gentled" them with a rolled-up newspaper, which he tapped on their noses if they misbehaved. He decried the fact that it was necessary to irritate the cats to provoke performance-level threatening and roaring; otherwise, he said, they were gentle creatures—though he learned never to turn his back on them. Moralito, the owner of the circus, whom Ernest also befriended, complained that the lions were his biggest draw but cost a lot to keep. He relied on a lion-taming team who worked cheap, and he constantly feared they would find out what more established circuses paid. Ernest joked that he would gladly work as Moralito's lion tamer if his employees deserted him. Ernest also told Mary and Ed Hotchner that he was planning such an act, and that Moralito was actually going to announce it, billing Ernest as the legendary North American lion tamer.

What happened next became a legend in Cuba. René Villarreal has given a fine account of the story: he says that he heard the circus owner announcing throughout the neighborhood that Mr. Ernest Hemingway, the American writer, would be appearing that evening as the lion tamer. René found Ernest in his bedroom rubbing some viscous potion from a whiskey bottle on his torso and arms. The potion was lion lard, rendered from the lions he had shot in Africa, Ernest told the boy, and he was rubbing it on himself so that he would smell like a lion to the circus beast. He was actually planning to appear that night with the circus. He refused to consider canceling his performance because it would look like he was backing out, he said. He put on his safari clothes and made his way to the circus tent, where he found Gonzalo and told him about the deal he had made with Moralito.

At this point, René said, both Moralito and Gonzalo urged Ernest not to go into the ring, but he insisted. The audience and the circus workers, somewhat astounded by this turn of events, wondered how far this was going to go. Even Ernest acknowledged to Moralito, before the event, that the crowds had come "to see how the lions maul Hemingway, not to see Hemingway tame the lions." What followed was a bit of an anticlimax. Gonzalo urged Ernest to stay right beside him when they went before the crowd. The tamer picked up a chair and a whip, and Ernest picked up another chair. Together they entered the ring. The lion lifted his paw and took a swipe at Gonzalo's chair, knocking it from the man's hand. Gonzalo, concentrating on the lion, told Ernest to walk quietly but quickly to the cage door and let himself out. Ernest complied. René's account ends here—but in another telling, Ernest demanded, and received, payment for his part in the performance.

After this escapade, Hotch noticed long, deep scratches on Ernest's forearms, which Ernest admitted had been made when he was "gentling" the cotsies—and which he also disclosed to Mary and Charlie Scribner. If they found this behavior peculiar, they did not say, Hotchner and Scribner confining themselves to protesting that he was endangering his livelihood and ought to stop. Mary extracted a promise from him, he sheepishly told Hotch and Charlie, that he would not work with the big cats again, and for the time being he kept it. But when the circus came to town the following year, Ernest, though he did not perform, again hung about the tent until he was allowed to talk to the bears and "gentle" the cats. He told a friend that he hoped to work before long with an elephant.

A number of factors seem to have been at work in Ernest's attempt at greater intimacy with dangerous animals. First was his belief in his own invincibility, fostered by years of accidents and close calls. Second was a kind of magical thinking at work; Ernest was a big believer in superstitions and also in some sorts of psychic phenomena. This was partly what drew him to bullfighting; like many *aficionados,* he believed the bullfighter must "understand" the bull if he was to be successful. Looked at in another way, Ernest's quest for intimacy with the circus animals was simply a natural outgrowth of the intimacy he had learned to feel with nature since boyhood, a kind of silent communion that is at work in several of the Nick Adams stories.

Perhaps the intimacy grew out of another tendency in his thought that was coming to the fore the summer that he turned fifty. Surrounded by yea-sayers who applauded all his actions at the same time as they depended on him financially and emotionally, Ernest had come to view the Finca as a sort of feudal domain, with himself as a local potentate with the very highest status in the local community. It is not surprising that, seeing himself as a quasi-patriarch, Ernest came to feel he was a sort of Lord of the Jungle.

In fact, this last element in his foolhardy attempt at intimacy with circus animals in the summer of 1949 suggests the grandiosity that was increasingly coming to dominate his thinking—which was becoming less and less rational as he grew more and more unhinged.

While mental illness had been lurking in Ernest's genes since birth, it had not previously predominated in his emotional life. In fact, he does not seem to have suffered earlier from full-blown mania, though his characteristic quickness, high self-regard, and sheer exuberance all might be seen as manic symptoms, responsible for, as in many talented and highly functional sufferers of the disease, his great productivity and, in a different aspect, even his charisma. The concomitant depressive episodes are a little easier to track; Ernest seems to have sunk into a major depression during, for example, the hundred-day separation from Pauline in 1926, when he threatened suicide.

What was happening to Ernest around 1949, when he turned fifty, was something more than a midlife crisis (though it partook of that quality as well). Rather, it seems to have marked the beginning of a manic cycle in his life on an order he had not before experienced. To many onlookers and those who loved him, the symptoms were not immediately recognizable, particularly as they seemed consonant with his generally excitable, voluble nature. In fact, Carlos Baker uses the term "rough exuberance" to describe the aspect his letters took on in this period. It was more than that, however.

Acknowledged symptoms of mania include any of the following: generalized excitement and happiness; racing thought and pressured speech; confusion; irritability; restlessness and insomnia; grandiosity or inflated view of self; poor judgment; reckless behavior; increased sex drive; overspending; self-destructive behavior; and, sometimes, hallucinations, paranoia, and catatonic behavior. In conditions like Ernest's, cycles of depression follow cycles of mania, but many sufferers cycle rapidly in and out of these conditions.

It is important to note, however, that what was wrong with Ernest would not necessarily have been recognized as a mental illness. His symptoms would be attributed not only to his personality—his "exuberance"—but also, perhaps, to drunkenness. They could effectively be explained away.

Many competent physicians would probably not have classified his behavior as manic depression; the disorder was not diagnosed often in those years, and not widely recognized until 1970, at the same time (strangely enough) lithium was found to treat the disease. Ernest's behavior would not definitively indicate mental illness—though some doctors took note that it increasingly found psychotic expression.

Ernest's midlife mania may have been triggered by any number of factors: Jack's marriage in June, which may have reminded him unpleasantly of the passage of time; he responded badly when Patrick subsequently announced his engagement to Henrietta Broyles, writing to Henny's parents, falsely, that his grandfather was a Son of the American Revolution and a member of the Order of the Cincinnati. Both his sons' marriages seemed to bring out a heretofore buried, clannish snobbery, learned from his mother and perhaps activated by his exposure to the Venetian aristocracy in 1949 and 1950.

At about the same time, Ernest received a letter that excited quite different emotions. It was from Arthur Mizener, asking him for information about Scott Fitzgerald. Now that the Fitzgerald revival was in full swing, Mizener, undertaking a major biography, was contacting friends and associates who knew Scott. Ernest answered Mizener's letter immediately, and would bombard him with letters about his old friend for the next year—some vitriolic.

The timing of Arthur Mizener's biography of F. Scott Fitzgerald, *The Far Side of Paradise*, which was published in early 1951, occasioned some of Ernest's most baroque remarks and some of his worst perfidy—though also some indications of his tender feelings toward his old friend. Mizener originally contacted Ernest just before his fiftieth birthday in July 1949, right at the onset of Ernest's crisis. Ernest told Mizener of his willingness to help him in gathering information and bemoaned the loss of his letters from Scott, destroyed by bugs in storage in Key West. His initial letter to the biographer established the parameters of his relationship with Scott for Mizener: Ernest really loved Scott, but he was impossible. "He had a very steep trajectory and was almost like a guided missile with no one guiding him," Ernest wrote, perceptively. Ernest did not say anything about his own large professional debt to Scott: the essential help Scott gave him early in his career—namely, touting his work at Scribner's and other places and making the much needed cut of the first twenty pages of *The Sun Also Rises*, and the edits he made in the rest of the manuscript. (Ernest did mention the suggestions Scott made about *A Farewell to Arms*, which he completely ignored, and which he frequently misrepresented so as to make Scott look

stupid.) In the picture Ernest painted for Mizener, he was always the dominant one in the relationship—thus the emphasis on Scott's case of hero
worship of him. He was trying to imprint this on the permanent record.

Ernest wrote seven letters to Mizener over the next year and a half,
in almost every one offering his help freely. "I never had any respect for
[Scott] ever," Ernest wrote in an April 1950 letter, "except for his lovely,
golden, wasted talent." In the same letter he passed on what he thought
was useful information, for instance, the story of Zelda asking Ernest if he
didn't think Al Jolson was greater than Jesus. Yet he closed the letter with a
touching and insightful paragraph that ended with a wish that Scott were
there. "He was romantic, ambitious, and Christ, Jesus, God knows how
talented." He was a "charming cheerful companion" except for "his tendency to hero-worship"—especially difficult, Ernest said, when you were
one of his heroes. "He was fragile Irish instead of tough Irish," he wrote.

A month later he explained the relevance of Scott's sexual inexperience:
"I think Scott in his strange mixed-up Irish catholic monogamy wrote for
Zelda and when he lost all hope in her and she destroyed his confidence in
himself he was through." He trotted out another favorite canard: that Scott
was hoping to live on advances for *The Last Tycoon*, never intending to
complete the novel. He offered his reading of Fitzgerald's output, observing, for instance, that he found *Gatsby* "OK with reservations."

Ernest wrote two back-to-back letters to Mizener in early June. The first
was mostly incoherent rambling about himself as a writer and contemporary of Scott, with observations about Joyce, Pound, Stein, and some critics. Edmund Wilson was on his mind—especially Wilson's theory about
Ernest's work, which was that Ernest wrote from a psychic wound (as much
as his physical wound in World War I) that shaped his entire sensibility and
his writing. In the second letter to Mizener he told one of his more gruesome stories of killing a German, one of 122 "sures," but Ernest added a
postscript that said the letter was never sent.

There was nothing of use about Scott in either of these letters. A week
later Ernest was explaining to Harvey Breit, a faithful correspondent,
that one of his activities was helping out Mizener with his biography: "I
try to give him the straight dope on Scott because he, Scott, was crazy
about immortality etc. and I was very fond of him even though he was a
horses ass."

*   *   *

The novel that came out of Ernest's long manic period was *Across the River
and into the Trees,* born, without a doubt, from Ernest's deep fears about

his writing future and his reputation. *For Whom the Bell Tolls* had appeared almost ten years before; he had not published a book since. Word had leaked out that he was writing the "Big Book," the one he envisioned as the Land, Air, and Sea book—or, alternately, a trilogy. So far, however, he had produced only a desultory series of sketches about the sea, using an autobiographical stand-in, Roger Hudson, Hudson's adventures in Bimini, and his relationship with his sons. Ernest had broken off the Sea novel to begin *The Garden of Eden,* the gender-bending story of an idyll (the main character had been a pilot during World War I, so perhaps the project grew out of a larger Air piece), and he was floundering with this one as well. He also believed it was unpublishable for its sexual content and, presumably, what it revealed about his own inner landscape. As Robert Trogdon has pointed out, two other factors relating to Ernest's writing life were in play: one was the fact that he owed *Cosmopolitan* the money Ed Hotchner had gotten as an advance for two short stories. He could fulfill his obligations to the magazine by letting them serialize what had taken shape as a novel. Furthermore, he may have felt the heat of competition from new sources: a wave of young postwar writers, including Norman Mailer.

Many of these concerns came together around Ernest's birthday on July 21, 1949, when he turned fifty. Before and after that date he very often referred to himself as "half a hundred"; so too does the fifty-year-old protagonist in *Across the River and into the Trees.* The new book was all about the colonel's mortality, clearly a projection of Ernest's very real fears—fears that were not unfounded, given his medical history. *Across the River* presents a chilling, if off-putting, portrait of a man at the end of his rope, clear even in the bonhomie of sections set in the Gritti and with Renata. The colonel bears a close resemblance to characters in earlier stories like "The Battler," "The Undefeated," and "The Snows of Kilimanjaro," moving inexorably toward their rendezvous with death, although only the last has a protagonist as self-aware as Colonel Cantwell. What was new was Ernest's willingness to present his character at such an extreme of emotional vulnerability. Yet Ernest seems to have had little artistic control over his portrait of the colonel; the sureness of his earlier work is not there. The novel presents the death throes of a character deeply identified with his creator—but his creator may have had no idea how autobiographical his portrait was.

In this sense, Ernest plunged into mania to cheat death. Over the next year or so he told enormous lies; he spent outrageous amounts of money; he got into terrible fights, some physical; he displayed outsize egotism and delusions of grandeur; his moods fluctuated wildly, commented on by almost everyone who knew him; he made bad decisions; he fell in love with an inappropriate woman; he seemed to have inexhaustible supplies of energy that fueled all sorts of complicated schemes and projects. By the time those around him were able to tell something was wrong, his mania was full-blown and there was no reasoning with him. It is not clear how he would have responded were someone to have intervened. The idea of psychiatry, it seems, was not broached until the last year of his life. Shock treatments were familiar to him through Patrick's illness, and Gregory would undergo many such treatments in future. Lithium would not be available in the United States until 1970, nine years after Ernest's suicide. Finally, it is not entirely clear that these options were not discussed by Ernest and those around him; in his last illness great care was taken to ensure secrecy, and similar concerns may have been operative long before.

Those in the grip of mania often lose a sense of proportion, becoming grandiose and making poor choices. Perhaps worst of all, Ernest lost all critical judgment when it came to his writing. And he was writing poorly, his words powered by his manic delusions rather than any real inspiration or even storytelling impulse. *Across the River and into the Trees* is riddled with flaws, from the colonel's fundamental unlikability to the unreality of a young, lovely, nobly born woman having fallen in love with a cantankerous and garrulous fifty-year-old whose only subjects are war, food, and their very dubious love affair. Mostly, the writing is repetitive and indulgent: the colonel asks "Daughter" repeatedly if she loves him, and she tells him she does. Everything is done "ably," "truly," or by way of some other adverb applied with thudding "significance": Renata "chewed well and solidly on her steak" (*ARIT*, 127). The book is sloppy, unedited, or unpruned, or all three: Hemingway describes the Grand Canal in a cold wind, "with the houses as clear and sharp as on a winter day, which, of course, it was" (*ARIT*, 48).

What the book shows most starkly is the extent of Hemingway's self-delusion. To take just one example: the colonel really believes that the eighteen-year-old countess loves him, just as Ernest believed the eighteen-year-old Adriana Ivancich loved him. When Ernest did the bulk of the writing, he had seen Adriana several times but had probably not declared his love, except playfully, and had included Mary and an Ivancich family member at each meeting. It is clear he wanted more, and a second visit to Venice by Ernest and Mary the following year seems to have been planned with his escalated courtship of Adriana in mind. In an explicit love scene in *Across the River and into the Trees* the colonel masturbates Renata in a gondola and later makes love to her in his room in the Gritti Palace, scenarios Ernest on some level believed plausible for himself and his real-life Venetian paramour.

In a manic phase, people believe their thoughts are brilliant and want only to get others to listen; there is no mistaking this quality in Ernest's statements about the manuscript during the writing of the novel, its editing, and even throughout its poor reception. He told Charlie Scribner, in a moment of relative calm, "It is a very fine novel, written to beat all comers, and written as well or better as I can write." He went on a little more defensively, "It is a better novel than any other son of a bitch, alive or dead, can write. . . . It is a beauty of a novel." He enjoyed describing his accomplishment in inflated sports metaphors, comparing, for instance, his talent at this point in his career to a racehorse: "It was not until I was half one hundred years old that I realized had never turned the horse loose and let him run." At the same time, he began claiming imaginary sporting feats: he told Scribner he had gone foxhunting, riding on an English saddle for the first time; in another letter he said he had ridden through the "chutes" in a "bear trap saddle," for $100, presumably in a rodeo; extending sports prowess to Greg, he said the boy could ride anything bareback expertly enough to keep a postcard between his ass and the horse. Ernest claimed that as a young man he had hit a home run out of the park in the largest ballpark in the "upper Michigan league," and had the photo to prove it. All of this fed into his increasingly grandiose expectations for his new book: as he told an interviewer, he was not trying for a no-hitter with *Across the River and into the Trees:* "Going to win maybe twelve to nothing or twelve to eleven."

Sports—especially boxing—and writing, for Ernest, had somehow become one and the same. In a letter to Charlie Scribner shortly after his fiftieth birthday, he imagined himself in the ring with other writers; he knew he could never beat "Mr. Shakespeare" or "Mr. Anonymous," but he had beaten Mr. Turgenev and Mr. Maupassant, and thought he had a chance against Mr. Tolstoy. He continued in this vein the next month in his Sherry-Netherland suite in New York where Lillian Ross interviewed him for a *New Yorker* profile. He had refined the analogy in the intervening month, telling Ross, "I started out very quiet and beat Mr. Turgenev. Then I trained hard and I beat Mr. de Maupassant. I've fought two draws with Mr. Stendhal, and I think I had an edge in the last one." He was still uncertain about Tolstoy, this time saying he was not yet ready to get in the ring with the quintessential war novelist.

In a similar vein, Ernest began to rewrite his military history, implying he had fought in both world wars, when he had fought in neither in any official capacity. In one sense, this was nothing new—in the immediate aftermath of his wounding as an ambulance driver in Italy in 1918 he claimed that he had fought not only with the Italian army but with the Arditi. In spite of the fact that he had gotten into some trouble for arming himself when a war correspondent in World War II, he now bragged freely about his experiences with the Free French. He began to boast of the number of German soldiers he had killed.

In one such letter written in 1948 he told Archie MacLeish that he had been a captain with the Free French; that Buck Lanham had appointed him a second lieutenant at Hürtgenwald; that he had seen 104 days of combat; that he had got twenty-six "Krauts," all armed, "sures." He described killing a seventeen-year-old German in some detail (in other letters to different recipients he recounted other such individual killings, sometimes described in quite gruesome fashion).

Ernest made several other distortions of history in these months, many of them inexplicable and vaguely malevolent: he said, for instance, that his sister Carol was assaulted, knocked out, and raped by a sexual "pervert"; that he had a Cheyenne great-grandmother and that he had ancestors in the Crusades; that he had "read" law one winter, and that he and his brothers and sisters learned German as children. Ernest was seldom a sexual braggart, in part because his actual experience was less than his legend claimed, but in 1949–50 he told Scribner that on his birthday he had "fucked three times"; and in another letter he said he could "fuck better" now than at the age of twenty-five, and that he had, in addition to three countesses in Venice, a "lovely" new whore in Cuba. (This was one of the few periods in his life when Ernest patronized, or claimed to patronize, prostitutes.)

His letters were full of threats, some indirect but others more forthright and disturbing. He told Cardinal Spellman, in an unsent June 1949 letter, that the cardinal would not become pope as long as he, Ernest, was around. He challenged Senator Joe McCarthy to come down to Cuba and fight him "for free, without any publicity . . . would knock you on your ass the best day you ever lived." In a letter to Ingrid Bergman, a member of his chaste harem, he promised to kill Roberto Rossellini, presumably for impregnating Bergman and then not marrying her, swearing he would shoot Rossellini in various organs and in his face. When Ernest received a form letter from a committee set up to honor FDR's birthday in 1949, signed by Averell Harriman, whom he knew from Sun Valley days, Ernest wrote a polite letter declining the invitation. But he also dictated a bombastic letter to Harriman by way of his new secretary, Nita Jensen, in which he declared his unwillingness to honor "a rich and spoiled paralytic," whom he had personally found to be a "bore." (He directed Nita to keep this one in his files.)

Those around Ernest at this time noted other kinds of strange behavior as well. He was spending large amounts of money. He borrowed $10,000 from Charlie Scribner, half of it to buy a mink coat for Mary. She noted in her autobiography that they had installed a new electric stove and refrigerator in the Finca in 1949. More worryingly, however, was the fact that Ernest apparently discovered mail order shopping, possibly in the face of the difficulty of finding much that was desirable in Havana stores. Scribner had recently sent Ernest a "talk machine," which enabled him to dictate letters (and orders) through Nita. Perhaps in a nod to his new secretary's Mexican background, he ordered cases of El Paso enchilada dinners, pinto beans with red sauce, and Mexican tortillas. As his fiftieth birthday approached, be bought presents for the Finca or the *Pilar,* spending $15.95 for an alphabet's worth of marine signal flags from a Topeka, Kansas, company; an inexpensive sextant and books on celestial navigation; two quarts of an anti-mildew cleaner; a Navy ship's clock; and a waterproof floating flashlight for 98 cents. He evidently did not want to create the impression that he was buying things only for himself, having Nita send off an order to Hammacher Schlemmer for eight Currier & Ives dinner plates. At another point, however, Mary noted, in a record she showed Ernest to warn him of his excessive expenditures, that he had spent $258.90 on shirts—not a small sum in 1950 (about $2,500 today). Mary also noted another odd, house-related purchase that other observers of the Finca in those years remember as well: two miniature iron cannons that shot off good imitations of real shells, which coated operator and bystanders with black soot and made an impressive din. Firing the cannons became a ritual, according to Mary, staged for esteemed visitors.

Onlookers were noting some other elements of Ernest's behavior with alarm or concern. Mary noted some strange moods, in which Ernest appeared to make little sense: "At table Papa was ebullient, said he would marry me, even if I didn't go to bed with him." (They had married in 1946.) In her diary on October 5 she observed that Ernest was "nervous and tired" on finishing *Across the River;* soon after, she wrote, "His weariness blurred his personality." She noted behavior that Ross would observe in her *New Yorker* profile: "He was making constant repetitions of his philosophies and catchphrases and jokes, and omitting his customary beguiling grace notes. . . . I had heard him say 'truly' in solemn voice too often, and 'daughter,' voice benign, and 'when the chips are down' and 'how do you like it now, gentlemen?'" Ernest was drinking too much as well, Mary observed, and he was talking about his will. This is the one point at which the idea of seeing a psychiatrist was introduced: Mary wrote that, because in the fall of 1950 he seemed "restless and unhappy," she tried to persuade him to talk to the psychiatrist whom they consulted in Patrick's case, whom the boy had liked—to no avail.

Other health issues had arisen by this time: in February 1949, while in Venice, he developed a serious skin infection, erysipelas, his face swelling up and an ugly red. Erysipelas on the face can sometimes spread into the eye, which it evidently did in Ernest's case, as the infection was attributed to a scratch on the eye from road dust or wadded remnants of a shotgun shell. From the eye it can travel to the brain; it is a serious disease, often leading to blood poisoning. Indeed, Ernest was hospitalized in Padua for ten days for blood poisoning and received massive doses of penicillin. He was not exaggerating when he said that his life was in danger. *The New York Times* ran an article that said the infection had spread "so rapidly and virulently" that his doctors "despaired," and gave him "only a short time to live."

But these episodes perhaps obscure the point that his general health was not good. Peter Viertel, commenting on Ernest's condition in the fall of 1949, would remark, "Alcohol was obviously responsible for the deterioration of his health," though Viertel was perhaps underestimating the recovery time after the blood poisoning episode. He noted that Ernest had begun what was to be an ongoing habit of collecting and saving urine samples, urinating in a glass in the early morning and later in the day holding the urine up to the light. He kept ten or twenty such glasses in his bathroom at the Finca.

Ernest's medical records include his drug regimen in 1949, cited by Dr. Cucu Kohly. They included mannitol hexanitrate (an early drug to lower blood pressure, also used in explosives); Wychol, which prevents fat buildup in the liver; Seconal (a barbiturate); Combex (vitamin B complex); and ataxin, drops for the eyes that contain vitamin A. The regimen did not include any medication for his manic states.

All the while, however, most of Ernest's odd behavior, his inflated claims, and his hyperbolic language surrounded the novel he was writing. Those who had a glimpse of it, or more, were beginning to suspect that he was setting himself up for a big disappointment, and that his assessment of the novel as the best he'd ever written was misguided—if not deluded. Mary wrote in her autobiography that she was unhappy with the love story at the heart of the novel. "It made me feel disloyal," she wrote, "but I was finding Colonel Cantwell's and his girl's conversations banal beyond reason and their obsession with food and the ploy of the emeralds a mysterious lapse in judgment." But she kept quiet, she said, hoping that "someone at Scribner's" would help him with the manuscript.

Meanwhile, Charlie Scribner and his editors were hoping that Ernest would somehow wake up and see how bad the work was. Ed Hotchner had edited the manuscript for serialization in *Cosmopolitan,* where it began to appear in February 1950. Scribner's was getting a second, revised, manuscript from Hotchner, and what they were reading was not encouraging. Wallace Meyer was working closely with Ernest because he had gained the writer's trust, having handled advertising for *The Sun Also Rises* and copyedited *For Whom the Bell Tolls.* When he received the last *Cosmopolitan* installment, Meyer wrote Charlie Scribner that he could not be encouraging: "The basic trouble is that the book hasn't the idea of a novel." It should have been a short story, the operative word being "short." He hoped, he said, the same thing Charlie did, "that Ernest, when the manuscript has grown cold for him, as it must have done by now, would see the passages and aspects as padding, and would manage somehow to rework and rewrite to give the whole depth a reality."

Yet no one at the firm seems to have said anything critical to Ernest; Charlie Scribner wired him in February, "TRULY DELIGHTED WITH WHAT I HAVE READ OF REVISED VERSION OF NOVEL STOP IT IS NOW BECOMING YOU AT YOUR BEST." Despite this message, Ernest picked up on Meyer's and Scribner's doubts and wrote that Charlie should tell him what scenes he had trouble with so he could "fix" them. He admitted that the scene between the colonel and the Gritti headwaiter needed to be cut, but that he had gone on at such length "because it was fun." When Meyer saw the final version of the novel, however, he was dismayed anew. As he wrote Scribner, "The manuscript is not changed in any fundamental respect," though Ernest had "cleaned it up," taking out four-letter words and personal allusions—mostly scabrous comments about the colonel's ex-wife, clearly based on Martha Gellhorn. He also softened—but not by much—a thinly disguised take-down of Sinclair Lewis, whom Ernest and Mary had encountered at the Gritti.

Nobody was to do anything to his work except to fix his punctuation and spelling—at anything much more he balked, as Charlie Scribner found out when he discovered a technical error: Cantwell had addressed his driver as Sergeant, when elsewhere he identified him as having the rank of T5, which, "if you will go back to your manuals of marching," he told Ernest, was the rank of a corporal. Charlie was positively gleeful about this, feeling sure that Ernest would laugh about his technical "boner" and the publisher's diligence in catching it. He had miscalculated, however; Ernest wrote him a blistering letter in response. Scribner and his crew backed off once they saw the kind of reaction even the mildest criticism would provoke. Still, it is hard not to believe that Max would have intervened before publication if it became clear that Ernest was making no further changes to improve the novel. Instead, the new regime pushed through the book, determined to make it a best seller regardless of the critical response.

Concurrently with the publication of *Across the River and into the Trees,* Scribner's was trying to finesse another area of Ernest's poor judgment: his inability to see that a spate of poems written in 1949 were unfit for publication—though Wallace Meyer did say he found them, at first glance, "strange and individual and deeply moving," noting that he guessed Ernest was in some kind of "transition phase." Ernest, giving some thought to his reputation at the time of publication of his Venice novel, advised Scribner to bring out a volume of his stories and poems. The latter included recent poems like "Poetry" (1944) and "Defense of Luxembourg" (1945); the passive-aggressive "Poem to Mary" (1944); and a 1946 poem to one of the Finca's cats, "To Crazy Christian." It is not clear just what stories Ernest was recommending that Scribner's publish, but they no doubt included "The Good Lion" and "The Faithful Bull," two very brief fablelike stories published in *Holiday* in January 1950. In October Ernest told Charlie Scribner he thought he was making a mistake in not bringing out a collection. He wrote Charlie again in December saying that Charlie was just "wrong" in assessing the stories.

One letter to Ed Hotchner written in the run-up to publication of *Across the River and into the Trees* suggests that in more sober moments Ernest was having some doubts about his writing future—or at least that he was picking up on Hotch's anxieties. Ernest wrote, "Please don't think any chance of this being a secondary or not top-drawer book." He had been "throwing in [his] armour," he said, adding, "Brooklyn Tolstois grab your laurels." The reference to "Brooklyn Tolstois" was to Norman Mailer, who had been called the "Brooklyn Tolstoy" after the publication of his 1948 war novel, *The Naked and the Dead.* The recent spate of war novels was making Ernest anxious indeed; he, after all, was the war novelist par excellence, he believed (even including Stendhal, as his boxing ring fantasies make clear). Pretenders like Mailer, all of them younger, included, by now, John Horne Burns (*The Gallery,* 1947), Gore Vidal (*Williwaw,* 1946), and Vance Bourjaily (*The End of My Life,* 1947); Martha Gellhorn also published a war novel in 1948, *The Wine of Astonishment.* Another contender, closer to Ernest's age, was Irwin Shaw, who as Mary's erstwhile boyfriend was already suspect, and whose *The Young Lions* drew critical praise in 1948; that it contained characters based on Ernest, Mary, and Ernest's brother Leicester made Shaw's success even more galling. In his own time Ernest had seen contemporaries like E.E. Cummings and Dos Passos make their reputations on their novels about World War I and knew well what might lie ahead for the chroniclers of the next war. Perhaps his competitive anxieties fueled the inclusion of the colonel's war experiences as a plot element in *Across the River;* Ernest too felt he had to weigh in with a World War II novel—no matter that his account was an afterthought, and that the war was only incidental to the plot.

Across the River and into the Trees appeared first in *Cosmopolitan* in the winter and spring of 1950, then in book form in September. Beyond the editorial staff at Scribner's and Ernest's family and closest friends, those around him had few indications of what was on the horizon. One major exception was Martha Gellhorn's response after reading the novel in serialization: "I feel quite sick. . . . Shivering sick," she told Time-Life correspondent William Walton, then her lover, just as he had once been Mary Welsh's (though Ernest probably never knew this). "To me, it has a loud sound of madness and a terrible smell as of decay," she added. Another exception was John Dos Passos, who wrote to Edmund Wilson, after *Cosmopolitan*'s last installment, "*Across the River and into the Trees* brought out the goose pimples. . . . How can a man in his senses leave such bullshit on the page?"

This is not to say that those around him weren't having doubts on the eve of the novel's publication. On May 13, Lillian Ross's disturbing profile, "Portrait of Hemingway: 'How Do You Like It Now, Gentlemen?'" appeared in *The New Yorker.* The writer had first met Ernest in the winter of 1947–48, when she was working on a profile of matador Sidney Franklin. Undertaking her piece about Ernest, Ross did the bulk of her interviewing in New York in November 1949, when Ernest and Mary were on their way to Venice for a second visit, this time for a six-month stay. Ross met them at the airport with their fourteen pieces of luggage; once in the Hemingways' room at the Sherry-Netherland, Ernest ordered caviar and champagne, declaring that he meant to celebrate the completion of his novel.

Ross's profile followed Ernest for two days in New York, describing Ernest and Mary in their hotel room, entertaining Marlene Dietrich ("the Kraut") and Patrick Hemingway, visiting from Harvard. Ross accompanied Ernest on a shopping expedition to Abercrombie & Fitch, where he had a joyful reunion with Winston Guest. She joined a party of Ernest, Patrick, and Mary in a trip to the Metropolitan Museum, where they viewed El Greco's *View of Toledo* and paintings by Cézanne and Degas. Ross also reported on the Hemingways' room service lunch with Charlie Scribner, where Ernest told Charlie he had been "jamming, like a rider in a six-day bike race" (Ross, 53). Ross's profile captured the manic quality of Ernest's activity—most notably, in his statements about the novel. He reminisced about his pitching days, when he needed to conserve his arm for throwing fast balls (Ross, 17); he told Ross about having once lived with a bear in Montana and gotten drunk with him (Ross, 9). He forced an Abercrombie & Fitch salesclerk's hand into a fist and struck his own tensed belly with it, then punched himself, twice, as well (Ross, 40). Seeing Cézanne's work prompted him to say he wrote not only like Cézanne but also like "Mr. Johann Sebastian Bach," a new claim (Ross, 51). Moreover, Ross quoted long swaths of Ernest's speech in what she called "joke 'Indian' talk he had invented with his wife and friends," dropping his articles and pronouns in "a kind of shorthand" that she thought he employed because time was short, philosophically speaking (Ross, 60). And she showed him drinking, virtually without cease: two double bourbons before leaving the airport; champagne in the Sherry-Netherland between meals and Tavel rosé with lunch; something unnamed from a flask in the museum.

After the story appeared, Ross later wrote, disingenuously, it came to the "complete surprise of Hemingway, the *New Yorker*'s editors, and herself, [that] her profile had been very controversial." She had thought that readers would see the profile as a "sympathetic piece," as she and Ernest did (Ross, xix), and when some said they had found the piece "devastating," she said they evidently disapproved of him having a good time (Ross, xx–xxi).

Ernest, indeed, when sent the page proofs, worried mildly to Ross that she had made him sound "conceited," but then seems to have made up his mind to what he believed were Ross's good intentions, and went on to enjoy a long friendship with her. Others, however, were horrified—by the brutal forthrightness of the piece and by what it revealed about its subject. Selden Rodman, a critic who thought highly of Hemingway, flatly called the profile "a lethal exposure of posturing vanity," although he left aside Ross's motivations in so presenting Ernest. Ernest's old friend Alice B. Toklas wrote to Fernanda Pivano, Gertrude Stein's Italian translator (also Ernest's), that she was dismayed to read the profile: "It has strange revelations and exposures by himself and his wife—which were partially explained by Janet Flanner's telling me that he was mortally ill." The news had affected her "strangely," she told Pivano: "It is painful to know the

With Peter Viertel (middle) and A. E. Hotchner (right) in Paris, 1950

present situation and the horror it must hold for him." As one of those who had known him longest, and a godmother of his eldest son, she had no doubt that Ross's dire portrait was accurate.

The Hemingways, meanwhile, were eager to escape the New York literary scene. They crossed the Atlantic with Jigee Viertel, who was joined in Paris by her husband; they also met Hotch there, sent by *Cosmopolitan* to collect the manuscript of the novel, whose closing pages Ernest wrote in Paris. Afterward, Ernest showed more profligate generosity, twice dividing piles of French francs among his friends—first some unexpected French royalties and next some winnings from the horse racing at Auteuil. Both Peter and Mary detected a relationship between their spouses that went beyond flirtation, but after traveling through Avignon, Nîmes, Aix-en-Provence, Arles, and Nice, the Viertels and Hotch left the Hemingways on their own. Mary observed that "missing his cortege," Ernest was "miserable."

As they had the previous winter, Mary and Ernest split their time between Venice and Cortina. Mary, who had broken her right ankle the previous year on the ski slopes, this season broke her left one. Ernest's confidence in his forthcoming book remained unshakable, and was given a boost when the Italian publisher Mondadori reported that he was a favorite for the Nobel Prize. He also returned to spending as much time as he could in the company of Adriana. His chivalry was alive; he could at least see that readers might "mistake" Renata, the colonel's lover in *Across the River*, for his young friend, so he enjoined publication of the novel in Italy for two years. But because the hoped-for romance did not seem to progress, he decided that Adriana and her mother should pay a visit to the Finca in order to see how Gianfranco, who had been installed in the guest bedroom there, was managing in his job with the shipping company. Mary decided that etiquette dictated she issue the formal invitation; she asked Dora Ivancich over lunch at Harry's Bar, and Dora later accepted.

Leaving Venice for Paris in March, Ernest, already ecstatic that Adriana would be coming to Cuba, was further delighted to learn that she would be in Paris when he and Mary were there, furthering her studies in art. She had somewhat fancifully drawn up a cover illustration for Ernest's novel, a small sketch in watercolor of a Venice canal, complete with gondola. Charlie Scribner and his wife, traveling in Europe, met the Hemingways in Paris, and confirmed that Adriana's drawing would be used on the dust jacket—which, of course, excited Ernest further. He took the occasion to find a time and place where he and Adriana could be alone to talk. He began by telling her that, like many men—men who were not stupid—who wanted to marry her, he, himself not stupid, wanted to marry her as well. Adriana protested that he already had a wife. Ernest said, "Ah, yes, Mary. She is nice of course, and solid and courageous." But two people can sometimes come to a crossroads where one will go one way, and the other a different way, he said. "I love you in my heart," he went on, "and I cannot do anything about it." Finally, seeing Adriana's dismay, he concluded his pitch: "I would ask you to marry me, if I didn't know that you would say no." When she did not respond, Ernest smiled and said, "Now let us take a walk along the Seine." On March 21, Adriana accompanied Ernest and Mary to Le Havre and saw them off on the *Île de France*, headed for Havana.

Meanwhile, as an act in Ernest's drama with Adriana was ending, Scribner's set about planning the launch of Ernest's new novel, apparently having put aside their doubts. The previous fall they had written a press release, which announced Ernest's infection and subsequent blood poisoning in the winter of 1949, which they described as life-threatening: "Expecting the present novel to be his final work, Mr. Hemingway determined to make it the finest of his writing career. Those who have read the manuscript feel that this novel will rank above anything he has ever written." Yet they kept pushing back the publication date, which had originally been given as

March 1. Just before the installments began to run in *Cosmopolitan,* Scribner's told Ernest they expected to publish the first week of August. In May they said they would publish September 7; Ernest said this was all right with him, but he warned them to make sure they had not changed the date "because there was something wrong with the book." Ernest was enough of a publishing veteran to know that for a publication date to be pushed back this often was unusual. Moreover, he was preternaturally adept at reading meanings in the behavior and words of others; he "had an unfailing instinct," observed Peter Viertel, "about what was going through the minds of people around him." But his momentary doubts were lost in the roar inside his head.

No amount of delays, however, and no amount of money—Scribner's spent $35,000 on promotion—could forestall the novel's calamitous critical reception. Though many reviewers were but mildly disapproving—Malcolm Cowley felt it was "below the level of his earlier novels," and Richard Rovere in *Harper's* called it "a disappointing novel"—others went to extremes. Maxwell Geismar, in *The Saturday Review of Literature,* wrote, "It is not only Hemingway's worst novel; it is a synthesis of everything that is bad in his previous work and it throws a doubtful light on the future." Alfred Kazin, in *The New Yorker,* noted his own "embarrassment, even pity, that so important a writer can make such a travesty of himself." Cyril Connolly conceded that every writer can write "one thoroughly bad book," but criticized the colonel as "a drink-sodden and maundering old bore." Morton Dauwen Zabel gave a nod to the disastrous Ross profile in titling his review, "A Good Day for Mr. Tolstoy," and went on to say *Across the River and into the Trees* was "the poorest thing its author has ever done." *Time* called it a "parody" of Hemingway.

One significant exception was as effusive as other reviews were vitriolic: John O'Hara, who was a great admirer of Ernest's work, and may have wanted to signal Ernest he would like them to be better friends, wrote on the front page of *The New York Times Book Review,* "The most important author living today, the outstanding author since the death of Shakespeare, has brought out a new novel." Even Ernest knew this was bombast. Other reviewers were milder in their praise, and a handful pronounced themselves mystified by the barrage of negative reviews. Evelyn Waugh, for instance, accused reviewers of "high supercilious caddishness," and asked, "Why do they all hate him so?" Ben Redman, writing two months after the book appeared, similarly tried to find a reason for the critics' heated response: "Perhaps we really do know too much about Hemingway, or at least his public poses, to judge his work impartially."

Another set of positive remarks was more interesting and insightful, if somewhat idiosyncratically so. Tennessee Williams wrote a travel piece called "A Writer's Quest for Parnassus," which appeared in *The New York Times* in August, suggesting that he had seen a prepublication copy of the book. He was writing about Italy as a new destination for expatriate American writers and his own preference for Rome. On Venice he had this to say: "I could not go to Venice, now, without hearing the haunted cadences of Hemingway's new novel. It is the saddest novel in the world about the saddest city, and when I say I think it is the best and most honest work that Hemingway has done, you may think me crazy." He predicted (rightly) that while *Across the River* would be poorly received critically, it would be popular with readers. "But its hauntingly tired cadences," he went on, "are the direct speech of a man's heart who is speaking that directly for the first time, and that makes it, for me, the finest thing Hemingway has done."

Ernest never referred to this praise and perhaps never knew of it. He was surprised by all the negative reviews—hardly unexpectedly, given his outsize admiration for his own novel. The day the review in *Time* appeared, he lashed out at Charlie Scribner: "Isn't it sort of customary to tell an author about how things go and what people say when a book comes out that he has bet his shirt on and worked his heart out on nor missed a deadline nor failed to keep a promise?" As the other reviews came in, he sent some off to Buck Lanham and told him what O'Hara had written, which sent him off on a rant, saying O'Hara could not have understood the novel as "he had not known the kind of people I have known. . . . I do know fighting people of all kinds, painters, diplomats, thieves, gangsters, politicians, jockeys, trainers, bull fighters, many beautiful women, great ladies, the beau monde" and so forth. He went on for several pages, no doubt mystifying Buck:

Also have more than a battalion of bartenders and at least a platoon of priests and both the B.T.s and the Priests have loaned me money and been repaid. . . . When I was 19 Count Greppi who was a contemporary of Metternich and the Duke of Bronte who was a descendant of Nelson, both over ninety, were trying to bring me up.

With this jumbled flight of fancy, Ernest confirmed that the mania that had held him in its grip since his fiftieth birthday in the previous year had in no way abated.

TWENTY-EIGHT

Mary was handling Ernest very carefully in the wake of *Across the River and into the Trees*. His disappointment with its reviews was replaced by jubilation over its sales, just as Scribner's fears over the book's quality were replaced by marketing objectives and a large advertising campaign (the firm spent around $15,000 on post-publication advertising). The novel was on the best-seller list for twenty-one weeks, in first place for seven. Ernest made about $136,000, or over a million dollars today, including $85,000 paid by *Cosmopolitan* for the serialization, according to Robert Trogdon. (As for the reviews, he comforted himself by reasoning, as he told Mary, "It must have something to arouse such hysterical attack and defense.")

Nonetheless, Ernest seems to have been waiting for praise, which never came for this particular book. Mary wrote, "He was a simmering, restless stew of impatience." This was compounded by the arrival, eagerly awaited, of Adriana and her mother in late October. This year, Mary noted, "My husband needed friendship, sympathy and, if I could summon it, compassion, more than at any other time I'd known him." Coming down from his pre-publication euphoria, he told Mary he was "a desperate old man."

Adriana, who arrived on October 27, did much to dissipate his bleak mood. He first took her and Dora to the top of the recently built tower to see the view of Havana; Adriana, now very serious about art, set up a makeshift studio up there, in Ernest's unused study. Then and there, she and Ernest formed a "corporation" called "The White Tower, Inc."—which had no stated purpose. One of Ernest's enthusiasms was starting such spurious entities; he and Hotch had formed the Hem/Hotch Syndicate, which meant little more than that they placed horse-racing bets together, and in his fiction the colonel in *Across the River* joined in a mysterious brotherhood with the Gritti headwaiter.

Ernest showed Adriana all his Cuban haunts, from Cojimar and the Cerro Hunting Club to the Club de Cazadores; they went pigeon shooting and deep-sea fishing. She and her mother were happy to be reunited with Gianfranco, who vacated the guest bedroom in the Finca and moved out to the little house, the *casita* where the children always stayed, to be with his mother and sister. He had made friends with an array of Cuban residents, beginning with those associated with the Italian embassy in Havana and at Sidarma, the Italian shipping company where he worked. Between his contacts and the Hemingways', Adriana and Dora were introduced to the Cuban equivalent of a social elite—with the result that Adriana had more suitors than she could manage.

Aside from enjoying the attentions of a famous writer, the reason Dora and Adriana made the trip to Cuba is unclear. Perhaps part of Dora's motivation was to make a good match for her daughter from the Cuban aristocracy, or perhaps Gianfranco had identified some possible suitors in the Italian community in Havana. But Dora could likely have arranged a much better match for her daughter in Venice, or, failing that, in any one of the European capitals. Patrick evidently believed the Ivanciches were hoping for a match between Adriana and Ernest; when he was visiting the Finca at Christmas with his new wife, he made a point of hinting broadly to Adriana's mother that Ernest was not nearly as rich as he might seem. Meanwhile, Dora and Adriana were glad for the chance to see Gianfranco and debate his future. He soon left the shipping company and announced that he wanted to be a writer; if that was his real ambition, obviously Ernest would be a valuable connection. Dora was also investigating businesses she might fund for her son, as well as existing businesses she might buy for him. If any of Gianfranco's career endeavors bore fruit, possibly she intended that she and Adriana would join him in Cuba.

René Villarreal, the young Cuban who had witnessed Ernest's activities with the circus, saw Adriana's visit through different eyes, for he maintains that he had a love affair with her during her three-month visit, rendezvousing with her by the swimming pool almost every night after everyone had gone to sleep. Photographs of René, twenty at the time, show a handsome dark-skinned man with a sculptured physique, sporting a pencil mustache. He has told a convincing, detailed story about the horse-riding date that kicked off the romance, and leaves the impression that they made love at their late-night meetings. There is no way to ascertain the truth of his claims.

Another romance may have been afoot at the Finca that fall and winter. Mary and Gianfranco, whom she described as "Slim as a cypress, and with the deep dark eyes of his sister," seem to have been carrying on a bit of a flirtation, though the Italian was twelve years younger. Though now he was in the *casita,* he had been living at the Finca in the guest room, once the cats' room but heretofore called, because of Gianfranco's tenancy, the Venetian room, since early 1949, and would continue to live with the Hemingways off and on for fifteen years, becoming one of Mary's lifelong friends. An undated note from Mary to Gianfranco (whom she called Bunney, because he was short and slim), among Carlos Baker's papers at Princeton, reads, fairly suggestively,

> Bunney-Binney—
> It is curious how it doesn't get any better—the hurting and the longing in the bones and blood and skin and eyes and ears and nose. Sometimes, hurting strong, I ask myself "Was it worth this—that joy, this misery?" And the answer is always "yes," *Dearest Huomino.*

Baker attached a notation reading, in part, "Not to be read by scholars until after Mary Hemingway's death."

Though Ernest was absorbed in Adriana, he appears to have picked up on the romantic overtones between Mary and Gianfranco. One evening she brought her typewriter out to the living room to help Gianfranco with his application for a U.S. visa (he hoped to accompany his mother and sister on a visit to the mainland). Ernest picked up the typewriter and dashed it to the floor, and subsequently threw a glass of wine in Mary's face, leaving a burgundy smear on the white wall behind her.

By then, however, Ernest barely needed a pretext to attack Mary. The Ivanciches' visit coincided with some of his most abusive treatment of his wife. Perhaps motivated by his frustrated passion for Adriana and his jealousy of Gianfranco, his behavior was in no way inhibited by the presence of their visitors. His accusations were often enigmatic, seemingly based on an illogic all his own. One night he told Mary she had the face of a Torquemada, the Grand Inquisitor, while at another time he took her to task for the dark outfit she was wearing, calling it "your hangman's suit. Your executioner's suit," adding, as they all left for the movies in Havana, "You've sabotaged it." On another occasion, Ernest questioned Mary about a bruise on her arm; she said that Gianfranco had taken hold of it too roughly. Ernest called it "your badge of shame," shot out a light outside the front door, and threatened to shoot off Gianfranco's offending arm.

Mary thought of leaving Ernest several times. She wrote a long letter to Charlie Scribner (surely not the best confidant) saying Ernest had been "truculent, brutal, abusive and extremely childish." If anything displeased him at a meal, he would wordlessly put his laden plate on the floor. He had destroyed, she wrote, any residual feeling of loyalty to him. This treatment was especially cruel, she said, as she had just learned definitively she could not bear a child—which he threw up in her face. Not long after, Mary made a decision: though he seemed to be goading her to leave with his behavior, she resolved to stay, no matter what the provocation, unless he came to her in the morning, sober, and told her expressly that he wanted her to go. That did not stop the abuse—soon after, on New Year's Eve, perhaps because Adriana was out with a beau, he threw Mary's Venetian ashtray out the door, where it crashed on the tiled terrace. But making the resolution at least gave Mary some relief from the constant vacillation over what to do.

In the new year a crisis brought about Adriana and Dora's departure; they were headed to visit New York before sailing home to Italy. Dora received a letter from Venice mentioning that the word there was that Adriana was the model for Renata in Hemingway's recent novel. Despite the fact that *Across the River and into the Trees* had not yet been translated into Italian, the news spread unchecked. Rumors to this effect had been circulating even before the book came out; in fact, it is not clear why anyone was surprised. But Dora felt the insult to Adriana's reputation was potentially grave, and she and her daughter moved to a Havana hotel. They stayed in Cuba long enough, however, to attend a formal party for over two hundred guests in early February that the Hemingways were holding in Adriana's honor. Mother and daughter left Cuba soon after, on the 7th, with Mary accompanying them to show them parts of Florida and the South before they headed north alone. As a concession to Dora's worries, Ernest, who had eagerly planned to go along on this trip, stayed in Cuba.

Ernest, whose correspondence indicates he was still on a manic high, had been writing steadily since Adriana and her mother arrived; in fact, he later told Adriana that her presence made this stretch of work possible. By January 8 he could report to Buck Lanham that he had finished the Sea book—though he would still be adding sections of it through the spring; most of this would become the posthumously published *Islands in the Stream*. Just after Christmas he started something new; a story that he had heard from the *Pilar*'s erstwhile mate, Carlos Gutiérrez, about an old man who, over a period of four days and nights, battled and finally killed an enormous marlin from a skiff. The old man tied the dead fish to his boat, but sharks ate the carcass before he could get it to shore. Ernest had told the story in brief in April 1936, in an article he wrote for *Esquire* called "On the Blue Water."

Set in a town very like Cojimar, Ernest's fictional account featured an old man named Santiago and a young boy who is his friend, Manolin, the latter based on a Cojimar child he knew. Ernest wrote the story in exceedingly simple and terse prose, initially as a coda for the Sea novel, but he soon saw that it could stand on its own. Nevertheless, he held on to the story for some time. When Charlie and Vera Scribner visited later that spring, Charlie read a draft of it and said, somewhat noncommittally, "Very interesting."

Even more than his earlier work, *The Old Man and the Sea* was a story suffused with the presence of death. The same can be said for its predecessor, *Across the River.* Why a man of fifty had become so preoccupied with the end of life is a difficult question—though there were many possible reasons why. One of these, surely, was the confluence of several deaths of people who had played a large role in his life, and a reminder of another.

Arthur Mizener's *The Far Side of Paradise,* his biography of Fitzgerald, was published in early 1951. Ernest received an early copy, and soon after read an excerpt from it in *Life* magazine. Though it was obviously fruitless to comment further on Scott to Mizener at this point, Ernest amplified on a tired subject, the Callaghan-Hemingway bout in a Paris gym in 1929 at which Scott was scorekeeper. In the first of two letters after receiving the book, Ernest took a more thoughtful direction than the self-serving letters with which he had previously been plying Mizener. "You know it is a horrible thing to be somebody's hero," he wrote, "and have them attribute all sorts of qualities to you when you are only a man trying to work at it as well as you can." If he was harsh to Scott about his writing, it was only "because I wanted him to write perfectly and straighten up and fly right." This letter is not particularly critical of Mizener, though Ernest did refer to the biographer's having "buried" Scott, but Mizener either took offense or, more likely, got wind of the blistering comments Ernest was making to others about the *Life* excerpt from Mizener's book. In a January 11 letter, Ernest responded to what was evidently a letter from Mizener, with an apology for being so harsh. Mizener's book reported much about Scott that was new to Ernest, which was fine, he wrote, but "you can see how I would feel to see Scott . . . lying naked and dead in the market place." (By the time of his last letter to Mizener, a week later, he had decided that the biographer should be hanged.) In spite of the distortions he freely made of their relationship, Ernest's observations were in the main born out of regret that Scott had not been tougher and able to overcome the many adversities in his life, most of his own making. Ernest was angry at Scott, actually, for dying. In short, he very much, very keenly, wished his friend were still with him.

His feelings were easily as complicated when he learned, on June 29, that his mother had died. "I have been thinking how beautiful she was when she was young," he wrote Carlos Baker, "before everything went to hell in our family and about how happy we all were as children before it all broke up." Grace Hall Hemingway was seventy-nine at her death. She had been at Oak Park Hospital recovering from a head injury after a wheelchair accident had caused severe memory loss and then senile dementia. Her third daughter, Sunny, now living in Memphis, brought Grace to live with her. When Ernest heard of this he wrote Sunny very frankly saying that while it might seem cold-hearted on his part not to have assumed at least part of Grace's care, he was unable to: he couldn't have her in his presence, he said. By the end Grace could not recognize Sunny, but the night before she went into Memphis Hospital at the end she played classical compositions on the piano with great spirit, dying a few weeks later.

Her longtime companion, Ruth Arnold, had married in 1926; her husband, Harry Meehan, died after five years of marriage, at which point Ruth moved into Grace's River Forest home. The children, writing to their mother as adults, often asked Grace to give their love to Ruth—though Ernest did not. At Marcelline's instigation, the children also made a financial gift to Ruth—though there is no record Ernest pitched in. For undocumented reasons, Ernest violently disapproved of how Marcelline was handling the estate, and withheld his signatures to crucial documents for as long as he could, apparently just to hold things up and annoy his older sister. Sunny at one point was acting as a go-between for Marcelline and Ernest until he told her that he did not want to hear any more on the subject, because it bothered him while he was working. Several times as the estate was being settled he beseeched Sunny to get him his grandmother Hall's paintings—one of a barque (as he repeatedly spelled the word for "boat"), and another a seascape; he pointedly said he wanted these rather than any of his mother's paintings. He said Grace had probably thrown the ones out he wanted—unless Marcelline took them, he added.

A letter Grace wrote Ernest around the time of his fiftieth birthday, when his mania was at its most florid, had unleashed a torrent of abuse in his letters to others. He rehearsed with relish his exchange with his mother after Ed Hemingway's death about who was threatening whom, adding, "I hate her guts and she hates mine." This is the only reference to his mother hating him—which, the exaggeration aside, seems to have been partly true. At the very least, for a proper woman brought up in the Victorian age, she showed no conventional feelings toward her adult son, and often expressed her resentment openly; in the 1940s she tried more than once to sell her copies of the high school newspaper and literary magazine that contained Ernest's early writing. While this certainly does not mean she did not love him, it is fair to say she was not sentimental or tenderhearted so far as her son was concerned. In general, her earlier piety gave way as she aged to spiritualism, for which she became a tiresome proselytizer, annoying even the filial Marcelline.

Yet the extent to which Ernest had once been trapped in her orbit, as if she were a planet and he a moon, was impossible to deny. In 1949, at the height of his emotional instability, Grace, evidently cleaning house, had sent her son her baby books for his earliest years. Each of Ernest's baby books was at least two inches thick; all five of them would have made for an impressive package. Ernest immediately put them in a bureau drawer so that Mary could not see them. On the night of his mother's death Bill Walton was visiting, and late at night, probably over drinks, Ernest took him into the Venetian room for privacy and pulled out the baby books. Walton later called them "terribly revelatory." The story as told in the books began with Ernest in dresses and outfits that matched his sister Marcelline's—in Grace's effort to "twin" the brother and sister. The chronology ended with copies of the *Tabula* and his graduation program. The story the books told was not so much about the love of a mother for a son, but rather about her obsession. For the massive scrapbooks, assembled painstakingly *by* Grace, were finally *about* Grace, her career as a mother. They cannot have been of much comfort that night at the Finca after the news reached Ernest of her death.

The least expected development of 1951 was the death of Pauline, at fifty-six, on October 1, of a rare tumor of the adrenal gland, pheochromocytoma (though the cause of death would not be known to Ernest and his sons for nine years). Her illness and death unfolded in a rather extraordinary way—an event that sheds a great deal of light on Ernest's life as a husband and father. Pauline's death radically transformed his relationship with his two sons from that marriage.

Now in their young adulthood, none of Ernest's sons was following conventional trajectories. Jack, or Bumby, was probably the least complicated, but that does not mean relations between him and his father were easy, or worry-free. Jack had a hard time with jobs after his dramatic military career during the war. He never completed his education, begun at Dartmouth, though he attended the University of Montana. Fly-fishing was the passion of his life from an early age, and his first occupation was running a small fly-tying business in San Francisco with a partner. His marriage and the birth of Joan, his first child (two more daughters were to follow, Margot in 1955 and Mariel in 1961), brought him around to thinking of steadier work. Unsure of what to do, he went back on active duty with the Army and was currently stationed in Berlin; in the countryside he fished less than he hunted, most memorably wild boar. In 1951, he and Puck had just lost an infant son.

Patrick, Ernest's second son, had attended Stanford for two years and got his BA at Harvard in history and literature. He too was unsure how to make a living. He painted for a time, apparently very well. After his marriage in June 1950, he and Henny left for Europe, later traveling to Africa. Ernest and Pauline had been greatly relieved when Patrick made a full recovery from his 1947 brain injury. Ernest, however, could not resist blaming Pauline for her failure to seek medical treatment for Patrick's concussion immediately, though such accusations between divorced parents are hardly remarkable in this respect. Ernest told Hotchner that Pauline had told Patrick stories about his illness that had caused Patrick to become estranged from him.

Jack Hemingway would later describe how his father viewed his sons with some accuracy: "I think he saw me as a kind of, well, blah, a nice kid, smart enough, but, let's face it, never going to be a world beater. I think in Patrick he saw the tremendous intellectual potential. I think he recognized in Gregory so much more of himself, the capacity for good and evil." In fact, Ernest would make any number of conflicting statements about Greg, sometimes seeing him as the son with the brightest future, who had then turned out almost diametrically otherwise, he said. Mostly, however, he said terrible things about his youngest son. He wrote Jack, for instance, when Mary thought she might be pregnant, that he was happy about it, he told his son, because another child would "take the taste of Gregory out of my mouth."

But then Gregory could be very trying. He had enrolled at St. John's University in Annapolis, a highly regarded college with a rigorous "Great Books" curriculum. He did not take well to the structured quality, however, and by 1951 had dropped out and was studying with L. Ron Hubbard, whose 1950 blueprint for Scientology, *Dianetics,* was currently on the best-seller list. Greg later said that he had been looking for a "cure" for his cross-dressing habit all along, but letters between Ernest and Greg indicate that the subject was not mentioned between them during this time (though a number of Ernest's letters to his sons are still sealed to researchers). Greg married on April 29, receiving a wire the next day stating that his father explicitly did *not* give his consent. When Pauline heard that Ernest was not attending the wedding, she scolded him roundly: "I really don't know [how] you can behave so badly about the women your sons marry. They have had to take four [wives] of yours, and I think they have been damned cooperative and well mannered about it. So you don't like them—act like you do." Ernest would eventually come around to Patrick's and Jack's wives, but the matter would be more complicated in Greg's case, in ways that went beyond cross-dressing.

Greg and his new wife, Jane, settled in Venice, California, where he was working at Douglas Aircraft. On September 30 Pauline, then living in San Francisco, received a call saying that Greg had been arrested in the women's bathroom of a Los Angeles movie theater. She immediately flew down to Los Angeles, where she stayed with her sister, Jinny, and Jinny's partner, Laura Archera, and presumably got Greg released on bail. She had cabled Ernest, and that night around nine they had an acrimonious shouting match over the phone, according to Jinny's later report to Greg. Pauline, who had been experiencing headaches and fatigue in the weeks prior, woke up in agony in the middle of the night and was rushed to the hospital, where she died on the operating table.

Months later Greg and Jane visited the Finca in November. At a happy moment, when he and his father were getting along, Greg referred to his arrest on the West Coast that fall, saying, "It wasn't so bad, really, Papa." "No?" Ernest thundered. "Well, it killed Mother." Of course, Greg could say the same to his father. And that is how it was left for nine years. The family believed that Pauline had died of shock on the operating table. In 1960, when Greg was in medical school, he sent for his mother's autopsy report and learned about the tumor of the adrenal gland that caused Pauline's death. When this tumor is present, it can send blood pressure and the heart rate soaring, often rupturing an artery; many factors can cause the tumor to "fire off," to use Greg's term, among them emotional upset. Greg told his father what he had learned; in his memoir Greg said that according to "a person who was with [Ernest]" in Havana when he got Greg's letter, "he raged at first and then walked around the house in silence for the rest of the day."

Because Patrick and Greg were Pauline's heirs (she left Jack $10,000), Ernest's relationship with them changed significantly after her death—the cause of her death aside. The money freed them, at least for the time, from financial dependence on their father. Pauline's boys and Ernest jointly owned the Key West property, including the two-story pool house that had housed Ernest's studio—Ernest holding forty shares and Greg and Patrick thirty each. Joint ownership kept them financially linked for years, however—a state of affairs exacerbated by the furniture and possessions in the house, never properly dispersed, and by its being managed as a rental property, the latter keeping father and sons in nearly constant contact.

"She was a fine brave girl, and everyone misses her," Sara Murphy wrote to Ernest about Pauline about a year after her death; Sara was always one of Pauline's champions. Because Greg's arrest was all tied up with her death, Ernest's reaction was confusion. He wrote to Charlie Scribner three times on the two days following Pauline's death. In one he referred to Gregory as "corrupt." In another he confessed, in a rather masterful analogy, to being overwhelmed: "The wave of remembering has finally risen so that it has broken over the jetty that I built to protect the open roadstead of my heart." Now, he writes, "I have the full sorrow of Pauline's death with all the harbor scum of what caused it. I loved her very much for many years and to hell with her faults." The single person in Ernest's life who loved him unequivocally was, without a doubt, Pauline, and the loss was incalculable.

*   *   *

Ernest had been holding on to the manuscript of *The Old Man and the Sea,* intending to use it as a coda to his tripartite Sea novel, but as that manuscript kept growing, and kept growing more unruly, Ernest began to look at the story of the Cuban fisherman as a stand-alone piece of work—a novel or story, he wasn't sure which.

About a year after Ernest completed it, Charlie Scribner died, another great blow in a year of losses. Ernest explained to Wallace Meyer that he had seen that Charlie was having a difficult time filling Max's shoes and had thus made the decision to give him and the publishing house "absolute loyalty." He loved Charlie, he told Meyer. Charles Scribner IV (always known as Charles Jr.) took over capably enough, though the transfer of the reins inevitably eroded the close personal ties Ernest had to the house. Charlie hadn't been that excited by *The Old Man and the Sea* when he first saw it in February 1951; now, when Ernest dusted it off again, he considered it more carefully.

Slim Hayward, one of Ernest's chaste handmaidens, had known him for many years, ever since she and Howard Hawks, her first husband, visited in Key West when Hawks was interested in directing a film version of *To Have and Have Not.* Slim (later Slim Keith) said that an instant attraction sprang up between her and Ernest, but that on her end it was entirely because of his intelligence. While he was physically appealing in photographs, she later said, he was different in person: "Ernest never seemed clean or bathed to me. His beard was scraggly. He'd wear the same clothes for five days." She got to know him better in Sun Valley, where he admired her

Slim Hayward, 1940s

shooting skill. Late one afternoon in front of a fire at the resort, she was brushing her wet hair. Ernest asked if he could take over, and brushed her hair until it was dry. His heart was won.

In February 1952 Slim was vacationing in Cuba with her second husband, Leland Hayward, a Hollywood agent and producer with an eye for literary properties. On an evening at the Finca, Ernest shyly asked Slim if she wanted to read the typescript. Back in their room at the Hotel Nacional, Leland read it over her shoulder, both of them captivated. Leland, a consummate promoter and dealmaker, convinced Ernest that the story was so powerful that it rated something more than the usual methods of publication. *The New Yorker* had recently published John Hersey's *Hiroshima* in its entirely; Leland said *Life* should publish Ernest's entire piece, with illustrations.

At some point Ernest became convinced of the desirability of publishing *The Old Man and the Sea* as a stand-alone novella—or novel, as he and Scribner's both began to call it. In a frank letter to Wallace Meyer, he indicated that he had given thought to how this new book might strike the critics, who had turned on him for his last one. "Tactically," Ernest wrote, "publishing it now will get rid of the school of criticism that I am through as a writer." That, in fact, was the fundamental point of *The Old Man and the Sea*—at least as far as Ernest's reputation was concerned.

The Old Man and the Sea appeared in *Life* on September 1, with copies for sale August 28; as a Scribner's book on September 8; and as a Book-of-the-Month Club dual selection on September 9. Amazingly enough, the publication was a success in all three formats. *Life*, for example, sold 5,300,000 copies in two days. Scribner's was pleased to find that the magazine publication was itself news, worthy of its own press release. The book appeared on the best-seller list and stayed there for twenty-six weeks. The general conclusion, however, was that magazine publication hurt book sales in the end, just because the sheer number of readers who read the novella in *Life* was far larger than Scribner's sales, representing potential buyers of the book.

If 1950 saw the publication of a book that nearly all the critics hated, *Across the River and into the Trees*, 1952 produced *The Old Man and the Sea*—which was nearly unanimously hailed. "No phony glamour girls and no bullying braggarts sentimentalized almost to parody," the *New York Times* reviewer wrote, nearly chortling with relief. "Here is the master technician once more at the top of his form, doing superbly what he can do better than anyone else."

Ernest deployed two reviewers on whom he thought he could rely for positive notices. One was Harvey Breit, a writer and reviewer whose *New York Times* piece on Ernest in September 1950 marked the beginning of a mostly epistolary friendship. Writing in *The Nation*, Breit found *The Old Man and the Sea* "a great and true novel, touching and terrible, tragic and happy." The other reviewer was Carlos Baker, a Princeton professor who was writing a book about Ernest and his work. First swearing "to not aid, and to impede in every way, including legal" any such book, Ernest got Baker to agree to leave out anything biographical from what would be his 1952 book of criticism, *Hemingway: The Writer as Artist*. Ernest was wary of Baker, but thought he could be counted on for a good review. Indeed, Baker reviewed the book in *The Saturday Review*, calling Hemingway "one of the few genuine tragic writers of modern times."

Reviewers noticed that the hero of the fable, Santiago, was in some ways an autobiographical portrait. Ernest had hoped to avoid this; in fact, he had hoped that publication of the book would "destroy the school of criticism that claims I can write about nothing except myself and my own experiences." But as Robert Gorham Davis, in *The New York Times Book Review*, reminded readers, "Hemingway we know was himself a champion." Santiago had been eighty-four days without a fish, just as Hemingway had weathered a streak of bad luck. Joe DiMaggio, the baseball player who was a symbolic touchstone in the book, was, like Santiago and Hemingway, a champion who staged a comeback. Davis said, "It is a tale superbly told and in the telling Ernest Hemingway uses all the craft his disciplined trying over so many years has given him." In a victory of sorts, about which he may not even have heard, his old nemesis, Fanny Butcher, said in his hometown paper, the *Chicago Sunday Tribune,* that the book was "a great American classic of man's battle with a Titan of the sea." Reviewers spoke of Hemingway's maturity; consciously or not, they saw in Santiago's discipline and tenacity what they believed they were seeing in Ernest's career.

Not everyone was so positive. Critics—who recall, of course, the sharks who destroy the old man's marlin—derided the too obvious Christ symbolism, the childish exchanges about baseball, the mock-serious tone. Delmore Schwartz wrote an intelligent piece about the novel and its reception in *Partisan Review.* He detected "a note of insistence in the praise and a note of relief. *Across the River and into the Trees* was extremely bad in an ominous way." Readers and critics were reassured of Hemingway's talent. "This work is not so much good in itself as a virtuoso performance which reminds us of Hemingway at its best," wrote Schwartz.

A lot of people made a lot of money on the book and would continue to do so. Robert Trogdon has determined that Ernest might have made about $137,000 from *Life,* Scribner's, and the Book-of-the-Month Club combined. He sold the film rights to Leland Hayward for about $150,000; the amount included a fee for his services as a consultant on fishing. Scribner's made about $38,000 on the book in 1952. Sales would continue to be very strong after the novella was awarded a Pulitzer Prize in 1953.

The Old Man and the Sea, in fact, *reminds* us, as Schwartz said, of Hemingway's talent, but the novel merely showcases it rather than being a genuine, earned representation of his art. It gave his career a greatly needed boost, as Ernest himself recognized; what is unclear is what it did for Hemingway the man, beyond making him a lot of money. The novel's success made him a little less hostile to the critics, but a deep, joyless cynicism set in. His manic phase mostly over, he seems to have slid into depression—or, more accurately, a "mixed" state, a depression with manic features.

Ernest put his inner life on display in one arena that year: evaluating his fellow writers. His constant need to compare himself to his peers, always to his advantage, was a recurrent thread running through his psyche in the 1950s. The novelists of World War II were a particular sore spot. Ernest was one of the all-time-great war novelists, as *A Farewell to Arms* and *For Whom the Bell Tolls* made clear. He had not really written a World War II novel, however; *Across the River and into the Trees* was only loosely speaking "about" that war. Though many of the novelists of the recent war were his age, some were younger, and he must have feared he would be viewed as a hoary chronicler of a long-ago strife. Ernest was especially vexed by the cleverness of the "Brooklyn Tolstoy," Norman Mailer. In all Ernest's talk about the literary boxing ring, he never claimed to have won his bout with "Mr. Tolstoy."

It was James Jones, however, who really ate at him. When *From Here to Eternity* was published in 1951, it immediately made its way to the top of the best-seller list and stayed there, and it won the National Book Award for 1952. It was especially irksome that Jones was a Scribner's author—and that Ernest's name appeared three times in the novel, one character "sound[ing] like a page out of Hemingway." Jones was younger than Ernest by twenty-two years, and had written his book at a writers' colony run by an older woman (and Jones's lover), Lowney Handy, which readers of *Life* magazine learned from a nine-page spread about Jones and the colony. Jones had enlisted in the Army and been posted first to Pearl Harbor and later to Guadalcanal, where he was wounded by mortar fire and seems to have suffered something like shell shock or PTSD, and subsequently went AWOL. The *Life* reporter said that the experience left Jones "a whimpering neurotic," which Ernest thought established that he was a "psycho," not a soldier. He jumped all over Jones. He immediately assured Charlie Scribner that Jones would commit suicide, an oddly specific and irrational charge he repeated several times over several letters. Ernest came to believe Jones had not done his duty as a soldier, maintaining that *From Here to Eternity* "will do great damage to our country." He thought perhaps he should reread it to be sure. "But I do not have to eat an entire bowl of scabs to know they are scabs; nor suck a boil to know it is a boil. . . . If you give [Jones] a literary tea you might ask him to drain a bucket of snot and then suck the piss out of a dead nigger's ear." (A rough draft of this letter, preserved among Hemingway's papers, is even more scurrilous and bizarre.)

The occasion of Jones's book, in fact, sent Ernest into another, though more contained, episode of mania. He had suffered another concussion the previous summer when he slipped and fell on the *Pilar*, which could not have helped his mental state. In a letter to Charlie written over several days that month he was moved to review his own war experiences—as before, claiming a lot of imagined achievements and supplying details he seemingly invented. He implored Charlie to see that his contempt for complainers and "incorrigibles" came from an honored source: his own sacrifice in the first war. This led him into a tall tale for the record books. In the first war, he wrote, inmates from the Joliet Penitentiary who had volunteered were allowed to fight in Europe, where Ernest encountered them. One of the inmates allegedly approached him, saying he had heard Ernest was from Chicago. Ernest told the convict to leave before he castrated him and shoved his testicles in his mouth. He then told Charlie to take the mention of his name out of Jones's book because it "is a good fighting name back to 1700's." He gave his son Jack's bona fides, declaring he did not want his name "used sneeringly by a coward."

Ernest's imaginary flights—the mention of Joliet Penitentiary (in Illinois) suggests a childhood fantasy—were a sure sign that he was entering another unbalanced phase. The letters to Charlie from this period contain diatribes about Cardinal Spellman, a Scribner's author, to whom Ernest had written a threatening letter during his last manic phase; a rambling story about being constipated as a boy and subsequently plugging up a toilet at a track meet. This story was followed by a statement seemingly out of nowhere that he had been captain of his high school water polo team. Charlie evidently wrote him a concerned letter, as Ernest told him not to worry about his not eating—that bears don't eat all winter and the boxer Harry Wills fasted for a month every year. Charlie must have been flabbergasted.

TWENTY-NINE

By the time he published *The Old Man and the Sea,* Ernest, now fifty-three, was no longer moving his writing forward but was engaged in a kind of holding pattern, in the sense that he was not working on anything he deemed publishable in the near future. He had temporarily shelved *The Garden of Eden.* After publishing *The Old Man and the Sea,* which he had always meant to be part of the Sea book, he was thrown into confusion about the other parts of that book and simply put them aside.

It could be said that Ernest was instead scrambling to protect his rear flank, as books about his work and his life began to appear, much to his dismay. He was familiar with the approach favored by some of these writers, who came in three varieties: journalists, biographers, and critics. The lines of the three areas could be indistinct, however. Malcolm Cowley might today be classified as a literary critic, but he began his career as a poet and novelist. With *Exile's Return* (1934), he made his mark as an essayist about 1920s artists in Paris. By the end of the 1940s he was a literary jack-of-all-trades, supplementing his earnings as an editor with occasional journalism like his 1949 biographical profile of Ernest in *Life.* Ernest had cooperated with Cowley, supplying many details himself (often in misleading fashion) and putting him in touch with people like Buck Lanham. The result emphasized Ernest's activities in World War II: his sub-hunting adventures in the Caribbean and his exploits as a war correspondent and unofficial soldier in Europe late in the war. Yet Ernest complained that the *Life* piece opened the way for more searching biographical inquiries. Such investigation was extremely dicey in Ernest's case, since life and work were so intertwined. Ernest resented what he saw as the invasion of his privacy but also seems to have felt that allowing others to write about his life "used up" the material, making it impossible for him to use it in his fiction. "The Cowley piece," he told his newspaperman friend John Wheeler, "made me feel bad to lose things I was happy about because nobody knew them."

Cowley's profile was reprinted in the first book on Ernest's work, a collection of essays edited by John K. M. McCaffery, *Ernest Hemingway: The Man and His Work*, published in 1950. Close on its heels came inquiries from scholars Charles Fenton (at Yale), Philip Young (at NYU), and Carlos Baker (at Princeton). While Baker promptly agreed to exclude biography from his critical study, Young's critical theories depended on biographical fact: like Edmund Wilson before him, Young argued in his 1952 book that Hemingway's work was best understood in light of the physical and psychic wounds he suffered in World War I. Ernest decried both the detective work and the psychological interpretation that informed such theories and explored how he might prevent these books from appearing. He looked into his means of recourse, and, frustrated by the lack of legal measures to prevent such works, he took on these writers personally, entering into correspondence in which he was at times encouraging—though more often combative—but always, at least in the cases of Baker, Fenton, and Young, generous with his time. Cowley himself first told Ernest about Philip Young's work, as he knew the editor at Rinehart who was working with Young to revise his PhD dissertation into a commercial book. Ernest tried to deal with Young by the simple expedience of denying the scholar permission to quote from his work, but when Young told him that his career depended on the book's publication, Ernest capitulated and granted the scholar permission. That did not keep him from grumbling, complaining that a diagnosis of neurosis in this day and age was as damning as one of "tertiary syphilis."

Fenton was the writer who most engaged Ernest's attention, and he would be, perhaps not coincidentally, the author of the finest of these early books, *The Apprenticeship of Ernest Hemingway.* A handsome Yale professor and former RAF pilot (he had gone to Canada to enlist early), Fenton deftly fielded one of Ernest's complaints about his personal questions, writing that his own private life was "too engrossing to give me time to take on someone else's." Fenton was interested in Ernest's growth as a writer, focusing on the period from high school up until *In Our Time.* He alarmed Ernest at the outset, for one of his first findings was Ernest's use of the John Hadley pseudonym used when he was reporting from Europe for the *Toronto Star Weekly* and the International News Service at the same time, receiving payment from both. Ernest was genuinely afraid of being caught and punished for long-ago offenses like this journalistic double-dealing. He also worried obsessively about writers uncovering his shooting of a blue heron in 1915 near Windemere in violation of game laws—despite the fact that it had been decades since he appeared before a judge and paid a $15 fine. As time went by, his fear of punishment for real or, increasingly, imagined offenses only increased, however, anticipating and at times partaking of his paranoia in the last year or two of his life.

Perhaps to forestall any such revelations, Ernest began to pass on to these writers complicated fictions about his past in such endeavors as sports, romance and sexual activity, and warfare—the most colorful and multitudinous being those about his service in the two wars, including his sub hunting during World War II. In fact, his stories were so good he hated to give them away to chroniclers like Fenton. On July 13, 1952, Ernest sent Fenton a threatening letter, enclosing a check for $200 to pay the scholar's fare to Cuba. When Fenton protested that he could neither take the money nor afford such a trip himself, Ernest apologized, but then wrote an aggressive letter telling him to cease and desist, on the grounds that his critics too often came up with false data or interpretations of data, and that it was not worth his while to write lengthy letters helping critics like Fenton in their work.

Another letter to Fenton in August was remarkable in its length and the provision of details from his past. Yet the letter was rambling and nearly incoherent. Ernest began by critiquing Fenton's contacts at the *Kansas City Star*, who told him stories about Ernest's days on the paper. He abruptly changed the subject to his son Jack's World War II record and his own service in World War I, describing in detail his medal from Italy. On his return from World War I, he told Fenton, he was elected president of the Chicago chapter of the Unione Siciliano. Yet again, he rehearsed the story of his boxing bout with Morley Callaghan. Perhaps reminding himself that he must be firm with Fenton, he told one of his favorite stories: how he handled his mother after his father's death. Grace had told Ernest never to threaten her, saying his father had tried that once and regretted it. Ernest answered with a threatening letter saying that he was not his father, and that he never made threats but made promises. He then went on to describe his participation in World War II, telling Fenton that he had received orders to fight, ripped them up (so as not to incriminate those who wrote them), and joined in combat. He would have been given the Distinguished Service Cross, he said, but for the fact that he was "technically" a civilian. He moved on to his sub-hunting activities, alleging that he had been deputized by John Thomason, a Marine colonel, as a "pirate" who was given no orders but told to improvise.

Ernest then described a plan he had devised whereby he and Fenton could collaborate on a series of books about his life, with Ernest supplying letters that Fenton could publish alongside his investigative results, the two of them splitting the profits. He outlined how the second book could shape up: he would help Fenton research the Paris years, supplying details in long letters, some of which they could include as documents. He promised anecdotes about Stein, Pound, and Joyce. Using the military term "gen," shorthand for "intelligence" and thus one of his favorite words, Ernest told Fenton that he would feel better about writing such a long letter if the two of them were going to write up the "gen" in a book and make a lot of money from it. Though it seems Ernest made this proposal to collaborate in all seriousness, just as he had suggested to Peter Viertel that they cowrite a novel about sub hunting, nothing came of it; Fenton held his own and published his book in 1952.

Though it was not a story Ernest told chroniclers like Fenton, Buck Lanham remembered a particularly odd story dating from around this time about Ernest's experience in the Spanish Civil War. The Moors on the Nationalist side, Ernest recounted, were said to be so brutal that the Republicans decided those of their wounded who were unable to walk were better off dead than captured. Because Ernest could do what needed to be done, as he told Buck, he was designated to dispatch the wounded before the Nationalists moved on. What is remarkable here is not so much the content of the fantastic invention but the fact that Ernest seems to have had no censoring mechanism at this time to warn him that the story was too bizarre to be believable. He seemed not to care any longer whether his stories were believed—an ironic pass for a fiction writer to come to.

In the early 1950s Ernest continued to follow the working habits of long standing. He wrote from early in the morning until around noon. But very often now the sound of the typewriter meant only more and longer letters, addressed to all and sundry. Ernest had always been a keen letter writer; it is estimated that he wrote from eight thousand to ten thousand letters in his lifetime. After he moved to Cuba he picked up the pace, his letters becoming sloppier and more prolix, just as his writing did. In the summer and fall of 1952 he wrote densely typed letters not just to Fenton but to Young, Baker, Wallace Meyer, and Charles Scribner (who had succeeded his father) at Scribner's, as well as to Archie MacLeish, the last accompanied by a long letter to Archie's wife, Ada. His favorite correspondent in these months was Bernard Berenson. The art critic was a lively letter writer, full of literary and artistic observations; quasi-philosophical thoughts; complaints about reviews; and just plain gossip. Ernest reciprocated in kind. Mary had briefly known Berenson in Florence in 1949; Ernest never met him, though he told Berenson repeatedly that both he and Mary loved him. Unfortunately, another of Berenson's correspondents was Martha Gellhorn—so Ernest suggested that they steer clear of that topic.

In one letter, Ernest frankly and vividly described the relation of the fiction writer to the truth, providing a romantic view of the qualifications a good writer of fiction brings to the job, a view that is helpful in understanding why Ernest wrote:

Writers of fiction are only super-liars who if they know enough and are disciplined can make their lies truer than the truth. If you have fought and diced and served at court and gone to the wars and know navigation, sea-manship, the bad world and the great world and the different countries and other things then you have good knowledge to lie out of. That is all a writer of fiction is.

Fiction for Ernest, at times, provided a way to master the past so that the actual events—like World War I and its aftermath, or family life in Michigan—were bearable for him. In that sense, in this essentially adaptive character of his psyche and his work, fiction served him well for most of his life, partly because he wrote so well, thus not only managing the past but finding in it powerful stories.

On the other hand, Ernest was working in isolation. As his overreaction to James Jones makes clear, he had little but scorn for contemporary writers. His best writing took strength from life around him, but beyond the Sea book he was drawing very little from Cuba. At a time when it might have been salubrious for him to engage in some way with his environment, he was retreating further. His trips to Africa and Spain were essentially nostalgic in nature, and he seemed content to stay in his personal fiefdom at the Finca.

The Old Man and the Sea aside, his writing was stalled. Hoping to recall more fecund times, he turned to his old hero, Nick Adams, and began a tale about an escape into the Michigan forest of Nick and his little sister, known as Littless. The incident of the blue heron, when he was sought by the game warden, intruded itself on his consciousness—surely because of his preoccupation with Fenton et al.—and he thought to master it by writing about it, as he had with so many incidents in his past. In Ernest's retelling, which was published as a short story, "The Last Good Country," after his death, Nick is in trouble for violation of the game laws and is pursued by the warden and a man from "downstate." Because Littless insists, she joins him in the forest after cutting her hair so she can pass as a boy. Much of the story is about the preparation for their flight into an old hemlock forest, with a stream that provides as much trout as they can eat. The fragment we have of this story (titled by Mary Hemingway) suggests Ernest had a novel in mind.

But the story got away from him. The plot hinges on a game warden and a second official called in because Nick is a repeat offender; they intend to wait Nick out at his family home, for days if necessary; they follow up clues and leads as if on a criminal investigation. Surely only in childhood fantasies have game wardens so assiduously stalked an adolescent offender. By the time Ernest was well into his story, the pursuit had heated up, with violent plot developments seeming inevitable; one critic believed the plot was headed for a scene in which Littless is raped—by the pursuing authorities, it seems. Ernest seemed to be working from a memory that aroused great anxiety in him, but he was unable to tame it and shape it into fiction. Judging from dates on manuscript pages, it seems he took it up again the following year, and the year after that, never making significant headway.

* * *

The genesis of Ernest's second safari was in his son Patrick's decision to go to East Africa with his new wife to find some property and settle there. Ernest wrote him a letter of introduction to Philip "Pop" Percival, the white hunter he had met on his first expedition, now almost twenty years in the past. When Patrick's letters, filled with rapturous descriptions of the land and its inhabitants, began to arrive, Ernest started to think of moving there himself, and decided to make another safari to see what it would be like. He told Percival in another letter that his Cuban property was surrounded by all kinds of urban and suburban development; he could once hunt within walking distance of the Finca, but no more. Where he had previously never locked the door to his house, he now got out his guns to defend the place against a rash of burglaries that showed no sign of abating. Ernest took it into his head to revisit his past in Spain as well, spurred by the news that the last of his friends who had been imprisoned after the civil war were now freed. So he decided they would go on to Spain both before and after the safari. He gave Mary copies to read of Gerald Brenan's books on Spain and Isak Dinesen's *Out of Africa*. In other preparations for the trip, they concentrated on hunting rather than fishing in the winter and spring of 1953. They were getting into shape. Somehow Bill Lowe, an editor at *Look* magazine, got wind of the coming trip (probably through Hotchner) and convinced Ernest to let a photographer, Earl Theisen, follow him on the safari. The deal was clinched with an offer of $15,000 for expenses and $10,000 for a 3,500-word story.

It was an elaborate trip, requiring planning more commonly seen in a military campaign. Ernest and Mary first flew to Key West to check on the Whitehead Street property, now a rental, before traveling by train to New York, where they arranged the shipments of guns and ammunition to Africa and Ernest took in a Yankees game. They sailed on the *Flandre* for France on June 24. Gianfranco Ivancich, who had only months before returned to Venice after four years as a guest at the Finca, met them at Le Havre with Adamo, a driver, in Gianfranco's Lancia B10 sedan, car and driver both supplied by Ernest's friend Count Carlo Kechler. Adamo took them to Paris and, a few days later, to Pamplona, where Ernest and Mary joined friends for a rainy Festival of San Fermín, which Ernest had not celebrated for almost twenty-five years. Fellow *aficionado*s introduced him to Antonio Ordóñez, a talented young matador and the son of Niño de la Palma, the bullfighter who had been the model for Pedro Romero in *The Sun Also Rises*. From Pamplona Adamo took them to Madrid (where Ernest and Mary stayed in Ernest's old room at the Hotel Florida) and Valencia and, after a dash back to Paris, to Marseille. They sailed on the *Dunnottar Castle*, which took them through the Suez Canal and around the horn of Africa to Mombasa. Percival, who had come out of retirement to join the Hemingways on the safari, met them at the port and took them for a short stay at his Kitanga Farm just south of Nairobi. They were joined by their wealthy Cuban friend, Mario (Mayito) Menocal, son of the former president of Cuba, who would accompany them on safari.

The Hemingways and Menocal first went to the Southern Game Preserve in the Kajiado District in Kenya, where they would hunt for the month of September. Everywhere they went in Kenya and Tanganyika, they were given special treatment, for anything Hemingway might write about East Africa, it was hoped, would help bring back the tourists and hunting parties who had been frightened off by the ongoing Mau Mau uprising. They were met in the Kajiado preserve by Denis Zaphiro, a twenty-seven-year-old British game warden with the Kenya Game Department, who had a serious case of hero worship and immediately struck up a rapport with the couple. Before they started out, they met the rest of their retinue, from guides to cooks to drivers, most of them members of the Kamba tribe. Ernest, who had thus far been operating, in Paris, Pamplona, and Madrid, as if determined to relive the past, seemed blind to the many changes in those European spots and in Africa as well. It helped that Percival had met them on their arrival. When Ernest met his gun bearer, N'Gui, he asked the man's age and then decided he was the son of M'Cola, his gun bearer on his previous safari; Mary was dubious about this. Similarly, he pointed out to Mary, during a flight above the Serengeti Plain, the spot where, he said, "my previous and lovely wife Miss Pauline" had killed a lion, as well as the site where he killed a lion and a hyena.

Ernest was nowhere near as successful on this safari as he had been on the previous expedition, however. Menocal was outshooting him. The Cuban was in fact shocked by Ernest's poor shooting, later telling his son that Ernest couldn't have hit the side of a barn; all hands were similarly shocked by the deterioration in Ernest's hunting prowess, he said. His poor shooting, said Menocal, made him drink more, and he starting telling outlandish lies about his exploits. Ernest got his first lion in laborious fashion, wounding him and thus having to stalk him; when he and Denis found the beast, they fired two shots apiece into him. Days later Menocal downed a five-hundred-pound black-maned lion with one shot. A little further south, Ernest and Menocal each put a bullet into a leopard, a development welcomed by Theisen, the *Look* photographer, who had thus far been unable to get a decent shot of Ernest with a trophy animal. While Mary protested that the leopard might have easily been the Cuban's kill, Theisen snapped his photo. For weeks afterward the ambiguous kill was a bone of contention between Ernest and Mary.

In October, at an area newly opened to hunting called Fig Tree Camp near Kimana Swamp, Menocal left for Tanganyika, Theisen flew home, and Percival briefly returned to Kitanga Farm. For a period of weeks Ernest and Mary did little shooting except for birds, preferring instead to be driven out to watch the animals; at dusk they watched herds of elephants headed for a water hole in the river. Mary adopted a Grant's gazelle abandoned by its mother. Surely in part because of his bad luck shooting, Ernest was far more receptive to the idea of looking rather than hunting—which may have harked back to childhood with a father who was as much a naturalist as he was a hunter, or perhaps to his own misguided, and dangerous, obsession about working with lions and bears as their friends. But he and Mary loved coexisting with the animals during this period. Both felt gentler, as their letters and Mary's diaries make clear. They found themselves enjoying "little private carnivals" at nights in one of their cots, she later wrote, making up "games and secret names and joyous jokes."

After a visit to Patrick and Henny in Tanganyika, where the hunting was cut short by the rains, they returned to Kimana Swamp for another seven weeks of hunting. Mary finally—with Denis Zaphiro's help—got her lion. Otherwise, Ernest continued to have bad luck; he fell out of the Land Rover, cut his face, and bruised his right side, spraining his shoulder; the hunting did not improve either. But the nights continued to be idyllic, and Ernest and Mary discovered new pleasures that seem to have involved sexual role-playing. Mary recorded in her diary an imaginary interview between Ernest and a reporter that he invented for Mary's amusement, the reporter asking, "Is it true that your wife is a lesbian?" Ernest answering, "Of course not. Mrs. Hemingway is a boy." With great merriment, they imagined telling the reporter that one of their favorite sports was sodomy. One night Ernest, commandeering Mary's diary, wrote his own entry, which read, in part,

> [Mary] has always wanted to be a boy and thinks as a boy without ever losing any femininity. . . . She loves me to be her girls, which I love to be. . . . Mary has never had one lesbian impulse but has always wanted to be a boy. Since I have never cared for any man and dislike any tactile contact with men except the Spanish abrazo or embrace . . . I loved feeling the embrace of Mary which came to me as something quite new and outside all tribal law.

On the night of December 19, Ernest wrote, signing and dating the entry, "We worked out these things and I have never been happier."

In mid-December Mary flew to Nairobi for a haircut (much celebrated in subsequent sexual play, according to her diary) and some Christmas shopping. Meanwhile, Ernest was doing everything he could to become a Kamba himself. He shaved his head, which showed off his many scars, and dyed some of his clothes the rusty yellowish color the Kamba achieved by rubbing grease and red earth on their clothing. Mary took this transformation in stride, and she and Ernest celebrated Christmas by decorating a thorn tree with candles and feasting on spaghetti and cherry pie. Denis Zaphiro by then had returned with William Hale, chief of the Game Department of Kenya. Hale forbade them shooting any more animals for trophies, but also appointed Ernest honorary game warden, which negated any disappointment Ernest might have felt at having his hunting curtailed. The appointment would loom large in his fantasy life in the months to come, becoming a prominent feature of what he called "the African book," which he would begin after he and Mary left the country. He compared being a game warden (acting as though he had a real appointment) to taking command of members of the Free French, whom he called his Irregulars, at Rambouillet in World War II, and as with that imagined memory, the authority he wielded in Africa became an obsession.

As honorary game warden, Ernest was still allowed to kill, as were members of his party, such animals as hyenas and jackals and whatever else might threaten the population or otherwise need to be removed. The first problem brought to him was the destruction of a cornfield by marauding elephants. Traditionally an elephant was killed and its carcass left as a warning to the others, but Ernest had no desire to kill an elephant and instead reimbursed the farmer for the lost crop. His manner of adjudicating another dispute makes clear how far he thought his authority extended and how he wielded it:

> I told the elders that as far as I was concerned it was better for the young men to exercise at the use of their spears than to drink Golden Jeep sherry in Loitokitok. But that I was not the law and the father must take his son and present him to the police in that village. He should also have the wounds checked there and should be given penicillin. (*UK*, 28)

It is not clear how this scene could have taken place, given that Ernest did not know Swahili or Masai and most Kamba knew little English. Ernest later said he taught the tribe Spanish and they conversed in that language.

Ernest's life as a Kamba provided occasion for elaborate fantasies in the African book, all of them with some basis in reality. As he related them in these manuscripts, which would be edited and posthumously published, first as *True at First Light* and later *Under Kilimanjaro,* his stories are characterized by the wry, often elusive humor that is a feature of his later writing. Once, the Kamba got hold of a magazine the Hemingways had brought with them, which had artists' renditions of saber-tooth tigers, woolly mastodons, and brontosauruses—which the tribespeople then assumed Ernest had hunted in America. Inevitably, much of this material borders on the automatic racism and colonialism of this particular period and context; Ernest so enthusiastically assumed the role of Great White Father that he referred to Mary in the African book as "memsahib," confusing his continents. It is ironic that he was doing so at the same time as the Mau Mau rebellion and other anticolonialist uprisings.

He also eagerly learned how to hunt with a spear and went after game, as the Kamba did, at night, claiming to have successfully killed wild dogs, hyenas, jackals, and wild pigs in this manner. As if to actuate his fantasies of being a real Kamba, and probably inflamed by the realization of some of his gender fantasies with Mary, he committed himself to take as his wife a Kamba woman, Debba. He boasted in a letter to Harvey Breit that Debba was an heiress in her tribe, "like Brenda Frazier." She was "black and very beautiful," he said, later telling Archie she looked like Marilyn Monroe, although dark. Debba's family brought him presents of corn and beer while he gave them some lard and the haunch of a warthog. "My girl is completely impudent," he told Harvey. "Her face is impudent in repose, but absolutely loving and delicate rough." Mary, he wrote, was "understanding and wonderful."

Even if based in reality, his immersion in these fantasies suggests that Ernest was once again in a manic phase—one that would extend through the months ahead as he worked on the African book. In *Under Kiliman-jaro,* he re-created conversations with Mary that revealed her fears about his mental state. In his capacity as honorary game warden, Ernest took it on himself to distribute whatever medicines his party had with them. "You're getting a lot of practice as an amateur doctor," Mary said. "Do you think you can cure yourself?" "Of what?" Ernest replied, to which she responded, "Of whatever you get sometimes. I don't mean just physical things" (*UK,* 28). In another conversation he told Mary that Percival said he was crazy and had always been crazy. Mary and Ernest went on to discuss whether writers were crazy; Ernest said he believed that they were. Mary asked if it was true of all writers, and Ernest replied, "Only the good ones" (*UK,* 115–16). Mary was worried by Ernest's fantasies about the Kamba—which the tribespeople seemed to be playing along with, perhaps because, given the language barrier, they didn't know what Ernest was talking about. She warned Ernest, "When it is all fantastic and you . . . make up your lies and live in this strange world you all have then it is just fantastic and charming sometimes and I laugh at you. I feel superior to such nonsense and to the unrealness" (*UK* 84).

Ernest's Christmas present to Mary was a plane trip north and west over the Belgian Congo into Uganda, stopping overnight at Bakavu and Entebbe and then going on to Murchison Falls. Roy Marsh, the owner of their Cessna 180, was an experienced bush pilot, but he got in trouble circling a third time over the falls so that Mary could get better photographs: suddenly a flock of ibis appeared in the path of the plane. He tried to dive under them but hit some defunct telegraph wires, damaging one propeller and the tail of the plane. He was forced to land in deep bush, about three miles south of the falls, on a Nile tributary. The party consulted a map, finding they were forty miles from the nearest village, which might or might not have a telephone. The Cessna's antenna seemed to be broken, but Marsh tried to radio for help. As an afterthought, Mary and Ernest assessed their injuries: Mary, her heart pounding and feeling very queasy, seemed to be in shock; Ernest's back was hurt. They found a sandy spot on a knoll where they could camp for the night, carrying up from the plane water, leftover half-eaten sandwiches, and beer and whiskey.

New York Daily Mirror, January 25, 1954

The next day, rising at five, they rekindled their fire and ate whatever odds and ends they could find among the plane's stores. Incredibly, Ernest, looking around on a short walk, reported seeing a boat on the usually deserted river; it was the *Murchison,* a charter launch that Marsh and the Hemingways discovered, to their delight, was the boat John Huston had used in filming *The African Queen* (1951). Dropped at the town of Butiaba on Lake Albert, they were met by another bush pilot, Reggie Cartwright, and a local policeman. Cartwright and the policeman had been flying over the area looking for bodies, as someone had spotted the wrecked Cessna and presumed the pilot and passengers were dead. A wire service story had gone out on January 24, announcing Hemingway's death—which likely seemed to thousands of readers a shocking end, to be sure, but hardly a surprise, given how often he had seemingly courted his own demise. Cartwright offered to fly the Hemingways and Marsh out in his creaky twin-engine de Havilland to Entebbe.

Though it was getting dark, Cartwright started down the seriously uneven Butiaba airstrip. The plane lifted and dropped again, bumping its way down the runway. Suddenly the starboard engine and fuel tank burst into flames, which leapt to the cabin as the plane came to a stop. Marsh managed to kick out a window through which he and Mary escaped. Ernest, too big to fit through that space, found the door was pinned closed by a piece of wreckage, and, unable to kick it open, butted it open using his head; Cartwright exited last, kicking out another window. The plane burned to cinders, taking Mary's Hasselblad along with all her film, Marsh's pilot license, the Hemingways' passports, eyeglasses, money, and a $15,000 letter of credit. The policeman drove them to the nearby town of Masindi, where in the Railway Hotel they each gulped down much welcomed drinks. Too tired to wash, they fell into bed and slept.

Ernest awakened the next morning to see that a wound in his scalp behind his right ear had leaked a clear liquid—cerebral fluid—on the pillowcase. The local doctor cleaned the wounds on Ernest's and Mary's legs. Mary had a gash on her knee and two broken ribs. The extent of Ernest's injuries was not detected until they got to Nairobi; they included a dislocated shoulder, a collapsed lower intestine, two crushed lumbar vertebrae, a severely damaged liver and kidney, impairment of hearing in his right ear and of sight in his right eye. There was blood in his urine and his sphincter was paralyzed, which meant that when he coughed he would involuntarily defecate. When he saw Peter Viertel, he added a permanent erection to his list of injuries, somewhat convincingly explaining that this was due to the compression of his vertebrae.

But the damage to his head was the most serious. It was his fifth major concussion and probably the worst of any of them; Ernest was groggy and confused and suffered double vision. He managed to remain a little bit drunk throughout his recuperation. In a letter to Berenson a week later, after talking about languages in Africa, he observed, "This is a funny thing. Maybe—concussion is very strange—and I have been studying it. Double vision; hearing comes and goes, your capacity for scenting (smelling something) can become acute beyond belief." Lucidity seems to have come and gone as well. Ernest's head would never really clear.

Bill Lowe from *Look* promised Ernest $20,000 for an exclusive article on the crash. Ever the professional, Ernest agreed. From their room in the New Stanley Hotel in Nairobi, where Ernest and Mary were recuperating, he dictated the story to the wife of an RAF pilot. It was called "The Christmas Gift" (the tour by Cessna being Ernest's present for Mary), and it ran in two issues of the magazine. A rambling account, marked by the garrulousness (and humor) that characterizes all of Hemingway's writings on Africa, the story featured commentaries on such subjects as Gordon's gin (an antiseptic and restorative), Senator Joseph McCarthy, the sounds of the bush at night, dreams of making love to a lioness, and reading one's premature obituaries.

Ernest seems to have been experiencing manic episodes before the accident, but afterward it was evident that his brain injury had affected him profoundly, reactivating the worst of his mental illness, his mood swinging wildly between mania and depression. His fantasies multiplied. In a representative letter to Hotchner, he added expertise with airplanes to his battery of imaginary skills. He admitted that flying had once bothered him, but now he asked who started all the talk that he was wary of flying. Now able to manage aeronautical navigation, he told Hotch he had flown a B-25, a Mosquito, Hurricane gliders, and all manner of "kites" (ever since he "pranged" in his "kite," he was fond of pilot lingo). He boasted of buzzing the shamba (he wanted to do "slow rolls" over it, but said he refrained) and clipping with his propellers the flag flying over the police headquarters of the local town. In the same letter he waxed expansive, moreover, about his duties as honorary game warden, backed up by a group he called "Honest Ernies"; and he described the fine points of his engagement to Debba.

Ernest was performing, both for the readers of *Look* and for Hotch. He was trying out new tall tales, and urged Hotch to keep the letter so he could use it in a future story. He was proud that he had managed to dictate sixteen thousand words for *Look* and hoped that what he had written was funny. Discretion and inhibitions, heretofore a check on the worst of his excesses, seem to have all but vanished. When he chose not to dwell on his injuries and carp at Mary, he appeared to be having a fine time. Yet he knew something was very wrong, and when he was able to detach and watch himself, he was troubled. He told Berenson he heard in his head the mistakes he was making—the repeated words, the strange and angry statements—all because of his hurt head.

Meanwhile, Mary had gone on to Mombasa, where she and Ernest had previously chartered a fishing boat out of the town of Shimoni, intending a fishing holiday with Patrick and Henny and a party that included the Percivals, Denis Zaphiro, and Roy Marsh; Ernest joined them on February 21. Just days after arriving he witnessed a brushfire in the small fishing village and helped to put it out, but because of his physical condition, lost his balance and severely burned his legs, trunk, left hand, and right forearm. His injuries, from the fire but more so from the crash, were too extensive to permit much fishing, so he stationed himself on the veranda of their rented cottage. There, wrote Mary later, "he resumed [a] continuous conversation with whoever was around, repeating oft-told jokes, proud/humble heroics, homemade philosophies." He went out in the boat only once or twice, otherwise holding forth from his "command post" on the veranda about "becoming 'blood brothers' with his Wakamba friends among our safari servants." One morning, under questioning from Ernest, Patrick said the bait was "more or less in order" and Ernest exploded, starting in by saying "I don't permit 'more or less in order.'" He went on a tirade to Patrick about responsibility and the absolute necessity of doing things right, until Henny burst into tears and Patrick walked out and left for Mombasa, later sending back for Henny and their luggage. That day's fishing was off. It was just as well. The Hemingways had been having no better luck with their fishing than they had with their hunting.

Ernest and Mary went on to Venice by way of the *Africa* as planned. On arrival they checked into the Gritti, where Ernest received visitors—including Adriana—from his bed, and was later thoroughly checked out by a string of doctors at the local hospital. Ernest admitted that Mary had borne the brunt of his rancorous recuperation and sent her off to London, Paris, and Spain, planning to join her in Madrid. Lonely in Venice, he summoned Hotchner, who checked in to the Gritti on May 2, and together they went on to Spain. Adamo drove the two of them in the Lancia, where they caught up with Mary, who had been attending the bullfights with Peter Viertel and British *aficionado* Rupert Bellville, a former RAF pilot and playboy, a friend of Ernest's since 1937. Arriving in time for the festival of San Isidro, they took in that year's lusterless bullfights, afterward visiting the ranch of matador Luis Miguel Dominguín, the brother-in-law of rival Antonio Ordóñez, where they met Dominguín's current amour, Ava Gardner (still legally married to Frank Sinatra). Ernest described Dominguín as a cross between Don Juan and Hamlet.

Ernest and Ava Gardner became friends this spring. Inevitably, he became Papa and she became Daughter, but in this case Gardner was touched by it, for her own father had always addressed her as Daughter. She had starred in the widely acclaimed 1946 film *The Killers,* now considered a noir classic, whose plot, much of it in flashbacks, was derived from Ernest's story; Ava played Swede's girlfriend in the backstory. In the less successful *Snows of Kilimanjaro* she played a role that was invented for the film. That spring the actress was hospitalized for an attack of kidney stones; Ernest came to visit her and sat on her bed chatting. "*The Killers* was okay," he said. "But the only good things in *Snows of Kilimanjaro* were you and the dead cat," referring to the dead leopard found up on the titular mountain. After Ava passed the kidney stones Ernest, somewhat oddly, asked her if he could have one of them for a good-luck charm. She agreed, and he carried the object with him for years. A few years later, after she played Lady Brett Ashley in the 1957 *The Sun Also Rises,* she said, "I always felt close to Papa's women."

Viertel later wrote about the visit the party made to Dominguín's ranch; he commented that Ava and Dominguín "made a handsome couple—the young movie queen and her bullfighter."

After Ernest, Mary, and Bellville left for a bullfight in Madrid, Viertel and the matador started talking about Hemingway. Dominguín said that Ernest had made a remark to him about Peter that disturbed him. Ernest had said that Peter had talent, but probably would never write anything important. Dominguín could not forgive this: "Even if this is true, it is not a remark you make about a friend," he told Peter. A few days later they discussed the incident some more, Dominguín saying that the remark had disillusioned him, and put Peter on notice that Papa had a "mean streak." Peter gave some thought to Ernest's "duplicity," deciding that Ernest made the remark because he saw Peter as an interloper into his territory, the bullfight, about which he was exceedingly proprietary. Perhaps with the luxury of hindsight, Peter saw this as a sign of Ernest's growing paranoia, "for how could he," Peter wrote, "the greatest Anglo-Saxon expert on the *fiesta brava,* be at all concerned about a challenge from a neophyte like me?"

When Ernest and Mary were at the Palace Hotel, they were visited by George Plimpton, a tall and striking-looking young American writer. A well-born New Yorker, Plimpton, with degrees from Harvard and Cambridge, had just joined the staff of a recently founded literary magazine, *The Paris Review.* Plimpton had met Ernest in Paris in 1953 on the Hemingways' way to Africa, where he had convinced Hemingway to sit for a *Paris Review* interview, one of the earliest interviews in the magazine's "Writers at Work" series. Plimpton now turned up in Madrid, where he attempted, without much success, to conduct the interview. In the late mornings, Ernest would receive Plimpton in bed, Ava Gardner and Dominguín often sprawled across it; Hotchner would appear with a pitcher of iced martinis. The interview stalled and would not be completed until March 1957.

At the Finca on his return, in the summer of 1954, Ernest seemed an old man. When Hotchner saw him, for the first time since the plane crash, he was surprised: "What was shocking to me now was how he had aged. . . . He appeared to have diminished somewhat—I don't mean physically diminished, but some of the aura of massiveness seemed to have gone out of him." His hair was growing back in (almost completely white), but the collection of scars on his scalp was still visible, some of them alarming-looking. As before, Ernest kept his beard cropped close, a grizzled half-inch stubble, because recurrent skin problems made shaving difficult. As his hair grew in, he kept it combed straight back, as he had done since he was around forty-eight, when his hairline began seriously receding and his remaining hair thinned. (He liked to wear his hair long, all cut to the same length in back.) More often than not, he wore steel-rimmed spectacles. His grin showed rows of even teeth; it was in no way a twinkling or contented smile unless he was laughing; otherwise it looked vaguely frightening, and, indeed, he was said to show displeasure by visibly gritting his teeth. Slim Hayward saw a lot of him as the filming of *The Old Man and the Sea* approached, and to her, he retained much of his "massiveness." "Papa was a big man, and that alone kept you afraid most of the time," she later wrote. "He could have swatted you dead with one swat if he wanted to. He had a way of narrowing his eyes when he was angry, or ignoring you utterly."

Mary gave some indication of Ernest's post-plane-crash infirmities that summer in her diary, where she recorded an account of their first outing on the *Pilar* after their return:

The first time we went fishing my throat tightened while my husband slowly, determinedly let himself over the *Pilar*'s side into her cockpit. Although the day was warm, he wore a safari jacket in the breeze of the Gulf Stream instead of going topless, as was his custom. Whatever we caught was of no great importance or great strain and for once I was thankful for little success. That evening Ernest read peacefully in his chair. It had been a day of true triumph.

Few people, including those close to him, understood how severe the damage was.

Ernest had seen a doctor in Spain who had prescribed continued rest and limited alcohol, and Ernest tried to follow his instructions; for a time Mary insisted on an intake of one glass of whiskey and three glasses of wine a day. He was fond of saying alcohol had always been a "giant-killer" for him, but for all his talk of his friend Fitzgerald's having been a "rummy" he seemed unable to see that alcohol was taking as heavy a toll on him and on his writing as it had in Scott's life. Like many alcoholics, he had developed elaborate rationalizations for his behavior. "Rummies are rummies and can't help themselves and shouldn't drink," he told Charles Poore. "But if you learned to drink before you were fourteen and drank ever since and love to drink and can still write well at 53 do you rate as an alcoholic?" Years before, he had spelled out just what alcohol meant to him in a letter to Ivan Kashkin, his first critical champion in the Soviet Union:

> Don't you drink? I notice you speak slightingly of the bottle. I have drunk since I was fifteen and few things have given me more pleasure. When you work hard all day with your head and know you must work again the next day what else can change your ideas and make them run on a different plane like whiskey? When you are cold and wet what else can warm you? Before an attack who can say anything that gives you the momentary well being that rum does? I would as soon not eat at night as not to have red wine and water.

The trajectory of Ernest's engagement with alcohol is not hard to delineate. For years a simple pleasure, it was a feature of the good life in Hemingway's youth; he and his contemporaries were suspicious of anyone who *didn't* drink. This began to change for him, however, starting about, roughly, 1940. Soon it had become a daily necessity; in Cuba he generally had his first drink before noon, sometimes on awakening. In Africa on the second safari Ernest drank a quart of beer every day before breakfast. Denis Zaphiro told a biographer that Ernest drank two bottles of hard liquor a day—surely an exaggeration, though his son Patrick said his father drank a quart of whiskey a day from about 1940 on. Yet Ernest never seemed to get falling-down drunk. "I suppose he was drunk the whole time," said Zaphiro, but added that he seldom showed it. Mayito Menocal observed, "Gradually alcohol began to dominate him more and more until he became controlled by it." From 1954 on, doctors warned him that he was risking his life by continuing to drink as he did, and there were several periods when Ernest would severely restrict his drinking, sometimes cutting out drinks after dinner, say, or everything but wine. (Whether he followed his announced regimens is open to question.) He seems never to have cut out liquor entirely, however, not even at the last.

Alcohol played a part in almost all of Ernest's many accidents, from pulling the chain that brought a skylight down on his head, scarring his face for life, to his next-to-last concussion, sustained when he slipped aboard the *Pilar,* gashing open his head. There is no question that drinking in the wake of his many brain injuries made their effects worse, and drinking was also disastrous for his psychiatric problems, feeding his manic highs and darkening his depressive lows. As he aged, alcohol not only compromised his health, it contributed to the falling off in his creative powers. *Across the River and into the Trees* was the product not only of a mental disorder, but also of alcoholism. By the time he was fifty, Ernest was writing markedly less than he had in his twenties or thirties, and what he was writing was progressively weaker. He seems to have been lost in the "Big Book," now several books in various states of disarray.

* * *

For a long time Ernest had been tracking the awarding of the Nobel Prize for Literature, even as early as 1930, when Sinclair Lewis became the first American recipient. He told Archie MacLeish that he had always thought of the Nobel as something that came when you were very old; thus, he said, it "was a hell of a blow to me" when Lewis won at age forty-five—which is a curious choice of words. The remark indicates he had been shocked that Lewis, to whom he had heretofore given little thought as a competitor, had taken the prize and Ernest had not. He had had some time to get used to Lewis since then, but when Faulkner was awarded the Nobel in 1950, it rankled. Still, Faulkner never got under his skin in the way that Scott Fitzgerald or James Jones had. The two writers had kept their distance from each other, until Ernest got wind of a 1947 interview in which Faulkner said that of all contemporary writers Hemingway took the fewest risks in his writing; he even used the word "coward." Faulkner meant stylistic experimentation, but Ernest took it (understandably enough) as a comment on his courage and, somewhat strangely, had Buck Lanham write Faulkner about the bravery he had seen in Ernest during the war. Faulkner apologized to Ernest, saying he should have looked over the interview before allowing it to be printed. There was another minor flap when Harvey Breit, who seems to have thrived on stirring up literary intrigue, suggested that Faulkner review *The Old Man and the Sea*. In the interim Faulkner had won the Nobel, and in a letter to Breit Ernest accused Faulkner of having to drink to feel all right about his having the prize as long as Ernest was still alive. Meanwhile, Faulkner gave the novel a gracious review in the literary magazine *Shenandoah*, writing, "Time may show it to be the best single piece of any of us."

All of October 1954 the word was that Ernest was to be that year's Nobel Prize winner. On October 5 *The New York Times* said the only other contender was Halldór Laxness, an Icelandic writer. The newspaper later asserted, not very flatteringly, that Ernest was a prime candidate because of the scare about his death after the first plane crash in Africa.

Ernest received a phone call early on the morning of October 28, telling him he had won the prize; he woke Mary first and then called Buck Lanham to tell him the news. The press had been on hand for the past day or two, and Ernest stepped out of the Finca and talked to them on the steps and the terrace, welcoming about a dozen in for lunch and more for the afternoon. A former *Havana Post* writer and *Time* stringer, Henry F. Wallace, noted that Ernest was drinking gin-and-tonics and described him as "rolling to starboard like an old freighter." Ernest claimed he was on a regimen of rigid abstinence, but that he was "breaking training" that day. He named for reporters the three writers he thought deserved the prize: Isak Dinesen, Bernard Berenson, and Carl Sandburg, the Chicago poet he had known and admired in his youth. He also took the opportunity to plead for the release of his old friend, Ezra Pound, then in St. Elizabeths, the Washington, D.C., psychiatric hospital, confined because of pro-Fascist broadcasts he made in Italy during World War II. At three o'clock Ernest delivered a short speech he had written out. Mary's record of it makes little sense: "I am a man without politics. This is a great defect but it is preferable to arteriosclerosis," he began. "I like the [fighting] cocks and the Philharmonic Orchestra. . . . Now excuse some jokes and a legitimate admonition which follows and which one sees every morning in the mirror. Lacking are those types by which one can see the good which is humanity and those who manage to eat their failures." He went on to say that he was giving the medal to the Virgen de Cobre, Cuba's national saint, to be kept in her shrine outside Santiago de Cuba—which is where, indeed, it would ultimately come to rest (though it was stolen in the 1980s, recovered, and put in safe storage by the Catholic Church). He got belligerent about the prize money, $35,000, which he made a point of telling reporters and onlookers was not in his possession yet, taking the opportunity to rail against all the burglaries he had endured in the past year. He told reporters he did not expect to live five more years—a shocking statement that no doubt expressed his sense of his own physical vulnerability.

Ernest was too beat up to consider traveling to Sweden to accept the prize, which was convenient, because he hated public speaking. The medal itself was awarded the day after the announcement at the Finca, where Mary served a formal lunch. The official statement that accompanied the award praised Ernest's "mastery of the art of narrative, most recently demonstrated in *The Old Man and the Sea*." The American ambassador to Sweden, John Cabot, received the prize for him at the formal ceremony in Stockholm on December 10. Ernest recorded his acceptance speech for the occasion, which was short and eloquent. Some of what he said was curious, however, notably the following: "Writing, at its best, is a lonely life. . . . [The writer] grows in public stature as he sheds his loneliness and often his work deteriorates. For he does his work alone and if he is a good enough writer he must face eternity, or the lack of it, each day." Of all the possible ways Ernest could have accepted the Nobel, it seems downright contrary—not to say revealing—for him to speak of a writer growing in stature while his work deteriorates. For it was becoming all too clear that this was exactly what was happening to him.

THIRTY

Ernest devoted the rest of 1954, almost all of 1955, and the beginning months of 1956 to writing "the African book"—what would become a sheaf of about 850 pages, which he never did finish to his satisfaction. It is not clear exactly what he intended this book to be; different editors have seen different books in it, and Ernest himself took a big chunk of it out to put into *The Garden of Eden*. Sometime in 1956 he locked the manuscript away in a safe deposit box in a Havana bank, referring to it many times as his life insurance, the proceeds to go to his widow on publication (*UK*, viii). Excerpts appeared in *Sports Illustrated* in 1971 and 1972, and Patrick Hemingway edited and published *True at First Light*, a novel he carved out of the manuscript, in 1999, while *Under Kilimanjaro*, a much longer version, edited by Robert Lewis and Robert Fleming, appeared in 2005. Of these iterations, the last is closest to what Ernest left behind. As such it is not so much a novel, memoir, or work of nonfiction as it is simply a compendium, an outsize sequel of sorts to his account of the 1933–34 safari, *Green Hills of Africa*. In it are collected his dreams; memories of baseball games; meditations on the soul; stories about his childhood; the racket that safaris had become by this time (he rails against wealthy hunters, happy the Mau Mau scares have kept them away); his brother Leicester's novel; a reminiscence of Jane Mason; thoughts about Ezra Pound and Ford Madox Ford. The "plot" combines his adventures as a game warden, Mary's hunt for her lion, and his involvement with the Kamba and his African "fiancée," Debba. It shares with Ernest's later writing verbosity and insufficiently modulated detail: he throws in everything, and goes on about it at great length, as if he were unable to judge what was important and what was not. Though his usual working method was to spend infinite time composing carefully crafted sentences, rather than to get everything down on paper that he thought might go into a finished manuscript, it is of course possible that he was now working according to the latter technique, intending to cut it drastically, perhaps even to shape a novel from it, as Patrick Hemingway attempted to do.

Except for this—yet another ambitious, stalled project—Ernest's creative life in the 1950s was taken up by projects like the film version of *The Old Man and the Sea,* and, more dramatically, the update of *Death in the Afternoon* he planned to write for *Life* in 1959, in which he would focus on two matadors. Both projects were frustrating and the results of each pained and angered him. It is hard to tell how much was due to the nature of the projects and how much to the injuries he had sustained in the 1954 plane crash, especially the injuries to his brain. Perhaps triggered by this latest traumatic brain injury, he suffered further episodes of mental disturbance, mostly in the form of mania, though the depressions, if briefer, seemed to penetrate his psyche more deeply.

In the summer of 1955, still hard at work on the Africa book, Ernest became enmeshed in the film version of *The Old Man and the Sea.* Peter Viertel, who was writing the screenplay, came down to Cuba twice that summer—once with the Haywards and once on his own—to begin what he called his "indoctrination." In what seems to have been his version of Method acting for writers, Ernest felt that Peter needed to be immersed in the story of the Cuban fisherman if he was to write a convincing script. To that end he had the *Pilar* tow an open boat out to sea, in which Peter spent a long hour to get inside the skin of the old fisherman. He then had Peter spend the night in a room over La Terraza, his favorite café in Cojimar, the fishing village where the *Pilar* was berthed and the setting of his novella. He wanted Peter to rise at five in the morning with the fishermen, to better understand the old man's daily routine. Peter did indeed find the early-morning ritual memorable, as dozens of fishermen made their way down the dusty road to their boats before dawn, their path lit by lanterns.

Filming began in September. Initially Spencer Tracy had been slated to do the voice-over for the film, with a real Cuban fisherman as the old man, but Tracy soon made it clear he wanted to take on the role. When Hayward and Viertel were both in Cuba in May, Peter tried to dispel tensions between Ernest and the producer with a lame joke about Santiago going out on the eighty-fifth day and *not* catching a fish. Ernest, narrowing his eyes and speaking through gritted teeth, said, "The Jews have always had a superior attitude toward fishing—probably because fish has never been part of their diet." Peter, angry himself, hissed that he thought Ernest had gotten beyond his anti-Semitism with *The Sun Also Rises.* Ernest, who often became very contrite after lashing out at someone he cared about, assured Peter he had never been anti-Semitic, and matters were smoothed over.

Ernest's moods, however, were becoming unpredictable—and frightening. Slim Hayward, visiting in the fall, enjoyed a mild flirtation with Peter. Ernest did not comment, but no doubt he picked up on the charged atmosphere. He went outside every evening and sat on the steps of the Finca, very close to the guesthouse where she was staying, and sang "sad, romantic" songs like "Greensleeves." Slim, terrified that he might come into her room, pretended to be asleep. "Ernest grew more and more difficult," she wrote about her stay and the early days of filming the movie. "He not only gave me my first taste of his irrational side, he began to show the craziness that was in him. There was no verbal abuse, but when he looked at me, his eyes became smaller, sharper, meaner. It was obvious he was pissed off. In conversation, he was cold."

One evening they were all to go to the Floridita for a drink. Ernest had made no move to change his clothes before leaving, still barefoot and wearing his customary oversized shorts with his "Gott mit uns" belt, a Nazi souvenir from the war, fastened over them (the belt, which he wore almost constantly, would not fit through the loops of most of his clothes). When Slim looked up from her newspaper, he undid the belt, sucked in his gut, and allowed his shorts to fall down around his ankles. She and Peter were horrified.

The next day, when Slim was on her way to the airport, Peter handed her a manila envelope containing the first part of his screenplay for her to deliver to Leland. Ernest suspected some "skullduggery" about the script, Slim later wrote, "and he went absolutely crazy with rage." Showing him that the contents of the envelope were copies of the pages Peter had given him did no good. In June Peter had witnessed another unpleasant scene when a beggar encountered Ernest outside the Finca. The beggar did not leave immediately, and Ernest "flew into a rage," shouting, "Que se vaya!" Peter was chilled. Slim later commented sadly on her last visit to the Finca: "The judgment, wisdom, and sanity that had attracted me and held me in their spell were all receding, vanishing as I watched."

The filming began in September, though the director, Fred Zinnemann, was not present: a camera crew were to document the landing of the thousand-plus-pound marlin, the fish Santiago would catch in the film. Ernest took his role as fishing consultant very seriously, going out every day with the crew and spending long hours on the bridge of the *Pilar,* sipping tequila. Yet the only marlin they caught weighed just a few hundred pounds—not enough for the needed behemoth. Ernest invited George

Brown, the owner of the New York boxing gym that he frequented when in town, to come down and oversee his "training." Brown gave him massages when Ernest returned from a day's cruise and generally provided needed encouragement. (While Ernest was at sea with the crew, he directed Brown to give Peter daily boxing lessons on the tennis court.)

Filming was suspended for the winter and resumed in the spring of 1956. Spencer Tracy came down on a visit with Katharine Hepburn, whom Ernest had met on an Atlantic crossing on the *Paris* in 1934. A brouhaha developed promptly on their arrival: Tracy, an alcoholic, was nervous about his challenging role and Ernest's reputation. He had been drinking on the plane ride down, which frightened everyone, and showed up at the Finca clutching two bottles of Dubonnet, one half empty. Ernest and Zinnemann scolded Tracy "as if he were a truant schoolboy," said Peter. Hepburn leapt to Tracy's defense, saying he had not touched a drink for ten years. Ernest said he knew, as a matter of fact—and here he was passing on something Peter had told him in confidence—that Tracy had been drunk in Colorado on the set of his last film. (This nearly cost Viertel his friendship with Hepburn.)

Meanwhile, Ernest had begun to goad Tracy. He started in on the actor's drinking—or his *not* drinking. "What are you, a rummy?" Ernest said. "Can't you just have a drink or two? Do you have to go on till you're insensible? Is that your problem?" Tracy took a drink. Ernest kept bringing up Tracy's weight; the actor had been told to lose some of his 210 pounds and hadn't done so yet. He was "too fat and rich" for the role, Ernest said. "[He] can make money playing fat men now, or he can always get by in those toad-and-grasshopper films with Miss Hepburn, but he is a complete and terrible liability to the picture," Ernest would later say.

Meanwhile, because they could not get the needed fishing footage, in April 1956 a crew moved to the waters off Cabo Blanco, Peru, said to abound with huge marlin. Ernest brought Mary with him, and Elicio Arguelles, a noted Cuban sportsman (and cousin of Mayito Menocal), who would join Ernest in trying to land big fish; they also brought along the *Pilar*'s captain, Gregorio, to see to tackle and bait, among other duties. They were not much more successful there. One of the fish caught was big enough, at around a thousand pounds, but shots of the fish jumping over the surface were needed, and the fish did not cooperate. The movie was already way over budget, so after a month the Peruvian fishing expedition broke up. With Ernest elsewhere, director Zinnemann was able to proceed in shooting Tracy's scenes in Cuba, though not without incident. Zinnemann would soon be replaced by John Sturges (coincidentally, from Oak Park).

Eventually, footage of a huge marlin was secured elsewhere, and models of marlins would eventually be used as well—despite Ernest's sharp comment to Leland, "No movie made with a goddamn rubber fish ever made a goddamn dime."

*　*　*

While Ernest was giving his attention to the film in 1955 and 1956, life at the Finca was not proceeding smoothly. Slim Hayward provided a brief glimpse of the atmosphere in her memoir. Slim, who was fastidious and stylish, did not have much use for Mary; she found Ernest's wife "however you cut it, a badly groomed, unkempt woman." Nevertheless, she was appalled by the way Ernest treated Mary. "Poor Mary!" she wrote. "At the best of times Ernest was sweet to Mary in the way you might be with a child. But when he was in one of his moods he dumped on her. While I was at the Finca, Ernest had become increasingly abusive to her—so rude, belligerent, and cruel it was painful to witness." During one of Slim's visits, Mary returned from the hairdresser with her hair a reddish blond. When Peter asked her about it, she said, "I've had my hair dyed the color of Slim's." Peter and Slim, comparing notes later, decided this was "pitiful." They chalked it up to jealousy—when it was just as likely that Mary was trying out that color in accordance with Ernest's sexual fantasies about blondness—that is, it had nothing to do with her wanting to look like Slim.

Slim was quite right, however, that the Hemingways' life veered between sincere affection and happy physical intimacy on the one hand, and on the other disturbing cruelty—largely on Ernest's part. Mary and Ernest were both strong-willed, opinionated people with hair-trigger tempers. The extensive correspondence between them—even when living together, each wrote many "in-house" letters to the other—suggests considerable affection on both sides. They had many interests in common. Mary was almost as equally avid as Ernest for hunting and fishing, and both were enthusiastic swimmers. She called him Lamb or Papa, and he called her Kittner or Pickle. He sent her homemade cards, especially Valentines, and often decorated his letters with little drawings. He provided considerable financial and emotional support for the care of Mary's increasingly ailing and difficult parents, which required her to make frequent trips to the States. Though Mary sometimes wished their social life included visits to nightclubs and expensive restaurants—not just the Floridita—Ernest was for the most part financially generous, encouraging her to buy clothes and making several gifts of jewelry—especially after they quarreled.

It seems that only once, in 1946, did Mary complain about their sex life; their sexual interest in each other seldom flagged, and Mary indulged Ernest's fantasies about hair with alacrity. She also entertained his fantasies about gender roles, which they acted out, evidently with enthusiasm on her part, and especially after their intimacies on the African safari. She called him "you wonder boy-girl," and sent him love "from half a woman—or half a boy." When they were apart, Ernest often described erections he would experience while writing to her, especially in thinking about her hair. Though his letters sometimes verge on the pornographic, not so much in their sexual explicitness as their ritual repetition of fantasies, he also was capable of profoundly lyrical expressions of love. He liked to describe how beautiful he found her while she slept: like a leopard, he once observed, and not one in captivity—comparison to a big cat in the wild being perhaps his highest praise.

In turn, Mary not only entertained and participated in acting out his sexual fantasies, she evidently provided much needed reassurance that there was nothing wrong with the way those fantasies took shape. It is possible that Ernest had been seeking this kind of reassurance for some time; though, to be fair to his previous wives, it does seem that Mary was the first he allowed to see the full range of what made him happy sexually. At one point after their return from Africa, he declared his determination to get his ears pierced to show himself a member of the Kamba tribe (this despite the fact that it was over a year since the African trip). He wanted to wear gold earrings as Mary did, he said, and asked her to pierce his ears with a sterilized needle and a cork. Mary demurred, and afterward wrote him an in-house letter of explanation that was a masterpiece of supportive tact:

> For the well-being of both of us, I ask you please to reconsider having your ears pierced. . . . It would be flouting the mores of western civilization. I do not defend the modern idea that men, except for a few sailors, rakish fellows, do not wear earrings—but I think we should recognize that it exists. Everything you do sooner or later gets into print . . . and your wearing earrings will have a deleterious effect on your reputation.

She gently pointed out that getting his ears pierced would not make him a Kamba, and suggested there were other ways to show his brotherhood with the tribe. "And you know," she added, in a spirit of sexual playfulness, "that I love the fun of make-believe as much as you do." His desire must have privately horrified and dismayed her—needless to say, it was not at all common for Western men, in the 1950s, to wear earrings—but her handling of her husband was loving and thoughtful.

Increasingly, however, their friends and acquaintances were struck by the abusiveness of the relationship. Buck Lanham came to be appalled by Ernest's treatment of Mary, and his wife wrote Carlos Baker, "She really had to eat a lot of dirt to hold on to her position all those years." Mary might well have left Ernest were it not for her financial dependence on him; she also no doubt felt that she would have difficulty finding work because of her age. Ernest's youngest son assessed the situation with devastating accuracy in a 1952 letter to his father: "Because of the truly terrible way that you treat her, she would have left you long ago but she's too old now—couldn't make her way in the newspaper world anymore—you have to sleep with people to get the important stories, you know. It would be pretty hard going for her, so she sticks it out with you." Mary had said as much to Greg, he told his father. Many accounts, however, reveal Mary to have been a handful herself, gamely fighting back in kind. In part, she may have been taking out on her husband her frustration at having to stick with him. Ernest complained of being harangued by her in the middle of the night (she claimed he did it too), and scolded him in front of his friends, which he found mortifying, he said. And every time, he went on, she would deny any ill treatment of him, saying she had the best disposition in the world.

Mary must have known when she married Ernest that if she were to stay married to him she would have to become his caretaker in his old age. But that eventuality must have seemed far away when they met, given the vigorous and spirited man she married. Though she perhaps should have taken better note of his alcohol consumption, she was an enthusiastic drinker herself and they enjoyed drinking together—especially, during their courtship, champagne. Most important, she had not known she was signing on for someone whose severe mental illness would make itself felt within the first five years of their marriage. The signs were there had she chosen to see them—his shooting the photograph of her then husband, Noel Monks, in a toilet at the Ritz, to take just one example—but then again she would have had no reason to look for them. Not only did Ernest exude good health, he was a hugely successful author, an admired legend. Severe mood swings were apparent even before his first full-blown manic episode in 1949, when he turned fifty, but she and others around him mistook them for the ordinary highs and lows of an unusual man's daily life.

Ernest's son Jack noticed the change in Ernest in the mid-1950s. "Papa had undergone drastic changes from the man I had viewed all my life as my number one hero," he later wrote. He still could be "gentle," and "warm," but less often, "and his mood generally seemed to me plaintive, occasionally truculent, often so with Mary, and with an underlying bitterness." What Jack called "one of the most memorable moments of my lifelong relationship with my father" was an occasion on which they set themselves up on the rooftop of the Finca's tower with one gun, pitchers of martinis, and some strict shooting rules, and took turns shooting down great quantities of buzzards—no easy feat, for shooting big birds like buzzards or geese is tricky, according to Jack. Father and son knocked off after three pitchers of martinis, then repaired to the living room to watch *Casablanca*, Ernest waxing rhapsodic over "the Swede," as he called Ingrid Bergman. "It was totally maudlin and wonderfully close and human all at once," Jack wrote.

Ernest's flashes of anger were interspersed with his depression and a sort of creeping listlessness. Peter Viertel kept on his mantel a photograph of Ernest on the *Pilar* taken in May 1955, when Ernest was in his mid-fifties but looking, Peter said, twenty years older: "Despite his sturdy legs and arms, his eyes already have the detached look that people acquire as they near the end of their lives, and although Papa is grinning happily for the benefit of the photographer, his gray hair and his stooped posture are that of a much older man." When Hotchner flew down to meet Ernest and Mary in Key West that summer, where they were staying at the currently unoccupied pool house on Whitehead Street, he found that Ernest had gained "considerable" weight, mostly around his middle. "He looked old," observed Hotch, who had last seen Ernest in the spring of 1954, just a few months after the plane crash. "There were lines on his face I had not seen before, especially the vertical lines between his eyes." Moreover, he walked differently: where he had always walked on the balls of his feet— a characteristic noted by many observers—he now walked flat-footed, limping slightly. He came down with prickly heat and a swollen lymph node under his arm—very minor complaints, to be sure, but it seemed both to Hotch and to Mary that he had lost his previously enormous powers of recuperation. While he had recovered from the plane crash injuries, including those to his kidneys and spleen, his back continued to bother him. To sit comfortably, he often placed a board behind him and oversized books to either side. "I have to take so many pills," he told *Time* magazine after the Nobel Prize, "they have to fight among themselves if I take them too close together."

His blood pressure had been a concern since 1947, when in the wake of Patrick's stressful illness the reading was 225/125, with 130–140/80–90 being a desirable reading for someone his size. His weight fluctuated, as it always had, though now the degree of excess weight was worrisome. It went up as high as 256, and he struggled to keep it down to 225, though an ideal weight would have been less than 200. His cholesterol, left unchecked, rocketed to 380. Beginning in 1954, Ernest kept a daily penciled record of his weight and blood pressure on the walls of his bathroom at the Finca.

These ills in themselves required strict dieting to control, and Ernest worked at this. Almost every day he performed what he called "bellies," sit-ups that theoretically whittled away at his girth, and he and Mary both swam laps daily, sometimes as long as half a mile. In addition to painkillers for his back, he took two sleeping pills a night when he was writing ("The doctor says I am not nervously constructed so I could [not] become addicted to anything," he assured Charlie Scribner). In the same letter he said he took six vitamin B_1 capsules daily to combat the effects of alcohol, adding that he never drank after dinner and never had hangovers. As early as 1952, he told Harvey Breit that he took a tablet a day of methyltestosterone, dissolved under his tongue, not for potency but for overall health; it helped to counteract "the gloominess everyone gets."

All this attention to his physical health ignored the elephant in the room, which was Ernest's worsening alcoholism. In Key West in 1955, Hotch noted, "He drank constantly, the most I had ever seen him drink." When Hotch was fixing his breakfast, Ernest was sipping from a cold bottle of vodka from the refrigerator. His consumption had increased in part to dull the pain of his back injuries, but he was more and more drinking around the clock just to maintain. Beginning in 1954 with his visit to Dr. Juan Madinaveitia in Madrid, Ernest was periodically either forbidden alcohol or told to severely limit his intake.

Poor health plagued both Hemingways in 1955 and 1956, disrupting a trip to Europe and forcing them to cancel a planned trip to Africa, to which they had very much looked forward. Anemia had been bothering Mary for some time, and they hoped a change of climate would help. They sailed on the *Île de France* in August. Not Adamo but another Venetian friend of Gianfranco Ivancich drove them from Paris to Madrid by way of Logroño. They met Hotchner in Zaragoza for the *feria* in October, where the matador Ernest much admired, Antonio Ordóñez, was fighting. They were joined by their friends from the circuit in 1954, Rupert Bellville and Peter Buckley; also among the party were the maharajah of Cooch Behar and his maharani. Ernest and Mary booked passage to Mombasa, delighted to include Antonio and Carmen Ordóñez; they planned a six-week safari with Patrick as guide and white hunter.

Hotch noted that Ernest drank heavily every night in Zaragoza and showed distressingly little interest in anything but sitting for hours telling stories, not really caring who was listening to him, "sipping his drinks and talking, first coherently, then as the alcohol dissolved all continuity, his talk becoming repetitive, his speech slurred and disheveled." After they moved on to the Hotel Felipe II on the Escorial in Madrid, Hotchner noted that Ernest was still drinking too much, though he adhered to a strict diet of fish, salad, vegetables, and calves' liver and no beer, starch, or red meat; he allowed himself unlimited scotch. In Madrid Ernest again saw Juan Madinaveitia, who confirmed the presence of liver disease and also found an inflamed aorta—lowering the boom, as Ernest told Hotch, and insisting on just six ounces of whiskey a day and two glasses of wine with each meal (a generous allowance, by most standards), putting him on a new diet and, according to Ernest, forbidding sex, the latter for reasons Ernest did not reveal. Mary's health was not improving either, and they reluctantly canceled what would have been their third African safari, already complicated by the political crisis touched off by the closing of the Suez Canal.

When they arrived at the Ritz in Paris for a month's stay, Ernest immediately put himself under the care of a doctor, who kept him on his regimen, seeing him once a week. The Hemingways went to the races at Auteuil whenever the weather permitted, but Ernest was unhappy with the strict rationing of alcohol, especially at Christmastime. On their return trip, again on the *Île de France,* Ernest was treated by Dr. Jean Monnier, who gave him vitamin injections and cholesterol-lowering medication. Monnier stayed in touch with Ernest for two years, constantly telling him it was "of utmost importance" that Ernest "*must stop* drinking," underlining his words twice.

Ernest decided not to get off in New York (Mary debarked to visit her mother in Minnesota), instead summoning George Brown to join him on the *Île de France* for a West Indian cruise, which conveniently featured a stop in Cuba. Presumably, the idea was that Brown would give him massages and get him in shape on the way home; Ernest's goal was to get healthy. Brown would henceforth become a fixture in Ernest's life, presumably paid to "train" him, but perhaps also to keep him from drinking and out of fights. Unfortunately, the presence of Brown often seemed to remind him of boxing—which in effect encouraged his pugilism.

On his return to Cuba in March Ernest saw a new doctor, Rafael Ballestero, who put him on a wide range of medications, including Methiscol, for a fatty liver; Geriplex, a dietary supplement strong in B vitamins; and Primotest Depot intramuscular injections, or testosterone, every four weeks. He also was prescribed a new antipsychotic drug. Reserpine was derived from snakeroot (*Rauwolfia serpentina*), used for centuries in India for the treatment of insanity; Gandhi is said to have used it as a tranquilizer.

Reserpine was isolated in 1952 and FDA-approved in 1954; a contemporary ad for Ciba touted Serpasil, or reserpine, as "good for neuropsychiatric, neurological, and related disorders: Schizophrenia; Manic states; Paranoid stress; Delirium tremens; Arteriosclerosis and senile psychoses; Anxiety states; Some Cases of Depression." The other pharmacological breakthrough in treating mental illness in the 1950s was the similar drug chlorpromazine, sold as Thorazine—like reserpine, isolated in 1952 and approved in 1954, although it would later become far more widely used.

"Pills for Mental Illness?" asked a 1954 headline in *Time* magazine, the postwar news delivery system of choice for the Hemingways, as for many U.S. expatriates. The article went on to describe reserpine. For decades the only available treatments for mental illness were insulin shock therapy, hydrotherapy, lobotomy, and ECT—electroconvulsive therapy or shock treatment—the latter familiar to Ernest and Mary as the treatment that restored Patrick to sanity in 1947. Many of these treatments were used in combination, mostly on institutionalized patients. Otherwise, almost all of the mentally ill were still locked away in those years, on so-called back wards; it was these antipsychotic medications that would lead to the massive, and controversial, deinstitutionalization of mental patients in the 1960s. But in 1954, the idea that pills could be used to treat mental illness was completely novel; it is hard to overestimate how strange it would have seemed for many patients and their families. It is hard as well to imagine the promise these medications seemed to hold out.

At the same time that reserpine emerged as an antipsychotic, it was being studied as an antihypertensive, emerging as an effective agent in lowering high blood pressure. It should be noted that a 1955 editorial about reserpine in the prestigious *Annals of Internal Medicine* mentioned the drug's antihypertensive properties only in passing, recommending reserpine for psychiatric use. Because Ernest suffered from high blood pressure in addition to his mental illness, however, determining exactly why the drug was prescribed in his case is difficult, as well as how he used it. Which condition was it prescribed for? Was its efficacy in treating the two conditions he suffered from considered a bonus, or an afterthought?

Of perhaps greater interest in understanding Ernest biographically, what was he told about reserpine? Was he told it would make him less "nervous," or that it would calm him down? For that matter, what did his doctors understand of what was wrong with him mentally at this point, and did they tell him what they thought? Given the stigma attached to mental illness and the difficulty of discussing it, perhaps especially with the patient, might they have taken advantage of the drug's efficacy in treating hypertension and told him the reserpine was for his high blood pressure? Or was this simply what Ernest—and Mary—chose to believe? Certainly that was what they both told friends and family. At the end of his life, when he was hospitalized at the Mayo Clinic, the official line would be that Ernest was being treated for high blood pressure. If this is what Ernest came to believe, for how long was he in denial? To what extent did those around him, perhaps with the best of intentions, participate in what seems to have been a charade? It is possible too that in the mid-1950s Ernest's soaring blood pressure was the greater concern, and he, his doctors, and his family and friends, focused on this. Still, lest this discussion seem far afield, it is important to note that the dual properties of reserpine may have greatly affected his treatment and well-being.

Nor should the effects of Ernest's brain injuries be passed over at this point. Doctors knew very little about their effects, and could depend for diagnosis only on the stories of witnesses and/or the patient; MRIs and such tools were not available then. Today, repeated traumatic brain injuries have been found to lead to a condition called chronic traumatic encephalopathy, or CTE, which is a progressive degenerative disease whose symptoms are primarily dementia. Despite all the problems attendant to speculation about such a condition, it seems fair to say that Ernest's head injuries continued to be a factor as his life began to come apart.

Reserpine was but one of many drugs Ballestero prescribed for Ernest. He continued him on Wychol (for protection of the liver), and on the methyltestosterone he had been taking for several years; he prescribed Doriden, or glutethimide, a sedative or sleeping aid; and Ritalin, a newly introduced stimulant that was given in the late 1950s to counteract depression and/or the depressive or sedative effects of other medications. (And just a year before, Manuel Infiesta Bages, a Cuban doctor, also prescribed, in addition to Wychol, Seconal and Ecuanil—barbiturates—and Meonine, or methionine, for liver damage.) Some of these drugs had side effects and interactions that were poorly understood at the time; it is safe to say, however, that doctors today would recommend avoiding alcohol while taking most of these drugs.

Liver disease was a frightening development, an indication that alcohol had wreaked considerable damage. Beginning in 1956, Ernest's showed positive on the Maclagan test, also known as the thymol turbidity test, and Hanger's test, a measurement of cirrhosis devised by Franklin McCue Hanger in 1938. The tests showed his liver functioning was compromised; he needed to stop drinking. He interpreted the doctors' rationing of alcohol variously. He told Archie he was first restricted to two glasses of "light" red wine—however that was defined—with meals. After he returned to Cuba, the Hanger's test was still positive, however, so he had to cut out everything but one glass of wine with the evening meal. He admitted to Archie that the doctors said he must quit drinking completely, "but they do not want to treat the nervous system too violently," evidently trying to forestall symptoms of withdrawal like delirium tremens; perhaps the Doriden was prescribed for this reason.

Ernest stopped mentioning his diet and liquor allowance in his correspondence by the fall of 1957, though his persistent glumness indicated that he was still rationing his alcohol. When a young female editor from *The Atlantic Monthly* showed up in Cuba asking Ernest to contribute to their hundred-year anniversary issue, he agreed, writing two of the most perfunctory stories he ever produced. The first, "Get a Seeing-Eyed Dog," is about a man who has recently gone blind and heroically sends his wife away so he can get used to it alone, saying he does not want her to be his "seeing-eyed dog" (the wife corrects the phrase to "seeing-eye," but the protagonist insists on his version, "seeing-eyed," for no particular reason—and this is the spelling used in the title). The other story, more interesting but somewhat bizarre, was "A Man of the World," about a blind man who frequents a couple of gambling saloons in Nevada, taking a cut of 25 cents whenever he hears anyone win on the slot machines. The proprietor tells the horrific, graphically violent story of how the blind man lost his sight; during a bar fight, one of his eyes was dangling on his cheek, and an onlooker exhorted his opponent to bite it off "like a grape."

The stories were a direct expression of Ernest's newest obsession, which was that he was going blind. The blood poisoning that had nearly killed him in Cortina in 1949 had begun with erysipelas, a skin infection that in his case spread to the eyes. The plane crash in Africa in 1954 had temporarily blinded him in the right eye. Hypertension can also affect vision. Blindness is a terrible fate for a writer, and it struck close to home. It was reading he worried most about, however, because he had become familiar with, if not happy about, dictation.

Sunny evidently wrote Mary in some alarm, asking about Ernest's eyesight, for Mary wrote Sunny in December assuring her that Ernest could see just fine. "He got the idea," she explained to Sunny, "or the story grew up in him, from an entirely different story, about a young man who was blinded in a hunting accident." Mary's explanation raises other, more disturbing questions: was Ernest again manic, or experiencing a mixed manic state, where depression cycles rapidly with mania? Ernest's preoccupation with his sight is in the nature of an obsession, and Mary's description of it as "a story [that] grew up in him" is strikingly apt. But there is a suggestion that his mental state was beginning to be characterized by paranoia, that his imaginative state was becoming dissociated from reality.

Gregory Hemingway was himself going through a very rough time in 1957. He and Ernest had not seen each other since they quarreled over Pauline's death in 1951. Dressing as a woman was just one of Greg's many problems. He had moved on from Dianetics, or Scientology, working briefly as an airline mechanic and taking classes at UCLA; he soon divorced his first wife, Jane. After receiving his inheritance from Pauline, he had spent a lot of time in Africa, later claiming he shot eighteen elephants in the space of one month. Intending to be a white hunter like his brother Patrick, he applied for a game license but was rejected because of drunkenness. He was drafted in 1956 and inducted into the U.S. Army, signing up as a paratrooper with the 82nd Airborne, but ended up in a psychiatric ward at Fort Bragg. He was hospitalized twice in 1957, receiving shock treatments each time; he was misdiagnosed as schizophrenic, later diagnosed as suffering from manic-depressive illness.

Though in his later memoir of his father Greg would give the impression that he and Ernest were estranged from 1951 until his father's death in 1961, in fact they saw each other in 1957, after Greg's hospitalizations. Greg had showed up in Key West in a fairly confused state, Ernest told Patrick. "When I saw him," he went on, "Greg was in bad shape and very dirty"—Ernest couldn't get him to wash. (Greg did indeed lead a shambolic existence, according to his third wife and their son John—often surrounded by considerable disorder and personally disheveled.) Greg wanted treatment, Ernest said, and was getting it. Aside from this encounter, Ernest and his youngest son were in close contact by letter, and he often provided Greg with financial support. Ernest's correspondence with others about Greg runs the gamut. Sometimes he covered up his son's problems and emphasized his small successes, but most often he spoke cruelly and dismissively about his youngest son. As early as 1952, he told Harvey Breit that Greg, who had showed such promise, had turned out to be completely useless. In 1955 he told Marlene Dietrich that he loved two of his kids but that he found the presence of one son unbearable. In letters to Greg, he railed at his son for not writing letters frequently enough, for illegible handwriting and disgraceful spelling, for wasting Pauline's money and acting as if he had a right to his father's.

Greg gave as good as he got, recognizing that he shared with his father more than bad spelling: he too was manic-depressive, gender dsyphoric, and an alcoholic. Calling his father Ernestine, Greg wrote, brutally, "When it's all added up, papa it will be: he wrote a few good stories, had a novel and fresh approach to reality and he destroyed five persons—Hadley, Pauline, Marty, Patrick, and possibly myself." His father, he said, was a "gin-soaked abusive monster." He accused Ernest of surrounding himself with syco-phants and called Mary "your present whipping post." He threatened to "beat the shit" out of his father. His most succinct accusation was blunt and brutal—and contained flashes of insight:

> You'll never write that great novel because you're a sick man—sick in the head and too fucking proud and scared to admit it. In spite of the critics, that last one was as sickly a bucket of sentimental slop as was ever scrubbed off a barroom floor. There's nothing I'd rather see than you write a beauty and there's nothing I'd rather see than you act intel-ligently, but until you do I'm going to give you just what you deserve, and in extra large handfuls to make up for the trouble you've caused me.

At the heart of Greg's ambivalence about his father was an abiding admira-tion and love for him, as even this damning passage makes clear. Ernest loved his son no less. The result was tragic hurt on both sides.

Another concern of Ernest's in 1957 was the cause of his old friend Ezra Pound, confined in St. Elizabeths. Ernest and Archie MacLeish had urged that Pound be adjudged insane and unfit to stand trial, which spared the poet a certain prison sentence. Various efforts were made to release Pound over the years, with many writers visiting and showing their support (T. S. Eliot intervened to get Pound more grounds privileges, for example). This culminated in the award of the Bollingen Prize in Poetry in 1948, the first year it was given, which was as controversial as Pound's support-ers expected. Ernest wrote to Dorothy Pound asking her to congratulate her husband, and to pass on an assessment that every writer loves to hear: that he most admired Pound's *recent* work. Over the years Ernest referred to Ezra in his correspondence with great affection, notwithstanding his grievous wrongs. He told Bernard Berenson in a 1953 letter, "I liked Pound very much. He had this great pretense to universal knowledge and he got to be un-bearable. But the things he did know he knew very well and he had a lovely heart until he turned bitter." Ernest was aware of his immense personal and professional debt to Pound, who promoted him ceaselessly in the 1920s, and who, by virtue of being one of the "founders" of modern-ism, assured Ernest of a place in the artistic forefront.

Pound took pleasure in recalling their friendship too, it seems. Back in 1951 Hemingway had endorsed Ballantine Ale, and the company ran a two-page spread with a large photograph of Ernest sitting outdoors with a book in front of him and a glass of beer at his elbow. The caption under the photo reads "In every refreshing glass, Purity, Body, and Flavor." Somebody brought this ad to Pound in the psychiatric hospital, and he was delighted by it, folding it so under the photo of Ernest were the words "Purity, Body, and Flavor," which he found extremely funny.

When Ernest received the Nobel Prize, he did his best to bring Ezra into the many remarks and interviews that appeared in the press. He told a *Time* reporter "fiercely" that Ezra was a great poet and should be freed. In July 1956, he sent Ezra a check for a thousand dollars and told him he was giving Ezra the Nobel Prize medal. (Ernest did not end up sending it.) In his letter to Pound, Ernest gave him a moving tribute, calling him "our greatest living poet," and citing him as "an old tennis opponent, the man who founded *Bel Esprit* [the committee formed in 1921 to support T. S. Eliot], and the man who taught me, gently, to be merciful and tried to teach me to be kind." He could not stand the thought, he said, of his old friend being locked up.

Ernest wrote this letter in 1956, just when Pound's friends began to agitate for his release. MacLeish, Robert Frost, and Hemingway were instrumental in engineering Pound's release in April 1958, with MacLeish deserving most of the credit and Frost taking it. Pound left to live in Italy soon after, and Ernest never saw or wrote to him again. But he continued to speak highly of his old friend.

Other, more quotidian troubles bothered Mary and Ernest in 1957. The summer in Cuba was infernally hot, and the Gulf Stream seemed to be fished out for the time being. Ernest was having knotty troubles with his finances, which were themselves labyrinthine; his affairs were managed for years by New York lawyer Maurice Speiser, who died in 1948 and bequeathed management of Ernest's affairs to another lawyer in his firm, Alfred Rice. Particularly troublesome was the amount of income tax Ernest had to pay. One biographer has estimated that in the 1950s Ernest was paying income taxes of $60,000–80,000 per year on a gross income of less than $200,000—a shocking percentage. The problem was his foreign sales: Rice was receiving almost all of Ernest's foreign royalty payments in Ernest's account rather than leaving them in the foreign banks until either Ernest could collect them in person, or they could be received in the U.S. at more financially propitious times. Because he earned royalties, Ernest needed to make quarterly tax payments that were often a strain on his finances, and he had Rice set up a separate account for taxes. For these reasons, Ernest commonly collected cash in francs from his French publisher,

Gallimard, when in France, and in 1959 he had Gianfranco Ivancich buy him with lira a new Lancia in Italy and meet him in Spain, the car intended to be for Ernest's use in Europe. These kinds of financial details would come to obsess Ernest in the months ahead.

Matters were complicated by such details as the Key West rental, Ernest's deductible expenses (he itemized the costs of almost all travel, for instance), payments for Mary's parents' care, and movie deals. Fortunately, Ernest was realizing a healthy income from television rights. Hotchner had developed a thriving trade adapting Hemingway's work—principally the short stories—for film and the stage but mostly for television. One of the earliest and oddest of these efforts was adapting Ernest's story "The Capital of the World" for ballet; the production was staged at the Metropolitan Opera House in 1953. His adaptations for television were more successful. Television was a new medium and programming was still fluid: like many others, Hotchner learned as TV developed. Many of these productions were critically acclaimed, and an added benefit was that Ernest's name was kept before the public.

It helped too that Ernest had a new writing project, and one more commercially promising than the Africa book: a memoir of his life in Paris in the 1920s. He was spurred to write about his early days on his and Mary's stay in Paris in December of the previous year, on the last leg of their trip back from Africa via Venice and Spain. The management of the Ritz in Paris informed him that two trunks he had left there long ago were still in the hotel's baggage room. When he retrieved and opened them, Ernest found, in addition to some old clothes and similar belongings, more than ten notebooks and hundreds of loose manuscript pages containing writings from his earliest days in Paris. (Also included were manuscripts of early short stories he could sell to collectors for ready cash.) Reading these absorbed Ernest for much of his time in Paris, and he went out and bought Louis Vuitton luggage to get the pages back to Cuba safely.

Ernest had long been thinking about writing about Paris. When Gertrude Stein's *Autobiography of Alice B. Toklas,* with its unflattering remarks about him, came out in 1933, he wrote Max Perkins, "I'm going to write damned good memoirs when I write them because I'm jealous of no one, have a rat trap memory and the documents." As early as 1936, in "The Snows of Kilimanjaro," he included flashbacks to the Paris days, and later lamented "using up" so much material in this way. He *hadn't* used it up, however, as the memoir he began in 1957 makes clear. Calling it a memoir, however, is problematic; "Paris Sketches" would have been an accurate subtitle. For while the wonderful anecdotes with which Ernest studded his manuscript are meant to have the weight of fact, some of them are invented entirely, while in others the truth is twisted in such a way as either to make someone look bad or himself look good.

Old scores get settled: he reveals overhearing an intimate moment between Stein and Toklas that was a gross invasion of their privacy and quite possibly imagined. He also dismisses Stein as a writer concerned only with her reputation and who approved only of those writers who advanced it. He retails some of the nastiest Scott stories in his extensive repertoire, all meant to hammer home that his friend was a hopeless alcoholic destroyed by Zelda. Though the story about Scott's insecurity about his penis size does seem to have had its roots in fact, many of the details in that anecdote seem designed to make the story more amusing and Scott more ridiculous. He conjured up many incidents that conveyed that impression, such as a scene set in the U.S. in which Ernest seems to be (rather desperately) trying to make Scott look like an idiot for not putting enough oil in his car.

Ernest knew as much when he wrote Charles Scribner, Jr., in the last months of his life that the book was not fair to Scott, but his feelings were more complex and more affectionate than he suggests. It was unfair in the same way that telling a rollicking good story about a friend who is out of the room is unfair. His portrait of Scott in *A Moveable Feast* is very funny, tender in many ways, and finally loving. The trip to Lyon, for instance, sounds like one of the best road trips of all time, one that makes both men look like charming fools as they drunkenly bumble along and get to know one another. Ernest must be superior, and he must point out how silly Scott was, but beyond that, the memoir paints a portrait of a man he loved, whom he very much missed. Scott and Ernest had outgrown each other; certainly their artistic paths diverged dramatically. Their separate experiences with wives and women? Not much common ground there. They would have had little to say to each other in middle age or old age; their time together had been youth. Yet Ernest had come to regret, perhaps to his surprise, that Scott—and the youth they shared—had vanished.

If *A Moveable Feast*—Ernest never came up with a title, and this one was supplied posthumously by Mary and Hotchner—has a hero, it is unquestionably Ernest, or rather his younger self. The young writer, poor but happy; composing his stories in cafés to keep warm; having adventures on a shoestring with his loving, clever, and beautiful wife Hadley; aiming to write one true sentence; and looking at art to learn to "paint" in prose: this character is one of Ernest's most lasting and best-loved creations. He ventures that perhaps his worst offenses in Stein's eyes, in fact, were "youth and loving my wife" (*AMF*, 30).

Ernest agonized over what he was doing as he wrote the Paris sketches: not because of his cattiness and meanness, but because he knew his hero was largely fictive. The young writer had not been poor in Paris, but was supported by Hadley's trust fund, to give just one example. Perhaps worst of all, he redrew the emotional outlines of their marriage, placing the blame for its breakup on Pauline's shoulders, accepting none for himself. Ernest and Hadley were easy prey, as he chose to present it: "When you have two people who love each other, are happy and gay and really good work is being done by one or both of them, people are drawn to them as surely as migrating birds are drawn at night to a powerful beacon" (*AMF,* 214). But the real predator was Pauline, and the best relationship of his life was with Hadley. Ernest needed to believe that he had once been lucky in love: happy, fulfilled, productive, and loved for himself. Not only was he writing what purported to be a love story, he was rewriting his emotional history, because the record of his failures at relationships was not tolerable to him. To mangle a line from Joan Didion, *A Moveable Feast* was a story he told himself in order to live—or so he hoped.

Ernest also agonized over what to call his book, whether it was fiction or, like most memoirs, nonfiction. The original, 1964 edition of *A Moveable Feast* is prefaced with a curious statement: "If the reader prefers, this book may be regarded as fiction. But there is always the chance that such a book of fiction may throw some light on what has been written as fact." The "restored," 2009 edition appends, from the manuscript pages in the Hemingway archive, several statements on this subject. These include the following: "This book is fiction. I have left out much and changed and eliminated and I hope Hadley understands"; "This book is all fiction and the fiction may throw some light on what has been written as fact"; and "It was necessary to write as fiction rather than as fact and Hadley would understand I hope why it was necessary to use certain materials or fiction rightly or wrongly" (*AMF,* 229–30). It is one of the many ironies of Ernest's life that one of his most enduring late works would question reality and fiction in this way, in what he thought was a quest for "the true."

It is important to note, however, that the actual writing of *A Moveable Feast* was the best he had done for some time—lean, evocative, vivid. No doubt this was in part because he had rehearsed the story so many times—in his head, to friends, and in letters to scholars and biographers. And while much of his account was embroidered, he didn't have the increasingly intractable burden of creating a fictional narrative: the story was his life. Also, the project took him out of the creative isolation he had been working in for some time, and back to a period when he had been part of an artistic community. Whatever the drawbacks of the Paris scene, he had benefited from the proximity and friendship of the "moderns" and had perhaps nurtured their work as well. Nothing could have been a greater contrast to his present state as the undisputed lord at the Finca—and no doubt he knew it.

*   *   *

Paying his income tax, letter-writing campaigns for Ezra Pound, the memoir—all this activity propped up a man who had become a legend but who was personally falling apart. His white beard, his smile, even his bulk—all made him instantly recognizable, and strangers hailed him as Papa almost everywhere he went, even abroad—especially in Spain, where he was a popular hero (if not an official one; Franco was still in power). Whether Ernest dreaded death, accepted it, defied it, or embraced it, there is no question that in the late 1950s he returned again and again to thoughts of his own ending.

In Cuba, he remained a sort of local potentate, popular and generous, who brought a certain glamour to the island. But political conditions were changing as the year 1958 began. Fidel and Raúl Castro had amassed a rebel army that daily threatened the capital, setting off small bombs, one of which exploded outside the Finca. Dictator Batista's forces were striking back, and matters literally came home to the Hemingways when government patrols, looking for an escaped rebel fighter, killed Ernest's new dog, Machakos (named for a Kamba village). Days at the Finca Vigía no longer stretched into a tropical eternity, and Ernest and Mary began to think of other places where they might perch or nest.

THIRTY-ONE

Mary remembered that Ernest had loved the American West—Montana, Wyoming, and Idaho, and she wondered whether he might be happier there than he was in Cuba. First Mary, and then Ernest, wrote to Lloyd (Pappy) Arnold and his wife, Tillie, in August 1958 about coming to Sun Valley, or the neighboring town, Ketchum, for the fall and winter. The idea was to move out there while Ernest finished both his Paris sketches, now envisioned as a book, and *The Garden of Eden*, which he had taken up again toward the end of 1957. They would then go to Madrid for the San Isidro festival in the spring and spend the summer in Spain. On August 13, Mary said, "Papa decided that we better, pretty soon, get out of this climate for a while and head for Ketchum. We've had it too hot for too long and I feel sure the change would do him good." She wanted the Arnolds to find them a house to rent beginning October 1, or whenever the hunting season opened. Ernest wanted to try it for a month, anxious about whether Ketchum could offer a real escape from publicity. The Arnolds were convinced it could, and Tillie Arnold rented the Heiss house for them until December 15, when the Hemingways moved into the semi-finished Whicher House until March 15.

Life in Cuba was tense. As the Batista government's struggle against Castro's rebels became more desperate, the Hemingways feared the dictator might decide they were undesirables. Signs saying *"Cuba sí! Yanqui no!"* seemed to be everywhere. Ernest and Mary also came to fear lawlessness and the prospect of looters and other intruders. One spring morning about five months before the Hemingways decamped for Idaho, Ernest had Gregorio take him and Mary out fishing, directing him to take the *Pilar* farther and farther to sea. Once he deemed them far enough from land, he had Mary take the helm while he and Gregorio went below, removing from hiding places a remarkable array of weaponry, almost all of it presumably stashed there back in Ernest's sub-hunting days. According to Mary, they threw out "heavy rifles, sawed-off shotguns, and grenades and canisters and belts of ammunition for automatic rifles I had never known existed." It took them about half an hour, she said. The journalist Norberto Fuentes wrote that Gregorio told him about the various hiding places built into the boat back in the 1940s, and said that after the war, "We were allowed to keep all the weapons, including antitank guns, several bazookas and Papa's S&W magnum." "Stuff left over from the old days," Ernest told Mary. "My contribution to the revolution. Maybe we've saved a few lives. And please remember, Kitten, you haven't seen or heard anything." It seems he felt that disposing of the weapons, taking them out of circulation, meant that fewer people would be hurt or killed with them come the revolution. It is not known how or where Ernest amassed such a collection, or why he kept it on the relatively small, often crowded boat for so many years. It is surprising that Mary would have been unaware of its existence over the years as well.

The Hemingways left Cuba for their Idaho sojourn in October. Ernest got Toby Bruce and his wife, Betty, to drive out with him from Key West to Chicago, where they picked up Mary and headed for Ketchum, the Bruces to stay for a few days. Hotchner came out in November and found that Ernest "looked wonderful. . . . I couldn't believe his metamorphosis. He had become taut, the slack was gone, the smile back, the eyes were clear, and ten years had left his face."

Fall in Ketchum was a good time. The Hemingways bought four lots across the street from Pappy and Tillie Arnold, and Mary started drawing sketches for a house they would build, just as Grace Hemingway had done fifty years before. Hotch observed that Ernest "seemed content with the eating and drinking routines he had imposed on himself." The previous March, Ernest had added whiskeys to his daily ration of two glasses of wine. Now, Hotch observed, he had a glass of wine at dinner—a "moderate" amount—and "kept his evening Scotch down to two drinks." He and Hotch watched pro football on TV Sunday afternoons and the fights on Friday nights. Gary and Rocky Cooper came for a two-week visit. The two men hadn't seen each other in eleven years; sadly, soon after this reunion Cooper was diagnosed with prostate cancer. In February Ernest lost his good friend Taylor Williams, known as the Colonel, at seventy-two, his friendship with Ernest dating back to 1939 when Williams was a guide at Sun Valley in its opening season.

The news came in that as of New Year's Day, Castro had taken over in Cuba, an outcome that Ernest told a reporter he found "delightful." Mary got him to call the reporter back and change the quote to say he was "hopeful." While they would not know for some time how the change would affect their life at the Finca, Ernest evidently wanted to have a secure place to live. They decided not to build on their land, and in March bought the Bob Topping house, built on a perfect site on the Big Wood River with a staggering view revealed by large plate glass windows, then something of a novelty. The house was made of concrete, not yet stained brown. It looked impregnable. It was unfinished inside, the floors still plywood, and Mary made some crude furniture out of sheets of plywood and cinder blocks. She raved to the Hemingway sons about the bells and whistles of the new house: an "exhaust machine" over the stove, baseboard heating, an electric can opener, a contraption to hang the television from the ceiling.

So far, so good—but there were warning signs. Even so enthusiastic an observer as Pappy Arnold noted that when Ernest was at his friends' house for dinner, "it was now Papa's habit to take a little lie-down after a good evening meal"—perhaps before his "evening Scotches," a slightly disturbing sign in a man in his fifties. Moreover, Arnold said that after the winter of 1958–59, "I was intensely worried about my friend, and had been for some time." He hoped that it was attributable to the uncertainty of the Cuban situation: Arnold felt the situation "was a trigger . . . [for] the turmoil within," which came up all too often that winter. Arnold painted a vivid picture of Ernest staring into the middle distance, unfocused, "fingers hovering about his lower lip." Arnold said he would feel better about Ernest's state of mind if he and Mary would close up shop in Cuba and make the move to Idaho permanent. Yet Ernest's other Idaho friends noted Ernest's good health and spirits in the fall. And Leonard Bernstein wrote Martha Gellhorn that on meeting Ernest in January 1959 he had been unprepared for Ernest's "charm" and his "beauty." In fact, he noticed, even in the attenuated, diminished Ernest, those qualities that had served him so well in his youth; he remarked on Ernest's "lovely adolescent tenderness," adding, "And the voice and the memory, and the apparently genuine interest in every living soul: fantastic."

The Hemingways didn't feel they could stay away from the Finca for too long, and in March they left, Hotchner accompanying them, on a driving trip to New Orleans and then Key West, stopping in Arizona, where Ernest caught up with his old friend from Paris, the artist Waldo Peirce. In Las Vegas for two days, Ernest played the roulette wheel. They were at the Finca for less than a month, mainly to check on the property. Ernest had been in touch with his old friend Bill Davis, who was now living with his wife, Annie, and their two children, Teo and Nena, in Spain. The Davises had invited the Hemingways to La Consula, their house in Málaga, for the entire summer and into the fall. Ernest had only seen Bill a half dozen times (he and Martha had visited him in Mexico City), and Mary had never met the Davises.

Bill Davis was a fascinating man with more lives than a cat. With his wealthy first wife, Emily, he had been an avid art collector who concentrated on Jackson Pollock. The couple had split up and he had left the country with the Pollocks (and other art) and was said to stay away from the U.S. to keep them out of his wife's hands. Rumors floated about Bill, who was eight years younger than Ernest: that he had been with the OSS in World War II and, subsequently, been a CIA operative, for instance. He had remarried; his wife, Annie, was independently wealthy. Annie's sister Jeanie had been Cyril Connolly's first wife, but had left him for Laurence Vail, Peggy Guggenheim's first husband (Bill had had an affair with Peggy, Pollock's discoverer and patron). Bill was, according to a friend in those years, "a big, bald, shambolic man" who had "an air of controlled violence about him . . . cunning, coarse, a snob, moderately well-read"; the same commentator found Annie "bright and very kind." The writer and actress Elaine Dundy, married then to Kenneth Tynan, who was also in Málaga in the summer of 1959, said she had known Bill in Paris and that he had a bad reputation there, drinking and getting into fights, but that he had since mellowed. She compared La Consula to Villa America, the magical Provence home of Gerald and Sara Murphy, for whom every day was a fiesta; the Davises were latter-day Murphys. Though in many ways Málaga in 1959 was the 1950s version of France in the 1920s, the difference between the two scenes was as great as that between innocence and experience. Bill and Annie were attractive and gracious hosts, and La Consula was a lively and beautiful spot, but what was lost in the intervening years—as much as anything, youth itself—was hard to fathom.

While Mary hesitated to accept an invitation for such a long stay with people she did not know, Ernest assured her that La Consula was to be a base of operations for a summer of bullfights. He and Bill were great admirers of Antonio Ordóñez. Ernest and Mary had already planned to attend the San Isidro *feria* in Madrid in May, where Ordóñez was to fight. At the outset Ernest planned to write an "addendum" that would bring his 1932 *Death in the Afternoon* up to date; Scribner's had agreed to bring out a new, updated edition of the bullfighting classic in 1961. In retrospect, it seems probable that Scribner's was humoring Ernest, for it is unlikely they considered it a commercially worthwhile venture—though they must have been happy to have anything of his to plan on. As with *Across the River and into the Trees,* however, the unwillingness of Ernest's publisher to venture any editorial guidance to their prized author was disastrous to his career

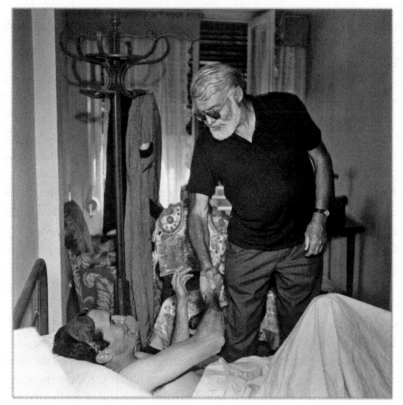

With bullfighter Luis Miguel Dominguín, summer 1959. Ernest is sixty years old.

and, more important in this case, to his psyche—though perhaps no one could foresee the latter.

Ernest would call the book that Scribner's eventually published *The Dangerous Summer.* A routinely bloody sport was even more so in the summer of 1959, with more brutal gorings than usual. The season was characterized by high winds, which meant the matadors often had trouble controlling the *muleta,* the scant obstacle between them and a lethal bull. The most dangerous feature of that summer, however, was that it was shaping up as a mano a mano contest between Ordóñez and his brother-in-law, Luis Miguel Dominguín, a celebrated fighter who had come out of retirement the year before. Rivalries of this sort often have bloody outcomes, as the less gifted matador often feels he must pull off the same risky moves and tricks of his opponent, which might or might not be possible; if he falters in any way, he usually fails, with disastrous results.

Ernest's last stay in the country he loved more than any other began in late May in Algeciras, after a crossing from New York on the *Constitution.* Bill Davis picked up Ernest and Mary in a dark pink Ford rental car, dubbed the Pembroke Coral after Ford's name for its odd color. He brought them to La Consula before they headed to Madrid for their first *corrida*. The 1835 house could not have been more welcoming. Elaine Dundy described it as

a beautiful white house with wide white verandas on a hill in a setting of trees and flowers. Inside were spacious white rooms hung with fine paintings and furnished with solid pieces of carved mahogany. Semi-invisible servants were there to make your beds, wash and iron and put away your clothes, to attend to your every need and desire and to cook delicious meals . . . . The swimming pool, in its beautiful setting, was redolent of the sweet, dry smell of the trees mixing with the flower-scented breeze.

There was no radio or telephone on the premises, though a phonograph often played Fats Waller. Colorful Pollocks joined the Goyas and a collection of antique maps on the white walls. Ernest was up early, writing a preface to a student edition of his stories. A siesta followed a vinous lunch, and in the early evening hosts and guests often repaired to the bar at the Miramar Hotel before a very late dinner at La Consula. Ernest's drinking was ratcheting up a notch, no doubt in response to the festive atmosphere.

On May 13 the Davises and Hemingways drove to Madrid in the Pembroke Coral for the ten days of the San Isidro bullfights. They were joined there by George Saviers and his wife; Saviers had become Ernest's doctor and good friend in Idaho the previous winter. Hotchner also joined them there, carrying a tape recorder that Ernest referred to as the "devil box." As an onlooker noted, Ernest had developed a phobia about publicity and specifically about being recorded. But Hotch, as usual, was able to get him to loosen up. "A tape recorder on anyone else would have been traitorous," a friend said. "With Hotch it was a cause for amusement." Judging from Hotchner's later memoir, he did a good deal of tape recording that summer.

The group went on to follow Ordóñez's fights in Córdoba, Sevilla, and Granada. The matador was gored at Aranjuez, and repaired to La Consula to recuperate. Mary and Annie returned to Málaga after Sevilla. Mary was finding the schedule and the concomitant alcohol consumption too tiring—lunch at four, dinner after eleven, with Ernest holding forth for hours at the dinner table into the early morning, long after the food was cleared away. She was none too pleased when Slim Hayward, then the top filly in Ernest's chaste stable, wired that she was in Granada with Lauren Bacall, and Ernest invited the two women to La Consula. That summer Bacall was infatuated with Ordóñez's rival, Dominguín, but that didn't stop her from turning on the charm when she met Ernest. Slim later wrote that she knew Mary was not pleased when the two showed up; indeed, Mary wrote that when they arrived, Slim flattered Ernest, saying, "Darling, you're so thin and beautiful," while Bacall breathed, "You're even bigger than I imagined." On the women's last night in Málaga, according to Slim, Mary approached Bacall holding two fists in front of her, asking the actress to choose one. After she did, Mary opened her hand to reveal a bullet. "That is for anyone who moves in on my man," she warned. Slim Hayward, who would see Ernest for the last time at the end of the summer, in Biarritz, wrote that he was by then "swinging between depression and madness."

Everywhere, however, Ernest seemed to pick up admirers. The second week of July the company (which included Ordóñez and his retinue, though he was not fighting there) headed to Pamplona for San Fermín. In Madrid a young and pretty Irish woman, Valerie Danby-Smith, had come to the Hotel Suecia to interview Ernest. (Valerie would later marry Ernest's son Gregory.) Convent-educated, Valerie was a would-be writer, a high-spirited seeker of adventure. Ernest was immediately smitten, inviting her to join the Hemingways' party in Pamplona. As the festival there drew to a close, he asked her to become his secretary and assistant for the remainder of the bullfighting season, and Valerie agreed.

Ordóñez was flattered and pleased that Hemingway, revered in Spain for his promotion of the bullfight and his clear love for the country, had formed an attachment to him. On Ernest's end, the handsome twenty-eight-year-old matador represented, as far as he was concerned, the height of the art. Ordóñez showed no fear in the bullring, where his cape work was "perfection" (DS, 72). In contrast, Dominguín, his great rival that summer, was thirty-four, plagued by an ungraceful stiff leg, and seemed to Ernest to have had his day; Ernest came to believe Dominguín relied too much on crowd-pleasing tricks and lacked Ordóñez's classical grace.

Bullfighters commonly tour with their own *cuadrilla,* or entourage—of trainers, wives and/or girlfriends, doctors, and the like. In the summer of 1959, it was hard to say whether the *cuadrilla* was following Antonio or Ernest. Juanito Quintana, the Pamplona innkeeper Ernest had befriended more than thirty years before (he appeared in *The Sun Also Rises* as Montoya), was employed as general factotum for the group, making reservations and otherwise handling logistics. Valerie had already joined the posse, and the men made an elaborate joke of "kidnapping" two young, good-looking Midwestern women they spotted at the *feria,* and who ended up doing the *corrida* circuit with the group. A young blond actress named Beverly Bentley, the star of a movie filmed in Spain that summer, signed on as well, and became fast friends with Valerie.

As Ernest customarily did in Pamplona, he led a group out to the nearby Irati River, where they picnicked and swam, Ernest delighted to have found it recovered from the logging that had left it so scarred on an earlier visit. Bottles of wine were chilled in the stream, and the younger women sunned in their bikinis. Mary was wading in the beautifully clear and deliciously cold river when she slipped and hurt a toe, which turned out to be broken in two places. Ernest was at first solicitous but became impatient when he realized Mary would need help getting back to their car and foresaw the attention she would be getting in the days to come—which would divert attention from him. In this, Valerie "observed a darker, meaner side of the writer." The break was slow to heal and seriously impeded Mary's ability to get around that summer. It did nothing for her temper either.

Not everything was thrilling or idyllic during the *cuadrilla*'s stay in Pamplona. Because the festival had become so popular (thanks in no small part to Ernest), the only accommodation that could fit all of them required the men to sleep in one dormitory-like room and the women in another. According to Annie Davis, in the early-morning hours Ernest walked in, naked and holding a bottle, and flipped the light on. "I'll show you girls how a real man is built," he said. Annie did not say how the women got him to leave.

The Pamplona festival preceded a landmark birthday for Ernest, his sixtieth. Bill and Annie Davis were happy to host a party at La Consula. Mary hired an orchestra and planned an elaborate menu and numerous entertainments, including a shooting gallery, flamenco dancers, and a fireworks display. She set up a long, narrow table, seating forty-five, on the second-floor veranda; fifteen servants waited table. Lanterns provided light and spotlights were trained on the gardens. Ernest's guests included, besides the *cuadrilla,* Buck Lanham; David and Evangeline Bruce (he had been the OSS officer close to Ernest during the war); two maharajas (one invited Ernest to a tiger shoot in India); Gianfranco Ivancich and his Cuban wife, Cristina (in Ernest's new cream-colored Lancia); and Peter Buckley and his wife, among others. Ordóñez was there, of course; in fact, the party was also meant to be a celebration of the thirtieth birthday of his wife, Carmen.

Provisions included six cases of rosé, four cases of champagne, and unspecified supplies of whiskey and gin; baked hams, codfish and shrimp dishes, fifty pounds of Chinese sweet-and-sour turkey (Ernest and Mary were fond of Chinese food); and an elaborate tiered cake. The party started at ten and didn't end until sunrise, when Bloody Marys were served around the pool. It proved to be a dangerous party. Sparks from the fireworks ignited the leaves of a tall palm tree and the fire department had to be called. Worse, Ernest got it into his head—or perhaps the idea originated with one of the less responsible members of his entourage—that he should substitute a .22 rifle for the air guns provided for the shooting gallery. He shot a lit cigarette from between Ordóñez's lips.

Buck Lanham couldn't help but notice the sharp mood swings to which his friend was subject. Late one night he made a show of giving Ernest an inscribed history of the 22nd Infantry Regiment. Ernest was overwhelmed and left the room in tears. Another night he had been at dinner for eight at the Hotel Miramar when he was walking behind Ernest's seat and side-swiped him, grazing his head. Ernest was furious and said loudly that no one was allowed to touch his head. Later, making peace with Buck, he explained that the comb-over he was wearing these days, in which hair from the back of his head was brushed over the front to cover his baldness, made bangs on his forehead. That made it imperative that no one disturb his hair. Sheepishly, he said he would go have his hair cut very short like his friend's, but Buck deflected him. Though he made it up with Ernest, bad feelings lingered.

More strange behavior was prompted by a telegram he received from movie producer David O. Selznick announcing that he was in Spain for a film festival. Ernest was furious. Selznick had recently telegraphed that he was making a new film of *A Farewell to Arms,* starring his wife, Jennifer Jones, as Catherine Barkley and Rock Hudson as Frederic Henry. Selznick offered to pay Ernest $50,000 out of the profits, which he didn't have to do: when Ernest sold the film rights thirty years before, he signed away the rights to any remakes as well. Selznick's offer only made this misjudgment further rankle. Ernest led Hotch to believe he wrote a scurrilous telegram in return. Valerie observed that Ernest often strode around with an open penknife, threatening to castrate Selznick if he showed up in Pamplona. Lauren Bacall appeared in Pamplona just at this time, however, and his obsession vanished.

The troupe was on to Valencia in a caravan, Bill Davis driving the Lancia with Valerie sitting in front between him and Ernest, and Buck and Hotch in the back. It was established that at the elaborate meals, Valerie would sit on Ernest's left and Ordóñez at his right. Valerie and Beverly Bentley sometimes became impatient, "irked by the incessant praise of Antonio and the nonstop regimen of eating and drinking that required our constant presence and attention."

Ordóñez and Dominguín finally met in a mano a mano on the fifth day of bullfights in Valencia. Dominguín was still recovering from a goring and his leg had been bothering him for several days. Ernest had cited the wind as another factor in this dangerous summer, and, indeed, during the *faena* the wind blew the *muleta* up and the bull charged into Dominguín's groin. The *cuadrilla* soldiered on, to Alicante, Murcia, and Granada. Mary had returned to La Consula with Annie in Annie's Volkswagen. Her toe made getting around difficult, and she noted that Ernest was drinking huge quantities of vodka and wine. Apart from that, however, she wrote,

> Something was changing in him or me or both of us. He was averaging three or four hours of sleep in twenty-four. . . . I was increasingly repelled by the dirty tables, the sour smell of spilled wine, the stupid chitchat with strangers and Ernest's endlessly repeated aphorisms, and I could not endure four hours of it before dinner at midnight.

No doubt the presence of Valerie was another aggravation—a repeat, potentially, of Ernest's infatuation with Adriana Ivancich. Valerie later wrote that Ernest talked to her about a future together, saying that his marriage to Mary was over and imagining that he and Valerie would marry and have the daughter he had wanted for so long. Valerie demurred. "I could not and did not take what he said seriously," she later wrote. "It was just another game, akin to the many games he liked to play—secret clubs, nicknames, imaginary assaults on enemies, and all the rest of his childish fantasy life, which for the most part, was charming, harmless, and endearing, but never to be confused with reality."

Sometime in May or June Will Lang of the Paris bureau of *Life* came to Spain, having heard Ernest was following the *corridas* for an addendum to or postscript for *Death in the Afternoon.* He convinced Ernest to let *Life* publish whatever he wrote. So Ernest kept making notes, and the bullfighters kept getting gored. After a spectacular mano a mano in Málaga, Dominguín went to Bilbao and was gored so badly that he was sidelined for the rest of the season. Antonio was hospitalized with a foot injury while fighting at Dax, just over the French border. On the way back to Madrid in the Lancia—La Barata, they called it, "the cheap one," because it was so expensive—Bill Davis fell asleep at the wheel with Ernest and Valerie beside him and drove the car off the road. No one was hurt, but the accident marked the beginning of the end of the dangerous summer. Ernest and Bill followed the bullfights to Cuenca, Murcia, Alicante, and Ronda. Hearing that Antonio had been barred from fighting for a month because of a rules infraction, they cut the trip short, spending two days in Madrid before returning to Málaga.

By mid-September Mary, still hobbling around with a broken toe, had had enough of bullfights and her husband. While Ernest, Bill, and Valerie continued on the circuit, Mary took a train to Paris with Annie, planning to meet Ernest and Bill at the Ritz for a couple of days. She would then fly home. Adding to her worries, Ernest had invited Antonio and Carmen to visit the Finca and then to drive the Hemingways to Idaho, where they could get in some shooting. Because Ernest and Mary had not yet moved into the Topping house in Ketchum, Mary was understandably concerned about having houseguests. The house was furnished, but it was not to her taste, and she had no idea how livable it was.

As his invitation to Ordóñez suggests, Ernest did not want the spirit of the *corridas* to end. Nevertheless, whenever Ernest and Mary were separated that summer, and especially after they parted in mid-September, Ernest wrote to her almost daily. In mid-August he complained about the road, the strain, and the hours; he told her he was drinking only wine. His need for her was becoming palpable. It was as if he calculated how he could manage life without her, and saw that it would not be possible. Valerie and the Davises toured the south of France with Ernest but, just as Adriana would not animate his fantasy of the aristocratic life in Venice, so Valerie could not re-create his past in Aigues-Mortes (where he had honeymooned with Pauline), in Le Grau-du-Roi (where he had set *The Garden of Eden*), or Arles (where he hunted down Van Gogh's whorehouse).

When Ernest and Mary, the Davises, and Valerie met up at the Ritz at the beginning of October, some of the magic was recaptured. Ernest gave the others a tour of his old haunts; he was checking addresses and recalling scenes for his Paris sketches. As he had done before with Jigee Viertel, Ernest fulfilled some idea of himself as a benevolent patriarch by taking his French royalties in franc notes and dividing the money into five bundles, which he then distributed to Mary, Bill and Annie, and Valerie. It was gambling money, he told them, and, after uncorking a bottle of champagne, he took them all to the races at Auteuil.

After they saw Mary off on October 4, it was back to Málaga, where Ernest began writing his account of the *corridas* on the 10th. But three days after he began, a letter from Mary arrived, a letter he had requested, assessing the summer's collateral damage to their marriage. Mary had returned to Cuba to find the Finca in disarray, the roof leaking after Hurricane Judith, a family of rats in the swimming pool pump. Setting the property to rights made her feel even more like a drudge with no other life outside of managing Ernest Hemingway and his residences. She wrote him with a tally of his bad behavior in the past five months; she had his attention, and she let fly. Ernest immediately sent her a telegram thanking her for the work she was doing at the Finca and telling her he disagreed with her conclusions about the summer. He said he still loved her. Consciously or not, he had married Mary partly against the day he would need a caretaker, and he had probably come to realize that the day was dawning.

Ernest followed his telegram with letters on October 13, 14, and 15. He was all contrition, but he wanted Mary to take note of his misery. His letters recall those he wrote to Pauline during their hundred-day separation, when his only message was how distraught he was. He told Mary he always seemed to get "Dear John" letters at bad times; Mary might have her hands full at the Finca, but he had to figure out finances and a way to raise tax money, "*so other people have their troubles too,*" he wrote, underlining his words. He did not want to fight by mail, he said, and he asked her what she wanted from Paris. His head was not in good shape, he said. He had a terrible pain in his neck and woke up every morning extremely depressed, "with deadly black ass," and yet made himself write every day. By then Mary was reaching some clarity: she had resolved to get an apartment in New York where she could carve out a life for herself, she said.

Ernest confessed his worries about his relationship with Mary to Hotchner, by now his closest confidant. He admitted that he had been guilty of neglect. "And she has a proper beef, you know. I was just having so much fun . . . well, it wasn't organized around her," he said, shifting a little of the blame. After Ernest saw her off to the States, however, he truly began to fret, in a way that anticipated his obsessive worries in the months to come—preoccupations that he often returned to in conversation. He had bought her a diamond pin at Cartier's, hoping this would smooth the way, and he asked Hotch and Valerie repeatedly if they thought it would win her over. He seemed to recognize, finally, that asking her to entertain the Ordóñezes in Havana and then in their newly occupied house in Ketchum meant a lot of work. While that might seem a paltry concession, he did appear to pick up on Mary's feelings of being taken for granted.

Yet he wanted to preserve his relationship with Valerie at the same time. Though she wrote later that in Spain that summer they barely touched, except for several bear hugs, she noted his penchant for walking arm-in-arm with her; he was still in the throes of what he believed was love. On one of their last nights in France, after Mary had flown home, Ernest asked Valerie to come to Cuba in January to stay with them at the Finca. He told her he was not able to work well without her, that he needed her presence emotionally. Valerie, who was not expecting this, said she would have to think about it. He went on, however, to say, she wrote, "Life without me at his side . . . was *nada*." He threatened to kill himself if she did not come. "My first reaction was anger," wrote Valerie. He had so often spoken of his father's suicide as the act of a coward (something he did not always admit he believed). She also, understandably, felt Ernest was subtly blackmailing her. An extremely kind-hearted and resourceful young woman, Valerie had taken the summer and her friendship with Ernest as a great adventure, and she had become enormously fond of him along the way. "Traveling with Ernest was never dull," she wrote. "He was a man of extremes." She had seen plenty of his dark side: his depressions, his rages, his massive egotism. "When he enjoyed life," however, "he enjoyed it to the fullest, and he had the gift of being able to impart his pleasure and enthusiasm to those around him. . . . He had the most inquiring mind of anyone I've ever met." Despite his infatuation, when Ernest told her he needed her in Cuba, she sensed that romantic love actually played very little part in it. He literally could not live without her, as a much needed assistant and secretary, as a companion, as someone who could accommodate his narcissistic requirements without the baggage of a spouse. Perhaps most important, he needed her as someone with whom he could fantasize a future when otherwise he saw only blackness before him.

Work on the bullfight piece was not going well, though the *Life* photographer, Larry Burrows, was able to get some impressive shots and stayed out of the way, Ernest told Hotchner approvingly. But there is some indication that Ernest was actually having trouble putting words on paper. Valerie wrote in her memoir that the requirements for her job were not only that she be a "critical reader." She also needed to be "a coherent writer, to be able to listen and discuss, to remember, and to take notes when necessary." When Hotchner flew back to the U.S., he left the "devil box" with Ernest. The machine was actually a Mohawk portable tape recorder, and Ernest and Hotch spoke often of Ernest making "Mohawk tapes" that could then be transcribed. Hotchner was working on a television production of "The Killers," and when he needed some bits of new writing from Ernest, Hotch told him to "speak onto one of your Mohawk tapes." Ernest was still not comfortable with the machine, but he grasped at this alternative to putting pen to paper—so difficult was he finding it to write. He had long been accustomed to dictating letters occasionally, and he saw "the box" as a way to get parts of the article to Hotchner, who could further help him with what he meant to say. Unfortunately, Ernest left the machine in Málaga. "If the box was here," he wrote Hotch, "I would just talk into it, send the things over & you could use it or not."

A running joke among the Hemingway-Ordóñez *cuadrilla* was to call

Bill Davis "el Negro"; no one really knew where the name came from, though some said it was given to him for his large lips. But a comment made by Ordóñez suggested a different source. *Hacer el negro* means to ghostwrite. Ordóñez joked, "Ernesto can't really write . . . Bill is his Negro. He tells the stories to Bill on trips or when they go into town and then Negro writes them. Now I know the trick." (Scribner's would excise the nickname when they published *The Dangerous Summer* in 1985.) While it is unlikely that those closest to Ernest did any actual writing for him, the sense that they were concerned about his ability to write at this time is unavoidable, as is the impression that they were picking up on his own anxieties. Writing no longer came naturally.

Those concerns and doubts proved to be deadly accurate. Ernest returned from Europe on the *Liberté,* arriving in New York on November 1. A few days later he and the Ordóñezes flew to Havana. Mary welcomed them to the Finca but left for Chicago soon after with her Jamaican maid, Lola, to buy household goods and furnishings before going on to Ketchum. The Ordóñezes and Ernest, with Roberto Herrera along to help with the driving, made the trek from Key West to Idaho in a new station wagon furnished by Buick (in exchange for allowing promotional photographs and giving endorsements—all arranged by Hotchner). Ernest told Hotchner that the trip did not go well (neither provided details) and that their guests felt far less at ease in Ketchum than they had in Spanish-speaking Cuba. Before they could get in a single day of duck hunting, Antonio took a call from his sister in Mexico and announced that a family emergency compelled his and Carmen's immediate departure. One imagines that Mary was relieved, but Ernest was crestfallen.

Ernest had given the manuscript of his Paris sketches to Charles Scribner, Jr., on his way through New York, and he wrote a few more in Ketchum, but he found he was unable to return to the *Garden of Eden* manuscript as he had hoped. It was not a good fall; for some reason Ernest's usual hunting companions were unable to join him in the field, so he took to shooting at clay targets with them in the parking area next to his house for an hour or so at lunchtime. On an early duck-hunting expedition, Mary took a bad fall on the frozen ground, managing to hold her gun aloft but shattering her elbow. Her arm needed delicate surgery; then, because it was not healing right, it needed to be rebroken and reset. Ernest was most uncharitable; in the car to the hospital after the accident, he scolded Mary for voicing pain, telling her soldiers never did that. Her recovery was long and arduous, and Ernest took it with ill grace.

Most ominously, he was becoming increasingly paranoid, so much so that he did not censor himself from mentioning his fears, as he had often done in the past. In early January, on the way to the Arnolds' for dinner, Ernest noticed the lights were on in the local bank, and became convinced that the FBI were checking his and Mary's accounts, finances having become an incessant preoccupation. The Arnolds had noticed some unusual behavior, especially some incidents where Ernest's anger seemed excessive, even for him. While in the bar at the Christiana, a local restaurant, a patron commented on his beard, and Ernest's enraged response silenced the room; Pappy Arnold only narrowly averted physical violence. Worse, that night Ernest could not let go of the incident, recalling it over and over afterward, as incensed as ever. Though Pappy did not specify, the Arnolds had been seeing more behavior that could be characterized as clinically psychotic. Referring to the Christiana incident, Pappy wrote, "We were not total strangers to occasional evidence of hallucinatory amblings, small inventions on this and that; nor of magnifications, overly-severe criticism." Mentally ill people can be hard to bear, and seldom do those who love them know just what to do, often hoping that someone else is dealing with the problem, or that it is only temporary: "Well, you say to yourself," Pappy wrote, "it can't be too long before a letup of tension is due."

The Hemingways returned to Cuba shortly after the holidays; in retrospect, Pappy found one of Ernest's parting remarks disturbing. He admitted he had come to like the Ketchum house now that he was used to it, adding, "But I bought it as a nest egg for Miss Mary."

*　*　*

Ernest left a terse description of the road leading up to his final breakdown, which began in the summer of 1959 and ended with his suicide in 1961. "Mary took wonderful care of me through a long bad time and working hard and with plenty of exercise I got healthy and sound again." Indeed, that winter at the Finca was quieter than any they had previously spent there, Mary later said. With the new government, and Washington's increasingly unfriendly stance toward it, almost none of the Hemingways' friends or relatives came to visit. According to Mary, Ernest did not bring up Valerie's joining them until late January. Mary readily agreed, for Ernest needed help desperately with his bullfight manuscript, now well over the ten thousand words *Life* wanted; she also hoped that Valerie's presence might cheer Ernest. Like Valerie, Mary understood Ernest's needs. While she had resolved to begin a new life for herself, over the months ahead, "I shelved the idea," she later wrote. "He seemed to have so many grave problems confronting him that I could not increase them." Besides, "Again he was addressing me as 'My dear Kittner.'"

Valerie arrived on January 27, moving into the guesthouse. She was fascinated by Cuba and immediately succumbed to the Finca's charms—though she noted its "slightly decaying air of mildew, humidity, and tiredness"—and easily adapted to the daily rhythms of the household. Ernest worked in the morning before his daily swim. Valerie joined him in late morning or early afternoon to take dictation of his letters, most of which she sent out in her handwriting, though business letters were typed. He would often talk about the bullfight manuscript, sometimes asking her if she remembered details of contests that eluded him. Mary gradually warmed to her, and they usually did the shopping in Havana's markets together; Mary enjoyed designing some lightweight tropical garments in bold prints for Valerie.

Everyone had two drinks before dinner, at which there was almost always a guest, usually Cuban. Different visitors came regularly on different nights; Dr. José Luis Herrera and his brother, Roberto, came on Mondays, for example. The doctor checked Ernest's blood pressure and his general physical shape; he also spent half an hour using an electric vibrator on Mary's still mending elbow. If there were no guests, Valerie and Ernest would often walk into the village after dinner, having a rum and soda with fresh lime at one of the outdoor cafés. Afterward, they would walk to the top of the hill on the property and look out over Havana at night, Ernest sometimes resting a hand on Valerie's shoulder (the other times they touched being when Ernest put his bare feet over hers at the dinner table).

Valerie remembers her early months in Cuba as being relatively worry-free; apparently the demons that had surfaced in Ketchum that winter were at bay. The Gulf Stream appeared to be nearly fished out but Ernest took the *Pilar* out nonetheless, usually on Wednesday afternoon and Saturday, Valerie more often accompanying him than Mary, whose elbow still inhibited her physically. They had a couple of pleasant visits: one was from Herbert Matthews, the *New York Times* reporter whom Ernest had first met in the Spanish Civil War. Matthews had next seen Ernest when he was covering Cuban politics in 1952. His biggest journalistic coup was locating and interviewing Castro in the Sierra Maestra in 1957, after Batista had declared him dead. Now he was one of the few American journalists inside Cuba, able to report the revolution and its aftermath from inside; Matthews soon came under fire for what were thought to be pro-Castro views. Ernest, in a notable exception to his treatment of old friends, was one of Matthews's most stalwart defenders. Matthews reminded Ernest of

With Fidel Castro, May 1960

a far less complicated time, and they had much to discuss about the Cuban situation. Another of the guests was an admirer with the Russian delegation to Cuba, another, less pleasant reminder of the changed atmosphere for an American living there.

The Cuban regime change unquestionably provoked a good deal of tension at the Finca. The American ambassador, Phil Bonsall, was a good friend and a regular dinner guest (Thursday was his night), and he kept Ernest and Mary up to date on the parlous state of diplomatic relations between the U.S. and Cuba. Though the U.S. officially recognized the new government right after the revolution, relations had deteriorated since, especially after Castro began nationalizing U.S.-owned businesses. Valerie, who provided accounts of Ernest's relations with Bonsall during this period, wrote that soon after her January arrival, the ambassador told Ernest to think seriously about leaving. The U.S. government wanted him to go, believing his departure would have great symbolic effect, signaling American disapproval of the Castro government. At the very least, Ernest should speak out against the new regime, Bonsall said. Ernest did not want to do either of these things. His objections were many: perhaps the most salient was that he loved the Cuban people and that he also loved and did not want to leave his home. He was a writer, unconcerned with politics, he said.

Then, on what was to be his last visit, Bonsall informed Ernest that he had been recalled; severance of U.S. ties with Cuba was imminent. It was even more important for Ernest to do what he had advised previously. Yet Ernest stayed on. He met Castro one day in May, fishing. The Hemingway Marlin Fishing Tournament had become an annual fixture in Cuba, popular with tourists. Castro joined in the two-day competition, fishing from a boat previously owned by Americans who had evacuated. When the fish were weighed at the end of the contest, Castro's haul was the heaviest, by all accounts a fair-and-square win. Since the competition was named for Ernest, he presented the silver trophy to the winner, no doubt an embarrassment to the eminences crafting Cuban policy in Washington. The mounting tension wore very heavily on Ernest. Once, when Peter Viertel asked Ernest where he would go if he had to leave Cuba, Ernest said he would probably take the *Pilar* out to where the water was eight hundred fathoms deep and jump off the stern.

His other obsession, that winter and spring, was the *Life* article, which grew and grew. The magazine had asked for ten thousand words. In March he had thirty thousand, and he told Hotchner to inform *Life* his new deadline was April 7. By then he had written 63,000 words, and he was still going. He was buried in the material, unable to see the forest for the trees. His first bullfighting book had been charming and accessible for those uninitiated into the *corrida.* For *aficionados,* on the other hand, it was a bible: a fine exposition of an impeccably ordered and incredibly dangerous ritual. With the *Life* article—which, by March, he was telling Scribner's could be published as a book, the original idea of reissuing an updated *Death in the Afternoon* with an addendum long dropped—he got bogged down and was creating something far more unwieldy and garrulous. He described almost every fight in great detail, unable to order his material or, it seems, his thoughts.

By June he was begging Hotch to come and help him; his friend knew he was needed long before this, but he was busy with television productions of Ernest's stories, the only moneymaking arm of the Hemingway concern that was still functioning. Ernest was now projecting a manuscript of 110,000 words; *Life* had agreed, one imagines none too happily, to run the article over three issues. Hotch arrived in Cuba on June 27. He described Ernest at lunch his first day there:

> He ate very little and half-filled his wine glass with water. He closed his eyes frequently and often pressed his fingers against them. His beard had not been trimmed for months; the forward part of his head had

become bald but he had covered it successfully by combing forward the long hair at the back of his head, giving himself the mien of a Roman emperor . . . . He looked thin. His chest and shoulders had lost their thrust and his upper arms were macilent and formless, as if his huge biceps had been pared down by an unskilled whittler.

Worst of all was his state of mind. He told Hotchner he felt he was living in a Kafka nightmare.

He proved completely unable to make cuts in the six-hundred-plus-page manuscript. When Hotch suggested excisions Ernest would not agree to them. Every detail, he said, was important. It took several marathon sessions, with Ernest constantly complaining that his eyes couldn't take it. When the manuscript was finally ready to go it was about 54,000 words, and Hotch and Ernest decided to let the *Life* editors take it from there. Hotchner brought the manuscript with him to New York and set out to negotiate a new deal for Ernest's work, since the relatively short article he had signed on for was now a three-part series. Hotchner got *Life* to agree to pay Ernest $90,000, with $10,000 more for rights to publish the series in *Life* in Spain.

The magazine had plans to publish beginning in September. Yet Ernest decided that he needed to return to Spain immediately to cover what was left of the 1960 summer's fights. Ordóñez and Dominguín were fighting on the same cartel at one event (though not mano a mano), and Ernest felt he should be there to support his friend, as well as to make necessary updates and corrections.

In the meantime, Hotchner had found a comfortable small apartment for Mary and Ernest at One East 62nd Street. Mary no longer had plans to live in the city by herself, but a New York foothold seemed like a good idea if they were to leave the Finca. Another worry about leaving Cuba was solved when Ernest and Mary decided to act on the Museum of Modern Art's long-standing request to borrow Ernest's Miró painting, *The Farm;* when the museum agreed, Mary promptly sent it off. It would have been difficult for the Hemingways to take the painting with them from Cuba, but a loan request made it possible for the Miró to leave the country. It was their most valuable possession, and their action showed they were making plans to leave Cuba for good.

Mary and Valerie came to New York with Ernest the first week of August, planning to stay at the new apartment for a week while Ernest flew off to Madrid on August 5. His time was spent conferring with Charles Scribner, Jr., about which to publish first, the Paris sketches or the bullfighting book, now to be called *The Dangerous Summer.* Scribner later said Ernest "agonized" over the choice, repeatedly making a decision and then reversing it. The editor loved the Paris sketches, but acknowledged that publication of *The Dangerous Summer* was time-sensitive. The decision was put off. Ernest's new fear, confided repeatedly to Hotch, was that his account had been too biased toward Ordóñez and not entirely fair to Dominguín.

Ernest was unused to traveling by jet, and he arrived in Málaga discombobulated by the time change. He was on a wide range of medications: Serpasil, or reserpine (for his mental disorder and/or his blood pressure); Wychol (a lipotropic for the liver); Equanil (a tranquilizer); and Doriden (a sedative). This combination did not seem to allay his psychic disorganization. He wrote or cabled Mary almost daily, complaining about his "bad head." It had been a mistake to come over, he said, and the thought of taking the next plane back was constantly on his mind. Optimistically, he told himself (and subsequently Mary) that he had felt this bad before, but had always pulled out of it into a "belle epoque," one of his favorite terms. Indeed, a highly productive and happy manic phase had always succeeded his blackest depressions; presumably, the pattern would repeat itself. "Never so dead in the head in my life," Ernest wrote Hotchner, but he hoped he would come out of it.

His attention—such as it was—was divided between taking notes on the current fights and lending Ordóñez his support, especially when the matador suffered a concussion and Carmen had a miscarriage, and worrying about the *Life* articles as they appeared. He was upset by the photographs that would accompany the series. *Life* had chosen the wrong ones, he saw with horror when the first issue came out. While he had carefully chosen photos that showed the bullfighters at their best, the ones the magazine used made their moves look clumsy; he feared publication of the photos would seriously injure his reputation "as an honest guy," and make him a "laughing stock" of the bullfight community, whose good opinion meant much to him. Should some Spanish readers miss his articles in American *Life*, Spanish *Life* would publish them soon enough. (As for the cover photo of Ernest accompanying the first installment of the series, it no doubt seemed to outsiders a classic "Papa" shot, but Ernest may have seen an old man, grizzled and grinning somewhat maniacally.)

Matters got worse. Ernest feared he was heading for a total breakdown, nervous as well as physical. It soon became clear he was right. He couldn't sleep and at one point estimated he had been awake for forty-four hours. His eyes were shot (though a New York doctor had pronounced them healthy). Worse, he was having bad dreams at night and, he told Mary, bad dreams in the daytime. She decided it would be a good idea if Valerie joined him, practically and emotionally, and Valerie, then in Paris on vacation, flew to Spain on August 30. When he accompanied her to her room in the Madrid hotel, she found him "tentative and ill at ease, tending to look over his shoulder as we passed through the lobby and entered the elevator in case someone was eavesdropping on our conversation," she said. "Angst was his inseparable companion." Hotchner came over as well to do a bit of business about the Nick Adams stories, and to him Ernest's suffering—and the trial for those around him—was palpable. When he came into Ernest's room at the Suecia in Madrid, he wrote, "Worry hung in the room like black crepe."

At the wheel of the (repaired) Lancia, La Barata, Bill Davis drove Valerie and a "sullen," taciturn Ernest around Spain to bullfights for a month. Then Ernest got it into his head that Bill was trying to kill him in a car accident. Valerie told him she was sure he was mistaken, but Ernest persisted in this delusion for the remainder of his time in Spain. Back at La Consula, he became so convinced that he was despised in the bullfighting world that he would not see anyone. He was either silent or talked obsessively about the *Life* photographs and the biases in the articles. He asked Valerie to sit by his bed at night until he fell asleep. He talked obsessively about suicide, but, he told her, he needed to be sure about her future. He developed an obsession about her status with the Office of Immigration; the Hemingways learned that Valerie's temporary visa had expired earlier, though this was inconsequential; Ernest began to fret that she had worked for him in Cuba in early 1960 without a work permit—how was he to pay her, both for her standing with the government and for his tax purposes? (Most of his obsessions and delusions had come to center around taxes and other financial matters.)

Everyone, Ernest included, hoped Hotchner's visit would help. But Ernest sounded the same note about the *Life* photographs and what Ordóñez and Dominguín would think of them. He began to complain of a kidney disorder, the Davises told Hotchner, and he was nearly silent most of the time. He was only drinking wine, but even really good wine seemed bad for him, he wrote Mary, "although it makes me cheerful and get awfully nervous without it." He felt poisoned, and wondered if his medications, combined with fatigue, had not built up to a toxic level; accordingly, he was cutting out some of them. Depending on which pills he eliminated, this might or might not have been a good idea.

The Davises, Hotchner, and Valerie had another struggle on their hands when it came time for Ernest to fly home. He worried that he would be barred from the plane because his luggage weighed too much, though calls to the airline made clear that Ernest's luggage was not overweight, and that in the event it was, it was a routine matter for passengers to pay for any excess weight when they checked in. Yet Ernest would not rest until Bill went out to the airport and received a signed letter from the airline saying Ernest would not be barred from embarking. He had booked the flight under Bill's name to throw off the press, and the details of straightening that out made him fret. He told Valerie he hoped the plane would crash so it would all be over. Hotchner assured him that he would be all right once he got to Ketchum and could again "breathe that good mountain air." Nobody believed it.

THIRTY-TWO

It did not end well. Between about 7:00 and 7:30 a.m. on July 2, 1961, Ernest arose and put on over his blue pajamas the brilliant red robe Mary had ordered to be made for him in Italy, which she called "the Emperor's robe." He took a key off the windowsill behind the kitchen sink in his Ketchum home, went down and unlocked the storeroom where the guns were stored. He selected a double-barreled Boss shotgun, put two shells in it, and took it upstairs to the entryway of the house. There he steadied the butt of the gun on the floor, leaned over, put his forehead on the gun barrels, and pulled the trigger.

* * *

By the time he did it, it seemed inevitable. From the day of Ernest's return to New York after the nightmarish trip to Spain to update the *Life* magazine articles, which needed no updating, his trajectory flattened, then headed straight down.

It is not clear whether he added any more words to the overstuffed yet severely pruned mass of words he had sent off to *Life* and brought to Scribner's before his last, short trip to Spain. If he did, they were not included in either version. By then the manuscript was seventy thousand words; *Life* further edited it down to thirty thousand. The final text, not published as a book until 1985, was about 45,000 words. Beyond his great distress as to how it would be received by the bullfight community and people in Spain, Ernest felt ashamed of the whole venture. He said it was one of the worst things he had ever written.

Ernest spent a week in New York in the East 62nd Street apartment with Mary. He barely went out, muttering that there were people lying in wait for him outside. Charles Scribner, Jr., commented on his meeting with Ernest in his last year: "He was failing visibly. He seemed almost frail; his arms weren't the old burly limbs. He was tentative in his movements." Peter Viertel, who saw Ernest last in October, also said he looked "gaunt," and observed, "His arms and chest [were] those of a very old man." His biceps had once measured eighteen inches around.

Mary and Ernest took the train from New York to Shoshone, the closest station to their Ketchum house. Once there, they saw few people. Ernest had become captive to several fears. First, he continued to be extremely worried about Valerie Danby-Smith—whether immigration officials had their eye on her since her lapsed temporary visitor's visa had been noticed in Key West the previous January. He was also still nervous about her lack of a work permit for her stay in Cuba, and whether payments he made to her in the U.S. could be traced to work she had done in Cuba. When Mary and Hotch managed to persuade him that Valerie was safe on both those counts, he decided that he would be apprehended for "impairing the morals of a minor"—his words. Hotchner noted his diction, sensing Ernest was drawn to the official sound of the words. It hardly mattered that he had been guilty of no such thing; in his delusion, he believed he could be pursued and worse for this. He also began fearing that as an Idaho property owner he was and had been liable for unpaid state taxes—to his mind, a most serious offense.

When Hotchner came to Ketchum in November, Ernest met him with a story of being followed to the airport. The car was bugged; so was his house and so was Hotchner's room at the Christiana Motor Lodge. They could talk safely only out in the woods, Ernest said. Mary had to jump through hoops to assure him that the IRS was not after him and that he had sufficient money in his bank accounts. One day that November she came across a letter addressed to Morgan Guaranty Bank in New York. After the salutation and the first sentence, Ernest had written gibberish—not in the English language or in any other she recognized.

Ernest's friend George Saviers had been a major presence in Ernest's life since becoming his doctor. He had originally met Ernest when he was working as an assistant guide in Sun Valley in 1940, when Saviers was twenty-five, which cemented the bond between them. The doctor came over every day around lunchtime to measure Ernest's blood pressure and check his general health; afterward, he and Ernest and Pappy Arnold often shot clay targets from the driveway. Saviers was aware of Ernest's delusional thinking and his marked depression, but he was at a loss as to what to do. "I'm just a country doctor," he told Hotchner, "and a pretty young one at that. I have the responsibility of knowing that Ernest needs immediate help that I can't provide." Yet, according to a letter to Buck about his wife's high blood pressure, Ernest strongly recommended she try reserpine; if it depressed her, she should try Ritalin with it. He said in the same letter, however, that Dr. Saviers now had him on Diuril (a diuretic and antihypertensive drug) for his high blood pressure. Indeed, Saviers told Carlos Baker that he was "weaning" Ernest off what he called "derivatives of Rauwolfia," by which he seems to have meant reserpine. By this time it had been reported that depression was emerging as a side effect of reserpine, which presumably led Saviers to discontinue it. As Saviers said, psychiatry was not his specialty, which seems to be why he did not consider prescribing other psychotropic drugs.

Though Ernest was isolated in the Ketchum community by preference, refusing (or refusing through Mary) to see many friends, and though the town itself was isolated, especially as the snow began to fall, two young professors from Montana State University in Bozeman, three hundred miles away, tracked Ernest down, turning up on his doorstep around nine one morning. One of them was the critic Leslie Fiedler, whose *Love and Death in the American Novel* was just published that year. His argument, then quite controversial, was that most American authors, Twain and Hemingway included, could, in Fiedler's words, "imagine an ennobling or redemptive love only between males in flight from women and civilization." Their fiction, he argued, was rife with homoerotic relationships. Ernest had not read the book (he asked Scribner's to send him a copy after Fiedler's visit), but he knew that an essay from it called "Come Back to the Raft Ag'in, Huck Honey" had caused a considerable stir when it appeared in *Partisan Review* in 1948.

Fiedler published a gossipy account of his meeting with Ernest just months after Hemingway's death, a generally thoughtful essay that enjoys the luxury of hindsight to make some fairly sharp points. The essay does, however, give us clues as to what those last months were like. Fiedler's first impression: "Hemingway . . . greeted us, framed by the huge black television screen that dominated the living room . . . an old man with spectacles slipping down his nose. An old man at sixty-one. . . . Fragile, I found myself thinking, breakable and broken—one time too often, broken beyond repair." Mostly, they talked about other writers, Ernest's contemporaries and those of a younger generation, but Ernest mostly spoke words of rather empty praise for each one who came up. He often fell silent. "It's hard enough for me to wr-write, much less—talk," he pleaded, twice. The conversation was fitful at best, and perhaps to ease the tension Ernest opened a bottle of Tavel, though it was just 9:30. At the end of the visit Fiedler was struck by Ernest's smile, "the teeth yellowish and widely spaced, but bared in all the ceremonious innocence of a boy's grin. He was suddenly, beautifully, twelve years old," Fiedler wrote. He remembered Gertrude Stein's story that Hemingway exclaimed that he was at twenty-three too young to be a father: "And I could hear him now in my inner ear crying out that he was too young to be an old man."

In Hotchner's account, he was the first of those around Ernest in the fall of 1960 to say he needed psychiatric treatment. It is impossible to know now who took the first steps to get him help. Duke MacMullen, a hunting friend, told Hotchner, "Hotch, you've got to do something. Nobody's doing anything," he went on, "and let me tell you, somebody has to *do* something." This had been the case for a shockingly long time, each of Ernest's friends hoping that someone else was doing something about his unmistakable deterioration. Worse, in some circles, acolytes, hangers-on, and even well-meaning friends too often enjoyed egging "Papa" on, encouraging him to drink more, regale them with stories, stay up late to tell the stories a second, even a third time, and applaud every rendition. The buck was repeatedly passed, and there was plenty of guilt to go around.

With Mary's consent, Hotchner called James Cottell, a New York psychiatrist he either knew or was told about in order to discuss Ernest's situation. Though Cottell emphasized that he had not met Ernest and could not diagnose or recommend treatment for him except in the most general way, he said he believed Ernest needed hospitalization and that the best place for him to go would be the Menninger Clinic in Topeka, Kansas. Hotchner, Mary, and Saviers knew Ernest would not consent to go to a psychiatric hospital, mostly because of the attendant publicity. Cottell then suggested the esteemed Mayo Clinic, which treated physical ailments as well as mental ones; it had been decided that a cover story could say that Ernest was there for treatment of his high blood pressure.

Hotchner's and Mary's accounts differ as to what Ernest was told that convinced him to go to the Mayo Clinic; Mary implied that Ernest knew the high blood pressure story was a fabrication, but Hotchner's account does not corroborate this. Given the possibility that Ernest had long told himself (or been told) that he was taking reserpine for his blood pressure rather than for his mental troubles, it is conceivable that he was not aware of the real purpose of his trip when he set out. It does not seem likely, however, that he could long sustain the illusion once he arrived at the clinic.

Larry Johnson, a pilot based in Hailey, Idaho, flew Ernest and Mary to Rochester, Minnesota, on November 30. There Ernest checked in as George Saviers to avoid any press. In a letter Howard Rome, Ernest's psychiatrist, wrote Ernest in January, the doctor told him that on admission his blood pressure was found to be 160/98 (the past month it had been as high as 250/125). His weight, 175 pounds, was noted to be ideal. Hugh R.

Butt, a liver specialist, found the "palpable left lobe of the liver . . . with a round edge." Rome also told Ernest that he might be suffering from hemochromatosis, a disease that can be inherited or can be caused by metabolic disorders; it is a buildup of iron in the patient's organs, often found with diabetes, cirrhosis, and bronze skin pigmentation (because excess iron builds up in the skin as well). Ernest definitely had liver disease and mild diabetes (diagnosed on his admission). Hemochromatosis, usually diagnosed in patients in their fifties, is easily treated and controlled by a medieval-sounding procedure—bleeding. Left long untreated, it is associated with organic brain damage and behavioral changes. While hemochromatosis—if he had it—was probably not directly related to Ernest's physical and mental decline, it was possibly a contributing factor.

In a letter to Mary in November 1961, written at her request to relieve her fears that she had done anything wrong in Ernest's care, as well as to let her know the Mayo doctors did not either, Dr. Rome seemed especially eager to establish that Ernest received psychotherapy—which is by no means clear in the available record. He described to her what he found when Ernest was first admitted to the clinic. Ernest and he had discussed suicide often, he told Mary, beginning when Ernest was first admitted and asked why he was put on a locked psychiatric unit.

In his January letter to Ernest, Dr. Rome said that some of his symptoms might be the result of the antihypertensive drug (reserpine) his Cuban doctors had prescribed, which the Mayo doctors were discontinuing because reports were showing that depression was a side effect of the drug. (This is difficult to square with Saviers's statement to Carlos Baker that he was "weaning" Ernest off reserpine, presumably at an earlier date.) It is not clear why the doctors did not replace reserpine with another antipsychotic—Thorazine, for example, which had many of the same effects as Serpasil, or Stelazine. Nor do they seem to have considered prescribing a tricyclic antidepressant like Tofranil, though Ernest was in a closed setting where doctors could have monitored the effects of any new course of medication.

Soon after his arrival at the Mayo, Ernest agreed to undergo a course of shock treatment. As Howard Rome said in his letter to Mary in November 1961, he found Ernest, on admission, to show clinical symptoms of agitated depression, loss of self-esteem, restlessness, ideas of worthlessness, was "unable to rely on" his lawyers and financial advisers (was Rome avoiding the word "paranoia"?), and guilt at failing Mary, his friends, his family, and others who relied on him. He said he had talked with Ernest about many of his preoccupations, like honor (in connection with gambling debts, bullfighting, and paying taxes), as well as his indecision about where he and Mary might live.

Ernest was, by now, familiar with ECT therapy because of its role in ending Patrick's terrible ordeal following his concussion in 1947—and because, ten years later, Greg, twice sent to a psychiatric hospital in 1957, had undergone two courses of ECT therapy, receiving thirty shock treatments that year. Though Greg would later be diagnosed with manic depression, and underwent scores more shock treatments, for the time being he had seemed to everyone, including his father, much better. Given his sons' positive experiences of electroshock, Ernest underwent the treatments willingly at first—though he came to object to them strongly because of a common side effect, the damage they were doing to his memory.

Howard Rome admitted in his later letter to Mary that the treatments were "an ordeal"—because the patient is concerned about the loss of control and is confused immediately afterward. Rome said Ernest told Rome he had to have things in control in order to write. His loss of memory worried him terribly. ECT affects short-term more than long-term memory; it was the latter that Ernest had always tapped so easily for his work. But in 1960–61, the memory loss caused by the treatments for his depression became in turn a source of his continued depression.

Ernest received eleven shock treatments in December, Hotchner said, and then they were "abruptly" stopped the first week in January. Hotchner visited Ernest again on January 13, and found he suffered from the same set of delusions as before: about Valerie, his finances, and so forth. The doctors, however, were pronouncing him much improved; they were most impressed by his statements about his work, which he said he was eager to resume. A little strangely, he went target shooting with Dr. Butt and one of his sons; he and Mary had spent Christmas with the doctor's family. On January 11 Kenneth McCracken, in the *Rochester Post-Bulletin,* broke the story that the George Saviers under treatment at the Mayo was actually Ernest Hemingway, and a raft of fan mail came from the resulting coverage, along with it scapulars and rosaries—presumably because the news account said he was in the clinic's St. Mary's Hospital, a Catholic facility.

Dr. Rome told Ernest, "It is my judgment that you have fully recovered from this experience and I see no reason to anticipate any further difficulty on this score." He told Ernest that reserpine *in its hypertensive capacity* caused his depression and agitation, which were made worse by the Ritalin prescribed to address those side effects. He advised Ernest to continue on the anti-anxiety drug Librium until Ernest returned "to a normal tenor of life," and added Tuinal, a sedative. (It isn't clear when

Ernest began taking Librium.) He said that he was withdrawing reserpine from his regimen because of what were thought to be at the time depressive side effects, and that he would not add it back "unless it becomes absolutely necessary"—whether in the event of increased blood pressure or more florid symptoms of mental illness is not clear. (As noted above, given recent findings that reserpine, or Serpasil, does *not* cause depression, Dr. Rome, like Dr. Saviers before him, may have done Ernest more harm than good in taking him off the drug—though no one could have known that then.) Again, it's hard to understand why the doctors at the Mayo Clinic did not prescribe tricyclic antidepressants like Tofranil, or antipsychotics like Stelazine or Thorazine.

Though the doctors said Ernest could go home in mid-January, the weather would not cooperate, and Ernest took advantage of the time to dictate answers to much of the fan mail, also dispatching letters to editor Harry Brague at Scribner's, George Plimpton, and the like. To almost everyone, he sent identical letters, saying that the doctors told him he could keep his blood pressure down if he maintained his weight at 175, and that he was going home as soon as there was good flying weather. Always canny about publicity, Ernest knew it was essential for his writing future to circulate good reports. In that sense, the doctors were right—he thought he might write again.

Ernest asked Harry Brague at Scribner's to send him, in addition to Leslie Fiedler's book, Isak Dinesen's *Shadows on the Grass;* Lawrence Durrell's *The Black Book; The Waste Makers* by Vance Packard, author of a controversial exposé of subliminal advertising; William Styron's *Set This House on Fire;* and the latest Herbert Gold novel. He even agreed to a request from the Modern Language Association to appear on a panel with Eliot, Camus, Sartre, Saint-John Perse (the winner of the 1960 Literature Nobel), and the Cuban poet Nicolás Guillén—a most unusual acceptance, considering his horror of public speaking and his mistrust of academia. Given this energetic and forward-looking behavior, the persistence of Ernest's delusions must have seemed no more than a messy detail.

Larry Johnson flew Ernest and Mary back to Ketchum on January 30. After the heartening plateau of January, however, Ernest's path continued downward. His weight was a bit of an issue, becoming an obsession with him. Certainly he was losing weight at a steady rate. Ernest was, since the war, usually over 200 pounds; he had once topped out at 260. In January he was told, "You can eat whatever you want, but stay at your current weight"—not the easiest advice to follow. Ernest should have resumed eating normally once he'd reached 178 pounds, the ideal weight for a six-foot-tall, heavy-boned man, but his weight kept dropping—from 171 in February to 166 in March to 164 in April. Dr. Rome, in his January letter to Ernest, mentioned Ernest's continued weight loss "despite eating." Dr. Saviers later said that Ernest had been concerned about his weight back in 1960, and avoided carbohydrates and beer. Dr. Rome told Mary that Ernest's need to watch his health made him "[eat] less than what the dieticians provided." That last sounds ominous in light of the weight charts Ernest began keeping in January.

On his bathroom wall at the Finca, Ernest had long kept a record of his weight down to the last half pound, as any visitor to the Finca can attest; those records, however, note only the date and weight. It is not known whether he made notes on the walls of the Ketchum house, but he did, starting in January, begin to keep pages and pages of records of his weight counts for each day. Yet these notes often contain more than one weight for each morning; he differentiates between his weight at several junctures: before or after breakfast, for example. Almost every day he records what he ate that morning (for instance, "4 slices toast, stewed fruit, egg, juice") as well as his bowel movement (small, big, normal, none). On a particular day, he might note: "March 16, 169 (stripped) in blue pajamas as at hospital—170—small movement." Or, on another day, "March 23, stripped before breakfast 167 with blue pajamas as at hospital 168 (practically no movement) after breakfast 3 slices toast, 1 slice ham, 1 egg—fruit juice, stewed fruit—coffee—milk—169 socks and underwear." If these were the notes of a teenage girl, we would immediately suspect anorexia or bulimia.

While those maladies may have played a very small part in Ernest's emotional makeup, it does seem clear that he saw his weight as a factor he could try to keep within his control. Certainly control had always been an issue for Ernest, part of his way to order the world. It will come as no surprise to a Hemingway fan that Dr. Rome later told Mary that one of Ernest's bogeymen was "a deep concern about his doing things the right way." The right way to do everything, from baiting a hook to running with the bulls to driving from Key West to Piggott, was an obsession with Ernest. As, with the onset of his illness, he saw himself losing control, he became obsessed with holding on to what was left. So, for instance, the shock treatments upset him profoundly; he lost control of his body and his memory. At the clinic, Dr. Rome told Mary, he taxed himself to make sure that everything was managed well; thus, Dr. Rome said, he criticized how the nurses took his blood pressure; thus he kept elaborate lists and records, especially toward the end; thus he fixated on the minutest detail of

The Hemingway house in Ketchum, Idaho, where Ernest killed himself in 1961

his taxes. Dr. Rome noted that when, according to regular practice at the clinic, he was given money, he took pains to account for every penny to the nurses later on; so too when the levels were marked in the wine bottles presented to him at meals he made a point of showing the nurses the level after the meal. Teased for these matters, he replied, "with an uncharacteristic absence of humor," Dr. Rome said, "that if this was the way to be able to get back to where we had no need to be concerned this would be the way he would do it."

That winter, according to Pappy Arnold, "There was a tired, worn and aged manner about him—an old, old man whom I definitely had not seen before." Ernest said he needed exercise, so Mary bought them snowshoes and they trekked out into the white fields. But he found the landscape too quiet and lonely. Eventually they settled on brisk walks north on Route 93, two miles up and two miles back. Every day, Ernest stood at a chest-high writing surface Pappy had set up for him in front of a window, spending a lot of time looking out at the Big Wood River. A cottonwood tree had fallen so as to create a natural bridge across the river, and he came to fret that one of his imagined pursuers could thus cross the river and find him.

But he mostly tinkered with the Paris book, unable to hit upon an ending, unable to come up with the all-important title—unable to add anything at all. He wrote some letters, mostly saying he was working. In a letter to Patrick—Mary had written to the children about what was happening—he said, tersely, "Things not good here nor about the Finca and am not feeling good." Before long, he told Scribner's to scrap all plans for the Paris book. He was unable to finish it, he feared libel suits, and he worried he had been unfair to Hadley, Pauline, and Scott Fitzgerald.

"Throughout the month of March," Mary wrote, "he turned more and more silent, his eyes more vacant." His delusions multiplied: he feared he would be punished for the method by which he paid the workers at the Finca. He directed Hotch and Valerie to put their letters to him in envelopes sent to Saviers at Sun Valley Hospital, Hotchner to use a return name that began with the letter O, Valerie one that began with A. His handwriting grew smaller and finally unreadable. He was again abusive toward Mary, as he had been in the months in the new house, when he would stand in the doorway of her room at bedtime and berate her for everything that had gone wrong—their exile from Cuba (the situation having become far worse with the Bay of Pigs incident); his inability to write; her moving them to Idaho and thus making his tax situation worse.

Dr. Rome later assured Mary that Ernest appreciated her tolerance: "He was especially proud of the fact that you had been able to share him with what he frequently referred to as that thing in his head—tapping his forefinger against his temple." Ernest told Dr. Rome that he had tried to let her know how much he loved and needed her but was afraid he never really put it right. "He often said that he was a difficult person to live with and that you had somehow or other acquired the knack." Mary hung on long after the faint of heart would have bailed out, showing extraordinary love and compassion—and a thick skin. It cannot have been easy.

On what should have been a happier occasion, the Hemingways and the Arnolds got together to watch the Oscars in April. Pappy found Ernest "frighteningly deteriorated." Gary Cooper, dying from prostate cancer, was getting an honorary award, and Jimmy Stewart proffered it with a tearful speech. After the show was over Mary decided they should call Cooper; when they finally reached him and Rocky, Mary chatted for ten minutes, and the Arnolds, old friends of the Coopers as they were of the Hemingways, talked to him for several minutes as well. But Ernest managed only about thirty seconds on the phone with his old hunting companion; legend has it that Cooper said, by way of goodbye, "Bet I make it to the barn before you do."

Mary came downstairs on April 18 at around eleven in the morning to find Ernest in a corner of the living room near the gun rack. He was holding a shotgun, and two shells lay on the nearest windowsill. Mary managed to talk to him encouragingly and softly, as one would calm an animal or a child, until George Saviers showed up at lunchtime for his daily visit. Saviers called another doctor, and together they gave Ernest sodium amytal and took him to Sun Valley Hospital. It was clear Ernest needed hospitalization again. As Saviers saw it, the situation was dire. Ernest would attempt suicide again if not readmitted to the Mayo Clinic.

Mary's and Ernest's friends had a terrible problem simply transporting him there. Again waiting for good flying weather, Ernest spent several days in Sun Valley Hospital. On the day he was to leave, his friend Don Anderson and nurse Joan Higgons took him back to his house to pack some things. Once he got there, Don close behind him, he grabbed a shotgun and attempted to load it. Don and Joan wrested it from him and then managed to get him on the plane. The trouble continued: when Larry Johnson brought the plane down in Rapid City to refuel, Ernest, allowed outside, ran into the hangar and began to rifle through drawers and closets looking for a weapon. Brought back to the plane by Don Anderson, he shook Don's arm off and started walking toward the whirring blades of a propeller plane, evidently meaning to kill himself by walking into the blades.

By the time Ernest was safely back in the Mayo Clinic, in St. Mary's Hospital, again Mary and Hotchner knew they needed a new approach. The shock treatments had provided only temporary improvement—and Mary was not even sure of that, suspecting Ernest had put on an act of being in good mental health for the doctors. This time they advised her not to accompany her husband, and Mary flew to New York and the apartment on 62nd Street.

Electroshock treatments were again administered, and Ernest again showed some improvement. He resumed his target shooting and promised Dr. Rome he would not kill himself while in the clinic, after he had pointed out he could easily do so. Again, no attempt was made to begin treatment with an antidepressant or antipsychotic.

Hotchner made another short visit to the clinic. Once again, Ernest would not talk until they retreated to a wooded hillside, where to Hotch's dismay he ran through the same delusions, repeating himself several times. Hotchner tried to interest him in the kinds of activities he had so loved: it was spring at the Auteuil racetrack, he reminded Ernest, and he could go on that tiger hunt the maharaja had promised him, for instance. Ernest outlined the reasons a man had for living: "Staying healthy. Working good. Eating and drinking with his friends. Enjoying himself in bed," Ernest said. "I haven't any of them." Before Hotchner could assure him these were all in the realm of the possible, Ernest launched anew into his litany of delusional worries. They said little more and Hotchner left later that afternoon, saying goodbye to, as he later wrote, "that thin, old, lovely man." He was never to see his best friend again.

In New York, late in May, Mary was able to meet Dr. Cottell in person; Hotchner also called on him after his return from Rochester. The doctor suggested that Ernest be sent to the Institute of Living in Hartford, Connecticut. One of the oldest psychiatric institutions in the country, the institute was highly esteemed, and, when Mary trekked up to Hartford to investigate, she liked what she saw. Dr. Cottell then contacted the doctors at the Mayo to suggest Ernest be sent there, but again ran up against Ernest's intransigency: "He would deny that he needed that," according to Mary. Without his consent, he could not be sent to another psychiatric facility.

Mary wrote a letter to Jack and Patrick saying that Ernest was now claiming she sent him to the clinic because she had a plan for getting his money away from him. He showed "intense hostility" to her, she said. He took her to task especially, she told the boys, for not allowing him to go to Pamplona for the running of the bulls in July. It may have seemed to him that he was cut off from yet another of the things he loved: "I feel very fine while [the bullfight] is going on," he had written in *Death in the Afternoon*, "and have a feeling of life and death and mortality and immortality, and after it is over I feel very sad but very fine" (*DIA*, 4). Perhaps he sought that same kind of clarity and perspective now. It was undoubtedly another blow to his spirit, but Mary knew better than to encourage the impossible.

In May the doctors contacted Mary to come in for a conjugal visit, which did not go well. A few days after she arrived, Dr. Rome called her into his office, where she found Ernest "dressed in street clothes, grinning like a Cheshire cat." The doctor told Mary her husband was ready to go home. Maybe Ernest had fooled the doctors again—Mary's interpretation. Perhaps, unwilling to admit that he had a gravely serious mental illness, he refused to stay any longer or undergo more shock treatments, a refusal that was his right. Mary wrote in her memoir that she did not feel that she could disagree with the doctor in Ernest's presence, presumably out of a sense of propriety or a reluctance to embarrass Ernest or herself. Unfortunate, maybe, but it most likely would have been futile in any case, given that Ernest wanted to leave.

Mary called on George Brown, Ernest's old boxing friend, who had accompanied Ernest on a short cruise of the Caribbean in 1957 and stayed on at the Finca to provide massage therapy and general support. Brown agreed to drive her and Ernest back to Ketchum in a rented car. For the trip, Mary routinely bought several bottles of wine. Ernest had always loved drinking in a car, whether as driver or passenger; everyone with him had observed the cocktail hour with drinks mixed on the road. He outfitted every car he owned with homemade drink holders—unheard of at the time. But on this trip he grew increasingly fearful that they would be pulled over and arrested for carrying alcohol. Nothing would quiet him until Mary left the unopened bottles in a ditch by the side of the road. It was a long and extremely difficult trip. James Corey, an admirer of Hemingway's who saw the writer emerge from his car and go into a roadside diner on this trip back to Idaho, was shocked by his appearance, noting his "desolated," skeletonlike frame. Hemingway, he said, could not walk unassisted. He seemed "drawn into himself, isolated, a man deadened by medications or resignation or both."

Ketchum was the same. By now, Ernest was almost mute, speaking seldom and only to register his delusional complaints. He was acting just as his father had before he shot himself in 1928. Ed Hemingway had become extremely irritable and distrustful; he began to keep his belongings under lock and key. He became irrationally attached to his younger son, Leicester. He desperately dwelled on financial fears. At the end he was, like his son, obsessed by taxes. His illness, his sister wrote, "confused his thinking." When he shot himself nobody was really surprised.

Mental illness coursed through the Hemingway family like one of the rivers Ernest wrote about with such beautiful economy, its incessant, implacable force pausing only in small eddies, where illness cursed individuals like Ed Hemingway, Ernest Hemingway, Greg Hemingway, and, later, some in the next generation, and, reportedly, in those after that. It took and continues to take the form of cycles of mania and psychotic depression; alcoholism and other addictions; and suicide. Many believe that three of Ed and Grace's six children—half of them—killed themselves.

Borne along with the river were many other qualities, not least good looks and charisma; Ed and Grace were compelling and handsome people with a beautiful and appealing brood. More important, the river carried as it rushed along artistic talent, even genius, as well as extraordinary personal charms. These qualities were apparent in Grace's musical gifts and, equally, in the incredible charisma she shared with her son. Hemingway descendants have written, painted, acted, and studied art history; one of Ernest's grandchildren wrote a book that was nominated for a Pulitzer Prize and a National Book Award. These strains were in the DNA that the river carried along just as surely as were mental illness and suicide.

On a Ketchum memorial to Hemingway's memory is an inscription that reads, "Best of all he loved the fall / The leaves yellow on the cottonwoods / Leaves floating on the trout streams / And above the hills / The high blue windless skies / . . . Now he will be a part of them forever." These are words Ernest wrote about another Sun Valley friend, Gene Van Guilder, for his funeral in 1939. While there is no question that autumn in the American West was one of the good times in one of the good places, it belonged to the second half of his life, and it took on for Ernest the bittersweet coloration of leave-taking.

In his last two years, in *A Moveable Feast*, he wrote again about the fall, this time in Paris in the 1920s, another good time in another good place. "You expected to be sad in the fall. Part of you died each year when the leaves fell from the trees and their branches were bare against the wind and the cold, wintery light" (*AMF,* 39). Yet fall during that period of his life was beautiful for what would inevitably follow: "You knew there would always be the spring, as you knew the river would flow again after it was frozen."

Acknowledgments

As befits my subject, the research and writing of this book has been an adventure, and I have many people to thank for help along the way. It's a pleasure to thank those friends who have read my manuscript or otherwise helped me in my labors: Marion Meade (my patient sounding board), Amanda Vaill, Carl Rollyson, and the other members of the New York University Biography Seminar. Also members of my unnamed hilltown biography group: Lina Bernstein, David Perkins, Polly Lyman, Heather Clark.

Also Teo Davis; John Dos Passos Coggin; Derek Donovan and Steve Paul at the *Kansas City Star;* Ruth Hawkins at the extraordinary Hemingway-Pfeiffer Museum and Educational Center; Valerie Hemingway; Hasty Hickok; Verna Kale; Elizabeth Kimbrel; Channy Lyons, Grace Hemingway's biographer; Ben Drabek and the Friends of the Archibald MacLeish Collections at Greenfield Community College; Mark Milburn, for matters Catholic and St. Louisan; Dennis Noble for suggestions for Cuba; Ken Panda, Jan Wheeler, and John Sanford for help with Hemingway's family; Raymond Steiner on the Art Students League; Symeon Waller and Bill Roworth on the history of Doncaster; and the late Allie Baker and her excellent website, the Hemingway Project, as well as members of the Hemingway listerv, who have enlivened and informed my days.

I must make special mention of the phenomenal Hemingway Letters Project, which is, under the general editor, Sandra Spanier, in the process of issuing a definitive edition of Ernest Hemingway's letters in a projected seventeen volumes. Volumes One and Two, which bring Hemingway up to 1925, have been invaluable in my research.

I have had significant help from archivists and librarians. Every Hemingway scholar is indebted to the matchless Ernest Hemingway Collection at the JFK Library and its staff, especially Susan Wrynn, Stephen Plotkin, Laurie Austin, and Connor Anderson—all of whom brought me materials, answered my questions, and generally made life easier for me. I am grateful for a Mellon Research Fellowship from the Harry Ransom Center, University of Texas at Austin, and to those who helped me with the Hemingway collection during my 2009 visit: Richard Workman, Pat Fox, Molly Schwartzburg, Thomas F. Staley, and Gregory Curtis. At Penn State, I was able to use the newly acquired collection of Hemingway's letters to his family; Bill Brockman, Bill Joyce, Sandra Spanier, and particularly Sandra Smelts, were excellent guides and resources there. The following provided help with documents and photographs in other collections: Bonnie Coles at the Library of Congress; Adrienne Sharpe at Yale; Pat Burdick at Colby College; Maryjo McAndrew at Knox College; Polly Armstrong at Stanford; and AnnaLee Pauls at Princeton.

The librarian who has helped me the most is my friend Liz Jacobson-Carroll, who runs the Buckland, Massachusetts, Public Library and has cheerfully facilitated scores of loans from far-flung libraries across the state, enabling intensive research and providing much-needed human interaction at the same time.

Other friends who provided hospitality or other kinds of support, great and small: Randi Parks, Robin Glenn, Beth Langan, Mary Campbell, the amazing Robert Nedlekoff, Zan Goncalves, Keith Nightenhelser, Tracy Dery, Meryl Altman, Lauren Krouk, Meredith Thomas, Tina Ruyter, and Freda Hamric. My family have been essential: Richard Dearborn and his wife Tommy, John T. G. Dearborn, John and Cristina Donnelly, and Ruah Donnelly.

I am grateful as always to my extraordinary agent, Georges Borchardt, and his wife, Anne. At Knopf Vicky Wilson has been an ideal editor, exacting and inspired. She has been ably assisted first by Audrey Silverman and more recently by Ryan Smernoff.

As always, I owe Eric Laursen the biggest debt of all. It wouldn't happen without him.

Notes

ABBREVIATIONS

AABT	Gertrude Stein, *The Autobiography of Alice B. Toklas*
AM	Archibald MacLeish
AMF	EH, *A Moveable Feast*
ARIT	EH, *Across the River and into the Trees*
ATH	Marcelline Hemingway Sanford, *At the Hemingways*
BEH	EH, *Byline: Ernest Hemingway*
CBP	Carlos Baker Papers, Archives of Charles Scribner's Sons, Special Collections, Princeton University, Princeton, New Jersey
CEH	Clarence Edward Hemingway
CS III	Charles Scribner III
CSS	EH, *The Complete Short Stories of Ernest Hemingway*
DIA	EH, *Death in the Afternoon*
DS	EH, *The Dangerous Summer*
EH	Ernest Hemingway
FSF	F. Scott Fitzgerald
FSF: ALL	Matthew J. Bruccoli, ed., *F. Scott Fitzgerald: A Life in Letters*
FTA	EH, *A Farewell to Arms*
GHH	Grace Hall Hemingway
HIW	Mary Welsh Hemingway, *How It Was*
HRC	Harry Ransom Center, University of Texas, Austin, Texas
HRH	Hadley Richardson Hemingway
IIS	EH, *Islands in the Stream*
JFK	Ernest Hemingway Collection, John F. Kennedy Presidential Library and Museum, Boston, Massachusetts
LEH	Sandra Spanier and Robert W. Trogdon, eds., *The Letters of Ernest Hemingway*
Lilly	Lilly Library, Indiana University, Bloomington, Indiana
LoC	Archibald MacLeish Papers, Owen Wister Papers, Library of Congress, Washington, DC
MG	Martha Gellhorn
MP	Maxwell Perkins
MWH	Mary Welsh Hemingway

PPH   Pauline Pfeiffer Hemingway
PSU   Special Collections Library, The Pennsylvania State University, State
          College, Pennsylvania
SL   Carlos Baker, ed., *Ernest Hemingway: Selected Letters, 1917–1961*
TMA   Martha Gellhorn, *Travels with Myself and Another*
UK   EH, *Under Kilimanjaro*
Yale   Beinecke Rare Book and Manuscript Library, Yale University, New
          Haven, Connecticut

PROLOGUE

5 male and female roles: In the intervening years, many Hemingway scholars had
  fallen on this idea with relish, producing such works as Mark Spilka's *Hemingway's Quarrel with Androgyny* (Lincoln: University of Nebraska, 1990), J. Gerald
  Kennedy's "Hemingway's Gender Trouble," *American Literature* 63 (June 1991),
  and Nancy Conley and Robert Scholes's *Hemingway's Genders: Rereading the
  Hemingway Text* (New Haven, CT: Yale University Press, 1994).

6 "I admired his combination": Harold Loeb, *The Way It Was* (New York: Criterion
  Books, 1959), 247.

7 "America's greatest": Norman Mailer, *Of a Fire on the Moon* (Boston: Little,
  Brown, 1959), 4.

7 "would be if": Norman Mailer, *Advertisements for Myself* (New York: G. P. Putnam's, 1959), 21.

9 The dangers of retrospective diagnosis: Today Hemingway is often said to have
  suffered from bipolar disorder, a term I have not used in the text precisely because
  of such dangers and because the term was not in use in Hemingway's time.

CHAPTER ONE

11 shaking Abraham Lincoln's hand: "Mrs. Anson Hemingway Dies," *Oak Leaves,*
   2/10/1923.

11 "much too large": Marcelline Hemingway Sanford, *At the Hemingways* (1962; rev.
   ed., Moscow: University of Idaho Press, 1999), 5. Hereafter *ATH.*

12 Another English family: Ernest Hall to GHH, 7/9/1904, HRC, Box 4, Folder 7.

12 Hall fought: Guy E. Logan, "Historical Sketch. First Regiment Iowa Volunteer
   Cavalry," *Roster and Record of Iowa Troops in the Rebellion,* vol. 4. Another Hancock daughter, Charlotte, died the year before the family emigrated. E-mails
   from Allen Goodwin to author, 10/17/2013 and 10/28/2013.

12 Jacob Hemingway was the first: Judith Ann Schiff, "Yale's First Student,"
   Yale Alumni Magazine, www.yalealumnimagazine.com/issues/2004_05/old_yale
   .html.

13 On his discharge: See Nagel, "Introduction," in *Ernest Hemingway: The Oak
   Park Legacy,* 6–9.

13 He came north: See http://a2z.my.wheaton.edu/alumni/anson-t-hemingway.

13 the only regrets she had: EH to Bernard Berenson, 4/22/1953, JFK, Box 50.

13 Anson Hemingway opened: Griffith, *Along with Youth,* 5. For Anson Hemingway and real estate, see "Anson T. Hemingway: Early Settler Celebrates His
   Eighty-Second Birthday Anniversaries—Recalls Memories of Days That Are

Gone," *Oak Leaves,* 8/28/1926; a reprint at Lilly. It is commonly thought that Anson Hemingway did not go into the real estate business until after his YMCA job, when he had in fact first opened such a practice in 1870. See, for example, Mellow, 7.

13 YMCA official: For Moody and the Civil War, see http://www.moody.edu/edu _MainPage.aspx?id=3472. See also Findlay, 101–5.

14 "Here are the things": Carol Hemingway Gardner, "Recollections," ed. Morris Buske, *Hemingway Review* 24 (Fall 2004), 26.

14 A "Rush doctor": See http://en.wikipedia.org/wiki/Rush_Medical_College; and http://www.rushu.rush.edu/servlet/Satellite?c=content_block&cid=11436615130 08&pagename=Rush/content_block/PrintContentBlockDetail.

15 Among Ernest Hall's: See doncasterhistory.co.uk/local-history-3/famous-don castrians/edward-miller/. See also Morris Buske, "What If Ernest Had Been Born on the Other Side of the Street?" in Nagel, ed., *Ernest Hemingway: The Oak Park Legacy,* 214.

15 His son, William: Symeon Waller to author, 2/1/2012. Thanks also to Bill Roworth on the Doncaster history page.

15 Grace later told: *ATH,* 54.

15 "prescribe for affection": GHH to CEH, 11/6/1893, HRC, Box 6, Folder 7.

16 "known all over": Louise Kapp-Young Cappiani, *Voice Culture,* p. 500, reprinted in Mary Kavanaugh Oldham Eagle, *The Congress of Women Held in the Women's Building: World's Columbian Exposition, Chicago 1893* (Chicago: W. B. Conkey, 1894). See http://digital.library.upenn.edu/women/eagle/congress/cappiani .html.

16 records show: Interview with Raymond J. Steiner, 10/22/2010. See Steiner; and Marchal E. Londgren, *Years of Art: The Story of the Art Students League of New York* (New York: Robert McBride, 1940).

16 "in upper Manhattan": Leicester Hemingway, *My Brother, Ernest Hemingway,* 1971 edition, 20. References hereafter to this edition unless otherwise noted.

16 Grace's correspondence: Mallinson Randall to GHH, 9/23/[n.d.]; Frances Randall to GHH, 12/13/1932, 2/15/1933, and [n.d.], HRC, Box 11, Folder 8. See Mallinson Randall, comp., *The Choirmaster's Guide to the Selections of Hymns and Anthems for the Services of the Church* (1900; no pub.).

16 "with any person": Quoted in Nagel, ed., "Introduction," *Ernest Hemingway: The Oak Park Legacy,* 13.

17 "The musically well-educated": See http://digital.library.upenn.edu/women/eagle /congress/cappiani.html.

17 "You have no idea": GHH to CEH, 6/2/1895, HRC, Box 6, Folder 7.

17 "a thousand dollars: *ATH,* 59. Bernice Kert was, it seems, the first to provide the $8/hour figure, p. 34.

17 At the age of seven: MWH, *How It Was,* 226. Hereafter *HIW.*

17 Apparently: Kert, 37.

17 "Living with Mother": Carol Hemingway Gardner, "Recollections," 24.

18 Daughter Marcelline: *ATH,* 65.

18 "burned the midnight oil": GHH to EH, 9/25/1949, JFK, Box 60.

18 "Beyond singing lullabies": Leicester Hemingway, 22.

18 "There is no use": *ATH,* 54.

19 "and said she was": Wilhelmina Corbett to Charles Fenton, 6/10/1952, JFK, Miscellaneous Accessions, Hem-14, Charles Fenton Correspondence.

19 He especially loved: Marguerite Bellows to GHH, 4/12/1907, HRC, Box 9, Folder 2.

19 "My mother was exempt": Carol Hemingway Gardner, "Recollections," 23.

19 "We planned": CEH to Carol Hemingway, 7/16/1919, HRC.

21 As a little baby: GHH to Sunny Hemingway, 4/15/1945, PSU, Box 2, Folder 22.

21 "Ernest shoots well": Scrapbook #2, JFK.

21 "that great hunter": Ernest Hall to GHH, 8/19/1903, HRC, Box 4, Folder 7.

21 The Agassiz Club: EH to CEH, [9/11/1910], Spanier and Trogdon, eds., *The Letters of Ernest Hemingway,* vol. 1, 10. Hereafter *LEH.*

22 But after the first: Lynn, 40. As late as World War I, the color pink was thought to be a "stronger" color than blue, and thus more suitable for boys. Beyond Grace's descriptions of the colors her children wore in the baby books, we cannot tell from black-and-white photos, of course, in what colors Marcelline and Ernest were dressed. See Marilyn Elkins, "The Fashion of *Machismo,*" in Wagner-Martin, ed., 112n5.

23 "He was quite fearful": Scrapbook #2, JFK.

24 "Mother always": *ATH,* 62.

25 "and one of them": Ibid., 111. The other Hemingway girls were similarly kept out of school for this year, though neither of the boys was. Mark Spilka, in *Hemingway's Quarrel with Androgyny,* 47, persuasively suggests that this practice was based on ideas about girls and menarche. I am extremely beholden to Mark Spilka's brilliant analysis of what was going on in the Hemingway household, a drama he situates in late-nineteenth-century popular reading habits.

25 "was a very big": Brian, 81.

26 "laying up stores": Ernest Hall to GHH, 7/16/1904, HRC, Box 4, Folder 7.

26 "I trust you are all": Ernest Hall to GHH, [n.d., 7/1901?], HRC, Box 4, Folder 5.

27 "controlled her terrible selfishness": EH to MWH, 9/13/1945, JFK, Box 48.

27 For "years": Kert, 30.

27 "careerist zeal": See Lynn, 31, 36.

28 "the doctor could both: See Kert, 30.

28 "severely modern": *ATH,* 105.

28 William Edward Miller: See http://www.library.manchester.ac.uk/searchresources/guidetospecialcollections/methodist/using/biographicalindex/mcallumtomylne/header-title-max-32-words-65766-en.html.

29 "unconventional": Corbett to Charles Fenton, 6/10/1952, JFK.

29 "Even at that age": Ibid.

30 "instantly": *ATH,* 31.

30 "My father's dimpled": *ATH,* 31.

31 "Try to forget": GHH to CEH, 10/17/1908, HRC, Box 6, Folder 8.

31 "You know, dear": GHH to CEH, 10/18/1908, HRC, Box 6, Folder 8.

31 "Don't you think": GHH to CEH, 10/17/1908, HRC Box 6, Folder 8.

32 "a pretty wretched physician": Ben Euwema to Baker, 11/28/1982, CBP.

32 "The Warners are": Dos Passos, *Chosen Country,* 60.

33 a young Bruce Barton: *ATH,* 147. For Bruce Barton as president, see "Christianity in Political World, *Ogden* (Utah) *Standard,* 1/3/1910; see http://chroniclingamerica.loc.gov/lccn/sn85058398/1910-01-03/ed-1/seq-7/.

33 of how you felt: Quoted in Baker, *Ernest Hemingway,* 11.

33 *The Call of the Wild*: Reynolds, *The Young Hemingway,* 109.

33 Ernest later said: Baker, p. 13. All Ernest's proclamations about his mother dominating his father, however, need to be read with skepticism.

CHAPTER TWO

35 *John Halifax, Gentleman:* For an especially illuminating discussion of the importance of this novel to the Hemingways, see Spilka, 17–42.

36 "Every man with": Ernest Hall to CEH, 8/13/1902, HRC, Box 4, Folder 4.

36 blue heron: The fullest accounts of the blue heron incident appear in Baker, *Ernest Hemingway,* 20–21; Linda Miller, ed., 51–53. See also Meyers, *Hemingway,* 15. Hemingway used the incident fictionally in "The Last Good Country."

37 "outspoken liberal": Fenton, 7.

37 A surviving letter: EH to Fannie Biggs, *LEH,* vol. 1, 38.

37 "as though the classroom": Griffin, *Along with Youth,* 25. Griffin seems to embroider on the facts, in some places more than others, but it is impossible to be conclusive because his documentation is so poor. This observation seems well grounded, however.

38 Bob Zuppke: See Baker, *Ernest Hemingway,* 431.

38 "were especially nice": Quoted in ibid., 27.

39 "Hemingway is reported": "A 'Ring Lardner' on the Bloomington Game," 11/24/1916, *The* (Oak Park) *Trapeze,* in Cynthia Maziarka and Donald Vogel, Jr., eds., *Hemingway at Oak Park High: The High School Writings of Ernest Hemingway* (Oak Park, IL: Oak Park and River Forest High School, 1993), 47.

39 "Dear Pashley": " 'Ring Lardner Junior' Writes About Swimming Meet. Oak Park Rivals Riverside," in Maziarka and Vogel, eds., *Hemingway at Oak Park High,* 60–61.

40 "some rather good additions": EH to unknown recipient, [ca. late September 1919], *LEH,* vol. 1, 208.

41 "Is this all we've got": See Morris Buske, "Early Hemingway Conflicts Foreshadow Later Ones," *Hemingway Review* 17 (Fall 1997), 81; and "Hemingway Faces God," *Hemingway Review* 22 (Fall 2002), 72–87. Buske consulted unpublished portions of the manuscript of Marcelline Hemingway Sanford's *At the Hemingways* at the Ernest Hemingway Foundation at Oak Park, from which he has taken this quotation.

42 He credited Fannie: Buske, "Early Hemingway Conflicts Foreshadow Later Ones," 83.

42 The father of another: Fannie Biggs, [n.d.], "For Mr. Fenton: Notes of Ernest Hemingway," JFK, Miscellaneous Accessions, Hem-14, Charles Fenton Correspondence.

42 "Neither of *my* parents": Buske, "Early Hemingway Conflicts Foreshadow Later Ones," 84. Buske says this letter is missing from Charles Fenton's papers at the Beinecke Library at Yale.

42 "Isn't that": EH to Hadley Richardson Hemingway, 4/24/1945, JFK.

43 "poets, musicians, diplomats": Fannie Biggs, [n.d.], "For Mr. Fenton: Notes of Ernest Hemingway," JFK, Miscellaneous Accessions, Hem-14, Charles Fenton Correspondence.

43 "was no particular prize": Wilhelmina Corbett to Charles Fenton, 6/10/1952, JFK, Miscellaneous Accessions, Hem-14, Charles Fenton Correspondence.

44 "unbrushed hair": Dos Passos, *Chosen Country,* 59.

44 "slovenly mess": Ursula Hemingway to EH, [n.d., 1933], JFK.

44 "unconventional": Lewis Clarahan in Matthew Bruccoli and C. E. Frazer Clarke, eds., *Fitzgerald/Hemingway Annual,* 1972, 137.

44 "Mrs. Santa Claus": Sue Lowry quoted in "Young Hemingway: A Panel," *Fitzgerald/Hemingway Annual,* 1972, 137.

46 Hemingway's train: Hemingway biographers, following Baker, 32, say Tyler Hemingway met Ernest at the train station, but Ernest explicitly writes to his family on October 17, "Carl Edgar met me the first evening I was here," *LEH,* vol, 1, 53.

46 "the best rules": Bruccoli, ed., *Conversations,* 21.

46 "Use short sentences": Quoted in Fenton, 31.

46 "can fail to write well": Bruccoli, ed., *Conversations,* 21.

46 where "you got accidents": Quoted in Fenton, 35.

47 A favorite doctor: See Griffin, *Along with Youth,* 49.

47 "I can tell Mayors": EH to Marcelline Hemingway, [ca. 1/30/1918], *LEH,* vol. 1, 79.

47 "developed a friendship": Quoted in Fenton, 36.

48 "magnificently sensational": EH to Charles Fenton, 8/2/1952, JFK, Box 50.

48 "Pure objective writing": Quoted in Fenton, 41.

49 the letter to his father: EH to CEH, 4/16/1918, *LEH,* vol. 1, 94.

50 Before too long: EH to GHH and CEH, [12/6/1917], *LEH,* vol. 1, 68.

50 Mary Wayne Marsh: Mae Marsh was born on November 9, 1894; Ernest's first wife Hadley's birthday was November 9, 1891. See http:// www.things-and-other -stuff.com/movies/profiles/mae-marsh.html.

51 "She is our dream": Kael quoted in Anthony Slide, *Silent Players: A Biographical and Autobiographical Study of 100 Silent Films* (Lexington: University Press of Kentucky, 2002), 246.

51 "the future Mrs. Hemingstein": EH to Marcelline Hemingway, [2/12/1918], *LEH,* vol. 1, 81.

52 "a wonder": EH to Marcelline Hemingway, [3/2/1918], *LEH,* vol. 1, 87.

53 Ernest's poor eyesight: Fifteen percent of those applying to the armed services in World War I were turned down because of problems with the "sense organs." Patrick W. Kelley, ed., *Military Preventive Medicine: Mobilization and Deployment,* Vol. 1 (Washington, DC: Borden Institute, 2003), p. 149. See http://www .bordeninstitute.army.mil/published_volumes/mpmvol1/pm1ch7.pdf.   Of course, it is impossible to tell how many never applied because of their eyesight, or, for that matter, how many circumvented the eye exam by memorizing the eye chart.

54 "a big, good-natured": Quoted in Fenton, 36.

54 "was that of a big": Theodore Brumback, "With Hemingway Before *A Farewell to Arms*," in Bruccoli, ed., *Ernest Hemingway: Cub Reporter*, 4.

CHAPTER THREE

55 "I can remember": Quoted in Baker, *Ernest Hemingway*, 38.

55 Paul Fussell has written: See Paul Fussell, *The Great War and Modern Memory* (New York: Oxford University Press, 1975), 27. See also Peter Stine, "Hemingway and the Great War," *Fitzgerald/Hemingway Annual*, 1979, 329.

56 "regular United States Army": EH to family, [5/14/1918], *LEH*, vol. 1, 97–98.

56 "a very poor": GHH to EH, 5/16/1918, HRC, Box 6.

57 he let Dale Wilson know: EH to Dale Wilson, 5/19/[1918], *LEH*, vol. 1, 105. At this point Mae Marsh, for all intents and purposes, disappeared from Ernest's life. In 1966, Wilson called Mae Marsh in Hermosa Beach, California. When he asked her about Ernest Hemingway, she said that she had never met him but "would have liked to." She said that she had married Lee Armes in New York in September 1918 and was still his wife. Dale Wilson to Donald Hoffman, [n.d.], CBP, Box 7. Biographers have commonly considered the Mae Marsh story a joke on EH's part, but a ca. 2/12/1918 letter to Marcelline that turned up recently at PSU, and was subsequently published in *LEH*, vol. 1, 80–82, provides more information on where they met. In general, the large amount of detail provided to several different people, over a period of months, would seem to militate against the friendship being an invention; whether it was a love affair is open to question. See Dale Wilson, "Hemingway in Kansas City," *Fitzgerald/Hemingway Annual*, 216.

57 "corporal of the 1st squad": EH to Hemingway family, [5/17–18/1918], in *LEH*, vol. 1, 100–101.

57 sometime in the third week: Accounts differ as to the exact date. See *LEH*, vol. 1, 103n2, for a useful summary of the differences.

58 "as if he'd been sent": Quoted in Baker, *Ernest Hemingway*, 40.

58 "cocky cap": EH to Hemingway family, [ca. 6/3/1918], *LEH*, vol. 1, 110.

58 "The color change": *Death in the Afternoon* (1932; rpt., New York: Scribner, 1960), 137. Subsequently cited in the text as *DIA*.

59 letter to "Al": Quoted in Griffin, *Along with Youth*, 70.

59 Around midnight: See C. E. Frazer Clarke, Jr., "American Red Cross Reports on the Wounding of Lieutenant Ernest M. Hemingway—1918," *Fitzgerald/Hemingway Annual*, 1974, 131–33.

60 "How splendidly": Quoted in Mellow, 62.

60 "complete with flies": Villard and Nagel, 24.

60 "That trip to Milan": EH to Jim Gamble, 12/12/1923, *SL*, 108.

60 "An enormous trench": Ted Brumback to CEH, 7/14/1918, JFK.

60 The Silver Medal: See Lynn, 80.

61 "Gravely wounded": Quoted in Lynn, 80.

61 "a dark-eyed": Unidentified newspaper clipping, PSU. This account says he received thirty-two .45-caliber bullets in his limbs and hands.

61 sexual encounter: Hotchner, *Papa Hemingway*, 89.

61 150 yards: As he says in a letter to his parents, 8/18/[1918], *LEH*, vol. 1, 131.

61 as one critic: Lynn, 84.

61 "any heroic act": *A Farewell to Arms* (1929; rpt., New York: Scribner, 1959), 63. Subsequently cited in the text as *FTA.*

61 "astonishing": Carpenter, 55.

62 Shell shock: See Caroline Alexander, "The Shock of War," *Smithsonian* (September 2010). In light of the effects of Hemingway's later brain injuries, it is interesting to note that recent findings suggest so-called blast injuries—sustained when soldiers are in proximity to an explosion—may be similar and/or related to CTE, or chronic traumatic encephalopathy, the dementia that results from repeated concussions. Some PTSD symptoms may in fact involve organic brain injury. For an overview, see Robert F. Worth, "What if PTSD Is More Physical than Psychological?" *New York Times,* 6/10/16.

63 "Ernest was badly": Quoted in Constance Cappel Montgomery, *Hemingway in Michigan* (New York: Fleet Publishing, 1966), 118.

63 Hemingway freely admitted: See, for example, EH to Arthur Mizener, 6/2/1950, *SL,* 697.

63 "It is an awfully": EH to Hemingway family, 10/18/[1918], *LEH,* vol. 1, 147.

63 "The Hemingway hero": Philip Young, *Ernest Hemingway: A Reconsideration* (1952; rpt., University Park: Penn State University Press, 1966), 55.

64 "Sure plenty trauma": EH to Harvey Breit, 7/23/1956, JFK.

64 It's as bad to say: EH to Carlos Baker, 6/4/52, Stanford, #370.

64 "I think the real explosion": Brian, 31.

66 "had hurt him severely": Villard and Nagel, 263.

66 Agnes von Kurowsky was bothered: Reynolds, *Hemingway's First War,* 182.

66 "Ernest never conceived": Villard and Nagel, 42.

66 She was tall and slim: Griffin, *Along with Youth,* 82.

67 "is far too fond": Agnes's diary entry for 8/27/1918, in Villard and Nagel, 73.

67 "holding court": Villard and Nagel, 14.

67 "and a few other": Ibid., 30.

68 "he was not an easy": Ibid., 27–28.

68 "completely spoiled": Ibid., 43.

68 To the Hemingway family: EH to Hemingway family, 11/11/[1918], *LEH,* vol. 1, 150.

69 "had seen little": Baker quotes from Dorman-Smith's unpublished memoir, 56, CBP.

69 "When I think": EH to Jim Gamble, 3/3/[1919], *LEH,* vol. 1, 168–69.

69 "You know how": Baker, *Ernest Hemingway,* 49.

69 "He was the kind": HRH quoted in Brian, 53.

70 "I didn't know": Donaldson, *By Force of Will,* 188.

70 "Oh gash may be fine": *A Moveable Feast,* Seán Hemingway, ed. (restored edn.; New York: Scribner, 2009), 28. Subsequently cited in the text as *AMF.*

70 "left in tears": Donaldson, *By Force of Will,* 188.

70 "My idea": Michael Reynolds, "Notes on Agnes von Kurowsky," JFK, Miscellaneous Accessions, Box 1.

70 "all sorts of wild things": Agnes von Kurowsky to EH, 12/15/[1918], quoted in Villard and Nagel, 142. All Kurowsky letters quoted are from this edition.

71 "Leaving Europe": Reynolds, *Hemingway's First War,* 204.

CHAPTER FOUR

72 "splendidly built": Wyndham Lewis quoted in Stock, 312–13.

72 "robust": Leff, 54.

72 "When she entered": Linda Miller, 91.

72 "large, handsome": Quoted in Kert, 37.

72 "formidable": Baker interview with Isabelle Simmons Godolphin, 10/22/1964, CBP.

72 "unforgettable": Kert, 43.

72 "Of course": GHH to CEH, 6/4/1896, HRC, Box 7, Folder 7.

73 no other evidence: Kert, 300, cites a circa April 1937 letter GHH wrote to EH or PPH; I was unable to locate this letter.

73 "could exhaust": Donaldson, *Archibald MacLeish*, 145.

74 Even literally so: See *LEH*, vol. 1, 178n7; and Griffin, *Along with Youth*, 104. Griffin says he saw "lecture cards."

74 "Has 227 wounds": Trogdon, ed., in *Ernest Hemingway: A Literary Reference*, reprints the 1/22/1919 *New York Sun* story, 16.

74 "Worst shot-up": Mellow, 88.

74 the *Oak Parker:* Leicester Hemingway, 53.

75 "now chuckles": EH to Bill Horne, [2/3/1919], *LEH*, vol. 1, 167.

75 "to the camouflaged": EH to Jim Gamble, 3/3/[1919], *LEH*, vol. 1, 169.

75 Ernest later told: See EH to Arthur Mizener, 6/2/1950, *SL*, 697.

75 a "festa": See "Italy's Gratitude," *Oak Parker,* 2/22/1919.

76 Written when: *ATH,* 190–92.

77 As one critic: Reynolds, *The Young Hemingway,* 57.

77 "Hemingway, we hail": Quoted in Mellow, 90.

77 Ernest repeated: See Reynolds, *The Young Hemingway,* 56.

77 "still very fond": Agnes von Kurowsky to EH, 3/7/1919, quoted in Villard and Nagel, 163.

78 "needs somebody": EH to Bill Horne, 3/30/[1919], *LEH*, vol. 1, 177.

78 "and bust all": This wording is Leicester Hemingway's, 52; EH's letter to Red Cross nurse Elsie Macdonald does not survive.

79 "These are all": EH to CEH, 10/28/[1919], *LEH*, vol. 1, 209.

80 "If you think": *ATH,* 195.

81 "I was always": Ruth Arnold to EH, 7/16/1951, JFK, Cuban Accession, Box 4. She added, "I have been in the family since you were seven."

81 Ruth was a member: See Elizabeth Burns Cord, "Peter Henry Fippinger, Pioneer Settler of Cook County," unpublished ms., for information about Ruth Arnold. Evidently Ruth or her sister provided Cord the manuscript with information about their association with Grace Hemingway, including Ruth caring for the remaining children when Grace took one of them to Nantucket; see p. 6. Cord seems to have picked up on the Arnold girls' decidedly mixed feelings about Dr. Hemingway. Elizabeth Arnold had a severe bout of tuberculosis in the 1920s, and Dr. Hemingway declared her case hopeless; the family sent Elizabeth to a sanitarium where she recovered; see p. 7. The document is no longer accessible on the Internet. Elizabeth Burns Cord, in an interview, 7/6/16, indicated that she

believed, as did other family members, that Ruth's relations with Grace Hemingway were platonic.

81 "unhappy and unsympathetic": GHH to CEH, [n.d.; marked "ans. to Aug. 2nd letter from CEH," 1919], HRC.

81 "I began loving": Ruth Arnold to GHH, [Saturday, 26]/1920, HRC, Box 8, Folder 6.

82 "can ever take": GHH to CEH, [n.d.; marked "ans. to Aug. 2nd letter from CEH," 1919], HRC.

82 "inquisitive": Marcelline Hemingway Sanford to GHH, [9/23/1919], HRC, Box 7, Folder 6.

82 "Dad does not": Marcelline Hemingway Sanford to GHH, 9/16/1919, HRC, Box 7, Folder 7.

82 "But Dad always": Marcelline Hemingway Sanford to GHH, 8/30/1919, HRC, Box 7, Folder 7.

82 "But Dad acts": Marcelline Hemingway Sanford to GHH, 8/31/1919, HRC, Box 7, Folder 7.

83 "I want to stand": Ruth Arnold to GHH, [n.d., Thursday, 1919], HRC, Box 8, Folder 6.

83 "but I could never": Ruth Arnold to GHH, 8/30/1919, HRC, Box 8, Folder 6.

83 "do the hauling": EH to CEH, [6/19/1919], *LEH,* vol. 1, 190.

83 "ever since I opposed": EH to Grace Quinlan, 8/8/1920, *LEH,* vol. 1, 238.

84 "By the sound": Ruth Arnold to GHH, [Saturday, 26]/1920, HRC, Box 8, Folder 6.

84 "I suppose Dr.": Ruth Arnold to GHH, 6/19/1920, HRC, Box 8, Folder 6.

84 "In the 1st place": GHH to Miss Marjory Andree and Mrs. Clara Havell, 7/10/1934, HRC, Box 6, Folder 5.

84 Ruth had married: Carol Hemingway Gardner did not know or did not wish to tell her interviewer that Ruth Arnold lived with her mother after Ruth's husband's death. See Morris Buske, ed., "Recollections," *Hemingway Review* 24 (Fall 2004), 29.

85 she did tell Ernest: GHH to EH, 1/23/1932, JFK.

85 "looks like the original": EH to Howell Jenkins, [12/20/1919], *LEH,* vol. 1, 219.

86 "aimed to give": Quoted in Fenton, 78.

86 "Hemingway could write": Quoted in Fenton, 81.

86 Ernest's first piece: *Byline: Ernest Hemingway* (1967; rpt., New York: Bantam, 1970), 3. Hereafter *BEH.*

CHAPTER FIVE

88 "just so someone": GHH to CEH, 7/27/1920, HRC.

89 "you don't like me": EH to Grace Quinlan, 9/30/[1920], *LEH,* vol. 1, 245.

90 Ed Hemingway wrote: Leicester Hemingway, 66.

90 "means of softening": Ibid., 67.

90 "I think Ernest": CEH to GHH, 7/22/1920, HRC, Box 6.

90 the Easter lily: Grace thanked Ernest effusively for an Easter lily sent that spring; see GHH to EH, 4/3/1920, JFK.

90 "Unless you": GHH to EH, 7/27/1920, quoted in Baker, *Ernest Hemingway,* 72.

91 masters of letter writing: Grace much later wrote her son about the talent for letter writing on her side of the family: "You know your mother, like your Abba Hall, always could write a masterly letter, when the occasion demanded it." GHH to EH, 10/2/1929, JFK, Box 60. It is unlikely that Ernest needed a reminder of his mother's skills in this line.

91 "I have written Ernest": CEH to GHH, 7/18/1920, HRC.

91 In all this hullabaloo: In Max Westbrook, "Grace Under Pressure: Hemingway and the Summer of 1920," in Nagel, ed., *Ernest Hemingway: The Writer in Context,* 77–106.

91 "unless we could do": GHH to CEH, 7/27/1920, HRC, Box 6, Folder 8.

92 "They will get into the game": CEH to GHH, 9/1/1920, HRC, Box 6, Folder 3.

92 "said he'd never open": GHH to CEH, 7/28/1920, HRC, Box 6, Folder 8.

92 "For false accusations": CEH to GHH, 9/15/1920, HRC, Box 6, Folder 4.

92 "doing the work": CEH to GHH, 7/28/1920, HRC, Box 6, Folder 8.

93 "That's another story": EH to Grace Quinlan, 8/8/1920, *LEH,* vol. 1, 238.

94 One was in answer: EH to *Chicago Daily Tribune,* [2/12/1920], *LEH,* vol. 1, 255.

94 The other letter: EH to *Chicago Daily Tribune,* 11/29[1920], *LEH,* vol. 1, 250.

94 "Big-hearted Y.K.": Quoted in Fenton, 99.

94 "He was pretty completely": Quoted in Fenton, 99.

95 "avail themselves": Quoted in *LEH,* vol. 1, 257n1.

95 "a cooperative thing": Quoted in Fenton, 98.

95 "his dark hair": Roy Dickey to Charles Fenton, 5/3/1952, JFK, Miscellaneous Accessions, Hem-14, Charles Fenton Correspondence.

95 "We had much fun": Quoted in Fenton, 108.

96 "Bull Gore": See Fenton, 108.

97 "a sort of cornbelt Florence": Fenton, 102.

97 Ernest's and Kenley's friends: See *LEH,* vol. 2, 237n1; see also html://press.uchicago .edu/Misc/Chicago/143783.html.

98 "could sit and listen": Townsend, 173. Fenton notes that while Ernest's roommates teased Anderson about such things as his flamboyant dress, Ernest was always deferential. See Fenton, 103–4.

98 a decidedly strange: EH, "Ultimately," *Ernest Hemingway: Complete Poems,* Nicholas Gerogiannis, ed., 39.

98 Ernest showed Marcelline: *ATH,* 210. Dates are confusing here. Marcelline remembers Ernest showing her the printed poem in the Chicago apartment, but "Ultimately" did not appear in *The Double Dealer* until 1922. On *The Double Dealer,* see http://www.knowla.org/entry.php?rec=662.

98 "fraternity-type horseplay": Fenton, 100.

98 "He was by far": Quoted in ibid.

98 Marcelline remembered: *ATH,* 208.

99 Bill Horne would later: "Young Hemingway: A Panel," *Fitzgerald/Hemingway Annual,* 1972.

99 "a difficult, controlling woman": Richard Usher (Florence's grandson) quoted in Diliberto, 3.

100 "My mother used to tell me": Quoted in Diliberto, 15.

100 "one long orgy": Quoted in Diliberto, viii and 27.

100 "I know that in their way": Quoted in Diliberto, 16.

100 "Being very suggestible": HRH to EH, 6/7/1921, quoted in Diliberto, 24.

101 "starved for people": Sokoloff, HRH/Alice Sokoloff Tapes, tape 11, http://www.thehemingwayproject.com/category/alice-hunt-sokoloff/.

101 "I was ready to go": Allie Baker, "Wasn't I a Knockout?" 4/21/2010, www.thehemingwayproject.com/, HRH/Alice Sokoloff Tapes, tape 3, http://www.thehemingwayproject.com/category/alice-hunt-sokoloff/.

101 "a pair of very red cheeks": Quoted in Diliberto, ix.

101 "You surprised me": Sokoloff, 17.

101 "hulky, bulky, masculine": HRH to EH, 1/23/1921, JFK.

102 "Ernest sort of knocked": HRH/Alice Sokoloff Tapes, tape 9.

102 "What have you been doing": Jim Gamble to EH, 12/27/1920, JFK.

102 "Rather go to Rome": EH to Jim Gamble, [ca. 12/27/1920], *LEH*, vol. 1, 260.

102 "I'm liable to leave": EH to HRH, [12/29/1920], *LEH*, vol. 1, 261.

102 "I would miss you": Quoted in Diliberto, 48.

102 comments she would make: See Brian, 53.

103 "filthy lucre": HRH to EH 3/30/1921, JFK.

103 "laid by the heels": HRH to EH, [8/21/1921], JFK.

103 "Why goodness no": HRH to EH, [7/5/1921], JFK.

103 "I ain't no good": HRH to EH, [n.d., 1921], JFK.

104 "Tremendous amount": HRH to EH, [8/10/1921], JFK.

104 "moments of sitting near you": HRH to EH, 8/6/1921, JFK.

104 Hadley's surviving sister: Fonnie's husband, Roland Usher, did not attend because he disliked Ernest, a development that might have reinforced Hadley's feeling that she was now out of her sister's sphere of influence. On the other hand, the wedding invitation was sent to "Mr. and Mrs. Roland Usher." See "Happy Anniversary, Ernie and Hadley," undated clipping from *The Graphic*, PSU.

104 "You have such": HRH to EH, [8/10/1921], JFK.

104 "gladly be slid": HRH to EH, [8/18/1921], JFK.

105 "I'm wild": HRH to EH, 6/5/1921, JFK.

105 "The world's a jail": HRH to EH, 6/3/1921, JFK.

105 "He trained me": Quoted in Diliberto, 89.

105 "to teach me about love": Quoted in Diliberto, 91.

105 "Well, I was just averse": Quoted in Diliberto, 92.

106 "Sherwood has the tenderest": HRH to EH, 8/23/1921, JFK.

106 "a young fellow": Quoted in Meyers, *Hemingway*, 56.

106 "instinctively in touch": Quoted in Baker, *Ernest Hemingway*, 83.

107 "a magnificent": Anderson, "They Come Bearing Gifts," *American Mercury*, October 1930, 129.

107 "Mr. Hemingway": Townsend, 228.

CHAPTER SIX

108 He was having such: EH to Bill Smith, [12/20/1921], *LEH*, vol. 1, 312.

108 Cuddy was fighting: *LEH*, vol. 1, 311n2.

108 Hadley mentioned: Cited in Diliberto, 97.

109 Ernest reported: EH to Howell Jenkins, 1/8/[1922], *SL*, 61.

111 "a very special point": HRH/Alice Sokoloff Tapes, tape 11.

111 his reading: EH to Jack Hirschman, 1/9/1953, Lilly.

112 Their rent: See Meyers, *Hemingway,* 64.

112 "The scum of Greenwich Village": EH, "American Bohemians in Paris," *BEH,* 21. The story originally appeared in the *Toronto Star Weekly,* 3/25/1922.

114 Before moving to Paris: See Tytell, 74, 167–68, 115–16.

115 "made more enemies": A. H. Orage, *New Age,* quoted in Stock, 235.

115 "resolved that at thirty": Quoted in Tytell, 18.

115 "With the rest of his time": Quoted in Lynn, 164–65.

115 Ernest and Hadley arrived: Joost states that Pound first met Hemingway at Sylvia Beach's Shakespeare and Company, where Pound said that Hemingway's first remark was "I have traveled four thousand miles to meet you." See Joost, *Ernest Hemingway and the Little Magazines,* 9.

115 "a queer duck": Nicholas Joost, *Scofield Thayer and* The Dial, 166.

115 The writer Ford Madox Ford: Moody, 113.

116 "There was a touch": Beach, 26.

116 "HELL": Ezra Pound to EH, 1/25/1927, JFK.

116 "This is a good story": Quoted in Lynn, 167.

116 "a young Chicago poet": Quoted in Gerogiannis, Introduction, *Complete Poems,* xi.

116 As the editor: Gerogiannis, Introduction, *Complete Poems,* xi.

117 Ernest evidently: For an excellent article on Hemingway's poetry, in which she surveys the critical response to it, see Verna Kale, "Hemingway's Poetry and the Paris Apprenticeship," *Hemingway Review* 26 (Spring 2007), 58–73. For Hemingway and Pound, see Jacqueline Tavernier-Curbon, "Ernest Hemingway and Ezra Pound," in Nagel, ed., *Ernest Hemingway: The Writer in Context,* 179–200.

118 "easily hurt": Brian, 52.

118 "He had no humor": Ibid., 43.

118 "five feet high": Quoted in Joost, *Scofield Thayer and* The Dial, 167–68.

118 Hemingway scholar Rose Marie Burwell: Burwell, 164–67.

119 "the most eminent": Thurber, "Excerpts from 'The Book-End,' 1923," in Michael Rosen, ed., *Collecting Himself: James Thurber on Writing and Writers, Humor, and Himself* (New York: HarperCollins, 1989), 32.

119 "the ravings of a lunatic": Quoted in Bridgman, 125.

119 "threw [his] typewriter": Quoted in McAlmon and Boyle, 21.

119 "For me the work": Sherwood Anderson, "Introduction," in Gertrude Stein, *Geography and Plays* (1922; rpt., Madison: University of Wisconsin Press, 1993), 8. Stein showed this to Hemingway at an early meeting; see EH to Sherwood Anderson, 3/9/[1922], *LEH,* vol. 1, 331.

119 "swell stuff": EH to Bill Smith, 2/26/1925, *LEH,* vol. 2, 258.

119 "I always wanted": EH to W. G. Rogers, 7/29/1948, *SL,* 650.

119 While Hemingway repeated: Despite his justified anger at being censored, it is curious why Ernest was reluctant to remove this story from any collection, or to change its language in any way. The sexual act in the story is portrayed in one description ("Jim had her dress up and was trying to do something to her") as well as Liz's protests ("You mustn't do it, Jim"). The most graphic of these is a

protest at the size of Jim's penis: "Oh, it's so big and it hurts so." This particular line was probably why the story was so *inaccrochable* to Stein. It is possible that Ernest did not want to remove this line because, in its comment on the size of Jim's penis, it was flattering to the writer.

120   "Can always tell": EH to Bill Smith, 2/26/1925, *LEH*, vol. 2, 258.

120   "We love Gertrude": EH to Sherwood Anderson, 3/9/[1922], *LEH*, vol. 1, 330.

120   "He is a delightful fellow": Quoted in Reynolds, *Hemingway: The Paris Years*, 36.

120   "You can do anything": Mary Dearborn, *Queen of Bohemia: The Life of Louise Bryant* (Boston: Houghton Mifflin, 1996), 33.

121   "to have the surest future": Kaplan, 264.

121   "He was an extraordinarily": Gertrude Stein, *Autobiography of Alice B. Toklas* (New York: Harcourt, Brace, 1933), 261.

121   "A splendidly built": Quoted in Stock, 312–13.

121   "the most beautiful": Eastman, 37.

121   "Robust, hulking": Shirer, 230.

121   "a priceless person": Quoted in Diliberto, 115.

121   Burton Rascoe said: See Raeburn, 21.

122   "Then suddenly his": Brian, 54.

122   "splendid looking": Arabella Hemingway to GHH and CEH, 8/14/1923, HRC, Box 8, Folder 1.

122   "Bones is called Binney": EH to Sherwood Anderson, 3/9/[1922], *LEH*, vol. 1, 331.

122   "they were prince": Diliberto, 61.

122   He once told his third wife: EH to MG, 7/7/[1943], JFK, Box 48.

123   "this harmless looking": Quoted in Reynolds, *Hemingway: The Paris Years*, 50.

123   Born in 1895: See Lavinia Greacen, *Chink: A Biography* (London: Macmillan, 1989), 55.

124   "Don't go back": EH, "A Veteran Visits the Old Front," in William White, ed., *Dateline Toronto: Hemingway's Complete* Toronto Star *Dispatches, 1920–1924* (New York: Scribner, 1985), 176. The article appeared in the *Star*, 7/22/1922.

126   "In the morning": "Old Constan," *BEH*, 4–48; the article appeared in the *Star*, 10/28/1922.

126   "It is a silent procession": "A Silent, Ghastly Procession," *BEH*, 46; the article appeared in the *Star*, 10/20/1922.

127   "Ernest was the only": Diliberto, 129.

128   "He had whored": "The Snows of Kilimanjaro," *The Compete Short Stories of Ernest Hemingway* (1987; rpt., New York: Scribner, 2003), 48. Hereafter all Hemingway's stories are cited in the text as *CSS*.

128   "As for Mrs. Bullet": EH to AM, 8/29/1927, quoted in Reynolds, *Hemingway: The Homecoming*, 137.

129   Hadley told an early: Sokoloff, *Hadley*, 57.

129   "the newsman's Nietzsche": Mellow, 203.

130   "kiked me so on money": EH to HRH, [11/28/1922], in *LEH*, vol. 1, 372. See 373n2 for EH's salary.

130   which a cable: EH to Frank Mason, [11/27/1922], *LEH*, vol. 1, 371.

130   "SUGGEST YOU UPSTICK": EH to Frank Mason, [ca. 12/15/1922], *LEH*, vol. 1, 378.

130   "Nobody noticed": Steffens, vol. 2, 834–35.

132 "I'm afraid the stuff": Lincoln Steffens to EH, 12/9/1922, JFK.

133 "act of Gawd": Ezra Pound to EH, 1/27/1923, JFK.

CHAPTER SEVEN

134 "You know, Mike": Brian, 41.

134 "was incapable": Quoted in Diliberto, 135.

134 "Whatever happened": Reynolds, *Hemingway: The Paris Years,* 90.

134 Frank Mason would find: Ibid., 93.

134 "Celto-Kike": EH to Ezra Pound, 1/23/[1923] and 1/29/[1923], *LEH,* vol. 2, 5–16.

137 Indeed, Ernest's letters: See, for example, EH to MWH, 5/3/1947, JFK, Box 48, in which he describes erections he gets while writing to her about her hair. The definitive account of his hair fetish is in Carl Eby, *Hemingway's Fetishism.*

137 "It looks a thousand": HRH to EH, [n.d., 1921], JFK.

138 "I am too young": Stein, *Autobiography,* 262.

138 she quoted it to Hadley: Sokoloff, 61.

138 "He felt deeply sorry": HRH/Alice Sokoloff Tapes, tape 12, http://www.thehemingwayproject.com/category/alice-hunt-sokoloff/.

138 "exuberant": Ibid., tape 3.

138 "as long as I promised": Quoted in Diliberto, 145.

138 Mike was a graduate: See "Henry Strater's Ogunquit Museum of American Art," http://www.someoldnews.com/?p=440.

140 "some years ago": Edward J. O'Brien, *The Dance of the Machines: The American Short Story and the Industrial Age* (New York: Macaulay, 1929), 240.

140 "Believe me": Glassco, 53.

141 when he was a young man: Smoller, *Adrift Among Geniuses,* 33.

141 according to her friend: Marianne Moore to John Moore, 2/20/1921, in Moore, 143.

141 "We neither of us": Bryher, 201.

142 "Maintaining that he chose": Smoller, *Nightinghouls,* quoted in Chris Bell, "50-Year Hangover: Remembering Robert McAlmon," www.wordsshiftminds.co.nz/tag/robert-mcalmon/.

142 McAlmon later said: Smoller, *Adrift Among Geniuses,* 36.

142 struck up separate friendships: Bryher was illegitimate; Sir John Ellerman did not marry Hannah Glover until after their daughter was born; a later son was legitimate.

142 "The fact of my being": McAlmon and Boyle, 3.

142 Ellerman knew of: Smoller, *Adrift Among Geniuses,* 89.

143 "the most honest": Ford, 34.

143 "a very charming man": T. S. Eliot to Scofield Thayer, 5/21/1921, in Valerie Eliot, ed., *The Letters of T. S. Eliot, Volume 1: 1898–1922* (London: Faber & Faber, 1928), 454.

143 "absolutely first-rate": Quoted in Ford, 55.

143 "certainly the most popular": Beach, 25.

144 Evidently Ernest sent: CEH to Ezra Pound, [11/1922], and GHH to Ezra Pound, [n.d., 11/1922], Princeton. CEH also thanked Pound "for all you've done to encourage my son."

144   "going places": Glassco, 53. This quotation is often attributed to Malcolm Cowley's *Second Flowering*, but that book was published in 1973, Glassco's *Memoirs of Montparnasse* in 1970. The movie *Limelight* didn't come out until 1952, but McAlmon clearly made his remark contemporaneously, so I have not capitalized "Limelight Kid." The expression is otherwise unknown, and the Chaplin film sheds no light on what it might mean; it seems McAlmon was talking metaphorically about the limelight used in theater.

144   "This was": Quoted in Reynolds, *Hemingway: The Paris Years*, 105.

145   "It's just like having": EH to Bill Horne, 7/17–18/1923, *SL*, 88.

146   McAlmon told the story: McAlmon and Boyle, 178–79.

147   Considerable tension: Almost all of Hemingway's biographers invoke McAlmon's bisexuality in this context, Kenneth Lynn wondering, for instance, whether McAlmon might have annoyed Ernest with his attentions to homosexual men he saw on the streets of the Spanish cities and towns. Lynn, 29.

147   "I was Vicky": Robert McAlmon to Norman Holmes Pearson, 2/28/1952, in Charles Fenton Papers, Yale. Pearson was a leader in the OSS in the Second World War and was instrumental in the formation of the American Studies Department at Yale, which some scholars have suggested was ideology-based. At the same time, they argue, the program was enlisting Yale students abroad in the CIA. See https://journals.ku.edu/index.php/amerstud/article/view File/2679/2638. Evidently Pearson employed H.D.'s daughter Perdita in some suspicious-sounding clerical work. It is not clear why McAlmon felt he could or should confide in Pearson, though he did know of Pearson's connection to Charles Fenton, the preeminent Hemingway scholar of his time, then teaching at Yale.

147   "It was clear": Glassco, 51.

147   "only in snarls": William Bird to Norman Pearson, 1/21/1963, Lilly.

148   "Hem making Bob": McAlmon and Boyle, 351.

148   "When a choice": Ibid., 352.

149   "The less publicity": EH, "Pamplona Letter," *transatlantic review* 2 (September 1924), 300–31; quoted in Raeburn, 18.

149   vignettes: See Lynn, 175–76, 193.

149   "the same gang": EH to Bill Horne, 7/17–18/1923, *LEH*, vol. 2, 37.

150   "Well I might as well say": Quoted in Diliberto, 154.

150   "It couldn't be": EH to Pound, [9/6–8/1923], *LEH*, vol. 2, 45.

150   "So many trips": HRH to CEH and GHH, 9/27/1923, JFK.

150   "sweetness in [Ernest's] smile": Callaghan quoted in Dana Cook, "Meeting Ernest Hemingway: A Miscellany of 50 First Encounters and Initial Impressions," *Hemingway Review* (Spring 1999), 5.

150   "appalled": Callaghan quoted in Fenton, 246.

151   "Ernest came in": HRH to CEH and GHH, [10/18/1923], JFK, Box 9.

151   "quite broke down": HRH to Isabelle Simmons Godolphin, quoted in Diliberto, 159.

151   "a corker": HRH to Isabelle Simmons Godolphin, 10/18/1923, JFK.

151   "because of the round": Quoted in Diliberto, 161.

151   "Feel that I'm": EH to Ezra Pound, 10/13/1923, *LEH*, vol. 2, 59.

152   "I feel like": CEH to EH and HRH, 1/10/1924, JFK.

CHAPTER EIGHT

153 "We have about the nicest place": EH to family, [5/7/1924], *LEH*, vol. 2, 119.

153 There was a small room: Guy Hickok, "Hemingway First Lives Wild Stories, Then Writes Them," undated and unattributed clipping, possibly from the *Brooklyn Eagle*, JFK, Box 61.

153 "like a Rolls Royce": EH to Bill Smith, 12/6/[1924], *LEH*, vol. 2, 186.

153 "She is keeping her piano": EH to Howell Jenkins, 11/9/1924, *LEH*, vol. 2, 177.

153 "People were happy": Quoted in Diliberto, 167.

155 "He had an extraordinary": Dos Passos, *The Best Times*, 162.

155 "Hemingway will be the best known": Bryher, 212.

156 That way, he told Ernest: Edwin Balmer to EH, 2/1/1920, CBP, Box 1.

156 He would later tell: EH to Arnold Gingrich, 8/18/[1934], JFK.

156 his first appearance: See *LEH*, vol. 1, 348n6. Audrey Hanneman notes in her bibliography of EH that this was his first piece published in an American magazine since his high school literary magazine.

157 "leave for London": *transatlantic review* (September 1924), 300.

157 "was a moody": Dos Passos, *The Best Times*, 161. When Dos Passos pointed out that perhaps Ernest was lucky to have missed college, Ernest laughed and agreed that it probably would have been the "ruination" of him.

157 "sphincter muscle": EH to Ezra Pound, 2/10/[1924], *LEH*, vol. 2, 98. On Thayer, see Dempsey, *The Tortured Life of Scofield Thayer*.

157 Hemingway's abuse of Seldes: Mellow, 253.

157 "And yet I want": EH to Edward O'Brien, 5/21/1923, *LEH*, vol. 2, 21.

158 the critic Allen Tate: Quoted in Dana Cook, "Meeting Ernest Hemingway: A Miscellany of 50 First Encounters and Initial Impressions, *Hemingway Review* (Spring 1999), 13.

158 "He's an experienced journalist": Quoted in Joost, *Ernest Hemingway and the Little Magazines*, 71.

158 "Eton-Oxford": Quoted in Meyers, *Hemingway*, 27.

159 often "rewriting": Quoted in Baker, *Ernest Hemingway*, 123.

159 "the long book": Quoted in Bridgman, 59. See Mary Dearborn, "*The Making of Americans* as an Ethnic Text," *Pocahontas's Daughters: Gender and Ethnicity in American Culture* (New York: Oxford University Press, 1986), 159–88.

160 "projects the moments": Quoted in Joost, *Ernest Hemingway and the Little Magazines*, 87.

160 "could get them to publish it": EH to Edmund Wilson 11/25/[1923], *LEH*, vol. 2, 80.

161 "one of the glibbest": Quoted in Lewis M. Dabney, *Edmund Wilson: A Life in Literature* (New York: Farrar, Straus & Giroux, 2005), 120.

161 "very silly": EH to Edmund Wilson, 10/18/1924, *LEH*, vol. 2, 165.

161 "His prose": Edmund Wilson, "Mr. Hemingway's Dry-Points," in *The Shores of Light*, 119–21.

161 As John Raeburn has pointed out: Raeburn, 14.

162 Ernest had let his family know: EH to GHH and CE, 11/4/1923, *LEH*, vol. 2, 66.

162 "grim look": *ATH*, 218–19.

162 "Goddam it": EH to Ezra Pound [5/2/1924], *LEH*, vol. 2, 114.

163 Shipman's first poems: See Robert Risch, "Evan Shipman: Friend and Foil," *Hemingway Review* 23 (Fall 2003), 42–57. After he enjoyed a close relationship with Ernest in the 1920s, Shipman would put distance between himself and Hemingway, and thus would be one of the few friends who would evade Ernest's wrath and escape being summarily dismissed. Ernest was close enough to him in the 1920s that he would dedicate his 1927 story collection to him. Shipman later became an intermittent journalist and horse race expert, and also played an important role with the Loyalists in the Spanish Civil War—all activities that made for common ground between the two men.

163 "You couldn't tell": EH, *The Nick Adams Stories* (1972; rpt., New York: Bantam, 1973), 219.

164 Hadley would later comment: Brian, 49.

164 "Now and then": Dos Passos, *The Best Times,* 160–61.

165 "He was hindered": Loeb, 194.

165 "Oscar Wilde and his lily": Ibid.

165 "overact[ing]": Ibid., 207.

166 "The godamdest": EH to Howell Jenkins, 11/9/1924, *LEH,* vol. 2, 175.

166 "around-the-clock": Stewart, 131.

166 This bit of legend: Baker, *Ernest Hemingway,* 129.

167 "The wildest damn country": EH to Howell Jenkins, 11/9/1924, *LEH,* vol. 2, 175.

167 "the Transatlantic killed": EH to Ezra Pound, 7/19/1924, *LEH,* vol. 2, 155.

167 George Breaker: For details, see Diliberto, 177–78. In 1928 Breaker would be indicted for embezzling $25,000 from his bank. Helen Breaker later came to Paris with her children and made her living as a photographer.

169 "the war, all mention of the war": EH, "The Art of the Short Story," *Paris Review* 23 (Spring 1981), 88.

169 "do the country": EH to Gertrude Stein and Alice B. Toklas, 8/15/[1924], *LEH,* vol. 2, 141.

170 "all that mental conversation": EH to Robert McAlmon, [11/15/1924], *SL,* 133.

CHAPTER NINE

171 manic behavior: A Hemingway scholar has called attention to a dramatic weight gain in 1924 that he suggests corresponded with an up cycle in Ernest's bipolar disease. A photograph taken between February and April 1924 shows a mustachioed Ernest with jowls, wearing a suit that looks two sizes too tight for him. Photographs from December 1923 and January 1925, Hays points out, show a much more healthy-looking Ernest, fit and lean. See Peter L. Hays, "Hemingway's Clinical Depression: A Speculation," *Hemingway Review* (Spring 1995). Hays is less convincing that the periods before and after this 1924 period were episodes of depression.

173 Horace Liveright: See Tom Dardis, *Firebrand: The Life of Horace Liveright* (New York: Random House, 1995), 251.

173 "low kike": Loeb, 227.

173 Don Stewart also: Walker Gilmer, *Horace Liveright: Publisher of the Twenties* (New York: David Lewis, 1970), 120.

174 He sent a new: EH to George Horace Lorimer, 1/21/1925, *LEH,* vol. 2, 221–22. Most of Van Loan's stories, however, were about baseball.

175 "I haven't felt": EH to Bill Smith, 12/6/[1924], *LEH,* vol. 2, 184.

176 "simultaneously kicked": EH to Harold Loeb, 2/27/1925, *LEH,* vol. 2, 260.

176 Isidor Schneider: For Loeb's version, see his "Hemingway's Bitterness" in Sara-son, ed., 118; and his *The Way It Was,* 238.

177 all of Hemingway's biographers: Ruth Hawkins, a recent biographer of Heming-way's second wife, Pauline Pfeiffer Hemingway, does call attention to this epi-sode; Hawkins, 39.

177 "There's a homosexual claque": EH to Bill Smith, 2/14/[1925], *LEH,* vol. 2, 248.

177 At this juncture: See Raeburn, 14.

178 "camp following eunochs": EH to Sherwood Anderson, 5/23/[1925], *LEH,* vol. 2, 339–40.

178 "I saw that old log": CEH to EH, 3/8/1925, JFK, Box 59.

178 "You cant do this": EH to CEH, 3/20/[1925], *LEH,* vol. 2, 286.

179 Kitty Cannell's version: Kitty Cannell, "Scenes with a Hero," in Sarason, ed., 148.

179 "petite with bright black eyes": Ibid., 146.

180 "his knees to his ears": Dos Passos, *The Best Times,* 160.

180 According to MacLeish's biographer: Donaldson, *Archibald MacLeish,* 145.

182 "the first step": Quoted in Bruccoli, *Some Sort of Epic Grandeur,* 221.

182 "really created": Quoted in James Mellow, *Charmed Circle: Gertrude Stein & Company* (New York: Praeger, 1974), 275.

183 "erotic dream": Quoted in Diliberto, 192.

183 "nobody is as male" Donnelly and Billings, 21.

183 "I notice": Milford, 149.

184 Hemingway was so elated: Eastman, 41.

184 didn't see: EH to Horace Liveright, 3/31/1925, *LEH,* vol. 2, 294–96.

184 "care about writing": EH to MP, 4/15/1925, *LEH,* vol. 2, 318.

185 "got all the fun": Dos Passos, *The Best Times,* 163.

185 "a swell Spanish Jew": EH to Dos Passos, 12/22/1925, *LEH,* vol. 2, 323.

185 "It aint a moral": EH to Bill Smith, 2/14/[1925], *LEH,* vol. 1, 249.

186 Because he would marry: The result has been some apocryphal stories that seem patently false—Scott Donaldson has said that in Kansas City (at the age of sev-enteen), Ernest was "known in every whorehouse in town" (*Death of a Rebel,* 74). Ernest loved to brag and he loved to write letters, so the absence of any correspondence to his buddies about going to whorehouses in this period mili-tates against the story. Furthermore, even if Ernest was frequenting such places, it's unlikely that in the six months he was in Kansas City he would visit "every" whorehouse often enough to become "known." Third, he does not seem to have visited whorehouses at any other point in his life (though he did number a cou-ple of whores among his acquaintances, most notably in Cuba), so even allowing for adolescent randiness it's simply not likely that Ernest was "known in every whorehouse in town."

186 hero without a penis: According to his friend A. E. Hotchner, Hemingway clari-fied just what part of Jake Barnes he had intended to have been shot off in the war. "His testicles were intact. That was all he had, but this made him capable of feeling everything a normal man feels but not able to do anything about it." Hotchner, *Papa Hemingway,* 49.

186 his sword on the marital bed: See Kert, 157.

186 "They were very much": Charters, 66–67. Charters said Pat Guthrie died not long after this summer by taking an overdose of sleeping "powder" on a drinking bout, 70.

187 "When she laughed": Kert, 158.

187 "Now for doubtful": Loeb, "Hemingway's Bitterness," in Sarason, ed., 120.

188 "As far as I know": EH to Harold Loeb, 6/21/[1925], *LEH*, vol. 2, 353.

188 "Pat broke the spell": Quoted in Kert, 161.

189 "You mean": Quoted in Kert, 162.

189 "and I wondered": Stewart, 143.

189 "a college reunion": Baker, *Ernest Hemingway*, 150.

189 One set of problems: Don Stewart to Baker, 2/20/51, CBP.

191 "I think it will be": EH to Jane Heap, [8/1925], CBP.

191 "hit like an upper-cut": Loeb, "Hemingway's Bitterness" in Sarason, ed., 126.

192 "Hemingway came to distort": Loeb, "Hemingway's Bitterness," in Sarason, ed., 134.

192 "The mean streak": Donald St. John, ed., "Interview with Donald Ogden Stewart," in Sarason, ed., 199.

CHAPTER TEN

194 "working very hard": Quoted in Diliberto, 201.

195 "I'm putting everyone in it": Quoted in Baker, *Ernest Hemingway*, 154. See also Reynolds, *Hemingway: The Paris Years*, 321, for a different version of this quotation.

195 "In [*A Story-Teller's Story*]": EH to Wyndham Lewis, 10/24/1927, *SL*, 264.

195 "was among the happiest": Townsend, 177.

196 "Ernest Hemingway has a": *NYT*, 10/18/1925.

196 "Ernest Hemingway is somebody": *Time*, 1/18/1926.

196 "Horseshit review": EH to Bill Smith, 12/3/1925, *LEH*, vol. 2, 429.

196 "What a lot of Blah Blah": EH to GHH, 12/14/[1925], *LEH*, vol. 2, 440,

196 Writing to his mother: EH to GHH, 10/19/1925, *LEH*, vol. 2, 403; and EH to GHH and CEH, 10/29/1925, *LEH*, vol. 2, 406.

197 "What have your family": EH to Isabelle Simmons Godolphin, 12/3/1925, *LEH*, vol. 2, 427.

197 "I wonder what": EH to family, [ca. 5/7/1924], *LEH*, vol. 2, 119.

197 "with interest": CEH to EH, 12/2/1925 and 12/9/1925, JFK, Box 59.

197 "I know what I'm doing": EH to CEH, 12/15/1925, *LEH*, vol. 2, 443–44.

197 "Hadley is better looking": EH to GHH, 9/11/1925, *LEH*, vol. 2, 389.

197 The following May: EH to CEH, 5/23/1926, *SL*, 207.

197 "A1 drinking": EH to Bill Smith, 12/3/1925, *LEH*, vol. 2, 429.

199 "There once was a prince": Stewart, 117.

199 "Living well": Calvin Tompkins, *Living Well Is the Best Revenge* (New York: Viking, 1971).

200 "I had never had": Dos Passos, *The Best Times*, 165.

200 "There *really* was": Gerald Murphy to the Fitzgeralds, 9/19/1925, Linda Miller, ed., 13.

200 when four-year-old Scottie: Turnbull, *Scott Fitzgerald*, 162.

200 "He was such an enveloping": Quoted in Vaill, *Everyone Was So Young*, 168.

201 "Sara and Gerald": Milford, 152–53.

201 "a nice, plain girl": Quoted in Vaill, *Everyone Was So Young*, 169.

201 "Conversation in the early twenties": Dos Passos, *The Best Times*, 157.

202 told a correspondent in 1953: EH to Charles Moore, 1/23/1953, American Heritage Center, University of Wyoming.

202 "He'd read it and we talked about it," EH to Sherwood Anderson, 5/6/1926, *SL*, 205.

202 "funny stuff": Quoted in Diliberto, 203.

202 "Was he deliberately writing": Dos Passos, *The Best Times*, 176–77.

203 "because I am something of a ballyhoo": FSF to Horace Liveright and T. R. Smith, [n.d., "Before 20 December 1925"], Bruccoli and Duggan, eds., *Correspondence of F. Scott Fitzgerald*, 183.

203 "You do not want it": EH to Horace Liveright, 12/7/1925, *LEH*, vol. 2, 435.

203 "You see I feel": EH to Sherwood Anderson, 5/21/1926, *SL*, 205.

203 "I thought [Anderson]": EH, "The Art of the Short Story." *Paris Review* 23 (Spring 1981), 100–101.

204 "a model of firmness": Horace Liveright to EH, 12/30/1925, quoted in Dardis, 259.

204 "REJECTING TORRENTS": Quoted in Dardis, 260.

204 "So I'm loose": EH to FSF, 12/31/1925–1/1/1926, *LEH*, vol. 2, 459.

205 As might be expected: See Hawkins, 17.

206 "Elevated Eyebrow": Hawkins, 26.

207 "wittiest person": Thomas Travisano, "Hemingway, Bishop and Key West: Two Writers' Perspectives," 6/15/2011, http://www.berfrois.com/2011/06/bishop-hemingway-connection-thomas-travisano/.

207 "Hadley was a likable": Eastman, 40.

207 "very sociable": Quoted in Gary Fountain and Peter Brazeau, eds., *Remembering Elizabeth Bishop* (Amherst: University of Massachusetts Press, 1994), 78.

207 "[Hadley] was nice": Eric (Chink) Dorman-O'Gowan to Baker, 11/13/1961, CBP.

208 "perhaps not coincidentally": Hawkins, 47.

208 "the adulation": Quoted in Diliberto, 195.

209 "Have an idea": EH to Isabelle Simmons Godolphin, 12/3/1925, *LEH*, vol. 2, 426–27.

209 calling himself Drum: Hawkins, 46.

209 "My dears": PPH to HRH, 1/21/1926, JFK.

210 "We wooda had": PPH to HRH, [1/12/1926], JFK.

210 "YOU CAN GET": FSF to MP, 1/8/1926, Bruccoli and Duggan, eds., *Correspondence of F. Scott Fitzgerald*, 187.

210 "PUBLISH NOVEL": These quotations and the details of these negotiations are from Donaldson, *Hemingway vs. Fitzgerald*, 74–75.

211 "temperamental in business": Donaldson, *Hemingway vs. Fitzgerald*, 77, FSF's emphasis.

212 "to [his] horror": FSF to MP, 12/30/1925, Turnbull, ed., *Letters of F. Scott Fitzgerald*, 217.

212 "too terrible": Quoted in Baker, *Ernest Hemingway*, 171.

CHAPTER ELEVEN

213 Gerald was elated: See Vaill, *Everyone Was So Young*, 172. Gerald remembered in a later interview that Hemingway used the phrase "grace under pressure" on this occasion. He may have misremembered, but in fact his is a good claim for the first appearance of the famous phrase; Hemingway used it in print for the first time a month later, in an April 10, 1926, letter to Fitzgerald (see *SL*, 200).

213 "We were all like": Dos Passos, *The Best Times*, 177–78.

214 On the trip: Diliberto, 216.

216 "[*Torrents*] is a joke": EH to Sherwood Anderson, 5/21/1926, *SL*, 205–6.

216 "possibly the most": Quoted in Baker, *Ernest Hemingway*, 171.

216 "'In Our Time' proved": Allen Tate, *Nation*, 7/28/1926.

216 "He is better": Harry Hansen, *New York World*, 5/30/1926.

217 Scott began the letter: FSF to EH, 6/1926, *Correspondence of F. Scott Fitzgerald*, 193–95, FSF's emphases.

217 "TO MY SON": EH to FSF, 4/20/1926, *SL*, 199.

218 "This is a novel": Quoted in Donaldson, *Hemingway vs. Fitzgerald*, 93.

219 "There is nothing": EH to MP, 6/5/1926, *SL*, 208.

220 "Did not realize": FSF to EH, [12/23/1926], Turnbull, ed., *Letters of F. Scott Fitzgerald*, 324–25.

221 "It would be a swell joke": HRH to EH, [5/21/1926], JFK, Box 69.

221 Pauline answered: PPH to EH, 5/20/1926, JFK.

222 "I work for the common good": HRH to EH, 5/24/1926, JFK.

222 "I had a terrible time": Quoted in Diliberto, 221.

222 "privately critical": Donnelly and Billings, 25.

222 "Here it was": Kert, 180–81.

222 "I came back": Quoted in Hawkins, 54.

223 "sexually spontaneous": Griffin, *Less Than a Treason*, 142–44. It is not clear where Griffin, who has since died, got his information. Diliberto, Hadley Hemingway's biographer, writes, 224, that Pauline one morning climbed into bed with Ernest and Hadley when Marie Cocotte brought their breakfast in, sharing their meal; she does not specify her source, which may have been Griffin's unsourced account.

223 But a letter: See PPH to EH, 9/24/1926, JFK. Pauline says that Ernest can even tell Hadley that they had slept together if it would help Hadley to understand.

223 "I never saw": Donaldson, *Archibald MacLeish*, 161.

224 writing to "Hadern": Gerald Murphy to HRH and EH [7/14/1926], Linda Miller, ed., 9.

224 "I'm going to get": PPH to EH, 7/1/1926, JFK.

225 as Scott noted: FSF to Ludlow Fowler, [Summer 1926], Bruccoli and Duggan, eds., *Correspondence of F. Scott Fitzgerald*, 200.

225 "The summer passed": Zelda Fitzgerald to FSF, [late summer 1930], Bruccoli and Duggan, eds., *Correspondence of F. Scott Fitzgerald*, 247. Zelda was writing a summary of her life with Scott, partly for therapeutic purposes. Scott would use this letter in composition of *Tender Is the Night* (1934), which drew in part on the story of his own marriage.

225 "We said to each other": Gerald and Sara Murphy to EH, [ca. fall 1926], Linda Miller, ed., 23–24.

225 "Hadley's tempo": Gerald Murphy to EH, [7/14/1926], Linda Miller, ed., 21–23.

226 "By writing you everything": PPH to EH, 9/24/1926, JFK.

227 "that it would be very natural": HRH to PPH, [n.d., 1926], JFK.

227 Ernest was "always": Diliberto, 236.

227 "I'm really just fold[ing]": PPH to EH, [10/17/1926], Box 61, JFK.

227 "Darling, you are very swell": All fall 1926 letters from PPH to EH are at JFK, Box 61, Series 3.

229 "I told him to relax": Drabeck and Ellis, eds., 29.

230 "If at the end": PPH to EH, [11]/2/1917. Hawkins points out that PPH's date on this letter, October 2, is incorrect, 288n29.

230 "You see when you went": EH to PPH, 11/12/1926 (the letter is misdated October 12), SL, 220–23. See 223n1 for the dating.

231 "I am *not* responsible": HRH to EH, 11/16/1926, JFK, HRH's emphasis.

231 "[You] are the best": EH to HRH, 11/18/1926, SL, 226–28.

231 immediately sent a telegram: Virginia Pfeiffer to EH, [n.d., 11/17?/1926], JFK.

231 "We are so lucky": PPH to EH, 11/23/1926, JFK.

231 "SUGGEST YOU SAIL": Quoted in Kert, 195.

231 "I love you so": EH to PPH, 12/3/1926, SL, 234–35.

CHAPTER TWELVE

233 "hat-in-the-air reviews": Cowley, A Second Flowering, 71.

233 "a most extraordinary perfume": MP to EH, 5/18/1926, Bruccoli, ed., The Only Thing That Counts, 38.

233 "a truly gripping story": New York Times Book Review, 10/31/1926.

233 "The dialogue is brilliant": New York Herald Tribune Books, 10/31/1926.

233 "Every sentence": New York Sun, 11/6/1926.

233 "as shallow as": Dial, 82 (1/1927).

233 "The Sun Also Rises is the kind of book": Chicago Daily Tribune, 11/27/1926.

233 "pretty interesting": EH to MP, [11/16/1926], Bruccoli, ed., The Only Thing That Counts, 50.

234 "best novel by one of my generation": EH told MP he saw the letter Wilson wrote to Bishop saying this. EH to MP, 12/21/1926, Bruccoli, ed., The Only Thing That Counts, 55. I could find no such letter.

234 "I imagine now": EH to MP, 12/21/1926, Bruccoli, ed., The Only Thing That Counts, 56.

234 "It's funny to write a book": EH to MP, [11/16/1926], Bruccoli, ed., The Only Thing That Counts, 50.

234 "as hollowed out": EH to MP, 12/7/1926, Bruccoli, ed., The Only Thing That Counts, 54–5.

234 The point of the book: EH to MP, 11/19/1926, Bruccoli, ed., The Only Thing That Counts, 51.

235 "hundreds of bright young men": Cowley, Exile's Return, 225.

235 "There was a time": Dorothy Parker, New Yorker, 10/29/1927, 92.

235 The critic Richmond Barrett: Quoted in Raeburn, 22.

235 "There is a story around": EH to FSF, 3/31/1927, *SL*, 249.

236 "I'm really tougher": Quoted in Kert, 196.

236 "The only thing was": EH to FSF, 10/15/1927, *SL*, 262.

236 According to Catholic procedure: E-mail, Mark Milburn to author, 1/15/2013.

236 "Italian tour": PPH to EH, 3/15/1927, JFK.

236 Meanwhile, Pauline found them: See Reynolds, *Hemingway: The Homecoming*, 113.

237 Ernest later claimed: EH to MP, [August 1929], Bruccoli, ed., *The Only Thing That Counts*, 115.

237 they did not attend the ceremony: Baker, *Ernest Hemingway*, 185.

237 "To see this farce": Quoted in Donaldson, *Archibald MacLeish*, 164. Ada's statement would seem to be at odds with the MacLeishes hosting the wedding breakfast.

237 "It certainly is an immense relief": Sara Murphy to PPH, 6/17/1927, CBP.

237 "Best to 'P the Pifer' ": Gerald Murphy to EH, 3/1927, quoted in Donnelly and Billings, 166.

238 when Don Stewart: See Stewart, 135.

239 "I should think I do": GHH to EH, 10/14/1927, JFK. Almost at the same moment, the expatriate newspaper *The Boulevardier* published a nasty satiric piece Ernest wrote about Spaniards in which his target was Bromfield. See Reynolds, *Hemingway: The Homecoming*, 138–40, 148.

239 "Mother was so pleased": CEH to EH, 1/27/1927, JFK.

240 "We have heard": GHH to EH, 12/4/1926, JFK.

240 "so I can deny": CEH to EH, 12/13/1926, JFK, Box 59.

240 "I am sure": CEH to EH, 12/18/1926, JFK, Box 59.

240 "on the rocks": GHH to EH, 2/20/1927, JFK, Box 59.

240 "Too bad!": CEH to EH, 3/6/1927, JFK, Box 59.

241 "in a comfortable": EH to family, 12/1/1926, *SL*, 233.

241 "Hadley and I have not": EH to GHH, 2/5/1927, *SL*, 243.

241 "I hope you may": CEH to EH, 8/8/1927, JFK, Box 59.

242 "I will never stop loving": EH to CEH, 9/14/1927, *SL*, 257–60.

242 "very depressed": GHH to EH, 12/14/1926, JFK.

242 the *Miami Herald*: See http://floridahistory.org/landboom.htm.

242 one letter refers: See GHH to EH, 3/24/1929, JFK.

243 "terse style": GHH to EH, 12/4/1926, JFK.

243 " 'technique' was wonderful": CEH to EH, 12/31/1926, JFK, Box 59.

243 "even a less important": GHH to EH, 10/14/1927, HRC.

244 "I *know* that I am not": EH to CEH, 9/14/1927, *SL*, 257–60, EH's emphasis.

244 That book had sold: Trogdon, *The Lousy Racket*, 49.

244 Perkins wanted to lead: Ibid., 57.

245 "promises [were] worthless": MP to EH, 10/14/1927, Bruccoli, ed., *The Only Thing That Counts*, 66.

245 "the softening feminine influence is absent": Virginia Woolf, *New York Herald Tribune*, 10/9/1927, quoted in Trogdon, ed., *Ernest Hemingway: A Literary Reference*, 80–87.

245 "The deliberate twisting": EH to MP, 11/1/1927, *SL*, 265.

245 "In his hands": *Nation*, 11/16/1927.

246 "Simple Annals": *Saturday Review of Literature*, 11/19/1927.

246 "With Mr. Hemingway": Quoted in Jeremy Lewis, *Cyril Connolly: A Life* (1998; rpt., New York: Random House, 2012), 179–80.

246 "drama almost always": Wilson, "The Sportsman's Tragedy," *The Shores of Light*, 341.

247 She observed what was happening: Dorothy Parker, *New Yorker*, 10/29/1927.

247 "I was touched": Dorothy Parker to EH, 11/3/1926, JFK.

248 "I don't like the Dotty poem": PPH to EH, 12/3/1926, JFK.

CHAPTER THIRTEEN

249 Jimmy Crane: Manuscript is Item 529b, JFK.

249 Hemingway had abandoned it: See Reynolds, *Hemingway: The Homecoming*, 148–54. Reynolds sees traces of Jimmy's father, the revolutionist, in Robert Jordan in *For Whom the Bell Tolls* and Thomas Hudson in the posthumous *Islands in the Stream*, 249n41.

250 which Ernest said was his remaining good eye: Though Ernest had poor eyesight and needed eyeglasses (which he seldom wore), there is no evidence that he had a bad eye.

251 "Hemingway was intrigued": Burwell, 108.

251 He told Archie MacLeish: EH to AM, 5/31/[1936], LoC.

251 "christ offal": EH to MP, 5/31/1928, *SL*, 278.

251 The Pfeiffers were rich: See Hawkins, 13.

252 "something seen in a dream": Quoted in McLendon, 20.

252 They sailed for Havana: In previous biographical accounts, the *Orita* was said to be a Royal Mail Steam Packet, but the Royal Mail did not have a vessel by that name. The U.K.'s Pacific Steam Navigation Company, called the Pacific Line, did have a vessel by that name that sailed from La Rochelle–Pallice to Havana. See http://www.theshipslist.com/ships/lines/royalmail.shtml and http://www.timetableimages.com/maritime/images/psn.htm.

252 "had a faintly": Dos Passos, *The Best Times*, 219–20.

253 "the only one": Ibid., 221.

254 Ernest sent a telegram: EH to CEH, 4/10/1928, PSU, Box 3, Folder 4. This telegram surfaced fairly recently; it has been assumed that Ernest ran into his parents on the Key West docks—an unlikely coincidence indeed.

254 "last evening": CEH to EH, 4/11/1928, JFK.

254 "I surely need a vacation": CEH to GHH, HRC, Box 6, Folder 3.

255 "My father changed": *ATH*, 228–32.

256 Ed brought up: See CEH to EH, 9/10/1928 and 9/20/1928, JFK.

256 "like a dream": CEH to EH, 4/11/1928, JFK.

257 "If you want me to attend": Quoted in Leicester Hemingway, 107–8.

258 "I wrote to Dad": EH to CEH and GHH, 7/4/1928, quoted in Leicester Hemingway, 290.

258 "and I've taken to": PPH to EH, 5/20/1928, JFK.

259 "hie away to the woods": Quoted in Hawkins, 95.

259 "The doctor said": Quoted in Hawkins, 95.

259 he compared the operation: Josephine Merck, "Stray Comments on Ernest Hemingway," JFK, Miscellaneous Accessions, Box 2.

259 "like a picador's horse": EH to Guy Hickok, [ca. 7/27/1928], *SL*, 280.

260 "This bull market": EH to MP, 5/31/1928, *SL*, 278.

260 "the last thing I want": EH to MP, 9/28/1928, *SL*, 286.

261 "the best story I've read in a hell of a time": EH to MP, 2/12/1928, *SL*, 272.

261 "Were I thirty": Quoted in *SL*, 255n2.

261 "that was so much": EH to Barklie McKee Henry, 8/15/1927, *SL*, 254–55, 255n2.

262 Then Wister and Ernest drove: See Darwin Payne, *Owen Wister: Chronicler of the West, Gentleman of the East* (Dallas: Southern Methodist University Press, 1985), 320; and Reynolds, *Hemingway: The Homecoming*, 94.

262 "a sweet old guy": EH to Waldo Peirce, 8/9/1928, *SL*, 282.

262 "young phoenix": Owen Wister to MP, quoted in Alan Price, " 'I'm Not an Old Fogey and You're Not a Young Ass': Owen Wister and Ernest Hemingway," *Hemingway Review* 9 (Fall 1989), 84.

262 "With you away": PPH to EH, 7/31/1928, JFK.

263 "Mother Hemingway": PPH to GHH, [12/6/1928], PSU, Box 1, Folder 63.

263 "the precious paintings": CEH to GHH, 1/16/1928, HRC, Box 6, Folder 3.

263 "Keep up the good work": CEH to GHH, 1/30/1928, HRC, Box 6, Folder 3.

263 "Let it all blow over": CEH to GHH, 1/30/1928, HRC, Box 6, Folder 3 (second of two letters written that day).

263 "claim for fame": "Exhibit of Note," *Oak Leaves*, 9/21/1928.

264 "these young writers": Bertha Fenberg, "Launches New Career After Raising Family," *Chicago Daily News*, 11/8/1927.

264 "frantic with worry": *ATH*, 130.

264 "I can't seem to think of a way": CEH to EH, 10/23/1928, JFK.

265 Mimi especially adored Ernest: See Donaldson, *Archibald MacLeish*, 163, 186.

265 "She ran to him": AM, *New and Collected Poems*, 23.

265 "made a shall we say nuisance": EH to FSF and Zelda Fitzgerald, 11/18/1928, *SL*, 290.

266 "FATHER DIED": Quoted in Reynolds, *Hemingway: The Homecoming*, 207.

266 "frantic worrying": *ATH*, 233.

267 "Dr. Hemingway was not": GHH to N. L. Bedford [n.d., 1933], HRC, Box 9, Folder 2.

267 Ed Hemingway went upstairs: Donald Junkins, "Conversations with Carol Hemingway Gardner at Ninety," *North Dakota Quarterly* 70 (Fall 2003).

268 "Praying him out of purgatory": Marcelline Hemingway to GHH, 4/4/1939, HRC, Box 7, Folder 7.

268 Ernest had told him to pray: Leicester Hemingway, 111.

269 "Never worry": EH to GHH, 3/11/1929, *SL*, 395.

270 "in desperation": Leicester Hemingway, 110–11.

270 Ernest seems to have saved: Reynolds, *Hemingway: The Homecoming*, 211. Reynolds's account of Ed Hemingway's death and the events surrounding it is by far the most thorough and thoughtful one we have.

270 he once again said: EH to Mary Pfeiffer, 12/13/[1928], Patrick Hemingway Papers, Princeton.

CHAPTER FOURTEEN

271 The house on South Street: Madelaine Hemingway Miller, *Ernie*, 112.

271 "I would give anything": See Berg, 139.

271 "I had one of the best": Quoted in Price, 85.

272 "It's a most beautiful book": MP to EH, 2/9/1929, Bruccoli, ed., *The Only Thing That Counts*, 86.

273 "blessed loyal children": GHH to EH, 2/2/1929, HRC.

273 "$25,000 insurance": EH to MP, 12/16/1928, *SL*, 292. But see GHH to EH, 2/24/1929, JFK, in which she gives $21,000 as the payment from "insurance."

273 "You will never know": GHH to EH, 2/24/1929, HRC.

273 He assured Grace: EH to GHH, [3/7/1929], PSU.

273 "Old Long John": GHH to EH, 2/24/1929, HRC.

274 "He was the best host": Quoted in Reynolds, *Hemingway: The 1930s*, 40.

274 "Dos Passos is the only": EH to HRH, 1/11/[?], JFK.

275 "He seems to me": "Rare Letter Shows Ernest Hemingway Championing Toronto's Morley Callaghan," thestar.com, 5/4/12; http://www.thestar.com/news /gta/2012/05/04/rare_letter_shows_ernest_hemingway_generously_champion ing_torontos_morley_callaghan.html.

275 "He did something": Callaghan, 121–23.

276 "If Ernest and I": Ibid., 211–13.

276 "He had been made": Ibid., 240.

276 "HAVE SEEN STORY": Ibid., 242.

277 "He sounded more like": Ibid., 249.

277 "When will you save me": FSF to EH, 12/28/1928; Bruccoli, *F. Scott Fitzgerald: A Life in Letters.* Hereafter *FSF: ALL*.

278 "delighted": FSF to MP, [ca. 3/1/1929], *FSF: ALL*, 161.

278 "pee-ed": EH to MP, 4/3/[1929], Bruccoli, ed., *The Only Thing That Counts*, 97.

278 "It is only fair": FSF to EH [11/30/1925], *FSF: ALL*, 130.

279 Ruth Goldbeck: See William Seabrook, "Sad Plight of the Cinderella Countess," *Milwaukee Sentinel*, 12/10/1941, http://news.google.com/newspapers?n id=1368&dat=19441209&id=HkJQAAAAIBAJ&sjid=BgoEAAAAIBAJ&pg =6270,5856119.

279 Scott thought: See FSF to EH, 9/9/1929, *FSF: ALL*, 168; and EH to FSF, 9/4/1929, *SL*, 304.

279 "[That spring] Ernest and I met": FSF to Zelda Fitzgerald, [Summer? 1930], *FSF: ALL*, 188.

279 "the great spots": Berg, 325.

280 "Not since": Quoted in Reynolds, *Hemingway: The Homecoming*, 193.

281 "Kiss my ass": FSF to EH, 6/1929, *FSF: ALL*, 164.

282 Ernest's alternate endings: See Seán Hemingway, ed., *A Farewell to Arms: The Hemingway Library Edition* (New York: Scribner, 2012).

283 "popular": Quoted in Hawkins, 107.

283 the two spent several days: See Franklin, 170–81. See also Paul, 72–74.

284 In 1933, when Franklin needed surgery: Paul, 95.

284 Immediately, he was writing: EH to AM, 12/1/1929, LoC.

284 "Maybe it is punk": EH to MP, [8/1929], Bruccoli, ed., *The Only Thing That Counts,* 114.

284 Ernest later claimed: See EH, "The Author's 1948 Introduction" in *A Farewell to Arms: The Hemingway Library Edition,* Seán Hemingway, ed., vii, ix. Hemingway makes the claim twice in his essay.

284 "It is beautiful": AM to EH, 9/1/[1929], in Winnick, ed., 230.

284 "I should need": Bishop and Dos Passos quoted in Mellow, 391.

284 "FIRST REVIEWS SPLENDID": Quoted in Baker, *Ernest Hemingway,* 204.

284 "a moving and beautiful book": *New York Times,* 9/29/1929.

284 "The writings of": *New Republic,* 10/9/1929.

285 "In its sustained": *Time,* 10/14/1929.

285 "a wider and deeper range": *Atlantic Monthly,* 11/1929.

285 "Mr. Ernest Hemingway": London *Times,* 11/15/1929.

285 "the most interesting novel": *Chicago Tribune,* 9/28/1929.

285 "Bourdon gauge": Edmund Wilson, "Hemingway: Gauge of Morale," 409.

285 "draw[ing] slowly: *New York Herald Tribune Books,* 10/6/1929.

286 "for the first time": *Bookwise* (November 1929).

286 by the end of October: MP to FSF, 10/30/1929, 157.

286 By Christmas: MP to FSF, 12/17/1929, Kuehl and Bryer, eds., 160.

286 "The danger now": MP to EH, 11/12/1929, Bruccoli, ed., *The Only Thing That Counts,* 122.

286 Stein said that during that talk: Stein, *Autobiography,* 270.

287 "She claims you": EH to FSF, 10/22/1929, *SL,* 308. Reynolds, in *Hemingway: The 1930s,* fixes the date definitively as October 22; previous accounts put it at the 22nd or the 29th. See 321n78.

287 "really created for the public": Stein, *Autobiography,* 268.

288 "She thinks the parts that fail": EH to FSF, [10/24 or 31/1929], *SL,* 309–10.

288 "a son of a bitch": EH to FSF, [ca. 12/24/1925], *LEH,* vol. 2, 455.

288 "unjustly treated": EH to MP, 10/3/[1929], Bruccoli, ed., *The Only Thing That Counts,* 119.

289 "mean things about Ernest": MP to FSF, 10/30/1929, Kuehl and Bryer, eds., 157–58.

289 "fairies": FSF to MP, [11/15/1929], Kuehl and Bryer, eds., 158–59.

289 "the soul of honor": EH to MP, 12/7/[1929] and 12/19/[1929], Bruccoli, ed., *The Only Thing That Counts,* 132–33.

289 Zelda apparently believed: FSF to Zelda Fitzgerald, [Summer]/1930, *FSF: ALL,* 189.

289 "I really loved him": FSF, *Notebooks,* #62, quoted in Bruccoli, *Some Sort of Epic Grandeur,* 289.

290 "I only wish to God": EH to FSF, 12/12/1929, *SL,* 312–14.

290 "[Scott] began to tell me": Callaghan, 206.

290 "had some need of": Ibid., 164.

CHAPTER FIFTEEN

291 "justice demanded": EH to GHH, 1/27/[1930], PSU, Box 1, Folder 72.

292 "It is beside the point": EH to GHH, 2/19/1930, PSU, Box 1, Folder 23, quoted in

http://news.psu.edu/story/190092/2008/03/06/letters-reveal-hemingways-lesser -known-facets.

292 "won't be corrupted": EH to Carol Hemingway, [10/1929], CBP.

293 "He's the one": Quoted in Brian, 81.

293 "What's simple in Paris": EH quoted in Reynolds, *Hemingway: The 1930s*, 39.

294 on this trip Ernest: See McLendon, 58.

294 "You won't have to spend": Quoted in Donaldson, *Archibald MacLeish*, 200.

295 "We'll go and purify": EH to AM, [Summer 1930], LoC.

295 "I like to shoot": EH to Janet Flanner, 4/8/1933, *SL*, 387.

295 The L-Bar-T: See Koch, 40.

295 "one of the choice": Eugene V. Moran, "Wild, Wild West: Ernest Hemingway in the Sunlight Basin of Wyoming," *Annals of Wyoming*, 77.

295 "a lovely, unharried wife": PPH to EH, [2/14/1932], JFK, PPH's emphasis.

295 "a real good sport": Quoted in Baker, *Ernest Hemingway*, 212.

295 "valued her literary judgment": Kert, 341–42.

296 "the sense of topography": Dos Passos, *The Best Times*, 226.

296 "an oblique spiral fracture": Baker, *Ernest Hemingway*, 217.

297 "He wasn't a very good invalid": Brian, 83.

297 "the most hair-raising": Quoted in Mellow, 403.

297 Ernest had a standing order: See statement by Cranston D. Raymond attesting to his actions on Hemingway's behalf, 7/4/1961, Hemingway Collection, Stanford, Box 3, Folder 23.

298 A "Talk of the Town" piece: "The Other Hemingways," *New Yorker*, 1/4/1930, 14. See Baker, *Ernest Hemingway*, 567, for the full names of the children. Marcelline, Sunny, and Carol did not have middle names.

298 He reported to Archie MacLeish: EH to AM, 3/14/[1931], LoC.

298 "May never be a gt. writer": EH to AM, 3/14/1931, *SL*, 338.

299 Shipman was an easy guest: EH to AM, [Spring 1931], LoC.

299 "splendidly": EH to Paul and Mary Pfeiffer, 1/28/[1931], Patrick Hemingway Papers, Princeton.

299 When Max Perkins showed up: Langer, 111–12.

299 "Look, the hero": Ibid., 111.

300 "the Lord Mayor": Ibid., 110.

300 "As long as people": Brian, 59.

300 It could be worse: Franklin, 170.

300 "fish knife": Carlos Baker, "Chub Weaver's Trip to Key West—Late December 1930–end of March, 1931," [n.d.], 2, CBP.

300 He often went: Ibid., 38–39.

300 He also carried a comb: Fuentes, 67.

301 "I am strong": EH to AM, 3/14/1931, *SL*, 338.

302 Sidney Franklin remembered Bumby: Franklin, 205.

302 "The boy had to repeat it": Crosby, 293.

302 But Ernest painted: EH to AM, [7/28/1931; LoC dates it 1932], LoC.

303 "some market": EH to MP, 8/1/1931, Scribner's Archive, Princeton, quoted in Reynolds, *Hemingway: The 1930s*, 72.

303 "Most bull displays lousy": EH to John Dos Passos, 6/26/1931, *SL*, 341–42.

304 The photographs are an essential part: The mystery is where these photographs came from; the photographer, or photographers, was highly skilled at close camera work in a very dangerous setting. Did Hemingway (or Gus Pfeiffer?) assemble these photographs without knowing the photographer(s), and if so, how? If he found the photographer(s) and had the photos taken, other questions arise.

305 "A Natural History of the Dead": Crosby did not end up publishing this piece.

305 "going Whitney": Stewart, 171.

306 "tall blonde, lovely": Quoted in Alane Salierno Mason, "A Comedy with Animals," *Boston Review* (February/March 2001). Interview with Alane Mason, 5/16/2013. See also her article, "To Love and Love Not," in *Vanity Fair* (July 1999). The *Boston Review* article is an expanded essay that reflects the author's discovery of her grandmother's draft of "Mr. and Mrs. Macomber," the other Hemingway fiction in which a character based on Jane Mason appeared. See also *Hemingway Review* 21 (Spring 2002), a special issue with Jane Mason's *Safari*, especially Bernice Kert, "Jane Mason and EH: A Biographer Reveals Her Notes."

306 wrote confidently to Archie: EH to AM, 12/9/[1931], LoC.

CHAPTER SIXTEEN

307 Ernest wrote his mother: Kert, 236–37.

307 "would cause her uterus": Gregory Hemingway, 17.

308 "Hemingway is one": MP to Marjorie Kinnan Rawlings, 6/10/1933, in Tarr, ed., 116n1.

308 "hellishly good": Quoted in Baker, *Ernest Hemingway*, 226.

309 "in some way a criticism": AM to EH, [4/7/1932], in Winnick, ed., 247.

309 "just practical": EH to AM, [April 1932], LoC.

309 "when Ernest seems insensitive": AM to Baker, 8/9/1963, CBP, Box 7, Folder 21.

310 "crushes" on new people: Donaldson, *Archibald MacLeish*, 162.

310 "temperament": AM to Baker, 8/9/1963, CBP, Box 7, Folder 21.

310 Ernest was quick: EH to AM, [April 1932], LoC.

310 "good, non-righteous": EH to AM, [May 1943], LoC, quoted in Meyers, *Hemingway*, 282.

311 "I suppose I have known it": AM to EH, [4/7/1932], in Winnick, ed., 247.

312 "became another kid brother": Kert, "Jane Mason and Ernest Hemingway: A Biographer Reviews Her Notes," *Hemingway Review* 21 (Spring 2002), 112.

313 "Pauline, you are the peak": Ibid.

313 That summer, when Jane: Jane Mason to EH, [n.d.; Summer 1932], JFK, Jane Mason Personal Papers, Box 1.

313 "Well Pauline is cock-eyed beautiful": EH to Guy Hickok, 10/14/1932, *SL*, 372.

313 there had been four cases: PPH to Don Carlos Guffey, [5/26/1932], JFK. The letter is dated "1931?" but on May 26, 1931, the Hemingways had left for Spain.

314 "a mean woman": See Reynolds, *Hemingway: The 1930s*, 189.

314 "great gal": Carol Hemingway to Jane Mason, [7/1932], JFK, Jane Mason Personal Papers, Box 1.

315 "like pink coral": Donnelly and Billings, 67–68.

315 "tasteless": Gerald Murphy to AM, 9/8/1932, Linda Miller, ed., 63–65.

316 "excellent reading": *Saturday Review of Literature*, 9/24/1932.

316 "It is a book": *New York Herald Tribune Books*, 9/25/1932.

316 "expresses some pretty": *New Yorker,* 10/1/1932.

316 10,300 copies: Leff, 160.

316 These "little pricks": EH to AM, 10/29/1932, LoC.

317 the film version of *A Farewell to Arms:* Paramount issued the film with a happy ending for the U.S. audience and released the film with an ending faithful to the book in Europe. However, the version that occasionally airs on U.S. television is the ending Hemingway intended. See http://www.imdb.com/title/tt0022879 /alternateversions.

317 As Pauline's biographer reports: See Hawkins, 144–48, for an excellent account of the film's opening.

317 "some of the coldest hours": See Baker, *Ernest Hemingway,* 235.

317 "very bad fall": PPH to Jane Mason, [12/21/1932], JFK, Jane Mason Personal Papers, Box 1.

318 "so [he] would not be lonely": EH to Arthur Mizener. 6/2/1950, *SL,* 697.

319 he slunk into a movie theater: Reynolds, *Hemingway: The 1930s,* 117–18.

319 a new magazine for men: See www.hearst.com/magazines/esquire.php.

320 "an overgrown boy scout": Elizabeth Lombardi, "Afterword," *Hemingway Review* 24 (Fall 2004), 49.

321 "the most superficial" Marcelline Hemingway to EH, [1/2/1934], in *ATH,* 341, Marcelline's emphasis.

321 "My dad was mortified": Elizabeth Lombardi quoted in Gail Sinclair, ed., "An Interview with Papa's Little Sister," *Hemingway Review* 24 (Fall 2004), 14.

321 "Only thing to have done": EH to Carol Hemingway Gardner, 1945, in Fuentes, Appendix I, 387.

321 "WOULD APPRECIATE": Gail Sinclair, "Carol and Ernest Hemingway: The Letters of Loss," *Hemingway Review* 24 (Fall 2004), 39.

321 "Gardnerism": Sinclair, 41–42.

322 Rollins College officials did know: See ibid., 39, 47n4, n5.

322 He compared Gardner: See ibid., 42–43.

322 Ernest called Jinny: EH to AM, 2/27/[1933], *SL,* 382.

322 "Ernie's done a great deal": Carol Hemingway to Jane Mason, 3/4/1933, JFK, Jane Mason Personal Papers, Box 1.

322 "hate[d] that guy": EH to Carol Hemingway Gardner, 1945, in Fuentes, 387. Denis Brian, 183–84, discusses Carol's reactions to hearing the letter, never mailed, read to her almost fifty years later.

322 When someone asked about Carol: Carol told this to Bernice Kert; see Kert, 335.

323 "sex pervert": Paul Johnson, "The Deep Waters of EH," in *Intellectuals* (New York: Harper & Row, 1988), 150. Johnson does not provide a source.

323 Carol flatly denied: Brian, 89.

323 "which proved me conclusively": EH to Janet Flanner, 4/8/1933, *SL,* 387–88.

324 "extraordinarily good-looking man": Stein, *Autobiography,* 261. Subsequently cited in the text as *AABT.*

324 "I always loved her": EH to W. G. Rogers, 7/29/1948, *SL,* 649.

324 "Gertrude Stein and me": EH to Sherwood Anderson, 3/9/[1922], *LEH,* vol. 1, 330.

325 "American Byron": Clifton Fadiman, "Ernest Hemingway: An American Byron," *Nation,* 1/18/1933, 63–64.

326   "It is of course a commonplace": Max Eastman, "Bull in the Afternoon," *New Republic*, 6/7/1933, Eastman's emphasis; rpt. in Trogdon, ed., *Ernest Hemingway: A Literary Reference*, 131–34.

326   "though he said so on paper": These remarks, said to be made in a letter from Hemingway to MacLeish dated 6/7/1933, are quoted in Leonard J. Leff, "A Thunderous Reception: Broadway, Hollywood, and *A Farewell to Arms*," *Hemingway Review* 15 (Spring 1996), 46. His article does not cite the location of this letter, however, and I have been unable to find it.

CHAPTER SEVENTEEN

327   But Jane did come unhinged: G. Grant Mason to Baker, 12/10/1966, CBP.

328   "Mrs. Parker": EH to AM, [6/1933], LoC.

328   "bleached by the sun": Josephine Merck, "Stray Comments on EH," JFK, Miscellaneous Accessions, Michael Reynolds Research.

328   "About your hair": PPH to EH, [July 1933], JFK.

328   "Ernest is a little subdued": PPH to Jane Mason, [8/11/1933], JFK, Jane Mason Personal Papers, Box 1.

329   "pale gold": PPH to EH, [9/22/1934], JFK, Box 61, Series 3.

329   "deep gold": PPH to EH, [9/15/1934], JFK, Box 61, Series 3.

329   She dyed her hair: EH to Jane Mason, 10/16/[1933], JFK, Jane Mason Personal Papers, Box 1.

329   The magazine's publishers: Merrill writes that 100,000 copies of the first issue were sent to men's clothing stores and 5,000 to newsstands, 45.

329   *Esquire* did not set out: Merrill writes, improbably, that the second issue of the magazine had a circulation of 400,000, 51.

329   twice the going rate: Lawrence Henry, "The Twentieth Century Gentleman," *American Spectator*, 3/5/2004; http://spectator.org/archives/2004/03/05/the-twentieth-century-gentleman/print.

330   "The general effect": Arnold Gingrich, "Scott, Ernest and Whoever," 3. Originally published in *Esquire*, December 1966.

330   "He edits best": http://wheneditorsweregods.typepad.com/when_editors_were_gods/2008/11/bio-arnold-gingrich.html.

330   "We . . . always operated": Arnold Gingrich, "Scott, Ernest and Whoever," 6.

331   Ernest spent most of the allotted space: EH, "A Paris Letter," *BEH*, 136.

331   "suburban": Quoted in Mellow, 429.

331   "We like him": Richard Ellman, *James Joyce* (1959; rpt., New York: Oxford University Press, 1974), 708.

331   "Pauline and I": McLendon, 99.

332   Later, when Ernest complained: Baker interview with Charles and Lorine Thompson, 3/28/1965, 6, CBP.

335   The piece made Ernest: Interview with David Gascoyne, May 2002; Fitch, *Sylvia Beach and the Lost Generation*, 343–44; see Meyers, *Hemingway*, 87.

335   "a dull-witted": Lewis, 302.

335   "steining of Hemingway": Ibid., 300.

336   Being compared to: For a brilliant comparison between Stein and Grace Hemingway, see Burwell, 164–68.

337 she was the mystery woman: See Anne Edwards, *A Remarkable Life: A Biography of Katharine Hepburn* (New York: William Morrow, 1985), 125. Paul Hendrickson, in *Hemingway's Boat,* believes the mystery woman who offered to pay for a second safari was Helen Hay Whitney.

338 "pull his weight": EH to GHH, 8/24/[1930], Lilly.

338 Ernest made up: EH to Carol Hemingway [n.d., 10/1929?], CBP. Ernest's work history may be accurate, but it is unlikely. His time while of school age is fairly well accounted for, and Ernest never mentioned this work elsewhere.

338 Leicester had to get a job: EH to GHH, 8/24/[1930], CBP.

338 Leicester dreamed of: "Sister Grace and Aunt Grace" to GHH and family, [n.d., 1929?], HRC.

338 Samuelson later wrote: Samuelson, 26–32.

339 "belle epoch": Leicester Hemingway, 146.

339 "Fishing had become": Samuelson, 94.

340 Charlie Thompson remembered: James Plath and Frank Simons, eds., *Remembering Ernest Hemingway* (Key West, FL: Ketch & Yawl Press, 1999), 8.

340 "a thrill of a lifetime": Samuelson, 142.

340 "disastrous": Ibid., 172.

340 "foam at the mouth": EH to MP, 4/19/1936, Bruccoli, ed., *The Only Thing That Counts,* 243.

341 "long bitch": EH to MP, 11/16/[1934], Bruccoli, ed., *The Only Thing That Counts,* 213.

342 "It is a swell thing": EH to MP, 11/20/1934, Bruccoli, ed., *The Only Thing That Counts,* 215–16, EH's emphasis.

342 "this long thing": EH to MP, 10/3/1934, Bruccoli, ed., *The Only Thing That Counts,* 212n2.

343 "that the book has": MP to EH, 4/4/1935, Bruccoli, ed., *The Only Thing That Counts,* 222.

343 "The tide runs against": MP to FSF, 10/28/1935, Kuehl and Bryer, eds., 225.

343 "WE TRY TO BE": Sara and Gerald Murphy to John and Katy Dos Passos and EH and PPH, 3/21/1935, Linda Miller, ed., 119.

343 "it is not as bad": EH to Gerald and Sara Murphy, 3/19/1935, Linda Miller, ed., 118.

344 "irascible": Katy Dos Passos to Gerald and Sara Murphy, [12/2/1934], Linda Miller, ed., 100.

344 "He had more crotchety moments": Dos Passos, *The Best Times,* 232.

346 "They come like express trains": Katy Dos Passos to Gerald Murphy, 6/20/1935, Linda Miller, ed., 132.

346 Mike blamed Ernest: See Michael Culver, "Sparring in the Dark: Hemingway, Strater and *The Old Man and the Sea,*" *Hemingway Review* (Spring 1992), 31–37. Strater says Hemingway used a sawed-off rifle rather than a machine gun. Based on Culver's interviews with Strater, but see also Baker, *Ernest Hemingway,* 273.

347 International Game Fish Association: See http://biminimuseum.com/sport_fishing.html.

347 "She looks simply marvelous": EH to Jane Mason, 6/3/1935, JFK, Jane Mason Personal Papers, Box 1, quoted in Hawkins, 178.

348 "You big fat slob": EH, *Islands in the Stream*, 37–40; Hendrickson, *Hemingway's Boat*, 236; Baker, 273.

348 an article to the Marxist-oriented *New Masses: New Masses*, 11/19/1935.

349 "had better" print: EH to Sara Murphy, 9/12/1935, Linda Miller, ed., 143.

CHAPTER EIGHTEEN

350 "Ernest—before he began": FSF, *Notebooks*, quoted in Mayfield, 156.

351 Ernest had agreed to meet: Edmund Wilson, *The Thirties: From Notebooks and Diaries of the Period* (New York: Farrar, Straus & Giroux, 1980), 301–3.

351 "as a person": Baker, "Talk with Edmund Wilson on Hemingway," 1/10/1953, CBP.

351 "Hemingway was now": Edmund Wilson, *The Bit Between My Teeth* (New York: Farrar, Straus & Giroux, 1939), 522.

351 "With Ernest I seem": FSF to Edmund Wilson, [1]/1933, *FSF: ALL*, 227.

351 "a terrible bat": FSF to MP, 1/19/1933, *FSF: ALL*, 226.

352 "Did you like the book?": FSF to EH, 5/10/1934, *FSF: ALL*, 259.

352 "I liked it and I didn't like it": EH to FSF, 5/28/1934, *SL*, 407–8. For the FSF–EH friendship at this time, see also Vaill, *Hotel Florida*, 203–4.

352 "skyophreniac": EH to Sara Murphy, 12/8/[1935], Linda Miller, ed., 149.

353 "It's amazing": EH to MP, 3/25/1939, *SL*, 483, EH's emphasis.

353 "Was delighted from the letter": EH to FSF, 12/16/1935, *SL*, 424–25.

353 "The Crack-Up": FSF, "Handle with Care," in *The Crack-Up*, ed. Edmund Wilson (New York: New Directions, 1945), 75.

354 "He seems to almost": EH to MP, [ca. 2/15/1936], Bruccoli, ed., *The Only Thing That Counts*, 237.

355 "some *damned* good": EH to MP, 4/6/[1936], Bruccoli, ed., *The Only Thing That Counts*, 239.

355 "God damn editor": Quoted in Gingrich, "Scott, Ernest, and Whoever," 6.

356 This manageable project: EH to MP, 7/11/[1936], Bruccoli, ed., *The Only Thing That Counts*, 244.

356 Moreover, Dos saw his first: Townsend Ludington, "Spain and the Hemingway–Dos Passos Relationship," *American Literature* 60 (May 1988), 270–73.

357 "absolutely the best thing": Quoted in Trogdon, *The Lousy Racket*, 110–11.

357 "cut the shit": EH to Dos Passos, 3/26/1932, *SL*, 355. On the Dos Passos–EH relationship at the time of EH's *To Have and Have Not*, see Vaill, *Hotel Florida*, 63–65.

357 "cut out all you objected to": EH to Dos Passos, 5/30/1932, *SL*, 360.

357 "chopping whole hunks": Gingrich, "Scott, Ernest and Whoever," 7.

358 "I cannot be a communist": EH to Ivan Kashkin, 8/19/1935, *SL*, 419.

360 Hemingway would lament: EH to Jack Whaler, 2/15/1949, JFK, Box 49.

362 "Let me tell you": FSF, "The Rich Boy," *The Short Stories of F. Scott Fitzgerald*, Matthew Bruccoli, ed. (New York: Scribner's, 1989), 318.

362 "the only difference": Berg, 385.

362 "Please lay off me": FSF to EH, 7/16/1936, *FSF: ALL*, 302.

362 Max Perkins noted: See Donaldson, *Hemingway vs. Fitzgerald*, 203.

362 "like a woman": Baker, *Ernest Hemingway*, 317.

362 "Croton mauler": See Mellow, 501.

362 "He is living at present": FSF to MP, 9/3/1927, Kuehl and Bryer, eds., 241.

363 "working on him": EH to Sara Murphy, [2/27/1936], *SL,* 439.

363 He told the story: EH to Dos Passos, 4/26/1937, *SL,* 446–47. "As I say," he added, "am always a perfectly safe man to tell any dirt to as it goes in one ear and out my mouth."

363 "I've *got* to go": EH to MP, 12/15/1936, *SL,* 455.

364 no way a "good" war: EH to Harry Sylvester, 2/5/1937, *SL,* 456.

364 Jinny Pfeiffer asked: Page, ed., *The Diaries of Dawn Powell,* 149.

364 "the leader of the Ingrates": EH to Paul and Mary Pfeiffer, 2/9/1937, *SL,* 457.

365 "the Syphilitic Baby": See Baker, *Ernest Hemingway,* 231.

365 In other countries critics: EH to Arnold Gingrich, 4/19/[1936], Scribner's Papers, Princeton.

365 "A writer is an outlier": EH to Ivan Kashkin, 8/19/1935, *SL,* 419.

366 "adventurer for all roads": Quoted in Mellow, 185.

366 "Mussolini is no fool": "Mussolini: Biggest Bluff in Europe," *BEH,* 54.

366 "but you can't preserve": EH to Paul and Mary Pfeiffer, 2/9/1937, *SL,* 457–58.

CHAPTER NINETEEN

368 So Hemingway claimed: EH to Bernard Berenson, 5/27/1953, JFK, Box 50.

368 "I had one lifelong rule": MG to Betsy Drake, 12/25/1987, Moorehead, ed., *Selected Letters of Martha Gellhorn,* 471.

369 "a young woman being charming": Quoted in Moorehead, ed., *Selected Letters of Martha Gellhorn,* 29.

370 "a large, dirty man": Quoted in Moorehead, *Gellhorn,* 101.

370 "beautiful blonde in a black dress": McLendon, 164–67.

370 "watch[ing] Miss Gellhorn": AM to Baker, 8/9/1962, CBP.

370 One biographer's detective work: See Reynolds, *Hemingway: The 1930s,* 244.

370 "Goodbye daughter": Moorehead, *Gellhorn,* 105.

370 "Ernestino": MG to PPH, 1/14/1937, *Selected Letters of Martha Gellhorn,* 47.

371 "Goddamn it": Donnelly and Billings, 114.

371 a family friend: Alice Lee Myers to EH, [2/6/1937], Linda Miller, ed., 187.

371 evidently only two letters: Quoted in Kert, 294. Even Caroline Moorehead, Gellhorn's authorized biographer, one of the very few people who have seen the restricted Gellhorn papers at Boston University, has not seen these letters, nor had Hemingway biographer Michael Reynolds.

372 "Beauty Problems": Moorehead, *Gellhorn,* 107.

372 "almost certainly": William Braasch Watson, "The Other Paris Years of Ernest Hemingway," in J. Gerald Kennedy and Jackson R. Bryer, *French Connections: Hemingway and Fitzgerald Abroad* (New York: St. Martin's, 1998), 145.

372 "as mild as your grandmother": Koch, 46.

372 "a high school boy": Ibid., 44.

372 While most gave $500: Schoots, 117. Meyers, *Hemingway,* 312, says the total cost of the film was $13,000, of which EH paid about one fourth. The amount of money Hemingway paid is confused rather than clarified by a subsequent quarrel with MacLeish over repayment of some of the funds and letters between

EH and AM, 7/28/1938; AM to EH, 7/29/1938; EH to Ralph "Mac" Ingersoll, 7/18/1938 and 7/27/1938, JFK.

373 "piece of fluff": William Braasch Watson, "Hemingway's Spanish Civil War Dispatches," *Hemingway Review* (Spring 1988), 13.

373 "the dirtiest of": Vernon, 19.

373 "After the first two weeks": EH to Mary Pfeiffer, 8/2/1937, *SL*, 461.

374 "I knew you'd get here": Quoted in Moorehead, *Gellhorn*, 131. See Vaill, *Hotel Florida*, 146–48, for MG's arrival in Spain and then Madrid.

374 restaurant, which was reserved: Franklin, 230.

374 while food shortages: Cowles, 26.

374 He also had outright rarities: Langer, 214; see Franklin, 231.

375 "idealists and mercenaries": Cowles, 31.

376 "was going to throw suspicion": Herbst, 154.

376 "He seemed to be embracing": Ibid., 151.

377 "You do that": Ludington, ed., Dos Passos, *The Fourteenth Chronicle*, 496.

377 a passionate account: Koch, 214. This partisan recounting unearths previously unknown details about this period and its characters; it is compromised, however, by the fact that Koch invented dialogue for several occasions.

377 "crackling with generosity": Herbst, 151.

377 "so no man": Kert, 297.

377 he told her the hotel: Moorehead, *Gellhorn*, 114.

378 "I wish you were here": PPH to EH, 4/29/1937, JFK.

378 she wasn't hard to look at: Franklin, 232.

378 "Don't stand there": Ibid., 220.

378 "sail[ing] in and out": Herbst, 138.

378 "got desperately greedy": Moorehead, *Gellhorn*, 120.

379 "all that objectivity shit": Ibid., 111. Moorehead believes the phrase was coined during the Spanish Civil War.

379 "Given that they longed": Moorehead, *Gellhorn*, 125. The definitive account on reporting the Spanish Civil War is Vaill's *Hotel Florida*.

379 "committed journalism": Vernon, 62.

380 "driver, secretary": McLendon, 145.

380 when Joris Ivens came down: See Schoots, 129.

380 MacLeish was chairing: Donaldson, *Archibald MacLeish*, 265.

380 "with the air": See Fitch, *Sylvia Beach and the Lost Generation*, 370–72.

381 "Why the hell am I": Donaldson, *Archibald MacLeish*, 265.

381 "It is very dangerous": Trogdon, ed., *Ernest Hemingway: A Literary Reference*, 195; Trogdon includes the entire speech, 193–96.

381 "each with his private blonde": Quoted in Reynolds, *Hemingway: The 1930s*, 270. Reynolds writes, without providing sources, that the fur was a gift from the Abraham Lincoln Brigade, which seems unlikely, unless they asked Ernest what she might want. But why a present in the first place, especially when funds were desperately needed?

381 "*too* noble": Louise Bogan to Morton Zabel, 8/22/1937; Limmer, ed., 161–62. Bogan's emphases.

381 "lapped up": Reynolds, *Hemingway: The 1930s*, 271.

382 "Remember me to the comrades": Quoted in Hawkins, 201.

382 "You effeminate boys": Interview in CBP, Box 2, Folder 25. Prudencio de Pereda, in a 6/22/1967 letter to Baker, disputed this story. See also http://www.wellesnet .com/?p=183, wherein Welles claims to have been "a very close friend" of Hemingway's, which was not the case.

382 Hemingway himself narrated: Schoots writes that Hemingway's narration was not recorded until some weeks later, after the film was shown in California; Schoots, 129.

382 "WHITE HOUSE STILL SAME COLOR": Quoted in Moorehead, *Gellhorn*, 132.

382 "enormously tall": EH to Mary Pfeiffer, 8/2/1937, *SL*, 460.

383 Pauline thought of joining him: PPH to Sara Murphy, 7/8/1937, Linda Miller, ed., 194.

383 That afternoon: Meade, 281. Lillian Hellman floated a story about tension between Scott and Ernest at a post-screening party after the showing; as Meade points out, Hellman had not yet met Hemingway. As Bart Paul writes, 167, Sidney Franklin sent a telegram to Ernest in California that closed with the words, "SALUD PAULINE JORIS," which indicates Pauline did make the trip, but Franklin may simply not have been informed of her last-minute decision not to go.

383 "I wish we could meet": FSF to EH, [6/5/1937], *FSF: ALL,* 324.

383 "THE PICTURE": FSF to EH, 7/13/1937, *FSF: ALL,* 332.

383 "nervous tensity": FSF to MP, 7/15/1937, Kuehl and Bryers, eds., 238.

384 Ernest was living in a world: FSF to MP, 9/3/1937, *FSF: ALL,* 335.

CHAPTER TWENTY

385 "In a war": Quoted in Vernon, 4. From EH, "Preface" to Gustav Regler, *The Great Crusade.*

386 "tall, handsome blonde": EH, "The Fifth Column" in *The Fifth Column and Four Stories of the Spanish Civil War* (1969; rpt., New York: Bantam, 1970), 4. Subsequent references to *Fifth Column* to be made in the text.

387 When he went out: EH made this comment in a recording whose source is unclear. See http://www.c-spanvideo.org/clip/3271458 for the clip. A contemporary account quoted the clip; see http://news.google.com/newspapers?nid=897& dat=19381011&id=ObBaAAAAIBAJ&sjid=7E8DAAAAIBAJ&pg=4615,6729673.

387 "The two rooms": http://theater.nytimes.com/2008/02/10/theater/10mcgr.html ?pagewanted=all&_r=0. The letter's date is not given. Hemingway scholar Gene Washington has compared this "dead angle" to the many "good places" in Hemingway's fiction; see his "Hemingway: *The Fifth Column* and the 'Dead Angle,'" *Hemingway Review* (Spring 2009).

387 Herbst, in her memoir of Spain: Herbst, 152.

388 "would be running away": Langer, 352n.

388 "I'd like to flatten": Langer, 352n. Pike told Langer this story.

388 "The very first time": Hotchner, *Papa Hemingway,* 133.

389 Bill Bird: Baker, *Ernest Hemingway,* 324.

389 "severe liver complaint": Ibid.

389 25,000 copies: Ibid., 320.

389 "morally odious": Connolly and Schwartz quoted in Meyers, *Hemingway*, 295–96.

389 "There is evidence": *New York Times*, 10/17/1937.

389 "tough racket": EH to MP, [mid-February 1938], Bruccoli, ed., *The Only Thing That Counts*, 256–57.

390 "Am in such": EH to MP, [mid-February 1938], Bruccoli, ed., *The Only Thing That Counts*, 257.

390 "All my love": PPH to EH, [4/15/1937], JFK, Box 61, Series 3.

390 "You can see that": PPH to EH, 4/29/1938, JFK, Box 61, Series 3.

391 That evening Pauline went ahead: McLendon, 185–87.

391 "BEST THING": EH to MP, [early January 1938], Bruccoli, ed., *The Only Thing That Counts*, 252.

392 "one of the most considerable achievements": *Nation*, 12/10/1938.

392 "I hope to live long": EH to Edmund Wilson, 12/10/1938, quoted in Mellow, 515.

392 "I'm in fine shape": PPH to EH, [9/2/1938], JFK, Box 61, Series 3.

392 "golden key": PPH to EH, [9/10/1938], JFK, Box 61, Series 3.

392 He vowed to Max Perkins: Quoted in Baker, *Ernest Hemingway*, 336.

393 "the mess everything's in": EH to MP, 10/28/1938, *SL*, 474.

393 "Hemingway . . . saw": Quoted in Vernon, 47.

393 she and Ernest were in fact in Paris: Vaill, *Hotel Florida*, 330–31.

394 "tenderness for others": MG to Leonard Bernstein, 1/14/1959, in Nigel Simeone, ed., *The Leonard Bernstein Letters* (New Haven, CT: Yale University Press, 2013), 412.

394 "In Spain, he was not tough": MG to David Gurewitch, 4/5/1950, Moorehead, ed., *Selected Letters of Martha Gellhorn*, 210.

394 "I think it was the only time": Kert, 299.

395 "ABSOLUTELY APPALLING": Quoted in Hawkins, 213.

395 "If you want": PPH to EH, 9/17/[1938]. JFK, Box 61, Series 3.

395 "I miss you very much": PPH to EH, 9/2/1938. JFK, Box 61, Series 3.

395 Grace had raised: GHH to EH, 2/6/1939, JFK.

395 a "generous" check: GHH to EH, 12/20/1938, JFK.

395 for three years: GHH to EH, 12/20/1938, JFK.

395 a year and a half: GHH to EH, 7/14/1938. JFK, Box 60.

395 "a very unkind": GHH to EH, 7/14/1938.

396 weaving tapestries: Kert, on p. 300, says Grace wrote Pauline in 1937 asking whether Ernest had ever received the tapestry she had woven for him. I have not been able to locate this letter.

396 Detroit *Social Register:* See Marcelline Hemingway to GHH, 10/29/1940, HRC, Box 7, Folder 8. Marcelline asked her mother not to tell her brothers and sisters, for "they would only laugh."

396 Marcelline wrote Ernest: Marcelline Hemingway to GHH, 4/14/1939, HRC, Box 7, Folder 7.

396 "If you go into the house": EH to Marcelline Hemingway, [7/1937], *ATH*, 349–51.

396 she had put in: Marcelline Hemingway to GHH [n.d., Spring 1941], HRC, Box 7, Folder 7.

397 "not only as a brilliant humorist": The Rev. W. Lucas Collins, M.A., Introduction, *Ancient Classics for English Readers,* Collins, ed., vol. 3: Aristophanes (London: William Blackwood, 1872).

398 "As if he took a delight": Theodore Alois Buckley, Introduction, *The Tragedies of Euripides,* vol. 1 (New York: Harper, 1968), vii.

398 "You may decorate your home": GHH, "The Analogy of Music and Color," HRC, Box 13, Folder 6, GHH's emphasis.

398 Ruth had been widowed: See [Elizabeth Burns Cord], "Peter Henry Fippinger, Pioneer Settler of Cook County," unpublished essay, 2006, p. 14.

399 "Let me know": GHH to "Duttons," 6/18/1939, Hemingway Collection, Stanford, Box 20, Item #494.

399 Martha's biographer suggests: Moorehead, *Gellhorn,* 157.

399 "what the French call 'reasonable' ": MG to Edna Gellhorn, 5/26/1938, Moorehead, ed., *Selected Letters of Martha Gellhorn,* 62.

399 "Also sweetie": PPH to EH, [6/23/1939], JFK.

399 "Relax and enjoy": PPH to EH, [7/9/1939], JFK.

402 "There are events which are so great": EH, Preface, in Regler, *The Great Crusade,* xi.

CHAPTER TWENTY-ONE

403 In great disrepair: See Rollyson, 113, for Jack Hemingway's description of the pink tennis court.

404 "slept on it": MG to Eleanor Roosevelt, 3/18/1939, Moorehead, ed., *Selected Letters of Martha Gellhorn,* 74.

404 "It is fine": EH to MP, [n.d. 1/14/1940], Bruccoli, ed., *The Only Thing That Counts,* 277.

404 "what we swore": PPH to EH, [3/17/1945], JFK.

404 tore up a letter: Ruth Hawkins interview with Allie Baker, 3/26/2013, http://www.thehemingwayproject.com/unbelievable-happiness-final-sorrow-the-hemingway-pfeiffer-marriage-an-interview-with-ruth-hawkins/.

405 "Oh Papa darling": PPH to EH, 8/11/[1939], JFK.

405 "You are the finest": Quoted in Hawkins, 219.

406 "Pauline hates me": EH to MP, [1/14/1940], Bruccoli, ed., *The Only Thing That Counts,* 277.

406 Paying alimony: EH to CS III, 9/6/1948, JFK, Box 48.

406 "any fool": Gregory Hemingway, 92.

407 "Mother Pfeiffer": EH to Mary Pfeiffer, 12/29/1939, *SL,* 499–500.

407 "This is the saddest Christmas": Mary Pfeiffer to EH [n.d.], *SL,* 500n.

407 initially Gus "upbraid[ed]": Dawn Powell, diary entry for 10/24/[1940], Page, ed., *The Diaries of Dawn Powell,* 182.

407 Ernest later claimed: See Lynn, 485.

407 Not long after: Gus Pfeiffer became demented before he died, and Ernest had to deal with a committee that represented Gus's interests when he tried to retrieve this manuscript. It was not easy to extract the manuscript, and Ernest spun paranoid fantasies about the committee members and their tactics. "Some of it is really spooky," he told his son Gregory, saying it involved an impostor arriving

in Cuba who identified himself as Gus Pfeiffer. See EH to Gregory Hemingway, 8/7/1954, in Fuentes, Appendix I: The Finca Vigía Papers, 400. The manuscript's current value is stratospheric.

407 Sun Valley: See http://sportsillustrated.cnn.com/vault/article/magazine/MAG 1076777/index.htmhttp://sportsillustrated.cnn.com/vault/article/magazine /MAG1076777/index.htm.

408 Steve Hannagan: See http://www.reviewjournal.com/news/steve-hannagan.

408 "Sun Valley, Society's Newest Winter Playground": http://community.seattle times.nwsource.com/archive/?date=19920407&slug=1485206.

408 he had not skied: It is not clear why EH abandoned skiing. According to Lloyd Arnold, 151, "Papa never so much as had on a pair of ski boots in Idaho."

408 what the resort offered: On Hemingway's time spent in Sun Valley and Idaho, see McLendon, 204–5; Martha Bellavance-Johnson, *Ernest Hemingway in Idaho: A Guide* (Ketchum, ID: The Computer Lab, 1997); and Lloyd Arnold, *High on the Wild with Hemingway.*

408 "I'd rather have": See "Tillie Arnold: The Sun Valley Years," in Plath and Simons, eds., 148.

409 "The book is what": MG to EH, 12/4/1939, Moorehead, ed., *Selected Letters of Martha Gellhorn,* 78.

409 "stinko deadly lonely": Moorehead, *Gellhorn,* 162; see also Baker, *Ernest Heming-way,* 344.

409 even shooting at coyotes: Baker, *Ernest Hemingway,* 344.

409 As usual: See McLendon, 198–200.

409 "guaranty": MG to "whom it may concern," 1/19/1940, Moorehead, ed., *Selected Letters of Martha Gellhorn,* 80–81.

410 On the dust jacket: See Meyers, *Hemingway,* 350.

410 "which is saying something": MG to Hortense (Flexner) and Wyncie King, 3/29/1940, Moorehead, ed., *Selected Letters of Martha Gellhorn,* 83.

410 Martha could say *fuck*: Jack Hemingway, 15.

410 Patrick considered her: Meyers, *Hemingway,* 349.

410 "She could talk of anything": Gregory Hemingway, 41.

410 Ernest wrote at a desk: See Rollyson, 113.

411 "That's my mermaid": Leicester Hemingway, 224.

411 In March, she was infuriated: See *Time,* 3/17/1940, and Moorehead, *Gellhorn,* 167.

411 "had decided to write as good": EH to HRH, 11/24/1939, *SL,* 496–97.

411 "the finest novel": Quoted in Moorehead, *Gellhorn,* 167.

411 "was the best": EH to MP [n.d., mid-April 1940], Bruccoli, ed., *The Only Thing That Counts,* 281.

411 "still in a kind of daze": MP to EH, 4/24/1940, Bruccoli, ed., *The Only Thing That Counts,* 283.

411 John Donne's: EH to MP, 4/21/1940, Bruccoli, ed., *The Only Thing That Counts,* 282.

412 "There isn't anybody smarter": Quoted in Donaldson, *Archibald MacLeish,* 333.

412 "contempt": AM, "Post-war Writers and Pre-war Readers," *New Republic,* 6/10/1940. AM's emphasis. EH, "War Writers on Democracy," *Life,* 6/24/1940, quoted in Donaldson, *Archibald MacLeish,* 335–36.

413 "the stamp of bourgeois approval": MP to FSF, 9/19/1940, in Kuehl and Bryer, eds., 266.

413 "Both of my husbands": Quoted in Kert, 343.

413 "an emotional instability": See Kert, 343.

413 "Dead-Shot Hemingway": See Arnold, 107.

414 he got to know Cooper: See Meyers, *Gary Cooper*, 171.

414 Cooper had gone on safari: Ibid., 173.

414 Rumors of a film version: See Trogdon, *The Lousy Racket*, 219.

414 "the Hemingway": Edmund Wilson, "Hemingway: Gauge of Morale," *The Portable Edmund Wilson*, 405; this is a 1941 update of the 1939 essay, with an updated title.

414 "Hemingway the artist": *New Republic*, 10/28/1940. Wilson was critical, however, of the novel's political stance—not surprisingly, as he was preoccupied with politics at the time.

414 "This is the best book": Quoted in Mellow, 521.

415 "I do not much care": Quoted in Mellow, 521–22.

415 "When they want to destroy you": EH to MP, 10/29/1940, Bruccoli, ed., *The Only Thing That Counts*, 298–99.

415 *Publishers Weekly* best-seller list: See http://en.wikipedia.org/wiki/Publishers _Weekly_list_of_bestselling_novels_in_the_United_States_in_the_1940s.

416 cumulative sales figure: Lynn, 484. Lynn does not cite a source.

416 "a work of this nature": See Trogdon, *The Lousy Racket*, 223–24.

416 "The miracle": Trogdon, *The Lousy Racket*, 226.

417 "We were giants": EH to Bernard Berenson, 5/37/1953, JFK, Box 50.

417 "wonderful to be legal": Quoted in Baker, *Ernest Hemingway*, 355.

417 "just a bad joke": EH to Edna Gellhorn, 9/21/1944, JFK, Box 48.

418 was deluded: EH to Bernard Berenson, 5/27/1953, JFK, Box 50.

418 "piles of books": Viertel, 9.

418 "You have never seen": Fred Spiegel, "Young Hemingway: A Panel," *Fitzgerald/ Hemingway Annual* (1972), 116.

418 Later, when cleaning house: Kert, 377.

418 "kept any and all": Fuentes, 80.

418 Ernest seldom bathed: Hotchner, *Papa Hemingway*, 86.

418 Gregory and Patrick joined them: See Baker, *Ernest Hemingway*, 352.

419 "It was wonderful for me": Jack Hemingway, 18–19.

CHAPTER TWENTY-TWO

420 "It is the most": MP to EH, 4/4/1931, Bruccoli, ed., *The Only Thing That Counts*, 307.

420 "I suppose the worms": EH to MP, 4/29/1941, Bruccoli, ed., *The Only Thing That Counts*, 309.

420 "Most of it has a deadness": EH to MP, 11/15/1941, *SL*, 528.

421 "By the beginning of 1941": MG, *Travels with Myself and Another* (1978; rpt., New York: Jeremy P. Tarcher, 2001), 11. Hereafter *TMA*.

422 "We are against people": Roger Starr, "*PM*: New York's Highbrow Tabloid," *City Journal* (Summer 1993), http://www.city-journal.org/article02.php?aid=1480.

422 Ingersoll agreed that: "Hemingway Reviewed by Ralph Ingersoll," *PM*, 6/9/1941, *BEH*, 270.

422 Ernest talked with Gary Cooper: Meyers, *Gary Cooper*, 177.

423 "spy mission": Peter Moreira, *Hemingway on the China Front: His WW II Spy Mission with Martha Gellhorn* (Washington, DC: Potomac Books, 2007), an otherwise excellent account.

423 "The Generalissimo": EH, "U.S. Aid to China," *PM*, 6/15/1941, *BEH*, 288–90.

425 Ernest told Max: EH to MP, 4/20/1926, *SL*, 202. He told Scott Fitzgerald he found the book "juvenile." See EH to FSF, [4/20/1926], *SL*, 200.

426 "I would rather listen": EH to MP, [2/11/1940 or 2/14/1940], *SL*, 501.

426 She had cleared the idea: MG to Charles Colebaugh, 7/17/[1941], Moorehead, ed., *Selected Letters of Martha Gellhorn*, 113. Baker, *Ernest Hemingway*, 372, says that there were about three thousand Falangists in Cuba.

427 "laziness": EH to CS III, 12/12/1941, *SL*, 532.

427 In 1940 Leicester: See Reynolds, *Hemingway: The Final Years*, 45. See also "The Case of Captain Gough," *Time*, 7/13/1942, an article reporting a development in Panama, which looks back to Leicester's trip.

427 told Leicester to get a haircut: EH to Leicester Hemingway, 6/28/1941, in Appendix One in Leicester Hemingway, *My Brother, Ernest Hemingway* (1961; rev. ed., Sarasota, FL: Pineapple Press, 1996), 300–31.

427 In 1942 the U.S. was losing: The numbers are from MG, *TMA*, 59–60. Statistics vary; see http://www.usmm.org/battleatlantic.html for a survey of these numbers.

428 "Dear guys": MG to Bill and Emily Davis, [6]/1942, Moorehead, ed., *Selected Letters of Martha Gellhorn*, 125. Moorehead incorrectly identifies Davis's then wife as Annie, though he did not marry Annie until the late 1940s.

428 He and Martha, however, were staying: Daniel Robinson, " 'My True Occupation Is That of a Writer': Hemingway's Passport Correspondence," *Hemingway Review* 25 (Spring 2005). Robinson's information comes from Department of State and CIA documents and correspondence concerning Hemingway's passport applications.

429 Perhaps they were talking: Baker, *Ernest Hemingway*, 372.

429 he claims he approached: Braden, 283. See also René and Raúl Villarreal, 44. Terry Mort's *The Hemingway Patrols* provides some important information, especially about World War II U-boats and nautical information in general, but his analysis is marred by idiosyncratic political views and an uncritical acceptance of Hemingway's statements.

429 Bob Joyce later told: Baker cites an April 1964 interview with Joyce; see *Ernest Hemingway*, p. 633.

429 Crook Factory: Baker, 372; see D. T. Max, "Ernest Hemingway's War Wounds," *New York Times*, Travel, 7/18/1999, http://www.nytimes.com/1999/07/18/magazine /ernest-hemingway-s-war-wounds.html; e-mails from Max to author, 9/25/2013.

429 "an ideal man to conduct this work": Quoted in Meyers, *Hemingway*, 373.

429 "wharf rats": Braden, 283.

429 Its first report: Thomas Fensch, *Behind Islands in the Stream: Hemingway, Cuba, the FBI and the Crook Factory*, reprints and edits Hemingway's FBI file.

430 He had heard it said: Nicholas Reynolds, "Ernest Hemingway, Wartime Spy," *Studies in Intelligence* 2002 (2012), 3. Reynolds credits the Joyce Papers at Yale for this information.

430 "Franco's Bastard Irish": Quoted in Meyers, *Hemingway*, 381.

430 Ellis Briggs pointed out: Meyers, *Hemingway*, 386. Ellis O. Briggs made this observation in his *Shots Heard Round the World: An Ambassador's Hunting Adventures of Four Continents* (New York: Viking, 1957), 57–58.

431 "throw beanbags down the hatch": Baker, *Ernest Hemingway*, 374.

431 Ernest told Braden: See Braden, 283–84.

431 "Friendless": Fuentes, 201.

431 Ernest's son Patrick: Patrick Hemingway, "*Islands in the Stream*: A Son Remembers," in Nagel, ed., *Ernest Hemingway: The Writer in Context*, 15.

431 Along the way: Leicester Hemingway, 231.

431 "war casualties": See Leddy memorandum, 10/8/1942, in Fensch, 15.

432 "We were just twenty-one": Quoted in D. T. Max, "Ernest Hemingway's War Wounds," 2.

432 "We had a bomb": Leicester Hemingway, 231–32.

432 Ernest drilled his shipmates: Fuentes, 193.

432 "probably the last, really great": Patrick Hemingway, in Nagel, ed., *Ernest Hemingway: The Writer in Context*, 15, 17.

433 The FBI, who still had: "FBI Memorandum for Mr. Ladd" was evidently prepared by C. H. Carson but reported the findings of agent Leddy. Because the same language and conclusions appear in reports prepared by Leddy, it is safe to assume that Carson submitted what Leddy gave him. An attached memorandum, also for Ladd and signed by Carson, notes that the main memorandum was "prepared by Mr. Leddy."

433 "a clique of celebrity hero worshippers": Arostegui died in 1944 at the age of thirty-nine of a kidney ailment. See *Time*, 2/7/1944, http://content.time.com /time/magazine/article/0,9171,791337,00.html.

434 "Hemingway is a man": Fensch, 57.

434 "rot and rubbish": See Kert, 385.

434 The discoveries were reported: See John Earl Haynes, Harvey Klehr, and Alexander Vassiliev, *Spies: The Rise and Fall of the KGB in America* (New Haven, CT: Yale University Press, 2009); Vassiliev was the former KGB agent who took notes on the Stalin-era files.

435 "The Soviet Union was not bound": EH, Preface, in Regler, ix.

436 "Our meetings with 'Argo' ": Quoted in Reynolds, *Hemingway: The Final Years*, 11.

437 "Excuse me if I talk politics": EH to Konstantin Simonov, 6/20/1946, *SL*, 608.

CHAPTER TWENTY-THREE

438 "Haven't written": EH to AM, 8/10/[1943], LoC.

438 *Men at War*: The book was originally compiled by William Kozlenko and published by Crown in 1942.

438 "limp" and "dead": EH to MP, 7/13/1940, Bruccoli, ed., *The Only Thing That Counts*, 285.

438   "He felt that he was entitled": Kert, 390. Patrick also told Kert that in his view Ernest was more afraid of dying in a war than Martha was—impossible to prove and somewhat unlikely.

439   "His idea of making Marty": Gregory Hemingway, 90–92.

439   "My man is another": MG to Hortense Flexner, 9/22/1941, Moorehead, ed., *Selected Letters of Martha Gellhorn*, 116.

439   "I wish we could stop it all now": MG to EH, 6/28/1943, Moorehead, ed., *Selected Letters of Martha Gellhorn*, 146.

440   "It had started at noon": EH, *Islands in the Stream* (1970; rpt., New York: Bantam, 1972), 202–3. Hereafter *IIS*.

440   "Papa would be just": Quoted in Reynolds, *Hemingway: The Final Years*, 83.

440   "demanded in his leisure hours": Dundy, 219.

440   "as long as people": Quoted in Brian, 59.

441   "He has the excessive need": MG to Leonard Bernstein, [1/14/1959], Nigel Simeone, ed., *The Leonard Bernstein Letters* (New Haven, CT: Yale University Press, 2013), 412.

441   Ernest vowed: EH to MG, 6/17/[1943], JFK, Box 48.

442   "damned lonely": EH to AM, 4/4/1943, LoC.

442   "very reluctant": Patrick Hemingway, "*Islands in the Stream*: A Son Remembers," in Nagel, ed., *Ernest Hemingway: The Writer in Context*, 15.

442   "so as to have": EH to AM, 8/10/1943, *SL*, 549.

442   "I won't urge you": MG to EH, 12/13/1943, Moorehead, ed., *Selected Letters of Martha Gellhorn*, 159.

443   reports Nicholas Reynolds: Nicholas Reynolds, 5–6. Details and quotes are from Nicholas Reynolds, who saw the CIA records.

444   "excitement and danger": Quoted in Kert, 391.

444   "just plain spoiled": EH to Edna Gellhorn, quoted in Moorehead, *Gellhorn*, 214.

444   "My crime really": Quoted in Kert, 391.

444   "They only fly men": Kert, 392.

444   "Take not the slightest": EH to MG, 1/31/1944, JFK, quoted in Andrea Lynn, *Shadow Loves: The Last Affairs of H. G. Wells* (Boulder, CO: Westview Press, 2001), 418.

445   "Q-boat play-acting": Kert, 398.

445   posh, quasi-British: See EH to MG, 8/5/1946, JFK, in a letter EH says he decided not to send.

445   "ARE YOU": Kert, 321.

445   "safe angle": See Washington, 128. For the Dorchester, see http://wwp.greenwich meantime.com/time-zone/europe/uk/england/london/west/london-w1/park -lane/dorchester.htm.

445   "the Dorch": This is in small part a surmise. Bernice Kert, who interviewed Martha Gellhorn extensively for *The Hemingway Women*, notes that Ernest was staying in a room "in a 'safe angle'" when Martha joined him at the Dorchester. Kert could only have known of the concept if Martha reported that the hotel room was situated in this way.

446   "glamour boys": See Elisa Mattiello, *An Introduction to English Slang: A Description of Its Morphology, Semantics and Sociology* (Polimetrica, 2008), 276. See also http://www.answers.com/topic/glamour-boy-slang-term.

446 John Pudney, one of the RAF's: See Meyers, *Hemingway*, 397.

446 "Set beside": Quoted in Baker, *Ernest Hemingway*, 393.

446 The two officers: Baker, *Ernest Hemingway*, 392.

446 "his collection of shotguns": Lambert, ed., 151. See also http://www.jot101 .com/2013/02/hemingway-at-mont-st-michel-1944.html.

447 "was a lot like reading Proust": Viertel, 11.

447 "the bearer . . . performed": Leicester Hemingway, 230; second ellipsis in original.

447 "useless and very expensive": Capa, 129.

447 Morris remembered: John G. Morris, *Get the Picture: A Personal History of Photo-journalism* (Chicago: University of Chicago Press, 2002), 75.

448 "His skull was split": Capa, 129. Capa said the wound was closed with forty-eight stitches, 131. Baker, *Ernest Hemingway*, 391, reports fifty-seven stitches.

448 "an Arab potentate": Morris, *Get the Picture*, 76.

448 "drinking with his pals": Quoted in Kert, 398.

448 "subdural hematoma": Baker, *Ernest Hemingway*, 447.

449 "What should have been done": EH to MWH, 4/14/1945, *SL*, 584.

451 "both stature and status": MWH, *HIW*, 96.

451 "newspapering sweatshop": Ibid., 29.

451 and covered: Ibid., 42.

451 "She was also having an affair": Shnayerson, 132. On McClure, see http://www .psywarrior.com/mcclure.html. Later promoted to major general, McClure went on to play a significant role in Cold War strategizing.

452 "the worst things he ever wrote": Meyers, *Hemingway*, 394.

453 Mary, assigned: MWH, *HIW*, 99.

453 Late at night: Donald Beistle, "EH's ETO Chronology," *Hemingway Review* (Fall 1994), 2.

453 "as though they were": EH, "Voyage to Victory," *Collier's*, 6/22/1944, *BEH*, 302.

454 "the day we took": Ibid., 300.

454 a colorful account: Leicester Hemingway, 243; William Van Dusen, "Hemingway's Longest Day," *True* (February 1963), 55, 62.

454 when he landed on the beaches: EH to Henry La Cossitt, 8/27/1945, JFK, Box 48.

454 "against [his] better judgment": See Baker, *Ernest Hemingway*, 396–99, for Ernest's coverage of the RAF. Pilot Peter Wykeham quoted on p. 399.

455 "abortion": Baker, *Ernest Hemingway*, 401.

455 "He spoke the same language": Quotations are from letters Kirkpatrick and Collingwood wrote to Meyers, quoted in Meyers's biography, *Hemingway*, 403–4.

455 "standing poised": Baker, "Hemingway-Lanham Chronology, 1944–45," CBP, Box 6.

455 On August 5: Though this injury is reported in all accounts and in EH's letters as a concussion, it is not known if he saw a doctor for the injury. The term SIS, or second-impact syndrome, was coined in 1984 to refer to such injuries, which follow a first injury before it has resolved.

456 "mysterious": Viertel, 19.

456 Ford shot film: See http://www.youtube.com/watch?v=uBSmGYpkFrs.

457 "good company, amusing, dogmatic": Quoted in Meyers, *Hemingway,* 403.

457 "When the mood was on him": Quoted in Meyers, *Hemingway,* 405.

457 "Are you sure": EH to John Westover, quoted in S. L. A. Marshall, "How Papa Liberated Paris," *American Heritage* (April 1962).

457 "Take his boots off": Beevor, 496.

457 Pinckney Ridgell: Shnayerson, 140.

458 "the entire Kraut MLR": Baker, *Ernest Hemingway,* 411.

458 Bruce later spoke highly: Mellow, 535.

458 "He was only a reporter": Brian, 158.

459 "could never take": Ibid., 160.

459 a contradictory report: See Meyers, *Hemingway,* 408. Vexingly, Meyers attributes this story to Andy Rooney as well; as I have argued, the confusion is typical of these stories.

459 "delirium": Baker, *Ernest Hemingway,* 417.

459 "Ernest and his boys": Hotchner, *Papa Hemingway,* 41.

460 Ernest sent his Irregulars: http://life.time.com/history/the-liberation-of-paris-a -photographers-story/#1. The story is told by *Life* photographer Ralph Morse.

460 "Papa took good hotel": Quoted in Raeburn, 117.

460 "Sit still": Quoted in Baker, *Ernest Hemingway,* 417.

460 his grandson has written: John D. Marshall, *Reconciliation Road: A Family Odyssey of War and Honor* (Syracuse, NY: Syracuse University Press, 1993).

461 Marshall himself provided: Marshall, "How Papa Liberated Paris."

461 "perfectly suited": Raeburn, 117.

CHAPTER TWENTY-FOUR

462 "red-headed Knickerbocker": Beevor, 345. The quotation is sourced to a Soviet war correspondent, Colonel Kraminov.

462 "truthiness": See, for instance, http://en.wikipedia.org/wiki/Truthiness; http:// www.urbandictionary.com/define.php?term ruthiness; and Paul Krugman, "Moment of Truthiness," *New York Times,* 10/15/2013. H. R. Stoneback applied this concept to EH in "Under Kilimanjaro—Truthiness at Late Light: Or, Would Oprah Kick Hemingway Out of Her Book Club," *Hemingway Review* (Spring 2006). Stoneback was writing before *The Colbert Report,* and his use of the concept, while extremely useful for his study, is very different from mine.

463 "I am ugly": EH to MG, 7/7/[1943], JFK, Box 48.

464 "sounded like an affectation": Viertel, 12–13.

464 "shameful, arrogant": Quoted in Meyers, *Hemingway,* 396.

464 "like a cobra": Moorehead, *Gellhorn,* 228.

464 Capa consoled her: Ibid., 229.

465 "You know, Papa": Whelan, 228.

465 "All hands despised her": Lanham to Baker, 8/13/1962, CBP, Box 6, Folder 18.

465 "She was a bitch": Brian, 177.

465 "Well, you can't shoot": See Baker, *Ernest Hemingway,* 441; Moorehead, *Gellhorn,* 230.

465 "a midmorning": MWH, *HIW,* 120–21.

465 He wanted Mary to see his Paris: EH to MWH, 11/22/[1944], JFK, Cuban Accessions, Box 1.

466 "You goddamn, smirking": MWH, *HIW,* 116.

466 "You ought to read a book": Ibid., 130–31.

466 "Something she did to your hair": Ibid., 132.

466 "He took a close interest": Moorehead, *Gellhorn,* 182.

467 "favorite and most frequent song": MWH, *HIW,* 128.

467 Buck Lanham brought Ernest: Ibid., 147. Baker, *Ernest Hemingway,* 443, says EH put the photograph on the back of the toilet before firing, but it seems unlikely EH would have missed the symbolic import of placing it in the bowl.

467 "I had never before": MWH, *HIW,* 117.

467 "on at least one occasion": Shnayerson, 143.

467 "as an armored column": MWH, *HIW,* 124, ellipses in original.

467 "We would be faithful": MWH, *HIW,* 126, emphasis MWH's.

467 In a letter soon after: EH to MWH, 12/27/1944, JFK.

468 "your sudden sunny gaiety": MWH to EH, n.d. [2/18/?], JFK.

468 "Go hang yourself": Quoted in Baker, *Ernest Hemingway,* 420.

468 later telling Carlos Baker: Baker, *Ernest Hemingway,* 425.

468 Ernest thought: EH to MWH, 11/16/1944, JFK, Cuban Accessions, Box 1.

469 Were he to lose his case: Baker, *Ernest Hemingway,* 429.

469 "There was considerable feeling": Quoted in Meyers, *Hemingway,* 407.

469 "Ernest, as a war correspondent": Quoted in Meyers, *Hemingway,* 406–7.

470 "no violation by him": See Meyers, *Hemingway,* 411. The quotation is from Malcolm Cowley, "A Portrait of Mr. Papa," *Life,* 1/10/1949.

470 he explained: EH to Charles Fenton, 1/2/1958, JFK, Box 50.

470 he dispatched Mary: EH to MWH, 11/25/1944, JFK, Cuban Accessions, Box 1.

471 describe Hürtgenwald: Stephen Ambrose, *Citizen Soldiers: The U.S. Army from the Normandy Beaches to the Bulge to the Surrender of Germany, June 7, 1944–May 7, 1945* (New York: Simon & Schuster, 1997), 177.

472 As Seán Hemingway: David Shields and Shane Salerno, *Salinger* (New York: Simon & Schuster, 2013), 114.

472 Equally dubious: Interview with Werner Kleeman, 2/12/2010. Kleeman says Salinger did "reveal" his testicular condition to Ernest in conversation, not through a physical demonstration. See also Noah Rosenberg, "Lifelong Pal Remembers J. D. Salinger," *Queens Courier,* 2/2/2010.

472 An Army psychiatrist: Baker, 435.

473 "an ignoramus": Reynolds, *Hemingway: The Final Years,* 121–22.

473 "He made me laugh more deeply": Brian, 155.

473 "He was a classic manic-depressive": Ibid., 302.

473 American troops finally: Ambrose, *Citizen Soldiers,* 177.

474 Ernest later told: EH to Charles Poore, 8/9/[ca. 1945?]), JFK, Box 49. In the same letter he quotes something that sounds like a de Beauvoir diary entry, which would hardly seem possible. She said or wrote, according to the letter, "Faut coucher avec Hem avant qu'il parte une autre fois au front. Peut-être tué." Or, roughly, "Must sleep with Hem before he leaves again for the front. Perhaps killed."

474 "that lousy Armenian": Quoted in Baker, *Ernest Hemingway,* 442.

474 "To Martha Gellhorn's Vagina": See Lanham to Baker, 9/25/1963, CBP. See Baker, *Ernest Hemingway,* 642n.

475 Mary, in her words: MWH, *HIW,* 150.

475 "I simply never want": Quoted in Moorehead, *Gellhorn,* 230.

475 Most of his complaints: These complaints are enumerated in a letter (unsent, according to a marginal comment) to MG, 8/5/1946, JFK.

475 "She had more ambition": *Across the River and into the Trees* (New York: Scribner's, 1950), 212. Hereafter *ARIT.*

475 "A cunt is a cunt": E-mail from Alan Sklar to the Hemingway listserv (heming-l @mtu.edu), 1/12/2009, reporting the inscription.

475 "Martha was a lovely girl": EH to CS III, 6/28/1947, *SL,* 623.

475 "The last time": EH to AH, [3/14/1955], DeFazio, ed., 184.

476 "Everybody friendly": EH to MG, [n.d., 1945], in Fuentes, 377–81.

477 "full of chest-beating": Lanham to Baker, 8/13/1962, CBP, Box 6, Folder 18.

CHAPTER TWENTY-FIVE

478 "is difficult on acct.": EH to Lanham, 6/9/1945, in Fuentes, 384.

478 He had plenty of material: EH to MP, 10/15/1944, Bruccoli, ed., *The Only Thing That Counts,* 333.

479 Jack was released: EH to MP, 7/23/1945, *SL,* 593.

479 "dazed": EH to MG, [n.d., 1943], JFK, Box 49.

479 boxing gym on West 47th Street: Greg Hemingway places the gym on 57th Street. See *Papa,* 33. But see "Author in the Forenoon," *Conversations with Ernest Hemingway,* 25. The article originally appeared in *The New Yorker,* where the fact-checkers are notoriously thorough.

479 put father and son: Patrick Hemingway, " 'Papa' Hemingway, as Seen by a Son," *Kansas City Star,* http://www.kcstar.com/hemingway/ehpapa.shtml.

480 Ernest was dubious: EH to MWH, 3/20/[1945], JFK, Box 48.

480 "those snot schools": Quoted in Lou Mandler, "The Hemingways at Canterbury," *Hemingway Review* (Spring 2010), 110.

480 "I Guess Everything": For the best account, see Robert C. Clark, *"Papa y El Tirador:* Biographical Parallels in Hemingway's 'I Guess Everything Reminds You of Something,' " *Hemingway Review* (Fall 2007), 89–106. Hendrickson, 497, treats the incident in great detail, though his specifics—the number of contestants, for instance—are different from those in Clark's account. Hendrickson's only source note says Clark's account "contains several important errors of fact," which he does not specify, nor does he provide a source note for his own details.

480 "El Pequeño Rey": Patrick Hemingway, *"Islands in the Stream:* A Son Remembers," in Nagel, ed., *Ernest Hemingway: The Writer in Context,* 14.

480 "The shoot was the turn": Quoted in Hendrickson, 396–97.

480 As a young boy: See Valerie Hemingway, 237. Hendrickson provides a thorough account of Greg's troubles; see also John Hemingway, one of Greg's sons, in *Strange Tribe.*

481 Mary discovered she was missing: Jeffrey Meyers, "The Hemingways: An American Tragedy," *Virginia Quarterly Review* (Spring 1999), http://www.vqronline .org/articles/1999/spring/meyers-hemingways-american-tragedy/.

481 Donald Junkins: See Nara Schoenberg, "The Son Also Falls," *Chicago Tribune,* 11/19/2001; http://ai.eecs.umich.edu/people/conway/TS/GregoryHemingway

Article.html. See also John Colapinto, "The Good Son," *Rolling Stone*, 9/5/2002, 60–65; he quotes Junkins.

481 "about twelve years old": Gerald Clarke, "The Sons Almost Rise," *Fame*, September 1989, 109.

481 "Giggy is better": EH to PPH, 6/9/1941, *SL*, 524.

483 Much has been made: Another Hemingway story seems to cry out for comment in this connection. The plot of "God Rest You Merry Gentlemen," which appeared in the 1933 collection *Winner Take Nothing*, is taken from a selection of letters Logan Clendening, a Kansas City doctor, showed Ernest when he was in that city for Gregory's birth in 1932. In the story, one doctor tells another about a boy he saw the day before Christmas who asked the doctor to castrate him because he could not stop "sinning"; on Christmas morning, the boy appeared in the emergency room having amputated his penis with a razor. It should be noted that "One Reader Writes," the other story Ernest wrote after reading one of Clendening's letters, was also rather gruesomely graphic; a woman wrote to the doctor asking what she should do about sexual relations with her husband, who had contracted syphilis while stationed in Shanghai.

483 "nicked in the scrotum": Hotchner, *Papa Hemingway*, 48.

483 "genito-urinary" ward: Bruccoli, ed., *Conversations with Ernest Hemingway*, 95.

485 In February 1946 he estimated: Mellow, 540.

486 "the happiness of the garden": EH to Lanham, 6/12/1948, CBP; quoted in Burwell, 97.

486 homosexual desires: See, for example, Christopher Lehmann-Haupt, "Was Hemingway Gay? There's More to His Story" (review of Comley and Scholes's *Hemingway's Genders*), *New York Times*, 11/10/1994.

486 "If anyone knew": Quoted in Burwell, 57.

487 gender issues: Interestingly, one of the first friends Ernest made in France raised transgender questions when interviewed by Carlos Baker. "Was there, perhaps," Lewis Galantière asked, "some vein in Hemingway which could have made him better satisfied to be a woman? Was his carefully cultivated hardy masculinity a means of concealing from others, and perhaps even from himself, the inward wish to be, or to know how it would be to be, a woman?" "Hemingway: Aspects of His Character and Appearance," Carlos Baker interview with Lewis Galantière, 1/13/1964, CBP.

487 "our one and only life": MWH, *HIW*, 114.

488 "as a present": Ibid., 170.

488 "no debt": Ibid., 184.

488 "Papa has been kind": Ibid., 179.

488 "I had been an entity": Ibid., 162.

488 The way Ernest: MWH to EH, [n.d., 10/1945 or 11/1945], JFK.

488 In one such letter: EH to MWH, 1/19/1946, JFK. See also Shnayerson, 132.

489 "straight out of the Napoleonic code": MWH, *HIW*, 183.

489 "small, furious earthquake": Ibid., 184.

489 "veterans from the 12th Brigade": Dawn Shumaitis, "Life with Papa," *New Jersey Monthly*, 2/6/2008, http://njmonthly.com/articles/lifestyle/people/life-with-papa.html.

489   "stooge": Mayito Menocal to Baker, 11/18/1970, CBP.

490   "the ideal subaltern": See Baker, *Ernest Hemingway,* 382.

490   "Can it be that I am becoming": EH to AM, [n.d., 12/1940], quoted in Donaldson, *Archibald MacLeish,* 336. See also EH to AM, 4/4/1943 and [n.d., 5/1943], LoC.

490   he had always wanted: EH to AM, 8/27/1948; this was the letter AM sealed for fifty years, because of, he said, EH's bragging about the war; see AM to Baker, 8/9/1963, CBP.

490   "Archie, apparently unperturbed": AM, "Years of the Dog," *New and Collected Poems,* 377.

490   "Archie was fine": AM to Sara Murphy, 8/14/1941, quoted in Donnelly and Billings, 177.

491   "You have to be familiar": Drabeck and Ellis, eds., 63.

491   a 1945 letter to Buck: EH to Lanham, 6/30/1945, CBP.

491   "good old Monster": Dos Passos to Sara Murphy, 9/8/1948, Linda Miller, ed., 307.

491   "He's killed her off": Quoted in Kert, 486; Kert cites a 1978 interview with Patrick Hemingway as her source.

491   "He followed up": EH to Dos Passos, 1/22/[1948], JFK, Cuban Accessions, Box 2.

491   "60 kikes": Tytell, 269.

492   "vile, absolutely idiotic drivel": EH to AM, 8/10/1943, *SL,* 548.

492   In fact, most of the credit: See E. Fuller Torrey, *The Roots of Treason: Ezra Pound and the Secret of St. Elizabeths* (New York: McGraw-Hill, 1984), 254.

492   "All he was": Quoted in Bruccoli, *Some Sort of Epic Grandeur,* 494.

492   "the book has that deadness": EH to MP, 11/15/1941, *SL,* 527–28.

492   "I know [*sic*] him": EH to MP, 2/25/1944, *SL,* 556–57.

493   "completely uneducated": EH to MP, 7/23/1945, *SL,* 594.

CHAPTER TWENTY-SIX

494   "I don't want to compete": EH to MWH, [n.d., 11/1944], in Fuentes, 369.

494   "Also would like": EH to MP, [ca. 1/14/1940], Bruccoli, ed., *The Only Thing That Counts,* 277.

495   "My father had wanted": Gregory Hemingway, 17.

495   earlier abortions: Biographer Moorehead estimates four abortions in MG's life, one after her marriage to EH; see 42–43, 59, 198, 262–63. EH would not learn the truth until Charlie Scribner told him years later, and he would be furious when he heard it.

495   "Slumming Across God's Country": MWH, *HIW,* 188.

495   "Lucky it was in Casper": Quoted in Baker, *Ernest Hemingway,* 190.

496   According to Tunney: "EH: Down for the Count," *Fine Books and Collections,* 9/4/2009, http://www.finebooksmagazine.com/fine_books_blog/2009/09/ernest-hemingway-down-for-the-count.phtml.

496   he had also heard: Lydia Monin, *From Poverty Bay to Broadway: The Story of Tom Heeney,* books.google.com/books?isbn=1459627814, 348–49.

497   George Brown was skeptical: Plimpton, 64.

497   Ernest didn't always fight fair: Ibid., 74.

497 "Do stop it": Clarence George, "Gene Tunney vs. Ernest Hemingway—Perfectly Charming," Boxing.com, 2/2/13, http://www.boxing.com/gene_tunney_vs._ernest_hemingwayperfectly_charming.html.

498 Dr. Herrera deemed Patrick's condition: Fuentes, 84.

498 The local priest: Hotchner says that Don Andrés got the nickname because he had been on the side of the Republic in Spain and thus, in Cuba, was assigned to the poorest parish. *Papa Hemingway*, 19.

499 "the high grade wife": Quoted in Hawkins, 252–53.

499 "with the liquor bottles": Fuentes, 84.

499 "In Pauline's family": EH to Hotchner, 3/14/[1955], DeFazio, ed., 186.

500 Ernest was able to report: EH to MWH, 7/8/1947, CBP, Box 4.

500 traumatic brain injury: See, for instance, T. W. McAllister, "Traumatic Brain Injury and Psychosis—What Is the Connection?," http://www.ncbi.nlm.nih.gov/pubmed/10085209; and A. David and M. Prince, "Psychosis Following Head Injury: A Critical Review," http://www.ncbi.nlm.nih.gov/pmc/articles/PMC1765686/.

500 Electroshock is still: See http://www.ncbi.nlm.nih.gov/pubmed/7796068; and R. Kant, A. M. Bogyi, N. W. Carosella, E. Fishman, V. Kane, and C. E. Coffey, "ECT as a Therapeutic Option in Severe Brain Injury," *Convulsive Therapy* 11 (March 1995), 45–50.

500 "Patrick is wonderful": PPH to EH, [11/1947], JFK, Box 48.

500 "what a source of strength": PPH to EH, [n.d., 1947], JFK, Box 61.

500 He liked imagining her: EH to MWH, [5/4/1947], JFK, Box 4.

501 Just writing these words: EH to MWH, 4/28/[1947], JFK, Box 4.

501 "He began to dream": EH to MWH, 5/6/[1947] and 6/7/[1947], JFK, Box 4.

501 "spooked shitless": Quoted in Eby, 203.

501 "Deeply rooted": MWH, *HIW*, 170.

502 "never cut a paragraph": EH to CS III, 6/28/1947, *SL*, 622.

503 "The alteration of a word": EH to Horace Liveright, 3/31/1925, *SL*, 154.

503 "The game of golf": EH to Horace Liveright, 5/22/1925, *SL*, 161.

503 "ventured an important criticism": MP to Marjorie Kinnan Rawlings, quoted in Tarr, ed., 373.

503 "It's a little like": Arnold Gingrich, "Scott, Ernest and Whoever," 6.

503 "When Max died": EH to Wallace Meyer, 2/21/1952, *SL*, 250.

503 "You are my most trusted friend": EH to MP, 6/10/1943, Bruccoli, ed., *The Only Thing That Counts*, 325.

504 Ernest replied: Leicester Hemingway, rev. ed. 1996, 305.

504 Strikingly handsome: EH to Lanham, 2/14/[1945], CBP, Box 6, Folder 20.

505 "Ernest was never very content": Leicester Hemingway, 130.

505 "an element of testing": Viertel, 12.

506 "a good yarn": Ibid., 34.

506 "to whore for Hollywood": Ibid., 54.

506 Writing back: Ibid., 55.

507 Papa Doble: Greene, 70, 76.

507 a small enough boat: EH to Peter Viertel, 6/10/1948, JFK, Box 48.

508 Ernest came to love Venice: Baker, *Ernest Hemingway*, 468.

509   At Fossalta: Details are from ibid., and Reynolds, *Hemingway: The Final Years*, 180–81. Information about EH's translator is from http://www.myvenice.org /print-512.html, "The Veneto of Ernest Hemingway in 90 Photos." See also http:// irenebrination.typepad.com/irenebrination_notes_on_a/2009/08/hemingway -the-beats-and-the-american-dream-tribute-to-fernanda-pivano-19172009.html.

511   "delightful . . . deep, dark eyes": MWH, *HIW,* 256.

511   "Ernest was weaving": Ibid., 254.

512   Some visitors had: René Villarreal, "Life with Papa," *New Jersey Monthly,* 2/6/2008, 2.

512   Both Lanhams had visited: Baker, 452.

CHAPTER TWENTY-SEVEN

514   Patrick Hemingway has stated: Carol Hemingway, "907 Whitehead Street," *Hemingway Review* (Fall 2003), 21.

514   "gut-shot": Baker, 379.

515   He owned dogs: Malcolm Cowley's count of the Finca's dogs and cats appeared in his *Life* article in January 1948, "A Portrait of Mister Papa," rpt. in McCaffery, ed., 34–56. In an 8/25–26/1949 letter full of exaggeration, Ernest told Charlie Scribner he had thirty-four cats and eleven dogs.

515   Peter Viertel later told: Viertel, 43.

515   Conversely, Tommy Shevlin's wife: Meyers, *Gary Cooper,* 175. Experts seem to be divided, however, as to whether a turtle will die if left on its back.

515   "Some people put the arm": Hotchner, *Papa Hemingway,* 8; see also, for example, Burgess, 94.

516   he used submarine guns: Dos Passos, *The Fourteenth Chronicle,* 421.

516   he shot coyotes: Baker, 344.

516   he once used: Tarr, ed., 245.

516   "[Ernest] was a great lover of nature": René Villarreal, "Life with Papa," 3.

516   He also told one: Valerie Hemingway, 72.

516   made love to a bear: EH to MWH, [7/1943], JFK, Box 48.

516   At another time: EH to Harvey Breit, 1/15/1953, JFK.

517   "I should get through to him": Hotchner, 30. Ernest also said he was part Indian—a falsehood—and that he had been talking "Indian talk."

517   René Villarreal has given: René and Raúl Villarreal, 110–15. René Villarreal claims that he volunteered to go into the cage with Ernest, and that he applied lion lard to his own body; Ernest then told the boy he couldn't let him go into the cage. For another, mostly apocryphal, version of the story, see Fuentes, 39–40.

518   work before long with an elephant: EH to Slim Hayward, 12/26/1952, JFK. Ernest told her he was going to approach the animal without irritating him, and he was sure that the elephant then wouldn't do anything Ernest wouldn't do.

519   "rough exuberance": *SL,* 661n3. Christopher Martin, a psychiatrist at Baylor University, believes Hemingway suffered from bipolar disorder: Christopher D. Martin, MD, "Ernest Hemingway: A Psychological Autopsy of a Suicide," *Psychiatry* (Winter 2006). Martin also found Ernest to be suffering from alcohol dependence, traumatic brain injury, and probable borderline and narcissistic personality traits.

520 writing to Henny's parents: EH to Mrs. Broyles, [n.d., 1950], JFK, Box 39. He said he was not attending the wedding because he was a "snob." This is a fragment of a letter that may not have been sent.

520 "He had a very steep trajectory": EH to Arthur Mizener, 7/6/1949, *SL*, 657.

521 "I never had any respect": EH to Arthur Mizener, 4/22/1950, *SL*, 691–92.

521 "I think Scott": EH to Arthur Mizener, 5/12/1950, *SL*, 694–95.

521 "I try to give him": EH to Harvey Breit, 7/9/1950, *SL*, 701.

524 "It is a very fine novel": EH to CS III, 8/24/1949. Princeton; quoted in Trogdon, *The Lousy Racket*, 230.

524 "It was not until": EH to CS, 9/6–7/1949, *SL*, 673–74.

524 he had gone foxhunting: EH to CS III, 8/19/1949, *SL*, 664.

524 "chutes": EH to CS III, 7/19/1950, *SL*, 706.

524 extending sports prowess: EH to CS III, 10/4/1949, *SL*, 679. This was observed when Gregory was seven, Ernest said.

524 "upper Michigan league": EH to CS III, 7/19/1950, *SL*, 706. Ernest did not play baseball in any league in Michigan.

524 "Going to win": Ross, 6.

524 "I started out very quiet": Ibid., 19.

525 Carol was assaulted: EH to CS III, 8/27/1949, *SL*, 670.

525 he had a Cheyenne: EH to CS III, 7/22/1949, *SL*, 659. In the same letter Ernest took Scribner to task on a point of etiquette: misaddressing an invitation to "Mr. Ernest Hemingway" when it should have gone to "Mr. and Mrs. Hemingway."

525 that he had "read" law: EH to CS III, 12/13/1949, Scribner's Papers, Princeton. See Trogdon, *The Lousy Racket*, 233.

525 he and his brothers and sisters: EH to CS III, 7/9–10/1950, *SL*, 704. He was comparing the Hemingway children to the Ivancich offspring, a claim probably also influenced by his new snobbism.

525 "fucked three times": EH to CS III, 7/22/1949, *SL*, 658.

525 "fuck better": EH to CS III, 8/25–26/1949, *SL*, 667.

525 He told Cardinal Spellman: EH to Cardinal Spellman, 7/28/1949, *SL*, 661.

525 "for free, without publicity": EH to Senator Joseph McCarthy, 5/8/1950, *SL*, 693. Baker notes that this was typed and signed twice by EH but "perhaps" not sent.

525 kill Roberto Rossellini: EH to Ingrid Bergman, 6/20/1950, JFK.

525 he also dictated a bombastic letter: EH to Averell Harriman, 9/9/1949, *SL*, 674. See EH to Harriman, 10/11/1949, *SL*, 674–75n1.

526 He borrowed $10,000: EH to CS III, 9/21/1949, Scribner's Papers, Princeton.

526 he had spent $258.90: MWH, *HIW*, 268.

526 two iron miniature cannons: Ibid., 241–42. See also Hendrickson, 308.

526 "At table": MWH, *HIW*, 243.

526 "nervous and tired": Ibid., 246.

526 "His weariness": Ibid., 248.

527 "restless and unhappy": Ibid., 275.

527 "so rapidly and virulently": *New York Times*, 10/13/1949, quoted in Meyers, *Hemingway*, 46.

527 "Alcohol was obviously responsible": Viertel, 90.

527 Wychol, which prevents fat buildup: The active agents in Wychol were choline

and inositol, lipotropics that aid in the breakdown of fats in the liver. Wychol is not manufactured any longer; choline and inositol are often ingredients in vitamin B complex supplements.

527   "It made me feel disloyal": MWH, *HIW,* 246.

528   "The basic trouble": Wallace Meyer to CS III, 3/13/1950, Scribner's Papers, Princeton, quoted in Trogdon, *The Lousy Racket,* 234.

528   "TRULY DELIGHTED": CS III to EH, 2/2/1950, Scribner's Papers, Princeton, quoted in Trogdon, *The Lousy Racket,* 233.

528   "because it was fun": EH to CS III, 3/14/1950, Scribner's Papers, Princeton, quoted in Trogdon, *The Lousy Racket,* 234.

528   "The manuscript is not changed": Wallace Meyer to CS III, 4/7/1950, quoted in Trogdon, *The Lousy Racket,* 235.

528   "if you will go back": CS III to EH, 7/18/50, Scribner's Papers, Princeton, quoted in Trogdon, *The Lousy Racket,* 237.

529   He had miscalculated: EH to CS III, 7/21/1950, Scribner's Papers, Princeton, quoted in Trogdon, *The Lousy Racket,* 239. EH let it be known that he was especially angry at having to write this letter on his birthday.

529   "strange and individual": Wallace Meyer to CS III, 8/7/1950, Scribner's Papers, Princeton, quoted in Trogdon, *The Lousy Racket,* 235.

529   "Please don't think": EH to Hotchner, 10/3/1949, DeFazio, ed., 49.

530   "To me, it has a loud sound": MG to William Walton, 2/3/1950, Moorehead, ed., *Selected Letters of Martha Gellhorn,* 204.

530   Another exception was John dos Passos: Dos Passos to Wilson, 7/19/1950. See Dos Passos, *The Fourteenth Chronicle,* 591.

531   "conceited": Ross to EH, 4/26/1950, JFK.

531   "a lethal exposure": Rodman, 52.

531   "It has strange revelations": Alice B. Toklas to Fernanda Pivano, [7/4/1950]; Edward Burns, ed., *Staying On Alone: Letters of Alice B. Toklas* (1973; rpt., New York: Vintage, 1975), 194.

532   "missing his cortege": MWH, *HIW,* 252.

533   He took the occasion: Kert, 450-51.

533   "Expecting the present novel": Trogdon, *The Lousy Racket,* 331-32.

534   "because there was something wrong": EH to CS III, 5/20/1950; quoted in Trogdon, *The Lousy Racket,* 237.

534   "had an unfailing instinct": Viertel, 81.

534   "below the level": *New York Herald Tribune Book Review,* 9/10/1950.

534   "a disappointing novel": *Harper's* (September 1950).

534   "It is not only": *Saturday Review of Literature,* 9/9/1950.

534   "embarrassment, even pity": *New Yorker,* 9/19/1950.

534   "one thoroughly bad book": London *Times,* 9/3/1950.

534   "the poorest thing": Quoted in Meyers, *Hemingway,* 458.

534   "parody": *Time,* 9/11/1950.

534   "The most important author": *New York Times Book Review,* 9/10/1950.

534   "high supercilious caddishness": *Commonweal,* 11/3/1950.

534   "Perhaps we really do know": *Saturday Review of Literature,* 10/28/1950.

535   "I could not go to Venice": "A Writer's Quest for Parnassus," *New York Times,* 8/13/1950.

535 "Isn't it sort of customary": EH to CS III, 9/9/1950, *SL*, 712–13.

535 "he had not known": EH to Lanham, 9/11/1950, *SL*, 715.

CHAPTER TWENTY-EIGHT

536 the best-seller list: DeFazio, ed., 91n.

536 Ernest made about $136,000: Trogdon, *The Lousy Racket*, 241.

536 "It must have something": MWH, *HIW*, 274.

536 "He was a simmering": Ibid., 271.

536 "My husband needed": Ibid., 272.

536 "a desperate old man": Ibid., 271.

537 Patrick evidently believed: Kert, 459. Kert does not provide a source for this point, but she cites interviews with and letters from Patrick elsewhere in the book.

537 "Slim as a": MWH, *HIW*, 246.

538 "Bunney-Binney": Burwell, 221n3. Baker probably restricted this letter to avoid embarrassment to Ivancich and MWH.

538 One evening she brought: MWH, *HIW*, 280.

538 "your hangman's suit": Ibid., 279.

538 "your badge of shame": Quoted in Reynolds, *Hemingway: The Final Years*, 232.

538 "truculent, brutal": MWH to CS III, 10/12/1950, Scribner's Papers, Princeton, quoted in Burwell, 205n25.

539 as she had just learned definitively: EH later wrote Bernard Berenson that he could not trust a woman who had not borne a child, 8/11/1953, JFK.

539 Despite the fact that: Ernest promised it would not appear in Italy for two years.

540 "Very interesting": MWH, *HIW*, 285.

540 "You know it is a horrible thing": EH to Arthur Mizener, 1/4/1951, *SL*, 717.

540 "you can see how": EH to Arthur Mizener, 1/11/1951, *SL*, 718.

540 By the time of his last letter: EH to Arthur Mizener, 1/18/1951, JFK, Box 49.

541 "before everything went to hell": EH to Baker, 6/30/1951, CBP, quoted in Mellow, 562.

541 he wrote Sunny: EH to Sunny Hemingway, 8/11/1949, JFK, Box 49.

541 the night before: See Kert, 460.

541 her husband: See [Elizabeth Burns Cord], "Peter Fippinger, Pioneer Settler of Cook County," unpublished essay, 2006, 14.

541 Ruth moved in: GHH's address on her letterhead was 551 Keystone Avenue, River Forest, Illinois. Marcelline Hemingway, in a letter to EH, 7/16/1951, referred to Ruth, "who will lose her home, 551 Keystone, at the age of 60." Grace had put the house in Marcelline's name in 1939; see Marcelline Hemingway to GHH, 4/19/1939 and 3/8/1941, HRC, Box 7, Folder 7. If Ruth was losing her home it seems that it was because Marcelline was evicting her.

541 Sunny at one point: EH to Sunny Hemingway, 5/29/1952, PSU, Box 2, Folder 11.

541 "I hate her guts": EH to CS, 8/27/1949, *SL*, 670.

542 "terribly revelatory": "Oral History Interview with William Walton," 3/30/1993, conducted by Megan Floyd Desnoyers, JFK.

542 The story as told in the books: The scrapbooks can be viewed online at http://www.jfklibrary.org/Research/The-Ernest-Hemingway-Collection/Hemingway

-Audiovisual-Materials.aspx. Grace assembled a sixth volume about Ernest as well, this one for his grandparents.

543 Pauline had told Patrick: Hotchner, *Papa Hemingway,* 126.

543 "I think he saw me": Hendrickson, "Hemingway's Older Sons," *Washington Post,* 7/30/1987.

543 "take the taste of Gregory": EH to Jack Hemingway, 12/16/1952, JFK, Box 50. Mary knew by this time that she could not have children, making this remark even odder.

543 "I really don't know": PPH to EH, [n.d., ca. 5/12/1950], JFK, Box 47.

544 "It wasn't so bad": Gregory Hemingway, 8.

544 mother's autopsy report: It is unlikely that Greg sent for or received an autopsy report. Autopsies are usually provided only when a family member requests them. In the unlikely event a Hemingway family member requested one, he or she would have seen it soon after Pauline's death in 1951. Greg must have been referring to his mother's death certificate, which cites "hemorrhage with Adrenal" as the direct cause of death; presumably this was enough for Greg, with his medical training, to determine she had died from an adrenal tumor. For the death certificate, see http://allanellenberger.com/sins-of-the-mother-the-story -of-pauline-hemingway/.

544 "a person who was with [Ernest]": Gregory Hemingway, 12.

545 "She was a fine brave girl": Sara Murphy to EH, [9/4/1952], JFK, Cuban Accession, Box 4.

545 "corrupt": Quoted in Hendrickson, 403.

545 "The wave of remembering": EH to CS III, 10/2/1951, *SL,* 737.

545 "Ernest never seemed clean": Keith, 43.

547 "Tactically": EH to Wallace Meyer, 3/4/1952 and 2/7/1952, *SL,* 758.

547 "No phony glamour girls": Orville Prescott, *New York Times,* 8/28/1950.

547 "a great and true novel": *Nation,* 9/6/1952.

547 "to not aid": EH to Baker, 2/17/1951, Stanford, 353.

547 "one of the few genuine": *Saturday Review,* 9/6/1952.

547 "destroy the school": EH to Wallace Meyer, 3/4/1952 and 3/7/1952, *SL,* 758.

548 "Hemingway we know": *New York Times Book Review,* 9/7/1952.

548 "a great American classic": *Chicago Sunday Tribune,* 9/7/1952.

548 "a note of insistence": *Partisan Review,* 11/1952.

548 about $137,000": Trogdon, *The Lousy Racket,* 253.

548 He sold the film rights: Mellow, 581.

549 "sound[ing] like a page": A. B. C. Whipple, "James Jones and His Angel," *Life,* 5/7/1951. Presumably EH had an early copy of *Life,* for on April 11–12, 1951, he refers to, and quotes from, the article.

549 "a whimpering neurotic": EH to CS III, 4/11–12/1951, *SL,* 722.

549 A rough draft: Undated fragment, presumably a draft of the 5/4/1951 letter to CS III, JFK, Box 51.

550 "is a good fighting name": EH to CS III, 4/11–12/1951, *SL,* 724.

CHAPTER TWENTY-NINE

551 "The Cowley piece": EH to John Wheeler, 2/15/1949, JFK, Box 49. Wheeler, who owned many syndicates, published the story in several newspapers; see,

for instance, *The Ottawa Journal*, 3/9/1949. Wheeler had hired EH to write for NANA during the Spanish Civil War. See his *I've Got News for You* (New York: E. P. Dutton, 1961).

552 That did not keep him: EH to Baker, 6/4/1952, Stanford, #370. For Young's account of his relationship with EH, see his introduction in Philip Young, *Ernest Hemingway: A Reconsideration* (University Park: Pennsylvania State University Press, 1966).

552 "tertiary syphilis": EH to Baker, 6/4/1952, Stanford, #370.

552 "too engrossing": Quoted in Donaldson, *The Death of a Rebel*, 56.

553 Ernest sent Fenton: EH to Fenton, 7/13/1952, JFK.

553 Another letter to Fenton: EH to Fenton, 8/2/1952, JFK, Box 50.

554 The Moors on the Nationalist side: Baker, "Hemingway-Lanham Chronology 1944–45," 18, CBP.

554 Ernest had always been: See, for instance, Celestine Bohlen, "Hide This Until You Die. Very Truly Yours, Ernest," *New York Times*, 5/4/2002.

555 "Writers of fiction": EH to Bernard Berenson, 10/14/1952, *SL*, 789.

555 The incident of the blue heron: See Donald R. Johnson, " 'The Last Good Country': Again the End of Something," in Jackson J. Benson, ed., *New Critical Approaches to the Short Stories of Ernest Hemingway*, 318. Johnson believes the story was meant to be the first page of Hemingway's Michigan novel, 315.

557 Lancia B10 sedan: For a photo of EH with the Lancia, see http://www.veloceto day.com/lifestyle/lifestyle_46.php.

557 They were met in the Kajiado preserve: Mayito Menocal to Baker, 11/18/1970, CBP.

558 "my previous and lovely wife": "The Christmas Gift," *Look*, 4/20/1954 and 5/4/1954, *BEH*, 377.

558 Ernest's poor shooting: Mayito Menocal Jr. to Baker, 11/16/1964, CBP.

558 But he and Mary loved: See Carey Voeller, " 'He Only Looked the Same Way I Felt': The Textual Confessions of Hemingway's Hunters," *Hemingway Review* (Fall 1995).

558 Both felt gentler: MWH, *HIW*, 351.

559 "Is it true": Ibid., 368–69.

559 "[Mary] has always wanted": From this account and several admittedly fictive scenes in *The Garden of Eden*, it seems Mary somehow penetrated Ernest anally, the two of them playing at switching their genders. See, for example, Carl Eby, " 'He Felt the Change So That It Hurt Him All Through': Sodomy and Transvestic Hallucination in Hemingway," *Hemingway Review* (Fall 2005), or his *Hemingway's Fetishism*.

560 "I told the elders": EH, *Under Kilimanjaro*, Robert W. Lewis and Robert E. Fleming, eds. (Kent, OH: Kent State University Press, 2007), 29. Hereafter *UK*.

560 Inevitably, much of this material: See, for example, Josep Armengol-Carrera, "Raceing Hemingway: Revisions of Masculinity and/as Whiteness in Hemingway's *Green Hills of Africa* and *Under Kilimanjaro*," *Hemingway Review* (Fall 2011).

560 "like Brenda Frazier": EH to Harvey Breit, 1/3/1954, *SL*, 826–27.

560 Marilyn Monroe: EH to AM, 3/29/1953, LoC.

563 The plane burned: See Reynolds, *Hemingway: The Final Years*, 274; MWH, *HIW*, 384.

563 Ernest's injuries: Viertel, 222.

563 "This is a funny thing": EH to Bernard Berenson, 2/2/1954, *SL*, 828. In his defense, Ernest may have had in mind a subject he wrote about repeatedly in the African book: the incredible sense of smell of the Kamba, who could identify a man's ethnicity, nationality, or tribe by smell alone.

564 His fantasies multiplied: EH to Hotchner, 3/14/1954, DeFazio, ed., 154–60.

564 He told Berenson: EH to Bernard Berenson, 4/4/1954, JFK, Box 50.

564 "he resumed": MWH, *HIW*, 389.

565 "more or less in order": Ibid., 391.

565 visiting the ranch of matador: Lee Server, *Ava Gardner: "Love Is Nothing"* (New York: St. Martin's, 2006), 281.

565 Inevitably, he became Papa: Ibid., 291.

565 *The Killers* was OK": Quoted in ibid., 290.

565 After Ava passed the kidney stones: Server, 292.

566 "I always felt close": Ibid., 342.

566 "made a handsome couple": Viertel, 225.

566 "Even if this is true": Ibid., 228.

566 "What was shocking to me": Hotchner, *Papa Hemingway*, 83.

567 His grin showed rows: Viertel, 233.

567 "Papa was a big man": Keith, 143.

567 "The first time we went fishing": MWH, *HIW*, 407.

567 Ernest had seen a doctor: René and Raúl Villarreal, 97.

567 "Rummies are rummies": EH to Charles Poore, 1/30/1953, JFK, Box 50, quoted in Dardis, 157.

568 "Don't you drink?": EH to Ivan Kashkin, 8/19/1935, *SL*, 420.

568 "I suppose he was drunk": Quoted in Meyers, *Hemingway*, 508.

568 "Gradually alcohol began": Mayito Menocal, Jr., to Baker, 11/18/1970, CBP.

569 "was a hell of a blow": EH to AM, 11/22/1930, *SL*, 331.

569 "coward": Quoted in Earl Rovit and Arthur Waldhorn, eds., *Hemingway and Faulkner in Their Time* (New York: Continuum, 2005), 164.

569 "Time may show it": Quoted in Mellow, 588.

570 "rolling to starboard": *Time*, 11/8/1954.

570 "I am a man without politics": See Tom Miller, "Off the Shelf: The Day Hemingway's Nobel Prize Came Out of Hiding," *Los Angeles Times*, 10/4/2009, text:http://www.latimes.com/entertainment/news/arts/la-caw-off-the-shelf42009 octo4,0,7529902.story#axzz2uA827yPF.

570 "mastery of the art of narrative": http://www.nobelprize.org/nobel_prizes/litera ture/laureates/1954/.

570 "Writing, at its best": http://www.nobelprize.org/nobel_prizes/literature/laure ates/1954/hemingway-speech.html.

CHAPTER THIRTY

572 Sometime in 1956: *UK*, viii.

573 "The Jews have always had": Viertel, 255.

574 "Ernest grew more and more": Keith, 144.

574 "skullduggery": Ibid., 145–46.

574 "flew into a rage": Viertel, 258.

574 "The judgment, wisdom, and sanity": Keith, 150.

575 "as if he were a truant schoolboy": Viertel, 278–79.

575 "What are you, a rummy?": Edwards, 303.

575 "[H]e can make money": James Curtis, *Spencer Tracy: A Biography* (New York: Alfred A. Knopf, 2011), 732.

575 The movie was already: The budget was $2 million, but the film ended up costing $5 million. Spencer Tracy would be nominated for an Oscar.

576 "No movie made": Viertel, 255.

576 "however you cut it": Keith, 146–47.

576 "I've had my hair dyed": Viertel, 269–70.

576 It seems that only once: MWH to EH, 6/23/[1946], JFK. Mary complained he was only good for chores "and release of your sex functions which has long been almost totally mechanical."

577 "you wonder boy-girl": MWH to EH, 11/25/[1948], JFK, Box 60.

577 "from half a woman": MWH to EH, [n.d., 1953?], JFK, Box 60.

577 like a leopard: EH to MWH, [9/1948?], JFK, Box 48.

577 "For the well-being": MWH to EH, 10/4/1955, JFK, Box 69. Mary quotes from the letter in *HIW,* 426–27; the versions are slightly different.

578 "She really had to eat": Pete (Mary) Lanham to Baker, 5/10/[1966], CBP.

578 "Because of the truly terrible": Gregory Hemingway to EH, 11/13/1952, quoted in John Hemingway, 118.

578 "Papa had undergone": Jack Hemingway, 131–33. MWH also describes this occasion, *HIW,* 427.

579 "Despite his sturdy": Viertel, 254.

579 "He looked old": Hotchner, *Papa Hemingway,* 156.

579 "I have to take": "Books: An American Storyteller," *Time,* 12/13/1954.

579 It went up as high: Dardis, 193.

580 "The doctor says I am not": EH to CS III, 5/19/1951, *SL,* 727.

580 "the gloominess": EH to Harvey Breit, 2/24/1952, *SL,* 753.

580 "He drank constantly": Hotchner, *Papa Hemingway,* 158.

580 "sipping his drinks": Ibid., 173.

581 "of utmost importance": Jean Monnier to EH, 3/18/[1957], JFK. Strangely, Monnier tells Ernest in this letter not to dwell on the liver test results; Ernest must have written him a worried letter.

582 "good for neuropsychiatric": 1955 advertisement, in EH's Medical Files, JFK.

582 a 1954 headline: "Pills for Mental Illness?" *Time,* 11/8/1954.

582 a 1955 editorial: "Editorial: Reserpine in the Treatment of Neuropsychiatric Disorders," *Annals of Internal Medicine* 43 (September 1955).

583 and Ritalin: "In 1957, Ciba Pharmaceutical Company began marketing methylphenidate as Ritalin to treat chronic fatigue, depression, psychosis associated with depression, narcolepsy, and to offset the sedating effects of other medications." See http://www.cesar.umd.edu/cesar/drugs/ritalin.asp. On August 15, before Ernest left for the 1956 trip to Spain, Dr. Manuel Infiesta Bages gave him a statement to carry with him on the journey saying EH had been prescribed Seconal, Equanil, Wychol, and Meonine.

583 And just a year: Dr. Manuel Infiesta Bages, statement, 8/15/1956, JFK, Medical Files. Some of these "statements" were addressed "To whom it may concern," for EH to carry with him on trips overseas.

583 He told Archie: EH to AM, 6/28/1957, SL, 877.

584 "He got the idea": MWH to Sunny Hemingway, 12/8/1957, PSU, Box 2, Folder 19.

585 After receiving his inheritance: Gregory Hemingway, 110. Greg later told Paul Hendrickson, 428, that the story about the elephants was a fiction.

585 "When I saw him": EH to Patrick Hemingway, 4/2/1957 and 9/4/1957, Patrick Hemingway Papers, Princeton.

585 In 1955 he told: EH to Marlene Dietrich, 4/15/1955, JFK, Box 50.

585 "When it's all added up": Gregory Hemingway to EH, 11/13/1952, quoted in John Hemingway, 116.

586 "You'll never write": Gregory Hemingway to EH, 11/14/1952, quoted in John Hemingway, 119–20.

586 Ernest wrote to Dorothy Pound: EH to Dorothy Pound, 8/22/1951, SL, 741–42. In that year Ernest wrote, in a keen assessment, that release could not be secured in the present political climate and that in fact Ezra might be found sane and retried. Furthermore, Pound couldn't as an American citizen be deported to Italy, which was one possibility that Ernest supported. See EH to D.D. Paige, 10/22/1951, SL, 739–41.

586 "I liked Pound": EH to Bernard Berenson, 3/20–22/1953, SL, 815.

587 "In every refreshing glass": See Tytell, 311.

587 He told a Time reporter: Robert Manning, "An American Storyteller," Time, 12/13/1954.

587 Ernest did not end up: Burwell, 183, reports that EH left a check with Bill Davis in Spain in the summer of 1959 to help Pound move from Italy to Spain. Pound did not move, and it is unclear whether he got the check. Burwell cites a letter at Lilly Library from Brigit Patmore to Joyce and Geoffrey Bridson, 1/8/1962.

587 "our greatest living poet": EH to Ezra Pound, 7/19/1956, SL, 865.

587 MacLeish, Robert Frost, and Hemingway: Though Frost used his connections and pleaded Ezra's case to President Eisenhower, MacLeish got Frost involved in the first place, and wielded his considerable connections more effectively than Frost. See Tytell, 325; and Donaldson, Archibald MacLeish, 447–49. Tytell, e-mail to author, 4/15/2014, believes Frost's connections were superior to AM's, but acknowledges that AM "instigated and organized" the campaign, 325.

587 Because he earned royalties: For financial details, see Reynolds, Hemingway: The Final Years, 302–6.

588 Hotchner had developed: For Hotchner's Hemingway adaptations, see his comprehensive list in his introduction to DeFazio, ed., 8.

588 When he retrieved: See Burwell, 152, for a letter EH wrote to collector Lee Samuels about this material.

588 Reading these: Scholars have pointed out that there are many different stories about these trunks and their contents, and some argue that they never existed. For the fullest discussion, see Jacqueline Tavernier-Courbin, Ernest Hemingway's A Moveable Feast: The Making of Myth (Boston: Northeastern University

Press, 1991); and Gerry Brenner, *A Comprehensive Companion to Hemingway's A Moveable Feast: Annotation to Interpretation* (Lewiston, NY: Edwin Mellen Press, 2000). Leonard Lyons, Ernest's gossip columnist friend, reported Ernest's discovery of the manuscripts in his column in the *New York Post* in 1957.

588 "I'm going to write": EH to MP, 10/16/1933, *SL*, 396.

589 Ernest knew as much: EH to CS IV, 4/18/1961, Scribner's Papers, Princeton. Reynolds says this letter was not mailed, *Hemingway: The Final Years*, 406n54.

590 "This book is fiction": EH thought he needed to apologize to Hadley, it seems, first, because he was writing about their personal lives; second, because he described the story of her losing his manuscripts, for which she was deeply sorry. Third, Hadley, who was not a stupid woman, would have recognized what Ernest was doing: falsely portraying their years together as idyllically simple. It is also possible that EH apologized thinking that her husband, Paul Mowrer, would mind, but this would have been totally out of character for Mowrer.

CHAPTER THIRTY-ONE

592 "Papa decided that we better": MWH to Tillie and Lloyd Arnold, 8/13/1958, in Arnold, 205.

592 "heavy rifles": MWH, *HIW*, 450.

593 "We were allowed to keep": Fuentes, 201.

593 "Stuff left over": MWH, *HIW*, 450.

593 "looked wonderful": Hotchner, *Papa Hemingway*, 191.

593 "seemed content": Ibid., 194.

593 "delightful": MWH, *HIW*, 459.

594 She raved: MWH to "Fellas" [John, Patrick, and Gregory Hemingway], 1/13/1959, Bernice Kert Papers, JFK, Box 26. The residence had a three-car garage on the basement level, and a cinder-block guesthouse.

594 "it was now Papa's habit": Arnold, 257, 271.

594 "lovely adolescent tenderness": Leonard Bernstein to Martha Gellhorn, 1/7/1959, in Simeone, ed., 410.

595 Rumors floated: Numerous accounts say Bill Davis worked for the CIA, but none can be confirmed. See, for example, Ben Sonnenberg, *Lost Property* (New York: Counterpoint, 1999), 116. Teo Davis thinks the story is probably true. Interview with Teo Davis, 11/15/2010; interview with Valerie Hemingway, 11/19/2010. Davis mentions the CIA in a letter to EH, [6/8/1950], JFK, Cuban Accession, Box 2.

595 Annie's sister Jeanie: Peggy Guggenheim said Bill Davis was the best lover she ever had. See Mary Dearborn, *Mistress of Modernism: The Life of Peggy Guggenheim* (Boston: Houghton Mifflin, 2004), 236.

595 "a big, bald, shambolic man": Jonathan Gathorne-Hardy, *Half an Arch: A Memoir* (London: Timewell Press, 2004), 220.

597 "a beautiful white house": Dundy, 188.

597 "A tape recorder": Valerie Hemingway, 46.

598 "Darling, you're so thin": MWH, *HIW*, 466.

598 "That is for anyone": Keith, 186–87.

598 "swinging between depression": Ibid., 198.

599 "observed a darker, meaner": Valerie Hemingway, 31.

599 "I'll show you girls": Annie Davis interview with Bernice Kert, 7/21/1959, Kert Papers, JFK, Box 23.

600 He shot a lit cigarette: Megh Testerman, who has studied photographs from that summer very closely, believes EH was using an air gun. See http://www .pri.org/stories/2013–08–12/photos-ernest-hemingways-dangerous-summer. Ordóñez told Jeffrey Meyers that EH used a pellet gun to shoot the cigarette at the party, but that "later, at Escorial outside Madrid, he shot cigarettes out of my mouth with real bullets," Meyers, *Hemingway*, 529. Valerie Hemingway, 40, writes that "to the horror and fascination of the onlookers," Ernest used a .22.

600 Another night he had been: Baker, *Ernest Hemingway*, 548.

600 More strange behavior: According to Hotchner, *Papa Hemingway*, 217–18, Ernest told Selznick that if his film, starring the forty-one-year-old Jones, were to make that much money in profit Selznick should change the amount into nickels and shove them up his ass until they came out his ears.

600 "irked by the incessant praise": Valerie Hemingway, 41.

601 "Something was changing": MWH, *HIW*, 471. MWH made this observation at Pamplona.

601 "I could not and did not": Valerie Hemingway, 85.

603 "*so other people*": EH to MWH, 10/13/1959, JFK, Box 51, EH's emphasis.

603 "And she has a proper beef": Hotchner, *Papa Hemingway*, 231, ellipsis in original.

603 "Life without me": Valerie Hemingway, 82.

604 "Traveling with Ernest": Ibid., 73.

604 "critical reader": Ibid., 47.

604 "Mohawk tapes": Hotchner to EH, 9/23/1959, DeFazio, ed., 269.

604 "If the box was here": EH to AEH, 10/3/1959, DeFazio, ed., 271.

605 "Ernesto can't really": Mandel, 112.

605 in exchange for allowing: See EH to Hotchner, 12/19/1959, DeFazio, ed., 275.

605 Ernest was most uncharitable: MWH, *HIW*, 481.

606 "We were not total strangers": Arnold, 290.

606 "But I bought it as a nest egg": Ibid., 297.

606 "Mary took wonderful care of me": EH, *The Dangerous Summer* (1960; rpt., New York: Touchstone, 1997), 59. Hereafter *DS*.

606 "I shelved the idea": MWH, *HIW*, 485.

607 "slightly decaying air": Valerie Hemingway, 95.

607 If there were no guests: Ibid., 104–6.

607 one was from Herbert Matthews: See Anthony DePalma, *The Man Who Invented Fidel: Castro, Cuba, and Herbert L. Matthews of the* New York Times (New York: PublicAffairs, 2006), 197–98.

609 "Ernest said he would probably take: Viertel, 242.

609 "He ate very little": Hotchner, *Papa Hemingway*, 241–2.

611 He was on a wide range: A list of medications to be taken with him in travel, prepared by José Luis Herrera, JFK. The previous April, Herrera listed Serpasil, Ritalin, Doriden, Combex, Seconal, Equanil, Diuril, Wychol, and Afaxin (a topical eye treatment), JFK. Diuril is for high blood pressure, which suggests he was taking the Serpasil (reserpine) for its psychiatric properties rather than its function as an antihypertensive.

611   "belle epoque": Quoted in MWH, *HIW,* 489.

611   "Never so dead": EH to AEH, 9/8/1960, DeFazio, ed., 298.

611   "as an honest guy": EH to Hotchner, 9/17/1960, DeFazio, ed., 299–301.

612   "tentative and ill at ease": Valerie Hemingway, 141.

612   "Worry hung": Hotchner, *Papa Hemingway,* 252.

612   Then Ernest got it into his head: Valerie Hemingway, 141–43.

612   "although it makes me": Quoted in MWH, *HIW,* 489. William Styron, another heavy-drinking writer who suffered from depression, wrote in his 1990 *Darkness Visible* about the onset of a major depression, at the beginning of which he developed an aversion to alcohol, which worried him as much as any other symptom. His account reveals some similarities to EH's experience.

612   He worried: Valerie Hemingway, 148.

613   "breathe that good mountain air": Hotchner, *Papa Hemingway,* 263.

CHAPTER THIRTY-TWO

614   "the Emperor's robe": Baker interview with Dr. Scott Earle, 8/7/1964, CBP.

614   He took a key: Mary later explained why she left the keys to the locked storeroom easily accessible: "I thought of hiding the keys, and decided that no one had a right to deny a man access to his possessions"—a statement that has led at least one biographer to question her motives. Jeffrey Meyers writes, 560, "It seems . . . [Mary] behav[ed] with classic ambivalence: she locked the guns in the basement but left the keys in the kitchen." This seems unfair; also, Mary went on to say, "I also assumed that Ernest would not remember the storeroom." *HIW,* 502. Her statement should be given some weight in connection with EH's recent problems with short-term memory—in other words, it is conceivable that she believed he would have forgotten where the keys were kept.

614   "He was failing visibly": Charles Scribner, Jr., *In the Company of Writers,* 75.

614   "gaunt": Viertel, 384.

615   "impairing the morals": Hotchner, *Papa Hemingway,* 269.

615   After the salutation: Ibid., 273–74.

615   He had originally met Ernest: Baker interview with George Saviers, 8/6/1964, CBP.

615   "I'm just a country doctor": Hotchner, *Papa Hemingway,* 274.

615   Yet, according to a letter: EH to Lanham, 12/1/1960, JFK.

616   "weaning": Baker, interview with George Saviers, 8/6/1964, CBP.

616   "imagine an ennobling": Leslie Fiedler, "An Almost Imaginary Interview: Hemingway in Ketchum," in Leslie Fiedler, *A Leslie Fiedler Reader* (New York: Stein & Day, 1977), 153–64; the essay was originally published in 1962.

617   "Hotch, you've got to do something": Hotchner, *Papa Hemingway,* 268. In a footnote in DeFazio, ed., Hotchner identifies Forrest (Duke) McMullen as a hunting companion and "man Friday" to Ernest. It is not clear what he meant by that. It seems that a number of those around Ernest at the end, like George Brown, were in the Hemingways' employ, but there is no way to be sure.

617   With Mary's consent: Hotchner, *Papa Hemingway,* gives a pseudonym, "Dr. Renown" (275), but Bernice Kert (499) and MWH (499) provide his name.

617   In a letter Howard Rome: Howard Rome to EH, 1/19/1961, JFK, Medical Files.

617 Hugh R. Butt: Baker, *Ernest Hemingway,* 556.

618 hemochromatosis, a disease: See Susan Beegel, "Hemingway and Hemochromatosis," *Hemingway Review* (Fall 1990). See also Nancy C. Andrews, "Disorders of Iron Metabolism," *New England Journal of Medicine* 341 (1999); and Massimo Franchini, "Hereditary Iron Overload: Update on Pathophysiology, Diagnosis, and Treatment," *American Journal of Hematology* 81, no. 3 (2006), http://www.mayoclinic.com/health/hemochromatosis/DS00455/DSECTION.

618 In a letter to Mary: Howard Rome to MWH, 11/1/6, JFK, Medical Files.

618 This is difficult to square: Ernest may not have told Rome that he was no longer taking reserpine, or Ernest might have disobeyed Saviers's advice. Saviers did not indicate to Baker when he took Ernest off the drug, but it would almost certainly have been before Ernest's first hospitalization. In fact, the decision not to replace reserpine with another antipsychotic when reserpine's side effects were being reported presents a sound argument that either Ernest was taking reserpine for its antihypertensive properties alone, or believed he was. His Cuban doctors and Saviers may have wanted to avoid telling Ernest that he needed to be put on a new antipsychotic drug—which would have entailed telling him that he had been taking reserpine for psychiatric purposes.

619 Greg, twice sent to a psychiatric hospital: Valerie Hemingway, 235. Greg came to believe ECT therapy was very good for him and boasted of undergoing it often, telling a reporter in 1987 that he had been given ninety-eight shock treatments, an estimate given fourteen years before his death in 2001, which suggests his lifetime total may have been yet higher. See Paul Hendrickson, "Papa's Boys," *Washington Post,* 7/29–30/1987. As Valerie Danby-Smith, who went on to become Greg Hemingway's wife, has written, Greg "maintained that shock treatments made him see things clearly. . . . Throughout his life he had needed the shocks to keep his brain in shape as well as to destroy the bad memories that crippled him and caused depression." Valerie Hemingway, 241.

619 Though Greg would later be diagnosed: See, for example, EH to Greg Hemingway, 2/4/1958, in John Hemingway, 143.

619 Ernest received eleven: Hotchner, *Papa Hemingway,* 276.

619 A little strangely: Baker, *Ernest Hemingway,* 557.

619 On January 11: Charles W. Mayo, *Mayo: The Story of My Family and My Career* (Garden City, NY: Doubleday, 1968), 302.

619 "It is my judgment": Howard Rome to EH, 1/19/1961, JFK, Medical Files.

620 Dr. Rome, like Dr. Saviers: That is, Ernest may have returned to a psychotic depression totally unrelated to his blood pressure. One of the remaining effective antipsychotic drugs was Thorazine, which does not have the side effect of depression (though that drug would prove to have crippling side effects of its own) that Serpasil was thought to have.

620 Ernest asked Harry Brague: EH to Baker, 1/16/1961, Hemingway Collection, Stanford. He asked Baker to contact the MLA for him.

621 Dr. Rome, in his January letter: Howard Rome to EH, 1/19/1961, JFK, Medical Files.

621 Dr. Saviers later said: Baker interview with George Saviers, 8/6/1964, CBP. It is important to note, however, that recent findings show that depression is *not* a

side effect of reserpine, after all—that is, that the earlier reports were false. In other words, with hindsight it seems that it perhaps would have been best to have continued Ernest on reserpine, though that was not considered best practice at the time.

621 Dr. Rome told Mary: Howard Rome to MWH, 11/1/1961, JFK, Medical Files.

621 begin to keep pages and pages: These notes are from the page for March 13 through March 26. JFK, Medical Files.

621 "a deep concern about his doing things": Howard Rome to MWH, 11/1/1961, JFK, Medical Files.

622 "There was a tired, worn": Arnold, 326.

623 "Things not good here": EH to Patrick Hemingway, 3/22/1961, SL, 919.

623 "Throughout the month of March": MWH, HIW, 496.

623 His handwriting grew smaller: Those who have read EH's handwritten letters will have noticed that the handwriting toward the end of his life becomes impossibly cramped and tiny; see Hotchner, Papa Hemingway, 284. This may have been due to a side effect of reserpine. See E. Lorenc-Koci, K. Ossowska, J. Wardas, and J. Wolfarth, "Does Reserpine Induce Parkinsonian Rigidity?," Journal of Neural Transmission 9 (1995), 211–23, http://www.ncbi.nlm.nih.gov/pubmed/8527005.

623 "He was especially proud": Howard Rome to MWH, 11/1/1961, JFK, Medical Files.

624 "Bet I make it": Arnold, 333. Pappy Arnold felt Cooper's remark did not sound like him; he also felt that Ernest would have been visibly upset by the words. Cooper died May 13.

624 Brought back to the plane: Pappy Arnold registered his disbelief of this story (probably told by Ketchum local Don Anderson), arguing that Larry Johnson, the pilot, would have told him about any such incident. Arnold, 336.

625 "Staying healthy": Hotchner, Papa Hemingway, 299.

625 "He would deny that he needed that": MWH, HIW, 500.

625 He took her to task: MWH to Jack and Patrick Hemingway, 6/7/1961, JFK.

625 "dressed in street clothes": MWH, HIW, 500.

626 "desolated": James Corey, "An Encounter with Hemingway," Hemingway Review (Fall 1992), 77–79.

626 "confused his thinking": ATH, 231.

Bibliography

Altman, Billy. *Laughter's Gentle Soul: The Life of Robert Benchley.* New York: W. W. Norton, 1997.

Arnold, Lloyd R. *High on the Wild with Hemingway.* Caldwell, ID: Caxton Printers, 1968.

Aschan, Ulf. *The Man Who Women Loved: The Life of Bror Blixen.* New York: St. Martin's, 1987.

Baker, Carlos. *Ernest Hemingway: A Life Story.* New York: Scribner's, 1969.

———. *Hemingway: The Writer as Artist.* Princeton, NJ: Princeton University Press, 1963.

———, ed. *Ernest Hemingway: Selected Letters,* 1917–1961. London: Granada, 1981.

———, ed. *Hemingway and His Critics: An International Anthology.* New York: Hill & Wang, 1961.

Beach, Sylvia. *Shakespeare and Company.* New York: Harcourt, Brace, 1959.

Beevor, Antony. *D-Day: The Battle for Normandy.* New York: Viking, 2009.

Berg, A. Scott. *Max Perkins: Editor of Genius.* 1978; rpt., New York: Pocket Books, 1979.

Bishop, Elizabeth. *One Art: Letters, Selected and Edited.* Robert Giroux, ed. New York: Farrar, Straus & Giroux, 1994.

———. *Poems, Prose, and Letters.* New York: Library of America, 2008.

Braden, Spruille. *Diplomats and Demagogues: The Memoirs of Spruille Braden.* New Rochelle, NY: Arlington House, 1971.

Brenner, Carlene Fredericka. *Hemingway's Cats.* Sarasota, FL: Pineapple Press, 2011.

Brian, Denis. *The True Gen: An Intimate Portrait of Ernest Hemingway by Those Who Knew Him.* New York: Delta Books, 1988.

Bridgman, Richard. *Gertrude Stein in Pieces.* New York: Oxford University Press, 1970.

Bruccoli, Matthew J. *Scott and Ernest: The Authority of Failure and the Authority of Success.* New York: Random House, 1978.

———. *Some Sort of Epic Grandeur: The Life of Scott Fitzgerald.* New York: Harcourt Brace Jovanovich, 1981.

———, ed. *Conversations with Ernest Hemingway.* Jackson: University Press of Mississippi, 1986.

———, ed. *Ernest Hemingway: Cub Reporter:* Kansas City Star *Stories.* Pittsburgh: University of Pittsburgh Press, 1970.

———, ed. *F. Scott Fitzgerald: A Life in Letters.* New York: Scribner's, 1994.

————, ed., *Hemingway and the Mechanism of Fame.* Columbia: University of South Carolina Press, 2006.

————, ed. *The Only Thing That Counts: The Ernest Hemingway–Maxwell Perkins Correspondence.* Columbia: University of South Carolina Press, 1996.

————, and Margaret Duggan, eds. *Correspondence of F. Scott Fitzgerald.* New York: Random House, 1980.

Bryher. *The Heart to Artemis: A Writer's Memories.* New York: Harcourt, Brace & World, 1962.

Buckley, Peter. *Ernie.* New York: Dial, 1978.

Burgess, Anthony. *Ernest Hemingway.* New York: Thames & Hudson, 1978.

Burwell, Rose Marie. *Hemingway: The Postwar Years and the Posthumous Novels.* Cambridge: Cambridge University Press, 1996.

Callaghan, Morley. *That Summer in Paris: Memories of Tangled Friendships with Hemingway, Fitzgerald, and Some Others.* New York: Dell, 1964.

Capa. Robert. *Slightly Out of Focus.* 1947; rpt., New York: Modern Library, 2001.

Carpenter, Humphrey. *Geniuses Together: American Writers in Paris in the 1920s.* Boston: Houghton Mifflin, 1988.

Carr, Virginia Spencer. *Dos Passos: A Life.* Garden City, NY: Doubleday, 1984.

Castillo-Puche, Jose Luis. Helen R. Lane, trans. *Hemingway in Spain.* Garden City, NY: Doubleday, 1974.

Cavedo, Keith. "(De)Constructions of Masculinity in the Hemingway Myth." In Bob Batchelor, *Cult Pop Culture: How the Fringe Became Mainstream.* Vol. 2, Literature and Music. New York: Praeger, 2012, 29–46.

Charters, Jimmie, as told to Morrill Cody. *This Must Be the Place: Memoirs of Montparnasse.* Introduction by Ernest Hemingway. 1934; rpt., New York: Collier Macmillan, 1989.

Conant, Jennet. *The Irregulars: Roald Dahl and the British Spy Ring in Wartime Washington.* New York: Simon & Schuster, 2008.

Conrad, Harold. *Dear Muffo: 35 Years in the Fast Lane.* New York: Stein & Day, 1982.

Cooper, Artemis, and Antony Beevor. *Paris After the Liberation: 1944–1949.* New York: Doubleday, 1994.

Cowles, Virginia. *Looking for Trouble.* New York: Harper, 1941.

Cowley, Malcolm. *And I Worked at the Writer's Trade: Chapters of Literary History, 1918–1978.* New York: Viking, 1978.

————. *Exile's Return: A Literary Odyssey of the 1920s.* New York: Viking, 1934.

————. *A Second Flowering: Works and Days of the Lost Generation.* New York: Viking, 1973.

Crosby, Caresse. *The Passionate Years.* 1953; rpt., Carbondale: University of Southern Illinois Press, 1968.

Curnutt, Kirk, and Gail D. Sinclair, eds. *Key West: A Reassessment.* Gainesville: University Press of Florida, 2009.

Dardis, Tom. *The Thirsty Muse: Alcohol and the American Writer.* New York: Ticknor & Fields, 1989.

de Beauvoir, Simone. *Hard Times; The Force of Circumstance, 1952–1962 (The Autobiography of Simone de Beauvoir).* 1963; rpt., Cambridge, MA: Da Capo, 1994.

DeFazio, Albert J. III, ed. *Dear Papa, Dear Hotch: The Correspondence of Ernest Hemingway and A. E. Hotchner.* Columbia: University of Missouri Press, 2005, 184.

Dempsey, James. *The Tortured Life of Scofield Thayer.* Gainesville: University Press of Florida, 2014.

Diliberto, Gioia. *Hadley.* New York: Ticknor & Fields, 1992.

Donaldson, Scott. *Archibald MacLeish: An American Life.* Boston: Houghton Mifflin, 1992.

———. *By Force of Will: The Life and Art of Ernest Hemingway.* New York: Viking, 1977.

———. *Death of a Rebel: The Charlie Fenton Story.* Madison, NJ: Lexington Books, 2012.

———. *Hemingway vs. Fitzgerald: The Rise and Fall of a Literary Friendship.* Woodstock, NY: Overlook Press, 1999.

Donnelly, Honoria Murphy, with Richard N. Billings. *Sara and Gerald: Villa America and After.* 1982; rpt., New York: Holt, Rinehart & Winston/Owl, 1984.

Dos Passos, John. *The Best Times: An Informal Memoir.* 1966; rpt., New York: Signet, 1968.

———. *Century's Ebb: The Thirteenth Chronicle.* Boston: Gambit, 1975.

———. *Chosen Country.* Boston: Houghton Mifflin, 1951.

———. *The Fourteenth Chronicle: Letters and Diaries of John Dos Passos.* Townsend Ludington, ed. Boston: Gambit, 1973.

———. "Madrid Under Siege." In *Travel Books and Other Writings, 1916–1941.* New York: Library of America, 2003, 463–71.

———. *The Theme Is Freedom.* New York: Dodd, Mead, 1956.

Drabeck, Bernard A., and Helen Ellis, eds. *Archibald MacLeish: Reflections.* Amherst: University of Massachusetts Press, 1986.

Dundy, Elaine. *Life Itself!* London: Virago, 2001.

Eastman, Max. *Einstein, Trotsky, Hemingway, Freud and Other Great Companions.* 1959; rpt., New York: Collier, 1962.

Eby, Carl. *Hemingway's Fetishism: Psychoanalysis and the Mirror of Manhood.* SUNY Series, Psychoanalysis and Culture. Albany, NY: SUNY Press, 1998.

Fensch, Thomas, ed. *Behind* Islands in the Stream: *Hemingway, Cuba, the FBI and the Crook Factory.* New York: iUniverse, 2010.

Fenton, Charles. *The Apprenticeship of Ernest Hemingway: The Early Years.* 1954; rpt., New York: Viking, 1965.

Findlay, James F. Jr. *Dwight L. Moody: American Evangelist, 1837–1899.* Chicago: University of Chicago Press, 1969.

Fitch, Noel Riley. *Sylvia Beach and the Lost Generation: A History of Literary Paris.* New York: W. W. Norton, 1983.

———. *Walks in Hemingway's Paris: A Guide to Paris for the Literary Traveler.* 1989; rev. ed., New York: St. Martin's, 1992.

Ford, Hugh. *Published in Paris: American and British Writers, Printers, and Publishers in Paris, 1920–1939.* 1975; rpt., Yonkers, NY: Pushcart Press, 1980.

Franklin, Sidney. *Bullfighter from Brooklyn: An Autobiography of Sidney Franklin.* Englewood Cliffs, NJ: Prentice-Hall, 1952.

Fuentes, Norberto. *Hemingway in Cuba.* Secaucus, NJ: Lyle Stuart, 1984.

Gardner, Martin. "Ernest Hemingway and Jane." In *Are Universes Thicker than Black-berries?* New York: W. W. Norton, 2003, 135–43.

Gellhorn, Martha. *Travels with Myself and Another.* New York: Dodd, Mead, 1979.

Gerogiannis, Nicholas, ed., *Ernest Hemingway: Complete Poems.* Lincoln: University of Nebraska Press, 1992.

Glassco, John. *Memories of Montparnasse.* 1970; rpt., New York: New York Review of Books, 2007, 53.

Greene, Philip. *To Have and to Have Another: A Hemingway Cocktail Companion.* New York: Perigee, 2012.

Griffin, Peter. *Along with Youth: Hemingway, The Early Years.* New York: Oxford University Press, 1985.

———. *Less Than a Treason: Hemingway in Paris.* New York: Oxford University Press, 1990.

Hanneman, Audre. *Ernest Hemingway: A Comprehensive Bibliography.* Princeton, NJ: Princeton University Press, 1967.

Hawkins, Ruth A. *Unbelievable Sadness and Early Sorrow: The Hemingway/Pfeiffer Marriage.* Fayetteville: University of Arkansas Press, 2012.

Hemingway, Gregory. *Papa: A Personal Memoir.* 1976; rpt., New York: Paragon House, 1988.

Hemingway, Jack. *A Life Worth Living: The Adventures of a Passionate Sportsman.* Guilford, CT: Lyons Press, 2002.

Hemingway, John. *Strange Tribe: A Family Memoir.* Guilford, CT: Lyons Press, 2007.

Hemingway, Leicester. *My Brother, Ernest Hemingway.* New York: World, 1971.

———. *My Brother, Ernest Hemingway.* 1961; rev. ed., Sarasota, FL: Pineapple Press, 1996.

Hemingway, Mary Welsh. *How It Was.* New York: Alfred A. Knopf, 1976.

Hemingway, Valerie. *Running with the Bulls: My Years with the Hemingways.* New York: Ballantine, 2004.

Hendrickson, Paul. *Hemingway's Boat: Everything He Loved in Life, and Lost, 1934–1961.* New York: Alfred A. Knopf, 2011.

Herbst, Josephine. *The Starched Blue Sky of Spain and Other Memoirs.* New York: HarperCollins, 1991.

Hotchner, A. E. *Choice People: The Greats, Near-Greats, and Ingrates I Have Known.* New York: William Morrow, 1984.

———. *Papa Hemingway: A Personal Memoir.* New York: Random House, 1966.

Johnson, Paul. "The Deep Waters of Ernest Hemingway." In *Intellectuals.* New York: Harper & Row, 1988, 138–72.

Joost, Nicholas. *Ernest Hemingway and the Little Magazines: The Paris Years.* Barre, MA: Barre Publishers, 1968.

———. *Scofield Thayer and The Dial.* Carbondale: University of Southern Illinois Press, 1964.

Josephson, Matthew. *Infidel in the Temple: A Memoir of the Nineteen-Thirties.* New York: Alfred A. Knopf, 1967.

Kaplan, Justin. *Lincoln Steffens: A Biography.* New York: Simon & Schuster, 1974.

Kazin, Alfred. *An American Procession.* New York: Alfred A. Knopf, 1984.

Keith, Slim. *Slim: Memories of a Rich and Imperfect Life.* 1990; rpt., New York: Warner, 1991.

Kennedy, J. Gerald and Jackson R. Bryer, eds. *French Connections: Hemingway and Fitzgerald Abroad.* New York: St. Martin's, 1998.

Kershaw, Alex. *Blood and Champagne: The Life and Times of Robert Capa.* New York: St. Martin's, 2002.

Kert, Bernice. *The Hemingway Women.* New York: W. W. Norton, 1983.

Koch, Stephen. *The Breaking Point: Hemingway, Dos Passos, and the Murder of José Robles.* New York: Counterpoint, 2005.

Kuehl, John, and Jackson Bryer, eds. *Dear Scott, Dear Max: The Fitzgerald–Perkins Correspondence.* New York: Scribner's, 1971.

Lambert, Gavin, ed. *The Ivan Moffat File: Life Among the Beautiful and Damned in London, Paris, New York, and Hollywood.* New York: Pantheon, 2004.

Langer, Elinor. *Josephine Herbst.* Boston: Little, Brown, 1984.

Leff, Leonard. *Hemingway and His Conspirators: Hollywood, Scribner's, and the Making of American Celebrity Culture.* Lanham, MD: Rowman & Littlefield, 1997.

Leibowitz, Herbert. *"Something Urgent I Have to Say to You": The Life and Works of William Carlos Williams.* New York: Farrar, Straus & Giroux, 2011.

Lewis, Wyndham. "The Dumb Ox," *American Review* (June 1934).

Limmer, Ruth, ed. *What the Woman Lived: Selected Letters of Louise Bogan, 1920–1979.* New York: Harcourt Brace Jovanovich, 1973.

Loeb, Harold. *The Way It Was.* New York: Criterion Books, 1959.

Lottman, Herbert R. *The Left Bank: Writers, Artists, and Politics from the Popular Front to the Cold War.* Boston: Houghton Mifflin, 1982.

Lynn, Kenneth S. *Hemingway.* New York: Simon & Schuster, 1987.

MacLeish, Archibald. *New and Collected Poems, 1917–1976.* Boston: Houghton Mifflin, 1976.

Mandel, Miriam. *Hemingway's Dangerous Summer: The Complete Annotations.* Metuchen, NJ: Scarecrow Press, 2008.

Matthews, Herbert L. *A World in Revolution: A Newspaperman's Memoir.* New York: Scribner's, 1971.

Mayfield, Sara. *Exiles from Paradise: Zelda and Scott Fitzgerald.* New York: Delacorte Press, 1971.

McAlmon, Robert, and Kay Boyle. *Being Geniuses Together, 1920–1930.* San Francisco: North Point Press, 1984.

McCaffery, John K. M., ed. *Ernest Hemingway: The Man and His Work.* 1950; rpt., New York: Cooper Square, 1969.

McLendon, James. *Papa: Hemingway in Key West.* 1970; rpt., Key West: Langley Press, 2002.

Meade, Marion. *Dorothy Parker: What Fresh Hell Is This?* 1988; rpt., New York: Penguin, 1989.

Mellow, James. *Hemingway: A Life Without Consequences.* Boston: Houghton Mifflin, 1992.

Merrill, Hugh. *Esky: The Early Years at Esquire.* New Brunswick, NJ: Rutgers University Press, 1995.

Meyers, Jeffrey. *Gary Cooper: American Hero.* New York: William Morrow, 1998.

―――. *Hemingway: A Biography.* New York: Harper & Row, 1985.

Milford, Nancy. *Zelda.* 1970; rpt., New York: Avon, 1971.

Miller, Brett C. *Elizabeth Bishop: Life and the Memory of It.* Berkeley: University of California Press, 1993.

Miller, Linda, ed. *Letters from the Lost Generation: Gerald and Sara Murphy and Friends.* New Brunswick, NJ: Rutgers University Press, 1991.

Miller, Madelaine Hemingway: *Ernie: Hemingway's Sister "Sunny" Remembers.* New York: Crown, 1975.

Moody, A. David. *Ezra Pound: Poet: A Portrait of the Man and His Work.* Vol. 1: *The Young Genius, 1885–1920.* New York: Oxford University Press, 2007.

Moore, Marianne. *Selected Letters of Marianne Moore.* Bonnie Costello, Celeste Goodridge, and Cristanne Miller, eds. New York: Alfred A. Knopf, 1997.

Moorehead, Caroline. *Gellhorn: A Twentieth-Century Life.* New York: Henry Holt, 2003.

―――, ed. *Selected Letters of Martha Gellhorn.* 2006; rpt., New York: Henry Holt/ Owl, 2007.

Mort, Terry. *The Hemingway Patrols: Ernest Hemingway and His Hunt for U-boats.* New York: Scribner, 2009.

Nagel, James, ed. *Ernest Hemingway: The Oak Park Legacy.* Tuscaloosa: University of Alabama Press, 1996.

―――, ed. *Ernest Hemingway: The Writer in Context.* Madison: University of Wisconsin Press, 1984.

Ondaatje, Christopher. *Hemingway in Africa: The Last Safari.* Woodstock, NY: Overlook Press, 2004.

Page, Tim. *Dawn Powell: A Biography.* New York: Henry Holt, 1998.

―――, ed. *The Diaries of Dawn Powell.* South Royalton, VT: Steerforth Press, 1995.

―――, ed. *Selected Letters of Dawn Powell, 1913–1965.* New York: Henry Holt, 1999.

Parker, Dorothy. "The Artist's Reward." *New Yorker,* 11/30/29, 28–31.

Paul, Bart. *Double-Edged Sword: The Many Lives of Hemingway's Friend, the American Matador Sidney Franklin.* Lincoln: University of Nebraska Press, 2009.

Plath, James, and Frank Simons, eds. *Remembering Ernest Hemingway.* Key West, FL: Ketch & Yawl Press, 1999.

Plimpton, George. *Shadow Box.* 1977; rpt., Guilford, CT: Lyons Press, 2003.

Poli, Bernard J. *Ford Madox Ford and the Transatlantic Review.* Syracuse, NY: Syracuse University Press, 1967.

Price, Reynolds. *A Common Room: Essays, 1954–1987.* New York: Atheneum, 1987.

Raeburn, John. *Fame Became of Him: Hemingway as Public Writer.* Bloomington: Indiana University Press, 1984.

Regler, Gustav. *The Great Crusade.* Preface by Ernest Hemingway. Translated by Whittaker Chambers and Barrows Mussey. New York: Longmans, Green, 1940.

Reynolds, Michael. *Hemingway: An Annotated Chronology.* Detroit: Omnigraphics, Inc., 1991.

―――. *Hemingway: The Final Years.* New York: W. W. Norton, 1999.

―――. *Hemingway's First War: The Making of* A Farewell to Arms. 1976; rpt., New York: Basil Blackwell, 1987.

―――. *Hemingway: The Homecoming.* 1992; rpt., New York: W. W. Norton, 1999.

————. *Hemingway: The 1930s.* 1997; rpt., New York: W. W. Norton, 1998.

————. *Hemingway: The Paris Years.* 1989; rpt., New York: W. W. Norton, 1999.

————. *The Young Hemingway.* 1986; rpt., New York: W. W. Norton, 1988.

Reynolds, Nicholas. "Ernest Hemingway, Wartime Spy." *Studies in Intelligence* 56 (Extracts, June 2012).

Rodman, Seldon. *Tongues of Fallen Angels: Conversations with Jorge Luis Borges, Among Others.* New York: New Directions, 1974.

Rollyson, Carl. *Beautiful Exile: The Life of Martha Gellhorn.* London: Aurum Press, 2001.

Ross, Lillian. "Portrait of Hemingway." *New Yorker* (5/13/50). rpt., New York: Modern Library, 1999.

Samuelson, Arnold. *With Hemingway: A Year in Key West and Cuba.* New York: Random House, 1984.

Sanford, Marcelline Hemingway. *At the Hemingways: With Fifty Years of Correspondence Between Ernest and Marcelline Hemingway.* Moscow: University of Idaho Press, 1999.

Sarason, Bertram, ed. *Hemingway and the Sun Set.* Washington, DC: Microcard Editions, 1972.

Schoots, Hans. *Living Dangerously: A Biography of Joris Ivens.* Amsterdam: Amsterdam University Press, 2000.

Scribner, Charles Jr. *In the Company of Writers: A Life in Publishing.* Based on the oral history by Joel R. Gardner. New York: Scribner's, 1990.

————. *In the Web of Ideas: The Education of a Publisher.* New York: Scribner's, 1993.

Shi, David E. *Matthew Josephson: Bourgeois Bohemian.* New Haven, CT: Yale University Press, 1981.

Shirer, William. *Twentieth-Century Journey.* Vol. 1, *The Start.* Boston: Little, Brown, 1976.

Shnayerson. Michael. *Irwin Shaw: A Biography.* New York: G. P. Putnam, 1989.

Smoller, Sanford J. *Adrift Among Geniuses: Robert McAlmon, Writer and Publisher of the Twenties.* University Park: Penn State University Press, 1975.

————, ed. *The Nightinghouls of Paris.* By Robert McAlmon. Champaign: University of Illinois Press, 2007.

Sokoloff, Alice Hunt. *Hadley: The First Mrs. Hemingway.* New York: Dodd, Mead, 1973.

Sonnenberg, Ben. *Lost Property: Memoirs and Confessions of a Bad Boy.* New York: Summit, 1991.

Spanier, Sandra, and Robert W. Trogdon, eds. *The Letters of Ernest Hemingway,* Vol. 1, 1907–1922. New York: Cambridge University Press, 2011.

————, eds. *The Letters of Ernest Hemingway.* Vol. 2, 1923–1925. New York: Cambridge University Press, 2013.

Spilka, Mark. *Hemingway's Quarrel with Androgyny.* Lincoln: University of Nebraska Press, 1990.

Spurrock, Donald. *Storyteller: The Authorized Biography of Roald Dahl.* New York: Simon & Schuster, 2010.

Steffens, Lincoln. *The Autobiography of Lincoln Steffens.* 2 vols. 1931; rpt., New York: Harcourt Brace Jovanovich, 1958.

Stein, Gertrude. *The Autobiography of Alice B. Toklas*. New York: Harcourt, Brace, 1933.

Steiner, Raymond J. *The Art Students League of New York: A History*. Saugerties, NY: CSS Publications, 1999.

Stewart, Donald Ogden. *By a Stroke of Luck! An Autobiography*. New York: Paddington Press, 1975.

Stock, Noel. *The Life of Ezra Pound*. 1970; rpt., New York: Penguin, 1974.

Tarr, Rodger L., ed. *Max and Marjorie: The Correspondence Between Maxwell E. Perkins and Marjorie Kinnan Rawlings*. Gainesville: University Press of Florida, 1999.

Tavernier-Courbin, Jacqueline. *Ernest Hemingway's* A Moveable Feast: *The Making of Myth*. Boston: Northeastern University Press, 1991.

Thurber, James, in Michael Rosen, ed. *Collecting Himself: James Thurber on Writing and Writers, Humor, and Himself*. New York: HarperCollins 1989.

Townsend, Kim. *Sherwood Anderson: A Biography*. Boston: Houghton Mifflin, 1987.

Travisano, Thomas, ed., with Saskia Hamilton. *Words in Air: The Complete Correspondence of Elizabeth Bishop and Robert Lowell*. New York: Farrar, Straus & Giroux, 2008.

Trogdon, Robert. *The Lousy Racket: Hemingway, Scribners, and the Business of Literature*. Kent, OH: Kent State University Press, 2007.

———, ed., *Ernest Hemingway: A Literary Reference*. 1999; rpt., New York: Carroll & Graf, 2002.

Turnbull, Andrew. *Scott Fitzgerald: A Biography*. 1962; rpt., New York: Ballantine, 1971.

———, ed. *Letters of F. Scott Fitzgerald*. 1963; rpt., New York: Dell, 1966.

Tynan, Kathleen. *The Life of Kenneth Tynan*. New York: William Morrow, 1987.

Tytell, John. *Ezra Pound: Solitary Volcano*. New York: Anchor, 1987.

Vaill, Amanda. *Everyone Was So Young: Gerald and Sara Murphy, A Lost Generation Love Story*. 1998; rpt., New York: Broadway Books, 1999.

———. *Hotel Florida: Truth, Love, and Death in the Spanish Civil War*. New York: Farrar, Straus & Giroux, 2014.

Vernon, Alex. *Hemingway's Second War: Bearing Witness to the Spanish Civil War*. Iowa City: University of Iowa Press, 2011.

Viertel, Peter. *Dangerous Friends: At Large with Hemingway and Huston in the Fifties*. New York: Doubleday, 1992.

Villard, Henry S., and James Nagel. *Hemingway in Love and War: The Lost Diary of Agnes von Kurowsky, Her Letters, and Correspondence of Ernest Hemingway*. Boston: Northeastern University Press, 1989.

Villarreal, René, and Raúl Villarreal. *Hemingway's Cuban Son: Reflections on the Writer by His Longtime Majordomo*. Kent, OH: Kent State University Press, 2009.

Wagner-Martin, Linda, ed. *A Historical Guide to Ernest Hemingway*. New York: Oxford University Press, 2000.

Weber, Ronald. *News of Paris: American Journalists in the City of Light Between the Wars*. Chicago: Ivan R. Dee, 2006.

Whelan, Richard. *Robert Capa: A Biography*. New York: Alfred A. Knopf, 1985.

Wickes, George. *Americans in Paris*. 1969; rpt., New York: Da Capo, 1980.

Wilson, Dale. "Hemingway in Kansas City." In *Fitzgerald/Hemingway Annual*, 1976, Matthew J. Bruccoli, ed., 211–16.

Wilson, Edmund. "Hemingway: Gauge of Morale." In *The Portable Edmund Wilson,* Lewis M. Dabney, ed. New York: Penguin, 1983.

————. *The Shores of Light: A Literary Chronicle of the Twenties and Thirties.* 1952: rpt., New York: Vintage, 1961.

Winnick, R. H., ed. *Letters of Archibald MacLeish: 1907–1982.* Boston: Houghton Mifflin, 1983.

Index

Initials EH refer to Ernest Hemingway in this index.
Page numbers followed by *f* indicate a figure.

Across the River and into the Trees
(Hemingway), 117, 475, 513, 521–24,
533–36, 549, 568–69
critical reception of, 534–36
dust jacket drawing for, 533
sales of, 536
serialization of, 528, 532, 536
signs of EH's mania in, 523–24,
527–29
Adams, Hamilton, 293, 344
Adams, J. Donald, 389, 414
Addams, Jane, 52
advertising work, 95–96
the African book (unfinished)
(Hemingway), 559–62, 572–73
The African Queen (Huston), 562
African safaris, 294–95, 306, 310–11,
330–36, 556–65
airplane crashes in, 561–64, 573, 584
EH's Kamba fantasy and, 559–61, 565,
572, 577
EH's writing on, 332–33, 339, 341–43
funding of, 294, 311
guides for, 332–33, 334, 556, 557
hunting and, 334, 414, 558–60
Look magazine's photography of, 556,
558
"After the Storm" (Hemingway), 318
Agassiz, Louis, 14
Agassiz Club, 14, 21–22
Aiken, Conrad, 233

Albert, Prince Consort of England, 11
Aldington, Richard, 114
Alfonso XIII, King of Spain, 303
Alger, Horatio, 36–37
Allen, Jay, 371, 414
Allington, Floyd, 296
All Quiet on the Western Front
(Remarque), 286
"An Alpine Idyll" (Hemingway), 116,
212
American Field Service (AFS), 53
American Red Cross, 53
American Writers' Congress, 380, 429
"America Was Promises" (MacLeish),
411–12
Anders, Glenn, 326
Anderson, Bob, 453–54
Anderson, Don, 624
Anderson, Margaret, 97
Anderson, Sherwood, 96–98, 140, 195,
324
EH's parody of, 172, 201–3, 216
EH's reviews of, 178, 195
on Gertrude Stein, 119
influence on EH of, 156
literary connections of, 106–11, 113,
177, 196
memoir of, 178
Anderson, Tennessee, 106, 108
Antheil, George, 184–85
anthroposophy, 320–21

antisemitism
    of EH, 139, 173–79, 191–92, 194–95,
        248, 573–74
    of Ezra Pound, 173, 491–92, 570
The Apes of God (Lewis), 335
The Apprenticeship of Ernest Hemingway
    (Fenton), 552–54
Areito, Félix, 498
Arguelles, Elicio, 575
Armies of the Night (Mailer), 339
Arnold, Lloyd "Pappy," 408–9, 418, 463,
    496, 592–94, 606, 622–24
Arnold, Ruth "Bobbie," 29, 81–85, 88,
    250, 267, 398, 541
Arnold, Tillie, 408, 496, 592–93, 606,
    623–24
Arostegui, Cathleen Vanderbilt, 433–34
"The Art of the Short Story"
    (Hemingway), 169–70
Asch, Nathan, 163, 167, 174, 300
Atatürk, Mustafa Kemal, 125, 131, 425
Atkinson, Joseph, 86
The Atlantic Monthly, 244, 268, 323–24,
    336, 584
At the Hemingways (Sanford), 268–69
Auchinleck, Claude, 513
Autobiography (Williams), 142
The Autobiography of Alice B. Toklas
    (Stein), 287, 323–25, 336, 588
An Autumn Penitent (Callaghan), 275

Babbitt (Lewis), 112
Bacall, Lauren, 597–98, 600
Baker, Carlos, 69, 389, 440, 449, 472,
    508, 519, 538
    critical study of EH by, 4, 63–64, 547,
        552
    review of *The Old Man and the Sea*
        of, 547
    sources of, 457
Ballantine Ale, 586–87
Ballestero, Rafael, 581, 583
Balmer, Edwin, 156
"A Banal Story" (Hemingway), 244, 247
Barea, Arturo, 378–79

Barnes, Djuna, 162, 250
Barnett, Lawrence, 79
Barney, Natalie, 108, 380
Barrett, Richmond, 235
Barton, Bruce, 32–33
Barton, Raymond O. "Tubby," 455, 465
Barton, William E., 32–33, 243
Batista, Fulgencio, 339–40, 433, 437, 591,
    592
"The Battler" (Hemingway), 176, 184,
    522
Beach, Sylvia, 111, 143, 155, 250, 335, 380
    on Ezra Pound, 116
    Shakespeare and Company and,
        111–12, 149, 168, 180
The Beautiful and Damned (Fitzgerald),
    182
Beauvoir, Simone de, 474
Beaverbrook, Max Aitken, Lord,
    451–52
Being Geniuses Together (Boyle/
    McAlmon), 145–46, 147–48
Bellville, Rupert, 565–66, 580
Belmonte, Juan, 145
Beloved Traitor, 52
Benchley, Robert, 188, 247, 383
Benítez, Manuel, 433
Bentley, Beverly, 598–99, 600
Berenson, Bernard, 417–18, 508, 554–55,
    570
Berg, A. Scott, 502
Bergman, Ingrid, 421, 470, 496, 525, 579
"Bernice Bobs Her Hair" (Fitzgerald),
    181
Bernstein, Leonard, 594
The Best American Short Stories series
    (ed. O'Brien), 139–40, 144, 160, 261
Bianchi, Don Giuseppi, 60, 236
Biggs, Fannie, 37–38, 42–43
The Big Money (Dos Passos), 358
"The Big Two-Hearted River"
    (Hemingway), 22, 62–63, 169–70,
    172
Billingsley, Sherman, 496
A Bill of Divorcement, 337
Bimini, 344–48, 357, 380, 383

biographies of EH, 3–5, 324, 551–54
  by Carlos Baker, 4, 547, 552
  by EH's family members, 90, 268,
    480, 495
  EH's opposition to, 64, 551–53
  by Malcolm Cowley, 360–61, 551–52
  on Scott Fitzgerald, 350–51
  on wound theory, 63–64
  See also critical writing on EH;
    reviews and articles
bipolar disorder. *See* mental illness
Bird, Bill, 120, 124, 132, 389
  publishing of EH by, 139–40, 143–44,
    149, 159–60, 184, 197
  Three Mountains Press, 158, 173
  travel with EH of, 145–48, 166–67
Bird, Sally, 124, 166
The Birth of a Nation, 50
Bishop, John Peale, 234, 284, 287, 351
Bishop, Margaret, 287
The Black Book (Durrell), 620
Blackburn, Jack, 43
BLAST, 115
Blixen-Finecke, Bror von, 334–35, 347
Blixen-Finecke, Eva von, 347
Bloomsbury group, 157, 245
Bocher, Main, 204–5
Bogan, Louise, 381
Bollingen Prize in Poetry, 586
Bone, John, 106, 125, 150
Boni and Liveright, 160, 165, 173,
    176–79, 184, 201–4, 210–11, 216–17
Bonsall, Phil, 608–9
Book-of-the-Month Club, 412–13,
    415–16, 547
Borgatti, Renata, 251
Bourjaily, Vance, 502, 529
Bowen, Stella, 158
Bowers, Claude, 423, 435
Boyer, Charles, 496
Boyle, Kay, 147–48
Braden, Spruille, 429–34, 447, 448
Bradfield, Ruth, 104
Brague, Harry, 620
Braun, Mathilde, 172
Breaker, George, 104, 167–68

Breaker, Helen, 104, 167–68, 250
Breit, Harvey, 64, 521, 547, 569
Brenan, Gerald, 556
Brian, Denis, 473
Brickell, Herschel, 316
The Bridge, 173
Bridge of San Luis Rey (Wilder), 260
Bridges, Robert, 212, 262
Briggs, Ellis O., 429, 430
Bromfield, Louis, 202, 211, 238–39
Brooks, George, 252
Brooks, Romaine, 380
Broom, 165, 184
Browder, Earl, 380
Brown, Bob, 119
Brown, George, 479, 497, 574–75, 581,
    626
Broyles, Henrietta, 520, 543
Bruce, Betty, 593
Bruce, David, 457–58, 469, 599
Bruce, Evangeline, 599
Bruce, Toby, 293, 380, 409, 593
Brumback, Ted, 53–54, 56–58, 60, 88,
    91–92, 238
Bryant, Louise, 128–29
Bryher (Winifred Ellerman), 141–47, 155,
    163, 167, 288
Buckley, Henry, 393
Buckley, Peter, 580, 599
bullfighting
  EH's travel for, 143f, 145–49, 166–67,
    185, 194, 220–25, 228–29, 243,
    274, 283–84, 298, 301–5, 557, 565,
    580–81, 595–605
  EH's writing on, 172, 174, 184–85,
    194–95, 246–47, 274, 284, 303–6,
    316
  Pamplona's Fiesta of San Fermín,
    148–49, 166, 171, 187–90, 194–95,
    223–24, 274, 283–84, 557, 598–600
  rivalries among matadors in,
    596–601
  See also *Death in the Afternoon*
"Bullfighting, Sport and Industry"
    (Hemingway), 284
Bullitt, William, 128, 380

Bumby. *See* Hemingway, John Hadley Nicanor
Bump, Georgiana, 89
Bump, Marjorie, 85, 89
Burke, Michael, 446, 474
Burne Holiday (character), 138
Burnett, Frances Hodgson, 22
Burns, John Horne, 529
Burroughs, Edgar Rice, 78
Burrows, Larry, 604
Burton, Harry, 411
Burwell, Rose Marie, 118, 136, 250
Bush, George W., 462
Buske, Morris, 41
Butcher, Fanny, 285, 548
Butler, Dorothy, 124
Butler, Nicholas Murray, 416
Butt, Hugh R., 617–19

Cabot, John, 570
Cadwalader, Charles, 337
Caldwell, Taylor, 502
Callaghan, Loretto, 275, 289–90
Callaghan, Morley, 150, 275–77, 289, 540, 553
The Call of the Wild (London), 33
Camus, Albert, 620
"A Canary for One" (Hemingway), 225
Cannell, Kitty, 165, 173, 179–80, 187, 195, 207
The Canyon (Viertel), 505
Capa, Robert, 393, 413, 445, 447–48, 456, 460, 464–65, 505
"The Capital of the World" (Hemingway), 588
Capote, Truman, 67
Cappiani, Louisa Kapp-Young, 16–17
Carpenter, Humphrey, 61
Cartwright, Reggie, 562–63
Casablanca, 579
Castro, Fidel, 7, 591, 592–94, 607, 608*f,* 609
Castro, Raúl, 591
Cather, Willa, 160, 182

Catherine Barkley (character), 66, 223, 258–62, 283
"Cat in the Rain" (Hemingway), 135, 168, 172, 281
Cézanne, Paul, 169–70, 531
"Champs d'Honneur" (Hemingway), 116–17
Chamson, André, 380
Chaplin, Duncan, 181
charisma, 72–74
Charters, Jimmie, 186–87
"Che Ti Dice La Patria" (Hemingway), 244, 247
Chiang Kai-shek, 421, 423–24
Chicago, 93–99, 365
"Chicago" (Sandburg), 96
Chicago Daily Tribune, 94
Chicago Poems (Sandburg), 96
Chicago World's Fair/Columbian Exposition of 1893, 16–17
Chicherin, George, 131
Child, Julia, 512
children of EH. *See* Hemingway, Gregory Hancock; Hemingway, John Hadley Nicanor; Hemingway, Patrick
China, 421–25, 438
Chosen Country (Dos Passos), 32, 43–44, 491
Chou Enlai, 423
"The Christmas Gift" (Hemingway), 563–64
circus animals, 516–19
Civil War, 12–13
Clarahan, Lewis, 36, 44
Clark, Greg, 86, 307
Clarke, Gerald, 481
"A Clean, Well-Lighted Place" (Hemingway), 75, 317–18
Coates, Frances, 43
Coates, Robert, 316
Cockburn, Claud, 374–75
Cocteau, Jean, 199, 316
Cohn, Louis Henry, 319–20
Colbert, Stephen, 462
Colebaugh, Charles, 426

Coleman, Emily, 250
Colette, 368
Collier's, 443–44
  EH's reporting for, 443–44, 453–61,
    468–69, 474
  Gellhorn's reporting for, 372, 378,
    392–95, 408–9, 421–26, 434, 444,
    475
Collingwood, Charles, 454–55, 456–57
Collins, Seward, 316
Colum, Mary, 362
"Come Back to the Raft Ag'in, Huck
  Honey" (Fiedler), 616
A Companion Volume (McAlmon),
  142
Complete Poems (Hemingway), 116
Connable, Dorothy, 85–86
Connable, Ralph, Jr., 85–86
Connable, Ralph, Sr., 85–86
Connolly, Cyril, 246, 389, 534, 595
Conrad, Joseph, 48, 143, 157, 167
Contact Editions, 133, 141–44, 149, 173,
  275, 299
Contact journal, 141, 143
Contemporary Historians, 372, 380
Cook, Lawrence, 451
Coolidge, Grace, 305
Cooper, Dick, 306, 312, 319, 332, 489
Cooper, Gary
  in *A Farewell to Arms* (Hemingway),
    401
  friendship with EH of, 408, 414, 416,
    418, 505, 515, 593, 623–24
  photo of, 415*f*
  in *For Whom the Bell Tolls,* 421
Cooper, Rocky, 414, 593, 623–24
Co-operative Commonwealth, 94–96, 106,
  167
Co-operative Society of America, 94–96,
  106
Corbett, Wilhelmina, 43–44
Corey, James, 626
Cosmopolitan, 130, 260–61, 341, 355, 411,
  507, 522, 528, 532, 536
Cottell, James, 617, 625
Cowles, Virginia, 375, 378

Cowley, Malcolm, 121, 163, 235, 515
  on *Across the River and into the Trees,*
    534
  essay of EH by, 360–61, 551–52
  on *A Farewell to Arms,* 285–86
  on *To Have and Have Not,* 389
Cox, James, 365
"The Crack-Up" (Fitzgerald), 353–54,
  361, 420
The Crack-Up (Fitzgerald), 492
Craik, Dinah Mulock, 35
Crane, Hart, 173
Crane, Stephen, 342
Cranston, J. Herbert, 86, 150
Crash of 1929, 286, 325, 347
Criqui, Eugène, 162
Critchfield's, 95
The Criterion, 157
critical writing on EH
  by Carlos Baker, 4, 63–64, 547, 552
  by Charles Fenton, 552–54
  on EH's interest in hair and gender,
    136, 250–51
  by John McCaffery, 551–52
  by Leslie Fiedler, 616
  by Philip Young, 552
  on wound theory, 63–64
  See also biographies of EH; reviews
    and articles
Cronin, A. J., 416
Crosby, Caresse, 302, 305, 319
"Cross-Country Snow" (Hemingway),
  135, 169, 172
Crouse, Russel, 48
Cuba, 311–12, 327–28, 399–402, 487–90,
  606–10
  Adriana and Gianfranco Ivancich in,
    510–11, 533, 536–39
  circus in, 517–19
  cockfighting in, 515–16
  EH's anti-Nazi campaign in, 425–37
  EH's cats and dogs in, 514–15, 591
  EH's Nobel Prize in, 570
  EH's *Pilar* in, 404
  EH's social circle in, 431–34, 440, 445,
    453, 489–90, 498–99, 503–4

Cuba *(continued)*
  EH's study in, 511–12
  fishing in, 327, 329, 340, 391, 488
  Floridita bar in, 429, 440
  Hemingway Marlin Fishing
    Tournament in, 608*f,* 609
  political unrest in, 339–40, 411, 433,
    437, 505–6, 591
  revolution of, 592–94, 606–9, 623
Cuddy, Henry, 108
Cummings, E. E., 112, 160, 163, 530
Curzon, Lord, 129, 131, 134

Dahl, Roald, 444
Danby-Smith, Valerie, 598–604, 606–13,
    615
The Dance of the Machines (O'Brien),
    140
The Dangerous Summer (Hemingway),
    145, 595–96, 601, 605, 606, 609–11,
    614
D'Annunzio, Gabriele, 436
Dark Laughter (Anderson), 202, 216
Davidson, Jo, 120
Davies, Dorothy, 43
Davis, Annie, 594–95, 599, 602, 612–13
Davis, Bill, 428, 594–613
Davis, Emily, 428, 595
Davis, Robert Gorham, 548
dead dog incident, 146
Death in the Afternoon (Hemingway), 5,
    58, 145–48, 185, 274
  critical reception of, 316, 325–26,
    362–63
  EH's addendum to, 573, 595–96, 601,
    605, 606, 609–11, 614
  EH's research for, 303–5
  John Dos Passos's suggestions for,
    356–57
  Old Lady character in, 304, 316,
    357
  publication of, 284
  sales of, 316
  taxonomy of the dead in, 305, 319
  writing of, 295, 297, 298, 306, 308

Debba, 560–61, 572
Debs, Eugene V., 365
Decan, Jean, 471
Deceit (Henry), 261
"Defense of Luxembourg"
    (Hemingway), 529
Degas, Edgar, 531
de la Palma, Niño, 557
Dell, Floyd, 97
Delmer, Sefton, 375
Dempsey, Jack, 184, 496
Derain, André, 324
Development (Bryher), 141
De Voto, Bernard, 286
The Dial, 115, 117, 157, 177, 233
"The Diamond as Big as the Ritz"
    (Fitzgerald), 181
Dianetics (Hubbard), 543, 585
Dickey, Roy, 95
Didion, Joan, 590
Dietrich, Marlene, 336, 470–71, 506,
    530
Dilworth, Wesley, 257
DiMaggio, Joe, 548
Dinesen, Isak, 334, 556, 570, 620
"A Divine Gesture" (Hemingway), 97,
    156
Dixon, Margaret, 37–38
"The Doctor and the Doctor's Wife"
    (Hemingway), 170, 172, 178, 197
Dodd, Lee Wilson, 246
Dominguín, Luis Miguel, 565–66, 596,
    598–601, 610–12
Donaldson, Arthur, 86
Donnelly, Eleanor, 259–60
Doodab (Loeb), 165, 173
Doolittle, Hilda "HD," 114, 141–42, 163
Doran, George H., 173
Dorman-Smith, Eric E. "Chink," 69,
    123–25, 129, 134, 154–55, 166, 305
  on EH and Hadley, 207
  military career of, 455, 513
D'Orn, Roger, 404
Dos Passos, John, 32, 112, 155, 412, 530
  EH's fictional portrayals of, 202,
    356–58

on EH's temperament, 157, 300
on EH's works, 284, 308, 356–57
expatriate American circle of,
    199–201
fame of, 358
friendship with EH of, 163–64, 166,
    168, 180, 213, 252–53, 274, 296, 308,
    340, 377, 435, 437, 491
in Key West, 344
literary reputation of, 274
marriage of, 251, 274, 294
photos of, 164f, 214f
published works of, 43–44, 164, 167,
    356, 357–58, 390
Spanish Civil War and, 372, 375–77,
    385, 390, 392
Dos Passos, Katy Smith, 32, 36, 44, 46,
    253, 308
in Chicago, 94, 98, 101, 104
death of, 491
on EH's temperament, 344, 377
marriage of, 251, 274, 294
photo of, 89f
in St. Louis, 179
The Double Dealer, 97, 156
Dreiser, Theodore, 96–97, 329
Dudek, Al, 338
Duhamel, Alain, 380
"The Dumb Ox" (Lewis), 335
Duñabeitia, Juan "Sinsky," 431–32, 489,
    498–99
Dundy, Elaine, 595, 597
Dunn, Clara, 250
Durán, Bonte, 514
Durán, Gustavo, 429–31, 514
Duranty, Walter, 380
Durrell, Lawrence, 620

Eastman, Max, 119, 120–21, 184, 325–26,
    362–63, 392
Eby, Carl, 136
Edgar, Carl, 36, 44, 46, 50, 56, 104
The Egoist, 115
Eisenhower, Dwight, 445, 459
Eisenstein, Sergei, 372

Eliot, T. S., 115, 117, 235, 586–87, 620
EH's views of, 157, 167, 316
on McAlmon, 143
published works of, 116, 157, 173
on Scott Fitzgerald's Great Gatsby, 182,
    280
Ellerman, Hannah, 142
Ellerman, John, 141–43
Ellis, Havelock, 103
"The End of Something" (Hemingway),
    168, 172
The English Review, 158
The Enormous Room (Cummings), 163
Ernest Hemingway: The Man and His
    Work (ed. McCaffery), 552
"Ernest Hemingway: A Tragedy of
    Draftsmanship" (Kashkin), 358–59
Ernst, Connie, 450
erysipelas, 527, 584
Esquire, 319–20, 329–31, 337
contributors to, 329
EH's "letters" series in, 229–331, 340,
    346, 366
EH's stories in, 354f, 355–57, 399,
    539–40
Scott Fitzgerald's work in, 353–54, 361
Eugénie, Empress of France, 11
exaggerations. See fabrications by EH
The Executioner's Song (Mailer), 339
Exile's Return (Cowley), 163, 551–52
Explorations (McAlmon), 142

fabrications by EH
for biographers, 553–54
on boxing, 108
on Ed Hemingway's suicide, 269–70
EH's head injuries and, 462–63,
    564–65
on Gregory Hemingway's birth, 307
on the Kamba, 559–61, 565, 572, 577
on the liberation of Paris, 456–61
on Paris life, 112
"truthiness" in, 402, 462–63, 468
on war experiences, 61–64, 68, 140,
    476–77, 524–25, 550, 553–54

Fadiman, Clifton, 325
"The Faithful Bull" (Hemingway), 529
A Farewell to Arms (Hemingway), 5, 66,
    68, 126, 252, 258–61, 271–72, 412,
    508
    banning in Boston of, 282
    Broadway production of, 326
    critical reception of, 284–86
    dedication of, 283
    EH's earnings from, 291
    ending of, 282–83
    film versions of, 287*f*, 317, 319, 414,
        600
    Fitzgerald's and Wister's critiques of,
        280–83, 520–21
    on haircuts, 135, 484
    Italian translation of, 508–9
    sales of, 286
    Scribner's serialization of, 212, 260–61,
        271–72, 282–83
The Farm (Miró), 165, 410, 610
Farrington, Kip, 346–47
The Far Side of Paradise (Mizener),
    520–21, 540
Fascism, 409, 421, 435–37
    in Cuba, 411, 426–37
    EH's speaking on, 380–83
    of Ezra Pound, 491–92, 570
    in Germany, 392, 395
    in Italy, 129, 236, 355, 366
    Spanish Civil War and, 363–67,
        371–83, 385–95, 412, 435
    For Whom the Bell Tolls and,
        416–17
    See also World War II
Faulkner, William, 140, 173, 316, 569
Federal Bureau of Investigation (FBI),
    429–30, 433
Fenberg, Bertha, 264
Fenton, Charles, 37, 42–43, 63–64,
    97–98, 470, 552–54
Fiedler, Leslie, 616–17
Fielding, Henry, 202–3
Fiesta of San Fermín (Pamplona),
    148–49, 166, 171, 187–90, 194–95,
    223–24, 274, 283–84, 557, 598–600

The Fifth Column (Hemingway),
    386–89, 391–92
    portrayal of Martha Gellhorn in,
        386–88, 445, 453
    Theatre Guild's performance of, 391,
        395
*The Fifth Column and the First Forty-
    nine Stories* (Hemingway), 355, 392,
    416
"Fifty Grand" (Hemingway), 40, 195,
    212, 244, 246–47
Finca Vigía, 7, 403–5, 410–11, 418, 430,
    441–42, 444–45, 526, 602–3, 607
Finney, Ben, 411
"First Poem to Mary" (Hemingway),
    452, 474
Fitzgerald, F. Scott, 138, 140, 158,
    199–200, 221, 248, 589
    alcohol use by, 225, 265–66, 278, 280,
        351–52, 567
    death of, 420
    on EH's works, 196, 203, 217–19,
        280–83, 353, 361–63
    friendship with EH of, 219–20, 225,
        267, 276–82, 286–90, 350–54,
        362–63, 383–84, 492–93
    Max Perkins and, 217, 266, 278–79,
        420, 492, 502
    Mizener's biography of, 520–21, 540
    photo of, 182*f*
    published works of, 182–83, 280,
        286–87, 325, 352–54, 420, 492
    references in EH's fiction to, 202,
        361–63, 420
    rumors of homosexuality of, 289
    Scribner's contacts of, 210–12
Fitzgerald, Scottie, 181, 200, 278
Fitzgerald, Zelda, 181–83, 199–200, 221,
    225, 265, 287, 493
    marriage of, 350–51, 521, 589
    mental illness of, 219–20, 280
    photo of, 182*f*
Fix Bayonets! (Thomason), 425
Flagler, Henry, 254, 293
Flanner, Janet, 250–51, 295, 323, 329, 335,
    380, 531

Flechtheim, Alfred, 117, 184–85
Fleischman, Leon, 173–79
Fleming, Robert, 572
Flynn, Errol, 375
Foley, Edith, 94
Folly Ranch, 259
Ford, Ford Madox, 115–16, 572
    EH's fictional portrayal of, 235–36
    literary teas and dances of, 158, 163,
        168
    Oak Park Hemingways and, 239
    the transatlantic review of, 158–159,
        162–63, 167–68, 174, 177–78, 324
Ford, John, 456–57
The Forgotten Threshold (O'Brien),
    139
The 42nd Parallel (Dos Passos), 274
For Whom the Bell Tolls (Hemingway),
    33–34, 379, 399–402, 435, 438,
    522
    Book-of-the-Month Club sales of,
        412–13, 415–16
    critical reception of, 414–16
    film version of, 401, 414, 421
    on haircuts, 135, 484
    manuscript of, 407
    on military tactics, 385
    sales of, 415–16
    writing of, 408–9, 411–13
Fowler, Henry, 337
Franchetti, Nanuk, 509–10
Franco, Francisco, 364, 374, 385–88,
    393–94, 430, 591
Frank, Waldo, 97, 184
Franklin, Sidney, 283, 300, 302, 330, 371,
    373–78, 530
Frederic Henry (character), 61, 66, 258,
    281–83, 414
Free French forces, 458–60, 525, 559
Freytag-Loringhoven, Elsa von, 167
Friede, Donald, 414
Friend, Krebs and Elizabeth, 167
From Here to Eternity (Jones), 549–50
Frost, Robert, 587
Fuentes, Gregorio, 404, 431–32, 488, 575,
    592–93

Fuentes, Norberto, 593
Fussell, Paul, 55

Galantière, Lewis, 106, 109–10, 117, 124,
    172, 174, 445
Galsworthy, John, 158
Gamble, Jim, 59, 60, 68–71, 75, 102
"The Gambler, the Nun, and the Radio"
    (Hemingway), 318
The Garden of Eden (Hemingway), 3, 7,
    237–38, 482–87, 522, 551, 572, 592,
    605
    on gender fluidity, 484–87
    on hair and sexuality, 135–36, 223,
        500
Gardner, Ava, 470, 565–66
Gardner, John Fentress "Jack," 320–23,
    494
Geismar, Maxwell, 534
Gellhorn, Edna, 368–70, 413, 444
Gellhorn, George, 368–69
Gellhorn, Martha, 452, 495, 555
    affair with EH of, 368–82, 390–99,
        403–11
    in Cuba, 403–4, 426–27, 442, 444,
        488
    on EH, 394, 441
    EH's fictional portrayals of, 386–88,
        445, 453, 475, 513, 528
    family background of, 368
    marriage to EH of, 417–19
    photos of, 369f
    published works of, 369–70, 408,
        410–11, 421, 424–25, 434, 442, 529
    reporting for *Collier's* of, 372, 378,
        392–95, 408–9, 421–25, 426, 434,
        475
    separation and divorce from EH
        of, 439–41, 444–45, 449, 463–65,
        474–76
    Spanish Civil War and, 371–79, 386,
        392–95
    in Sun Valley, 407–8
    World War II reporting of, 421–25,
        439–43, 453

gender questions, 7, 482–87
  cultural constructions of masculinity
    and, 3–5, 185–86
  EH's childhood twinning and, 22–25,
    251, 482
  EH's declining potency and, 450,
    463
  EH's explorations of androgyny and,
    3, 24, 135–37, 251, 482–84, 577
  EH's hair fetish and, 24, 120, 128,
    135–37, 172, 328–29, 347, 400, 401,
    466–67, 482–85, 500–501, 559,
    576–77
  EH's interest in lesbians and, 250–51,
    470–71, 559
  EH's possible homosexual
    relationships and, 68–71, 75,
    147–48, 289, 323–26
  eroticized Fiesta of San Fermín and,
    171–72
  Grace Hemingway's emasculation of
    Ed Hemingway and, 170
  Gregory Hemingway's crossdressing
    and, 481–83, 495, 543
Geneva Conventions, 458, 469
Geography and Plays (Stein), 119, 145,
  160
George H. Doran and Company, 173
"Get a Seeing-Eyed Dog" (Hemingway),
  584
"The G.I. and the General"
  (Hemingway), 455, 469
Gingrich, Arnold, 156, 300, 319–20,
  329–30, 340, 355–57, 361, 390,
  440–41, 503
Glaser, Benjamin, 395
"God Rest Ye Merry Gentlemen"
  (Hemingway), 54, 319
Gold, Herbert, 620
Goldbeck, Ruth and Walter, 236–37,
  278–79
Golder, Lloyd, 39
Golos, Jacob, 434–35
Gone with the Wind (Mitchell), 416
"The Good Lion" (Hemingway), 529

Gordon, Caroline, 287–88
Gorer, Peter, 448
Graebner, Walter, 451
Grant, Bruce, 459, 469
The Great Gatsby (Fitzgerald), 182–83,
  280, 286–87, 420, 492, 521
Greb, Harry, 43
Greco-Turkish War, 125–28, 130–31, 134,
  139, 425
Green, Julien, 260
Green Hills of Africa (Hemingway),
  332–34, 339–43, 572
Griffin, Peter, 64, 223
Gris, Juan, 185
Guest, Winston "Wolfie," 431–34, 440,
  441f, 453, 489–90, 496, 508, 530
Guffey, Don Carlos, 259
Guggenheim, Peggy, 595
Guillén, Nicolás, 620
Guthrie, Pat, 186–90, 236
Gutiérrez, Carlos, 327, 339, 539

Haines, Lett, 187
Hale, William, 559
Hall, Caroline Hancock, 12, 14–15, 19,
  307
Hall, Ernest, 11–12, 14–16, 25–26, 30, 36
Hall, Grace. See Hemingway, Grace Hall
Hall, Leicester, 12, 15, 26
Hamilton, Bill, 408
The Hamlet of A. MacLeish (MacLeish),
  316
Hancock, Alexander, 12
Hancock, Annie, 12
Hancock, Benjamin Tyley, 12, 15, 25–26,
  30
Handy, Lowney, 549
Hanger, Franklin McCue, 583
Hannagan, Steve, 408
Hansen, Harry, 216
Harding, Warren G., 365
Hardy, Thomas, 158
Harriman, Averell, 407, 445, 525
Harris, Harry, 459

Harry Ransom Center, 73, 91, 397
Hartley, Marsden, 143–44
Haskell, Henry J., 45
A Hasty Bunch (McAlmon), 142
Hawks, Howard, 545
"Hawks Do Not Share" (Hemingway), 183
Haynes, Grace, 50, 422
Hayward, Leland, 546, 548, 573–74, 576
Hayward, Slim, 470, 545–46, 567, 573–76, 597–98
head injuries, 448–50, 455–56, 461–63, 487, 549
   in Africa, 563–65, 573
   chronic traumatic encephalopathy and dementia from, 583
   of Patrick Hemingway, 497–501, 523, 543
   on the *Pilar,* 568
Heap, Jane, 139
Hearst, William Randolph, Jr., 458–59
The Heart of Another (Gellhorn), 408, 442
Hecht, Ben, 97, 216
Heeney, Tom, 347, 496–97
Hellman, Lillian, 372
Hemingway, Adelaide Edmonds, 11–13, 25
Hemingway, Allen, 12
Hemingway, Anson, 12–14, 25, 32, 242, 267, 273–74
Hemingway, Arabella, 46, 122, 259
Hemingway, Carol, 298, 525
   EH's nickname for, 39
   EH's relationship with, 16–26, 239, 269, 291–93, 299, 320–23
   marriage of, 320–22, 494
Hemingway, Clarence "Ed," 13–16, 53, 162
   EH's relationship with, 92–93, 238–44, 254–58, 264–65, 269–70
   on EH's writing, 162, 178, 197, 242–44

evangelical religion of, 30, 32–34, 75, 88, 268–69
family and home life of, 19–34, 79–81, 88–93, 178
financial challenges of, 272–73
health challenges of, 254–55, 263–64
medical practice of, 28, 32, 254
photos of, 20*f,* 256*f*
political engagement of, 365
psychological challenges of, 30–32, 82, 170, 242, 255, 267
suicide of, 21, 84, 242, 255, 266–70, 401, 626–27
Hemingway, Ernest Miller
   adolescence of, 34–45
   alcohol and drug use by, 7, 45, 146, 172, 197–98, 239, 329, 351–52, 418, 440–42, 450, 461, 464, 487, 526–27, 567–69, 580–84
   Catholicism of, 221, 235, 268–69, 303, 364
   childhood of, 3, 18–34
   children of. *See* names of EH's children
   Civil War gun of, 267, 273–74
   education of, 79–80, 85, 111–12
   fame of, 6–8, 72, 297–98, 325, 390
   family background of, 11–18
   financial status of, 239, 260–61, 291–92, 310–11, 587–88
   gender insecurity of. *See* gender questions
   head injuries of. *See* head injuries
   health of, 7–9, 11–12, 53, 62–64, 250, 296–98, 324, 333–34, 343, 447–50, 461, 463, 474, 527, 563–67, 579–85, 594, 617–18
   letter-writing correspondence of, 554–55
   love affairs of. *See* love interests
   marriages of. *See* names of EH's wives
   mental health challenges of. *See* mental illness
   Nobel Prize of, 569–71, 587

Hemingway, Ernest Miller (*continued*)
"Papa" nickname of, 223, 463–64, 470, 507, 591
personal traits and temperament of, 41–42, 54, 68, 71–74, 98, 117–18, 122, 155, 157, 164, 171–72, 200–201, 280–81, 297, 300, 310, 315, 320, 418, 444–45, 494–95
photos of, 20*f*, 21*f*, 23*f*, 65*f*, 83*f*, 89*f*, 109*f*, 198*f*, 214*f*, 256*f*, 272*f*, 308*f*, 415*f*, 449*f*, 456*f*, 471*f*, 532*f*, 596*f*, 608*f*
physical appearance of, 54, 67, 72, 76–77, 107, 121, 463, 566–67, 579, 591, 593, 609–10, 614–15, 626
poetry of, 98, 116–17, 130–31, 135, 156–57, 452–53, 474, 529, 627
political engagement of, 6, 358–59, 363–67, 371–95, 409, 416–17, 421, 435–37
portraits of, 138
religious practices of, 32–34
sports and outdoor activities of, 21–22, 36, 38, 43, 55, 73, 135, 165–67, 180, 262, 274–77, 293–96, 314–16, 515–19
suicide of, 7–8, 21, 33, 614
Hemingway, George, 254–55, 267, 270, 273
Hemingway, Grace Hall, 12, 14–36, 118, 298, 413
archive of, 73, 91, 397
art career of, 243, 263–64, 396
death of, 541
EH's relationship with, 26–27, 41–42, 45, 79, 83–84, 88–93, 105, 238–44, 254–57, 264, 291–93, 299, 395–99, 541–42
on EH's writing, 162, 196–97, 242–43
financial challenges of, 272–73, 291–92
health challenges of, 15
lecturing activities of, 397–98
marriage of, 15–18
motherhood and family life of, 18–33, 79

musical career of, 15–18, 24, 26–28, 33, 72, 243
personal traits and temperament of, 17–18, 72–74, 170, 178, 504
photos of, 20*f*
religious practices of, 32–33, 88
Ruth Arnold and, 80–85, 88, 250, 398, 541
Hemingway, Gregory Hancock, 307, 406
adult life of, 523, 543–45, 544–45, 585–86
childhood of, 313–14, 330, 335, 391, 397, 409, 480–81
crossdressing by, 481–83, 495, 543, 585
on EH, 438–40, 480, 495
EH's fictional portrayal of, 345, 478–79, 482
marriages of, 543–44, 598
on Martha Gellhorn, 410
on Mary Hemingway, 578
mental illness of, 585, 619, 626–27
photos of, 345*f*
visits to EH by, 410, 413, 418, 432–33, 440, 479–80, 488, 495–96
Hemingway, Hadley. *See* Richardson, Hadley
Hemingway, Harriet Louisa Tyler, 12
Hemingway, Jacob, 12
Hemingway, Jane, 544
Hemingway, Joan "Muffet," 512, 542–43
Hemingway, John (grandson), 585
Hemingway, John Hadley Nicanor "Bumby/Jack" (son), 151–54, 172–73
adult life of, 512, 542–43, 578–79
childhood of, 220–22, 330, 395, 419
children of, 512
EH's fictional portrayal of, 345, 478–79
godmothers of, 119, 154–55, 286, 324
marriage of, 512, 520
photos of, 154*f*, 198*f*, 345*f*
visits to EH by, 266, 271, 295, 301–2, 313, 391, 410–11, 495–96

WWII service of, 427, 443, 470, 479, 553
Hemingway, Leicester, 18, 39, 255–56, 267
  biography of EH by, 268
  Caribbean patrols of, 427
  EH's relationship with, 239, 269, 291, 337–39, 411, 421, 427, 504–5
  on Jane Mason, 312
  personal traits and temperament of, 504–5
  World War II of, 446–48, 454, 504
  writing and reporting of, 90, 421, 504, 572
Hemingway, Madelaine "Sunny," 18–26, 36, 39, 298, 541
  adolescence of, 91–92
  EH's relationship with, 239, 266, 271
  photos of, 20f, 83f
Hemingway, Marcelline Doris. See Sanford, Marcelline Hemingway
Hemingway, Margot, 542–43
Hemingway, Mariel, 543
Hemingway, Marietta, 12
Hemingway, Mary (aunt), 82
Hemingway, Mary Welsh (wife), 447–48, 526
  affair with EH of, 450–54, 463–68, 474, 487–89
  on African safari, 557–65
  autobiography of, 527–28
  in Cuba, 487–90
  on EH's mental illness, 526–28
  EH's mistreatment of, 466–67, 476–77, 512, 538–39, 576–79, 599, 602–3, 623
  family background of, 451, 497
  Gianfranco Ivancich and, 537–38
  hair and sex play of, 136–37, 466–67, 485, 488, 500–501, 512, 559, 576–77
  health challenges of, 580–81, 599–601, 605, 607
  journalism career of, 451–52, 468, 488
  in Ketchum, 593–94
  marriage to EH of, 489
  NYC apartment of, 610–11

  Pauline Pfeiffer and, 499
  on posthumous works of EH, 589
  pregnancy of, 495
  Valerie Danby-Smith and, 601, 606–10
Hemingway, Patrick, 8, 259, 295, 307, 407, 514
  adult life of, 537, 543, 544–45
  in Africa, 556, 558, 564–65, 585
  childhood of, 260–63, 271, 295, 313–14, 330, 335, 391, 397, 409
  on EH, 438–39, 442, 568
  EH's fictional portrayal of, 345, 478–79
  EH's unfinished African book and, 560, 572–73
  head injury of, 497–501, 519, 523, 543
  marriage of, 520, 585
  on Martha Gellhorn, 410
  photos of, 345f
  visits to EH by, 410, 413, 418, 432–33, 440, 479–80, 488, 495–96, 530–31
Hemingway, Pauline. See Pfeiffer, Pauline
Hemingway, Ralph, 12
Hemingway, Seán, 136, 283, 472
Hemingway, Tyler, 45–46, 259
Hemingway, Ursula, 18–26, 35, 39, 75–76, 298
  adolescence of, 91–92
  EH's relationship with, 239, 271, 318, 363
  photos of, 20f, 83f
Hemingway, Willoughby, 33, 82, 254
Hemingway-Callaghan boxing match, 275–77, 289, 540, 553
Hemingway code, 3
Hemingway Collection at the JFK Library, 136
Hemingway Marlin Fishing Tournament, 609
Hemingway: The Writer as Artist (Baker), 547
hemochromatosis, 618
Henry, Barklie McKee, 261
Hepburn, Katharine, 336–37, 575

Herbst, Josephine, 163, 174, 294, 299–300, 374–78, 387–88
Herrera, Roberto, 432, 489, 498–99, 605, 607
Herrera Sotolongo, José Luis, 449–50, 498–99, 607
Herrmann, John, 163, 174, 294, 299–300, 427
Herrold, Matthew, 206
Hersey, John, 546
Hewlett, Maurice, 85
Hickok, Guy, 130, 132, 153, 167, 236, 283–84
Hicks, Granville, 348
Hicks, Wilson, 48, 56
Higgons, Joan, 624
"Hills Like White Elephants" (Hemingway), 244, 246–47, 281, 322
Hindmarsh, Harry, 150–51
Hiroshima (Hersey), 546
Hitler, Adolf, 392, 423–24
Holiday, 529
"Homage to Ezra Pound" (Hemingway), 115
"Homage to Switzerland" (Hemingway), 318
Hoover, Herbert, 259, 365
Hoover, J. Edgar, 429–30
Hopkins, Charles, 56, 104, 238
Hopkins, Harry, 368
Horne, Bill, 57–59, 66–67, 74
  friendship with EH of, 93–94, 104, 259–60, 296, 308–9
  on Hadley Richardson, 99
  Oak Park Hemingways and, 238
Horne, Bunny, 296, 308
Hotchner, A. E. "Ed," 506–7
  at Cosmopolitan, 507, 522, 528
  friendship with EH of, 459–60, 475–76, 518, 565, 579–81, 593–94, 603, 609–10, 612–13, 615, 617, 619, 624–25
  photo of, 532f
  on posthumous works of EH, 589
  tape recording of EH by, 597, 604

TV adaptations of EH's works and, 588
"How to Live on Practically Nothing a Year" (Fitzgerald), 200
Hubbard, L. Ron, 543
Huckleberry Finn (Twain), 342
Hudson, Rock, 600
"Hugh Selwyn Mauberley" (Pound), 113, 235
Hugo, Victor, 436
Huston, Evelyn, 505
Huston, John, 505–6, 515, 562
Hutchison, Percy, 284

Ibarlucia, Paxtchi, 432, 453
iceberg principle, 104, 155, 169–70, 318, 416
"I Guess Everything Reminds You of Something" (Hemingway), 480
Imagism, 113–14
"I Must Try to Write the History of Belmonte" (Stein), 145
"In Another Country" (Hemingway), 61–62, 244, 246
"Indian Camp" (Hemingway), 159–60, 170
individualism, 55
Infiesta Bages, Manuel, 583
Ingersoll, Ralph, 421–22
Inönü, Ismet, 129
In Our Time (Hemingway), 53–54, 126, 139, 159–60, 173, 176–79, 184, 192, 552
  critical reception of, 195–97
  publication of, 195
"In Our Time" (Hemingway), 149
International Game Fish Association (IGFA), 347
"In the Station of the Metro" (Pound), 114
Intolerance, 50
Islands in the Stream (Hemingway), 345, 347, 478–79, 482, 539–40
Ivancich, Adriana, 509–11, 523–24, 533–34, 536–39, 565

Ivancich, Anton Luigi, 510
Ivancich, Carlo, 510–11
Ivancich, Cristina, 599
Ivancich, Dora, 510–11, 533, 536–39
Ivancich, Gianfranco, 510–11, 533, 537–38, 557, 580, 588, 599
Ivens, Joris, 372, 373f, 377–83

Jackson, Henry, 319
Jackson, Stonewall, 513
Jake Barnes (character), 186, 194, 217, 235, 483–84
James, Henry, 148, 158, 262, 280, 342
James, William, 119
Jazz Age, 181–82
Jenkins, Howell, 57–59, 93, 104, 238, 309
Jensen, Nita, 525–26
Jessup, Elsie, 70
John Halifax: Gentleman (Craik), 35
Johnson, Larry, 617, 620, 624
Johnston, Dossie, 175
Johnston, William Dawson, 175
Jolson, Al, 496
Jones, James, 502, 549–50, 555
Jones, Jennifer, 600
Jordan, Lillie, 262
Jorgensen, Christine, 486
journalism of EH, 37–39
    in Chicago, 93–99, 106
    Gertrude Stein's advice on, 120, 129
    on the Greco-Turkish War, 125–28
    in high school, 38–39, 41–42
    in Kansas City, 34, 45–54, 93
    on the Lausanne peace conference, 130–34
    for the Toronto Star, 93, 106–7, 110, 112–13, 120–21, 124–30, 139, 144, 150–52
    for the Toronto Star Weekly, 86–87, 150–51
Jouvenel, Bertrand de, 368, 370–71
Joyce, Bob, 429–30, 439–43
Joyce, James, 108, 111, 115, 143, 159, 229, 246, 331, 335

Joyce, Jane, 429
Joyce, Nora, 331
"The Judgment of Manitou" (Hemingway), 37
Junkins, Donald, 481
Justin, Elaine "Pinky," 445, 447–48

Kael, Pauline, 50–51
Kahle, Hans, 393
Kansas City Star, 34, 45–54, 93, 553
    EH's fictional portrayals of, 53–54
    house style of, 46
Kashkin, Ivan, 358–59, 568
Kauffman, Bea, 176–77
Kazin, Alfred, 389, 534
Kechler, Carlo, 509–10, 557
Kechler, Federico, 508
Ken magazine, 390, 392–93
Kert, Bernice, 187, 295, 371
Ketchum, Idaho, 592–93, 605–6, 614–27
    Hemingway house in, 593–94, 605, 622f
    Hemingway memorial in, 627
    MacDonald Cabins in, 496, 505
    Sun Valley in, 407–9, 413–14, 592
Key, Jakie, 293
The Keys of the Kingdom (Cronin), 416
Key West, 252–58, 266, 271–74, 275f, 298–301, 307–11
    cats in, 514
    EH's departure from, 409
    as EH's personal fiefdom, 300–301, 344, 436
    EH's Pilar in, 337–40, 346
    EH's social circle in, 293
    EH's visitors in, 298–300, 307–11, 338, 344, 579
    fishing trips from, 293–94, 299–300, 308, 311, 344–48, 380
    marlin fishing in, 253, 312, 327, 334, 337–40
    Martha Gellhorn's visit to, 369–71

Key West (continued)
  Sloppy Joe's bar in, 293, 301, 369–70,
      391
  trips to Cuba from, 311–12, 327–28
  Whitehead Street house in, 301,
      307–8, 344, 380, 407, 544–45, 557,
      588
"The Killers" (Hemingway), 40, 212,
      216, 243, 246
The Killers (film), 565
Kipling, Rudyard, 48, 97
Kirkpatrick, Helen, 456–57, 460
Kirstein, Lincoln, 316
Kleeman, Werner, 472
Klein, Herb, 388
Knapp, Joseph Fairchild, 348
Knight, Clifford, 48
Knopf, 173
Kohly, Carlos "Cucu" M., 497–98,
      527
Kreymborg, Alfred, 165
Krutch, Joseph Wood, 245–46
Kulcsar, Ilse, 378–79
Kurowsky, Agnes von, 64–71, 77–78, 89,
      127–28, 162, 258

La Consula, 595–97, 599–601, 612
La Cossitt, Henry, 454
"Lady Poets with Foot Notes"
      (Hemingway), 184–85
The Lake, 337
Lang, Will, 601
Langer, Elinor, 387–88
Lanham, Charles "Buck," 553, 578
  friendship with EH of, 455, 496, 512,
      535, 551–52, 569, 599–600
  World War II and, 455, 456f, 465,
      467–68, 472–73, 476–77, 513, 525
Lanham, Mary "Pete," 512
Lardner, Jim, 393
Lardner, Ring, 38–40, 97, 140, 162
"The Last Good Country"
      (Hemingway), 484, 555–56
The Last Tycoon (Fitzgerald), 420, 492,
      521

Laughlin, James, 492
Lawrence, D. H., 158, 195, 196
Laxness, Halldór, 569
L-Bar-T Ranch, 295–96, 347, 405, 419
League of American Writers, 380
Leclerc, Philippe, 458–60
Leddy, Raymond, 429, 433–34
Leff, Leonard, 316
Léger, Fernand, 199
Lent, Walther, 172
Leopold, Nathan, 322
Lerner, Helen, 347
Lerner, Mike, 347
Levine, Isaac Don, 365
Lewis, Robert, 572
Lewis, Sinclair, 112, 569
Lewis, William R., 14
Lewis, Wyndham, 115, 121, 158, 335–36
Liana (Gellhorn), 442
Liebling, A. J., 456
Life magazine, 408, 412–13, 453, 573
  Cowley's essay on EH in, 360–61,
      551–52
  EH's bullfighting piece for, 601, 604,
      606, 609–11, 614
  The Old Man and the Sea in,
      546–47
Lincoln, Abraham, 11
Lindsay, Vachel, 96–97
literary modernism, 11
Little Lord Fauntleroy (Burnett), 22
The Little Review, 97, 117, 135, 139, 149,
      160
Liveright, Horace, 173, 176–79, 184,
      201–4, 210–11, 216–17, 330, 502–3
Livingston, Grace, 338
Lloyd George, David, 150
Loeb, Harold, 165–66
  Duff Twysden and, 187–90
  EH's enmity toward, 194–95, 204
  EH's fictional portrayal of, 4, 190–93,
      236
  on EH's temper, 191–93
  friendship with EH of, 173–79, 192,
      220
Long, Ray, 130, 260

Longan, George, 46
Longfield, 35–36
Look Homeward, Angel (Wolfe), 319
Look magazine, 556, 558, 563–64
Loomis, Bob, 91
Loomis, Elizabeth, 91
Loos, Anita, 225
Lorimer, George Horace, 172, 219, 353
"Lost Generation," 118, 234, 325
Love and Death in the American Novel
    (Fiedler), 616
love interests, 463
    Adriana Ivancich, 509–11, 523–24,
        533–34, 536–39, 565
    Agnes von Kurowsky, 64–71, 77–78,
        89, 127–28, 162
    Debba, 560–61, 572
    Jane Kendall Mason, 306, 311–13,
        327–28, 572
    Jim Gamble, 68–71, 75, 102
    Louise Bryant, 128–29
    Mae Marsh, 50–52, 56–57
    Martha Gellhorn, 368–82, 386–88,
        390–99, 403–5
    Mary Welsh, 450–54, 463, 464–68,
        474, 487–89
    Pauline Pfeiffer, 195, 197–99, 202,
        206–15, 221–32, 590
    Valerie Danby-Smith, 598–604,
        606–13, 615
"The Love Song of J. Alfred Prufrock"
    (Eliot), 115
Lowe, Bill, 556, 563
Lowell, Amy, 114, 184–85
Lower Ranch, 259
Lowry, Malcolm and Ruth White, 259
Loy, Mina, 143–44
Luce, Clare Boothe, 466
Ludington, Townsend, 377
Lunar Baedecker (Loy), 144
Lynn, Kenneth, 3, 350
Lyons, Leonard, 496

Macadam, John, 446
MacDonald, Elsie, 78

Machado, Gerardo, 339, 505–6
MacLeish, Ada, 166, 180, 237, 248, 265,
    310, 329, 490
MacLeish, Archibald, 73, 117, 128, 166,
    196, 476, 587
    on EH's works, 284
    at *Fortune* magazine, 284, 293–94,
        299–300, 308, 311
    friendship with EH of, 180, 223,
        225–27, 237, 248, 265, 294, 297,
        308–11, 326, 330, 338–39, 412, 442,
        490–91
    Jane Mason and, 328
    as Librarian of Congress, 411, 491–92
    on Martha Gellhorn, 370
    personal traits and temperament of,
        309–10
    photo of, 180*f*
    Second American Writers' Conference
        of, 380
    Spanish Civil War and, 372
    Uphill Farm of, 265
    World War II politics of, 411–12, 423
    writing of, 310–11, 316
MacLeish, Ken, 265
MacLeish, Mimi, 265
MacMullen, Duke, 617
Madill, George, 40
Madinaveitia, Juan, 580–81
Magruder, John, 443
Mailer, Norman, 5, 339, 529, 549
Main Street (Lewis), 112
Maison des Amis des Livres, 111
The Making of Americans (Stein), 159,
    324
Malatesta, Sigismondo, 137–38
Malraux, André, 366
Mance de Mores, Paul, 279
Manhattan Transfer (Dos Passos), 164,
    356
manic-depressive disorder. *See* mental
    illness
The Man Nobody Knows (B. Barton),
    32–33
"A Man of the World" (Hemingway),
    584

Man's Fate (Malraux), 366

Many Marriages (Anderson), 178

Mao Tse-tung, 421–25

March, Fredric, 383

Marigny, Nancy de, 512

marriages of convenience, 141–42

marriages of EH. *See* Gellhorn, Martha; Hemingway, Mary Welsh; Pfeiffer, Pauline; Richardson, Hadley

Marsh, Mae, 50–52, 56–57

Marsh, Roy, 561–64

Marshall, S. L. A., 459–60

Maskin, Major, 472–73

Mason, Frank, 125, 130, 134

Mason, G. Grant, Jr., 306, 311–12, 327, 340

Mason, Jane Kendall, 305–6, 311–14, 327–28, 340, 572
  affairs of, 306, 312, 355–56
  Carol Hemingway and, 320, 322
  EH's fictional portrayal of, 356, 357, 359
  photo of, 313*f*

Mason, Tony, 327

Masters, Edgar Lee, 96–97

Masterson, Bat, 206

Mata Hari, 61

"A Matter of Colour" (Hemingway), 43

Matthews, Herbert, 375, 378, 386, 392–93, 607–8

Matthews, T. S., 284–85

Maugham, Somerset, 421

Maurois, André, 380

Mayo Clinic, 617–26

McAlmon, Robert, 141–49, 174, 324
  Contact Editions of, 133, 141–44, 149, 173, 275, 299
  friendship with EH of, 145–49, 161, 166–67, 184, 289, 305
  memoir of, 145–48
  publishing of EH by, 133, 140–44, 149–50, 155, 158
  as writer, 163, 167, 191, 288–89

McCaffery, John K. M., 551–52

McCarthy, Joseph, 525, 564

McCloy, John, 442

McClure, John, 156, 489

McClure, Robert A., 452

McCracken, Kenneth, 617–19

McDaniel, Marion, 42

McKey, Edward, 60

M'Cola, 333, 557

McWine, Turner, 443

Meehan, Harry William, 398, 541

"Melanctha" (Stein), 119

Mencken, H. L., 173, 184, 202

Menocal, Mario "Mayito," 489–90, 557–58, 568

mental illness, 7, 18, 31, 171–72, 473, 561, 598, 606–7, 611–27
  depression in, 579, 594, 603, 619
  drugs for, 581–83, 615–20
  electroshock treatments for, 618–21, 624–25
  familial tendencies toward, 18, 585, 619, 626–27
  hair-trigger temper and, 172, 191–93, 300, 391, 538–39, 579, 600
  head injuries and, 448–50, 455–56, 461–63, 549, 563–65, 568, 573
  hemochromatosis in, 618
  manic grandiosity of, 518–28, 531, 535, 549–50, 573, 578
  paranoid delusions of, 553, 566, 584–85, 605–6, 612–13, 615–16, 619–23, 625–26
  shell shock and, 61–64
  suicide attempts and, 624
  talk of suicide in, 230, 401, 519, 604, 612–13, 618

Men Without Women (Hemingway), 54, 244–47

"The Mercenaries" (Hemingway), 78, 86

Merck, Josephine, 328

Mesa, Fernando, 432

Meyer, Art, 104

Meyer, Wallace, 528–29

Meyers, Jeffrey, 324, 481

Millay, Edna St. Vincent, 184–85

Miller, Edward, 15

Miller, Henry, 15, 485

Miller, William Edward, 15, 28
Miró, Joan, 165, 410, 610
Missouri National Guard, 53
Mizener, Arthur, 520–21, 540
Moddelmog, Debra, 136
Modern Language Association, 620
Moffat, Ivan, 446
Mogaman, Munro, 296
Moise, Lionel, 48
Mola, Emilio, 386
Mondadori, Alberto, 508, 532–33
Monks, Mary Welsh, 447–48
    See also Hemingway, Mary Welsh
Monks, Noel, 451, 467, 487, 489, 578
Monnier, Adrienne, 111, 155–56, 250
Monnier, Jean, 581
Monroe, Harriet, 97, 115, 132
Moody, Dwight, 13, 30
Moore, Marianne, 141, 172
Moorehead, Alan and Lucy, 508
Moorhead, Ethel, 172, 176
Moralito (circus owner), 517–18
Morford, Edwin, 81
Morgan, Pat and Maude, 299–300
Morgenthau, Henry, Jr., 423, 425
Morison, Samuel Eliot, 442
Morris, Cedric, 187
Morris, John, 447
A Moveable Feast (Hemingway), 24, 112,
    185, 405, 588–92, 605, 623, 627
    2009 edition of, 590
    on Hadley Richardson, 226,
        589–90
    on haircuts, 24, 136–37, 483
    lost manuscript of, 129–35
    on Pauline Pfeiffer, 198–99, 206–9,
        590
    posthumous additions to, 136
    on Rapallo, 138–39
    on Scott Fitzgerald, 181–83, 219–20,
        350–51, 589
    on Wyndham Lewis, 336
Mowrer, Paul, 266, 269, 419, 512
"Mr. and Mrs. Elliot" (Hemingway),
    172, 176
Murphy, Baoth, 199, 314, 343–44

Murphy, Gerald and Sara, 166, 199–203,
    208, 300, 352
    children of, 199, 314, 343–44, 371
    on EH's marriages, 225–26, 237
    photos of, 214f
    travel and holidays with, 204–5, 213,
        220–25, 314–15, 343–44
    Villa America of, 199–201, 220–21,
        224–25, 595
Murphy, Honoria, 199, 222, 314–15,
    371
Murphy, Patrick, 199, 314, 343–44, 371
Musselman, Morris, 40
Mussolini, Benito, 129, 355, 366, 508
My Brother, Ernest Hemingway (L.
    Hemingway), 90
Myers, Alice Lee, 371
"My Old Man" (Hemingway), 40,
    120–21, 130, 132, 140, 160, 170

Nagel, James, 66
The Naked and the Dead (Mailer),
    529
Napoleon III, Emperor of France, 11
"A Natural History of the Dead"
    (Hemingway), 305, 319
Nerone, Nick, 76, 105
Nevill, W. P., 55
The New Age, 115
The New Freewoman, 115
New Masses, 348–49, 355, 358, 381
The New Yorker, 298, 329
    Hersey's Hiroshima in, 546
    Ross's portrait of EH in, 40, 524,
        530–32, 534
N'Gui, 557
Nick Adams stories, 22, 87, 113, 168–70,
    327, 555–56, 612
    haircuts in, 484
    impact of war on, 62–63
    publication of, 159–60, 176
    sexual exploits in, 89
"Night Before Battle" (Hemingway),
    392, 399
1919 (Dos Passos), 308, 357

NKVD, 434–36
Nobel Prize for Literature, 533, 569–71, 587, 620
Les Noces (Stravinsky), 199–201
Nordquist, Lawrence and Olive, 295, 298, 361, 363
North, Henry, 446, 474
North American Committee for Spain, 372
North American Newspaper Alliance (NANA), 367, 371, 385–86, 388
Notebooks (Fitzgerald), 350
Nothing Is Sacred (Herbst), 299
"Now I Lay Me" (Hemingway), 62–63, 244, 246–47

Oak Park, Illinois, 12, 19–20
    EH's childhood home in, 27–29
    EH's World War I lectures in, 75–77
Oberlin College, 13–14, 30, 44–45
O'Brien, Edward, 139–40, 144, 157–58, 161, 261
The Office (Asch), 163
Office of Strategic Services (OSS), 428, 442–43, 446, 456–57, 469–70, 510, 595
O'Hara, John, 492, 534–35
Ohlsen, Ray, 36, 39, 41–42
The Old Man and the Sea (Hemingway), 7, 539–40, 545–48, 570
    critical reception of, 547–48, 569
    film rights of, 548
    film version of, 567, 573–76
    sales of, 547
O'Neil, Dave, 134–35
O'Neil, George, 166, 169
One Man's Initiation (Dos Passos), 164
"One Trip Across" (Hemingway), 341, 355–56
"On the Blue Water" (Hemingway), 539–40
"On the Quai at Smyrna" (Hemingway), 126
Ordóñez, Antonio, 557, 565, 580, 595–602, 605, 610–12

Ordóñez, Carmen, 580, 602, 605, 611
Ordóñez, Cayetano, 189, 190
Orlov, Alexander, 435
Orr, Elaine, 163
"The Other Hemingways," 298
Other Voices, Other Rooms (Capote), 67
Ottoman Empire, 125–27
The Outline of History (Wells), 166
Out of Africa (Dinesen), 556

Pacciardi, Randolfo, 393–94
Packard, Vance, 620
Palfrey, John, 454
Paris, 106–33, 152–54, 274–83, 301, 331
    EH's development as writer in, 155–70, 172
    EH's income in, 112
    EH's literary connections in, 106–20, 158–66, 168, 174
    EH's memoir of, 24, 112–13, 129–37, 405, 588–92, 605, 623, 627
    EH's reputation in, 120–22
    marriages of convenience in, 141–42
    See also A Moveable Feast
"Paris 1922" (Hemingway), 135
The Paris Review, 566
Paris Was Our Mistress (Putnam), 277
Parker, Dorothy, 140, 235, 247–48, 305, 319, 383, 413–14, 492
Parker, Harrison, 94–95, 106
Parsons, Louella, 206
Pascual y Baguer, Miguel, 403
Paterson, Isabel, 276
Paton, Alan, 502
Patton, George, 455, 460
Paulhan, Jean, 380
Pearson, Norman Holmes, 146
Peirce, Alzira, 293
Peirce, Waldo, 253, 265, 274, 293, 363, 594
Pelkey, Archie "Red," 455–57, 460
Pentecost, Jack, 104
Percival, Philip, 332–34, 342, 359, 556–58, 561, 564
Pereda, Prudencio de, 371, 381

Perkins, Max, 116, 163, 265, 280–81, 317, 362, 372
authors of, 502
on the crash of 1929, 286
death of, 501–3
on EH, 308, 340–41
on John Thomason's stories, 425
photo of, 272f
publishing of EH's works by, 183–84, 201, 210–12, 228, 233, 244, 280–83, 304, 318–19, 330, 343, 355, 389
Robert McAlmon and, 288–89
Scott Fitzgerald and, 217, 266, 278–79, 420, 492, 502
Thomas Wolfe and, 319, 502
visits to Key West by, 271–72, 293–94, 299, 343
on For Whom the Bell Tolls, 411, 413
See also Scribner's
Perse, Saint-John, 620
Personae (Pound), 113
Pfeiffer, Gus, 205–6, 208, 251–52, 283
funding of EH's and Pauline by, 236–37, 252, 291, 294, 301, 304, 311
the Hemingway's divorce and, 406–7
photo of, 302f
visits with EH and Pauline of, 265, 298, 301, 319
Pfeiffer, Karl, 251
Pfeiffer, Louise, 298
Pfeiffer, Mary, 204–5, 229–31, 251–52, 258–60, 263, 406–7, 413
Pfeiffer, Paul, 205, 251–52, 258, 406–7
Pfeiffer, Pauline, 179–80, 204–10, 262, 371
on African safari, 330–36, 558
biography of, 208
Catholicism of, 205–6, 209, 221, 303, 364, 406, 479–80
death of, 542–45
EH's affair with, 195, 197–99, 202, 206–15, 221–32, 590
EH's fictional portrayals of, 208, 332, 341–42, 360, 405
EH's hair fetish and, 328–29, 347
on EH's writing, 248, 295, 406

family background and wealth of, 205–6, 251–52, 291
Jane Mason and, 311–13
in Key West and Cuba, 252–53, 298–301, 307–8, 338, 345, 391
marriage to EH of, 236–38, 241–42
Martha Gellhorn and, 370–71, 378, 380, 390, 392, 395
Mary Hemingway and, 499
motherhood and home life of, 250–63
in Paris, 274, 278–79, 287
Patrick's illness and, 497–500, 543
photos of, 205f, 308f
pregnancies of, 250, 253–54, 258–59, 301–2, 306–7
separation and divorce from EH of, 399, 404–9, 417–18
in Spain, 301–2
Spanish Civil War and, 388–89
Vogue assignment of, 179, 204, 206, 229
on western trips, 260, 295, 391
Pfeiffer, Virginia "Jinny," 204, 213–14, 236–37, 244
as caregiver for Patrick, 262–63
Catholicism of, 364
on the Hemingway's divorce, 406–7
interactions with the Hemingways of, 283–84, 307, 314, 317, 320, 322, 330, 335, 371
social world of, 250–51
Phelan, Janet, 129
Phelan, Mab, 129
Picasso, Pablo, 185, 199, 225
Pictorial Review, 157–58
Pike, William, 388
the Pilar, 337–40, 346, 380, 404, 515
EH's concussion on, 549
log of, 433
Q-boat hunting in, 430–37, 506
weaponry on, 592–93
Pinder, Bread, 344
Pivano, Fernanda, 508–9, 531
Platt, Frank, 37
Plimpton, George, 566, 620
PM newspaper, 421–24, 438

"Poem to Mary" (Hemingway), 529
"Poetry" (Hemingway), 529
Poetry: A Magazine of Verse, 97, 115, 116–17, 132
Pollock, Jackson, 428, 595, 597
Ponzi, Charles, 95
Poore, Charles, 474
Poor White (Anderson), 106
The Portable F. Scott Fitzgerald (ed. Parker), 492
Porter, Cole and Linda, 199
"Portrait of Hemingway" (Ross), 530–32
Post-Adolescence (McAlmon), 142
post-traumatic stress disorder, 63
Pound, Dorothy, 236, 586
Pound, Ezra, 40, 97, 106, 113–18, 132–33, 150, 329, 572, 586–87
    antisemitism and Fascism of, 173, 491–92, 570
    EH's satire of, 117–18
    EH's tribute to, 176
    existential pessimism of, 235
    friendship with EH, 121, 156, 161–62, 165, 236
    honors and awards, 586
    Imagism of, 113–14
    literary connections of, 114–17, 144, 156, 158–159, 173
    photos of, 114*f*
    physical appearance of, 115–16
    in Rapallo, 137–39
Powell, Dawn, 381, 407
Primo de Rivera, Miguel, 302–3
Prohibition, 112
psychiatric challenges. *See* mental illness
Pudney, John, 446
Pulitzer Prize for fiction, 416
"A Pursuit Race" (Hemingway), 54
Putnam, Samuel, 277

Der Querschnitt, 117, 172, 184
Quinlan, Grace, 89, 93

Quinn, John, 158, 167
Quintana, Juanito, 188, 598
Quintanilla, Pepe, 387

Raeburn, John, 160, 461
Ramona, 50
Randall, Mallinson, 16
Randall, William, 12
Rapallo (Italy), 137–45
Rapallo, Constance, 100
Rapallo, Edna, 100
Rascoe, Burton, 160, 233
Rawlings, Marjorie Kinnan, 502–3
Reconciliation Road (Marshall), 460–61
Redbook, 78–79, 156
Redman, Ben, 316, 534
Reed, John, 120, 128, 365
Regler, Gustav, 402, 428, 435
Reid, Marjorie, 159–60
Remarque, Erich Maria, 286
reserpine, 581–83, 615–20
reviews and articles
    of *Across the River and into the Trees,* 534–35, 536
    of *Death in the Afternoon,* 316, 325–26, 362–63
    by Edmund Wilson, 160–61, 177, 234, 246, 285, 414, 521
    on EH himself, 325–26, 340, 341*f,* 348, 354*f,* 358–59, 360–61, 380–81, 390, 464, 507, 524, 527, 530–32, 551–52, 616–17, 619
    of *A Farewell to Arms,* 284–86
    of *The Fifth Column and the First Forty-nine Stories,* 392
    of *To Have and Have Not,* 389–90
    by Lillian Ross, 40, 524, 530–32, 534
    of *Men Without Women,* 244–47
    of *The Old Man and the Sea,* 547–48, 569
    of *In Our Time,* 195–97
    of *The Sun Also Rises,* 233–36

of *Three Stories and Ten Poems,* 149, 160

of *For Whom the Bell Tolls,* 414–16

by Wyndham Lewis, 335–36

Reynolds, Nicholas, 443

Rice, Alfred, 587–88

Richardson, Clifford, 99

Richardson, Florence, 99–101, 103

Richardson, Hadley, 24, 40, 98–107, 189, 305, 368, 419, 512

  biographies of, 189

  courtship and wedding of, 102–4

  education of, 100–101

  on EH's appearance, 69

  EH's hair fetish and, 135–37, 483

  in EH's memoirs, 589–90

  family background of, 99–100

  financial independence of, 103, 112

  loss of EH's manuscripts by, 129–35, 485

  loyalty to EH of, 104–5

  marriage to Paul Mowrer of, 266, 269

  Paris life of, 108–12, 122–33, 153–55, 179–80, 187, 194, 199–202, 589–90

  Pauline Pfeiffer and, 206–15, 221–32, 590

  photos of, 109*f,* 198*f,* 207

  pregnancy of, 138–39, 144, 149–50, 207

  separation and divorce from EH of, 225–27, 231–32, 236, 240–41, 260

  See also Paris

Richardson, James, 99–100

Richardson, James, Sr., 103

"The Rich Boy" (Fitzgerald), 362

Riddle, Georgia, 103

Ridgell, Pinckney, 457

"The Right Honorable the Strawberries" (Wister), 261

RMS *Lusitania,* 52

Robert Jordan (character), 400–402, 411, 412, 414, 484

  as anti-Fascist hero, 416–17, 437, 438

  suicide of, 33–34

Robinson, Daniel, 428

Robles Pazos, José, 375–78, 390, 401, 435, 491

Rodman, Selden, 531

Rogers, W. G., 324

Rohrbach, Marie Cocotte, 112, 153, 167–68, 222–24, 266

Rome, Howard, 617–26

Rooney, Andy, 459

Roosevelt, Eleanor, 368, 382, 423, 434

Roosevelt, Franklin D., 365, 368, 382, 423, 430, 525–26

Roosevelt, Theodore, 261–62, 332

Roscoe, Burton, 121

Rosenfeld, Paul, 195, 196

Rosinante to the Road Again (Dos Passos), 356

Ross, Lillian, 40, 464, 524, 530–32, 534

Ross, Mary, 285

Rossellini, Roberto, 525

Rouse, Bobby, 94

Rovere, Richard, 534

Royce, Smokey, 296

Ruggles of Red Gap (Wilson), 86

Ruspoli, Camilo, 433–34

Russell, Joe "Josie," 293, 312, 327, 330, 409, 425

The Russian Revolution (Levine), 365

Ryall, William Bolitho, 129–30

Saint-Exupéry, Antoine de, 375

Salinger, J. D., 472

Sampson, Harold, 37, 40, 41, 43

Samuels, Lee, 475

Samuelson, Arnold "Mice," 293, 338–40

Sánchez, Thorwald, 432

Sandburg, Carl, 96–98, 570

Sanford, Marcelline Hemingway, 12, 18, 39, 238

  adult life of, 82, 273, 298, 321

  education of, 44–45, 50, 79

  EH's relationship with, 25, 43, 92, 239, 267–69, 396–97, 541

  Loomis cottage of, 257–58

  memoir of, 24–25, 76–77, 162, 268–69

Sanford, Marcelline Hemingway
　　(continued)
　　photos of, 20f, 23f, 83f, 89f
　　twinning with EH of, 22–25, 251, 482
Sanford, Sterling, 273
Santiago (character), 540, 547–48,
　　563–64
Saroyan, William, 446–47, 474
Sartre, Jean-Paul, 474, 620
The Saturday Evening Post, 78–79, 156,
　　158, 172, 181, 219
Sauer, Martha, 207
Saunders, Bra, 253, 293, 318, 337, 338
Saunders, Burge, 293, 299–300
Saviers, George, 597, 615–21, 624
Saxon, Don, 432
Scherman, Dave, 447
Scherschel, Frank, 447
Schneider, Isidor, 176–77
Schoenberg, Nara, 481
Schulberg, Budd, 505
Schwartz, Delmore, 389, 548
Scientology, 543, 585
Scribner, Charles III, 501–3, 518, 531, 533
　　death of, 545
　　on EH's later writing, 528–29, 540
　　loans to EH by, 526
Scribner, Charles IV "Jr.," 545, 550,
　　610–11, 614
Scribner, Vera, 540
Scribner's, 5, 163, 181–84, 201
　　Martha Gellhorn's work for, 475
　　payments to EH by, 260–61, 272, 337
　　publishing of EH, 183–84, 210–12,
　　　216–17, 415–16, 595–96
　　See also Perkins, Max
Scribner's Magazine, 212, 243, 244, 411
　　editor of, 262
　　EH's works in, 212, 260–61, 271–72,
　　　282–83, 318
　　Scott Fitzgerald's works in, 352–53
"The Sea Change" (Hemingway), 318
Second American Writers' Congress,
　　380, 429
"Second Poem to Mary" (Hemingway),
　　452, 474

Secret Intelligence (SI), 443
"Secret Pleasures" (Hemingway),
　　136–37
Segura, Pedro Cardinal, 303
Seidl, Anton, 16
Seldes, George, 120, 157, 172
Selznick, David O., 600
"Sepi Jingam" (Hemingway), 37
Sergeant York, 416
Set This House on Fire (Styron), 620
7th Missouri Infantry of the National
　　Guard, 53
sexuality. See gender questions
Shadows on the Grass (Dinesen), 620
Shakespear, Dorothy, 115, 137
Shakespear, Olivia, 115
Shakespeare and Company, 111–12, 149,
　　168, 180
Shaw, Irwin, 446–47, 450–52, 456, 460,
　　467, 489, 504, 529–30
Sheean, Vincent, 393, 445
shell shock, 61–64
Shephardson, Whitney, 428, 442–43
Shevlin, Tommy, 347, 432, 433–34, 440,
　　489, 508
Shipman, Evan, 163, 244, 289, 299, 373,
　　427
Shirer, William, 121
"The Short Happy Life of Francis
　　Macomber" (Hemingway), 333, 355,
　　359, 392
Silver Medal of Military Valor, 60–61
Simmons, Isabelle, 129, 134–35, 151,
　　196–97
Sinclair, Gail, 321–22
Sino-Japanese War, 421–25
Six Red Months in Russia (Bryant), 128
Slocombe, George, 120, 130
Smart, David, 319, 390
Smith, Bill, 94, 305
　　friendship with EH of, 44–45, 108,
　　　170, 174–75, 185, 188–89, 253, 309
　　Loeb and, 194–95
　　at Walloon Lake, 36
Smith, Doodles, 94, 98, 174–75
Smith, Katy. See Dos Passos, Katy Smith

Smith, Yeremiah Kenley (Y.K.), 44,
94–99, 102, 174–75, 365
Snows of Kilimanjaro (film), 565
"The Snows of Kilimanjaro"
(Hemingway), 8, 126–28, 208, 354*f*,
359–63, 405, 522
fictional portrayals of EH's friends in,
66, 361–63, 420
Katharine Hepburn and, 337
Paris flashbacks in, 588
Sokoloff, Alice, 189
Solano, Solita, 335
"Soldier's Home" (Hemingway), 61–62,
172
Soldier's Pay (Faulkner), 173
Some Do Not (Ford), 167
"The Soul of Spain with McAlmon and
Bird the Publishers" (Hemingway),
184
Soviet Union
Spanish Civil War and, 381, 385,
392–93, 435, 437
World War II and, 408, 428, 434–36
Spackman, Spike, 408
Spain, 145–49, 557
EH's fame in, 591, 598
EH's final visits to, 595–605, 611–13
EH's love of, 247–48, 306, 363–64,
400
nonintervention treaties of, 372, 385
Pamplona's Fiesta of San Fermín in,
148–49, 166, 171, 187–90, 194–95,
223–24, 274, 283–84, 598–600
political unrest in, 302–3, 330–31
See also bullfighting; Spanish Civil
War
Spain in Flames, 371–72
Spanier, Sandra, 108
Spanish Civil War, 284, 357, 363–67,
371–95, 426, 554
EH's play on, 386–87, 391–92
EH's reporting on, 371–79, 385–86,
390–95, 412, 423
EH's speaking on, 380–83, 429
Guernica massacre of, 379
International Brigade in, 393, 428, 435

John Dos Passos and, 375–77
Joris Ivens's filming of, 372–74,
377–79
observers and reporters of, 375
Republican exiles from, 428–29, 432
Soviet involvement in, 381, 385,
392–93, 435, 437
See also For Whom the Bell Tolls
The Spanish Earth, 372–83, 490, 505
Spear-O-Wigwam Ranch, 260
Speiser, Maurice, 357, 414, 587
Spellman, Francis Joseph, Cardinal, 525,
550
Spender, Stephen, 380
Spewack, Sam, 120
Spiegel, Fred, 445
Spilka, Mark, 136
Sports Illustrated, 572
Stalin, Josef, 408, 428, 435
The Starched Blue Sky of Spain (Herbst),
377
Steffens, Lincoln, 120–21, 130–32
Stein, Gertrude, 106, 118–22, 131–32, 138,
156, 246, 250–51, 616–17
on bullfighting, 145, 324
as Bumby's godmother, 119, 154–55,
286, 324
death of, 512
EH's relationship with, 120, 129,
286–88, 323–25
EH's views on, 119–20, 159, 588–89
on EH's works, 149, 160–61, 288, 324
on *The Great Gatsby,* 182
memoir of, 323–25, 336, 588
photo of, 154*f*
published works of, 119, 145, 159, 160,
167
references in EH's fiction to, 202
Wyndham Lewis's views of, 335–36
Steiner, Rudolf, 320–21
Stern, Ada, 313–14, 330, 335, 391, 480–81
Stevens, George, 446
Stevens, Wallace, 363
Stewart, Bea, 305
Stewart, Donald Ogden
on EH's temper, 192, 199

Stewart, Donald Ogden *(continued)*
    friendship with EH of, 163, 166–67,
        173–76, 185, 188–90, 225, 248, 305
    Oak Park Hemingways and, 238
    Second American Writers' Conference
        and, 380
Stewart, Jimmy, 623
A Story Teller's Story (Anderson), 178,
    195
"A Strange Country" (Hemingway), 132
Strasberg, Lee, 391
Strater, Maggie, 138, 144
Strater, Mike, 118, 162, 253
    bullfighting interest of, 145
    on EH's lost manuscripts, 134
    friendship with EH of, 138, 144, 265,
        274, 294, 299–300, 308, 330, 344,
        346
A Stricken Field (Gellhorn), 410–11
Stringer, Bill, 456
Sturges, John, 575
Styron, William, 620
subdural hematomas, 448–50
Sullivan, J. B., 293
The Sun Also Rises (Hemingway), 4, 172,
    189–95, 260
    critical reception of, 220, 233–36
    ending of, 282
    epigrams in, 234
    fictional portrayals of EH's friends in,
        186–90, 195, 235–36, 483, 557, 598
    film version of, 566
    Jake Barnes in, 186, 194, 217, 235,
        483–84
    publication of, 209–12
    as revenge fiction, 192–93
    Robert Cohn in, 4, 190–93, 195,
        218–19
    sales of, 244
    Scott Fitzgerald's editing of, 217–20,
        280, 353, 520
Sunday, Billy, 43
Sun Valley, Idaho, 407–9, 413–14, 592
    See also Ketchum, Idaho
Sweeny, Charles, 425–26, 455
Sylvester, Harry, 364

Tabula magazine, 37, 156, 398–99
"Talk of the Town" piece, 298
Tate, Allen, 97, 158, 196, 216, 287–88
Ten Days That Shook the World (Reed),
    128, 365
Tender Buttons (Stein), 119
Tender Is the Night (Fitzgerald), 286, 325,
    352–53, 420, 492
"Ten Indians" (Hemingway), 195, 216
That Summer in Paris (Callaghan),
    275–77, 290
Thayer, Scofield, 115, 117, 118, 157, 163,
    172
Theatre Guild, 391, 395
Theisen, Earl, 556, 558
"They Come Bearing Gifts" (Anderson),
    106–7
"They Made Peace—What Is Peace?"
    (Hemingway), 131–32
This Quarter, 172, 176
This Side of Paradise (Fitzgerald), 138,
    181, 253, 287
Thomason, John W., 425–27, 430–31, 553
Thompson, Charles, 252–53, 293–94,
    312, 315–16, 370, 391
    on the Depression, 340
    EH's fictional portrayal of, 332, 341–42
    travel with EH of, 330–36, 338–39
Thompson, Ed, 447
Thompson, Lorine, 253, 266, 297, 301,
    335, 338, 391
Thorazine, 582, 618
Thornton, James, 469–70
"The Three-Day Blow" (Hemingway),
    168–69, 172
Three Lives (Stein), 119
Three Mountains Press, 158, 173, 178
Three Soldiers (Dos Passos), 164, 356, 412
Three Stories and Ten Poems
    (Hemingway), 133, 149, 160–61, 173
Thurber, James, 119, 478
Tift, Asa, 301
Tighe, Katherine, 217
Time magazine, 359, 381, 390, 411, 421
"The Time Now, the Place Spain"
    (Hemingway), 390

"To a Tragic Poetess" (Hemingway), 247–48
"To Crazy Christian" (Hemingway), 529
"Today Is Friday" (Hemingway), 216, 247
To Have and Have Not (Hemingway), 305–6, 354–57, 361, 371, 380, 383
   critical reception of, 389–90
   film version of, 545
   sales of, 389
Toklas, Alice, 118–20, 131–32, 145, 155, 250, 286, 512, 531–32, 589
Tolstoy, Leo, 436
Tone, Franchot, 391
Toomer, Jean, 97
Topping, Bob, 594
Toronto Star, 93
   EH's European assignment for, 106–7, 110, 112–13, 120–21, 124–30, 139, 144, 365
   EH's pseudonym in, 125, 552
   EH's work in Toronto for, 144, 150–52
Toronto Star Weekly, 86–87, 150–51
The Torrents of Spring (Hemingway), 172, 201–3, 207, 210–11, 216–17, 503
the Tortugas, 293–94, 299–300, 308, 311, 344–48
Tracy, Spencer, 573, 575
"The Tradesman Returns" (Hemingway), 355–56
the transatlantic review, 149, 158–64, 167–68, 174, 177–78, 324
transgenderism, 486
traumatic brain injury, 448–50
   See also head injuries
Travels with Myself and Another (Gellhorn), 421, 424–25, 434
"Treachery in Aragon" (Hemingway), 390
Trexler trilogy (Herbst), 299
Trogdon, Robert, 108, 416, 522, 536
Tropic of Cancer (Miller), 485
The Trouble I've Seen (Gellhorn), 369
True at First Light (ed. P. Hemingway), 560, 572

Tunney, Gene, 496–97
Turgenev, Ivan, 97, 202
Twain, Mark, 40, 48, 342, 616
Twysden, Duff, 185–90, 193, 236
Twysden, Roger Thomas, 186
Tynan, Kenneth, 595
Tzara, Tristan, 199

"Ultimately" (Hemingway), 97, 156
Ulysses (Joyce), 115, 149
"The Undefeated" (Hemingway), 172, 174, 184–85, 243, 244, 246, 522
Under Kilimanjaro (Hemingway), 560–61, 572
Untzaín, Andrés "the Black Priest," 489, 498–99
"Up in Michigan" (Hemingway), 111, 119–20, 132, 176
U.S.A. trilogy (Dos Passos), 164, 274, 357–58, 390
U.S. Film Corps, 446–47

Vail, Jeanie and Laurence, 595
Vaill, Amanda, 343, 388
Valéry, Paul, 380
Vance, Arthur, 140
Vanderbilt, Alfred, 334–35
Van Dusen, Bill, 454
Van Guilder, Gene, 408, 627
Van Loan, Charles E., 172
Venice, 508–11, 513, 532–33, 535, 565
Verlaine, Paul, 110
Vernon, Alex, 378
"A Very Short Story" (Hemingway), 162
Victoria, Queen of England, 11
Vidal, Gore, 529
Viertel, Peter
   friendship with EH of, 446–47, 505–7, 515, 527, 565–66, 579, 609, 614
   The Old Man and the Sea screenplay by, 573–75
   photo of, 532*f*
Viertel, Salka and Berthold, 505

Viertel, Virginia "Jigee," 505–6, 532, 602
View of Toledo (El Greco), 531
Villa America, 199–201, 220–21, 224–25, 595
Villalta, Nicanor, 151
Villard, Henry, 66, 67
Villarreal, René, 430, 489, 497, 517–18, 537
The Virginian (Wister), 261

Wallace, George, 57
Wallace, Henry F., 570
Wallace, Ivan, 296
Walsh, Ernest, 142–43, 172, 175–76
Walton, Bill, 448, 454, 456, 465, 471, 473–74, 542
"War in the Siegfried Line" (Hemingway), 469
The Wasteland (Eliot), 116, 157, 173, 235
The Waste Makers (Packard), 620
Waugh, Evelyn, 534
"A Way You'll Never Be" (Hemingway), 318, 327
Weaver, Leland Stanford "Chub," 296, 298–99, 300
Wedderkop, Hermann von, 117
Welles, Orson, 382
Wellington, C. G. "Pete," 46–48, 54
Wells, H. G., 158, 166, 369
Welsh, Adeline, 451
Welsh, Mary. *See* Hemingway, Mary Welsh
Welsh, Tom, 451
Wertenbaker, Charles, 445, 450–51, 456, 460, 475
Wertenbaker, Lael, 445, 448
Wescott, Glenway, 177, 235, 260
Westbrook, Max, 91
western trips, 259–60, 313–16, 363, 391, 405–7, 495–96, 592–93
    bear hunting in, 315–16, 319
    friends from, 296, 298–99, 496
    L-Bar-T Ranch, 295–96, 347, 405, 419
    See also Ketchum, Idaho
We Were Strangers (Huston), 505–6

Wharton, Edith, 182, 280
What Mad Pursuit (Gellhorn), 368
Wheaton College, 13, 14
Wheeler, John, 367, 371
White, Bud, 312
Whitney, Jock and Jean, 305
Wilde, Oscar, 165
Wilder, Thornton, 260
Williams, Taylor, 408–9, 593
Williams, Tennessee, 535
Williams, William Carlos, 141–44, 167, 174
Wilson, Dale, 48, 51, 57
Wilson, Earl, 496
Wilson, Edmund "Bunny," 174, 177, 196, 217, 420
    editing of Scott Fitzgerald by, 353–54
    on EH's temperament, 351
    on Gertrude Stein's memoir, 336
    reviews of EH's works by, 160–61, 234, 246, 285, 392, 414, 521
Wilson, Harry Leon, 86
Wilson, Woodrow, 52, 57, 365
Winchell, Walter, 366–67
Windemere at Walloon Lake, Michigan, 20–21, 29, 156, 257–58, 552–53
    EH's flirtations at, 88–89, 92–93, 105
    EH's honeymoon at, 104–5
    EH's shooting a heron at, 36, 552, 555
    family quarrels over, 268–69, 396–97
    farming at, 35–36, 45, 80
    Grace Cottage and, 80–85
The Wine of Astonishment (Gellhorn), 529
"The Wine of Wyoming" (Hemingway), 263, 293, 318
Winesburg, Ohio (Anderson), 106
"Wings over Africa" (Hemingway), 355
Winner Take Nothing (Hemingway), 54, 318–19, 340, 380
Wister, Owen, 261–62, 280–83
"With Pascin at the Dôme" (Hemingway), 185
Wittlesey, Byra "Puck," 512
Wolfe, Thomas, 319, 502
Wolfert, Ira, 456, 460

Wong, Ramón, 488
Woolf, Virginia, 245
"The Woppian Way" (Hemingway), 79,
   85, 156
World War I, 34, 52–53, 508–9
   EH's ambulance driver service in, 35,
      53, 55–64, 68
   EH's injuries and trauma from, 11–12,
      59–68, 169–70, 318, 483, 524–25
   EH's speaking and writing on, 73–80,
      85–86
   EH's views on, 61–62
   EH's visit to battlefields of, 124
   literature of disillusionment after, 113
   Nick Adams stories and, 169–70
   Treaty of Versailles, 128
   U.S. entry into, 52
World War II, 408, 419, 524–25
   D-Day of, 453–54
   EH's head injuries in, 447–50, 455–56,
      461–63
   EH's reporting on, 438, 443–44,
      453–61, 465, 468–75
   EH's stories of, 462–63, 476–77
   EH's volunteer espionage of, 425–37,
      442–43, 506
   Free French forces of, 458–60, 525, 559
   Jack Hemingway's service in, 427, 443,
      470, 479, 553
   legend of EH and, 461
   liberation of Paris of, 457–61,
      469–70
   Martha Gellhorn's reporting on,
      421–25, 439–44, 453
   novels on, 529–30, 549
   Sino-Japanese war and, 421–25, 438
   S.L.A. Marshall's accounts of, 460–61
   Soviet Union and, 428, 434–36
   U.S. Film Corps in, 446–47
wound theory, 63–64
Wright, Don, 94–99
"A Writer's Quest for Parnassus"
   (Williams), 535
Wykeham, Peter, 474
Wyman, Arthur, 103, 112

"Years of the Dog" (MacLeish), 490
Yeats, William, 115
You Know Me Al (Lardner), 38
Young, Philip, 63–64, 552
The Young Lions (Shaw), 504

Zabel, Morton Dauwen, 412, 534
Zaphiro, Denis, 557–59, 564, 568
Zinnemann, Fred, 574–75
Zuppke, Bob, 38

Illustration Credits

All photographs are courtesy of the Ernest Hemingway Collection, John F. Kennedy Presidential Library and Museum, Boston, Massachusetts, with the exception of those listed below.

Star newsroom © Anderson photographs, Wilborn and Associates

Ernest Hemingway in hospital © Villard, John F. Kennedy Presidential Library and Museum

Hemingway children in water © Pennsylvania State University

Sherwood Anderson © Alfred Steiglitz, Library of Congress

Ezra Pound © Alvin Langdon Coburn/Contributor/Getty Images

Robert McAlmon © Sylvia Beach Collection, Princeton University

Ada and Archibald MacLeish © Beinecke Library, Yale University

F. Scott and Zelda Fitzgerald © Universal Images Group / Getty Images

Pauline Pfeiffer © Princeton University

Hemingway naked © Colby College

Movie poster of *A Farewell to Arms* © Grosset and Dunlap, Random House

Hemingway with a broken arm © Knox College, Special Collections

Jane Mason in "Secrets of a Smart Sun-Tan" ad © Edward Steichen

Paper dolls © *Vanity Fair,* March 1934

"Snows of Kilimanjaro" story © Esquire

Movie poster of *The Spanish Earth* © University of South Carolina Ernest Hemingway Speiser and Easterling-Hallman Foundation Collection

With Gary Cooper © Getty Images

Winston Guest © Getty Images

Hemingway at St. George's Hospital, photo by Robert Capa © International Center of Photography/Magnum Photos

A NOTE ON THE TYPE

This book was set in Adobe Garamond. Desined for the Adobe corporation by Robert Slimbach, the fonts are based on types first cut by Claude Garamond (c. 1480–1561). Garamond was a pupil of Geoffroy Tory and is believed to have followed the Venetian models, although he introduced a number of important differences, and it is to him that we owe the letter we now know as "old style." He gave to his letters a certain elegance and feeling of movement that won their creator an immediate reputation and the patronage of Francis I of France.

Composed by North Market Street Graphics, Lancaster, Pennsylvania
Printed and bound by Berryville Graphics, Berryville, Virginia
Designed by Iris Weinstein